Literature
Across Cultures

FIFTH EDITION

Sheena Gillespie

Tony Pipolo

Terezinha Fonseca

Queensborough Community College
City University of New York

Longman

Boston Columbus Indianapolis New York San Francisco Upper Saddle River
Amsterdam Cape Town Dubai London Madrid Milan Munich Paris
Montreal Toronto Delhi Mexico City São Paulo Sydney
Hong Kong Seoul Singapore Taipei Tokyo

To Terezinha Fonseca, James Geasor, Ridley Gunderson, Laura Kuehn, Susan Madera, and Catherine Stolfi with affection and gratitude.

—Sheena Gillespie

To all the students whose lives and minds have touched mine and made teaching one of life's great learning experiences.

—Tony Pipolo

To Aïla de Oliveira Gomes, whose intellectual and spiritual vocation has inspired generations of Brazilian students.

—Terezinha Fonseca

Acquisitions Editor: *Matthew Wright*
Development Editor: *Heidi Jacobs*
Executive Marketing Manager: *Megan Galvin-Fak*
Senior Supplements Editor: *Donna Campion*
Production Manager: *Ellen MacElree*
Project Coordination, Text Design, and Electronic Page Makeup: *TexTech International*
Cover theme inspired by the artwork of Jim Geasor.
Senior Manufacturing Buyer: *Alfred C. Dorsey*
Printer and Binder: *Courier, Stoughton*
Cover Printer: *Courier, Stoughton*

For permission to use copyright material, grateful acknowledgment is made to the copyright holders on pp. 1031–1034, which are hereby made part of this copyright page.

Library of Congress Cataloging-in-Publication Data

Gillespie, Sheena.
  Literature across cultures / Sheena Gillespie, Tony Pipolo, Terezinha Fonseca. — 5th ed.
      p.   cm.
  Includes bibliographical references and index.
  ISBN 13: 978-0-205-18468-2   ISBN 10: 0-205-18468-5
  1. Literature—collections.   I. Pipolo, Tony.   II. Fonseca, Terezinha.   III. Title.
PN6014.G43 2008
808'.8—dc22   2007013255

This book includes 2009 MLA guidelines.

Longman
is an imprint of

1 2 3 4 5 6 7 8 9 10—CRS—14 13 12 11

ISBN 13: 978-0-205-18468-2
ISBN 10:   0-205-18468-5

www.pearsonhighered.com

Contents

PART TWO: *Gender and Identity* 281

FICTION

ESSAYS

POETRY

PART THREE: *War and Violence* 459

PART FOUR: *Race and Culture*   **579**

DRAMA

PART FIVE: *Individualism and Community* 769

FICTION

ESSAYS

POETRY

Preface for Instructors

> No one can deny the persisting continuities of long traditions, sustained
> habitations, national languages, and cultural geographies, but there seems
> no reason except fear and prejudice to keep insisting on their separation
> and distinctiveness, as if that were all human life were about. Survival in
> fact is about connections between things.
>
> —Edward Said

Literature Across Cultures invites students and instructors to explore "connections between things," particularly the literature of the past and present, in contexts that go beyond traditional boundaries in an attempt to recognize, respect, and learn from the increasing heterogeneity of contemporary human experience. Like its predecessors, the fifth edition of *Literature Across Cultures* continues to highlight its most distinguished and identifying features: the promotion of conversation with traditional, multicultural, and contemporary voices through a study of thematic topics.

This book focuses on the political, sociocultural, and multicultural aspects of literary debates related to the dialectics of roots and rebellions, self and society, gender and identity, and the causes and effects of war and violence, as well as issues of class, race, ethnicity, and sexual preference. These features have distinguished this volume among other thematic anthologies.

ORGANIZATION OF THE TEXT

Following the tradition of the previous editions, the fifth edition of *Literature Across Cultures* is organized around an introduction, five thematic parts, and four pedagogical appendices. The first chapter addresses reading and writing as a social act, highlighting the relevance of a collaborative classroom approach. We provide instructors and students with interactive strategies for reading and writing, with the goal of producing multiple meanings generated by close textual analysis, analytical student writings, peer critiques, and checklists that promote self-monitoring practices.

Each of the five thematic parts consists of fiction, essays, poetry, drama, a film unit, discussion questions, writing assignments, and research topics. The poetry section groups poems in clusters of two or three to help students explore the multi-cultural diversity and commonality of the poetic experience. Our choice of reading texts draws on the rich literary and ethnic perspectives from different historical periods. Included works explore topics such as roots, identity, gender, sexuality, war, violence, race, social class, culture, the self, the family, and the community.

These vital issues were chosen to stimulate class discussion, to promote comprehensive responses to literature in reading and writing, and to develop critical and argumentative skills. The four appendices—A. "An Introduction to the Elements of Fiction, Nonfiction, Poetry, and Drama"; B. "Writing a Research Paper"; C. "Researching Literary Sources"; and D. "Critical Approaches: A Case Study of *Hamlet*"—provide a stimulating apparatus for understanding the literary genres, the research paper, the Internet, and literary criticism. The book also includes a diverse range of teaching resources for instructors and students.

ENDURING FEATURES

The fifth edition is built on the following features of the four previous editions:

- An emphasis on the **multicultural aspects of literature** leads students beyond their literary and cultural traditions.
- The presentation of **fiction, nonfiction, poetry, and drama** as cultural productions suggests ways of combining the study of literature with cultural perspectives and interpretations.
- A stimulating focus on **five thematic units** suggests different ways of understanding and responding to literary reading strategies.
- **Discussion questions, collaborative group questions, and research topics** introduce students to the writing process, presenting strategies for writing the research paper, and information on locating critical sources.
- The presentation of a **concise and proven pedagogical apparatus** motivates students to acquire the critical and analytical skills they need to read and write about literature.

Each of the foregoing features was created to provide instructors and students with a variety of strategies for a rewarding and stimulating teaching/learning experience.

NEW FEATURES OF THE FIFTH EDITION

The fifth edition of *Literature Across Cultures* incorporates many excellent critiques and suggestions from our editors, reviewers, colleagues, and students. The new features also reflect our commitment to making *Literature Across Cultures* pedagogically, culturally, and historically useful to college students in their reading of texts, in group work with their peers, and in their various written responses.

Revised Titles and Contexts of the Thematic Parts

Part One, "Origins and Insights," has been replaced by "Roots and Rebellions" to more accurately reflect the rites of passage of writers and students as they speculate on the influence of tradition and culture, the degree to which the past informs the present, the interaction of personal and cultural memories, and the multiple effects of generational conflicts on familial and individual identities. Students will converse, for example, with writers from different generations and cultural heritages on the degree to which myths and folktales have informed their relationships, hopes, fears, and dreams. They will trace connections between past and present in the interweaving of myth, history, and family stories that have contributed to the roots as well as the rebellions of many writers, from ancient cultures to the present day. In still other texts, they will reflect on the complex role of memory as writers seek to understand their individual and cultural roots. Some readings present the fusion of memory and imagination in creating continuity between past and present; others capture the precarious balance between remembering and forgetting as an essential part of immigrant experiences as well as the gains and losses of Diaspora experiences.

"Gender and Identity" texts in Part Two provide not only a starting point for a more open debate on gender differences, but also an opportunity to explore issues of gender through readings about same-sex relationships and marriages (i.e., same-sex relationships are not just about sexual preference; there are also cultural aspects). Many writers of both genders examine the crucial links between gender and identity, including the necessity of freeing men and women from the constraints of traditional concepts and definitions of masculinity and femininity and stereotypical gender roles in various historical and cultural contexts. This part also includes texts from the literature of AIDS because this condition finds emotional correlatives in the fiction, poetry, and drama of our time as well as being a current relevant topic.

The "War and Violence" selections in Part Three present similarities and differences between these issues. Although all wars are violent, not all violence is linked to war, yet many texts in this part pose questions about war as a cause and effect of the daily violence that occurs in every society, in homes and on the streets in communities around the world. The tragic events of 9/11 have brought the violence of terrorism closer to home for Americans and for millions of people throughout the world. Issues of terrorism and violence have been added to the conversation through texts and films in this revision. The texts also suggest ways by which students may reevaluate historical and contemporary heroic myths of war and examine new sensibilities promoting the merits of political negotiation and citing the misuses of power in a global, pluralistic society.

Part Four, formerly "Race and Difference," has been reconfigured and renamed "Race and Culture" to include more discussions of ethnicity and social class. The texts invite students to understand better the sociohistorical realities of personal indignities and social injustices resulting from individual, institutional, and societal discrimination toward ethnicity, race, gender, sexuality, and socioeconomic class. This part includes also texts that focus on the current debate on immigration and the anger and disillusionment of illegal immigrants from their sense of entrapment and exclusion from the North American mainstream. Other voices use prose and poetry to wrestle with the complexities of what it means to be bilingual and bicultural in the United States. Students are invited to add their voices to conversations about the linguistic pain of transition from the private world to the public, and whether or not mastery of the dominant language will erase the rich stories and traditions of their multilingual, indigenous cultures.

The "Individualism and Community" texts in Part Five explore the implications of the dialectic of self and society, examining the degree to which our ability to say "I" is predicated on our need and willingness to say "we." Students are asked to seek answers to questions such as these: What constitutes a community? How do the sociocultural and sociohistorical characteristics of a community change over time? How do the tenets of a community relate to individuals, some of whom submit and some of whom rebel? To what extent does the Japanese proverb "the nail that sticks out is hammered down" resonate or conflict with your concept of community? What are an individual's responsibilities to the larger community?

Total Revision of the Introduction, "Reading and Writing as a Social Act"

The Introduction has been reconfigured and recast to reflect more accurately our commitment to the concept of reading and writing as a social act by inviting students at the outset to think of themselves as members of a community of readers and writers. We have separated the strategies for reading and writing to highlight more clearly the steps involved in each process and to increase possibilities for student engagement and interactions. The Strategies for Reading Literature section emphasizes the importance of student responses, close textual reading, cultural contexts, and collaborative peer discussions by focusing more directly on the production of multiple meanings. To illustrate how this might be done, we offer discussions of the historical and cultural contexts of Kate Chopin's "The Story of an Hour" and include examples of students' collaborative and diverse textual and cultural analyses of this story.

A writing as a social act section has also been included to better promote students' engagement in the writing process by including them as full partners as they respond to and critique an analytical essay on "The Unforgetting" by Chinese American writer Lan Samantha Chang. To cover the essential elements of this process, we show how one student, Catherine Stolfi, responds to the writing process, reacts to peer critiques, and uses an evaluation checklist for composing her final draft. Instead of providing students with prescriptive strategies for the revision of the first draft, this section's newly enhanced pedagogy inspires them to expand their understanding of the revision process by suggesting ways in which they can interact, collaborate, and respond to writing that is socially and culturally constructed by audience peer groups.

As part of this socially constructed rationale to expand the possibilities for production of meaning, we have included in each part of the anthology samples of different kinds of student writing. Part One, for example, features an analytical paper on Langston Hughes and Robert Hayden and includes a section on generating ideas, a formal outline, a first draft, peer critiques, and a final version. Part Two presents students' journal entries on a short story by Haruki Murakami; Part Three includes a research paper on the Vietnam War, including the student-writer's description of the steps he followed in selecting his topic and using the library and the Internet. Part Four offers a student's journal entry on an essay by May Sarton, and Part Five features a student's brainstorming exercise for an essay on the poetry of Wallace Stevens and Leo Romero.

Revised Introductions to the Reading Selections

The introductions to the five parts have been extensively revised to highlight the ethnicities of the authors, to update background information, and to intensify the relevance of the cultural contexts of the texts.

New and Revised Discussion Questions

The new and revised discussion questions following each short story, each cluster of poems, and each play are meant to assist students in making informed responses to the reading selections. Their aim is to suggest multiple possibilities for the production of meaning. Specifically, this fifth edition devises a progression from close textual analysis to critical thinking and include **Journal Entries** suggestions, **Textual Considerations** questions, and **Cultural Contexts** questions, which expose students not only to cultural interactions with the sociohistorical realities of the literary texts, but also to interactive engagement with their peers.

Revision of Film Angles

The purpose of a separate film unit for each section of the book is to demonstrate not only thematic continuity with the literature selections but also the distinctive ways in which films affect society, mirroring—in both positive and negative ways—the moral, political, social, and psychological conflicts within society. To a great extent, this cultural impact is created directly by the sheer power of movies, their audio and visual impact. The film angles are designed to sensitize students and teachers to that impact by calling attention to the artistic, stylistic, and technological uniqueness of the medium, the specific means it employs to achieve its ends. We do not honor short stories, novels, poems, and plays simply because they treat important subjects; the very best examples are the ones that make the most of the formal and stylistic possibilities available to the writer. In the same sense, an important subject does not automatically make a film good; the films that we admire and see again and that warrant study are those that embody their subjects in the "language" of cinema—not only the screenplay or the dialogue, but also the audio and visual "grammar" of the medium, that which turns it into art. The relevant terms of this language, like those pertinent to dramatic or poetic forms, are defined in the glossary.

In some cases, the film units can be used in direct conjunction with the literature selections. In Part One: "Roots and Rebellion" and Part Four: "Race and Culture," for example, several film versions of *Hamlet* and *Othello* are discussed. Most units provide historical overviews that consider how the subjects of the unit (e.g., gender, race, and war) have been treated throughout film history. This is followed by attention to specific films that exemplify each theme. The questions are designed to prompt students to think about how the nature of the film experience affects the comprehension of the themes in question and how this differs from the reading of literature. Films were selected to reflect both popular and serious tastes. This is because cultural attitudes toward subjects such as class, race, gender, war, violence, and sexual difference are often more discernible in genre movies with mass appeal than they are in highbrow art films. This is not to dismiss the latter so much as it is to recognize the former as a more revealing barometer of how feelings and convictions change within a society.

In Part One of this edition, for example, a new stress on the coming-of-age or rite of passage film illustrates how this universal theme infiltrates virtually every film genre. Because genre films throughout film history have always attracted the biggest audiences, the ones that deal with the coming of age story have the potential, at least, of disseminating insights and lessons more widely. Students who find Shakespeare difficult or inaccessible may be pleased to learn that many of the themes that concerned them are also traceable in less daunting works of literature and film. Taking genre films seriously should not replace Shakespeare but can provide another pathway for them.

Inevitably, social events dictate how we look at the world. Since the tragedy of 9/11 and the ensuing war in Iraq, Americans and people everywhere have been forced to admit fear of terrorism and the troubling awareness of other cultures and mindsets into their everyday lives. It is inevitable that such concerns affect not only the way we live, but the way we read and look at movies—and, indeed, often determine *what* we read and which movies we see. Part Three: "War and Violence" tries to reflect these concerns with a consideration of three films about the events of 9/11.

Other changes in the film angles of this edition include a weaving together of the issues and film discussions of gender and sexual difference, so that some of the material that once belonged to "Race and Difference" (now "Race and Culture") has been incorporated into Part Two: "Gender and Identity."

Performance Exercises

This edition presents a series of Performance Exercises—interactive, collaborative work that encourages peer responses to the interrelationship between students and the dramatic text.

New and Revised Topics

The new and revised writing topics at the end of each thematic section are meant to provide students with engaging assignments and relevant research topics.

Revised Appendices

This edition includes revised versions of the following appendices:

Appendix A: "An Introduction to the Elements of Fiction, Nonfiction, Poetry, and Drama"
- Explores the complexities of the literary genres
- Provides a list of revised and new topics—sixty-seven in all—that discuss literature as cultural productions and address currently relevant issues in twenty-first-century society

Appendix B: "Writing a Research Paper"
- A streamlined approach that encourages students to concentrate on the validity of their writing, such as developing a concise thesis, and the critical aspects of drafting a research paper
- New sections include clear explanations of how to engage in dialogue using literary criticism, as well as an updated component on the research process

Appendix C: "Researching Literary Sources"
- Focuses on having the students use the library and the Internet as a combined unit of research
- With added emphasis on the Internet, the new content explores the use of search engines and the value of doing research online
- An in-depth view of the strengths and weaknesses of using the Internet as a research tool and the reliability of online resources

Appendix D: "Critical Approaches: A Case Study of *Hamlet*"
- Includes a discussion of several approaches to the play, including psychoanalytic, psychosocial, new-critical, reader-response, feminist, and new historical perspectives
- Engages the play from various critical viewpoints

A Paragraph on Deconstruction

At a time of great turmoil in Shakespearean studies, marked as much by the Royal Shakespeare Company's multicultural production of Shakespeare's plays (2006–07 season) as by scholars' rejection of a single, unified Shakespearean text (Arden III publication of three equally accepted versions of Hamlet, 2006), we have added a section on deconstruction.

SUPPLEMENTS
For the Instructor

New, Revised Instructor's Manual
A revised Instructor's Manual includes strategies for discussing literature in an interactive classroom, selected critical biographies, audio/visual teaching resources,

internet resources organized according to author, a sample syllabus, teaching suggestions, expanded discussion of film, and expanded filmographies.

The Longman Printed Testbank for Literature, by Heidi L. M. Jacobs
The Longman Electronic Testbank for Literature, by Heidi L. M. Jacobs
This test bank features various objective questions on the major works of fiction, short fiction, poetry, and drama. A versatile and handy resource, this easy-to-use Testbank can be used for all quizzing and testing needs. The user-friendly CD-ROM allows instructors to choose questions from the electronic test bank, and then print out the completed test for distribution. Print ISBN: 0-321-14312-4; CD ISBN: 0-321-14314-0

Teaching Literature On-line Second Edition, by Dan Kline
Concise and practical, Teaching Literature On-line provides instructors with strategies and advice for incorporating elements of computer technology into the literature classroom. Offering a range of information and examples, this manual provides ideas and activities for enhancing literature courses with the help of technology. ISBN: 0-321-10618-0

MyLiteratureLab Faculty Teaching Guide
This helpful guide gives instructors step-by-step advice for integrating the features of MyLiteratureLab into their classroom, including detailed instructions in how to use Exchange, Longman's online writing review tool. ISBN: 0-321-33213-X

For the Student

MyLiteratureLab.com
MyLiteratureLab.com is a Web-based state-of-the-art interactive learning system designed to accompany *Literature Across Cultures* and help students in their literature course. It adds a new dimension to the study of literature with Longman Lectures—evocative, richly illustrated audio readings along with advice on how to read, interpret, and write about literary works from our roster of Longman authors. This powerful program also features Diagnostic Tests, Interactive Readings with clickable prompts, sample student papers, Literature Timelines, Avoiding Plagiarism, Research Navigator ™ research tools, and Exchange, an electronic instructor/peer feedback tool. *MyLiteratureLab.com* can be delivered within Course Compass, Web CT, or Blackboard course management systems, enabling instructors to administer their entire course online.

Analyzing Literature, Second Edition, by Sharon James McGee
This brief supplement provides critical reading strategies, writing advice, and sample student papers to help students interpret and discuss literary works in a variety of genres. Suggestions for collaborative activities and online research on literary topics are also featured, as well as numerous exercises and writing assignments. ISBN: 0-321-09338-0

Responding to Literature: A Writer's Journal, by Daniel Kline

This beautiful spiral-bound journal provides students with their own personal space for recording their reactions to the literature they read. Guided writing prompts, suggested writing assignments, and overviews of literary terms provide students with the tools—and ideas—they need for responding to fiction, poetry, and drama. ISBN: 0-321-09542-1

The Longman Researcher's Journal

The Longman Researcher's Journal is designed to help students work through the steps involved in writing a research paper. Each section contains record-keeping strategies, checklists, graphic organizers, and pages for taking notes from sources or for a student's own thoughts and reactions. ISBN: 0-321-09530-8

Screening Shakespeare: Using Film to Understand Plays, by Michael Greer

This brief guide is an accessible introduction to Shakespeare's most popular plays on film. It provides analytical tools and rubrics for responding to films, with discussion questions and writing prompts that move from formal analysis to considerations of historical and cultural contexts. ISBN: 0-321-19479-9

Evaluating a Performance, by Michael Greenwald

Designed to look like a Playbill, this is the perfect tool for the student assigned to review a local theater production. This free supplement offers students a convenient place to record their evaluation of the staging, acting, costuming, set design, and so on. Useful tips and suggestions of things to consider when evaluating a production are included. ISBN: 0-321-09541-3

Evaluating Plays on Film and Video, by Anne Marie Welsh and Martin Morawski

This guide steps students through the process of analyzing and writing about plays on film, whether in a short review or a longer essay. Four appendices include writing and editing tips and a glossary of film terms. Worksheets aid students in organizing their notes and thoughts before they begin writing. ISBN: 0-321-18794-6

Literature Timeline, by Heidi L. M. Jacobs

This laminated four-page timeline provides students with a chronological overview of the major literary works that have been written throughout history. In addition, the timeline also lists major sociocultural and political events to provide students with historical and contextual insights into the impact historical events have had on writers and their works . . . and vice versa. ISBN: 0-321-14315-9

Handbook of Literary Terms—Literature, Language, Theory, by X. J. Kennedy, Dana Gioia, and Mark Bauerlein

From the author team of the discipline's most widely used literature anthology comes this practical and instructive guide to the language of literary study. Featuring an engaging and accessible writing style, this brief manual explains over 400 literary terms with clear, concise definitions, culturally diverse examples, and a pronunciation guide to help students use unfamiliar words in class discussions. ISBN: 0-321-20207-4

Glossary of Literary and Critical Terms, by Heidi L. M. Jacobs

The Glossary of Literary and Critical Terms is a quick, reliable, and portable resource for students of Literature and Creative Writing. This easy-to-use glossary includes definitions, explanations, and examples for over 100 literary and critical terms which students commonly encounter in their readings or hear in their lectures and class discussions. In addition to basic terms related to form and genre, the glossary also includes terms and explanations related to literary history, criticism, and theory. ISBN: 0-321-12691-2

Penguin Putnam Novel Discount Program

In cooperation with Penguin Putnam, Inc., one of our sibling companies, Longman is proud to offer a variety of Penguin paperbacks at a significant discount when packaged with any Longman title. Excellent additions to any literature course, Penguin titles give students the opportunity to explore contemporary and classical fiction and drama. The available titles include works by authors as diverse as Toni Morrison, Julia Alvarez, Mary Shelley, and Shakespeare. To review the complete list of titles available, visit the Longman-Penguin-Putnam website at: http://www.ablongman.com/penguin.

Video Program

For qualified adopters, an impressive selection of videotapes is available to enrich students' experience of literature. One video per 100 students per semester, with a limit of 5. List of videos available on Clubhouse. Contact your local Longman/Pearson sales representative for details.

ACKNOWLEDGMENTS

I am grateful to Erika Berg, our editor, who guided us through most of this project, and to Joseph Terry who completed it. Heidi Jacobs was our excellent developmental editor and offered valuable critiques on the several sections that were totally revised. Special thanks are due to Ridley Gunderson and James Geasor, who completely revised Appendices B and C and assisted with the revision of the introduction, "Reading and Writing as a Social Act." Several students, including Catherine Stolfi, Laura Kuehn, and James Geasor, contributed essays and descriptions of their writing process, and others provided valuable peer critiques, journal entries, and brainstorming exercises. Terezinha Fonseca revised Appendix D and the Performance Exercises, and Tony Pipolo updated the Film Angles and Filmographies for the Instructor's Manual. Susan Madera added and updated the biographical endnotes, and Anna Howard and Betty Tseng assisted with the preparation of the manuscript, as did Gianna Negovetti, Patty Gorton, and Gladys DeBuccio. Isabel

Pipolo typed the Instructor's Manual. We also received invaluable suggestions from our colleagues at Queensborough Community College, many of whom have used our text since the first edition.

Finally, we would like to thank the following reviewers: Billie Bennett, University of Georgia; Emily Dial-Driver, Rogers State University; Carey Emmons, Utah State University; Susan Smith Nash, Excelsior College; Zivah Perel, Queensborough Community College; Tracy Schaelen, Southwestern College; Georgeanna Sellers, High Point University; Jeffery H. Taylor, Metropolitan State College of Denver.

Preface for Students

> People and their cultures perish in isolation, but they are born or reborn
> in contact with other men and women, with men and women of another
> culture, another creed, another race. If we do not recognize our humanity
> in others, we will not recognize it in ourselves.
>
> —Carlos Fuentes

As teachers and students of literature, we believe that one of the most effective ways to understand peoples of other cultures, creeds, and races is through language; a person's words are the windows through which we gain access to his or her world. In this anthology, we invite you to travel with us to worlds beyond your own, to engage in a conversation among cultures, to explore unfamiliar traditions, and to evaluate human relationships in an attempt to understand better the meanings of community in our own pluralistic society and the multicultural society of the twenty-first century.

We hope that as you listen to these voices, past and present, you will feel compelled to enter the conversation, to add your own voice and your own words. You will soon realize that literature will provide you with one of the most stimulating channels to enrich your sense of self, expand your creative power, question your own assumptions about the world, and challenge you to become an active member of your society. In brief, by fostering your encounter with the human condition, the study of literature will help you grow as a student and as a human being. As you engage in dialogue with the selections, both in writing and in discussion with your fellow students, you will experiment with new ways of looking at yourself and enlarging the windows from which you view the world. The journey we invite you to share will be challenging—many of the voices that you will encounter, both classical and contemporary, respond to the human capacity for learning and transmitting knowledge to succeeding generations through language and abstract thought and to the way different cultures assimilate while retaining their separate identities.

In Part One, "Roots and Rebellions," you will encounter many cultural variations: the oral traditions and affinity with the worlds of nature and the spirit of Native Americans; the love of language, family, and ethnic pride of Hispanic Americans; the emphasis on ancestors, kinship, and music in the literature of African Americans; the generational affiliations and conflicts of Asian Americans; the fierceness of familial and cultural loyalties among Italian Americans. Many of the younger writers in Part One focus also on their rebellions, which are caused by the complexities of the transitions implicit in being second or third generation, including the ramifications of the immigrant experience, bilingualism, acculturation, ethnic identity, dislocation, and parental expectations.

In Part Two, "Gender and Identity," you will be invited to examine traditional cross-cultural concepts of masculinity and femininity and to evaluate the degree to which they have affected both men and women in their individual quests for identity. Some of the voices will ask you whether gender conflicts should be confronted or avoided; others will challenge your preconceptions about sexual preference, including your views on expanding your concept of marriage to include same-sex partnerships. The focus of Part Two is to pose possibilities for freeing both sexes from the confines of traditional roles, so that men and women may become more dynamic and fulfilled selves.

In Part Three, "War and Violence," you will be asked to think about the similarities and differences between these issues, particularly because the tragic events of 9/11 have brought the violence of terrorism closer to home for millions of people throughout the world. You will also evaluate older heroic myths of war and violence from other cultures, as well as newer sensibilities advocating compromise as the desirable outcome of political conflict. You may also debate on the misuses of power in a global, pluralistic society. Primarily, you will be asked to consider whether the recognition of our shared humanity will ever enable us to look beyond war and violence to peace.

In Part Four, "Race and Culture," you will be asked to participate in what Henry Louis Gates Jr. calls "a conversation among different voices" and to reexamine many of the racial and cultural stereotypes with which we have all grown up. Some of these voices from diverse ethnic groups will invite you to share the anguish and anger of exclusion; others will challenge your preconceptions about social class, racial and cultural differences, and monolingualism, and still others will ask whether conversations on these issues should be silenced or articulated, respected or shunned. Carlos Fuentes reminds us that embracing multiculturalism involves a choice: "To be with others or to be alone? Isolation means death. Encounter means birth, even rebirth."

In Part Five, "Individualism and Community," you will confront the conflict, experienced in every culture, between the needs and desires of our individual selves and the needs and desires of the community. Many voices in this part debate the issue of individual freedom versus social responsibility; others advocate that solo voices join in the discord and harmony of the human chorus.

The fifth edition of *Literature Across Cultures* also provides you with new features, such as Performance Exercises and Film Angles, that will enrich your enjoyment of literature and help you make connections between literature and the dramatic and cinematographic arts.

Finally, we invite you to think of yourself as joining a community of readers and writers, in which you and your fellow students will become engaged in what we call "reading and writing as a social act." As you converse with the voices in this anthology, both old and new, you will travel into unchartered territories—into real and imagined worlds where many of the familiar guideposts will no longer apply. And a vital part of this process will be the different kinds of writing you will produce by yourself and with your peers, as you respond personally and analytically to the issues raised by the writers of the various texts. Being part of the global village of the twenty-first century requires that your generation sharpen its definition of an educated person. By adding your voice to these cultural conversations, you will begin that process, perhaps leaving the familiar in favor of the unfamiliar.

Sheena Gillespie
Tony Pipolo
Terezinha Fonseca

Reading and Writing as a Social Act

Why do writers read and write? Emily Dickinson, a nineteenth-century poet, viewed reading as a means of traveling to far-off places: "There is no Frigate like a Book." Jorge Luis Borges (1899–1986), a twentieth-century Latin American novelist, thought of reading as a way of revitalizing the self: "I have always come to life after coming to books." African American writer Toni Morrison (1931–), a Nobel Prize–winning author, believes in the power of narrative to help us understand ourselves and others: "Narrative is radical, creating us at the very moment it is being created." Morrison is particularly concerned that the writer's words and stories be the windows through which both writer and reader gain knowledge not only of the self, but also of the self in relation to people of other ethnic groups and cultures. In other words, writers write to be read; they write for you, their audience. They communicate their insights to you in the hope that you will recognize aspects of your own thoughts and experiences in their essays and stories.

Although many students express skepticism about finding meanings in the literature of the past, most acknowledge readily that human beings throughout history have had experiences in common. According to the novelist Albert Camus (1913–1960), "Every great work of art makes the human face more admirable and richer." His suggestion is that as we share in reading of the sufferings and joys of others, we better understand our own. The novelist James Baldwin (1924–1987) also reminds us of the continuity of human experiences in his short story "Sonny's Blues":

> For while the tale of how we suffer, and how we are delighted, and how we may triumph is never new, it always must be heard. There isn't any other tale to tell. It's the only light we've got in all this darkness.

We invite you to approach the reading of the texts in this anthology from the vantage points suggested by Camus and Baldwin. Perhaps thinking about fiction, poetry, and drama as expressions of human suffering, delight, and triumph will make it possible for you to understand Medea's anger at being abandoned by her husband in favor of a younger woman; to empathize with Hamlet's attempt to find his real identity; and to share in the triumph of a contemporary Puerto Rican housewife's daring choice to reclaim her ethnic heritage. You might even discover something about yourself. As the novelist Toni Morrison reminds us, interacting with literature is a dynamic process engaging both reader and writer: "The imagination that produces work which bears and invites rereading, which points to future readings as well as contemporary ones, implies a shareable world and an especially flexible language. Readers and writers both struggle to interpret and perform within a common language shareable imaginative worlds."

THE MEANING OF LITERATURE

What is literature? Traditionally set apart from other kinds of discourse, literature has been defined by the *Webster's Universal Unabridged Dictionary* as "all writings in prose or verse, especially those of an imaginative or critical character." Although this definition, like many others, has proved to be incomplete, it does highlight the presence of two major features of literature: its language and its imaginative character. When combined, these two elements produce a fictional world that reflects and evokes reality.

One story in this anthology can be used to illustrate this power of literature. The introduction to "The Sniper" transports us, not to the real world of urban guerrillas in Dublin, but to the fictional atmosphere of a Dublin that Liam O'Flaherty especially recreated as a unique literary experience:

> The long June twilight faded into night, Dublin lay enveloped in darkness but for the dim light of the moon that shone through fleecy clouds, casting a pale light as of approaching dawn over the streets and the dark waters of the Liffey. Around the beleaguered Four Courts the heavy guns roared. Here and there through the city, machine-guns and rifles broke the silence of the night, spasmodically, like dogs barking on lone farms. Republicans and Free Staters were waging civil war.
> —"The Sniper"

Although O'Flaherty might have modeled his portrayal of Dublin on a factual description of this Irish city caught in the civil war between the Republicans and Free Staters, his city, in strictly literary terms, is fictional. His text articulates imaginatively and creatively the significance of an actual historical event.

In O'Flaherty's text, atmosphere and imagery provide insights into events that we have not experienced directly. Characterization is another way literature can broaden our experience. You will observe, in other texts in this volume, how characters such as Antigone, Hamlet, Eveline, and Roselily have dramatized across the centuries some of the most terrifying and stimulating possibilities of human experience. In this sense, literature can be defined as the enactment of human possibilities, or as a vehicle that will help us to discover more about ourselves and the meaning we can make of life. For the French philosopher Jean-Paul Sartre (1905–1980), the function of literature is to search for the meaning of life and to speculate about the role of human beings in the world.

Perhaps the best way to define literature is in practice, encountering the literary experience face-to-face through the readings in this anthology. In the process, you may notice that a literary work leads you to encounter not one precise, correct reading but a range of meanings evoked by the interaction of the text with your own experience as a reader. For instance, *Hamlet*, a work that is widely discussed from different critical perspectives, illustrates the variety of meanings that Shakespeare's readers have produced in the process of interpreting this play. In fact, one appendix in this anthology is devoted to exploring some of these various critical approaches and responses, including psychoanalytic, formalist, reader-response, feminist, and New Historical (see Appendix D, "Critical Approaches: A Case Study of *Hamlet*.").

THE FUNCTION OF LITERATURE

Following the literary tradition that the Latin poet Horace (65–8 B.C.) established for poetry, some scholars emphasize "to instruct" or "to delight," or both, as the major functions of literature. Recent scholarly opinion indicates that another function of literature is to actively shape our culture. For example, some literary historians believe that human beings learned how to cultivate a romantic idea of love only after reading works of literature that portrayed love in this light rather than as a social or sexual arrangement between a man and a woman. Both ancient and modern approaches emphasize two of literature's major functions: to construct and articulate sociocultural realities and to involve you as the reader in an invigorating interaction with these realities.

When you address the questions we formulate under "Cultural Contexts" in this anthology, you will be asked to interact with your classmates, to take sides, to make decisions, and to add your voice to various cultural and political issues related to class, race, gender, war, and violence.

Compare, for example, the responses of two contemporary American poets on their visits to the Vietnam War Memorial in Washington, D.C. Jeffrey Harrison writes, "As we touch the name the stone absorbs our grief./ It takes us in—we see ourselves inside it." For Yusef Komunyakaa, a Vietnam veteran, the experience brings angry tears. "I said I wouldn't,/ dammit:/ No tears/ I'm stone. I'm flesh." By presenting such viewpoints, literature can empower us—it can promote our active engagement with the world through our encounters with the poems' disclosure of the reality and effects of violence caused by war. Thus literature can fulfill a major cultural function in society.

"Why read literature?" is a question many instructors pose during the first session of an introduction to literature class. Because we have found student journal entries to be excellent catalysts for exploring this topic, we thought you would find it interesting to compare your journal responses to "Why read literature?" with an excerpt from a journal entry by one of our students, Yoon A. Choi.

Reading helps me escape the mundane and my sense of normalcy. It makes me strong and weak, spiteful and remorseful. Books can comprehensively illustrate the complex nature of human relationships and the plight of the human condition, survival, pain and sufferings, sacrifices, and the fight for justice. Reading opens my eyes to the beauty and expression of thoughts into words. It makes me wonder about the important things in life. Books awaken my inner spirit and intellect. I also feel that reading improves my writing skills. The more I read, the more I become familiarized with new vocabularies and writing strategies. I believe that reading can make you a better person.

Reread your journal entry and Yoon A. Choi's, and highlight similarities and differences in your responses. What did you find most provocative about Yoon's ideas on reading? What did you identify with or disagree with in what she wrote? What kind of conversation can you imagine having with Yoon? What new thoughts about reading and its relationship to writing emerged from this assignment?

Now imagine yourself as a writer reading Yoon's and your journal entries. How might you respond? Remember that writers create for audiences because they wish to share their thoughts and emotions with potential readers and establish a relationship with them.

In an interview about her novel *Jazz*, Toni Morrison described *Jazz* as a "talking book," in which the writer talks to you as the reader. Most writers also leave "space" for readers to enter the conversation by bringing their own experiences, ideas, and points of view to the texts. Responding to a student who sent Steinbeck a paper on Steinbeck's novel *The Grapes of Wrath*, the author wrote that the purpose of a book is to "amuse, interest, instruct but its warmer purpose is just to associate with the reader. . . . The circle is not closed until the trinity is present—the writer, the book, and his reader." Although Steinbeck was referring specifically to novels, his words point out an essential similarity between literary texts in general and other kinds of writing; a short story or a novel, a poem or a play is incomplete until a reader makes it his or her own.

But Steinbeck's substitution of book for subject also suggests a significant difference between literary and other kinds of writing. The primary purpose of a storyteller or a poet is to close the circle, to intensify the sense of association between writer and reader through their shared experience of the written word. Whatever the subject matter of a story or poem or play, what draws the writer and reader together is the story itself.

One reason for writing about literature is to participate more actively in this "warmer" association. You as a reader will probably not close the circle with an author this directly, but you might broaden the circle by sharing your understanding of a book with other readers and so building a sense of community between the writer, the text, and other readers, including your classmates.

There are other reasons for writing about literature. Scholars write about literary texts to explore the insights they offer into the history, culture, and values of the people who produced them. Critics write to inform readers of new developments in literature and to measure these developments against the literature of the past.

Students are often asked to write about literary texts because such writing helps them develop into more active readers of all kinds of texts, both literary and nonliterary. When you read as well as when you write, you compose meaning out of your perceptions and knowledge of the world around you. Writing about literature is a particularly effective way of fine-tuning this skill because literary texts have no overt point to make, no stated thesis to explain, no explicit argument to develop. Because stories are told and poems are sung, in this sense for their own sake, such writing invites—indeed, requires—a reader's interpretations more obviously than expository prose. When you summarize the thesis of an essay, you clarify the essay's meaning. But a summary of a short story is only a retelling of the story's plot; what the story means, finally, depends on the reader's point of view and the judgments it leads him or her to make about the story.

Reading and writing about literature is indeed a social act, and as you continue, as a member of a community of readers and writers, to explore the meanings that a story, poem, or play holds for you, you will share your understanding of the text with others who have read it, including your instructor and your peers.

STRATEGIES FOR READING LITERATURE

Think of yourself as an active reader beginning a conversation between you and the writer who has created a literary text such as a short story for you—his or her audience. Reading and analyzing a short story with the intent of writing about it is something you are already familiar with from high school. You are aware that studying literature requires a particularly alert response from a reader. In a short story, every word or sentence seems to play a vital role in the unfolding of the characters' lives or the development of the narrative of events. The reader must approach the text of a story with a kind of Janus mask—looking behind and ahead at the same time, trying to establish some pattern or meaning or significance that will make the story coherent to you and to other readers.

Previewing

Before you read a text, preview it by asking yourself questions and looking for clues provided by the author. Here are some examples:

- What does the title suggest?
- Have I heard of this author before?

While reading the text, keeping the following questions in mind and trying to answer them as you read will help to give you better insight into the story:

- Does my anthology provide any information about the text and the author?
- What point of view does the author use?
- What is his or her purpose?

- How important is setting and chronology?
- What clues does the author provide to define theme through symbols, imagery, dialogue, and tone?

Highlighting

Read the text carefully, and highlight or underline the sections that particularly strike you about the author's style, structure, ideas, characterization, or any other key feature you have observed as a reader. Notice, for example, that in the following passage from James Joyce's short story "Eveline," the repetition of the verb form "used to" (here highlighted in bold type) indicates repeated action in the past. What does identifying such a pattern suggest about Eveline's relationship to the past? What do you infer about her psychological ability to accept change in the future?

> One time there **used to** be a field there in which they **used to** play every evening with other people's children. Then a man from Belfast bought the field and built houses in it—not like the little brown houses but bright brick houses with shining roofs. The children of the avenue **used to** play together in that field—the Devines, the Waters, the Dunns, little Keogh the cripple, she and her brothers and sisters. Ernest, however, never played: he was too grown up. Her father **used** often **to** hunt them in out of the field with his blackthorn stick; but **usually** little Keogh **used to** keep *nix* and call out when he saw her father coming. Still they seemed to have been rather happy then . . .

Annotating

Annotating means making marginal notes on the book's pages or using a pad or note cards. Once you reach this phase, you are also involved in the critical process of selecting and summarizing. After a second and third reading, your notes will eventually lead you to respond to the literary and cultural impact of the text by identifying its words, imagery, and themes. Responding actively to the text therefore becomes a challenge for you as a reader because you will interact with it and define its meanings on the basis of both the factual evidence that you find there and your own insights and experiences.

The following guided reading of Kate Chopin's "The Story of an Hour" should help you to understand what we mean by interaction between the reader and the text. After previewing, highlighting, and annotating the text, you might consider approaching your analysis of the "Textual Considerations" of "The Story of an Hour" as a detective trying to solve a crime. Arm yourself with a dictionary and thesaurus, and be on the alert for the many textual hints and clues that the writer has supplied for you. Pay close attention to the text, including the words we have highlighted in bold type, by examining how the author uses nouns, adjectives, images, and symbols to construct plot and to build characterization.

GUIDED READING

Kate Chopin (1851-1904) The Story of an Hour

"The Story of an Hour"

1. Knowing that **Mrs. Mallard** was afflicted with a heart trouble, great care was taken to break to her as gently as possible the news of her husband's death.

2. It was her sister Josephine who told her, in broken sentences, veiled hints that revealed in half concealing. Her husband's friend Richards was there, too, near her. It was he who had been in the newspaper office when intelligence of the railroad disaster was received, with Brently Mallard's name leading the list of "killed." He had only taken the time to assure himself of its truth by a second telegram, and had hastened to forestall any less careful, less tender friend in bearing the sad message.

3. She did not hear the story as many women have heard the same, with a paralyzed inability to accept its significance. She wept at once, with sudden, **wild abandonment**, in her sister's arms. When the storm of grief had spent itself she went to her room alone. She would have no one follow her.

4. There stood, facing the open window, a comfortable, roomy armchair. Into this she sank, pressed down by a physical exhaustion that haunted her body and seemed to reach into her soul.

Textual Considerations

■ *What kinds of expectations does the opening paragraph raise in the reader about the protagonist and the plot of the story? Have you noticed that the protagonist is addressed as Mrs. Mallard and that the starting point of the story is "the news of her husband's death"?*

■ *Respond to Josephine's and Richards's attitude about breaking the news to Mrs. Mallard.*

■ *Focus on paragraph 3. What does the phrase "wild abandonment" suggest? Are you surprised by Mrs. Mallard's insistence on being left alone after hearing such bad news? Explain.*

■ *What examples do you find of images of freedom and repression in paragraphs 4 and 5? Comment on these examples.*

5. She could see in the open square before her house the **tops of trees that were all aquiver with the new spring life. The delicious breath of rain was in the air**. In the street below a peddler was crying his wares. The notes of a distant song which some one was singing reached her faintly, and countless sparrows were twittering in the eaves.

6. There were patches of blue sky showing here and there through the clouds that had met and piled above the other in the west facing her window.

7. She sat with her head thrown back upon the cushion of the chair quite motionless, except when a sob came up into her throat and shook her, as a child who has cried itself to sleep continues to sob in its dreams.

8. She was **young**, with a **fair**, calm face, whose **lines bespoke repression** and even a certain strength. But now there was a dull stare in her eyes, whose gaze was fixed away off yonder on one of those patches of blue sky. It was not a **glance of reflection**, but rather indicated a **suspension of intelligent thought**.

9. There was **something coming to her** and she was waiting for it, fearfully. What was it? She did not know; it was too subtle and elusive to name. But she felt it, creeping out of the sky, reaching toward her through the sounds, the scents, the color that filled the air.

10. Now her bosom rose and fell tumultuously. She was beginning to recognize this thing that was approaching to possess her, and she was striving to beat it back with her will—as powerless as her two white slender hands would have been.

■ *Writers frequently use nature to open a symbolic level for the text. What is unusual about the text's emphasis on spring, given the events of the story thus far? What other aspects of nature emerge in paragraphs 5 and 6? What do they suggest about Mrs. Mallard's state of mind? What kind of expectations do they raise in the reader?*

■ *Characterize your response to paragraphs 7 and 8.*

■ *What new aspects of Mrs. Mallard's personality occur in paragraph 8? To what might "the lines of repression" be attributable? Consider the difference between a "glance of reflection" and a "suspension of intelligent thought."*

■ *What dramatic pattern is the text shaping in terms of plot (events, to rising action), characterization (Mrs. Mallard's reaction), and your own response as a reader? Focus on paragraphs 9 and 10.*

11. When she abandoned herself a little word escaped her **slightly parted lips**. She said it over and over under her breath: "**Free**, free, free!" **The vacant stare** and the look of terror that had followed it went from her eyes. They stayed keen and bright. Her **pulses beat fast**, and the coursing **blood warmed** and relaxed every inch of her body.

■ *What does "the vacant stare" suggest? What does "the look of terror" convey? Contrast the descriptions of Mrs. Mallard's bodily responses in paragraphs 4 and 11. To what extent are these physical and psychological reversals gender based (characteristic of women more than men)?*

12. She did not stop to ask if it were not a **monstrous** joy that held her. A clear and exalted perception enabled her to dismiss the suggestion as trivial.

■ *Check your thesaurus for various connotations of "monstrous." Speculate about Chopin's description of Mrs. Mallard's joy as "monstrous" in paragraph 12.*

13. She knew that she would weep again when she saw the kind tender hands folded in death; the face that had never looked save with love upon her, fixed and gray and dead. But she saw beyond that **bitter moment a long procession of years to come** that would belong to her absolutely. And she opened and spread her arms out to them in welcome.

■ *Notice how Mrs. Mallard contrasts the "bitter moment" of the present with "a long procession of years to come." To what extent does this contrast suggest her desire to rewrite her personal history? To what extent does the world of closed windows and fixed gender identities versus the evocations of freedom and self-discovery create narrative suspense?*

14. There would be no one to live for during those coming years: **she would live for herself. There would be no powerful will bending her in** that blind persistence with which men and women believe they have a right to impose a private will upon a fellow-creature. A kind intention or a cruel intention made the act seem no less a crime as she looked upon it in that brief moment of illumination.

■ *Does Mrs. Mallard surprise you with her realistic portrait of male and female relations? What does this moment of illumination amount to?*

15. And yet she had loved him— sometimes. Often she had not. What did it matter! What could love, the unsolved mystery, count for in face of this possession of self-assertion which she suddenly recognized as the strongest impulse of her being!

■ *To what extent do you empathize with Mrs. Mallard's desire for autonomy and psychological space?*

16. "Free! Body and soul free!" she kept whispering.

17. Josephine was kneeling before the closed door with her lips to the keyhole, imploring for admission. "**Louise**, open the door! I beg; open the door—you will make yourself ill. What are you doing, Louise? For heaven's sake open the door."

18. "Go away. I am not making myself ill." No; she was drinking in the very elixir of life through that open window.

19. Her fancy was running riot along **those days ahead of her**. Spring days, and summer days, and all sorts of days that would be her own. She breathed a quick prayer that life might be long. It was only **yesterday she** had thought with a shudder that life might be long.

20. She arose at length and opened the door to her sister's importunities. There was a feverish triumph in her eyes, and she carried herself unwittingly like a goddess of Victory. She clasped her sister's waist, and together they descended the stairs. Richards stood waiting for them at the bottom.

21. Some one was opening the front door with a **latchkey**. It was Brently Mallard who entered, a little travel-stained, composedly carrying his **gripsack** and **umbrella**. He had been far from the scene of the accident, and did not even know there had been one. He stood amazed at Josephine's piercing cry: at Richards's quick motion to screen him from the view of his **wife**. But Richards was too late.

22. When the doctors came they said that she had died of heart disease—**of joy that kills**.

■ *How do you characterize Mrs. Mallard's emotional outburst?*

■ *Explain why Chopin withholds the protagonist's first name until paragraph 17.*

■ *Identify the two voices that interact in this paragraph.*

■ *React to the way the text juxtaposes the repression of the past and the possibilities of the future. Such a pattern culminates in paragraph 20 in the image that Mrs. Mallard "carried herself unwittingly like a goddess of Victory." To what extent does Chopin suggest that Mrs. Mallard's triumph will be transitory?*

■ *Read this paragraph carefully. Comment on the images of "latchkey," "gripsack," and "umbrella." What significance do you attach to Louise being referred to as "his wife"? To what extent does Richard's inability to protect Mrs. Mallard destabilize the action of the story? What kind of suspense or expectation does this paragraph create in the reader?*

■ *How do you account for the ironic turn of the last sentence? Is it appropriate that the doctors misread the true cause of Mrs. Mallard's death? Explain.*

Read "The Story of an Hour" again at least twice. More ideas will no doubt surface at each new reading, and you will react to more details concerning the arrangement of the events, Mrs. Mallard's reactions and expectations, and your own ability as a reader to produce more meanings in response to the text. As you deepen your understanding of the story, you will also become more aware of its cultural implications. To assist your interaction with the cultural possibilities of Chopin's text, you may discuss gender-related questions such as the ones listed in the following "Cultural Contexts."

1. To what extent does "The Story of an Hour" reflect a feminist outlook on the roles of women? What evidence is there that the story is told from the perspective of a female narrator?
2. Consider what the text reveals about marriage as an institution. Is the concept of marriage that Chopin's text explores still applicable to contemporary gender relations?
3. Are men and women today more liberated than they were a century ago? Discuss the differences you see between then and now in their socially defined roles and "fixed gender identities" (identities determined by gender and social roles).

The following are some literature students' responses to the two literary and cultural topics listed below.

1. Respond to Kate Chopin's use of nature imagery in "The Story of an Hour."
2. React to the new meanings "The Story of an Hour" evokes as you think about the issues of gender and identity. Does this text reaffirm traditional ideas about gender relations, or does it provoke readers to discover different truths about gender relations?

In their responses to topic 1, Chopin's use of nature imagery, the students previewed, highlighted, and annotated the text before they outlined how Chopin's suggestive use of imagery communicates Mrs. Mallard's new expectations about her future:

> Kate Chopin uses a great deal of imagery in "The Story of an Hour." Her description of "the tops of trees that were all aquiver with the new spring life" in paragraph 5 is a good example of her use of a nature image to communicate Mrs. Mallard's new feeling toward life, blooming, and rebirth.
>
> In paragraph 8, the image of "those patches of blue sky," showing that even though the dominant color of the sky might be gray it possesses "patches of blue," suggests that the color blue is also an indicator of new spring life. In spring the color of the sky is blue. However, it is important to realize that Chopin's reference to the clouds can function as a fore- shadowing, indicating that the blue sky is as far off as Mrs. Mallard's expectations of freedom.
>
> —Danielle Lucas

Kate Chopin's reference to "the new spring life," "the notes of a distant song," "the delicious breath of rain," and "sparrows twittering" obviously suggests how Mrs. Mallard begins to respond to life. She is born again like new spring life, and she is ready to take in a new clean breath like "the delicious breath of rain." Her aspiration is to live her own life like the sparrow who is free to fly. Chopin uses the "patches of blue sky . . . through the clouds" as an image of a clearing in Mrs. Mallard's life. Gone is the husband with his "powerful will bending her in." There is a clearing of "blue sky" for her.

Chopin says that Mrs. Mallard drinks in the very "elixir of life through the open window." Such an image supports the idea that Chopin uses nature imagery to show the freedom that Mrs. Mallard has now acquired.

—Mary Ellen Hogan

Two other students, Mike Lonergan and Robert Longstreet, also covered the preliminary reading strategies before they analyzed the issue of gender and identity as part of the larger cultural network Chopin's text evokes:

"The Story of an Hour" by Kate Chopin reaffirms traditional ideas about gender relations with a riptide that illuminates the reader.

Mr. and Mrs. Mallard portray a typical married couple of the late 1800s. Brently Mallard, the husband, is the head of the household, while Louise Mallard, his wife, is his possession. To quote Emily Dickinson, Louise "rose to his requirement . . . to take the honorable work of women, and of wife" (Poem 172).

Like a typical wife of this era, Mrs. Mallard was supposed to obey her husband without any rebukes. Knowing nothing different, Mrs. Mallard accepted these social norms of her time.

However, Chopin's "The Story of an Hour" reveals the aged wrinkle in this status quo arrangement by showing how, subconsciously, Mrs. Mallard's inner self and soul were being repressed and sentenced to death by lack of use.

—Mike Lonergan

"The Story of an Hour" is not a story that reaffirms traditional ideas about gender relations. In fact, Kate Chopin's text does just the opposite. It shows that no matter what your gender is, you should never lose your identity. The story suggests that instead of ignoring the restrictions of gender relations or hiding from them, you should try to eliminate them.

—Robert Longstreet

Notice that the following texts also focus on perceptive and provocative peer group discussions of "The Story of an Hour." Read each response carefully, and in your reading journal write a summary comparing and contrasting the points that were raised. Did your group agree or disagree, for example, with group 1's equating marriage with the loss of individual identity, or group 2's disagreement with the doctors' interpretation that Louise dies of sadness?

You will notice that group 3 focuses on Chopin's treatment of time in the story. Although the actual events take place within a time frame of sixty minutes, the students compare and contrast the past, present, and future of Mrs. Mallard's life. They juxtapose the weight of time that Mrs. Mallard experienced while her husband was alive with the anticipation of freedom that characterized her response to his death. What point was Chopin trying to make about chronological and psychological time? What new meanings about time emerged from your group's discussion? What are your own thoughts about time?

Group 4, in contrast concludes that both Mr. and Mrs. Mallard were victims of their historical time period, when great emphasis was placed on the traditional roles expected of husbands and wives. They raise the important issue of chronology pertinent to this particular text, as Chopin wrote at a time when the "woman question" was being widely debated by male and female writers in the United States and Europe. To what extent do current gender relationships focus more on individual identity and the "space" necessary to create it? Is conforming to traditional gender roles less prevalent in contemporary relationships? What new ideas emerged from reading the group responses and discussions with your own peers?

> The Mallards' marriage is the marriage of two to make up one. In fact, their marriage can be represented as A + B = C. As in the chemical reaction necessary to human survival, wherein a molecule of glucose must give up a portion of itself to become a part of a larger molecule (dehydration synthesis), so it is in marriage. One part of the self must be given up to form the sacred union of marriage. It is an unfortunate circumstance of marriage that identity and the self must be its sacrificial lamb.
>
> Our group concluded that it is not possible to have a "successful" marriage without some loss of self. Mr. and Mrs. Mallard have just such a marriage: a "successful" one.
>
> —Recorded by Karen Digirolano

> Mr. Mallard was a typical husband, who never thought twice about his wife's thoughts or wishes. Neither did he think about the imposition of his own will over hers. Their marriage seemed a typical one. Mrs. Mallard, in fact, even "loved him—sometimes." For all intents and purposes, Mrs. Mallard seemed to have been a dutiful wife.
>
> When informed of the news that her husband was dead, she acted as any woman would at her loss. However, when alone in her room, Mrs. Mallard came to know a feeling foreign to her: "There would be no one to live for during those coming years: she would live for herself. There would be no powerful will bending her in." She found herself looking forward to "those days ahead of her" which would truly be hers and no one else's. She even "spread her arms out to them in welcome."

The doctors were wrong when they said that Mrs. Mallard died of "the joy that kills." The shock to her weak heart was of sadness. When she saw her husband, she realized that her freedom was lost—once again.

—Recorded by Rina Russo

When Mrs. Mallard moves away from the past and the present to think of the days ahead in the future, she is obviously elated. She prays to live a long life, whereas before her husband died she had prayed for a short one. Mrs. Mallard's first reactions show us that when her husband was alive, she had no optimistic outlook on the future. She only wanted to die.

After his death, she drinks from the elixir of the open window, or from all the freedom (the birds, the trees, and the blue sky) that she witnesses outside. Through all these revelations, we can see how Mrs. Mallard evaluates her life in the past, present, and future.

—Recorded by Mary Ellen Hogan

We got the impression that even though Mrs. Mallard had an identity of her own, she was above all Mr. Mallard's wife. Thus, it was their nineteenth-century marriage that held Mrs. Mallard back from being the individual she really was: "She was young with a calm face whose lines bespoke repression."

Our group concluded that Mr. Mallard, like most husbands of his time, did not know how his wife felt. He probably thought he was a good husband to his wife. In fact, she sometimes loved him and "she knew that she would weep again when she saw the kind, tender hands folded in death." Our conclusion is that Mr. and Mrs. Mallard both were victims of the time they lived in.

—Recorded by Damien Donohue

STRATEGIES FOR WRITING ABOUT LITERATURE

We move now from reading as a social act to writing as a social act in order to consider various strategies for enhancing interactions between you as an individual writer and your peer group. Your goal is to incorporate what you learned as an active reader and apply it to this new task of writing an essay on the meaning or significance that a short story holds for you by demonstrating how and why you arrived at your understanding of this text.

As a way of showing the many ways a writer may respond to a story and the different perspectives a reader many bring to a text, we explore various approaches to arranging, writing, and revising a literary analysis. As an illustration, we examine "The Unforgetting," by Lan Samantha Chang—a contemporary Chinese American writer—in Part One, "Roots and Rebellions."

Before we begin our discussion of writing as a social act, we want to review a number of central concepts related to reading and writing literature critically. Writers who explain both what a story means to them and how their point of view reflects particular elements in their frame of reference offer their audience the opportunity to understand their interpretations in the broadest possible contexts. At the same time, they establish a unique bridge with their audience. By inviting their readers to look at the story from one particular angle, such writers acknowledge that there are other equally valid vantage points and other plausible interpretations of a text. As you develop your ideas about a particular text, try to add some information about the perspective (or perspectives) you are bringing to bear on the story. Analyze not only the details of the story but consider the elements of your frame of reference, which may have had an effect on how you saw or understood these details. Acknowledging your frame of reference is also an effective way to communicate to your audience the possibilities for creating multiple meanings and accepting interpretations that may differ from their own.

FRAMES OF REFERENCE

As a prelude to our exploration of the various stages involved in the writing process, let us review the various frames of reference you brought to your reading of "The Story of an Hour" and to your evaluations of the comments from the four peer groups.

Factors that influence how you read a particular work include your personal perspective (comprising your family background and your individual life experiences), your social perspective (including your ethnicity, social class, and work experiences), your cultural perspective (your previous reading experiences, education, and religion, as well as your knowledge of the media and other aspects of popular culture), and your literary perspective (the result of your study of literary elements, including techniques, structures, and literary traditions).

GENERATING IDEAS

Rather than just diving right in to writing a paper, first take your frames of reference into consideration, and then find ways to generate your own ideas about this particular story. Here are some ways to generate ideas:

- Freewriting in your journal about your initial responses to the text.
- Posing and answering questions about the story.
- Brainstorming on your own or with your peer group.
- Collecting evidence from the text—as you did in your reading of Chopin's short story—to support the ideas that you develop.

Your audience consists of other informed readers in the sense that they too have read the story, but their perspectives on what happens will, no doubt, differ from yours. Expressing your experience of the story leads to the production of multiple meanings. It is the discussion and realization of these multiple meanings that makes writing about literature such an important and valuable social act.

Other useful prewriting strategies are brainstorming and clustering.

Brainstorming

To brainstorm, simply list details of the story along with any questions or comments that may occur to you. You can do this on your own and then compare your list with those of your peer group. Or you can work with your group initially, with each member contributing to the list and commenting on it, playing off and reacting to the contributions of others.

Clustering

Clustering is a variation of brainstorming that has the added advantage of visually representing the relationships among the brainstormed ideas. You can cluster by yourself or in a group. To cluster on your own, review your brainstorming list and try clustering your observations and ideas. What shaping idea might they lead to in developing a thesis for your paper? What additional material might you need to illustrate and explain this shaping idea? In group clustering, the topic is written in the middle of the board, and as the group brainstorms, the ideas are clustered around it in related groups.

Remember that because you are a unique person and a unique writer, not all of these techniques will work for you. By giving each a serious try, however, you might discover a tool that will make you a more comfortable and effective writer. When you find a strategy that works, incorporate it into your writing process.

FINDING A THESIS

We asked Catherine Stolfi, one of our students, to write a description of her composing process, including how she found and formulated her thesis on the paper she wrote on "The Unforgetting."

> The way I go about choosing my topic is to first make a column listing the themes of the story. This may seem tedious, but it is well worth the effort. In doing this, I am not only listing the themes that most appeal to me but I am also beginning to write a portion of my essay. Then I try to list as many themes as possible, but most likely my top three themes are the best to choose from because they were the most engaging to me.
>
> Once I choose my topic, I jot down some more notes about it. As I do this, I also try to start thinking of a thesis statement. My thesis statement normally is an overall statement about the theme of my essay as a whole, usually on a controversial issue. From my extra notes, I pick the best two or three topics. These will be the main themes for the body paragraphs of my essay. Once I have my thesis statement, I keep it at the top of my sheet or computer screen.

Here is the brainstorming list she created to help formulate her thesis:

Being removed from your homeland
Maintaining a culture in a new land

Memories
The American Dream
Making sacrifices for your children
Father/son relationship
Generational conflicts
Learning a new language
Father interested in chemistry; son chose to major in history
Adapting to the food and popular culture of a new country
Parents' decision to forget the past to make assimilation easier for their son
Ironies of their choices

Thesis Statement

Many immigrants, to live the American Dream, leave the
traditions of their homeland culture behind, thus leaving
a part of themselves.

Review Catherine's brainstorming list with your group and try clustering the themes that she incorporated into her thesis statement. Remember that the thesis should state directly and clearly what the paper will be about. It should not be too narrow because it must encompass the scope of the writer's ideas. To what extent does Catherine's thesis meet these criteria? Which items on her brainstorming list would not make an effective thesis?

DEVELOPING A ROUGH DRAFT WITH PEER EDITING

Having created her thesis, Catherine describes her next steps in developing a rough draft:

I find the best thing to do is to have all my notes (and thesis statement) in front of me and then just start free-form writing. I keep my focus in mind the whole time. I write my introduction first, with the ideas of my body paragraphs in mind. The introduction is just a preparation for what I am to write in my body paragraphs. I write my body paragraphs one at a time, based on the two or three topics I wrote down in my notes.

Here is the first draft of Catherine's paper on "The Unforgetting." Read it over carefully with your group, keeping in mind that the framework of a critical paper is a narrative of your process of reading a story and responding to its details. It should include exposition in order to summarize, to explain, and to interpret parts of the story; to analyze their effect as you explore what meanings the story holds; and to draw some generalized conclusion about the results of your exploration.

Many immigrants, in order to live the American Dream,
leave the traditions of their homeland culture behind,

thus leaving a part of themselves. They usually make this kind of sacrifice in order to give their children a better chance to live a good American life. There are both good and bad repercussions to this decision. Is it worth losing the cultural traditions of your homeland and the memories of your past to better adapt to an American life? Perhaps an answer to this question can be found in "The Unforgetting," by Lan Samantha Chang. The loss of the language of the parents' homeland and the rejection of memories of the past is what leads to the complete loss of the parents' identities and the Americanization of their son, Charles.

In "The Unforgetting," by Lan Samantha Chang, the father, Ming, made many sacrifices for his son to live a good American life. His father, always glancing at his physics and chemistry handbook, gave up his dream of gaining a Ph.D. and becoming a scientist to work as a copy machine repair man. He did this for his son. His son began to excel in school, but not in math or science like he had hoped, but in history. The father had also forbid his wife and son to speak Chinese at home and encouraged his whole family to speak English at all times. By doing this, his son picked up the English language very well and it helped steer him toward his humanities interest. The father felt somewhat betrayed. He thought his son would carry on his legacy in the field of science. However, he truly adapted to the American culture, even being accepted into Harvard, the most famous of all American Ivy League schools. The parents were shocked to find out that their son was leaving them to pursue his own American dream. The father is in part to blame, though. He encouraged his whole family to leave their Chinese language behind and pursue the adoption of the American language, English.

Both parents, Ming and Sansan, denied the past of their lives in China. The mother, Sansan, would read stories of Chinese classics and romances but because they wanted the English language to be spoken more often than Chinese at home, she put them away. Since she stopped reading the stories, she describes how the stories slipped away from her. The narrator says, "The tales were pushed into a smaller and smaller part of her mind." Ming, also, constantly denied his past and never passed on the stories of his homeland because, as the title of the story tells, he felt it was better to forget China to live a better life here. He even avoided talking about China with other people, such as his co-workers. He denied his memories of his grandfather and Beijing, where he grew up and used to live. As the narrator says, "He replaced such useless memories with thoughts of Charles." However, how useless were these memories? As the story progresses, he drifts apart from his son because of the cultural barrier he puts up. His relationship with his wife also suffers because of their denial of their past. Ming and Sansan gave up so much of themselves for their son, but their son ends up completely embracing his life here in America.

Yet an amount of bitterness was gained toward their son. Instead of being proud of his achievements, they could only focus on how Americanized he had become. If only they hadn't denied their past, then he maybe would have grown up with an amount of appreciation for his culture while also embracing the great opportunities here in America.

The "American Dream" can sometimes be confused with the need to leave behind the old homeland in order to fully embrace a new one. The great thing about America that should be remembered, though, is that people from different countries have the freedom to practice their countries' traditions and maintain their culture while still embracing their new life in America.

By working with peer groups, Catherine was able to get a wide range of ideas and feedback, not only on her essay, but also on Lan Samantha Chang's story. Such is the advantage of working with peer groups. By sharing her essay with these groups, Catherine expressed and explained what she found most meaningful to her in "The Unforgetting." The groups reciprocated by giving Catherine their views on what she should emphasize in the story. Hence, both Catherine and her audience, the peer groups, were engaging in the important social act of creating and exchanging views on the multiple meanings found in Chang's work.

Peer Group Critiques

Group 1. Overall, this is a well-organized and clear essay. However, the student should be including more insight into the author's *purpose* for writing the story. She says in her introduction, for example, that "perhaps an answer to this question can be found." We think the author's purpose is not to answer a question but rather to help us understand the struggles of many immigrants. The student should include in the introduction and conclusion an overall feel of the story and its purpose.

Group 2. The student does not do enough with the meaning of the *title*, which is always an important clue that the author provides. She only mentions the title in paragraph three, when she talks about how the father avoided talking about the past with his co-workers.
She should delve a little deeper into the meaning of the title and its importance to the story, and especially to the parents.

Group 3. The student could include more about the *father/son* relationship. She needs to emphasize how the son was so distant from his father throughout the story and how his father didn't know how to handle his American independent child.
She should mention and analyze why Charles wants to go away to school and why, although he excelled in English, he hardly communicated with his father. She should explain why he even closed the door in his father's face during a conversation. If she mentions more examples like these, her paper should get an A.

Group 4. This student should remember to go outside the story. She could probably write an entire essay on the author's purpose behind the story. She could also improve the conclusion and mention other topics besides "the American Dream."

Group 5. This essay should discuss Chang's juxtaposition of Ming's and Sansan's desire to forget the past versus Charles's search to learn about the past. She should mention the irony found in the fact that although Ming and Sansan tried to forget their pasts for their son to be able to live a better life in the United States, their rejection of the past created a large rift in the family and, in part, drove their son to leave home for university.

A review of the five peer critiques illustrates how much can be learned from a community of active readers working collaboratively on an assignment. Look over the critiques again and highlight the comments you agree with. Is there anything else you would add to improve Catherine's first draft? Write a journal entry on what you found most useful about this process.

REVISING THE ROUGH DRAFT AND WRITING THE FINAL PAPER

After reviewing her peer critiques, Catherine realized that to incorporate all of their suggestions (most of which she agreed with) would involve extensive revision of her paper. Her initial response was to focus only on elaborating on the father-and-son conflict. A second reading of her paper and of her critiques, however, convinced her that taking into account more of the groups' comments would make her paper more comprehensive by including some of the different possible meanings "The Unforgetting" holds. Catherine decided to include four of the five critiques in her final paper. Although all were equally valid, she decided that including group 5's ideas would involve extensive explanation outside the main scope of her paper, causing her paper to lose focus.

Catherine decided that it might also be helpful to review the "Checklist for Revising Your Interpretative Essay" distributed by her professor before starting on her final draft. She responded to each question in her journal and made several changes in her first draft.

Checklist for Revising Your Interpretive Essay

1. How clearly did you establish a shaping idea or thesis?
2. Did you provide your readers with an adequate context for understanding the personal, social, cultural, or literary perspectives you brought to the story?
3. How effectively did you organize your interpretation of the story? Did you proceed logically from one element of the story to another or one thematic concern to another?
4. Do you think your interpretation makes a real contribution to your readers' understanding and appreciation of the story's meaning and value? How might you improve your interpretation of the story?
5. Were you able to relate your interpretation to some broader context or perspective as a way of showing the story's relevance or significance to a contemporary reader?
6. If you quoted from the story, does your quotation highlight some important point in the story that is vital to your interpretation?

Review the professor's checklist. Which questions do you find most interesting? Which do you think Catherine found most helpful?

The Final Draft

> Many immigrants, in order to live the American Dream,
> leave the traditions of their homeland culture behind,
> thus leaving a part of themselves. They usually make this

kind of sacrifice in order to give their children a better chance to live a good American life. There are both good and bad repercussions to this decision. Is it worth losing the cultural traditions of your homeland and the memories of your past to better adapt to an American life? In "The Unforgetting," the author of the story, Lan Samantha Chang, presents the experiences of two Chinese immigrants. The loss of the language of the parents' homeland and the rejection of memories of the past is what leads to the complete loss of the parents' identities and their Americanization of their son, Charles.

In "The Unforgetting," by Lan Samantha Chang, the father, Ming, makes many sacrifices for his son to live a good American life. His father, always glancing at his physics and chemistry handbook, gave up his dream of gaining a Ph.D and becoming a scientist to work as a copy machine repair man. He does this for his son. His son began to excel in school, but not in math or science like he had hoped, but in history. The father had also forbid his wife and son to speak Chinese at home and encouraged his whole family to speak English at all times. By doing this, his son picked up the English language very well and it helped steer him toward his humanities interest.

The father, however, feels somewhat betrayed. He thinks his son would carry on his legacy in the field of science. However, Charles adapts to the American culture and is even accepted into Harvard, the most famous of all American Ivy League schools. The parents are shocked to find out that their son is leaving them to pursue his own American Dream. The father is in part to blame, though. He encouraged his whole family to leave their Chinese language behind and pursue the adoption of the American language, English.

Both parents, Ming and Sansan, denied the past of their lives in China. The mother, Sansan, would read stories of Chinese classics and romances but because they wanted the English language to be spoken more often at home, she put them away. Since she stopped reading the stories, they slipped away from her. The narrator says,

"The tales were pushed into a smaller and smaller part of her mind." Ming, also, constantly denied his past and never passed on the stories of his homeland because, as the title of the story tells, he felt it was better to forget China in order to live a better life here. He even avoided talking about China with other people, such as his co-workers. As the story progresses, Ming drifts apart from his son because of the barrier he puts up. Charles was excelling in English at school yet he barely spoke to his father when he was home, and even closed the door of his room during a conversation with his father. His relationship with his wife also suffered because of the denial from the both of them of their past. Ming and Sansan give up so much of themselves for their son, and their son ends up completely embracing his life here in America. Yet, an amount of bitterness was gained towards their son. Instead of being proud of his achievements, they could only focus on how Americanized he had become. If only they hadn't denied their past, then maybe their son would have grown up with an amount of appreciation for his culture while also embracing the great opportunities here in America.

The title is very significant to the story. The parents try to forget their past but this seemed almost impossible. There are certain things, such as an embedded culture, that can't be forgotten, or "unforgotten." To deny your past is to also deny a part of yourself. The "American Dream" can also be confused with the need to leave behind the old homeland in order to fully embrace a new one. The great thing about America that should be remembered, though, is that people from different countries have the freedom to practice their countries' traditions and maintain their culture while still embracing their new life in America.

Read Catherine's revised essay carefully. How did she incorporate the comments and critiques offered by her peer groups? Did she do so effectively?

You are now ready to write your own paper on "The Unforgetting." You might find it helpful to know that the author included this story in a collection entitled *Hunger*.

You might also think about whether the generational conflicts in this story are attributable only to the immigrant experience or whether they are part of the normal process of growing up. In any case, it will be interesting to compare and contrast the emphases in your paper not only with Catherine's but with those of your peers. The different emphases illustrate how multiple meanings can be found by readers and writers working as a community, and they also demonstrate the value and effectiveness of reading and writing as a social act.

PART ONE

ROOTS AND REBELLIONS

Fiction

The Unforgetting, Lan Samantha Chang ◆ *Roman Fever*, Edith Wharton ◆
Father and I, Pär Lagerkvist ◆ *The Watch*, Elie Wiesel ◆ *Powder*, Tobias Wolff

Essays

The Nobel Lecture in Literature, Toni Morrison ◆ *The Allegory of the Cave*, Plato ◆
The Way to Rainy Mountain, N. Scott Momaday ◆ From *Imaginary Homelands*,
Salman Rushdie ◆ *I Get Born*, Zora Neale Hurston

Poetry

The Negro Speaks of Rivers, Langston Hughes ◆ *First Light*, Linda Hogan ◆
warm heart contains life, Evangelina Vigil-Piñón ◆ *Going Home*, Maurice
Kenny ◆ *Street Kid*, Duane Niatum ◆ *In the Tree House at Night*, James Dickey ◆
Mid-term Break, Seamus Heaney ◆ *The Possessive*, Sharon Olds ◆ *Breaking
Tradition*, Janice Mirikitani ◆ *Fern Hill*, Dylan Thomas ◆ *If I could only live
at the pitch that is near madness*, Richard Eberhart ◆ *My Grandmother's Hands*,
Maria Mazziotti Gillan ◆ *Beads*, James Geasor ◆ *Poem for My Father*, Eric
Chock ◆ *The Gift*, Li-Young Lee ◆ *Fishermen*, James A. Emanuel ◆ *Frederick
Douglass*, Robert Hayden ◆ *Tour 5*, Robert Hayden ◆ *Those Winter Sundays*,
Robert Hayden ◆ *Runagate Runagate*, Robert Hayden

Drama

Oedipus Rex, Sophocles ◆ *The Tragedy of Hamlet, Prince of Denmark*, William
Shakespeare

The artist's imagination has always been captivated by the idea of the past and its relationship with the present. Stories from oral traditions of ancient cultures as well as our own evoke the power and mysteries of the past by portraying a time in which myths, fables, legends, and archetypes dictated the values of human actions within the community. As the Filipino American writer Carlos Bulosan relates, "when they started singing Philippine songs their voices were so sad, so full of yesterday and the haunting presence of familiar seas. . . ."

The ritual of storytelling was an integral part of Native American life, too—connecting, as contemporary writer Simon Ortiz reminds us, the people, the land, and the stories. "If anything is most vital, essential, and absolutely important in native cultural philosophy, it is this concept of interdependence: the fact that without land there is no life, and without a responsible social and cultural outlook by humans, no life-sustaining land is possible." Thus, as tribal members from the oldest to the youngest listened to, received, or retold stories about creation, nature, good and evil, war and peace, and life and death, they reflected on the myths and rituals of their cultural past and their relevance to the present and the future.

Folklore also helps explain human relationships, hopes, fears, and dreams. Folktales and myths are not culturally or ethnically bound; people from all over the world use them to explain their cultures, religions, traditions, and social customs. Many of the Native American writers you will encounter in Part One cherish their roots. N. Scott Momaday, for example, in "The Way to Rainy Mountain" celebrates his tribal heritage by creating a tapestry in which he interweaves myth, history, and family stories, uniting them through the traditional journey motif that links the actual journey of his tribe, the Kiowas, and his own quest to discover his roots and identity, which he describes as "many journeys in one." In contrast, two contemporary Native American poets, Maurice Kenny and Duane Niatum, focus on their journeys of rejection and rebellion, which preceded their eventual acceptance of and pride in their ethnic heritage.

How can we understand the past? What can we learn from it? Why are memories so important to our private and communal selves? Zora Neale Hurston, through her extensive writings on folklore and anthropology, records a part of her African American culture that interested very few of her literary contemporaries—the language, religion, life, and spirit of ordinary people immersed in the richness of the oral tradition and folklore. In "I Get Born," an excerpt from her autobiography, she fuses memory, folk, and imagination to create a vivid and humorous account of her birth that includes an analysis and dramatization of her father's reaction to the event.

Lan Samantha Chang, in contrast, captures the precarious balances between remembering and forgetting as an essential part of the immigrant experience, as well as the gains and losses of the Diaspora. In her short story "The Unforgetting," her protagonists decide that repressing their unpleasant memories of their native China is necessary for their family's survival in the United States. Ironically, this choice, intended to expedite and assure the assimilation of their only son, causes generational conflicts, rebellion, and ultimately rejection.

Other writers in Part One begin with what Toni Morrison calls "sites of memory"—places that have affected these writers' lives because of the emotional, intellectual, or sensory associations with them. Contemporary Indian writer Salman Rushdie, now residing in the United States, refers in his "Imaginary Homelands" to his native Bombay as a city in which "the past is home, albeit a lost home in a lost city in the midst of lost time." And the speaker in Dylan Thomas's poem "Fern Hill" also takes us back to the past and the Welsh landscapes and summer experiences that framed his childhood.

People who have influenced our lives are often important catalysts in reconstructing and understanding our stories. Many texts in Part One are concerned with the relationships among siblings and other family members. In his poem "In the Tree House at Night," James Dickey celebrates the spiritual presence of his now dead brother, and in their poems, Sharon Olds and Janice Mirikitani confront the reality of their adolescent daughters' transitions to adulthood. In "The Gift," Li-Young Lee recalls a tender moment with his father; Eric Chock wrestles with his father's expectations for his son in "Poem for My Father."

Historical places such as Williamsburg, Ellis Island, and the Martin Luther King Jr. Memorial—or even photographs of a grandparent's birthplace—are also important sites of memory. They can motivate us to listen to the voices of the past or to search for our roots in an attempt to establish a dialogue with our past selves as we explore our own terrain further. To what extent is it important for us to try to under- stand our histories? Is it plausible to say that our identities and our individual lives are sometimes shaped by a fixed historical reality? Some of the writers in Part One speculate about these questions by examining the conditions under which people become particularly aware of historical identities. African American poet Robert Hayden celebrates the life and struggles of former slave Frederick Douglass in one poem, and in "Runagate Runagate" he reconstructs what it means to be a renegade caught in the grim historical reality that shaped the destiny of African slaves in the United States. In "The Watch," Holocaust survivor Elie Wiesel explores his protagonist's attempt to retrieve a watch that symbolizes the past—"the soul and memory of that time" of war and holocaust. "Once more," says the protagonist as he attempts to defy time and to retrieve the past, "I am the mitzvah child . . . I get ready to re-enact the scene my memory recalls."

Shakespeare's *Hamlet* offers us another example of how men and women can identify themselves with the past. One major question you will explore in the play is why the Danish prince wavers between remembering and forgetting the past that seems to link him and the political future of Denmark. What do people do when they realize that they carry the burden of the past with them or that the past can become an obstacle to their growth and to a redefinition of themselves? In Sophocles' *Oedipus Rex*, the protagonist's journey backward into the past of blindness and transgression leads forward into the narrative present of self-knowledge, recognition, and revelation. In *Oedipus Rex*, the past also emerges as dramatic spectacle, controlling and shaping human destiny through the inexorable grip of the unconscious.

Native American Linda Hogan uses the metaphor of "First Light" to recreate the pristine beauty of her ancestral past; Langston Hughes charts the historical and symbolic journey of his people from slavery to freedom in "The Negro Speaks of Rivers." In both texts we encounter yet another aspect of the past that voices the private and collective myths of the racial memory.

As you explore these and other texts from the sites of memory, consider them catalysts for your own recollections and discoveries of your personal and communal past, for as Oscar Wilde reminds us, "Memory is the diary that we carry about with us."

FICTION

Lan Samantha Chang

The Unforgetting

On the summer day in 1967 when Ming Hwang first saw the eastern Iowa hills, he pulled his car off the road and stopped the engine. He felt overwhelmed, as if he had arrived once more at the sea that he had crossed to reach America and his destiny lay again upon some faraway shore. The neat, green fields rolled out to meet the sky. The narrow strip of highway looked barely navigable. Surely no Chinese man could ever have laid eyes upon this place before.

Beside him, Sansan stirred and squinted into the hazy light. "This is beautiful," she said. "Why did you stop?"

For a minute Ming could not reply. He wanted to say, "This place has nothing to do with us." Instead, he pointed out the windshield. "Do you see that water over there? That's Mercy Lake. The town is only a mile away." He added, "Maybe it will bring us luck."

When she didn't answer, he turned to examine her smooth, brown face and knew that she also was afraid. He looked over his shoulder to make sure that Charles was still asleep and would not hear the conversation. "Is something wrong?" he asked.

"We're getting old," she said. "How will we make the space in our minds for everything we'll need to learn here?"

Without a pause, he answered her, "We will forget."

Sansan's dark eyes flickered; then she nodded. Ming glanced back again at his son. He turned the key in the ignition and fixed his gaze upon the road.

And so the Hwangs forgot what they no longer needed. In the basement, inside the yellow carpetbag that Sansan had carried from Beijing, were six rice bowls that Sansan's mother said had once been used in the emperor's household. They were plain white bowls; Sansan said she thought they were only from the servants' quarters. Still, she had held onto them, imagining that their thin-edged beauty might sustain her when she grew tired of living in the present. But once the Hwangs had settled in Mercy Lake, she never used the bowls; she rarely even mentioned them.

They forgot what they could no longer bear to hope for. In the basement of their house, behind a sliding panel in his desk, stood Ming's old copy of the *Handbook of Chemistry and Physics*. It was the Twenty-sixth Edition, published in 1943, the only book that he had carried in his suitcase out of China. The *Handbook*'s deep brown cover was cracked and stained; its information had grown outdated. Ming had once believed that some day Charles might find it interesting, and so he had saved the heavy volume, even though its Periodic Table listed only ninety-two elements. In 1958, when Charles was born, the table of known elements had grown to 101, and Ming had lost track of chemistry, had given up his hope of studying science. In Mercy Lake he started his new job as a photocopy machine repairman, and the *Handbook* stayed on its shelf.

They learned what they needed to know. Photocopy machines were still so new that people had trouble maintaining them—mostly due to fear. They would call about the slightest problems: a toner cartridge, a paper jam. Ming possessed a delicate touch. He quickly grasped the ins and outs of the different models. He could sense which button or lever to press and how to get at the most difficult jams. While he fiddled around, a clerk or secretary often stood nearby, curious and wary, watching his face and hands, remarking on the infallibility and effectiveness of carbon paper. Ming would listen and nod, affecting sympathy, but privately he disagreed. He needed to believe in the future, when every office would have a new machine. And he found comfort in the presence of such effortless reproduction. He brought home photocopied samples to show Sansan how the machines could trace the shapes of drawings or letters, handwritten or typed. Sometimes, on the weekend, he took Charles to the office. To the inside cover of his logbook he taped a photocopy of Charles's little hand.

When Charles finished fourth grade, the Hwangs received a letter from his teacher, Mrs. Carlsen. She said he was doing excellent work in math and science, but his vocabulary was below average. He also had trouble pronouncing words. Did they speak Chinese in their house? She suggested that they not require him to speak Chinese, for the time being at least.

"I *do* speak English," Ming insisted, after he and Sansan had told Charles his usual bedtime story and sent him off to bed.

Charles had always been quiet and slow to speak. But Ming had assumed that he was cautious, reasoning out what he said. Now Ming began to worry that he might get lost between his two languages. The day after they received the letter, Ming came home early and watched Charles trudge up the driveway, his blue backpack heavy with books he could not read. Sansan kissed him at the door, helped him remove the backpack and poured him a bowl of sweet bean porridge. After his snack, he bent over his reader at the kitchen table. He breathed with effort, sounding out each English word so slowly that Ming did not see how he could remember what he had read.

The sight of him lit a fear in Ming's mind. "If you pay him less attention, he might want to stay in school instead of flying home to you," he told Sansan.

She said, "You don't know about children."

"I was not so coddled by my mother."

"The other children make fun of him."

Ming frowned. He reread the teacher's letter. That evening, when Charles had finished his bath and climbed into Ming and Sansan's bed for his nighttime ritual, Ming told his son there would be no bedtime story.

Charles sat perfectly still. "No story?"

"Daddy thinks we should speak English for a while," Sansan explained.

Ming watched his son's face. Recently, Charles had developed an expression of careful solitude. "I can read to you from your schoolbook," Ming said.

Charles shook his head.

"Do you understand why you need to learn English?" Ming asked.

Charles nodded. In the next few months, he gradually stopped speaking Chinese. Since they did not test him, Ming never knew how long it took for all of those words to be forgotten.

Many other things passed out of memory without their noticing. Sansan stopped reading her Chinese classics and romances. When they'd first moved to Mercy Lake, she had reread them until their bindings buckled, shredded, and fell off. She had even tried to get Ming to skim the books, so she would have someone to talk to, but Ming was busy at work. Then came Charles's letter from Mrs. Carlsen. Eventually, the tales were pushed into a smaller and smaller part of her mind, until the characters and stories only came up now and then, usually in her dreams, and when they did, she said to Ming, they seemed almost quaint, exotic. The novels found their way onto a shelf, in the basement, where they stood next to a red-bound history text that Ming and Sansan had kept in order to remind themselves of their culture and the importance of their race.

Instead of reading, Sansan practiced her English by watching television. She also took good care of Ming and Charles. She laundered Ming's new work clothes: permanent-press shirts with plastic tabs inserted in the stiff, pointed collars; bright, wide ties. Ming needed to dress well, because he had found a second calling as a salesman. He had discovered that clients were comforted by his appearance and his accent, which went together, in some way, with his efficiency and mechanical know-how. He began persuading them to buy larger, more expensive machines. He asked for and received a commission for each machine he sold. These extra monies, he and Sansan agreed, would go into a savings account for Charles's education at the University of Iowa.

In the kitchen, Sansan learned to cook with canned and frozen foods. She made cream of tomato soup for lunch, and stored envelopes of onion soup mix for meat loaf or quick onion dip. More often as Ming's career improved, Sansan consulted the Betty Crocker cookbook and made something for him to bring to an office party or to entertain a coworker at home. She kept a filebox listing everything she made, with annotations reminding her which dishes the Americans liked and didn't like.

She bought air freshener in a plastic daisy, and a jello mold shaped like a fish. They taught Charles to use a knife and fork, and they ate their meals off brittle plastic plates that they had chosen at the discount store: bright, hard disks, flat and cheerful, the color of candy: scarlet, lime green, yellow, and white.

They forgot some things deliberately; they wanted to forget. Ming won a trip for two to Chicago, based on his annual sales, and he did not protest when Sansan bought an expensive new suitcase rather than open her old yellow carpetbag and confront the six white rice bowls. At work, Ming avoided one well-meaning coworker who had once asked, "What was it like in China? It must be different from here." How could he answer that question without remembering the smell of fresh rolls sold on the street, or the scent of his grandfather's pipe?

Ming forgot the delicate taste of his grandfather's favorite fruit, the yellow watermelon. He forgot his grandfather's hopes that he might study hard and rebuild China. He forgot the fact that he had once desired to earn a Ph.D., to work in a laboratory, to discover great things and add to the body of humanity's scientific knowledge.

He replaced such useless memories with thoughts of Charles. It was for Charles that Ming had taken his job in Iowa and bought his house, because he had believed, since Charles was born, that he could make a new life in America. He struggled through clumsy conversations at the office and employee "happy hours," practicing his English. For Charles, he read the local newspaper and mowed the lawn. With Charles in mind, he struggled out of bed on winter mornings, fighting sleepiness and persistent dreams. He maintained the new Chevrolet sedan—changed the oil, followed the tune-up dates, and kept good records of all repairs.

He labored on the yard. They had moved into a neighborhood so new that at certain times the air was redolent of cow, and Ming would dream that he was being watched by large, calm eyes, and that their house had been surrounded by those strange and fragrant animals. The soil itself seemed exotic to Ming; it looked so coarse, so rich and reddish-purple—not exhausted by three thousand years of farming, like the Chinese earth, but exuberant and wild. Ming could sense the rolling fields that pressed upon their house. Mutinous seeds opposed the lawn: tall leaves of pale new wheat, foamy milkweed, Queen Anne's lace. He fussed over his spears of frail bluegrass. In the autumn he reseeded and raked, pruned back the shrubs, hid Sansan's yellow rosebush under its protective cone; but in the spring, when the melting snow lay bare his lawn, he watched and held his breath. He did not quite trust the land. He did not know what he might find. On warm spring nights, he lay awake and listened to a distant hum amidst the silence; it might have been the wind over ten thousand acres of fields, or the hatching of a thousand insects. He did not want to miss these changes. He wanted nothing taking place behind his back.

Charles's English did improve. To Ming's surprise, he read all the time: after school, in front of the television, on Saturday mornings, over meals, and even, his teachers told Ming and Sansan, during recess. In fifth grade, his teachers were pleased. In sixth grade, they were excited, and by the time he entered seventh grade, his level of achievement was, they said, phenomenal.

Even more, the teachers said, he seemed to find a pure pleasure in learning—an almost obsessive pleasure. He once failed to hear a fire drill bell while reading a biography of Thomas Paine. He wrote his papers, they said, with such articulate and righteous passion that his assignments more than compensated for his lack of class participation. He was drawn to the humanities and he seemed to be developing a passion for examining the past; he possessed a truly unusual mind.

Why the humanities? Ming wondered. What intricate foldings lay behind his son's quiet face; what opinions had formed beneath his stiff-mown hair? The autumn of Charles's eighth-grade year, Ming bought him a wooden desk and a sturdy lamp with a metal shade. He adjusted his chair and bolted a steel pencil sharpener into the wall. Then he and Sansan drove to the discount store and heaped a shopping cart with blue spiral notebooks (his favorite color) as well as blue pencils, a blue cloth-covered binder, and an enormous blue eraser. Charles brought these things to school in his backpack, and after that, Ming glimpsed them only now and then, evidence of his son's mysterious passions.

One winter evening, while Charles was helping his mother set the dining room table, Ming said, "I think I understand your interest in history. I used to like to read the history of science. I used to love science." He allowed his mind a glimpse—only a glimpse—into the basement, through the sliding panel of his desk, at the *Handbook of Chemistry and Physics*. "Do you like science?"

Charles looked up, the silverware clutched in his hand. "Not really," he said quickly. "But in history, I learned about trains." He began to talk about the European and American-born pioneers who had settled the land and made it into fields and towns. Ming watched him gesture, still holding their three forks in one brown hand, his wrists grown out of his last year's shirtsleeves. He described how the use of trains had sped the populating of the West, and how the transcontinental railroad had been built by Chinese immigrants. Then, to Ming's dismay, he asked, "Why was China so poor that people had to come to the U.S. and work on the railroads?"

Ming did not know how to tackle this enormous question. "Well," he said finally, "I'm not certain of that, but the country has always been poor."

"Why is that? Did you learn about it when you were in school?"

"We studied history."

"Did you like history?"

Ming stood and thought for a moment. "To tell you the truth," he said, "I can't remember."

That careful, lonely look came into Charles's face. He went into the kitchen and left Ming standing at the table, regretting how he had ended the conversation. He found himself envying the easy way that Charles reached for the past. How could he explain to his son that the past was his enemy? That his memories dogged him, filled his thoughts and plans with silt? They rose up in his dreams, the way that in the spring the Mercy Lake flooded through its margins, leaving the fishing huts surrounded by water.

He could not forget the colors of the Beijing sky. At night, in bed, he remembered the burning smell on winter nights from the thousand coal fires that burned in kitchens and under old-fashioned brick beds, the thousand pale streams of smoke that rose into the darkness. He recalled the grit of the spring dust storms catching in his throat, and the loose slat on the wall of the noodle-making shop that had enabled him to peer inside at the man who thinned the noodles by hand.

Ming could not forget one warm and beautiful summer evening in 1932, when he had helped his Uncle Lu pack up his belongings. The family was leaving Beijing, for what they thought would be only a few years, the duration of the war. Uncle Lu, his father's youngest brother, had never taken a real job but had remained in the family house, supported by his brothers and sisters, like an invalid, long after his beard indicated that he should have had a family of his own. As far as Ming could recall, his Uncle Lu was only interested in the practice of calligraphy. He had no other desires, it seemed, but to sit before a well-lit table, the brush upright in his hand, a gentle hand unfit for more practical tasks. That night, when they were not half finished, his uncle had sat down at his desk, helplessly, and looked about his little room, with tears rolling down his cheeks. Ming had turned away in embarrassment and hurried to pack the precious brushes and rolls of soft, white paper—the only things Uncle Lu wanted brought with him.

Where had those brushes and papers gone? What had become of the scrolls that Lu had painted and saved, so carefully? Nothing remained except Ming's recollection of them. Charles had never even seen a photograph of his great uncle. Like everyone else, Lu had died. He had suffered a stroke the night after the family left Beijing, the first casualty in a long line of lost and missing. Only a few cousins were living now, and they were scattered. Any photographs had been lost. Sometimes, Ming wondered if it were possible—that of the over two dozen members of that household everyone was scattered and gone. He could not believe that of the grandparents, uncles and aunts, cousins, and so many others, that this family had dwindled into the slender thread of his own memory.

By the time Charles entered high school he had impressed his teachers as a young man with a singular determination and potential. They said he needed to relax more, that was all. They said he seemed "like a fish out of water" during lunch period. Academically, he continued to excel. In his World History class, he developed an interest in World War II and, in particular, the Pacific theater.

One spring night Ming went to Charles's room to ask his son if he wanted a bowl of sweet bean porridge. He trudged down the hall, with no particular expectation, but was surprised to find his son's door closed. He stood dumbly for a moment and then, without thinking, he put his hand on the knob. The door was locked.

He knocked, foolishly, a little angry. After a moment, he heard the creak of a mattress, three steps toward the door. The lock clicked open.

"Charles?"

They were of a height, he noticed. Charles was so young that even when weary, he looked fresh. Ming observed his son, in whose narrow face he recognized his own; he noted the smooth, brown skin Charles had inherited from Sansan. What did he have to be weary about? "What are you doing?" Ming asked, despite the fact that he could see the books and papers strewn over the bed.

"What do you mean?"

Ming retreated. "I came up to see if you would like some *lu dou tang*."

"No, not right now, thanks." With such politeness Ming was thus rebuffed. Charles closed the door in his face and Ming stood there, blank for a moment. Then he turned and went back to the kitchen. Halfway down the hall he heard the lock click shut again.

That night, his dreams kept bringing him down the hallway, and he stood once again before his son's locked door. The next day he could not concentrate at work. The image of the door disturbed him, as if Charles had access to another world inside that room, as if he might disappear at will, might float from their second-story windows and vanish into the shimmering, yellow Iowa light.

He used a Phillips screwdriver to take apart the doorknobs and disable the locks on Charles's bedroom, the bathrooms, and the upstairs closets. Charles said nothing to him. But later Ming heard him ask his mother, "What did Dad do to my lock?" Ming caught these words one morning on his way out and paused to listen. "That's all right," Sansan said. Ming heard the squeak of a kiss. "Things get old sometimes. Don't tell Daddy—you'll make him feel bad."

Later he attempted to defend himself. A family, he told Sansan, should need no windows and no doors. In China there had been no locks on children's rooms. True, they had come to America—but even in this country, what obedient child would *need* to lock his parents from his room? "He doesn't respect me," Ming insisted.

"Of course he does."

"He's my son—I can tell from his voice, the shape of his face. But sometimes I wonder if he's my son!"

"Hush," said Sansan. She cocked her head, gesturing toward Charles's room. They both listened, but the house was absolutely quiet. The comforting odor of fried rice lingered in the air. Ming listened more closely. Beyond the house, from the land, he could hear the distant hum of early spring.

Despite their efforts, they could not forget their language, the musical pitch of Mandarin tones, the shapes of phrases. Over and over, they reached for certain words that had no equivalents in English. Sansan could find no substitute for the word *yiwei*, which meant that a person "had once assumed, but incorrectly." And no matter how much he drilled himself, Ming could not instinctively convert the measure *wan* to "ten thousand," rather than "a thousand."

In English, Sansan seemed to hide from her more complicated thoughts. "So much is missing," she told Ming. Her English world was limited to the clipped and casual rhythm of daily plans. "Put on your tie." "Did you turn on the rice?" "Be home by five o'clock."

Later that spring, there came a rainy evening when Charles looked up from his book and said, "Tomorrow I can't be home until ten."

"Is there a school event of yours that we should go to?" Ming asked.

"No." Charles flipped his book out of its jacket and folded it back. "It's college night," he said, finally. "The guidance counselor is ordering pizza. Then a man is coming to talk to us about college."

Ming nudged Sansan. "We like you to come home for dinner," Sansan said. "We don't get to see you otherwise."

Charles moved his lips for a moment, then looked up at them. "Sometime I'll have to go to college," he said. Then he stopped.

Ming jumped in. "We've been saving for you to go to college! I wanted to go to college, myself. You know that!" His voice cracked. He frowned at Sansan. "Why are you looking at me like that?"

She said, "Let's talk about this later."

A painful knot, the size of a cherry stone, formed inside Ming's throat and stayed there. Sansan turned on the television. Neither spoke until Charles had gone back to his room. Then they went to their own bedroom and undressed in silence.

In bed, in the dark, Sansan turned to him. "It's funny," she said. "I am very proud of Charles. But lately, I've been thinking it's not enough."

Ming swallowed and nodded in the dark.

"Do you remember the second Taipei flood?" she asked, cautiously, in Mandarin this time.

Ming muttered, "Maybe—not too well. Maybe you should remind me."

Her words, in Mandarin, came slowly at first and then more easily, low and wondering, as if she were marveling at her ability to speak. Her murmuring voice flowed with the steady drumming of the storm.

"Remember how poor we were? We were so poor that we could only afford one vegetable with the rice. We had to live with my mother's old Aunt Green Blossom in her flat over that restaurant, the Drunken Moon. On the day of the storm, the restaurant was serving flounder. A big catch must have just come in. When you got home for lunch, the scent of ginger and garlic sprouts, with oil, had soaked into our room."

He knew she spoke to comfort him, but his eyes had filled with tears.

"The smell from the restaurant made us quarrel with each other," she said. "That afternoon, the rains began; we holed ourselves inside and watched the commotion from the window. It rained until the streets were rivers. And you had a wonderful idea."

He smiled then. "It wasn't wonderful; it was scientific logic. The Drunken Moon was only one step up."

"We waited; we watched the water rise, then trickle over the step. All the customers left. The neighborhood was as flooded as a rice paddy. And then you went downstairs and asked them if they needed a dry place to store their food!" She laughed. "How well we ate that night!"

Ming looked at his wife. He could barely see her profile in the glow from their bedside clock. She lay on her back now, gazing at the ceiling. "Lately," she said, "I've been dreaming about that meal. Over and over. And I wonder why the food we eat now doesn't taste as good."

Their memories seeped under the doors and sifted through the keyhole. They had taken root in the earth itself, as tough and stubborn as the weeds in the garden. It seemed to Ming that after seven years in Mercy Lake, the world of his past had grown every day larger and more vivid until it pressed against his mind, beautiful and shining. And he wondered if perhaps this world had pushed his own son out of his house—if they had lost their son because of their stubborn inability to forget.

One evening he came home early. Sansan had gone to the library. In the mailbox was a letter from the guidance counselor at Charles's high school; he wanted to congratulate Charles's parents for his high test scores, and he was certain that their son would be an excellent student at the prestigious East Coast college that he had applied to, early admission. Ming read this letter; he pushed his glasses up his nose, and read it again, the paper weightless in his hands.

Ming went to his son's room. Everything lay neatly under the lamplight: the desk, the piles of books, the plain blue bedspread. Charles sat at his desk, surrounded by piles of homework. A college brochure lay open before him.

"The best state school is only an hour away," Ming said.

Charles took a deep breath. "But I don't want to go to the state school," he said. This fact drowned out all sound for a moment, but when Ming's thoughts cleared he grew aware that Charles was still talking. Charles was saying, Did they realize how little he knew about the world? He needed to know what the world was like, the world outside of their house, outside of Iowa, so that for the rest of his life he would not remain entirely lost.

"Why didn't you tell me?" Ming asked.

"I knew you didn't want me to leave."

"Why do you want to leave, then?"

Charles looked at him. "Because I know I have to go," he said.

Ming said nothing. Charles turned his attention to his brochure. After a few minutes Ming realized that his son had ended the conversation. He stood, bewildered, and walked out, closing the door behind him. When he reached the foot of the stairs, he stopped and glanced again at the closed door.

After this, it seemed to Ming that the very passage of days imprisoned him. Each morning, alone in the small bathroom, he cleared his throat and blew his nose—he had developed an allergy to ragweed over the years. His cough rang off the tiles. In the kitchen, his tea steamed sour against his upper lip. He left the house, and climbed into the Chevrolet. These habits built around him a dark and airless riddle. Charles was a part of it; even Sansan was a part of it.

On the day after they learned that Charles had been accepted early to Harvard, Sansan cooked a celebratory dinner. Afterward, they waited all evening for their son to go upstairs, their eyes bright and voices low, deliberate, and harsh. Ming tidied the messy coffee table with shaking hands. Sansan folded laundry, gripping the center of the sheets between her teeth. Charles vanished off to bed, as if he could smell the sulfur in the air. He stepped out of the room so quietly they would never have noticed if they had not been waiting.

Later, they turned off the television and faced each other. The air between them quivered as if they had been waiting to make love.

Sansan shrugged. "What did you expect?" she asked. "Sons in this country leave their parents and make their own homes, with their women." Her voice was tense, accusatory.

Ming took a sharp breath. "And that is all you have to say?"

"Isn't this what you wanted for him? That he should become like them?" Her voice grew higher. "No, I have nothing else to say."

"What *I* wanted?" Ming's voice rose. "So this is all my fault?"

"It is what you wanted! It was your idea to get a job here, in the middle of nowhere—your idea!"

"It's your fault as much as mine!"

She was standing before him, her knees bent and both feet planted, her face distorted, shouting suddenly, "You're lying!" Then, without taking her eyes from him, she moved backward, toward the dishrack. She reached blindly for a brittle, plastic plate, raised it slowly into the air, as if she were casting a spell, then flung it against the kitchen floor.

For a moment Ming stood, arrested by the sight of the red disk hurtling downward, surprised to see it breaking into pieces against the floor. He had not known such goods could shatter. Then he walked slowly to the cabinet, his heavy fingers tingling at his sides.

They broke every plate on the shelf, plus the china pencil holder and the good teapot. Sansan stood with knees bent and both feet planted, near the dishrack, jerking her arm downward to emphasize a point, tears flying as she shook her head from side to side. She shouted, *"You are the cause of this! You have ruined me! You have trapped me into this life!"* "I should go downstairs and get those rice bowls!" Ming threatened. "Go ahead!" she shouted. "Why did we save them, anyway?" The words flew from their mouths, whirled through the kitchen. Colorful disks flew through the air, cracked and bounced against the walls, the chairs, the cabinets.

When they had finished, they stood transfixed, breathing hard, admiring their handiwork. The broken pieces made a bright mosaic on the floor.

A certain quality to the silence made them both look up.

The kitchen door had somehow been left open. There stood Charles in his pajamas, squinting in the light. He whispered, "I wish you would be happy for me."

In that moment, Ming understood that Charles was indeed his son. There was no question about it. The resemblance wasn't in the shape of his face. It was in his look of sorrow.

After Charles left the room, they turned once more toward each other. Sansan's face was rigid and blank. What had happened to them? Ming wondered. What would happen? He had no one to ask—no friends, no parents—no one who could have understood the language of his thoughts.

Now Sansan stood by the back door, holding her jacket. "I want to go back," she said. Her voice was shaking. "Why did you have to bring me here?"

She turned and quietly left the house, clicking the door shut behind her. Ming stood inside. He made out her shape in the dim garage as she got into the Chevrolet, backed it out in one quick motion, and drove west, toward the highway.

For an hour, he sat at the kitchen table. He had switched off the lights, and the blackness soothed his mind. He fixed his gaze upon the square of faint streetlight that lay upon the counter.

He was alone. What kind of cruelty had held him back from saying what she most desired to hear? That he needed her. That even with Charles gone, they would endure.

The Chevrolet moved like a comet in his mind. Sansan, never a confident driver, veering left onto Polk Avenue. The neighborhood houses prim on either side of her, reflecting the pale car in their dark windows. She would list over the center line and then correct herself. She would enter the freeway, careening down the empty entrance ramp; she would turn north, away from the new commercial area, and toward the country roads that stretched among the winter fields, the dried-up stalks of corn, the earth rich and softly dark, scattered with snow and bits of wheat and chaff from the harvest. He knew his wife. For a long time, he had suspected that a part of her longed simply to disappear into those fields. The car would jounce a bit as she turned onto the gravel, then into the simplest two-tire track in the dirt. And there she might sit amidst the harvested soy beans, surrounded by silence, resting. Why did so many farmers grow soy beans? Ming wondered. No one in a hundred miles would dream of buying soy sauce. He imagined the local people were secure in their desires for steak and milk, protected by their barns, their tractors, and their slumbering cows.

Would she leave him? Perhaps she would leave, now that they had glimpsed their fate. Perhaps she would be able to forget—free and clear, wiped clean at last. Ming imagined her leaving the dirt roads and heading across the local highway to join the night traffic on the interstate, merging silently into the stream of traffic.

But even as he envisioned this, he knew it would not happen. Sansan had nowhere else to go. Nothing remained of the stories and meals and people they'd known, nothing but what they remembered. Their world lived in them, and they would be the end of it. They had no solace, and no burden, but each other.

The next morning, as he warmed up the car, he stooped to examine the tires. He found mud and grains of yellow wheat embedded deep into the treads.

[1998]

Journal Entry

Brainstorm on the story's title. How many multiple meanings did you generate regarding possible themes?

Textual Considerations

1. In the second section of the story, Chang uses repetition in each of her three topic sentences. To what effect? Be specific.
2. Characterize Charles. What contributes to his look of "careful solitude"? Does Ming understand Charles despite the fact that they seldom talk? Explain.
3. Chang's story contains multiple ironies. Cite two or three that impressed you and show how irony enhances theme.
4. Explain the symbolic significance of Charles's locking his door. How does the author use it to foreshadow other decisions that Charles makes?

Cultural Contexts

1. "In English, Sansan seemed to hide from her more complicated thoughts." Discuss with your group the role of one's native tongue in preserving culture, identity, memory, and roots. To what extent does the necessity of learning English contribute to their later alienation from one another?
2. "The Unforgetting" is part of a collection of stories titled *Hunger*. What evidence of various kinds of hunger do you find in the story? What does the story imply about the gains and losses of the immigrant experience? Summarize your group's responses.

Edith Wharton

Roman Fever

I

From the table at which they had been lunching two American ladies of ripe but well-cared-for middle age moved across the lofty terrace of the Roman restaurant and, leaning on its parapet, looked first at each other, and then down on the outspread glories of the Palatine and the Forum, with the same expression of vague but benevolent approval.

As they leaned there a girlish voice echoed up gaily from the stairs leading to the court below. "Well, come along, then," it cried, not to them but to an invisible companion, "and let's leave the young things to their knitting"; and a voice as fresh laughed back: "Oh, look here, Babs, not actually *knitting*—" "Well, I mean figuratively," rejoined the first. "After all, we haven't left our poor parents much else to do . . ." and at that point the turn of the stairs engulfed the dialogue.

The two ladies looked at each other again, this time with a tinge of smiling embarrassment, and the smaller and paler one shook her head and colored slightly.

"Barbara!" she murmured, sending an unheard rebuke after the mocking voice in the stairway.

The other lady, who was fuller, and higher in color, with a small determined nose supported by vigorous black eyebrows, gave a good-humored laugh. "That's what our daughters think of us!"

Her companion replied by a deprecating gesture. "Not of us individually. We must remember that. It's just the collective modern idea of Mothers. And you see—" Half-guiltily she drew from her handsomely mounted black handbag a twist of crimson silk run through by two fine knitting needles. "One never knows," she murmured. "The new system has certainly given us a good deal of time to kill; and sometimes I get tired just looking—even at this." Her gesture was now addressed to the stupendous scene at their feet.

The dark lady laughed again, and they both relapsed upon the view, contemplating it in silence, with a sort of diffused serenity which might have been borrowed from the spring effulgence of the Roman skies. The luncheon hour was long past, and the two had their end of the vast terrace to themselves. At its opposite extremity a few groups, detained by a lingering look at the outspread city, were gathering up guidebooks and fumbling for tips. The last of them scattered, and the two ladies were alone on the air-washed height.

"Well, I don't see why we shouldn't just stay here," said Mrs. Slade, the lady of the high color and energetic brows. Two derelict basket chairs stood near and she pushed them into the angle of the parapet, and settled herself in one, her gaze upon the Palatine. "After all, it's still the most beautiful view in the world."

"It always will be, to me," assented her friend Mrs. Ansley, with so slight a stress on the "me" that Mrs. Slade, though she noticed it, wondered if it were not merely accidental, like the random underlinings of old-fashioned letter writers.

"Grace Ansley was always old-fashioned," she thought; and added aloud, with a retrospective smile: "It's a view we've both been familiar with for a good many years. When we first met here we were younger than our girls are now. You remember?"

"Oh, yes, I remember," murmured Mrs. Ansley, with the same undefinable stress. "There's that headwaiter wondering," she interpolated. She was evidently far less sure than her companion of herself and of her rights in the world.

"I'll cure him of wondering," said Mrs. Slade, stretching her hand toward a bag as discreetly opulent-looking as Mrs. Ansley's. Signing to the headwaiter, she explained that she and her friend were old lovers of Rome, and would like to spend the end of the afternoon looking down on the view—that is, if it did not disturb the service? The headwaiter, bowing over her gratuity, assured her that the ladies were most welcome, and would be still more so if they would condescend to remain for dinner. A full-moon night, they would remember. . . .

Mrs. Slade's black brows drew together, as though references to the moon were out of place and even unwelcome. But she smiled away her frown as the headwaiter retreated. "Well, why not? We might do worse. There's no knowing, I suppose, when the girls will be back. Do you even know back from *where*? I don't!"

Mrs. Ansley again colored slightly. "I think those young Italian aviators we met at the Embassy invited them to fly to Tarquinia for tea. I suppose they'll want to wait and fly back by moonlight."

"Moonlight—moonlight! What a part it still plays. Do you suppose they're as sentimental as we were?"

"I've come to the conclusion that I don't in the least know what they are," said Mrs. Ansley. "And perhaps we didn't know much more about each other."

"No; perhaps we didn't."

Her friend gave her a shy glance. "I never should have supposed you were sentimental, Alida."

"Well, perhaps I wasn't." Mrs. Slade drew her lids together in retrospect; and for a few moments the two ladies, who had been intimate since childhood, reflected how little they knew each other. Each one, of course, had a label ready to attach to the other's name; Mrs. Delphin Slade, for instance, would have told herself, or anyone who asked her, that Mrs. Horace Ansley, twenty-five years ago, had been exquisitely lovely—no, you wouldn't believe it, would you?. . . though, of course, still charming, distinguished. . . . Well, as a girl she had been exquisite; far more beautiful than her daughter Barbara, though certainly Babs, according to the new standards at any rate, was more effective—had more *edge*, as they say. Funny where she got it, with those two nullities as parents. Yes; Horace Ansley was—well, just the duplicate of his wife. Museum specimens of old New York. Good-looking, irreproachable, exemplary. Mrs. Slade and Mrs. Ansley had lived opposite each other—actually as well as figuratively—for years. When the drawing-room curtains in No. 20 East 73rd Street were renewed, No. 23, across the way, was always aware of it. And of all the movings, buyings, travels, anniversaries, illnesses—the tame chronicle of an estimable pair. Little of it escaped Mrs. Slade. But she had grown bored with it by the time her husband made his big *coup* in Wall Street, and when they bought in upper Park Avenue had already begun to think: "I'd rather live opposite a speakeasy for a change; at least one might see it raided." The idea of seeing Grace raided was so amusing that (before the move) she launched it at a woman's lunch. It made a hit, and went the rounds—she sometimes wondered if it had crossed the street, and reached Mrs. Ansley. She hoped not, but didn't much mind. Those were the days when respectability was at a discount, and it did the irreproachable no harm to laugh at them a little.

A few years later, and not many months apart, both ladies lost their husbands. There was an appropriate exchange of wreaths and condolences, and a brief renewal of intimacy in the half-shadow of their mourning; and now, after another interval, they had run across each other in Rome, at the same hotel, each of them the modest appendage of a salient daughter. The similarity of their lot had again drawn them together, lending itself to mild jokes, and the mutual confession that, if in old days it must have been tiring to "keep up" with daughters, it was now, at times, a little dull not to.

No doubt, Mrs. Slade reflected, she felt her unemployment more than poor Grace ever would. It was a big drop from being the wife of Delphin Slade to being his widow. She had always regarded herself (with a certain conjugal pride) as his equal in social gifts, as contributing her full share to the making of the exceptional couple they were: but the difference after his death was irremediable. As the wife of the famous corporation lawyer, always with an international case or two on hand, every day brought its exciting and unexpected obligation: the impromptu entertaining of eminent colleagues from abroad, the hurried dashes on legal business to London, Paris or Rome, where the entertaining was so handsomely reciprocated; the amusement of hearing in her wake: "What, that handsome woman with the good clothes and the eyes is Mrs. Slade—*the* Slade's wife? Really? Generally the wives of celebrities are such frumps."

Yes; being *the* Slade's widow was a dullish business after that. In living up to such a husband all her faculties had been engaged; now she had only her daughter to live up to, for the son who seemed to have inherited his father's gifts had died suddenly in boyhood. She had fought through that agony because her husband was there, to be helped and to help; now, after the father's death, the thought of the boy had become unbearable. There was nothing left but to mother her daughter; and dear Jenny was such a perfect daughter that she needed no excessive mothering. "Now with Babs Ansley I don't know that I *should* be so quiet," Mrs. Slade sometimes half-enviously reflected; but Jenny, who was younger than her brilliant friend, was that rare accident, an extremely pretty girl who somehow made youth and prettiness seem as safe as their absence. It was all perplexing—and to Mrs. Slade a little boring. She wished that Jenny would fall in love—with the wrong man, even; that she might have to be watched, out-maneuvered, rescued. And instead, it was Jenny who watched her mother, kept her out of drafts, made sure that she had taken her tonic. . . .

Mrs. Ansley was much less articulate than her friend, and her mental portrait of Mrs. Slade was slighter, and drawn with fainter touches. "Alida Slade's awfully brilliant; but not as brilliant as she thinks," would have summed it up; though she would have added, for the enlightenment of strangers, that Mrs. Slade had been an extremely dashing girl; much more so than her daughter, who was pretty, of course, and clever in a way, but had none of her mother's—well, "vividness," someone had once called it.

Mrs. Ansley would take up current words like this, and cite them in quotation marks, as unheard-of audacities. No; Jenny was not like her mother. Sometimes Mrs. Ansley thought Alida Slade was disappointed; on the whole she had had a sad life. Full of failures and mistakes; Mrs. Ansley had always been rather sorry for her. . . .

So these two ladies visualized each other, each through the wrong end of her little telescope.

II

For a long time they continued to sit side by side without speaking. It seemed as though, to both, there was a relief in laying down their somewhat futile activities in the presence of the vast Memento Mori which faced them. Mrs. Slade sat quite still, her eyes fixed on the golden slope of the Palace of the Caesars, and after a while Mrs. Ansley ceased to fidget with her bag, and she too sank into meditation. Like many intimate friends, the two ladies had never before had occasion to be silent together, and Mrs. Ansley was slightly embarrassed by what seemed, after so many years, a new stage in their intimacy, and one with which she did not yet know how to deal.

Suddenly the air was full of that deep clangor of bells which periodically covers Rome with a roof of silver. Mrs. Slade glanced at her wristwatch. "Five o'clock already," she said, as though surprised.

Mrs. Ansley suggested interrogatively: "There's bridge at the Embassy at five." For a long time Mrs. Slade did not answer. She appeared to be lost in contemplation, and Mrs. Ansley thought the remark had escaped her. But after a while she said, as if speaking out of a dream: "Bridge, did you say? Not unless you want to. . . . But I don't think I will, you know."

"Oh, no," Mrs. Ansley hastened to assure her. "I don't care to at all. It's so lovely here; and so full of old memories, as you say." She settled herself in her chair, and almost furtively drew forth her knitting. Mrs. Slade took sideway note of this activity, but her own beautifully cared-for hands remained motionless on her knee.

"I was just thinking," she said slowly, "what different things Rome stands for to each generation of travelers. To our grandmothers, Roman fever; to our mothers, sentimental dangers—how we used to be guarded!—to our daughters, no more dangers than the middle of Main Street. They don't know it—but how much they're missing!"

The long golden light was beginning to pale, and Mrs. Ansley lifted her knitting a little closer to her eyes. "Yes; how we were guarded!"

"I always used to think," Mrs. Slade continued, "that our mothers had a much more difficult job than our grandmothers. When Roman fever stalked the streets it must have been comparatively easy to gather in the girls at the danger hour; but when you and I were young, with such beauty calling us, and the spice of disobedience thrown in, and no worse risk than catching cold during the cool hour after sunset, the mothers used to be put to it to keep us in—didn't they?"

She turned again toward Mrs. Ansley, but the latter had reached a delicate point in her knitting. "One, two, three—slip two; yes, they must have been," she assented, without looking up.

Mrs. Slade's eyes rested on her with a deepened attention. "She can knit—in the face of *this*! How like her. . . ."

Mrs. Slade leaned back, brooding, her eyes ranging from the ruins which faced her to the long green hollow of the Forum, the fading glow of the church fronts beyond it, and the outlying immensity of the Colosseum. Suddenly she thought: "It's all very well to say that our girls have done away with sentiment and moonlight. But if Babs Ansley isn't out to catch that young aviator—the one who's a Marchese—then I don't know anything. And Jenny has no chance beside her. I know that too. I wonder if that's why Grace Ansley likes the two girls to go everywhere together? My poor Jenny as a foil—!" Mrs. Slade gave a hardly audible laugh, and at the sound Mrs. Ansley dropped her knitting.

"Yes—?"

"I—oh, nothing. I was only thinking how your Babs carries everything before her. That Campolieri boy is one of the best matches in Rome. Don't look so innocent, my dear—you know he is. And I was wondering, ever so respectfully, you understand . . . wondering how two such exemplary characters as you and Horace had managed to produce anything quite so dynamic." Mrs. Slade laughed again, with a touch of asperity.

Mrs. Ansley's hands lay inert across her needles. She looked straight out at the great accumulated wreckage of passion and splendor at her feet. But her small profile was almost expressionless. At length she said: "I think you overrate Babs, my dear."

Mrs. Slade's tone grew easier. "No; I don't. I appreciate her. And perhaps envy you. Oh, my girl's perfect; if I were a chronic invalid I'd—well, I think I'd rather be in Jenny's hands. There must be times . . . but there! I always wanted a brilliant daughter . . . and never quite understood why I got an angel instead."

Mrs. Ansley echoed her laugh in a faint murmur. "Babs is an angel too."

"Of course—of course! But she's got rainbow wings. Well, they're wandering by the sea with their young men; and here we sit . . . and it all brings back the past a little too acutely."

Mrs. Ansley had resumed her knitting. One might almost have imagined (if one had known her less well, Mrs. Slade reflected) that, for her also, too many memories rose from the lengthening shadows of those august ruins. But no; she was simply absorbed in her work. What was there for her to worry about? She knew that Babs would almost certainly come back engaged to the extremely eligible Campolieri. "And she'll sell the New York house, and settle down near them in Rome, and never be in their way . . . she's much too tactful. But she'll have an excellent cook, and just the right people in for bridge and cocktails . . . and a perfectly peaceful old age among her grandchildren."

Mrs. Slade broke off this prophetic flight with a recoil of self-disgust. There was no one of whom she had less right to think unkindly than of Grace Ansley. Would she never cure herself of envying her? Perhaps she had begun too long ago.

She stood up and leaned against the parapet, filling her troubled eyes with the tranquilizing magic of the hour. But instead of tranquilizing her the sight seemed to increase her exasperation. Her gaze turned toward the Colosseum. Already its golden flank was drowned in purple shadow, and above it the sky curved crystal clear, without light or color. It was the moment when afternoon and evening hang balanced in mid-heaven.

Mrs. Slade turned back and laid her hand on her friend's arm. The gesture was so abrupt that Mrs. Ansley looked up, startled.

"The sun's set. You're not afraid, my dear?"

"Afraid—?"

"Of Roman fever or pneumonia? I remember how ill you were that winter. As a girl you had a very delicate throat, hadn't you?"

"Oh, we're all right up here. Down below, in the Forum, it does get deathly cold, all of a sudden . . . but not here."

"Ah, of course you know because you had to be so careful." Mrs. Slade turned back to the parapet. She thought: "I must make one more effort not to hate her." Aloud she said: "Whenever I look at the Forum from up here, I remember that story about a great-aunt of yours, wasn't she? A dreadfully wicked great-aunt?"

"Oh, yes; great-aunt Harriet. The one who was supposed to have sent her young sister out to the Forum after sunset to gather a night-blooming flower for her album. All our great-aunts and grandmothers used to have albums of dried flowers."

Mrs. Slade nodded. "But she really sent her because they were in love with the same man—"

"Well, that was the family tradition. They said Aunt Harriet confessed it years afterward. At any rate, the poor little sister caught the fever and died. Mother used to frighten us with the story when we were children."

"And you frightened *me* with it, that winter when you and I were here as girls. The winter I was engaged to Delphin."

Mrs. Ansley gave a faint laugh. "Oh, did I? Really frightened you? I don't believe you're easily frightened."

"Not often; but I was then. I was easily frightened because I was too happy. I wonder if you know what that means?"

"I—yes . . ." Mrs. Ansley faltered.

"Well, I suppose that was why the story of your wicked aunt made such an impression on me. And I thought: 'There's no more Roman fever, but the Forum is deathly cold after sunset—especially after a hot day. And the Colosseum's even colder and damper'."

"The Colosseum—?"

"Yes. It wasn't easy to get in, after the gates were locked for the night. Far from easy. Still, in those days it could be managed; it *was* managed, often. Lovers met there who couldn't meet elsewhere. You knew that?"

"I—I dare say. I don't remember."

"You don't remember? You don't remember going to visit some ruins or other one evening, just after dark, and catching a bad chill? You were supposed to have gone to see the moon rise. People always said that expedition was what caused your illness."

There was a moment's silence; then Mrs. Ansley rejoined: "Did they? It was all so long ago."

"Yes. And you got well again—so it didn't matter. But I suppose it struck your friends—the reason given for your illness, I mean—because everybody knew you were so prudent on account of your throat, and your mother took such care of you. . . . You *had* been out late sight-seeing, hadn't you, that night?"

"Perhaps I had. The most prudent girls aren't always prudent. What made you think of it now?"

Mrs. Slade seemed to have no answer ready. But after a moment she broke out: "Because I simply can't bear it any longer—!"

Mrs. Ansley lifted her head quickly. Her eyes were wide and very pale. "Can't bear what?"

"Why—your not knowing that I've always known why you went."

"Why I went—?"

"Yes. You think I'm bluffing, don't you? Well, you went to meet the man I was engaged to—and I can repeat every word of the letter that took you there."

While Mrs. Slade spoke Mrs. Ansley had risen unsteadily to her feet. Her bag, her knitting and gloves, slid in a panic-stricken heap to the ground. She looked at Mrs. Slade as though she were looking at a ghost.

"No, no—don't," she faltered out.

"Why not? Listen, if you don't believe me. 'My one darling, things can't go on like this. I must see you alone. Come to the Colosseum immediately after dark tomorrow. There will be somebody to let you in. No one whom you need fear will suspect'—but perhaps you've forgotten what the letter said?"

Mrs. Ansley met the challenge with an unexpected composure. Steadying herself against the chair she looked at her friend, and replied: "No; I know it by heart too."

"And the signature? 'Only *your* D.S.' Was that it? I'm right, am I? That was the letter that took you out that evening after dark?"

Mrs. Ansley was still looking at her. It seemed to Mrs. Slade that a slow struggle was going on behind the voluntarily controlled mask of her small quiet face. "I shouldn't have thought she had herself so well in hand," Mrs. Slade reflected, almost resentfully. But at this moment Mrs. Ansley spoke. "I don't know how you knew. I burnt that letter at once."

"Yes; you would, naturally—you're so prudent!" The sneer was open now. "And if you burnt the letter you're wondering how on earth I know what was in it. That's it, isn't it?"

Mrs. Slade waited, but Mrs. Ansley did not speak.

"Well, my dear, I know what was in that letter because I wrote it!"

"You wrote it?"

"Yes."

The two women stood for a minute staring at each other in the last golden light. Then Mrs. Ansley dropped back into her chair. "Oh," she murmured, and covered her face with her hands.

Mrs. Slade waited nervously for another word or movement. None came, and at length she broke out: "I horrify you."

Mrs. Ansley's hands dropped to her knee. The face they uncovered was streaked with tears. "I wasn't thinking of you. I was thinking—it was the only letter I ever had from him!"

"And I wrote it. Yes; I wrote it! But I was the girl he was engaged to. Did you happen to remember that?"

Mrs. Ansley's head drooped again. "I'm not trying to excuse myself . . . I remembered. . . ."

"And still you went?"

"Still I went."

Mrs. Slade stood looking down on the small bowed figure at her side. The flame of her wrath had already sunk, and she wondered why she had ever thought there would be any satisfaction in inflicting so purposeless a wound on her friend. But she had to justify herself.

"You do understand? I found out—and I hated you, hated you. I knew you were in love with Delphin—and I was afraid; afraid of you, of your quiet ways, your sweetness . . . your . . . well, I wanted you out of the way, that's all. Just for a few weeks; just till I was sure of him. So in a blind fury I wrote that letter . . . I don't know why I'm telling you now."

"I suppose," said Mrs. Ansley slowly, "it's because you've always gone on hating me."

"Perhaps. Or because I wanted to get the whole thing off my mind." She paused. "I'm glad you destroyed the letter. Of course I never thought you'd die."

Mrs. Ansley relapsed into silence, and Mrs. Slade, leaning above her, was conscious of a strange sense of isolation, of being cut off from the warm current of human communion. "You think me a monster!"

"I don't know. . . . It was the only letter I had, and you say he didn't write it?"

"Ah, how you care for him still!"

"I cared for that memory," said Mrs. Ansley.

Mrs. Slade continued to look down on her. She seemed physically reduced by the blow—as if, when she got up, the wind might scatter her like a puff of dust. Mrs. Slade's jealousy suddenly leapt up again at the sight. All these years the woman had been living on that letter. How she must have loved him, to treasure the mere memory of its ashes! The letter of the man her friend was engaged to. Wasn't it she who was the monster?

"You tried your best to get him away from me, didn't you? But you failed; and I kept him. That's all."

"Yes. That's all."

"I wish now I hadn't told you. I'd no idea you'd feel about it as you do; I thought you'd be amused. It all happened so long ago, as you say; and you must do me the justice to remember that I had no reason to think you'd ever taken it seriously. How could I, when you were married to Horace Ansley two months afterward? As soon as you could get out of bed your mother rushed you off to Florence and married you. People were rather surprised—they wondered at its being done so quickly; but I thought I knew. I had an idea you did it out of *pique*—to be able to say you'd got ahead of Delphin and me. Girls have such silly reasons for doing the most serious things. And your marrying so soon convinced me that you'd never really cared."

"Yes. I suppose it would," Mrs. Ansley assented.

The clear heaven overhead was emptied of all its gold. Dusk spread over it, abruptly darkening the Seven Hills. Here and there lights began to twinkle through the foliage at their feet. Steps were coming and going on the deserted terrace—waiters looking out of the doorway at the head of the stairs, then reappearing with trays and napkins and flasks of wine. Tables were moved, chairs straightened. A feeble string of electric lights flickered out. Some vases of faded flowers were carried away, and brought back replenished. A stout lady in a dust coat suddenly appeared, asking in broken Italian if anyone had seen the elastic band which held together her tattered Baedeker. She poked with her stick under the table at which she had lunched, the waiters assisting.

The corner where Mrs. Slade and Mrs. Ansley sat was still shadowy and deserted. For a long time neither of them spoke. At length Mrs. Slade began again: "I suppose I did it as a sort of joke—"

"A joke?"

"Well, girls are ferocious sometimes, you know. Girls in love especially. And I remember laughing to myself all that evening at the idea that you were waiting around there in the dark, dodging out of sight, listening for every sound, trying to get in—Of course I was upset when I heard you were so ill afterward."

Mrs. Ansley had not moved for a long time. But now she turned slowly toward her companion. "But I didn't wait. He'd arranged everything. He was there. We were let in at once," she said.

Mrs. Slade sprang up from her leaning position. "Delphin there? They let you in?—Ah, now you're lying!" she burst out with violence.

Mrs. Ansley's voice grew clearer, and full of surprise. "But of course he was there. Naturally he came—"

"Came? How did he know he'd find you there? You must be raving!"

Mrs. Ansley hesitated, as though reflecting. "But I answered the letter. I told him I'd be there. So he came."

Mrs. Slade flung her hands up to her face. "Oh, God—you answered! I never thought of your answering. . . ."

"It's odd you never thought of it, if you wrote the letter."

"Yes. I was blind with rage."

Mrs. Ansley rose, and drew her fur scarf about her. "It is cold here. We'd better go . . . I'm sorry for you," she said, as she clasped the fur about her throat.

The unexpected words sent a pang through Mrs. Slade. "Yes; we'd better go." She gathered up her bag and cloak. "I don't know why you should be sorry for me," she muttered.

Mrs. Ansley stood looking away from her toward the dusky secret mass of the Colosseum. "Well—because I didn't have to wait that night."

Mrs. Slade gave an unquiet laugh. "Yes; I was beaten there. But I oughtn't to begrudge it to you, I suppose. At the end of all these years. After all, I had everything; I had him for twenty-five years. And you had nothing but that one letter that he didn't write."

Mrs. Ansley was again silent. At length she turned toward the door of the terrace. She took a step, and turned back, facing her companion.

"I had Barbara," she said, and began to move ahead of Mrs. Slade toward the stairway.

[1936]

Journal Entry

Explore the literal and symbolic meanings of the story's title. What different kinds of fevers are presented? Explain. *illness, love & passion*

Textual Considerations

1. Analyze the implications of Wharton's choice of Rome as the "site of memory." Consider, for example, whether the events that occur there could have taken place elsewhere.
2. What are the literal and figurative meanings of the story's title?
3. Find as many examples as you can of foreshadowing, and analyze Wharton's use of this technique to prepare the reader for the ending.
4. Both women have kept secret essential choices in their pasts. What do you think prompted their disclosures? How do you respond to their revelations?
5. Contrast the attitudes of the protagonists toward aging and widowhood. To what extent are they reconciled to their present? How have their pasts affected their attitudes toward the present?

Cultural Contexts

1. "Roman Fever" explores the urge that human beings sometimes feel to return to the past in an attempt to reconcile its contradictions with the present. Working with your group, make a list of the features and traits that Mrs. Slade uses to unravel the mysteries and enigmas of the past.
2. Discuss with members of your group the deep implications of the "metaphor of place." To what extent can a place—a historical or cultural site or a new country, for example—influence people's ability to act and make choices? Think of the role place has played in your lives.

Pär Lagerkvist

Father and I

When I was getting on toward ten, I remember, Father took me by the hand one Sunday afternoon, as we were to go out into the woods and listen to the birds singing. Waving good-bye to Mother, who had to stay at home and get the evening meal, we set off briskly in the warm sunshine. We didn't make any great to-do about this going to listen to the birds, as though it were something extra special or wonderful; we were sound, sensible people, Father and I, brought up with nature and used to it. There was nothing to make a fuss about. It was just that it was Sunday afternoon and Father was free. We walked along the railway line, where people were not allowed to go as a rule, but Father worked on the railway and so he had a right to. By doing this we could get straight into the woods, too, without going a round-about way.

Soon the bird song began and all the rest. There was a twittering of finches and willow warblers, thrushes and sparrows in the bushes, the hum that goes on all around you as soon as you enter a wood. The ground was white with wood anemones, the birches had just come out into leaf, and the spruces had fresh shoots;

there were scents on all sides, and underfoot the mossy earth lay steaming in the sun. There was noise and movement everywhere; bumblebees came out of their holes, midges swarmed wherever it was marshy, and birds darted out of the bushes to catch them and back again as quickly.

All at once a train came rushing along and we had to go down on to the embankment. Father hailed the engine driver with two fingers to his Sunday hat and the driver saluted and extended his hand. It all happened quickly; then on we went, taking big strides so as to tread on the sleepers and not in the gravel, which was heavy going and rough on the shoes. The sleepers sweated tar in the heat, everything smelled, grease and meadowsweet, tar and heather by turns. The rails glinted in the sun. On either side of the line were telegraph poles, which sang as you passed them. Yes, it was a lovely day. The sky was quite clear, not a cloud to be seen, and there couldn't be any, either, on a day like this, from what Father said.

After a while we came to a field of oats to the right of the line, where a crofter we knew had a clearing. The oats had come up close and even. Father scanned them with an expert eye and I could see he was satisfied. I knew very little about such things, having been born in a town. Then we came to the bridge over a stream, which most of the time had no water to speak of but which now was in full spate. We held hands so as not to fall down between the sleepers. After that it is not long before you come to the platelayer's cottage lying embedded in greenery, apple trees and gooseberry bushes. We called in to see them and were offered milk, and saw their pig and hens and fruit trees in blossom; then we went on. We wanted to get to the river, for it was more beautiful there than anywhere else; there was something special about it, as farther upstream it flowed past where Father had lived as a child. We usually liked to come as far as this before we turned back, and today, too, we got there after a good walk. It was near the next station, but we didn't go so far. Father just looked to see that the semaphore was right—he thought of everything.

We stopped by the river, which murmured in the hot sun, broad and friendly. The shady trees hung along the banks and were reflected in the backwater. It was all fresh and light here; a soft breeze was blowing off the small lakes higher up. We climbed down the slope and walked a little way along the bank, Father pointing out the spots for fishing. He had sat here on the stones as a boy, waiting for perch all day long; often there wasn't even a bite, but it was a blissful life. Now he didn't have time. We hung about on the bank for a good while, making a noise, pushing out bits of bark for the current to take, throwing pebbles out into the water to see who could throw farthest; we were both gay and cheerful by nature, Father and I. At last we felt tired and that we had had enough, and we set off for home.

It was beginning to get dark. The woods were changed—it wasn't dark there yet, but almost. We quickened our steps. Mother would be getting anxious and waiting with supper. She was always afraid something was going to happen. But it hadn't; it had been a lovely day, nothing had happened that shouldn't. We were content with everything.

The twilight deepened. The trees were so funny. They stood listening to every step we took, as if they didn't know who we were. Under one of them was a glow-worm. It lay down there in the dark staring at us. I squeezed Father's hand, but he didn't see the strange glow, just walked on. Now it was quite dark. We came to the bridge over the stream. It roared down there in the depths, horribly, as though it wanted to swallow us up; the abyss yawned below us. We trod carefully on the sleepers, holding each other tightly by the hand so as not to fall in. I thought Father would carry me across, but he didn't say anything; he probably wanted me to be like him and think nothing of it.

We went on. Father was so calm as he walked there in the darkness, with even strides, not speaking, thinking to himself. I couldn't understand how he could be so calm when it was so murky. I looked all around me in fear. Nothing but darkness everywhere. I hardly dared take a deep breath, for then you got so much darkness inside you, and that was dangerous. I thought it meant you would soon die. I remember quite well that's what I thought then. The embankment sloped steeply down, as though into chasms black as night. The telegraph poles rose, ghostly, to the sky. Inside them was a hollow rumble, as though someone were talking deep down in the earth and the white porcelain caps sat huddled fearfully together listening to it. It was all horrible. Nothing was right, nothing real; it was all so weird.

Hugging close to Father, I whispered, "Father, why is it so horrible when it's dark?"

"No, my boy, it's not horrible," he said, taking me by the hand.

"Yes, Father, it is."

"No, my child, you mustn't think that. Not when we know there is a God."

I felt so lonely, forsaken. It was so strange that only I was afraid, not Father, that we didn't think the same. And strange that what he said didn't help me and stop me from being afraid. Not even what he said about God helped me. I thought he too was horrible. It was horrible that he was everywhere here in the darkness, down under the trees, in the telegraph poles which rumbled—that must be he—everywhere. And yet you could never see him.

We walked in silence, each with his own thoughts. My heart contracted, as though the darkness had got in and was beginning to squeeze it.

Then, as we were rounding a bend, we suddenly heard a mighty roar behind us! We were awakened out of our thoughts in alarm. Father pulled me down on to the embankment, down into the abyss, held me there. Then the train tore past, a black train. All the lights in the carriages were out, and it was going at frantic speed. What sort of train was it? There wasn't one due now! We gazed at it in terror. The fire blazed in the huge engine as they shovelled in coal; sparks whirled out into the night. It was terrible. The driver stood there in the light of the fire, pale, motionless, his features as though turned to stone. Father didn't recognize him, didn't know who he was. The man just stared straight ahead, as though intent on rushing into the darkness, far into the darkness that had no end.

Beside myself with dread, I stood there panting, gazing after the furious vision. It was swallowed up by the night. Father took me up on to the line; we hurried home. He said, "Strange, what train was that? And I didn't recognize the driver." Then we walked on in silence.

But my whole body was shaking. It was for me, for my sake. I sensed what it meant: it was the anguish that was to come, the unknown, all that Father knew nothing about, that he wouldn't be able to protect me against. That was how this world, this life, would be for me; not like Father's, where everything was secure and certain. It wasn't a real world, a real life. It just hurtled, blazing, into the darkness that had no end.

[1954]

Journal Entry

What images, memories, associations, or experiences with the word *father* can you bring to your reading of this text?

Textual Considerations

1. What qualities of the family males does the narrator stress in the first paragraph?
2. At what point does the son begin to feel that his father cannot protect him from the unknown? What foreshadows his fear?
3. What objects and experiences that formed part of their daytime walk are repeated at night? How do they differ?
4. How does the narrator's use of pronouns differ in the day and night sections of the story? How does this difference underline meaning?
5. Why doesn't the father react to the dark in the same way as the son? What is his reaction to the black train?

Cultural Contexts

1. Review the last paragraph of the story with the members of your group. What does the black train symbolize for the son? Is it temporary? Will he one day be as "secure and certain" as his father? Explain.
2. "Father and I" is a story about the rite of passage when children become adolescents and realize they can no longer depend on parents for protection. Are the two trains effective metaphors for what the narrator wants to convey? What other metaphors might he have used? Create a list of such metaphors with your group.

Elie Wiesel

The Watch

For my bar mitzvah, I remember, I had received a magnificent gold watch. It was the customary gift for the occasion, and was meant to remind each boy that henceforth he would be held responsible for his acts before the Torah and its timeless laws.

But I could not keep my gift. I had to part with it the very day my native town became the pride of the Hungarian nation by chasing from its confines every single one of its Jews. The glorious masters of our municipality were jubilant: they were rid of us, there would be no more kaftans on the streets. The local newspaper was brief and to the point: from now on, it would be possible to state one's place of residence without feeling shame.

The time was late April, 1944.

In the early morning hours of that particular day, after a sleepless night, the ghetto was changed into a cemetery and its residents into gravediggers. We were digging feverishly in the courtyard, the garden, the cellar, consigning to the earth, temporarily we thought, whatever remained of the belongings accumulated by several generations, the sorrow and reward of long years of toil.

My father took charge of the jewelry and valuable papers. His head bowed, he was silently digging near the barn. Not far away, my mother, crouched on the damp ground, was burying the silver candelabra she used only on Shabbat eve; she was moaning softly, and I avoided her eyes. My sisters burrowed near the cellar. The youngest, Tziporah, had chosen the garden, like myself. Solemnly shoveling, she declined my help. What did she have to hide? Her toys? Her school notebooks? As for me, my only possession was my watch. It meant a lot to me. And so I decided to bury it in a dark, deep hole, three paces away from the fence, under a poplar tree whose thick, strong foliage seemed to provide a reasonably secure shelter.

All of us expected to recover our treasures. On our return, the earth would give them back to us. Until then, until the end of the storm, they would be safe.

Yes, we were naïve. We could not foresee that the very same evening, before the last train had time to leave the station, an excited mob of well-informed friendly neighbors would be rushing through the ghetto's wide-open houses and courtyards, leaving not a stone or beam unturned, throwing themselves upon the loot.

Twenty years later, standing in our garden, in the middle of the night, I remember the first gift, also the last, I ever received from my parents. I am seized by an irrational, irresistible desire to see it, to see if it is still there in the same spot, and if defying all laws of probability, it has survived—like me—by accident, not knowing how or why. My curiosity becomes obsession. I think neither of my father's money nor of my mother's candlesticks. All that matters in this town is my gold watch and the sound of its ticking.

Despite the darkness, I easily find my way in the garden. Once more I am the bar mitzvah child; here is the barn, the fence, the tree. Nothing has changed. To my left, the path leading to the Slotvino Rebbe's house. The Rebbe, though, had changed: the burning bush burned itself out and there is nothing left, not even smoke. What could he possibly have hidden the day we went away? His phylacteries? His prayer shawl? The holy scrolls inherited from his famous ancestor Rebbe Meirl of Premishlan? No, probably not even that kind of treasure. He had taken everything along, convinced that he was thus protecting not only himself but his disciples as well. He was proved wrong, the wonder rabbi.

But I mustn't think of him, not now. The watch, I must think of the watch. Maybe it was spared. Let's see, three steps to the right. Stop. Two forward. I recognize the place. Instinctively, I get ready to re-enact the scene my memory recalls. I fall on my

[handwritten margin notes: "fast-paced" "like tempo rhythm" "watch" "fast heart-rate" "suspense"]

knees. What can I use to dig? There is a shovel in the barn; its door is never locked. But by groping around in the dark I risk stumbling and waking the people sleeping in the house. They would take me for a marauder, a thief, and hand me over to the police. They might even kill me. Never mind, I'll have to manage without a shovel. Or any other tool. I'll use my hands, my nails. But it is difficult; the soil is hard, frozen, it resists as if determined to keep its secret. Too bad, I'll punish it by being the stronger.

Feverishly, furiously, my hands claw the earth, impervious to cold, fatigue and pain. One scratch, then another. No matter. Continue. My nails inch ahead, my fingers dig in, I bear down, my every fiber participates in the task. Little by little the hole deepens. I must hurry. My forehead touches the ground. Almost. I break out in a cold sweat, I am drenched, delirious. Faster, faster. I shall rip the earth from end to end, but I must know. Nothing can stop or frighten me. I'll go to the bottom of my fear, to the bottom of night, but I will know.

What time is it? How long have I been here? Five minutes, five hours? Twenty years. This night was defying time. I was laboring to exhume not an object but time itself, the soul and memory of that time. Nothing could be more urgent, more vital.

Suddenly a shiver goes through me. A sharp sensation, like a bite. My fingers touch something hard, metallic, rectangular. So I have not been digging in vain. The garden is spinning around me, over me. I stand up to catch my breath. A moment later, I'm on my knees again. Cautiously, gently I take the box from its tomb. Here it is, in the palm of my hand: the last relic, the only remaining symbol of everything I had loved, of everything I had been. A voice inside me warns: Don't open it, it contains nothing but emptiness, throw it away and run. I cannot heed the warning; it is too late to turn back. I need to know, either way. A slight pressure of my thumb and the box opens. I stifle the cry rising in my throat: the watch is there. Quick, a match. And another. Fleetingly, I catch a glimpse of it. The pain is blinding: could this thing, this object, be my gift, my pride? My past? Covered with dirt and rust, crawling with worms, it is unrecognizable, revolting. Unable to move, wondering what to do, I remain staring at it with the disgust one feels for love betrayed or a body debased. I am angry with myself for having yielded to curiosity. But disappointment gives way to profound pity: the watch too lived through war and holocaust, the kind reserved for watches perhaps. In its way, it too is a survivor, a ghost infested with humiliating sores and obsolete memories. Suddenly I feel the urge to carry it to my lips, dirty as it is, to kiss and console it with my tears, as one might console a living being, a sick friend returning from far away and requiring much kindness and rest, especially rest.

I touch it, I caress it. What I feel, besides compassion, is a strange kind of gratitude. You see, the men I had believed to be immortal had vanished into fiery clouds. My teachers, my friends, my guides had all deserted me. While this thing, this nameless, lifeless thing had survived for the sole purpose of welcoming me on my return and providing an epilogue to my childhood. And there awakens in me a desire to confide in it, to tell it my adventures, and in exchange, listen to its own. What had happened in my absence: who had first taken possession of my house, my bed? Or rather, no; our confidences could wait for another time, another place: Paris, New York, Jerusalem. But first I would entrust it to the best jeweler in the world, so that the watch might recover its luster, its memory of the past.

It is growing late. The horizon is turning a deep red. I must go. The tenants will soon be waking, they will come down to the well for water. No time to lose. I stuff the watch into my pocket and cross the garden. I enter the courtyard. From under the porch a dog barks. And stops at once: he knows I am not a thief, anything but a thief. I open the gate. Halfway down the street I am overcome by violent remorse: I have just committed my first theft.

I turn around, retrace my steps through courtyard and garden. Again I find myself kneeling, as at Yom Kippur services, beneath the poplar. Holding my breath, my eyes refusing to cry, I place the watch back into its box, close the cover, and my first gift once more takes refuge deep inside the hole. Using both hands, I smoothly fill in the earth to remove all traces.

Breathless and with pounding heart, I reach the still deserted street. I stop and question the meaning of what I have just done. And find it inexplicable.

In retrospect, I tell myself that probably I simply wanted to leave behind me, underneath the silent soil, a reflection of my presence. Or that somehow I wanted to transform my watch into an instrument of delayed vengeance: one day, a child would play in the garden, dig near the tree and stumble upon a metal box. He would thus learn that his parents were usurpers, and that among the inhabitants of his town, once upon a time, there had been Jews and Jewish children, children robbed of their future.

The sun was rising and I was still walking through the empty streets and alleys. For a moment I thought I heard the chanting of schoolboys studying Talmud; I also thought I heard the invocations of Hasidim reciting morning prayers in thirty-three places at once. Yet above all these incantations, I heard distinctly, but as though coming from far away, the tick-tock of the watch I had just buried in accordance with Jewish custom. It was, after all, the very first gift that a Jewish child had once been given for his very first celebration.

Since that day, the town of my childhood has ceased being just another town. It has become the face of a watch.

[1964]

Journal Entry

Is there an object that you cherish as Wiesel did the gold watch? Describe why it has symbolic value for you.

Textual Considerations

1. What prompts Wiesel to dig up the watch twenty years later? What does he mean when he says that he was laboring to exhume "time itself, the soul and memory of that time"?
2. Discuss Wiesel's use of such literary devices as repetition, symbolism, and fragmented sentences to convey the narrator's attachment to his watch.

3. Identify the climactic scene in the text, and speculate on the meaning it carries for the narrator.
4. Except for the opening section of the essay, most of the narrative is written in the present tense. Where in the account of his return to his native town does Wiesel revert to the past tense? Why does he do so? What effect does he achieve?
5. Discuss whether the image of the neighbors looting the ghetto might have unconsciously influenced the protagonist to place the watch back inside the hole. What does this image, preceded by the expression "Yes, we were naïve," indicate about his attitude about human beings in the context of this story?

Cultural Contexts

1. Consider how "The Watch" explores the concept that human beings may personally be entrapped by a historical event. To what extent has the narrator in Wiesel's story come to terms with his historical past?
2. Discuss with your group the degree to which our personal past contributes to our present selves, and debate whether understanding our pasts is necessary for self-realization. Is it important to write about significant past experiences? What consensus did your group reach?

Tobias Wolff

Powder

Just before Christmas my father took me skiing at Mount Baker. He's had to fight for the privilege of my company, because my mother was still angry with him for sneaking me into a night-club during our last visit, to see Thelonious Monk.

He wouldn't give up. He promised, hand on heart, to take good care of me and have me home for dinner on Christmas Eve, and she relented. But as we were checking out of the lodge that morning it began to snow, and in this snow he observed some quality that made it necessary for us to get in one last run. We got in several last runs. He was indifferent to my fretting. Snow whirled around us in bitter, blinding squalls, hissing like sand, and still we skied. As the life bore us to the peak yet again, my father looked at his watch and said, "Criminey. This'll have to be a fast one."

By now I couldn't see the trail. There was no point in trying. I stuck to him like white on rice and did what he did and somehow made it to the bottom without sailing off a cliff. We returned our skis and my father put chains on the Austin-Healy while I swayed from foot to foot, clapping my mittens and wishing I were home. I could see everything. The green tablecloth, the plates with the holly pattern, the red candles waiting to be lit.

We passed a diner on our way out. "You want some soup?" my father asked. I shook my head. "Buck up," he said. "I'll get you there. Right, doctor?"

I was supposed to say, "Right, doctor," but I didn't say anything.

A state trooper waved us down outside the resort. A pair of sawhorses were blocking the road. The trooper came up to our car and bent down to my father's window. His face was bleached by the cold. Snowflakes clung to his eyebrows and to the fur trim of his jacket and cap.

"Don't tell me," my father said.

The trooper told him. The road was closed. It might get cleared, it might not. Storm took everyone by surprise. So much, so fast. Hard to get people moving. Christmas Eve. What can you do?

My father said, "Look. We're talking about four, five inches. I've taken this car through worse than that."

The trooper straightened up, boots creaking. His face was out of sight but I could hear him. "The road is closed."

My father sat with both hands on the wheel, rubbing the wood with his thumbs. He looked at the barricade for a long time. He seemed to be trying to master the idea of it. Then he thanked the trooper, and with a weird, old-maidy show of caution turned the car around. "Your mother will never forgive me for this," he said.

"We should have left before," I said, "Doctor."

He didn't speak to me again until we were both in a booth at the diner, waiting for our burgers. "She won't forgive me," he said, "Do you understand? Never."

"I guess," I said, but no guesswork was required; she wouldn't forgive him.

"I can't let that happen." He bent toward me. "I'll tell you what I want. I want us to be together again. Is that what you want?"

I wasn't sure, but I said, "Yes, sir."

He bumped my chin with his knuckles. "That's all I needed to hear."

When we finished eating he went to the pay phone in the back of the diner, then joined me in the booth again. I figured he'd called my mother, but he didn't give a report. He sipped at his coffee and stared out the window at the empty road. "Come on!" When the trooper's car went past, lights flashing, he got up and dropped some money on the check. "Okay. *Vamanos.*"

The wind had died. The snow was falling straight down, less of it now; lighter. We drove away from the resort, right up to the barricade. "Move it," my father told me. When I looked at him he said, "What are you waiting for?" I got out and dragged one of the sawhorses aside, then pushed it back after he drove through. When I got inside the car he said, "Now you're an accomplice. We go down together." He put the car in gear and looked at me. "Joke, doctor."

"Funny, doctor."

Down the first long stretch I watched the road behind us, to see if the trooper was on our tail. The barricade vanished. Then there was nothing but snow: snow on the road, snow kicking up from the chains, snow on the trees, snow in the sky; and our trail in the snow. I faced around and had a shock. The lie of the road behind us had been marked by our own tracks, but there were no tracks ahead of us. My father was breaking virgin snow between a line of tall trees. He was humming "Stars Fell on Alabama." I felt snow brush along the floorboards under my feet. To keep my hands from shaking I clamped them between my knees.

My father grunted in a thoughtful way and said, "Don't ever try this yourself."

"I won't."

"That's what you say now, but someday you'll get your license and then you'll think you can do anything. Only you won't be able to do this. You need, I don't know—a certain instinct."

"Maybe I have it."

"You don't. You have your strong points, but not . . . you know. I only mention it because I don't want you to get the idea this is something just anybody can do. I'm a great driver. That's not a virtue, okay? It's just a fact, and one you should be aware of. Of course you have to give the old heap some credit, too—there aren't many cars I'd try this with. Listen!"

I listened. I heard the slap of the chains, the stiff, jerky rasp of the wipers, the purr of the engine. It really did purr. The car was almost new. My father couldn't afford it, and kept promising to sell it, but here it was.

I said, "Where do you think that policeman went to?"

"Are you warm enough?" He reached over and cranked up the blower. Then he turned off the wipers. We didn't need them. The clouds had brightened. A few sparse, feathery flakes drifted into our slipstream and were swept away. We left the trees and entered a broad field of snow that ran level for a while and then tilted sharply downward. Orange stakes had been planted at intervals in two parallel lines and my father ran a course between them, though they were far enough apart to leave considerable doubt in my mind as to where exactly the road lay. He was humming again, doing little scat riffs around the melody.

"Okay, then. What are my strong points?"

"Don't get me started," he said. "It'd take all day."

"Oh, right. Name one."

"Easy. You always think ahead."

True. I always thought ahead. I was a boy who kept his clothes on numbered hangers to ensure proper rotation. I bothered my teachers for homework assignments far ahead of their due dates so I could make up schedules. I thought ahead, and that was why I knew that there would be other troopers waiting for us at the end of our ride, if we got there. What I did not know was that my father would wheedle and plead his way past them—he didn't sing "O Tannenbaum" but just about—and get me home for dinner, buying a little more time before my mother decided to make the split final. I knew we'd get caught; I was resigned to it. And maybe for this reason I stopped moping and began to enjoy myself.

Why not? This was one for the books. Like being in a speedboat, only better. You can't go downhill in a boat. And it was all ours. And it kept coming, the laden trees, the unbroken surface of snow, the sudden white vistas. Here and there I saw hints of the road, ditches, fences, stakes, but not so many that I could have found my way. But then I didn't have to. My father in his forty-eighth year, rumpled, kind, bankrupt of honor, flushed with certainty. He was a great driver. All persuasion, no coercion. Such subtlety at the wheel, such tactful pedalwork. I actually trusted him. And the best was yet to come—switchbacks and hairpins impossible to describe. Except maybe to say this: if you haven't driven fresh powder, you haven't driven.

[1996]

Journal Entry

How effective is the title of the story? Write a journal entry on the images that come to mind when you think of powder.

Textual Considerations

1. Characterize the narrator's attitude toward his father. How would you describe their relationship? Cite evidence from the text to justify your answer.
2. How does the dialogue between the characters in "Powder" affect your interpretation of their relationship? How does the father's position toward responsibility affect the son? Be specific.
3. Compare the language and imagery the narrator uses to describe his relationship with his mother to that of his father. How has the separation of his parents affected him? What do you see as the likely outcome of their breakup on the son?
4. While driving down the mountain, the narrator observed, "The lie of the road behind us had been marked by our own tracks, but there were no tracks ahead of us." How would you relate this observation to their relationship?
5. What is the son's attitude toward his father by the end of the story? Does the story end on a positive note? Explain your answer.

Cultural Contexts

1. Many authors write about father-and-son relationships. It is an important topic in that it can give the reader revealing glimpses into how diverse cultures deal with the subject on social, ethnic, and historical levels. Discuss with your group the father-and-son relationship in "Powder." How does it compare with other stories you may have read in part one (e.g., "Father and I," "The Unforgetting")? Discuss with your group your own relationship with your father or with a "father figure" you may have known growing up.
2. In contemporary societies, divorce is a fact of life. For children who come from broken homes, this is or could be a difficult adjustment. What is unusual regarding the nature of the characters in "Powder"? Record your group's responses.

ESSAYS

Toni Morrison

The Nobel Lecture in Literature

Your Majesties, Your Highnesses, Ladies and Gentlemen:

Narrative has never been merely entertainment for me. It is, I believe, one of the principal ways in which we absorb knowledge. I hope you will understand, then, why I begin these remarks with the opening phrase of what must be the oldest sentence in the world, and the earliest one we remember from childhood: "Once upon a time . . . "

"Once upon a time there was an old woman. Blind but wise." Or was it an old man? A guru, perhaps. Or a *griot* soothing restless children. I have heard this story, or one exactly like it in the lore of several cultures.

"Once upon a time there was an old woman. Blind Wise."

In the version I know the woman is the daughter of slaves, black, American, and lives alone in a small house outside of town. Her reputation for wisdom is without peer and without question.

Among her people she is both the law and its transgression. The honor she is paid and the awe in which she is held reach beyond her neighborhood to places far away, to the city where the intelligence of rural prophets is the source of much amusement.

One day the woman is visited by some young people who seem to be bent on disproving her clairvoyance and showing her up for the fraud they believe she is. Their plan is simple: they enter her house and ask the one question the answer to which rides solely on her difference from them, a difference they regard as a profound disability: her blindness. They stand before her, and one of them says,

"Old woman, I hold in my hand a bird. Tell me whether it is living or dead." She does not answer, and the question is repeated. "Is the bird I am holding living or dead?" Still she does not answer. She is blind and cannot see her visitors, let alone what is in their hands. She does not know their color, gender or homeland. She only knows their motive. The old woman's silence is so long; the young people have trouble holding their laughter.

Finally she speaks and her voice is soft but stern. "I don't know," she says. "I don't know whether the bird you are holding is dead or alive, but what I do know is that it is in your hands. It is in your hands."

Her answer can be taken to mean: if it is dead, you have either found it that way or you have killed it. If it is alive, you can still kill it. Whether it is to stay alive is your decision. Whatever the case it is your responsibility.

For parading their power and her helplessness, the young visitors are reprimanded, told they are responsible not only for the act of mockery but also for the

60

small bundle of life sacrificed to achieve its aims. The blind woman shifts attention away from the assertions of power to the instrument through which that power is exercised.

Speculation on what (other than its own frail body) that bird in the hand might signify has always been attractive to me, but especially so now, thinking as I have been about the work I do that has brought me to this company. So I choose to read the bird as language and the woman as a practiced writer.

She is worried about how the language she dreams in, given to her at birth, is handled, put into service, even withheld from her for certain nefarious purposes. Being a writer, she thinks of language partly as a system, partly as a living thing over which one has control, but mostly as agency—as an act with consequences. So the question the children put to her, "Is it living or dead?" is not unreal, because she thinks of language as susceptible to death, erasure; certainly imperiled and salvageable only by an effort of the will. She believes that if the bird in the hands of her visitors is dead, the custodians are responsible for the corpse. For her a dead language is not only one no longer spoken or written, it is unyielding language content to admire its own paralysis. Like statist language, censored and censoring, ruthless in its policing duties, it has no desire or purpose other than to maintain the free range of its own narcotic narcissism, its own exclusively and dominance. However moribund, it is not without effect, for it actively thwarts the intellect, stalls conscience, suppresses human potential. Unreceptive to interrogation, it cannot form or tolerate new ideas, shape other thoughts, tell another story, fill baffling silences. Official language smitheried to sanction ignorance and preserve privilege is a suit of armor, polished to shocking glitter, a husk from which the knight departed long ago. Yet there it is, dumb, predatory, sentimental: exciting reverence in schoolchildren, providing shelter for despots, summoning false memories of stability, harmony among the public.

She is convinced that when language dies, out of carelessness, disuse, indifference, and absence of esteem, or killed by fiat, not only she herself but all users and makers are accountable for its demise. In her country children have bitten their tongues off and use bullets instead to iterate the void of speechlessness, of disabled and disabling language, of language adults have abandoned altogether as a device for grappling with meaning, providing guidance, or expressing love. But she knows tongue-suicide is not only the choice of children. It is common among the infantile heads of state and power merchants whose evacuated language leaves them with no access to what is left of their human instincts, for they speak only to those who obey, or in order to force obedience.

The systematic looting of language can be recognized by the tendency of its users to forgo its nuanced, complex, mid-wifery properties, replacing them with menace and subjugation. Oppressive language does more than represent violence; it is violence; does more than represent the limits of knowledge; it limits knowledge. Whether it is obscuring state language or the faux language of mindless media; whether it is the round but calcified language of the academy or the commodity-driven language of science; whether it is the malign language of law-without-ethics, or language designed for the estrangement of minorities, hiding its racist plunder in its literary cheek—it must be rejected, altered, and exposed. It is the language that drinks blood, laps vulnerabilities, tucks its fascist boots under crinolines of respectability and patriotism as it moves relentlessly toward the bottom line and the bottomed-out mind. Sexist language, racist language, theistic language—all are typical of the policing languages of mastery, and cannot, do not, permit new knowledge or encourage the mutual exchange of ideas.

The old woman is keenly aware that no intellectual mercenary or insatiable dictator, no paid-for politician or demagogue, no counterfeit journalist would be persuaded by her thoughts. There is and will be rousing language to keep citizens armed and arming; slaughtered and slaughtering in the malls, courthouses, post offices, playgrounds, bedrooms and boulevards; stirring, memorializing language to mask the pity and waste of needless death. There will be more diplomatic language to countenance rape, torture, assassination. There is and will be more seductive, mutant language designed to throttle women, to pack their throats like pate-producing geese with their own unsayable, transgressive words; there will be more of the language of surveillance disguised as research; of politics and history calculated to render the suffering of millions mute; language glamorized to thrill the dissatisfied and bereft into assaulting their neighbors; arrogant pseudo-empirical language crafted to lock creative people into cages of inferiority and hopelessness.

Underneath the eloquence, the glamour, the scholarly associations, however stirring or seductive, the heart of such language is languishing, or perhaps not beating at all—if the bird is already dead.

She has thought about what could have been the intellectual history of any discipline if it had not insisted upon, or been forced into, the waste of time and life that rationalizations for and representation of dominance required—lethal discourses of exclusion blocking access to cognition for both the excluder and the excluded.

The conventional wisdom of the Tower of Babel story is that the collapse was a misfortune. That it was the distraction or the weight of many languages that precipitated the tower's failed architecture. That one monolithic language would have expedited the building and heaven would have been reached. Whose heaven, she wonders? And what kind? Perhaps the achievement of Paradise was premature, a little hasty if no one could take the time to understand other languages, other views, other narratives. Had they, the heaven they imagined might have been found at their feet. Complicated, demanding, yes, but a view of heaven as life; not heaven as post-life.

She would not want to leave her young visitors with the impression that language should be forced to stay alive merely to be. The vitality of language lies in its ability to limn the actual, imagined, and possible lives of its speakers, readers, writers. Although its poise is sometimes in displacing experience, it is not a substitute for it. It arcs toward the place where meaning may lie. When a President of the United States thought about the graveyard his country had become, and said, "The world will little note nor long remember what we say here. But it will never forget what they did here." His simple words were exhilarating in their life-sustaining properties because they refused to encapsulate the reality of 600,000 dead men in a cataclysmic race war. Refusing to monumentalize, disdaining the "final word," the precise "summing up," acknowledging their words signal deference to the uncapturability of the life it mourns. It is the deference that moves her, that recognition that language can never live up to life once and for all. Nor should it. Language can never "pin down" slavery, genocide, war. Nor should it yearn for the arrogance to be able to do so. Its force, its felicity, is in its reach toward the ineffable.

Be it broad or slender, burrowing, blasting, or refusing to sanctify; whether it laughs out loud or is a cry without an alphabet, the choice word or the chosen silence, unmolested language surges toward knowledge, not its destruction. But who does not know of literature banned because it is interrogative; discredited because it is critical; erased because alternate? And how many are outraged by the thought of a self-ravaged tongue?

Word-work is sublime, she thinks, because it is generative; it makes meaning that secures our difference, our human difference—the way in which we are like no other life.

We die. That may be the meaning of life. But we do language. That may be the measure of our lives.

"Once upon time . . ." Visitors ask an old woman a question. Who are they, these children? What did they make of that encounter? What did they hear in those final words: "the bird is in your hands"? A sentence that gestures toward possibility, or one that drops a latch? Perhaps what the children heard was, "It is not my problem. I am old, female, black, blind. What wisdom I have now is in knowing I cannot help you. The future of language is yours."

They stand there. Suppose nothing was in their hands. Suppose the visit was only a ruse, a trick to get to be spoken to, taken seriously, as they have not been before. A chance to interrupt, to violate the adult world, its miasma of discourse about them. Urgent questions are at stake, including the one they have asked: "Is the bird we hold living or dead?" Perhaps the question meant: "Could someone tell us what is life? What is death?" No trick at all, no silliness. A straightforward question worthy of the attention of a wise one. An old one. And if the old and wise who have lived life and faced death cannot describe either, who can?

But she does not; she keeps her secret, her good opinion of herself, gnomic pronouncements, her art without commitment. She keeps her distance, enforces it and retreats into the singularity of isolation, in sophisticate privileged space.

Nothing, no word follows her declaration of transfer. That silence is deep, deeper than the meaning available in the words she has spoken. It shivers this silence, and the children, annoyed, fill it with language invented on the spot.

"Is there no speech," they ask her, "no words you can give us that help us break through your dossier of failures?" through the education you have just given us that is no education at all because we are paying close attention to what you have done as well as to what you have said? to the barrier you have erected between generosity and wisdom?

"We have no bird in our hands, living or dead." We have only you and our important question. Is the nothing in our hands something you could not bear to contemplate, to even guess? Don't you remember being young, when language was magic without meaning? When what you could say, could not mean? When the invisible was what imagination strove to see? When questions and demands for answers burned so brightly you trembled with fury at not knowing?

"Do we have to begin consciousness with a battle heroes and heroines like you have already fought and lost, leaving us with nothing in our hands except what you have imagined is there? Your answer is artful, but its artfulness embarrasses us and ought to embarrass you. Your answer is indecent in its self-congratulation. A made-for-television script that makes no sense if there is nothing in our hands."

"Why didn't you reach out, touch us with your soft fingers, delay the sound bite, the lesson, until you knew who we were? Did you so despise our trick, our *modus operandi*, that you could not see that we were baffled about how to get your attention? We are young. Unripe. We have heard all our short lives that we have to be responsible. What could that possibly mean in the catastrophe this world has become; where, as a poet said, 'nothing needs to be exposed since it is already barefaced'? Our inheritance is an affront. You want us to have your old blank eyes and see only cruelty and mediocrity." Do you think we are stupid enough to perjure ourselves again and again with the fiction of nationhood? How dare you talk to us of duty when we stand waist deep in the toxins of your past?

"You trivialize us and trivialize the bird that is not in our hands. Is there no context for our lives? No song, no literature, no poem full of vitamins, no history connected to experience that you can pass along to help us start strong? You are an adult. The old one, the wise one. Stop thinking about saving your face. Think of our lives and tell us your particularized world. Make up a story. Narrative is radical, creating us at the very moment it is being created. We will not blame you if your reach exceeds your grasp; if love so ignites your words that they go down in flames and nothing is left but their scald. Or if, with the reticence of a surgeon's hands, your words suture only the places where blood might flow. We know you can never do it properly—once and for all. Passion is never enough; neither is skill. But try. For our sake and yours forget your name in the street; tell us what the world has been to you in the dark places and in the light. Don't tell us what to believe, what to fear. Show us belief's wide skirt and the stitch that unravels fear's caul. You, old woman, blessed with blindness, can speak the language that tells us what only language can: how to see without pictures. Language alone protects us from the scariness of things with no names. Language alone is meditation."

"Tell us what it is to be a woman so that we may know what it is to be a man. What moves at the margin. What it is to have no home in this place. To be set adrift from the one you knew. What it is to live at the edge of towns that cannot bear your company."

"Tell us about ships turned away from shorelines at Easter, placental in a field. Tell us about a wagonload of slaves, how they sang so softly their breath was indistinguishable from the falling snow. How they knew from the hunch of the nearest shoulder that the next stop would be their last. How, with hands prayered in their sex, they thought of heat, then sun. Lifting their faces as though it was there for the taking. Turning as though there for the taking. They stop at an inn. The driver and his mate go in with the lamp, leaving them humming in the dark. The horses void steams into the snow beneath its hooves and the hiss and melt are the envy of the freezing slaves."

"The inn door opens: a girl and a boy step away from its light. They club into the wagon bed. The boy will have a gun in three years, but now he carries a lamp and a jug of warm cider. They pass it from mouth to mouth. The girl offers bread, pieces of meat and something more, a glance into the eyes of the one she serves.

One helping for each man, two for each woman. And a look. They look back. The next stop will be their last. But not this one. This one is warmed."

It's quiet again when the children finish speaking, until the woman breaks into the silence.

"Finally," she says. "I trust you now. I trust you with the bird that is not in your hands because you have truly caught it. Look. How lovely it is, this thing we have done—together."

I entered this hall pleasantly haunted by those who have entered it before me. That company of laureates is both daunting and welcoming, for among its lists are names of persons whose work has made whole worlds available to me. The sweep and specificity of their art have sometimes broken my heart with the courage and clarity of its vision. The astonishing brilliance with which they practiced their craft has challenged and nurtured my own. My debt to them rivals the profound one I owe to the Swedish Academy for having selected me to join that distinguished alumni.

Early in October an artist friend left a message which I kept on the answering service for weeks and played back every once in a while just to hear the trembling pleasure in her voice and the faith in her words. "My dear sister," she said, "the prize that is yours is also ours and could not have been placed in better hands." The spirit of her message with its earned optimism and sublime trust marks this day for me.

I will leave this hall, however, with a new and much more delightful haunting than the one I felt upon entering: this is the company of the laureates yet to come. Those who, even as I speak, are mining, sifting and polishing languages for illuminations none of us has dreamed of. But whether or not anyone of them secures a place in this pantheon, the gathering of these writers is unmistakable and mounting. Their voices bespeak civilizations gone and yet to be; the precipice from which their imagination's gaze will rivet us; they do not blink or turn away. It is therefore mindful to the gifts of my predecessors, the blessing of my sisters, in joyful anticipation of writers to come that I accept the honor the Swedish Academy has done me, and ask you to share what is for me a moment of grace.

[1993]

Journal Entry

What memories, images, and emotions does the phrase "Once upon a time" evoke for you?

Textual Considerations

1. What is a guru or a griot? Is it significant that the old woman is blind? Explain.
2. Why does she reprimand the young people?
3. Review paragraph 11 and identify the deadening characteristics of the statist language to which Morrison refers.
4. Who does she blame for the looting of language in paragraph 13?
5. In paragraph 18 Morrison states that language can never be a substitute for life itself. What does she mean by her statement, "Its force, its felicity, is in its reach toward the ineffable"?
6. What is the significance of the questions the young people ask?
7. What does their story about slaves in a wagon mean to the old woman?
8. What is it that they have "done together"?

Cultural Contexts

1. Explain the significance of Morrison's allusion to the Tower of Babel. What is your response to monolingualism as opposed to multilingualism?
2. In another context, Morrison has posed this challenge to your generation: "Although you don't have complete control of the narrative—no author does—you can nevertheless, create it. . . . The theme you choose may change or elude you, but being your story means you can always choose the tone, the style. It also means you can invent the language to say who you are and what you mean." Discuss this proposition with your group. What elements would you include in your narrative thus far?

Plato

The Allegory of the Cave

And now, I said, let me show in a figure how far our nature is enlightened or unenlightened: Behold! human beings living in an underground den, which has a mouth open towards the light and reaching all along the den; here they have been from their childhood, and have their legs and necks chained so that they cannot move, and can only see before them, being prevented by the chains from turning round their heads. Above and behind them a fire is blazing at a distance, and between the fire and the prisoners there is a raised way; and you will see, if you look, a low wall built along the way, like the screen which marionette players have in front of them, over which they show the puppets.

I see.

And do you see, I said, men passing along the wall carrying all sorts of vessels, and statues and figures of animals made of wood and stone and various materials, which appear over the wall? Some of them are talking, others silent.

You have shown me a strange image, and they are strange prisoners.

Like ourselves, I replied; and they see only their own shadows, or the shadows of one another, which the fire throws on the opposite wall of the cave?

True, he said; how could they see anything but the shadows if they were never allowed to move their heads?

And of the objects which are being carried in like manner they would only see the shadows?

Yes, he said.

And if they were able to converse with one another, would they not suppose that they were naming what was actually before them?

Very true.

And suppose further that the prison had an echo which came from the other side, would they not be sure to fancy when one of the passers-by spoke that the voice which they heard came from the passing shadow?

No question, he replied.

To them, I said, the truth would be literally nothing but the shadows of the images.

That is certain.

And now look again, and see what will naturally follow if the prisoners are released and disabused of their error. At first, when any of them is liberated and compelled suddenly to stand up and turn his neck round and walk and look towards the light, he will suffer sharp pains; the glare will distress him and he will be unable to see the realities of which in his former state he had seen the shadows; and then conceive some one saying to him, that what he saw before was an illusion, but that now, when he is approaching nearer to being and his eye is turned towards more real existence, he has a clearer vision—what will be his reply? And you may further imagine that his instructor is pointing to the objects as they pass and requiring him to name them—will he not be perplexed? Will he not fancy that the shadows which he formerly saw are truer than the objects which are now shown to him?

Far truer.

And if he is compelled to look straight at the light, will he not have a pain in his eyes which will make him turn away to take refuge in the objects of vision which he can see, and which he will conceive to be in reality clearer than the things which are now being shown to him?

True, he said.

And suppose once more, that he is reluctantly dragged up a steep and rugged ascent, and held fast until he is forced into the presence of the sun himself, is he not likely to be pained and irritated? When he approaches the light his eyes will be dazzled and he will not be able to see anything at all of what are now called realities.

Not all in a moment, he said.

He will require to grow accustomed to the sight of the upper world. And first he will see the shadows best, next the reflections of men and other objects in the water, and then the objects themselves; then he will gaze upon the light of the moon and the stars and the spangled heaven; and he will see the sky and the stars by night better than the sun or the light of the sun by day?

Certainly.

Last of all he will be able to see the sun, and not mere reflections of him in the water, but he will see him in his own proper place, and not in another; and he will contemplate him as he is.

Certainly.

He will then proceed to argue that this is he who gives the season and the years, and is the guardian of all that is in the visible world, and in a certain way the cause of all things which he and his fellows have been accustomed to behold.

Clearly, he said, he would first see the sun and then reason about him.

And when he remembered his old habitation, and the wisdom of the den and his fellow-prisoners, do you not suppose that he would felicitate himself on the change, and pity them?

Certainly, he would.

And if they were in the habit of conferring honors among themselves on those who were quickest to observe the passing shadows and to remark which of them went before, and which followed after, and which were together; and who were therefore best able to draw conclusions as to the future, do you think that he would care for such honors and glories, or envy the possessors of them? Would he not say with Homer,

Better to be the poor servant of a poor master,

and to endure anything, rather than think as they do and live after their manner?

Yes, he said, I think that he would rather suffer anything than entertain these false notions and live in this miserable manner.

Imagine once more, I said, such an one coming suddenly out of the sun to be replaced in his old situation; would he not be certain to have his eyes full of darkness?

To be sure, he said.

And if there were a contest, and he had to compete in measuring the shadows with the prisoners who had never moved out of the den, while his sight was still weak, and before his eyes had become steady (and the time which would be needed to acquire this new habit of sight might be very considerable) would he not be ridiculous? Men would say of him that up he went and down he came without his eyes; and that it was better not even to think of ascending; and if any one tried to loose another and lead him up to the light, let them only catch the offender, and they would put him to death.

No question, he said.

This entire allegory, I said, you may now append, dear Glaucon, to the previous argument; the prison-house is the world of sight, the light of the fire is the sun, and you will not misapprehend me if you interpret the journey upwards to be the ascent of the soul into the intellectual world according to my poor belief, which, at your desire, I have expressed—whether rightly or wrongly God knows. But, whether true or false, my opinion is that in the world of knowledge the idea of good appears last of all, and is seen only with an effort; and, when seen, is also inferred to be the universal author of all things beautiful and right, parent of light and of the lord of light in this visible world, and the immediate source of reason and truth in the intellectual; and that this is the power upon which he who would act rationally either in public or private life must have his eye fixed.

I agree, he said, as far as I am able to understand you.

Moreover, I said, you must not wonder that those who attain to this beatific vision are unwilling to descend to human affairs; for their souls are ever hastening into the upper world where they desire to dwell; which desire of theirs is very natural, if our allegory may be trusted.

Yes, very natural.

And is there anything surprising in one who passes from divine contemplations to the evil state of man, misbehaving himself in a ridiculous manner; if, while his eyes are blinking and before he has become accustomed to the surrounding darkness, he is compelled to fight in courts of law, or in other places, about the images or the shadows of images of justice, and is endeavouring to meet the conceptions of those who have never yet seen absolute justice?

Anything but surprising, he replied.

Any one who has common sense will remember that the bewilderments of the eyes are of two kinds, and arise from two causes, either from coming out of the light or from going into the light, which is true of the mind's eye, quite as much as of the bodily eye; and he who remembers this when he sees any one whose vision is perplexed and weak, will not be too ready to laugh; he will first ask whether that soul of man has come out of the brighter life, and is unable to see because unaccustomed to the dark, or having turned from darkness to the day is dazzled by excess of light. And he will count the one happy in his condition and state of being, and he will pity the other; or, if he have a mind to laugh at the soul which comes from below into the light, there will be more reason in this than in the laugh which greets him who returns from above out of the light into the den.

That, he said, is a very just distinction.

[c. 340 B.C.]

Journal Entry

Do you agree with Plato that human beings are often reluctant to confront unpleasant realities and prefer to fantasize and avoid them? What examples can you think of to support or refute his point of view?

Textual Considerations

1. An **allegory**, or **parable**, is a concrete story on one level and an explication of abstract, moral truths on another. Plato explains at the end what each part of history symbolizes on the moral level. What correspondences does he establish?
2. If we assume the people in the cave represent humankind, why does Plato call them "prisoners"? Although Plato does not specify who placed the people in chains, who seems to be the jailer when the freed prisoner returns to free the others?
3. Plato equates making the "journey upwards" on the story level with gaining knowledge on the **abstract** level. Why, instead of making the ascent, would people prefer to remain in the cave with illusions of what is real? Do you agree with Plato's analysis of human nature here? Explain.
4. Plato's essay is presented as a dialogue between teacher and student. What contribution to structure and theme is made by the student's brief comments?
5. Review Plato's concluding paragraph. Is his final comment on the allegory necessary, or would you have been able to fit together his meaning without this ending? Explain.

Cultural Contexts

1. Plato says of the man who returns to the cave after seeing the sun that if the prisoners could lay hands on him, they would kill him. Are there historical or contemporary situations that fulfill this prediction?
2. Discuss with your group Plato's concept that human beings are often reluctant to confront reality. How does his viewpoint compare with Emily Dickinson's "Tell all the truth but tell it slant" (Part Five)? What examples can you think of to support or refute Plato's thesis?

N. Scott Momaday

The Way to Rainy Mountain

A single knoll rises out of the plain in Oklahoma, north and west of the Wichita Range. For my people, the Kiowas, it is an old landmark, and they gave it the name Rainy Mountain. The hardest winter in the world is there. Winter brings blizzards, hot tornadic winds arise in the spring, and in summer the prairie is an anvil's edge. The grass turns brittle and brown, and it cracks beneath your feet. There are green belts along the rivers and creeks, linear groves of hickory and pecan, willow and witch hazel. At a distance in July or August, the steaming foliage seems almost to writhe in fire. Great green and yellow grasshoppers are everywhere in the tall grass, popping up like corn to sting the flesh, and tortoises crawl about on the red earth, going nowhere in the plenty of time. Loneliness is an aspect of the land. All things in the plain are isolate; there is no confusion of objects in the eye, but *one* hill or *one* tree or *one* man. To look upon that landscape in the early morning, with the sun at your back, is to lose the sense of proportion. Your imagination comes to life, and this, you think, is where Creation was begun.

I returned to Rainy Mountain in July. My grandmother had died in the spring, and I wanted to be at her grave. She had lived to be very old and at last infirm. Her only living daughter was with her when she died, and I was told that in death her face was that of a child.

I like to think of her as a child. When she was born, the Kiowas were living the last great moment of their history. For more than a hundred years they had controlled the open range from the Smoky Hill River to the Red, from the headwaters of the Canadian to the fork of the Arkansas and Cimarron. In alliance with the Comanches, they had ruled the whole of the southern Plains. War was their sacred business, and they were among the finest horsemen the world has ever known. But warfare for the Kiowas was pre-eminently a matter of disposition rather than of survival, and they never understood the grim, unrelenting advance of the U.S. Cavalry. When at last, divided and ill-provisioned, they were driven onto the Staked Plains in the cold rains of autumn, they fell into panic. In Palo Duro Canyon they abandoned their crucial stores to pillage and had nothing then but their lives. In order to save themselves, they surrendered to the soldiers of Fort Sill and were imprisoned in the old stone corral that now stands as a military museum. My grandmother was spared the humiliation of those high gray walls by eight or ten years, but she must have known from birth the affliction of defeat, the dark brooding of old warriors.

Her name was Aho, and she belonged to the last culture to evolve in North America. Her forebears came down from the high country in western Montana nearly three centuries ago. They were a mountain people, a mysterious tribe of hunters whose language has never been positively classified in any major group. In the late seventeenth century they began a long migration to the south and east. It was a journey toward the dawn, and it led to a golden age. Along the way the Kiowas were befriended by the Crows, who gave them the culture and religion of the Plains. They acquired horses, and their ancient nomadic spirit was suddenly free of the ground. They acquired Tai-me, the sacred Sun Dance doll, from that moment the object and symbol of their worship, and so shared in the divinity of the sun. Not least, they acquired the sense of destiny, therefore courage and pride. When they entered upon the southern Plains they had been transformed. No longer were they slaves to the simple necessity of survival; they were a lordly and dangerous society of fighters and thieves, hunters and priests of the sun. According to their origin myth, they entered the world through a hollow log. From one point of view, their migration was the fruit of an old prophecy, for indeed they emerged from a sunless world.

Although my grandmother lived out her long life in the shadow of Rainy Mountain, the immense landscape of the continental interior lay like memory in her blood. She could tell of the Crows, whom she had never seen, and of the Black Hills, where she had never been. I wanted to see in reality what she had seen more perfectly in the mind's eye, and traveled fifteen hundred miles to begin my pilgrimage.

Yellowstone, it seemed to me, was the top of the world, a region of deep lakes and dark timber, canyons and waterfalls. But, beautiful as it is, one might have the sense of confinement there. The skyline in all directions is close at hand, the high wall of the woods and deep cleavages of shade. There is a perfect freedom in the mountains, but it belongs to the eagle and the elk, the badger and the bear. The Kiowas reckoned their stature by the distance they could see, and they were bent and blind in the wilderness.

Descending eastward, the highland meadows are a stairway to the plain. In July the inland slope of the Rockies is luxuriant with flax and buckwheat, stonecrop and larkspur. The earth unfolds and the limit of the land recedes. Clusters of trees, and animals grazing far in the distance, cause the vision to reach away and wonder to build upon the mind. The sun follows a longer course in the day, and the sky is immense beyond all comparison. The great billowing clouds that sail upon it are shadows that move upon the grain like water, dividing light. Farther down, in the land of the Crows and Blackfeet, the plain is yellow. Sweet clover takes hold of the hills and bends upon itself to cover and seal the soil. There the Kiowas paused on their way; they had come to the place where they must change their lives. The sun is at home on the plains. Precisely there does it have the certain character of a god. When the Kiowas came to the land of the Crows, they could see the dark lees of the hills at dawn across the Bighorn River, the profusion of light on the grain shelves, the oldest deity ranging after the solstices. Not yet would they veer southward to the caldron of the land that lay below; they must wean their blood from the northern winter and hold the mountains a while longer in their view. They bore Tai-me in procession to the east.

A dark mist lay over the Black Hills, and the land was like iron. At the top of the ridge I caught sight of Devil's Tower upthrust against the gray sky as if in the birth of time the core of the earth had broken through its crust and the motion of the world was begun. There are things in nature that engender an awful quiet in the heart of man; Devil's Tower is one of them. Two centuries ago, because they could not do otherwise, the Kiowas made a legend at the base of the rock. My grandmother said:

> Eight children were there at play, seven sisters and their brother. Suddenly the boy was struck dumb; he trembled and began to run upon his hands and feet. His fingers became claws, and his body was covered with fur. Directly there was a bear where the boy had been. The sisters were terrified; they ran, and the bear ran after them. They came to the stump of a great tree, and the tree spoke to them. It bade them climb upon it, and as they did so it began to rise into the air. The bear came to kill them, but they were just beyond its reach. It reared against the tree and scored the bark all around with its claws. The seven sisters were borne into the sky, and they became the stars of the Big Dipper.

From that moment, and so long as the legend lives, the Kiowas have kinsmen in the night sky. Whatever they were in the mountains, they could be no more. However tenuous their well-being, however much they had suffered and would suffer again, they had found a way out of the wilderness.

My grandmother had a reverence for the sun, a holy regard that now is all but gone out of mankind. There was a wariness in her, and an ancient awe. She was a Christian in her later years, but she had come a long way about, and she never forgot her birthright As a child she had been to the Sun Dances; she had taken part in those annual rites, and by them she had learned the restoration of her people in the presence of Tai-me. She was about seven when the last Kiowa Sun Dance was held in 1887 on the Washita River above Rainy Mountain Creek. The buffalo were gone. In order to consummate the ancient sacrifice—to impale the head of a buffalo bull upon the medicine tree—a delegation of old men journeyed into Texas, there to beg and barter for an animal from the Goodnight herd. She was ten when the Kiowas came together for the last time as a living Sun Dance culture. They could find no buffalo; they had to hang an old hide from the sacred tree Before the dance could begin, a company of soldiers rode out from Fort Sill under orders to disperse the tribe. Forbidden without cause the essential act of their faith, having seen the wild herds slaughtered and left to rot upon the ground, the Kiowas backed away forever from the medicine tree. That was July 20, 1890, at the great bend of the Washita. My grandmother was there. Without bitterness, and for as long as she lived, she bore a vision of deicide.

Now that I can have her only in memory, I see my grandmother in the several postures that were peculiar to her: standing at the wood stove on a winter morning and turning meat in a great iron skillet; sitting at the south window, bent above her beadwork, and afterwards, when her vision had failed, looking down for a long time into the fold of her hands; going out upon a cane, very slowly as she did when the weight of age came upon her; praying. I remember her most often at prayer. She made long, rambling prayers out of suffering and hope, having seen many things. I was never sure that I had the right to hear, so exclusive were they of all mere custom and company. The last time I saw her she prayed standing by the side of her bed at night, naked to the waist, the light of a kerosene lamp moving upon her dark skin. Her long, black hair, always drawn and braided in the day, lay upon her shoulders and against her breasts like a shawl. I do not speak Kiowa, and I never understood her prayers, but there was something inherently sad in the sound, some merest hesitation upon the syllables of sorrow. She began in a high and descending pitch, exhausting her breath to silence; then again and again—and always the same intensity of effort, of something that is, and is not, like urgency in the human voice. Transported so in the dancing light among the shadows of her room, she seemed beyond the reach of time. But that was illusion; I think I knew then that I should not see her again.

[1967]

Journal Entry

What memories of grandparents can you bring to Momaday's memoir?

Textural Considerations

1. According to tribal myth, the Kiowa "entered the world through a hollow log." From what sort of world did they consider themselves to have emerged? How might this tradition have shaped the Kiowas's attitude toward life and death?
2. Momaday says his grandmother regarded the last Kiowa Sun Dance (1887) as "a vision of deicide," or god killing. Do you agree? Was it the death of a god or of a people?
3. What portrait of Momaday's grandmother emerges from the essay? How would you describe their relationship?
4. What is the significance of Momaday's equating family with tribe?
5. How does Momaday use description of the setting (the mountains and plains, the great spaces of the West) to control the mood and tone of his essay?

Cultural Contexts

1. "To be ourselves we must have ourselves—possess, if need be, repossess, our life stories." Discuss this statement by psychologist Oliver Sachs and apply it to Momaday's memoir and your own experience. To what extent, for example, does Momaday's journey to his grandmother's house help "recollect" himself?
2. If there were a sound track to Momaday's essay, what would it be? Or create one with your group and record a song that you hear.

Salman Rushdie

From *Imaginary Homelands*

An old photograph in a cheap frame hangs on a wall of the room where I work. It's a picture dating from 1946 of a house into which, at the time of its taking, I had not yet been born. The house is rather peculiar—a three-storied gabled affair with tiled roofs and round towers in two corners, each wearing a pointy tiled hat.

"The past is a foreign country," goes the famous opening sentence of L. P. Hartley's novel *The Go-Between*, "they do things differently there." But the photograph tells me to invert this idea; it reminds me that it's my present that is foreign, and that the past is home, albeit a lost home in a lost city in the mists of lost time.

A few years ago I revisited Bombay, which is my lost city, after an absence of something like half my life. Shortly after arriving, acting on an impulse, I opened the telephone directory and looked for my father's name. And, amazingly, there it was; his name, our old address, the unchanged telephone number, as if we had never gone away to the unmentionable country across the border. It was an eerie discovery. I felt as if I were being claimed, or informed that the facts of my faraway life were illusions, and that this continuity was the reality. Then I went to visit the house in the photograph and stood outside it, neither daring nor wishing to announce myself to its new owners. (I didn't want to see how they'd ruined the interior.) I was overwhelmed. The photograph had naturally been taken in black and white; and my memory, feeding on such images as this, had begun to see my childhood in the same way, monochromatically. The colors of my history had seeped out of my mind's eye; now my other two eyes were assaulted by colors, by the vividness of the red tiles, the yellow-edged green of cactus-leaves, the brilliance of bougainvillaea creeper. It is probably not too romantic to say that that was when my novel *Midnight's Children* was really born; when I realized how much I wanted to restore the past to myself, not in the faded grays of old family-album snapshots, but whole, in CinemaScope and glorious Technicolor.

Bombay is a city built by foreigners upon reclaimed land; I, who had been away so long that I almost qualified for the title, was gripped by the conviction that I, too, had a city and a history to reclaim.

It may be that writers in my position, exiles or emigrants or expatriates, are haunted by some sense of loss, some urge to reclaim, to look back, even at the risk of being mutated into pillars of salt. But if we do look back, we must also do so in the knowledge—which gives rise to profound uncertainties—that our physical alienation from India almost inevitably means that we will not be capable of reclaiming precisely the thing that was lost; that we will, in short, create fictions, not actual cities or villages, but invisible ones, imaginary homelands, Indias of the mind.

Writing my book in North London, looking out through my window onto a city scene totally unlike the ones I was imagining onto paper, I was constantly plagued by this problem, until I felt obliged to face it in the text, to make clear that (in spite of my original and I suppose somewhat Proustian ambition to unlock the gates of lost time so that the past reappeared as it actually had been, unaffected by the distortions of memory) what I was actually doing was a novel of memory and about memory, so that my India was just that: "my" India, a version and no more than one version of all the hundreds of millions of possible versions. I tried to make it as imaginatively true as I could, but imaginative truth is simultaneously honorable and suspect, and I knew that my India may only have been one to which I (who am no longer what I was, and who by quitting Bombay never became what perhaps I was meant to be) was, let us say, willing to admit I belonged.

This is why I made my narrator, Saleem, suspect in his narration; his mistakes are the mistakes of a fallible memory compounded by quirks of character and of circumstances and his vision is fragmentary. It may be that when the Indian writer who writes from outside India tries to reflect that world, he is obliged to deal in broken mirrors, some of whose fragments have been irretrievably lost.

But there is a paradox here. The broken mirror may actually be as valuable as the one which is supposedly unflawed. Let me again try and explain this from my own experience. Before beginning *Midnight's Children*, I spent many months trying simply to recall as much of the Bombay of the 1950s and 1960s as I could; and not only Bombay—Kashmir, too, and Delhi and Aligarh, which, in my book, I've moved to Agra to heighten a certain joke about the Taj Mahal. I was genuinely amazed by how much came back to me. I found myself remembering what clothes people had worn on certain days, and school scenes, and whole passages of Bombay dialogue verbatim, or so it seemed; I even remembered advertisements, film posters, the neon Jeep sign on Marine Drive, toothpaste ads for Binaca and for Kolynos, and a footbridge over the local railway line which bore, on one side, the legend "Esso puts a tiger in your tank" and, on the other, the curiously contradictory admonition: "Drive like Hell and you will get there." Old songs came back to me from nowhere. . . .

I knew that I had tapped a rich seam; but the point I want to make is that of course I'm not gifted with total recall, and it was precisely the partial nature of these memories, their fragmentation, that made them so evocative for me. The shards of memory acquired greater status, greater resonance, because they were *remains*; fragmentation made trivial things seem like symbols, and the mundane acquired numinous qualities. There is an obvious parallel here with archaeology. The broken pots of antiquity, from which the past can sometimes, but always provisionally, be reconstructed, are exciting to discover, even if they are pieces of the most quotidian objects.

It may be argued that the past is a country from which we have all emigrated, that its loss is part of our common humanity. Which seems to me self-evidently true; but I suggest that the writer who is out-of-country and even out-of-language may experience this loss in an intensified form. It is made more concrete for him by the physical fact of discontinuity, of his present being in a different place from his past, of his being "elsewhere." This may enable him to speak properly and concretely on a subject of universal significance and appeal.

But let me go further. The broken glass is not merely a mirror of nostalgia. It is also, I believe, a useful tool with which to work in the present.

John Fowles begins *Daniel Martin* with the words: "Whole sight: or all the rest is desolation." But human beings do not perceive things whole; we are not gods but wounded creatures, cracked lenses, capable only of fractured perceptions. Partial beings, in all the senses of that phrase. Meaning is a shaky edifice we build out of scraps, dogmas, childhood injuries, newspaper articles, chance remarks, old films, small victories, people hated, people loved; perhaps it is because our sense of what is the case is constricted from such inadequate materials that we defend it so fiercely, even to the death. The Fowles position seems to me a way of succumbing to the guru-illusion. Writers are no longer sages, dispensing the wisdom of the centuries. And those of us who have been forced by cultural displacement to accept the provisional nature of all truths, all certainties, have perhaps had modernism forced upon us. We can't lay claim to Olympus, and are thus released to describe our worlds in the way in which all of us, whether writers or not, perceive it from day to day. . . .

The Indian writer, looking back at India, does so through guilt-tinted spectacles. (I am of course, once more, talking about myself.) I am speaking now of those of us who emigrated . . . and I suspect that there are times when the move seems wrong to us all, when we seem, to ourselves, post-lapsarian men and women. We are Hindus who have crossed the black water; we are Muslims who eat pork. And as a result—as my use of the Christian notion of the Fall indicates—we are now partly of the West. Our identity is at once plural and partial. Sometimes we feel that we straddle two cultures; at other times, that we fall between two stools. But however ambiguous and shifting this ground may be, it is not an infertile territory for a writer to occupy. If literature is in part the business of finding new angles at which to enter reality, then once again our distance, our long geographical perspective, may provide us with such angles.

[1991]

Journal Entry

Rushdie describes Bombay as his "lost city." If you have such a place, write about a memory that conveys your emotional attachment to it.

Textual Considerations

1. Review the first paragraph of Rushdie's essay, and explain what the photograph represents to him.
2. Paragraph 7 begins, "But there is a paradox here. The broken mirror may actually be as valuable as the one which is supposedly unflawed." What is the meaning of the paradox to which Rushdie refers?
3. What points does Rushdie make concerning memory in paragraph 8? Review paragraphs 9–12 and explain.
4. What connections does Rushdie make between memory and the writer? Explain.
5. Identify some of the references Rushdie makes to literary works, including his own. To what extent do these references help shape his theme of "lost time," "lost city," and "loss of self" in his text? How do they help him define his feelings about Bombay?

Cultural Contexts

1. Rushdie writes that all immigrants have an identity that is both "plural and partial." What does he mean? If you share his experience as an immigrant, explain how this experience has affected your identity.
2. Brainstorm with your group on your associations with homeland. Are these common motifs? How would you distinguish between real and imaginary homelands?

Zora Neal Hurston

I Get Born

This is all hear-say. Maybe some of the details of my birth as told me might be a little inaccurate, but it is pretty well established that I really did get born.

The saying goes like this. My mother's time had come and my father was not there. Being a carpenter, successful enough to have other helpers on some jobs, he was away often on building business, as well as preaching. It seems that my father was away from home for months this time. I have never been told why. But I did hear that he threatened to cut his throat when he got the news. It seems that one daughter was all that he figured he could stand. My sister, Sarah, was his favorite child, but that one girl was enough. Plenty more sons, but no more girl babies to wear out shoes and bring in nothing. I don't think he ever got over the trick he felt that I played on him by getting born a girl, and while he was off from home at that. A little of my sugar used to sweeten his coffee right now. That is a Negro way of saying his patience was short with me. Let me change a few words with him—and I am of the word-changing kind—and he was ready to change ends. Still and all, I looked more like him than any child in the house. Of course, by the time I got born, it was too late to make any suggestions, so the old man had to put up with me. He was nice about it in a way. He didn't tie me in a sack and drop me in the lake, as he probably felt like doing.

People were digging sweet potatoes, and then it was hog-killing time. Not at our house, but it was going on in general over the country like, being January and a bit cool. Most people were either butchering for themselves, or off helping other folks do their butchering, which was almost just as good. It is a gay time. A big pot of hass-slits cooking with plenty of seasoning, lean slabs of fresh-killed pork frying for the helpers to refresh themselves after the work is done. Over and above being neighborly and giving aid, there is the food, the drinks and the fun of getting together.

So there was no grown folks close around when Mama's water broke. She sent one of the smaller children to fetch Aunt Judy, the mid-wife, but she was gone to Woodbridge, a mile and a half away, to eat at a hog-killing. The child was told to go over there and tell Aunt Judy to come. But nature, being indifferent to human arrangements, was impatient. My mother had to make it alone. She was too weak after I rushed out to do anything for herself, so she just was lying there, sick in the body, and worried in mind, wondering what would become of her, as well as me. She was so weak, she couldn't even reach down to where I was. She had one consolation. She knew I wasn't dead, because I was crying strong.

Help came from where she never would have thought to look for it. A white man of many acres and things, who knew the family well, had butchered the day before. Knowing that Papa was not at home, and that consequently there would be no fresh meat in our house, he decided to drive the five miles and bring a half of a shoat, sweet potatoes, and other garden stuff along. He was there a few minutes after I was born. Seeing the front door standing open, he came on in, and hollered,

"Hello, there! Call your dogs!" That is the regular way to call in the country because nearly everybody who has anything to watch has biting dogs.

Nobody answered, but he claimed later that he heard me spreading my lungs all over Orange County, so he shoved the door open and bolted on into the house.

He followed the noise and then he saw how things were, and, being the kind of a man he was, he took out his Barlow Knife and cut the navel cord, then he did the best he could about other things. When the mid-wife, locally known as a granny, arrived about an hour later, there was a fire in the stove and plenty of hot water on. I had been sponged off in some sort of a way, and Mama was holding me in her arms.

As soon as the old woman got there, the white man unloaded what he had brought, and drove off cussing about some blankety-blank people never being where you could put your hands on them when they were needed.

He got no thanks from Aunt Judy. She grumbled for years about it. She complained that the cord had not been cut just right, and the bellyband had not been put on tight enough. She was mighty scared I was going to have a weak back, and that I would have trouble holding my water until I reached puberty. I did.

The next day or so a Mrs. Neale, a friend of Mama's, came in and reminded her that she had promised to let her name the baby in case it was a girl. She had picked up a name somewhere which she thought was very pretty. Perhaps she had read it somewhere, or somebody back in those woods was smoking Turkish cigarettes. So I became Zora Neale Hurston.

There is nothing to make you like other human beings so much as doing things for them. Therefore, the man who grannied me was back next day to see how I was coming along. Maybe it was a pride in his own handiwork, and his resourcefulness in a pinch, that made him want to see it through. He remarked that I was a God-damned fine baby, fat and plenty of lung-power. As time went on, he came infrequently, but somehow kept a pinch of interest in my welfare. It seemed that I was spying noble, growing like a gourd vine, and yelling bass like a gator. He was the kind of man that had no use for puny things, so I was all to the good with him. He thought my mother was justified in keeping me.

But nine months rolled around, and I just would not get on with the walking business. I was strong, crawling well, but showed no inclination to use my feet. I might remark in passing, that I still don't like to walk. Then I was over a year old, but still I would not walk. They made allowances for my weight, but yet, that was no real reason for my not trying.

They tell me that an old sow-hog taught me how to walk. That is, she didn't instruct me in detail, but she convinced me that I really ought to try.

It was like this. My mother was going to have collard greens for dinner, so she took the dishpan and went down to the spring to wash the greens. She left me sitting on the floor, and gave me a hunk of cornbread to keep me quiet. Everything was going along all right, until the sow with her litter of pigs in convoy came abreast of the door. She must have smelled the cornbread I was messing with and scattering crumbs about the floor. So, she came right on in, and began to nuzzle around.

My mother heard my screams and came running. Her heart must have stood still when she saw the sow in there, because hogs have been known to eat human flesh.

But I was not taking this thing sitting down. I had been placed by a chair, and when my mother got inside the door, I had pulled myself up by that chair and was getting around it right smart.

As for the sow, poor misunderstood lady, she had no interest in me except my bread. I lost that in scrambling to my feet and she was eating it. She had much less intention of eating Mama's baby, than Mama had of eating hers.

With no more suggestions from the sow or anybody else, it seems that I just took to walking and kept the thing a-going. The strangest thing about it was that once I found the use of my feet, they took to wandering. I always wanted to go. I would wander off in the woods all alone, following some inside urge to go places. This alarmed my mother a great deal. She used to say that she believed a woman who was an enemy of hers had sprinkled "travel dust" around the doorstep the day I was born. That was the only explanation she could find. I don't know why it never occurred to her to connect my tendency with my father, who didn't have a thing on his mind but this town and the next one. That should have given her a sort of hint. Some children are just bound to take after their fathers in spite of women's prayers.

[1942]

Journal Entry

What stories about your own birth can you bring to your reading of Hurston's memoir?

Textual Considerations

1. What is Hurston's father's reaction to the birth of his daughter?
2. Hurston explains in the third and fourth paragraphs the unusual circumstances surrounding her birth. What else does she add to the essay's meaning in the third paragraph?
3. Why does Hurston include the episode of her learning to walk? What do we find out about her from this inclusion?
4. What is the significance of the essay's last line, and how does it contribute to meaning?

Cultural Contexts

1. Discuss with your group the extent to which Hurston's use of humor reinforces the importance of folk elements in her essay. How is her choice of words appropriate to her subject matter? Cite examples you considered effective.
2. Discuss with your group your responses to the intervention of the white man and Aunt Judy's complaints about him. What does he add to the memoir?

POETRY

Langston Hughes

The Negro Speaks of Rivers

I've known rivers:
I've known rivers ancient as the world and older than the flow of
    human blood in human veins.

My soul has grown deep like the rivers.

I bathed in the Euphrates when dawns were young.   5
I built my hut near the Congo and it lulled me to sleep.
I looked upon the Nile and raised the pyramids above it.

I heard the singing of the Mississippi when Abe Lincoln
    went down to New Orleans, and I've seen its muddy
    bosom turn all golden in the sunset.   10

I've known rivers:
Ancient, dusky rivers.

My soul has grown deep like the rivers.

[1926]

Linda Hogan

First Light

for Robin

In early morning
I forget I'm in this world
with crooked chiefs
who make federal deals.

80

6. Characterize the relation between the past and the future in Vigil-Piñón's "warm heart contains life." To what extent does the speaker's bilingual text contribute to the poem's meaning? Explain.
7. Speculate on the thematic implications of the title of Vigil-Piñón's poem.
8. Compare and contrast the meaning of "rivers," "first light," and "warm hearts" in "The Negro Speaks of Rivers," "First Light," and "warm heart contains life." What do these images reveal about the speakers' attitudes toward their roots and the past?

Cultural Contexts

1. According to paleontologist Loven Eiseley, "to grow is to gain, an enlargement of life . . . yet it is also a departure. There is something lost that will not return." Create a response by Hughes and Hogan, and add a sentence or two expressing your views on Eiseley's statement.
2. In a text she edited in 1983 entitled *Woman of Her Word: Hispanic Women Writers*, Vigil-Piñón describes the Latina writer: "As a person in the literature, the Latina is a woman of her word—*mujer de su palabra*. In this role, the Latina is self-sacrificing to her family as a mother and wife. She conveys values to her family members by way of example, and through the oral tradition, and, as such, she represents a tie to the cultural past." Discuss with your group how oral tradition functions in Vigil-Piñón's poem.

Maurice Kenny

Going Home

The book lay unread in my lap
snow gathered at the window
from Brooklyn it was a long ride
the Greyhound followed the plow
from Syracuse to Watertown   5
to country cheese and maples
tired rivers and closed paper mills
home to gossipy aunts . . .
their dandelions and pregnant cats . . .
home to cedars and fields of boulders   10
cold graves under willow and pine

home from Brooklyn to the reservation
that was not home
to songs I could not sing
to dances I could not dance   15
from Brooklyn bars and ghetto rats
to steaming horses stomping frozen earth
barns and privies lost in blizzards
home to a Nation, Mohawk
to faces, I did not know   20
and hands which did not recognize me
to names and doors
my father shut

[1987]

Duane Niatum

Street Kid

I stand before the window that opens
to a field of sagebrush—
California country northeast of San Francisco.

Holding to the earth and its shield of silence,
The sun burns my thirteen years into the hill.
The white breath of twilight   5
Whirrs with insects crawling down the glass
Between the bars. But it is the meadowlark
Warbling at the end of the fence
That sets me apart from the rest of the boys,
The cool toughs playing ping pong   10
And cards before lock-up.
When this new home stops calling on memory,
As well as my nickname, Injun Joe,
Given to me by the brothers,   15
The Blacks, the Chicanos, the others growing
Lean as this solitude, I step
From the window into the darkness
Reach my soul building a nest against the wall.

[1978]

Journal Entry

What experiences of feeling isolated or alienated can you bring to your reading of these texts?

Textual Considerations

1. Contrast Kenny's associations with Brooklyn as opposed to the reservation. Which best communicate his feelings of homelessness?
2. What is the thematic effect of omitting periods in the poem?
3. How does Niatum use setting to enhance theme in "Street Kid"?
4. Comment on the use of nature imagery in the text to mirror the protagonist's emotional state. How does his identification with the meadowlark help us better understand him?

Cultural Contexts

1. Discuss with your group the causes of alienation and entrapment experienced by the speakers in both poems.
2. Speculate on the multiple meanings of the titles of both texts. To what extent are they ironic? Explain.

DICKEY AND HEANEY

James Dickey

In the Tree House at Night

And now the green household is dark.
The half-moon completely is shining
On the earth-lighted tops of the trees.
To be dead, a house must be still.
The floor and the walls wave me slowly;   5
I am deep in them over my head.
The needles and pine cones about me

Are full of small birds at their roundest,
Their fists without mercy gripping
Hard down through the tree to the roots   10
To sing back at light when they feel it.
We lie here like angels in bodies,
My brothers and I, one dead,
The other asleep from much living,

In mid-air huddled beside me.   15
Dark climbed to us here as we climbed
Up the nails I have hammered all day
Through the sprained, comic rungs of the ladder
Of broom handles, crate slats, and laths
Foot by foot up the trunk to the branches   20
Where we came out at last over lakes

Of leaves, of fields disencumbered of earth
That move with the moves of the spirit.
Each nail that sustains us I set here;
Each nail in the house is now steadied   25
By my dead brother's huge, freckled hand.
Through the years, he has pointed his hammer
Up into these limbs, and told us

That we must ascend, and all lie here.
Step after step he has brought me,   30
Embracing the trunk as his body,
Shaking its limbs with my heartbeat,
Till the pine cones danced without wind

And fell from the branches like apples.
In the arm-slender forks of our dwelling   35

I breathe my live brother's light hair.
The blanket around us becomes
As solid as stone, and it sways.
With all my heart, I close
The blue, timeless eye of my mind.   40
Wind springs, as my dead brother smiles
And touches the tree at the root;

A shudder of joy runs up
The trunk; the needles tingle;
One bird uncontrollably cries.   45
The wind changes round, and I stir
Within another's life. Whose life?
Who is dead? Whose presence is living?
When may I fall strangely to earth,

Who am nailed to this branch by a spirit?   50
Can two bodies make up a third?
To sing, must I feel the world's light?
My green, graceful bones fill the air
With sleeping birds. Alone, alone
And with them I move gently.   55
I move at the heart of the world.

[1961]

Seamus Heaney

Mid-term Break

I sat all morning in the college sick bay
Counting bells knelling classes to a close.
At two o'clock our neighbors drove me home.

In the porch I met my father crying—   5
He had always taken funerals in his stride—
And Big Jim Evans saying it was a hard blow.

The baby cooed and laughed and rocked the pram
When I came in, and I was embarrassed
By old men standing up to shake my hand   10

And tell me they were "sorry for my trouble,"
Whispers informed strangers I was the eldest,
Away at school, as my mother held my hand

In hers and coughed out angry tearless sighs.
At ten o'clock the ambulance arrived   15
With the corpse, stanched and bandaged by the nurses.

Next morning I went up into the room. Snowdrops
And candles soothed the bedside; I saw him
For the first time in six weeks. Paler now,

Wearing a poppy bruise on his left temple,   20
He lay in the four foot box as in his cot.
No gaudy scars, the bumper knocked him clear.

A four foot box, a foot for every year.

[1966]

Journal Entry

What experiences, images, or associations with the death of a sibling can you bring to your
reading of these texts?

Textual Considerations

1. "To be dead, a house must be still." In Dickey's "In the Tree House at Night," does the
   speaker picture the tree house as dead or alive? What physical description of the tree
   house does the speaker include?
2. What role does the dead brother play in "In the Tree House at Night"? What emotions
   does the speaker reveal about his other brother?
3. How do the birds function symbolically in Dickey's poem? Why do they have to grip the
   root of the tree with their "fists" to "sing back at light"? What is the meaning of "light"
   throughout "In the Tree House at Night"?
4. What is Heaney's "Mid-term Break" about? How does the speaker's tone affect your
   understanding of the poem?
5. What images does the title "Mid-term Break" evoke?
6. What lines in "Mid-term Break" most contradict these images?
7. The speaker expresses his grief through understatement in "Mid-term Break." What
   examples do you find most effective? How does the speaker's expression of grief compare
   and contrast with the speaker's feeling of dejection in "In the Tree House at Night"?
   Which one has most affected you?

Cultural Contexts

1. Review stanzas 4 and 5 of Dickey's poem with your group. What lines indicate that the
   tree house has a symbolic meaning? What connections does the poet establish between

the tree house and his dead brother? Between the tree house and himself? What do the questions in the seventh and eighth stanzas contribute?

2. Discuss with members of your group the mourning rituals you are most familiar with. How do law and custom affect them? Whose attitude toward death reflects yours—Dickey's or Heaney's? Explain.

OLDS AND MIRIKITANI

Sharon Olds

The Possessive

My daughter—as if I
owned her—that girl with the
hair wispy as a frayed bellpull

has been to the barber, that knife grinder,
and had the edge of her hair sharpened.   5

Each strand now cuts
both ways. The blade of new bangs
hangs over her red-brown eyes
like carbon steel.

       All the little   10
spliced ropes are sliced, the curtain of
dark paper-cuts veils the face that
started from next to nothing in my body—

My body. My daughter. I'll have to find
another word. In her bright helmet   15
she looks at me as if across a
great distance. Distant fires can be
glimpsed in the resin light of her eyes:

the watch fires of an enemy, a while before
the war starts.   20

[1980]

Janice Mirikitani

Breaking Tradition

for my Daughter

My daughter denies she is like me,
Her secretive eyes avoid mine.
   She reveals the hatreds of womanhood
   already veiled behind music and smoke and telephones.

I want to tell her about the empty room
of myself.
This room we lock ourselves in
where whispers live like fungus,
giggles about small breasts and cellulite,
where we confine ourselves to jealousies,
bedridden by menstruation.
This waiting room where we feel our hands
are useless, dead speechless clamps
that need hospitals and forceps and kitchens
and plugs and ironing boards to make them useful.
I deny I am like my mother. I remember why:
She kept her room neat with silence,
defiance smothered in requirements to be otonashii,
  passion and loudness wrapped in an obi,
  her steps confined to ceremony,
  the weight of her sacrifice she carried like
  a foetus. Guilt passed on in our bones.
I want to break tradition—unlock this room
  where women dress in the dark.
  Discover the lies my mother told me.
  The lies that we are small and powerless,
  that our possibilities must be compressed
  to the size of pearls, displayed only as
  passive chokers, charms around our neck.
Break Tradition.
  I want to tell my daughter of this room
  of myself
  filled with tears of violins,
  the light in my hands,
  poems about madness,
  the music of yellow guitars—
  sounds shaken from barbed wire and
  goodbyes and miracles of survival.
  This room of open window where daring ones escape.
My daughter denies she is like me
  her secretive eyes are walls of smoke
  and music and telephones,
  her pouting ruby lips, her skirts
  swaying to salsa, teena marie and the stones,
  her thighs displayed in carnavals of color.
  I do not know the contents of her room.
  She mirrors my aging.
  She is breaking tradition.

[1987]

Journal Entry

What experiences or knowledge of mother-and-daughter relationships can you bring to your reading of these texts?

Textual Considerations

1. Explain the thematic significance of the title of Olds's poem. What are your associations with the word *possessive*? Are mothers usually possessive of their daughters?
2. Identify images of war in "The Possessive." Why does the mother consider her daughter an enemy?
3. Is hair usually a source of conflict between mothers and daughters? Explain.
4. Is the conflict resolved by the end of the poem? How?
5. How does the daughter in Mirikitani's poem express her rebellion?
6. Why doesn't the speaker in "Breaking Tradition" want to be like her mother?
7. Characterize the tone of the speaker in Mirikitani's poem.
8. What does she mean by "she mirrors my aging"?

Cultural Contexts

1. To what extent are both poems about breaking traditions? What traditions are being broken? By whom? How do you and your group members respond to their conflicts? Do adolescents always break traditions? Explain.
2. With members of your group, create a portrait of both mothers. Which mother appeals to you more? Did your group reach a consensus?

THOMAS AND EBERHART

Dylan Thomas

Fern Hill

Now as I was young and easy under the apple boughs
About the lilting house and happy as the grass was green,
  The night above the dingle° starry,
   Time let me hail and climb
  Golden in the heydays of his eyes,   5
And honored among wagons I was prince of the apple towns
And once below a time I lordly had the trees and leaves
   Trail with daisies and barley
  Down the rivers of the windfall light.

And as I was green and carefree, famous among the barns 10
About the happy yard and singing as the farm was home,
  In the sun that is young once only,
   Time let me play and be
  Golden in the mercy of his means,
And green and golden I was huntsman and herdsman, the calves 15
Sang to my horn, the foxes on the hills barked clear and cold,
   And the sabbath rang slowly
  In the pebbles of the holy streams.

All the sun long it was running, it was lovely, the hay
Fields high as the house, the tunes from the chimneys, it was air 20
   And playing, lovely and watery
    And fire green as grass.
   And nightly under the simple stars
As I rode to sleep the owls were bearing the farm away,
All the moon long I heard, blessed among stables, the nightjars 25
  Flying with the ricks, and the horses
   Flashing into the dark.

And then to awake, and the farm, like a wanderer white
With the dew, come back, the cock on his shoulder: it was all
  Shining, it was Adam and maiden,
   The sky gathered again   30
  And the sun grew round that very day.

So it must have been after the birth of the simple light
In the first, spinning place, the spellbound horses walking warm
    Out of the whinnying green stable   35
      On to the fields of praise.

And honored among foxes and pheasants by the gay house
Under the new made clouds and happy as the heart was long,
    In the sun born over and over,
      I ran my heedless ways,   40
    My wishes raced through the house high hay
And nothing I cared, at my sky blue trades, that time allows
In all his tuneful turning so few and such morning songs
    Before the children green and golden
      Follow him out of grace,   45

Nothing I cared, in the lamb white days, that time would take me
Up to the swallow thronged loft by the shadow of my hand,
    In the moon that is always rising,
      Nor that riding to sleep
    I should hear him fly with the high fields   50
And wake to the farm forever fled from the childless land.
Oh as I was young and easy in the mercy of his means,
    Time held me green and dying
    Though I sang in my chains like the sea.

                                   [1946]

3 dingle: Wooded valley.

Richard Eberhart

If I could only live at the pitch that is near madness

If I could only live at the pitch that is near madness
When everything is as it was in my childhood
Violent, vivid, and of infinite possibility:
That the sun and the moon broke over my head.

Then I cast time out of the trees and fields,   5
Then I stood immaculate in the Ego;
Then I eyed the world with all delight,
Reality was the perfection of my sight.

And time has big handles on the hands,
Fields and trees a way of being themselves.
I saw battalions of the race of mankind
Standing stolid, demanding a moral answer.

I gave the moral answer and I died
And into a realm of complexity came
Where nothing is possible but necessity
And the truth wailing there like a red babe.

10

15

[1960]

[handwritten margin notes: "childlike innocence red", "hearts truths painful, left unattended even;"]

Journal Entry

Write a short vignette focusing on a memorable moment in your childhood. Include as many sensory and visual images as you can recall to capture what makes it so significant.

Textual Considerations

1. How does Thomas's use of color reinforce meaning in "Fern Hill"? How do his references to music also contribute to the poem's meaning?
2. In stanza 4 the speaker compares his childhood to the garden of Eden. How does his comparison reinforce his concept of childhood innocence? How does it compare with the speaker's childhood in "Fern Hill"?
3. The speaker in "Fern Hill" sounds an ominous note for the first time in stanza 5. What **foreshadowings** of this danger can you find in earlier stanzas?
4. Explain the paradox in the last two lines of "Fern Hill."
5. Do you agree with Eberhart's description of childhood as "violent, vivid, and of infinite possibility"? Explain.
6. What further descriptions of childhood are added by each of the four lines in the second stanza of Eberhart's poem?
7. The third stanza contrasts with the first two. What has happened to time in line 9? To the fields and trees in line 10? What does he mean by a "moral answer" in line 12?

Cultural Contexts

1. The title of Thomas's poem refers to his aunt's house in Wales, where he obviously spent many carefree summers. Is there a "site of memory" that has shaped your historical past? Describe it to your group, and discuss the extent to which we are influenced by the landscapes of our pasts.
2. Eberhart equates adulthood with the "moral answer" and "the realm of complexity." Is he suggesting that in childhood people are more imaginative and more likely to think of possibilities as opposed to limitations? Discuss these ideas with members of your group and record your findings.

[handwritten margin notes: "loss of innocence soon proved as;" "soon of leaving", "eve (paradise lost)"]

GILLAN AND GEASOR

Maria Mazziotti Gillan

My Grandmother's Hands

I never saw them.
Once she sent a picture of herself,
skinny as a hook, her backdrop
a cobbled street and a house
of stones, an arched doorway.   5
In a black dress and black stockings,
she smiles over toothless gums,
old—years before she should have been,
buttoned neck to shin in heavy black.
Her eyes express an emotion   10
it is difficult to read.

I think of my mother's mother
and her mother's mother, traced
back from us on the thin thread of memory.
In that little mountain village,   15
the beds where the children
were born and the old ones died
were passed from one generation
to the next, but when my mother married,
she left her family behind. The ribbon   20
between herself and the past
ended with her,
though she tried to pass it on:

And my own children cannot understand
a word of the old language,   25
the past of the village so far
removed that they cannot find
the connection between it
and themselves, will not pass it on.
They cannot possess it,   30
not in the way that we possessed it,
in the 17th street kitchen
where the Italian stories and the words
fell over us like confetti.

All the years of our growing,   35
my mother's arms held us.
secure in that tenement kitchen,
the old stories weaving connections
between ourselves and the past,
teaching us so much about love   40
and the gift of self
and I wonder: Did I fail
my own children? Where
is the past I gave to them
like a gift? I have tried   45
to love them so that always,
they will imagine that love
wrapping them, like a cashmere sweater
warm and soothing on their skin.
The skein of the past spun from that love,   50
stretches back from them to me to my mother,
the old country, the old language lost,
but in this new world, saved and cherished:
the tablecloth my grandmother made,
the dresser scarves she crocheted,   55
and the love she taught us to weave
a thread of woven silk
to lead us home.

                                                    [1985]

James Geasor

Beads

They sit atop the dresser
on the veil that she used
to cover her head with on Sundays
still and curled
like a cat napping on a carpet   5

she's been gone twelve years now
but I can no longer bring myself to move them
in fact, I only held them in my hands
once

and that was after her first birthday had passed   10
after she had past
passed from past
its quaintness fails
                    to move me

black as habit   15
oily from the daily supplication
herfingerstremblinglikehereyelidstremblinglikeherlipstrembling
to pray for those less fortunate than her
she would kneel and clutch the beads
as if they were the lifeline   20
to eternity
but to eternity she's gone
and only the beads remain

                                                            [2006]

Journal Entry

What associations, emotions, and memories of grandmothers do you bring to your reading
of these poems?

Textual Considerations

1. What metaphors does Gillan use to connect her grandmother's and mother's past and
   present? Which do you find most effective?
2. Why does she ask if she failed her own children? How would you answer her question?
3. What multiple meanings does the title of Geasor's poem generate?
4. Comment on the structure of the poem. How does it enhance theme?
5. Cite examples of visual and sensory images in both texts.

Cultural Contexts

1. Discuss with your group the portrait of her mother that emerges in Gillan's poem. With
   what losses does she connect her? To what extent is loss inevitably involved in the immigrant experience? Explain.
2. Create you own portrait of a grandmother, mother, or aunt using visual and sensory
   imagery. Share your portrait with your group for peer critiques.

CHOCK, LEE, AND EMANUEL

Eric Chock

Poem for My Father

I lie dreaming
when my father comes to me and says,
I hope you write a book someday.
He thinks I waste my time,
but outside, he spends hours over stones,   5
gauging the size and shape a rock will take
to fill a space,
to make a wall of dreams around our home.
In the house he built with his own hands
I wish for the lure that catches all fish   10
or girls with hair like long moss in the river.
His thoughts are just as far and old
as the lava chips like flint off his hammer,
and he sees the mold of dreams
taking shape in his hands.   15
His eyes see across orchids on the wall,
into black rock, down to the sea,
and he remembers the harbor full of fish,
orchids in the hair of women thirty years before
he thought of me, this home, these stone walls.   20
Some rocks fit perfectly, slipping into place
with light taps of his hammer.
He thinks of me inside
and takes a big slice of stone,
and pounds it into the ground   25
to make the corner of the wall.
I cannot wake until I bring
the fish and the girl home.

[1989]

Li-Young Lee

The Gift

To pull the metal splinter from my palm
my father recited a story in a low voice.
I watched his lovely face and not the blade.
Before the story ended, he'd removed
the iron sliver I thought I'd die from.   5

I can't remember the tale,
but hear his voice still, a well
of dark water, a prayer.
And I recall his hands,
two measures of tenderness   10
he laid against my face,
the flames of discipline
he raised above my head.

Had you entered that afternoon
you would have thought you saw a man   15
planting something in a boy's palm,
a silver tear, a tiny flame.
Had you followed that boy
you would have arrived here,
where I bend over my wife's right hand.   20

Look how I shave her thumbnail down
so carefully she feels no pain.
Watch as I lift the splinter out.
I was seven when my father
took my hand like this,   25

and I did not hold that shard
between my fingers and think,
Metal that will bury me,
christen it Little Assassin,
Ore Going Deep for My Heart,   30
And I did not lift up my wound and cry,
Death visited here!
I did what a child does
when he's given something to keep.
I kissed my father.

[1986]

James A. Emanuel

Fishermen

When three, he fished these lakes,
Curled sleeping on a lip of rock,
Crib blankets tucked from ants and fishbone flies,
Twitching as the strike of bass and snarling reel
Uncoiled my shouts not quit   5
Till he jerked blinking up on all-fours,
Swaying with the winking leaves.
Strong awake, he shook his cane pole like a spoon
And dipped among the wagging perch
Till, tired, he drew his silver rubber blade   10
And poked the winding fins that tugged our string,
Or sprayed the dimpling minnows with his plastic gun,
Or, rainstruck, squirmed to my armpit in the poncho.

Ten years uncurled him, thinned him hard.
Now, far he casts his line into the wrinkled blue   15
And easy toes a rock, reel on his thigh
Till bone and crank cry out the strike
He takes with manchild chuckles, cunning
In his play of zigzag line and plunging silver.

Now fishing far from me, he strides through rain, shoulders   20
A spiny ridge of pines, and disappears
Near lakes that cannot be, while I must choose
To go or stay: bring blanket, blade, and gun,
Or stand a fisherman.

[1968]

Journal Entry

What associations, memories, or experiences do you have that relate to the bond between fathers and sons? To what extent are they reinforced or contradicted in the three poems?

Textual Considerations

1. How does the father in Chock's poem spend his days?
2. What are his dreams and memories? How do they affect his dreams for his son?
3. How does the speaker link past and present in Lee's "The Gift"?
4. What does Lee's poem make you see? Consider the images the speaker uses to describe his father's hands. Does he also reveal anything about his character? In which lines of the poem?

5. Why does the speaker include the scene with his wife? Would the poem's meaning change without it? Explain.
6. Compare and contrast the three fishing trips in Emanuel's poem.
7. Explain the significance of the last line of the poem.

Cultural Contexts

1. Assess the father-and-son relationship in each text. Which best reflects your experiences? Are conflicts between fathers and sons inevitable? Explain.
2. "Fishermen" is told from the point of view of the father; the other two poems are narrated from the point of view of the sons. To what extent does that fact affect your responses to the texts? Explain.

Robert Hayden

Frederick Douglass°

When it is finally ours, this freedom, this liberty, this beautiful
and terrible thing, needful to man as air,
usable as earth; when it belongs at last to all,
when it is truly instinct, brain matter, diastole, systole,
reflex action; when it is finally won; when it is more   5
than the gaudy mumbo jumbo of politicians:
this man, this Douglass, this former slave, this Negro
beaten to his knees, exiled, visioning a world
where none is lonely, none hunted, alien,
this man, superb in love and logic, this man   10
shall be remembered. Oh, not with statues' rhetoric,
not with legends and poems and wreaths of bronze alone,
but with the lives grown out of his life, the lives
fleshing his dream of the beautiful, needful thing.

[1947]

Frederick Douglass: Born a slave, Douglass (1817–95) escaped and became an important spokesman for the abolitionist movement and later for civil rights for African Americans.

Robert Hayden

Tour 5

The road winds down through autumn hills
in blazonry of farewell scarlet
and recessional gold,
past cedar groves, through static villages
whose names are all that's left   5
of Choctaw, Chickasaw.°

We stop a moment in a town
watched over by Confederate sentinels,

buy gas and ask directions of a rawboned man
whose eyes revile us as the enemy.   10

Shrill gorgon silence breathes behind
his taut civility
and in the ever-tautening air,
dark for us despite its Indian summer glow.
We drive on, following the route   15
of highwaymen and phantoms,

Of slaves and armies.
Children, wordless and remote,
wave at us from kindling porches.
And now the land is flat for miles,   20
the landscape lush, metallic, flayed,
its brightness harsh as bloodstained swords.

[1962]

6 **Choctaw, Chickasaw:** American Indian tribes, originally of Mississippi.

Robert Hayden

Those Winter Sundays

Sundays too my father got up early
and put his clothes on in the blueblack cold,
then with cracked hands that ached
from labor in the weekday weather made
banked fires blaze. No one ever thanked him.   5

I'd wake and hear the cold splintering, breaking.
When the rooms were warm, he'd call,
and slowly I would rise and dress,
fearing the chronic angers of that house,   10

Speaking indifferently to him,
who had driven out the cold
and polished my good shoes as well.
What did I know, what did I know
of love's austere and lonely offices?

[1962]

Robert Hayden

Runagate Runagate — *fugitive, vagabond*

I.

Runs falls rises stumbles on from darkness into darkness
and the darkness thicketed with shapes of terror
and the hunters pursuing and the hounds pursuing
and the night cold and the night long and the river
to cross and the jack-muh-lanterns beckoning beckoning   5
and blackness ahead and when shall I reach that somewhere
morning and keep on going and never turn back and keep on going

       Runagate
           Runagate
               Runagate   10

Many thousands rise and go
many thousands crossing over

                     O mythic North
                O star-shaped yonder Bible city

Some go weeping and some rejoicing   15
some in coffins and some in carriages
some in silks and some in shackles

       Rise and go or fare you well

No more auction block for me
no more driver's lash for me   20

       If you see my Pompey, 30 yrs of age,
       new breeches, plain stockings, negro shoes;
       if you see my Anna, likely young mulatto
       branded E on the right cheek, R on the left,
       catch them if you can and notify subscriber,   25
       Catch them if you can, but it won't be easy.
       They'll dart underground when you try to catch them,
       plunge into quicksand, whirlpools, mazes,
       turn into scorpions when you try to catch them.

And before I'll be a slave   30
I'll be buried in my grave

North star and bonanza gold
I'm bound for the freedom, freedom-bound
and oh Susyanna don't you cry for me
    Runagate   35

       Runagate

II.
Rises from their anguish and their power,

          Harriet Tubman,

          woman of earth, whipscarred,
          a summoning, a shining   40

          Mean to be free

And this was the way of it, brethren brethren,
way we journeyed from Can't to Can.

          Moon so bright and no place to hide,
          the cry up and the patterollers riding,   45
          hound dogs belling in bladed air.
          And fear starts a-murbling, Never make it,
          we'll never make it. *Hush that now,*
          and she's turned upon us, levelled pistol
          glinting in the moonlight: 50

       Dead folks can't jaybird-talk she says:
       you keep on going now or die, she says.

Wanted   Harriet Tubman   alias The General
alias Moses   Stealer of Slaves

In league with Garrison   Alcott   Emerson   55
Garrett   Douglass   Thoreau   John Brown

Armed and known to be Dangerous

Wanted   Reward   Dead or Alive

       Tell me, Ezekiel, oh tell me do you see
       mailed Jehovah coming to deliver me?   60

Hoot-owl calling in the ghosted air,
five times calling to the hants in the air.
Shadow of a face in the scary leaves,
shadow of a voice in the talking leaves:
Come ride-a my train   65

Oh that train, ghost-story train
through swamp and savanna movering movering,

over trestles of dew, through caves of the wish,
Midnight Special on a sabre track movering movering,
first stop Mercy and the last Hallelujah.   70

Come ride-a my train

Mean mean mean to be free.

[1985]

Journal Entry

Freewrite on your associations, images, or concepts of freedom. To what extent is freedom related to ethnicity? Explain.

Textual Considerations

1. According to Hayden, when and how will Douglass be remembered?
2. Research the origins of "mumbo jumbo" in line 6 of "Frederick Douglass." How does Hayden's use affect the poem's meaning?
3. What is the effect of delaying the subject of the first sentence until line 7 and the verb until line 11 in "Frederick Douglass"?
4. Does Hayden imply that there will come a time when freedom will belong to all? Do you agree? Why or why not?
5. Describe the effects of stopping for gas in "Tour 5."
6. Contrast the language of the first and last stanzas of "Tour 5." What is the effect on the poem's mood and meaning?
7. Characterize the father in "Those Winter Sundays." What is the effect of using *too* in the first line?
8. How does the son attempt to subdue the "chronic angers" of the house? How does the use of repetition in line 13 of "Those Winter Sundays" reinforce meaning?
9. What kind of relationship do father and son share in "Those Winter Sundays"? Explain the meaning of "offices" in the last line.
10. Consult a dictionary for the various meanings of *runagate*. What effect is gained by repeating it in the title, "Runagate Runagate"?
11. How do the visual effects in "Runagate Runagate" contribute to its sense of movement as the slaves attempt to escape to the North through the Underground Railroad?
12. What is the effect of juxtaposing the thoughts and feelings of the runagate with the slave owner's handbill providing reward for his capture?
13. If you are unfamiliar with Harriet Tubman or others mentioned in part II of "Runagate Runagate," research their contribution to the abolitionist movement.

Cultural Contexts

1. Construct with your group a brief narrative on the abolitionist movement based on your responses to question 13. To what extent does this statement apply to Hayden's poems in this anthology?
2. How does Frederick Douglass's idea expressed in his autobiography that "we have to do with the past only as it is useful for the present and the future" apply to the poem by Hayden? To what extent is the past always with us?

DRAMA

<svg/triangular decorative border>

Sophocles

Oedipus Rex

CHARACTERS

OEDIPUS, *King of Thebes, supposed son of Polybos and Merope,*
  King and Queen of Corinth
IOKASTE, *wife of Oedipus and widow of the late King Laios*
KREON, *brother of Iokaste, a prince of Thebes*
TEIRESIAS, *a blind seer who serves Apollo*
PRIEST
MESSENGER, *from Corinth*
SHEPHERD, *former Servant of Laios*
SECOND MESSENGER, *from the palace*
CHORUS OF THEBAN ELDERS
CHORAGOS, *leader of the Chorus*
ANTIGONE *and* ISMENE, *young daughters of Oedipus and Iokaste.*
  They appear in the Exodos but do not speak.
Suppliants, Guards, Servants

SCENE. *Before the palace of* OEDIPUS, *King of Thebes. A central door and two lateral doors open onto a platform which runs the length of the facade. On the platform, right and left, are altars; and three steps lead down into the orchestra, or chorus-ground. At the beginning of the action these steps are crowded by suppliants who have brought branches and chaplets of olive leaves and who sit in various attitudes of despair.* OEDIPUS *enters.*

PROLOGUE

OEDIPUS: My children, generations of the living
In the line of Kadmos,° nursed at his ancient hearth:
Why have you strewn yourselves before these altars
In supplication, with your boughs and garlands?
The breath of incense rises from the city   5
With a sound of prayer and lamentation.
                                        Children,

I would not have you speak through messengers,

---

2. **Kadmos:** founder of Thebes, according to legend.

And therefore I have come myself to hear you—
I, Oedipus, who bear the famous name.
(*To a* PRIEST.) You, there, since you are eldest in the company,   10
Speak for them all, tell me what preys upon you,
Whether you come in dread, or crave some blessing:
Tell me, and never doubt that I will help you
In every way I can; I should be heartless
Were I not moved to find you suppliant here.   15
PRIEST: Great Oedipus, O powerful king of Thebes!
You see how all the ages of our people
Cling to your altar steps: here are boys
Who can barely stand alone, and here are priests
By weight of age, as I am a priest of God,   20
And young men chosen from those yet unmarried;
As for the others, all that multitude,
They wait with olive chaplets in the squares,
At the two shrines of Pallas,° and where Apollo°
Speaks in the glowing embers.

                           Your own eyes   25
Must tell you: Thebes is tossed on a murdering sea
And cannot lift her head from the death surge.
A rust consumes the buds and fruits of the earth;
The herds are sick; children die unborn,
And labor is vain. The god of plague and pyre   30
Raids like detestable lightning through the city,
And all the house of Kadmos is laid waste,
All emptied, and all darkened: Death alone
Battens upon the misery of Thebes.

You are not one of the immortal gods, we know;   35
Yet we have come to you to make our prayer
As to the man surest in mortal ways
And wisest in the ways of God. You saved us
From the Sphinx,° that flinty singer, and the tribute
We paid to her so long; yet you were never   40
Better informed than we, nor could we teach you:
A god's touch, it seems, enabled you to help us.

Therefore, O mighty power, we turn to you:
Find us our safety, find us a remedy,

---

24. Pallas: Pallas Athena, Zeus's daughter; goddess of wisdom;   **24. Apollo:** Zeus's son, god of the sun, truth, and poetry.   **39. Sphinx:** a monster with the body of a lion, the wings of a bird, and the face of a woman. The Sphinx had challenged Thebes with a riddle, killing those who failed to solve it. When Oedipus answered correctly, the Sphinx killed herself.

Whether by counsel of the gods or of men.   45
A kin of wisdom tested in the past
Can act in a time of troubles, and act well.
Noblest of men, restore
Life to your city! Think how all men call you
Liberator for your boldness long ago;   50
Ah, when your years of kingship are remembered,
Let them not say *We rose, but later fell*—
Keep the State from going down in the storm!
Once, years ago, with happy augury,
You brought us fortune; be the same again!   55
No man questions your power to rule the land:
But rule over men, not over a dead city!
Ships are only hulls, high walls are nothing,
When no life moves in the empty passageways.

OEDIPUS: Poor children! You may be sure I know   60
All that you longed for in your coming here.
I know that you are deathly sick; and yet,
Sick as you are, not one is as sick as I.
Each of you suffers in himself alone
His anguish, not another's; but my spirit   65
Groans for the city, for myself, for you.

I was not sleeping, you are not waking me.
No, I have been in tears for a long while
And in my restless thought walked many ways.
In all my search I found one remedy,   70
And I have adopted it: I have sent Kreon,
Son of Menoikeus, brother of the queen,
To Delphi,° Apollo's place of revelation,
To learn there, if he can,
What act or pledge of mine may save the city.   75
I have counted the days, and now, this very day,
I am troubled, for he has overstayed his time.
What is he doing? He has been gone too long.
Yet whenever he comes back, I should do ill
Not to take any action the god orders.   80

PRIEST: It is a timely promise. At this instant
They tell me Kreon is here.

OEDIPUS: O Lord Apollo!
May his news be fair as his face is radiant!

PRIEST: Good news, I gather! he is crowned with bay,
The chaplet is thick with berries.

---

73. Delphi: location of the prophetic oracle, regarded as the keeper of religious truth.

OEDIPUS: We shall soon know;   85
  He is near enough to hear us now. (*Enter* KREON.) O prince:
  Brother: son of Menoikeus:
  What answer do you bring us from the god?
KREON: A strong one. I can tell you, great afflictions
  Will turn out well, if they are taken well.   90
OEDIPUS: What was the oracle? These vague words
  Leave me still hanging between hope and fear.
KREON: Is it your pleasure to hear me with all these
  Gathered around us? I am prepared to speak,
  But should we not go in?
OEDIPUS: Speak to them all,   95
  It is for them I suffer, more than for myself.
KREON: Then I will tell you what I heard at Delphi.
  In plain words
  The god commands us to expel from the land of Thebes
  An old defilement we are sheltering.   100
  It is a deathly thing, beyond cure;
  We must not let it feed upon us longer.
OEDIPUS: What defilement? How shall we rid ourselves of it?
KREON: By exile or death, blood for blood. It was
  Murder that brought the plague-wind on the city.   105
OEDIPUS: Murder of whom? Surely the god has named him?
KREON: My Lord: Laios once ruled this land,
  Before you came to govern us.
OEDIPUS: I know;
  I learned of him from others; I never saw him.
KREON: He was murdered; and Apollo commands us now   110
  To take revenge upon whoever killed him.
OEDIPUS: Upon whom? Where are they? Where shall we find a clue
  To solve that crime, after so many years?
KREON: Here in this land, he said. Search reveals
  Things that escape an inattentive man.   115
OEDIPUS: Tell me: Was Laios murdered in his house,
  Or in the fields, or in some foreign country?
KREON: He said he planned to make a pilgrimage.
  He did not come home again.
OEDIPUS: And was there no one,
  No witness, no companion, to tell what happened?   120
KREON: They were all killed but one, and he got away
  So frightened that he could remember one thing only.
OEDIPUS: What was that one thing? One may be the key
  To everything, if we resolve to use it.
KREON: He said that a band of highwaymen attacked them,   125
  Outnumbered them, and overwhelmed the king.

OEDIPUS: Strange, that a highwayman should be so daring—
   Unless some faction here bribed him to do it.
KREON: We thought of that. But after Laios' death
   New troubles arose and we had no avenger.   130
OEDIPUS: What troubles could prevent your hunting down the killers?
KREON: The riddling Sphinx's song
   Made us deaf to all mysteries but her own.
OEDIPUS: Then once more I must bring what is dark to light.
   It is most fitting that Apollo shows,   135
   As you do, this compunction for the dead.
   You shall see how I stand by you, as I should,
   Avenging this country and the god as well,
   And not as though it were for some distant friend,
   But for my own sake, to be rid of evil.   140
   Whoever killed King Laios might—who knows?—
   Lay violent hands even on me—and soon.
   I act for the murdered king in my own interest.

   Come, then, my children: leave the altar steps,
   Lift up your olive boughs!
              One of you go   145
   And summon the people of Kadmos to gather here.
   I will do all that I can; you may tell them that.   (*Exit a* PAGE.)
   So, with the help of God,
   We shall be saved—or else indeed we are lost.
PRIEST: Let us rise, children. It was for this we came,   150
   And now the king has promised it.
   Phoibos° has sent us an oracle; may he descend
   Himself to save us and drive out the plague.

        (*Exeunt*° OEDIPUS *and* KREON *into the palace by the central door. The* PRIEST
        and the SUPPLIANTS *disperse right and left. After a short pause the* CHORUS
        enters the orchestra.)

PARODOS

STROPHE 1

CHORUS: What is God singing in his profound
   Delphi of gold and shadow?
   What oracle for Thebes, the Sunwhipped city?
   Fear unjoints me, the roots of my heart tremble.
   Now I remember, O Healer, your power, and wonder: 5
   Will you send doom like a sudden cloud, or weave it

---

152. Phoibos: Apollo.   **s.d. Exeunt:** Latin term meaning "they exit."

Like nightfall of the past?
Speak to me, tell me, O
Child of golden Hope, immortal Voice.

ANTISTROPHE 1

Let me pray to Athene, the immortal daughter of Zeus,   10
And to Artemis° her sister
Who keeps her famous throne in the market ring,
And to Apollo, archer from distant heaven—
O gods, descend! Like three streams leap against
The fires of our grief, the fires of darkness;   15
Be swift to bring us rest!
As in the old time from the brilliant house
Of air you stepped to save us, come again!

STROPHE 2

Now our afflictions have no end,
Now all our stricken host lies down   20
And no man fights off death with his mind;
The noble plowland bears no grain,
And groaning mothers cannot bear—
See, how our lives like birds take wing,
Like sparks that fly when a fire soars,   25
To the shore of the god of evening.

ANTISTROPHE 2

The plague burns on, it is pitiless,
Though pallid children laden with death
Lie unwept in the stony ways,
And old gray women by every path   30
Flock to the strand about the altars
There to strike their breasts and cry
Worship of Phoibos in wailing prayers:
Be kind, God's golden child!

STROPHE 3

There are no swords in this attack by fire,
No shields, but we are ringed with cries.   35
Send the besieger plunging from our homes
Into the vast sea-room of the Atlantic
Or into the waves that foam eastward of Thrace—

11. **Artemis:** goddess of the hunt.

For the day ravages what the night spares—   40
Destroy our enemy, lord of the thunder!
Let him be riven by lightning from heaven!

ANTISTROPHE 3

Phoibos Apollo, stretch the sun's bowstring,
That golden cord, until it sing for us,
Flashing arrows in heaven!
                 Artemis, Huntress,   45
Race with flaring lights upon our mountains!
O scarlet god,° O golden-banded brow,
O Theban Bacchos in a storm of Maenads,°

     (*Enter* OEDIPUS, *center.*)

Whirl upon Death, that all the Undying hate!
Come with blinding torches, come in joy!   50

SCENE I

OEDIPUS: Is this your prayer? It may be answered. Come,
Listen to me, act as the crisis demands,
And you shall have relief from all these evils.

Until now I was a stranger to this tale,
As I had been a stranger to the crime.   5
Could I track down the murderer without a clue?
But now, friends,
As one who became a citizen after the murder,
I make this proclamation to all Thebans:
If any man knows by whose hand Laios, son of Labdakos,   10
Met his death, I direct that man to tell me everything,
No matter what he fears for having so long withheld it.
Let it stand as promised that no further trouble
Will come to him, but he may leave the land in safety.
Moreover: If anyone knows the murderer to be foreign,   15
Let him not keep silent: he shall have his reward from me.
However, if he does conceal it; if any man
Fearing for his friend or for himself disobeys this edict,
Hear what I propose to do:

I solemnly forbid the people of this country,   20
Where power and throne are mine, ever to receive that man

---

47. scarlet god: Bacchos, god of wine and revelry.   **48. Maenads:** female attendants of Bacchos.

Or speak to him, no matter who he is, or let him
Join in sacrifice, lustration, or in prayer.
I decree that he be driven from every house,
Being, as he is, corruption itself to us: the Delphic   25
Voice of Apollo has pronounced this revelation.
Thus I associate myself with the oracle
And take the side of the murdered king.

As for the criminal, I pray to God—
Whether it be a lurking thief, or one of a number—   30
I pray that that man's life be consumed in evil and wretchedness.
And as for me, this curse applies no less
If it should turn out that the culprit is my guest here,
Sharing my hearth.
                              You have heard the penalty.
I lay it on you now to attend to this   35
For my sake, for Apollo's, for the sick
Sterile city that heaven has abandoned.
Suppose the oracle had given you no command:
Should this defilement go uncleansed for ever?
You should have found the murderer: your king,   40
A noble king, had been destroyed!
                        Now I,
Having the power that he held before me,
Having his bed, begetting children there
Upon his wife, as he would have, had he lived—
Their son would have been my children's brother,   45
If Laios had had luck in fatherhood!
(And now his bad fortune has struck him down)—
I say I take the son's part, just as though
I were his son, to press the fight for him
And see it won! I'll find the hand that brought   50
Death to Labdakos' and Polydoros' child,
Heir of Kadmos' and Agenor's line.°
And as for those who fail me,
May the gods deny them the fruit of the earth,
Fruit of the womb, and may they rot utterly!   55
Let them be wretched as we are wretched, and worse!

For you, for loyal Thebans, and for all
Who find my actions right, I pray the favor
Of justice, and of all the immortal gods.
CHORAGOS: Since I am under oath, my lord, I swear   60
    I did not do the murder, I cannot name

51–52. Labdakos, Polydoros, Kadmos, and **Agenor:** ancestors of Laios.

The murderer. Phoibos ordained the search;
Why did he not say who the culprit was?

OEDIPUS: An honest question. But no man in the world
Can make the gods do more than the gods will.   65

CHORAGOS: There is an alternative, I think—

OEDIPUS: Tell me.
Any or all, you must not fail to tell me.

CHORAGOS: A lord clairvoyant to the lord Apollo,
As we all know, is the skilled Teiresias.
One might learn much about this from him, Oedipus.   70

OEDIPUS: I am not wasting time:
Kreon spoke of this, and I have sent for him—
Twice, in fact; it is strange that he is not here.

CHORAGOS: The other matter—that old report—seems useless.

OEDIPUS: What was that? I am interested in all reports.   75

CHORAGOS: The king was said to have been killed by highwaymen.

OEDIPUS: I know. But we have no witnesses to that.

CHORAGOS: If the killer can feel a particle of dread,
Your curse will bring him out of hiding!

OEDIPUS: No.
The man who dared that act will fear no curse.   80

(*Enter the blind seer* TEIRESIAS, *led by a* PAGE.)

CHORAGOS: But there is one man who may detect the criminal.
This is Teiresias, this is the holy prophet
In whom, alone of all men, truth was born.

OEDIPUS: Teiresias: seer: student of mysteries,
Of all that's taught and all that no man tells,   85
Secrets of Heaven and secrets of the earth:
Blind though you are, you know the city lies
Sick with plague; and from this plague, my lord,
We find that you alone can guard or save us.

Possibly you did not hear the messengers?   90
Apollo, when we sent to him,
Sent us back word that this great pestilence
Would lift, but only if we established clearly
The identity of those who murdered Laios.
They must be killed or exiled.

                                Can you use   95
Birdflight° or any art of divination
To purify yourself, and Thebes, and me
From this contagion? We are in your hands.

---

96. Birdflight: the flight of birds was one sign used to predict the future.

There is no fairer duty
Than that of helping others in distress.   100
TEIRESIAS: How dreadful knowledge of the truth can be
When there's no help in truth! I knew this well,
But did not act on it; else I should not have come.
OEDIPUS: What is troubling you? Why are your eyes so cold?
TEIRESIAS: Let me go home. Bear your own fate, and I'll   105
Bear mine. It is better so: trust what I say.
OEDIPUS: What you say is ungracious and unhelpful
To your native country. Do not refuse to speak.
TEIRESIAS: When it comes to speech, your own is neither temperate
Nor opportune. I wish to be more prudent.   110
OEDIPUS: In God's name, we all beg you—
TEIRESIAS: You are all ignorant.
No; I will never tell you what I know.
Now it is my misery; then, it would be yours.
OEDIPUS: What! You do know something, and will not tell us?
You would betray us all and wreck the State?   115
TEIRESIAS: I do not intend to torture myself, for you.
Why persist in asking? You will not persuade me.
OEDIPUS: What a wicked old man you are! You'd try a stone's
Patience! Out with it! Have you no feeling at all?
TEIRESIAS: You call me unfeeling. If you could only see   120
The nature of your own feelings . . .
OEDIPUS: Why,
Who would not feel as I do? Who could endure
Your arrogance toward the city?
TEIRESIAS: What does it matter?
Whether I speak or not, it is bound to come.
OEDIPUS: Then, if "it" is bound to come, you are bound to tell me.   125
TEIRESIAS: No, I will not go on. Rage as you please.
OEDIPUS: Rage? Why not!
                                        And I'll tell you what I think:
You planned it, you had it done, you all but
Killed him with your own hands: if you had eyes,
I'd say the crime was yours, and yours alone.   130
TEIRESIAS: So? I charge you, then,
Abide by the proclamation you have made:
From this day forth
Never speak again to these men or to me;
You yourself are the pollution of this country.   135
OEDIPUS: You dare say that! Can you possibly think you have
Some way of going free, after such insolence?
TEIRESIAS: I have gone free. It is the truth sustains me.
OEDIPUS: Who taught you shamelessness? It was not your craft.

TEIRESIAS: You did. You made me speak. I did not want to.　140

OEDIPUS: Speak what? Let me hear it again more clearly.

TEIRESIAS: Was it not clear before? Are you tempting me?

OEDIPUS: I did not understand it. Say it again.

TEIRESIAS: I say that you are the murderer whom you seek.

OEDIPUS: Now twice you have spat out infamy. You'll pay for it!　145

TEIRESIAS: Would you care for more? Do you wish to be really angry?

OEDIPUS: Say what you will. Whatever you say is worthless.

TEIRESIAS: I say you live in hideous shame with those
　　Most dear to you. You cannot see the evil.

OEDIPUS: Can you go on babbling like this for ever?　150

TEIRESIAS: I can, if there is power in truth.

OEDIPUS:　　　　　　　　　　　　There is:
　　But not for you, not for you,
　　You sightless, witless, senseless, mad old man!

TEIRESIAS: You are the madman. There is no one here
　　Who will not curse you soon, as you curse me.　155

OEDIPUS: You child of total night! I would not touch you;
　　Neither would any man who sees the sun.

TEIRESIAS: True: it is not from you my fate will come.
　　That lies within Apollo's competence,
　　As it is his concern.

OEDIPUS:　　　　　　Tell me, who made　160
　　These fine discoveries? Kreon? or someone else?

TEIRESIAS: Kreon is no threat. You weave your own doom.

OEDIPUS: Wealth, power, craft of statemanship!
　　Kingly position, everywhere admired!
　　What savage envy is stored up against these,　165
　　If Kreon, whom I trusted, Kreon my friend,
　　For this great office which the city once
　　Put in my hands unsought—if for this power
　　Kreon desires in secret to destroy me!

　　He has bought this decrepit fortune-teller, this　170
　　Collector of dirty pennies, this prophet fraud—
　　Why, he is no more clairvoyant than I am!

　　　　　　　　　　　　　　Tell us:
　　Has your mystic mummery ever approached the truth?
　　When that hellcat the Sphinx was performing here,　175
　　What help were you to these people?
　　Her magic was not for the first man who came along:
　　It demanded a real exorcist. Your birds—
　　What good were they? or the gods, for the matter of that?
　　But I came by,
　　Oedipus, the simple man, who knows nothing—　180

I thought it out for myself, no birds helped me!
And this is the man you think you can destroy,
That you may be close to Kreon when he's king!
Well, you and your friend Kreon, it seems to me,
Will suffer most. If you were not an old man,   185
You would have paid already for your plot.

CHORAGOS: We cannot see that his words or yours
    Have been spoken except in anger, Oedipus,
    And of anger we have no need. How to accomplish
    The god's will best: that is what most concerns us.   190

TEIRESIAS: You are a king. But where argument's concerned
    I am your man, as much a king as you.
    I am not your servant, but Apollo's.
    I have no need of Kreon or Kreon's name.

    Listen to me. You mock my blindness, do you?   195
    But I say that you, with both your eyes, are blind:
    You cannot see the wretchedness of your life,
    Nor in whose house you live, no, nor with whom.
    Who are your father and mother? Can you tell me?
    You do not even know the blind wrongs   200
    That you have done them, on earth and in the world below.
    But the double lash of your parents' curse will whip you
    Out of this land some day, with only night
    Upon your precious eyes.
    Your cries then—where will they not be heard?   205
    What fastness of Kithairon° will not echo them?
    And that bridal-descant of yours—you'll know it then,
    The song they sang when you came here to Thebes
    And found your misguided berthing.
    All this, and more, that you cannot guess at now,   210
    Will bring you to yourself among your children.

    Be angry, then. Curse Kreon. Curse my words.
    I tell you, no man that walks upon the earth
    Shall be rooted out more horribly than you.

OEDIPUS: Am I to bear this from him?—Damnation   215
    Take you! Out of this place! Out of my sight!

TEIRESIAS: I would not have come at all if you had not asked me.

OEDIPUS: Could I have told that you'd talk nonsense, that
    You'd come here to make a fool of yourself, and of me?

TEIRESIAS: A fool? Your parents thought me sane enough.   220

OEDIPUS: My parents again!—Wait: who were my parents?

TEIRESIAS: This day will give you a father and break your heart.

---

206. Kithairon: mountain where the infant Oedipus was left for dead.

OEDIPUS: Your infantile riddles! Your damned abracadabra!
TEIRESIAS: You were a great man once at solving riddles.
OEDIPUS: Mock me with that if you like; you will find it true.   225
TEIRESIAS: It was true enough. It brought about your ruin.
OEDIPUS: But if it saved this town?
TEIRESIAS (*to the* PAGE):   Boy, give me your hand.
OEDIPUS: Yes, boy; lead him away.
                                   —While you are here
    We can do nothing. Go; leave us in peace.
TEIRESIAS: I will go when I have said what I have to say.   230
    How can you hurt me? And I tell you again:
    The man you have been looking for all this time,
    The damned man, the murderer of Laios,
    That man is in Thebes. To your mind he is foreign-born,
    But it will soon be shown that he is a Theban,   235
    A revelation that will fail to please.
                                   A blind man,
    Who has his eyes now; a penniless man, who is rich now;
    And he will go tapping the strange earth with his staff.
    To the children with whom he lives now he will be
    Brother and father—the very same; to her   240
    Who bore him, son and husband—the very same
    Who came to his father's bed, wet with his father's blood.
    Enough. Go think that over.
    If later you find error in what I have said,
    You may say that I have no skill in prophecy.   245

                    (*Exit* TEIRESIAS, *led by his* PAGE. OEDIPUS *goes into the palace.*)

ODE 1

STROPHE 1

CHORUS: The Delphic stone of prophecies
    Remembers ancient regicide
    And a still bloody hand.
    That killer's hour of flight has come.
    He must be stronger than riderless   5
    Coursers of untiring wind,
    For the son of Zeus° armed with his father's thunder
    Leaps in lightning after him;
    And the Furies° hold his track, the sad Furies.

---

7. son of Zeus: Apollo.   **9. Furies:** female spirits who avenged evil deeds.

ANTISTROPHE 1

Holy Parnassos° peak of snow   10
Flashes and blinds that secret man,
That all shall hunt him down:
Though he may roam the forest shade
Like a bull gone wild from pasture
To rage through grooms of stone.   15
Doom comes down on him; flight will not avail him;
For the world's heart calls him desolate,
And the immortal voices follow, forever follow.

STROPHE 2

But now a wilder thing is heard
From the old man skilled at hearing Fate in the wing-beat of a bird.   20
Bewildered as a blown bird, my soul hovers and cannot find
Foothold in this debate, or any reason or rest of mind.
But no man ever brought—none can bring
Proof of strife between Thebes' royal house,
Labdakos' line, and the son of Polybos°;   25
And never until now has any man brought word
Of Laios' dark death staining Oedipus the King.

ANTISTROPHE 2

Divine Zeus and Apollo hold
Perfect intelligence alone of all tales ever told;
And well though this diviner works, he works in his own night;   30
No man can judge that rough unknown or trust in second sight,
For wisdom changes hands among the wise.
Shall I believe my great lord criminal
At a raging word that a blind old man let fall?
I saw him, when the carrion woman° faced him of old,   35
Prove his heroic mind. These evil words are lies.

SCENE II

KREON: Men of Thebes:
I am told that heavy accusations
Have been brought against me by King Oedipus.

I am not the kind of man to bear this tamely.

---

10. Parnassos: holy mountain, dwelling place of Zeus, king of the gods.   **25. Polybos:** Oedipus' adoptive father, king of Corinth.   **35. woman:** the Sphinx.

If in these present difficulties   5
He holds me accountable for any harm to him
Through anything I have said or done—why, then,
I do not value life in this dishonor.
It is not as though this rumor touched upon
Some private indiscretion. The matter is grave.   10
The fact is that I am being called disloyal
To the State, to my fellow citizens, to my friends.

CHORAGOS: He may have spoken in anger, not from his mind.

KREON: But did you not hear him say I was the one
Who seduced the old prophet into lying?   15

CHORAGOS: The thing was said; I do not know how seriously.

KREON: But you were watching him! Were his eyes steady?
Did he look like a man in his right mind?

CHORAGOS: I do not know.
I cannot judge the behavior of great men.
But here is the king himself.

      (*Enter* OEDIPUS.)

OEDIPUS: So you dared come back.   20
Why? How brazen of you to come to my house,
You murderer!
           Do you think I do not know
That you plotted to kill me, plotted to steal my throne?
Tell me, in God's name: am I coward, a fool,
That you should dream you could accomplish this?   25
A fool who could not see your slippery game?
A coward, not to fight back when I saw it?
You are the fool, Kreon, are you not? hoping
Without support or friends to get a throne?
Thrones may be won or bought: you could do neither.   30

KREON: Now listen to me. You have talked; let me talk, too.
You cannot judge unless you know the facts.

OEDIPUS: You speak well: there is one fact; but I find it hard
To learn from the deadliest enemy I have.

KREON: That above all I must dispute with you.   35

OEDIPUS: That above all I will not hear you deny.

KREON: If you think there is anything good in being stubborn
Against all reason, then I say you are wrong.

OEDIPUS: If you think a man can sin against his own kind
And not be punished for it, I say you are mad.   40

KREON: I agree. But tell me: what have I done to you?

OEDIPUS: You advised me to send for that wizard, did you not?

KREON: I did. I should do it again.

OEDIPUS: Very well. Now tell me:

How long has it been since Laios—

KREON: What of Laios?

OEDIPUS: Since he vanished in that onset by the road?   45

KREON: It was long ago, a long time.

OEDIPUS: And this prophet,
Was he practicing here then?

KREON: He was; and with honor, as now.

OEDIPUS: Did he speak of me at that time?

KREON: He never did,
At least, not when I was present.

OEDIPUS: But . . . the enquiry?
I suppose you held one?

KREON: We did, but we learned nothing.   50

OEDIPUS: Why did the prophet not speak against me then?

KREON: I do not know; and I am the kind of man
Who holds his tongue when he has no facts to go on.

OEDIPUS: There's one fact that you know, and you could tell it.

KREON: What fact is that? If I know it, you shall have it.   55

OEDIPUS: If he were not involved with you, he could not say
That it was I who murdered Laios.

KREON: If he says that, you are the one that knows it!—
But now it is my turn to question you.

OEDIPUS: Put your questions. I am no murderer.   60

KREON: First, then: You married my sister?

OEDIPUS: I married your sister.

KREON: And you rule the kingdom equally with her?

OEDIPUS: Everything that she wants she has from me.

KREON: And I am the third, equal to both of you?

OEDIPUS: That is why I call you a bad friend.   65

KREON: No. Reason it out, as I have done.
Think of this first: would any sane man prefer
Power, with all a king's anxieties,
To that same power and the grace of sleep?
Certainly not I.   70
I have never longed for the king's power—only his rights.
Would any wise man differ from me in this?
As matters stand, I have my way in everything
With your consent, and no responsibilities.
If I were king, I should be a slave to policy.   75
How could I desire a scepter more
Than what is now mine—untroubled influence?
No, I have not gone mad; I need no honors,
Except those with the perquisites I have now.
I am welcome everywhere; every man salutes me,   80
And those who want your favor seek my ear,

Since I know how to manage what they ask.
Should I exchange this ease for that anxiety?
Besides, no sober mind is treasonable.
I hate anarchy   85
And never would deal with any man who likes it.
Test what I have said. Go to the priestess
At Delphi, ask if I quoted her correctly.
And as for this other thing: if I am found
Guilty of treason with Teiresias,   90
Then sentence me to death. You have my word
It is a sentence I should cast my vote for—
But not without evidence!
           You do wrong
When you take good men for bad, bad men for good.
A true friend thrown aside—why, life itself   95
Is not more precious!
           In time you will know this well:
For time, and time alone, will show the just man,
Though scoundrels are discovered in a day.

CHORAGOS: This is well said, and a prudent man would ponder it.
Judgments too quickly formed are dangerous.   100

OEDIPUS: But is he not quick in his duplicity?
And shall I not be quick to parry him?
Would you have me stand still, hold my peace, and let
This man win everything, through my inaction?

KREON: And you want—what is it, then? To banish me?   105

OEDIPUS: No, not exile. It is your death I want,
So that all the world may see what treason means.

KREON: You will persist, then? You will not believe me?

OEDIPUS: How can I believe you?

KREON: Then you are a fool.

OEDIPUS: To save myself?

KREON: In justice, think of me.   110

OEDIPUS: You are evil incarnate.

KREON: But suppose that you are wrong?

OEDIPUS: Still I must rule.

KREON: But not if you rule badly.

OEDIPUS: O city, city!

KREON: It is my city, too!

CHORAGOS: Now, my lords, be still. I see the queen,
Iokaste, coming from her palace chambers;   115
And it is time she came, for the sake of you both.
This dreadful quarrel can be resolved through her.

(*Enter* IOKASTE.)

IOKASTE: Poor foolish men, what wicked din is this?
   With Thebes sick to death, is it not shameful
   That you should rake some private quarrel up?   120
   (*To* OEDIPUS.) Come into the house.

                      —And you, Kreon, go now:
   Let us have no more of this tumult over nothing.
KREON: Nothing? No, sister: what your husband plans for me
   Is one of two great evils: exile or death.
OEDIPUS: He is right.

               Why, woman, I have caught him squarely   125
   Plotting against my life.
KREON: No! Let me die
   Accurst if ever I have wished you harm!
IOKASTE: Ah, believe it, Oedipus!
   In the name of the gods, respect this oath of his
   For my sake, for the sake of these people here!   130

STROPHE 1

CHORAGOS: Open your mind to her, my lord. Be ruled by her, I beg you!
OEDIPUS: What would you have me do?
CHORAGOS: Respect Kreon's word. He has never spoken like a fool,
   And now he has sworn an oath.
OEDIPUS: You know what you ask?
CHORAGOS: I do.
OEDIPUS: Speak on, then.
CHORAGOS: A friend so sworn should not be baited so,   135
   In blind malice, and without proof.
OEDIPUS: You are aware, I hope, that what you say
   Means death for me, or exile at the least.

STROPHE 2

CHORAGOS: No, I swear by Helios, first in heaven!
   May I die friendless and accurst,   140
   The worst of deaths, if ever I meant that!
   It is the withering fields
     That hurt my sick heart:
   Must we bear all these ills,
   And now your bad blood as well?   145
OEDIPUS: Then let him go. And let me die, if I must,
   Or be driven by him in shame from the land of Thebes.
   It is your unhappiness, and not his talk,
   That touches me.
           As for him—
Wherever he goes, hatred will follow him.   150

KREON: Ugly in yielding, as you were ugly in rage!
  Natures like yours chiefly torment themselves.
OEDIPUS: Can you not go? Can you not leave me?
KREON: I can.
  You do not know me; but the city knows me,
  And in its eyes I am just, if not in yours.   (*Exit* KREON.)   155

> ANTISTROPHE 1

CHORAGOS: Lady Iokaste, did you not ask the King to go to his chambers?
IOKASTE: First tell me what has happened.
CHORAGOS: There was suspicion without evidence; yet it rankled.
  As even false charges will.
IOKASTE: On both sides?
CHORAGOS: On both.
IOKASTE: But what was said?   160
CHORAGOS: Oh let it rest, let it be done with!
  Have we not suffered enough?
OEDIPUS: You see to what your decency has brought you:
  You have made difficulties where my heart saw none.

> ANTISTROPHE 2

CHORAGOS: Oedipus, it is not once only I have told you—   165
  You must know I should count myself unwise
  To the point of madness, should I now forsake you—
        You, under whose hand,
          In the storm of another time,
          Our dear land sailed out free.   170
      But now stand fast at the helm!
IOKASTE: In God's name, Oedipus, inform your wife as well:
  Why are you so set in this hard anger?
OEDIPUS: I will tell you, for none of these men deserves
  My confidence as you do. It is Kreon's work,   175
  His treachery, his plotting against me.
IOKASTE: Go on, if you can make this clear to me.
OEDIPUS: He charges me with the murder of Laios.
IOKASTE: Has he some knowledge? Or does he speak from hearsay?
OEDIPUS: He would not commit himself to such a charge,   180
  But he has brought in that damnable soothsayer
  To tell his story.
IOKASTE: Set your mind at rest.
  If it is a question of soothsayers, I tell you
  That you will find no man whose craft gives knowledge
  Of the unknowable.
                      Here is my proof: 185

An oracle was reported to Laios once
(I will not say from Phoibos himself, but from
His appointed ministers, at any rate)
That his doom would be death at the hands of his own son—
His son, born of his flesh and of mine!   190

Now, you remember the story: Laios was killed
By marauding strangers where three highways meet;
But his child had not been three days in this world
Before the king had pierced the baby's ankles
And left him to die on a lonely mountainside.   195
Thus, Apollo never caused that child
To kill his father, and it was not Laios' fate
To die at the hands of his son, as he had feared.
This is what prophets and prophecies are worth!
Have no dread of them.

           It is God himself   200
Who can show us what he wills, in his own way.

OEDIPUS: How strange a shadowy memory crossed my mind,
   Just now while you were speaking; it chilled my heart.

IOKASTE: What do you mean? What memory do you speak of?

OEDIPUS: If I understand you, Laios was killed   205
   At a place where three roads meet.

IOKASTE: So it was said;
   We have no later story.

OEDIPUS: Where did it happen?

IOKASTE: Phokis, it is called: at a place where the Theban Way
   Divides into the roads toward Delphi and Daulia.

OEDIPUS: When?

IOKASTE: We had the news not long before you came   210
   And proved the right to your succession here.

OEDIPUS: Ah, what net has God been weaving for me?

IOKASTE: Oedipus! Why does this trouble you?

OEDIPUS: Do not ask me yet.
   First, tell me how Laios looked, and tell me
   How old he was.

IOKASTE: He was tall, his hair just touched   215
   With white; his form was not unlike your own.

OEDIPUS: I think that I myself may be accurst
   By my own ignorant edict.

IOKASTE: You speak strangely.
   It makes me tremble to look at you, my king.

OEDIPUS: I am not sure that the blind man cannot see.   220
   But I should know better if you were to tell me—

IOKASTE: Anything—though I dread to hear you ask it.

OEDIPUS: Was the king lightly escorted, or did he ride
    With a large company, as a ruler should?

IOKASTE: There were five men with him in all: one was a herald;   225
    And a single chariot, which he was driving.

OEDIPUS: Alas, that makes it plain enough!
                                   But who—
Who told you how it happened?
                      A household servant,

IOKASTE: The only one to escape.

OEDIPUS: And is he still
    A servant of ours?

IOKASTE: No; for when he came back at last   230
    And found you enthroned in the place of the dead king,
    He came to me, touched my hand with his, and begged
    That I would send him away to the frontier district
    Where only the shepherds go—
    As far away from the city as I could send him.   235
    I granted his prayer; for although the man was a slave,
    He had earned more than this favor at my hands.

OEDIPUS: Can he be called back quickly?

IOKASTE: Easily.
    But why?

OEDIPUS: I have taken too much upon myself
    Without enquiry; therefore I wish to consult him.   240

IOKASTE: Then he shall come.
                    But am I not one also
    To whom you might confide these fears of yours?

OEDIPUS: That is your right; it will not be denied you,
    Now least of all; for I have reached a pitch
    Of wild foreboding. Is there anyone   245
    To whom I should sooner speak?

    Polybos of Corinth is my father.
    My mother is a Dorian: Merope.
    I grew up chief among the men of Corinth
    Until a strange thing happened—   250
    Not worth my passion, it may be, but strange.
    At a feast, a drunken man maundering in his cups
    Cries out that I am not my father's son!
    I contained myself that night, though I felt anger
    And a sinking heart. The next day I visited   255
    My father and mother, and questioned them. They stormed,
    Calling it all the slanderous rant of a fool;
    And this relieved me. Yet the suspicion
    Remained always aching in my mind;

I knew there was talk; I could not rest;   260
And finally, saying nothing to my parents,
I went to the shrine at Delphi.

The god dismissed my question without reply;
He spoke of other things.
              Some were clear,
Full of wretchedness, dreadful, unbearable: 265
As, that I should lie with my own mother, breed
Children from whom all men would turn their eyes;
And that I should be my father's murderer.
I heard all this, and fled. And from that day
Corinth to me was only in the stars   270
Descending in that quarter of the sky,
As I wandered farther and farther on my way
To a land where I should never see the evil
Sung by the oracle. And I came to this country
Where, so you say, King Laios was killed.   275

I will tell you all that happened there, my lady.
There were three highways
Coming together at a place I passed;
And there a herald came towards me, and a chariot
Drawn by horses, with a man such as you describe   280
Seated in it. The groom leading the horses
Forced me off the road at his lord's command;
But as this charioteer lurched over towards me
I struck him in my rage. The old man saw me
And brought his double goad down upon my head   285
As I came abreast.
           He was paid back, and more!
Swinging my club in this right hand I knocked him
Out of his car, and he rolled on the ground.
                I killed him.

I killed them all.   290
Now if that stranger and Laios were—kin,
Where is a man more miserable than I?
More hated by the gods? Citizen and alien alike
Must never shelter me or speak to me—
I must be shunned by all.
           And I myself   295
Pronounced this malediction upon myself!

Think of it: I have touched you with these hands,
These hands that killed your husband. What defilement!

Am I all evil, then? It must be so,
Since I must flee from Thebes, yet never again
See my own countrymen, my own country,   300
For fear of joining my mother in marriage
And killing Polybos, my father.
                             Ah,
If I was created so, born to this fate,
Who could deny the savagery of God?   305
O holy majesty of heavenly powers!
May I never see that day! Never!
Rather let me vanish from the race of men
Than know the abomination destined me!
CHORAGOS: We too, my lord, have felt dismay at this.
But there is hope: you have yet to hear the shepherd.   310
OEDIPUS: Indeed, I fear no other hope is left me.
IOKASTE: What do you hope from him when he comes?
OEDIPUS: This much:
If his account of the murder tallies with yours,
Then I am cleared.
IOKASTE: What was it that I said
Of such importance?
OEDIPUS: Why, "marauders," you said,   315
Killed the king, according to this man's story.
If he maintains that still, if there were several,
Clearly the guilt is not mine: I was alone.
But if he says one man, singlehanded, did it,
Then the evidence all points to me.   320
IOKASTE: You may be sure that he said there were several;
And can he call back that story now? He cannot.
The whole city heard it as plainly as I.
But suppose he alters some detail of it:
He cannot ever show that Laios' death   325
Fulfilled the oracle: for Apollo said
My child was doomed to kill him; and my child—
Poor baby!—it was my child that died first.

No. From now on, where oracles are concerned,
I would not waste a second thought on any.   330
OEDIPUS: You may be right.
                        But come: let someone go
For the shepherd at once. This matter must be settled.
IOKASTE: I will send for him.
I would not wish to cross you in anything,
And surely not in this.—Let us go in.   (*Exeunt into the palace.*)   335

ODE 2

STROPHE 1

CHORUS: Let me be reverent in the ways of right,
Lowly the paths I journey on;
Let all my words and actions keep
The laws of the pure universe
From highest Heaven handed down.   5
For Heaven is their bright nurse,
Those generations of the realms of light;
Ah, never of mortal kind were they begot,
Nor are they slaves of memory, lost in sleep:
Their Father is greater than Time, and ages not.   10

ANTISTROPHE 1

The tyrant is a child of Pride
Who drinks from his great sickening cup
Recklessness and vanity,
Until from his high crest headlong
He plummets to the dust of hope.   15
That strong man is not strong.
But let no fair ambition be denied;
May God protect the wrestler for the State
In government, in comely policy,
Who will fear God, and on his ordinance wait.   20

STROPHE 2

Haughtiness and the high hand of disdain
Tempt and outrage God's holy law;
And any mortal who dares hold
No immortal Power in awe
Will be caught up in a net of pain: 25
The price for which his levity is sold.
Let each man take due earnings, then,
And keep his hands from holy things,
And from blasphemy stand apart—
Else the crackling blast of heaven   30
Blows on his head, and on his desperate heart.
Though fools will honor impious men,
In their cities no tragic poet sings.

ANTISTROPHE 2

Shall we lose faith in Delphi's obscurities,
We who have heard the world's core   35
Discredited, and the sacred wood
Of Zeus at Elis praised no more?
The deeds and the strange prophecies
Must make a pattern yet to be understood.
Zeus, if indeed you are lord of all,   40
Throned in light over night and day,
Mirror this in your endless mind:
Our masters call the oracle
Words on the wind, and the Delphic vision blind!
Their hearts no longer know Apollo,   45
And reverence for the gods has died away.

SCENE III

(*Enter* IOKASTE.)

IOKASTE: Princes of Thebes, it has occurred to me
    To visit the altars of the gods, bearing
    These branches as a suppliant, and this incense.
    Our king is not himself: his noble soul
    Is overwrought with fantasies of dread,   5
    Else he would consider
    The new prophecies in the light of the old.
    He will listen to any voice that speaks disaster,
    And my advice goes for nothing. (*She approaches the altar, right.*)
                            To you, then, Apollo,
    Lycean lord, since you are nearest, I turn in prayer   10
    Receive these offerings, and grant us deliverance
    From defilement. Our hearts are heavy with fear
    When we see our leader distracted, as helpless sailors
    Are terrified by the confusion of their helmsman.

(*Enter* MESSENGER.)

MESSENGER: Friends, no doubt you can direct me: 15
    Where shall I find the house of Oedipus,
    Or, better still, where is the king himself?
CHORAGOS: It is this very place, stranger; he is inside.
    This is his wife and mother of his children.
MESSENGER: I wish her happiness in a happy house,   20
    Blest in all the fulfillment of her marriage.
IOKASTE: I wish as much for you: your courtesy
    Deserves a like good fortune. But now, tell me:

Why have you come? What have you to say to us?

MESSENGER: Good news, my lady, for your house and your husband.   25

IOKASTE: What news? Who sent you here?

MESSENGER: I am from Corinth.
The news I bring ought to mean joy for you,
Though it may be you will find some grief in it.

IOKASTE: What is it? How can it touch us in both ways?

MESSENGER: The word is that the people of the Isthmus   30
Intend to call Oedipus to be their king.

IOKASTE: But old King Polybos—is he not reigning still?

MESSENGER: No. Death holds him in his sepulchre.

IOKASTE: What are you saying? Polybos is dead?

MESSENGER: If I am not telling the truth, may I die myself.   35

IOKASTE (*to a* MAIDSERVANT):   Go in, go quickly; tell this to your master.
O riddlers of God's will, where are you now!
This was the man whom Oedipus, long ago,
Feared so, fled so, in dread of destroying him—
But it was another fate by which he died.   40

(*Enter* OEDIPUS *center.*)

OEDIPUS: Dearest Iokaste, why have you sent for me?

IOKASTE: Listen to what this man says, and then tell me
What has become of the solemn prophecies.

OEDIPUS: Who is this man? What is his news for me?

IOKASTE: He has come from Corinth to announce your father's death!   45

OEDIPUS: Is it true, stranger? Tell me in your own words.

MESSENGER: I cannot say it more clearly: the king is dead.

OEDIPUS: Was it by treason? Or by an attack of illness?

MESSENGER: A little thing brings old men to their rest.

OEDIPUS: It was sickness, then?

MESSENGER: Yes, and his many years.   50

OEDIPUS: Ah!
Why should a man respect the Pythian hearth,° or
Give heed to the birds that jangle above his head?
They prophesied that I should kill Polybos,
Kill my own father; but he is dead and buried,   55
And I am here—I never touched him, never,
Unless he died of grief for my departure,
And thus, in a sense, through me. No. Polybos
Has packed the oracles off with him underground.
They are empty words.

IOKASTE: Had I not told you so?   60

---

51. Pythian hearth: Delphi; the alternative name came from the dragon Python, which once guarded Delphi until Apollo vanquished it.

OEDIPUS: You had; it was my faint heart that betrayed me.

IOKASTE: From now on never think of those things again.

OEDIPUS: And yet—must I not fear my mother's bed?

IOKASTE: Why should anyone in this world be afraid,
Since Fate rules us and nothing can be foreseen?   65
A man should live only for the present day.

Have no more fear of sleeping with your mother:
How many men, in dreams, have lain with their mothers!
No reasonable man is troubled by such things.   70

OEDIPUS: That is true; only—
If only my mother were not still alive!
But she is alive. I cannot help my dread.

IOKASTE: Yet this news of your father's death is wonderful.

OEDIPUS: Wonderful. But I fear the living woman.   75

MESSENGER: Tell me, who is this woman that you fear?

OEDIPUS: It is Merope, man; the wife of King Polybos.

MESSENGER: Merope? Why should you be afraid of her?

OEDIPUS: An oracle of the gods, a dreadful saying.

MESSENGER: Can you tell me about it or are you sworn to silence?   80

OEDIPUS: I can tell you, and I will.
Apollo said through his prophet that I was the man
Who should marry his own mother, shed his father's blood
With his own hands. And so, for all these years
I have kept clear of Corinth, and no harm has come—   85
Though it would have been sweet to see my parents again.

MESSENGER: And is this the fear that drove you out of Corinth?

OEDIPUS: Would you have me kill my father?

MESSENGER: As for that
You must be reassured by the news I gave you.

OEDIPUS: If you could reassure me, I would reward you.   90

MESSENGER: I had that in mind, I will confess: I thought
I could count on you when you returned to Corinth.

OEDIPUS: No: I will never go near my parents again.

MESSENGER: Ah, son, you still do not know what you are doing—

OEDIPUS: What do you mean? In the name of God tell me!   95

MESSENGER: —If these are your reasons for not going home.

OEDIPUS: I tell you, I fear the oracle may come true.

MESSENGER: And guilt may come upon you through your parents?

OEDIPUS: That is the dread that is always in my heart.

MESSENGER: Can you not see that all your fears are groundless?   100

OEDIPUS: Groundless? Am I not my parents' son?

MESSENGER: Polybos was not your father.

OEDIPUS: Not my father?

MESSENGER: No more your father than the man speaking to you.

OEDIPUS: But you are nothing to me!

MESSENGER: Neither was he.

OEDIPUS: Then why did he call me son?

MESSENGER: I will tell you:

   Long ago he had you from my hands, as a gift.   105

OEDIPUS: Then how could he love me so, if I was not his?

MESSENGER: He had no children, and his heart turned to you.

OEDIPUS: What of you? Did you buy me? Did you find me by chance?

MESSENGER: I came upon you in the woody vales of Kithairon.

OEDIPUS: And what were you doing there?

MESSENGER: Tending my flocks.   110

OEDIPUS: A wandering shepherd?

MESSENGER: But your savior, son, that day.

OEDIPUS: From what did you save me?

MESSENGER: Your ankles should tell you that.

OEDIPUS: Ah, stranger, why do you speak of that childhood pain?

MESSENGER: I pulled the skewer that pinned your feet together.

OEDIPUS: I have had the mark as long as I can remember.   115

MESSENGER: That was why you were given the name you bear.°

OEDIPUS: God! Was it my father or my mother who did it?

   Tell me!

MESSENGER: I do not know. The man who gave you to me

   Can tell you better than I.

OEDIPUS: It was not you that found me, but another?   120

MESSENGER: It was another shepherd gave you to me.

OEDIPUS: Who was he? Can you tell me who he was?

MESSENGER: I think he was said to be one of Laios' people.

OEDIPUS: You mean the Laios who was king here years ago?

MESSENGER: Yes; King Laios; and the man was one of his herdsmen.   125

OEDIPUS: Is he still alive? Can I see him?

MESSENGER: These men here

   Know best about such things.

OEDIPUS: Does anyone here

   Know this shepherd that he is talking about?

   Have you seen him in the fields, or in the town?

   If you have, tell me. It is time things were made plain.   130

CHORAGOS: I think the man he means is that same shepherd

   You have already asked to see. Iokaste perhaps

   Could tell you something.

OEDIPUS: Do you know anything

   About him, Lady? Is he the man we have summoned?

   Is that the man this shepherd means?

IOKASTE: Why think of him?   135

116. the name you bear: "Oedipus" translates as "the one with a swollen foot."

Forget this herdsman. Forget it all.
This talk is a waste of time.

OEDIPUS: How can you say that,
When the clues to my true birth are in my hands?

IOKASTE: For God's love, let us have no more questioning!   140
Is your life nothing to you?
My own is pain enough for me to bear.

OEDIPUS: You need not worry. Suppose my mother a slave,
And born of slaves: no baseness can touch you.

IOKASTE: Listen to me, I beg you: do not do this thing!

OEDIPUS: I will not listen; the truth must be made known.   145

IOKASTE: Everything that I say is for your own good!

OEDIPUS: My own good
Snaps my patience, then; I want none of it.

IOKASTE: You are fatally wrong! May you never learn who you are!

OEDIPUS: Go, one of you, and bring the shepherd here.
Let us leave this woman to brag of her royal name.   150

IOKASTE: Ah, miserable!
That is the only word I have for you now.
That is the only word I can ever have.   (*Exit into the palace.*)

CHORAGOS: Why has she left us, Oedipus? Why has she gone
In such a passion of sorrow? I fear this silence: 155
Something dreadful may come of it.

OEDIPUS: Let it come!
However base my birth, I must know about it.
The Queen, like a woman, is perhaps ashamed
To think of my low origin. But I
Am a child of Luck; I cannot be dishonored.   160
Luck is my mother; the passing months, my brothers,
Have seen me rich and poor.

                        If this is so,
How could I wish that I were someone else?
How could I not be glad to know my birth?

ODE 3

STROPHE

CHORUS: If ever the coming time were known
To my heart's pondering,
Kithairon, now by Heaven I see the torches
At the festival of the next full moon,
And see the dance, and hear the choir sing   5
A grace to your gentle shade:
Mountain where Oedipus was found,
O mountain guard of a noble race!

May the god° who heals us lend his aid,
And let that glory come to pass   10
For our king's cradling-ground.

ANTISTROPHE

Of the nymphs that flower beyond the years,
Who bore you,° royal child,
To Pan° of the hills or the timberline Apollo,
Cold in delight where the upland clears,   15
Or Hermes° for whom Kyllene's° heights are piled?
Or flushed as evening cloud,
Great Dionysos,° roamer of mountains,
He—was it he who found you there,
And caught you up in his own proud   20
Arms from the sweet god-ravisher
Who laughed by the Muses'° fountains?

SCENE IV

OEDIPUS: Sirs: though I do not know the man,
I think I see him coming, this shepherd we want:
He is old, like our friend here, and the men
Bringing him seem to be servants of my house.
But you can tell, if you have ever seen him.   5

   (*Enter* SHEPHERD *escorted by* SERVANTS.)

CHORAGOS: I know him, he was Laios' man. You can trust him.
OEDIPUS: Tell me first, you from Corinth: is this the shepherd
   We were discussing?
MESSENGER: This is the very man.
OEDIPUS (*to* SHEPHERD):   Come here. No, look at me. You must answer
Everything I ask.—You belonged to Laios?   10
SHEPHERD: Yes: born his slave, brought up in his house.
OEDIPUS: Tell me: what kind of work did you do for him?
SHEPHERD: I was a shepherd of his, most of my life.
OEDIPUS: Where mainly did you go for pasturage?
SHEPHERD: Sometimes Kithairon, sometimes the hills near-by.   15
OEDIPUS: Do you remember ever seeing this man out there?

---

9. god: Apollo.   **13. Who bore you:** The Chorus wonders whether Oedipus might be the son of a nymph and a god: Pan, Apollo, Hermes, or Dionysus.   **14. Pan:** God of nature; from the waist up, he is human, from the waist down, a goat.   **16. Hermes:** Zeus's son, messenger of the gods;   **16. Kyllene:** sacred mountain, the birthplace of Hermes.   **18. Dionysos:** (Dionysus) god of wine, sometimes called Bacchos.   **22. Muses:** nine goddesses, sisters, who are the patronesses of poetry, music, art, and the sciences.

SHEPHERD: What would he be doing there? This man?

OEDIPUS: This man standing here. Have you ever seen him before?

SHEPHERD: No. At least, not to my recollection.

MESSENGER: And that is not strange, my lord. But I'll refresh   20
His memory. He must remember when we two
Spent three whole seasons together, March to September,
On Kithairon or thereabouts. He had two flocks;
I had one. Each autumn I'd drive mine home
And he would go back with his to Laios' sheepfold.—   25
Is this not true, just as I have described it?

SHEPHERD: True, yes; but it was all so long ago.

MESSENGER: Well, then: do you remember back in those days,
That you gave me a baby boy to bring up as my own?

SHEPHERD: What if I did? What are you trying to say?   30

MESSENGER: King Oedipus was once that little child.

SHEPHERD: Damn you, hold your tongue!

OEDIPUS: No more of that!
It is your tongue needs watching, not this man's.

SHEPHERD: My king, my master, what is it I have done wrong?

OEDIPUS: You have not answered his question about the boy.   35

SHEPHERD: He does not know . . . He is only making trouble . . .

OEDIPUS: Come, speak plainly, or it will go hard with you.

SHEPHERD: In God's name, do not torture an old man!

OEDIPUS: Come here, one of you; bind his arms behind him.

SHEPHERD: Unhappy king! What more do you wish to learn?   40

OEDIPUS: Did you give this man the child he speaks of?

SHEPHERD: I did.
And I would to God I had died that very day.

OEDIPUS: You will die now unless you speak the truth.

SHEPHERD: Yet if I speak the truth, I am worse than dead.

OEDIPUS (to ATTENDANT):   He intends to draw it out, apparently—   45

SHEPHERD: No! I have told you already that I gave him the boy.

OEDIPUS: Where did you get him? From your house? From somewhere else?

SHEPHERD: Not from mine, no. A man gave him to me.

OEDIPUS: Is that man here? Whose house did he belong to?

SHEPHERD: For God's love, my king, do not ask me any more!   50

OEDIPUS: You are a dead man if I have to ask you again.

SHEPHERD: Then . . . Then the child was from the palace of Laios.

OEDIPUS: A slave child? or a child of his own line?

SHEPHERD: Ah, I am on the brink of dreadful speech!

OEDIPUS: And I of dreadful hearing. Yet I must hear.   55

SHEPHERD: If you must be told, then . . .
                                        They said it was Laios' child;
But it is your wife who can tell you about that.

OEDIPUS: My wife—Did she give it to you?

SHEPHERD: My lord she did.

OEDIPUS: Do you know why?

SHEPHERD: I was told to get rid of it.

OEDIPUS: Oh heartless mother!

SHEPHERD: But in dread of prophecies . . .   60

OEDIPUS: Tell me.

SHEPHERD: It was said that the boy would kill his own father.

OEDIPUS: Then why did you give him over to this old man?

SHEPHERD: I pitied the baby, my king,
And I thought that this man would take him far away
To his own country.

                He saved him—but for what a fate!   65
For if you are what this man says you are,
No man living is more wretched than Oedipus.

OEDIPUS: Ah God!
It was true!

        All the prophecies!

                —Now,
O Light, may I look on you for the last time!   70
I, Oedipus,
Oedipus, damned in his birth, in his marriage damned,
Damned in the blood he shed with his own hand!

(He rushes into the palace.)

ODE 4

STROPHE 1

CHORUS: Alas for the seed of men.
What measure shall I give these generations
That breathe on the void and are void
And exist and do not exist?
Who bears more weight of joy   5
Than mass of sunlight shifting in images,
Or who shall make his thought stay on
That down time drifts away?
Your splendor is all fallen.
O naked brow of wrath and tears,   10
O change of Oedipus!
I who saw your days call no man blest—
Your great days like ghosts gone.

ANTISTROPHE 1

That mind was a strong bow.
Deep, how deep you drew it then, hard archer,   15
At a dim fearful range,
And brought dear glory down!
You overcame the stranger°—
The virgin with her hooking lion claws—
And though death sang, stood like a tower   20
To make pale Thebes take heart.
Fortress against our sorrow!
True king, giver of laws,
Majestic Oedipus!
No prince in Thebes had ever such renown,   25
No prince won such grace of power.

STROPHE 2

And now of all men ever known
Most pitiful is this man's story:
His fortunes are most changed; his state
Fallen to a low slave's   30
Ground under bitter fate.
O Oedipus, most royal one!
The great door° that expelled you to the light
Gave at night—ah, gave night to your glory:
As to the father, to the fathering son.   35
All understood too late.
How could that queen whom Laios won,
The garden that he harrowed at his height,
Be silent when that act was done?

ANTISTROPHE 2

But all eyes fail before time's eye,   40
All actions come to justice there.
Though never willed, though far down the deep past,
Your bed, your dread sirings,
Are brought to book at last.
Child by Laios doomed to die,   45
Then doomed to lose that fortunate little death,
Would God you never took breath in this air
That with my wailing lips I take to cry:

18. **stranger:** the Sphinx.   33. **door:** refers to the birth process.

For I weep the world's outcast.
I was blind, and now I can tell why: 50
Asleep, for you had given ease of breath
To Thebes, while the false years went by.

EXODOS°

(Enter, from the palace, SECOND MESSENGER.)

SECOND MESSENGER: Elders of Thebes, most honored in this land,
What horrors are yours to see and hear, what weight
Of sorrow to be endured, if, true to your birth,
You venerate the line of Labdakos!
I think neither Istros nor Phasis, those great rivers,   5
Could purify this place of all the evil
It shelters now, or soon must bring to light—
Evil not done unconsciously, but willed.
The greatest griefs are those we cause ourselves.

CHORAGOS: Surely, friend, we have grief enough already;   10
What new sorrow do you mean?
SECOND MESSENGER: The queen is dead.
CHORAGOS: O miserable queen! But at whose hand?
SECOND MESSENGER: Her own.
The full horror of what happened you cannot know,
For you did not see it; but I, who did, will tell you
As clearly as I can how she met her death.   15

When she had left us,
In passionate silence, passing through the court,
She ran to her apartment in the house,
Her hair clutched by the fingers of both hands.
She closed the doors behind her; then, by that bed   20
Where long ago the fatal son was conceived—
That son who should bring about his father's death—
We heard her call upon Laios, dead so many years,
And heard her wail for the double fruit of her marriage,
A husband by her husband, children by her child.   25
Exactly how she died I do not know:
For Oedipus burst in moaning and would not let us
Keep vigil to the end: it was by him
As he stormed about the room that our eyes were caught.
From one to another of us he went, begging a sword,   30

Exodos: final scene.

Hunting the wife who was not his wife, the mother
Whose womb had carried his own children and himself.
I do not know: it was none of us aided him,
But surely one of the gods was in control!
For with a dreadful cry   35
He hurled his weight, as though wrenched out of himself,
At the twin doors: the bolts gave, and he rushed in.
And there we saw her hanging, her body swaying
From the cruel cord she had noosed about her neck.
A great sob broke from him, heartbreaking to hear,   40
As he loosed the rope and lowered her to the ground.

I would blot out from my mind what happened next!
For the king ripped from her gown the golden brooches
That were her ornament, and raised them, and plunged them down
Straight into his own eyeballs, crying, "No more,   45
No more shall you look on the misery about me,
The horrors of my own doing! Too long you have known
The faces of those whom I should never have seen,
Too long been blind to those for whom I was searching!
From this hour, go in darkness!" And as he spoke,   50
He struck at his eyes—not once, but many times;
And the blood spattered his beard,
Bursting from his ruined sockets like red hail.
So from the unhappiness of two this evil has sprung,
A curse on the man and woman alike. The old   55
Happiness of the house of Labdakos
Was happiness enough: where is it today?
It is all wailing and ruin, disgrace, death—all
The misery of mankind that has a name—
And it is wholly and for ever theirs.   60

CHORAGOS: Is he in agony still? Is there no rest for him?

SECOND MESSENGER: He is calling for someone to open the doors wide
So that all the children of Kadmos may look upon
His father's murderer, his mother's—no,
I cannot say it!
                     And then he will leave Thebes,   65
Self-exiled, in order that the curse
Which he himself pronounced may depart from the house.
He is weak, and there is none to lead him,
So terrible is his suffering.
                     But you will see:
Look, the doors are opening; in a moment   70
You will see a thing that would crush a heart of stone.

(The central door is opened, OEDIPUS, *blinded, is led in.)*

CHORAGOS: Dreadful indeed for men to see.
  Never have my own eyes
  Looked on a sight so full of fear.

  Oedipus!   75
  What madness came upon you, what demon
  Leaped on your life with heavier
  Punishment than a mortal man can bear?
  No: I cannot even
  Look at you, poor ruined one.   80
  And I would speak, question, ponder,
  If I were able. No.
  You make me shudder.
OEDIPUS: God. God.
  Is there a sorrow greater?
  Where shall I find harbor in this world?   85
  My voice is hurled far on a dark wind.
  What has God done to me?—
CHORAGOS: Too terrible to think of, or to see.

STROPHE 1

OEDIPUS: O cloud of night,   90
  Never to be turned away: night coming on,
  I cannot tell how: night like a shroud!
  My fair winds brought me here.
                   O God. Again
  The pain of the spikes where I had sight,
  The flooding pain   95
  Of memory, never to be gouged out.
CHORAGOS: This is not strange.
  You suffer it all twice over, remorse in pain,
  Pain in remorse.

ANTISTROPHE 1

OEDIPUS: Ah dear friend   100
  Are you faithful even yet, you alone?
  Are you still standing near me, will you stay here,
  Patient, to care for the blind?
                  The blind man!
  Yet even blind I know who it is attends me,
  By the voice's tone—   105
  Though my new darkness hide the comforter.

CHORAGOS: Oh fearful act!
    What god was it drove you to rake black
    Night across your eyes?

STROPHE 2

OEDIPUS: Apollo. Apollo. Dear   110
    Children, the god was Apollo.
    He brought my sick, sick fate upon me.
    But the blinding hand was my own!
    How could I bear to see
    When all my sight was horror everywhere?   115
CHORAGOS: Everywhere; that is true.
OEDIPUS: And now what is left?
    Images? Love? A greeting even,
    Sweet to the senses? Is there anything?
    Ah, no, friends: lead me away.   120
    Lead me away from Thebes.
                      Lead the great wreck
    And hell of Oedipus, whom the gods hate.
CHORAGOS: Your misery, you are not blind to that.
    Would God you had never found it out!

ANTISTROPHE 2

OEDIPUS: Death take the man who unbound   125
    My feet on that hillside
    And delivered me from death to life! What life?
    If only I had died,
    This weight of monstrous doom
    Could not have dragged me and my darlings down.   130
CHORAGOS: I would have wished the same.
OEDIPUS: Oh never to have come here
    With my father's blood upon me! Never
    To have been the man they call his mother's husband!
    Oh accurst! Oh child of evil,   135
    To have entered that wretched bed—
                    the selfsame one!
    More primal than sin itself, this fell to me.
CHORAGOS: I do not know what words to offer you.
    You were better dead than alive and blind.
OEDIPUS: Do not counsel me any more. This punishment   140
    That I have laid upon myself is just.
    If I had eyes,
    I do not know how I could bear the sight

Of my father, when I came to the house of Death,
Or my mother: for I have sinned against them both   145
So vilely that I could not make my peace
By strangling my own life.
             Or do you think my children,
Born as they were born, would be sweet to my eyes?
Ah never, never! Nor this town with its high walls,
Nor the holy images of the gods.
                    For I,   150
Thrice miserable!—Oedipus, noblest of all the line
Of Kadmos, have condemned myself to enjoy
These things no more, by my own malediction
Expelling that man whom the gods declared
To be a defilement in the house of Laios.   155
After exposing the rankness of my own guilt,
How could I look men frankly in the eyes?
No, I swear it,
If I could have stifled my hearing at its source,
I would have done it and made all this body   160
A tight cell of misery, blank to light and sound:
So I should have been safe in my dark mind
Beyond external evil.
            Ah Kithairon!
Why did you shelter me? When I was cast upon you,
Why did I not die? Then I should never   165
Have shown the world my execrable birth.

Ah Polybos! Corinth, city that I believed
The ancient seat of my ancestors: how fair
I seemed, your child! And all the while this evil
Was cancerous within me!
             For I am sick   170
In my own being, sick in my origin.
O three roads, dark ravine, woodland and way
Where three roads met; you, drinking my father's blood,
My own blood, spilled by my own hand: can you remember
The unspeakable things I did there, and the things   175
I went on from there to do?
             O marriage, marriage!
The act that engendered me, and again the act
Performed by the son in the same bed—
                  Ah, the net
Of incest, mingling fathers, brothers, sons,
With brides, wives, mothers: the last evil   180
That can be known by men: no tongue can say

How evil!

No. For the love of God, conceal me
Somewhere far from Thebes; or kill me; or hurl me
Into the sea, away from men's eyes for ever.   185

Come, lead me. You need not fear to touch me.
Of all men, I alone can bear this guilt.

(*Enter* KREON.)

CHORAGOS: Kreon is here now. As to what you ask,
He may decide the course to take. He only
Is left to protect the city in your place.
OEDIPUS: Alas, how can I speak to him? What right have I   190
To beg his courtesy whom I have deeply wronged?
KREON: I have not come to mock you, Oedipus,
Or to reproach you, either.
(*To* ATTENDANTS.)   —You, standing there:
If you have lost all respect for man's dignity,   195
At least respect the flame of Lord Helios:
Do not allow this pollution to show itself
Openly here, an affront to the earth
And Heaven's rain and the light of day. No, take him
Into the house as quickly as you can.   200
For it is proper
That only the close kindred see his grief.
OEDIPUS: I pray you in God's name, since your courtesy
Ignores my dark expectation, visiting
With mercy this man of all men most execrable: 205
Give me what I ask—for your good, not for mine.
KREON: And what is it that you turn to me begging for?
OEDIPUS: Drive me out of this country as quickly as may be
To a place where no human voice can ever greet me.
KREON: I should have done that before now—only,   210
God's will had not been wholly revealed to me.
OEDIPUS: But his command is plain: the parricide
Must be destroyed. I am that evil man.
KREON: That is the sense of it, yes; but as things are,
We had best discover clearly what is to be done.   215
OEDIPUS: You would learn more about a man like me?
KREON: You are ready now to listen to the god.
OEDIPUS: I will listen. But it is to you
That I must turn for help. I beg you, hear me.

The woman is there—   220
Give her whatever funeral you think proper:

She is your sister.
          —But let me go, Kreon!
Let me purge my father's Thebes of the pollution
Of my living here, and go out to the wild hills,
To Kithairon, that has won such fame with me,
The tomb my mother and father appointed for me,   225
And let me die there, as they willed I should.
And yet I know
Death will not ever come to me through sickness
Or in any natural way: I have been preserved
For some unthinkable fate. But let that be.   230

As for my sons, you need not care for them.
They are men, they will find some way to live.
But my poor daughters, who have shared my table,
Who never before have been parted from their father—
Take care of them, Kreon; do this for me.   235

And will you let me touch them with my hands
A last time, and let us weep together?
Be kind, my lord,
Great prince, be kind!
          Could I but touch them,
They would be mine again, as when I had my eyes.   240

       (*Enter* ANTIGONE *and* ISMENE, *attended.*)

Ah, God!
Is it my dearest children I hear weeping?
Has Kreon pitied me and sent my daughters?
KREON: Yes, Oedipus: I knew that they were dear to you
In the old days, and know you must love them still.   245
OEDIPUS: May God bless you for this—and be a friendlier
Guardian to you than he has been to me!

Children, where are you?
Come quickly to my hands: they are your brother's—
Hands that have brought your father's once clear eyes   250
To this way of seeing—
          Ah dearest ones,
I had neither sight nor knowledge then, your father
By the woman who was the source of his own life!
And I weep for you—having no strength to see you—,
I weep for you when I think of the bitterness   255
That men will visit upon you all your lives.
What homes, what festivals can you attend
Without being forced to depart again in tears?

And when you come to marriageable age,
Where is the man, my daughters, who would dare   260
Risk the bane that lies on all my children?
Is there any evil wanting? Your father killed
His father; sowed the womb of her who bore him;
Engendered you at the fount of his own existence!
That is what they will say of you.

                            Then, whom   265
Can you ever marry? There are no bridegrooms for you,
And your lives must wither away in sterile dreaming.

O Kreon, son of Menoikeus!
You are the only father my daughters have,
Since we, their parents, are both of us gone for ever.   270
They are your own blood: you will not let them
Fall into beggary and loneliness;
You will keep them from the miseries that are mine!
Take pity on them; see, they are only children,
Friendless except for you. Promise me this,   275
Great prince, and give me your hand in token of it.

         (KREON *clasps his right hand.*)

Children.
I could say much, if you could understand me,
But as it is, I have only this prayer for you:
Live where you can, be as happy as you can—   280
Happier, please God, than God has made your father.

KREON: Enough. You have wept enough. Now go within.

OEDIPUS: I must; but it is hard.

KREON: Time eases all things.

OEDIPUS: You know my mind, then?

KREON: Say what you desire.

OEDIPUS: Send me from Thebes!

KREON: God grant that I may!   285

OEDIPUS: But since God hates me . . .

KREON: No, he will grant your wish.

OEDIPUS: You promise?

KREON: I cannot speak beyond my knowledge.

OEDIPUS: Then lead me in.

KREON: Come now, and leave your children.

OEDIPUS: No! Do not take them from me!

KREON: Think no longer
That you are in command here, but rather think   290
How, when you were, you served your own destruction.

(*Exeunt into the house all but the* CHORUS; *the* CHORAGOS *chants directly to the audience.*)

CHORAGOS: Men of Thebes: look upon Oedipus.

This is the king who solved the famous riddle
And towered up, most powerful of men.
No mortal eyes but looked on him with envy,   295
Yet in the end ruin swept over him.

Let every man in mankind's frailty
Consider his last day; and let none
Presume on his good fortune until he find
Life, at his death, a memory without pain.   300

                                                    [430 B.C.]

Journal Entry

Assume the persona of Iokaste and write a brief explanation of why you gave away your infant son.

Textual Considerations

1. Cite specific examples of Sophocles' use of dramatic **irony** throughout the play and discuss their thematic significance.
2. What are the functions of the chorus? What do they provide besides the spectacle of music, poetry, and dance? How effective is the chorus from the dramatic viewpoint?
3. What is the thematic significance of the plague as the background of the drama? Who inflicts the plague on Thebes? Why?
4. Discuss the thematic relevance of the metaphor of blindness versus sight as well as its counterpart of darkness versus light. Include Oedipus's tug of war with Teiresias, as well as Oedipus's blinding of himself in your discussion. Explain why Oedipus's removal of his eyes takes place off stage.
5. What role does Iokaste play in *Oedipus Rex*? What position does she assume in relation to the oracle? To Oedipus's downfall? Explain.
6. To what extent can we explain Oedipus's character in terms of *hubris*, or human pride? Do you empathize with him? Why or why not?

Cultural Contexts

1. Does Sophocles present the play as ordained by divine forces? Is Oedipus responsible for his own downfall? Is he a victim of fate or a victim of his own unconscious? Read Freud's interpretation of this play (Appendix D), and discuss these issues with members of your group.
2. Sophocles' play culminates with the revelation that Oedipus has committed parricide and incest. Working with your group, attack or defend the thesis that by using his reason to destroy the Sphinx's savagery, Oedipus promotes humanism, progress, and social order.

Performance Exercises

PERFORMANCE EXPRESS (40 MINUTES)

To discuss the use of masks in performance, design full or half masks for Oedipus, Iokaste, Kreon, and Teiresias before this exercise is due. On the day of the performance, ask the masked actors to act out scenes 1, 2, and 3 in an improvisational and spontaneous style, and invite the whole class to react to the performance. How helpful is the use of a mask to amplify and hide emotions or show the character's real self? Do masks help the actors distance themselves from the audience? Could the actors have used their real faces as masks? What other acting resources did the masked actors have to develop in their performance? Explain.

PERFORMANCE PROJECTS

1. To learn about Greek theater production in the fifth century b.c., research through the Internet the production of *Oedipus Rex* with Tyrone Guthrie at Stratford, Canada, 1954. Then stage one scene of *Oedipus Rex* using classical costumes, and a chorus with chants and music. Notice that for the sake of clarity, most modern producers of ancient Greek drama distribute the lines of the chorus among the performers rather than having them speak in unison.
2. To test the dramatic effectiveness of ancient drama, act out one scene of *Oedipus Rex* in postmodern style. Decide on the use of costumes and the choices of time, place, and sets that evoke the tragic atmosphere of the play in the twentieth-first century. React to the possibility of using costumes connected with sets such as your college gym.

William Shakespeare

The Tragedy of Hamlet, Prince of Denmark

CHARACTERS

CLAUDIUS, *King of Denmark*
HAMLET, *son to the late and nephew to the present king*
POLONIUS, *lord chamberlain*
HORATIO, *friend to Hamlet*
LAERTES, *son to Polonius*
VOLTIMAND
CORNELIUS
ROSENCRANTZ ⎱ *courtiers*
GUILDENSTERN ⎰
OSRIC
A GENTLEMAN
A PRIEST
MARCELLUS ⎱ *officers*
BERNARDO ⎰
FRANCISCO, *a soldier*
REYNALDO, *servant to Polonius*
PLAYERS
TWO CLOWNS, *grave-diggers*
FORTINBRAS, *Prince of Norway*
A CAPTAIN
ENGLISH AMBASSADORS
GERTRUDE, *Queen of Denmark, and mother to Hamlet*
OPHELIA, *daughter to Polonius*
GHOST *of Hamlet's father*
(LORDS, LADIES, OFFICERS, SOLDIERS, SAILORS, MESSENGERS, AND OTHER
    ATTENDANTS)

SCENE. Denmark.

ACT I

SCENE I

(Elsinore. A platform° before the castle.)

(Enter BERNARDO *and* FRANCISCO, *two sentinels.)*

BERNARDO: Who's there?
FRANCISCO: Nay, answer me°: stand, and unfold yourself.

I.i. s.d. platform: a level space on the battlements of the royal castle at Elsinore, a Danish seaport; now Helsingör. **2. me:** this is emphatic, since Francisco is the sentry.

BERNARDO: Long live the king!°
FRANCISCO: Bernardo?
BERNARDO: He.   5
FRANCISCO: You come most carefully upon your hour.
BERNARDO: 'Tis now struck twelve; get thee to bed, Francisco.
FRANCISCO: For this relief much thanks: 'tis bitter cold,
    And I am sick at heart.
BERNARDO: Have you had quiet guard?
FRANCISCO: Not a mouse stirring.   10
BERNARDO: Well, good night.
    If you do meet Horatio and Marcellus,
    The rivals° of my watch, bid them make haste.

            (*Enter* HORATIO *and* MARCELLUS.)

FRANCISCO: I think I hear them. Stand, ho! Who is there?
HORATIO: Friends to this ground.
MARCELLUS: And liegemen to the Dane.   15
FRANCISCO: Give you° good night.
MARCELLUS: O, farewell, honest soldier:
    Who hath reliev'd you?
FRANCISCO: Bernardo hath my place.
    Give you good night.   (*Exit* FRANCISCO.)
MARCELLUS: Holla! Bernardo!
BERNARDO: Say,
    What, is Horatio there?
HORATIO: A piece of him.
BERNARDO: Welcome, Horatio: welcome, good Marcellus.   20
MARCELLUS: What, has this thing appear'd again to-night?
BERNARDO: I have seen nothing.
MARCELLUS: Horatio says 'tis but our fantasy,
    And will not let belief take hold of him.
    Touching this dreaded sight, twice seen of us: 25
    Therefore I have entreated him along
    With us to watch the minutes of this night;
    That if again this apparition come,
    He may approve° our eyes and speak to it.
HORATIO: Tush, tush, 'twill not appear.
BERNARDO: Sit down awhile;   30
    And let us once again assail your ears,
    That are so fortified against our story
    What we have two nights seen.

---

3. Long live the king!: either a password or greeting; Horatio and Marcellus use a different one in line 15.
13. rivals: partners.   **16. Give you:** God give you.   **29. approve:** corroborate.

HORATIO: Well, sit we down,
And let us hear Bernardo speak of this.
BERNARDO: Last night of all,   35
When yond same star that's westward from the pole°
Had made his course t' illume that part of heaven
Where now it burns, Marcellus and myself,
The bell then beating one,—

(*Enter* GHOST.)

MARCELLUS: Peace, break thee off; look, where it comes again!   40
BERNARDO: In the same figure, like the king that's dead.
MARCELLUS: Thou art a scholar°; speak to it, Horatio.
BERNARDO: Looks 'a not like the king? mark it, Horatio.
HORATIO: Most like: it harrows° me with fear and wonder.
BERNARDO: It would be spoke to.°
MARCELLUS: Speak to it. Horatio.   45
HORATIO: What art thou that usurp'st this time of night,
Together with that fair and warlike form
In which the majesty of buried Denmark°
Did sometimes march? by heaven I charge thee, speak!
MARCELLUS: It is offended.
BERNARDO: See it stalks away!   50
HORATIO: Stay! speak, speak! I charge thee, speak!   (*Exit* GHOST.)
MARCELLUS: 'Tis gone, and will not answer.
BERNARDO: How now, Horatio! you tremble and look pale:
Is not this something more than fantasy?
What think you on 't?   55
HORATIO: Before my God, I might not this believe
Without the sensible and true avouch
Of mine own eyes.
MARCELLUS: Is it not like the king?
HORATIO: As thou art to thyself:
Such was the very armour he had on   60
When he the ambitious Norway combated;
So frown'd he once, when, in an angry parle,
He smote° the sledded Polacks° on the ice.
'Tis strange.
MARCELLUS: Thus twice before, and jump° at this dead hour,   65
With martial stalk hath he gone by our watch.

36. pole: polestar.   **42. scholar:** exorcisms were performed in Latin, which Horatio as an educated man
would be able to speak.   **44. harrows:** lacerates the feelings.   **45. It . . . to:** a ghost could not speak until
spoken to.   **48. buried Denmark:** the buried king of Denmark.   **63. smote:** defeated.   **63. sledded
Polacks:** Polanders using sledges.   **65. jump:** exactly.

HORATIO: In what particular thought to work I know not;
    But in the gross and scope° of my opinion,
    This bodes some strange eruption to our state.

MARCELLUS: Good now,° sit down, and tell me, he that knows,   70
    Why this same strict and most observant watch
    So nightly toils° the subject° of the land,
    And why such daily cast° of brazen cannon,
    And foreign mart° for implements of war;
    Why such impress° of shipwrights, whose sore task   75
    Does not divide the Sunday from the week;
    What might be toward, that this sweaty haste
    Doth make the night joint-labourer with the day:
    Who is't that can inform me?

HORATIO: That can I;
    At least, the whisper goes so. Our last king,   80
    Whose image even but now appear'd to us,
    Was, as you know, by Fortinbras of Norway,
    Thereto prick'd on° by a most emulate° pride,
    Dar'd to the combat; in which our valiant Hamlet—
    For so this side of our known world esteem'd him—   85
    Did slay this Fortinbras; who, by a seal'd compact,
    Well ratified by law and heraldry,°
    Did forfeit, with his life, all those his lands
    Which he stood seiz'd° of, to the conqueror:
    Against the which, a moiety competent°   90
    Was gaged by our king; which had return'd
    To the inheritance of Fortinbras,
    Had he been vanquisher; as, by the same comart,°
    And carriage° of the article design'd,
    His fell to Hamlet. Now, sir, young Fortinbras,   95
    Of unimproved° mettle hot and full,°
    Hath in the skirts of Norway here and there
    Shark'd up° a list of lawless resolutes,°
    For food and diet,° to some enterprise
    That hath a stomach in't; which is no other—   100
    As it doth well appear unto our state—
    But to recover of us, by strong hand

---

68. gross and scope: general drift.   **70. Good now:** an expression denoting entreaty or expostulation.
72. toils: causes or makes to toil.   **72. subject:** people, subjects.   **73. cast:** casting, founding.
74. mart: buying and selling, traffic.   **75. impress:** impressment.   **83. prick'd on:** incited.   **83. emulate:** rivaling.   **87. law and heraldry:** heraldic law, governing combat.   **89. seiz'd:** possessed.
90. moiety competent: adequate or sufficient portion.   **93. comart:** joint bargain.   **94. carriage:** import, bearing.   **96. unimproved:** not turned to account.   **96. hot and full:** full of fight.
98. Shark'd up: got together in haphazard fashion.   **98. resolutes:** desperadoes.   **99. food and diet:** no pay but their keep.

And terms compulsatory, those foresaid lands
So by his father lost: and this, I take it,
Is the main motive of our preparations, 105
The source of this our watch and the chief head
Of this post-haste and romage° in the land.
BERNARDO: I think it be no other but e'en so:
Well may it sort° that this portentous figure
Comes armed through our watch; so like the king 110
That was and is the question of these wars.
HORATIO: A mote° it is to trouble the mind's eye.
In the most high and palmy state° of Rome,
A little ere the mightiest Julius fell,
The graves stood tenantless and the sheeted dead 115
Did squeak and gibber in the Roman streets:
As stars with trains of fire° and dews of blood,
Disasters° in the sun; and the moist star°
Upon whose influence Neptune's empire° stands
Was sick almost to doomsday with eclipse: 120
And even the like precurse° of fear'd events,
As harbingers preceding still the fates
And prologue to the omen coming on,
Have heaven and earth together demonstrated
Unto our climatures and countrymen.— 125

(*Enter* GHOST.)

But soft, behold! lo, where it comes again!
I'll cross° it, though it blast me. Stay, illusion!
If thou hast any sound, or use of voice,
Speak to me! (*It° spreads his arms.*)
If there be any good thing to be done, 130
That may to thee do ease and grace to me,
Speak to me!
If° thou art privy to thy country's fate,
Which, happily, foreknowing may avoid,
O, speak! 135
Or if thou hast uphoarded in thy life
Extorted treasure in the womb of earth,
For which, they say, you spirits oft walk in death, (*The cock crows.*)
Speak of it: stay, and speak! Stop it, Marcellus.

---

107. **romage:** bustle, commotion.   109. **sort:** suit.   112. **mote:** speck of dust.   113. **palmy state:** triumphant sovereignty.   117. **stars . . . fire:** i.e., comets.   118. **Disasters:** unfavorable aspects.   118. **moist star:** the moon, governing tides.   119. **Neptune's empire:** the sea.   121. **precurse:** heralding.   127. **cross:** meet, face, thus bringing down the evil influence on the person who crosses it. 129. **It:** the Ghost, or perhaps Horatio.   133–139. **If . . . :** in the following seven lines, Horatio recites the traditional reasons why ghosts might walk.

MARCELLUS: Shall I strike at it with my partisan?° 140

HORATIO: Do, if it will not stand.

BERNARDO: 'Tis here!

HORATIO: 'Tis here!

MARCELLUS: 'Tis gone! (*Exit* GHOST.)

We do it wrong, being so majestical,
To offer it the show of violence;
For it is, as the air, invulnerable, 145
And our vain blows malicious mockery.

BERNARDO: It was about to speak, when the cock crew.°

HORATIO: And then it started like a guilty thing
Upon a fearful summons. I have heard,
The cock, that is the trumpet to the morn, 150
Doth with his lofty and shrill-sounding throat
Awake the god of day; and, at his warning,
Whether in sea or fire, in earth or air,
Th' extravagant and erring° spirit hies
To his confine°: and of the truth herein 155
This present object made probation.°

MARCELLUS: It faded on the crowing of the cock.
Some say that ever 'gainst° that season comes
Wherein our Saviour's birth is celebrated,
The bird of dawning singeth all night long: 160
And then, they say, no spirit dare stir abroad;
The nights are wholesome; then no planets strike,°
No fairy takes, nor witch hath power to charm,
So hallow'd and so gracious° is that time.

HORATIO: So have I heard and do in part believe it. 165
But, look, the morn, in russet mantle clad,
Walks o'er the dew of yon high eastward hill:
Break we our watch up; and by my advice,
Let us impart what we have seen to-night
Unto young Hamlet; for, upon my life, 170
This spirit, dumb to us, will speak to him.
Do you consent we shall acquaint him with it,
As needful in our loves, fitting our duty?

MARCELLUS: Let's do 't, I pray; and I this morning know
Where we shall find him most conveniently. (*Exeunt.*) 175

---

140. partisan: long-handled spear with a blade having lateral projections. **147. cock crew:** according to traditional ghost lore, spirits returned to their confines at cockcrow. **154. extravagant and erring:** wandering. Both words mean the same thing. **155. confine:** place of confinement. **156. probation:** proof, trial. **158. 'gainst:** just before. **162. planets strike:** it was thought that planets were malignant and might strike travelers by night. **164. gracious:** full of goodness.

SCENE II

(*A room of state in the castle.*)

(*Flourish. Enter* CLAUDIUS, *King of Denmark*, GERTRUDE *the Queen*, COUNCILORS, POLONIUS *and his Son* LAERTES, HAMLET, *cum aliis*° [*including* VOLTIMAND *and* CORNELIUS].)

KING: Though yet of Hamlet our dear brother's death
   The memory be green, and that it us befitted
   To bear our hearts in grief and our whole kingdom
   To be contracted in one brow of woe,
   Yet so far hath discretion fought with nature   5
   That we with wisest sorrow think on him,
   Together with remembrance of ourselves.
   Therefore our sometime sister, now our queen,
   Th' imperial jointress° to this warlike state,
   Have we, as 'twere with a defeated joy,—   10
   With an auspicious and a dropping eye,
   With mirth in funeral and with dirge in marriage,
   In equal scale weighing delight and dole,—
   Taken to wife: nor have we herein barr'd
   Your better wisdoms, which have freely gone   15
   With this affair along. For all, our thanks.
   Now follows, that° you know, young Fortinbras,
   Holding a weak supposal° of our worth,
   Or thinking by our late dear brother's death
   Our state to be disjoint° and out of frame,°   20
   Colleagued° with this dream of his advantage,°
   He hath not fail'd to pester us with message,
   Importing° the surrender of those lands
   Lost by his father, with all bands of law,
   To our most valiant brother. So much for him.   25
   Now for ourself and for this time of meeting:
   Thus much the business is: we have here writ
   To Norway, uncle of young Fortinbras,—
   Who, impotent and bed-rid, scarcely hears
   Of this his nephew's purpose,—to suppress   30
   His further gait° herein; in that the levies,
   The lists and full proportions, are all made

I.ii. s.d. cum aliis: with others.   **9. jointress:** woman possessed of a jointure, or, joint tenancy of an estate.   **17. that:** that which.   **18. weak supposal:** low estimate.   **20. disjoint:** distracted, out of joint.
20. frame: order.   **21. Colleagued:** added to.   **21. dream . . . advantage:** visionary hope of success.
23. Importing: purporting, pertaining to.   **31. gait:** proceeding.

Out of his subject°: and we here dispatch
You, good Cornelius, and you, Voltimand,
For bearers of this greeting to old Norway;   35
Giving to you no further personal power
To business with the king, more than the scope
Of these delated° articles allow.
Farewell, and let your haste commend your duty.

CORNELIUS: ⎫
VOLTIMAND: ⎭ In that and all things will we show our duty.   40

KING: We doubt it nothing: heartily farewell.

(*Exeunt* VOLTIMAND *and* CORNELIUS.)

And now, Laertes, what's the news with you?
You told us of some suit; what is't, Laertes?
You cannot speak of reason to the Dane,°
And lose your voice°: what wouldst thou beg, Laertes,   45
That shall not be my offer, not thy asking?
The head is not more native° to the heart,
The hand more instrumental° to the mouth,
Than is the throne of Denmark to thy father.
What wouldst thou have, Laertes?

LAERTES: My dread lord,   50
Your leave and favour to return to France;
From whence though willingly I came to Denmark,
To show my duty in your coronation,
Yet now, I must confess, that duty done,
My thoughts and wishes bend again toward France   55
And bow them to your gracious leave and pardon.°

KING: Have you your father's leave? What says Polonius?

POLONIUS: He hath, my lord, wrung from me my slow leave
By laboursome petition, and at last
Upon his will I seal'd my hard consent: 60
I do beseech you, give him leave to go.

KING: Take thy fair hour, Laertes; time be thine,
And thy best graces spend it at thy will!
But now, my cousin° Hamlet, and my son,—

HAMLET (*aside*):   A little more than kin, and less than kind!°   65

KING: How is it that the clouds still hang on you?

---

33. Out of his subject: at the expense of Norway's subjects (collectively).   **38. delated:** expressly stated.
44. the Dane: Danish king.   **45. lose your voice:** speak in vain.   **47. native:** closely connected, related.
48. instrumental: serviceable.   **56. leave and pardon:** permission to depart.   **64. cousin:** any kin not
of the immediate family.   **65. A little . . . kind:** i.e., my relation to you has become more than kinship
warrants; it has also become unnatural.

HAMLET: Not so, my lord; I am too much in the sun.°
QUEEN: Good Hamlet, cast thy nighted colour off,
  And let thine eye look like a friend on Denmark.
  Do not for ever with thy vailed lids   70
  Seek for thy noble father in the dust:
  Thou know'st 'tis common; all that lives must die,
  Passing through nature to eternity.
HAMLET: Ay, madam, it is common.°
QUEEN: If it be,
  Why seems it so particular with thee?   75
HAMLET: Seems, madam! nay, it is; I know not "seems."
  'Tis not alone my inky cloak, good mother,
  Nor customary suits° of solemn black,
  Nor windy suspiration° of forc'd breath,
  No, nor the fruitful river in the eye,   80
  Nor the dejected 'haviour of the visage,
  Together with all forms, moods, shapes of grief,
  That can denote me truly: these indeed seem,
  For they are actions that a man might play:
  But I have that within which passeth show;   85
  These but the trappings and the suits of woe.
KING: 'Tis sweet and commendable in your nature, Hamlet,
  To give these mourning duties to your father:
  But, you must know, your father lost a father;
  That father lost, lost his, and the survivor bound   90
  In filial obligation for some term
  To do obsequious° sorrow: but to persever
  In obstinate condolement° is a course
  Of impious stubbornness; 'tis unmanly grief;
  It shows a will most incorrect° to heaven,   95
  A heart unfortified, a mind impatient,
  An understanding simple and unschool'd:
  For what we know must be and is as common
  As any the most vulgar thing° to sense,
  Why should we in our peevish opposition   100
  Take it to heart? Fie! 'tis a fault to heaven,

---

67. **I am . . . sun:** the senses seem to be: I am too much out of doors, I am too much in the sun of your grace (ironical), I am too much of a son to you. Possibly an allusion to the proverb "Out of heaven's blessing into the warm sun"; i.e., Hamlet is out of house and home in being deprived of the kingship. 74. **Ay . . . common:** i.e., it is common, but it hurts nevertheless; possibly a reference to the commonplace quality of the queen's remark.   78. **customary suits:** suits prescribed by custom for mourning. 79. **windy suspiration:** heavy sighing.   92. **obsequious:** dutiful.   93. **condolement:** sorrowing. 95. **incorrect:** untrained, uncorrected.   99. **vulgar thing:** common experience.

A fault against the dead, a fault to nature,
To reason most absurd; whose common theme
Is death of fathers, and who still hath cried,
From the first corse till he that died to-day, 105
"This must be so." We pray you, throw to earth
This unprevailing° woe, and think of us
As of a father: for let the world take note,
You are the most immediate° to our throne;
And with no less nobility° of love 110
Than that which dearest father bears his son,
Do I impart° toward you. For your intent
In going back to school in Wittenberg,°
It is most retrograde° to our desire:
And we beseech you, bend you° to remain 115
Here, in the cheer and comfort of our eye,
Our chiefest courtier, cousin, and our son.
QUEEN: Let not thy mother lose her prayers, Hamlet:
I pray thee, stay with us; go not to Wittenberg.
HAMLET: I shall in all my best obey you, madam. 120
KING: Why, 'tis a loving and a fair reply:
Be as ourself in Denmark. Madam, come;
This gentle and unforc'd accord of Hamlet
Sits smiling to my heart: in grace whereof,
No jocund health that Denmark drinks to-day, 125
But the great cannon to the clouds shall tell,
And the king's rouse° the heaven shall bruit again,°
Re-speaking earthly thunder. Come away.

(Flourish. Exeunt all but HAMLET.*)*

HAMLET: O, that this too too sullied flesh would melt,
Thaw and resolve itself into a dew! 130
Or that the Everlasting had not fix'd
His canon 'gainst self-slaughter! O God! God!
How weary, stale, flat and unprofitable,
Seem to me all the uses of this world!
Fie on't! ah fie! 'tis an unweeded garden, 135
That grows to seed; things rank and gross in nature
Possess it merely.° That it should come to this!
But two months dead: nay, not so much, not two:
So excellent a king; that was, to this,

---

107. **unprevailing:** unavailing. 109. **most immediate:** next in succession. 110. **nobility:** high degree. 112. **impart:** the object is apparently love (1.110). 113. **Wittenberg:** famous German university founded in 1502. 114. **retrograde:** contrary. 115. **bend you:** incline yourself; imperative. 127. **rouse:** draft of liquor. 127. **bruit again:** echo. 137. **merely:** completely, entirely.

Hyperion° to a satyr; so loving to my mother   140
That he might not beteem° the winds of heaven
Visit her face too roughly. Heaven and earth!
Must I remember? why, she would hang on him,
As if increase of appetite had grown
By what it fed on: and yet, within a month—   145
Let me not think on't—Frailty, thy name is woman!—
A little month, or ere those shoes were old
With which she followed my poor father's body,
Like Niobe,° all tears:—why she, even she—
O God! a beast, that wants discourse of reason,°   150
Would have mourn'd longer—married with my uncle,
My father's brother, but no more like my father
Than I to Hercules: within a month:
Ere yet the salt of most unrighteous tears
Had left the flushing in her galled° eyes,   155
She married. O, most wicked speed, to post
With such dexterity° to incestuous sheets!
It is not nor it cannot come to good:
But break, my heart; for I must hold my tongue.

(*Enter* HORATIO, MARCELLUS, *and* BERNARDO.)

HORATIO: Hail to your lordship!   160
HAMLET: I am glad to see you well:
  Horatio!—or I do forget myself.
HORATIO: The same, my lord, and your poor servant ever.
HAMLET: Sir, my good friend; I'll change that name with you°:
  And what make you from Wittenberg, Horatio?   165
  Marcellus?
MARCELLUS: My good lord—
HAMLET: I am very glad to see you. Good even, sir.
  But what, in faith, make you from Wittenberg?
HORATIO: A truant disposition, good my lord.   170
HAMLET: I would not hear your enemy say so,
  Nor shall you do my ear that violence,
  To make it truster of your own report
  Against yourself: I know you are no truant.
  But what is your affair in Elsinore?   175
  We'll teach you to drink deep ere you depart.

140. Hyperion: God of the sun in the older regime of ancient gods.   **141. beteem:** allow.
149. Niobe: Tantalus's daughter, who boasted that she had more sons and daughters than Leto; for this
Apollo and Artemis slew her children. She was turned into stone by Zeus on Mount Sipylus.   **150. discourse of reason:** process or faculty of reason.   **155. galled:** irritated.   **157. dexterity:** facility.
164. I'll . . . you: I'll be your servant, you shall be my friend; also explained as "I'll exchange the name of
friend with you."

HORATIO: My lord, I came to see your father's funeral.

HAMLET: I prithee, do not mock me, fellow-student;

    I think it was to see my mother's wedding.

HORATIO: Indeed, my lord, it follow'd hard° upon.   180

HAMLET: Thrift, thrift, Horatio! the funeral bak'd meats°

    Did coldly furnish forth the marriage tables.

    Would I had met my dearest° foe in heaven

    Or ever I had seen that day, Horatio!

    My father!—methinks I see my father.   185

HORATIO: Where, my lord!

HAMLET: In my mind's eye, Horatio.

HORATIO: I saw him once; 'a° was a goodly king.

HAMLET: 'A was a man, take him for all in all,

    I shall not look upon his like again.

HORATIO: My lord, I think I saw him yesternight.   190

HAMLET: Saw? who?

HORATIO: My lord, the king your father.

HAMLET: The king my father!

HORATIO: Season your admiration° for a while

    With an attent ear, till I may deliver,

    Upon the witness of these gentlemen,   195

    This marvel to you.

HAMLET: For God's love, let me hear.

HORATIO: Two nights together had these gentlemen,

    Marcellus and Bernardo, on their watch,

    In the dead waste and middle of the night,

    Been thus encount'red. A figure like your father,   200

    Armed at point exactly, cap-a-pe,°

    Appears before them, and with solemn march

    Goes slow and stately by them: thrice he walk'd

    By their oppress'd° and fear-surprised eyes,

    Within his truncheon's° length; whilst they, distill'd°   205

    Almost to jelly with the act° of fear,

    Stand dumb and speak not to him. This to me

    In dreadful secrecy impart they did;

    And I with them the third night kept the watch;

    Where, as they had deliver'd, both in time,   210

    Form of the thing, each word made true and good,

    The apparition comes: I knew your father;

---

180. hard: close.   **181. bak'd meats:** meat pies.   **183. dearest:** direst; the adjective *dear* in Shakespeare has two different origins: O.E. *deore,* "beloved," and O.E. *deor,* "fierce." *Dearest* is the superlative of the second.   **187. 'a:** he.   **193. Season your admiration:** restrain your astonishment.   **201. cap-a-pe:** from head to foot.   **204. oppress'd:** distressed.   **205. truncheon:** officer's staff.   **205. distill'd:** softened, weakened.   **206. act:** action.

These hands are not more like.

HAMLET: But where was this?

MARCELLUS: My lord, upon the platform where we watch'd.

HAMLET: Did you not speak to it?

HORATIO: My lord, I did; 215
But answer made it none: yet once methought
It lifted up it° head and did address
Itself to motion, like as it would speak;
But even then the morning cock crew loud,
And at the sound it shrunk in haste away, 220
And vanish'd from our sight.

HAMLET: 'Tis very strange.

HORATIO: As I do live, my honour'd lord, 'tis true;
And we did think it writ down in our duty
To let you know of it.

HAMLET: Indeed, indeed, sirs, but this troubles me. 225
Hold you the watch to-night?

MARCELLUS: }
BERNARDO: } We do, my lord.

HAMLET: Arm'd, say you?

MARCELLUS: }
BERNARDO: } Arm'd, my lord.

HAMLET: From top to toe?

MARCELLUS: }
BERNARDO: } My lord, from head to foot.

HAMLET: Then saw you not his face? 230

HORATIO: O, yes, my lord; he wore his beaver° up.

HAMLET: What, look'd he frowningly?

HORATIO: A countenance more
In sorrow than in anger.

HAMLET: Pale or red?

HORATIO: Nay, very pale.

HAMLET: And fix'd his eyes upon you?

HORATIO: Most constantly.

HAMLET: I would I had been there. 235

HORATIO: It would have much amaz'd you.

HAMLET: Very like, very like. Stay'd it long?

HORATIO: While one with moderate haste might tell a hundred.

MARCELLUS: }
BERNARDO: } Longer, longer.

HORATIO: Not when I saw't.

HAMLET: His beard was grizzled,—no? 240

HORATIO: It was, as I have seen it in his life,

217. it: its.   **231. beaver:** visor on the helmet.

A sable° silver'd.

HAMLET: I will watch to-night;
   Perchance 'twill walk again.

HORATIO: I warr'nt it will.

HAMLET: If it assume my noble father's person,
   I'll speak to it, though hell itself should gape   245
   And bid me hold my peace. I pray you all,
   If you have hitherto conceal'd this sight,
   Let it be tenable in your silence still;
   And whatsoever else shall hap to-night,
   Give it an understanding, but no tongue: 250
   I will requite your loves. So, fare you well:
   Upon the platform, 'twixt eleven and twelve,
   I'll visit you.

ALL: Our duty to your honour.

HAMLET: Your loves, as mine to you: farewell.   (*Exeunt all but* HAMLET.)
   My father's spirit in arms! all is not well;   255
   I doubt° some foul play: would the night were come!
   Till then sit still, my soul: foul deeds will rise,
   Though all the earth o'erwhelm them, to men's eyes.   *Exit.*

SCENE III

(*A room in* POLONIUS'S *house.*)

(*Enter* LAERTES *and* OPHELIA, *his Sister.*)

LAERTES: My necessaries are embark'd: farewell:
   And, sister, as the winds give benefit
   And convoy is assistant,° do not sleep,
   But let me hear from you.

OPHELIA: Do you doubt that?

LAERTES: For Hamlet and the trifling of his favour,   5
   Hold it a fashion° and a toy in blood,°
   A violet in the youth of primy° nature,
   Forward,° not permanent, sweet, not lasting,
   The perfume and suppliance of a minute°;
   No more.

OPHELIA: No more but so?

LAERTES: Think it no more: 10
   For nature, crescent,° does not grow alone

---

242. **sable:** black color.   256. **doubt:** fear.   I.iii. 3. **convoy is assistant:** means of conveyance are available.   6. **fashion:** custom, prevailing usage.   6. **toy in blood:** passing amorous fancy.   7. **primy:** in its
prime.   8. **Forward:** precocious.   9. **suppliance of a minute:** diversion to fill up a minute.   11. **crescent:** growing, waxing.

In thews° and bulk, but, as this temple° waxes,
The inward service of the mind and soul
Grows wide withal. Perhaps he loves you now,
And now no soil° nor cautel° doth besmirch   15
The virtue of his will: but you must fear,
His greatness weigh'd,° his will is not his own;
For he himself is subject to his birth:
He may not, as unvalued persons do,
Carve for himself; for on his choice depends   20
The safety and health of this whole state;
And therefore must his choice be circumscrib'd
Unto the voice and yielding° of that body
Whereof he is the head. Then if he says he loves you,
It fits your wisdom so far to believe it   25
As he in his particular act and place
May give his saying deed°; which is no further
Than the main voice of Denmark goes withal.
Then weigh what loss your honour may sustain,
If with too credent° ear you list his songs,   30
Or lose your heart, or your chaste treasure open
To his unmast'red° importunity.
Fear it, Ophelia, fear it, my dear sister,
And keep you in the rear of your affection,
Out of the shot and danger of desire.   35
The chariest° maid is prodigal enough,
If she unmask her beauty to the moon:
Virtue itself 'scapes not calumnious strokes:
The canker galls the infants of the spring,°
Too oft before their buttons° be disclos'd,°   40
And in the morn and liquid dew° of youth
Contagious blastments° are most imminent.
Be wary then; best safety lies in fear:
Youth to itself rebels, though none else near.
OPHELIA: I shall the effect of this good lesson keep,   45
As watchman to my heart. But, good my brother,
Do not, as some ungracious° pastors do,
Show me the steep and thorny way to heaven;
Whiles, like a puff'd° and reckless libertine,
Himself the primrose path of dalliance treads,   50

---

12. thews: bodily strength. **12. temple:** body. **15. soil:** blemish. **15. cautel:** crafty device. **17. greatness weigh'd:** high position considered. **23. voice and yielding:** assent, approval. **27. deed:** effect. **30. credent:** credulous. **32. unmast'red:** unrestrained. **36. chariest:** most scrupulously modest. **39. The canker . . . spring:** the cankerworm destroys the young plants of spring. **40. buttons:** buds. **40. disclos'd:** opened. **41. liquid dew:** i.e., time when dew is fresh. **42. blastments:** blights. **47. ungracious:** graceless. **49. puff'd:** bloated.

And recks° not his own rede.°

(*Enter* POLONIUS.)

LAERTES: O, fear me not.
    I stay too long: but here my father comes.
    A double° blessing is a double grace;
    Occasion° smiles upon a second leave. 55

POLONIUS: Yet here, Laertes? aboard, aboard, for shame!
    The wind sits in the shoulder of your sail,
    And you are stay'd for. There; my blessing with thee!
    And these few precepts° in thy memory
    Look thou character.° Give thy thoughts no tongue, 60
    Nor any unproportion'd° thought his act.
    Be thou familiar, but by no means vulgar.°
    Those friends thou hast, and their adoption tried,
    Grapple them to thy soul with hoops of steel;
    But do not dull thy palm with entertainment 65
    Of each new-hatch'd, unfledg'd° comrade. Beware
    Of entrance to a quarrel, but being in,
    Bear't that th' opposed may beware of thee.
    Give every man thy ear, but few thy voice;
    Take each man's censure, but reserve thy judgement. 70
    Costly thy habit as thy purse can buy,
    But not express'd in fancy°; rich, not gaudy;
    For the apparel oft proclaims the man,
    And they in France of the best rank and station
    Are of a most select and generous chief in that.° 75
    Neither a borrower nor a lender be;
    For loan oft loses both itself and friend,
    And borrowing dulleth edge of husbandry.°
    This above all: to thine own self be true,
    And it must follow, as the night the day, 80
    Thou canst not then be false to any man.
    Farewell: my blessing season° this in thee!

LAERTES: Most humbly do I take my leave, my lord.

POLONIUS: The time invites you; go; your servants tend.

LAERTES: Farewell, Ophelia; and remember well 85
    What I have said to you.

OPHELIA: 'Tis in my memory lock'd,

---

51. recks: heeds. **51. rede:** counsel. **54. double:** i.e., Laertes has already bade his father good-by. **55. Occasion:** opportunity. **59. precepts:** many parallels have been found to the series of maxims which follows, one of the closer being that in Lyly's *Euphues*. **60. character:** inscribe. **61. unproportion'd:** inordinate. **62. vulgar:** common. **66. unfledg'd:** immature. **72. express'd in fancy:** fantastical in design. **75. Are . . . that:** chief is usually taken as a substantive meaning "head," "eminence." **78. husbandry:** thrift. **82. season:** mature.

And you yourself shall keep the key of it.

LAERTES: Farewell.   (*Exit* LAERTES.)

POLONIUS: What is 't, Ophelia, he hath said to you?

OPHELIA: So please you, something touching the Lord Hamlet.   90

POLONIUS: Marry, well bethought:
   'Tis told me, he hath very oft of late
   Given private time to you; and you yourself
   Have of your audience been most free and bounteous:
   If it be so, as so 't is put on° me.   95
   And that in way of caution, I must tell you,
   You do not understand yourself so clearly
   As it behooves my daughter and your honour.
   What is between you? give me up the truth.

OPHELIA: He hath, my lord, of late made many tenders°   100
   Of his affection to me.

POLONIUS: Affection! pooh! you speak like a green girl,
   Unsifted° in such perilous circumstance.
   Do you believe his tenders, as you call them?

OPHELIA: I do not know, my lord, what I should think.   105

POLONIUS: Marry, I will teach you: think yourself a baby;
   That you have ta'en these tenders° for true pay,
   Which are not sterling.° Tender° yourself more dearly;
   Or—not to crack the wind° of the poor phrase,
   Running it thus—you'll tender me a fool.°   110

OPHELIA: My lord, he hath importun'd me with love
   In honourable fashion.

POLONIUS: Ay, fashion° you may call it; go to, go to.

OPHELIA: And hath given countenance° to his speech, my lord,
   With almost all the holy vows of heaven.   115

POLONIUS: Ay, springes° to catch woodcocks.° I do know,
   When the blood burns, how prodigal the soul
   Lends the tongue vows: these blazes, daughter,
   Giving more light than heat, extinct in both,
   Even in their promise, as it is a-making,   120
   You must not take for fire. From this time
   Be somewhat scanter of your maiden presence;
   Set your entreatments° at a higher rate
   Than a command to parley.° For Lord Hamlet,
   Believe so much in him,° that he is young,   125

---

95. put on: impressed on.   **100, 104. tenders:** offers.   **103. Unsifted:** untried.   **107. tenders:** promises to pay.   **108. sterling:** legal currency.   **108. Tender:** hold.   **109. crack the wind:** i.e., run it until it is broken-winded.   **110. tender . . . fool:** show me a fool (for a daughter).   **113. fashion:** mere form, pretense.   **114. countenance:** credit, support.   **116. springes:** snares.   **116. woodcocks:** birds easily caught, type of stupidity.   **123. entreatments:** conversations, interviews.   **124. command to parley:** mere invitation to talk.   **125. so . . . him:** this much concerning him.

And with a larger tether may he walk
Than may be given you: in few,° Ophelia,
Do not believe his vows; for they are brokers°;
Not of that dye° which their investments° show,
But mere implorators of° unholy suits,   130
Breathing° like sanctified and pious bawds,
The better to beguile. This is for all;
I would not, in plain terms, from this time forth,
Have you so slander° any moment leisure,
As to give words or talk with the Lord Hamlet.   135
Look to 't, I charge you: come your ways.

OPHELIA: I shall obey, my lord.   (*Exeunt.*)

SCENE IV

(*The platform.*)

(*Enter* HAMLET, HORATIO, *and* MARCELLUS.)

HAMLET: The air bites shrewdly; it is very cold.
HORATIO: It is a nipping and an eager air.
HAMLET: What hour now?
HORATIO: I think it lacks of twelve.
MARCELLUS: No, it is struck.
HORATIO: Indeed? I heard it not: then it draws near the season   5
Wherein the spirit held his wont to walk.

(*A flourish of trumpets, and two pieces go off.*)

What does this mean, my lord?
HAMLET: The king doth wake° to-night and takes his rouse,°
Keeps wassail,° and the swagg'ring up-spring° reels°;
And, as he drains his draughts of Rhenish° down,   10
The kettle-drum and trumpet thus bray out
The triumph of his pledge.°
HORATIO: Is it a custom?
HAMLET: Ay, marry, is 't:
But to my mind, though I am native here
And to the manner born,° it is a custom   15
More honour'd in the breach than the observance.

---

127. **in few:** briefly. **128. brokers:** go-betweens, procurers. **129. dye:** color or sort. **129. investments:** clothes. **130. implorators of:** solicitors of. **131. Breathing:** speaking. **134. slander:** bring disgrace or reproach upon. **I.iv. 8. wake:** stay awake, hold revel. **8. rouse:** carouse, drinking bout. **9. wassail:** carousal. **9. up-spring:** last and wildest dance at German merry-makings. **9. reels:** reels through. **10. Rhenish:** rhine wine. **12. triumph . . . pledge:** his glorious achievement as a drinker. **15. to . . . born:** destined by birth to be subject to the custom in question.

This heavy-headed revel east and west
Makes us traduc'd and tax'd of other nations:
They clepe° us drunkards, and with swinish phrase°
Soil our addition°; and indeed it takes   20
From our achievements, though perform'd at height,
The pith and marrow of our attribute.°
So, oft it chances in particular men,
That for some vicious mole of nature° in them,
As, in their birth—wherein they are not guilty,   25
Since nature cannot choose his origin—
By the o'ergrowth of some complexion,
Oft breaking down the pales° and forts of reason,
Or by some habit that too much o'er-leavens°
The form of plausive° manners, that these men,   30
Carrying, I say, the stamp of one defect,
Being nature's livery,° or fortune's star,°—
Their virtues else—be they as pure as grace,
As infinite as man may undergo—
Shall in the general censure take corruption   35
From that particular fault: the dram of eale°
Doth all the noble substance of a doubt
To his own scandal.°

(*Enter* GHOST.)

HORATIO: Look, my lord, it comes!
HAMLET: Angels and ministers of grace° defend us!
Be thou a spirit of health or goblin damn'd,   40
Bring with thee airs from heaven or blasts from hell,
Be thy intents wicked or charitable,
Thou com'st in such a questionable° shape
That I will speak to thee: I'll call thee Hamlet,
King, father, royal Dane: O, answer me!   45
Let me not burst in ignorance; but tell
Why thy canoniz'd° bones, hearsed° in death,
Have burst their cerements°; why the sepulchre,
Wherein we saw thee quietly interr'd,

---

19. clepe: call.   **19. with swinish phrase:** by calling us swine.   **20. addition:** reputation.   **22. attribute:** reputation.   **24. mole of nature:** natural blemish in one's constitution.   **28. pales:** palings (as of a fortification).   **29. o'er-leavens:** induces a change throughout (as yeast works in bread).   **30. plausive:** pleasing.   **32. nature's livery:** endowment from nature.   **32. fortune's star:** the position in which one is placed by fortune, a reference to astrology. The two phrases are aspects of the same thing.   **36. dram of eale:** has had various interpretations, the preferred one being probably, "a dram of evil.   **36–38. the dram . . . scandal:** a famous crux.   **39. ministers of grace:** messengers of God.   **43. questionable:** inviting question or conversation.   **47. canoniz'd:** buried according to the canons of the church.   **47. hearsed:** coffined.   **48. cerements:** grave-clothes.

Hath op'd his ponderous and marble jaws,   50
To cast thee up again. What may this mean,
That thou, dead corse, again in complete steel
Revisits thus the glimpses of the moon,°
Making night hideous; and we fools of nature°
So horridly to shake our disposition
With thoughts beyond the reaches of our souls?   55
Say, why is this? wherefore? what should we do?

       (GHOST *beckons* HAMLET.)

HORATIO: It beckons you to go away with it,
  As if it some impartment° did desire
  To you alone.
MARCELLUS: Look, with what courteous action
  It waves you to a more removed° ground: 60
  But do not go with it.
HORATIO: No, by no means.
HAMLET: It will not speak; then I will follow it.
HORATIO: Do not, my lord!
HAMLET: Why, what should be the fear?
  I do not set my life at a pin's fee;
  And for my soul, what can it do to that,   65
  Being a thing immortal as itself?
  It waves me forth again: I'll follow it.
HORATIO: What if it tempt you toward the flood, my lord,
  Or to the dreadful summit of the cliff
  That beetles o'er° his base into the sea,   70
  And there assume some other horrible form,
  Which might deprive your sovereignty of reason°
  And draw you into madness? think of it:
  The very place puts toys of desperation,°
  Without more motive, into every brain   75
  That looks so many fathoms to the sea
  And hears it roar beneath.
HAMLET: It waves me still.
  Go on; I'll follow thee.
MARCELLUS: You shall not go, my lord.
HAMLET: Hold off your hands!
HORATIO: Be rul'd; you shall not go.   80
HAMLET: My fate cries out,

---

53. glimpses of the moon: the earth by night.   **54. fools of nature:** mere men, limited to natural knowledge.   **59. impartment:** communication.   **61. removed:** remote.   **71. beetles o'er:** overhangs threateningly.   **73. deprive . . . reason:** take away the sovereignty of your reason. It was thought that evil spirits would sometimes assume the form of departed spirits in order to work madness in a human creature.   **75. toys of desperation:** freakish notions of suicide.

And makes each petty artere° in this body
As hardy as the Nemean lion's° nerve.°
Still am I call'd. Unhand me, gentlemen.
By heaven, I'll make a ghost of him that lets° me!
I say, away! Go on; I'll follow thee.   (*Exeunt* GHOST *and* HAMLET.) 85
HORATIO: He waxes desperate with imagination.
MARCELLUS: Let's follow; 'tis not fit thus to obey him.
HORATIO: Have after. To what issue° will this come?
MARCELLUS: Something is rotten in the state of Denmark.
HORATIO: Heaven will direct it.°   90
MARCELLUS: Nay, let's follow him.   (*Exeunt.*)

SCENE V

(*Another part of the platform.*)

(*Enter* GHOST *and* HAMLET.)

HAMLET: Whither wilt thou lead me? speak; I'll go no further.
GHOST: Mark me.
HAMLET: I will.
GHOST: My hour is almost come,
   When I to sulphurous and tormenting flames
   Must render up myself.
HAMLET: Alas, poor ghost!
GHOST: Pity me not, but lend thy serious hearing
   To what I shall unfold.   5
HAMLET: Speak; I am bound to hear.
GHOST: So art thou to revenge, when thou shalt hear.
HAMLET: What?
GHOST: I am thy father's spirit,
   Doom'd for a certain term to walk the night,
   And for the day confin'd to fast° in fires,   10
   Till the foul crimes done in my days of nature
   Are burnt and purg'd away. But that I am forbid
   To tell the secrets of my prison-house,
   I could a tale unfold whose lightest word
   Would harrow up thy soul, freeze thy young blood,   15
   Make thy two eyes, like stars, start from their spheres,°
   Thy knotted° and combined° locks to part

---

82. artere: artery.   **83. Nemean lion's:** Nemean lion was one of the monsters slain by Hercules.
83. nerve: sinew, tendon. The point is that the arteries which were carrying the spirits out into the body
were functioning and were as stiff and hard as the sinews of the lion.   **85. lets:** hinders.   **89. issue:** outcome.   **91. it:** i.e., the outcome.   **I.v. 11. fast:** probably, do without food. It has been sometimes taken
in the sense of doing general penance.   **17. spheres:** orbits.   **18. knotted:** perhaps intricately
arranged.   **18. combined:** tied, bound.

And each particular hair to stand an end,
Like quills upon the fretful porpentine°:   20
But this eternal blazon° must not be
To ears of flesh and blood. List, list, O, list!
If thou didst ever thy dear father love—
HAMLET: O God!
GHOST: Revenge his foul and most unnatural° murder.   25
HAMLET: Murder!
GHOST: Murder most foul, as in the best it is;
But this most foul, strange and unnatural.
HAMLET: Haste me to know't, that I, with wings as swift
As meditation or the thoughts of love,   30
May sweep to my revenge.
GHOST: I find thee apt;
And duller shouldst thou be than the fat weed°
That roots itself in ease on Lethe wharf,°
Wouldst thou not stir in this. Now, Hamlet, hear:
'Tis given out that, sleeping in my orchard,   35
A serpent stung me; so the whole ear of Denmark
Is by a forged process of my death
Rankly abus'd: but know, thou noble youth,
The serpent that did sting thy father's life
Now wears his crown.
HAMLET: O my prophetic soul!   40
My uncle!
GHOST: Ay, that incestuous, that adulterate° beast,
With witchcraft of his wit, with traitorous gifts,—
O wicked wit and gifts, that have the power
So to seduce!—won to his shameful lust   45
The will of my most seeming-virtuous queen:
O Hamlet, what a falling-off was there!
From me, whose love was of that dignity
That it went hand in hand even with the vow
I made to her in marriage, and to decline   50
Upon a wretch whose natural gifts were poor
To those of mine!
But virtue, as it never will be moved,
Though lewdness court it in a shape of heaven,
So lust, though to a radiant angel link'd,   55
Will sate itself in a celestial bed,

20. **porpentine:** porcupine.   21. **eternal blazon:** promulgation or proclamation of eternity, revelation of the hereafter.   25. **unnatural:** i.e., pertaining to fratricide.   32. **fat weed:** many suggestions have been offered as to the particular plant intended, including asphodel; probably a general figure for plants growing along rotting wharves and piles.   33. **Lethe wharf:** bank of the river of forgetfulness in Hades. 42. **adulterate:** adulterous.

And prey on garbage.
But, soft! methinks I scent the morning air;
Brief let me be. Sleeping within my orchard,
My custom always of the afternoon,   60
Upon my secure° hour thy uncle stole,
With juice of cursed hebona° in a vial.
And in the porches of my ears did pour
The leperous° distilment; whose effect
Holds such an enmity with blood of man   65
That swift as quicksilver it courses through
The natural gates and alleys of the body,
And with a sudden vigour it doth posset°
And curd, like eager° droppings into milk,
The thin and wholesome blood: so did it mine;   70
And a most instant tetter bark'd about,
Most lazar-like,° with vile and loathsome crust,
All my smooth body.
Thus was I, sleeping, by a brother's hand
Of life, of crown, of queen, at once dispatch'd°:   75
Cut off even in the blossoms of my sin,
Unhous'led,° disappointed,° unanel'd,°
No reck'ning made, but sent to my account
With all my imperfections on my head:
O, horrible! O, horrible! most horrible!°   80
If thou hast nature in thee, bear it not;
Let not the royal bed of Denmark be
A couch for luxury° and damned incest.
But, howsomever thou pursues this act,
Taint not thy mind,° nor let thy soul contrive   85
Against thy mother aught: leave her to heaven
And to those thorns that in her bosom lodge,
To prick and sting her. Fare thee well at once!
The glow-worm shows the matin° to be near,
And 'gins to pale his uneffectual fire°:   90
Adieu, adieu, adieu! remember me.   (*Exit.*)
HAMLET: O all you host of heaven! O earth! what else?
And shall I couple° hell? O, fie! Hold, hold, my heart;

---

61. **secure:** confident, unsuspicious.   62. **hebona:** generally supposed to mean henbane, conjectured hemlock; ebenus, meaning "yew."   64. **leperous:** causing leprosy.   68. **posset:** coagulate, curdle. 69. **eager:** sour, acid.   72. **lazar-like:** leperlike.   75. **dispatch'd:** suddenly bereft.   77. **Unhous'led:** without having received the sacrament.   77. **disappointed:** unready, without equipment for the last journey.   77. **unanel'd:** without having received extreme unction.   80. **O, . . . horrible:** many editors give this line to Hamlet; Garrick and Sir Henry Irving spoke it in that **part**.   83. **luxury:** lechery. 85. **Taint . . . mind:** probably, deprave not thy character, do nothing except in the pursuit of a natural revenge.   89. **matin:** morning.   90. **uneffectual fire:** cold light.

And you, my sinews, grow not instant old,
But bear me stiffly up. Remember thee!   95
Ay, thou poor ghost, whiles memory holds a seat
In this distracted globe.° Remember thee!
Yea, from the table of my memory
I'll wipe away all trivial fond records,
All saws° of books, all forms, all pressures° past,   100
That youth and observation copied there;
And thy commandment all alone shall live
Within the book and volume of my brain,
Unmix'd with baser matter; yes, by heaven!
O most pernicious woman!   105
O villain, villain, smiling, damned villain!
My tables,°—meet it is I set it down,
That one may smile, and smile, and be a villain;
At least I am sure it may be so in Denmark: (*Writing.*)
So, uncle, there you are. Now to my word°;   110
It is "Adieu, adieu! remember me,"
I have sworn't.

        (*Enter* HORATIO *and* MARCELLUS.)

HORATIO: My lord, my lord—
MARCELLUS: Lord Hamlet,—
HORATIO: Heavens secure him!
HAMLET: So be it!
MARCELLUS: Hillo, ho, ho,° my lord!   115
HAMLET: Hillo, ho, ho, boy! come, bird, come.
MARCELLUS: How is't, my noble lord?
HORATIO: What news, my lord?
HAMLET: O, wonderful!
HORATIO: Good my lord, tell it.
HAMLET: No; you will reveal it.   120
HORATIO: Not I, my lord, by heaven.
MARCELLUS: Nor I, my lord.
HAMLET: How say you, then; would heart of man once think it?
    But you'll be secret?
HORATIO: ⎫
MARCELLUS: ⎬   Ay, by heaven, my lord.
HAMLET: There's ne'er a villain dwelling in all Denmark
    But he's an arrant° knave.   125

---

93. couple: add.   **97. distracted globe:** confused head.   **100. saws:** wise sayings.   **100. pressures:**
impressions stamped.   **107. tables:** probably a small portable writing-tablet carried at the belt.
110. word: watchword.   **115. Hillo, ho, ho:** a falconer's call to a hawk in air.   **125. arrant:** thorough-
going.

HORATIO: There needs no ghost, my lord, come from the grave
   To tell us this.
HAMLET: Why, right; you are in the right;
   And so, without more circumstance at all,
   I hold it fit that we shake hands and part:
   You, as your business and desire shall point you;   130
   For every man has business and desire,
   Such as it is; and for my own poor part,
   Look you, I'll go pray.
HORATIO: These are but wild and whirling words, my lord.
HAMLET: I am sorry they offend you, heartily;   135
   Yes, 'faith, heartily.
HORATIO: There's no offence, my lord.
HAMLET: Yes, by Saint Patrick,° but there is, Horatio,
   And much offence too. Touching this vision here,
   It is an honest° ghost, that let me tell you:
   For your desire to know what is between us,   140
   O'ermaster't as you may. And now, good friends,
   As you are friends, scholars and soldiers,
   Give me one poor request.
HORATIO: What is 't, my lord? we will.
HAMLET: Never make known what you have seen to-night.   145
HORATIO: ⎫
MARCELLUS: ⎬ My lord, we will not.
HAMLET: Nay, but swear 't.
HORATIO: In faith,
   My lord, not I.
MARCELLUS: Nor I, my lord, in faith.
HAMLET: Upon my sword.°
MARCELLUS: We have sworn, my lord, already.
HAMLET: Indeed, upon my sword, indeed. (GHOST *cries under the stage.*) 150
GHOST: Swear.
HAMLET: Ah, ha, boy! say'st thou so? art thou there, truepenny?°
   Come on—you hear this fellow in the cellarage—
   Consent to swear.
HORATIO: Propose the oath, my lord.
HAMLET: Never to speak of this that you have seen,   155
   Swear by my sword.
GHOST (*beneath*):   Swear.
HAMLET: Hic et ubique?° then we'll shift our ground.
   Come hither, gentlemen,
   And lay your hands again upon my sword: 160

137. Saint Patrick: St. Patrick was keeper of Purgatory and patron saint of all blunders and confusion.
139. honest: i.e., a real ghost and not an evil spirit.   **149. sword:** i.e., the hilt in the form of a cross.
152. truepenny: good old boy, or the like.   **158. Hic et ubique?:** here and everywhere?

Swear by my sword,
Never to speak of this that you have heard.
GHOST (*beneath*):   Swear by his sword.
HAMLET: Well said, old mole! canst work i' th' earth so fast?
A worthy pioner!° Once more remove, good friends.   165
HORATIO: O day and night, but this is wondrous strange!
HAMLET: And therefore as a stranger give it welcome.
There are more things in heaven and earth, Horatio,
Than are dreamt of in your philosophy.
But come;   170
Here, as before, never, so help you mercy,
How strange or odd soe'er I bear myself,
As I perchance hereafter shall think meet
To put an antic° disposition on,
That you, at such times seeing me, never shall,   175
With arms encumb'red° thus, or this head-shake,
Or by pronouncing of some doubtful phrase,
As "Well, well, we know," or "We could, an if we would,"
Or "If we list to speak," or "There be, an if they might,"
Or such ambiguous giving out,° to note°   180
That you know aught of me: this not to do,
So grace and mercy at your most need help you,
Swear.
GHOST (*beneath*):   Swear
HAMLET: Rest, rest, perturbed spirit! (*They swear.*) So, gentlemen, 185
With all my love I do commend me to you:
And what so poor a man as Hamlet is
May do, t' express his love and friending° to you,
God willing, shall not lack. Let us go in together;
And still your fingers on your lips, I pray.   190
The time is out of joint: O cursed spite,
That ever I was born to set it right!
Nay, come, let's go together.   (*Exeunt.*)

ACT II

SCENE I (*A room in* POLONIUS's *house.*)

(*Enter old* POLONIUS *with his man* [REYNALDO].)

POLONIUS: Give him this money and these notes, Reynaldo.
REYNALDO: I will, my lord.

---

165. pioner: digger, miner.   **174. antic:** fantastic.   **176. encumb'red:** folded or entwined.   **180. giving out:** profession of knowledge.   **180. to note:** to give a sign.   **188. friending:** friendliness.

REYNALDO: I shall, my lord.   70

POLONIUS: And let him ply his music.°

REYNALDO: Well, my lord.

POLONIUS: Farewell!   (*Exit* REYNALDO.)

         (*Enter* OPHELIA.)

                How now, Ophelia! what's the matter?

OPHELIA: O, my lord, my lord, I have been so affrighted!

POLONIUS: With what, i' th' name of God?

OPHELIA: My lord, as I was sewing in my closet,°   75

  Lord Hamlet, with his doublet° all unbrac'd°;

  No hat upon his head; his stockings foul'd,

  Ungart'red, and down-gyved° to his ankle;

  Pale as his shirt; his knees knocking each other;

  And with a look so piteous in purport   80

  As if he had been loosed out of hell

  To speak of horrors,—he comes before me.

POLONIUS: Mad for thy love?

OPHELIA: My lord, I do not know;

  But truly, I do fear it.

POLONIUS: What said he?

OPHELIA: He took me by the wrist and held me hard;   85

  Then goes he to the length of all his arm;

  And, with his other hand thus o'er his brow,

  He falls to such perusal of my face

  As 'a would draw it. Long stay'd he so;

  At last, a little shaking of mine arm   90

  And thrice his head thus waving up and down,

  He rais'd a sigh so piteous and profound

  As it did seem to shatter all his bulk°

  And end his being: that done, he lets me go:

  And, with his head over his shoulder turn'd,   95

  He seem'd to find his way without his eyes;

  For out o'doors he went without their helps,

  And, to the last, bended their light on me.

POLONIUS: Come, go with me: I will go seek the king.

  This is the very ecstasy of love,   100

  Whose violent property° fordoes° itself

  And leads the will to desperate undertakings

  As oft as any passion under heaven

  That does afflict our natures. I am sorry.

---

71. ply his music: probably to be taken literally.   **75. closet:** private chamber.   **76. doublet:** close-fiting coat.   **76. unbrac'd:** unfastened.   **78. down-gyved:** fallen to the ankles (like gyves or fetters).   **93. bulk:** body.   **101. property:** nature.   **101. fordoes:** destroys.

What, have you given him any hard words of late?   105
OPHELIA: No, my good lord, but, as you did command,
    I did repel his letters and denied
    His access to me.
POLONIUS: That hath made him mad.
    I am sorry that with better heed and judgement
    I had not quoted° him: I fear'd he did but trifle,   110
    And meant to wrack thee; but, beshrew my jealousy!°
    By heaven, it is as proper to our age
    To cast beyond° ourselves in our opinions
    As it is common for the younger sort
    To lack discretion. Come, go we to the king: 115
    This must be known; which, being kept close, might move
    More grief to hide than hate to utter love.°
    Come.   (*Exeunt.*)

SCENE II

(*A room in the castle.*)

(*Flourish. Enter* KING *and* QUEEN, ROSENCRANTZ, *and* GUILDENSTERN
[*with others*].)

KING: Welcome, dear Rosencrantz and Guildenstern!
    Moreover that° we much did long to see you,
    The need we have to use you did provoke
    Our hasty sending. Something have you heard
    Of Hamlet's transformation; so call it,   5
    Sith° nor th' exterior nor the inward man
    Resembles that it was. What it should be,
    More than his father's death, that thus hath put him
    So much from th' understanding of himself,
    I cannot dream of: I entreat you both,   10
    That, being of so young days° brought up with him,
    And sith so neighbour'd to his youth and haviour,
    That you vouchsafe your rest° here in our court
    Some little time: so by your companies
    To draw him on to pleasures, and to gather,   15
    So much as from occasion you may glean,
    Whether aught, to us unknown, afflicts him thus,

---

110. **quoted:** observed.   111. **beshrew my jealousy:** curse my suspicions.   113. **cast beyond:** over-
shoot, miscalculate.   116–117. **might . . . love:** i.e., I might cause more grief to others by hiding the
knowledge of Hamlet's love to Ophelia than hatred to me and mine by telling of it.   **II.ii. 2. Moreover
that:** besides the fact that.   6. **Sith:** since.   11. **of . . . days:** from such early youth.   13. **vouchsafe
your rest:** please to stay.

That, open'd, lies within our remedy.
QUEEN: Good gentlemen, he hath much talk'd of you;
And sure I am two men there are not living   20
To whom he more adheres. If it will please you
To show us so much gentry° and good will
As to expend your time with us awhile,
For the supply and profit° of our hope,
Your visitation shall receive such thanks   25
As fits a king's remembrance.
ROSENCRANTZ: Both your majesties
Might, by the sovereign power you have of us,
Put your dread pleasures more into command
Than to entreaty.
GUILDENSTERN: But we both obey,
And here give up ourselves, in the full bent°   30
To lay our service freely at your feet,
To be commanded.
KING: Thanks, Rosencrantz and gentle Guildenstern.
QUEEN: Thanks, Guildenstern and gentle Rosencrantz:
And I beseech you instantly to visit   35
My too much changed son. Go, some of you,
And bring these gentlemen where Hamlet is.
GUILDENSTERN: Heavens make our presence and our practices
Pleasant and helpful to him!
QUEEN: Ay, amen!

(*Exeunt* ROSENCRANTZ *and* GUILDENSTERN [*with some* ATTENDANTS].)

(*Enter* POLONIUS.)

POLONIUS: Th' ambassadors from Norway, my good lord,   40
Are joyfully return'd.
KING: Thou still hast been the father of good news.
POLONIUS: Have I, my lord? I assure my good liege,
I hold my duty, as I hold my soul,
Both to my God and to my gracious king: 45
And I do think, or else this brain of mine
Hunts not the trail of policy so sure
As it hath us'd to do, that I have found
The very cause of Hamlet's lunacy.
KING: O, speak of that; that do I long to hear.   50
POLONIUS: Give first admittance to th' ambassadors;
My news shall be the fruit to that great feast.
KING: Thyself do grace to them, and bring them in.   (*Exit* POLONIUS.)

22. gentry: courtesy.   **24. supply and profit:** aid and successful outcome.   **30. in . . . bent:** to the utmost degree of our mental capacity.

He tells me, my dear Gertrude, he hath found
The head and source of all your son's distemper, 55
QUEEN: I doubt° it is no other but the main°;
His father's death, and our o'erhasty marriage.
KING: Well, we shall sift him.

(*Enter* AMBASSADORS VOLTIMAND *and* CORNELIUS, *with* POLONIUS.)

Welcome, my good friends!
Say, Voltimand, what from our brother Norway?
VOLTIMAND: Most fair return of greetings and desires. 60
Upon our first, he sent out to suppress
His nephew's levies; which to him appear'd
To be a preparation 'gainst the Polack;
But, better look'd into, he truly found
It was against your highness: whereat griev'd, 65
That so his sickness, age and impotence
Was falsely borne in hand,° sends out arrests
On Fortinbras; which he, in brief, obeys;
Receives rebuke from Norway, and in fine°
Makes vow before his uncle never more 70
To give th' assay° of arms against your majesty.
Whereon old Norway, overcome with joy,
Gives him three score thousand crowns in annual fee,
And his commission to employ those soldiers,
So levied as before, against the Polack: 75
With an entreaty, herein further shown, (*giving a paper.*)
That it might please you to give quiet pass
Through your dominions for this enterprise,
On such regards of safety and allowance°
As therein are set down.
KING: It likes° us well; 80
And at our more consider'd° time we'll read,
Answer, and think upon this business.
Meantime we thank you for your well-took labour:
Go to your rest; at night we'll feast together:
Most welcome home!   (*Exeunt* AMBASSADORS.)
POLONIUS: This business is well ended. 85
My liege, and madam, to expostulate
What majesty should be, what duty is,
Why day is day, night night, and time is time,

---

56. doubt: fear.   **56. main:** chief point, principal concern.   **67. borne in hand:** deluded.   **69. in fine:** in the end.   **71. assay:** assault, trial (of arms).   **79. safety and allowance:** pledges of safety to the country and terms of permission for the troops to pass.   **80. likes:** pleases.   **81. consider'd:** suitable for deliberation.

Were nothing but to waste night, day and time.
Therefore, since brevity is the soul of wit,° 90
And tediousness the limbs and outward flourishes,°
I will be brief: your noble son is mad:
Mad call I it; for, to define true madness
What is 't but to be nothing else but mad?
But let that go.
QUEEN: More matter, with less art. 95
POLONIUS: Madam, I swear I use no art at all.
That he is mad, 'tis true: 'tis true 'tis pity;
And pity 'tis 'tis true: a foolish figure°;
But farewell it, for I will use no art.
Mad let us grant him, then: and now remains 100
That we find out the cause of this effect,
Or rather say, the cause of this defect,
For this effect defective comes by cause:
Thus it remains, and the remainder thus.
Perpend.° 105
I have a daughter—have while she is mine—
Who, in her duty and obedience, mark,
Hath given me this: now gather, and surmise. (*Reads the letter.*)
"To the celestial and my soul's idol, the most beautified Ophelia,"—
That's an ill phrase, a vile phrase; "beautified" is a vile phrase: but you shall hear. 110
Thus: (*Reads.*)
"In her excellent white bosom, these, & c."
QUEEN: Came this from Hamlet to her?
POLONIUS: Good madam, stay awhile; I will be faithful. (*Reads.*)
      "Doubt thou the stars are fire; 115
      Doubt that the sun doth move;
      Doubt truth to be a liar;
      But never doubt I love.
"O dear Ophelia, I am ill at these numbers°; I have not art to reckon° my groans:
but that I love thee best, O most best, believe it. Adieu. 120
"Thine evermore, most dear lady, whilst this machine° is to him, Hamlet."
This, in obedience, hath my daughter shown me,
And more above,° hath his solicitings,
As they fell out° by time, by means° and place,
All given to mine ear.
KING: But how hath she 125
Receiv'd his love?

---

90. wit: sound sense or judgment.   **91. flourishes:** ostentation, embellishments   **98. figure:** figure of speech.   **105. Perpend:** consider.   **119. ill . . . numbers:** unskilled at writing verses.   **119. reckon:** number metrically, scan.   **121. machine:** bodily frame.   **123. more above:** moreover.   **124. fell out:** occurred.   **124. means:** opportunities (of access).

POLONIUS: What do you think of me?
KING: As of a man faithful and honourable.
POLONIUS: I would fain prove so. But what might you think,
When I had seen this hot love on the wing—
As I perceiv'd it, I must tell you that,   130
Before my daughter told me—what might you,
Or my dear majesty your queen here, think,
If I had play'd the desk or table-book,°
Or given my heart a winking,° mute and dumb,
Or look'd upon this love with idle sight;   135
What might you think? No, I went round to work,
And my young mistress thus I did bespeak°:
"Lord Hamlet is a prince, out of thy star°;
This must not be": and then I prescripts gave her,
That she should lock herself from his resort,   140
Admit no messengers, receive no tokens.
Which done, she took the fruits of my advice;
And he, repelled—a short tale to make—
Fell into a sadness, then into a fast,
Thence to a watch,° thence into a weakness,   145
Thence to a lightness,° and, by this declension,°
Into the madness wherein now he raves,
And all we mourn for.
KING: Do you think 'tis this?
QUEEN: It may be, very like.
POLONIUS: Hath there been such a time—I would fain know that—   150
That I have positively said "'Tis so,"
When it prov'd otherwise?
KING: Not that I know.
POLONIUS (*pointing to his head and shoulder*):   Take this from this, if this be otherwise:
If circumstances lead me, I will find
Where truth is hid, though it were hid indeed   155
Within the centre.°
KING: How may we try it further?
POLONIUS: You know, sometimes he walks four hours together
Here in the lobby.
QUEEN: So he does indeed.   160
POLONIUS: At such a time I'll loose my daughter to him:
Be you and I behind an arras° then;
Mark the encounter: if he love her not

---

133. play'd . . . table-book: i.e., remained shut up, concealed this information.   **134. given . . . wink-ing:** given my heart a signal to keep silent.   **137. bespeak:** address.   **138. out . . . star:** above thee in position.   **145. watch:** state of sleeplessness.   **146. lightness:** lightheartedness.   **146. declension:** decline, deterioration.   **155. centre:** middle point of the earth.   **163. arras:** hanging, tapestry.

And be not from his reason fall'n thereon,° 165
Let me be no assistant for a state,
But keep a farm and carters.
KING: We will try it.

(*Enter* HAMLET [*reading on a book*].)

QUEEN: But, look, where sadly the poor wretch comes reading.
POLONIUS: Away, I do beseech you both, away:

(*Exeunt* KING *and* QUEEN [*with* ATTENDANTS].)

I'll board° him presently. O, give me leave. 170
How does my good Lord Hamlet?
HAMLET: Well, God-a-mercy.
POLONIUS: Do you know me, my lord?
HAMLET: Excellent well; you are a fishmonger.°
POLONIUS: Not I, my lord. 175
HAMLET: Then I would you were so honest a man.
POLONIUS: Honest, my lord!
HAMLET: 180 Ay, sir; to be honest, as this world goes, is to be one man picked out
of ten thousand.
POLONIUS: That's very true, my lord. 180
HAMLET: For if the sun breed maggots in a dead dog, being a good kissing car-
rion,°—Have you a daughter?
POLONIUS: I have, my lord.
HAMLET: 185 Let her not walk i' the sun°: conception° is a blessing: but as your
daughter may conceive—Friend, look to 't. 185
POLONIUS (*aside*):   How say you by° that? Still harping on my daughter: yet he
knew me not at first; 'a said I was a fishmonger: 'a is far gone, far gone: and
truly in my youth I suffered much extremity for love; very near this. I'll speak
to him again. What do you read, my lord?
HAMLET: Words, words, words. 190
POLONIUS: What is the matter,° my lord?
HAMLET: Between who?°
POLONIUS: I mean, the matter that you read, my lord.
HAMLET: Slanders, sir: for the satirical rogue says here that old men have grey
beards, that their faces are wrinkled, their eyes purging° thick amber and 195
plum-tree gum and that they have a plentiful lack of wit, together with most
weak hams: all which, sir, though I most powerfully and potently believe, yet I
hold it not honesty° to have it thus set down, for yourself, sir, should be old as I
am, if like a crab you could go backward.

---

164. thereon: on that account.   **170. board:** accost.   **174. fishmonger:** an opprobrious expression
meaning "bawd," "procurer."   **181–182. good kissing carrion:** i.e., a good piece of flesh for kissing (?).
184. i' the sun: in the sunshine of princely favors.   **184. conception:** quibble on "understanding" and
"pregnancy."   **186. by:** concerning.   **191. matter:** substance.   **192. Between who?:** Hamlet deliberately takes matter as meaning "basis of dispute."   **195. purging:** discharging.   **198. honesty:** decency.

POLONIUS (*aside*):   Though this be madness, yet there is method in 't.—Will you   200
walk out of the air, my lord?

HAMLET: Into my grave.

POLONIUS: Indeed, that's out of the air. (*Aside.*) How pregnant sometimes his
replies are! a happiness° that often madness hits on, which reason and sanity
could not so prosperously° be delivered of. I will leave him, and suddenly con-   205
trive the means of meeting between him and my daughter.—My honourable
lord, I will most humbly take my leave of you.

HAMLET: You cannot, sir, take from me any thing that I will more willingly part
withal: except my life, except my life, except my life.

(*Enter* GUILDENSTERN *and* ROSENCRANTZ.)

POLONIUS: Fare you well, my lord.   210

HAMLET: These tedious old fools!

POLONIUS: You go to seek the Lord Hamlet; there he is.

ROSENCRANTZ (*to* POLONIUS):   God save you, sir!   (*Exit* POLONIUS.)

GUILDENSTERN: My honoured lord!

ROSENCRANTZ: My most dear lord!   215

HAMLET: My excellent good friends! How dost thou, Guildenstern? Ah, Rosencrantz! Good lads, how do ye both?

ROSENCRANTZ: As the indifferent° children of the earth.

GUILDENSTERN: Happy, in that we are not over-happy;
On Fortune's cap we are not the very button.   220

HAMLET: Nor the soles of her shoe?

ROSENCRANTZ: Neither, my lord.

HAMLET: Then you live about her waist, or in the middle of her favours?

GUILDENSTERN: 'Faith, her privates° we.

HAMLET: In the secret parts of Fortune? O, most true; she is a strumpet. What's   225
the news?

ROSENCRANTZ: None, my lord, but that the world's grown honest.

HAMLET: Then is doomsday near: but your news is not true. Let me question more
in particular: what have you, my good friends, deserved at the hands of Fortune, that she sends you to prison hither?   230

GUILDENSTERN: Prison, my lord!

HAMLET: Denmark's a prison.

ROSENCRANTZ: Then is the world one.

HAMLET: A goodly one; in which there are many confines,° wards and dungeons,
Denmark being one o' the worst.   235

ROSENCRANTZ: We think not so, my lord.

HAMLET: Why, then, 'tis none to you; for there is nothing either good or bad, but
thinking makes it so: to me it is a prison.

---

204. happiness: felicity of expression.   **205. prosperously:** successfully.   **218. indifferent:** ordinary.
224. privates: i.e., ordinary men (sexual pun on private parts).   **234. confines:** places of confinement.

ROSENCRANTZ: Why then, your ambition makes it one; 'tis too narrow for your
   mind.   240
HAMLET: O God, I could be bounded in a nutshell and count myself a king of infinite space, were it not that I have bad dreams.
GUILDENSTERN: Which dreams indeed are ambition, for the very substance of the
   ambitious° is merely the shadow of a dream.
HAMLET: A dream itself is but a shadow.   245
ROSENCRANTZ: Truly, and I hold ambition of so airy and light a quality that it is but
   a shadow's shadow.
HAMLET: Then are our beggars bodies, and our monarchs and outstretched heroes
   the beggars' shadows. Shall we to the court? for, by my fay,° I cannot reason.°
ROSENCRANTZ: ⎫
GUILDENSTERN: ⎬ We'll wait upon° you.   250
HAMLET: No such matter: I will not sort° you with the rest of my servants, for, to
   speak to you like an honest man, I am most dreadfully attended.° But, in the
   beaten way of friendship,° what make you at Elsinore?
ROSENCRANTZ: To visit you, my lord: no other occasion.
HAMLET: Beggar that I am, I am ever poor in thanks; but I thank you: and sure, 255
   dear friends, my thanks are too dear a° halfpenny. Were you not sent for? Is it
   your own inclining? Is it a free visitation? Come, come, deal justly with me:
   come, come; nay, speak.
GUILDENSTERN: What should we say, my lord?
HAMLET: Why, any thing, but to the purpose. You were sent for; and there is a kind 260
   of confession in your looks which your modesties have not craft enough to
   colour: I know the good king and queen have sent for you.
ROSENCRANTZ: To what end, my lord?
HAMLET: That you must teach me. But let me conjure° you, by the rights of our
   fellowship, by the consonancy of our youth,° by the obligation of our ever- 265
   preserved love, and by what more dear a better proposer° could charge you
   withal, be even and direct with me, whether you were sent for, or no?
ROSENCRANTZ (*aside to* GUILDENSTERN):   What say you?
HAMLET (*aside*):   Nay, then, I have an eye of you.—If you love me, hold not off.
GUILDENSTERN: My lord, we were sent for.   270
HAMLET: I will tell you why; so shall my anticipation prevent your discovery,° and
   your secrecy to the king and queen moult no feather. I have of late—but
   wherefore I know not—lost all my mirth, forgone all custom of exercises; and
   indeed it goes so heavily with my disposition that this goodly frame, the earth,
   seems to me a sterile promontory, this most excellent canopy, the air, look you, 275
   this brave o'erhanging firmament, this majestical roof fretted° with golden fire,
   why, it appeareth nothing to me but a foul and pestilent congregation of

243–44. very . . . ambitious: that seemingly most substantial thing which the ambitious pursue.
249. fay: faith.   **249. reason:** argue.   **250. wait upon:** accompany.   **251. sort:** class.   **252. dreadfully
attended:** poorly provided with servants.   **254. in the . . . friendship:** as a matter of course among
friends.   **256. a:** i.e., at a.   **264. conjure:** adjure, entreat.   **265. consonancy of our youth:** the fact that
we are of the same age.   **266. better proposer:** one more skillful in finding proposals.   **271. prevent
your discovery:** forestall your disclosure.   **276. fretted:** adorned.

vapours. What a piece of work is a man! how noble in reason! how infinite in faculties!° in form and moving how express° and admirable! in action how like an angel! in apprehension° how like a god! the beauty of the world! the paragon of animals! And yet, to me, what is this quintessence° of dust? man delights not me: no, nor woman neither, though by your smiling you seem to say so.   280

ROSENCRANTZ: My lord, there was no such stuff in my thoughts.

HAMLET: Why did you laugh then, when I said "man delights not me"?   285

ROSENCRANTZ: To think, my lord, if you delight not in man, what lenten° entertainment the players shall receive from you: we coted° them on the way; and hither are they coming, to offer you service.

HAMLET: He that plays the king shall be welcome; his majesty shall have tribute of me; the adventurous knight shall use his foil and target°; the lover shall not sigh gratis; the humorous man° shall end his part in peace; the clown shall make those laugh whose lungs are tickle o' the sere°; and the lady shall say her mind freely, or the blank verse shall halt for 't.° What players are they?   290

ROSENCRANTZ: Even those you were wont to take delight in, the tragedians of the city.   295

HAMLET: How chances it they travel? their residence,° both in reputation and profit, was better both ways.

ROSENCRANTZ: I think their inhibition° comes by the means of the late innovation.°

HAMLET: Do they hold the same estimation they did when I was in the city? are they so followed?   300

ROSENCRANTZ: No, indeed, are they not.

HAMLET: How° comes it? do they grow rusty?

ROSENCRANTZ: Nay, their endeavour keeps in the wonted pace: but there is, sir, an aery° of children, little eyases,° that cry out on the top of question,° and are most tyrannically° clapped for 't: these are now the fashion, and so berattle° the common stages°—so they call them—that many wearing rapiers° are afraid of goose-quills° and dare scarce come thither.   305

---

279. faculties: capacity.   **279. express:** well-framed (?), exact (?).   **280. apprehension:** understanding.   **281. quintessence:** the fifth essence of ancient philosophy, supposed to be the substance of the heavenly bodies and to be latent in all things.   **286. lenten:** meager.   **287. coted:** overtook and passed beyond.   **290. foil and target:** sword and shield.   **291. humorous man:** actor who takes the part of the humor characters.   **292. tickle o' the sere:** easy on the trigger.   **293. the lady ... for 't:** the lady (fond of talking) shall have opportunity to talk, blank verse or no blank verse.   **296. residence:** remaining in one place.   **298. inhibition:** formal prohibition (from acting plays in the city or, possibly, at court).   **298. innovation:** the new fashion in satirical plays performed by boy actors in the "private" theaters.   **305–320. How ... load too:** the passage is the famous one dealing with the War of the Theatres (1599–1602); namely, the rivalry between the children's companies and the adult actors.   **304. aery:** nest.   **304. eyases:** young hawks.   **304. cry ... question:** speak in a high key dominating conversation; clamor forth the height of controversy; probably "excel" (cf. line 458); perhaps intended to decry leaders of the dramatic profession.   **305. tyrannically:** outrageously.   **305. berattle:** berate.   **306. common stages:** public theaters.   **306. many wearing rapiers:** many men of fashion, who were afraid to patronize the common players for fear of being satirized by the poets who wrote for the children.   **307. goose-quills:** i.e., pens of satirists.

HAMLET: What, are they children? who maintains 'em? how are they escoted?° Will they pursue the quality° no longer than they can sing?° will they not say afterwards, if they should grow themselves to common° players—as it is most like, if their means are no better—their writers do them wrong, to make them exclaim against their own succession?° 310

ROSENCRANTZ: 'Faith, there has been much to do on both sides; and the nation holds it no sin to tarre° them to controversy: there was, for a while, no money bid for argument,° unless the poet and the players went to cuffs° in the question.° 315

HAMLET: Is't possible?

GUILDENSTERN: O, there has been much throwing about of brains.

HAMLET: Do the boys carry it away?°

ROSENCRANTZ: Ay, that they do, my lord; Hercules and his load° too.

HAMLET: It is not very strange; for my uncle is king of Denmark, and those that would make mows° at him while my father lived, give twenty, forty, fifty, a hundred ducats° a-piece for his picture in little.° 'Sblood, there is something in this more than natural, if philosophy could find it out. 320

(*A flourish [of trumpets within].*)

GUILDENSTERN: There are the players.

HAMLET: Gentlemen, you are welcome to Elsinore. Your hands, come then: the appurtenance of welcome is fashion and ceremony; let me comply° with you in this garb,° lest my extent° to the players, which, I tell you, must show fairly outwards, should more appear like entertainment than yours. You are welcome: but my uncle-father and aunt-mother are deceived. 325

GUILDENSTERN: In what, my dear lord? 330

HAMLET: I am but mad north-north-west°: when the wind is southerly I know a hawk from a handsaw.°

(*Enter* POLONIUS.)

POLONIUS: Well be with you, gentlemen!

HAMLET: Hark you, Guildenstern; and you too: at each ear a hearer: that great baby you see there is not yet out of his swaddling-clouts.° 335

ROSENCRANTZ: Happily he is the second time come to them; for they say an old man is twice a child.

---

308. escoted: maintained. **309. quality:** acting profession. **309. no longer . . . sing:** i.e., until their voices change. **310. common:** regular, adult. **312. succession:** future careers. **314. tarre:** set on (as dogs). **315. argument:** probably, plot for a play. **315. went to cuffs:** came to blows. **315. question:** controversy. **318. carry it away:** win the day. **319. Hercules . . . load:** regarded as an allusion to the sign of the Globe Theatre, which was Hercules bearing the world on his shoulder. **321. mows:** grimaces. **322. ducats:** gold coins worth 9s. 4d. **322. in little:** in miniature. **326. comply:** observe the formalities of courtesy. **327. garb:** manner. **327. extent:** showing of kindness. **331. I am . . . north-north-west:** I am only partly mad, i.e., in only one point of the compass. **332. handsaw:** a proposed reading of hemshaw would mean "heron"; handsaw may be an early corruption of hernshaw. Another view regards hawk as the variant of hack, a tool of the pickax type, and handsaw as a saw operated by hand. **335. swaddling-clouts:** clothes in which to wrap a newborn baby.

HAMLET: I will prophesy he comes to tell me of the players; mark it.—You say right, sir: o' Monday morning°; 'twas then indeed.

POLONIUS: My lord, I have news to tell you. 340

HAMLET: My lord, I have news to tell you. When Roscius° was an actor in Rome,—

POLONIUS: The actors are come hither, my lord.

HAMLET: Buz, buz!°

POLONIUS: Upon my honour,— 345

HAMLET: Then came each actor on his ass,—

POLONIUS: The best actors in the world, either for tragedy, comedy, history, pastoral, pastoral-comical, historical-pastoral, tragical-historical, tragical-comical-historical-pastoral, scene individable,° or poem unlimited°: Seneca° cannot be too heavy, nor Plautus° too light. For the law of writ and the liberty,° these are 350 the only men.

HAMLET: O Jephthah, judge of Israel,° what a treasure hadst thou!

POLONIUS: What a treasure had he, my lord?

HAMLET: Why,

"One fair daughter, and no more, 355
The which he loved passing well."

POLONIUS (*aside*): Still on my daughter.

HAMLET: Am I not i' the right, old Jephthah?

POLONIUS: If you call me Jephthah, my lord, I have a daughter that I love passing° well. 360

HAMLET: Nay, that follows not.

POLONIUS: What follows, then, my lord?

HAMLET: Why,

"As by lot, God wot,"

and then, you know, 365

"It came to pass, as most like° it was,"—

the first row° of the pious chanson° will show you more; for look, where my abridgement comes.°

(*Enter the* PLAYERS.)

You are welcome, masters; welcome, all. I am glad to see thee well. Welcome, good friends. O, old friend! why, thy face is valanced° since I saw thee last: 370 comest thou to beard me in Denmark? What, my young lady and mistress!

339. o' Monday morning: said to mislead Polonius. **341. Roscius:** a famous Roman actor. **344. Buz, buz:** an interjection used at Oxford to denote stale news. **349. scene individable:** a play observing the unity of place. **349. poem unlimited:** a play disregarding the unities of time and place. **349. Seneca:** writer of Latin tragedies, model of early Elizabethan writers of tragedy. **350. Plautus:** writer of Latin comedy. **350. law . . . liberty:** pieces written according to rules and without rules, i.e., "classical" and "romantic" dramas. **352. Jephthah . . . Israel:** Jephthah had to sacrifice his daughter; see Judges 11. **359. passing:** surpassingly. **366. like:** probable. **367. row:** stanza. **367. chanson:** ballad. **368. abridgement comes:** opportunity comes for cutting short the conversation. **370. valanced:** fringed (with a beard).

By'r lady, your ladyship is nearer to heaven than when I saw you last, by the altitude of a chopine.° Pray God, your voice, like a piece of uncurrent° gold, be not cracked within the ring.° Masters, you are all welcome. We'll e'en to 't like French falconers, fly at any thing we see: we'll have a speech straight: come, give us a taste of your quality; come, a passionate speech. 375

FIRST PLAYER: What speech, my good lord?

HAMLET: I heard thee speak me a speech once, but it was never acted; or, if it was, not above once; for the play, I remember, pleased not the million; 'twas caviary to the general°: but it was—as I received it, and others, whose judgements in such matters cried in the top of° mine—an excellent play, well digested in the scenes, set down with as much modesty as cunning.° I remember, one said there were no sallets° in the lines to make the matter savoury, nor no matter in the phrase that might indict° the author of affectation; but called it an honest method, as wholesome as sweet, and by very much more handsome than fine.° One speech in 't I chiefly loved: 'twas Æneas' tale to Dido°; and thereabout of it especially, where he speaks of Priam's slaughter: if it live in your memory, begin at this line: let me see, let me see— 380

"The rugged Pyrrhus°, like th' Hyrcanian beast,"°—
'tis not so:—it begins with Pyrrhus:— 390
"The rugged Pyrrhus, he whose sable arms,
Black as his purpose, did the night resemble
When he lay couched in the ominous horse,°
Hath now this dread and black complexion smear'd
With heraldry more dismal; head to foot 395
Now is he total gules°; horridly trick'd°
With blood of fathers, mothers, daughters, sons,
Bak'd and impasted° with the parching streets,
That lend a tyrannous and a damned light
To their lord's murder: roasted in wrath and fire, 400
And thus o'er-sized° with coagulate gore,
With eyes like carbuncles, the hellish Pyrrhus
Old grandsire Priam seeks."
So, proceed you.

---

373. chopine: kind of shoe raised by the thickness of the heel; worn in Italy, particularly at Venice. **373. uncurrent:** not passable as lawful coinage. **374. cracked within the ring:** in the center of coins were rings enclosing the sovereign's head; if the coin was cracked within this ring, it was unfit for currency. **380. caviary to the general:** not relished by the multitude. **381. cried in the top of:** spoke with greater authority than. **382. cunning:** skill. **383. sallets:** salads: here, spicy improprieties. **384. indict:** convict. **385. as wholesome . . . fine:** its beauty was not that of elaborate ornament, but that of order and proportion. **386. Æneas' tale to Dido:** the lines recited by the player are imitated from Marlowe and Nashe's *Dido Queen of Carthage* (II.i. 214 ff.). They are written in such a way that the conventionality of the play within a play is raised above that of ordinary drama. **389. Pyrrhus:** a Greek hero in the Trojan War. **389. Hyrcanian beast:** the tiger; see Virgil, Aeneid, IV. 266. **393. ominous horse:** Trojan horse. **396. gules:** red, a heraldic term. **396. trick'd:** spotted, smeared. **398. impasted:** made into a paste. **401. o'er-sized:** covered as with size or glue.

POLONIUS: 'Fore God, my lord, well spoken, with good accent and good dis-   405
   cretion.
FIRST PLAYER: "Anon he finds him
   Striking too short at Greeks; his antique sword,
   Rebellious to his arm, lies where it falls,
   Repugnant° to command: Unequal match'd,   410
   Pyrrhus at Priam drives; in rage strikes wide;
   But with the whiff and wind of his fell sword
   Th' unnerved father falls. Then senseless Ilium,°
   Seeming to feel this blow, with flaming top
   Stoops to his base, and with a hideous crash   415
   Takes prisoner Pyrrhus' ear: for, lo! his sword
   Which was declining on the milky head
   Of reverend Priam, seem'd i' th' air to stick:
   So, as a painted tyrant,° Pyrrhus stood,
   And like a neutral to his will and matter,°   420
   Did nothing.
   But, as we often see, against° some storm,
   A silence in the heavens, the rack° stand still,
   The bold winds speechless and the orb below
   As hush as death, anon the dreadful thunder   425
   Doth rend the region,° so, after Pyrrhus' pause,
   Aroused vengeance sets him new a-work;
   And never did the Cyclops' hammers fall
   On Mars's armour forg'd for proof eterne°
   With less remorse than Pyrrhus' bleeding sword   430
   Now falls on Priam.
   Out, out, thou strumpet, Fortune! All you gods,
   In general synod,° take away her power;
   Break all the spokes and fellies° from her wheel,
   And bowl the round nave° down the hill of heaven,   435
   As low as to the fiends!"
POLONIUS: This is too long.
HAMLET: It shall to the barber's, with your beard. Prithee, say on: he's for a jig° or
   a tale of bawdry,° or he sleeps: say on: come to Hecuba.°
FIRST PLAYER: "But who, ah woe! had seen the mobled° queen—"   440
HAMLET: "The mobled queen?"
POLONIUS: That's good; "mobled queen" is good.
FIRST PLAYER: "Run barefoot up and down, threat'ning the flames

---

410. Repugnant: disobedient.   **413. Then senseless Ilium:** insensate Troy.   **419. painted tyrant:**
tyrant in a picture.   **420. matter:** task.   **422. against:** before.   **423. rack:** mass of clouds.
426. region: assembly.   **429. proof eterne:** external resistance to assault.   **433. synod:** assembly.
434. fellies: pieces of wood forming the rim of a wheel.   **435. nave:** hub.   **438. jig:** comic performance given at the end or in an interval of a play.   **439. bawdry:** indecency.   **439. Hecuba:** wife of
Priam, king of Troy.   **440. mobled:** muffled.

With bisson rheum°; a clout° upon that head
Where late the diadem stood, and for a robe,   445
About her lank and all o'er-teemed° loins,
A blanket, in the alarm of fear caught up;
Who this had seen, with tongue in venom steep'd
'Gainst Fortune's state would treason have pronounc'd°:
But if the gods themselves did see her then   450
When she saw Pyrrhus make malicious sport
In mincing with his sword her husband's limbs,
The instant burst of clamour that she made,
Unless things mortal move them not at all,
Would have made milch° the burning eyes of heaven,   455
And passion in the gods."
POLONIUS: Look, whe'r he has not turned° his colour and has tears in 's eyes.
    Prithee, no more.
HAMLET: 'Tis well; I'll have thee speak out the rest soon. Good my lord, will you
    see the players well bestowed? Do you hear, let them be well used; for they are 460
    the abstract° and brief chronicles of the time: after your death you were better
    have a bad epitaph than their ill report while you live.
POLONIUS: My lord, I will use them according to their desert.
HAMLET: God's bodykins,° man, much better: use every man after his desert, and
    who shall 'scape whipping? Use them after your own honour and dignity: the   465
    less they deserve, the more merit is in your bounty. Take them in.
POLONIUS: Come, sirs.
HAMLET: Follow him, friends: we'll hear a play tomorrow. (*Aside to* FIRST PLAYER.)
    Dost thou hear me, old friend; can you play the Murder of Gonzago?
FIRST PLAYER: Ay, my lord.   470
HAMLET: We'll ha 't to-morrow night. You could, for a need, study a speech of some
    dozen or sixteen lines,° which I would set down and insert in 't, could you not?
FIRST PLAYER: Ay, my lord.
HAMLET: Very well. Follow that lord; and look you mock him not.—My good   475
    friends, I'll leave you till night: you are welcome to Elsinore.
                                            (*Exeunt* POLONIUS *and* PLAYERS.)
ROSENCRANTZ: Good my lord   (*Exeunt* [ROSENCRANTZ *and* GUILDENSTERN.])
HAMLET: Ay, so, God bye to you.—Now I am alone.
    O, what a rogue and peasant° slave am I!
    Is it not monstrous that this player here,   480
    But in a fiction, in a dream of passion,

---

444. bisson rheum: blinding tears.   **444. clout:** piece of cloth.   **446. o'er-teemed:** worn out with bearing children.   **449. pronounc'd:** proclaimed.   **455. milch:** moist with tears.   **457. turned:** changed.   **461. abstract:** summary account.   **464. bodykins:** diminutive form of the oath "by God's body."   **473. dozen or sixteen lines:** critics have amused themselves by trying to locate Hamlet's lines. Lucianus's speech III.ii. 226–231 is the best guess.   **479. peasant:** base.

Could force his soul so to his own conceit
That from her working all his visage wann'd,°
Tears in his eyes, distraction in 's aspect,
A broken voice, and his whole function suiting 485
With forms to his conceit?° and all for nothing!
For Hecuba!
What's Hecuba to him, or he to Hecuba,
That he should weep for her? What would he do,
Had he the motive and the cue for passion 490
That I have? He would drown the stage with tears
And cleave the general ear with horrid speech,
Make mad the guilty and appall the free,
Confound the ignorant, and amaze indeed
The very faculties of eyes and ears. 495
Yet I,
A dull and muddy-mettled° rascal, peak,°
Like John-a-dreams,° unpregnant of° my cause,
And can say nothing; no, not for a king.
Upon whose property° and most dear life 500
A damn'd defeat was made. Am I a coward?
Who calls me villain? breaks my pate across?
Plucks off my beard, and blows it in my face?
Tweaks me by the nose? gives me the lie i' th' throat,
As deep as to the lungs? who does me this? 505
Ha!
'Swounds, I should take it: for it cannot be
But I am pigeon-liver'd° and lack gall
To make oppression bitter, or ere this
I should have fatted all the region kites° 510
With this slave's offal: bloody, bawdy villain!
Remorseless, treacherous, lecherous, kindless° villain!
O, vengeance!
Why, what an ass am I! This is most brave,
That I, the son of a dear father murder'd, 515
Prompted to my revenge by heaven and hell,
Must, like a whore, unpack my heart with words,
And fall a-cursing, like a very drab,°
A stallion!°

---

483. wann'd: grew pale. **485–486. his whole: . . . conceit:** his whole being responded with forms to suit his thought. **497. muddy-mettled:** dull-spirited. **497. peak:** mope, pine. **498. John-a-dreams:** an expression occurring elsewhere in Elizabethan literature to indicate a dreamer. **498. unpregnant of:** not quickened by. **500. property:** proprietorship (of crown and life). **508. pigeon-liver'd:** the pigeon was supposed to secrete no gall; if Hamlet, so he says, had had gall, he would have felt the bitterness of oppression, and avenged it. **510. region kites:** kites of the air. **512. kindless:** unnatural. **518. drab:** prostitute. **519. stallion:** prostitute (male or female).

Fie upon 't! foh! About,° my brains! Hum, I have heard   520
That guilty creatures sitting at a play
Have by the very cunning of the scene
Been struck so to the soul that presently
They have proclaim'd their malefactions;
For murder, though it have no tongue, will speak   525
With most miraculous organ. I'll have these players
Play something like the murder of my father
Before mine uncle: I'll observe his looks:
I'll tent° him to the quick: if 'a do blench,°
I know my course. The spirit that I have seen   530
May be the devil°: and the devil hath power
T' assume a pleasing shape; yea, and perhaps
Out of my weakness and my melancholy,
As he is very potent with such spirits,°
Abuses me to damn me: I'll have grounds   535
More relative° than this°: the play's the thing
Wherein I'll catch the conscience of the king.

                                                      (*Exit.*)

ACT III

Scene I

(*A room in the castle.*)

(*Enter* King, Queen, Polonius, Ophelia, Rosencrantz,
Guildenstern, Lords.)

King: And can you, by no drift of conference,°
   Get from him why he puts on this confusion,
   Grating so harshly all his days of quiet
   With turbulent and dangerous lunacy?
Rosencrantz: He does confess he feels himself distracted;
   But from what cause 'a will by no means speak.   5
Guildenstern: Nor do we find him forward° to be sounded,
   But, with a crafty madness, keeps aloof,
   When we would bring him on to some confession
   Of his true state.
Queen: Did he receive you well?
Rosencrantz: Most like a gentleman.   10
Guildenstern: But with much forcing of his disposition.°

---

520. About: about it, or turn thou right about.   **529. tent:** probe.   **529. blench:** quail, flinch.   **531. May be the devil:** Hamlet's suspicion is properly grounded in the belief of the time.   **534. spirits:** humors.   **536. relative:** closely related, definite.   **536. this:** i.e., the ghost's story.   **III.i. 1. drift of conference:** device of conversation.   **7. forward:** willing.   **12. forcing of his disposition:** i.e., against his will.

ROSENCRANTZ: Niggard of question°; but, of our demands,
   Most free in his reply.
QUEEN: Did you assay° him
   To any pastime?   15
ROSENCRANTZ: Madam, it so fell out, that certain players
   We o'er-raught° on the way; of these we told him;
   And there did seem in him a kind of joy
   To hear of it: they are here about the court,
   And, as I think, they have already order   20
   This night to play before him.
POLONIUS: 'Tis most true:
   And he beseech'd me to entreat your majesties
   To hear and see the matter.
KING: With all my heart; and it doth much content me
   To hear him so inclin'd.   25
   Good gentlemen, give him a further edge,°
   And drive his purpose into these delights.
ROSENCRANTZ: We shall, my lord.   (*Exeunt* ROSENCRANTZ *and* GUILDENSTERN.)
KING: Sweet Gertrude, leave us too;
   For we have closely° sent for Hamlet hither,
   That he, as 'twere by accident, may here   30
   Affront° Ophelia:
   Her father and myself, lawful espials,°
   Will so bestow ourselves that, seeing, unseen,
   We may of their encounter frankly judge,
   And gather by him, as he is behav'd,   35
   If 't be th' affliction of his love or no
   That thus he suffers for.
QUEEN: I shall obey you.
   And for your part, Ophelia, I do wish
   That your good beauties be the happy cause
   Of Hamlet's wildness°: so shall I hope your virtues   40
   Will bring him to his wonted way again,
   To both your honours.
OPHELIA: Madam, I wish it may.   (*Exit* QUEEN.)
POLONIUS: Ophelia, walk you here. Gracious,° so please you,
   We will bestow ourselves. (*To* OPHELIA.) Read on this book;
   That show of such an exercise° may colour°   45
   Your loneliness. We are oft to blame in this,—

---

13. Niggard of question: sparing of conversation.   **14. assay:** try to win.   **17. o'er-raught:** overtook.
26. edge: incitement.   **29. closely:** secretly.   **31. Affront:** confront.   **32. lawful espials:** legitimate
spies.   **40. wildness:** madness.   **43. Gracious:** your grace (addressed to the king).   **45. exercise:** act
of devotion (the book she reads is one of devotion).   **45. colour:** give a plausible appearance to.

'Tis too much prov'd—that with devotion's visage
And pious action we do sugar o'er
  The devil himself.
KING: (*Aside*) O, 'tis too true!
How smart a lash that speech doth give my conscience!   50
The harlot's cheek, beautied with plast'ring art,
Is not more ugly to° the thing° that helps it
Than is my deed to my most painted word:
O heavy burthen!
POLONIUS: I hear him coming: let's withdraw, my lord.   55
                       (*Exeunt* KING *and* POLONIUS.)

    (*Enter* HAMLET.)

HAMLET: To be, or not to be: that is the question:
  Whether 'tis nobler in the mind to suffer
  The slings and arrows of outrageous fortune,
  Or to take arms against a sea° of troubles,
  And by opposing end them? To die: to sleep;   60
  No more; and by a sleep to say we end
  The heart-ache and the thousand natural shocks
  That flesh is heir to, 'tis a consummation
  Devoutly to be wish'd. To die, to sleep;
  To sleep: perchance to dream: ay, there's the rub;   65
  For in that sleep of death what dreams may come
  When we have shuffled° off this mortal coil,°
  Must give us pause: there's the respect°
  That makes calamity of so long life°;
  For who would bear the whips and scorns of time,°   70
  Th' oppressor's wrong, the proud man's contumely,
  The pangs of despis'd° love, the law's delay,
  The insolence of office° and the spurns°
  That patient merit of th' unworthy takes,
  When he himself might his quietus° make   75
  With a bare bodkin?° who would fardels° bear,
  To grunt and sweat under a weary life,
  But that the dread of something after death,
  The undiscover'd country from whose bourn°

---

52. to: compared to. **52. thing:** i.e., the cosmetic. **59. sea:** the mixed metaphor of this speech has often been commented on; a later emendation, *siege* has sometimes been spoken on the stage. **67. shuffled:** sloughed, cast. **67. coil:** usually means "turmoil"; here, possibly "body" (conceived of as wound about the soul like rope); *clay, soil, veil,* have been suggested as emendations. **68. respect:** consideration. **69. of . . . life:** so long-lived. **70. time:** the world. **72. despis'd:** rejected. **73. office:** office-holders. **73. spurns:** insults. **75. quietus:** acquittance; here, death. **76. bare bodkin:** mere dagger; bare is sometimes understood as "unsheathed." **76. fardels:** burdens. **79. bourn:** boundary.

No traveller returns, puzzles the will   80
And makes us rather bear those ills we have
Than fly to others that we know not of?
Thus conscience° does make cowards of us all;
And thus the native hue° of resolution
Is sicklied o'er° with the pale cast° of thought,   85
And enterprises of great pitch° and moment°
With this regard° their currents° turn awry,
And lose the name of action—Soft you now!
The fair Ophelia! Nymph, in thy orisons°
Be all my sins rememb'red.

OPHELIA: Good my lord,   90
    How does your honour for this many a day?

HAMLET: I humbly thank you; well, well, well.

OPHELIA: My lord, I have remembrances of yours,
    That I have longed long to re-deliver;
    I pray you, now receive them.   95

HAMLET: No, not I;
    I never gave you aught.

OPHELIA: My honour'd lord, you know right well you did;
    And, with them, words of so sweet breath compos'd
    As made the things more rich: their perfume lost,   100
    Take these again; for to the noble mind
    Rich gifts wax poor when givers prove unkind.
    There, my lord.

HAMLET: Ha, ha! are you honest?°

OPHELIA: My lord?   105

HAMLET: Are you fair?

OPHELIA: What means your lordship?

HAMLET: That if you be honest and fair, your honesty° should admit no discourse
    to° your beauty.

OPHELIA: Could beauty, my lord, have better commerce° than with honesty?   110

HAMLET: Ay, truly; for the power of beauty will sooner transform honesty from
    what it is to a bawd than the force of honesty can translate beauty into his like-
    ness: this was sometime a paradox, but now the time° gives it proof. I did love
    you once.

OPHELIA: Indeed, my lord, you made me believe so.   115

---

83. conscience: probably, inhibition by the faculty of reason restraining the will from doing wrong.
84. native hue: natural color; metaphor derived from the color of the face.   **85. sicklied o'er:** given a
sickly tinge.   **85. cast:** shade of color.   **86. pitch:** height (as of falcon's flight).   **86. moment:** importance.   **87. regard:** respect, consideration.   **87. currents:** courses.   **89. orisons:** prayers.   **104–9. are
you honest . . . beauty:** honest meaning "truthful" and "chaste" and fair meaning "just, honorable" (line
106) and "beautiful" (line 108) are not mere quibbles; the speech has the irony of a double entendre.
108. your honesty: your chastity.   **109. discourse to:** familiar intercourse with.   **110. commerce:**
intercourse.   **113. the time:** the present age.

HAMLET: You should not have believed me; for virtue cannot so inoculate° our old
stock but we shall relish of it°: I loved you not.

OPHELIA: I was the more deceived.

HAMLET: Get thee to a nunnery; why wouldst thou be a breeder of sinners? I am
myself indifferent honest°; but yet I could accuse me of such things that it were   120
better my mother had not borne me: I am very proud, revengeful, ambitious,
with more offences at my beck° than I have thoughts to put them in, imagination to give them shape, or time to act them in. What should such fellows as I
do crawling between earth and heaven? We are arrant knaves, all; believe none
of us. Go thy ways to a nunnery. Where's your father?   125

OPHELIA: At home, my lord.

HAMLET: Let the doors be shut upon him, that he may play the fool no where but
in 's own house. Farewell.

OPHELIA: O, help him, you sweet heavens!

HAMLET: If thou dost marry, I'll give thee this plague for thy dowry: be thou as   130
chaste as ice, as pure as snow, thou shalt not escape calumny. Get thee to a nunnery, go: farewell. Or, if thou wilt needs marry, marry a fool; for wise men
know well enough what monsters° you make of them. To a nunnery, go, and
quickly too. Farewell.

OPHELIA: O heavenly powers, restore him!   135

HAMLET: I have heard of your° paintings too, well enough; God hath given you
one face, and you make yourselves another: you jig,° you amble, and you lisp;
you nick-name God's creatures, and make your wantonness your ignorance.°
Go to, I'll no more on 't; it hath made me mad. I say, we will have no more marriage: those that are married already, all but one,° shall live; the rest shall keep   140
as they are. To a nunnery, go.   *(Exit.)*

OPHELIA: O, what a noble mind is here o'er-thrown!
The courtier's, soldier's, scholar's, eye, tongue, sword;
Th' expectancy and rose° of the fair state,
The glass of fashion and the mould of form,°   145
Th' observ'd of all observers,° quite, quite down!
And I, of ladies most deject and wretched,
That suck'd the honey of his music vows,
Now see that noble and most sovereign reason,
Like sweet bells jangled, out of time and harsh;   150
That unmatch'd form and feature of blown° youth
Blasted with ecstasy°: O, woe is me,

---

116. inoculate: graft (metaphorical).   **117. but . . . it:** i.e., that we do not still have about us a taste of the
old stock, i.e., retain our sinfulness.   **120. indifferent honest:** moderately virtuous.   **122. beck:** command.   **133. monsters:** an allusion to the horns of a cuckold.   **136. your:** indefinite use.   **137. jig:** move
with jerky motion; probably allusion to the jig, or song and dance, of the current stage.   **138. make . . .
ignorance:** i.e., excuse your wantonness on the ground of your ignorance.   **140. one:** i.e., the king.
144. expectancy and rose: source of hope.   **145. The glass . . . form:** the mirror of fashion and the pattern of courtly behavior.   **146. observ'd . . . observers:** i.e., the center of attention in the court.
151. blown: blooming.   **152. ecstasy:** madness.

T' have seen what I have seen, see what I see!

(*Enter* KING *and* POLONIUS.)

KING: Love! his affections do not that way tend;
Nor what he spake, though it lack'd form a little,   155
Was not like madness. There's something in his soul,
O'er which his melancholy sits on brood;
And I do doubt° the hatch and the disclose°
Will be some danger: which for to prevent,
I have in quick determination   160
Thus set it down: he shall with speed to England,
For the demand of our neglected tribute:
Haply the seas and countries different
With variable° objects shall expel
This something-settled° matter in his heart,   165
Whereon his brains still beating puts him thus
From fashion of himself.° What think you on 't?

POLONIUS: It shall do well: but yet do I believe
The origin and commencement of his grief
Sprung from neglected love. How now, Ophelia!   170
You need not tell us what Lord Hamlet said;
We heard it all. My lord, do as you please;
But, if you hold it fit, after the play
Let his queen mother all alone entreat him
To show his grief: let her be round° with him;   175
And I'll be plac'd, so please you, in the ear
Of all their conference. If she find him not,
To England send him, or confine him where
Your wisdom best shall think.

KING: It shall be so: 180
Madness in great ones must not unwatch'd go.   (*Exeunt.*)

SCENE II

(*A hall in the castle.*)

(*Enter* HAMLET *and three of the* PLAYERS.)

HAMLET: Speak the speech, I pray you, as I pronounced it to you, trippingly on the
tongue: but if you mouth it, as many of your° players do, I had as lief the town-
crier spoke my lines. Nor do not saw the air too much with your hand, thus, but
use all gently; for in the very torrent, tempest, and, as I may say, whirlwind of

---

158. doubt: fear.   **158. disclose:** disclosure or revelation (by chipping of the shell).   **164. variable:** various   **165. something-settled:** somewhat settled.   **167. From . . . himself:** out of his natural manner.   **175. round:** blunt.   **III.ii. 2. your:** indefinite use.

your passion, you must acquire and beget a temperance that may give it   5
smoothness. O, it offends me to the soul to hear a robustious° periwig-pated°
fellow tear a passion to tatters, to very rags, to split the ears of the groundlings,°
who for the most part are capable of° nothing but inexplicable° dumb-shows
and noise: I would have such a fellow whipped for o'er-doing Termagant°; it
out-herods Herod°: pray you, avoid it.   10

FIRST PLAYER: I warrant your honour.

HAMLET: Be not too tame neither, but let your own discretion be your tutor: suit
the action to the word, the word to the action; with this special observance,
that you o'er-step not the modesty of nature: for any thing so overdone is from
the purpose of playing, whose end, both at the first and now, was and is, to   15
hold, as 't were, the mirror up to nature; to show virtue her own feature, scorn
her own image, and the very age and body of the time his form and pressure.°
Now this overdone, or come tardy off,° though it make the unskilful laugh,
cannot but make the judicious grieve; the censure of the which one° must in
your allowance o'erweigh a whole theatre of others. O, there be players that   20
I have seen play, and heard others praise, and that highly, not to speak it pro-
fanely, that, neither having the accent of Christians nor the gait of Christian,
pagan, nor man, have so strutted and bellowed that I have thought some of
nature's journeymen° had made men and not made them well, they imitated
humanity so abominably.

FIRST PLAYER: I hope we have reformed that indifferently° with us, sir.   25

HAMLET: O, reform it altogether. And let those that play your clowns speak no
more than is set down for them; for there be of° them that will themselves
laugh, to set on some quantity of barren° spectators to laugh too; though, in
the mean time, some necessary question of the play be then to be considered:
that's villanous, and shows a most pitiful ambition in the fool that uses it. Go,   30
make you ready.

                                           (*Exeunt* PLAYERS.)

(*Enter* POLONIUS, GUILDENSTERN, *and* ROSENCRANTZ.)

How now, my lord! will the king hear this piece of work?

POLONIUS: And the queen too, and that presently.

HAMLET: Bid the players make haste.   (*Exit* POLONIUS.)
Will you two help to hasten them?   35

ROSENCRANTZ: ⎫
               ⎬   We will, my lord.   (*Exeunt they two.*)
GUILDENSTERN: ⎭

---

6. **robustious:** violent, boisterous.   6. **periwig-pated:** wearing a wig.   8. **groundlings:** those who stood
in the yard of the theater.   8. **capable of:** susceptible of being influenced by.   8. **inexplicable:** of no significance worth explaining.   10. **Termagant:** a god of the Saracens; a character in the St. Nicholas play,
where one of his worshipers, leaving him in charge of goods, returns to find them stolen; whereupon he
beats the god (or idol), which howls vociferously.   10. **Herod:** Herod of Jewry; a character in The Slaughter of the Innocents and other cycle plays. The part was played with great noise and fury.   17. **pressure:**
stamp, impressed character.   18. **come tardy off:** inadequately done.   19. **the censure . . . one:** the
judgment of even one of whom.   23. **journeymen:** laborers not yet masters in their trade.   25. **indifferently:** fairly, tolerably.   27. **of:** i.e., some among them.   28. **barren:** i.e., of wit.

HAMLET: What ho! Horatio!

(*Enter* HORATIO.)

HORATIO: Here, sweet lord, at your service.

HAMLET: Horatio, thou art e'en as just° a man

   As e'er my conversation cop'd withal.   40

HORATIO: O, my dear lord,—

HAMLET: Nay, do not think I flatter;

   For what advancement may I hope from thee

   That no revenue hast but thy good spirits,

   To feed and clothe thee? Why should the poor be flatter'd?

   No, let the candied tongue lick absurd pomp,   45

   And crook the pregnant° hinges of the knee

   Where thrift° may follow fawning. Dost thou hear?

   Since my dear soul was mistress of her choice

   And could of men distinguish her election,

   S' hath seal'd thee for herself; for thou hast been   50

   As one, in suff'ring all, that suffers nothing,

   A man that fortune's buffets and rewards

   Hast ta'en with equal thanks: and blest are those

   Whose blood and judgement are so well commeddled,

   That they are not a pipe for fortune's finger   55

   To sound what stop° she please. Give me that man

   That is not passion's slave, and I will wear him

   In my heart's core, ay, in my heart of heart,

   As I do thee.—Something too much of this.—

   There is a play to-night before the king;   60

   One scene of it comes near the circumstance

   Which I have told thee of my father's death:

   I prithee, when thou seest that act afoot,

   Even with the very comment of thy soul°

   Observe my uncle: if his occulted° guilt   65

   Do not itself unkennel in one speech,

   It is a damned° ghost that we have seen,

   And my imaginations are as foul

   As Vulcan's stithy.° Give him heedful note;

   For I mine eyes will rivet to his face,   70

   And after we will both our judgments join

   In censure of his seeming.°

HORATIO. . . .   Well, my lord:

---

39. just: honest, honorable. **46. pregnant:** pliant. **47. thrift:** profit. **56. stop:** hole in a wind instrument for controlling the sound. **64. very . . . soul:** inward and sagacious criticism. **65. occulted:** hidden. **67. damned:** in league with Satan. **69. stithy:** smithy, place of stiths (anvils). **72. censure . . . seeming:** judgment of his appearance or behavior.

If 'a steal aught the whilst this play is playing,
And 'scape detecting, I will pay the theft.   75

> (*Enter trumpets and kettledrums*, KING, QUEEN, POLONIUS, OPHELIA,
> [ROSENCRANTZ, GUILDENSTERN, *and* OTHERS].)

HAMLET: They are coming to the play; I must be idle°: Get you a place.

KING: How fares our cousin Hamlet?

HAMLET: Excellent, i' faith; of the chameleon's dish°: I eat the air, promise-
crammed: you cannot feed capons so.

KING: I have nothing with° this answer, Hamlet; these words are not mine.°   80

HAMLET: No, nor mine now. (*To* POLONIUS.) My lord, you played once i' the university, you say?

POLONIUS: That did I, my lord; and was accounted a good actor.

HAMLET: What did you enact?

POLONIUS: I did enact Julius Cæsar: I was killed i' the Capitol; Brutus killed me.   85

HAMLET: It was a brute part of him to kill so capital a calf there. Be the players
ready?

ROSENCRANTZ: Ay, my lord; they stay upon your patience.

QUEEN: Come hither, my dear Hamlet, sit by me.

HAMLET: No, good mother, here's metal more attractive.   90

POLONIUS (*to the* KING):   O, ho! do you mark that?

HAMLET: Lady, shall I lie in your lap? (*Lying down at* OPHELIA's *feet*.)

OPHELIA: No, my lord.

HAMLET: I mean, my head upon your lap?

OPHELIA: Ay, my lord.   95

HAMLET: Do you think I meant country° matters?

OPHELIA: I think nothing, my lord.

HAMLET: That's a fair thought to lie between maids' legs.

OPHELIA: What is, my lord?

HAMLET: Nothing.

OPHELIA: You are merry, my lord.   100

HAMLET: Who, I?

OPHELIA: Ay, my lord.

HAMLET: O God, your only° jig-maker.° What should a man do but be merry? for
look you, how cheerfully my mother looks, and my father died within's two   105
hours.

OPHELIA: Nay, 'tis twice two months, my lord.

HAMLET: So long? Nay then, let the devil wear black, for I'll have a suit of sables.°
O heavens! die two months ago, and not forgotten yet? Then there's hope a

---

76. idle: crazy, or not attending to anything serious.   **78. chameleon's dish:** chameleons were supposed to feed on air. (Hamlet deliberately misinterprets the king's "fares" as "feeds.")   **80. have . . .
with:** make nothing of.   **80. are not mine:** do not respond to what I ask.   **96. country:** with a bawdy
pun.   **104. your only:** only your.   **104. jig-maker:** composer of jigs (song and dance).   **108. suit of
sables:** garments trimmed with the fur of the sable, with a quibble on sable meaning "black."

great man's memory may outlive his life half a year: but, by 'r lady, 'a must build   110
churches, then; or else shall 'a suffer not thinking on,° with the hobbyhorse,
whose epitaph is "For, O, for, O, the hobbyhorse is forgot."°

    (The trumpets sound. Dumb show follows.)

    (Enter a KING *and a* QUEEN *[very lovingly]; the* QUEEN *embracing him, and
he her. [She kneels, and makes show of protestation unto him.] He takes her
up, and declines his head upon her neck: he lies him down upon a bank of
flowers: she, seeing him asleep, leaves him. Anon comes in another man, takes
off his crown, kisses it, pours poison in the sleeper's ears, and leaves him. The*
QUEEN *returns; finds the* KING *dead, makes passionate action. The* POISONER,
*with some three or four come in again, seem to condole with her. The dead body
is carried away. The* POISONER *woos the* QUEEN *with gifts: she seems harsh
awhile, but in the end accepts love.)*

                                                                    (Exeunt.)

OPHELIA: What means this, my lord?
HAMLET: Marry, this is miching mallecho°; it means mischief.
OPHELIA: Belike this show imports the argument of the play.   115

    (Enter PROLOGUE.)

HAMLET: We shall know by this fellow: the players cannot keep counsel; they'll tell
    all.
OPHELIA: Will 'a tell us what this show meant?
HAMLET: Ay, or any show that you'll show him: be not you ashamed to show, he'll
    not shame to tell you what it means.   120
OPHELIA: You are naught, you are naught°: I'll mark the play.
PROLOGUE: For us, and for our tragedy,
    Here stooping° to your clemency,
    We beg your hearing patiently.   *(Exit.)*
HAMLET: Is this a prologue, or the posy° of a ring?   125
OPHELIA: 'Tis brief, my lord.
HAMLET: As woman's love.

    (Enter [two Players as] KING *and* QUEEN.)

PLAYER KING: Full thirty times hath Phoebus' cart gone round
    Neptune's salt wash° and Tellus'° orbed ground,
    And thirty dozen moons with borrowed° sheen   130
    About the world have times twelve thirties been,

---

111. suffer . . . on: undergo oblivion.   **112. "For . . . forgot":** verse of a song occurring also in *Love's
Labour's Lost,* III.i.30; the hobbyhorse was a character in the Morris Dance.   **114. miching mallecho:**
sneaking mischief.   **121. naught:** indecent.   **123. stooping:** bowing.   **125. posy:** motto.   **129. salt
wash:** the sea.   **129. Tellus:** goddess of the earth (orbed ground).   **130. borrowed:** i.e., reflected.

Since love our hearts and Hymen° did our hands
Unite commutual° in most sacred bands.

PLAYER QUEEN: So many journeys may the sun and moon
Make us again count o'er ere love be done! 135
But, woe is me, you are so sick of late,
So far from cheer and from your former state,
That I distrust° you. Yet, though I distrust,
Discomfort you, my lord, it nothing must:
For women's fear and love holds quantity°; 140
In neither aught, or in extremity.
Now, what my love is, proof hath made you know;
And as my love is siz'd, my fear is so:
Where love is great, the littlest doubts are fear;
Where little fears grow great, great love grows there. 145

PLAYER KING: 'Faith, I must leave thee, love, and shortly too;
My operant° powers their functions leave° to do:
And thou shalt live in this fair world behind,
Honour'd, belov'd; and haply one as kind
For husband shalt thou—

PLAYER QUEEN: O, confound the rest! 150
Such love must needs be treason in my breast:
In second husband let me be accurst!
None wed the second but who kill'd the first.

HAMLET (*aside*): Wormwood, wormwood.

PLAYER QUEEN: The instances that second marriage move 155
Are base respects of thrift, but none of love:
A second time I kill my husband dead,
When second husband kisses me in bed.

PLAYER KING: I do believe you think what now you speak;
But what we do determine oft we break. 160
Purpose is but the slave to memory,
Of violent birth, but poor validity:
Which now, like fruit unripe, sticks on the tree;
But fall, unshaken, when they mellow be.
Most necessary 'tis that we forget 165
To pay ourselves what to ourselves is debt:
What to ourselves in passion we propose,
The passion ending, doth the purpose lose.
The violence of either grief or joy
Their own enactures° with themselves destroy: 170
Where joy most revels, grief doth most lament;

---

132. Hymen: god of matrimony. **133. commutual:** mutually. **138. distrust:** am anxious about. **140. holds quantity:** keeps proportion between. **147. operant:** active. **147. leave:** cease. **170. enactures:** fulfillments.

Grief joys, joy grieves, on slender accident.
This world is not for aye,° nor 'tis not strange
That even our loves should with our fortunes change;
For 'tis a question left us yet to prove,   175
Whether love lead fortune, or else fortune love.
The great man down, you mark his favourite flies;
The poor advanc'd makes friends of enemies.
And hitherto doth love on fortune tend;
For who° not needs shall never lack a friend,   180
And who in want a hollow friend doth try,
Directly seasons° him his enemy.
But, orderly to end where I begun,
Our wills and fates do so contrary run
That our devices still are overthrown;   185
Our thoughts are ours, their ends° none of our own:
So think thou wilt no second husband wed;
But die thy thoughts when thy first lord is dead.
PLAYER QUEEN: Nor earth to me give food, nor heaven light!
Sport and repose lock from me day and night!   190
To desperation turn my trust and hope!
An anchor's° cheer° in prison be my scope!
Each opposite° that blanks° the face of joy
Meet what I would have well and it destroy!
Both here and hence pursue me lasting strife,   195
If, once a widow, ever I be wife!
HAMLET: If she should break it now!
PLAYER KING: 'Tis deeply sworn. Sweet, leave me here awhile;
My spirits grow dull, and fain I would beguile
The tedious day with sleep. (*Sleeps.*)
PLAYER QUEEN: Sleep rock thy brain;   200
And never come mischance between us twain!   (*Exit.*)
HAMLET: Madam, how like you this play?
QUEEN: The lady doth protest too much, methinks.
HAMLET: O, but she'll keep her word.
KING: Have you heard the argument? Is there no offence in 't?   205
HAMLET: No, no, they do but jest, poison in jest; no offence i' the world.
KING: What do you call the play?
HAMLET: The Mouse-trap. Marry, how? Tropically.° This play is the image of a
     murder done in Vienna: Gonzago° is the duke's name; his wife, Baptista: you

---

173. aye: ever.   180. who: whoever.   182. seasons: matures, ripens.   186. ends: results.   192. An
anchor's: an anchorite's.   192. cheer: fare; sometimes printed as chair.   193. opposite: adverse thing.
193. blanks: causes to *blanch* or grow pale.   208. Tropically: figuratively, *tropically* suggests a pun on
trap in *Mouse-trap* (1.211).   209. Gonzago: in 1538 Luigi Gonzago murdered the Duke of Urbano by
pouring poisoned lotion in his ears.

shall see anon; 't is a knavish piece of work: but what o' that? your majesty and   210
we that have free souls, it touches us not: let the galled jade° winch,° our with-
ers° are unwrung.°

(*Enter* LUCIANUS.)

This is one Lucianus, nephew to the king.

OPHELIA: You are as good as a chorus,° my lord.

HAMLET: I could interpret between you and your love, if I could see the puppets   215
dallying.°

OPHELIA: You are keen, my lord, you are keen.

HAMLET: It would cost you a groaning to take off my edge.

OPHELIA: Still better, and worse.°

HAMLET: So you mistake° your husbands. Begin, murderer; pox,° leave thy   220
damnable faces, and begin. Come: the croaking raven doth bellow for revenge.

LUCIANUS: Thoughts black, hands apt, drugs fit, and time agreeing;
Confederate° season, else no creature seeing;
Thou mixture rank, of midnight weeds collected,
With Hecate's° ban° thrice blasted, thrice infected,   225
Thy natural magic and dire property,
On wholesome life usurp immediately.

(*Pours the poison into the sleeper's ears.*)

HAMLET: 'A poisons him i' the garden for his estate. His name's Gonzago: the
story is extant, and written in very choice Italian: you shall see anon how the
murderer gets the love of Gonzago's wife.   230

OPHELIA: The king rises.

HAMLET: What, frighted with false fire!°

QUEEN: How fares my lord?

POLONIUS: Give o'er the play.

KING: Give me some light away!   235

POLONIUS: Lights, lights, lights!   (*Exeunt all but* HAMLET *and* HORATIO.)

HAMLET: Why, let the strucken deer go weep,
The hart ungalled play;
For some must watch, while some must sleep:
Thus runs the world away.°   240

---

211. galled jade: horse whose hide is rubbed by saddle or harness.   **211. winch:** wince.   **212. withers:**
the part between the horse's shoulder blades.   **212. unwrung:** not wrung or twisted.   **214. chorus:** in
many Elizabethan plays the action was explained by an actor known as the "chorus"; at a puppet show the
actor who explained the action was known as an "interpreter," as indicated by the lines following.
215–218. dallying: with sexual suggestion, continued in **keen** (sexually aroused), **groaning** (i.e., in pregnancy), and **edge** (i.e., sexual desire or impetuosity).   **219. Still . . . worse:** more keen, less decorous.
220. mistake: err in taking.   **220. pox:** an imprecation.   **223. Confederate:** conspiring (to assist the
murderer).   **225. Hecate:** the goddess of witchcraft.   **225. ban:** curse.   **232. false fire:** fireworks, or a
blank discharge.   **237–240. Why . . . away:** probably from an old ballad, with allusion to the popular
belief that a wounded deer retires to weep and die. Cf. *As You Like It*, II, i. 66.

Would not this,° sir, and a forest of feathers°—if the rest of my fortunes turn
Turk with° me—with two Provincial roses° on my razed° shoes, get me a
fellowship in a cry° of players,° sir?

HORATIO: Half a share.°

HAMLET: A whole one, I.   245
For thou dost know, O Damon dear,
   This realm dismantled° was
Of Jove himself; and now reigns here
   A very, very°—pajock.°

HORATIO: You might have rhymed.   250

HAMLET: O good Horatio, I'll take the ghost's word for a thousand pound.
Didst perceive?

HORATIO: Very well, my lord.

HAMLET: Upon the talk of the poisoning?

HORATIO: I did very well note him.   255

HAMLET: Ah, ha! Come, some music! come, the recorders!°
For if the king like not the comedy,
Why then, belike, he likes it not, perdy.°
Come, some music!

(*Enter* ROSENCRANTZ *and* GUILDENSTERN.)

GUILDENSTERN: Good my lord, vouchsafe me a word with you.   260

HAMLET: Sir, a whole history.

GUILDENSTERN: The king, sir,—

HAMLET: Ay, sir, what of him?

GUILDENSTERN: Is in his retirement marvelous distempered.

HAMLET: With drink, sir?   265

GUILDENSTERN: No, my lord, rather with choler.°

HAMLET: Your wisdom should show itself more richer to signify this to his doctor;
   for, for me to put him to his purgation would perhaps plunge him into far more
   choler.

GUILDENSTERN: Good my lord, put your discourse into some frame° and start not   270
   so wildly from my affair.

HAMLET: I am tame, sir: pronounce.

---

241. this: i.e., the play.   **241. feathers:** allusion to the plumes which Elizabethan actors were fond of
wearing.   **242. turn Turk with:** go back on.   **242. two Provincial roses:** rosettes of ribbon like the
roses of Provins near Paris, or else the roses of Provence.   **242. razed:** cut, slashed (by way of ornament).   **243. cry:** pack (as of hounds).   **243. fellowship . . . players:** partnership in a theatrical company.   **244. Half a share:** allusion to the custom in dramatic companies of dividing the ownership into
a number of shares among the householders.   **247. dismantled:** stripped, divested.   **246–249. For . . .
very:** probably from an old ballad having to do with Damon and Pythias.   **249. pajock:** peacock (a bird
with a bad reputation). Possibly the word was patchock, diminutive of patch, clown.   **256. recorders:**
wind instruments of the flute kind.   **258. perdy:** corruption of par dieu.   **266. choler:** bilious disorder,
with quibble on the sense "anger."   **270. frame:** order.

GUILDENSTERN: The queen, your mother, in most great affliction of spirit, hath
sent me to you.

HAMLET: You are welcome.   275

GUILDENSTERN: Nay, good my lord, this courtesy is not of the right breed. If it
shall please you to make me a wholesome° answer, I will do your mother's commandment; if not, your pardon and my return shall be the end of my business.

HAMLET: Sir, I cannot.

GUILDENSTERN: What, my lord?   280

HAMLET: Make you a wholesome answer; my wit's diseased: but, sir, such answer as
I can make, you shall command; or rather, as you say, my mother: therefore no
more, but to the matter°: my mother, you say,—

ROSENCRANTZ: Then thus she says; your behaviour hath struck her into amazement and admiration.   285

HAMLET: O wonderful son, that can so 'stonish a mother! But is there no sequel at
the heels of this mother's admiration? Impart.

ROSENCRANTZ: She desires to speak with you in her closet, ere you go to bed.

HAMLET: We shall obey, were she ten times our mother. Have you any further
trade with us?   290

ROSENCRANTZ: My lord, you once did love me.

HAMLET: And do still, by these pickers and stealers.°

ROSENCRANTZ: Good my lord, what is your cause of distemper? you do, surely, bar
the door upon your own liberty, if you deny your griefs to your friend.

HAMLET: Sir, I lack advancement.   295

ROSENCRANTZ: How can that be, when you have the voice° of the king himself for
your succession in Denmark?

HAMLET: Ay, sir, but "While the grass grows,"°—the proverb is something musty.

(*Enter the* PLAYERS *with recorders.*)

O, the recorders! let me see one. To withdraw° with you:—why do you go
about to recover the wind° of me, as if you would drive me into a toil?°   300

GUILDENSTERN: O, my lord, if my duty be too bold, my love is too unmannerly.°

HAMLET: I do not well understand that. Will you play upon this pipe?

GUILDENSTERN: My lord, I cannot.

HAMLET: I pray you.

GUILDENSTERN: Believe me, I cannot.   305

HAMLET: I beseech you.

GUILDENSTERN: I know no touch of it, my lord.

---

277. **wholesome:** sensible.   283. **matter:** matter in hand.   292. **pickers and stealers:** hands, so called
from the catechism "to keep my hands from picking and stealing."   296. **voice:** support.   298. **"While . . .
grows":** the rest of the proverb is "the silly horse starves." Hamlet may be destroyed while he is waiting for
the succession to the kingdom.   299. **withdraw:** speak in private.   300. **recover the wind:** get to the
windward side.   300. **toil:** snare.   301. **if . . . unmannerly:** if I am using an unmannerly boldness, it is my
love which occasions it.

HAMLET: 'Tis as easy as lying: govern these ventages° with your fingers and thumb, give it breath with your mouth, and it will discourse most eloquent music. Look you, these are the stops.   310

GUILDENSTERN: But these cannot I command to any utterance of harmony; I have not the skill.

HAMLET: Why, look you now, how unworthy a thing you make of me! You would play upon me; you would seem to know my stops; you would pluck out the heart of my mystery; you would sound me from my lowest note to the top of   315 my compass°: and there is much music, excellent voice, in this little organ°; yet cannot you make it speak. 'Sblood, do you think I am easier to be played on than a pipe? Call me what instrument you will, though you can fret° me, you cannot play upon me.

      (*Enter* POLONIUS.)

    God bless you, sir!   320

POLONIUS: My lord, the queen would speak with you, and presently.

HAMLET: Do you see yonder cloud that 's almost in shape of a camel?

POLONIUS: By the mass, and 'tis like a camel, indeed.

HAMLET: Methinks it is like a weasel.

POLONIUS: It is backed like a weasel.   325

HAMLET: Or like a whale?

POLONIUS: Very like a whale.

HAMLET: Then I will come to my mother by and by. (*Aside.*) They fool me to the top of my bent.°—I will come by and by.°

POLONIUS: I will say so.   (*Exit.*)   330

HAMLET: By and by is easily said.

    Leave me, friends.   (*Exeunt all but* HAMLET.)

    'Tis now the very witching time° of night,

    When churchyards yawn and hell itself breathes out

    Contagion to this world: now could I drink hot blood,   335

    And do such bitter business as the day

    Would quake to look on. Soft! now to my mother.

    O heart, lose not thy nature; let not ever

    The soul of Nero° enter this firm bosom:

    Let me be cruel, not unnatural: 340

    I will speak daggers to her, but use none;

    My tongue and soul in this be hypocrites;

---

308. ventages: stops of the recorders.   **316. compass:** range of voice.   **316. organ:** musical instrument, i.e., the pipe.   **318. fret:** quibble on meaning "irritate" and the piece of wood, gut, or metal which regulates the fingering.   **329. top of my bent:** limit of endurance, i.e., extent to which a bow may be bent.   **329. by and by:** immediately.   **333. witching time:** i.e., time when spells are cast.   **339. Nero:** murderer of his mother, Agrippina.

How in my words somever she be shent,°
To give them seals° never, my soul, consent!   (*Exit.*)

SCENE III

(*A room in the castle.*)

(*Enter* KING, ROSENCRANTZ, *and* GUILDENSTERN.)

KING: I like him not, nor stands it safe with us
To let his madness range. Therefore prepare you;
I your commission will forthwith dispatch,°
And he to England shall along with you:
The terms° of our estate° may not endure   5
Hazard so near us as doth hourly grow
Out of his brows.°

GUILDENSTERN: We will ourselves provide:
Most holy and religious fear it is
To keep those many many bodies safe
That live and feed upon your majesty.   10

ROSENCRANTZ: The single and peculiar° life is bound,
With all the strength and armor of the mind,
To keep itself from noyance°; but much more
That spirit upon whose weal depend and rest
The lives of many. The cess° of majesty   15
Dies not alone; but, like a gulf,° doth draw
What's near it with it: it is a massy wheel,
Fix'd on the summit of the highest mount,
To whose huge spokes ten thousand lesser things
Are mortis'd and adjoin'd; which, when it falls,   20
Each small annexment, petty consequence,
Attends° the boist'rous ruin. Never alone
Did the king sigh, but with a general groan.

KING: Arm° you, I pray you, to this speedy voyage;
For we will fetters put about this fear,   25
Which now goes too free-footed.

ROSENCRANTZ: We will haste us.
                    (*Exeunt* GENTLEMEN [ROSENCRANTZ *and* GUILDENSTERN].)

(*Enter* POLONIUS.)

POLONIUS: My lord, he's going to his mother's closet:

---

343. shent: rebuked.   **344. give them seals:** confirm with deeds.   **III.iii. 3. dispatch:** prepare.
5. terms: condition, circumstances.   **5. estate:** state.   **7. brows:** effronteries.   **11. single and peculiar:**
individual and private.   **13. noyance:** harm.   **15. cess:** decease.   **16. gulf:** whirlpool.   **22. Attends:** participates in.   **24. Arm:** prepare.

Behind the arras° I'll convey° myself,
To hear the process°; I'll warrant she'll tax him home°:
And, as you said, and wisely was it said,   30
'Tis meet that some more audience than a mother,
Since nature makes them partial, should o'erhear
The speech, of vantage.° Fare you well, my liege:
I'll call upon you ere you go to bed,
And tell you what I know.
KING: Thanks, dear my lord.   (*Exit* [POLONIUS].) 35
O, my offence is rank, it smells to heaven;
It hath the primal eldest curse° upon't,
A brother's murder. Pray can I not,
Though inclination be as sharp as will°:
My stronger guilt defeats my strong intent;   40
And, like a man to double business bound,
I stand in pause where I shall first begin,
And both neglect. What if this cursed hand
Were thicker than itself with brother's blood,
Is there not rain enough in the sweet heavens   45
To wash it white as snow? Whereto serves mercy
But to confront° the visage of offence?
And what's in prayer but this two-fold force,
To be forestalled° ere we come to fall,
Or pardon'd being down? Then I'll look up;   50
My fault is past. But, O, what form of prayer
Can serve my turn? "Forgive me my foul murder"?
That cannot be: since I am still possess'd
Of those effects for which I did the murder,
My crown, mine own ambition° and my queen.   55
May one be pardon'd and retain th' offence?°
In the corrupted currents° of this world
Offence's gilded hand° may shove by justice,
And oft 'tis seen the wicked prize° itself
Buys out the law: but 'tis not so above;   60
There is no shuffling,° there the action lies°
In his true nature; and we ourselves compell'd,
Even to the teeth and forehead° of our faults,

---

28. arras: screen of tapestry placed around the walls of household apartments.   **28. convey:** implication
of secrecy; *convey* was often used to mean "steal."   **29. process:** proceedings.   **29. tax him home:**
reprove him severely.   **33. of vantage:** from an advantageous place.   **37. primal eldest curse:** the
curse of Cain, the first to kill his brother.   **39. sharp as will:** i.e., his desire is as strong as his determination.   **47. confront:** oppose directly.   **49. forestalled:** prevented.   **55. ambition:** i.e., realization of
ambition.   **56. offence:** benefit accruing from offense.   **57. currents:** courses.   **58. gilded hand:**
hand offering gold as a bribe.   **59. wicked prize:** prize won by wickedness.   **61. shuffling:** escape by
trickery.   **61. lies:** is sustainable.   **63. teeth and forehead:** very face.

To give in evidence. What then? what rests?°
Try what repentance can: what can it not? 65
Yet what can it when one can not repent?
O wretched state! O bosom black as death!
O limed° soul, that, struggling to be free,
Art more engag'd!° Help, angels! Make assay!°
Bow, stubborn knees; and, heart with strings of steel, 70
Be soft as sinews of the new-born babe!
All may be well. (*He kneels.*)

(*Enter* HAMLET.)

HAMLET: Now might I do it pat,° now he is praying;
And now I'll do 't. And so 'a goes to heaven;
And so am I reveng'd. That would be scann'd°: 75
A villain kills my father; and for that,
I, his sole son, do this same villain send
To heaven.
Why, this is hire and salary, not revenge.
'A took my father grossly, full of bread°; 80
With all his crimes broad blown,° as flush° as May;
And how his audit stands who knows save heaven?
But in our circumstance and course° of thought,
'Tis heavy with him: and am I then reveng'd,
To take him in the purging of his soul, 85
When he is fit and season'd for his passage?°
No!
Up, sword; and know thou a more horrid hent°:
When he is drunk asleep,° or in his rage,
Or in th' incestuous pleasure of his bed; 90
At game, a-swearing, or about some act
That has no relish of salvation in 't;
Then trip him, that his heels may kick at heaven,
And that his soul may be as damn'd and black
As hell, whereto it goes. My mother stays: 95
This physic° but prolongs thy sickly days.   (*Exit.*)
KING (*rising*):   My words fly up, my thoughts remain below:
Words without thoughts never to heaven go.   (*Exit.*)

---

64. rests: remains.   **68. limed:** caught as with birdlime.   **69. engag'd:** embedded.   **69. assay:** trial.
73. pat: opportunely.   **75. would be scann'd:** needs to be looked into   **80. full of bread:** enjoying his
worldly pleasures (see Ezekiel 16:49).   **81. broad blown:** in full bloom.   **81. flush:** lusty.   **83. in . . .
course:** as we see it in our mortal situation.   **86. fit . . . passage:** i.e., reconciled to heaven by forgiveness of his sins.   **88. heat:** seizing; or more probably, occasion of seizure.   **89. drunk asleep:** in a
drunken sleep.   **96. physic:** purging (by prayer)

SCENE IV

(*The Queen's closet.*)

(*Enter* [QUEEN] GERTRUDE *and* POLONIUS.)

POLONIUS: 'A will come straight. Look you lay° home to him:
Tell him his pranks have been too broad° to bear with,
And that your grace hath screen'd and stood between
Much heat° and him. I'll sconce° me even here.
Pray you, be round° with him.   5
HAMLET (*within*):   Mother, mother, mother!
QUEEN: I'll warrant you,
Fear me not: withdraw, I hear him coming.

(POLONIUS *hides behind the arras.*)

(*Enter* HAMLET.)

HAMLET: Now, mother, what's the matter?
QUEEN: Hamlet, thou hast thy father much offended.
HAMLET: Mother, you have my father° much offended.   10
QUEEN: Come, come, you answer with an idle tongue.
HAMLET: Go, go, you question with a wicked tongue.
QUEEN: Why, how now, Hamlet!
HAMLET: What's the matter now?
QUEEN: Have you forgot me?
HAMLET: No, by the rood,° not so: 15
You are the queen, your husband's brother's wife;
And—would it were not so!—you are my mother.
QUEEN: Nay, then, I'll set those to you that can speak.
HAMLET: Come, come, and sit you down; you shall not budge;
You go not till I set you up a glass   20
Where you may see the inmost part of you.
QUEEN: What wilt thou do? thou wilt not murder me?
Help, help, ho!
POLONIUS (*behind*):   What, ho! help, help; help!
HAMLET (*drawing*):   How now! a rat? Dead, for a ducat, dead!

(*Makes a pass through the arras.*)
                                                                                               25
POLONIUS (*behind*):   O, I am slain! (*Falls and dies.*)
QUEEN: O me, what hast thou done?
HAMLET: Nay, I know not:

III.iv. **1. lay:** thrust.   **2. broad:** unrestrained.   **4. Much heat:** i.e., the king's anger.   **4. sconce:** hide.
5. round: blunt.   **9–10. thy father . . . my father:** i.e., Claudius, the elder Hamlet.   **14. rood:** cross.

Is it the king?

QUEEN: O, what a rash and bloody deed is this!

HAMLET: A bloody deed! almost as bad, good mother,
As kill a king, and marry with his brother.   30

QUEEN: As kill a king!

HAMLET: Ay, lady, it was my word.

(Lifts up the arras and discovers POLONIUS.)

Thou wretched, rash, intruding fool, farewell!
I took thee for thy better: take thy fortune;
Thou find'st to be too busy is some danger.
Leave wringing of your hands: peace! sit you down,   35
And let me wring your heart; for so I shall,
If it be made of penetrable stuff,
If damned custom have not braz'd° it so
That it be proof and bulwark against sense.

QUEEN: What have I done, that thou dar'st wag thy tongue   40
In noise so rude against me?

HAMLET: Such an act
That blurs the grace and blush of modesty,
Calls virtue hypocrite, takes off the rose
From the fair forehead of an innocent love
And sets a blister° there, makes marriage-vows   45
As false as dicers' oaths: O, such a deed
As from the body of contraction° plucks
The very soul, and sweet religion° makes
A rhapsody° of words: heaven's face does glow
O'er this solidity and compound mass   50
With heated visage, as against the doom
Is thought-sick at the act.°

QUEEN: Ay me, what act,
That roars so loud, and thunders in the index?°

HAMLET: Look here, upon this picture, and on this.
The counterfeit presentment° of two brothers.   55
See, what a grace was seated on this brow;
Hyperion's° curls; the front° of Jove himself;
An eye Mars, to threaten and command;
A station° like the herald Mercury
New-lightned on a heaven-kissing hill;   60

---

38. braz'd: brazened, hardened.   **45. sets a blister:** brands as a harlot.   **47. contraction:** the marriage contract.   **48. religion:** religious vows.   **49. rhapsody:** senseless string.   **49–52. heaven's . . . act:** heaven's face blushes to look down upon this world, compounded of the four elements, with hot face as though the day of doom were near, and thought-sick at the deed (i.e., Gertrude's marriage).   **53. index:** prelude or preface.   **55. counterfeit presentment:** portrayed representation.   **57. Hyperion's:** the sun god's.   **57. front:** brow.   **59. station:** manner of standing.

A combination and form indeed,
Where every god did seem to set his seal,
To give the world assurance° of a man:
This was your husband. Look you now, what follows:
Here is your husband; like a mildew'd ear,° 65
Blasting his wholesome brother. Have you eyes?
Could you on this fair mountain leave to feed,
And batten° on this moor?° Ha! have you eyes?
You cannot call it love; for at your age
The hey-day° in the blood is tame, it's humble, 70
And waits upon the judgment: and what judgment
Would step from this to this? Sense, sure, you have,
Else could you not have motion,° but sure, that sense
Is apoplex'd° for madness would not err.
Nor sense to ecstasy was ne'er so thrall'd° 75
But it reserv'd some quantity of choice,°
To serve in such a difference. What devil was't
Tha thus hath cozen'd° you at hoodman-blind?°
Eyes without feeling, feeling without sight,
Ears without hands or eyes, smelling sans° all, 80
Or but a sickly part of one true sense
Could not so mope.°
O shame! where is thy blush? Rebellious hell,
If thou canst mutine° in a matron's bones.
To flaming youth let virtue be as wax, 85
And melt in her own fire: proclaim no shame
When the compulsive ardor gives the charge,°
Since frost itself as actively doth burn
And reason panders will.°
QUEEN: O Hamlet, speak no more:
Thou turn'st mine eyes into my very soul; 90
And there I see such black and grained° spots
As will not leave their tinct.
HAMLET: Nay, but to live
In the rank sweat of an enseamed° bed,

---

63. assurance: pledge, guarantee.   **65. mildew'd ear:** see Genesis 41:5–7.   **68. batten:** grow fat.
68. moor: barren upland.   **70. hey-day:** state of excitement.   **72–73. Sense . . . motion:** sense and
motion are functions of the middle or sensible soul, the possession of sense being the basis of motion.
74. apoplex'd: paralyzed; mental derangement was thus of three sorts: apoplexy, ecstasy, and diabolic
possession.   **75. thrall'd:** enslaved.   **76. quantity of choice:** fragment of the power to choose.
78. cozen'd: tricked, cheated.   **78. hoodman-blind:** blindman's buff.   **80. sans:** without.   **82. mope:**
be in a depressed, spiritless state, act aimlessly.   **84. mutine:** mutiny, rebel.   **87. gives the charge:**
delivers the attack.   **89. reason panders will:** the normal and proper situation was one in which reason
guided the will in the direction of good; here, reason is perverted and leads in the direction of evil.
91. grained: dyed in grain.   **93. enseamed:** loaded with grease, greased.

Stew'd in corruption, honeying and making love
Over the nasty sty,—

QUEEN: O, speak to me no more;   95
These words, like daggers, enter in mine ears;
No more, sweet Hamlet!

HAMLET: A murderer and a villain:
A slave that is not twentieth part the tithe
Of your precedent lord°; a vice of kings°;
A cutpurse of the empire and the rule,   100
That from a shelf the precious diadem stole,
And put it in his pocket!

QUEEN: No more!

(Enter GHOST.*)*

HAMLET: A king of shreds and patches,°—
Save me, and hover o'er me with your wings,
You heavenly guards! What would your gracious figure?   105

QUEEN: Alas, he's mad!

HAMLET: Do you not come your tardy son to chide,
That, laps'd in time and passion,° lets go by
Th' important° acting of your dread command?
O, say!   110

GHOST: Do not forget: this visitation
Is but to whet thy almost blunted purpose.
But, look, amazement° on thy mother sits:
O, step between her and her fighting soul:
Conceit in weakest bodies strongest works: 115
Speak to her, Hamlet.

HAMLET: How is it with you, lady?

QUEEN: Alas, how is 't with you,
That you do bend your eye on vacancy
And with th' incorporal° air do hold discourse?
Forth at your eyes your spirits wildly peep;   120
And, as the sleeping soldiers in th' alarm,
Your bedded° hair, like life in excrements,°
Start up, and stand an° end. O gentle son,
Upon the heat and flame of thy distemper
Sprinkle cool patience. Whereon do you look?   125

99. precedent lord: i.e., the elder Hamlet.   **99. vice of kings:** buffoon of kings; a reference to the Vice, or clown, of the morality plays and interludes.   **103. shreds and patches:** i.e., motley, the traditional costume of the Vice.   **108. laps'd . . . passion:** having suffered time to slip and passion to cool; also explained as "engrossed in casual events and lapsed into mere fruitless passion, so that he no longer entertains a rational purpose."   **109. important:** urgent.   **113. amazement:** frenzy, distraction. **119. incorporal:** immaterial.   **122. bedded:** laid in smooth layers.   **122. excrements:** the hair was considered an excrement or voided part of the body.   **123. an:** on.

HAMLET: On him, on him! Look you, how pale he glares!
His form and cause conjoin'd,° preaching to stones,
Would make them capable.—Do not look upon me;
Lest with this piteous action you convert
My stern effects°: then what I have to do   130
Will want true colour°; tears perchance for blood.
QUEEN: To whom do you speak this?
HAMLET: Do you see nothing there?
QUEEN: Nothing at all; yet all that is I see.
HAMLET: Nor did you nothing hear?
QUEEN: No, nothing but ourselves.
HAMLET: Why, look you there! look, how it steals away!   135
My father, in his habit as he liv'd!
Look, where he goes, even now, out at the portal!   (*Exit* GHOST.)
QUEEN: This is the very coinage of your brain:
This bodiless creation ecstasy
Is very cunning in.
HAMLET: Ecstasy!   140
My pulse, as yours, doth temperately keep time,
And makes as healthful music; it is not madness
That I have utt'red: bring me to the test,
And I the matter will re-word,° which madness
Would gambol° from. Mother, for love of grace,   145
Lay not that flattering unction° to your soul,
That not your trespass, but my madness speaks:
It will but skin and film the ulcerous place,
Whiles rank corruption, mining° all within,
Infects unseen. Confess yourself to heaven;   150
Repent what's past; avoid what is to come°;
And do not spread the compost° on the weeds,
To make them ranker. Forgive me this my virtue°;
For in the fatness° of these pursy° times
Virtue itself of vice must pardon beg,   155
Yea, curb° and woo for leave to do him good.
QUEEN: O Hamlet, thou hast cleft my heart in twain.
HAMLET: O, throw away the worser part of it,
And live the purer with the other half.

---

127. **conjoin'd:** united.   129–30. **convert . . . effects:** divert me from my stern duty. For effects, possibly affects (affections of the mind).   131. **want true colour:** lack good reason so that (with a play on the normal sense of colour) I shall shed tears instead of blood.   144. **re-word:** repeat in words.   145. **gambol:** skip away.   146. **unction:** ointment used medicinally or as a rite; suggestion that forgiveness for sin may not be so easily achieved.   149. **mining:** working under the surface.   151. **what is to come:** i.e., the sins of the future.   152. **compost:** manure.   153. **this my virtue:** my virtuous talk in reproving you. 154. **fatness:** grossness.   154. **pursy:** short-winded, corpulent.   156. **curb:** bow, bend the knee.

Good night: but go not to my uncle's bed; 160
Assume a virtue, if you have it not.
That monster, custom, who all sense doth eat,
Of habits devil, is angel yet in this,
That to the use of actions fair and good
He likewise gives a frock or livery, 165
That aptly is put on. Refrain to-night,
And that shall lend a kind of easiness
To the next abstinence: the next more easy;
For use almost can change the stamp of nature,
And either . . . the devil, or throw him out° 170
With wondrous potency. Once more, good night:
And when you are desirous to be bless'd,°
I'll blessing beg of you. For this same lord, (*Pointing to* POLONIUS.)
I do repent: but heaven hath pleas'd it so,
To punish me with this and this with me, 175
That I must be their scourge and minister.
I will bestow him, and will answer well
The death I gave him. So, again, good night.
I must be cruel, only to be kind:
Thus bad begins and worse remains behind. 180
One word more, good lady.
QUEEN: What shall I do?
HAMLET: Not this, by no means, that I bid you do:
Let the bloat° king tempt you again to bed;
Pinch wanton on your cheek; call you his mouse;
And let him, for a pair of reechy° kisses, 185
Or paddling in your neck with his damn'd fingers,
Make you to ravel all this matter out,
That I essentially° am not in madness,
But mad in craft. 'Twere good you let him know;
For who, that's but a queen, fair, sober, wise, 190
Would from a paddock,° from a bat, a gib,°
Such dear concernings° hide? who would do so?
No, in despite of sense and secrecy,
Unpeg the basket on the house's top,
Let the birds fly, and like the famous ape,° 195
To try conclusions,° in the basket creep,

---

170. defective line usually emended by inserting *master* after *either*.   **172. be bless'd:** become blessed,
i.e., repentant.   **183. bloat:** bloated.   **185. reechy:** dirty, filthy.   **188. essentially:** in my essential
nature.   **191. paddock:** toad.   **191. gib:** tomcat.   **192. dear concernings:** important affairs.   **195.
the famous ape:** a letter from Sir John Suckling seems to supply other details of the story, otherwise not
identified: "It is the story of the jackanapes and the partridges; thou starest after a beauty till it be lost to
thee, then let'st out another, and starest after that till it is gone too."   **196. conclusions:** experiments.

And break your own neck down.
QUEEN: Be thou assur'd, if words be made of breath,
And breath of life, I have no life to breathe
What thou hast said to me.   200
HAMLET: I must to England; you know that?
QUEEN: Alack,
I had forgot: 'tis so concluded on.
HAMLET: There's letters seal'd: and my two schoolfellows,
Whom I will trust as I will adders fang'd,
They bear the mandate; they must sweep my way,°   205
And marshal me to knavery. Let it work;
For 'tis the sport to have the enginer°
Hoist° with his own petar°: and 't shall go hard
But I will delve one yard below their mines,
And blow them at the moon: O, 'tis most sweet,   210
When in one line two crafts° directly meet.
This man shall set me packing°:
I'll lug the guts into the neighbour room.
Mother, good night. Indeed this counsellor
Is now most still, most secret and most grave,   215
Who was in life a foolish prating knave.
Come, sir, to draw° toward an end with you.
Good night, mother.
                      (*Exeunt* [*severally;* HAMLET *dragging in* POLONIUS].)

ACT IV

SCENE I

(*A room in the castle*)

(*Enter* KING *and* QUEEN, *with* ROSENCRANTZ *and* GUILDENSTERN.)

KING: There's matter in these sighs, these profound heaves;
You must translate: 'tis fit we understand them.
Where is your son?
QUEEN: Bestow this place on us a little while.
                      (*Exeunt* ROSENCRANTZ *and* GUILDENSTERN.)
Ah, mine own lord, what have I seen to-night!   5

---

205. sweep my way: clear my path.   **207. enginer:** constructor of military works, or possibly, artillery-man.   **208. Hoist:** blown up.   **208. petar:** defined as a small engine of war used to blow in a door or make a breach, and as a case filled with explosive materials.   **211. two crafts:** two acts of guile, with quibble on the sense of "two ships."   **212. set me packing:** set me to making schemes, and set me to lugging (him), and, also, send me off in a hurry.   **217. draw:** come, with quibble on literal sense.

KING: What, Gertrude? How does Hamlet?
QUEEN: Mad as the sea and wind, when both contend
    Which is the mightier: in his lawless fit,
    Behind the arras hearing something stir,
    Whips out his rapier, cries, "A rat, a rat!"   10
    And, in this brainish° apprehension,° kills
    The unseen good old man.
KING: O heavy deed!
    It had been so with us, had we been there:
    His liberty is full of threats to all;
    To you yourself, to us, to every one.   15
    Alas, how shall this bloody deed be answer'd?
    It will be laid to us, whose providence°
    Should have kept short,° restrain'd and out of haunt,°
    This mad young man: but so much was our love,
    We would not understand what was most fit;   20
    But, like the owner of a foul disease,
    To keep it from divulging,° let it feed
    Even on the pith of life. Where is he gone?
QUEEN: To draw apart the body he hath kill'd:
    O'er whom his very madness, like some ore   25
    Among a mineral° of metals base,
    Shows itself pure; 'a weeps for what is done.
KING: O Gertrude, come away!
    The sun no sooner shall the mountains touch,
    But we will ship him hence: and this vile deed   30
    We must, with all our majesty and skill,
    Both countenance and excuse. Ho, Guildenstern!

(*Enter* ROSENCRANTZ *and* GUILDENSTERN.)

    Friends both, go join you with some further aid:
    Hamlet in madness hath Polonius slain,
    And from his mother's closet hath he dragg'd him: 35
    Go seek him out; speak fair, and bring the body
    Into the chapel. I pray you, haste in this.

(*Exeunt* ROSENCRANTZ *and* GUILDENSTERN.)

    Come, Gertrude, we'll call up our wisest friends;
    And let them know, both what we mean to do,
    And what's untimely done . . .°   40

IV.i. 11. brainish: headstrong, passionate.   **11. apprehension:** conception, imagination.   **17. providence:** foresight.   **18. short:** i.e., on a short tether.   **18. out of haunt:** secluded.   **22. divulging:** becoming evident.   **26. mineral:** mine.   **40.** defective line; some editors add: *so haply, slander*; others add: *for, haply, slander*; other conjectures.

Whose whisper o'er the world's diameter,°
As level° as the cannon to his blank,°
Transports his pois'ned shot, may miss our name,
And hit the woundless° air. O, come away!
My soul is full of discord and dismay.   (*Exeunt.*)   45

SCENE II

(*Another room in the castle.*)

(*Enter* HAMLET.)

HAMLET: Safely stowed.

ROSENCRANTZ
                    } (*within*):   Hamlet! Lord Hamlet!
GUILDENSTERN

HAMLET: But soft, what noise? Who calls on Hamlet? O, here they come.

(*Enter* ROSENCRANTZ *and* GUILDENSTERN.)

ROSENCRANTZ: What have you done, my lord, with the dead body?
HAMLET: Compounded it with dust, whereto 'tis kin.
ROSENCRANTZ: Tell us where 'tis, that we may take it thence   5
    And bear it to the chapel.
HAMLET: Do not believe it.
ROSENCRANTZ: Believe what?
HAMLET: That I can keep your counsel° and not mine own. Besides, to be
    demanded of a sponge! What replication° should be made by the son of a king?   10
ROSENCRANTZ: Take you me for a sponge, my lord?
HAMLET: Ay, sir, that soaks up the king's countenance, his rewards, his authorities.°
    But such officers do the king best service in the end: he keeps them, like an ape
    an apple, in the corner of his jaw; first mouthed, to be last swallowed: when he
    needs what you have gleaned, it is but squeezing you, and, sponge, you shall be   15
    dry again.
ROSENCRANTZ: I understand you not, my lord.
HAMLET: I am glad of it: a knavish speech sleeps in a foolish ear.
ROSENCRANTZ: My lord, you must tell us where the body is, and go with us to the
    king.   20
HAMLET: The body is with the king, but the king is not with the body.° The king is
    a thing—

---

41. diameter: extent from side to side.   **42. level:** straight.   **42. blank:** white spot in the center of a target.   **44. woundless:** invulnerable.   **IV.ii. 9. keep your counsel:** Hamlet is aware of their treachery but says nothing about it.   **10. replication:** reply.   **12. authorities:** authoritative backing.   **21. The body . . . body:** there are many interpretations; possibly, "The body lies in death with the king, my father; but my father walks disembodied"; or "Claudius has the bodily possession of kingship, but kingliness, or justice of inheritance, is not with him."

GUILDENSTERN: A thing, my lord!

HAMLET: Of nothing: bring me to him. Hide fox, and all after.°   (*Exeunt.*)

SCENE III

(*Another room in the castle.*)

(*Enter* KING, *and two or three.*)

KING: I have sent to seek him, and to find the body.
How dangerous is it that this man goes loose!
Yet must not we put the strong law on him:
He's lov'd of the distracted° multitude,
Who like not in their judgement, but their eyes;   5
And where 'tis so, th' offender's scourge° is weigh'd,°
But never the offence. To bear all smooth and even,
This sudden sending him away must seem
Deliberate pause°: diseases desperate grown
By desperate appliance are reliev'd,   10
Or not at all.

(*Enter* ROSENCRANTZ, [GUILDENSTERN,] *and all the rest.*)

          How now! what hath befall'n?

ROSENCRANTZ: Where the dead body is bestow'd, my lord,
We cannot get from him.

KING: But where is he?

ROSENCRANTZ: Without, my lord; guarded, to know your pleasure.

KING: Bring him before us.   15

ROSENCRANTZ: Ho! bring in the lord.

(*They enter* [with HAMLET].)

KING: Now, Hamlet, where's Polonius?

HAMLET: At supper.

KING: At supper! where?

Hamlet: Not where he eats, but where 'a is eaten: a certain convocation of politic°   20
worms° are e'en at him. Your worm is your only emperor for diet: we fat all
creatures else to fat us, and we fat ourselves for maggots: your fat king and your
lean beggar is but variable service,° two dishes, but to one table: that's the end.

KING: Alas, alas!

---

24. Hide . . . after: an old signal cry in the game of hide-and-seek.   **IV.iii. 4. distracted:** i.e., without power of forming logical judgments.   **6. scourge:** punishment.   **6. weigh'd:** taken into consideration.   **9. Deliberate pause:** considered action.   **20–21. convocation . . . worms:** allusion to the Diet of Worms (1521).   **20. politic:** crafty.   **23. variable service:** a variety of dishes.

HAMLET: A man may fish with the worm that hath eat of a king, and eat of the fish   25
    that hath fed of that worm.

KING: What dost thou mean by this?

HAMLET: Nothing but to show you how a king may go a progress° through the
    guts of a beggar.

KING: Where is Polonius?   30

HAMLET: In heaven; send thither to see: if your messenger find him not there, seek
    him i' the other place yourself. But if indeed you find him not within this
    month, you shall nose him as you go up the stairs into the lobby.

KING (*to some* ATTENDANTS):   Go seek him there.

HAMLET: 'A will stay till you come.   (*Exeunt* ATTENDANTS.)   35

KING: Hamlet, this deed, for thine especial safety,—
    Which we do tender,° as we dearly grieve
    For that which thou hast done,—must send thee hence
    With fiery quickness: therefore prepare thyself;
    The bark is ready, and the wind at help,   40
    Th' associates tend, and everything is bent
    For England.

HAMLET: For England!

KING: Ay, Hamlet.

HAMLET: Good.

KING: So is it, if thou knew'st our purposes.

HAMLET: I see a cherub° that sees them. But, come; for England! Farewell, dear
    mother.   45

KING: Thy loving father, Hamlet.

HAMLET: My mother; father and mother is man and wife; man and wife is one
    flesh; and so, my mother. Come, for England!   (*Exit.*)

KING: Follow him at foot°; tempt him with speed aboard;
    Delay it not; I'll have him hence to-night: 50
    Away! for every thing is seal'd and done
    That else leans on th' affair: pray you, make haste.

                    (*Exeunt all but the* KING.)

    And, England, if my love thou hold'st at aught—
    As my great power thereof may give thee sense,
    Since yet thy cicatrice° looks raw and red   55
    After the Danish sword, and thy free awe°
    Pays homage to us—thou mayst not coldly set
    Our sovereign process; which imports at full,
    By letters congruing to that effect,
    The present death of Hamlet. Do it, England;   60
    For like the hectic° in my blood he rages,

---

28. progress: royal journey of state.   **37. tender:** regard, hold dear.   **44. cherub:** cherubim are angels
of knowledge.   **49. at foot:** close behind, at heel.   **55. cicatrice:** scar.   **56. free awe:** voluntary show
of respect.   **61. hectic:** fever.

And thou must cure me; till I know 'tis done,
Howe'er my haps,° my joys were ne'er begun.   (*Exit.*)

SCENE IV

(*A plain in Denmark.*)

(*Enter* FORTINBRAS *with his Army over the stage.*)

FORTINBRAS: Go, captain, from me greet the Danish king;
Tell him that, by his license,° Fortinbras
Craves the conveyance° of a promis'd march
Over his kingdom. You know the rendezvous.
If that his majesty would aught with us,   5
We shall express our duty in his eye°;
And let him know so.
CAPTAIN: I will do't, my lord.
FORTINBRAS: Go softly° on.   (*Exeunt all but* CAPTAIN.)

(*Enter* HAMLET, ROSENCRANTZ, [GUILDENSTERN,] &c.)

HAMLET: Good sir, whose powers are these?   10
CAPTAIN: They are of Norway, sir.
HAMLET: How purpos'd, sir, I pray you?
CAPTAIN: Against some part of Poland.
HAMLET: Who commands them, sir?
CAPTAIN: The nephew to old Norway, Fortinbras.   15
HAMLET: Goes it against the main° of Poland, sir,
Or for some frontier?
CAPTAIN: Truly to speak, and with no addition,
We go to gain a little patch of ground
That hath in it no profit but the name.   20
To pay five ducats, five, I would not farm it°;
Nor will it yield to Norway or the Pole
A ranker rate, should it be sold in fee.°
HAMLET: Why, then the Polack never will defend it.
CAPTAIN: Yes, it is already garrison'd.   25
HAMLET: Two thousand souls and twenty thousand ducats
Will not debate the question of this straw°;
This is th'imposthume° of much wealth and peace,
That inward breaks, and shows no cause without
Why the man dies. I humbly thank you, sir.   30

---

63. haps: fortunes.   **IV.iv. 2. license:** leave.   **3. conveyance:** escort, convey.   **6. in his eye:** in his presence.   **9. softly:** slowly.   **16. main:** country itself.   **21. farm it:** take a lease of it.   **23. fee:** fee simple.   **27. debate . . . straw:** settle this trifling matter.   **28. imposthume:** purulent abscess or swelling.

CAPTAIN: God be wi' you, sir.   (*Exit.*)
ROSENCRANTZ: Will 't please you go, my lord?
HAMLET: I'll be with you straight. Go a little before.

(*Exeunt all except* HAMLET.)

How all occasions° do inform against° me,
And spur my dull revenge! What is a man,
If his chief good and market of his time°   35
Be but to sleep and feed? a beast, no more.
Sure, he that made us with such large discourse,
Looking before and after, gave us not
That capability and god-like reason
To fust° in us unus'd. Now, whether it be   40
Bestial oblivion, or some craven scruple
Of thinking too precisely on th' event,
A thought which, quarter'd, hath but one part wisdom
And ever three parts coward, I do not know
Why yet I live to say "This thing's to do";   45
Sith I have cause and will and strength and means
To do 't. Examples gross as earth exhort me:
Witness this army of such mass and charge
Led by a delicate and tender prince,
Whose spirit with divine ambition puff'd   50
Makes mouths at the invisible event,
Exposing what is mortal and unsure
To all that fortune, death and danger dare,
Even for an egg-shell. Rightly to be great
Is not to stir without great argument,   55
But greatly to find quarrel in a straw
When honour's at the stake. How stand I then,
That have a father kill'd, a mother stain'd,
Excitements of° my reason and my blood,
And let all sleep? while, to my shame, I see   60
The imminent death of twenty thousand men,
That, for a fantasy and trick° of fame,
Go to their graves like beds, fight for a plot°
Whereon the numbers cannot try the cause,
Which is not tomb enough and continent   65
To hide the slain? O, from this time forth,
My thoughts be bloody, or be nothing worth!   (*Exit.*)

---

33. occasions: incidents, events.   **33. inform against:** generally defined as "show," "betray" (i.e., his tardiness); more probably *inform* means "take shape," as in *Macbeth*, II.i.48.   **35. market of his time:** the best use he makes of his time, or, that for which he sells his time.   **40. fust:** grow moldy.   **59. Excitements of:** incentives to.   **62. trick:** toy, trifle,   **63. plot:** i.e., of ground.

SCENE V

(*Elsinore. A room in the castle.*)

(*Enter* HORATIO, [QUEEN] GERTRUDE, *and a* GENTLEMAN.)

QUEEN:	I will not speak with her.
GENTLEMAN:	She is importunate, indeed distract;

Her mood will needs be pitied.

QUEEN: What would she have?

GENTLEMAN: She speaks much of her father; says she hears
  There's tricks° i' th' world; and hems, and beats her heart°;   5
  Spurns enviously at straws°; speaks things in doubt,
  That carry but half sense: her speech is nothing,
  Yet the unshaped° use of it doth move
  The hearers to collection°; they yawn° at it,
  And botch° the words up fit to their own thoughts;   10
  Which, as her winks, and nods, and gestures yield° them,
  Indeed would make one think there might be thought,
  Though nothing sure, yet much unhappily.°

HORATIO: 'Twere good she were spoken with: for she may strew
  Dangerous conjectures in ill-breeding minds.°   15

QUEEN: Let her come in.   (*Exit* GENTLEMAN.)
  (*Aside.*) To my sick soul, as sin's true nature is,
  Each toy seems prologue to some great amiss°:
  So full of artless jealousy is guilt,
  It spills itself in fearing to be spilt.°   20

(*Enter* OPHELIA [*distracted*].)

OPHELIA: Where is the beauteous majesty of Denmark?

QUEEN: How now, Ophelia!

OPHELIA (*she sings*):   How should I your true love know
    From another one?
  By his cockle hat° and staff,   25
    And his sandal shoon.°

QUEEN: Alas, sweet lady, what imports this song?

IV.v. 5. tricks: deceptions.   **5. heart:** i.e., breast.   **6. Spurns . . . straws:** kicks spitefully at small objects in her path.   **8. unshaped:** unformed, artless.   **9. collection:** inference, a guess at some sort of meaning.   **9. yawn:** wonder.   **10. botch:** patch.   **11. yield:** deliver, bring forth (her words).   **13. much unhappily:** expressive of much unhappiness.   **15. ill-breeding minds:** minds bent on mischief.   **18. great amiss:** calamity, disaster.   **19–20. So . . . split:** guilt is so full of suspicion that it unskillfully betrays itself in fearing to be betrayed   **25. cockle hat:** hat with cockleshell stuck in it as a sign that the wearer has been a pilgrim to the shrine of St. James of Compostella; the pilgrim's garb was a conventional disguise for lovers.   **26. shoon:** shoes.

OPHELIA: Say you? nay, pray you mark.
  (*Song*) He is dead and gone, lady,
      He is dead and gone;   30
  At his head a grass-green turf,
      At his heels a stone.
  O, ho!
QUEEN: Nay, but, Ophelia—
OPHELIA: Pray you, mark   35
  (*Sings*.)   White his shroud as the mountain snow,—

            (*Enter* KING.)

QUEEN: Alas, look here, my lord.
OPHELIA (*Song*):   Larded° all with flowers;
  Which bewept to the grave did not go
      With true-love showers.   40
KING: How do you, pretty lady?
OPHELIA: Well, God 'ild° you! They say the owl° was a baker's daughter. Lord, we
  know what we are, but know not what we may be. God be at your table!
KING: Conceit upon her father.
OPHELIA: Pray let's have no words of this; but when they ask you what it means, say   45
  you this:
  (*Song*) To-morrow is Saint Valentine's day.
      All in the morning betime,
  And I a maid at your window,
      To be your Valentine.°   50
  Then up he rose, and donn'd his clothes,
      And dupp'd° the chamber-door;
  Let in the maid, that out a maid
      Never departed more.
KING: Pretty Ophelia!   55
OPHELIA: Indeed, la, without an oath, I'll make an end on 't:
  (*Sings*.) By Gis° and by Saint Charity,
      Alack, and fie for shame!
  Young men will do 't, if they come to 't;
      By cock,° they are to blame.   60
  Quoth she, before you tumbled me,
      You promis'd me to wed.
  So would I ha' done, by yonder sun,
      An thou hadst not come to my bed.
KING: How long hath she been thus?   65

---

38. Larded: decorated.   **42. God 'ild:** god yield or reward.   **42. owl:** reference to a monkish legend
that a baker's daughter was turned into an owl for refusing bread to the Savior.   **50. Valentine:** this
song alludes to the belief that the first girl seen by a man on the morning of this day was his valentine or
true love.   **52. dupp'd:** opened.   **57. Gis:** Jesus.   **60. cock:** perversion of "God" in oaths.

OPHELIA: I hope all will be well. We must be patient: but I cannot choose but
weep, to think they would lay him i' the cold ground. My brother shall know of
it: and so I thank you for your good counsel. Come, my coach! Good night,
ladies; good night, sweet ladies; good night, good night.   (*Exit.*)

KING: Follow her close; give her good watch, I pray you.   (*Exit* HORATIO.)   70
O, this is the poison of deep grief; it springs
All from her father's death. O Gertrude, Gertrude,
When sorrows come, they come not single spies,
But in battalions. First, her father slain:
Next your son gone; and he most violent author   75
Of his own just remove: the people muddied,
Thick and unwholesome in their thoughts and whispers,
For good Polonius' death; and we have done but greenly,°
In hugger-mugger° to inter him; poor Ophelia
Divided from herself and her fair judgement,   80
Without the which we are pictures, or mere beasts:
Last, and as much containing as all these,
Her brother is in secret come from France,
Feeds on his wonder, keeps himself in clouds,°
And wants not buzzers° to infect his ear   85
With pestilent speeches of his father's death;
Wherein necessity, of matter beggar'd,°
Will nothing stick° our person to arraign
In ear and ear.° O my dear Gertrude, this,
Like to a murd'ring-piece,° in many places   90
Gives me superfluous death. (*A noise within.*)

QUEEN: Alack, what noise is this?

KING: Where are my Switzers?° Let them guard the door.

          (*Enter a* MESSENGER.)

What is the matter?

MESSENGER: Save yourself, my lord:
The ocean, overpeering° of his list,°
Eats not the flats with more impiteous haste   95
Than young Laertes, in a riotous head,
O'erbears your officers. The rabble call him lord;
And, as the world were now but to begin,
Antiquity forgot, custom not known,
The ratifiers and props of every word,°   100

---

78. greenly: foolishly.   **79. hugger-mugger:** secret haste.   **84. in clouds:** invisible.   **85. buzzers:**
gossipers.   **87. of matter beggar'd:** unprovided with facts.   **88. nothing stick:** not hesitate.   **89. In
ear and ear:** in everybody's ears.   **90. murd'ring-piece:** small cannon or mortar; suggestion of numerous missiles fired.   **92. Switzers:** Swiss guards, mercenaries.   **94. overpeering:** overflowing.   **94. list:**
shore.   **100. word:** promise.

They cry "Choose we: Laertes shall be king":
Caps, hands, and tongues, applaud it to the clouds:
"Laertes shall be king, Laertes king!" (*A noise within.*)

QUEEN: How cheerfully on the false trail they cry!
O, this is counter,° you false Danish dogs!   105

KING: The doors are broke.

(*Enter* LAERTES *with others.*)

LAERTES: Where is this king? Sirs, stand you all without.

DANES: No, let's come in.

LAERTES: I pray you, give me leave.

DANES: We will, we will.   (*They retire without the door.*)

LAERTES: I thank you: keep the door. O thou vile king,   110
Give me my father!

QUEEN: Calmly, good Laertes.

LAERTES: That drop of blood that's calm proclaims me bastard,
Cries cuckold to my father, brands the harlot
Even here, between the chaste unsmirched brow
Of my true mother.   115

KING: What is the cause, Laertes,
That thy rebellion looks so giant-like?
Let him go, Gertrude; do not fear our person:
There's such divinity doth hedge a king,
That treason can but peep to° what it would,°   120
Acts little of his will. Tell me, Laertes,
Why thou art thus incens'd. Let him go, Gertrude.
Speak, man.

LAERTES: Where is my father?

KING: Dead.

QUEEN: But not by him.

KING: Let him demand his fill.   125

LAERTES: How came he dead? I'll not be juggled with:
To hell, allegiance! vows, to the blackest devil!
Conscience and grace, to the profoundest pit!
I dare damnation. To this point I stand,
That both the worlds I give to negligence,°   130
Let come what comes; only I'll be reveng'd
Most throughly° for my father.

KING: Who shall stay you?

LAERTES: My will,° not all the world's:

---

105. counter: a hunting term meaning to follow the trail in a direction opposite to that which the game has taken.   **120. peep to:** i.e., look at from afar off.   **120. would:** wishes to do.   **130. give to negligence:** he despises both the here and the hereafter.   **132. throughly:** thoroughly.   **133. My will:** he will not be stopped except by his own will.

And for my means, I'll husband them so well,
They shall go far with little.
KING: Good Laertes,   135
If you desire to know the certainty
Of your dear father, is 't writ in your revenge,
That, swoopstake,° you will draw both friend and foe,
Winner and loser?
LAERTES: None but his enemies.
KING: Will you know them then?   140
LAERTES: To his good friends thus wide I'll ope my arms;
And like the kind life-rend'ring pelican,°
Repast° them with my blood.
KING: Why, now you speak
Like a good child and a true gentleman.
That I am guiltless of your father's death,   145
And am most sensibly in grief for it,
It shall as level to your judgment 'pear
As day does to your eye.

> (*A noise within: "Let her come in."*)

LAERTES: How now! what noise is that?

> (*Enter* OPHELIA.)

O heat,° dry up my brains! tears seven times salt,   150
Burn out the sense and virtue of mine eye!
By heaven, thy madness shall be paid with weight,
Till our scale turn the beam. O rose of May!
Dear maid, kind sister, sweet Ophelia!
O heavens! is 't possible, a young maid's wits   155
Should be as mortal as an old man's life?
Nature is fine in love, and where 'tis fine,
It sends some precious instance of itself
After the thing it loves.
OPHELIA (*Song*):   They bore him barefac'd on the bier;   160
Hey non nonny, nonny, hey nonny;
And in his grave rain'd many a tear:—
Fare you well, my dove!
LAERTES: Hadst thou thy wits, and didst persuade revenge,
It could not move thus.   165
OPHELIA (*sings*):   You must sing a-down a-down,
An you call him a-down-a.

---

138. swoopstake: literally, drawing the whole stake at once, i.e., indiscriminately.   **142. pelican:** reference to the belief that the pelican feeds its young with its own blood.   **143. Repast:** feed.   **150. heat:** probably the heat generated by the passion of grief.

O, how the wheel° becomes it! It is the false steward,° that stole his master's
daughter.

LAERTES: This nothing's more than matter.   170

OPHELIA: There's rosemary,° that's for remembrance; pray you, love, remember:
and there is pansies,° that's for thoughts.

LAERTES: A document° in madness, thoughts and remembrance fitted.

OPHELIA: There's fennel° for you, and columbines°: there's rue° for you; and here's
some for me: we may call it herb of grace o' Sundays: O, you must wear your   175
rue with a difference. There's a daisy°: I would give you some violets,° but they
withered all when my father died: they say 'a made a good end,—
(*Sings*.) For bonny sweet Robin is all my joy.°

LAERTES: Thought° and affliction, passion, hell itself,
She turns to favour and to prettiness.   180

OPHELIA (*Song*):   And will 'a not come again?°
And will 'a not come again?
No, no, he is dead:
Go to thy death-bed:
He never will come again.   185
His beard was as white as snow,
All flaxen was his poll°:
He is gone, he is gone,
And we cast away° moan:
God ha' mercy on his soul!   190
And of all Christian souls, I pray God. God be wi' you.   (*Exit.*)

LAERTES: Do you see this, O God?

KING: Laertes, I must commune with your grief,
Or you deny me right.° Go but apart,
Make choice of whom your wisest friends you will,   195
And they shall hear and judge 'twixt you and me:
If by direct or by collateral° hand
They find us touch'd,° we will our kingdom give,
Our crown, our life, and all that we call ours,
To you in satisfaction; but if not,   200
Be you content to lend your patience to us,

---

168. **wheel:** spinning wheel as accompaniment to the song refrain.   168–69. **false steward . . . daughter:** the story is unknown.   171. **rosemary:** used as a symbol of remembrance both at weddings and at
funerals.   172. **pansies:** emblems of love and courtship. Cf. French *pensées*.   173. **document:** piece of
instruction or lesson.   174. **fennel:** emblem of flattery.   174. **columbines:** emblem of unchastity (?) or
ingratitude (?).   174. **rue:** emblem of repentance. It was usually mingled with holy water and then known
as herb of grace. Ophelia is probably playing on the two meanings of rue "repentant" and "even for Ruth
(pity)"; the former signification is for the queen, the latter for herself.   176. **daisy:** emblem of dissem-
bling, faithlessness.   176. **violets:** emblems of faithfulness.   178. **For . . . joy:** probably a line from a
Robin Hood ballad.   179. **Thought:** melancholy thought.   181. **And . . . again:** this song appeared in
the songbooks as "The Merry Milkmaids' Dumps."   187. **poll:** head.   189. **cast away:** shipwrecked.
194. **right:** my rights.   197. **collateral:** indirect.   198. **touch'd:** implicated.

And we shall jointly labour with your soul
To give it due content.
LAERTES: Let this be so;
His means of death, his obscure funeral—
No trophy, sword, nor hatchment° o'er his bones,   205
No noble rite nor formal ostentation—
Cry to be heard, as 'twere from heaven to earth,
That I must call 't in question.
KING: So you shall;
And where th' offence is let the great axe fall.
I pray you, go with me.   (*Exeunt.*) 210

SCENE VI

(*Another room in the castle.*)

(*Enter* HORATIO *and others.*)

HORATIO: What are they that would speak with me?
GENTLEMAN: Sea-faring men, sir: they say they have letters for you.
HORATIO: Let them come in.   (*Exit* GENTLEMAN.)
I do not know from what part of the world
I should be greeted, if not from lord Hamlet.   5

(*Enter* SAILORS.)

FIRST SAILOR: God bless you, sir.
HORATIO: Let him bless thee too.
FIRST SAILOR: 'A shall sir, an 't please him. There's a letter for you, sir; it comes
from the ambassador that was bound for England; if your name be Horatio, as
I am let to know it is.   10
HORATIO (*reads*):   "Horatio, when thou shalt have overlooked this, give these fellows some means° to the king: they have letters for him. Ere we were two days
old at sea, a pirate of very warlike appointment gave us chase. Finding ourselves too slow of sail, we put on a compelled valour, and in the grapple I
boarded them: on the instant they got clear of our ship; so I alone became their 15
prisoner. They have dealt with me like thieves of mercy°: but they knew what
they did; I am to do a good turn for them. Let the king have the letters I have
sent; and repair thou to me with as much speed as thou wouldst fly death. I
have words to speak in thine ear will make thee dumb; yet are they much too
light for the bore° of the matter. These good fellows will bring thee where I 20
am. Rosencrantz and Guildenstern hold their course for England: of them I
have much to tell thee. Farewell.
                      "He that thou knowest thine, Hamlet."

---

205. hatchment: tablet displaying the armorial bearings of a deceased person. **IV.vi. 12. means:**
means of access. **16. thieves of mercy:** merciful thieves. **20. bore:** caliber, importance.

Come, I will give you way for these your letters;
And do 't the speedier, that you may direct me   25
To him from whom you brought them.   (*Exeunt.*)

Scene VII

(*Another room in the castle.*)

(*Enter* King *and* Laertes.)

KING: Now must your conscience° my acquittance seal,
And you must put me in your heart for friend,
Sith you have heard, and with a knowing ear,
That he which hath your noble father slain
Pursued my life.
LAERTES: It well appears: but tell me   5
Why you proceeded not against these feats,
So criminal and so capital° in nature,
As by your safety, wisdom, all things else,
You mainly° were stirr'd up.
KING: O, for two special reasons;
Which may to you, perhaps, seem much unsinew'd,°   10
But yet to me th' are strong. The queen his mother
Lives almost by his looks; and for myself—
My virtue or my plague, be it either which—
She's so conjunctive° to my life and soul,
That, as the star moves not but in his sphere,°   15
I could not but by her. The other motive,
Why to a public count° I might not go,
Is the great love the general gender° bear him;
Who, dipping all his faults in their affection,
Would, like the spring° that turneth wood to stone,   20
Convert his gyves° to graces; so that my arrows,
Too slightly timber'd° for so loud° a wind,
Would have reverted to my bow again,
And not where I had aim'd them.
LAERTES: And so have I a noble father lost;   25
A sister driven into desp'rate terms,°
Whose worth, if praises may go back° again,

IV.vii. **1. conscience:** knowledge that this is true.   **7. capital:** punishable by death.   **9. mainly:** greatly.
10. unsinew'd: weak.   **14. conjunctive:** conformable (the next line suggesting planetary conjunction).
15. sphere: the hollow sphere in which, according to Ptolemaic astronomy, the planets were supposed
to move.   **17. count:** account, reckoning.   **18. general gender:** common people.   **20. spring:** i.e.,
one heavily charged with lime.   **21. gyves:** fetters; here, faults, or possibly, punishments inflicted (on
him).   **22. slightly timber'd:** light.   **22. loud:** strong.   **26. terms:** state, condition.   **27. go back:**
i.e., to Ophelia's former virtues.

Stood challenger on mount° of all the age°
For her perfections: but my revenge will come.
KING: Break not your sleeps for that: you must not think   30
That we are made of stuff so flat and dull
That we can let our beard be shook with danger
And think it pastime. You shortly shall hear more:
I lov'd your father, and we love ourself;
And that, I hope, will teach you to imagine—   35

(*Enter a* MESSENGER *with letters.*)

How now! what news?
MESSENGER: Letters, my lord, from Hamlet:
These to your majesty; this to the queen.°
KING: From Hamlet! who brought them?
MESSENGER: Sailors, my lord, they say; I saw them not:
They were given me by Claudio°; he receiv'd them   40
Of him that brought them.
KING: Laertes, you shall hear them.
Leave us.   (*Exit* MESSENGER.)
(*Reads:*) "High and mighty, You shall know I am set naked° on your kingdom. To-
morrow shall I beg leave to see your kingly eyes: when I shall, first asking your
pardon thereunto, recount the occasion of my sudden and more strange return.   45
                                                        "Hamlet."

What should this mean? Are all the rest come back?
Or is it some abuse, and no such thing?
LAERTES: Know you the hand?
KING: 'Tis Hamlet's character. "Naked!"
And in a postscript here, he says "alone."   50
Can you devise° me?
LAERTES: I'm lost in it, my lord. But let him come;
It warms the very sickness in my heart,
That I shall live and tell him to his teeth,
"Thus didst thou."   55
KING: If it be so, Laertes—
As how should it be so? how otherwise?°—
Will you be rul'd by me?
LAERTES: Ay, my lord;
So you will not o'errule me to a peace.
KING: To thine own peace. If he be now return'd,

---

28. on mount: set up on high, mounted (on horseback).   **28. of all the age:** qualifies *challenger* and not
mount.   **37. to the queen:** one hears no more of the letter to the queen.   **40. Claudio:** this character
does not appear in the play.   **43. naked:** unprovided (with retinue).   **51. devise:** explain to.   **56. As . . .
otherwise?** how can this (Hamlet's return) be true? (yet) how otherwise than true (since we have the evidence of his letter)? Some editors read "How should it not be so," etc., making the words refer to Laertes's
desire to meet with Hamlet.

As checking at° his voyage, and that he means 60
No more to undertake it, I will work him
To an exploit, now ripe in my device,
Under the which he shall not choose but fall:
And for his death no wind of blame shall breathe,
But even his mother shall uncharge the practice° 65
And call it accident.

LAERTES: My lord, I will be rul'd;
The rather, if you could devise it so
That I might be the organ.°

KING: It falls right.
You have been talk'd of since your travel much,
And that in Hamlet's hearing, for a quality 70
Wherein, they say, you shine: your sum of parts
Did not together pluck such envy from him
As did that one, and that, in my regard,
Of the unworthiest siege.°

LAERTES: What part is that, my lord?

KING: A very riband in the cap of youth, 75
Yet needful too; for youth no less becomes
The light and careless livery that it wears
Than settled age his sables° and his weeds,
Importing health and graveness. Two months since,
Here was a gentleman of Normandy:— 80
I have seen myself, and serv'd against, the French,
And they can well° on horseback: but this gallant
Had witchcraft in 't; he grew unto his seat;
And to such wondrous doing brought his horse,
As had he been incorps'd and demi-natur'd° 85
With the brave beast: so far he topp'd° my thought,
That I, in forgery° of shapes and tricks,
Come short of what he did.

LAERTES: A Norman was 't?

KING: A Norman.

LAERTES: Upon my life, Lamord.° 90

King: The very same.

LAERTES: I know him well: he is the brooch indeed
And gem of all the nation.

KING: He made confession° of you,
And gave you such a masterly report 95

---

60. checking at: used in falconry of a hawk's leaving the quarry to fly at a chance bird; turn aside.
65. uncharge the practice: acquit the stratagem of being a plot.   **68. organ:** agent, instrument.
74. siege: rank.   **78. sables:** rich garments.   **82. can well:** are skilled.   **85. incorps'd and demi-natur'd:** of one body and nearly of one nature (like the centaur).   **86. topp'd:** surpassed.   **87. forgery:** invention.   **90. Lamord:** this refers possibly to Pietro Monte, instructor to Louis XII's master of the horse.   **94. confession:** grudging admission of superiority.

For art and exercise° in your defence°
And for your rapier most especial,
That he cried out, 'twould be a sight indeed,
If one could match you: the scrimers° of their nation, 100
He swore, had neither motion, guard, nor eye,
If you oppos'd them. Sir, this report of his
Did Hamlet so envenom with his envy
That he could nothing do but wish and beg
Your sudden coming o'er, to play° with you.
Now, out of this,—
LAERTES: What out of this, my lord? 105
KING: Laertes, was your father dear to you?
Or are you like the painting of a sorrow,
A face without a heart?
LAERTES: Why ask you this?
KING: Not that I think you did not love your father;
But that I know love is begun by time; 110
And that I see, in passages of proof,°
Time qualifies the spark and fire of it.
There lives within the very flame of love
A kind of wick or snuff that will abate it;
And nothing is at a like goodness still; 115
For goodness, growing to a plurisy,°
Dies in his own too much°: that we would do,
We should do when we would; for this "would" changes
And hath abatements° and delays as many
As there are tongues, are hands, are accidents°; 120
And then this "should" is like a spendthrift° sigh,
That hurts by easing. But, to the quick o' th' ulcer°:—
Hamlet comes back: what would you undertake,
To show yourself your father's son in deed
More than in words? 125
LAERTES: To cut his throat i' th' church.
KING: No place, indeed, should murder sanctuarize°;
Revenge should have no bounds. But, good Laertes,
Will you do this, keep close within your chamber.
Hamlet return'd shall know you are come home: 130
We'll put on those shall praise your excellence
And set a double varnish on the fame

---

96. art and exercise: skillful exercise.   **96. defence:** science of defense in sword practice.
99. scrimers: fencers.   **104. play:** fence.   **111. passages of proof:** proved instances.   **116. plurisy:**
excess, plethora.   **117. in his own too much:** of its own excess.   **119. abatements:** diminutions.
120. accidents: occurrences, incidents.   **121. spendthrift:** an allusion to the belief that each sigh cost
the heart a drop of blood.   **122. quick o' th' ulcer:** heart of the difficulty.   **127. sanctuarize:** protect
from punishment; allusion to the right of sanctuary with which certain religious places were invested.

The Frenchman gave you, bring you in fine together
And wager on your heads: he, being remiss,
Most generous and free from all contriving,   135
Will not peruse the foils; so that, with ease,
Or with a little shuffling, you may choose
A sword unbated,° and in a pass of practice°
Requite him for your father.

LAERTES: I will do 't:
And, for that purpose, I'll anoint my sword.   140
I bought an unction of a mountebank,°
So mortal that, but dip a knife in it,
Where it draws blood no cataplasm° so rare,
Collected from all simples° that have virtue
Under the moon,° can save the thing from death   145
That is but scratch'd withal: I'll touch my point
With this contagion, that, if I gall° him slightly,
It may be death.

KING: Let's further think of this;
Weigh what convenience both of time and means
May fit us to our shape°: if this should fail,   150
And that our drift look through our bad performance,°
'Twere better not assay'd: therefore this project
Should have a back or second, that might hold,
If this should blast in proof.° Soft! let me see:
We'll make a solemn wager on your cunnings°:   155
I ha't:
When in your motion you are hot and dry—
As make your bouts more violent to that end—
And that he calls for drink, I'll have prepar'd him
A chalice° for the nonce, whereon but sipping,   160
If he by chance escape your venom'd stuck,°
Our purpose may hold there. But stay, what noise?

              (*Enter* QUEEN.)

QUEEN: One woe doth tread upon another's heel,
    So fast they follow: your sister's drown'd, Laertes.
LAERTES: Drown'd! O, where?   165
QUEEN: There is a willow° grows askant° the brook,
    That shows his hoar° leaves in the glassy stream;

---

138. unbated: not blunted, having no button.   **138. pass of practice:** treacherous thrust.   **141. mountebank:** quack doctor.   **143. cataplasm:** plaster or poultice.   **144. simples:** herbs.   **145. Under the moon:** i.e., when collected by moonlight to add to their medicinal value.   **147. gall:** graze, wound.   **150. shape:** part we propose to act.   **151. drift . . . performance:** intention be disclosed by our bungling.   **154. blast in proof:** burst in the test (like a cannon).   **155. cunnings:** skills.   **160. chalice:** cup.   **161. stuck:** thrust (from *stoccado*).   **166. willow:** for its significance of forsaken love.   **166. askant:** askant.   **167. hoar:** white (i.e., on the underside).

There with fantastic garlands did she make
Of crow-flowers,° nettles, daisies, and long purples°
That liberal° shepherds give a grosser name,   170
But our cold maids do dead men's fingers call them:
There, on the pendent boughs her crownet° weeds
Clamb'ring to hang, an envious sliver° broke;
When down her weedy° trophies and herself
Fell in the weeping brook. Her clothes spread wide;   175
And, mermaid-like, awhile they bore her up:
Which time she chanted snatches of old lauds°;
As one incapable° of her own distress,
Or like a creature native and indued°
Upon that element: but long it could not be   180
Till that her garments, heavy with their drink,
Pull'd the poor wretch from her melodious lay
To muddy death.
LAERTES: Alas, then, she is drown'd?
QUEEN: Drown'd, drown'd.
LAERTES: Too much of water hast thou, poor Ophelia,   185
And therefore I forbid my tears: but yet
It is our trick°; nature her custom holds,
Let shame say what it will: when these are gone,
The woman will be out.° Adieu, my lord:
I have a speech of fire, that fain would blaze,   190
But that this folly drowns it.   (*Exit.*)
KING: Let's follow, Gertrude:
How much I had to do to calm his rage!
Now fear I this will give it start again;
Therefore let's follow.   (*Exeunt.*)

ACT V

SCENE I

(*A churchyard.*)

(*Enter two* CLOWNS° [*with spades, &c*].)

FIRST CLOWN: Is she to be buried in Christian burial when she wilfully seeks her
   own salvation?

---

169. crow-flowers: buttercups.   **169. long purples:** early purple orchids.   **170. liberal:** probably,
free- spoken.   **172. crownet:** coronet; made into a chaplet.   **173. sliver:** branch.   **174. weedy:** i.e., of
plants.   **177. lauds:** hymns.   **178. incapable:** lacking capacity to apprehend.   **179. indued:** endowed
with qualities fitting her for living in water.   **187. trick:** way.   **188–189. when. . . out:** when my tears
are all shed, the woman in me will be satisfied.   **Vi.i. s.d. clowns:** the word *clown* was used to denote
peasants as well as humorous characters; here applied to the rustic type of clown.

SECOND CLOWN: I tell thee she is; therefore make her grave straight°: the crowner°
  hath sat on her, and finds it Christian burial.

FIRST CLOWN: How can that be, unless she drowned herself in her own defence? 5

SECOND CLOWN: Why, 'tis found so.

FIRST CLOWN: It must be "se offendendo"°; it cannot be else. For here lies the
  point: if I drown myself wittingly,° it argues an act: and an act hath three
  branches°; it is, to act, to do, and to perform: argal,° she drowned herself wittingly. 10

SECOND CLOWN: Nay, but hear you, goodman delver,°—

FIRST CLOWN: Give me leave. Here lies the water; good; here stands the man;
  good: if the man go to this water, and drown himself, it is, will he, nill he, he
  goes,—mark you that; but if the water come to him and drown him, he drowns
  not himself: argal, he that is not guilty of his own death shortens not his own 15
  life.

SECOND CLOWN: But is this law?

FIRST CLOWN: Ay, marry, is 't; crowner's quest° law.

SECOND CLOWN: Will you ha' the truth on 't? If this had not been a gentle-woman,
  she should have been buried out o' Christian burial. 20

FIRST CLOWN: Why, there thou say'st°: and the more pity that great folk should
  have countenance° in this world to drown or hang themselves, more than their
  even° Christian. Come, my spade. There is no ancient gentlemen but gardeners, ditchers, and grave-makers: they hold up° Adam's profession.

SECOND CLOWN: Was he a gentleman? 25

FIRST CLOWN: 'A was the first that ever bore arms.

SECOND CLOWN: Why, he had none.

FIRST CLOWN: What, art a heathen? How dost thou understand the Scripture?
  The Scripture says "Adam digged": could he dig without arms? I'll put another
  question to thee: if thou answerest me not to the purpose, confess thyself°— 30

SECOND CLOWN: Go to.°

FIRST CLOWN: What is he that builds stronger than either the mason, the shipwright, or the carpenter?

SECOND CLOWN: The gallows-maker; for that frame outlives a thousand tenants. 35

FIRST CLOWN: I like thy wit well, in good faith: the gallows does well; but how does
  it well? it does well to those that do ill: now thou dost ill to say the gallows is
  built stronger than the church: argal, the gallows may do well to thee. To 't
  again, come.

SECOND CLOWN: Who builds stronger than a mason, a shipwright, or a carpenter? 40

---

3. straight: straightway, immediately; some interpret "from east to west in a direct line, parallel with the
church." **3. crowner:** coroner. **7. "se offendendo"** for se defendendo, term used in verdicts of justifiable homicide. **8. wittingly:** intentionally. **8–9. three branches:** parody of legal phraseology.
9. argal: corruption of ergo, therefore. **11. delver:** digger. **18. quest:** inquest. **21. there thou
say'st:** that's right. **22. countenance:** privilege. **23. even:** fellow. **24. hold up:** maintain, continue.
30–31. confess thyself: "and be hanged" completes the proverb. **32. Go to:** perhaps, "begin," or
some other form of concession.

FIRST CLOWN: Ay, tell me that, and unyoke.°
SECOND CLOWN: Marry, now I can tell.
FIRST CLOWN: To 't.
SECOND CLOWN: Mass,° I cannot tell.

(*Enter* HAMLET *and* HORATIO [*at a distance*].)

FIRST CLOWN: Cudgel thy brains no more about it, for your dull ass will not mend   45
his pace with beating; and, when you are asked this question next, say "a grave-
maker": the houses he makes lasts till doomsday. Go, get thee in, and fetch me
a stoup° of liquor.   (*Exit* SECOND CLOWN.)

(*Song.* [*He digs.*])

In youth, when I did love, did love,
    Methought it was very sweet,   50
To contract—O—the time, for—a—my behove,°
    O, methought, there—a—was nothing—a—meet.
HAMLET: Has this fellow no feeling of his business, that 'a sings at gravemaking?
HORATIO: Custom hath made it in him a property of easiness.°
HAMLET: 'Tis e'en so: the hand of little employment hath the daintier sense.   55
FIRST CLOWN (*Song.*):   But age, with his stealing steps,
    Hath claw'd me in his clutch,
And hath shipped me into the land
    As if I had never been such. (*Throws up a skull.*)
HAMLET: That skull had a tongue in it, and could sing once: how the knave jowls°   60
it to the ground, as if 'twere Cain's jaw-bone,° that did the first murder! This
might be the pate of a politician,° which this ass now o'er-reaches;° one that
would circumvent God, might it not?
HORATIO: It might, my lord.
HAMLET: Or of a courtier; which could say "Good morrow, sweet lord! How dost   65
thou, sweet lord?" This might be my lord such-a-one, that praised my lord
such-a-one's horse, when he meant to beg it; might it not?
HORATIO: Ay, my lord.
HAMLET: Why, e'en so: and now my Lady Worm's; chapless,° and knocked about
the mazzard° with a sexton's spade: here's fine revolution, an we had the trick   70
to see 't. Did these bones cost no more the breeding, but to play at loggats°
with 'em? mine ache to think on 't.
FIRST CLOWN (*Song.*):   A pick-axe, and a spade, a spade,
    For and° a shrouding sheet:

---

41. unyoke: after this great effort you may unharness the team of your wits.   **44. Mass:** by the Mass.
48. stoup: two-quart measure.   **51. behove:** benefit.   **54. property of easiness:** a peculiarity that now
is easy.   **60. jowls:** dashes.   **61. Cain's jaw-bone:** allusion to the old tradition that Cain slew Abel with
the jawbone of an ass.   **62. politician:** schemer, plotter.   **62. o'er-reaches:** quibble on the literal sense
and the sense "circumvent."   **69. chapless:** having no lower jaw.   **70. mazzard:** head.   **71. loggats:** a
game in which six sticks are thrown to lie as near as possible to a stake fixed in the ground, or block of
wood on a floor.   **74. For and:** and moreover.

O, a pit of clay for to be made   75
   For such a guest is meet. (*Throws up another skull.*)

HAMLET: There's another: why may not that be the skull of a lawyer? Where be his
   quiddities° now, his quillities,° his cases, his tenures,° and his tricks? why does
   he suffer this mad knave now to knock him about the sconce° with a dirty
   shovel, and will not tell him of his action of battery? Hum! This fellow might   80
   be in 's time a great buyer of land, with his statutes, his recognizances,° his
   fines, his double vouchers,° his recoveries:° is this the fine° of his fines, and the
   recovery of his recoveries, to have his fine pate full of fine dirt? will his vouchers vouch him no more of his purchases, and double ones too, than the length
   and breadth of a pair of indentures?° The very conveyances of his lands will   85
   scarcely lie in this box; and must the inheritor° himself have no more, ha?

HORATIO: Not a jot more, my lord.

HAMLET: Is not parchment made of sheep-skins?

HORATIO: Ay, my lord, and of calf-skins° too.

HAMLET: They are sheep and calves which seek out assurance in that.° I will speak   90
   to this fellow. Whose grave's this, sirrah?

FIRST CLOWN: Mine, sir.

   (*Sings.*) O, a pit of clay for to be made
      For such a guest is meet.

HAMLET: I think it be thine, indeed; for thou liest in 't.   95

FIRST CLOWN: You lie out on 't, sir, and therefore 't is not yours: for my part, I do
   not lie in 't, yet it is mine.

HAMLET: Thou dost lie in 't, to be in 't and say it is thine: 'tis for the dead, not for
   the quick; therefore thou liest.

FIRST CLOWN: 'Tis a quick lie, sir; 'twill away again, from me to you.   100

HAMLET: What man dost thou dig it for?

FIRST CLOWN: For no man, sir.

HAMLET: What woman, then?

FIRST CLOWN: For none, neither,

HAMLET: Who is to be buried in 't?   105

FIRST CLOWN: One that was a woman, sir; but, rest her soul, she's dead.

HAMLET: How absolute° the knave is! we must speak by the card,° or equivoca-
   tion° will undo us. By the Lord, Horatio, these three years I have taken note of
   it, the age is grown so picked° that the toe of the peasant comes so near the

---

78. quiddities: subtleties, quibbles.   **78. quillities:** verbal niceties, subtle distinctions.   **78. tenures:**
the holding of a piece of property or office or the conditions or period of such holding.   **79. sconce:**
head.   **81. statutes, recognizances:** legal terms connected with the transfer of land.   **82. vouchers:**
persons called on to warrant a tenant's title.   **82. recoveries:** process for transfer of entailed estate.
82. fine: the four uses of this word are as follows: (1) end, (2) legal process, (3) elegant, (4) small.   **85.
indentures:** conveyances or contracts.   **86. inheritor:** possessor, owner.   **89. calf-skins:** parchments.
90. assurance in that: safety in legal parchments.   **107. absolute:** positive, decided.   **107. by the
card:** with precision, i.e., by the mariner's card on which the points of the compass were marked.
107–8. equivocation: ambiguity in the use of terms.   **109. picked:** refined, fastidious.

heel of the courtier, he galls° his kibe.° How long hast thou been a grave- 110
maker?

FIRST CLOWN: Of all the day i' the year, I came to 't that day that our last king
Hamlet overcame Fortinbras.

HAMLET: How long is that since?

FIRST CLOWN: Cannot you tell that? every fool can tell that: it was the very day that 115
young Hamlet was born; he that is mad, and sent into England.

HAMLET: Ay, marry, why was he sent into England?

FIRST CLOWN: Why, because 'a was mad: 'a shall recover his wits there; or, if 'a do
not, 'tis no great matter there.

HAMLET: Why? 120

FIRST CLOWN: 'Twill not be seen in him there; there the men are as mad as he.

HAMLET: How came he mad?

FIRST CLOWN: Very strangely, they say.

HAMLET: How strangely?

FIRST CLOWN: Faith, e'en with losing his wits. 125

HAMLET: Upon what ground?

FIRST CLOWN: Why, here in Denmark: I have been sexton here, man and boy,
thirty years.°

HAMLET: How long will a man lie i' the earth ere he rot?

FIRST CLOWN: Faith, i' a be not rotten before 'a die—as we have many pocky° 130
corses now-a-days, that will scarce hold the laying in—'a will last you some
eight year or nine year: a tanner will last you nine year.

HAMLET: Why he more than another?

FIRST CLOWN: Why, sir, his hide is so tanned with his trade, that 'a will keep out
water a great while; and your water is a sore decayer of your whoreson dead 135
body. Here's a skull now hath lain you i' th' earth three and twenty years.

HAMLET: Whose was it?

FIRST CLOWN: A whoreson mad fellow's it was: whose do you think it was?

HAMLET: Nay, I know not.

FIRST CLOWN: A pestilence on him for a mad rogue! 'a poured a flagon of Rhenish 140
on my head once. This same skull, sir, was Yorick's skull, the king's jester.

HAMLET: This?

FIRST CLOWN: E'en that.

HAMLET: Let me see. (*Takes the skull.*) Alas, poor Yorick! I knew him, Horatio: a
fellow of infinite jest, of most excellent fancy: he hath borne me on his back a 145
thousand times; and now, how abhorred in my imagination it is! my gorge rises
at it. Here hung those lips that I have kissed I know not how oft. Where be
your gibes now? your gambols? your songs? your flashes of merriment, that
were wont to set the table on a roar? Not one now, to mock your own grinning? quite chap-fallen? Now get you to my lady's chamber, and tell her, let her 150

---

110. galls: chafes.   **110. kibe:** chilblain.   **128. thirty years:** this statement with that in line 116 shows
Hamlet's age to be thirty years.   **130. pocky:** rotten, diseased.

paint an inch thick, to this favour she must come; make her laugh at that.
Prithee, Horatio, tell me one thing.

HORATIO: What's that, my lord?

HAMLET: Dost thou think Alexander looked o' this fashion i' the earth?

HORATIO: E'en so.   155

HAMLET: And smelt so? pah! (*Puts down the skull.*)

HORATIO: E'en so, my lord.

HAMLET: To what base uses we may return, Horatio! Why may not imagination
trace the noble dust of Alexander, till'a find it stopping a bunghole?

HORATIO: 'Twere to consider too curiously,° to consider so.   160

HAMLET: No, faith, not a jot; but to follow him thither with modesty enough, and
likelihood to lead it: as thus: Alexander died, Alexander was buried, Alexander
returneth into dust; the dust is earth; of earth we make loam°; and why of that
loam, whereto he was converted, might they not stop a beer-barrel?

    Imperious° Cæsar, dead and turn'd to clay,   165
    Might stop a hole to keep the wind away:
    O, that that earth, which kept the world in awe,
    Should patch a wall t'expel the winter's flaw!°

But soft! but soft awhile! here comes the king.

    (*Enter* KING, QUEEN, LAERTES, *and the Corpse of* [OPHELIA, *in procession,*
    with PRIEST, LORDS, *etc.*].)

The queen, the courtiers: who is this they follow?   170
And with such maimed rites? This doth betoken
The corse they follow did with desp'rate hand
Fordo° it° own life: 'twas of some estate.
Couch° we awhile, and mark.   (*Retiring with* HORATIO.)

LAERTES: What ceremony else?

HAMLET: That is Laertes,   175
A very noble youth: mark.

LAERTES: What ceremony else?

FIRST PRIEST: Her obsequies have been as far enlarg'd°
As we have warranty: her death was doubtful;
And, but that great command o'ersways the order,   180
She should in ground unsanctified have lodg'd
Till the last trumpet; for charitable prayers,
Shards,° flints and pebbles should be thrown on her:
Yet here she is allow'd her virgin crants,°
Her maiden strewments° and the bringing home   185

---

160. curiously: minutely.   **163. loam:** clay paste for brickmaking.   **165. Imperious:** imperial.   **168.
flaw:** gust of wind.   **173. Fordo:** destroy.   **173. it:** its.   **174. Couch:** hide, lurk.   **178. enlarg'd:**
extended, referring to the fact that suicides are not given full burial rites.   **183. Shards:** broken bits of
pottery.   **184. crants:** garlands customarily hung upon the biers of unmarried women.   **185. strew-
ments:** traditional strewing of flowers.

Of bell and burial.°

LAERTES: Must there no more be done?

FIRST PRIEST: No more be done:
  We should profane the service of the dead
  To sing a requiem and such rest to her
  As to peace-parted° souls.   190

LAERTES: Lay her i' th' earth:
  And from her fair and unpolluted flesh
  May violets spring! I tell thee, churlish priest,
  A minist'ring angel shall my sister be,
  When thou liest howling.°

HAMLET: What, the fair Ophelia!   195

QUEEN: Sweets to the sweet: farewell! (*Scattering flowers.*)
  I hop'd thou shouldst have been my Hamlet's wife;
  I thought thy bride-bed to have deck'd, sweet maid,
  And not have strew'd thy grave.

LAERTES: O, treble woe
  Fall ten times treble on that cursed head,   200
  Whose wicked deed thy most ingenious sense°
  Depriv'd thee of! Hold off the earth awhile,
  Till I have caught her once more in mine arms: (*Leaps into the grave.*)
  Now pile your dust upon the quick and dead,
  Till of this flat a mountain you have made,   205
  T' o'ertop old Pelion,° or the skyish head
  Of blue Olympus.

HAMLET: (*Advancing.*) What is he whose grief
  Bears such an emphasis? whose phrase of sorrow
  Conjures the wand'ring stars,° and makes them stand
  Like wonder-wounded hearers? This is I,   210
  Hamlet the Dane. (*Leaps into the grave.*)

LAERTES: The devil take thy soul! (*Grappling with him.*)

HAMLET: Thou pray'st not well,
  I prithee, take thy fingers from my throat;
  For, though I am not splenitive° and rash,   215
  Yet have I in me something dangerous,
  Which let thy wisdom fear: hold off thy hand.

KING: Pluck them asunder.

QUEEN: Hamlet, Hamlet!

ALL: Gentlemen,—

185–86. bringing . . . burial: the laying to rest of the body, to the sound of the bell.   **190. peace-parted:** allusion to the text "Lord, now lettest thy servant depart in peace."   **195. howling:** i.e., in hell.
201. ingenious sense: mind endowed with finest qualities.   **206. Pelion:** Olympus, Pelion, and Ossa are mountains in the north of Thessaly.   **209. wand'ring stars:** planets.   **215. splenitive:** quick-tempered.

HORATIO: Good my lord, be quiet.

(*The* ATTENDANTS *part them, and they come out of the grave.*)

HAMLET: Why, I will fight with him upon this theme   220
   Until my eyelids will no longer wag.°
QUEEN: O my son, what theme?
HAMLET: I lov'd Ophelia: forty thousand brothers
   Could not, with all their quantity° of love,
   Make up my sum. What wilt thou do for her?   225
KING: O, he is mad, Laertes.
QUEEN: For love of God, forbear° him.
HAMLET: 'Swounds,° show me what thou 'lt do:
   Woo 't weep? woo 't fight? woo 't fast? woo 't tear thyself?
   Woo 't drink up eisel?° eat a crocodile?   230
   I'll do 't. Dost thou come here to whine?
   To outface me with leaping in her grave?
   Be buried quick with her, and so will I:
   And, if thou prate of mountains, let them throw
   Millions of acres on us, till our ground,   235
   Singeing his pate against the burning zone,°
   Make Ossa like a wart! Nay, an thou 'lt mouth,
   I'll rant as well as thou.
QUEEN: This is mere madness:
   And thus awhile the fit will work on him;   240
   Anon, as patient as the female dove.
   When that her golden couplets° are disclos'd,
   His silence will sit drooping.
HAMLET: Hear you, sir;
   What is the reason that you use me thus?   245
   I lov'd you ever: but it is no matter;
   Let Hercules himself do what he may,
   The cat will mew and dog will have his day.
KING: I pray thee, good Horatio, wait upon him.   (*Exit* HAMLET *and* HORATIO.)
(*To* LAERTES.) Strengthen your patience in° our last night's speech;   250
   We'll put the matter to the present push.°
   Good Gertrude, set some watch over your son.
   This grave shall have a living° monument:

---

221. wag: move (not used ludicrously).   **224. quantity:** some suggest that the word is used in a depreca-
tory sense (little bits, fragments).   **227. forbear:** leave alone.   **228. 'Swounds:** oath, "God's
wounds."   **229. Woo 't:** with thou.   **230. eisel:** vinegar. Some editors have taken this to be the name of
a river, such as the Yssel, the Weissel, and the Nile.   **236. burning zone:** sun's orbit.   **242. golden
couplets:** the pigeon lays two eggs; the young when hatched are covered with golden down.   **250. in:**
by recalling.   **251. present push:** immediate test.   **253. living:** lasting; also refers (for Laertes' benefit) to the plot against Hamlet.

An hour of quiet shortly shall we see;
Till then, in patience our proceeding be. (*Exeunt.*) 255

SCENE II

(*A hall in the castle.*)

(*Enter* HAMLET *and* HORATIO.)

HAMLET: So much for this, sir: now shall you see the other:
You do remember all the circumstance?
HORATIO: Remember it, my lord!
HAMLET: Sir, in my heart there was a kind of fighting,
That would not let me sleep: methought I lay 5
Worse than the mutines° in the bilboes.° Rashly,°
And prais'd be rashness for it, let us know,
Our indiscretion sometime serves us well,
When our deep plots do pall°: and that should learn us
There's a divinity that shapes our ends, 10
Rough-hew° them how we will,—
HORATIO: That is most certain.
HAMLET: Up from my cabin,
My sea-gown° scarf'd about me, in the dark
Grop'd I to find out them; had my desire,
Finger'd° their packet, and in fine° withdrew 15
To mine own room again; making so bold,
My fears forgetting manners, to unseal
Their grand commission; where I found, Horatio,—
O royal knavery!—an exact command,
Larded° with many several sorts of reasons 20
Importing Denmark's health and England's too,
With, ho! such bugs° and goblins in my life,°
That, on the supervise,° no leisure bated,°
No, not to stay the grinding of the axe,
My head should be struck off.
HORATIO: Is 't possible? 25
HAMLET: Here's the commission: read it at more leisure.
But wilt thou hear me how I did proceed?

V.ii. **6. mutines:** mutineers. **6. bilboes:** shackles. **6. Rashly:** goes with line 12. **9. pall:** fail.
11. Rough-hew: shape roughly; it may mean "bungle." **13. sea-gown:** "A sea-gown, or a corase,
high-collered, and short-sleeved gowne, reaching down to the mid-leg, and used most by seamen and
saylors" (Cotgrave, quoted by Singer). **15. finger'd:** pilfered, filched. **15. in fine:** finally.
20. Larded: enriched. **22. bugs:** bug-bears. **22. such . . . life:** such imaginary dangers if I were
allowed to live. **23. supervise:** perusal. **23. leisure bated:** delay allowed.

HORATIO: I beseech you.

HAMLET: Being thus be-netted round with villanies,—

Ere I could make a prologue to my brains,   30

They had begun the play°—I sat me down,

Devis'd a new commission, wrote it fair;

I once did hold it, as our statists° do,

A baseness to write fair° and labour'd much

How to forget that learning, but, sir, now   35

It did me yeoman's° service: wilt thou know

Th' effect of what I wrote?

HORATIO: Ay, good my lord.

HAMLET: An earnest conjuration from the king,

As England was his faithful tributary,

As love between them like the palm might flourish,   40

As peace should still her wheaten garland° wear

And stand a comma° 'tween their amities,

And many such-like 'As'es° of great charge,°

That, on the view and knowing of these contents,

Without debatement further, more or less,   45

He should the bearers put to sudden death,

Not shriving-time° allow'd.

HORATIO: How was this seal'd?

HAMLET: Why, even in that was heaven ordinant.°

I had my father's signet in my purse,

Which was the model of that Danish seal;   50

Folded the writ up in the form of th' other,

Subscrib'd it, gave 't th' impression, plac'd it safely,

The changeling never known. Now, the next day

Was our sea-fight; and what to this was sequent°

Thou know'st already.   55

HORATIO: So Guildenstern and Rosencrantz go to 't.

HAMLET: Why, man, they did make love to this employment;

They are not near my conscience; their defeat

Does by their own insinuation° grow:

'Tis dangerous when the baser nature comes   60

Between the pass° and fell incensed° points

Of mighty opposites.

HORATIO: Why, what a king is this!

30–31. prologue: . . . play: i.e., before I could begin to think, my mind had made its decision.   **33. stat-
ists:** statesmen.   **34. fair:** in a clear hand.   **36. yeoman's:** i.e., faithful.   **41. wheaten garland:** symbol of
peace.   **42. comma:** smallest break or separation. Here amity begins and amity ends the period, and peace
stands between like a dependent clause. The comma indicates continuity, link.   **43. 'As'es:** the "where-
ases" of a formal document, with play on the word ass.   **43. charge:** import, and burden.   **47. shriving-
time:** time for absolution.   **48. ordinant:** directing.   **54. sequent:** subsequent.   **59. insinuation:**
interference.   **61. pass:** thrust.   **61. fell incensed:** fiercely angered.

HAMLET: Does it not, think thee, stand° me now upon—
He that hath kill'd my king and whor'd my mother,
Popp'd in between th' election° and my hopes,   65
Thrown out his angle° for my proper life,
And with such coz'nage°—is 't not perfect conscience,
To quit° him with this arm? and is 't not to be damn'd,
To let this canker° of our nature come
In further evil?   70
HORATIO: It must be shortly known to him from England
What is the issue of the business there.
HAMLET: It will be short: the interim is mine;
And a man's life's no more than to say "One."
But I am very sorry, good Horatio,   75
That to Laertes I forgot myself;
For, by the image of my cause, I see
The portraiture of his: I'll court his favours:
But, sure, the bravery° of his grief did put me
Into a tow'ring passion.
HORATIO: Peace! who comes here?   80

(*Enter a* COURTIER [OSRIC].)

OSRIC: Your lordship is right welcome back to Denmark.
HAMLET: I humbly thank you, sir. (*To* HORATIO.) Dost know this water-fly?°
HORATIO: No, my good lord.
HAMLET: Thy state is the more gracious; for 'tis a vice to know him. He hath much
    land, and fertile: let a beast be lord of beasts,° and his crib shall stand at the   85
    king's mess°: 'tis a chough°; but, as I say, spacious in the possession of dirt.
OSRIC: Sweet lord, if your lordship were at leisure, I should impart a thing to you
    from his majesty.
HAMLET: I will receive it, sir, with all diligence of spirit. Put your bonnet to his
    right use; 'tis for the head.   90
OSRIC: I thank you lordship, it is very hot.
HAMLET: No, believe me, 'tis very cold; the wind is northerly.
OSRIC: It is indifferent° cold, my lord, indeed.
HAMLET: But yet methinks it is very sultry and hot for my complexion.
OSRIC: Exceedingly, my lord; it is very sultry,—as 'twere,—I cannot tell how. But,   95
    my lord, his majesty bade me signify to you that 'a has laid a great wager on
    your head: sir, this is the matter,—

---

63. stand: become incumbent.   **65. election:** the Danish throne was filled by election.   **66. angle:**
fishing line.   **67. coz'nage:** trickery.   **68. quit:** repay.   **69. canker:** ulcer, or possibly the worm which
destroys buds and leaves.   **79. bravery:** bravado.   **82. water-fly:** vain or busily idle person.   **85. lord
of beasts:** cf Genesis 1:26, 28.   **85–86. his crib . . . mess:** he shall eat at the king's table, i.e., be one of
the group of persons (usually four) constituting a mess at a banquet.   **86. chough:** probably, chattering
jackdaw; also explained as chuff, provincial boor or churl.   **93. indifferent:** somewhat.

HAMLET: I beseech you, remember°—

(HAMLET *moves him to put on his hat.*)

OSRIC: Nay, good my lord; for mine ease,° in good faith. Sir, here is newly come to court Laertes; believe me, an absolute gentleman, full of most excellent differ-ences, of very soft° society and great showing°: indeed, to speak feelingly° of him, he is the card° or calendar of gentry,° for you shall find in him the conti-nent of what part a gentleman would see.

HAMLET: Sir, his definement° suffers no perdition° in you; though, I know, to divide him inventorially° would dozy° the arithmetic of memory, and yet but yaw° neither, in respect of his quick sail. But, in the verity of extolment, I take him to be a soul of great article°; and his infusion° of such dearth and rareness,° as, to make true diction of him, his semblable° is his mirror; and who else would trace° him, his umbrage,° nothing more.

OSRIC: Your lordship speaks most infallibly of him.

HAMLET: The concernancy,° sir? why do we wrap the gentleman in our more rawer breath?°

OSRIC: Sir?

HORATIO (*aside to* HAMLET):   Is 't not possible to understand in another tongue?° You will do 't, sir, really.

HAMLET: What imports the nomination° of this gentleman?

OSRIC: Of Laertes?

HORATIO (*aside to* HAMLET):   His purse is empty already; all 's golden words are spent.

HAMLET: Of him, sir.

OSRIC: I know you are not ignorant—

HAMLET: I would you did, sir; yet, in faith, if you did, it would not much approve° me. Well, sir?

OSRIC: You are not ignorant of what excellence Laertes is—

HAMLET: I dare not confess that, lest I should compare with him in excellence; but to know a man well, were to know himself.°

OSRIC: I mean, sir, for his weapon; but in the imputation° laid on him by them, in his meed° he's unfellowed.

HAMLET: What's his weapon?

OSRIC: Rapier and dagger.

98. **remember:** i.e., remember thy courtesy; conventional phrase for "Be covered." 99. **mine ease:** conventional reply declining the invitation of "Remember thy courtesy." 101. **soft:** gentle. 101. **showing:** distinguished appearance. 101. **feelingly:** with just perception. 102. **card:** chart, map. 102. **gentry:** good breeding. 104. **definement:** definition. 104. **perdition:** loss, diminution. 105. **divide him inventorially:** i.e., enumerate his graces. 105. **dozy:** dizzy. 106. **yaw:** to move unsteadily (of a ship). 107. **article:** moment or importance. 107. **infusion:** infused temperament, character imparted by nature. 107. **dearth and rareness:** rarity. 108. **semblable:** true likeness. 109. **trace:** follow. 109. **umbrage:** shadow. 111. **concernancy:** import. 112. **breath:** speech. 114. **Is 't . . . tongue?:** i.e., can one converse with Osric only in this outlandish jargon? 116. **nomination:** naming. 121. **approve:** command. 125. **but . . . himself:** but to know a man as excellent were to know Laertes. 126. **imputation:** reputation. 127. **meed:** merit.

HAMLET: That's two of his weapons: but, well.   130

OSRIC: The king, sir, hath wagered with him six Barbary horses: against the which he has impawned,° as I take it, six French rapiers and poniards, with their assigns, as girdle, hangers,° and so: three of the carriages, in faith, are very dear to fancy,° very responsive° to the hilts, most delicate° carriages, and of very liberal conceit.°

HAMLET: What call you the carriages?   135

HORATIO (*aside to* HAMLET):   I knew you must be edified by the margent° ere you had done.

OSRIC: The carriages, sir, are the hangers.

HAMLET: The phrase would be more german° to the matter, if we could carry cannon by our sides: I would it might be hangers till then. But, on: six Barbary horses   140 against six French swords, their assigns, and three liberal-conceited carriages; that's the French bet against the Danish. Why is this "impawned," as you call it?

OSRIC: The king, sir, hath laid, that in a dozen passes between yourself and him, he shall not exceed you three hits: he hath laid on twelve for nine; and it would   145 come to immediate trial, if your lordship would vouchsafe the answer.

HAMLET: How if I answer "no"?

OSRIC: I mean, my lord, the opposition of your person in trial.

HAMLET: Sir, I will walk here in the hall: if it please his majesty, it is the breathing time° of day with me; let the foils be brought, the gentleman willing, and the   150 king hold his purpose, I will win for him as I can; if not, I will gain nothing but my shame and the odd hits.

OSRIC: Shall I re-deliver you e'en so?

HAMLET: To this effect, sir; after what flourish your nature will.

OSRIC: I commend my duty to your lordship.   155

HAMLET: Yours, yours. (*Exit* OSRIC.) He does well to commend it himself; there are no tongues else for 's turn.

HORATIO: This lapwing° runs away with the shell on his head.

HAMLET: 'A did comply, sir, with his dug,° before 'a sucked it. Thus has hey—and many more of the same bevy that I know the drossy° age dotes on—only got   160 the tune° of the time and out of an habit of encounter°; a kind of yesty° collection, which carries them through and through the most fann'd and winnowed° opinions; and do but blow them to their trial, the bubbles are out.°

(*Enter a* LORD.)

132. he has impawned: he has wagered.   **133. hangers:** straps on the sword belt from which the sword hung.   **133. dear to fancy:** fancifully made.   **134. responsive:** probably, well balanced, corresponding closely.   **134. delicate:** i.e., in workmanship.   **134. liberal conceit:** elaborate design.   **136. margent:** margin of a book, place for explanatory notes.   **139. german:** germane, appropriate.   **149–50. breathing time:** exercise period.   **158. lapwing:** peewit; noted for its wiliness in drawing a visitor away from its nest and its supposed habit of running about when newly hatched with its head in the shell; possibly an allusion to Osric's hat.   **159. did comply . . . dug:** paid compliments to his mother's breast.   **160. drossy:** frivolous.   **161. tune:** temper, mood.   **161. habit of encounter:** demeanor of social intercourse.   **161. yesty:** frothy.   **162. fann'd and winnowed:** select and refined   **163. blow . . . out:** i.e., put them to the test, and their ignorance is exposed.

LORD: My lord, his majesty commended him to you by young Osric, who brings
        back to him, that you attend him in the hall: he sends to know if your pleasure   165
        hold to play with Laertes, or that you will take longer time.

HAMLET: I am constant to my purposes; they follow the king's pleasure: if his fit-
        ness speaks, mine is ready; now or whensoever, provided I be so able as now.

LORD: The king and queen and all are coming down.

HAMLET: In happy time,°   170

LORD: The queen desires you to use some gentle entertainment to Laertes before
        you fall to play.

HAMLET: She well instructs me.   (*Exit* LORD.)

HORATIO: You will lose this wager, my lord.

HAMLET: I do not think so; since he went into France, I have been in continual   175
        practice; I shall win at the odds. But thou wouldst not think how ill all 's here
        about my heart: but it is no matter.

HORATIO: Nay, good my lord,—

HAMLET: It is but foolery; but it is such a kind of gain-giving,° as would perhaps
        trouble a woman.   180

HORATIO: If your mind dislike any thing, obey it: I will forestall their repair hither,
        and say you are not fit.

HAMLET: Not a whit, we defy augury: there's a special providence in the fall of a
        sparrow. If it be now, 'tis not to come; if it be not to come, it will be now; if it be
        not now, yet it will come: the readiness is all°: since no man of aught he leaves   185
        knows, what is 't to leave betimes? Let be.

> (*A table prepared.* [*Enter*] *Trumpets, Drums, and Officers with cushions;*
> KING, QUEEN, [OSRIC,] *and all the State; foils, daggers,* [*and wine borne in;*]
> *and* LAERTES.)

KING: Come, Hamlet, come, and take this hand from me.

> (*The* KING *puts* LAERTES*'s hand into* HAMLET*'s.*)

HAMLET: Give me your pardon, sir: I have done you wrong;
        But pardon 't as you are a gentleman.
        This presence° knows,   190
        And you must needs have heard, how I am punish'd
        With a sore distraction. What I have done,
        That might your nature, honour and exception°
        Roughly awake, I here proclaim was madness.
        Was 't Hamlet wrong'd Laertes? Never Hamlet: 195
        If Hamlet from himself be ta'en away.
        And when he's not himself does wrong Laertes,
        Then Hamlet does it not, Hamlet denies it.
        Who does it, then? His madness: if 't be so,

---

170. in happy time: a phrase of courtesy.   **179. gain-giving:** misgiving.   **185. all:** all that matters.
190. presence: royal assembly.   **193. exception:** disapproval.

Hamlet is of the faction that is wrong'd; 200
His madness is poor Hamlet's enemy.
Sir, in this audience,
Let my disclaiming from a purpos'd evil
Free me so far in your most generous thoughts,
That I have shot mine arrow o'er the house, 205
And hurt my brother.

LAERTES: I am satisfied in nature,°
Whose motive, in this case, should stir me most
To my revenge: but in my terms of honour
I stand aloof; and will no reconcilement,
Till by some elder masters, of known honour, 210
I have a voice° and precedent of peace,
To keep my name ungor'd. But till that time,
I do receive your offer'd love like love,
And will not wrong it.

HAMLET: I embrace it freely;
And will this brother's wager frankly play. 215
Give us the foils. Come on.

LAERTES: Come, one for me.

HAMLET: I'll be your foil,° Laertes: in mine ignorance
Your skill shall, like a star i' th' darkest night,
Stick fiery off° indeed.

LAERTES: You mock me, sir.

HAMLET: No, by this hand. 220

KING: Give them the foils, young Osric. Cousin Hamlet,
You know the wager?

HAMLET: Very well, my lord;
Your grace has laid the odds o' th' weaker side.

KING: I do not fear it; I have seen you both;
But since he is better'd, we have therefore odds. 225

LAERTES: This is too heavy, let me see another.

HAMLET: This likes me well. These foils have all a length?

(They prepare to play.)

OSRIC: Ay, my good lord.

KING: Set me the stoups of wine upon that table.
If Hamlet give the first or second hit, 230
Or quit in answer of the third exchange,
Let all the battlements their ordnance fire;

---

206. nature: i.e., he is personally satisfied, but his honor must be satisfied by the rules of the code of honor.   **211. voice:** authoritative pronouncement.   **217. foil:** quibble on the two senses: "background which sets something off," and "blunted rapier for fencing."   **219. Stick fiery off:** stand out brilliantly

The king shall drink to Hamlet's better breath;
And in the cup an union° shall he throw,
Richer than that which four successive kings   235
In Denmark's crown have worn. Give me the cups;
And let the kettle° to the trumpet speak,
The trumpet to the cannoneer without,
The cannons to the heavens, the heavens to earth,
"Now the king drinks to Hamlet." Come begin: (*Trumpets the while.*)   240
And you, the judges, bear a wary eye.

HAMLET: Come on, sir.

LAERTES: Come, my lord. (*They play.*)

HAMLET: One.

LAERTES: No.

HAMLET: Judgment.

OSRIC: A hit, a very palpable hit.

(*Drums, trumpets, and shot. Flourish. A piece goes off.*)

LAERTES: Well; again.

KING: Stay; give me drink. Hamlet, this pearl° is thine;
Here's to thy health. Give him the cup.   245

HAMLET: I'll play this bout first; set it by awhile.
Come. (*They play.*) Another hit; what say you?

LAERTES: A touch, a touch, I do confess 't.

KING: Our son shall win.

QUEEN: He's fat,° and scant of breath.
Here, Hamlet, take my napkin, rub thy brows: 250
The queen carouses° to thy fortune, Hamlet.

HAMLET: Good madam!

KING: Gertrude, do not drink.

QUEEN: I will, my lord; I pray you, pardon me. (*Drinks.*)

KING (*aside*):   It is the poison'd cup: it is too late.

HAMLET: I dare not drink yet, madam; by and by.   255

QUEEN: Come, let me wipe thy face.

LAERTES: My lord, I'll hit him now.

KING: I do not think 't.

LAERTES (*aside*):   And yet 'tis almost 'gainst my conscience.

HAMLET: Come, for the third, Laertes: you but dally;
I pray you, pass with your best violence;   260
I am afeard you make a wanton° of me.

LAERTES: Say you so? come on. (*They play.*)

---

234. union: pearl.   **237. kettle:** kettledrum.   **244. pearl:** i.e., the poison.   **249. fat:** not physically fit, out of training. Some earlier editors speculated that the term applied to the corpulence of Richard Burbage, who originally played the part, but the allusion now appears unlikely. "Fat" may also suggest "sweaty."   **251. carouses:** drinks a toast.   **261. wanton:** spoiled child.

OSRIC: Nothing, neither way.

LAERTES: Have at you now!

(LAERTES *wounds* HAMLET; *then, in scuffling, they change rapiers,*° *and*
HAMLET *wounds* LAERTES.)

KING: Part them; they are incens'd.

HAMLET: Nay, come again.   (*The* QUEEN *falls.*)

OSRIC: Look to the queen there, ho!   265

HORATIO: They bleed on both sides. How is it, my lord?

OSRIC: How is 't, Laertes?

LAERTES: Why, as a woodcock° to mine own springe,° Osric;
   I am justly kill'd with mine own treachery.

HAMLET: How does the queen?

KING: She swounds° to see them bleed.   270

QUEEN: No, no, the drink, the drink,—O my dear Hamlet,—
   The drink, the drink! I am poison'd.   (*Dies.*)

HAMLET: O villany! Ho! let the door be lock'd:
   Treachery! Seek it out.   (LAERTES *falls.*)

LAERTES: It is here, Hamlet: Hamlet, thou art slain;   275
   No med'cine in the world can do thee good;
   In thee there is not half an hour of life;
   The treacherous instrument is in thy hand,
   Unbated° and envenom'd: the foul practice
   Hath turn'd itself on me; lo, here I lie,   280
   Never to rise again: thy mother's poison'd:
   I can no more: the king, the king's to blame.

HAMLET: The point envenom'd too!
   Then, venom, to thy work. (*Stabs the* KING.)

ALL: Treason! treason!   285

KING: O, yet defend me, friends; I am but hurt.

HAMLET: Here, thou incestuous, murd'rous, damned Dane.
   Drink off this potion. Is thy union here?
   Follow my mother.   (KING *dies.*)

LAERTES: He is justly serv'd;
   It is a poison temper'd° by himself.   290
   Exchange forgiveness with me, noble Hamlet:
   Mine and my father's death come not upon thee,
   Nor thine on me!   (*Dies.*)

HAMLET: Heaven make thee free of it! I follow thee.
   I am dead, Horatio. Wretched queen, adieu!   295

s.d. in scuffling, they change rapiers: according to a widespread stage tradition, Hamlet receives a
scratch, realizes that Laertes's sword is unbated (not blunted), and accordingly forces an exchange.
268. woodcock: as type of stupidity or as decoy.   **268. springe:** trap, snare.   **270. swounds:** swoons.
279. Unbated: Not blunted with a button.   **290. temper'd:** mixed.

You that look pale and tremble at this chance,
That are but mutes° or audience to this act,
Had I but time—as this fell sergeant,° Death,
Is strict in his arrest—O, I could tell you—
But let it be. Horatio, I am dead;   300
Thou livest; report me and my cause aright
To the unsatisfied.

HORATIO: Never believe it:
I am more an antique Roman° than a Dane:
Here's yet some liquor left.

HAMLET: As th' art a man,
Give me the cup: let go, by heaven, I'll ha 't.   305
O God! Horatio, what a wounded name,
Things standing thus unknown, shall live behind me!
If thou didst ever hold me in thy heart,
Absent thee from felicity awhile,
And in this harsh world draw thy breath in pain,   310
To tell my story. (*A march afar off.*)
                  What warlike noise is this?

OSRIC: Young Fortinbras, with conquest come from Poland,
To the ambassadors of England gives
This warlike volley.

HAMLET: O, I die, Horatio;
The potent poison quite o'er-crows° my spirit: 315
I cannot live to hear the news from England;
But I do prophesy th' election lights
On Fortinbras: he has my dying voice;
So tell him, with th' occurrents,° more and less,
Which have solicited.° The rest is silence.   (*Dies.*) 320

HORATIO: Now cracks a noble heart. Good night, sweet prince;
And flights of angels sing thee to thy rest!
Why does the drum come hither? (*March within.*)

(*Enter* FORTINBRAS, *with the* [*English*] AMBASSADORS [*and others*].)

FORTINBRAS: Where is this sight?
HORATIO: What is it you would see?
If aught of woe or wonder, cease your search.   325

FORTINBRAS: This quarry° cries on havoc.° O proud Death,
What feast is toward in thine eternal cell,
That thou so many princes at a shot

---

297. **mutes:** performers in a play who speak no words.   298. **sergeant:** sheriff's officer.   303. **Roman:**
it was the Roman custom to follow masters in death.   315. **o'er-crows:** triumphs over.   319. **occur-**
rents: events, incidents.   320. **solicited:** moved, urged.   326. **quarry:** heap of dead.   326. **cries on:**
havoc proclaims a general slaughter.

So bloodily hast struck?

FIRST AMBASSADOR:　　　　　The sight is dismal;
And our affairs from England come too late:　　　　　　　　　330
The ears are senseless that should give us hearing,
To tell him his commandment is fulfill'd,
That Rosencrantz and Guildenstern are dead:
Where should we have our thanks?

HORATIO:　　　　　　　　　　　Not from his mouth,°
Had it th' ability of life to thank you:　　　　　　　　　335
He never gave commandment for their death.
But since, so jump° upon this bloody question,°
You from the Polack wars, and you from England,
Are here arriv'd, give order that these bodies
High on a stage° be placed to the view;　　　　　　　　　340
And let me speak to th' yet unknowing world
How these things came about: so shall you hear
Of carnal, bloody, and unnatural acts,
Of accidental judgements, casual slaughters,
Of deaths put on by cunning and forc'd cause,　　　　　　　345
And, in this upshot, purposes mistook
Fall'n on th' inventors' heads: all this can I
Truly deliver.

FORTINBRAS:　　Let us haste to hear it,
And call the noblest to the audience.
For me, with sorrow I embrace my fortune:　　　　　　　　350
I have some rights of memory° in this kingdom,
Which now to claim my vantage doth invite me.

HORATIO:　　Of that I shall have also cause to speak,
And from his mouth whose voice will draw on more°:
But let this same be presently perform'd,　　　　　　　　　355
Even while men's minds are wild; lest more mischance,
On° plots and errors, happen.

FORTINBRAS:　　　　　　　　Let four captains
Bear Hamlet, like a soldier, to the stage;
For he was likely, had he been put on,
To have prov'd most royal: and, for his passage,°　　　　　360
The soldiers' music and the rites of war
Speak loudly for him.
Take up the bodies: such a sight as this
Becomes the field,° but here shows much amiss.

---

334. his mouth: i.e., the king's.　**337. jump:** precisely.　**337. question:** dispute.　**340. stage:** platform.　**351. of memory:** traditional, remembered.　**354. voice . . . more:** vote will influence still others.　**357. On:** on account of, or possibly, on top of, in addition to.　**360. passage:** death.　**364. field:** i.e., of battle.

Go, bid the soldiers shoot.   365

> (*Exeunt [marching, bearing off the dead bodies; after which a peal of ordnance is shot off].*)

[c. 1600]

Journal Entry

Is there a character in *Hamlet* with whom you identify? What is it about his or her personality or situation that interests you?

Textual Considerations

1. In act 2, Hamlet tries to discover the facts about Claudius's guilt while the king attempts to uncover the truth about Hamlet's madness. Explain what their plans have in common. How do they culminate in the "mousetrap," the play within the play? What purpose does the "mousetrap" serve? Explain.
2. Discuss the degree to which Hamlet's bitterness and sorrow are attributable to his mother's remarrying rather than to his father's death. What role does Gertrude play in King Hamlet's death? What arguments does Hamlet use against her when he confronts her in act 3, scene 4?
3. To what extent is Laertes a **foil** to Hamlet? Compare, for example, their responses to their fathers' murders. What do Hamlet's soliloquies reveal about his relationship with his father? Which of Hamlet's soliloquies do you find more interesting? Explain.
4. Investigate the dramatic impact of the play from its two extremes—the ghost's urge to disclose his story to Hamlet in act 1, scene 5, and Hamlet's plea for Horatio to tell his story in act 5, scene 2. What do these scenes reveal about Old Hamlet's and Hamlet's attitudes toward their origins? How effectively do these scenes enhance the dramatic action of the play?
5. Review Hamlet's interview with Ophelia in act 3, scene 1. Consider what his comments disclose about the motives and attitudes that prompt him to cast Ophelia, rather than Claudius, as his antagonist. Why does Ophelia commit suicide? What does Hamlet's letter to Ophelia reveal about him and his attitude toward women before his father's death?
6. Why does Hamlet delay in avenging his father's death? Discuss how Hamlet's act of remembering and forgetting the ghost—or his ambivalence toward the ghost's plea for revenge—informs his actions throughout the play.
7. Do you think *Hamlet* would lose much of its dramatic power if Shakespeare had cut out the role of Fortinbras? Speculate as to why some productions of *Hamlet* omit the Fortinbras role.

Cultural Contexts

1. What can we infer about Ophelia's and Gertrude's roles in *Hamlet*? Do these feminine characters merely fulfill the gender roles in the play, or do they also add to our understanding of Hamlet's character? Investigate also how Ophelia and Gertrude narrate the past, and how they establish a dramatic dialogue with the present and the future. How do Hamlet's attacks on these characters and on women in general affect your response to the drama?

2. Explore the father-and-son relationship in Hamlet. In your discussion, debate with members of your group whether Hamlet, by inheriting the past and his father's designs, is also forced to inherit his father's moral law.

Performance Exercises

PERFORMANCE EXPRESS (45 MINUTES)

1. Following a long tradition established by actresses like Sarah Bernhardt (1844–1923) who played the role of Hamlet, select a female classmate and cast her in the role of Hamlet. Ask her to deliver an improvised and spontaneous version of the nursery scene (3.1.90–153) in which she interacts with Ophelia, who could be played by a woman or a man. Invite the whole class to discuss the dramatic effectiveness of this gender-reversal performance.

2. Peter Brooks, a British stage director, proposes the following performance exercise in his book *The Empty Space* (London: MacGibbon & Kee, 1968): "Take the two lines 'To be or not to be, That is the question' and give them to ten actors, one word each. The actors stand in a closed circle and endeavor to play the words one after the other trying to produce a living phrase. . . . When after long work the sentence suddenly flows, a thrilling freedom is experienced by everyone. They see in a flash the possibility of group playing, and the obstacles to it." Working with your group, follow Brooks's directions to deliver the same line above. Discuss your response to this exercise.

PERFORMANCE PROJECTS

1. British critic John Dover Wilson once stated that "we were never intended to reach the heart of Hamlet's mystery." Using Internet resources, read about John Gielgud's (1930s), Laurence Olivier's (1937), Michael Redgrave's (1950), and Richard Burton's (1964) performances of *Hamlet*. Then, working with your group, stage one key scene of *Hamlet* that clearly defines *your* approach to Hamlet's mysterious character. Does your group want to cast Hamlet as an idealist, a lunatic, or a neurotic or psychotic character? Which lines would you cut to suit your stage production? Decide on time period, costumes, props, and stage actions.

2. Discuss with your group the possibility of transferring the setting of *Hamlet* to the United State in the twenty-first century. Watch Ethan Hawke's and Campbell Scott's performances of *Hamlet* on video before you decide how you would stage one of the scenes of the play. Besides considering your Hamlet's physical appearance, dominant traits, and costumes, also decide whether you would lean toward a Freudian or a non-Freudian interpretation of the play. Explain your reasons. (See Appendix D on the Freudian interpretation of *Hamlet*.)

COMPOSING PROCESS AND PEER CRITIQUES: PART ONE

We asked our student Laura Kuehn briefly to describe her writing process and write a paper on one of the topics for Discussion and Writing at the end of Part One. She chose number 4 because she enjoys writing about the intersection of past and present. As you read her composing process, highlight what seems helpful to you.

After choosing to write about poets Langston Hughes and Robert Hayden, my next step was to do research and brainstorm. I went online to look up their biographies as I knew very little about either of them. Then I read and reread the poems, concentrating on the meaning of each word. While reading, I jotted down any thoughts and ideas on a piece of scrap paper. When I finally felt confident, I constructed a simple outline using the brainstorming notes on the scrap paper. Using the outline and referring constantly to the poems, I wrote a first draft. I put the paper aside for a couple of days and reviewed it with a fresh perspective, paying close attention to grammatical errors and checking the paper's coherence.

OUTLINE FOR ESSAY

Introduction

I. Hughes and Hayden influential in movement.
   a. popular poets
   b. inspired by Harlem Renaissance
   c. voice for African American community

Body

I. "The Negro Speaks of Rivers" by Hughes
   a. connects nature and human experience
   b. relates past and present
   c. rivers are mighty, enduring, have life of their own
   d. Hughes associates river with physiological attributes
   e. Remembering a time before slavery
   f. Never uses words "slave" or "slavery"

II.   "Frederick Douglass" by Hayden
    a. perception of freedom from conceptual to tangible
    b. immediate stress that struggle is still prevalent
    c. physiological references and notes use of political tool
    d. poem describes Douglass's trials and tribulations
    e. give brief synopsis of who Douglass was
    f. Hayden wants Douglass's legacy to be continuing the fight for freedom

Conclusion

I.   Hughes and Hayden more than writers.
    a. intelligent and insightful
    b. maintain fight.
    c. message in both poems
    d. freedom is a prerequisite for living

Kuehn 1

Laura Kuehn
Professor Gillespie
EN 101
Fall 2004

An Analysis of Two Poems by
Hughes and Hayden

Langston Hughes and Robert Hayden were two
of the most influential writers who examined the
struggles of the African American community. Both
men recognized that silence meant submission and
that the economic and social inequalities
bestowed on the African American people needed to
be told. Hughes and Hayden were determined to
give a strong voice to an otherwise often
oppressed people. They were fortunate to be
living and creating during the era of the Harlem
Renaissance, which gave them much to stand on and
allowed for a wider range of audience. The surge
of interest that sprung from the Renaissance
undoubtedly fueled much of the poets' creativity.
A brief analysis of two popular poems, one
written by each author, will shed light on how
passionate both Hughes and Hayden were when it
came to preserving their people's culture and
pride.

In the poem "The Negro Speaks of Rivers,"
Langston Hughes draws a connection between
nature and the human experience while
simultaneously relating the past with the
present in respect to the narrator who is
African American. Metaphorically speaking,
a river is thought to be mighty and enduring
with a palpable sense of having a life of its

ancient as the world and older than the flow of
human blood in human veins." The idea that the
narrator has "known rivers" is a powerful notion,
but by associating rivers with physiological
attributes, Hughes allows for the reader to
appreciate the concept. In the fifth, sixth, and
seventh lines the narrator proceeds to tell of
the time before slavery, a time reminiscent of
African strength and empowerment. He makes
references to three specific rivers that played
vital roles for successful African civilization.
The first river mentioned, the Euphrates, bears
important biblical meaning as well, because
according to Genesis 2:14, it flows from the
Garden of Eden, The second and third African
rivers mentioned, the Congo and Nile, were
lifelines that provided surrounding fertile lands
and were spiritually revered. However all of
these significant rivers would turn out to be
lifelines of another sort when they became
integral routes for the Atlantic slave trade.
Without losing nuance, Hughes is then able to
jolt the reader ahead many years by writing,
"I heard the singing of the Mississippi when Abe
Lincoln went down to New Orleans.' Although the
poem never mentions the words *slave* or *slavery*,
the reader conjures up thoughts of years of
oppression and struggle, and then eventual
emancipation. In essence, the narrator and his
people have journeyed from free to bondage and
back to free again. Hughes ends the poem with the
narrator repeating that he "has grown deep like
the rivers," meaning that he has lived long and
hard but will continue to go on.

Kuehn 3

In Robert Hayden's poem "Frederick Douglas,"
he examines how the perception of freedom from
past to present has changed from conceptual to
seemingly tangible. The first few words that say
"when it is finally ours" immediately stress that
true liberty for the African American people has
yet to be achieved, that the struggle is far from
over. The first stanza declares that freedom is
as "needful to man as air." Hayden makes
physiological references also to *diastole* and
systole, which refer to the rhythmic flow of
blood pumping through the heart and vessels.
These lines are incredibly impressive because
they imply that freedom is as vital and necessary
to life as the blood that flows through the body.
Hayden also longs for the day when the freedom of
African Americans is "more than the gaudy mumbo
jumbo of politicians," used as a political tool
throughout history when so few were genuine or
sincere. The eighth, ninth, and tenth lines are
poignant because they tell of the trials and
tribulations of Frederick Douglass himself; "a
former slave . . . beaten to his knees, exiled,
visioning a world where none is lonely, none
hunted, or alien." Douglass was an integral part
of the abolitionist movement during the Civil War
era. The eleventh line proclaims, "This man shall
be remembered." And he has been. His story has
been told numerous times, taught among
classrooms, and his image immortalized by
countless statues. Yet Hayden insists that
Douglass not simply be remembered by this but
rather by "the lives grown out of his, the lives
fleshing his dream of the beautiful." By this

Hayden is stating that Douglass's legacy is the African American men and women that follow in his footsteps and continue to fight for equality and freedom. Hayden's poem asserts a sense of animosity but for a purpose. He, like Douglass, envisions much more for his people. He's willing to play the antagonist to motivate others to keep up the fight, which he perceives as very much attainable. And perhaps he is right, and one day the beauty of freedom and liberty will finally be universal.

Hughes and Hayden were more than mere writers. They were intelligent and insightful men who took a stand for what they believed in. Each was active in the fight to maintain a strong and empowering African American community. Realizing that words can be a powerful tool, Hughes and Hayden used their writings to motivate others. In both poems, "The Negro Speaks of Rivers" and "Frederick Douglass," there is a message, one that expresses the sentiment that freedom is imperative. Without it a person is not human, he or she does not exist. Freedom, above all else, is a prerequisite for living.

TOPICS FOR DISCUSSION
AND WRITING

Writing Topics

1. The understanding of parent by child or child by parent is the focus of several poems in Part One. Write an analysis of the father-and-son or mother-and-daughter relationship portrayed by Lee, Olds, Hayden, Chock, Mirikitani, or Emanuel. What insights did the speakers gain through their recollections of family? To what extent are their relationships characterized by conflicting emotions? Choose any three poems.

2. A particular place evokes significant reflections for the characters in the stories by Wharton, Wolff, Chang, and Wiesel. Analyze the interactions between people and places in one of the stories that made these insights possible.

3. Several short stories focus on the passage of time and changes that occur in the lives of the characters. Using "The Watch," "Powder," or "The Unforgetting," compare and contrast the attitudes that any two characters in two of the stories take toward the passing of time.

4. Hughes and Hayden focus on the heritage of African Americans. Analyze the interactions of past and present in "The Negro Speaks of Rivers" and "Runagate Runagate." Include the role of setting in your analysis.

5. Rewrite Hamlet's dilemma from Horatio's point of view, and discuss the degree to which his viewpoint corresponds to or differs from yours.

6. The protagonists in "The Unforgetting," "The Watch," and "Father and I" are involved in literal and symbolic journeys. Trace the journeys in any two texts, and analyze their emotional, physical, or psychological significance for the characters' lives. To what extent did their journeys include a new awareness of solitude?

7. Past experiences are important to Momaday, Hurston, and Rushdie. Does the fact that each essay is about their particular cultures and traditions have any relevance to their theme and purpose? Compare and contrast their attitudes toward their roots. Is rebellion a part of their experiences? Choose two texts and write an essay on these issues.

8. Contrast portrayals of childhood with premonitions of adulthood in the poems by Eberhart and Thomas. How does each poet use imagery to enhance theme?

9. At the outset of the play *Oedipus Rex*, Oedipus as king is attempting to answer an objective question: Who murdered King Laios? As the drama progresses, however, Oedipus as an individual is confronted with the subjective question: Who am I? Explain what he learns about himself as he seeks to answer both questions.

10. Analyze Hamlet's psychological state at the outset of the drama. To what extent does his state of mind contribute to his later actions in play? Cite specific examples.

11. Several texts in Part One focus on the relationship between father and son, including the stories by Lagerkvist, Chang, and Wolff. Choose two stories and compare and contrast the portrayals of this relationship. To what extent was rebellion part of this tie?

12. How are the gods and their prophecies presented in *Oedipus Rex*? Does the fact that the oracle decreed that Oedipus will kill his father and marry his mother absolve him of guilt for his actions? Write an analytical essay responding to these questions.

13. Several texts in Part One communicate the validity of past experiences and explore the role that memory plays in the interactions of roots and rebellions as past and present intersect. Write an analysis of any two texts that present these themes.

14. Hamlet and Ophelia's relationship is problematic. Was Hamlet really in love with her, or does she become the victim of his rebellion against Claudius and his mother? To what extent is Hamlet to blame for Ophelia's madness and death? Write a paper responding to these questions that includes an analysis of their love affair.

Research Topics

1. Carry out a research project on your family history: Tape interviews with family members and collect old family photos, letters, diaries, memoirs, or any other family records that you might use as supporting evidence. Then check library sources, such as newspapers and magazines, to identify the major sociohistorical events that were part of your family's history. In writing the paper, consider assuming the personal voice of a family member and narrating your family history from his or her point of view.

2. *Oedipus Rex* and *Hamlet* have inspired diverse literary, psychological, and cultural responses. One of the most frequent interpretations of these plays concerns Sigmund Freud's psychoanalytic theory known as the Oedipus complex. To understand more about this theory, consult the references to psychoanalytic criticism in Appendix D, as well as sources such as Ernest Jones's *Hamlet and Oedipus* (New York: Norton, 1976) and Edmond Lowell's *Oedipus: The Ancient Legend and Its Later Analogues* (Baltimore: Johns Hopkins University Press, 1985). Applying Freud's theory to both dramas, write a research paper arguing whether the Oedipus complex helps explain the mental processes of the protagonists.

3. Several writers in Part One focus on the passage of time and the generational changes that occur in families and/or or in attitudes toward ethnic and cultural roots. Select an ethnic group represented by one of the authors, and using library and Internet sources, identify the major sociohistorical events that are part of its history. Using supporting evidence and your responses to the texts of the author you chose, write a paper that explores the causes and effects of generational and/or cultural rebellions.

FILM ANGLES

Because the themes of this unit, embodied in such works as *Oedipus Rex*, and *Hamlet*, are among the most enduring in the history of literature, it is not surprising that they can also be found in films. These include not only films based on literature (e.g., there are several film versions of *Oedipus* and *Hamlet*) but those with original screenplays that deal with characters' quests for origins or roots and insights into their lives. As in the case of Oedipus, this search often takes the form of an investigation into the past in an effort to determine one's true identity or simply to better understand one's self. As the tragic fate of Oedipus attests, however, the insight gained from such a search does not always bring greater happiness.

Just as many of the themes found in literature can be found in films, certain narrative techniques are shared by both media, although the forms they take, of course, are different. Films that tell stories, like novels and short stories, have narrative structures, plots, characters, dialogue, and a specific point of view. Some films have dramatic "three-act" structures, like plays. Many films also have complex visual structures equivalent to imagery in poetry: The repetition of certain objects or colors or specific techniques can accumulate meaning by association, just as the repetition of such things in poems does. Although films are usually more visual than linguistic, they can create such things as metaphors through the artful juxtaposition of images in which two gestures, objects, or actions are compared in a particular context.

The object of the film units is to encourage you to identify and appreciate the similarities between narrative films and literature as well as to learn how to look at films for the unique ways in which they create expression and meaning. These ways are the formal aspects of film style and technique; they appear in the text in boldface and are defined in the glossary of film terms at the back of the book.

FILM HISTORY AND GENRES

The range of movies that can be profitably examined with regard to the themes of roots and rebellion is wide, ranging from recognized masterpieces (e.g., *Citizen Kane* (d. Orson Welles, 1941) and biographical dramas (e.g., *Freud*, d. John Huston, 1962; and *The Miracle Worker*, d. Arthur Penn, 1962), to science fiction adventures (e.g., *Back to the Future*, d. Robert Zemeckis, 1985) and teenage melodramas (e.g., *Rebel Without a Cause*, d. Nicholas Ray, 1955).

In each case, the type of movie—the **genre** it belongs to—affects the way the theme emerges. A biographical drama often structures the narrative in light of a central fact about its real-life subject. For example, the story line in *Freud* concerns how Sigmund Freud's investigation of the origins of his own sufferings led to his groundbreaking insights into the workings of the unconscious. Although this approach does not give us a complete biographical portrait, using such a dramatic or thematic hook allows the filmmaker to organize the material toward a specific goal so the protagonist is engaged on a quest toward insights into his or her life. By structuring a film in this way, the viewer becomes actively involved in the quest as well, although one should remember that the structure—like the quest—is an artificial framework, not the real life of the biographical subject.

THE COMING-OF-AGE FILM

Many popular films, although belonging to distinct genres, are also coming-of-age narratives, a fictional type found in literature and film. So although *Back to the Future* and *Terminator 2* (d. James Cameron, 1991) are science fiction films in that they include time travel, they also feature young protagonists who must come to terms with who they are in relation to real or symbolic parental figures. And although it would be delimiting to label either *Hamlet* or *Oedipus the King* coming-of-age dramas, the role of parents in how each tragic figure has formed his identity and view of the world is a determinant factor.

As the phrase indicates, the coming-of-age film is usually about protagonists entering adolescence, a period of life that generally provokes questioning the roots from which we have sprung and the people—namely, parents—whose values we have inherited. Sometimes this leads to an intense conflict with the adult world and brings about such a shattering of childhood ideals that nothing less than revolt seems an adequate response. But although words such as *revolt* and *rebellion* conjure up images of aggressive, even violent, behavior, the transformation that is implied can also be quietly assertive, informed by an inner change rather than a lashing out. The following films are a few of the excellent examples across many genres that can be fruitfully studied in conjunction with the literature and themes of this unit.

Rebel Without a Cause (d. Nicholas Ray, 1955), largely famous for the performance of James Dean, a teenage icon of the 1950s, remains a strong dramatization of alienated youth. Dean's own premature death in an automobile accident made him almost the cinematic prototype of this concept. The character he portrays is a sensitive loner, misunderstood by a controlling, overemotional mother and a weak father, a situation that parallels the absent or non-nurturing parents of two other leading characters: the girl who loves him and the boy who idolizes him. To prove his manhood and be accepted by his peers, he engages in dangerous teenage rituals that lead to the death of another boy. In one of the film's strongest scenes, the role of the ineffectual parent in the crisis of alienation is powerfully conveyed when the Dean character tells his parents that they are "tearing him apart" and begs his father to be a man and stand up for him.

Whereas *Rebel* is set in the teeming city of Los Angeles, the action in *Hud* (d. Martin Ritt, 1963) is limited to a small Texas town and the cattle ranch owned by the title character's father. Hud is a cynic and a womanizer, but when his father calls him an "unprincipled man," we wonder how much of what he is results from his father's withdrawal of love and respect. In the course of the story, Hud is a role model for his nephew, whose father (Hud's brother) was killed in an accident for which Hud feels guilty. By observing how Hud treats his grandfather and the woman housekeeper, the boy slowly recognizes the weaknesses of the man he admires and, in the end, he rejects him as a failed image of a man. The inner struggle that leads to the boy's decision to leave Hud behind to pursue a life of his own is never flamboyantly dramatized, but it is no less a form of rebellion.

The Return (d. Andrey Zvyagintsev, 2004) is a powerful Russian tale of two young boys whose father suddenly returns after an unexplained absence of many years. In an effort to assert his presence and authority in their lives, he takes them on a journey to an island where he has buried something years before. The film leaves this and other details unexplained to stress the moral and psychological struggle that ensues between the father and his sons, the youngest of whom violently objects to the way the man treats them, suspects he is not really their father, and fears he will kill them. Although the film is realistic, it works as an allegory of contemporary Russian history and achieves a mythic stature with its allusions to the Bible (e.g., the story of Abraham and Isaac) and the primal emotions of Freud's Oedipal theory.

Steven Spielberg's *Hook* (1991) might be considered a variation of the coming-of-age story, in its reimagining of the Peter Pan legend, whereby a businessman in the real world must enter a fantasy adventure world and rediscover his childhood in order to be a better father.

Yet another interesting variation of this unit's themes—of special relevance to the dominance of the media in contemporary society—is the Jim Carrey vehicle *The Truman Show* (d. Peter Weir, 1998). The emerging consciousness of the main character involves his recognition that his entire life has been literally "programmed" by the media and is on view for millions of television addicts. Truman's determination to find the "real" world beyond the fabricated one in which he lives is a heroic struggle that ends in a step into the unknown. Here, the confrontation is extended beyond parental values to an awareness that everything in the environment and every "relation" with others is artificial. Could the characterization of one's roots be any more disastrous? Could the effort to discover something real beyond it be any more courageous?

Questions to Consider

1. Compare any two of the films mentioned in this section, and consider how in each case the main character achieves his or her insights within the conventions of the genre.
2. Look at a biographical film and try to identify the *hook*, the thematic premise that becomes the goal of the character's life and the central focus of the film. Does this key idea reduce the biographical subject too simplistically? Is the idea effective in organizing the film? Would the film lose its coherence and be less appealing without it? Can you think of a better hook for the film?
3. Can Oedipus's struggle to discover the truth of his origins be compared with the struggles of the protagonists in any of the coming-of-age films discussed here?
4. Coming-of-age stories often involve a recognition that neither the people we love nor the world around us is quite as ideal as we believed. This is often described as a loss of innocence. Does this idea still seem pertinent or has the age we live in rendered the notion of innocence irrelevant? Consider any of the films in the coming-of-age category in this light.
5. Given the artificiality of his entire environment, how is Truman able to imagine another world? In what way is his decision to leave the only world he knows an act of rebellion?
6. Is Truman's quest and the film a metaphor for the limitations of false constructs about the world that all of us may have to confront in our lives?

CASE STUDIES

Note: The films singled out under this category in each unit are recommended for study because (1) they are recognized as superior examples of film art, (2) they are especially effective in illustrating how the themes of the unit have been translated into cinematic terms, and (3) they are readily available on DVD and VHS for classroom use or for individual student research.

In some cases, the film or films chosen may be versions of a work of literature in the unit (e.g., *Hamlet* in this unit; *Othello* in the Race and Culture unit). In other cases, the films may be used as *separate but equivalent texts* in a different medium that deal with the themes of the unit in unique ways (e.g., *Citizen Kane* in this unit; *Full Metal Jacket* in the War and Violence unit; *All That Heaven Allows* in the Gender and Identity unit). By making use of these films, you will learn (1) how important themes are handled in the very powerful and influential art form of motion pictures, (2) that even popular films are vehicles for such important themes, and (3) that thematic links between film and literature are much closer than is often imagined.

Citizen Kane

Sometimes, the quest for roots is initiated by a secondary character. In Orson Welles's *Citizen Kane* (1941), regarded as one of the greatest movies ever made, a newspaper reporter is assigned to investigate the meaning of "Rosebud," the last word uttered by the film's protagonist, Charles Foster Kane, before his death. The reporter interviews people who were close to Kane, but neither they nor he discovers who or what "Rosebud" is. The secret is revealed at the end of the film but only to the audience, who must then weigh its significance in the light of what has been learned about the character throughout the film. The tracing of origins and gathering of insights, therefore, is the subject of the film, determining both its **flashback** narrative structure and its multiple **point of view**.

One of the film's many stylistic patterns is its consistent use of **deep-focus cinematography**, a way of filming that keeps all planes of action—foreground, middle ground, and background—and aspects of the **mise-en-scene** in sharp focus and in clear relation to each other. In *Citizen Kane*, this technique is repeatedly used to reveal the way the protagonist (Kane) relates to the significant people in his life. For example, in the important childhood scene in which Kane's mother sends him away to be raised by a banker, the boy Kane is seen through a window in the background playing outside in the snow while negotiations determining his future are being made by his parents and the banker in the foreground. This becomes a model **composition** in the film that both reiterates his childhood origins and provides continued insight into his character makeup. In the light of this early experience in his childhood, the adult Kane's behavior in wanting everything his way more and more resembles that of a man who has never grown up and still needs to rebel. Examining a number of the film's deep-focus shots reveals how Kane's early childhood experience is reenacted in his later life. It also teaches us how cinematic composition and **visual motifs** produce and reinforce meaning in a film.

Questions to Consider

1. Although the character of Kane remains somewhat enigmatic, a compelling portrait of him can be drawn from the recollections of those who knew him. What features of Kane's personality help fill in that portrait?
2. If Kane is emotionally immature and incapable of insight into his own character, as some characters suggest, does this explain why we are not given his own point of view? If Kane were to have his own flashback, what do you think it would include? What would it exclude?
3. Locate and analyze several deep-focus shots in the film. What do they reveal about Kane's relationship with the other character(s) in the shot?

Hamlet

Note: Because *Hamlet* is a major text 0in the literature section of this book, some background information is provided to help you approach film versions of the play.

Language and Film

Shakespeare's plays have attracted filmmakers since the silent era. Sound versions often fail, however, because of the difficulty of the language and of finding film actors who can speak it convincingly and because certain stage conventions, such as the soliloquy, do not transfer well to the screen. On stage the actor plays off of, and establishes an intimacy with, a live audience, whereas on screen the same actor speaking the same soliloquy can seem artificial and remote. Innovative filmmakers have tried to solve these problems in a variety of ways—for example, by magnifying the actor's body language and physical features through close-ups, telegraphing small facial expressions and slight movements of the eyes that capture subtle nuances and convey feelings that might substitute for some of the language.

Some filmmakers reduce the language to a minimum, stressing narrative clarity over psychological and poetic depth. Others offset the language with contemporary settings and topical action: e.g., Baz Luhrmann's *Romeo and Juliet* (1996) makes use of gang wars and ultra-hip set design. Still others eliminate the language altogether and adapt the story to contemporary tastes: The musical *West Side Story* (1960), also based on *Romeo and Juliet*, is a famous example.

In *Titus* (1999), her film version of Shakespeare's *Titus Andronicus*, Julie Taymor uses all the technical resources of the cinema while staging the drama in a fictional fusion of several historical epochs that links the cruelties and tyrannies of ancient Rome (the play's setting) with those of fascism in the last century. The final scene is set in the Colosseum as a way of acknowledging the play as a violent spectacle. The result is a blend of theater and film that evades questions of realism and credibility because it unfolds within the **theater of the imagination**, an effective corollary to Shakespeare's wildly excessive text.

Even the most eloquent and successful film treatments by noted Shakespearean actors and directors–for example, Laurence Olivier and Orson Welles—trim the language to avoid inordinate length. Kenneth Branagh's complete *Hamlet* (1996) runs four hours. Something is lost when lines and parts of soliloquies are cut, but their meanings are often supplied through a film's visual vocabulary.

One way filmmakers have solved the problem of the soliloquy is through the technique of **voice-over**, which preserves the intimate quality of an interior monologue. It is used in Olivier's *Hamlet*, in Grigory Kozintsev's Russian *Hamlet* of 1964, and in Michael Almeyrada's modern dress *Hamlet* of 2000. In Olivier's film, voice-over accentuates the character's isolation and loneliness and is often accompanied by close-ups of the actor's tormented face. In Kozintsev we often hear Hamlet's inner thoughts while he is around other people—as in the scene with the visiting players—so he seems to be commenting internally at the moment he witnesses something rather than later in retrospect. In each case, the filmmaker has found a way to incorporate the soliloquy into the film's world without sacrificing either intimacy or its privileged position in Shakespeare's text.

Question to Consider

Select a soliloquy from one of the film versions of *Hamlet* and examine carefully the way it is handled. Do you find the actor's delivery convincing? Has the soliloquy been shortened? Why and how? What film techniques has the director used either to enliven the scene or to compensate for any cuts?

Hamlets on Film

Hamlet has been the subject of films from the early 1900s. Since 1990 there have been four film versions, including Branagh's period spectacle and Almeyrada's contemporary reading set in New York. Thanks to the technology of VHS and DVD, such famous stage performances as those of Richard Burton and Nicol Williamson from the 1960s and 1970s are also available for study.

Perhaps the most curious film version of *Hamlet* is the silent Danish/German film of 1920, based on historical sources as well as Shakespeare's play. Hamlet is not only played by a woman (Asta Nielsen), but the character *is* a woman raised as a man because of political exigencies. This approach has fascinating implications for the character and the plot, culminating in the death scene when Horatio, while embracing the expiring "prince," suddenly realizes his friend's true sexual identity and love for him.

Laurence Olivier, one of the twentieth century's most honored actors, directed and starred in the first full-length film of *Hamlet*, which won the Academy Award for Best Picture of 1948. It can be productively compared to two more action-oriented costume versions, the first directed by Franco Zeffirelli in 1990 with Mel Gibson, and the second directed by and starring Kenneth Branagh in 1996. Because many versions of *Hamlet* exist on VHS and DVD, you can examine the variable ways in which the character—perhaps the most psychologically and morally complex in all literature—can be interpreted. Just as critical and theoretical approaches (see Appendix D in this textbook) shed light on different ways of looking at the play, seeing Hamlet portrayed by such different actors as Olivier, Branagh, and Gibson, along with Richard Burton, Nicol Williamson, Ethan Hawke, Kevin Kline, and Campbell Scott (the latter two in less available video versions), lets us *see* the many angles from which the character can be approached and appreciate the subtle differences of gestures and line readings that alter our understanding of the same text.

Question to Consider

Though the Asta Nielsen film had a narrative rationale for Hamlet's being played by a woman, in fact several noted actresses (e.g., Sarah Bernhardt) have played the prince as a man on stage. What impressions or behavioral or psychological aspects of Hamlet's character might lend themselves to this approach? Would it be possible for a woman to play Hamlet in a film or on stage in today's culture? Why or why not?

Scene Comparisons

Comparing two or more screen versions in terms of their treatment of the same scene in the play not only illuminates the often contradictory potential meanings the play can have but is instructive in highlighting interpretive and ideological approaches and how they reflect critical fashions of the time. For example, an interpretation of Hamlet's behavior that once dominated dramatic criticism and stage performances was the Freudian one (see Appendix D). Freudian psychoanalysis had its strongest hold on American and British culture between the late 1930s and the late 1950s, during which time novels and films were rife with psychological symbolism and frequent allusions to such concepts as the Oedipus complex.

Olivier's *Hamlet*, made in the midst of this period, manifests this influence, although because it was the *only* film version for decades, it was easy to forget it was a specific reading of the play. Key scenes and speeches are composed and delivered in ways that make the Oedipal conflict central to the action and the primary cause of Hamlet's delay in avenging his father's murder. This approach is worked out in the film both through the use of **subjective camera** work that renders Hamlet's key soliloquies truly introspective experiences (note the "To be or not to be" speech, for example) and through Olivier's sensitive performance, which emphasizes the prince's cultivated nature—his affinity with the arts and the best of human instincts—that make the vengeful task before him seem all the more intolerable. In contrast to Olivier's subjective approach, Branagh's Hamlet is a more active, demonstrative character, even in the soliloquies, which are often set against vast scenic backdrops that make them seem less interior than public.

Questions to Consider

1. Compare the bedroom scene between Hamlet and his mother in the Olivier film with the way it is handled in the Zeffirelli version, which also sees the character in Oedipal terms. In the Zeffirelli, Hamlet kisses his mother on the mouth. How does this gesture affect the scene and the appearance of his father's ghost? Because the Oedipus complex is an *unconscious* phenomenon, how can it explain so literal a gesture? Discuss the implications of this treatment in comparison with Olivier's. Which version do you think is truest to the play? Which is the most effective? Why?

2. Examine the same soliloquy in both the Olivier and Branagh versions. What similarities or differences can you identify? What seems to be the director's intention in each case? What do the differences in approach reveal about the character of Hamlet?

3. In Olivier's film, the play within the play is filmed with dramatic camera angles and dark, moody lighting to stress the play's affect on Claudius and dramatically reveal his guilt. Compare Olivier's treatment to the way that scene is presented in the Branagh or Zeffirelli version or any of the others available. Discuss how this illustrates the power of filmic design, cinematography, lighting, and sound in establishing the meaning of a scene and the interpretation of the work.

Hamlet *in Modern Dress*

The Olivier, Zeffirelli, and Branagh films are all period costume spectacles. Some filmmakers reject that approach and choose to modernize the play, a decision that must deal with a wholly different set of problems, not the least of which is having people who look and act just like people today speaking Elizabethan verse. However, this approach stresses the relevance of the play's conflicts and themes to contemporary society. In the Almeyrada film, Hamlet is the son of a businessman who has been murdered by his brother who takes over the company. The power struggles of royalty are replaced by the ambitions and rivalries of the corporate world in a modern metropolis.

Question to Consider

Study the Almeyrada film and consider the pros and cons of doing Hamlet in modern dress. The film uses many aspects of the contemporary world to give new twists and meanings to the text. For example, in Ophelia's mad scene, she scatters Polaroid photos instead of flowers. What other touches can you find, consistent with today's world, that give a modern edge to lines or ideas in the play?

Research Topics

1. The films *Back to the Future* and *Terminator 2* manipulate time, suggesting that if we could see into the future or back into the past, we could change our lives. How do such fantasies affect the way insights are ordinarily achieved in life? What do they tell us about the conflicts and needs that are particular to childhood and adolescence and how to deal with them?

2. *Memento* (d. Christopher Nolan, 2001) also plays with time and narrative, so the viewer continually wonders who and what can be trusted. How is the viewer's position analogous to that of the protagonist? Are we in a better position to gain insight into the character? How does the character's memory problem affect his ability to have any reliable

insights? Does he ever learn where his problem originated? Is the film a metaphor for how people often forget or deny things that are unpleasant?

3. Is the protagonist of *Citizen Kane* a tragic figure? Does he share any character traits with Oedipus or Hamlet? In classic tragedy, as defined by Aristotle, the tragic hero must be a noble character with a tragic flaw (usually pride) who recognizes his errors in the end and accepts responsibility. Given these conditions, is the film a classic tragedy? Why or why not? If Kane does not fit the description of a tragic figure, does this make it difficult for the viewer to sympathize with him?

4. *The Truman Show* raises questions about the manipulation of the media, especially television, and its influence on people's lives. Do you see any connection or thematic relationship between the film's fabrication of an entire world, which the main character believes is "real," and the so-called reality shows on television?

5. Compare one or two soliloquies from two different film versions of *Hamlet*. How does each compare with the soliloquy in the play? Has the filmmaker made cuts in the soliloquy? Has he used mise-en-scène (e.g., **setting and lighting**) or film techniques (e.g., camera angles and **camera movement**) to prevent the scene from becoming static? Has the director **edited** the scene in a way to make the speech more dynamic? As a result of your examination, what have you learned (1) about the soliloquy and its importance in Shakespeare's plays and (2) about the differences between film and theater?

6. Compare Olivier's *Hamlet* with Branagh's by closely examining one or two identical scenes in each. Identify specific performative aspects—for example, voice, delivery, and body language—in each version that convey different impressions of the characters and the scenes. What specific cinematic elements—setting, lighting, framing of shots, editing, camera movements—has the director used in each version, and what effects do they have on the overall impression of the scene and the meanings we perceive?

7. What is the nature of the origins and insights in *Hamlet*? Does his situation provoke his soul searching? Do his speculations on the relationship between thought and action produce insights for the reader and viewer? How are these complex ideas effectively conveyed in any of the film versions?

8. One traditional interpretation of Hamlet's character stresses his procrastination—that is, his inability to take action against Claudius until circumstances push him to it at the end. This would suggest he is a character more prone to thought than action. How can such a view be reconciled with such different film approaches as those of Olivier, Zeffirelli, and Branagh?

9. The Richard Burton, Nicol Williamson, and Kevin Kline *Hamlets* are actually records of live performances rather than true films. Examine one of these and consider what is gained or lost in retaining the limitations of the stage. Study a particular scene or soliloquy and compare it to the way the same scene or soliloquy is treated in one of the more cinematic versions discussed in this unit.

10. Compare any film version of *Hamlet* with the experience of *reading* the play. What are some of the obvious differences? If you read the play before seeing any version of it, what impressions of the character of Hamlet (or any others) did you bring to your viewing of the film? Did those impressions conflict with what you saw? Illustrate your response with specific examples. Were you inclined to revise your understanding or feelings about any of the characters as a result of seeing a film version of the play?

PART TWO

GENDER AND IDENTITY

Fiction

On Seeing the 100% Perfect Girl One Beautiful April Morning, Haruki Murakami
♦ *The Storm*, Kate Chopin ♦ *Roselily*, Alice Walker ♦ *The Yellow Wallpaper*,
Charlotte Perkins Gilman ♦ *Another Evening at the Club*, Alifa Rifaat ♦ *Fountains
in the Rain*, Yukio Mishima ♦ *The Smells of Home*, Sandip Roy

Essays

Professions for Women, Virginia Woolf ♦ *An Amateur Marriage*, Steve Tesich ♦
The Power of Marriage, David Brooks ♦ *The Fraternal Bond as a Joking Relation-
ship*, Peter Lyman ♦ *Sex, Lies, and Conversation: Why Is It So Hard for Men and
Women to Talk to Each Other?*, Deborah Tannen

Poetry

Woman's Constancy, John Donne ♦ *The Sun Rising*, John Donne ♦ *For My Lover,
Returning to His Wife*, Anne Sexton ♦ *Adultery*, James Dickey ♦ *Ragazza*, Mary-
frances Wagner ♦ *Borders*, Pat Mora ♦ *Home Burial*, Robert Frost ♦ *The Harlem
Dancer*, Claude McKay ♦ *What Lips My Lips Have Kissed*, Edna St. Vincent Millay ♦
Colours, Yevgeny Yevtushenko ♦ *I Knew a Woman*, Theodore Roethke ♦ *Oranges*,
Gary Soto ♦ *My Last Duchess*, Robert Browning ♦ *My Ex-Husband*, Gabriel Spera ♦
AIDS, May Sarton ♦ *How to Watch Your Brother Die*, Michael Lassell ♦ *To His Coy
Mistress*, Andrew Marvell ♦ *The Willing Mistress*, Aphra Behn ♦ *Bright Star*, John
Keats ♦ *She Proves the Inconsistency of the Desires and Criticism of Men Who Accuse
Women of What They Themselves Cause*, Sor Juana Inés de la Cruz ♦ *Sonnet 30*
"When to the Sessions of Sweet Silent Thought," William Shakespeare ♦ *Sonnet 116*
"Let Me Not to the Marriage of True Minds," William Shakespeare ♦ *Sonnet 129*
"Th' Expense of Spirit in a Waste of Shame," William Shakespeare ♦ *Sonnet 130*
"My Mistress' Eyes are Nothing Like the Sun," William Shakespeare

Drama

Medea, Euripides ♦ *Kiss of the Spider Woman*, Manuel Puig

$\mathcal{F}$ew aspects of contemporary life in North America and other parts of the world have changed more radically in the last two decades than those that focus on women in the workplace, gender roles in marriage, women's sexuality, new definitions of masculinity, divorce, communication between men and women, child custody, and sexual preference.

The culturally diverse texts in Part Two invite you to join in the conversation with writers from various cultures and traditions as they explore the degree to which gender has shaped individual and cultural identities from ancient times to the present. The texts present a number of points of view on the relationships between men and women and their perceptions of each other. The writers explore, among other topics, why various cultures have constructed different images of men and women at various points in their history.

They invite you to examine these changing cross-cultural concepts of masculinity and femininity and to evaluate the degree to which they have affected both men and women in their individual quests for identity, as well as radical changes in the structure of the family. Some of the writers ask you to decide whether gender conflicts should be confronted or avoided; others pose possibilities for freeing both sexes from the confines of traditional roles.

The most recurrent and controversial aspects of gender relations found in these texts is the debate between patriarchs and feminists. In some, the traditional idea of male supremacy has left its mark, and in others, it is vigorously rejected, shattering intrapersonal and intracultural harmony.

Looking back, we discover several traditions that have created images of women to represent specific models of male–female relations. Major among these is the idealizing tradition, which portrays women as different and superior beings. For example, the Greek story of Pygmalion—the legendary sculptor who fell in love with the female statue he carved according to his own inspired view of beauty— illustrates an extreme idealization of the notion of women. Such an idealization often transforms a woman into a love object that men can use to escape immediate reality. Other idealizing traditions, such as platonic love and courtly love, also explore the Pygmalion model of gender relations. English romantic poet John Keats, in his sonnet "Bright Star" (1819), for example, evokes a romantic concept of women in the poet's transformation of his mistress into an image of permanence essential to his orderly view of the world. In contrast, English dramatist and poet William Shakespeare, in his sonnet "My Mistress' Eyes Are Nothing Like the Sun," playfully rejects the idealizing tradition; he views his lover more realistically, in keeping with the rational trend of Renaissance tradition.

The destructive effects of dominance in gender relationships are the focus of *Medea*, Euripides' classical play, written centuries ago but presenting emotional issues that resonate with contemporary audiences. The drama reinforces the myth of woman as femme fatale by dramatizing the story of a forsaken woman, driven by sexual jealousy and the loss of her husband to a younger woman, who resorts to extreme revenge to reestablish her sense of justice.

By the late nineteenth century, "the woman question" had become a matter of public debate in Europe and the United States as both male and female writers rebelled against the Victorian ideal of woman as "the angel in the house" and exposed the limitations of marriages in which traditional gender roles were obediently observed. In 1879, for example, Norwegian audiences were outraged by Henrik Ibsen's drama *A Doll House*, in which the protagonist, Nora, moves from negotiation to open confrontation with her husband and decides that finding her own identity as a person is more important than her roles of wife and even mother. British readers responded in a similar fashion to novelist George Gissing's sympathetic portrayal of women struggling to define themselves as educated persons in pursuit of economic independence in *The Odd Women* (1866), and in the United States, southern writer Kate Chopin's novel *The Awakening* (1899) was banned a few months after publication because the author dared to focus explicitly on women's sexual pleasure and adultery. Although they were mainly condemned in their own time as immoral and irresponsible, contemporary critics view these writers as courageous pioneers who pointed the way to freeing men and women from the confinements of traditional gender roles.

Other texts focus on the complexities that men and women often encounter in trying to communicate their emotions to one another. Deborah Tannen, a professor of linguistics at Georgetown University, in her essay "Sex, Lies and Conversation: Why Is It So Hard for Men and Women to Talk to Each Other?" (1990), contrasts the ways men and women communicate with one another and the misunderstandings that occur when either partner fails to "listen" to the other. In her short story, "Another Evening at the Club," contemporary Egyptian writer Alifa Rifaat, despite opposition from her Muslim family, explores the extent to which feminine domesticity and financial dependence have restricted the identities of both genders.

Japanese novelist and short story writer Haruki Murakami reflects on his narrator's lost opportunity to introduce himself to the "100% Perfect Girl"; David Brooks and Steve Tesich present radically different concepts of marriage. Several male poets, including Yevgeny Yevtushenko, Theodore Roethke, and Gary Soto, focus on vulnerability in gender relationships, and female poets, including Aphra Behn, Anne Sexton, and Edna St. Vincent Millay, emphasize the issue of women's sexuality.

Sexual orientation and sexual preference are current controversies, particularly in queer theory in which scholars propose that human sexuality is a social construct based on culture rather than nature. They argue that in many cultures outside of the United States bisexuality and homosexuality are accepted, releasing both males and females from the restrictions of traditional sexual roles. Obviously, such reconsiderations are complex, involving not only individual and social values but moral and religious beliefs.

Argentinian playwright Manuel Puig in *Kiss of the Spider Woman* and Indian fiction writer Sandip Roy in "The Smells of Home" focus on the social and political exclusion of lesbians and homosexuals. May Sarton's poem AIDS and Michael Lassell's "How to Watch Your Brother Die" explore sexual preference and the gay community's capacity for grief, rage, and desire for connection.

As you join the debate here between feminists and patriarchs in these and other texts from various cultures and traditions, you will be invited to speculate on questions such as these: Are men rightly in charge of the family and the tribe? Should women be accorded the same personal, political, and economic rights as men? How have both men and women used traditional concepts of sexuality, femininity, and masculinity to manipulate each other? How have traditional societal and cultural expectations affected gender identity? What new possibilities are there for healthier gender relationships and more fulfilled individual selves? For despite the difficulties involve in forming relationships, one theme remains constant in all of these texts: We are social beings whose personal and cultural identities are rooted in our need for relatedness.

FICTION

Haruki Murakami

On Seeing the 100% Perfect Girl One Beautiful April Morning

Translated by Jay Rubin

One beautiful April morning, on a narrow side street in Tokyo's fashionable. Harajuku neighborhood, I walk past the 100% perfect girl.

Tell you the truth, she's not that good-looking. She doesn't stand out in any way. Her clothes are nothing special. The back of her hair is still bent out of shape from sleep. She isn't young, either—must be near thirty, not even close to a "girl," properly speaking. But still, I know from fifty yards away: She's the 100% perfect girl for me. The moment I see her, there's a rumbling in my chest, and my mouth is as dry as a desert.

Maybe you have your own particular favorite type of girl—one with slim ankles, say, or big eyes, or graceful fingers, or you're drawn for no good reason to girls who take their time with every meal. I have my own preferences, of course. Sometimes in a restaurant I'll catch myself staring at the girl at the table next to mine because I like the shape of her nose.

But no one can insist that his 100% perfect girl correspond to some preconceived type. Much as I like noses, I can't recall the shape of hers—or even if she had one. All I can remember for sure is that she was no great beauty. It's weird.

"Yesterday on the street I passed the 100% perfect girl," I tell someone.

"Yeah?" he says. "Good-looking?"

"Not really."

"Your favorite type, then?"

"I don't know. I can't seem to remember anything about her—the shape of her eyes or the size of her breasts."

"Strange."

"Yeah. Strange."

"So anyhow," he says, already bored, "what did you do? Talk to her? Follow her?"

"Nah. Just passed her on the street."

She's walking east to west, and I west to east. It's a really nice April morning.

Wish I could talk to her. Half an hour would be plenty: just ask her about herself, tell her about myself, and—what I'd really like to do—explain to her the complexities of fate that have led to our passing each other on a side street in Harajuku on a beautiful April morning in 1981. This was something sure to be crammed full of warm secrets, like an antique clock built when peace filled the world.

After talking, we'd have lunch somewhere, maybe see a Woody Allen movie, stop by a hotel bar for cocktails. With any kind of luck, we might end up in bed.

Potentiality knocks on the door of my heart.

Now the distance between us has narrowed to fifteen yards.

How can I approach her? What should I say?

"Good morning, miss. Do you think you could spare half an hour for a little conversation?"

Ridiculous. I'd sound like an insurance salesman.

"Pardon me, but would you happen to know if there is an all-night cleaners in the neighborhood?"

No, this is just as ridiculous. I'm not carrying any laundry, for one thing. Who's going to buy a line like that?

Maybe the simple truth would do. "Good morning. You are the 100% perfect girl for me."

No, she wouldn't believe it. Or even if she did, she might not want to talk to me. Sorry, she could say, I might be the 100% perfect girl for you, but you're not the 100% perfect boy for me. It could happen. And if I found myself in that situation, I'd probably go to pieces. I'd never recover from the shock. I'm thirty-two, and that's what growing older is all about.

We pass in front of a flower shop. A small, warm air mass touches my skin. The asphalt is damp, and I catch the scent of roses. I can't bring myself to speak to her. She wears a white sweater, and in her right hand she holds a crisp white envelope lacking only a stamp. So: She's written somebody a letter, maybe spent the whole night writing, to judge from the sleepy look in her eyes. The envelope could contain every secret she's ever had.

I take a few more strides and turn: She's lost in the crowd.

Now, of course, I know exactly what I should have said to her. It would have been a long speech, though, far too long for me to have delivered it properly. The ideas I come up with are never very practical.

Oh, well. It would have started "Once upon a time" and ended "A sad story, don't you think?"

Once upon a time, there lived a boy and a girl. The boy was eighteen and the girl sixteen. He was not unusually handsome, and she was not especially beautiful. They were just an ordinary lonely boy and an ordinary lonely girl, like all the others. But they believed with their whole hearts that somewhere in the world there lived the 100% perfect boy and the 100% perfect girl for them. Yes, they believed in a miracle. And that miracle actually happened.

One day the two came upon each other on the corner of a street.

"This is amazing," he said. "I've been looking for you all my life. You may not believe this, but you're the 100% perfect girl for me."

"And you," she said to him, "are the 100% perfect boy for me, exactly as I'd pictured you in every detail. It's like a dream."

They sat on a park bench, held hands, and told each other their stories hour after hour. They were not lonely anymore. They had found and been found by their 100% perfect other. What a wonderful thing it is to find and be found by your 100% perfect other. It's a miracle, a cosmic miracle.

As they sat and talked, however, a tiny, tiny sliver of doubt took root in their hearts: Was it really all right for ones dreams to come true so easily?

And so, when there came a momentary full in their conversation, the boy said to the girl, "Let's test ourselves—just once. If we really are each other's 100% perfect lovers, then sometime, somewhere, we will meet again without fail. And when that happens, and we know that we are the 100% perfect ones, we'll marry then and there. What do you think?"

"Yes," she said, "that is exactly what we should do."

And so they parted, she to the east, and he to the west.

The test they had agreed upon, however, was utterly unnecessary. They should never have undertaken it, because they really and truly were each other's 100% perfect lovers, and it was a miracle that they had ever met. But it was impossible for them to know this, young as they were. The cold, indifferent waves of fate proceeded to toss them unmercifully.

One winter, both the boy and the girl came down with the season's terrible influenza, and after drifting for weeks between life and death they lost all memory of their earlier years. When they awoke, their heads were as empty as the young D. H. Lawrence's piggy bank.

They were two bright, determined young people, however, and through their unremitting efforts they were able to acquire once again the knowledge and feeling that qualified them to return as full-fledged members of society. Heaven be praised, they became truly upstanding citizens who knew how to transfer from one subway line to another, who were fully capable of sending a special-delivery letter at the post office. Indeed, they even experienced love again, sometimes as much as 75% or even 85% love.

Time passed with shocking swiftness, and soon the boy was thirty-two, the girl thirty.

One beautiful April morning, in search of a cup of coffee to start the day the boy was walking from west to east, while the girl, intending to send a special-delivery letter, was walking from east to west, both along the same narrow street in the Harajuku neighborhood of Tokyo. They passed each other in the very center of the street. The faintest gleam of their lost memories glimmered for the briefest moment in their hearts. Each felt a rumbling in the chest. And they knew:

She is the 100% perfect girl for me.

He is the 100% perfect boy for me.

But the glow of their memories was far too weak, and their thoughts no longer had the clarity of fourteen years earlier. Without a word, they passed each other, disappearing into the crowd. Forever.

A sad story, don't you think?

Yes, that's it, that is what I should have said to her.

[1993]

Journal Entry

Write a journal entry responding to the title of the story. Why do you think the author quantifies love? Is it really possible and practical to do so?

Textual Considerations

1. Identify examples of imagery that you thought most effective. How does his use of imagery contribute to the meanings of the story?
2. Why does the character not approach the girl? Do you find his reasons justifiable? Or do you think he is just making excuses? Cite evidence to support your answer.
3. Identify several instances in which the speaker contrasts the conditions of younger versus older people. What points he is trying to make? With which do you agree or disagree?
4. Although the narrator describes what he would like to do and talk about with the girl, does he ever allude to anything permanent? Does this imply anything about his personality and priorities? Explain.

Cultural Contexts

1. Discuss with your group the various references to fate in the story. What do they imply about the speaker's attitudes toward fate? How are they similar or different from those of your group? Record your responses to these questions.
2. Time is mentioned several times in the story. How does the speaker manipulate time, and what does he achieve by so doing? To what extent are his ideas about time similar to or different from yours? Did your group reach a consensus on this issue?

Kate Chopin

The Storm

I

The leaves were so still that even Bibi thought it was going to rain. Bobinôt, who was accustomed to converse on terms of perfect equality with his little son, called the child's attention to certain sombre clouds that were rolling with sinister intention from the west, accompanied by a sullen, threatening roar. They were at Friedheimer's store and decided to remain there till the storm had passed. They sat within the door on two empty kegs. Bibi was four years old and looked very wise.

"Mama'll be 'fraid, yes," he suggested with blinking eyes.

"She'll shut the house. Maybe she got Sylvie helpin' her this evenin'," Bobinôt responded reassuringly.

"No; she ent got Sylvie. Sylvie was helpin' her yistiday," piped Bibi.

Bobinôt arose and going across to the counter purchased a can of shrimps, of which Calixta was very fond. Then he returned to his perch on the keg and sat stolidly holding the can of shrimps while the storm burst. It shook the wooden store and seemed to be ripping great furrows in the distant field. Bibi laid his little hand on his father's knee and was not afraid.

II

Calixta, at home, felt no uneasiness for their safety. She sat at a side window sewing furiously on a sewing machine. She was greatly occupied and did not notice the approaching storm. But she felt very warm and often stopped to mop her face on which the perspiration gathered in beads. She unfastened her white sacque at the throat. It began to grow dark, and suddenly realizing the situation she got up hurriedly and went about closing windows and doors.

Out on the small front gallery she had hung Bobinôt's Sunday clothes to air and she hastened out to gather them before the rain fell. As she stepped outside, Alcée Laballière rode in at the gate. She had not seen him very often since her marriage, and never alone. She stood there with Bobinôt's coat in her hands, and the big rain drops began to fall. Alcée rode his horse under the shelter of a side projection where the chickens had huddled and there were plows and a harrow piled up in the corner.

"May I come and wait on your gallery till the storm is over, Calixta?" he asked.

"Come 'long in, M'sieur Alcée."

His voice and her own startled her as if from a trance, and she seized Bobinôt's—vest. Alcée, mounting to the porch, grabbed the trousers and snatched Bibi's braided jacket that was about to be carried away by a sudden gust of wind. He expressed an intention to remain outside, but it was soon apparent that he might as well have been out in the open: the water beat in upon the boards in driving sheets, and he went inside, closing the door after him. It was even necessary to put something beneath the door to keep the water out.

"My! what a rain! It's good two years since it rain' like that," exclaimed Calixta as she rolled up a piece of bagging and Alcée helped her to thrust it beneath the crack.

She was a little fuller of figure than five years before when she married; but she had lost nothing of her vivacity. Her blue eyes still retained their melting quality; and her yellow hair, dishevelled by the wind and rain, kinked more stubbornly than ever about her ears and temples.

The rain beat upon the low, shingled roof with a force and clatter that threatened to break an entrance and deluge them there. They were in the dining room—the sitting room—the general utility room. Adjoining was her bed room, with Bibi's couch along side her own. The door stood open, and the room with its white, monumental bed, its closed shutters, looked dim and mysterious.

Alcée flung himself into a rocker and Calixta nervously began to gather up from the floor the lengths of a cotton sheet which she had been sewing.

"If this keeps up, *Dieu sait*[1] if the levees goin' to stan' it!" she exclaimed.

"What have you got to do with the levees?"

---

[1] God knows.

"I got enough to do! An' there's Bobinôt with Bibi out in that storm—if he only didn't left Friedheimer's!"

"Let us hope, Calixta, that Bobinôt's got sense enough to come in out of a cyclone."

She went and stood at the window with a greatly disturbed look on her face. She wiped the frame that was clouded with moisture. It was stiflingly hot. Alcée got up and joined her at the window, looking over her shoulder. The rain was coming down in sheets obscuring the view of far-off cabins and enveloping the distant wood in a gray mist. The playing of the lightning was incessant. A bolt struck a tall chinaberry tree at the edge of the field. It filled all visible space with a blinding glare and the crash seemed to invade the very boards they stood upon.

Calixta put her hands to her eyes, and with a cry, staggered backward. Alcée's arm encircled her, and for an instant he drew her close and spasmodically to him.

"*Bonté!*"[2] she cried, releasing herself from his encircling arm and retreating from the window, "the house'll go next! If I only knew w'ere Bibi was!" She would not compose herself; she would not be seated. Alcée clasped her shoulders and looked into her face. The contact of her warm palpitating body when he had unthinkingly drawn her into his arms, had aroused all the old-time infatuation and desire for her flesh.

"Calixta," he said, "don't be frightened. Nothing can happen. The house is too low to be struck, with so many tall trees standing about. There! aren't you going to be quiet? say, aren't you?" He pushed her hair back from her face that was warm and steaming. Her lips were as red and moist as pomegranate seed. Her white neck and a glimpse of her full, firm bosom disturbed him powerfully. As she glanced up at him the fear in her liquid blue eyes had given place to a drowsy gleam that unconsciously betrayed a sensuous desire. He looked down into her eyes and there was nothing for him to do but to gather her lips in a kiss. It reminded him of Assumption.

"Do you remember—in Assumption, Calixta?" he asked in a low voice broken by passion. Oh! she remembered; for in Assumption he had kissed her and kissed and kissed her; until his senses would well nigh fail, and to save her he would resort to a desperate flight. If she was not an immaculate dove in those days, she was still inviolate; a passionate creature whose very defenselessness had made her defense, against which his honor forbade him to prevail. Now—well, now—her lips seemed in a manner free to be tasted, as well as her round, white throat and her whiter breasts.

They did not heed the crashing torrents, and the roar of the elements made her laugh as she lay in his arms. She was a revelation in that dim, mysterious chamber; as white as the couch she lay upon. Her firm, elastic flesh that was knowing for the first time its birthright, was like a creamy lily that the sun invites to contribute its breath and perfume to the undying life of the world.

The generous abundance of her passion, without guile or trickery, was like a white flame which penetrated and found response in depths of his own sensuous nature that had never yet been reached.

---

[2] "Goodness!"

When he touched her breasts they gave themselves up in quivering ecstasy, inviting his lips. Her mouth was a fountain of delight. And when he possessed her, they seemed to swoon together at the very borderland of life's mystery.

He stayed cushioned upon her, breathless, dazed, enervated, with his heart beating like a hammer upon her. With one hand she clasped his head, her lips lightly touching his forehead. The other hand stroked with a soothing rhythm his muscular shoulders.

The growl of the thunder was distant and passing away. The rain beat softly upon the shingles, inviting them to drowsiness and sleep. But they dared not yield.

The rain was over; and the sun was turning the glistening green world into a palace of gems. Calixta, on the gallery, watched Alcée ride away. He turned and smiled at her with a beaming face; and she lifted her pretty chin in the air and laughed aloud.

III

Bobinôt and Bibi, trudging home, stopped without at the cistern to make themselves presentable.

"My! Bibi, w'at will yo' mama say! You ought to be ashame'. You oughtn' put on those good pants. Look at 'em! An' that mud on yo' collar! How you got that mud on yo' collar, Bibi? I never saw such a boy!" Bibi was the picture of pathetic resignation. Bobinôt was the embodiment of serious solicitude as he strove to remove from his own person and his son's the signs of their tramp over heavy roads and through wet fields. He scraped the mud off Bibi's bare legs and feet with a stick and carefully removed all traces from his heavy brogans. Then, prepared for the worst—the meeting with an over-scrupulous housewife, they entered cautiously at the back door.

Calixta was preparing supper. She had set the table and was dripping coffee at the hearth. She sprang up as they came in.

"Oh, Bobinôt! You back! My! but I was uneasy. W'ere you been during the rain? An' Bibi? he ain't wet? he ain't hurt?" She had clasped Bibi and was kissing him effusively. Bobinôt's explanations and apologies which he had been composing all along the way, died on his lips as Calixta felt him to see if he were dry, and seemed to express nothing but satisfaction at their safe return.

"I brought you some shrimps, Calixta," offered Bobinôt, hauling the can from his ample side pocket and laying it on the table.

"Shrimps! Oh, Bobinôt! you too good fo' anything!" and she gave him a smacking kiss on the cheek that resounded. "*J'vous réponds,*[3] we'll have a feas' tonight! umph-umph!"

Bobinôt and Bibi began to relax and enjoy themselves, and when the three seated themselves at table they laughed much and so loud that anyone might have heard them as far away as Laballière's.

---

[3] "I tell you."

IV

Alcée Laballière wrote to his wife, Clarisse, that night. It was a loving letter, full of tender solicitude. He told her not to hurry back, but if she and the babies liked it at Biloxi, to stay a month longer. He was getting on nicely; and though he missed them, he was willing to bear the separation a while longer—realizing that their health and pleasure were the first things to be considered.

V

As for Clarisse, she was charmed upon receiving her husband's letter. She and the babies were doing well. The society was agreeable; many of her old friends and acquaintances were at the bay. And the first free breath since her marriage seemed to restore the pleasant liberty of her maiden days. Devoted as she was to her husband, their intimate conjugal life was something which she was more than willing to forego for a while.

So the storm passed and everyone was happy.

[1899]

Journal Entry

What memories, associations, and experiences of storms, both literal and metaphorical, do you bring to your reading of the story?

Textual Considerations

1. What evidence does "The Storm" offer about the past relationship of Calixta and Alcée? Is it important for the reader to know about this relationship? Explain your answer.
2. How does Chopin use point of view to develop characterization in the first two sections of the story?
3. What is the symbolic significance of the storm? What chain of events does it set in motion?
4. Pay particular attention to Chopin's use of language in the story. Do her images reflect her attitude toward her characters? Does her choice of words imply judgment or empathy? Select evidence from the text to justify your point of view.

Cultural Contexts

1. Discuss with your group your responses to the last sentence of the story. Do you agree with her conclusion? Why or why not? Summarize your group's responses. Did you reach a consensus?
2. Chopin chose not to publish this story during her lifetime. How might readers in the 1890s have responded to her lack of condemnation of adultery or to the fact that both Calixta and Alcée enjoy their sexual encounter as equals? Working with your group, debate whether you accept or reject Calixta's and Alcee's attitudes toward marriage and infidelity.

Alice Walker

Roselily

Dearly Beloved

She dreams; dragging herself across the world. A small girl in her mother's white robe and veil, knee raised waist high through a bowl of quicksand soup. The man who stands beside her is against this standing on the front porch of her house, being married to the sound of cars whizzing by on highway 61.

we are gathered here

Like cotton to be weighed. Her fingers at the last minute busily removing dry leaves and twigs. Aware it is a superficial sweep. She knows he blames Mississippi for the respectful way the men turn their heads up in the yard, the women stand waiting and knowledgeable, their children held from mischief by teachings from the wrong God. He glares beyond them to the occupants of the cars, white faces glued to promises beyond a country wedding, noses thrust forward like dogs on a track. For him they usurp the wedding.

in the sight of God

Yes, open house. That is what country black folks like. She dreams she does not already have three children. A squeeze around the flowers in her hands chokes off three and four and five years of breath. Instantly she is ashamed and frightened in her superstition. She looks for the first time at the preacher, forces humility into her eyes, as if she believes he is, in fact, a man of God. She can imagine God, a small black boy, timidly pulling the preacher's coattail.

to join this man and this woman

She thinks of ropes, chains, handcuffs, his religion. His place of worship. Where she will be required to sit apart with covered head. In Chicago, a word she hears when thinking of smoke, from his description of what a cinder was, which they never had in Panther Burn. She sees hovering over the heads of the clean neighbors in her front yard black specks falling, clinging, from the sky. But in Chicago. Respect, a chance to build. Her children at last from underneath the detrimental wheel. A chance to be on top. What a relief, she thinks. What a vision, a view, from up so high.

in holy matrimony.

Her fourth child she gave away to the child's father who had some money. Certainly a good job. Had gone to Harvard. Was a good man but weak because good language meant so much to him he could not live with Roselily. Could not abide TV in the living room, five beds in three rooms, no Bach except from four to six on Sunday afternoons. No chess at all. She does not forget to worry about her son among his father's people. She wonders if the New England climate will agree with him. If he will ever come down to Mississippi, as his father did, to try to right the country's wrongs. She wonders if he will be stronger than his father. His father cried off and on throughout her pregnancy. Went to skin and bones. Suffered nightmares, retching and falling out of bed. Tried to kill himself. Later told his wife he found the right baby through friends. Vouched for, the sterling qualities that would make up his character.

It is not her nature to blame. Still, she is not entirely thankful. She supposes New England, the North, to be quite different from what she knows. It seems right somehow to her that people who move there to live return home completely changed. She thinks of the air, the smoke, the cinders. Imagines cinders big as hail-stones; heavy, weighing on the people. Wonders how pressure finds it way into the veins, roping the springs of laughter.

If there's anybody here that knows a reason why

But of course they know no reason why beyond what they daily have come to know. She thinks of the man who will be her husband, feels shut away from him because of the stiff severity of his plain black suit. His religion. A lifetime of black and white. Of veils. Covered head. It is as if her children are already gone from her. Not dead, but exalted on a pedestal, a stalk that has no roots. She wonders how to make new roots. It is beyond her. She wonders what one does with memories in a brand-new life. This had seemed easy, until she thought of it. "The reasons why . . . the people who" . . . she thinks, and does not wonder where the thought is from.

these two should not be joined

She thinks of her mother, who is dead. Dead, but still her mother. Joined. This is confusing. Of her father. A gray old man who sold wild mink, rabbit, fox skins to Sears, Roebuck. He stands in the yard, like a man waiting for a train. Her young sisters stand behind her in smooth green dresses, with flowers in their hands and hair. They giggle, she feels, at the absurdity of the wedding. They are ready for something new. She thinks the man beside her should marry one of them. She feels old. Yoked. An arm seems to reach out from behind her and snatch her backward. She thinks of cemeteries and the long sleep of grandparents mingling in the dirt. She believes that she believes in ghosts. In the soil giving back what it takes.

together

In the city. He sees her in a new way. This she knows, and is grateful. But is it new enough? She cannot always be a bride and virgin, wearing robes and veil. Even now her body itches to be free of satin and voile, organdy and lily of the valley. Memories crash against her. Memories of being bare to the sun. She wonders what it will be like.

Not to have to go to a job. Not to work in a sewing plant. Not to worry about learning to sew straight seams in workingmen's overalls, jeans, and dress pants. Her place will be in the home, he has said, repeatedly, promising her rest she had prayed for. But now she wonders. When she is rested, what will she do? They will make babies—she thinks practically about her fine brown body, his strong black one. They will be inevitable. Her hands will be full. Full of what? Babies. She is not comforted.

let him speak

She wishes she had asked him to explain more of what he meant. But she was impatient. Impatient to be done with sewing. With doing everything for three children, alone. Impatient to leave the girls she had known since childhood, their children growing up, their husbands hanging around her, already old, seedy. Nothing about them that she wanted, or needed. The fathers of her children driving by, waving, not waving; reminders of times she would just as soon forget. Impatient to see the South Side, where they would live and build and be respectable and respected and free. Her husband would free her. A romantic hush. Proposal. Promises. A new life! Respectable, reclaimed, renewed. Free! In robe and veil.

or forever hold

She does not even know if she loves him. She loves his sobriety. His refusal to sing just because he knows the tune. She loves his pride. His blackness and his gray car. She loves his understanding of her *condition*. She thinks she loves the effort he will make to redo her into what he truly wants. His love of her makes her completely conscious of how unloved she was before. This is something; though it makes her unbearably sad. Melancholy. She blinks her eyes. Remembers she is finally being married, like other girls. Like other girls, women? Something strains upward behind her eyes. She thinks of the something as a rat trapped, concerned, scurrying to and fro in her head, peering through the windows of her eyes. She wants to live for once. But doesn't know quite what that means. Wonders if she has ever done it. If she ever will. The preacher is odious to her. She wants to strike him out of the way, out of her light, with the back of her hand. It seems to her he has always been standing in front of her, barring her way.

his peace.

The rest she does not hear. She feels a kiss, passionate, rousing, within the general pandemonium. Cars drive up blowing their horns. Firecrackers go off. Dogs come from under the house and begin to yelp and bark. Her husband's hand is like the clasp of an iron gate. People congratulate. Her children press against her. They look with awe and distaste mixed with hope at their new father. He stands curiously apart, in spite of the people crowding about to grasp his free hand. He smiles at them all but his eyes are as if turned inward. He knows they cannot understand that he is not a Christian. He will not explain himself. He feels different, he looks it.

The old women thought he was like one of their sons except that he had somehow got away from them. Still a son, not a son. Changed.

She thinks how it will be later in the night in the silvery gray car. How they will spin through the darkness of Mississippi and in the morning be in Chicago, Illinois. She thinks of Lincoln, the president. That is all she knows about the place. She feels ignorant, *wrong*, backward. She presses her worried fingers into his palm. He is standing in front of her. In the crush of well-wishing people, he does not look back.

[1973]

Journal Entry

A rose is traditionally associated with sexual passion, whereas a lily connotes sexual purity. Is Roselily an appropriate name for Walker's protagonist? Why or why not?

Textual Considerations

1. What effects does Walker achieve by using the text of the marriage service to interrupt Roselily's thoughts? What do we learn about her past and her ambivalence about the future?
2. Characterize her husband by listing his faults and his virtues. What is his attitude toward marriage? How does he envision Roselily's role? What is her response?
3. Religion plays an important role in the story. Why does Roselily think of the preacher as someone who is always "barring her way"?
4. What is her husband's attitude toward *his* religion?
5. Roselily wants freedom, yet at the end of the ceremony, "her husband's hand is like the clasp of an iron gate." Cite and explain other images of entrapment.

Cultural Contexts

1. Contrasts form the basis of this story. How does Walker use differences in setting, characterization, religion, family, and community to heighten potential conflicts in the relationship? To what extent are Roselily's needs for freedom and respectability resolved?
2. Roselily reflects on the father of her fourth child, who is white and who she met during the civil rights movement in the 1960s. Why does Walker focus on him? What do we know about him? How does Roselily feel about having given him the child? What is your group's response to her action?

Charlotte Perkins Gilman

The Yellow Wallpaper

It is very seldom that mere ordinary people like John and myself secure ancestral halls for the summer.

A colonial mansion, a hereditary estate, I would say a haunted house, and reach the height of romantic felicity—but that would be asking too much of fate!

Still I will proudly declare that there is something queer about it.

Else, why should it be let so cheaply? And why have stood so long untenanted?

John laughs at me, of course, but one expects that in marriage.

John is practical in the extreme. He has not patience with faith, an intense horror of superstition, and he scoffs openly at any talk of things not to be felt and seen and put down in figures.

John is a physician, and *perhaps*—(I would not say it to a living soul, of course, but this is dead paper and a great relief to my mind)—*perhaps* that is one reason I do not get well faster.

You see he does not believe I am sick!

And what can one do?

If a physician of high standing, and one's own husband, assures friends and relatives that there is really nothing the matter with one but temporary nervous depression—a slight hysterical tendency—what is one to do?

My brother is also a physician, and also of high standing, and he says the same thing.

So I take phosphates or phosphites—whichever it is, and tonics, and journeys, and air, and exercise, and am absolutely forbidden to "work" until I am well again.

Personally, I disagree with their ideas.

Personally, I believe that congenial work, with excitement and change, would do me good.

But what is one to do?

I did write for a while in spite of them, but it *does* exhaust me a good deal—having to be so sly about it, or else meet with heavy opposition.

I sometimes fancy that in my condition if I had less opposition and more society and stimulus—but John says the very worst thing I can do is to think about my condition, and I confess it always makes me feel bad.

So I will let it alone and talk about the house.

The most beautiful place! It is quite alone, standing well back from the road, quite three miles from the village. It makes me think of English places that you read about, for there are hedges and walls and gates that lock, and lots of separate little houses for the gardeners and people.

There is a *delicious* garden! I never saw such a garden—large and shady, full of box-bordered paths, and lined with long grape-covered arbors with seats under them.

There were greenhouses, too, but they are all broken now.

There was some legal trouble, I believe, something about the heirs and coheirs; anyhow, the place has been empty for years.

That spoils my ghostliness, I am afraid, but I don't care—there is something strange about the house—I can feel it.

I even said so to John one moonlight evening, but he said what I felt was a *draught*, and shut the window.

I get unreasonably angry with John sometimes. I'm sure I never used to be so sensitive. I think it is due to this nervous condition.

But John says if I feel so, I shall neglect proper self-control; so I take pains to control myself—before him, at least, and that makes me very tired.

I don't like our room a bit. I wanted one downstairs that opened on the piazza and had roses all over the window, and such pretty old-fashioned chintz hangings! But John would not hear of it.

He said there was only one window and not room for two beds, and no near room for him if he took another.

He is very careful and loving, and hardly lets me stir without special direction.

I have a schedule prescription for each hour in the day; he takes all care from me, and so I feel basely ungrateful not to value it more.

He said we came here solely on my account, that I was to have perfect rest and all the air I could get. "Your exercise depends on your strength, my dear," said he, "and your food somewhat on your appetite, but air you can absorb all the time." So we took the nursery at the top of the house.

It is a big, airy room, the whole floor nearly, with windows that look all ways, and air and sunshine galore. It was nursery first and then playroom and gymnasium, I should judge; for the windows are barred for little children, and there are rings and things in the walls.

The paint and paper look as if a boys' school had used it. It is stripped off—the paper—in great patches all around the head of my bed, about as far as I can reach, and in a great place on the other side of the room low down. I never saw a worse paper in my life.

One of those sprawling flamboyant patterns committing every artistic sin.

It is dull enough to confuse the eye in following, pronounced enough to constantly irritate and provoke study, and when you follow the lame uncertain curves for a little distance they suddenly commit suicide—plunge off at outrageous angles, destroy themselves in unheard of contradictions.

The color is repellent, almost revolting; a smoldering unclean yellow, strangely faded by the slow-turning sunlight.

It is a dull yet lurid orange in some places, a sickly sulphur tint in others.

No wonder the children hated it! I should hate it myself if I had to live in this room long.

There comes John, and I must put this away,—he hates to have me write a word.

We have been here two weeks, and I haven't felt like writing before, since that first day.

I am sitting by the window now, up in this atrocious nursery, and there is nothing to hinder my writing as much as I please, save lack of strength.

John is away all day, and even some nights when his cases are serious.

I am glad my case is not serious!

But these nervous troubles are dreadfully depressing.

John does not know how much I really suffer. He knows there is no *reason* to suffer, and that satisfies him.

Of course it is only nervousness. It does weigh on me so not to do my duty in any way!

I meant to be such a help to John, such a real rest and comfort, and here I am a comparative burden already!

Nobody would believe what an effort it is to do what little I am able,—to dress and entertain, and order things.

It is fortunate Mary is so good with the baby. Such a dear baby!

And yet I *cannot* be with him, it makes me so nervous.

I suppose John never was nervous in his life. He laughs at me so about this wall-paper!

At first he meant to repaper the room, but afterwards he said that I was letting it get the better of me, and that nothing was worse for a nervous patient than to give way to such fancies.

He said that after the wall-paper was changed it would be the heavy bedstead, and then the barred windows, and then that gate at the head of the stairs, and so on.

"You know the place is doing you good," he said, "and really, dear, I don't care to renovate the house just for a three months' rental."

"Then do let us go downstairs," I said, "there are such pretty rooms there."

Then he took me in his arms and called me a blessed little goose, and said he would go down to the cellar, if I wished, and have it whitewashed into the bargain.

But he is right enough about the beds and windows and things.

It is an airy and comfortable room as any one need wish, and, of course, I would not be so silly as to make him uncomfortable just for a whim.

I'm really getting quite fond of the big room, all but that horrid paper.

Out of one window I can see the garden, those mysterious deepshaded arbors, the riotous old-fashioned flowers, and bushes and gnarly trees.

Out of another I get a lovely view of the bay and a little private wharf belonging to the estate. There is a beautiful shaded lane that runs down there from the house. I always fancy I see people walking in these numerous paths and arbors, but John has cautioned me not to give way to fancy in the least. He says that with my imaginative power and habit of story-making, a nervous weakness like mine is sure to lead to all manner of excited fancies, and that I ought to use my will and good sense to check the tendency. So I try.

I think sometimes that if I were only well enough to write a little it would relieve the press of ideas and rest me.

But I find I get pretty tired when I try.

It is so discouraging not to have any advice and companionship about my work. When I get really well, John says we will ask Cousin Henry and Julia down for a long visit; but he says he would as soon put fireworks in my pillow-case as to let me have those stimulating people about now.

I wish I could get well faster.

But I must not think about that. This paper looks to me as if it *knew* what a vicious influence it had!

There is a recurrent spot where the pattern lolls like a broken neck and two bulbous eyes stare at you upside down.

I get positively angry with the impertinence of it and the everlastingness. Up and down and sideways they crawl, and those absurd, unblinking eyes are everywhere. There is one place where two breadths didn't match, and the eyes go all up and down the line, one a little higher than the other.

I never saw so much expression in an inanimate thing before, and we all know how much expression they have! I used to lie awake as a child and get more entertainment and terror out of blank walls and plain furniture than most children could find in a toy-store.

I remember what a kindly wink the knobs of our big, old bureau used to have, and there was one chair that always seemed like a strong friend.

I used to feel that if any of the other things looked too fierce I could always hop into that chair and be safe.

The furniture in this room is no worse than inharmonious, however, for we had to bring it all from downstairs. I suppose when this was used as a playroom they had to take the nursery things out, and no wonder! I never saw such ravages as the children have made here.

The wall-paper, as I said before, is torn off in spots, and it sticketh closer than a brother—they must have had perseverance as well as hatred.

Then the floor is scratched and gouged and splintered, the plaster itself is dug out here and there, and this great heavy bed which is all we found in the room, looks as if it had been through the wars.

But I don't mind it a bit—only the paper.

There comes John's sister. Such a dear girl as she is, and so careful of me! I must not let her find me writing.

She is a perfect and enthusiastic housekeeper, and hopes for no better profession. I verily believe she thinks it is the writing which made me sick!

But I can write when she is out, and see her a long way off from these windows.

There is one that commands the road, a lovely shaded winding road, and one that just looks off over the country. A lovely country, too, full of great elms and velvet meadows.

This wall-paper has a kind of sub-pattern in a different shade, a particularly irritating one, for you can only see it in certain lights, and not clearly then.

But in the places where it isn't faded and where the sun is just so—I can see a strange, provoking, formless sort of figure, that seems to skulk about behind that silly and conspicuous front design.

There's sister on the stairs!

Well, the Fourth of July is over! The people are all gone and I am tired out. John thought it might do me good to see a little company, so we just had mother and Nellie and the children down for a week.

Of course I didn't do a thing. Jennie sees to everything now.

But it tired me all the same.

John says if I don't pick up faster he shall send me to Weir Mitchell[1] in the fall.

But I don't want to go there at all. I had a friend who was in his hands once, and she says he is just like John and my brother, only more so!

Besides, it is such an undertaking to go so far.

---

[1] Dr. Silas Weir Mitchell, a renowned specialist in women's nervous diseases.

I don't feel as if it was worth while to turn my hand over for anything, and I'm getting dreadfully fretful and querulous.

I cry at nothing, and cry most of the time.

Of course I don't when John is here, or anybody else, but when I am alone.

And I am alone a good deal just now. John is kept in town very often by serious cases, and Jennie is good and lets me alone when I want her to.

So I walk a little in the garden or down that lovely lane, sit on the porch under the roses, and lie down up here a good deal.

I'm getting really fond of the room in spite of the wall-paper. Perhaps *because* of the wall-paper.

It dwells in my mind so!

I lie here on this great immovable bed—it is nailed down, I believe—and follow that pattern about by the hour. It is as good as gymnastics, I assure you. I start, we'll say, at the bottom, down in the corner over there where it has not been touched, and I determine for the thousandth time that I *will* follow that pointless pattern to some sort of a conclusion.

I know a little of the principle of design, and I know this thing was not arranged on any laws of radiation, or alternation, or repetition, or symmetry, or anything else that I ever heard of.

It is repeated, of course, by the breadths, but not otherwise.

Looked at in one way each breadth stands alone, the bloated curves and flourishes—a kind of "debased Romanesque" with *delirium tremens*—go waddling up and down in isolated columns of fatuity.

But, on the other hand, they connect diagonally, and the sprawling outlines run off in great slanting waves of optic horror, like a lot of wallowing seaweeds in full chase.

The whole thing goes horizontally, too, at least it seems so, and I exhaust myself in trying to distinguish the order of its going in that direction.

They have used a horizontal breadth for a frieze, and that adds wonderfully to the confusion.

There is one end of the room where it is almost intact, and there, when the crosslights fade and the low sun shines directly upon it, I can almost fancy radiation after all—the interminable grotesques seem to form around a common centre and rush off in headlong plunges of equal distraction.

It makes me tired to follow it. I will take a nap I guess.

I don't know why I should write this.

I don't want to.

I don't feel able.

And I know John would think it absurd. But I *must* say what I feel and think in some way—it is such a relief!

But the effort is getting to be greater than the relief.

Half the time now I am awfully lazy, and lie down ever so much.

John says I mustn't lose my strength, and has me take cod liver oil and lots of tonics and things, to say nothing of ale and wine and rare meat.

Dear John! He loves me very dearly, and hates to have me sick. I tried to have a real earnest reasonable talk with him the other day, and tell him how I wish he would let me go and make a visit to Cousin Henry and Julia.

But he said I wasn't able to go, nor able to stand it after I got there; and I did not make out a very good case for myself, for I was crying before I had finished.

It is getting to be a great effort for me to think straight. Just this nervous weakness I suppose.

And dear John gathered me up in his arms, and just carried me upstairs and laid me on the bed, and sat by me and read to me till it tired my head.

He said I was his darling and his comfort and all he had, and that I must take care of myself for his sake, and keep well.

He says no one but myself can help me out of it, that I must use my will and self-control and not let any silly fancies run away with me.

There's one comfort, the baby is well and happy, and does not have to occupy this nursery with the horrid wall-paper.

If we had not used it, that blessed child would have! What a fortunate escape! Why, I wouldn't have a child of mine, an impressionable little thing, live in such a room for worlds.

I never thought of it before, but it is lucky that John kept me here after all, I can stand it so much easier than a baby, you see.

Of course I never mention it to them any more—I am too wise,—but I keep watch of it all the same.

There are things in that paper that nobody knows but me, or ever will.

Behind that outside pattern the dim shapes get clearer every day.

It is always the same shape, only very numerous.

And it is like a woman stooping down and creeping about behind that pattern. I don't like it a bit. I wonder—I begin to think—I wish John would take me away from here!

It is so hard to talk with John about my case, because he is so wise, and because he loves me so.

But I tried it last night.

It was moonlight. The moon shines in all around just as the sun does.

I hate to see it sometimes, it creeps so slowly, and always comes in by one window or another.

John was asleep and I hated to waken him, so I kept still and watched the moonlight on that undulating wall-paper till I felt creepy.

The faint figure behind seemed to shake the pattern, just as if she wanted to get out.

I got up softly and went to feel and see if the paper *did* move, and when I came back John was awake.

"What is it, little girl?" he said. "Don't go walking about like that—you'll get cold."

I thought it was a good time to talk, so I told him that I really was not gaining here, and that I wished he would take me away.

"Why darling!" said he, "our lease will be up in three weeks, and I can't see how to leave before.

"The repairs are not done at home, and I cannot possibly leave town just now. Of course if you were in any danger, I could and would, but you really are better, dear, whether you can see it or not. I am a doctor, dear, and I know. You are gaining flesh and color, your appetite is better, I feel really much easier about you."

"I don't weigh a bit more," said I, "nor as much; and my appetite may be better in the evening when you are here, but it is worse in the morning when you are away!"

"Bless her little heart!" said he with a big hug, "she shall be as sick as she pleases! But now let's improve the shining hours by going to sleep, and talk about it in the morning!"

"And you won't go away?" I asked gloomily.

"Why, how can I, dear? It is only three weeks more and then we will take a nice little trip of a few days while Jennie is getting the house ready. Really dear you are better!"

"Better in body perhaps—" I began, and stopped short, for he sat up straight and looked at me with such a stern, reproachful look that I could not say another word.

"My darling," said he, "I beg of you, for my sake and for our child's sake, as well as for your own, that you will never for one instant let that idea enter your mind! There is nothing so dangerous, so fascinating, to a temperament like yours. It is a false and foolish fancy. Can you not trust me as a physician when I tell you so?"

So of course I said no more on that score, and we went to sleep before long. He thought I was asleep first, but I wasn't, and lay there for hours trying to decide whether that front pattern and the back pattern really did move together or separately.

On a pattern like this, by daylight, there is a lack of sequence, a defiance of law, that is a constant irritant to a normal mind.

The color is hideous enough, and unreliable enough, and infuriating enough, but the pattern is torturing.

You think you have mastered it, but just as you get well underway in following, it turns a back-somersault and there you are. It slaps you in the face, knocks you down, and tramples upon you. It is like a bad dream.

The outside pattern is a florid arabesque, reminding one of a fungus. If you can imagine a toadstool in joints, an interminable string of toadstools, budding and sprouting in endless convolutions—why, that is something like it.

That is, sometimes!

There is one marked peculiarity about this paper, a thing nobody seems to notice but myself, and that is that it changes as the light changes.

When the sun shoots in through the east window—I always watch for that first long, straight ray—it changes so quickly that I never can quite believe it.

That is why I watch it always.

By moonlight—the moon shines in all night when there is a moon—I wouldn't know it was the same paper.

At night in any kind of light, in twilight, candle light, lamplight, and worst of all by moonlight, it becomes bars! The outside pattern I mean, and the woman behind it is as plain as can be.

I didn't realize for a long time what the thing was that showed behind, that dim sub-pattern, but now I am quite sure it is a woman.

By daylight she is subdued, quiet. I fancy, it is the pattern that keeps her so still. It is so puzzling. It keeps me quiet by the hour.

I lie down ever so much now. John says it is good for me, and to sleep all I can.

Indeed he started the habit by making me lie down for an hour after each meal.

It is a very bad habit I am convinced, for you see I don't sleep.

And that cultivates deceit, for I don't tell them I'm awake—O no!

The fact is I am getting a little afraid of John.

He seems very queer sometimes, and even Jennie has an inexplicable look.

It strikes me occasionally, just as a scientific hypothesis,—that perhaps it is the paper!

I have watched John when he did not know I was looking, and come into the room suddenly on the most innocent excuses, and I've caught him several times *looking at the paper!* And Jennie too. I caught Jennie with her hand on it once.

She didn't know I was in the room, and when I asked her in a quiet, a very quiet voice, with the most restrained manner possible, what she was doing with the paper—she turned around as if she had been caught stealing, and looked quite angry—asked me why I should frighten her so!

Then she said that the paper stained everything it touched, that she had found yellow smooches on all my clothes and John's, and she wished we would be more careful!

Did not that sound innocent? But I know she was studying that pattern, and I am determined that nobody shall find it out but myself!

Life is very much more exciting now than it used to be. You see I have something more to expect, to look forward to, to watch. I really do eat better, and am more quiet than I was.

John is so pleased to see me improve! He laughed a little the other day, and said I seemed to be flourishing in spite of my wall-paper.

I turned it off with a laugh. I had no intention of telling him it was *because* of the wall-paper—he would make fun of me. He might even want to take me away.

I don't want to leave now until I have found it out. There is a week more, and I think that will be enough.

I'm feeling ever so much better! I don't sleep much at night, for it is so interesting to watch developments; but I sleep a good deal in the daytime.

In the daytime it is tiresome and perplexing.

There are always new shoots on the fungus, and new shades of yellow all over it. I cannot keep count of them, though I have tried conscientiously.

It is the strangest yellow, that wall-paper! It makes me think of all the yellow things I ever saw—not beautiful ones like buttercups, but old foul, bad yellow things.

But there is something else about that paper—the smell! I noticed it the moment we came into the room, but with so much air and sun it was not bad. Now we have had a week of fog and rain, and whether the windows are open or not, the smell is here.

It creeps all over the house.

I find it hovering in the dining-room, skulking in the parlor, hiding in the hall, lying in wait for me on the stairs.

It gets into my hair.

Even when I go to ride, if I turn my head suddenly and surprise it—there is that smell!

Such a peculiar odor, too! I have spent hours in trying to analyze it, to find what it smelled like.

It is not bad—at first, and very gentle, but quite the subtlest, most enduring odor I ever met.

In this damp weather it is awful, I wake up in the night and find it hanging over me.

It used to disturb me at first. I thought seriously of burning the house—to reach the smell.

But now I am used to it. The only thing I can think of that it is like is the *color* of the paper! A yellow smell.

There is a very funny mark on this wall, low down, near the mopboard. A streak that runs round the room. It goes behind every piece of furniture, except the bed, a long, straight, even *smooch*, as if it had been rubbed over and over.

I wonder how it was done and who did it, and what they did it for. Round and round and round—round and round and round—it makes me dizzy!

I really have discovered something at last.

Through watching so much at night, when it changes so, I have finally found out.

The front pattern *does* move—and no wonder! The woman behind shakes it!

Sometimes I think there are a great many women behind, and sometimes only one, and she crawls around fast, and her crawling shakes it all over.

Then in the very bright spots she keeps still, and in the very shady spots she just takes hold of the bars and shakes them hard.

And she is all the time trying to climb through. But nobody could climb through that pattern—it strangles so; I think that is why it has so many heads.

They get through, and then the pattern strangles them off and turns them upside down, and makes their eyes white!

If those heads were covered or taken off it would not be half so bad.

I think that woman gets out in the daytime!

And I'll tell you why—privately—I've seen her!

I can see her out of every one of my windows!

It is the same woman, I know, for she is always creeping, and most women do not creep by daylight.

I see her on that long road under the trees, creeping along, and when a carriage comes she hides under the blackberry vines.

I don't blame her a bit. It must be very humiliating to be caught creeping by daylight!

I always lock the door when I creep by daylight. I can't do it at night, for I know John would suspect something at once.

And John is so queer now, that I don't want to irritate him. I wish he would take another room! Besides, I don't want anybody to get that woman out at night but myself.

I often wonder if I could see her out of all the windows at once.

But, turn as fast as I can, I can only see out of one at one time.

And though I always see her, she *may* be able to creep faster than I can turn!

I have watched her sometimes away off in the open country, creeping as fast as a cloud shadow in a high wind.

If only that top pattern could be gotten off from the under one! I mean to try it, little by little.

I have found out another funny thing, but I shan't tell it this time! It does not do to trust people too much.

There are only two more days to get this paper off, and I believe John is beginning to notice. I don't like the look in his eyes.

And I heard him ask Jennie a lot of professional questions about me. She had a very good report to give.

She said I slept a good deal in the daytime.

John knows I don't sleep very well at night, for all I'm so quiet!

He asked me all sorts of questions, too, and pretended to be very loving and kind. As if I couldn't see through him!

Still, I don't wonder he acts so, sleeping under this paper for three months.

It only interests me, but I feel sure John and Jennie are secretly affected by it.

Hurrah! This is the last day, but it is enough. John to stay in town over night, and won't be out until this evening.

Jennie wanted to sleep with me—the sly thing! but I told her I should undoubtedly rest better for a night all alone.

That was clever, for really I wasn't alone a bit! As soon as it was moonlight and that poor thing began to crawl and shake the pattern, I got up and ran to help her.

I pulled and she shook, I shook and she pulled, and before morning we had peeled off yards of that paper.

A strip about as high as my head and half around the room.

And then when the sun came and that awful pattern began to laugh at me, I declared I would finish it to-day!

We go away to-morrow, and they are moving all my furniture down again to leave things as they were before.

Jennie looked at the wall in amazement, but I told her merrily that I did it out of pure spite at the vicious thing.

She laughed and said she wouldn't mind doing it herself, but I must not get tired.

How she betrayed herself that time!

But I am here, and no person touches this paper but me—not *alive!*

She tried to get me out of the room—it was too patent! But I said it was so quiet and empty and clean now that I believed I would lie down again and sleep all I could; and not to wake me even for dinner—I would call when I woke.

So now she is gone, and the servants are gone, and the things are gone, and there is nothing left but that great bedstead nailed down, with the canvas mattress we found on it.

We shall sleep downstairs to-night, and take the boat home to-morrow.

I quite enjoy the room, now it is bare again.

How those children did tear about here!

This bedstead is fairly gnawed!

But I must get to work.

I have locked the door and thrown the key down into the front path.

I don't want to go out, and I don't want to have anybody come in, till John comes.

I want to astonish him.

I've got a rope up here that even Jennie did not find. If that woman does get out, and tries to get away, I can tie her!

But I forgot I could not reach far without anything to stand on!

This bed will *not* move!

I tried to lift and push it until I was lame, and then I got so angry I bit off a little piece at one corner—but it hurt my teeth.

Then I peeled off all the paper I could reach standing on the floor. It sticks horribly and the pattern just enjoys it! All those strangled heads and bulbous eyes and waddling fungus growths just shriek with derision!

I am getting angry enough to do something desperate. To jump out of the window would be admirable exercise, but the bars are too strong even to try.

Besides I wouldn't do it. Of course not. I know well enough that a step like that is improper and might be misconstrued.

I don't like to *look* out of the windows even—there are so many of those creeping women, and they creep so fast.

I wonder if they all come out of that wall-paper as I did?

But I am securely fastened now by my well-hidden rope—you don't get *me* out in the road there!

I suppose I shall have to get back behind the pattern when it comes night, and that is hard!

It is so pleasant to be out in this great room and creep around as I please!

I don't want to go outside. I won't, even if Jennie asks me to.

For outside you have to creep on the ground, and everything is green instead of yellow.

But here I can creep smoothly on the floor, and my shoulder just fits in that long smooch around the wall, so I cannot lose my way.

Why there's John at the door!

It is no use, young man, you can't open it!

How he does call and pound!

Now he's crying for an axe.

It would be a shame to break down that beautiful door!

"John dear!" said I in the gentlest voice, "the key is down by the front steps, under a plantain leaf!"

That silenced him for a few moments.

Then he said—very quietly indeed, "Open the door, my darling!"

"I can't," said I. "The key is down by the front door under a plantain leaf!"

And then I said it again, several times, very gently and slowly, and said it so often that he had to go and see, and he got it of course, and came in. He stopped short by the door.

"What is the matter?" he cried. "For God's sake, what are you doing?"

I kept on creeping just the same, but I looked at him over my shoulder.

"I've got out at last," said I, "in spite of you and Jane. And I've pulled off most of the paper, so you can't put me back!"

Now why should that man have fainted? But he did, and right across my path by the wall, so that I had to creep over him every time!

[1891]

Journal Entry

Soon after Gilman's story was published in 1891, a Boston physician declared, "Such a story ought not to be written, . . . it was enough to drive anyone mad to read it" (*The Forerunner*, October 1913). Respond to the emotional impact of the story as a whole. What does the story say to you as a reader?

Textual Considerations

1. Prepare a profile of John, listing his good and bad points. Is he responsible for his wife's emotional state? Why or why not? To what extent do you agree with John that she should not write?

2. Analyze the connection between meaning and symbolism in the story. Consider, for example, the physical description of the bedroom, particularly the wallpaper. How does the narrator's description of it and feelings toward it change? Why is the color appropriate? What pattern does she discover, and what does it represent?

3. How does the author use stylistic changes to mirror the narrator's mental disintegration? Cite examples from the text.

4. Explain the narrator's statement "I've got out at last" in the next-to-last paragraph. To what extent is this true? Is there any sense in which madness can be liberating? Explain.

5. Gilman declared that her drive to write "The Yellow Wallpaper" was to save people from insanity. Do you think the story succeeds in fulfilling Gilman's wish? Cite evidence from the text to support your position.

Cultural Contexts

1. Discuss with your group the reasons for the current popularity of "The Yellow Wall-paper."

2. The rest cure prescribed by the narrator's doctor and physician-husband was standard treatment in Victorian medical theory for what is now known as postpartum depression. Discuss with your group how this so-called cure might affect emotional depression and sense of identity.

Alifa Rifaat

Another Evening at the Club

In a state of tension, she awaited the return of her husband. At a loss to predict what would happen between them, she moved herself back and forth in the rocking chair on the wide wooden veranda that ran along the bank and occupied part of the river itself, its supports being fixed in the river bed, while around it grew grasses and reeds. As though to banish her apprehension, she passed her fingers across her hair. The specters of the eucalyptus trees ranged along the garden fence rocked before her gaze, with white egrets slumbering on their high branches like huge white flowers among the thin leaves.

The crescent moon rose from behind the eastern mountains and the peaks of the gently stirring waves glistened in its feeble rays, intermingled with threads of light leaking from the houses of Manfalout scattered along the opposite bank. The colored bulbs fixed to the trees in the garden of the club at the far end of the town stood out against the surrounding darkness. Somewhere over there her husband now sat, most likely engrossed in a game of chess.

It was only a few years ago that she had first laid eyes on him at her father's house, meeting his gaze that weighed up her beauty and priced it before offering the dowry. She had noted his eyes ranging over her as she presented him with the coffee in the Japanese cups that were kept safely locked away in the cupboard for important guests. Her mother had herself laid them out on the silver-plated tray with its elaborately embroidered spread. When the two men had taken their coffee, her father had looked up at her with a smile and had told her to sit down, and she had seated herself on the sofa facing them, drawing the end of her dress over her knees and looking through lowered lids at the man who might choose her as his wife. She had been glad to see that he was tall, well-built and clean-shaven except for a thin greying moustache. In particular she noticed the well-cut coat of English tweed and the silk shirt with gold links. She had felt herself blushing as she saw him returning her gaze. Then the man turned to her father and took out a gold case and offered him a cigarette.

"You really shouldn't, my dear sir," said her father, patting his chest with his left hand and extracting a cigarette with trembling fingers. Before he could bring out his box of matches Abboud Bey had produced his lighter.

"No, after you, my dear sir," said her father in embarrassment. Mingled with her sense of excitement at this man who gave out such an air of worldly self-confidence was a guilty shame at her father's inadequacy.

After lighting her father's cigarette Abboud Bey sat back, crossing his legs, and took out a cigarette for himself. He tapped it against the case before putting it in the corner of his mouth and lighting it, then blew out circles of smoke that followed each other across the room.

"It's a great honor for us, my son," said her father, smiling first at Abboud Bey, then at his daughter, at which Abboud Bey looked across at her and asked:

"And the beautiful little girl's still at secondary school?"

She lowered her head modestly and her father had answered:

"As from today she'll be staying at home in readiness for your happy life together. Allah permitting," and at a glance from her father she had hurried off to join her mother in the kitchen.

"You're a lucky girl," her mother had told her. "He's a real find. Any girl would be happy to have him. He's an Inspector of Irrigation though he's not yet forty. He earns a big salary and gets a fully furnished government house wherever he's posted, which will save us the expense of setting up a house—and I don't have to tell you what our situation is—and that's beside the house he owns in Alexandria where you'll be spending your holidays."

Samia had wondered to herself how such a splendid suitor had found his way to her door. Who had told him that Mr. Mahmoud Barakat, a mere clerk at the Court of Appeal, had a beautiful daughter of good reputation?

The days were then taken up with going the rounds of Cairo's shops and choosing clothes for the new grand life she would be living. This was made possible by her father borrowing on the security of his government pension. Abboud Bey, on his part, never visited her without bringing a present. For her birthday, just before they were married, he bought her an emerald ring that came in a plush box bearing the name of a well-known jeweler in Kasr el-Nil Street. On her wedding night, as he put a diamond bracelet round her wrist, he had reminded her that she was marrying someone with a brilliant career in front of him and that one of the most important things in life was the opinion of others, particularly one's equals and seniors. Though she was still only a young girl she must try to act with suitable dignity.

"Tell people you're from the well-known Barakat family and that your father was a judge," and he went up to her and gently patted her cheeks in a fatherly, re-assuring gesture that he was often to repeat during their times together.

Then, yesterday evening, she had returned from the club somewhat light-headed from the bottle of beer she had been required to drink on the occasion of someone's birthday. Her husband, noting the state she was in, hurriedly took her back home. She had undressed and put on her nightgown, leaving her jewelry on the dressing table, and was fast asleep seconds after getting into bed. The following morning, fully recovered, she slept late, then rang the bell as usual and had breakfast brought to her. It was only as she was putting her jewelry away in the wooden and mother-of-pearl box that she realized that her emerald ring was missing.

Could it have dropped from her finger at the club? In the car on the way back? No, she distinctly remembered it last thing at night, remembered the usual difficulty she had in getting it off her finger. She stripped the bed of its sheets, turned over the mattress, looked inside the pillow cases, crawled on hands and knees under the bed. The tray of breakfast lying on the small bedside table caught her eye and she remembered the young servant coming in that morning with it, remembered the noise of the tray being put down, the curtain being drawn, the tray then being lifted up again and placed on the bedside table. No one but the servant had entered the room. Should she call her and question her?

Eventually, having taken two aspirins, she decided to do nothing and await the return of her husband from work.

Directly he arrived she told him what had happened and he took her by the arm and seated her down beside him:

"Let's calm down and go over what happened."

She repeated, this time with further details, the whole story.

"And you've looked for it?"

"Everywhere. Every possible and impossible place in the bedroom and the bathroom. You see, I remember distinctly taking it off last night."

He grimaced at the thought of last night, then said:

"Anybody been in the room since Gazia when she brought in the breakfast?"

"Not a soul. I've even told Gazia not to do the room today."

"And you've not mentioned anything to her?"

"I thought I'd better leave it to you."

"Fine, go and tell her I want to speak to her. There's no point in your saying anything but I think it would be as well if you were present when I talk to her."

Five minutes later Gazia, the young servant girl they had recently employed, entered behind her mistress. Samia took herself to a far corner of the room while Gazia stood in front of Abboud Bey, her hands folded across her chest, her eyes lowered.

"Yes, sir?"

"Where's the ring?"

"What ring are you talking about, sir?"

"Now don't make out you don't know. The one with the green stone. It would be better for you if you hand it over and then nothing more need be said."

"May Allah blind me if I've set eyes on it."

He stood up and gave her a sudden slap on the face. The girl reeled back, put one hand to her cheek, then lowered it again to her chest and made no answer to any of Abboud's questions. Finally he said to her:

"You've got just fifteen seconds to say where you've hidden the ring or else, I swear to you, you're not going to have a good time of it."

As he lifted up his arm to look at his watch the girl flinched slightly but continued in her silence. When he went to the telephone Samia raised her head and saw that the girl's cheeks were wet with tears. Abboud Bey got through to the Superintendent of Police and told him briefly what had occurred.

"Of course I haven't got any actual proof but seeing that no one else entered the room, it's obvious she's pinched it. Anyway I'll leave the matter in your capable hands—I know your people have their ways and means."

He gave a short laugh, then listened for a while and said: "I'm really most grateful to you."

He put down the receiver and turned to Samia:

"That's it, my dear. There's nothing more to worry about. The Superintendent has promised me we'll get it back. The patrol car's on the way."

The following day, in the late afternoon, she'd been sitting in front of her dressing-table rearranging her jewelry in its box when an earring slipped from her grasp and fell to the floor. As she bent to pick it up she saw the emerald ring stuck between the leg of the table and the wall. Since that moment she had sat in a state of panic awaiting her husband's return from the club. She even felt tempted to walk down to the water's edge and throw it into the river so as to be rid of the unpleasantness that lay ahead.

At the sound of the screech of tires rounding the house to the garage, she slipped the ring onto her finger. As he entered she stood up and raised her hand to show him the ring. Quickly, trying to choose her words but knowing that she was expressing herself clumsily, she explained what an extraordinary thing it was that it should have lodged itself between the dressing-table and the wall, what an extraordinary coincidence she should have dropped the earring and so seen it, how she'd thought of ringing him at the club to tell him the good news but . . .

She stopped in mid-sentence when she saw his frown and added weakly: "I'm sorry. I can't think how it could have happened. What do we do now?"

He shrugged his shoulders as though in surprise.

"Are you asking me, my dear lady? Nothing of course."

"But they've been beating up the girl—you yourself said they'd not let her be till she confessed."

Unhurriedly, he sat himself down as though to consider this new aspect of the matter. Taking out his case, he tapped a cigarette against it in his accustomed manner, then moistened his lips, put the cigarette in place and lit it. The smoke rings hovered in the still air as he looked at his watch and said:

"In any case she's not got all that long before they let her go. They can't keep her for more than forty-eight hours without getting any evidence or a confession. It won't kill her to put up with things for a while longer. By now the whole town knows the servant stole the ring—or would you like me to tell everyone: 'Look, folks, the fact is that the wife got a bit tiddly on a couple sips of beer and the ring took off on its own and hid itself behind the dressing-table'? What do you think?"

"I know the situation's a bit awkward . . . "

"Awkward? It's downright ludicrous. Listen, there's nothing to be done but to give it to me and the next time I go down to Cairo I'll sell it and get something else in its place. We'd be the laughing-stock of the town."

He stretched out his hand and she found herself taking off the ring and placing it in the outstretched palm. She was careful that their eyes should not meet. For a moment she was on the point of protesting and in fact uttered a few words:

"I'd just like to say we could . . . "

Putting the ring away in his pocket, he bent over her and with both hands gently patted her on the cheeks. It was gesture she had long become used to, a gesture that promised her that this man who was her husband and the father of her child had also taken the place of her father who, as though assured that he had found her a suitable substitute, had followed up her marriage with his own funeral. The gesture told her more eloquently than any words that he was the man, she the woman, he the one who carried the responsibilities, made the decisions, she the one whose role it was to be beautiful, happy, carefree. Now, though, for the first time in their life together the gesture came like a slap in the face.

Directly he removed his hands her whole body was seized with an uncontrollable trembling. Frightened he would notice, she rose to her feet and walked with deliberate steps towards the large window. She leaned her forehead against the comforting cold surface and closed her eyes tightly for several seconds. When she opened them she noticed that the café lights strung between the trees on the opposite shore had been turned on and that there were men seated under them and a waiter moving among the tables. The dark shape of a boat momentarily blocked out the café scene; in the light from the hurricane lamp hanging from its bow she saw it cutting through several of those floating islands of Nile waterlilies that, rootless, are swept along with the current.

Suddenly she became aware of his presence alongside her.

"Why don't you go and change quickly while I take the car out? It's hot and it would be nice to have supper at the club."

"As you like. Why not?"

By the time she had turned round from the window she was smiling.

[1983]

Journal Entry

Rifaat is from Cairo, Egypt, where the tradition of arranged marriages is still observed. What knowledge or experience of such marriages can you bring to your reading of this text? Imagine yourself as the wife of the Inspector of Irrigation. How would your responses to your husband be similar to or different from Samia's?

Textual Considerations

1. To analyze "Another Evening at the Club" in terms of its narrative structure, consider Rifaat's use of **flashbacks** at several points in the story. Cite two or three examples and discuss their relation to the story's meaning.
2. Analyze how Rifaat uses the language of gazes, glances, slaps, and gestures to reinforce the story's theme. What evidence can you find of the influence of other cultures on the characters' beliefs and behavior? What examples do you find most effective?
3. Comment on the role of the servant girl. To what extent is she Samia's victim as well as Abboud Bey's?
4. Examine the bonds that tie the young wife to her husband. To what extent has marriage enhanced her sense of identity and autonomy? Explain how Samia's role as a wife upholds Abboud Bey's male identity.
5. What is the significance of the story's title? How does it relate to the concluding paragraph of the text? How do you respond to the title?

Cultural Contexts

1. Feminists, including the French writer Simone de Beauvoir, have suggested that men have occupied the position of subject, or actor, while women have occupied the position of marginalized object, or one acted upon. Identify and discuss with your group the cultural and economic forces that have contributed to a similar model of gender relations in Rifaat's text. Consider, too, how the wife's presence as object affects her husband's masculine identity.

2. Share with your classmates what you know about marriage traditions in different cultures. Then debate the merits of marriage customs centered on the "dowry" or the "sponsalia." Consider, too, the extent to which such traditions have affected Samia's and other women's views of themselves.

Yukio Mishima

Fountains in the Rain

Translated by John Bester

The boy was tired of walking in the rain dragging the girl, heavy as a sandbag and weeping continually, around with him.

A short while ago, in a tea shop in the Marunouchi Building, he had told her he was leaving her.

The first time in his life that he'd broken with a woman!

It was something he had long dreamed of; it had at last become a reality.

It was for this alone that he had loved her, or pretended to love her; for this alone he had assiduously undermined her defenses; for this alone he'd furiously sought the chance to sleep with her, slept with her—till lo, the preparations were complete and it only remained to pronounce the phrase he had longed just once to pronounce with his own lips, with due authority, like the edict of a king:

"It's time to break it off!"

Those words, the mere enunciation of which would be enough to rend the sky asunder. . . . Those words that he had cherished so passionately even while half-resigned to the impossibility of the fact. . . . That phrase, more heroic, more glorious than any other in the world, which would fly in a straight line through the heavens like an arrow released from its bow. . . . That spell which only the most human of humans, the most manly of men, might utter. . . . In short:

"It's time to break it off!"

All the same, Akio felt a lingering regret that he'd been obliged to say it with such a deplorable lack of clarity, with a rattling noise in the throat, like an asthmatic with a throatful of phlegm, which even a preliminary draft of soda pop through his straw had failed to avert.

At the time, his chief fear had been that the words might not have been heard. He'd have died sooner than be asked what he'd said and have to repeat it. After all, if a goose that for years had longed to lay a golden egg had found it smashed before anyone could see it, would it promptly have laid another?

Fortunately, however, she had heard. She'd heard, and he hadn't had to repeat it, which was a splendid piece of luck. Under his own steam, Akio had crossed the pass over the mountains that he'd gazed at for so long in the distance.

Sure proof that she'd heard had been vouchsafed in a flash, like chewing gum ejected from a vending machine.

The windows were closed because of the rain, so that the voices of the customers talking around them, the clatter of dishes, the ping of the cash register clashed with each other all the more violently, rebounding subtly off the clammy condensation on the inside of the panes to create a single, mind-fuddling commotion.

Akio's muffled words had no sooner reached Masako's ears through the general uproar than her eyes—wide, staring eyes that seemed to be trying to shove her surroundings away from her thin, unprepossessing features—opened still wider. They were no longer eyes so much as an embodiment of disaster, irretrievable disaster. And then, all at once, the tears had burst forth.

There was no business of breaking into sobs; nor did she bawl her head off: the tears simply gushed, expressing nothing, and with a most impressive force.

Akio naturally assumed that waters of such pressure and flow would soon cease. And he marveled at the peppermint freshness of mind with which he contemplated the phenomenon. This was precisely what he had planned, worked to encompass, and brought to reality: a splendid achievement, though admittedly somewhat mechanical.

It was to witness this, he told himself again, that he had made love to Masako: he, who had always been free from the dominance of desire.

And the tearful face of the woman now in front of him—this was reality! A genuine forsaken woman—forsaken by himself, Akio!

Even so, Masako's tears went on for so long with no sign of abating that the boy began to worry about the people around them.

Masako, still wearing her light-colored raincoat, was sitting upright in her chair. The collar of a red blouse showed at the neck of the coat. She looked as though set in her present position, with her hands pressed down on the edge of the table, a tremendous force in both of them.

She stared straight ahead, letting the tears flow unchecked. She made no move to take out a handkerchief to wipe them. Her breath, catching in her thin throat, gave out a regular wheeze like new shoes, and the mouth that with student perverseness she refused to paint turned up disconsolately, quivering continually.

The older customers were looking at them curiously, with stares of a kind calculated to disturb Akio's newfound sense of maturity.

The abundance of Masako's tears was a genuine cause for astonishment. Not for a moment did their volume diminish. Tired of watching, Akio dropped his gaze and looked at the tip of the umbrella he had stood against a chair. The raindrops running from it had formed a small, darkish puddle on the old-fashioned, tile mosaic floor. Even the puddle began to look like Masako's tears to him.

Abruptly, he grabbed the bill and stood up.

The June rains had been falling steadily for three days. As he left the Marunouchi Building and unfurled his umbrella, the girl came silently after him. Since she had no umbrella herself, he had no choice but to let her share his. It reminded him of the way older people, for the benefit of the outside world, went on pretending even after they'd stopped feeling anything. Now he too had acquired the same habit; to share an umbrella with a girl once you'd made the move to break with her was just a gesture for other people's benefit. It was simply being cut-and-dried about things. Yes: to be cut-and-dried (even when it took such subtle forms) suited Akio's nature. . . .

As they wandered along the broad sidewalk in the direction of the Imperial Palace, the problem foremost in his mind was finding somewhere to dump this tearbag he was saddled with.

I wonder—he thought vaguely to himself—if the fountains work even when it's raining?

Why should the idea of fountains have occurred to him? Another few paces, and he realized the physical pun in his own train of thought.

The girl's wet raincoat, which he was touching—remotely, of course, and unfeelingly—in the cramped space beneath the umbrella, had the texture of a reptile. But he bore with it, forcing his mind to follow the pun to its logical conclusion.

Yes: fountains in the rain. He'd bring the fountains and Masako's tears into confrontation. Even Masako would surely find her match there. For one thing, the fountains were the type that used the same water over and over again, so the girl, whose tears all ran to waste, could hardly compete with them. A human being was scarcely a match for a reflex fountain; almost certainly, she'd give up and stop crying. Then he'd be able somehow to get rid of this unwanted baggage. The only question was whether the fountains would be working as usual in the rain.

Akio walked in silence. Masako, still weeping, followed doggedly under the same umbrella. Thus, while it was difficult to shake her off, it was easy to drag her along where he wanted.

What with the rain and the tears, Akio felt as if his whole body was getting wet. It was all right for Masako in her white boots, but his own socks, inside his loafers, felt like thick, wet seaweed around his feet.

There was some time still before the office workers came out, and the sidewalk was deserted. Traversing a pedestrian crossing, they made their way toward Wadakura Bridge, which crossed the palace moat. When they reached the end of the bridge with its old-fashioned wooden railings topped by pointed knobs, they could see on their left a swan floating on the moat in the rain and, to the right, on the other side of the moat, the white tablecloths and red chairs of a hotel dining room, dimly visible through rain-blurred glass. They crossed the bridge. Passing between high stone ramparts, they turned left and emerged in the small garden with the fountains.

Masako, as ever, was crying soundlessly.

Just inside the garden was a large Western-style summer-house. The benches under its roof, which consisted of a kind of blind of fine reeds, were protected to some extent from the rain, so Akio sat down with his umbrella still up and Masako sat down next to him, at an angle, so that all he could see, right in front of his nose, was a shoulder of her white raincoat and her wet hair. The rain on the hair, repelled by the oil on it, looked like a scattering of fine white dew. Still crying, with her eyes wide open, she might almost have been in some kind of coma, and Akio felt an urge to give the hair a tug, to bring her out of it.

She went on crying, endlessly. It was perfectly clear that she was waiting for him to say something, which made it impossible, as a matter of pride, for him to break the silence. It occurred to him that since that one momentous sentence he hadn't spoken a single word.

Not far away, the fountains were throwing up their waters in profusion, but Masako showed no inclination to look at them.

Seen from here, head on, the three fountains, two small and one large, were lined up one behind the other, and the sound, blotted out by the rain, was distant and faint, but the fact that their blurring of spray was not visible at a distance gave the lines of water, dividing up in various directions, a clearly defined look like curved glass tubes.

Not a soul was in sight anywhere. The lawn on this side of the fountains and the low ornamental hedge were a brilliant green in the rain.

Beyond the garden, though, there was a constant procession of wet truck hoods and bus roofs in red, white, or yellow; the red light of a signal at a crossing was clearly visible, but when it changed to the lower green, the light disappeared in a cloud of spray from the fountains.

The act of sitting down and remaining still and silent aroused an indefinable anger in the boy. With it, amusement at his little joke of a while ago disappeared.

He couldn't have said what he was angry about. Not long before, he had been on a kind of high, but now, suddenly, he was beset with an obscure sense of dissatisfaction. Nor was his inability to dispose of the forever crying Masako the whole extent of the frustration.

Her? I could easily deal with *her* if I cared to, he told himself. I could just shove her in the fountain and do a bunk—and that would be the end of it. The thought restored his earlier elation. No, the only trouble was the absolute frustration he felt at the rain, the tears, the leaden sky that hung like a barrier before him. They pressed down on him on all sides, reducing his freedom to a kind of damp rag.

Angry, the boy gave in to a simple desire to hurt. Nothing would satisfy him now till he had got Masako thoroughly soaked in the rain and given her a good eyeful of the fountains.

Getting up suddenly, he set off running without so much as a glance back; raced on along the gravel path that encircled the fountains outside and a few steps higher than the walk around the fountains themselves; reached a spot that gave a full view of that; and came to a halt.

The girl came running through the rain. Checking herself just as she was about to collide with him, she took a firm grip of the umbrella he was holding up. Damp with tears and rain, her face was pale.

"Where are you going?" she said through her gasps.

Akio was not supposed to reply, yet found himself talking as effortlessly as though he'd been waiting for her to ask this very thing.

"Just look at the fountains. Look! You can cry as much as you like, but you're no match for *them*."

And the two of them tilted the umbrella and, freed from the need to keep their eyes on each other, stared for a while at the three fountains: the central one imposing, the other two slighter, like attendants flanking it on both sides.

Amidst the constant turmoil of the fountains and the pool around them, the streaks of rain falling into the water were almost indistinguishable. Paradoxically, the only sound that struck the ear was the fitful drone of distant cars; the noise of the fountains wove itself so closely into the surrounding air that unless you made an effort to hear you seemed to be enclosed in perfect silence.

First, the water at the bottom bounced in isolated drops off the huge shallow basin of black granite, then ran in a continual drizzle over the black rim.

Another six jets of water, describing far-flung radiating arcs in the air, stood guard around the main column that shot upward from the center of each basin.

This column, if you watched carefully, did not always achieve the same height. In the almost complete absence of a breeze, the water spouted vertically and undisturbed toward the gray, rainy sky, varying from time to time in the height of its summit. Occasionally, ragged water would be flung up to an astonishing height before finally dispersing into droplets and floating to earth again.

The water near the summit, shadowed by the clouds that were visible through it, was gray with an admixture of chalky white, almost too powdery-looking for real water, and a misty spray clung about it, while around the column played a mass of foam in large white flakes mingling like snow with the rain.

But Akio was less taken with the three main columns of water than with the water that shot out in radiating curves all around.

The jets from the big central fountain in particular leaped far above the marble rim, flinging up their white manes only to dash themselves gallantly down again onto the surface of the pool. The sight of their untiring rushing to the four quarters threatened to usurp his attention. Almost before he knew it, his mind, which till now had been with him in this place, was being taken over by the water, carried away on its rushing, cast far away. . . .

It was the same when he watched the central column.

At first glance, it seemed as neat, as motionless, as a sculpture fashioned out of water. Yet watching closely he could see a transparent ghost of movement moving upward from bottom to top. With furious speed it climbed, steadily filling a slender cylinder of space from base to summit, replacing each moment what had been lost the moment before, in a kind of perpetual replenishment. It was plain that at heaven's height it would be finally frustrated; yet the unwaning power that supported unceasing failure was magnificent.

The fountains he had brought the girl to see had ended by completely fascinating the boy himself. He was still dwelling on their virtues when his gaze, lifted higher, met the sky from which the all-enveloping rain was falling.

He got rain on his eyelashes.

The sky, hemmed in by dense clouds, hung low over his head; the rain fell copiously and without cease. The whole scene was filled with rain. The rain descending on his face was exactly the same as that falling on the roofs of the red-brick buildings and hotel in the distance. His own almost beardless face, smooth and shiny, and the rough concrete that floored the deserted room of one of those buildings were no more than two surfaces exposed, unresisting, to the same rain. From the rain's point of view, his cheeks and the dirty concrete roof were quite identical.

Immediately, the image of the fountains there before his eyes was wiped from his mind. Quite suddenly, fountains in the rain seemed to represent no more than the endless repetition of a stupid and pointless process.

Before long, he had forgotten both his joke of a while ago and the anger that had followed it, and felt his mind steadily becoming empty.

Empty, save for the falling rain. . . .

Aimlessly, the boy started walking.

"Where are you going?" She fell into step with him as she spoke, this time keeping a firm hold on the handle of the umbrella.

"Where? That's my business, isn't it? I told you quite plainly some time ago, didn't I?"

"What did you tell me?"

He gazed at her in horror, but the rain had washed away the traces of tears from the drenched face, and although the damp, reddened eyes still showed the aftermath of weeping, the voice in which she spoke was no longer shaky.

"What do you mean, 'what'? I told you a while back, didn't I?—that we'd better split up."

Just then, the boy spotted, beyond her profile as it moved through the rain, some crimson azalea bushes blooming, small and grudgingly, here and there on the lawn.

"Really? Did you say that? I didn't hear you." Her voice was normal.

Almost bowled over by shock, the boy managed a few steps further before an answer finally came and he stammered.

"But—in that case, what did you cry for? I don't get it."

She didn't reply immediately. Her wet little hand was still firmly attached to the umbrella handle.

"The tears just came. There wasn't any special reason."

Furious, he wanted to shout something at her, but at the crucial moment it came out as an enormous sneeze.

If I'm not careful I'm going to get a cold, he thought.

[1963]

Journal Entry

Write a journal entry on your responses to the narrator and Masako. Does their youth account for their behavior? Explain.

Textual Considerations

1. Analyze Akio and Masako's relationship. Why does Akio engage in it just to cut it off?
2. Characterize Masako's reactions to Akio's actions. Why does she follow him?
3. Comment on the motif of boredom in the story. How does the daily routine erode any triumph that Akio tried to achieve? Are boredom and routine avoidable? Why or why not?
4. What is the significance of the story's title? How do Akio's descriptions of the fountains apply to himself and to young people in general?

Cultural Contexts

1. Discuss with your group how Mishima uses setting to enhance meaning. What other literary devices does he use? To what effect?
2. Create a conversation between Murakami and Mishima on youth and fate. On what points do they agree and disagree? What factors, besides chronology, might account for differences in their points of view?

Sandip Roy

The Smells of Home

When she was seven years old Savitri's aunt visited from England. She brought her boxes of delicious chocolates filled with strawberries and hazelnuts and lots of pretty dresses. But what Savitri loved best was to bury her head in her aunt's suitcase and breathe in the fragrance of her clothes and cosmetics.

"Lavender, lilac, rosemary," she would whisper to herself making a daisychain of flowers she had never seen.

It was a scorchingly hot summer even by Delhi standards. In the afternoons her aunt would draw the blinds and take a nap. Savitri would tiptoe into the dark room and carefully open the suitcase. Then she would bury her head in the soft cottons and smooth silks and breathe deeply and surreptitiously. It was like a little corner of England trapped in there. She would feel herself falling through it and leaving the hot parched Delhi streets and the cruel blue Indian skies far behind. It smelled cool and fresh—so unlike the ripe kitchen smells that clung to her mother's sari— turmeric and sweat and stale talcum powder.

"Foxglove, primrose, daffodil."

She was now walking down a little cobbled street past houses like the picture on her tin of chocolates. She was going home to have scones and strawberries and cream. Her house had a pointed tiled roof and a chimney. And ivy on the walls or was it honeysuckle?

"Honeysuckle, bluebells, forget-me-not."

Crouched near the suitcase, like a little mouse, Savitri wished she could pack herself in with the soft nighties and synthetic saris. She imagined waking up and finding she was in England.

"Savi," her mother's shrill voice could be heard from downstairs. "Where is that girl? Savi, you haven't finished your rice. Come down or the cat will eat it up."

Savitri decided that when she grew up she would go to England.

Avinash was not quite from England. He was from New York. Well, not New York, New York but some small university town in the northern part of the state where he was just finishing his Ph.D. in Economics or something like that. It all sounded very difficult to Savitri. She liked to read Wordsworth and Keats. Not even Byron—there was something too hot and sunny about Byron, something sinewy and dangerous seemed to lurk beneath his poetry. For her Keats and Wordsworth had a watercolor feel about them which she found very soothing. Their colors were more muted. Savitri had never liked bright harsh colors—pinks and oranges and yellows.

"Look at that girl," her mother would say. "Only seventeen and dresses like a widow."

Avinash seemed the perfect match for her. Serious, academic and sober—he didn't wear hot pinks and sunny yellows either.

"My son," said his mother to Savitri's mother over a cup of tea, "has always been the top boy in his class. A model student his principal called him. Never one to wander the streets like these other roadside Romeos. That was why I never had the slightest fear of sending him to America. You know Mrs. Dutt, it's all about upbringing and family. If you bring him up right, then why should you fear?"

Savitri's mother nodded wisely.

"Everyone told me," continued his mother, "See one day he'll call and announce he wants to marry some American girl. But I said 'I trust my Avi. He would not break his mother's heart.' Arre, he is my only son. He knows his duty. Ever since his poor father died I have brought him up myself. It was not easy on a schoolteacher's salary. But I had faith and see him now. Do you know he has had papers published in important journals. Why, my friend Sulata said to me, 'Look Bani, mark my words if your Avi does not get the Nobel Prize one day.'"

In the pause that ensued as all assembled digested this piece of information, Savitri's aunt jumped in.

"So how old is Avinash exactly?"

"Well," said his mother defensively, "he's thirty-three. But what's age in a man? My husband was eleven years older than me. I don't believe in all this same-age marriages that go on these days. You need some difference in age to maintain a balance in the household. And tell me, how can you respect your husband if you are the same age as him?

"I've been telling him for so long now—get married, get married. But he keeps saying, 'First I must finish my Master's.' Then it was, 'Oh I must complete my Ph.D. and get a job, Ma. How will I have a family on a student's income?' So responsible, no? The day he got his professorship I said 'Enough Avi. Now I have to see you settled down with a good girl. Then only can I shut my eyes in peace.' He said 'But I don't have tenure yet' and I said *'Bas.* I will not listen anymore to your excuses.' We are not running after looks in my family," she said glancing at Savitri who was a little plain. "Good family and education is what we value. Avi's father was a renowned professor you know—he wrote three books. And I hear your Savitri has an M.A. in English Literature."

Avinash took Savitri out for dinner once. He was a thin quiet man with thinning hair and owlish glasses. He smelt faintly of lemony aftershave. They did not have much in common. She knew nothing about Economics, he had long forgotten his Wordsworth. They concentrated instead on the food and discussed the merits of the Tandoori chicken. When they exhausted that topic, they ate in silence listening to the ebb and flow of conversation at the tables around them.

"What was he like?" asked her mother.

"All right, I suppose," she answered. Though she had not found much in common with him she had not found anything objectionable either. At least he did not wear those loud colorful shirts with big flowers that she had seen American tourists wear.

Only once she said, almost wistfully, "You know I really wanted to go to England."

Her father laughed and said, "Savi, Wordsworth's England is long dead. In your grandfather's time people would go to England for then England still had power and glory. Now it is truly a nation of shopkeepers. And most of the shopkeepers are Indian anyway. You are lucky, you are going to the richest country in the world."

"And such a brilliant husband," added her mother.

"And so courteous and well-mannered," added her aunt. "I hope my daughter is as lucky as you."

"Heather, daisy, larkspur," Savitri said under her breath, playing with the words as if they were prayer beads.

Savitri was amazed at how easily she left India behind. As the airplane left Delhi airport she looked out of the window at the lights of Delhi growing smaller and smaller. She had a sense of her past, her ties, her home all falling away behind her like an unraveling sari. "Perhaps," she thought sipping her Coca-Cola, "I was not meant to be Indian at all." She glanced over at Avinash, seated next to her, absorbed in the latest issue of *Time*. He glanced up at her and finding himself caught in her gaze looked away guiltily. Then he said quietly "How do you imagine America?"

"America—I don't know," she said wonderingly. "Big buildings, fast cars, movies."

"Washing machines," she added as an afterthought. "Lawnmowers, microwaves."

"You never thought of America as freedom?"

"Freedom?" she said perplexed. "No not really." Then she smiled slightly and said, "Maybe it was for you when you went there as a student. But I am going there as your wife."

"That's true," he replied.

"Are you afraid that now I am going with you, you will lose your freedom?" she asked half-teasingly.

"Who is really free anyway?" he answered without looking at her and returned to the magazine. She opened her mouth to speak but he seemed to have drawn curtains around himself.

Savitri hated America from the moment she stepped off that plane. The accents jarred her—they had none of the clean crispness of the BBC World Service programs she so loved and listened to on her father's prized short-wave radio. The freeways with their whizzing cars and many lanes terrified her. She could not imagine ever being able to drive on them. Yet Avinash had told her that if you didn't know how to drive here you were a prisoner. She was confused by all the machines she needed to handle and all the buttons she had to press whether to get money from the bank or to buy a roll of stamps. But most of all she missed having people to talk to.

Avinash spent long hours at school sometimes coming home after she had gone to bed. She would lie in the dark hearing the purr of the microwave as he warmed his dinner. Her mother always waited for her father to come home before she had dinner. But Savitri invariably got a headache if she let herself go hungry too long. She would leave his dinner on the table in front of the jar of Priya mango pickles. She would lie in bed and try and figure out what he was eating.

"He must be finished with the dal, he is probably on the chicken now." She would hear him open the refrigerator as he got some Coke. They needed to get more Coke and detergent and something else. She knitted her brows and tried to remember what. Soon she knew she would hear the tap running as he rinsed the dishes and then the clank of the dishes being loaded into the dishwasher. That was when she closed her eyes and turned on her side, away from his side of the bed. It was her way of punishing him for being late again. But he did not seem to mind. She would feel the bed as he climbed onto it. Then the sharp minty smell of toothpaste. In a little while she would hear his gentle easy breathing and she would lie awake angry, making grocery lists in her head.

Everyday she would run downstairs at two o'clock and check the mail. She had even come to know the postman. He always said, "Hi, how's it going?" But no one ever wrote to her. All she got were catalogs from department stores. She would spend the afternoon reading about furniture sales and installment plans to buy home entertainment systems. Apart from that all they seemed to get were bills and coupons from pizza-joints. She had written two letters home but had not gotten anything from India. Mail from India could take twenty days Avinash told her. Once she found a personal letter from India. In her excitement at seeing an Indian stamp she tore it open before she realized the letter was for Avinash. Though she did not read it he was very annoyed.

"I am your wife. We share the same bank account," she said.

"You don't understand," he replied, "letters are different. It could be, could be anything."

Savitri remembered the day she got her first letter. It had been raining all day—a fine dispiriting drizzle. She had wanted to walk down to the library but was stuck indoors since Avinash for some reason had left the umbrella in his office. Frustrated she had spent the whole day rearranging her spices. She had poured them into individual little spice-jars and then labeled the jars in her best handwriting. For a while she debated whether to write the Hindi names or the English ones—haldi, jeera, and dhania or turmeric, cumin, coriander? She finally decided on "Turmeric," "Cumin," "Coriander." But she did not know the word for methi so she left it blank. She smelt her hands—and suddenly remembered her mother cooking and then wiping her hands on her sari. Her old saris always had turmeric stains.

She wiped her hands on a paper towel and ran downstairs to get the mail. And there it was, a neat little envelope with Mrs. Mitra written on it in an almost childish uneven handwriting. She turned it over but there was no sender's name or address. The postmark was local. Puzzled she climbed up the stairs slowly trying to figure out who it was.

She put Avinash's mail on the dining table and pulled out the Kashmiri letter-cutter her friend Leena had given her and slit open the envelope. There was just one sheet in there—a yellow ruled sheet torn from a writing pad.

Dear Mrs. Mitra, (it said)

You don't know me but I have been dreading your arrival for months now. I have been your husband's lover for over two years now. I always knew I would have to keep it a secret but I didn't expect this. Avi said he is merely doing his duty and his mother would kill herself otherwise. Maybe that is so. I don't know too much about Indians. Avi never introduced me to his friends. I am no longer his lover. I couldn't bear the hypocrisy and I did not want to share. He thought we could carry on just as before except it would have to be at my place now. He can't understand why I would make such a fuss. After all, it had always been a secret from everyone else. Now we'd just keep it a secret from you too. Avi said, "It's not as if I promised to marry you or something." That's true, so why am I writing you this? Especially since I have broken up with him? I'd like to think I want to warn you and save you. But I think it's just my own vindictiveness and selfishness. I wanted to make him understand what he is doing to you and me. I wanted to hurt Avinash and the only way I knew how was through you. Forgive me if you can.

Sincerely,
John Elwood

She tore the letter up with shaking hands. Then she sat and put the pieces back together as if she could rearrange the words to say something else. Four times she lifted the receiver to call Avinash. Four times she put it down. She sat and stared at the neatly arranged spices and tried to remember the English for methi. Maybe she should just write methi. She wondered what would happen to her now. How much did a one-way fare to India cost? She sat and watched one television program after another letting the images drip meaninglessly in front of her. When Avinash came home she was already in bed.

"It's only nine o'clock," he said, "are you all right?"

She lay curled up on her side, her fists clenched in her mouth to prevent herself from screaming. She buried her face in the pillow and tried to summon up the old familiar smells of home.

"Turmeric, coriander, cumin," she whispered fiercely as if in exorcism.

But all she could smell was the happy lemon-lime spring-fresh smell of freshly laundered sheets. She buried herself deeper trying desperately to go home.

She felt him approaching the bed.

Mustard, poppyseed, methi. She was drawing a ring of spices to protect her.

She felt his hand on her forehead—cold and clammy. She shrank away from his touch.

Turmeric, coriander, methi.

Flies buzzing round her head.

Turmeric, coriander, methi.

Falling, falling, falling . . .
Her mother in the kitchen . . .
Her father reading the newspaper . . .
Old Sushila chopping the fish . . .
Haldi, dhania, methi
Haldi, dhania, methi . . .

[1996]

Journal Entry

What meanings, memories, and emotions do you bring that deepen the significance of the story's title?

Textual Considerations

1. Characterize Savitri. How does the author use visual, auditory, and sensory imagery to reveal Savitri's emotions to the reader?
2. Avinash's mother is sure that her son "would not break his mother's heart." To what extent do the events of the story contradict or affirm her point of view? What is your response to Avinash?
3. Identify and analyze the central conflict of the story.
4. What is your response to the story's ending? Where does the author use irony to foreshadow the contents of the letter?
5. How does Savitri change during the story?

Cultural Contexts

1. Avinash associates America with personal freedom, whereas Savitri relates it to big buildings, fast cars, movies, and microwaves. What kind of freedom might Avinash be seeking? Does he find it? Are Savitri's expectations more attainable? Why or why not?
2. Discuss with your group your responses to the letter from John Elwood. Where does the author use irony to foreshadow the contents of the letter?

ESSAYS

Virginia Woolf

Professions for Women

When your secretary invited me to come here, she told me that your Society is concerned with the employment of women and she suggested that I might tell you something about my own professional experiences. It is true I am a woman; it is true I am employed, but what professional experiences have I had? It is difficult to say. My profession is literature; and in that profession there are fewer experiences for women than in any other, with the exception of the stage—fewer, I mean, that are peculiar to women. For the road was cut many years ago—by Fanny Burney, by Aphra Behn, by Harriet Martineau, by Jane Austen, by George Eliot—many famous women, and many more unknown and forgotten, have been before me, making the path smooth, and regulating my steps. Thus, when I came to write, there were very few material obstacles in my way. Writing was a reputable and harmless occupation. The family peace was not broken by the scratching of a pen. No demand was made upon the family purse. For ten and sixpence one can buy paper enough to write all the plays of Shakespeare—if one has a mind that way. Pianos and models, Paris, Vienna and Berlin, masters and mistresses, are not needed by a writer. The cheapness of writing paper is, of course, the reason why women have succeeded as writers before they have succeeded in the other professions.

But to tell you my story—it is a simple one. You have only got to figure to yourselves a girl in a bedroom with a pen in her hand. She had only to move that pen from left to right—from ten o'clock to one. Then it occurred to her to do what is simple and cheap enough after all—to slip a few of those pages into an envelope, fix a penny stamp in the corner, and drop the envelope in the red box at the corner. It was thus that I became a journalist; and my effort was rewarded on the first day of the following month—a very glorious day it was for me—by a letter from an editor containing a check for one pound ten shillings and sixpence. But to show you how little I deserve to be called a professional woman, how little I know of the struggles and difficulties of such lives, I have to admit that instead of spending that sum upon bread and butter, rent, shoes and stockings, or butcher's bills, I went out and bought a cat—a beautiful cat, a Persian cat, which very soon involved me in bitter disputes with my neighbors.

What could be easier than to write articles and to buy Persian cats with the profits? But wait a moment. Articles have to be about something. Mine, I seem to remember, was about a novel by a famous man. And while I was writing this review, I discovered that if I were going to review books I should need to do battle with a certain phantom. And the phantom was a woman, and when I came to know her better I called her after the heroine of a famous poem, The Angel in the House. It was she who used to come between me and my paper when I was writing reviews. It was she who bothered me and wasted my time and so tormented me that at last I killed her. You who come of a younger and happier generation may not have heard of her—you may not know what I mean by the Angel in the House. I will describe her as shortly as I can. She was intensely sympathetic. She was immensely charming. She was utterly unselfish. She excelled in the difficult arts of family life. She sacrificed herself daily. If there was chicken, she took the leg; if there was a draught she sat in it—in short she was so constituted that she never had a mind or a wish of her own but preferred to sympathize always with the minds and wishes of others. Above all—I need not say it—she was pure. Her purity was supposed to be her chief beauty—her blushes, her great grace. In those days—the last of Queen Victoria— every house had its Angel. And when I came to write I encountered her with the very first words. The shadow of her wings fell on my page; I heard the rustling of her skirts in the room. Directly, that is to say, I took my pen in hand to review that novel by a famous man, she slipped behind me and whispered: "My dear, you are a young woman. You are writing about a book that has been written by a man. Be sympathetic; be tender; flatter; deceive; use all the arts and wiles of our sex. Never let anybody guess that you have a mind of your own. Above all, be pure." And she made as if to guide my pen. I now record the one act for which I take some credit to myself, though the credit rightly belongs to some excellent ancestor of mine who left me a certain sum of money—shall we say five hundred pounds a year?—so that it was not necessary for me to depend solely on charm for my living. I turned upon her and caught her by the throat. I did my best to kill her. My excuse, if I were to be had up in a court of law, would be that I acted in self-defense. Had I not killed her she would have killed me. She would have plucked the heart out of my writing. For, as I found, directly I put pen to paper, you cannot review even a novel without having a mind of your own, without expressing what you think to be the truth about human relations, morality, sex. And all these questions, according to the Angel in the House, cannot be dealt with freely and openly by women; they must charm, they must conciliate, they must—to put it bluntly—tell lies if they are to succeed. Thus, whenever I felt the shadow of her wing or the radiance of her halo upon my page, I took up the inkpot and flung it at her. She died hard. Her fictitious nature was of great assistance to her. It is far harder to kill a phantom than a reality. She was always creeping back when I thought I had despatched her. Though I flatter myself that I killed her in the end, the struggle was severe; it took much time that had better have been spent upon learning Greek grammar; or in roaming the world in search of adventures. But it was a real experience; it was an experience that was bound to befall all women writers at that time. Killing the Angel in the House was part of the occupation of a woman writer.

But to continue my story. The Angel was dead; what then remained? You may say that what remained was a simple and common object—a young woman in a bedroom with an inkpot. In other words, now that she had rid herself of falsehood, that young woman had only to be herself. Ah, but what is "herself"? I mean, what is a woman? I assure you, I do not know. I do not believe that you know. I do not believe that anybody can know until she has expressed herself in all the arts and professions open to human skill. That indeed is one of the reasons why I have come here—out of respect for you, who are in process of showing us by your experiments what a woman is, who are in process of providing us, by your failures and successes, with that extremely important piece of information.

But to continue the story of my professional experiences. I made one pound ten and six by my first review; and I bought a Persian cat with the proceeds. Then I grew ambitious. A Persian cat is all very well, I said; but a Persian cat is not enough. I must have a motor car. And it was thus that I became a novelist—for it is a very strange thing that people will give you a motor car if you will tell them a story. It is a still stranger thing that there is nothing so delightful in the world as telling stories. It is far pleasanter than writing reviews of famous novels. And yet, if I am to obey your secretary and tell you my professional experiences as a novelist, I must tell you about a very strange experience that befell me as a novelist. And to understand it you must try first to imagine a novelist's state of mind. I hope I am not giving away professional secrets if I say that a novelist's chief desire is to be as unconscious as possible. He has to induce in himself a state of perpetual lethargy. He wants life to proceed with the utmost quiet and regularity. He wants to see the same faces, to read the same books, to do the same things day after day, month after month, while he is writing, so that nothing may break the illusion in which he is living—so that nothing may disturb or disquiet the mysterious nosings about, feelings round, darts, dashes and sudden discoveries of that very shy and illusive spirit, the imagination. I suspect that this state is the same both for men and women. Be that as it may, I want you to imagine me writing a novel in a state of trance. I want you to figure to yourselves a girl sitting with a pen in her hand, which for minutes, and indeed for hours, she never dips into the inkpot. The image that comes to my mind when I think of this girl is the image of a fisherman lying sunk in dreams on the verge of a deep lake with a rod held out over the water. She was letting her imagination sweep unchecked round every rock and cranny of the world that lies submerged in the depths of our unconscious being. Now came the experience, the experience that I believe to be far commoner with women writers than with men. The line raced through the girl's fingers. Her imagination had rushed away. It had sought the pools, the depths, the dark places where the largest fish slumber. And then there was a smash. There was an explosion. There was foam and confusion. The imagination had dashed itself against something hard. The girl was roused from her dream. She was indeed in a state of the most acute and difficult distress. To speak without figure she had thought of something, something about the body, about the passions which it was unfitting for her as a woman to say. Men, her reason told her, would be shocked. The consciousness of what men will say of a woman who speaks the truth about her passions had roused her from her artist's state of unconsciousness. She could write no more. The trance was over. Her imagination could work no longer. This I believe to be a very common experience with women writers—they are impeded by the extreme conventionality of the other sex. For though men sensibly allow themselves great freedom in these respects, I doubt that they realize or can control the extreme severity with which they condemn such freedom in women.

These then were two very genuine experiences of my own. These were two of the adventures of my professional life. The first—killing the Angel in the House—I think I solved. She died. But the second, telling the truth about my own experiences as a body, I do not think I solved. I doubt that any woman has solved it yet. The obstacles against her are still immensely powerful—and yet they are very difficult to define. Outwardly, what is simpler than to write books? Outwardly, what obstacles are there for a woman rather than for a man? Inwardly, I think the case is very different; she has still many ghosts to fight, many prejudices to overcome. Indeed it will be a long time still, I think, before a woman can sit down to write a book without finding a phantom to be slain, a rock to be dashed against. And if this is so in literature, the freest of all professions for women, how is it in the new professions which you are now for the first time entering?

Those are the questions that I should like, had I time, to ask you. And indeed, if I have laid stress upon these professional experiences of mine, it is because I believe that they are, though in different forms, yours also. Even when the path is nominally open—when there is nothing to prevent a woman from being a doctor, a lawyer, a civil servant—there are many phantoms and obstacles, as I believe, looming in her way. To discuss and define them is I think of great value and importance; for thus only can the labor be shared, the difficulties be solved. But besides this, it is necessary also to discuss the ends and the aims for which we are fighting, for which we are doing battle with these formidable obstacles. Those aims cannot be taken for granted; they must be perpetually questioned and examined. The whole position, as I see it—here in this hall surrounded by women practising for the first time in history I know not how many different professions—is one of extraordinary interest and importance. You have won rooms of your own in the house hitherto exclusively owned by men. You are able, though not without great labor and effort, to pay the rent. You are earning your five hundred pounds a year. But this freedom is only a beginning; the room is your own, but it is still bare. It has to be furnished; it has to be decorated; it has to be shared. How are you going to furnish it, how are you going to decorate it? With whom are you going to share it, and upon what terms? These, I think, are questions of the utmost importance and interest. For the first time in history you are able to ask them; for the first time you are able to decide for yourselves what the answers should be. Willingly would I stay and discuss those questions and answers—but not tonight. My time is up; and I must cease.

[1931]

Journal Entry

Born in London of upper-middle-class parents, Woolf has emerged as one of the most important feminist writers and critics. Originally delivered as a talk in 1931, Woolf's "Professions for Women" raises questions that still resonate. What, for example, does having your own space mean to you? How will you decide "With whom are you going to share it, and upon what terms"?

Textual Considerations

1. What reasons does Woolf provide to support her thesis that "writing was a reputable and harmless occupation" for women?

2. What do Woolf's arguments suggest about a woman's place in her society?
3. What does the Angel in the House encourage Woolf to do? Is *angel* an appropriate term? Why or why not?
4. Consider Woolf's statement concerning the angel: "Had I not killed her she would have killed me." Is the angel still present today?
5. Do you agree that a woman must kill the angel to survive, both personally and professionally?

Cultural Contexts

1. Discuss with your group Woolf's concept that "it is far harder to kill a phantom than a reality." Why is this so? What forms do these phantoms take in contemporary culture?
2. How do you think Woolf's audience might have reacted to her speech? How would a postmodern female audience respond to her speech today? How do you respond? What cultural and economic tensions in Woolf's 1931 address have been resolved in your view? Which remain unresolved? Can your group reach a consensus?

Steve Tesich

An Amateur Marriage

Everyone told me that when I turned 16 some great internal change would occur. I truly expected the lights to go down on my former life and come up again on a new, far more enchanting one. It didn't work. Nothing happened.

When asked by others, I lied and said that, yes, I did feel a great change had taken place. They lied and told me that they could see it in me.

They lied again when I turned 18. There were rumors that I was now a "man." I noticed no difference, but I pretended to have all the rumored symptoms of manhood. Even though these mythical milestones, these rituals of passage, were not working for me, I still clung to the belief that they should, and I lied and said they were.

My 21st birthday was the last birthday I celebrated. The rituals weren't working, and I was tired of pretending I was changing. I was merely growing—adding on rooms for all the kids who were still me to live in. At 21, I was single but a family man nevertheless.

All these birthday celebrations helped to prepare me for the greatest myth of all: marriage. Marriage comes with more myths attached to it than a six-volume set of ancient Greek history. Fortunately for me, by the time I decided to get married I didn't believe in myths anymore.

It was a very hot day in Denver, and I think Becky and I decided to get married because we knew the city hall was air-conditioned. It was a way of hanging around a cool place for a while. I had forgotten to buy a wedding ring, but Becky was still wearing the ring from her previous marriage, so we used that one. It did the job. She had to take it off and then put it back on again, but it didn't seem to bother anyone. The air-conditioners were humming.

I felt no great change take place as I repeated our marriage vows. I did not feel any new rush of "commitment" to the woman who was now my wife, nor did I have any plans to be married to her forever. I did love her, but I saw no reason why I should feel that I had to love her forever. I would love her for as long as I loved her. I assumed she felt the same way. The women I saw on my way out of city hall, a married man, did not look any less beautiful than the women I saw on my way in. It was still hot outside. We walked to our car carrying plastic bags containing little samples of mouthwash, toothpaste, shampoo and aspirin, gifts from the Chamber of Commerce to all newlyweds.

And so my marriage began—except that I never really felt the beginning. I had nothing against transforming myself into a married man, but I felt no tidal pull of change. I assumed Becky had married me and not somebody else, so why should I become somebody else? She married a family of kids of various ages, all of them me, and I married a family of kids of various ages, all of them her. At one time or another I assumed some of them were bound to get along.

Marriage, I was told, required work. This sounded all wrong to me from the start. I couldn't quite imagine the kind of "work" it required, what the hours were, what the point was. The very idea of walking into my apartment and "working" on my marriage seemed ludicrous. My apartment was a place where I went to get away from work. The rest of life was full of work. If marriage required "work," I would have to get another apartment just for myself where I could go and rest. Since I couldn't afford that at the time, I said nothing to Becky about working on our marriage. She said nothing about it herself. We were either very wise or very lazy.

We are led to believe that the harder we try, the better we get. This "aerobic dancing theory" of life may apply to certain things, but I don't think marriage is one of them. You can't go to a gym and pump marriage. It can't be tuned-up like a car. It can't be trained like a dog. In this century of enormous scientific breakthroughs, there have been no major marriage breakthroughs that I know of.

Progress junkies find this a frustrating state of affairs. They resist the notion that marriage is essentially an amateur endeavor, not a full-time profession, and they keep trying to work on their marriages and make them better. The only way to do that is to impose a structure on the marriage and then fiddle and improve the structure. But that has nothing to do with the way you feel when the guests have left the house and it's just the two of you again. You are either glad you're there with that person or you're not. I've been both.

This need to improve, the belief that we can improve everything, brings to mind some of my friends who are constantly updating their stereo equipment until, without being aware of it, they wind up listening to the equipment and not to the music. You can do the same thing to friendship, to marriage, to life in general. Let's just say I have chosen to listen to the music, such as it is, on the equipment on hand.

The best trips that I have taken were always last-minute affairs, taken as a lark. When I've sent off for brochures and maps, the trips always turned into disappointments. The time I invested in planning fed my expectations, and I traveled to fulfill my expectations rather than just to go somewhere I hadn't been. I consider my marriage one of those trips taken as a lark. I have become rather fond of the sheer aimlessness of the journey. It's a choice. I know full well that people do plan journeys to the Himalayas, they hire guides, they seek advice, and when they get there, instead of being disappointed, they experience a kind of exhilaration that I never will. My kind of marriage will never reach Mount Everest. You just don't go there as a lark, nor do you get there by accident.

I'm neither proud nor ashamed of the fact that I've stayed married for 13 years. I don't consider it an accomplishment of any kind. I have changed; my wife has changed. Our marriage, however, for better or worse, is neither better nor worse. It has remained the same. But the climate has changed.

I got married on a hot day a long time ago, because it was a way of cooling off for a while. Over the years, it's also become a place where I go to warm up when the world turns cold.

[1984]

Journal Entry

Why does Tesich begin his essay by mentioning his sixteenth, eighteenth, and twentieth birthdays?

Textual Considerations

1. Tesich reacts very strongly to society's ideas that marriage is work. Are his reasons convincing? To what extent did he convince you?
2. Tesich uses the metaphor of a journey to present his views on marriage. What elements do you find most effective?
3. What point is Tesich making about his marriage by relating it to the fact that the best trips he took were at the last minute rather than carefully planned?
4. Explain the meaning of the essay's title.

Cultural Contexts

1. Discuss with your group Tesich's statement that "marriage comes with more myths attached to it than a six-volume set of ancient Greek history." What myths regarding marriage would you add to the conversation?
2. Do you consider Tesich's views of marriage controversial? Was his purpose to persuade his readers? Record your group's responses. What consensus did you reach?

David Brooks

The Power of Marriage

Anybody who has several sexual partners in a year is committing spiritual suicide. He or she is ripping the veil from all that is private and delicate in oneself, and pulverizing it in an assembly line of selfish sensations.

But marriage is the opposite. Marriage joins two people in a sacred bond. It demands that they make an exclusive commitment to each other and thereby takes two discrete individuals and turns them into kin.

Few of us work as hard at the vocation of marriage as we should. But marriage makes us better than we deserve to be. Even in the chores of daily life, married couples find themselves, over the years, coming closer together, fusing into one flesh. Married people who remain committed to each other find that they reorganize and deepen each other's lives. They may eventually come to the point when they can say to each other: "Love you? I am you."

Today marriage is in crisis. Nearly half of all marriages end in divorce. Worse, in some circles, marriage is not even expected. Men and women shack up for a while, produce children and then float off to shack up with someone else.

Marriage is in crisis because marriage, which relies on a culture of fidelity, is now asked to survive in a culture of contingency. Today, individual choice is held up as the highest value: choice of lifestyles, choice of identities, choice of cellphone rate plans. Freedom is a wonderful thing, but the culture of contingency means that the marriage bond, which is supposed to be a sacred vow till death do us part, is now more likely to be seen as an easily canceled contract.

Men are more likely to want to trade up, when a younger trophy wife comes along. Men and women are quicker to opt out of marriages, even marriages that are not fatally flawed, when their "needs" don't seem to be met at that moment.

Still, even in this time of crisis, every human being in the United States has the chance to move from the path of contingency to the path of marital fidelity—except homosexuals. Gays and lesbians are banned from marriage and forbidden to enter into this powerful and ennobling institution. A gay or lesbian couple may love each other as deeply as any two people, but when you meet a member of such a couple at a party, he or she then introduces you to a "partner," a word that reeks of contingency.

You would think that faced with this marriage crisis, we conservatives would do everything in our power to move as many people as possible from the path of contingency to the path of fidelity. But instead, many argue that gays must be banished from matrimony because gay marriage would weaken all marriage. A marriage is between a man and a woman, they say. It is women who domesticate men and make marriage work.

Well, if women really domesticated men, heterosexual marriage wouldn't be in crisis. In truth, it's moral commitment, renewed every day through faithfulness, that "domesticates" all people.

Some conservatives may have latched onto biological determinism (men are savages who need women to tame them) as a convenient way to oppose gay marriage. But in fact we are not animals whose lives are bounded by our flesh and by our gender. We're moral creatures with souls, endowed with the ability to make covenants, such as the one Ruth made with Naomi: "Where you go I will go, and where you stay I will stay. Your people will be my people and your God my God. Where you die I will die, and there I will be buried."

The conservative course is not to banish gay people from making such commitments. It is to expect that they make such commitments. We shouldn't just allow gay marriage. We should insist on gay marriage. We should regard it as scandalous that two people could claim to love each other and not want to sanctify their love with marriage and fidelity.

When liberals argue for gay marriage, they make it sound like a really good employee benefits plan. Or they frame it as a civil rights issue, like extending the right to vote.

Marriage is not voting. It's going to be up to conservatives to make the important, moral case for marriage, including gay marriage. Not making it means drifting further into the culture of contingency, which, when it comes to intimate and sacred relations, is an abomination.

Journal Entry

Write a journal entry responding to the title of Brooks's essay on marriage.

Textual Considerations

1. In paragraph 4, Brooks states that "marriage is in crisis." What evidence does he cite that best supports his point of view? To what extent do you agree with him? What reasons would you offer to support or refute him?
2. According to Brooks, we have replaced a "culture of fidelity" with "a culture of contingency" in regard to marriage. How are they different? Similar? Do you share his opinion? Why or why not?
3. "Today individual choice is held up as the highest value." Do you agree with this statement? How does this value affect gender relationships according to the author?

Cultural Contexts

1. Review the first paragraph of Brooks's essay with your group. With which points do you agree or disagree? Technically, is this an effective introduction? Explain.
2. In the latter part of his essay, Brooks offers several reasons for supporting gay marriage. Highlight those you consider most and least convincing. Prepare with your group a list of your reasons for or against gay marriage.

Peter Lyman

The Fraternal Bond as a Joking Relationship

One evening during dinner, forty-five fraternity men suddenly broke into the dining room of a nearby campus sorority, surrounded the thirty women residents, and forced them to watch while one pledge gave a speech on Freud's theory of penis envy as another demonstrated various techniques of masturbation with a rubber penis. The women sat silently staring downward at their plates listening for about ten minutes, until a woman law student who was the graduate resident in charge of the house walked in, surveyed the scene, and demanded, "Please leave immediately!" As she later described that moment, "There was a mocking roar from the men, 'It's tradition.' I said, 'That's no reason to do something like this, please leave!' And they left. I was surprised. Then the women in the house started to get angry. And the guy who made the penis envy speech came back and said to us, 'That was funny to me. If that's not funny to you I don't know what kind of sense of humor you have, but I'm sorry.'"

That night the women sat around the stairwell of their house discussing the event, some angry and others simply wanting to forget the whole thing. They finally decided to ask the university to require the men to discuss the event. When university officials threatened to take action, the men agreed to the meeting. I was asked by both the men and women involved to attend the discussion as a facilitator, and was given permission to write about the event as long as I concealed their identities.

In the women's view, the joke had not failed because of its subject; they considered sexual jokes to be a normal part of the erotic joking relationship between men and women. They criticized the emotional structure, the mixture of sexuality with aggression and the atmosphere of physical intimidation in the room. Although many of the men individually regretted the damage to their relationship with women friends in the group, they argued that the special group solidarity created by the initiation was a unique form of masculine friendship that justified the inconvenience caused the women.

Fraternal group bonding in everyday life frequently takes the form of *joking relationships*, in which men relate to each other by exchanging insults and jokes in order to create a feeling of solidarity that negotiates the latent tension and aggression they feel toward each other (Radcliffe-Brown, 1959). The humor of joking relationships is generally sexual and aggressive, and frequently consists of sexist or racist jokes. As Freud (1960:99) observed, the jokes men direct *toward* women are generally sexual, tend to be clever (like double entendres), and have a seductive purpose; but the jokes that men tell *about* women in the presence of other men tend to be sexist rather than intimate or erotic, and use hostile and aggressive rather than clever verbal forms. In this case study, joking relationships will be analyzed to uncover the emotional dynamics of fraternal groups and the impact of fraternal bonding upon relationships between men and women.

The Girls' Story

The women had frequently been the target of fraternity initiation rites in the past, and generally enjoyed this joking relationship with the men, if with a certain ambivalence. "There was the naked Christmas Carol event, they were singing 'We wish you a Merry Christmas,' and 'Bring on the hasty pudding' was the big line they liked to yell out. And they had five or six pledges who had to strip in front of the house and do naked jumping jacks on the lawn, after all the women in the house were lined up on the steps to watch." The women did not think these events were hostile because they had been invited to watch, and the men stood with them watching, suggesting that the pledges, not the women, were the targets of the joke. This defined the joke as sexual, not sexist, and part of the normal erotic joking relation between "guys and girls." Still, these jokes were ritual events, not real social relationships. One woman said, "We were just supposed to watch, and the guys were watching us watch. The men set the stage and the women are brought along to observe. They were the controlling force, then they jump into the car and take off."

At the meeting with the men, two of the women spoke for the group while eleven others sat silently in the center, surrounded by almost thirty men. The first woman began, "Your humor was pretty funny as long as it was sexual, but when it went beyond sexual to sexist, then it became painful. You were saying 'I'm better than you.' When you started using sex as a way of proving your superiority, it hurt me and made me angry."

The second woman said that the fraternity's raid had the tone of a rape. "I admit we knew you were coming over, and we were whispering about it. But it went too far, and I felt afraid to say anything. Why do men always think about women in terms of violating them, in sexual imagery? You have to understand that the combination of a sexual topic with the physical threat of all of you standing around terrified me. I couldn't move. You have to realize that when men combine sexuality and force, it's terrifying to women."

Many of the women began by saying, "I'm not a feminist, but . . . ," to reassure the men that although they felt angry, they hoped to reestablish the many individual friendships that had existed between men and women in the two groups. In part the issue was resolved when the women accepted the men's construction of the event as a joke, although a failed joke, transforming a discussion about sexuality and force into a debate about good and bad jokes.

For an aggressive joke to be funny, and most jokes must contain some hostility, the joke teller must send the audience a cue that says "this is meant as a joke." If accepted, the cue invokes special social rules that "frame" the hostile words that are typical of jokes, ensuring they will not be taken seriously. The men had implicitly sent such a cue when they stood *next* to the women during the naked jumping jacks. Verbal aggression mediated by the joke form will generally be without later consequences in the everyday world, and will be judged in terms of the formal intention of jokes, shared play and laughter.

In accepting construction of the event as "just a joke" the women absolved the men of responsibility for their actions by calling them "little boys." One woman said, "It's not wrong, they're just boys playing a prank. They're little boys, they don't know what they're doing. It was unpleasant, but we shouldn't make a big deal out of it." In appealing to the rules of the joke form (as in saying "That was funny to me, I don't know what kind of sense of humor you have"), the men sacrificed their personal friendships with the women in order to protect the feelings of fraternal solidarity it produced. In calling the men "little boys" the women were bending the rules of friendship, trying to preserve their relationships to the guys by playing a patient and nurturing role.

The Guys' Story

Aside from occasional roars of laughter, the men interrupted the women only once. When a woman began to say that the men had obviously intended to intimidate them, the men loudly protested that the women couldn't possibly judge their intentions, that they intended the whole event only as a joke, and the intention of a joke is, by definition, just fun.

At this point the two black men in the fraternity intervened to explain the rules of making joking relationships to the women. In a sense, they said, they agreed with the women, being the object of hostile jokes is painful. As they described it, the collective talk of the fraternity at meals and group events was entirely hostile joking, including many racist jokes. One said, "I'd had to listen to things in the house that I'd have hit someone for saying if I'd heard them outside." The guys roared with laughter, for the fraternal joking relation consisted almost entirely of aggressive words that were barely contained by the convention that joke tellers are not responsible for what they say.

One woman responded, "Maybe people should be hit for saying those things, maybe that's the right thing to do." But the black speaker was trying to explain the rules of male joke culture to the women. "If you'd just ignored us, it wouldn't have been any fun." To ignore a joke, even though it makes you feel hurt or angry, is to be cool, one of the primary masculine ideals of the group.

Another man tried to explain the failure of the joke in terms of the difference between the degree of "crudeness" appropriate "between guys" and between "guys and girls." He said, "As I was listening to the speech I was both embarrassed and amused. I was standing at the edge of the room, near the door, and when I looked at the guys I was laughing but when I looked at the girls I was embarrassed. I could see both sides at the same time. It was too crude for your sense of propriety. We have a different sense of crudeness you don't have. That's a cultural aspect of the difference between girls and guys."

The other men laughed as he mentioned "how crude we are at the house," and one of the black men added, "You wouldn't believe how crude it gets." Many of the men later said that although they individually found the jokes about women vulgar, the jokes were justified because they were necessary for the formation of the fraternal bond. These men thought that the mistake had been to reveal their crudeness to the women; this was "in bad taste."

In part the crudeness was a kind of "signifying" or "dozens," a ritual exchange of intimate insults that creates group solidarity. "If there's one theme that goes on it's the emphasis on being able to take a lot of ridicule, of shit, and not getting upset about it. Most of the interaction we have is verbally abusing each other, making disgusting references to your mother's sexuality, or the women you were seen with, or your sex organ, the size of your sex organ. And you aren't cool unless you can take it without trying to get back." Being cool is an important male value in other settings as well, like sports or work; the joking relationship is a kind of training that, in one guy's words, "teaches you how to keep in control of your emotions."

But the guys themselves would not have described their group as a joking relationship or fraternal bond, they called it friendship. One man said that he had found perhaps a dozen guys in the house who were special friends, "guys I could cry in front of." Another said, "I think the guys are very close, they would do nearly any-thing for each other, drive each other places, give each other money. I think when they have problems about school, their car, or something like that, they can talk to each other. I'm not sure they can talk to each other about women though." Although the image of crying in front of the other guys was mentioned as an example of the intimacy of the fraternal bond, no one could actually recall anyone in the group ever crying. In fact crying would be an admission of vulnerability which would violate the ideals of "strength" and "being cool."

The women interpreted the sexist jokes as a sign of vulnerability. "The thing that struck me the most about our meeting together," one said, "was when the men said they were afraid of trusting women, afraid of being seen as jerks." One of the guys added, "I think deep down all the guys would love to have satisfying relation-ships with women. I think they're scared of failing, of having to break away from the group they've become comfortable with. I think being in a fraternity, having close relationships with men is a replacement for having close relationships with women. It'd be painful for them because they'd probably fail." These men preferred to relate to women as a group at fraternity parties, where they could take women back to their rooms for quick sex without commitments.

Sexist jokes also had a social function, policing the boundaries of the group, making sure that guys didn't form serious relationships with girls and leave the fra-ternity (cf. Slater, 1963). "One of the guys just acquired a girlfriend a few weeks ago. He's someone I don't think has had a woman to be friends with, maybe ever, at least in a long time. Everybody has been ribbing him intensely the last few weeks. It's good natured in tone. Sitting at dinner they've invented a little song they sing to him. People yell questions about his girlfriend, the size of her vagina, does she have big breasts." Thus, in dealing with women, the group separated intimacy from sex, defining the male bond as intimate but not sexual (homosocial), and relationships with women as sexual but not intimate (heterosexual).

The Fraternal Bond in Men's Life Cycle

Men often speak of friendship as a group relationship, not a dyadic one, and men's friendships often grow from the experience of shared activities or risk, rather than from self-disclosing talk (cf. Rubin, 1983:130). J. Glenn Gray (1959:89–90) distin-guishes the intimate form of friendship from the comradeship that develops from the shared experience of suffering and danger of men at war. In comradeship, he argues, the individual's sense of self is subordinated to a group identity, whereas friendship is based upon a specific feeling for another that heightens a sense of individuality.

In this case, the guys used joking relationships to suspend the ordinary rules and responsibilities of everyday life, placing the intimacy of the fraternal group in competition with heterosexual friendships. One of the men had been inexpressive as he listened to the discussion, but spoke about the fraternity in a voice filled with emotion: "The penis envy speech was a hilarious idea, great college fun. That's what I joined the fraternity for, a good time. College is a stage in my life to do crazy and humorous things. In ten years when I'm in the business world I won't be able to carry on like this [loud laughter from the men]. The initiation was intended to be humorous. We didn't think through how sensitive you women were going to be."

This speech gives the fraternal bond a specific place in the life cycle. The joking relationship is a ritual bond that creates a male group bond in the transition between boyhood and manhood: after the separation from the family where the authority of mothers limits fun, but before becoming subject to the authority of work. One man later commented on the transitional nature of the fraternal bond, "I think a lot of us are really scared of losing total control over our own lives. Having to sacrifice our individuality. I think we're scared of work in the same way we're scared of women." The jokes expressed hostility toward women because an intimate friendship with a woman was associated with "loss of control," namely the responsibility for work and family.

Most, but not all, of the guys in the fraternity were divided between their group identity and a sense of personal identity that was expressed in private friendships with women. Some of the guys, like one who could "see both sides" as he stood on the edge of the group during the initiation, had reached the point of leaving the fraternity because they couldn't reconcile the tension between his group identity and the sense of self that he felt in his friendships with women.

Ultimately the guys justified the penis envy joke because it created a special kind of male intimacy. But although the fraternal group was able to appropriate the guys' needs for intimacy and commitment it is not clear that it was able to satisfy those needs, because it defined strength as shared risk taking rather than a quality of individual character or personality. In Gray's terms, the guys were constructing comradeship through an erotic of shared activities with an element of risk, shared danger, or rule breaking such as sports, paramilitary games, wild parties, and hostile jokes. In these contexts, strength implied the substitution of a group identity for a personal code that might extend to commitment and care for others (cf. Bly 1982).

In the guys' world, aggression was identified with strength, and defined as loss of control only if it was angry. The fraternal bond was built upon an emotional balance between aggression and anger, for life of the group centered upon the mobilization of aggressive energies in rule-governed activities, especially sports and games. In each arena, aggression was defined as strength (toughness) only when it was rule-governed (cool). Getting angry was called "losing control," and the guys thought they were most likely to lose control when they experienced themselves as personally dependent, that is, in relationships with women and at work. The sense of order within fraternal groups is based upon the belief that all members are equally dependent upon the rules, and that no *personal* dependence is created within the group. This is not true of the family or of relations with women, both of which are intimate, and, from the guys' point of view, are "out of control" because they are governed by emotional commitments.

The guys recognized the relationship between their male bond and the work world by claiming that "high officials of the University know about the way we act, and they understand what we are doing." Although this might be taken as evidence that the guys were internalizing their fathers' norms and thus inheriting the rights of patriarchy, the guys described their fathers as slaves to work and women, not as patriarchs. It is striking that the guys would not accept the notion that men have more power than women; to them it is not men who rule, but work and women that govern men.

[1987]

References

Bly, Robert. (1982) "What men really want: An interview with Keith Thompson." *New Age* 30–37, 50–51.

Freud, Sigmund. (1960) *Jokes and Their Relation to the Unconscious*. New York, NY: W. W. Norton.

Gray, Glenn J. (1959) *The Warriors: Reflections on Men in Battle*. New York, NY: Harper.

Radcliffe-Brown, Alfred. (1959) *Structure and Function in Primitive Society*. Glencoe: The Free Press.

Rubin, Lillian. (1983) *Intimate Strangers*. New York, NY: Harper & Row.

Slater, Philip. (1963) "On Social Regression." *The American Sociological Review* 28:339–364.

Journal Entry

Respond to the concept that societal stereotypes of masculinity often result in men's masking their real emotions.

Textual Considerations

1. Summarize the incident that Lyman describes in the first part of the essay.
2. At the meeting Lyman attended, both groups expressed their views on the fraternity initiation incident. List the important differences between male and female attitudes toward joke culture that emerged from the discussion. With which responses do you agree or disagree? Explain.
3. What did the comments of the black fraternity members add to the debate?
4. To what extent did the responses of both male and female students conform to sexual stereotypes? Explain.
5. Make a list of the arguments you identify with in Lyman's text, and argue in their defense.
6. Comment on how Lyman's division of the text into three parts adds to its overall impact.

Cultural Contexts

1. What gender roles exist only in the United States? In some countries, for example, it is not unusual for men to express affection for one another or even to cry in public. Discuss how cultural experience affects gender stereotypes.
2. Working with your group, discuss male and female concepts of friendship. How are they similar? Different? What are some of the implications of the differences you have noted? According to Lyman, how did the fraternity members distinguish between intimacy and friendship?

Deborah Tannen

Sex, Lies and Conversation: Why Is It So Hard for Men and Women to Talk to Each Other?

I was addressing a small gathering in a suburban Virginia living room—a women's group that had invited men to join them. Throughout the evening, one man had been particularly talkative, frequently offering ideas and anecdotes, while his wife sat silently beside him on the couch. Toward the end of the evening, I commented that women frequently complain that their husbands don't talk to them. This man quickly concurred. He gestured toward his wife and said, "She's the talker in our family." The room burst into laughter; the man looked puzzled and hurt. "It's true," he explained. "When I come home from work I have nothing to say. If she didn't keep the conversation going, we'd spend the whole evening in silence."

This episode crystallizes the irony that although American men tend to talk more than women in public situations, they often talk less at home. And this pattern is wreaking havoc with marriage.

The pattern was observed by political scientist Andrew Hacker in the late '70s. Sociologist Catherine Kohler Riessman reports in her new book *Divorce Talk* that most of the women she interviewed—but only a few of the men—gave lack of communication as the reason for their divorces. Given the current divorce rate of nearly 50 percent, that amounts to millions of cases in the United States every year—a virtual epidemic of failed conversation.

In my own research, complaints from women about their husbands most often focused not on tangible inequities such as having given up the chance for a career to accompany a husband to his, or doing far more than their share of daily life-support work like cleaning, cooking, social arrangements and errands. Instead, they focused on communication: "He doesn't listen to me," "He doesn't talk to me." I found, as Hacker observed years before, that most wives want their husbands to be, first and foremost, conversational partners, but few husbands share this expectation of their wives.

In short, the image that best represents the current crisis is the stereotypical cartoon scene of a man sitting at the breakfast table with a newspaper held up in front of his face, while a woman glares at the back of it, wanting to talk.

Linguistic Battle of the Sexes

How can women and men have such different impressions of communication in marriage? Why the widespread imbalance in their interests and expectations?

In the April [1990] issue of *American Psychologist*, Stanford University's Eleanor Maccoby reports the results of her own and others' research showing that children's development is most influenced by the social structure of peer interactions. Boys and girls tend to play with children of their own gender, and their sex-separate groups have different organizational structures and interactive norms.

I believe these systematic differences in childhood socialization make talk between women and men like cross-cultural communication, heir to all the attraction and pitfalls of that enticing but difficult enterprise. My research on men's and women's conversations uncovered patterns similar to those described for children's groups.

For women, as for girls, intimacy is the fabric of relationships, and talk is the thread from which it is woven. Little girls create and maintain friendships by exchanging secrets; similarly, women regard conversation as the cornerstone of friendship. So a woman expects her husband to be a new and improved version of a best friend. What is important is not the individual subjects that are discussed but the sense of closeness, of a life shared, that emerges when people tell their thoughts, feelings, and impressions.

Bonds between boys can be as intense as girls', but they are based less on talking, more on doing things together. Since they don't assume talk is the cement that binds a relationship, men don't know what kind of talk women want, and they don't miss it when it isn't there.

Boy's groups are larger, more inclusive, and more hierarchical, so boys must struggle to avoid the subordinate position in the group. This may play a role in women's complaints that men don't listen to them. Some men really don't like to listen, because being the listener makes them feel one-down, like a child listening to adults or an employee to a boss.

But often when women tell men, "You aren't listening," and the men protest, "I am," the men are right. The impression of not listening results from misalignment in the mechanics of conversation. The misalignment begins as soon as a man and a woman take physical positions. This became clear when I studied videotapes made by psychologist Paul Dorval of children and adults talking to their same-sex best friends. I found that at every age, the girls and women faced each other directly, their eyes anchored on each other's faces. At every age, the boys and men sat at angles to each other and looked elsewhere in the room, periodically glancing at each other. They were obviously attuned to each other, often mirroring each other's movements. But the tendency of men to face away can give women the impression they aren't listening even when they are. A young woman in college was frustrated: Whenever she told her boyfriend she wanted to talk to him, he would lie down on the floor, close his eyes, and put his arm over his face. This signaled to her, "He's taking a nap." But he insisted he was listening extra hard. Normally, he looks around the room, so he is easily distracted. Lying down and covering his eyes helped him concentrate on what she was saying.

Analogous to the physical alignment that women and men take in conversation is their topical alignment. The girls in my study tended to talk at length about one topic, but the boys tended to jump from topic to topic. The second-grade girls exchanged stories about people they knew. The second-grade boys teased, told jokes, noticed things in the room and talked about finding games to play. The sixth-grade girls talked about problems with a mutual friend. The sixth-grade boys talked about 55 different topics, none of which extended over more than a few turns.

Listening to Body Language

Switching topics is another habit that gives women the impression men aren't listening, especially if they switch to a topic about themselves. But the evidence of the 10th-grade boys in my study indicates otherwise. The 10th-grade boys sprawled across their chairs with bodies parallel and eyes straight ahead, rarely looking at each other. They looked as if they were riding in a car, staring out the windshield. But they were talking about their feelings. One boy was upset because a girl had told him he had a drinking problem, and the other was feeling alienated from all his friends.

Now, when a girl told a friend about a problem, the friend responded by asking probing questions and expressing agreement and understanding. But the boys dismissed each other's problems. Todd assured Richard that his drinking was "no big problem" because "sometimes you're funny when you're off your butt." And when Todd said he felt left out, Richard responded, "Why should you? You know more people than me."

Women perceive such responses as belittling and unsupportive. But the boys seemed satisfied with them. Whereas women reassure each other by implying, "You shouldn't feel bad because I've had similar experiences," men do so by implying, "You shouldn't feel bad because your problems aren't so bad."

There are even simpler reasons for women's impression that men don't listen. Linguist Lynette Hirschman found that women make more listener-noise, such as "mhm," "uhuh," and "yeah," to show "I'm with you." Men, she found, more often give silent attention. Women who expect a stream of listener-noise interpret silent attention as no attention at all.

Women's conversational habits are as frustrating to men as men's are to women. Men who expect silent attention interpret a stream of listener-noise as overreaction or impatience. Also, when women talk to each other in a close, comfortable setting, they often overlap, finish each other's sentences and anticipate what the other is about to say. This practice, which I call "participatory listenership," is often perceived by men as interruption, intrusion, and lack of attention.

A parallel difference caused a man to complain about his wife, "She just wants to talk about her own point of view. If I show her another view, she gets mad at me." When most women talk to each other, they assume a conversationalist's job is to express agreement and support. But many men see their conversational duty as pointing out the other side of an argument. This is heard as disloyalty by women, and refusal to offer the requisite support. It is not that women don't want to see other points of view, but that they prefer them phrased as suggestions and inquiries rather than as direct challenges.

In his book *Fighting for Life*, Walter Ong points out that men use "agonistic" or warlike, oppositional formats to do almost anything; thus discussion becomes debate, and conversation a competitive sport. In contrast, women see conversation as a ritual means of establishing rapport. If Jane tells a problem and June says she has a similar one, they walk away feeling closer to each other. But this attempt at establishing rapport can backfire when used with men. Men take too literally women's ritual "troubles talk," just as women mistake men's ritual challenges for real attack.

The Sounds of Silence

These differences begin to clarify why women and men have such different expectations about communication in marriage. For women, talk creates intimacy. Marriage is an orgy of closeness: you can tell your feelings and thoughts, and still be loved. Their greatest fear is being pushed away. But men live in a hierarchical world, where talk maintains independence and status. They are on guard to protect themselves from being put down and pushed around.

This explains the paradox of the talkative man who said of his silent wife, "She's the talker." In the public setting of a guest lecture, he felt challenged to show his intelligence and display his understanding of the lecture. But at home, where he has nothing to prove and no one to defend against, he is free to remain silent. For his wife, being home means she is free from the worry that something she says might offend someone, or spark disagreement, or appear to be showing off; at home she is free to talk.

The communication problems that endanger marriage can't be fixed by mechanical engineering. They require a new conceptual framework about the role of talk in human relationships. Many of the psychological explanations that have become second nature may not be helpful, because they tend to blame either women (for not being assertive enough) or men (for not being in touch with their feelings). A sociolinguistic approach by which male–female conversation is seen as cross-cultural communication allows us to understand the problem and forge solutions without blaming either party.

Once the problem is understood, improvement comes naturally, as it did to the young woman and her boyfriend who seemed to go to sleep when she wanted to talk. Previously, she had accused him of not listening, and he had refused to change his behavior, since that would be admitting fault. But then she learned about and explained to him the differences in women's and men's habitual ways of aligning themselves in conversation. The next time she told him she wanted to talk, he began, as usual, by lying down and covering his eyes. When the familiar negative reaction bubbled up, she reassured herself that he really was listening. But then he sat up and looked at her. Thrilled she asked why. He said, "You like me to look at you when we talk, so I'll try to do it." Once he saw their differences as cross-cultural rather than right and wrong, he independently altered his behavior.

Women who feel abandoned and deprived when their husbands won't listen to or report daily news may be happy to discover their husbands trying to adapt once they understand the place of small talk in women's relationships. But if their husbands don't adapt, the women may still be comforted that for men, this is not a failure of intimacy. Accepting the difference, the wives may look to their friends or family for that kind of talk. And husbands who can't provide it shouldn't feel their wives have made unreasonable demands. Some couples will still decide to divorce, but at least their decisions will be based on realistic expectations.

In these times of resurgent ethnic conflicts, the world desperately needs cross-cultural understanding. Like charity, successful cross-cultural communication should begin at home.

[1990]

Journal Entry

According to Tannen, "Women's conversational habits are as frustrating to men as men's are to women." Do you agree? Cite examples from your experience.

Textual Considerations

1. According to Tannen, the causes of communication difficulties between men and women are rooted in childhood patterns of socialization. What evidence does she provide to support her thesis?
2. How accurately does Tannen's hypothesis about communication between men and women reflect your own experience as a child and as an adult?
3. What solutions does Tannen offer to improve communication between the sexes?
4. What is your interpretation of and response to "cross-cultural communication"?
5. Is Tannen's purpose to inform, or does she also wish to persuade her readers? How do style and tone contribute to her purpose? Cite specific examples.

Cultural Contexts

1. Discuss the degree to which society and culture influence our concepts of masculinity and femininity. To what extent is it possible or desirable to go beyond stereotypical definitions?
2. With your group, discuss Tannen's question posed in the essay's title, and analyze carefully the components of sex, lies, and conversation. How do the responses for your generation compare to those cited in Tannen's research? How do you account for differences that exist?

POETRY

John Donne

Woman's Constancy

Now thou hast loved me one whole day,
To-morrow when thou leavest, what wilt thou say?
Wilt thou then antedate some new-made vow?
    Or say that now
We are not just those persons which we were?   5
Or that oaths made in reverential fear
Of Love, and his wrath, any may forswear?
Or, as true deaths true marriages untie,
So lovers' contracts, images of those,
Bind but till sleep, death's image, them unloose?   10
    Or, your own end to justify,
For having purposed change and falsehood, you
Can have no way but falsehood to be true?
Vain lunatic, against these 'scapes I could
    Dispute, and conquer, if I would;   15
    Which I abstain to do,
For by to-morrow I may think so too.

[1633]

346

John Donne

The Sun Rising

Busy old fool, unruly Sun,
    Why dost thou thus,
Through windows, and through curtains call on us?
Must to thy motions lovers' seasons run?
        Saucy pedantic wretch, go chide   5
        Late school boys and sour prentices,°
    Go tell Court-huntsmen, that the King will ride,
    Call country ants to harvest offices°;
Love, all alike, no season knows, nor clime,°
Nor hours, days, months, which are the rags of time.   10

        Thy beams, so reverend, and strong
        Why shouldst thou think?°
I could eclipse and cloud them with a wink,
But that I would not lose her sight so long;
        If her eyes have not blinded thine,   15
        Look, and tomorrow late, tell me,
    Whether both the Indias of spice and Mine°
    Be where thou leftst them, or lie here with me.
Ask for those kings whom thou saw'st yesterday,
And thou shalt hear, All here in one bed lay.   20

        She'is° all States, and all Princes, I,
        Nothing else is.
Princes do but play us; compared to this,
All honor's mimic; all wealth alchemy.°
        Thou, sun, art half as happy'as° we,   25
        In that the world's contracted thus;
    Thine age asks ease, and since thy duties be
    To warm the world, that's done in warming us.
Shine here to us, and thou art everywhere;
This bed thy center° is, these walls, thy sphere.   30

[1633]

---

6 prentices: apprentices   **8 Call . . . offices:** i.e., notify the country's ants to carry out the duty of eating the harvest of grain and produce.   **9 clime:** climate   **11, 12 Thy beams . . . think?:** i.e., why shouldst thou think that thy beams are so reverend and strong?   **17 Indias of spice and Mine:** The India of "spice" is the East Indies; the India of "Mine" (gold) is the West Indies.   **21 She'is:** For scansion, these two words are to be considered one syllable ("shé's").   **24 all wealth alchemy:** i.e., all wealth is false because it has been created by alchemists.   **25 happy'as:** to be scanned as a trochee ("háppy̆ăz").   **30 center:** the earth, around which the sun revolves (according to the Ptolemaic view of the solar system).

Journal Entry

What is your concept of the ideal gender relationship? How does it compare to Donne's view of the man–woman relationship in "Woman's Constancy" and "The Sun Rising"?

Textual Considerations

1. Describe the argumentative structure of "Woman's Constancy." Why does the speaker criticize his mistress for her supposed faithlessness? Identify the arguments the speaker uses to build the image of his mistress in this lyric meditation.
2. Where does the speaker change his tone throughout the text? Explain his mood or attitude in lines 14–17. Does he surprise the reader at the end of the poem?
3. How are the lovers in "Woman's Constancy" affected by time? How important are the speaker's references to "Now" (line 1), and "Tomorrow" (lines 2, 17)? Is time connected with any major theme of the lyric? Explain.
4. How effective is the speaker's image of the sun in "The Sun Rising"? Explain how he develops and expands this image. How does he use this image to create his ideal world of love?
5. Contrast the views of love expressed in "The Sun Rising" (lines 9–10) and "Woman's Constancy." How do they differ? What statements do these lyrics make about love, time, and the role of the mistress?

Cultural Contexts

1. Working with your group, try to identify some of today's popular love songs that use images of the cosmos, politics, and lovers' physical surroundings (like the bedroom in "The Sun Rising") to explore the theme of love.
2. How do today's love songs address the theme of love, including the dichotomy of the body and soul, sexuality, and the issue of time? How do they compare with John Donne's treatment of love in "Woman's Constancy" and "The Sun Rising"?

SEXTON AND DICKEY

Anne Sexton

For My Lover, Returning to His Wife

She is all there.
She was melted carefully down for you
and cast up from your childhood,
cast up from your one hundred favorite aggies.°

She has always been there, my darling.   5
She is, in fact, exquisite.
Fireworks in the dull middle of February
and as real as a cast-iron pot.

Let's face it, I have been momentary.
A luxury. A bright red sloop in the harbor.   10
My hair rising like smoke from the car window.
Littleneck clams out of season.

She is more than that. She is your have to have,
has grown you your practical your tropical growth.
This is not an experiment. She is all harmony.   15
She sees to oars and oarlocks for the dinghy,

has placed wild flowers at the window at breakfast,
sat by the potter's wheel at midday,
set forth three children under the moon,
three cherubs drawn by Michelangelo,   20

done this with her legs spread out
in the terrible months in the chapel.
If you glance up, the children are there
like delicate balloons resting on the ceiling.

She has also carried each one down the hall   25
after supper, their heads privately bent,
two legs protesting, person to person,
her face flushed with a song and their little sleep.

I give you back your heart.
I give you permission——   30

for the fuse inside her, throbbing
angrily in the dirt, for the bitch in her

and the burying of her wound——
for the burying of her small red wound alive——

for the pale flickering flare under her ribs,   35
for the drunken sailor who waits in her left pulse,
for the mother's knee, for the stockings,
for the garter belt, for the call——

the curious call
when you will burrow in arms and breasts   40
and tug at the orange ribbon in her hair
and answer the call, the curious call.

She is so naked and singular.
She is the sum of yourself and your dream.
Climb her like a monument, step after step.   45
She is solid.

As for me, I am a watercolor.
I wash off.

                                                                    [1967]

4 aggies: Colorful playing marbles.

James Dickey

Adultery

We have all been in rooms
We cannot die in, and they are odd places, and sad
Often Indians are standing eagle-armed on hills

In the sunrise   open wide to the Great Spirit
Or gliding in canoes   or cattle are browsing on the walls   5
Far away   gazing down with the eyes of our children

Not far away   or there are men driving
The last railspike, which has turned
Gold in their hands. Gigantic forepleasure lives

Among such scenes, and we are alone with it   10
At last. There is always some weeping
Between us   and someone is always checking

A wrist watch by the bed to see how much
Longer we have left. Nothing can come
Of this   nothing can come   15

Of us: of me with my grim techniques
Or you who have sealed your womb
With a ring of convulsive rubber:

Although we come together,
Nothing will come of us. But we would not give   20
It up, for death is beaten

By praying Indians   by distant cows   historical
Hammers   by hazardous meetings that bridge
A continent. One could never die here

Never die   never die   25
While crying. My lover, my dear one
I will see you next week

When I'm in town. I will call you
If I can. Please get hold of   please don't
Oh God, Please don't any more I can't bear . . . Listen: 30

We have done it again   we are
Still living. Sit up and smile,
God bless you. Guilt is magical.

[1966]

Journal Entry

Brainstorm on your associations with adultery. Do you connect it with passion, desire, or love? Is guilt an element?

Textual Considerations

1. Discuss how Sexton's use of contrasting images of the wife and mistress contribute to the transience of the love affair the poem describes.
2. With whom do you empathize—the mistress or the wife—in "For My Lover, Returning to His Wife"? Cite evidence from the text to support your position. What does the poem reveal about the husband? What is your attitude toward him?
3. How does Dickey describe the "rooms we cannot die in" in "Adultery"? Characterize the scenes on the walls.
4. Why do the two lovers check their wrist watches in "Adultery"? If "nothing can come of this," why do they continue to meet?
5. How does the structure of "Adultery" help emphasize the speaker's ambivalent feelings? In what ways do both poems build to a climax? What change in rhythm occurs in the last three lines of Dickey's text? What is the effect of Sexton's contrasting images in the last six lines?

Cultural Contexts

1. Discuss the significance of the references to children in both poems. How do they contribute to the theme? What effect do they have on your attitudes to the affairs?
2. Working with your group, speculate about attitudes toward adultery. How do different cultures react toward this issue? How does your generation respond to marital infidelity? Is fidelity an intimate relationship or an unrealistic expectation, given the emphasis on sexuality in the present culture? Can your group reach a consensus on this issue?

Maryfrances Wagner

Ragazza

A good Italian woman
will cover her dust-free house
with crocheted doilies,
bear dark-eyed sons,
know what to do   5
with artichokes and chick peas.
Her floors will shine.
She will serve tender brucaluni
in her perfect sauce,
make her own cannoli shells,   10
bake biscottas for every wedding.
Supper will be hot at six o'clock.
She will always wear dresses.
She will not balance the checkbook.
He can doze behind the paper   15
when she washes dishes.
Because she will never leave him,
he will forgive her bulging thighs.
Because he will never leave her,
she won't notice unfamiliar stains.   20

Italian men always know *ragazze*
who work the fields in Bivona.
For airfare one will come.
In time she will learn English.
In time they may learn to love.   25

[1983]

Pat Mora

Borders

My research suggests that men and women
may speak different languages that they
assume are the same. —Carol Gilligan

If we're so bright,
why didn't we notice?

I

The side-by-side translations
were the easy ones.
Our tongues tasted *luna*   5
chanting, chanting to the words
it touched; our lips circled
moon sighing its longing.
We knew: similar but different.

II

And we knew of grown-up talk,   10
how even in our own home
like became unlike,
how the child's singsong

                              I want, I want
burned our mouth   15
when we whispered in the dark.

III

But us? You and I
who've talked for years
tossing words back and forth

                              success, happiness   20

back and forth
over coffee, over wine
at parties, in bed
and I was sure you heard,
    understood,   25
though now I think of it
I can remember screaming
to be sure.

So who can hear
the words we speak
you and I, like but unlike, 30
and translate us to us
side by side?

[1986]

Robert Frost

Home Burial

He saw her from the bottom of the stairs
Before she saw him. She was starting down,
Looking back over her shoulder at some fear.
She took a doubtful step and then undid it
To raise herself and look again. He spoke 5
Advancing toward her: "What is it you see
From up there always?—for I want to know."
She turned and sank upon her skirts at that,
And her face changed from terrified to dull.
He said to gain time: "What is it you see?" 10
Mounting until she cowered under him.
"I will find out now—you must tell me, dear."
She, in her place, refused him any help,
With the least stiffening of her neck and silence.
She let him look, sure that he wouldn't see, 15
Blind creature; and awhile he didn't see.
But at last he murmured, "Oh," and again, "Oh."

"What is it—what?" she said.

                                   "Just that I see."

"You don't," she challenged. "Tell me what it is." 20

"The wonder is I didn't see at once.
I never noticed it from here before.
I must be wonted to it—that's the reason.
The little graveyard where my people are!
So small the window frames the whole of it. 25
Not so much larger than a bedroom, is it?
There are three stones of slate and one of marble,
Broad-shouldered little slabs there in the sunlight
On the sidehill. We haven't to mind *those*.

But I understand: it is not the stones,   30
But the child's mound ——"

                                   "Don't, don't, don't, don't," she cried.

She withdrew, shrinking from beneath his arm
That rested on the banister, and slid downstairs;
And turned on him with such a daunting look,   35
He said twice over before he knew himself:
"Can't a man speak of his own child he's lost?"

"Not you!—Oh, where's my hat? Oh, I don't need it!
I must get out of here. I must get air.—
I don't know rightly whether any man can."   40

"Amy! Don't go to someone else this time.
Listen to me. I won't come down the stairs."
He sat and fixed his chin between his fists.
"There's something I should like to ask you, dear."

"You don't know how to ask it."   45

                                "Help me, then."

Her fingers moved the latch for all reply.

"My words are nearly always an offense.
I don't know how to speak of anything
So as to please you. But I might be taught,   50
I should suppose. I can't say I see how.
A man must partly give up being a man
With womenfolk. We could have some arrangement
By which I'd bind myself to keep hands off
Anything special you're a-mind to name.   55
Though I don't like such things 'twixt those that love.
Two that don't love can't live together without them.
But two that do can't live together with them.
Don't carry it to someone else this time.
Tell me about it if it's something human.   60
Let me into your grief. I'm not so much
Unlike other folks as your standing there
Apart would make me out. Give me my chance.
I do think, though, you overdo it a little.
What was it brought you up to think it the thing   65
To take your mother-loss of a first child
So inconsolably—in the face of love.
You'd think his memory might be satisfied—"

"There you go sneering now!"

                               "I'm not, I'm not!   70

You make me angry. I'll come down to you.
God, what a woman! And it's come to this,
A man can't speak of his own child that's dead."

"You can't because you don't know how to speak.
If you had any feelings, you that dug   75
With your own hand—how could you?—his little grave;
I saw you from that very window there,
Making the gravel leap and leap in air,
Leap up, like that, like that, and land so lightly
And roll back down the mound beside the hole.   80
I thought, Who is that man? I didn't know you.
And I crept down the stairs and up the stairs
To look again, and still your spade kept lifting.
Then you came in. I heard your rumbling voice
Out in the kitchen, and I don't know why,   85
But I went near to see with my own eyes.
You could sit there with the stains on your shoes
Of the fresh earth from your own baby's grave
And talk about your everyday concerns.
You had stood the spade up against the wall   90
Outside there in the entry, for I saw it."

"I shall laugh the worst laugh I ever laughed.
I'm cursed. God, if I don't believe I'm cursed."

"I can repeat the very words you were saying:
'Three foggy mornings and one rainy day   95
Will rot the best birch fence a man can build.'
Think of it, talk like that at such a time!
What had how long it takes a birch to rot
To do with what was in the darkened parlor?
You *couldn't* care! The nearest friends can go   100
With anyone to death, comes so far short
They might as well not try to go at all.
No, from the time when one is sick to death,
One is alone, and he dies more alone.
Friends make pretense of following to the grave,   105
But before one is in it, their minds are turned
And making the best of their way back to life
And living people, and things they understand.
But the world's evil. I won't have grief so
If I can change it. Oh, I won't, I won't!"   110

"There, you have said it all and you feel better.
You won't go now. You're crying. Close the door.
The heart's gone out of it: why keep it up?
Amy! There's someone coming down the road!"

"*You*—oh, you think the talk is all. I must go—
Somewhere out of this house. How can I make you—"

"If—you—do!" She was opening the door wider.
"Where do you mean to go? First tell me that.
I'll follow and bring you back by force. I *will!*—"

[1930]

Journal Entry

Many linguists agree that indirectness is a characteristic of human communication. How does this concept apply to the texts by Wagner, Mora, and Frost?

Textual Considerations

1. Explain the significance of the titles of the poems by Wagner, Mora, and Frost. What does the title reveal about the theme of each poem and the speaker's attitude toward life? How do you respond to each of these poems? Would the poems evoke a different response if we changed their titles? Explain.
2. Identify the images that state the accomplishments of the "good Italian woman" in "Ragazza," and contrast them with what she will not do (lines 14, 17, and 20). Explain how language defines the ragazza's identity as a wife.
3. Discuss the speaker's concepts of personal identity in "Borders." How does the speaker develop this concept in stanzas I and II? Identify images that express this concept in the poem. How does language play a role in the speaker's identity as wife and mother?
4. Explain the dramatic situation of "Home Burial," citing in detail the events that lead to the confrontation on the stairs. According to Amy, why does her husband merit her anger?
5. To what extent does Amy succeed in being "heard" in "Home Burial"? Do you agree that the father feels the loss of the child less than the mother does? Explain.
6. Review the last lines of "Ragazza," "Borders," and "Home Burial." How effective are the speakers in communicating their moods? With whom do you empathize, and why?

Cultural Considerations

1. Apply Carol Gilligan's thesis (see p. 000) to "Borders." What does she mean by "different languages"? Review lines 50–55 of "Home Burial." What do these lines suggest about the husband's attitude toward his wife, toward communication within their relationship, and toward love? Characterize your response to the husband. How is Gilligan's thesis also relevant to "Home Burial"?
2. Working with your group, argue in favor of or against the conclusions of the three poems. What does each poem reveal about gender relations, sexuality, and cultural identity?

Claude McKay

The Harlem Dancer

Applauding youths laughed with young prostitutes
And watched her perfect, half-clothed body sway;
Her voice was like the sound of blended flutes
Blown by black players upon a picnic day.
She sang and danced on gracefully and calm,   5
The light gauze hanging loose about her form;
To me she seemed a proudly-swaying palm
Grown lovelier for passing through a storm.
Upon her swarthy neck black shiny curls
Luxuriant fell; and tossing coins in praise,   10
The wine-flushed, bold-eyed boys, and even the girls,
Devoured her shape with eager, passionate gaze;
But looking at her falsely-smiling face,
I knew her self was not in that strange place.

[1917]

Edna St. Vincent Millay

What Lips My Lips Have Kissed

What lips my lips have kissed, and where, and why,
I have forgotten, and what arms have lain
Under my head till morning; but the rain
Is full of ghosts tonight, that tap and sigh
Upon the glass and listen for reply,   5
And in my heart there stirs a quiet pain
For unremembered lads that not again
Will turn to me at midnight with a cry.
Thus in the winter stands the lonely tree,
Nor knows what birds have vanished one by one,   10
Yet knows its boughs more silent than before:
I cannot say what loves have come and gone,

> I only know that summer sang in me
> A little while, that in me sings no more.
>
> [1923]

Journal Entry

What knowledge of the Harlem Renaissance and the culture of the Jazz Age can you bring to your reading of these texts?

Textual Considerations

1. What words and images does the speaker use to contrast his perceptions of the dancer with those of her audience in McKay's poem?
2. What evidence does the speaker cite to justify his conclusion in the last line of "The Harlem Dancer"? Do you agree with his judgment? Why or why not? Is the speaker reliable, or does he romanticize the dancer's position?
3. State the theme of the first eight lines of Millay's poem. Do the speaker's gender and her inability to remember her individual lovers affect your response? How?
4. How effective is Millay's use of nature imagery to communicate meaning in the sonnet's sestet? Cite examples to justify your point of view.
5. How is the image of the tree in each poem consistent with the emotions each speaker expresses? Explain.

Cultural Contexts

1. What do both poems suggest about the relation between sexuality and identity and between sexuality and youth? To what extent is McKay's portrayal of gender relations relevant to today's society?
2. Working with your group, assess what you know about Harlem in the early 1920s, when it was the center of American jazz. How does "The Harlem Dancer" capture the experience of the Harlem Renaissance in the 1920s? Explain. What does "What Lips My Lips Have Kissed" suggest about the changing roles of women with respect to personal freedom and sexual identity in the 1920s?

Yevgeny Yevtushenko

Colours

When your face
appeared over my crumpled life
at first I understood
only the poverty of what I have.
Then its particular light   5
on woods, on rivers, on the sea,
became my beginning in the coloured world
in which I had not yet had my beginning.
I am so frightened, I am so frightened,
of the unexpected sunrise finishing,   10
of revelations
and tears and the excitement finishing,
I don't fight it, my love is this fear,
I nourish it who can nourish nothing,
love's slipshod watchman.   15
Fear hems me in.
I am conscious that these minutes are short
and that the colours in my eyes will vanish
when your face sets.

[1962]

Theodore Roethke

I Knew a Woman

I knew a woman, lovely in her bones,
When small birds sighed, she would sigh back at them;
Ah, when she moved, she moved more ways than one:
The shapes a bright container can contain!
Of her choice virtues only gods should speak,   5
Or English poets who grew up on Greek
(I'd have them sing in chorus, cheek to cheek).

How well her wishes went! She stroked my chin,
She taught me Turn, and Counter-turn, and Stand;
She taught me Touch, that undulant white skin;   10
I nibbled meekly from her proffered hand;
She was the sickle; I, poor I, the rake,
Coming behind her for her pretty sake
(But what prodigious mowing we did make).

Loves like a gander, and adores a goose: 15
Her full lips pursed, the errant note to seize;
She played it quick, she played it light and loose,
My eyes, they dazzled at her flowing knees;
Her several parts could keep a pure repose,
Or one hip quiver with a mobile nose   20
(She moved in circles, and those circles moved).

Let seed be grass, and grass turn into hay:
I'm martyr to a motion not my own;
What's freedom for? To know eternity.
I swear she cast a shadow white as stone.   25
But who would count eternity in days?
These old bones live to learn her wanton ways:
(I measure time by how a body sways).

[1954]

Gary Soto

Oranges

The first time I talked
With a girl, I was twelve,
Cold, and weighted down
With two oranges in my jacket.
December. Frost cracking   5
Beneath my steps, my breath
Before me, then gone,
As I walked toward
Her house, the one whose
Porch light burned yellow   10
Night and day, in any weather.
A dog barked at me, until
She came out pulling

At her gloves, face bright
With rouge. I smiled,
Touched her shoulder, and led   15
Her down the street, across
A used car lot and a line
Of newly planted trees,
Until we were breathing   20
Before a drugstore. We
Entered, the tiny bell
Bringing a saleslady
Down a narrow aisle of goods.
I turned to the candies   25
Tiered like bleachers
And asked what she wanted—
Light in her eyes, a smile
Starting at the corners
Of her mouth. I fingered   30
A nickel in my pocket,
And when she lifted a chocolate
That cost a dime,
I didn't say anything.
I took the nickel from   35
My pocket, then an orange,
And set them quietly on
The counter. When I looked up,
The lady's eyes met mine.
And held them, knowing   40
Very well what it was all
About.

    Outside,
A few cars hissing past,
Fog hanging like old   45
Coats between the trees.
I took my girl's hand
In mine for two blocks,
Then released it to let
Her unwrap the chocolate.   50
I peeled my orange
That was so bright against
The grey of December
That, from some distance,
Someone might have thought   55
I was making a fire in my hands.

[1985]

Journal Entry

What memories and emotions of your first love do you bring to your understanding and appreciation of these poems?

Textual Considerations

1. On what metaphor is Yevtushenko's entire poem based? At what points does his use of comparisons seem particularly effective?
2. Why is the speaker's life "crumpled" and "impoverished" in "Colours"? In what sense is it black and white, without color?
3. What aspect of the woman's physical being does the speaker emphasize throughout "I Knew a Woman"? Does his description ever go beyond the physical?
4. What is the effect of the imagery in lines 2, 4, 5–7, 12–14, 22, and 23 in Roethke's poem?
5. "Oranges" is a narrative poem. What elements of a traditional story can you identify?
6. What visual and sensory images enhance theme?
7. Reread lines 35–40 and comment on the effects of using eye contact instead of language. What made this possible?

Cultural Contexts

1. Soto's autobiographical poem is narrated in the first person. Working with your group, retell the story from the point of view of the saleslady or that of the young girl.
2. Are the speakers in all three poems romantics? Does it surprise you that male speakers portray vulnerability? What gender stereotypes do the poems contradict? Summarize your group's discussion.

BROWNING AND SPERA

Robert Browning

My Last Duchess

Ferrara

That's my last Duchess painted on the wall,
Looking as if she were alive; I call
That piece a wonder, now: Frà Pandolf's° hands
Worked busily a day, and there she stands.
Will't please you sit and look at her? I said   5
"Frà Pandolf" by design, for never read
Strangers like you that pictured countenance,
The depth and passion of its earnest glance,
But to myself they turned (since none puts by
The curtain I have drawn for you, but I)   10
And seemed as they would ask me, if they durst,
How such a glance came there; so, not the first
Are you to turn and ask thus. Sir,'twas not
Her husband's presence only, called that spot
Of joy into the Duchess' cheek: perhaps   15
Frà Pandolf chanced to say "Her mantle laps
Over my Lady's wrist too much," or "Paint
Must never hope to reproduce the faint
Half-flush that dies along her throat": such stuff
Was courtesy, she thought, and cause enough   20
For calling up that spot of joy. She had
A heart—how shall I say?—too soon made glad,
Too easily impressed; she liked whate'er
She looked on, and her looks went everywhere.
Sir, 'twas all one! My favor at her breast,   25
The dropping of the daylight in the West,
The bough of cherries some officious fool
Broke in the orchard for her, the white mule
She rode with round the terrace—all and each
Would draw from her alike the approving speech,   30
Or blush, at least. She thanked men,—good; but thanked
Somehow—I know not how—as if she ranked
My gift of a nine-hundred-years-old name
With anybody's gift. Who'd stoop to blame
This sort of trifling? Even had you skill   35

In speech—(which I have not)—to make your will
Quite clear to such an one, and say, "Just this
Or that in you disgusts me; here you miss,
Or there exceed the mark"—and if she let
Herself be lessoned so, nor plainly set   40
Her wits to yours, forsooth, and made excuse,
—E'en then would be some stooping, and I choose
Never to stoop. Oh, Sir, she smiled, no doubt,
Whene'er I passed her; but who passed without
Much the same smile? This grew; I gave commands;   45
Then all smiles stopped together. There she stands
As if alive. Will't please you rise? We'll meet
The company below, then. I repeat,
The Count your Master's known munificence
Is ample warrant that no just pretence   50
Of mine for dowry will be disallowed;
Though his fair daughter's self, as I avowed
At starting, is my object. Nay, we'll go
Together down, Sir! Notice Neptune, though,
Taming a sea-horse, thought a rarity,   55
Which Claus of Innsbruck° cast in bronze for me.

                                                         [1842]

3 **Frá Pandolf's:** a fictitious artist.   56 **Claus of Innsbruck:** also a fictitious artist.

Gabriel Spera

My Ex-Husband

That's my ex-husband pictured on the shelf,
Smiling as if in love. I took it myself
With his Leica, and stuck it in that frame
We got for our wedding. Kind of a shame
To waste it on him, but what could I do?   5
(Since I haven't got a photograph of you.)
I know what's on your mind—you want to know
Whatever could have made me let him go—
He seems like any woman's perfect catch,
What with his ruddy cheeks, the neat mustache,   10
Those close-set, piercing eyes, that tilted grin.
But snapshots don't show what's beneath the skin!

Sure, he'd a certain charm, charisma, style,
That passionate, earnest glance he struck, meanwhile
Whispering the sweetest things, like, "Your lips   15
Are like plump rubies, eyes like diamond chips,"
Could flush the throat of any woman, not
Just mine. He knew the most romantic spots
In town, where waiters, who all knew his face,
Reserved an intimately dim-lit place   20
Half-hidden in a corner nook. Such stuff
Was all too well rehearsed, I soon enough
Found out. He had an attitude—how should
I put it—smooth, self-satisfied, too good
For the rest of the world, too easily   25
Impressed with his officious self. And he
Flirted—fine! but flirted somehow a bit
Too ardently, too blatantly, as if,
If someone ever noticed, no one cared
How slobbishly he carried on affairs.   30
Who'd lower herself to put up with shit
Like that? Even if you'd the patience—which
I have not—to go and see some counselor
And say, "My life's a living hell," or
"Everything he does disgusts, the lout!"—   35
And even if you'd somehow worked things out,
Took a long trip together, made amends,
Let things get back to normal, even then
You'd still be on the short end of the stick;
And I choose never ever to get stuck.   40
Oh, no doubt, it always made my limbs go
Woozy when he kissed me, but what bimbo
In the steno pool went without the same
Such kisses? So, I made some calls, filed some claims,
All kisses stopped together. There he grins,   45
Almost lovable. Shall we go? I'm in
The mood for Chez Pierre's, perhaps, tonight,
Though anything you'd like would be all right
As well, of course, though I'd prefer not to go
To any place with checkered tables. No,   50
We'll take my car. By the way, have I shown
You yet these lovely champagne flutes, hand blown,
Imported from Murano, Italy,
Which Claus got in the settlement for me!

[1992]

Journal Entry

What images, memories, experiences, or situations do you associate with jealousy? Why does it surface so often in gender relationships? Cite reasons.

Textual Considerations

1. What crime has the Duke's last Duchess committed in "My Last Duchess"?
2. Characterize the dramatic situation in "My Last Duchess." Consider the setting, the Duke's character, and the poem's final image of Neptune taming a sea-horse. What is the significance of the Neptune statue?
3. Discuss how Browning's use of dramatic irony in "My Last Duchess" results in our learning more about the Duke than he understands about himself. Consider, for example, his motivation for ordering the duchess's death. Cite evidence to show how the Duchess became a projection of the Duke's fears and insecurities.
4. How do you respond to Spera's parody of Browning's poem in "My Ex-Husband"? Do you think the parallels Spera draws in terms of tone and theme lead to a greater appreciation of Browning's "My Last Duchess"? Explain.
5. Why does Spera's speaker assume a female persona? Does gender reversal from Browning's male speaker to Spera's female voice add anything to the humorous tone of the poem? Explain.
6. Who is the speaker in "My Ex-Husband" addressing—her lover or her reader? Or is she engaging in a dialogue with herself? Cite evidence to support your point of view.

Cultural Contexts

1. Discuss the causes of the violence against spouses in Browning's and Spera's poems.
2. Working with your group, analyze the role of social class in each poem. Consider, for example, the extent to which the Duchess was aware of class distinctions, and how her attitude toward other people affected the Duke. In "My Ex-Husband," focus on the role that Spera's updated setting plays in identifying the lovers' social class.

SARTON AND LASSELL

May Sarton

AIDS

We are stretched to meet a new dimension
Of love, a more demanding range
Where despair and hope must intertwine.
How grow to meet it? Intention
Here can neither move nor change   5
The raw truth. Death is on the line.
It comes to separate and estrange
Lover from lover in some reckless design.
Where do we go from here?

Fear.   Fear.   Fear.   Fear.   10

Our world has never been more stark
Or more in peril.

It is very lonely now in the dark.
Lonely and sterile.

And yet in the simple turn of a head   15
Mercy lives. I heard it when someone said
"I must go now to a dying friend.
Every night at nine I tuck him into bed,
And give him a shot of morphine,"
And added, "I go where I have never been."   20
I saw he meant into a new discipline
He had not imagined before, and a new grace.

Every day now we meet face to face.
Every day now devotion is the test.
Through the long hours, the hard, caring nights   25
We are forging a new union. We are blest.
As closed hands open to each other
Closed lives open to strange tenderness.
We are learning the hard way how to mother.
Who says it is easy? But we have the power.   30
I watch the faces deepen all around me.
It is the time of change, the saving hour.
The word is not fear, the word we live,

But an old word suddenly made new,
As we learn it again, as we bring it alive: 35

Love. Love. Love. Love.

[1988]

Michael Lassell

How to Watch Your Brother Die

When the call comes, be calm
Say to your wife, "My brother is dying. I have
to fly to California."
Try not to be shocked that he already looks like a cadaver.
Say to the young man sitting by your brother's side,   5
"I'm his brother."
Try not to be shocked when the young man says,
"I'm his lover. Thanks for coming."

Listen to the doctor with a steel face on.
Sign the necessary forms.   10
Tell the doctor you will take care of everything.
Wonder why doctors are so remote.

Watch the lover's eyes as they stare into
your brother's eyes as they stare into
space.   15
Wonder what they see there.
Remember the time he was jealous and
opened your eyebrows with a sharp stick.
Forgive him out loud
even if he can't understand you.   20
Realize the scar will be
all that's left of him.

Over coffee in the hospital cafeteria
say to the lover, "You're an extremely good-looking
young man."   25
Hear him say,
"I never thought I was good enough looking to
deserve your brother."
Watch the tears well up in his eyes. Say,
"I'm sorry. I don't know what it means to be   30
the lover of another man."

Hear him say,
"It's just like a wife, only the commitment is
deeper because the odds against you are so much
greater."
Say nothing, but
take his hand like a brother's.

Drive to Mexico for unproven drugs that might
help him live longer.
Explain what they are to the border guard.
Fill with rage when he informs you,
"You can't bring those across."
Begin to grow loud.
Feel the lover's hand on your arm,
restraining you. See in the guard's eye
how much a man can hate another man.
Say to the lover, "How can you stand it?"
Hear him say, "You get used to it."
Think of one of your children getting used to
another man's hatred.

Call your wife on the telephone. Tell her
"He hasn't much time.
I'll be home soon." Before you hang up, say,
"How could anyone's commitment be deeper than
a husband and wife?" Hear her say,
"Please, I don't want to know all the details."

When he slips into an irrevocable coma
hold his lover in your arms while he sobs,
no longer strong. Wonder how much longer
you will be able to be strong.
Feel how it feels to hold a man in your arms
whose arms are used to holding men.
Offer God anything to bring your brother back.
Know you have nothing God could possibly want.
Curse God, but do not
abandon Him.

Stare at the face of the funeral director
when he tells you he will not
embalm the body for fear of
contamination. Let him see in your eyes
how much a man can hate a man.

Stand beside a casket covered in flowers,
white flowers. Say,

35

40

45

50

55

60

65

70

"Thank you for coming" to each of several hundred men
who file past in tears, some of them   75
holding hands. Know that your brother's life
was not what you imagined. Overhear two mourners say,
"I wonder who'll be next."

Arrange to take an early flight home.
His lover will drive you to the airport.   80
When your flight is announced say,
awkwardly, "If I can do anything, please
let me know." Do not flinch when he says,
"Forgive yourself for not wanting to know him
after he told you. He did."   85
Stop and let it soak in. Say,
"He forgave me, or he knew himself?"
"Both," the lover will say, not knowing what else
to do. Hold him like a brother while he
kisses you on the cheek. Think that   90
you haven't been kissed by a man since
your father died. Think,
"This is no moment not to be strong." Fly
first class and drink scotch. Stroke
your split eyebrow with a finger   95
and think of your brother alive. Smile
at the memory and think
how your children will feel in your arms,
warm and friendly and without challenge.

                                                                            [1985]

Journal Entry

What attitudes, opinions, or knowledge of AIDS do you bring to your reading of these texts?

Textual Considerations

1. To what extent do you agree with the speaker in "AIDS" that "Our world has never been more stark / Or more in peril"?
2. How do you respond to the idea that words like *fear*, *mercy*, and *love* evoke new meanings in the context of AIDS?
3. What is the difference between "separate" and "estranged"?
4. Explain the effects of spacing, capitalizing, and repeating "Love" in the last line of the text.
5. Lassell uses contrasting images of love and hate in "How to Watch Your Brother Die." Cite examples of each.
6. Analyze the function of dialogue in Lassell's poem. Consider, for example, what the speaker's "conversations" reveal about himself, his wife, and his relationship to his brother and to his brother's lover.

7. Explain the last two words of Lassell's poem. How does it compare with the last line of Sarton's poem?

Cultural Contexts

1. Are homosexuals an oppressed group in the United States? Make a list of the arguments and evidence you would offer to support or refute this thesis.
2. Review with your group your responses to question 4. What do the various conversations suggest about the relationship of the gay community to the larger society? Make a list of the images that you associate with gays and lesbians. To what extent do you agree that people should be free to express their sexual preferences?

MARVELL AND BEHN

Andrew Marvell

To His Coy Mistress

Had we but world enough, and time,
This coyness, lady, were no crime.
We would sit down, and think which way
To walk, and pass our long love's day.
Thou by the Indian Ganges'° side   5
Shouldst rubies find; I by the tide
Of Humber° would complain. I would
Love you ten years before the flood,
And you should, if you please, refuse
Till the conversion of the Jews.   10
My vegetable love should grow
Vaster than empires and more slow;
An hundred years should go to praise
Thine eyes, and on thy forehead gaze;
Two hundred to adore each breast,   15
But thirty thousand to the rest;
An age at least to every part,
And the last age should show your heart.
For, lady, you deserve this state,
Nor would I love at lower rate.   20
    But at my back I always hear
Time's wingèd chariot hurrying near;
And yonder all before us lie
Deserts of vast eternity.

Thy beauty shall no more be found;   25
Nor, in thy marble vault, shall sound
My echoing song; then worms shall try
That long-preserved virginity,
And your quaint honor turn to dust,
And into ashes all my lust: 30
The grave's a fine and private place,
But none, I think, do there embrace.
    Now therefore, while the youthful hue
Sits on thy skin like morning dew
And while thy willing soul transpires   35

At every pore with instant fires,
Now let us sport us while we may,
And now, like amorous birds of prey,
Rather at once our time devour
Than languish in his slow-chapped power.   40
Let us roll all our strength and all
Our sweetness up into one ball,
And tear our pleasures with rough strife
Through the iron gates of life:
Thus, though we cannot make our sun   45
Stand still, yet we will make him run.

[1681]

5 Ganges: river in northern India.   **7 Humber:** estuary in northern England formed by the Ouse
and Trent rivers.

Aphra Behn

The Willing Mistress

Amyntas led me to a grove,
    Where all the trees did shade us;
The sun itself, though it had strove,
    It could not have betrayed us.
The place secured from human eyes   5
    No other fear allows
But when the winds that gently rise
    Do kiss the yielding boughs.

Down there we sat upon the moss,
    And did begin to play   10
A thousand amorous tricks, to pass
    The heat of all the day.
A many kisses did he give
    And I returned the same,
Which made me willing to receive   15
    That which I dare not name.

His charming eyes no aid required
    To tell their softening tale;
On her that was already fired
    'Twas easy to prevail.   20

> He did but kiss and clasp me round,
>   Whilst those his thoughts expressed:
> And laid me gently on the ground;
>   Ah who can guess the rest?

[1673]

Journal Entry

The rituals of courtship have long been associated with male leadership. How does Behn's text, written in 1673, reverse this tradition? How do you respond to her text?

Textual Considerations

1. How do you respond to the titles of the poems? What do they suggest about the images men create of women? Do these concepts of gender relationships seem out of date to you? Why or why not?
2. Explain what the image "I would/Love you ten years before the flood" in lines 7–8 of Marvell's poem suggests about the speaker's attitude toward time.
3. How do the images Marvell uses in the second and third sections of "To His Coy Mistress" mirror or contradict those in the first section?
4. How does the speaker in "To His Coy Mistress" characterize himself as a lover?
5. How does the speaker's gender and use of humor affect your response to "The Willing Mistress"?
6. Discuss female and male attitudes toward love in "To His Coy Mistress" and "The Willing Mistress."

Cultural Contexts

1. Aphra Behn, a seventeenth-century British writer, freely discussed female desire and issues concerning gender roles in her works. To what extent does she explore these issues in "The Willing Mistress"? Is it relevant that the lovers in the poem create a world of love ("a grove . . . secured from human eyes") separated from the outside world? Explain.
2. "To His Coy Mistress" is known as one of the most celebrated erotic poems in English literature. Working with your group, cite evidences of erotic elements in the poem.

KEATS AND DE LA CRUZ

John Keats

Bright Star

Bright star, would I were steadfast as thou art—
  Not in lone splendor hung aloft the night
And watching, with eternal lids apart,
  Like nature's patient, sleepless Eremite,°
The moving waters at their priestlike task   5
  Of pure ablution round earth's human shores,
Or gazing on the new soft fallen mask
  Of snow upon the mountains and the moors—
No—yet still steadfast, still unchangeable,
  Pillowed upon my fair love's ripening breast,   10
To feel forever its soft fall and swell,
  Awake forever in a sweet unrest,
Still, still to hear her tender-taken breath,
And so live ever—or else swoon to death.

[1819]

4 Eremite: hermit, devotee.

Sor Juana Inés de la Cruz

She Proves the Inconsistency of the Desires and Criticism of Men Who Accuse Women of What They Themselves Cause

Foolish men who accuse
women unreasonably,
you blame yet never see
you cause what you abuse.

You crawl before her, sad,   5
begging for a quick cure;

why ask her to be pure
when you have made her bad?

You combat her resistance   10
and then with gravity,
you call frivolity
the fruit of your intents.

In one heroic breath
your reason fails, like a wild   15
bogeyman made up by a child
who then is scared to death.

With idiotic pride
you hope to find your prize:
a regal whore like Thaïs°   20
and Lucretia° for a bride.

Has anyone ever seen
a stranger moral fervor:
you who dirty the mirror
regret it is not clean?   25

You treat favor and disdain
with the same shallow mocking voice: love you and you squawk,
demur and you complain.

No answer at her door   30
will be a proper part:
say no—she has no heart,
say yes—and she's a whore.

Two levels to your game
in which *you* are the fool: 35
one you blame as cruel,
one who yields, you shame.

How can one not be bad
the way your love pretends
to be? Say no and she offends.   40
Consent and you are mad.

With all the fury and pain
your whims cause her, it's good
for her who has withstood
you. Now go and complain!

You let her grief take flight   45
and free her with new wings.

Then after sordid things
you say she's not upright.

Who is at fault in all   50
this errant passion? She
who falls for his pleas, or he
who pleads for her to fall?

Whose guilt is greater in
this raw erotic play?   55
The girl who sins for pay
or man who pays for sin?

So why be shocked or taunt
her for the steps you take?
Care for her as you make   60
her, or shape her as you want,

but do not come with pleas
and later throw them in
her face, screaming of sin
when you were at her knees.   65

You fight us from birth
with weapons of arrogance.
Between promise and pleading stance,
you are devil, flesh, and earth.

[1680]

19 Thaïs: an Athenian courtesan who was the mistress of Alexander the Great.   **20 Lucretia:**
daughter of Prefect of Kone who was raped by the son of King Tanquinius Superbus.

Journal Entry

What associations do you have with the romantic concept of woman as goddess? Is it out-
moded in the postmodern age? Why or why not? How might such a concept affect the identify of both men and women?

Textual Considerations

1. The "Bright Star" is the North Star, a traditional symbol of permanence also used by
   other poets, such as Shakespeare. Compare and contrast the ways Keats uses this symbol
   in the octave and the sestet of the sonnet. Discuss the appeal of the image. What meanings does it suggest, and what emotions does it rouse in the reader?
2. Comment on the speaker's desire for steadfastness in lines 11, 12, and 14 of "Bright Star."
   What kind of permanence does the speaker aspire to? How central is the image of the star
   to express the speaker's romantic aspirations?

3. Summarize the key points of de la Cruz's arguments. To what extent do you agree or disagree with the logic and point of view she develops in the poem?
4. Describe the tone of de la Cruz's poem. Is the speaker sarcastic, angry, bitter, or objective? How does it compare with the tone of Keats's poem? Cite examples to support your answer.
5. Argue in favor of or against de la Cruz's statement that men "fight" women from birth "with weapons of arrogance."
6. Analyze the title of de la Cruz's poem. What does it reveal about the speaker? Does it seem to have been written by a Catholic nun in seventeenth-century Mexico? Explain.

Cultural Contexts

1. How would you describe the effects of such stereotypes as goddess, madonna, or whore on women's identity? To what extent do these stereotypes promote a male-dominated model of gender relations? Explain.
2. Working with your group, discuss the degree to which Keats's romantic aspiration for the "fair love's ripening breast" of an idealized mistress in nineteenth-century England and de la Cruz's protest against the debasing view of women as demons and whores in seventeenth-century Mexico are relevant to women's position in society today.

SHAKESPEARE

William Shakespeare

30

When to the sessions of sweet silent thought
I summon up remembrance of things past,
I sigh the lack of many a thing I sought,
And with old woes new wail my dear time's waste.
Then can I drown an eye, unused to flow,   5
For precious friends hid in death's dateless night,
And weep afresh love's long since cancelled woe,
And moan th'expense of many a vanished sight.
Then can I grieve at grievances foregone,
And heavily from woe to woe tell o'er   10
The sad account of fore-bemoanèd moan,
Which I new pay as if not paid before.
   But if the while I think on thee, dear friend,
   All losses are restored, and sorrows end.

[c. 1609]

William Shakespeare

116

Let me not to the marriage of true minds
Admit impediments. Love is not love
Which alters when it alterations find,
Or bends with the remover to remove.
O no, it is an ever-fixèd mark   5
That looks on tempests and is never shaken;
It is the star to every wand'ring bark,
Whose worth's unknown, although his height be taken.
Love's not time's fool, though rosy lips and cheeks
Within his bending sickle's compass come.   10
Love alters not with his brief hours and weeks,

But bears it out ev'n to the edge of doom.
 If this be error and upon me proved,
 I never writ, nor no man ever loved.

[c. 1609]

William Shakespeare

129

Th'expense of spirit in a waste of shame
Is lust in action, and till action, lust
Is perjur'd, murd'rous, bloody, full of blame,
Savage, extreme, rude, cruel, not to trust,
Enjoy'd no sooner but despisèd straight,   5
Past reason hunted, and no sooner had,
Past reason hated as a swallowed bait
On purpose laid to make the taker mad:
[Mad] in pursuit and in possession so,
Had, having, and in quest to have, extreme,   10
A bliss in proof, and prov'd, [a] very woe,
Before, a joy propos'd, behind, a dream.
 All this the world well knows, yet none knows well
 To shun the heaven that leads men to this hell.

[c. 1609]

William Shakespeare

130

My mistress' eyes are nothing like the sun;
Coral is far more red than her lips' red;
If snow be white, why then her breasts are dun;
If hairs be wires, black wires grow on her head.
I have seen roses damasked,° red and white,   5
But no such roses see I in her cheeks;
And in some perfumes is there more delight
Than in the breath that from my mistress reeks.
I love to hear her speak, yet well I know
That music hath a far more pleasing sound;   10

> I grant I never saw a goddess go°;
> My mistress, when she walks, treads on the ground.
> And yet, by heaven, I think my love as rare
> As any she belied with false compare.

[c. 1609]

5 damasked: variegated. **11 a goddess go:** walk.

Journal Entry

What is your definition of *true love*? How would you distinguish it from *falling in love* or *romantic love*? How do your definitions of love compare to those of Shakespeare?

Textual Considerations

1. Discuss the speaker's use of comparisons involving the past versus the present in sonnet 30. How do the losses the speaker suffered in the past (lines 6, 7, and 8) compare to what he gains in the present?
2. What is the theme of sonnet 116? Comment on the negative statements in lines 2, 4, and 9, and 11. What purpose do they serve to establish the theme of the sonnet? Explain.
3. Sonnet 116, stating the speaker's strong wish that true love might last forever, seems to be a favorite among Shakespeare's readers. Which of the four sonnets do you like best? Explain why, citing evidence from the text.
4. How does the speaker define "lust in action" in sonnet 129? How does he define lust before it becomes action and after it becomes action? What does the reversal in the sonnet's couplet (the last two lines of the poem) convey regarding the speaker's feeling about lust? To what extent do you agree or disagree with the speaker's point of view in this sonnet and in sonnets 30, 116, and 130?
5. Make a list of the eight major similes the speaker uses to describe his mistress's physical attributes in sonnet 130. What kind of portrait emerges in the sonnet? What does it reveal about the speaker's attitude toward his mistress?

Cultural Contexts

1. What does sonnet 130 reveal about Shakespeare's use of the convention of the literary mistress? What does it reveal about the idealization of women? What does it do to sustain or collapse this literary convention?
2. Working with your group, write a love sonnet in which you update the images that Shakespeare uses in sonnet 130. Start with a list of similes to portray your mistress's beauty; develop a theme, such as loss of love, aspirations toward true love, or sexual anxiety, for example; and aim at a fourteen-line poem. What does your poem reveal about cultural changes from Shakespeare's days to ours?

DRAMA

Euripides

Medea

Translated by Moses Hadas and John McLean

CHARACTERS

NURSE
CREON, *King of Corinth*
CHILDREN OF MEDEA
MEDEA
TUTOR
JASON
CHORUS, *Corinthian Women*
AEGEUS, *King of Athens*
MESSENGER

The scene represents the home of Medea at Corinth.

(*Enter* NURSE.)

NURSE: How I wish that the ship Argo[1] had never winged its way through the gray Clashing Rocks to the land of the Colchians! How I wish the pines had never been hewn down in the glens of Pelion, to put oars into the hands of the Heroes who went to fetch for Pelias the Golden Fleece! Then Medea my mistress would not have sailed to the towers of Iolcus, her heart pierced through and through with love for Jason, would not have prevailed on the daughters of Pelias to murder their father, would not now be dwelling here in Corinth with her husband and children. When she fled here she found favor with the citizens to whose land she had come and was herself a perfect partner in all things for Jason. (And therein lies a woman's best security, to avoid conflict with her husband.) But now there is nothing but enmity, a blight has come over their great love.

Jason has betrayed his own children and my mistress to sleep beside a royal bride, the daughter of Creon who rules this land, while Medea, luckless Medea, in her desolation invokes the promises he made, appeals to the pledges in which she put her deepest trust, and calls Heaven to witness the sorry

---

[1] **Argo:** Jason's ship on the expedition of the Argonauts, sent by Pelias, king of Iolcus in Thessaly (Jason's uncle, who had usurped the throne), to Colchis on the Black Sea. The Symplegades were clashing rocks, one of the obstacles along the way. Pelion is a mountain in Thessaly. Medea was a princess of Colchis who fell in love with Jason and followed him back to Greece.

recompense she has from Jason. Ever since she realized her husband's perfidy, she has been lying there prostrated, eating no food, her whole frame subdued to sorrow, wasting away with incessant weeping. She has not lifted an eye nor ever turned her face from the floor. The admonitions of her friends she receives with unhearing ears, like a rock or a wave of the sea. Only now and then she turns her white neck and talks to herself, in sorrow, of her dear father and her country and the home which she betrayed to come here with a husband who now holds her in contempt. Now she knows, from bitter experience, how sad a thing it is to lose one's fatherland. She hates her own children and has no pleasure at the sight of them. I fear she may form some new and horrible resolve. For hers is a dangerous mind, and she will not lie down to injury. I know her and she frightens me [lest she make her way stealthily into the palace where his couch is spread and drive a sharp sword into his vitals or even kill both the King and the bridegroom and then incur some greater misfortune.] She is cunning. Whoever crosses swords with her will not find victory easy, I tell you.

But here come the children, their playtime over. Little thought have they of their mother's troubles. Children do not like sad thoughts.

(*Enter* TUTOR, *with boys.*)

TUTOR: Ancient household chattel of my mistress, why are you standing here all alone at the gates, muttering darkly to yourself? What makes Medea want you to leave her alone?

NURSE: Aged escort of Jason's children, when their master's affairs go ill, good slaves find not only their misfortune but also their heart's grief. My sorrow has now become so great that a longing came over me to come out here and tell to earth and sky the story of my mistress's woes.

TUTOR: What? Is the poor lady not yet through with weeping?

NURSE: I wish I had your optimism. Why, her sorrow is only beginning, it's not yet at the turning point.

TUTOR: Poor foolish woman!—if one may speak thus of one's masters. Little she knows of the latest ills!

NURSE: What's that, old man? Don't grudge me your news.

TUTOR: It's nothing at all. I'm sorry I even said what I said.

NURSE: Please, I beg of you, don't keep it from a fellow slave. I'll keep it dark, if need be.

TUTOR: I had drawn near the checkerboards where the old men sit, beside the sacred water of Pirene, and there, when nobody thought I was listening, I heard somebody say that Creon the ruler of this land was planning to expel these children *and* their mother from Corinth. Whether the tale is true or not I do not know. I would wish it were not so.

NURSE: But will Jason ever allow his children to be so treated, even if he is at variance with their mother?

TUTOR: Old loves are weaker than new loves, and that man is no friend to this household.

NURSE: That's the end of us then, if we are to ship a second wave of trouble before we are rid of the first.

TUTOR: Meanwhile you keep quiet and don't say a word. This is no time for the mistress to be told.

NURSE: O children, do you hear what love your father bears you? Since he is my master, I do not wish him dead, but he is certainly proving enemy of those he should love.

TUTOR: Like the rest of the world. Are you only now learning that every man loves himself more than his neighbor? [Some justly, others for profit, as] now for a new bride their father hates these children.

NURSE: Inside, children, inside. It will be all right. (*To the* TUTOR.) And you keep them alone as much as you can, and don't let them near their mother when she's melancholy. I have already noticed her casting a baleful eye at them as if she would gladly do them mischief. She'll not recover from her rage, I know well, till the lightning of her fury has struck somebody to the ground. May it be enemies, not loved ones, that suffer!

MEDEA (*within*):   Oh! my grief! the misery of it all! Why can I not die?

NURSE: What did I tell you, dear children? Your mother's heart is troubled, her anger is roused. Hurry indoors, quick. Keep out of her sight, don't go near her. Beware of her fierce manner, her implacable temper. Hers is a selfwilled nature. Go now, get you inside, be quick. Soon, it is clear, her sorrow like a gathering cloud will burst in a tempest of fury. What deed will she do then, that impetuous, indomitable heart, poisoned by injustice?

(Exeunt children with TUTOR.)

MEDEA (*within*):   O misery! the things I have suffered, cause enough for deep lamentations! O you cursed sons of a hateful mother, a plague on you! And on your father! Ruin seize the whole household!

NURSE: Ah me, unhappy me! Why will you have your sons partake of their father's guilt? Why hate them? Ah children, your danger overwhelms me with anxiety. The souls of royalty are vindictive; they do not easily forget their resentment, possibly because being used to command they are seldom checked. It is better to be used to living among equals. For myself, at any rate, I ask not greatness but a safe old age. Moderation! Firstly, the very name of it is excellent; to practise it is easily the best thing for mortals. Excess avails to no good purpose for men, and if the gods are provoked, brings greater ruin on a house.

(Enter CHORUS.)

CHORUS: *I heard a voice, I heard a cry. It was the unhappy Colchian woman's. She is not yet calm. Pray tell us, old woman. From the court outside I heard her cries within. I do not rejoice, woman, in the griefs of this house. Dear, dear it is to me.*

NURSE: It is a home no more; the life has gone out of it. Its master a princess' bed enthralls, while the mistress in her chamber is pining to death, and her friends have no words to comfort her heart.

MEDEA (*within*):   Oh! Would that a flaming bolt from Heaven might pierce my brain! What is the good of living any longer? O Misery! Let me give up this life I find so hateful. Let me seek lodging in the house of death.

CHORUS: *O Zeus, O Earth, O Light, hear what a sad lament the hapless wife intones. What is this yearning, rash woman, after that fearful bed? Will you hasten to the end that is Death? Pray not for that. If your husband worships a new bride, it is a common event; be not exasperated. Zeus will support your cause. Do not let grief for a lost husband waste away your life.*

MEDEA (*within*):   Great Zeus and Lady Themis, see you how I am treated, for all the strong oaths with which I bound my cursed husband? May I live to see him and his bride, palace and all, in one common destruction, for the wrongs that they inflict, unprovoked, on me! O father, O country, that I forsook so shamefully, killing my brother, my own!

NURSE: Hear what she says, how she cries out to Themis of Prayers and to Zeus whom mortals regard as the steward of oaths. With no small revenge will my mistress bate her rage.

CHORUS: *I wish she would come into our presence and hear the sound of the words we would speak. Then she might forget the resentment in her heart and change her purpose. May my zeal be ever at the service of my friends. But bring her here, make her come forth from the palace. Tell her that here too are friends. Make haste before she does any harm to those within. Furious is the surge of such a sorrow.*

NURSE: I shall do so, though I am not hopeful of persuading the mistress. But I freely present you with the gift of my labor. Yet she throws a baleful glare, like a lioness with cubs, at any servant who approaches her as if to speak. Blunderers and fools! that is the only proper name for the men of old who invented songs to bring the joy of life to feasts and banquets and festive boards, but never discovered a music of song or sounding lyre to dispel the weary sorrows of humanity, that bring death and fell havoc and destruction of homes. Yet what a boon to man, could these ills be cured by some! At sumptuous banquets why raise a useless strain? The food that is served and the satisfaction that comes to full men, that in itself is pleasure enough.

(*Exit* NURSE.)

CHORUS: *I hear a cry of grief and deep sorrow. In piercing accents of misery she proclaims her woes, her ill-starred marriage and her love betrayed. The victim of grievous wrongs, she calls on the daughter of Zeus, even Themis, Lady of Vows, who led her through the night by difficult straits across the briny sea to Hellas.*

(*Enter* MEDEA.)

MEDEA: Women of Corinth, do not criticize me, I come forth from the palace. Well I know that snobbery is a common charge, that may be levelled against recluse and busy man alike. And the former, by their choice of a quiet life, acquire an extra stigma: they are deficient in energy and spirit. There is no justice in the eyes of men; a man who has never harmed them they may hate at sight, without ever knowing anything about his essential nature. An alien, to be sure, should adapt himself to the citizens with whom he lives. Even the citizen is to be condemned if he is too selfwilled or too uncouth to avoid offending his fellows. So I . . . but this unexpected blow which has befallen me has broken my heart.

It's all over, my friends; I would gladly die. Life has lost its savor. The man who was everything to me, well he knows it, has turned out to be the basest of men. Of all creatures that feel and think, we women are the unhappiest species. In the first place, we must pay a great dowry to a husband who will be the tyrant of our bodies (that's a further aggravation of the evil); and there is another fearful hazard: whether we shall get a good man or a bad. For separations bring disgrace on the woman and it is not possible to renounce one's husband. Then, landed among strange habits and regulations unheard of in her own home, a woman needs second sight to know how best to handle her bedmate. And if we manage this well and have a husband who does not find the yoke of intercourse too galling, ours is a life to be envied. Otherwise, one is better dead. When the man wearies of the company of his wife, he goes outdoors and relieves the disgust of his heart [having recourse to some friend or the companions of his own age], but we women have only one person to turn to.

They say that we have a safe life at home, whereas men must go to war. Nonsense! I had rather fight three battles than bear one child. But be that as it may, you and I are not in the same case. You have your city here, your paternal homes; you know the delights of life and association with your loved ones. But I, homeless and forsaken, carried off from a foreign land, am being wronged by a husband, with neither mother nor brother nor kinsman with whom I might find refuge from the storms of misfortune. One little boon I crave of you, if I discover any ways and means of punishing my husband for these wrongs: your silence. Woman in most respects is a timid creature, with no heart for strife and aghast at the sight of steel; but wronged in love, there is no heart more murderous than hers.

LEADER: Do as you say, Medea, for just will be your vengeance. I do not wonder that you bemoan your fate. But I see Creon coming, the ruler of this land, bringing tidings of new plans.

(*Enter* CREON.)

CREON: You there, Medea, looking black with rage against your husband; I have proclaimed that you are to be driven forth in exile from this land, you and your two sons. Immediately. I am the absolute judge of the case, and I shall not go back to my palace till I have cast you over the frontier of the land.

MEDEA: Ah! Destruction, double destruction is my unhappy lot. My enemies are letting out every sail and there is no harbor into which I may flee from the menace of their attack. But ill-treated and all, Creon, still I shall put the question to you: Why are you sending me out of the country?

CREON: I am afraid of you—there's no need to hide behind a cloak of words— afraid you will do my child some irreparable injury. There's plenty logic in that fear. You are a wizard possessed of evil knowledge. You are stung by the loss of your husband's love. And I have heard of your threats—they told me of them— to injure bridegroom and bride and father of the bride. Therefore before anything happens to me, I shall take precautions. Better for me now to be hateful in your eyes than to relent and rue it greatly later.

MEDEA: Alas! Alas! Often ere now—this is not the first time—my reputation has hurt me and done me grievous wrong. If a man's really shrewd, he ought never to have his children taught too much. For over and above a name for uselessness that it will earn them, they incur the hostility and envy of their fellow men. Offer clever reforms to dullards, and you will be thought a useless fool yourself. And the reputed wiseacres, feeling your superiority, will dislike you intensely. I myself have met this fate. Because I have skill, some are jealous of me, others think me unsociable. But my wisdom does not go very far. However, you are afraid you may suffer something unpleasant at my hands, aren't you? Fear not, Creon; it is not my way to commit my crimes against kings. What wrong have you done me? You have only bestowed your daughter on the suitor of your choice. No, it is my husband I hate. You, I dare say, knew what you were doing in the matter. And now I don't grudge success to your scheme. Make your match, and good luck to you. But allow me to stay in this country. Though foully used, I shall keep my peace, submitting to my masters.

CREON: Your words are comforting to hear, but inside my heart there is a horrible fear that you are plotting some mischief, which makes me trust you even less than before. The hot-tempered woman, like the hot-tempered man, is easier to guard against than the cunning and silent. But off with you at once, make no speeches. My resolve is fixed; for all your skill you will not stay amongst us to hate me.

MEDEA: Please no, I beseech you, by your knees, by the young bride . . .

CREON: You are wasting your words; you will never convince me.

MEDEA: Will you drive me out and have no respect for my prayers?

CREON: Yes, for I love you less than I love my own family.

MEDEA: O fatherland, how strongly do I now remember you!

CREON: Yes, apart from my children, that is *my* dearest love.

MEDEA: Alas! the loves of men are a mighty evil.

CREON: In my opinion, that depends on the circumstances.

MEDEA: O Zeus, do not forget the author of this wickedness.

CREON: On your way, vain woman, and end my troubles.

MEDEA: The troubles are mine, I have no lack of troubles.

CREON: In a moment you will be thrust out by the hands of servants.

MEDEA: No, no, not that. But Creon I entreat you . . .

CREON: You seem to be bent on causing trouble, woman.

MEDEA: I shall go into exile. It is not *that* I beg you to grant me.

CREON: Why then are you clinging so violently to my hand?

MEDEA: Allow me to stay for this one day to complete my plans for departure and get together provision for my children, since their father prefers not to bother about his own sons. Have pity on them. You too are the father of children. It is natural that you should feel kindly. Stay or go, I care nothing for myself. It's them I weep for in their misfortune.

CREON: My mind is not tyrannical enough; mercy has often been my undoing. So now, though I know that it is a mistake, woman, you will have your request. But I give you warning: if tomorrow's divine sun sees you and your children inside the borders of this country, you die. True is the word I have spoken. [Stay, if you must, this one day. You'll not have time to do what I dread.]

(*Exit* CREON.)

CHORUS: *Hapless woman! overwhelmed by sorrow! Where will you turn? What stranger will afford you hospitality? God has steered you, Medea, into an unmanageable surge of troubles.*

MEDEA: Ill fortune's everywhere, who can gainsay it? But it is not yet as bad as that, never think so. There is still heavy weather ahead for the new bride and groom, and no little trouble for the maker of the match. Do you think I would ever have wheedled the king just now except to further my own plans? I would not even have spoken to him, nor touched him either. But he is such a fool that though he might have thwarted my plans by expelling me from the country he has allowed me to stay over for this one day, in which I shall make corpses of three of my enemies, father and daughter and my own husband.

My friends, I know several ways of causing their death, and I cannot decide which I should turn my hand to first. Shall I set fire to the bridal chamber or make my way in stealthily to where their bed is laid and drive a sword through their vitals? But there is one little difficulty. If I am caught entering the palace or devising my bonfire I shall be slain and my enemies shall laugh. Better take the direct way and the one for which I have the natural gift. Poison. Destroy them with poison. So be it.

But suppose them slain. What city will receive me? Whose hospitality will rescue me and afford me a land where I shall be safe from punishment, a home where I can live in security? It cannot be. I shall wait, therefore, a little longer and if any tower of safety shows up I shall carry out the murders in stealth and secrecy. However, if circumstances drive me to my wits' end, I shall take a sword in my own hands and face certain death to slay them. I shall not shirk the difficult adventure. No! by Queen Hecate[2] who has her abode in the recesses of my hearth—her I revere above all gods and have chosen to assist me—never shall any one of them torture my heart with impunity. I shall make their marriage a torment and grief to them. Bitterly shall they rue the match they have made and the exile they inflict on me.

But enough! Medea, use all your wiles; plot and devise. Onward to the dreadful moment. Now is the test of courage. Do you see how you are being

---

[2] **Hecate:** Greek goddess of mysterious origins who brought good luck to sailors.

treated? It is not right that the seed of Sisyphus[3] and Aeson should gloat over you, the daughter of a noble sire and descendant of the Sun. But you realize that. Moreover by our mere nature we women are helpless for good, but adept at contriving all manner of wickedness.

CHORUS: *Back to their sources flow the sacred rivers. The world and morality are turned upside-down. The hearts of men are treacherous; the sanctions of Heaven are undermined. The voice of time will change, and our glory will ring down the ages. Womankind will be honored. No longer will ill-sounding report attach to our sex.*

The strains of ancient minstrelsy will cease, that hymned our faithlessness. Would that Phoebus, Lord of Song, had put into woman's heart the inspired song of the lyre. Then I would have sung a song in answer to the tribe of males. History has much to tell of the relations of men with women.

You, Medea, in the mad passion of your heart sailed away from your father's home, threading your way through the twin rocks of the Euxine, to settle in a foreign land. Now, your bed empty, your lover lost, unhappy woman, you are being driven forth in dishonor into exile.

Gone is respect for oaths. Nowhere in all the breadth of Hellas is honor any more to be found; it has vanished into the clouds. Hapless one, you have no father's house to which you might fly for shelter from the gales of misfortune; and another woman, a princess, has charmed your husband away and stepped into your place.

(*Enter* JASON.)

JASON: Often and often ere now I have observed that an intractable nature is a curse almost impossible to deal with. So with you. When you might have stayed on in this land and in this house by submitting quietly to the wishes of your superiors, your forward tongue has got you expelled from the country. Not that your abuse troubles *me* at all. Keep on saying that Jason is a villain of the deepest dye. But for your insolence to royalty consider yourself more than fortunate that you are only being punished by exile. I was constantly mollifying the angry monarch and expressing the wish that you be allowed to stay. But in unabated folly you keep on reviling the king. That is why you are to be expelled.

But still, despite everything, I come here now with unwearied goodwill, to contrive on your behalf, Madam, that you and the children will not leave this country lacking money or anything else. Exile brings many hardships in its wake. And even if you do hate me, I could never think cruelly of you.

MEDEA: Rotten, heart-rotten, that is the word for you. Words, words, magnificent words. In reality a craven. You come to me, you come, my worst enemy! This isn't bravery, you know, this isn't valor, to come and face your victims. No! it's

---

[3] **Sisyphus:** In Greek mythology, a son of Aeolus and founder of the city of Ephyre, later Corinth. Sisyphus appears as a rogue and a trickster in numerous classical legends. He is best known for the punishment he received for revealing Zeus's rape of Aegina to her father, the river Asopus: in Hades he is condemned to roll a huge stone up a hill, only to have it roll down again each time.

the ugliest sore on the face of humanity, Shamelessness. But I thank you for coming. It will lighten the weight on my heart to tell your wickedness, and it will hurt you to hear it. I shall begin my tale at the very beginning.

I saved your life, as all know who embarked with you on the Argo, when you were sent to master with the yoke the fire-breathing bulls and to sow with dragon's teeth that acre of death. The dragon, too, with wreathed coils, that kept safe watch over the Golden Fleece and never slept—I slew it and raised for you the light of life again. Then, forsaking my father and my own dear ones, I came to Iolcus where Pelias reigned, came with you, more than fond and less than wise. On Pelias too I brought death, the most painful death there is, at the hands of his own children. Thus I have removed every danger from your path.

And after all those benefits at my hands, you basest of men, you have betrayed me and made a new marriage, though I have borne you children. If you were still childless, I could have understood this love of yours for a new wife. Gone now is all reliance on pledges. You puzzle me. Do you believe that the gods of the old days are no longer in office? Do you think that men are now living under a new dispensation? For surely you know that you have broken all your oaths to me. Ah my hand, which you so often grasped, and oh my knees, how all for nothing have we been defiled by this false man, who has disappointed all our hopes.

But come, I shall confide in you as though you were my friend, not that I expect to receive any benefit from you. But let that go. My questions will serve to underline your infamy. As things are now, where am I to turn? Home to my father? But when I came here with you, I betrayed my home and my country. To the wretched daughters of Pelias? They would surely give me a royal welcome to their home; I only murdered their father. For it is how it is. My loved ones at home have learned to hate me; the others, whom I need not have harmed, I have made enemies to oblige you. And so in return for these services you have made me envied among the women of Hellas! A wonderful, faithful husband I have in you, if I must be expelled from the country into exile, deserted by my friends, alone with my friendless children! A fine story to tell of the new bridegroom, that his children and the woman who saved his life are wandering about in aimless beggary! O Zeus, why O why have you given to mortals sure means of knowing gold from tinsel, yet men's exteriors show no mark by which to descry the rotten heart?

LEADER: Horrible and hard to heal is the anger of friend at strife with friend.

JASON: It looks as if I need no small skill in speech if, like a skilful steersman riding the storm with close-reefed sheets, I am to escape the howling gale of your verbosity, woman. Well, since you are making a mountain out of the favors you have done me, I'll tell *you* what I think. It was the goddess of Love and none other, mortal or immortal, who delivered me from the dangers of my quest. You have indeed much subtlety of wit, but it would be an invidious story to go into, how the inescapable shafts of Love compelled you to save my life. Still, I shall not put too fine a point on it. If you helped me in some way or other, good and well. But as I shall demonstrate, in the matter of my rescue you got more than you gave.

In the first place, you have your home in Greece, instead of in a barbarian land. You have learned the blessings of Law and Justice, instead of the Caprice of the Strong. And all the Greeks have realized your wisdom, and you have won great fame. If you had been living on the edges of the earth, nobody would ever have heard of you. May I have neither gold in my house nor skill to sing a sweeter song than Orpheus if my fortune is to be hid from the eyes of men. That, then, is my position in the matter of the fetching of the Fleece. (It was you who proposed the debate.)

There remains my wedding with the Princess, which you have cast in my teeth. In this connection I shall demonstrate, one, my wisdom; two, my rightness; three, my great service of love to you and my children. (Be quiet please.) When I emigrated here from the land of Iolcus, dragging behind me an unmanageable chain of troubles, what greater windfall could I have hit upon, I an exile, than a marriage with the king's daughter? Not that I was weary of your charms (that's the thought that galls you) or that I was smitten with longing for a fresh bride; still less that I wanted to outdo my neighbors in begetting numerous children. Those I have are enough, there I have no criticism to make. No! what I wanted, first and foremost, was a good home where we would lack for nothing (well I knew that the poor man is shunned and avoided by all his friends); and secondly, I wanted to bring up the children in a style worthy of my house, and, begetting other children to be brothers to the children born of you, to bring them all together and unite the families. Then my happiness would be complete. What do *you* want with more children? As for me, it will pay me to advance the children I have by means of those I intend to beget. Surely that is no bad plan? You yourself would admit it, if jealousy were not pricking you.

You women have actually come to believe that, lucky in love, you are lucky in all things, but let some mischance befall that love, and you will think the best of all possible worlds a most loathsome place. There ought to have been some other way for men to beget their children, dispensing with the assistance of women. Then there would be no trouble in the world.

LEADER: Jason, you arrange your arguments very skillfully. And yet in my opinion, like it or not, you have acted unjustly in betraying your wife.

MEDEA: Yes! I do hold many opinions that are not shared by the majority of people. In my opinion, for example, the plausible scoundrel is the worst type of scoundrel. Confident in his ability to trick out his wickedness with fair phrases he shrinks from no depth of villainy. But there is a limit to his cleverness. As there is also to yours. You may well drop that fine front with me, and all that rhetoric. One word will floor you. If you had been an honorable man, you would have sought my consent to the new match and not kept your plans secret from your own family.

JASON: And if I had announced to you my intention to marry, I am sure I would have found you a most enthusiastic accomplice. Why! even now you cannot bring yourself to master your heart's deep resentment.

MEDEA:　That's not what griped you. No! your foreign wife was passing into an old age that did you little credit.

JASON:　Accept my assurance, it was not for the sake of a woman that I made the match I have made. As I told you once already, I wanted to save you and to beget princes to be brothers to my own sons, thereby establishing our family.

MEDEA:　May it never be mine . . . a happiness that hurts, a blessedness that frets my soul.

JASON:　Do you know how to change your prayer to show better sense? "May I regard nothing useful as grievous, no good fortune as ill."

MEDEA:　Insult me. *You* have a refuge, but I am helpless, faced with exile.

JASON:　It was your own choice. Don't blame anyone else.

MEDEA:　What did I do? Did I betray you and marry somebody else?

JASON:　You heaped foul curses on the king.

MEDEA:　And to your house also I shall prove a curse.

JASON:　Look here, I do not intend to continue this discussion any further. If you want anything of mine to assist you or the children in your exile, just tell me. I am ready to give it with an ungrudging hand and to send letters of introduction to my foreign friends who will treat you well. If you reject this offer, woman, you will be a great fool. Forget your anger, and you will find it greatly to your advantage.

MEDEA:　I would not use your friends on any terms or accept anything of yours. Do not offer it. The gifts of the wicked bring no profit.

JASON:　At any rate, heaven be my witness that I am willing to render every assistance to you and the children. But you do not like what is good for you. Your obstinacy repulses your friends; it will only aggravate your suffering.

MEDEA:　Be off with you. As you loiter outside here, you are burning with longing for the girl who has just been made your wife. Make the most of the union. Perhaps, god willing, you are making the kind of marriage you will some day wish unmade.

(*Exit* JASON.)

CHORUS:　*Love may go too far and involve men in dishonor and disgrace. But if the goddess comes in just measure, there is none so rich in blessing. May you never launch at me, O Lady of Cyprus, your golden bow's passion-poisoned arrows, which no man can avoid.*

　　May Moderation content me, the fairest gift of Heaven. Never may the Cyprian pierce my heart with longing for another's love and bring on me angry quarrelings and never-ending recriminations. May she have respect for harmonious unions and with discernment assort the matings of women.

　　O Home and Fatherland, never, never, I pray, may I be cityless. It is an intolerable existence, hopeless, piteous, grievous. Let me die first, die and bring this life to a close. There is no sorrow that surpasses the loss of country.

　　My eyes have seen it; not from hearsay do I speak. You have neither city nor friend to pity you in your most terrible trials. Perish, abhorred, the man who never brings himself to unbolt his heart in frankness to some honored friends! Never shall such a man be a friend of mine.

(Enter AEGEUS, *in traveler's dress.*)

AEGEUS: Medea, good health to you. A better prelude than that in addressing one's friends, no man knows.

MEDEA: Good health be yours also, wise Pandion's son, Aegeus. Where do you come from to visit this land?

AEGEUS: I have just left the ancient oracle of Phoebus.

MEDEA: What sent you to the earth's oracular hub?

AEGEUS: I was enquiring how I might get children.

MEDEA: In the name of Heaven, have you come thus far in life still childless?

AEGEUS: By some supernatural influence I am still without children.

MEDEA: Have you a wife or are you still unmarried?

AEGEUS: I have a wedded wife to share my bed.

MEDEA: Tell me, what did Phoebus tell you about offspring?

AEGEUS: His words were too cunning for a mere man to interpret.

MEDEA: Is it lawful to tell me the answer of the god?

AEGEUS: Surely. For, believe me, it requires a cunning mind to understand.

MEDEA: What then was the oracle? Tell me, if I may hear it.

AEGEUS: I am not to open the cock that projects from the skin . . .

MEDEA: Till you do what? Till you reach what land?

AEGEUS: Till I return to my ancestral hearth.

MEDEA: Then what errand brings your ship to this land?

AEGEUS: There is one Pittheus, king of Troezen . . .

MEDEA: The child of Pelops, as they say, and a most pious man.

AEGEUS: To him I will communicate the oracle of the god.

MEDEA: Yes, he is a cunning man and well-versed in such matters.

AEGEUS: Yes, and of all my comrades in arms the one I love most.

MEDEA: Well, good luck to you, and may you win your heart's desire.

AEGEUS: Why, what's the reason for those sad eyes, that wasted complexion?

MEDEA: Aegeus, I've got the basest husband in all the world.

AEGEUS: What do you mean? Tell me the reason of your despondency, tell me plainly.

MEDEA: Jason is wronging me; I never did him wrong.

AEGEUS: What has he done? Speak more bluntly.

MEDEA: He has another wife, to lord it over me in our home.

AEGEUS: You don't mean that he has done so callous, so shameful a deed!

MEDEA: Indeed he did. Me that used to be his darling he now despises.

AEGEUS: Has he fallen in love? Does he hate your embraces?

MEDEA: Yes, it's a grand passion! He was born to betray his loved ones.

AEGEUS: Let him go, then, since he is so base, as you say.

MEDEA: He became enamored of getting a king for a father-in-law.

AEGEUS: Who gave him the bride? Please finish your story.

MEDEA: Creon, the ruler of this Corinth.

AEGEUS: In that case, Madam, I can sympathize with your resentment.

MEDEA: My life is ruined. What is more, I am being expelled from the land.

AEGEUS: By whom? This new trouble is hard.

MEDEA: Creon is driving me out of Corinth into exile.

AEGEUS: And does Jason allow this? I don't like that either.

MEDEA: He says he does not, but he'll stand it. Oh! I beseech you by this beard, by these knees, a suppliant I entreat you, show pity, show pity for my misery. Do not stand by and see me driven forth to a lonely exile. Receive me into your land, into your home and the shelter of your hearth. So may the gods grant you the children you desire, to throw joy round your deathbed. You do not know what a lucky path you have taken to me. I shall put an end to your childlessness. I shall make you beget heirs of your blood. I know the magic potions that will do it.

AEGEUS: Many things make me eager to do this favor for you, Madam. Firstly, the gods, and secondly, the children that you promise will be born to me. In that matter I am quite at my wits' end. But here is how I stand. If you yourself come to Athens, I shall try to be your champion, as in duty bound. This warning, however, I must give you! I shall not consent to take you with me out of Corinth. If you yourself come to my palace, you will find a home and a sanctuary. Never will I surrender you to anybody. But your own efforts must get you away from this place. I wish to be free from blame in the eyes of my hosts also.

MEDEA: And so you shall. But just let me have a pledge for these services, and I shall have all I could desire of you.

AEGEUS: Do you not trust me? What is your difficulty?

MEDEA: I do trust you. But both the house of Pelias and Creon are my enemies. Bound by oaths, you would never hand me over to them if they tried to extradite me. But with an agreement of mere words, unfettered by any sacred pledge, you might be won over by their diplomatic advances to become *their* friend. For I have no influence or power, whereas they have the wealth of a royal palace.

AEGEUS: You take great precautions, Madam. Still, if you wish, I will not refuse to do your bidding. For me too it will be safer that way, if I have some excuse to offer to your enemies, and *you* will have more security. Dictate the oath.

MEDEA: Swear by the Floor of Earth, by the Sun my father's father, by the whole family of the gods, one and all——

AEGEUS: To do or not do what? Say on.

MEDEA: Never yourself to cast me out of your country and never, willingly, during your lifetime, to surrender me to any of my foes that desire to seize me.

AEGEUS: I swear by the Earth, by the holy majesty of the Sun, and by all the gods, to abide by the terms you propose.

MEDEA: Enough! And if you abide not by your oath, what punishment do you pray to receive?

AEGEUS: The doom of sacrilegious mortals.

MEDEA: Go and fare well. All is well. I shall arrive at your city as soon as possible, when I have done what I intend to do, and obtained my desire.

LEADER (*as* AEGEUS *departs*):   May Maia's son, the Lord of Journeys,[4] bring you safe to Athens, and may you achieve the desire that hurries you homeward; for you are a generous man in my esteem.

---

[4] **Maia's Son, the Lord of Journeys:** Mercury.

MEDEA: O Zeus and his Justice, O Light of the Sun! The time has come, my friends, when I shall sing songs of triumph over my enemies. I am on my way. Now I can hope that my foes will pay the penalty. Just as my plans were most storm-tossed at sea, this man has appeared, a veritable harbor, where I shall fix my moorings, when I get to the town and citadel of Pallas.

Now I shall tell you all my plans; what you hear will not be said in fun. I shall send one of my servants to ask Jason to come and see me. When he comes, I shall make my language submissive, tell him I approve of everything else and am quite contented [with his royal marriage and his betrayal of me, that I agree it is all for the best]; I shall only ask him to allow my children to remain. Not that I wish to leave them in a hostile land [for my enemies to insult]. No! I have a cunning plan to kill the princess. I shall send them with gifts to offer to the bride, to allow them to stay in the land—a dainty robe and a headdress of beaten gold. If she takes the finery and puts it on her, she will die in agony. She and anyone who touches her. So deadly are the poisons in which I shall steep my gifts.

But now I change my tone. It grieves me sorely, the horrible deed I must do next. I shall murder my children, these children of mine. No man shall take them away from me. Then when I have accomplished the utter overthrow of the house of Jason, I shall flee from the land, to escape the consequences of my own dear children's murder and my other accursed crimes. My friends, I cannot bear being laughed at by my enemies.

So be it. Tell me, what has life to offer them. They have no father, no home, no refuge from danger.

My mistake was in leaving my father's house, won over by the words of a Greek. But, as god is my ally, he shall pay for his crime. Never, if I can help it, shall he behold his sons again in this life. Never shall he beget children by his new bride. She must die by my poisons, die the death she deserves. Nobody shall despise *me* or think me weak or passive. Quite the contrary. I am a good friend, but a dangerous enemy. For that is the type the world delights to honor.

LEADER: You have confided your plan in me, and I should like to help you, but since I also would support the laws of mankind, I entreat you not to do this deed.

MEDEA: It is the only way. But I can sympathize with your sentiments. You have not been wronged like me.

LEADER: Surely you will not have the heart to destroy your own flesh and blood?

MEDEA: I shall. It will hurt my husband most that way.

LEADER: But it will make you the unhappiest woman in the world.

MEDEA: Let it. From now on all words are superfluous. (*To the* NURSE.) Go now, please, and fetch Jason. Whenever loyalty is wanted, I turn to you. Tell him nothing of my intentions, as you are a woman and a loyal servant of your mistress.

(*Exit* NURSE.)

CHORUS: *The people of Erechtheus have been favored of Heaven from the beginning. Children of the blessed gods are they, sprung from a hallowed land that no foeman's foot has trodden. Their food is glorious Wisdom. There the skies are always clear, and lightly do they walk in that land where once on a time blonde Harmony bore nine chaste daughters, the Muses of Pieria.*

Such is the tale, which tells also how Aphrodite sprinkled the land with water from the fair streams of Cephissus and breathed over it breezes soft and fragrant. Ever on her hair she wears a garland of sweet-smelling roses, and ever she sends the Loves to assist in the court of Wisdom. No good thing is wrought without their help.

How then shall that land of sacred rivers, that hospitable land receive you the slayer of your children? It would be sacrilege for you to live with them. Think. You are stabbing your children. Think. You are earning the name of murderess. By your knees we entreat you, by all the world holds sacred, do not murder your children.

Whence got you the hardihood to conceive such a plan? And in the horrible act, as you bring death on your own children, how will you steel your heart and hand? When you cast your eyes on them, your own children, will you not weep that you should be their murderess? When your own children fall at your feet and beg for mercy, you will never be able to dye your hands with their blood. Your heart will not stand it.

(*Enter* JASON, *followed by the* NURSE.)

JASON: I come at your bidding. Though you hate me, I shall not refuse you an audience. What new favor have you to ask of me, woman?

MEDEA: Jason, please forgive me for all I said. After all the services of love you have rendered me before, I can count on you to put up with my fits of temper. I have been arguing the matter out with myself. Wretched woman (thus I scolded myself), why am I so mad as to hate those that mean me well, to treat as enemies the rulers of this land and my husband who, in marrying a princess and getting brothers for my children, is only doing what is best for us all? What is the matter with me? Why am I still furious, when the gods are showering their blessings on me? Have I not children of my own? Am I forgetting that I am an exile from my native land, in sore need of friends? These reflections let me see how very foolish I have been and how groundless is my resentment. Now, I want to thank you. I think you are only doing the right thing in making this new match. I have been the fool. I ought to have entered into your designs, helped you to accomplish them, even stood by your nuptial couch and been glad to be of service to the new bride. But I am what I am . . . to say no worse, a woman. You ought not therefore to imitate me in my error or to compete with me in childishness. I beg your pardon, and confess that I was wrong then. But now I have taken better counsel, as you see.

Children, children, come here, leave the house, come out and greet your father as I do. Speak to him. Join your mother in making friends with him, forgetting our former hate. It's a truce; the quarrel is over. Take his right hand. Alas! my imagination sickens strangely. My children, will you stretch out loving arms like that in the long hereafter? My grief! How quick my tears are! My fears brim over. It is that long quarrel with your father, now done with, that fills my tender eyes with tears.

LEADER: From my eyes, too, the burning tears gush forth. May Sorrow's advance proceed no further.

JASON: That is the talk I like to hear, woman. The past I can forgive. It is only natural for your sex to show resentment when their husbands contract another marriage. But your heart has now changed for the better. It took time, to be sure, but you have now seen the light of reason. That's the action of a wise woman. As for you, my children, your father has not forgotten you. God willing, he has secured your perfect safety. I feel sure that you will yet occupy the first place here in Corinth, with your brothers. Merely grow up. Your father, and any friends he has in heaven, will see to the rest. May I see you, sturdy and strong, in the flower of your youth, triumphant over my enemies.

   You there, why wet your eyes with hot tears, and avert your pale cheek? Why are you not happy to hear me speak thus?

MEDEA: It's nothing. Just a thought about the children here.

JASON: Why all this weeping over the children? It's too much.

MEDEA: I am their mother. Just now when you were wishing them long life, a pang of sorrow came over me, in case things would not work out that way.

JASON: Cheer up, then. I shall see that they are all right.

MEDEA: Very well, I shall not doubt your word. Women are frail things and naturally apt to cry. But to return to the object of this conference, something has been said, something remains to be mentioned. Since it is their royal pleasure to expel me from the country—oh yes! it's the best thing for me too, I know well, not to stay on here in the way of you and the king; I am supposed to be their bitter enemy—*I* then shall go off into exile. But see that the children are reared by your own hand, ask Creon to let *them* stay.

JASON: I don't know if he will listen to me, but I shall try, as I ought.

MEDEA: At least you can get your wife to intercede with her father on their behalf.

JASON: Certainly, and I imagine I shall persuade her.

MEDEA: If she is a woman like the rest of us. In this task, I too shall play my part. I shall send the children with gifts for her, gifts far surpassing the things men make to-day [a fine robe, and a head-dress of beaten gold]. Be quick there. Let one of my maids bring the finery here. What joy will be hers, joys rather, joys innumerable, getting not only a hero like you for a husband, but also raiment which the Sun, my father's father, gave to his children. (MEDEA *takes the casket from a maid who has brought it, and hands it to the* CHILDREN.) Here, my children, take these wedding gifts in your hands. Carry them to the princess, the happy bride, and give them to her. They are not the kind of gifts she will despise.

JASON: Impetuous woman! Why leave yourself thus empty-handed? Do you think a royal palace lacks for raiment and gold? Keep these things for yourself, don't give them away. If my wife has any regard for me at all, she will prefer me to wealth, I'm sure.

MEDEA: Please let me. They say that gifts persuade even the gods, and gold is stronger than ten thousand words. Hers is the fortune of the hour; her now is god exalting. She has youth, and a king for a father. And to save my children from exile, I would give my very life, let alone gold.

   Away, my children, enter the rich palace and entreat your father's young wife, my mistress, to let you stay in Corinth. Give her the finery. That is most important. She must take these gifts in her hands. Go as fast as you can. Success attend your mission, and may you bring back to your mother the tidings she longs to hear.

(*Exeunt* CHILDREN *with* TUTOR *and* JASON.)

CHORUS: *Now are my hopes dead. The children are doomed. Already they are on the road to death. She will take it, the bride will take the golden diadem, and with it will take her ruin, luckless girl. With her own hands she will put the precious circlet of death on her blonde hair.*

The beauty of it, the heavenly sheen, will persuade her to put on the robe and the golden crown. It is in the halls of death that she will put on her bridal dress forthwith. Into that fearful trap she will fall. Death will be her portion, hapless girl. She cannot overleap her doom.

And you, poor man. Little luck your royal father-in-law is bringing you. Unwittingly, you are bringing death on your children, and on your wife an awful end. Illstarred man, what a way you are from happiness.

And now I weep for your sorrow, hapless mother of these children. You will slaughter them to avenge the dishonor of your bed betrayed, criminally betrayed by your husband who now sleeps beside another bride.

(*Enter* CHILDREN *with their* TUTOR.)

TUTOR: Mistress, here are your children, reprieved from exile. Your gifts the royal bride took gladly in her hands. The children have made their peace with *her*. What's the matter? Why stand in such confusion, when fortune is smiling? [Why do you turn away your cheek? Why are you not glad to hear my message?]

MEDEA: Misery!

TUTOR: That note does not harmonize with the news I have brought.

MEDEA: Misery, and again Misery!

TUTOR: Have I unwittingly brought you bad news? I thought it was good. Was I mistaken?

MEDEA: Your message was . . . your message. It is not you I blame.

TUTOR: Why then are your eyes downcast and your tears flowing?

MEDEA: Of necessity, old man, of strong necessity. This is the gods' doing, and mine, in my folly.

TUTOR: Have courage. Some day your children will bring you too back home.

MEDEA: Ah me! Before that day I shall bring others to another home.

TUTOR: You are not the first woman to be separated from her children. We are mortals and must endure calamity with patience.

MEDEA: That I shall do. Now go inside and prepare their usual food for the children.

(*Exit* TUTOR.)

O my children, my children. For you indeed a city is assured, and a home in which, leaving me to my misery, you will dwell for ever, motherless. But I must go forth to exile in a strange land, before I have ever tasted the joy of seeing *your* happiness, before I have got you brides and bedecked your marriage beds and held aloft the bridal torches. Alas! my own self-will has brought me to misery. Was it all for nothing, my children, the rearing of you, and all the ago-nizing labor, all the fierce pangs I endured at your birth? Ah me, there was a time when I had strong hopes, fool as I was, that you would tend my old age and with your own hands dress my body for the grave, a fate that the world might envy. Now the sweet dream is gone. Deprived of you, I shall live a life of pain and sorrow. And you, in another world altogether will never again see your mother with your dear, dear eyes.

O the pain of it! Why do your eyes look at me, my children? Why smile at me that last smile? Ah! What can I do? My heart is water, women, at the sight of my children's bright faces. I could never do it. Goodbye to my former plans. I shall take my children away with me. Why should I hurt their father by *their* misfortunes, only to reap a double harvest of sorrow myself? No! I cannot do it. Goodbye to my plans.

And yet . . . what is the matter with me? Do I want to make myself a laughing-stock by letting my enemies off scot-free? I must go through with it. What a coward heart is mine, to admit those soft pleas. Come, my children, into the palace. Those that may not attend my sacrifices can see to it that they are absent. I shall not let my hand be unnerved.

Ah! Ah! Stop, my heart. Do not you commit this crime. Leave them alone, unhappy one, spare the children. Even if they live far from us, they will bring you joy. No! by the unforgetting dead in hell, it cannot be! I shall not leave my chil-dren for my enemies to insult. [In any case they must die. And if die they must, *I* shall slay them, who gave them birth.] My schemes are crowned with success. She shall not escape. Already the diadem is on her head; wrapped in the robe the royal bride is dying, I know it well. And now I am setting out on a most sorrowful road [and shall send these on one still more sorrowful]. I wish to speak to my children. Give your mother your hands, my children, give her your hands to kiss.

O dear, dear hand. O dear, dear mouth, dear shapes, dear noble faces, hap-piness be yours, but not here. Your father has stolen this world from you. How sweet to touch! The softness of their skin, the sweetness of their breath, my babies! Away, away, I cannot bear to see you any longer. (*Children retire within.*) My misery overwhelms me. O I *do* realize how terrible is the crime I am about, but passion overrules my resolutions, passion that causes most of the misery in the world.

CHORUS: *Often ere now I have grappled with subtle subjects and sounded depths of argu-ment deeper than woman may plumb. But, you see, we also have a Muse who teaches us philosophy. It is a small class—perhaps you might find one in a thousand—the women that love the Muse.*

And I declare that in this world those who have had no experience of paternity are happier than the fathers of children. Without children a man does not know whether they are a blessing or a curse, and so he does not miss a joy he has never had and he escapes a multitude of sorrows. But them that have in their home young, growing children that they love, I see them consumed with anxiety, day in day out, how they are to rear them properly, how they are to get a livelihood to leave to them. And, after all that, whether the children for whom they toil are worth it or not, who can tell?

And now I shall tell you the last and crowning sorrow for all mortals. Suppose they have found livelihood enough, their children have grown up, and turned out honest. Then, if it is fated that way, death carries their bodies away beneath the earth. What then is the use, when the love of children brings from the gods this crowning sorrow to top the rest?

MEDEA: My friends, all this time I have been waiting for something to happen, watching to see what they will do in the royal palace. Now I see one of Jason's attendants coming this way. His excited breathing shows that he has a tale of strange evils to tell.

(*Enter* MESSENGER.)

MESSENGER: What a horrible deed of crime you have done, Medea. Flee, flee. Take anything you can find, sea vessel or land carriage.

MEDEA: Tell me, what has happened that I should flee.

MESSENGER: The princess has just died. Her father Creon, too, killed by your poisons.

MEDEA: Best of news! From this moment and for ever you are one of my friends and benefactors.

MESSENGER: What's that? Are you sane and of sound mind, woman? You have inflicted a foul outrage on a king's home, yet you rejoice at the word of it and are not afraid.

MEDEA: I too have a reply that I might make to you. But take your time, my friend. Speak on. How did they die? You would double my delight, if they died in agony.

MESSENGER: When your children, both your offspring, arrived with their father and entered the bride's house, we rejoiced, we servants who had been grieved by your troubles. Immediately a whisper ran from ear to ear that you and your husband had patched up your earlier quarrel. And one kisses your children's hands, another their yellow hair. I myself, in my delight, accompanied the children to the women's rooms. The mistress, whom we now respect in your place, did not see the two boys at first, but cast a longing look at Jason. Then, however, resenting the entrance of the children, she covered her eyes with a veil and averted her white cheek.

Your husband tried to allay the maiden's angry resentment, saying, "You must not hate your friends. Won't you calm your temper, and turn your head this way? You must consider your husband's friends your own. Won't you accept the gifts and ask your father to recall their sentence of exile, for my sake?" Well, when she saw the finery, she could not refrain, but promised her husband everything, and before Jason and your children were far away from the house she took the elaborate robes and put them on her. She placed the golden diadem on her clustering locks and began to arrange her coiffure before a shining mirror, smiling at her body's lifeless reflection. Then she arose from her seat and walked through the rooms, stepping delicately with her fair white feet, overjoyed with the gifts. Time and time again, standing erect, she gazes with all her eyes at her ankles.

But then ensued a fearful sight to see. Her color changed, she staggered, and ran back, her limbs all atremble, and only escaped falling by sinking upon her chair. An old attendant, thinking, I suppose, it was a panic fit, or something else of divine sending, raised a cry of prayer, until she sees a white froth drooling from her mouth, sees her rolling up the pupils of her eyes, and all the blood leaving her skin. Then, instead of a cry of prayer, she let out a scream of lamentation. Immediately one maid rushed to Creon's palace, another to the new bridegroom, to tell of the bride's misfortune. From end to end, the house echoed to hurrying steps. A quick walker, stepping out well, would have reached the end of the two hundred yard track, when the poor girl, lying there quiet, with closed eyes, gave a fearful groan and began to come to. A double plague assailed her. The golden diadem on her head emitted a strange flow of devouring fire, while the fine robes, the gifts of your children, were eating up the poor girl's white flesh. All aflame, she jumps from her seat and flees, shaking her head and hair this way and that, trying to throw off the crown. But the golden band held firmly, and after she had shaken her hair more violently, the fire began to blaze twice as fiercely. Overcome by the agony she falls on the ground, and none but her father could have recognized her. The position of her eyes could not be distinguished, nor the beauty of her face. The blood, clotted with fire, dripped from the crown of her head, and the flesh melted from her bones, like resin from a pinetree, as the poisons ate their unseen way. It was a fearful sight. All were afraid to touch the corpse, taught by what had happened to her.

But her father, unlucky man, rushed suddenly into the room, not knowing what had happened, and threw himself on the body. At once he groaned, and embracing his daughter's form he kissed it and cried, "My poor, poor child, what god has destroyed you so shamefully? Who is it deprives this aged tomb of his only child? Ah! let me join you in death, my child." Then, when he ceased his weeping and lamentation and sought to lift his aged frame upright, he stuck to the fine robes, like ivy to a laurel bush. His struggles were horrible. He would try to free a leg, but the girl's body stuck to his. And if he pulled violently, he tore his shrunken flesh off his bones. At last his life went out; doomed, he gave up the ghost. Side by side lie the two bodies, daughter and old father. Who would not weep at such a calamity?

It seems to me . . . I need not speak of what's in store for you; you yourself will see how well the punishment fits the crime . . . it's not the first time the thought has come, that the life of a man is a shadow. [I might assert with confidence that the mortals who pass for philosophers and subtle reasoners are most to be condemned.] No mortal man has lasting happiness. When the tide of fortune flows his way, one man may have more prosperity than another, but happiness never.

(*Exit* MESSENGER.)

LEADER: It seems that this day Fate is visiting his sins on Jason. Unfortunate daughter of Creon, we pity your calamity. The love of Jason has carried you through the gates of death.

MEDEA: My friends, I am resolved to act, and act quickly [to slay the children and depart from the land]. I can delay no longer, or my children will fall into the murderous hands of those that love them less than I do. In any case they must die. And if they must, I shall slay them, who gave them birth. Now, my heart, steel yourself. Why do we still hold back? The deed is terrible, but necessary. Come, my unhappy hand, seize the sword, seize it. Before you is a course of misery, life-long misery; on now to the starting post. No flinching now, no thinking of the children, the darling children, that call you mother. This day, this one short day, forget your children. You have all the future to mourn for them. Aye, to mourn. Though you mean to kill them, at least you loved them. Oh! I am a most unhappy woman.

(*Exit* MEDEA.)

CHORUS: *O Earth, O glorious radiance of the Sun, look and behold the accursed woman. Stop her before she lays her bloody, murderous hands on her children. Sprung are they from your golden race, O Sun, and it is a fearful thing that the blood of a god should be spilt by mortals. Nay, stop her, skyborn light, prevent her. Deliver the house from the misery of slaughter, and the curse of the unforgetting dead.*

Gone, gone for nothing, are your maternal pangs. For nothing did you bear these lovely boys, O woman, who made the inhospitable passage through the gray Clashing Rocks! Why let your spleen poison your heart? Why this murderlust, where love was? On the man that spills the blood of kinsmen the curse of heaven descends. Go where he may, it rings ever in his ears, bringing sorrows and tribulations on his house.

(*The* CHILDREN *are heard within.*)

Listen, listen. It is the cry of the children. O cruel, ill-starred woman.

ONE OF THE CHILDREN (*within*): Ah me! What am I to do? Where can I escape my mother's murderous hands?

THE OTHER (*within*): I know not, my dear, dear brother. She is killing us.

CHORUS: *Should we break in? Yes! I will save them from death.*

ONE OF THE CHILDREN (*within*): Do, for god's sake. Save us. We need your help.

THE OTHER (*within*): Yes, we are already in the toils of the sword.

CHORUS: *Heartless woman! Are you made of stone or steel? Will you slaughter the children, your own seed, slaughter them with your own hands?*

Only one woman, only one in the history of the world, laid murderous hands on her children, Ino whom the gods made mad, driven from home to a life of wandering by the wife of Zeus. Hapless girl, bent on that foul slaughter, she stepped over a precipice by the shore and fell headlong into the sea, killing herself and her two children together. What crime, more horrible still, may yet come to pass? O the loves of women, fraught with sorrow, how many ills ere now have you brought on mortals!

(*Enter* JASON, *attended.*)

JASON: You women there, standing in front of this house, is Medea still within, who wrought these dreadful deeds? Or has she made her escape? I tell you, she had better hide under the earth or take herself off on wings to the recesses of the sky, unless she wishes to give satisfaction to the family of the king. Does she think she can slay the rulers of the land and get safely away from this house? But I am not so anxious about her as I am about the children. The victims of her crimes will attend to her. It's my own children I am here to save, in case the relatives of the king do them some injury, in revenge for the foul murders their mother has committed.

LEADER: Jason, poor Jason, you do not know the sum of your sorrows, or you would not have said these words.

JASON: What is it? She does not want to kill me too, does she?

LEADER: Your children are dead, slain by their mother's hand.

JASON: For pity's sake, what do you mean? You have slain me, woman.

LEADER: Your children are dead, make no mistake.

JASON: Why, where did she slay them? Indoors or out here?

LEADER: Open the doors and you will see their bodies.

JASON: Quick, servants, loosen the bolts, undo the fastenings. Let me see the double horror, the dead bodies of my children, and the woman who . . . oh! let me punish her.

>   MEDEA *appears aloft in a chariot drawn by winged dragons. She has the bodies of the* CHILDREN.

MEDEA: What's all this talk of battering and unbarring? Are you searching for the bodies and me who did the deed? Spare yourself the trouble. If you have anything to ask of me, speak if you will, but never shall you lay a hand on me. I have a magic chariot, given me by the Sun, my father's father, to protect me against my enemies.

JASON: You abominable thing! You most loathsomest woman, to the gods and me and all mankind. You had the heart to take the sword to your children, you their mother, leaving me childless. And you still behold the earth and the sun, you who have done this deed, you who have perpetrated this abominable outrage. My curses on you! At last I have come to my senses, the senses I lost when I brought you from your barbarian home and country to a home in Greece, an evil plague, treacherous alike to your father and the land that reared you. There is a fiend in you, whom the gods have launched against me. In your own home you had already slain your brother when you came aboard the Argo, that lovely ship. Such was your beginning. Then you married me and bore me children, whom you have now destroyed because I left your bed. No Greek woman would ever have done such a deed. Yet I saw fit to marry you, rather than any woman of Greece, a wife to hate me and destroy me, not a woman at all, but a tigress, with a disposition more savage than Tuscan Scylla.[5] But why all this?

---

[5] **Scylla:** the daughter of Hecate who was originally human but was turned into a monster by a rival in love. She survived by eating fish but also devoured sailors if their ships came near her cave.

Ten thousand reproaches could not sting you; your impudence is too engrained. The devil take you, shameless, abominable murderess of your children. I must bemoan my fate; no joy shall I have of my new marriage, and I shall never see alive the children I begot and reared and lost.

MEDEA: I might have made an elaborate rebuttal of the speech you have made, but Zeus the Father knows what you received at my hands and what you have done. You could not hope, nor your princess either, to scorn my love, make a fool of me, and live happily ever after. Nor was Creon, the matchmaker, to drive me out of the country with impunity. Go ahead, then. Call me tigress if you like, or Scylla that haunts the Tuscan coast. I don't mind, now I have got properly under your skin.

JASON: You too are suffering. You have your share of the sorrow.

MEDEA: True, but it's worth the grief, since you cannot scoff.

JASON: O children, what a wicked mother you got!

MEDEA: O children, your father's sins have caused your death.

JASON: Yet it was not *my* hand that slew them.

MEDEA: No, it was your lust, and your new marriage.

JASON: Because your love was scorned you actually thought it right to murder.

MEDEA: Do you think a woman considers that a small injury?

JASON: Good women do. But you are wholly vicious.

MEDEA: The children here are dead. That will sting you.

JASON: No! they live to bring fierce curses on your head.

MEDEA: The gods know who began it all.

JASON: They know, indeed, they know the abominable wickedness of your heart.

MEDEA: Hate me then. I despise your bitter words.

JASON: And I yours. But it is easy for us to be quit of each other.

MEDEA: How, pray? Certainly I am willing.

JASON: Allow me to bury these bodies and lament them.

MEDEA: Certainly not. I shall bury them with my own hands, taking them to the sanctuary of Hera of the Cape, where no enemy may violate their tombs and do them insult. Here in the land of Sisyphus we shall establish a solemn festival, and appoint rites for the future to expiate their impious murder. I myself shall go to the land of Erechtheus, to live with Aegeus, the son of Pandion. You, as is proper, will die the death you deserve, [struck on the head by a fragment of the Argo,] now you have seen the bitter fruits of your new marriage.

JASON: May you be slain by the Curse of your children, and Justice that avenges murder!

MEDEA: What god or power above will listen to you, the breaker of oaths, the treacherous guest?

JASON: Oh! abominable slayer of children.

MEDEA: Get along to the palace and bury your wife.

JASON: I go, bereft of my two sons.

MEDEA: You have nothing yet to bemoan. Wait till you are old.

JASON: My dear, dear children!

MEDEA: Yes, dear to their mother, not to you.

JASON: And yet you slew them.

MEDEA: I did, to hurt you.

JASON: Alas! my grief! I long to kiss their dear mouths.

MEDEA: Now you speak to them, now you greet them, but in the past you spurned them.

JASON: For god's sake, let me touch my children's soft skin.

MEDEA: No! You have gambled and lost.

JASON: O Zeus, do you hear how I am repelled, how I am wronged by this foul tigress, that slew her own children? But such lament as I may and can make, I hereby make. I call upon the gods. I invoke the powers above to bear me witness that you slew my children and now prevent me from embracing their bodies and giving them burial. Would that I had never begotten them, to live to see them slain at your hands.

CHORUS: *Zeus on Olympus hath a wide stewardship. Many things beyond expectation do the gods fulfil. That which was expected has not been accomplished; for that which was unexpected has god found the way. Such was the end of this story.*

(Exeunt.)

[431 B.C.]

Journal Entry

Is Medea a moral monster or a helpless victim of passion? Is Jason's infidelity the catalyst for her crime? Cite evidence to explain or justify Medea's and Jason's actions.

Textual Considerations

1. How would you characterize Jason, based on the portraits the nurse and Medea draw of him? What does the nurse's first speech reveal about Jason's mythological background? What contrast does she establish between Jason's roles in the past and the present? What does Medea's speech to the women of Corinth (pages 387–388) reveal about Jason?

2. Identify images in Medea's memorable language that are especially effective in communicating her view of love, hate, and violence. Analyze what such a language reveals about Medea's magical power and her sense of self as a woman, lover, wife, and mother.

3. What does Medea's encounter with Creon reveal about male status in the play? Characterize Creon as a ruler. What makes him change his "fixed resolve" to exile Medea? What kinds of weapons does Medea use against Creon?

4. The chorus of Corinthian women plays an important role in *Medea*. What is the chorus's view of gender relationships? To what extent does it empathize with Medea? What is its attitude toward Jason, love, and gender relations?

5. To what extent do you consider Jason's decision to abandon Medea justifiable? Are his arguments convincing? Why or why not?

Cultural Considerations

1. Consider the psychological depth of *Medea* by applying to Medea's tragedy the definition of love as an irresistible passion that overpowers reason and eventually destroys itself.

2. The concept of preserving communal values emerges as an important aspect of ancient Greek culture. To what extent does Euripides present Jason and Medea as tearing apart the social fabric of the family and community? To what extent does the play explore the issues of exogamy (marriage outside of a specific group) and endogamy (marriage within a specific group)? Does your group hold Jason and Medea accountable for their actions? Why or why not?

Performance Exercises

PERFORMANCE EXPRESS (45 MINUTES)

To create a dynamic group *ensemble*, cast one of your classmates as Medea and have her stand on a chair, surrounded by several other classmates who, sitting on the floor, will play the roles of Jason, Creon, the nurse, Aegeus, and Medea's children. Ask the actors sitting in the circle to question Medea about her origins, her skills as a sorcerer, her status as a barbarian in Corinth, the golden fleece myth, Jason's motives for deserting her, or any other plot or characterization issue.

PERFORMANCE PROJECTS

1. Use the Internet to carry out research on the style of acting in ancient Greece, focusing primarily on the use of masks and the choreography of the chorus. Then, working with your group, stage one of *Medea's* key scenes in both ancient Greek and contemporary staging styles. Think about costumes, scenic designs, the use of masks, and the choreography of the chorus. What aspects of the play have been lost or highlighted in each staging? Think about the dramatic purpose of the scene you have selected and how you can best portray it.

2. In her speech to the chorus (pages 387–388), Medea delivers a manifesto about the status of women in ancient Greece. To stage this scene, cast one of your classmates in the role of a feminist Medea. Decide on the costume and scene design you would use to recreate this highly emotional character. Notice that your choices about Medea's costumes can help you evoke her status as a foreign barbarian, a formidable feminist, or a cold-blooded murderer.

Manuel Puig

Kiss of the Spider Woman°

Translated by Allan J. Baker

ACT I

SCENE I

(SCENE: *A small cell in the Villa Devoto prison in Buenos Aires. The stage is in total darkness. Suddenly two overhead white spots light up the heads of the two men. They are sitting down, looking in opposite directions.*)

MOLINA: You can see there's something special about her, that she's not any ordinary woman. Quite young . . . and her face more round than oval, with a little pointy chin like a cat's.

VALENTIN: And her eyes?

MOLINA: Most probably green. She looks up at the model, the black panther lying down in its cage in the zoo. But she scratches her pencil against the sketch pad and the panther sees her.

VALENTIN: How come it didn't smell her before?

MOLINA (*deliberately not answering*): But, who's that behind her? Someone trying to light a cigarette, but the wind blows out the match.

VALENTIN: Who is it?

MOLINA: Hold on. She flusters. He's no matinée idol but he's nice-looking, in a hat with a low brim. He touches the brim like he's saluting and says the drawing is terrific. She fiddles with the curls of her fringe.

VALENTIN: Go on.

MOLINA: He can tell she's a foreigner by her accent. She tells him that she came to New York when the war broke out. He asks her if she's homesick. And then it's like a cloud passes across her eyes and she tells him she comes from the mountains, someplace not far from Transylvania.

VALENTIN: Where Dracula comes from.

MOLINA: The next day he's in his office with some colleagues—he's an architect—and this girl, another architect he works with—and when the clock strikes three he just wants to drop everything and go to the zoo. It's right across the street. And the architect girl asks him why he's so happy. Deep down, she's really in love with him, no use her pretending otherwise.

VALENTIN: Is she a dog?

MOLINA: No, nothing out of this world: chestnut hair, but pleasant enough. But the other one, the one at the zoo, Irene—no, Irina—has disappeared. As time

Kiss of the Spider Woman: A play based on his novel of the same title.

goes by he just can't get her out of his mind until one day he's walking down this fashionable avenue and he notices something in the window of an art gallery. They're pictures by an artist who only paints . . . panthers. The guy goes in and there's Irina being congratulated by all the guests. And I don't remember what comes next.

VALENTIN: Try to remember . . .

MOLINA: Hold on a sec . . . Okay, . . . then the architect goes up and congratulates her too. She drops the critics and walks off with him. He tells her that he just happened to be passing by, really he was on his way to buy a present.

VALENTIN: For the girl architect.

MOLINA: Now he's wondering if he's got enough money with him to buy two presents. And he stops outside a shop and she gets a funny feeling when she sees what kind of shop it is. There are all different kinds of birds in little cages sipping fresh water from their bowls.

VALENTIN: Excuse me . . . is there any water in the bottle?

MOLINA: Yes, I filled it up when they let us out to the toilet.

> (*The white light which up till now has lit just their heads widens to fully light both actors: we see the cell for the first time.*)

VALENTIN: That's okay then.

MOLINA: Do you want some? It's nice and cool.

VALENTIN: No or we won't have enough for tea in the morning. Go on.

MOLINA: Don't exaggerate. We've got enough to last all day.

VALENTIN: Don't spoil me. I forgot to fetch some when they let us out to shower. If it wasn't for you we wouldn't have any.

MOLINA: Look, there's plenty . . . Anyway, when they go inside that shop it's like—I don't know what—it's like the devil just came in. The birds, blind with fear, fly into the wire mesh and hurt their wings. She grabs his hand and drags him outside. Straight away the birds calm down. She asks him to let her go home. When he comes back into the shop the birds are chirruping and singing just like normal and he buys one for the other girl's birthday. And then . . . it's no good, I can't remember what happens next, I'm pooped.

VALENTIN: Just a little more.

MOLINA: When I'm sleepy my memory goes. I'll carry on with the morning tea.

VALENTIN: No, it's better at night. During the day I don't want to bother with this trivia. There are more important things . . . (MOLINA *shrugs.*) If I'm not reading and I'm keeping quiet it's because I'm thinking. But don't take it wrong.

MOLINA (*upset by* VALENTIN'*s remark. With almost concealed irony*):   I shan't bother you. You can count on that!

VALENTIN: I see you understand. See you in the morning. (*He settles down to sleep.*)

MOLINA: Till tomorrow. Pleasant dreams of Irina. (MOLINA *settles down too, but he is troubled by something.*)

VALENTIN: I prefer the architect girl.

MOLINA: I'd already guessed that.

SCENE II

(SCENE: MOLINA *and* VALENTIN *are sitting in different positions. They do not look at one another. Only their heads are lit: seconds later the night light comes on.*)

MOLINA: So they go on seeing each other and they fall in love. She pampers him, cuddles up in his arms, but when he wants to hold her tight and kiss her she slips away from him. She asks him not to kiss her but to let her kiss him with her full lips, but she keeps her mouth shut tight. (VALENTIN *is about to interrupt but* MOLINA *forges ahead.*) So, on their next date they go to this quaint restaurant. He tells her she's prettier than ever in her shimmering black blouse. But she's lost her appetite, she can't manage a thing, and they leave. It's snowing gently. The noise of the city is muffled but far away you can just hear the growling of wild animals. The zoo's close, that's why. Barely in a whisper she says she's afraid to return to her house and spend the night alone. He hails a taxi and they go to his house. It's a huge place, all *fin de siècle*; it used to be his mother's.

VALENTIN: And what does he do?

MOLINA: Nothing. He lights up his pipe and looks over at her. You always guessed he had a kind heart.

VALENTIN: I'd like to ask you something: how do you picture his mother?

MOLINA: So you can make fun of her?

VALENTIN: I swear I won't.

MOLINA: I don't know . . . someone really charming. She made her husband happy and her children too. She's always well groomed.

VALENTIN: And do you picture her scrubbing floors?

MOLINA: No, she's always impeccable. The high-necked dress hides the wrinkles round her throat.

VALENTIN: Always impeccable. With servants. People with no other choice than to fetch and carry for her. And, of course, she was happy with her husband who also exploited her in his turn, kept her locked up in the house like a slave, waiting for him . . .

MOLINA: . . . Listen . . .

VALENTIN: . . . waiting for him to come home every night from his chambers or his surgery. And she condoned the system, fed all this crap to her son and now he trips over the panther woman. Serves him right.

MOLINA (*irritated*):   Why did you have to bring up all that? . . . I'd forgotten all about this dump while I was telling you the movie.

VALENTIN: I'd forgotten about it too.

MOLINA: Well, then . . . Why d'you have to go and break the spell?

VALENTIN: Let me explain. . . .

MOLINA: Fine, but not now, tomorrow. . . . Why did I get lumbered with you and not the panther woman's boyfriend?

VALENTIN: That's another story and one that doesn't interest me.

MOLINA: Are you frightened to talk about it?

VALENTIN: It bores me. I know all about it—even though you've never said a word.

MOLINA: Fine. I told you I got done for corruption of minors. There's nothing else to add. So don't come the psychologist with me.

VALENTIN (*shielding himself behind humor*): Admit that you like him because he smokes a pipe.

MOLINA: No, it's not that. It's because he's gentle and understanding.

VALENTIN: His mother castrated him, that's all.

MOLINA: I like him and that's that. And you like the architect girl—what's so Bolshy about her?

VALENTIN: I prefer her to the panther woman, that's for sure. But the guy with the pipe won't suit you.

MOLINA: Why not?

VALENTIN: Your intentions aren't exactly chaste, are they?

MOLINA: Of course not.

VALENTIN: Exactly. He likes Irina because she's frigid and he doesn't have to pounce on her and that's why he takes her to the house where his mother is still present even if she is dead.

MOLINA (*getting angrier and angrier*): Continue.

VALENTIN: If he's still kept all his mother's things it's because he wants to remain a child. He doesn't bring home a woman but a child to play with.

MOLINA: That's all in your head. I don't even know if the place is his mother's—I said that because I liked the place and since I saw antiques there I told you it belonged to his mother. For all I know he rents it furnished.

VALENTIN: So you're making up half the movie?

MOLINA: I'm not, I swear. But—you know—there are some things I add to fill it out for you. The house, for example. And, in any case, don't forget I'm a window dresser and that's almost like being an interior designer. . . . Well, she begins to tell him her story but I don't remember all the details. . . . I remember that in her village, a long time ago, there used to be panther-women. And these tales frightened her a lot when she was a little girl.

VALENTIN: And the birds? . . . Why were they afraid of her?

MOLINA: That's what the architect asks her. And what does she say? She doesn't say anything! And the scene ends with him in pyjamas and a dressing gown, good quality, no pattern, something serviceable—and he looks at her sleeping on the sofa from his bedroom door and he lights up his pipe and stands there . . . thoughtful.

VALENTIN: Do you know what I like about it? That it's like an allegory of women's fear of submitting to the male, because when it comes to sex, the animal part takes over. You see?

MOLINA (*he doesn't approve of* VALENTIN's *comments*): Irina wakes up, it's morning already.

VALENTIN: She wakes up because of the cold, like us.

MOLINA (*irritated*): I knew you were going to say that. . . . She's woken up by the canary, singing in its cage. At first she's afraid to go near it, but the little bird is chirpy so she dares to move a little closer. She heaves a big sigh of relief because the bird isn't frightened of her. And then she makes breakfast . . . toast and cereals and pancakes . . .

VALENTIN: Don't mention food.

MOLINA: . . . and pancakes . . .

VALENTIN: I'm serious. Neither food nor women.

MOLINA: She wakes him up and he's all happy to see her settling in and so he asks her to stay there forever and marry him. And she says, yes, from the bottom of her heart and she looks around and the curtains look so beautiful to her, they're made of thick dark velvet.

(*Aggressively*.) And now you can fully appreciate the *fin de siècle* decor. Then Irina asks him if he truly wants her to be his wife to give her just a little more time, just long enough for her to get over her fears.

VALENTIN: You can see what's going on with her, can't you?

MOLINA: Hold on. He agrees and they get married. And on their wedding night she sleeps in the bed and he sleeps on the couch.

VALENTIN: Looking at his mother's ornaments. Admit it, it's your ideal home, isn't it?

MOLINA: Of course it is! Now I've got to put up with you telling me the same thing they all say.

VALENTIN: What d'you mean? What do they all say?

MOLINA: They're all the same, they all tell me the same thing.

VALENTIN: What?

MOLINA: That I was fussed over as a kid and that's why I'm like I am now, that I was clinging to my mother's skirts, but it's never too late to straighten out and all I need is a good woman because there's nothing better than a good woman.

VALENTIN: And that's what they all tell you?

MOLINA: And this is what I tell them. . . . You're dead right! . . . and since there's nothing better than a woman . . . I want to be one! So spare me the advice please, because I know what I feel like and it's all as clear as day to me.

VALENTIN: I don't see it as clear—at least, not the way you've just put it.

MOLINA: I don't need you telling me what's what—if you want I'll go on with the picture, if not, ciao. . . . I'll just whisper it to myself, and *arrivederci*, Sparafucile!

VALENTIN: Who's Sparafucile?

MOLINA: You don't have a clue about opera. He's the hatchet man in *Rigoletto*. . . . Where were we?

VALENTIN: The wedding night. He hasn't laid a finger on her.

MOLINA: And I forgot to tell you that they'd agreed she'd go and see a psychoanalyst.

VALENTIN: Excuse me again . . . don't get upset.

MOLINA: What is it?

VALENTIN (*less communicative than ever, somber*):   I can't keep my mind on the story.

MOLINA: Is it boring you?

VALENTIN: No, it's not that. It's . . . My head is in a state. (*He talks more to himself than to* MOLINA.) I just want to be quiet for a while. I don't know if this has ever happened to you, that you're just about to understand something, you've got the end of the thread and if you don't yank it now . . . you'll lose it.

MOLINA: Why do you like the architect girl?

VALENTIN: It has to come out some way or other. . . . (*Self-contemptuous.*) Weakness, I mean . . .

MOLINA: Ttt . . . it's not weakness.

VALENTIN (*bitter, impersonally*):   Funny how you just can't avoid getting attached to something. It's . . . it's as if the mind just oozed sentiment constantly.

MOLINA: Is that what you believe?

VALENTIN: Like a leaky tap. Drips falling over anything.

MOLINA: Anything?

VALENTIN: You can't stop the drips.

MOLINA: And you don't want to be reminded of your girlfriend, is that it?

VALENTIN (*mistrustful*):   How do you know whether I have a girlfriend?

MOLINA: It's only natural.

VALENTIN: I can't help it. . . . I get attached to anything that reminds me of her. Anyway, I'd do better to get my mind on what I ought to, right?

MOLINA: Yank the thread.

VALENTIN: Exactly.

MOLINA: And if you get it all in a tangle, Missy Valentina, you'll flunk needlework.

VALENTIN: Don't worry on my account.

MOLINA: Okay, I won't say another word.

VALENTIN: And don't call me Valentina. I'm not a woman.

MOLINA: How should I know?

VALENTIN: I'm sorry, Molina, but I don't give demonstrations.

MOLINA: I wasn't asking for one.

SCENE III

(SCENE: *Night. The prison light is on.* MOLINA *and* VALENTIN *are sitting on the floor, eating.*)

VALENTIN (*speaking as soon as he finishes his last mouthful*):   You're a good cook.

MOLINA: Thank you, Valentin.

VALENTIN: It could cause problems later on. I'm getting spoiled.

MOLINA: You're crazy. Live for today!

VALENTIN: I don't believe in that live for today crap. We haven't earned that paradise yet.

MOLINA: Do you believe in Heaven and Hell?

VALENTIN: Hold on a minute. If we're going to have a discussion then we need a framework. Otherwise you'll just ramble on.

MOLINA: I'm not going to ramble.

VALENTIN: Okay. I'll state an opening proposition. Let me put it to you like this.

MOLINA: Put it any way you like.

VALENTIN: I can't live just for today. All I do is determined by the ongoing political struggle. D'you get me? Everything that I endure here, which is bad enough . . . is nothing if you compare it to torture . . . but you don't know what that's like.

MOLINA: I can imagine.

VALENTIN: No, Molina, you can't imagine what it's like. . . . Well, anyway, I can put up with all this because there's a blueprint. The essential thing is the social revolution and the pleasures of the senses come second. The greatest pleasure, well, it's knowing that I'm part of the most noble cause . . . my ideas, for instance . . . (*The prison lights go out. The* BLUE *nighttime light stays on.*) It's eight . . .

MOLINA: What do you mean "your ideas"?

VALENTIN: My ideals. Marxism. And that good feeling is one I can experience anywhere, even here in this cell, and even in torture. And that's my strength.

MOLINA: And what about your girlfriend?

VALENTIN: That has to be second too. And I'm second for her. Because she also knows what's most important. (MOLINA *remains silent.*) You don't look convinced.

MOLINA: Don't mind me. I'm going to turn in soon.

VALENTIN: You're mad! What about the panther-woman?

MOLINA: Tomorrow.

VALENTIN: What's up?

MOLINA: Look, Valentin, that's me. I get hurt easy. I cooked that food for you, with my supplies, and worse still I give you half my avocado—which is my favorite and could have eaten tomorrow . . . Result? You throw it in my face that I'm spoiling you. . . .

VALENTIN: Don't be so soft! It's just like a . . .

MOLINA: Say it!

VALENTIN: Say what?

MOLINA: I know what you were going to say, Valentin.

VALENTIN: Cut it out.

MOLINA: "It's just like a woman." That's what you were going to say.

VALENTIN: Yes.

MOLINA: And what's wrong with being soft like a woman? Why can't a man—or whatever—a dog, or a fairy—why can't he be sensitive if he feels like it?

VALENTIN: In excess, it can get in a man's way.

MOLINA: In the way of what? Of torturing someone?

VALENTIN: No, of getting rid of the torturers.

MOLINA: But if all men were like women then there'd be no torturers.

VALENTIN: And what would you do without men?

MOLINA: You're right. They're brutes, but I need them.

VALENTIN: Molina . . . you just said that if all men were like women there'd be no torturers. You've got a point there; kind of weird, but a point at least.

MOLINA: The way you say things. (*Imitating* VALENTIN.) "A point at least."

VALENTIN: I'm sorry I upset you.

MOLINA: I'm not upset.

VALENTIN: Well, cheer up, don't reproach me.

MOLINA: Do you want me to go on with the picture?

VALENTIN: Yeah, man, of course.

MOLINA: Man? What man? Tell me so he won't get away.

VALENTIN (*trying to hide that he finds this funny*):   Start.

MOLINA: Irina goes along to the psychoanalyst who's a ladykiller, real handsome.

VALENTIN: Tell me what you mean by real handsome. I'd like to know.

MOLINA: Well, let's get this straight, he isn't my type at all.

VALENTIN: Who's the actor?

MOLINA: I don't remember. Too skinny for my taste. With a pencil moustache. But there's something about him, so full of himself, he just puts you off. And he puts off Irina. She skips the next appointment, she lies to her husband and instead of going to the doctor's she puts on that black fleecy coat and goes to the zoo, to look at the panther. The keeper comes along, opens the cage, throws in the meat and closes the door again. But he's absent-minded and leaves the key in the lock. Irina sneaks up to the door and puts her hand on the key. And she just stands there, musing, rapt in her thoughts.

VALENTIN: What does she do then?

MOLINA: That's all for tonight. I'll continue tomorrow.

VALENTIN: At least, let me ask you something.

MOLINA: What?

VALENTIN: Who do you identify with? Irina or the architect girl?

MOLINA: With Irina—who do you think? *Moi*—always with the leading lady.

VALENTIN: Continue.

MOLINA: What about you? I guess you're stuck because the guy is such a wimp.

VALENTIN: Don't laugh—with the psychoanalyst. But I didn't say anything about your choice, so don't mock mine. . . . You know something? I'm finding it hard to keep my mind on it.

MOLINA: What's the problem?

VALENTIN: Nothing.

MOLINA: Come on, open up a little.

VALENTIN: When you said the girl was there in front of the cage, I imagined it was my girl who was in danger.

MOLINA: I understand.

VALENTIN: I shouldn't be telling you this, Molina. But I guess you've figured it all out for yourself anyhow. My girl is in the organization too.

MOLINA: So what.

VALENTIN: It's only that I don't want to burden you with information it's better you don't know.

MOLINA: With me, it's not a woman, a girlfriend I mean. It's my mother. She's got blood pressure and a weak heart.

VALENTIN: People can live for years with that.

MOLINA: Sure, but they don't need more aggravation, Valentin. Imagine the shame of having a son inside—and why.

VALENTIN: Look, the worst has already happened, hasn't it?

MOLINA: Yes, but the risk is ever-present inside her. It's that dodgy heart.

VALENTIN: She's waiting for you. Eight years'll fly by, what with remission and all that. . . .

MOLINA (*a little contrived*):   Tell me about your girlfriend if you like. . . .

VALENTIN: I'd give anything to hold her in my arms right now.

MOLINA: It won't be long. You're not in for life.

VALENTIN: Something might happen to her.

MOLINA: Write to her, tell her not to take chances, that you need her.

VALENTIN: Never. Impossible. If you think like that you'll never change anything in the world.

MOLINA (*not realizing he's mocking* VALENTIN):   And you think you're going to change the world?

VALENTIN: Yes, and I don't care that you laugh. It makes people laugh to hear this, but what I have to do before anything is to change the world.

MOLINA: Sure, but you can't do it just like that, *and* on your own.

VALENTIN: But I'm not on my own—that's it! I'm with her and all those other people who think like we do. That's the end of the thread that slips through my fingers . . . I'm not apart from my comrades—I'm with them, right now! . . . It doesn't matter whether I can see them or not.

MOLINA (*with a slight drawl, skeptically*):   If that makes you feel good, terrific!

VALENTIN: Christ, what a moron!

MOLINA: Sticks and stones . . .

VALENTIN: Don't provoke me then. I'm not some loudmouth who just spouts off about politics in a bar. The proof is that I'm in here.

MOLINA: I'm sorry.

VALENTIN: It's okay . . .

MOLINA (*pretending not to pry*):   You were going to tell me something . . . about your girlfriend.

VALENTIN: We'd better drop that.

MOLINA: As you like . . .

VALENTIN: Why it gets me so upset, I can't fathom.

MOLINA: Better not, then, if it upsets you . . .

VALENTIN: The one thing I shouldn't tell you is her name.

MOLINA: What sort of girl is she?

VALENTIN: She's twenty-four, two years younger than me.

MOLINA: Thirteen years younger than me. . . . No, I tell a lie, sixteen.

VALENTIN: She was always politically conscious. First it was . . . well, I needn't be shy with you, at first it was because of the sexual revolution.

MOLINA (*bracing himself for some saucy tidbit*):   That I wouldn't miss.

VALENTIN: She comes from a bourgeois family, not really wealthy, but comfortably off. But as a kid and all through her adolescence she had to watch her parents destroy each other. Her father was cheating her mother, you know what I mean?

MOLINA: No, I don't.

VALENTIN: Cheating her by not telling her he needed other relationships. I don't hold with monogamy.

MOLINA: But it's beautiful when a couple love each other for ever and ever.

VALENTIN: Is that what you'd like?

MOLINA: It's my dream.

VALENTIN: Why do you like men then?

MOLINA: What's that got to do with it? I want to marry a man—to love and to cherish, for ever and ever.

VALENTIN: So, basically, you're just a bourgeois man?

MOLINA: A bourgeois lady, please.

VALENTIN: If you were a woman you'd think otherwise.

MOLINA: The only thing I want is to live forever with a wonderful man.

VALENTIN: And that's impossible because . . . well, if he's a man, he wants a woman . . . you'll always be living in a fool's paradise.

MOLINA: Go on about your girlfriend. I don't want to talk about me.

VALENTIN: She was brought up to be the lady of the house. Piano lessons, French, drawing. . . . I'll tell you the rest tomorrow, Molina . . . I want to think about something I was studying today.

MOLINA: Now you're getting your own back.

VALENTIN: No, silly. I'm tired, too.

MOLINA: I'm not sleepy at all.

SCENE IV

(SCENE: *Night. The prison lights are on.* VALENTIN *is engrossed in a book.* MOLINA, *restless, is flicking through a magazine he already knows backwards.*)

VALENTIN (*lifting his head from the book*): Why are they late with dinner? Next door had it ages ago.

MOLINA (*ironic*): Is *that* all you're studying tonight? I'm not hungry, thank goodness.

VALENTIN: That's unusual. Don't you feel well?

MOLINA: No, just nerves.

VALENTIN: Listen . . . I think they're coming.

MOLINA: Hide the magazines or they'll pinch them.

VALENTIN: I'm famished.

MOLINA: Please Valentin, don't make a scene with the guards.

VALENTIN: No.

(*Through the grille in the door come two plates of porridge—one visibly more loaded than the other.* MOLINA *looks at* VALENTIN.)

VALENTIN: Porridge.

MOLINA: Yes. (MOLINA *looks at the two plates which* VALENTIN *has collected from the hatch. Exchanging an enigmatic glance with the invisible guard*). Thank you.

VALENTIN (*to guard*): What about this one? Why's it got less? (*To* MOLINA.) I didn't say anything for your sake. Otherwise I'd have thrown it in his face, this bloody glue.

MOLINA: What's the use of complaining?

VALENTIN: One plate's only got half as much as the other. That bastard guard, he's out of his fucking mind.

MOLINA: It's okay, Valentin, I'll take the small portion.

VALENTIN (*serving* MOLINA *the large one*):　No, you like porridge, you always lap it up.

MOLINA:　Skip the chivalry. You have it.

VALENTIN:　I told you no.

MOLINA:　Why should I have the big one?

VALENTIN:　Because I know you like porridge.

MOLINA:　But I'm not hungry.

VALENTIN:　Eat it, it'll do you good. (VALENTIN *starts eating from the small plate*.)

MOLINA:　No.

VALENTIN:　It's not too bad today.

MOLINA:　I don't want it.

VALENTIN:　Afraid of putting on weight?

MOLINA:　No.

VALENTIN:　Get stuck in then. This porridge à la glue isn't so bad today. This small plate is plenty for me.

MOLINA (*starts eating, overcoming his resistance; his voice nostalgic now*):　Thursday. Ladies day. The cinema in my neighborhood used to show a romantic triple feature on Thursdays. Years ago now.

VALENTIN:　Is that where you saw the panther-woman?

MOLINA:　No, that was in a smart little cinema in that German neighborhood where all those posh houses with gardens are. My house was near there, but in the rundown part. Every Monday they'd show a German-language feature. Even during the war. They still do.

VALENTIN:　Nazi propaganda films.

MOLINA:　But the musical numbers were fabulous!

VALENTIN:　You're touched. (*He finishes his dinner*.) They'll be turning off the lights soon, that's it for studying today. (*Unconsciously authoritarian*.) You can go on with the film now—Irina's hand was on the key in the lock.

MOLINA (*picking at his porridge*):　She takes the key out of the lock and gives it back to the keeper. The old fellow thanks her and she goes back home to wait for her husband. She's all out to kiss him, on the mouth this time.

VALENTIN (*absorbed*):　Mmmm . . .

MOLINA:　Irina calls him up at his office, it's getting late, and the girl architect answers. Irina hangs up. She's eaten up with jealousy. She paces up and down the apartment like a caged beast, and when she walks by the bird cage she notices that the bird's wings are flapping frenetically. She can't control herself and she opens the little door and puts her hand right inside the cage. The little bird drops stone dead before she even touches it. Irina panics and flees from the house looking for her husband, but, of course, she has to go past the bar on the corner and she sees them both inside. And she just wants to tear the other woman to shreds. Irina only wears black clothes but she's never again worn that blouse he liked so much, the one in the restaurant scene, with all the rhinestones.

VALENTIN:　What are they?

MOLINA (*shocked*):　Rhinestones! I don't believe this! You don't know . . . ?

VALENTIN:　I haven't the faintest.

MOLINA:　They're like diamonds only worthless; little pieces of glass that shine.

(*At this moment the cell light goes out.*)

VALENTIN: I'm going to turn in early tonight. I've had enough of all this drivel.

MOLINA (*overreacting, but deeply hurt*):   Thank goodness there's no light so I don't have to see your face. Don't ever speak another word to me!

> (*Note: The production must establish that when the blue light is on—meaning nighttime—THEY CANNOT SEE EACH OTHER, and so are free to express themselves as they like in gestures and body language.*)

VALENTIN: I'm sorry . . . (MOLINA *stays silent.*) Really, I'm sorry, I didn't think you'd get so upset.

MOLINA: You upset me because it's one of my favorite movies, you can't know . . . (*He starts to cry.*) . . . you didn't see it.

VALENTIN: Are you crazy? It's nothing to cry about.

MOLINA: I'll . . . I'll cry if I feel like it.

VALENTIN: Suit yourself. . . . I'm very sorry.

MOLINA: And don't get the idea you've made me cry. It's because today's my mother's birthday and I'm dying to be with her. . . . And not with you. (*Pause.*) Ay! . . . Ay! . . . I don't feel well.

VALENTIN: What's wrong?

MOLINA: Ay! . . . Ay!

VALENTIN: What is it? What's the matter?

MOLINA: The girl's fucked!

VALENTIN: Which girl?

MOLINA: Me, dummy. It's my stomach.

VALENTIN: Do you want to throw up?

MOLINA: The pain's lower down. It's in my guts.

VALENTIN: I'll call the guard, okay?

MOLINA: No, it'll pass, Valentin.

VALENTIN: The food didn't do anything to me.

MOLINA: I bet it's my nerves. I've been on edge all day. I think it's letting up now.

VALENTIN: Try to relax. Relax your arms and legs, let them go loose.

MOLINA: Yes, that's better. I think it's going.

VALENTIN: Do you want to go to sleep?

MOLINA: I don't know . . . Ugh! it's awful . . .

VALENTIN: Maybe it'd be better if you talk, it'll take your mind off the pain.

MOLINA: You mean the movie?

VALENTIN: Where had we got to?

MOLINA: Afraid I'm going to croak before we get to the end?

VALENTIN: This is for your benefit. We broke off when they were in the bar on the corner.

MOLINA: Okay . . . the two of them get up together to leave and Irina takes cover behind a tree. The architect girl decides to take the shortcut home through the park. He told her everything while they were in the bar, that Irina doesn't make love to him, that she has nightmares about panther-women and all. The other girl, who'd just got used to the idea that she'd lost him, now begins to think maybe she has a chance again. So she's walking along and then you hear heels clicking behind her. She turns round and sees the silhouette of a woman. And then the clicking gets faster and now, right, the girl begins to get frightened, because you know what it's like when you've been talking about scary things. . . . But she's right in the middle of the park and if she starts to run she'll be in even worse trouble . . . and, then, suddenly, you can't hear the human footsteps any-more. . . . Ay! . . . Ay! . . . it's still hurting me.

SCENE V

(SCENE: *Day.* VALENTIN *is lying down, doubled up with stomach pains.* MOLINA *stands looking on at him.*)

VALENTIN: You can't imagine how much it hurts. Like a stabbing pain.
MOLINA: Just what I had two days ago.
VALENTIN: And each time it gets worse, Molina.
MOLINA: You should go to the clinic.
VALENTIN: Don't be thick, I already told you I don't want to go.
MOLINA: They'll only give you a little Seconal. It can't harm you.
VALENTIN: Of course it can; you can get hooked on it. You don't have a clue.
MOLINA: About what?
VALENTIN: Nothing.
MOLINA: Go on, tell me. Don't be like that.
VALENTIN: It happened to one of my comrades once. They got him hooked, his will power just went. A political prisoner can't afford to end up in a prison hospital. You follow me? Never. Once you're in there they come along and interrogate you and you have no resistance. . . . Ay! . . . Ay! . . . It feels like my guts are splitting open. Aaargh!
MOLINA: I told you not to gobble down your food like that.
VALENTIN (*raising himself with difficulty*):   You were right. I'm ready to burst.
MOLINA: Stretch out a little.
VALENTIN: No, I don't want to sleep, I had nightmares all last night and this morn-ing.
MOLINA (*relenting, like a middle-class housewife*):   I swore I wouldn't tell you another film. I'll probably go to hell for breaking my word.
VALENTIN: Ay! . . . Oh, fucking hell . . . (MOLINA *hesitates.*) You carry on. Pay no attention if I groan.
MOLINA: I'll tell you another movie, one for tummy ache. Now, you seemed keen on those German movies, am I right?
VALENTIN: In their propaganda machine . . . but, listen, go on with the panther-woman. We left off where the architect girl stopped hearing the human foot-steps behind her in the park.
MOLINA: Well . . . she's shaking with fear, she won't dare turn around in case she sees the panther. She stops for a second to see if she still can't hear the woman's

footsteps, but there's nothing, absolute silence, and then suddenly she begins to notice this rustling noise coming from the bushes being stirred by the wind . . . or maybe by something else. . . . (MOLINA *imitates the actions he describes.*) And she turns round with a start.

VALENTIN: I think I want to go to the toilet again.

MOLINA: Shall I call them to open up?

VALENTIN: They'll catch on that I'm ill.

MOLINA: They're not going to whip you into hospital for a dose of the runs.

VALENTIN: It'll go away, carry on with the story.

MOLINA: Okay . . . (*Repeating the same actions.*) . . . she turns around with a start . . .

VALENTIN: Ay! . . . ay! the pain . . .

MOLINA (*suddenly*):   Tell me something: you never told me why your mother doesn't bring you any food.

VALENTIN: She's a . . . a difficult woman. That's why I don't talk about her. She could never stand my ideas—she believes she's entitled to everything she's got, her family's got a certain position to keep up.

MOLINA: The family name.

VALENTIN: Only second league, but a name all the same.

MOLINA: Let her know that she can bring you a week's supplies at a time. You're only spiting yourself.

VALENTIN: If I'm in here it's because I brought it on myself, it's got nothing to do with her.

MOLINA: My mother didn't visit lately 'cos she's ill, did I tell you?

VALENTIN: You never mentioned it.

MOLINA: She thinks she's going to recover from one minute to the next. She won't let anyone but her bring me food, so I'm in a pickle.

VALENTIN: If you could get out of this hole she'd improve, right?

MOLINA: You're a mind reader. . . . Okay, let's get on with it. (*Repeating the same action as before.*) She turns round with a start.

VALENTIN: Ay! . . . Ay! . . . What have I gone and done? I'm sorry.

MOLINA: No, no. . . hold still, don't clean yourself with the sheet, wait a second.

VALENTIN: No, not your shirt . . .

MOLINA: Here, take it, wipe yourself with it. You'll need the sheet to keep warm.

VALENTIN: No, you haven't got a change of shirt.

MOLINA: Wait . . . get up, that way it won't go through . . . like this . . . mind it doesn't soil the sheet.

VALENTIN: Did it go through?

MOLINA: Your underpants held it in. Here, take them off . . .

VALENTIN: I'm embarrassed . . .

MOLINA: Didn't you say you have to be a man . . . ? So what's all this about being embarrassed?

VALENTIN: Wrap my underpants up well, Molina, so they don't smell.

MOLINA: I know how to handle this. You see . . . all wrapped up in the shirt. It'll be easier to wash than the sheet. Take the toilet paper.

VALENTIN: No, not yours. You'll have none left.

MOLINA: You never had any. So cut it out.

VALENTIN: Thank you. (*He takes the tissue and wipes himself and hands the roll back to* MOLINA.)

MOLINA: You're welcome. Relax a little, you're shaking.

VALENTIN: It's with rage. I could cry . . . I'm furious for letting myself get caught.

MOLINA: Calm down. Pull yourself together. (VALENTIN *watches* MOLINA *wrap the shirt and soiled tissue in a newspaper.*)

VALENTIN: Good idea . . . so it won't smell, eh?

MOLINA: Clever, isn't it?

VALENTIN: I'm freezing.

MOLINA (*Meanwhile lighting the stove and putting water on to boil*): I'm just making some tea. We're down to the last little bag. It's camomile, good for the nerves.

VALENTIN: No, leave it, it'll go away now.

MOLINA: Don't be silly.

VALENTIN: You're crazy—you're using up all your supplies.

MOLINA: I'll be getting more soon.

VALENTIN: But your mother's sick and can't come.

MOLINA: I'll continue. (*With irony. Repeating the same gestures as before but without the same élan.*) She turns round with a start. The rustling noise gets nearer and she lets rip with a desperate scream, when . . . whack! the door of the bus opens in front of her. The driver saw her standing there and stopped for her. . . . The tea's almost ready. (MOLINA *pours the hot water.*)

VALENTIN: Thanks. I mean that sincerely. And I want to apologize. . . . sometimes I get too rough and hurt people without thinking.

MOLINA: Don't talk nonsense.

VALENTIN: Instead of a film, I want to tell you something real. About me. I lied when I told you about my girlfriend. I was talking about another one, someone I loved very much. I didn't tell you the truth about my real girlfriend, you'd like her a lot, she's just a sweet and simple kid, but really courageous.

MOLINA: Please don't tell me anything about her. I don't want to know anything about your political business.

VALENTIN: Don't be dumb. Who's going to question you about me?

MOLINA: They might interrogate me.

VALENTIN (*finishing his tea; much improved*): You trust me, don't you?

MOLINA: Yes . . .

VALENTIN: Well, then . . . Inside here it's got to be share and share alike.

MOLINA: It's not that . . .

VALENTIN (*he lies down on the pillow, relaxing*): There's nothing worse than feeling bad about having hurt someone. And I hurt her, I forced her to join the organization when she wasn't ready for it, she's very . . . unsophisticated.

MOLINA: But don't tell me anymore now. I'm doing the telling for the moment. Where were we? Where did we stop? . . . (*Hearing no response,* MOLINA *looks at* VALENTIN *who has fallen asleep.*) How did it continue? What comes next? (MOLINA *feels proud of having helped his fellow cellmate.*)

SCENE VI

(SCENE: *Daylight. Both* MOLINA *and* VALENTIN *are stretched out on their beds, lost in a private sorrow. In the distance we hear a bolero tune.*)

MOLINA (*singing softly*):   "My love, I write to you again
    The night brings an urge to inquire
    If you, too, dear, recall the tender pain
    And the sad dreams our love would inspire."

VALENTIN: What's that you're singing?

MOLINA: A bolero. "My letter."

VALENTIN: Only you would go for that stuff.

MOLINA: What's wrong with it?

VALENTIN: It's romantic eyewash, that's what. You're daft.

MOLINA: I'm sorry. I think I've put my foot in it.

VALENTIN: In what?

MOLINA: Well, after you got that letter you were really down in the dumps and here I am singing about sad love letters.

VALENTIN: It was some bad news. You can read it if you like.

MOLINA: Better not.

VALENTIN: Don't start all that again; no one's going to ask you anything. Besides, they read it through before I did. (*He unfolds the letter and reads it as he talks.*)

MOLINA: The handwriting's like hen's tracks.

VALENTIN: She didn't have much education. . . . One of the comrades was killed, and now she's leader of the group. It's all written in CODE.

MOLINA: Ah . . .

VALENTIN: And she writes that she's having relations with another of the lads, just like I told her.

MOLINA: What relations?

VALENTIN: She was missing me too much. In the organization we take an oath not to get too involved with someone because it can paralyze you when you go into action.

MOLINA: Into action?

VALENTIN: Direct action. Risking your life. . . . We can't afford to worry about someone who wants us to go on living because it makes you scared of dying. Well, maybe not scared exactly, but you hate the suffering it'll cause others. And that's why she's having a relationship with another comrade.

MOLINA: You said that your girlfriend wasn't really the one you told me about.

VALENTIN: Damn, staring at this letter has made me dizzy again.

MOLINA: You're still weak.

VALENTIN: I'm shivering and I feel queasy. (*He covers himself with the sheet.*)

MOLINA: I told you not to start taking food again.

VALENTIN: But I was famished. (MOLINA *helps* VALENTIN *wrap up well.*)

MOLINA: You were getting better yesterday and then you went and ate and got sick again. And today it's the same story. Promise me you won't touch a thing tomorrow.

VALENTIN: The girl I told you about, the bourgeois one, she joined the organization with me but she dropped out and tried to persuade me to split with her.

MOLINA: Why?

VALENTIN: She loved life too much and she was happy just to be with me, that's all she wanted. So we had to break up.

MOLINA: Because you loved each other too much.

VALENTIN: You make it sound like one of your boleros.

MOLINA: The truth is you mock those songs because they're too close to home. You laugh to keep from crying. As a tango says.

VALENTIN: I was lying low for a while in that guy's flat, the one they killed. With his wife and kid. I even used to change the kid's nappies. . . . And do you want to know what the worst of it is? I can't write to a single one of them without blowing them to the police.

MOLINA: Not even to your girlfriend?

VALENTIN (*struggling to hold back his tears*): Oh, God! . . . what a mess! . . . it's all so sad!

MOLINA: There's nothing you can do.

VALENTIN: Help me get my arm from under . . . the blanket.

MOLINA: What for?

VALENTIN: Give me your hand, Molina. Squeeze hard . . .

MOLINA: Hold it tight.

VALENTIN: There's something else. It's wrecking me. It's shameful, awful . . .

MOLINA: Tell me, get it off your chest.

VALENTIN: It's . . . the girl I want to hear from, the one I want to have next to me right now and hug and kiss . . . it's not the one in the movement, but the other one . . . Marta, that's her name . . .

MOLINA: If that's what you feel deep down . . . Oh, I forgot, if your stomach feels real empty, there's a few digestives I'd forgotten all about. (*Without taking his hand from* VALENTIN*'s he reaches for the packet of digestives.*)

VALENTIN: For all I shoot my mouth off about progress . . . when it comes to women, what I really like is a woman with class and I'm just like all the reactionary sons-of-bitches that killed my comrade. . . . The same, exactly the same . . .

MOLINA: That's not true . . .

VALENTIN: And sometimes I think maybe I don't even love Marta because of who she is but because she's got . . . class . . . I'm just like all the other class-conscious sons-of-bitches . . . in the world.

GUARD'S VOICE: Luis Alberto Molina! To the visiting room!

> (VALENTIN *and* MOLINA *let go of each other's hand as if caught in a shameful act. The cell door opens and* MOLINA *exits, but not before he's managed to slip the biscuits under* VALENTIN*'s blanket. Hereafter, the dialogue is on prerecorded tape. Meanwhile,* VALENTIN *remains on stage and takes the biscuits from under his covers, manages to find just three at the bottom of the large packet and begins to eat them, one at a time, savoring each one.*)

WARDEN'S VOICE: Stop shaking, man, no one's going to do anything to you.

MOLINA'S VOICE: I had a bad stomach ache before, sir, but I'm fine now.

WARDEN'S VOICE: You've got nothing to be afraid of. We've made it look like you've had a visitor. The other one won't suspect a thing.

MOLINA'S VOICE: No, he won't suspect anything.

WARDEN'S VOICE: At home last night I had dinner with your protector and he had some good news for you. Your mother is on the road to recovery . . . it seems the chance of your pardon is doing her good . . .

MOLINA'S VOICE: Are you sure?

WARDEN'S VOICE: What's the matter with you? Why are you trembling? . . . You should be jubilant. . . . Well, have you got any news for me yet? Has he told you anything? Is he opening up to you?

MOLINA'S VOICE: No, sir, not so far. You have to take these things a step at a time.

WARDEN'S VOICE: Didn't it help at all when we weakened him physically?

MOLINA'S VOICE: I had to eat the first plate of fixed food myself.

WARDEN'S VOICE: You shouldn't have done that.

MOLINA'S VOICE: The truth is he doesn't like porridge and since one portion was bigger than the other . . . he insisted I eat it. If I'd refused he might have got suspicious. You told me, sir, that the doctored food would be on the newest plate but they made a mistake piling it high like that.

WARDEN'S VOICE: Ah, well, in that case, I'm obliged to you, Molina. I'm sorry about the mistake.

MOLINA'S VOICE: Now you should let him get some of his strength back.

WARDEN'S VOICE (*irritated*):   That's for us to decide. We know what we're doing. And when you get back to your cell say you had a visit from your mother. That'll explain why you're so excited.

MOLINA'S VOICE: No, I couldn't say that, she always brings me a food parcel.

WARDEN'S VOICE: Okay, we'll send out for some groceries. Think of it as a reward for the trouble with the porridge. Poor Molina!

MOLINA'S VOICE: Thank you, Warden.

WARDEN'S VOICE: Reel off a list of what she usually brings. (*Pause.*) Now!

MOLINA'S VOICE: To you?

WARDEN'S VOICE: Yes, and be quick about it, I've got work to catch up with.

MOLINA'S VOICE (*as the curtain falls*):   A tin of treacle, a can of peaches . . . two roast chickens . . . a big bag of sugar . . . two packs of tea, one breakfast, one camomile . . . powdered milk, a bar of soap, bathsize . . . oh, let me think a second, my mind's a complete blank . . .

ACT II

SCENE VII

(SCENE: *Lighting as in previous scene. The cell door opens and* MOLINA *enters with a shopping bag.*)

MOLINA: Look what I've got!!!

VALENTIN: No! Your mother?

MOLINA: Yes!!

VALENTIN: So she's better now?

MOLINA: A little better. . . . And look what she brought me. Ooops! Sorry, brought us!

VALENTIN (*secretly flattered*): No, it's for you. Cut the nonsense.

MOLINA: Shut it, you're the invalid. The chickens are for you, they'll get you back on your feet.

VALENTIN: No, I won't let you do this.

MOLINA: It's no sacrifice. I can go without the chicken if it means I don't have to put up with your pong . . . No, listen, I'm being serious now, you've got to stop eating this pig swill they serve in here. At least for a day or two.

VALENTIN: You think so?

MOLINA: And then when you're better . . . Close your eyes. (VALENTIN *closes his eyes and* MOLINA *places a large tin in one of his hands.*) Three guesses . . .

VALENTIN: Ahem . . . er . . . er . . . (*Enjoying the game.* MOLINA *places an identical one in* VALENTIN'*s other hand.*)

MOLINA: The weight ought to help you . . .

VALENTIN: Heavy all right . . . I give up.

MOLINA: Open your eyes.

VALENTIN: Treacle!

MOLINA: But you can't have it yet, not until you're better. And this is for both of us.

VALENTIN: Marvellous.

MOLINA: First . . . we'll have a cup of camomile tea because my nerves are shot and you can have a drumstick, no, better not, it's only five. . . . Anyway, we can have tea and some biscuits, they're even lighter than those digestives.

VALENTIN: Please, can't I have one right away?

MOLINA: Why not! But no treacle on it—just marmalade! . . . Luckily, everything she brought is easy to get down so it won't give you any trouble. Except the treacle for the time being.

VALENTIN: Oh, Molina, I'm wilting with hunger. Why won't you let me have that chicken leg now?

MOLINA (*he hesitates a moment*): Here . . .

VALENTIN (*wolfing down the chicken*): Honest, I really was beginning to feel bad. . . . (*He devours the chicken.*) Thanks . . .

MOLINA: You're welcome.

VALENTIN (*his mouth full*): But there's just one thing missing to round off the picnic.

MOLINA: Tut, and I thought I was supposed to be the pervert here.

VALENTIN: Stop fooling around! What we need is a movie . . .

MOLINA: Ah! . . . Well, now there's a scene where Irina has a completely new hairstyle.

VALENTIN: Oh, I'm sorry, I don't feel too good, it's that dizziness again.

MOLINA: Are you positive?

VALENTIN: Yes, it's been threatening all night.

MOLINA: But it can't be the chicken. Maybe you're imagining it.

VALENTIN: I felt full up all of a sudden.

MOLINA: That's because you wolfed it down without even chewing.

VALENTIN: And this itching is driving me wild. I don't know when I last had a bath.

MOLINA: Don't even think about that. That freezing water in your present state! (*Pause.*) Anyway, she looks stunning here, you can see her reflection in a window-pane, it's drizzling and all the drops are running down the glass. She's got raven black hair and it's all scooped up in a bun. Let me describe it to you. . . .

VALENTIN: It's all scooped up, okay, never mind the silly details. . . .

MOLINA: Silly, my foot! And she's got a rhinestone flower in her hair.

VALENTIN (*very agitated now because of his itch*):   I know what rhinestones are so you can save your breath!

MOLINA: My, you are touchy today!

VALENTIN: Do you mind if I say something?

MOLINA: Go ahead.

VALENTIN: I feel all screwed up—and confused. If it's not too much trouble I'd like to dictate a letter to her. Would you mind taking it down? . . . I get dizzy if I try to focus my eyes too hard.

MOLINA: Let me get a pencil.

VALENTIN: You're very kind to me.

MOLINA: We'll do a rough draft first on a bit of paper.

VALENTIN: Here, take my pen-case.

MOLINA: Wait till I sharpen this pencil.

VALENTIN (*short-tempered*):   I told you! Use one of mine!

MOLINA: Okay, don't blow your top!

VALENTIN: I'm sorry, it's just that everything is going black.

MOLINA: Okay, ready, shoot . . .

VALENTIN (*very sad*):   Dear Marta . . . you don't expect this letter. . . . In your case, it won't endanger you. . . . I'm feeling . . . lonely, I need you, I want to be . . . near you . . . I want you to give me . . . a word of encouragement.

MOLINA: . . . "of encouragement" . . .

VALENTIN: . . . in this moment I couldn't face my comrades, I'd be ashamed of being so weak. . . . I have sores all over inside, I need somebody to pour some honey . . . over my wounds. . . . And only you could understand . . . because you too were brought up in a nice clean house to enjoy life to the full, . . . I can't accept becoming a martyr, it makes me angry to be one . . . or, it isn't that, I see it clearer now . . . I'm afraid because I'm sick, horribly afraid of dying . . . that it may just end here, that my life has amounted to nothing more than this, I never exploited anyone . . . and ever since I had any sense I've been struggling against the exploitation of my fellow man . . .

MOLINA: Go on.

VALENTIN: Where was I?

MOLINA: "My fellow man" . . .

VALENTIN: . . . because I want to go out into the street one day and not die. And sometimes I get this idea that never ever again will I be able to touch a woman, and I can't accept it, and when I think of women I only see you, and what a relief it would be to believe that right until I finish writing this letter you'll be thinking of me . . . and that you'll be running your hands over your body I so well remember . . .

MOLINA: Hold on, don't go so fast.

VALENTIN: over your body I so well remember, and you'll be thinking that it's my hand . . . it would be as if I were touching you, darling . . . because there's still something of me inside you, isn't that so? Just as your own scent has stayed in my nose . . . beneath my fingertips lies a sort of memory of your skin, do you understand me? Although it's not a matter of understanding . . . it's a matter of believing, and sometimes I'm convinced that I took something of you with me . . . and that I haven't lost it, and then sometimes not, I feel there's just me all alone in this cell . . . (*Pause.*)

MOLINA: Yes, "all alone in this cell" . . . Go on.

VALENTIN: . . . because nothing leaves any trace, and my luck in having had such happiness with you, of spending those nights and afternoons and mornings of sheer enjoyment, none of this is any use now, just the opposite, it all turns against me, because I miss you madly, and all I can feel is the torture of my loneliness, and in my nose there is only the stench of this cell, and of myself . . . and I can't have a wash because I'm ill, really weak, and the cold water would give me pneumonia and beneath my fingertips what I feel is the chill of my fear of death, I can feel it in my joints . . . what a terrible thing to lose hope and that's what's happened to me . . .

MOLINA: I'm sorry for butting in . . .

VALENTIN: What is it?

MOLINA: When you finish dictating the letter there's something I want to say.

VALENTIN (*wound up*):   What?

MOLINA: Because if you take one of those freezing showers it'll kill you.

VALENTIN (*almost hysterical*):   And? . . . So what? Tell me, for Christ's sake.

MOLINA: I could help you to get cleaned up. You see, we've got the hot water we were going to use to boil the potatoes and we've got two towels, so we lather one of them and you do your front and I'll do the back and then you can dry yourself with the other towel.

VALENTIN: And then I'd stop itching?

MOLINA: Sure. And we'd clean a bit at a time so you won't catch cold.

VALENTIN: And you'll help me?

MOLINA: Of course I will.

VALENTIN: When?

MOLINA: Now, if you like. The water's boiling, we can mix it with a little cold water. (MOLINA *starts to do this.*)

VALENTIN (*who can't believe in such happiness*):   And I'd be able to get to sleep without scratching?

MOLINA: Take your shirt off. I'll put some more water on. (*He mixes the hot and cold water.*)

VALENTIN: Give me the letter, Molina.

MOLINA: What for?

VALENTIN: Just hand it over.

MOLINA: Here. (VALENTIN *tears it up.*) What are you doing???

VALENTIN: This. (*He tears it into quarters.*) Let's not mention it again.

MOLINA: As you like . . .

VALENTIN: It's wrong to get carried away like that by despair.

MOLINA: But it's good to get it into the open. You said so yourself.

VALENTIN: But it's bad for me. I have to learn to restrain myself. (*Pause.*) Listen, I mean it, one day I'll thank you properly for all this. (MOLINA *puts more water on the stove.*) Are you going to waste all that water?

MOLINA: Yes . . . and don't be daft, there's no need to thank me. (MOLINA *signals to* VALENTIN *to turn around.*)

VALENTIN: Tell me, how does the movie end, just the last scene.

MOLINA (*scrubbing* VALENTIN's *back*):   It's either all or nothing.

VALENTIN: Why?

MOLINA: Because of the details. Her hairdo is important, it's the style that women wear, or used to wear, when they wanted to show that this was a crucial moment in their lives, because the hair all scooped up in a bun which left the neck bare, gave the woman's face a certain nobility. (VALENTIN, *despite the tensions and turmoil of the difficult day, changes his expression and smiles.*) Why have you got that mocking little grin on your face? I don't see anything to laugh at.

VALENTIN: Because my back doesn't itch anymore!

SCENE VIII

(SCENE: *Day.* MOLINA *is tidying up his belongings with extreme care so as not to wake* VALENTIN. VALENTIN, *nevertheless, wakes up. Both of them are charged with renewed energy and the dialogue begins at its normal pace but accelerates rapidly into tenseness.*)

VALENTIN: Good morning.

MOLINA: Good morning.

VALENTIN: What's the time?

MOLINA: Ten past ten. I call my mother "ten past ten," the poor dear, because of the way her feet stick out when she walks.

VALENTIN: It's late.

MOLINA: When they brought the tea round you just turned over and carried on sleeping.

VALENTIN: What were you saying about your old lady?

MOLINA: Look who's still sleeping. Nothing. Sleep well?

VALENTIN: I feel a lot better.

MOLINA: You don't feel dizzy?

VALENTIN: Lying in bed, no.

MOLINA: Great—why don't you try to walk a little?

VALENTIN: No—you'll laugh.

MOLINA: At what?

VALENTIN: Something that happens to a normal healthy man when he wakes up in the morning with too much energy.

MOLINA: You've got a hard-on? Well, God bless . . .

VALENTIN: But look away, please. I get embarrassed. (*He gets up to wash his face with water from the jug.*)

MOLINA (*he puts his hand over his eyes and looks away*):   My eyes are shut tight.

VALENTIN: It's all thanks to your food. My legs are a bit shaky still, but I don't feel queasy. You can look now. (*He gets back into bed.*) I'll lie down a bit more.

MOLINA (*overprotective and smothering*):   I'll put the water on for tea.

VALENTIN: No, just reheat the crap they brought us this morning.

MOLINA: I threw it out when I went to the loo. You must look after yourself properly if you want to get better.

VALENTIN: It embarrasses me to use up your things. I'm better now.

MOLINA: Button it.

VALENTIN: No, listen . . .

MOLINA: Listen nothing. My mother's bringing stuff again.

VALENTIN: Okay, thanks, but just for today. (*He collects his books together.*)

MOLINA: And no reading. Rest! . . . I'll start another film while I'm making the tea.

VALENTIN: I'd better try and study, if I can, now that I'm on form. (*He starts to read.*)

MOLINA: Won't it be too tiring?

VALENTIN: I'll give it a go.

MOLINA: You're a real fanatic.

VALENTIN (*throwing the book to the ground as his tenseness increases*):   I can't . . . the words are jumping around.

MOLINA: I told you so. Are you feeling dizzy?

VALENTIN: Only when I try to read.

MOLINA: You know what it is? It's probably just a temporary weakness—if you have a ham sandwich you'll be right as rain.

VALENTIN: Do you think so?

MOLINA: Sure, and then later, after you've had lunch and another little snooze you'll feel up to studying again.

VALENTIN: I feel lazy as hell. I'll just lie down.

MOLINA (*schoolmistressy*):   No, lying in bed only weakens the constitution, you'd be better standing or at least sitting up. (MOLINA *hands him the tea.*)

VALENTIN: This is the last day I'm taking any more of this.

MOLINA (*mistress of the situation*):   Ha! Ha! I already told the guard not to bring you any more tea in the morning.

VALENTIN: Listen, you decide what you want for yourself, but I want them to bring me the tea even if it is horse's piss.

MOLINA: You don't know the first thing about a healthy diet.

VALENTIN (*trying to control himself*):   I'm not joking Molina, I don't like other people controlling my life.

MOLINA (*counting on his fingers*):   Today is Wednesday . . . everything will hang on what happens on Monday. That's what my lawyer says. I don't believe in appeals and all that but if there's someone who can pull a few strings, maybe there's a chance.

VALENTIN: I hope so.

MOLINA (*with concealed cunning, as he makes more tea*):   If they let me out . . . who knows who you'll get as a cellmate.

VALENTIN: Haven't you had breakfast yet?

MOLINA: I didn't want to disturb you. You were sleeping. (*He takes* VALENTIN's *cup to refill it.*) Will you join me in another cup?

VALENTIN: No, thanks.

MOLINA (*opening a new packet, not letting* VALENTIN *see*):   Tell me, what are you going to study later on?

VALENTIN: What are you doing?

MOLINA: A surprise. Tell me what you're reading.

VALENTIN: Nothing . . .

MOLINA: Cat got your tongue? . . . And now . . . we untie the mystery parcel . . . which I had hidden about my person . . . and, what have we got here? . . . Something that goes a treat with tea . . . a cherry madeira!

VALENTIN: No, thanks.

MOLINA: What d'you mean "no"? . . . the kettle's on . . . Oh, I know why not—you want to go to the loo. Ask them to open up and then fly back here.

VALENTIN: For Christ's sake, don't tell me what to do!

MOLINA (*he squeezes* VALENTIN's *chin*):   Oh, come on, let me pamper you a little.

VALENTIN: That's enough . . . you prick!

MOLINA: Are you crazy? . . . What's the matter with you?

VALENTIN (*he hurls the teacup and the cake against the wall*):   Shut your fucking trap!

MOLINA: The cake . . . (VALENTIN *is silent.*) Look what you've done . . . if the stove's broke, we're done for. . . . (*Pause.*) . . . and the saucer . . . (*Pause.*) . . . and the tea . . .

VALENTIN: I'm sorry . . . (MOLINA *is silent now.*) I lost control . . . I'm really sorry. (MOLINA *remains silent.*) The stove is okay; but the paraffin spilled. (MOLINA *still doesn't answer.*) . . . I'm sorry I got carried away, forgive me. . . .

MOLINA (*deeply wounded*):   There's nothing to forgive.

VALENTIN: There is. A lot.

MOLINA: Forget it. Nothing happened.

VALENTIN: It did, I'm dying with shame. (MOLINA *says nothing.*) . . . I behaved like an animal. . . . Look, I'll call the guard and fill up the bottle while I'm at it. We're almost out of water. . . . Molina, please, look at me. Raise your head. (MOLINA *remains silent.*)

GUARD'S VOICE: Luis Alberto Molina. To the visiting room!

> (*The door opens and* MOLINA *exits. The recorded dialogue begins as soon as* MOLINA *moves toward the door.* MOLINA *returns with the provisions to find* VALENTIN *picking up the things he has just thrown on the floor.* MOLINA *starts to unpack the shopping bag. The recorded dialogue is heard while the action takes place on stage.*)

WARDEN'S VOICE: Today's Monday, Molina, what have you got for me?

MOLINA'S VOICE: Nothing, I'm afraid, sir.

WARDEN'S VOICE: Indeed.

MOLINA'S VOICE: But he's taking me more into his confidence.

WARDEN'S VOICE: The problem is they're putting pressure on me, Molina. From the top: from the President's private office. You understand what I'm saying to you, Molina? They want to try interrogation again. Less carrot, more stick.

MOLINA'S VOICE: Not that sir. It'd be even worse if you lost him in interrogation.

WARDEN'S VOICE: That's what I tell them, but they won't listen.

MOLINA'S VOICE: Just one more week, sir. Please. I have an idea . . .

WARDEN'S VOICE: What?

MOLINA'S VOICE: He's a hard nut but he has an emotional side.

WARDEN'S VOICE: So?

MOLINA'S VOICE: Well, if the guard were to come and say they're moving me to another block in a week's time because of the appeal, that might really soften him up.

WARDEN'S VOICE: What are you driving at?

MOLINA'S VOICE: Nothing, I swear. It's just a hunch. If he thinks I'm leaving soon he'll feel like opening up even more with me. Prisoners are like that, sir . . . when one of their pals is leaving they feel more defenseless than ever.

> (*At this moment* MOLINA *is back in the cell and he takes out the food as the* WARDEN'S VOICE *mentions each item.* VALENTIN *looks at* MOLINA.)

WARDEN'S VOICE: Guard, take this down: two roast chickens, four baked apples, one carton of coleslaw, one pound of bacon, one pound of cooked ham, four French loaves, four pieces of crystallized fruit (*the recorded voice begins to fade out*) . . . a carton of orange juice, two cherry madeiras . . .

MOLINA (*very calm and very sad; still upset by* VALENTIN'*s remarks*): This is the bacon and this one's the ham. I'm going to make a sandwich while the bread's fresh. You fix yourself whatever you want.

VALENTIN (*deeply ashamed*): Thank you.

MOLINA (*reserved, calm*): I'm going to cut this roll in half and spread it with butter and have a ham sandwich. And a baked apple.

VALENTIN: Sounds delicious.

MOLINA: If you'd like some of the chicken while it's still warm, go ahead. Feel free.

VALENTIN: Thank you, Molina.

MOLINA: We'll each fend for ourselves. Then I won't get on your nerves.

VALENTIN: If that's what you prefer.

MOLINA: There's some crystallized fruit, too. All I ask is you leave me the pumpkin. Otherwise, take what you want.

VALENTIN (*finding it hard to apologize*): I'm still embarrassed . . . because of that tantrum.

MOLINA: Don't be silly.

VALENTIN: If I got annoyed with you . . . it was because you were kind to me . . . and I didn't want . . . to treat you the same way.

MOLINA: Look, I've been thinking too and I remembered something you once said, right? . . . that when you're involved in a struggle like that, well, it's not too convenient to get fond of someone. Well, fond is maybe going too far. . . . Or, why not? Fond as a friend.

VALENTIN: That's a very noble way of looking at it.

MOLINA: You see, sometimes I do understand what you tell me.

VALENTIN: But are we so fettered by the world outside that we can't act like human beings just for a minute . . . ? Is the enemy out there that powerful?

MOLINA: I don't follow.

VALENTIN: Our persecutors are on the outside, not inside this cell. . . . The problem is I'm so brainwashed that it freaks me out when someone is nice to me without asking anything in return.

MOLINA: I don't know about that . . .

VALENTIN: About what?

MOLINA: Don't get me wrong, but if I'm nice to you, well, it's because I want you to be my friend . . . and why not admit it? . . . I want your affection. Just like I treat my mother well because she's a good person and I want her to love me. And you're a good person too, and unselfish because you're risking your life for an ideal . . . that I don't understand but, all the same, it's not just for yourself. . . . Don't look away like that, are you embarrassed?

VALENTIN: A bit. (*He looks* MOLINA *in the face.*)

MOLINA: And that's why I respect you and have warm feelings toward you . . . and why I want you to like me . . . because, you see, my mother's love is the only good thing I've felt in my life, because she likes me . . . just the way I am.

VALENTIN (*pointing to the loaf* MOLINA *put aside*):   Can I cut the loaf for you?

MOLINA: Of course . . .

VALENTIN (*cutting the loaf*):   And did you never have good friends that meant a lot to you?

MOLINA: My friends were all . . . screaming queens, like me, we never really count on each other because . . . how can I express it?—because we know we're so easily frightened off. We're always looking, you know, for friendship, or whatever, with somebody more serious, with a man, you see? And that just doesn't happen, right? Because what a man wants is a woman.

VALENTIN (*taking a slice of ham for* MOLINA'S *sandwich*):   And are all homosexuals like that?

MOLINA: Oh no, there are some who fall in love with each other. But me and my friends we're women. One hundred percent. We don't go in for those little games. We're normal women; *we* only go to bed with men.

VALENTIN (*too absorbed to see the funny side of this*):   Butter?

MOLINA: Yes, thanks. There's something I have to tell you.

VALENTIN: Of course, the movie . . .

MOLINA (*with cunning, but nervous all the same*):   My lawyer said things were looking up.

VALENTIN: What a creep I am! I didn't ask you.

MOLINA: And when there's an appeal pending, the prisoner gets moved to another block in the prison. They'll probably shift me within a week or so.

VALENTIN (*upset by this but dissimulating*):   That's terrific . . . you ought to be pleased.

MOLINA: I don't want to dwell on it too much, build my hopes. . . . Have some coleslaw.

VALENTIN: Should I?

MOLINA: It's very good.

VALENTIN: Your news made me lose my appetite. (*He gets up.*)

MOLINA: Pretend I didn't say anything, nothing's settled yet.

VALENTIN: No, it all looks good for you, we should be happy.

MOLINA: Have some salad.

VALENTIN: I don't know what's wrong, but all of a sudden I don't feel too good.

MOLINA: Is your stomach hurting?

VALENTIN: No . . . it's my head. I'm all confused.

MOLINA: About what?

VALENTIN: Let me rest for a while.

(VALENTIN *sits down again, resting his head in his palms. The light changes to indicate a shift to a different time—the two characters stay where they are: there is a special tension, a hypersensitivity in the air.*)

MOLINA: The guy is all muddled up, he doesn't know how to handle this freaky wife of his. She comes in, sees that he's dead serious and goes to the bathroom to put away her shoes, all dirty with mud. He says he went to the doctor's to look for her and found out that she didn't go anymore. Then she breaks into tears and tells him that she's just what she always feared, a mad woman with hallucinations or even worse, a panther-woman. Then he gives in and takes her in his arms and you were right, she's really just a little girl for him, because when he sees her so defenseless and lost, he feels again he loves her with all his heart and tells her that everything will sort itself out. . . . (MOLINA *sighs deeply.*) Ahhh . . . !

VALENTIN: What a sigh!

MOLINA: Life is so difficult. . . .

VALENTIN: What's the matter?

MOLINA: I don't know, I'm afraid of building up my hopes of getting out of here . . . and that I'll get put in some other cell and spend my life there with God knows what sort of creep.

VALENTIN: Don't lose sight of this. Your mother's health is the most precious thing to you, right?

MOLINA: Yes . . .

VALENTIN: Think about her recovery. Period!

MOLINA (*he laughs involuntarily in his distress*):   I don't want to think about it.

VALENTIN: What's wrong?

MOLINA: Nothing!

VALENTIN: Don't bury your head in the pillow.... Are you keeping something from me?

MOLINA: It's ...

VALENTIN: It's what? ... Look, when you get out of here you're going to be a free man. You can join a political organization if you like.

MOLINA: You're crazy! They won't trust a fag.

VALENTIN: But I can tell you who to speak to....

MOLINA (*suddenly forceful, raising his head from the pillow*): Promise me on whatever you hold most dear, never, never, you understand, never tell me anything about your comrades.

VALENTIN: But who would ever think you're seeing them?

MOLINA: They could interrogate me, whatever, but if I know nothing, I say nothing.

VALENTIN: In any case, there are all kinds of groups, of political action; there are even some who just sit and talk. When you get out things'll be different.

MOLINA: Things *won't* be different. That's the worst of it.

VALENTIN: How many times have I seen you cry? Come on, you annoy me with your sniveling.

MOLINA: It's just that I can't take any more.... I've had nothing but bad luck ... always. (*The prison light goes out.*)

VALENTIN: Lights out already? ... In the first place you must join a group, avoid being alone.

MOLINA: I don't understand any of that ... (*Suddenly grave.*) ... and I don't believe in it much either.

VALENTIN (*tough*): Then like it or lump it.

MOLINA (*still crying a little*): Let's ... skip it.

VALENTIN (*conciliatory*): Come on, don't be like that.... (*He pats* MOLINA *on the back affectionately.*)

MOLINA: I'm asking you ... please don't touch me.

VALENTIN: Can't a friend pat you on the back?

MOLINA: It makes it worse....

VALENTIN: Why? ... Tell me what's troubling you....

MOLINA (*with deep, deep feeling*): I'm so tired, Valentin.... I'm tired of suffering. I hurt all over inside.

VALENTIN: Where does it hurt you?

MOLINA: Inside my chest and my throat.... Why does sadness always get you there? It's choking me, like a knot....

VALENTIN: It's true, that's where people always feel it. (MOLINA *is quiet.*) Is it hurting you a lot, this knot?

MOLINA: Yes.

VALENTIN: Is it here?

MOLINA: Yes.

VALENTIN: Want me to stroke it ... here?

MOLINA: Yes.

VALENTIN (*after a short pause*): This is relaxing....

MOLINA: Why relaxing, Valentin?

VALENTIN: Not to think about myself for a while. Thinking about you, that you need me, and I can be of some use to you.

MOLINA: You're always looking for explanations. . . . You're crazy.

VALENTIN: I don't want events to get the better of me. I want to know why they happen.

MOLINA: Can I touch you?

VALENTIN: Yes . . .

MOLINA: I want to touch that mole—the little round one over your eye. (*Pause.* MOLINA *touches the mole*.) You're very kind.

VALENTIN: No, you're the one who's kind.

MOLINA: If you like you can do what you want with me . . . because I want it too. . . . If it won't disgust you . . .

VALENTIN: Don't say that—let's not say anything. (VALENTIN *goes under* MOLINA's *top sheet*.) Shift a bit closer to the wall. . . . (*Pause.*) You can't see a thing it's so dark.

MOLINA: Gently . . . (*Pause.*) No, it hurts too much like that. (*Pause.*) Slowly please . . . (*Pause.*) That's it . . . (*Pause.*) . . . thanks . . .

VALENTIN: Thank you, too. Are you feeling better?

MOLINA: Yes. And what about you, Valentin?

VALENTIN: Don't ask me. . . . I don't know anything anymore. . . .

MOLINA: Oh, . . . it's beautiful . . .

VALENTIN: Don't say anything . . . not for now . . .

MOLINA: It's just that I feel . . . such strange things. . . . Without thinking, I just lifted my hand to my eye, looking for that mole.

VALENTIN: What mole? . . . *I'm* the one with the mole, not you.

MOLINA: I know, but I just lifted up my hand . . . to touch the mole . . . I don't have.

VALENTIN: Ssh, try and keep quiet for a while. . . .

MOLINA: And do you know what else I felt, but only for a minute, no longer . . .

VALENTIN: Tell me, but keep still, like that. . . .

MOLINA: For just a minute, it felt like I wasn't here . . . not in here, nor anywhere else . . . (*Pause.*) It felt like I wasn't here, there was just you. . . . Or that I wasn't me anymore. As if I was . . . you.

SCENE IX

(SCENE: *Day.* MOLINA *and* VALENTIN *are in their beds*.)

VALENTIN: Good morning. (*He is reinvigorated, happy.*)

MOLINA (*also highly charged*):   Good morning, Valentin.

VALENTIN: Did you sleep well?

MOLINA: Yes. (*Calmly, not insisting.*) Would you like tea or coffee?

VALENTIN: Coffee. To wake me up well—and study. Try to get back into the swing of things. . . . What about you? Is the gloom over? Or not?

MOLINA: Yes it is, but I feel groggy. I can't think . . . my mind's a blank.

VALENTIN: I don't want to think about anything either, so I'm going to read. That'll keep my mind off things.

MOLINA: Off what? Feeling guilty about what happened?

VALENTIN: I'm more and more convinced that sex is innocence itself.

MOLINA: Can I ask you a favor? . . . Let's not discuss anything, just for today.

VALENTIN: Whatever you like.

MOLINA: I feel . . . fine and I don't want anything to rob me of that feeling. I haven't felt so good since I was a kid. Since my mother bought me some toy.

VALENTIN: Do you remember what toy you liked most?

MOLINA: A doll.

VALENTIN: Ay!! (*He starts to laugh.*)

MOLINA: What's funny about that?

VALENTIN: As a psychologist I would starve.

MOLINA: Why?

VALENTIN: Nothing . . . I was just wondering if there was any link between your favorite toy and . . . me.

MOLINA (*playing along*): It was your own fault for asking.

VALENTIN: Are you sure it wasn't a boy doll?

MOLINA: Absolutely. She had blond braids and a little Tyrolese folk dress. (*They laugh together, unself-consciously.*)

VALENTIN: One question. . . . Physically, you're as much a man as I am.

MOLINA: Ummm . . .

VALENTIN: Why then don't you behave like a man. . . . I don't mean with women if you're not attracted to them, but with another man?

MOLINA: It's not me. I only enjoy myself like that.

VALENTIN: Well, if you like being a woman. . . you shouldn't feel diminished because of that. (MOLINA *doesn't answer.*) I mean you shouldn't feel you owe anyone, or feel obliged to them because that's what you happen to like. . . . You shouldn't yield . . .

MOLINA: But if a man is . . . my husband, he has to be boss to feel good. That's only natural.

VALENTIN: No, the man and the woman should be equal partners inside the home. Otherwise, it's exploitation. Don't you see?

MOLINA: But there's no thrill in that.

VALENTIN: What?

MOLINA: Since you want to know about it. . . . The thrill is that when a man embraces you, you're a bit afraid.

VALENTIN: Who put that idea into your head? That's all crap.

MOLINA: But it's what I feel.

VALENTIN: It's not what you feel—it's what you were taught to feel. Being a woman doesn't make you . . . how should I say? . . . a martyr. And if I didn't think it would hurt like hell I'd ask you to do it to me, to show you that all this business about being macho doesn't give anyone rights over another person.

MOLINA (*now disturbed*): This is getting us nowhere.

VALENTIN: On the contrary, I want to talk about it.

MOLINA: Well, I don't, so that's it. I'm begging you, no more please.

GUARD'S VOICE: Prisoner Luis Alberto Molina! To the visiting room!

> (*The door opens and* MOLINA *exits.* VALENTIN, *contented, sorts through his books, lays out his pencil and paper and begins to read. Meanwhile, we hear the* WARDEN'S VOICE.)

WARDEN'S VOICE: Put me through to your boss, please. . . . How's it going? Nothing this end. Yes, that's why I called. He's on his way here now. . . . Yes, they need the information, I'm aware of that. . . . And if Molina still hasn't found out anything, what should I do with him? . . . Are you sure? . . . Let him out today? . . . But why today? . . . Yes, of course, there's no time to lose. Quite, and if the other one gives him a message Molina will lead us straight to the group. . . . I've got it, yes, we'll give him just enough time for the other to pass on the message. . . . The tricky thing will be if Molina catches on that he's under surveillance. . . . It's hard to anticipate the reactions of someone like Molina: a pervert after all.

> (*The cell door opens and* MOLINA *comes back in, totally deflated.*)

MOLINA: Poor Valentin, you're looking at my hands.

VALENTIN: I didn't mean to.

MOLINA: Your eyes give you away, poor love. . . .

VALENTIN: Such language . . .

MOLINA: I didn't get a parcel. You'll have to forgive me. . . . Ay! Valentin . . .

VALENTIN: What's wrong?

MOLINA: Ay, you can't imagine . . .

VALENTIN: What's up? Tell me!

MOLINA: I'm going.

VALENTIN: To another cell. . . . What a nuisance!

MOLINA: No, they're releasing me.

VALENTIN: No.

MOLINA: I'm out on parole.

VALENTIN (*exploding with unexpected happiness*):   But that's incredible!

MOLINA (*confused by the way* VALENTIN'*s taking this*):   You're very kind to be so pleased for me.

VALENTIN: I'm happy for you too, of course . . . but, it's terrific! And I guarantee there's not the slightest risk.

MOLINA: What are you saying?

VALENTIN: Listen, . . . I had to get urgent information out to my people and I was dying with frustration because I couldn't do anything about it. I was racking my brains trying to find a way. . . . And you come and serve it to me on a plate.

MOLINA (*as if he'd just had an electric shock*):   I can't do that, you're out of your head.

VALENTIN: You'll memorize it in a minute. That's how easy it is. All you have to do is tell them that Number Three Command has been knocked out and they have to go to Corrientes for new orders.

MOLINA: No, I'm on parole, they can lock me up again for anything.

VALENTIN: I give you my word there's no risk.

MOLINA: I'm pleading with you. I don't want to hear another word. Not who they are or where they are. Nothing.

VALENTIN: Don't you want me to get out one day too?

MOLINA: Of here?

VALENTIN: Yes, to be free.

MOLINA: There's nothing I want more. But listen to me, I'm telling you for your own good. . . . I'm not good at this sort of thing, if they catch me, I'll spill everything.

VALENTIN: I'll answer for my comrades. You just have to wait a few days and then call from a public telephone, and make an appointment with someone in some bogus place.

MOLINA: What do you mean "a bogus place"?

VALENTIN: You just give them a name in code, let's say the Ritz cinema, and that means a certain bench in a particular square.

MOLINA: I'm frightened.

VALENTIN: You won't be when I explain the procedure to you.

MOLINA: But if the phone's tapped I'll get in trouble.

VALENTIN: Not from a public callbox and if you disguise your voice. It's the easiest thing in the world, I'll show you how to do it. There are millions of ways—a sweet in your mouth, or a toothpick under your tongue . . .

MOLINA: No.

VALENTIN: We'll discuss it later.

MOLINA: No!!!

VALENTIN: Whatever you say. (MOLINA *flops on the bed, all done in, and buries his face in the pillow.*) Look at me please.

MOLINA (*not looking at* VALENTIN):   I made a promise, I don't know who to, maybe God, even though I don't much believe in that.

VALENTIN: Yes . . .

MOLINA: I swore that I'd sacrifice anything if I could only get out of here and look after my mother. And my wish has come true.

VALENTIN: It was very generous of you to put someone else first.

MOLINA: But where's the justice in it? I always get left with nothing . . .

VALENTIN: You have your mother and she needs you. You have to assume that responsibility.

MOLINA: Listen, my mother's already had her life, she's lived, been married, had a child . . . she's old now, and her life is almost finished. . . .

VALENTIN: But she's still alive. . . .

MOLINA: And so am I . . . But when is my life going to begin? . . . When is it my turn for something good to happen? To have something for myself?

VALENTIN: You can start a new life outside. . . .

MOLINA: All I want is to stay with you. . . . (VALENTIN *doesn't say anything.*) Does that embarrass you?

VALENTIN: No, . . . er, well, yes . . .

MOLINA: Yes what?

VALENTIN: That . . . it makes me a little embarrassed.

MOLINA: If I can relay the information will you get out sooner?

VALENTIN: It's a way of helping the cause.

MOLINA: But you won't get out quickly? You just think it'll bring the revolution a bit closer.

VALENTIN: Yes, Molinita. . . . Don't dwell on it, we'll discuss it later.

MOLINA: There's no time left to discuss.

VALENTIN: Besides, we have to finish the panther movie.

MOLINA: It's a sad ending.

VALENTIN: How?

MOLINA: She's a flawed woman. (*With his usual irony.*) All of us flawed women come to a sad ending.

VALENTIN (*laughing*):   And the psychoanalyst? Does he get her in the end?

MOLINA: She gets him! And good! No, it's not so terrible, she just tears him to pieces.

VALENTIN: Does she kill him?

MOLINA: In the movie, yes. In real life, no.

VALENTIN: Tell me.

MOLINA: Let's see. Irina goes from bad to worse, she's insanely jealous of the other girl and tries to kill her. But the other one's lucky like hell and she gets away. Then one day the husband, who's at his wits' end now, arranges to meet the psychoanalyst at their house while she's out. But things get all muddled up and when the psychoanalyst arrives she's there on her own. He tries to take advantage of the situation and throws himself at her and kisses her. And right there she turns into a panther. By the time the husband gets home the guy's bled to death. Meanwhile, Irina has made it to the zoo and she sidles up to the panther's cage. She's all alone, in the night. That afternoon she got the key when the keeper left it in the lock. It's like Irina's in another world. The husband is on his way with the cops at top speed. Irina opens the panther's cage and it pounces on her and mortally wounds her with the first blow. The animal is scared away by the police siren, it dashes out into the street, a car runs over it and kills it.

VALENTIN: I'm going to miss you, Molinita.

MOLINA: The movies, at least.

VALENTIN: At least.

MOLINA: I want to ask you for a going away present. Something that we never did, although we got up to worse.

VALENTIN: What?

MOLINA: A kiss.

VALENTIN: It's true. We never did.

MOLINA: But right at the end, just as I'm leaving.

VALENTIN: Okay.

MOLINA: I'm curious. . . . Did the idea of kissing me disgust you?

VALENTIN: Ummm . . . Maybe I was afraid you'd turn into a panther.

MOLINA: I'm not the panther-woman.

VALENTIN: I know.

MOLINA: It's not fun to be a panther-woman, no one can kiss you. Or anything else.

VALENTIN: You're the spider-woman who traps men in her web.

MOLINA (*flattered*):   How sweet! I like that!

VALENTIN: And now it's your turn to promise me something: that you'll make people respect you, that you won't let anybody take advantage of you. . . . Promise me you won't let anybody degrade you.

GUARD'S VOICE: Prisoner Luis Alberto Molina, be ready with your belongings!

MOLINA: Valentin . . .

VALENTIN: What?

MOLINA: Nothing, it doesn't matter. . . . (*Pause.*) Valentin . . .

VALENTIN: What is it?

MOLINA: Rubbish, skip it.

VALENTIN: Do you want . . . ?

MOLINA: What?

VALENTIN: The kiss.

MOLINA: No, it was something else.

VALENTIN: Don't you want your kiss now?

MOLINA: Yes, if it won't disgust you.

VALENTIN: Don't get me mad. (*He walks over to* MOLINA *and timidly gives him a kiss on the mouth.*)

MOLINA: Thank you.

VALENTIN: Thank you.

MOLINA (*after a long pause*):   And now give me the number of your comrades.

VALENTIN: If you want.

MOLINA: I'll get the message to them.

VALENTIN: Okay . . . Is that what you wanted to ask?

MOLINA: Yes.

VALENTIN (*he kisses* MOLINA *one more time*):   You don't know how happy you've made me. It's 323–1025.

> (*Bolero music starts playing: it chokes* VALENTIN'S *voice as he gives his instructions.* MOLINA *and* VALENTIN *separate slowly.* MOLINA *puts all his belongings into a duffel bag. They are now openly brokenhearted;* MOLINA *can hardly keep his mind on what he's doing.* VALENTIN *looks at him in total helplessness. Their taped voices are heard as all this action takes place on stage.*)

MOLINA'S VOICE: What happened to me, Valentin, when I got out of here?

VALENTIN'S VOICE: The police kept you under constant surveillance, listened in on your phone, everything. The first call you got was from an uncle, your godfather: he told you not to dally with minors again. You told him what he deserved, that he should go to hell, because in jail you'd learned what dignity was. Your friends telephoned and you called each other Greta and Marlene and Marilyn and the police thought maybe it was a secret code. You got a job as a window dresser and then finally one day you called my comrades. You took your mother to the movies and bought her some fashion magazines. And one day you went to meet my friends but the police were shadowing you and they arrested you. My friends opened fire and killed you from their getaway car as you'd asked them to if the police caught you. And that was all. . . . And what about me, Molina, what happened to me?

MOLINA'S VOICE: They tortured you a lot . . . and then your wounds turned septic. A nurse took pity on you and secretly he gave you some morphine and you had a dream.

VALENTIN'S VOICE: About what?

MOLINA'S VOICE: You dreamed that inside you, in your chest, you were carrying Marta and that you'd never ever be apart from one another. And she asked you if you regretted what had happened to me, my death, which she said was your fault.

VALENTIN'S VOICE: And what did I answer her?

MOLINA'S VOICE: You replied that I had died for a noble and selfless ideal. And she said that wasn't true, she said that I had sacrificed myself just so I could die like the heroine in a movie. And you said that only I knew the answer. And you dreamed you were very hungry when you escaped from prison and that you ended up on a savage island and in the middle of the jungle you met a spider woman who gave you food to eat. And she was so lonely there in the jungle but you had to carry on with your struggle and go back to join your comrades, and your strength was restored by the food the spider woman gave you.

VALENTIN'S VOICE: And, at the end, did I get away from the police or did they catch up with me?

MOLINA'S VOICE: No, at the end you left the island, you were glad to be reunited with your comrades in the struggle, because it was a short dream, but a pleasant one. . . .

(The door opens. MOLINA *and* VALENTIN *embrace one another with infinite sadness.* MOLINA *exits. The door closes behind him. Curtain.)*

[1981]

Journal Entry

Among many others issues, *Kiss of the Spider Woman* explores the appeal of film as pop culture. How is film represented in Puig's text? What is its relation to politics, ideology, and art?

Textual Considerations

1. Characterize Molina. What has his life been like? Why does he feel so deeply about the film he narrates? How and why does Valentin affect him?
2. Characterize Valentin. What has his life been like? What are his values? What political changes does he want to effect? How does he respond to the story of the panther woman? How and why does Molina affect him?
3. How does Puig use setting to enhance the theme of physical and symbolic imprisonment? How do the characters respond to the restrictions to which they are subjected? Consider, too, their emotional and psychological entrapments.
4. Although Molina is gay and Valentin is heterosexual, to what extent are their views about male–female relations stereotypical? Explain.
5. In what ways have Molina and Valentin changed by the end of the play? How has your attitude toward them changed? Explain.

Cultural Contexts

1. The play dramatizes the brutality of contemporary Latin American military regimes and their imprisonment of homosexuals and political dissidents, as well as the effects of surveillance and torture on political and sexual identity. What kind of political change does Puig advocate through the friendship between Molina and Valentin? Is Puig's drama mostly concerned with homosexuality? Why or why not?
2. Respond to the link that Puig establishes between the discourse of imprisonment and Theodore Roszak's idea that the "kind of woman who is most in need of liberation, and desperately so, is the woman every man keeps locked in the dungeons of his psyche" (Ronald Christ, "Last Interview With Manuel Puig").

Performance Exercises

Performance Express (45 minutes)

For your semester performance of *Kiss of the Spider Woman*, ask your classmates to audition for the roles of Molina and Valentin. Group students in pairs (women included), and ask them to select a dialogue, rehearse for about ten minutes, and render a spontaneous, improvised version of their scene to the whole class. The students who are not auditioning for the main roles should critique their classmates' performance constructively, considering their voice (is it audible, strong, colorful?), physical presence (Are their gestures controlled? Do they serve a purpose?), and emotions (Do they vary?), and finally should select the best actors for the semester's performance project.

Performance Projects

1. Expand the roles of Molina's mother, Valentin's girlfriend, and the prison's warden by recreating them as a Greek chorus. Make them speak in unison or alternate their voices as they comment on and make general observations on the dramatic action that unfolds before their eyes. Like the Greek chorus, their comments should lead the audience to realize the greater significance of the actions unfolding before their eyes.
2. Following the lead of the Broadway musical, choreograph a tango performance for *Kiss of the Spider Woman* in which your classmates, as Molina and Valentin, take turns dancing with the spider woman. Decide on the music, costumes, and makeup for a performance that should attempt to capture, through music and dancing, some of the major themes of Puig's text, including the original spider woman legend, in which, after coupling, she devours her partner.

STUDENT JOURNAL ENTRIES

The story "On Seeing the 100% Perfect Girl One Beautiful April Morning," is about a man walking the streets of Tokyo, whereupon he discovers a lady who he instantly falls in love with: "I know from fifty yards away: She's the 100% perfect girl for me." It is at this moment that he is faced with a choice which for him is more like a dilemma. He would like nothing more at this moment than a chance to speak to her. But the physiological response of his heart pounding through his chest is his nemesis. In this moment he begins to question himself about how to approach her and start a conversation; doubt and fear of rejection begin to seep into his core. He says, "I'd probably go to pieces" when thinking about his reaction if she rejected him. Tragically, he decides not to pursue her any further. His chance is lost, and looking back on it years later, he feels pangs of regret. This story is one that many readers can relate to. And it is realistic, unlike many Hollywood movies that we see. Whether a 100% perfect girl really exists or whether we are able to fall in love at first sight is irrelevant. What is relevant is the fact that his character passed up a chance on love because of the fear of failure. This story reminded me that nothing risked is nothing gained. The character years later realizes he felt alive in that short moment and not many things in life make you feel that way. Given another opportunity, I am sure he would have chosen to take a risk. After all, he already knows what he would say!

—Joseph Choi

With Murakami's straightforward style and simple story lines, I find it hard to believe that anyone would have trouble seeing the value of his short stories. Even "On Seeing the 100% Perfect Girl One Beautiful April Morning," which is the shortest in length and simplest story line of all the stories, can contain lessons in life or "wisdom from the Orient." The entire story is about a boy reminiscing about passing the girl of his dreams on a busy street one day and pondering all the actions he could have taken. As readers read this story, they inevitably evaluate what their own reactions would be. Some will conclude that a change is needed and do so; others will not see the need, confident in their decisions. An open mind sees these opportunities and is capable of change upon reevaluation. This is essentially what happens to the character in this story. Having an open mind allowed him to evaluate his past reaction, examine the alternatives, and finally decide on the best course of action were he ever to see her again. When looked at from this angle, the potential lesson learned from this simple story is an extremely powerful one. From another viewpoint, the moral of the story can simply be not to let chance opportunities slip away. Either way, even the simplest of his stories are deeply meaningful to an open-minded person. On the other hand, a closed-minded person might view the story as "feckless wandering" and "ending with a blank wall."

— John Pion

Do you agree with Joe, that the story is about the importance of taking risks, or with John, that we view experiences differently according to whether we have an open mind or a closed one? Write a journal entry on your interpretation of Murakami's short story.

TOPICS FOR DISCUSSION AND WRITING

Writing Topics

1. According to the French feminist Simone de Beauvoir in *The Second Sex*, "The word *love* has by no means the same sense for both sexes, and this is one of the most serious misunderstandings that divide them." Apply this thesis to any three texts in Part Two.

2. Several texts in this part portray a male vision of gender relationships as fragmented and commercialized. Apply this concept to the texts by Rifaat, Lyman, and Euripides.

3. Assume the role of therapist, and write an essay on your first session with Gilman's protagonist. Use examples of her viewpoint as the basis for your evaluation.

4. American linguist Deborah Tannen has observed that even though women usually start the conversation, it is men who control it. To what extent do you consider these linguistic differences a major factor in conversations between men and women?

5. Consider the functions that the myth of the perfect housewife or the cult of domesticity serves in society. In your discussion, consider the premise that such a myth, at its best, may fulfill women's highest aspirations and, at it worst, may contribute to women's low self-esteem. Use three texts from this part to support your arguments.

6. Analyze the sources of the woman's anger in "Home Burial," and write about the causes of her inability to accept that her husband also mourns their child's death. Review lines 92–93 and lines 100–105 before formulating your response.

7. Several authors representing diverse cultures focus on economics and gender. Compare and contrast the degree to which economics shapes gender relationships in "Another Evening at the Club" and "My Last Duchess."

8. Discuss the interplay of rationality and irrationality in "The Yellow Wallpaper" or *Medea*. Trace this theme in either text, pointing out its effects on the identity of the protagonist. Focus on the ironies and contradictions that the theme creates.

9. Apply to any three texts in this part the concept that women's worst enemy is the enemy inside themselves—in other words, their inability to change their own, ingrained psychological structure.

10. Several poets explore this issue of woman's sexuality from different vantage points. Compare and contrast the attitudes toward this issue in the texts by Sexton, Millay, Behn, and de la Cruz.

11. To focus on changing characteristics of masculinity, compare and contrast the attitudes toward male power in the poems by Browning, Marvell, Roethke, and Yevtushenko. Analyze the cultural forces that shape male identity in each text.

12. Write an essay discussing attitudes toward sexual and marital fidelity in the texts by Chopin, Sexton, and Dickev. How do they compare with your ideas on these issues?

13. Compare and contrast the role of setting in the stories by Murakami and Mishima. To what extent do both authors use it to enhance theme and characterization?

447

14. In *Kiss of the Spider Woman*, setting functions as the third character. Analyze the effects of the play's setting on the relationship of Molina and Valentin, as well as the dual themes of sexual and political oppression.

15. Analyze the thematic effects of Murakami's use of a first-person narrator with the juxtaposition of the fantasy speech told by an omniscient author. How did this change in narrator affect your responses as reader?

16. Write an essay comparing and contrasting the philosophies of Brooks and Tesich toward marriage. With what points did you most agree or disagree?

17. Several male poets from various historical periods and cultures explore gender relationships. Choose three from different eras and write an essay comparing and contrasting their attitudes toward women and fidelity. To what extent do they affirm or refute your point of view?

Research Topics

1. Several works in Part Two examine the history of women from different cultural viewpoints. To understand what these texts portray in light of the women's liberation movement, investigate the history of one of the following: Mary Wollstonecraft's *A Vindication of the Rights of Women* (1790), Olympe de Gourges's *Declaration of the Rights of Women and Female Citizens* (1791), the suffragette movement in nineteenth-century England, the movement of the American feminists in the 1970s, or the black women's movement in America in the last three decades. For sources, search under women—history, women—France, feminism, gender, American women and politics, African American women—history. You might also check:

   Krichmar, Albert. *The Women's Movement in the Seventies: An International English-Language Bibliography*.

   Sim, Janet. *The Progress of Afro-American Women: A Selected Bibliography and Resource Guide*.

   Williams, Ora. *American Black Women in the Arts and Social Sciences: A Bibliographic Survey*, revised and expanded edition.

2. Explore the relation of violence and possessive love in Browning's "My Last Duchess," *Medea*, and *Othello* (Part Four). Read a critical essay on each text and cite the essays as your secondary sources of information.

3. When interviewed by Ronald Christ in 1991, Manuel Puig stated,

   For me, the only natural sexuality is bisexuality: that is total sexuality. It's all a matter of sexuality, not homosexuality, not heterosexuality. . . . In a free society, though where women and men would stop acting within the limitations of roles, their children would be free too. But certainly, not people of our generation. ("A Last Interview" 578)

   Consult Ronald Christ's "A Last Interview with Manuel Puig" as well as the other articles on Puig in *World Literature Today: A Literary Quarterly of the University of Oklahoma* (Autumn 1991) to fully understand what Puig describes as "total sexuality." Examine the extent to which Puig succeeds in combining his theory of "total sexuality" to ideas related to politics, ideology, and film in *The Kiss of the Spider Woman*.

FILM ANGLES

The literature of this unit speaks of different images of women at different points in their history—as goddess, rebel, warrior, sex object, mother, wife, and "other." Just as these images and the themes of the unit can be found in such varied works as the Greek tragedy *Medea*, the poems "My Last Duchess" and "For My Lover Returning to His Wife," and a number of the short stories, movies—both popular and elitist—are cultural products that assimilate and reflect attitudes toward women prevalent at different historical periods. Increasingly, gender questions have also been raised in respect to men, examining an equally wide range of roles traditionally thought to be inherently masculine and challenging cultural assumptions that have long been reinforced by popular movies.

Although the subject of gender and its relationship to one's identity has been actively addressed over the last few decades, it is a mistake to assume that filmmakers of the past were ignorant of or indifferent to the topic. Hollywood cinema, from the silent period through the 1950s, is filled with examples of strong actresses playing strong female parts. In such classic comedies as *Bringing Up Baby* (d. Howard Hawks, 1938), *His Girl Friday* (d. Howard Hawks, 1940), *The Lady Eve* (d. Preston Sturges, 1941), *Adam's Rib* (d. George Cukor, 1949), and *Pat and Mike* (d. George Cukor, 1952), male and female stereotypes are investigated to illuminating, often hilarious effect.

The issue of gender identity was more of an implicit presence in classic Hollywood films, affecting the conventions and formulas of **genres** in terms of the way they often depict men and women. Action genres like the western and the war film were considered "male," whereas melodramas were "female"—in each case referring both to the protagonists who dominated the story line as well as the audience to which the films were thought to appeal. For this reason genre movies can be examined in respect to how they reflect and revise their conventions and formulas over time. For example, although *Thelma and Louise* (d. Ridley Scott, 1991), *The Silence of the Lambs* (d. Jonathan Demme, 1991), *Alien* (d. Ridley Scott, 1979) and its sequels, *Million Dollar Baby* (d. Clint Eastwood, 2004), and *Brokeback Mountain* (d. Ang Lee, 2005) all appropriate the conventions of genres—the western, the crime thriller, the horror film, the boxing drama, and science fiction—they draw attention to the role of gender by attributing actions, behavior, and feelings to the protagonists normally unassociated or unacknowledged in characters in classic examples of the genre.

In the following section and case studies of this unit, images of women range from the wives and mothers in *All That Heaven Allows* (d. Douglas Sirk, 1956), *Far from Heaven* (d. Todd Haynes, 2002), and *The Hours* (d. Stephen Daldry, 2002), to the goddesses and **femmes fatales** of **film noir**, and the warrior in the *Alien* films. Images of men in *All That Heaven Allows*, *Hud* (d. Martin Ritt, 1963), and *Brokeback Mountain* illustrate how the masculine stereotype is often associated with nature, the outdoors, and aggressive behavior, typically seen in westerns.

In studying these films, we remind you to look beyond the screenplay and the dialogue for important clues to how the films alter or revise the conventions of the genre. Underlying ideas can also be discerned in the visual style of a film, its **mise-en-scène**—that is, the way it is designed, framed, and composed—which often reveals aspects unstated in words but key to how we should interpret the film.

Question to Consider

Using a working definition of "gender" from the literature sections of this unit, think of a recent film that might be examined from this perspective. How is male or female identity represented in the film? Does it conform to familiar stereotypes (e.g., men associated with aggressive behavior, women with passive behavior)? Or does it question such rigid definitions?

FILM HISTORY AND GENRES

From the 1920s through the 1950s, the dominant source of American filmmaking was Hollywood's studio system. The films that came out of Hollywood influenced generations of viewers long before the arrival of television, and, for the most part, they were genre films: melodramas, horror films, science fiction, musicals, romantic comedies, war films, and westerns. Genre movies reach larger audiences and reflect popular taste and values. For this reason, genre studies are especially revealing of a society's attitudes about questions of gender at any specific historical moment. Changes in the conventions and rules of genre movies mirror changes in the social attitudes toward gender issues. Subjects once thought taboo or difficult to address in a classic Hollywood genre movie often find their way into the genre as it changes over time. Thus scholars concerned about gender issues have reexamined classic Hollywood movies in terms of how genre conventions reflected and reinforced the links between human behavior and prevailing social attitudes of any given time.

Melodrama

Perhaps the genre that most explicitly addressed the way gender roles functioned in society was the **melodrama**, sometimes derogatively referred to as the "soap opera." The appeal of the melodrama was so strong that it eventually became a fixture of daytime television and many popular evening programs.

The typical Hollywood melodrama tells a story of average people experiencing a crisis in their romantic lives, the resolution of which can either be happy or sad. Characters are generally ruled by one all-consuming wish, engaged in a single, all-involving situation, and governed by their emotions. Because they are rarely psychologically complex, the viewer can easily identify with their predicaments.

Whereas men dominated westerns, crime, war, horror, and science fiction genres, women were the privileged characters of the melodrama. Often the central theme was the choice a woman had to make between pursuing an independent career or accepting the social codes that mandated she could only do so at the expense of her supposedly true role as wife and mother, a dilemma faced by many women in American society during the 1930s, 1940s, and 1950s. Sacrificing one for the other was a constant theme in melodramas. In such classic examples as *Stella Dallas* (d. King Vidor, 1937), *Mildred Pierce* (d. Michael Curtiz, 1945), and *Letter from an Unknown Woman* (d. Max Ophuls, 1948), a woman's romantic prospects, career, personality, happiness, or misery structures the narrative. In *Letter from an Unknown Woman*, the woman's centrality to the narrative is reinforced by the director's efforts to recreate the fictional world in accordance with her sensibility and **point of view**, letting her voice tell her story on the soundtrack while **framing** shots and using **camera movements** to express and imitate her emotional states.

The men in classic melodramas often fell into stereotypical categories: Either they were the husbands working from nine to five and too exhausted to notice the boredom or misery of their wives; or as in two of the films just cited, they seduced and abandoned the female protagonists, leaving them to the fortunes of fate in an unforgiving sexist society and with an illegitimate child to rear. On the surface the men in melodramas seem to be in more powerful social positions, but they are often more stereotyped than the women, who are revealed as fuller, more complex human beings. There are, of course, exceptions to these examples. In *Now, Voyager* (d. Irving Rapper, 1942), a celebrated Bette Davis vehicle, two complex and intelligent men—a wise doctor and the married man she falls in love with—are instrumental in turning the repressed spinster that Davis plays into a strong-minded flesh-and-blood woman.

Questions to Consider

1. Choose a scene from *Letter from an Unknown Woman* and discuss the means by which the director establishes and reinforces the woman's point of view. How effective are these techniques in helping the viewer enter into the woman's mind? Can a male viewer do this as easily as a female? Why or why not?
2. Characterize one of the male characters in any of the films cited earlier. Is the character developed in a psychologically complex way? Or is he there simply as a backdrop to the woman's plight?
3. More recent melodramas include *The Bridges of Madison County* (d. Clint Eastwood, 1995) and *Far from Heaven* (d. Todd Haynes, 2002). Do these films conform to and/or modify the genre? What is the nature of the woman's dilemma in each case? Is the emphasis on her struggle to balance her emotional needs and her sense of social responsibility? How are these issues handled in the film?

Film Noir

Whereas women in melodramas were objects of idealization or pity, women in film noir were usually femmes fatales—deadly creatures who, like Clytemnestra or Medea of Greek tragedy, lured men to their doom, even at the expense of their own lives and happiness, in revenge for sexual betrayal or rejection.

These films—like their Greek prototypes—involve crime and retribution. The femme fatale is the inverse image of the suffering woman in the melodrama. Classics of this form include *Double Indemnity* (d. Billy Wilder, 1944), *Leave Her to Heaven* (d. John Stahl, 1945), *The Postman Always Rings Twice* (d. Tay Garnett, 1946), and *The Lady from Shanghai* (d. Orson Welles, 1948). In all of these, the male protagonist is presumably seduced into a relationship with a dangerous woman who will stop at nothing to possess him or uses him to escape from an intolerable situation with a controlling husband.

In both the melodrama and film noir, the concept of the woman as goddess was prevalent. Although this was not a purely American phenomenon, the Hollywood studios were its primary manufacturers. From the silent period, the making and exploitation of the glamorous star was a staple of the Hollywood system. In some melodramas or films noir, this often involved a contradiction when actresses with glamorous star appeal (e.g., Joan Crawford, Bette Davis, or Lana Turner) played unglamorous housewives. Just as often, however, the glamorous star was equated with the femme fatale (e.g., Rita Hayworth in *The Lady from Shanghai*), complicating her appeal as well as the moral perspective of the film.

Questions to Consider

1. Characterize the male figure in any of the films discussed. Is he a passive object of the woman's seduction? Or is he portrayed and developed in credible psychological terms? To what degree does your answer to either question indicate or rely on your understanding of (a) male and female stereotypes in movies and (b) the conventions of a movie genre?

2. Popular examples of film noir in recent decades include *Body Heat* (1981; a remake of *Double Indemnity*), *Fatal Attraction* (d. Adrian Lyne, 1987), *Basic Instinct* (d. Paul Verhoeven, 1992), *Mulholland Drive* (d. David Lynch, 2001), and *Femme Fatale* (d. Brian de Palma, 2002), all of which feature treacherous women who do not always pay for their crimes. Consider any of these films in conjunction with the story of Medea, who revenges herself on several people, and even murders her children, yet escapes "legal" punishment with the help of the gods.
3. Can this trend be tied to any contemporary attitudes toward strong women? Can it be seen as a backlash against feminist thinking and the challenges it posed to male/female relationships?
4. The phenomenon of the movie sex goddess goes back as far as the 1920s with such female characters as "the vamp." Later examples of the type included such stars as Kim Novak and Marilyn Monroe. Is the "sex goddess" a remnant of the past, or are there actresses in today's films that are deliberately publicized to fit this category? If so, what does this say about today's attitudes and values about sexual stereotyping?

Action and Crime Films

Both *The Silence of the Lambs* and *Thelma and Louise* rework genre formulas. The former pits a young female FBI trainee named Clarice against an awesome array of assertive male figures who challenge her self-esteem and identity in different ways: There is her dead father who continues to shape her life and aspirations, the seasoned FBI agents who challenge her confidence and courage, the psychotic mastermind Hannibal Lecter who plays mind games that arouse her innermost fears, and finally, the serial killer who is himself a confusion of genders.

Thelma and Louise takes two working-class women whose weekend escape from nagging husband and job turns into an episodic journey across the American landscape that evokes both the western and the road movie, two genres usually dominated by men and masculine ideals. In both, the openness of space and the ruggedness of the terrain connote freedom from social constraint and the challenge of the wilderness, two images and themes associated with male characters not only in movies but in American literature (e.g., the novels of James Fenimore Cooper). In both film and literary traditions, the women of those genres are associated with the home, social constrictions, and civilization—the very things Thelma and Louise are trying to escape.

Question to Consider

Consider any crime thriller or science fiction film of recent years (e.g., *X-Men*, *The Matrix*, *Matrix Reloaded*, *Terminator 2*, *Terminator 3*, *Hulk*) and discuss the concept of role playing. Is any distinction made between what men and women do vis-à-vis the action in the film? How is love interest integrated with the main action of the film?

CASE STUDIES

All That Heaven Allows

One of the finest examples of the melodrama, made by one of the genre's quintessential practitioners, Douglas Sirk's *All That Heaven Allows* has received extensive attention in the decades since its first release in 1956. It tells the story of a widow named Cary who falls in love with Ron, her young gardener, and must choose between her happiness and the hypocritical outrage the affair generates in her New England upper-middle-class social set and her own children. Both express repugnance and disrespect, cheapening her affections by suggesting she is only attracted by "a good set of muscles." Film scholars have studied the film for its subtle rendering of a situation faced by many middle-age women in American society, especially during the 1940s and 1950s, whose loneliness went unnoticed and whose potential for personal growth and happiness diminished every day. Even as a widow with her children grown, she was expected to be loyal to the memory of her dead husband and not tarnish the image of the sacrificing mother.

The woman's dilemma is well defined not only by the script but by the careful attention the director gives to the mise-en-scène. A constant visual motif, for example, is the way she is framed by various glass objects: windows, mirrors, and, at one critical point, a television screen. The sense of her being trapped within the very things in her home that constitute her comfortable middle-class life is stressed repeatedly by these motifs as well as by the use of color and shadows.

So endearing is the film that two major filmmakers virtually remade it, adopting it to different cultural circumstances and times. German director Rainer Werner Fassbinder's *Ali: Fear Eats the Soul* (1974) is about a German working-class widow who falls in love with a migrant Arab worker thirty years younger. The shock effect is intensified by racial difference. More recently, Todd Haynes's *Far from Heaven* (2002; also discussed in Part Four) pays homage to Sirk's film while complicating the situation. The woman is younger and lives what seems to be an exemplary upper-middle-class life with successful husband and two young children. When she discovers her husband's homosexuality, her life almost crumbles, and she takes comfort in her gardener, a black man and widower raising a young daughter.

Questions to Consider

1. How is the widow's situation initially presented in *All That Heaven Allows*? Do you get the impression that had the gardener not pursued her, she would have been content living the life she had? Why?

2. Describe the filmmaker's use of mirrors and windows in the film. What is the story context in each case? How does this framing device enrich our sense of Cary's situation and how she deals with it? How does the television scene fit into this imagery, and what does it add to our impressions?

3. How does Ron's association with nature function as a symbol in the film? What are the details of this association, and what is the significance of the references to Thoreau's *Walden* in this context? Do they make the character himself only a symbolic figure in Cary's life, or is he a believable flesh-and-blood man? What scenes or dialogue in the film might support the latter?

4. Look at either the Fassbinder or the Haynes film and compare it as a melodrama to the Sirk. Sirk's film was made at the height of the melodrama's success in Hollywood, whereas the others are products of more culturally aware times in terms of gender issues. What details of either film's narrative or style reflect this knowledge? Do you think the later versions are better in any way? Why?

The *Alien* Series

The issues of gender and identity have affected other Hollywood genres as well. For example, *Alien* (d. Ridley Scott, 1979), *Aliens* (d. James Cameron, 1986), and *Alien 3* (d. David Fincher, 1992) demonstrate an important shift in the adventure, science fiction, and **horror** genres. The films contain and fuse features of these genres, in all three of which men had traditionally been the primary agents of action and women were in the more passive roles of homemaker, helper, or romantic interest.

The protagonist of the *Alien* films is Ripley, a woman whose evolution—from victor over the monster and lone survivor of the space mission in *Alien*, to warrior mother who battles the formidable "bad mother" Alien Queen in *Aliens*, to savior of the human race in *Alien 3*—was a groundbreaking development. By making the woman the heroine of genres in which men were traditionally the heroes and decision makers, the filmmakers had radically revised the established formulas of action genres. An important contributing element to the unity and success of the films is the presence of the same actress in all three. Ripley, as portrayed by Sigourney Weaver, broke new ground in female incarnations and remains one of the most memorable and original screen creations of the last several decades.

Imagery and symbolism convey important ideas in the films. In *Alien*, set design gives visual form to many implied but unstated associations between the human body and various artificial simulations. When the film opens, the camera explores a spaceship run entirely by machines while the crew sleeps in incubator-like cavities, dressed in loincloths resembling diapers. Connotations of nesting, birth, and infancy are evoked again on the alien spaceship where the crew finds the eggs of the creatures in their prenatal state. The cavernous interior of the alien spaceship is even shaped like a huge womb. These links between the organic and nonorganic are epitomized by the alien creature itself, which is a fusion of the metallic and the biological and—with its phallic shape and ability to reproduce—has characteristics of both genders.

Questions to Consider

1. The *Alien* films propose that a woman can be both motherly and soldierly, aggressive and conciliatory, without compromising either function. What assumptions or expectations of the spectator are challenged by these facts? Can this challenge be applied to the way the spectator feels about male and female roles in society?

2. In *Alien*, why do we only see parts of the creature, rather than a fully satisfying look at its whole body, until the very end of the movie? Apart from keeping the viewer in suspense, could there be some other reason the director forces us to imagine how the creature's parts ultimately cohere?

3. One reason for the characters' and the spectator's fear in *Alien* is that the creature can effectively conceal itself on the spaceship. What features allow it to do so? What physical aspects of the spaceship does it resemble? How does this relate to the film's overall themes?

4. How is the imagery in *Alien*, especially the allusions to the male and female body, related to the film's genre changes and to the questions of gender and identity?

5. Can you find image patterns in *Aliens* and *Alien 3* similar to the ones in *Alien*? What ideas or aspects of each film's story and theme can they be connected to?

The Hours

Perhaps no figure in literary history embodies the concerns raised by gender studies more importantly than Virginia Woolf, whose novel *Mrs. Dalloway*, filmed in 1998, inspired Michael Cunningham's novel *The Hours*, made into a successful movie in 2002. *The Hours* relates Woolf's experience as she wrote the book, to the lives of two American women, one an unhappy Los Angeles housewife in 1949, the other a contemporary lesbian New York editor. Bridging time periods and cultures, it is a literary tour de force, revealing a continuity of sensibility among women of diverse backgrounds.

The Hours expands the role of homosexuality subtly implied in *Mrs. Dalloway* by suggesting an affinity directly tied to sexual difference between the lonely novelist haunted by suicide and two of the characters in the other stories: the Los Angeles housewife, who tries to kill herself following the surfacing of her repressed desires with a female neighbor, and the homosexual writer dying of AIDS.

The thematic structure of *The Hours* relies considerably on *framing* and **editing** techniques to telegraph and underline the parallels and similarities the filmmaker wants to make among the three principal female characters. This is noticeable from the beginning when the film cuts from a shot of Woolf to a shot of the editor making a similar gesture, each one shaking her head over a sink; or from a shot of the editor reaching for a vase that seems to be swept away (obviously a different one) by the husband of the housewife in the middle story. In such ways the filmmaker sustains the sense of continuity among all three stories and time periods.

Questions to Consider

1. Do you identify with any of the characters in *The Hours*? Which one? Which features of his or her personality and dilemma facilitate your capacity to identify?
2. Watch a brief scene that includes dialogue from the film. Listen carefully to the tones of the actors' voices and the rhythm of their speaking. What adjectives best describe the diction and speech patterns? What impressions do you form of the characters from these observations? Do they bear directly on gender and identity issues?
3. Are there techniques—visual, audio, or linguistic—that help bridge the time periods and experiences of the three characters and reinforce the parallels in *The Hours*? How do they add to your appreciation or understanding of the film's themes?
4. In certain sequences from *The Hours* we hear the voice of the Woolf character, speaking aloud lines from her novel *Mrs. Dalloway*, over shots or scenes from the other stories, a film technique known as **audio/visual montage**. Select one of these passages and examine closely how the words relate to the situations in the other stories. What is the purpose and effect of this technique? Does it establish Woolf as the dominant consciousness in the film?
5. What is the role of language in the film? How does it reflect the class and manners of the characters?

SEXUAL DIFFERENCE: HISTORY AND GENRE

An inevitable aspect of gender studies is the question of sexual difference. Among the groups whose identity has been the object of the "politics of exclusion" are homosexuals and lesbians. For decades, homosexuality was a taboo subject in Hollywood films. When Lillian Hellman's play *The Children's Hour* was filmed in 1936 as *These Three*, all references to lesbianism were eliminated. Instead, the scandal at the center of the story involved an alleged affair between a female teacher and her boyfriend. William Wyler, the director of that film, remade it in 1962, restoring the play's title and its original theme. But in other films of the same period—for example, *Tea and Sympathy* (d. Vincente Minnelli, 1956) and *Advise and Consent* (d. Otto Preminger, 1962)—the male homosexuality of the literary source was either awkwardly skirted or treated as a dirty secret.

In his book *The Celluloid Closet*, author Vito Russo notes that for decades in Hollywood movies, the taboos against male intimacy and homosexual behavior were so strong that dozens of scripts were sanitized to avoid such implications in the establishment of male camaraderie.

Nevertheless, emotional bonding between men can be seen in many genre films—especially westerns, war films, action, crime, and gangster films—often overshadowing heterosexual relationships in the same films. The term *buddy movie* describes films in which the relationship between two male characters is the dominant one, a phenomenon discernible as far back as the silent version of *Ben-Hur* (d. Fred Niblo, 1926) and manifested in such popular movies as the 1959 *Ben-Hur* (d. William Wyler), *Butch Cassidy and the Sundance Kid* (d. George Roy Hill, 1969), *Midnight Cowboy* (d. John Schlesinger, 1969), and the *Lethal Weapon* series. Many of the actors in these films have admitted that they deliberately played scenes with an intensity that implied a homoerotic undercurrent that could not be acknowledged.

The subject has been equally delicate in foreign films in which the homosexual is a marginalized figure—as in *Rules of the Game* (d. Jean Renoir, France, 1939) and *Ossessione* (d. Luchino Visconti, Italy, 1942)—and homosexual desire is a forbidden theme—as in Visconti's *Rocco and His Brothers* (Italy, 1960). Both *Victim* (d. Basil Dearden, 1961) and *Sunday, Bloody Sunday* (d. John Schlesinger, 1971) were breakthrough British films—the former about a lawyer who risks his reputation confronting the gang that caused his ex-lover's death, and the latter about a married couple both in love with the same man. Later films from Britain have continued the trend with *My Beautiful Laundrette* (d. Stephen Frears, 1985) and *Beautiful Thing* (d. Hettie MacDonald, 1996). Only recently has Chinese cinema dealt with homosexuality—for example, in *Happy Together* (d. Wong Kar-wai, 1997).

Although the subject has been treated more openly in recent decades, it is still rare to find a commercial mainstream film with a nonstereotypical homosexual main character—like Al Pacino's bank robber in *Dog Day Afternoon* (d. Sidney Lumet, 1975), Mariel Hemingway's Olympic athlete in *Personal Best* (d. Robert Towne, 1982), or Tom Hanks's lawyer afflicted with AIDS in *Philadelphia* (d. Jonathan Demme, 1993). It is all too common to see homosexuals as flamboyant objects of humor—as in *La Cage aux Folles* (d. Eduardo Molinaro, Italy/France, 1978) and its Hollywood remake, *The Birdcage* (d. Mike Nichols, 1996).

As films over the last decade attest, sexual difference is a more viable, but still provocative subject. In such films as *The Crying Game* (d. Neil Jordan, Great Britain, 1992), *Boys Don't Cry* (d. Kimberly Pierce, 1999), *Tarnation* (d. Jonathan Caouette, 2004), *Breakfast on Pluto* (d. Neil Jordan, Great Britain, 2005), and *Transamerica* (d. Duncan Tucker, 2005), the issue is posed in terms of gender confusion, in which the boundaries of masculinity and femininity are explored and where the protagonists are men who want to be women and women who play at being men. These films, however, are independent productions—along with *My Own Private Idaho* (d. Gus van Sant, 1991) and *Gods and Monsters* (d. Bill Condon, 1998)—rather than mainstream. Only time will tell whether the recent success of *Brokeback Mountain* (d. Ang Lee, 2005) bodes a change in this tendency. Ironically, in the last decade homosexuals became more visible on television, both in the "safer" comic contexts of regular network shows such as *Will and Grace* and in a more serious and explicit vein in cable programs such as *Six Feet Under* and *Queer as Folk*.

Question to Consider

In mainstream Hollywood films of the past, a homosexual character was often stereotyped as a guilt-ridden tragic figure who had to suffer exclusion and shame and be purged from so-called normal social life—as in the 1962 version of *The Children's Hour* in which the lesbian commits suicide. Is such treatment tenable in today's society? What social changes affect the way homosexuals are now portrayed in movies? Are there other movie stereotypes of gay people?

CASE STUDY

Brokeback Mountain

Ang Lee's film is adapted from a short story by Annie Proulx about two modern-day cowboys who fall in love while tending sheep on Brokeback Mountain in Montana. Proulx describes her characters—Jack Twist and Ennis del Mar—as "high school dropout country boys with no prospects, brought up to hard work and privation, both rough-mannered, rough-spoken, inured to the stoic life." This is hardly the stereotype of homosexual men as many movies have portrayed them. Although both men initially deny the implications of their sexual encounter—"I'm not no queer," says Ennis; "Me neither," says Jack—and put it down to boredom, drink, and the cold night air, they continue to act on their urges throughout the summer, even in broad daylight. When the first snows fall and they go their separate ways, both marry and have children. Nevertheless, as time passes, they resume the affair, meeting periodically but briefly, an unsatisfying situation for Jack who has developed strong feelings for Ennis and wants more. Eventually both marriages fail; and Jack, who has been reduced to anonymous sexual encounters with other men, is savagely murdered by a homophobic gang of thugs. Only at the end, when Ennis visits Jack's parents and sees two old shirts—his and Jack's—hung together one inside the other that Jack had kept for years, does he realize the full meaning of what happened between them.

Ang Lee's film is a faithful adaptation of the story, set in the beautiful outdoors associated with traditional westerns. This fact alone makes the film a good example of how a genre's conventions have been revised. The film's situation evokes many classic westerns in which men spend months on end together herding cattle from one part of the country to another. In none of those films do we detect a glimpse of the sexual deprivation or frustrated longings that might lead to the situation dramatized in *Brokeback Mountain*.

As with many controversial films, critical and popular reception of *Brokeback Mountain* is a telling indicator of its success. Although the film is a breakthrough, it did exceptionally well in many parts of the country, was nominated for several Academy Awards, and was named Best Picture of the Year by many critical groups. However, many critics, in an attempt to normalize it for the mainstream, effectively denied its difference, underplaying the homosexuality by suggesting that the film is simply a universal love story in which the characters just happen to be gay. But as the astute Daniel Mendelsohn put it (in *The New York Review of Books*, February 23, 2006), the film is not just a love story, but "a tragedy about the specifically gay phenomenon of the 'closet'—about the disastrous emotional and moral consequences of erotic self-expression and of the social intolerance that first causes and then exacerbates it." Ang's film stresses the continuance of homophobic hate and violence in society when it flashes images of Jack's murder on the screen, recalling the newspaper photos of the beating and death of Matthew Shepard in 1998.

Questions to Consider

1. *Brokeback Mountain* was a box office success but mostly in big cities like Boston, New York, Los Angeles, and San Francisco. What do you think accounts for this? Do you think it would have been received differently if the characters and the actors who play them had manifested more stereotypical gay behavior?
2. The film achieves many of its effects from subtle wordless interactions between the two male characters. Examine a scene that illustrates this and shows how acting and directing is often about letting small gestures communicate important underlying emotions.

3. Consider the film in the light of any classical Hollywood western you may have seen. What conventions does it borrow from this genre, and what images or scenes do you think contradict those conventions? How does the concept of the "buddy movie" apply or not to the film?

Research Topics

1. Select any classic example of a Hollywood genre—comedy, melodrama, western, crime, horror, musical, or science fiction—and discuss the ways in which it portrays gender roles. What changes in society's attitudes toward gender have occurred since the film was made? Try to reimagine the same film by making changes in the story or treatment to accommodate the changes you have identified in today's society.
2. The melodramas *All That Heaven Allows* and *Far from Heaven*, made more than forty years apart, present different views of the same decade—the 1950s. Discuss the differences in subject matter, style, point of view, and theme that reflect each period in which the film was made. How is the female protagonist represented in each film? Is she more active than passive in either case? Is the resolution of the story in each case believable?
3. Do a close study of a film whose first-person narrator is a woman—for example, *Letter from an Unknown Woman*, *Mrs. Dalloway* (d. Marleen Gorris, Great Britain, 1998), *Clueless* (d. Amy Heckerling, 1995), or a recent film you've seen. What is the effect of the voice-over technique? Does the woman's voice always confirm and verify what we see, or is there sometimes a disparity between what the voice tells us and what we see? What is the function of this disparity?
4. Seek out one of the film versions of the Greek tragedy *Medea* and compare it with the play. Does the film capture the intensity of the drama? Analyze Medea's character as she appears in both play and film. What features are emphasized in the film version?
5. Alfred Hitchcock's *Vertigo* (1958) is a powerful psychological study of a man obsessed with turning a woman into the perfect embodiment of his ideal. Examine the film in terms of how it relates to the Pygmalion myth and speaks to one of the issues addressed by feminist studies concerning the "traditional" male's desire for the perfect woman.
6. Several foreign language films over the last decade have dealt openly with gender issues: *Raise the Red Lantern* (d. Zhang Yimou, Hong Kong, 1992), *Leila* (d. Dariush Mehrjui, Iran, 1997), *Kadosh* (d. Amos Gitai, Israel, 2000), *Y Tu Mamá También* (d. Alfonso Cuaron, Mexico, 2002), *Talk to Her* (d. Pedro Almodovar, Spain, 2002), and *Late Marriage* (d. Dover Kosashvili, Israel, 2002). Examine a few of these films and compare their views on women, marriage, and relationships.
7. Research and examine some reviews of *Brokeback Mountain*, and determine how the film's reception was in some ways related to the playing down of the homosexuality of the two men. Why was this necessary? What does it indicate about the readiness of mainstream culture to accept this kind of film or the behavior it reflects?

PART THREE

WAR AND VIOLENCE

459

Why do nations go to war? What causes individuals to engage in violence? What is the relation between power and violence? Why do poets, artists, musicians, and filmmakers create images celebrating the glories of war? What causes so many people to prefer conflict and tension to stability and calm? According to German American social philosopher Hannah Arendt (1906–75), a major cause of war throughout human history is the conflict between freedom and tyranny. Paul Fussell, an expert on modern warfare, laments, "The drift of modern history seems to imply that the power of the human mind to learn principles of human restraint and reform from modern wars is extremely limited. What people learn from wars seems to be this: the techniques for making each extremely efficient—that is, destructive and vicious." Even more ironic, in the name of freedom, innocent people are tortured, strangled, exiled, and murdered.

Why has the human imagination always been captivated by heroism and the horrors of war? And why do so few literary works celebrate the virtues and possibilities of peace? In his recent book, *War Is a Force That Gives Us Meaning*, Chris Hedges writes that "the myth of war is essential to justify the horrible sacrifices required in war, the destruction and death of innocents." In fact, ordinary people often bear a greater share of the human costs of war than do their leaders who initiate the conflicts. The writers of many of the texts in Part Three try to make sense of a world where violence is perpetrated not only by the horrors of war but also by the racial and ethnic conflicts erupting almost daily in cities throughout the United States and other countries of the world.

The texts in this part pose many questions about the nature and consequences of war and violence. Some, such as Walt Whitman's "The Dying Veteran," celebrate the glory and victory of war, whereas others, such as Wilfred Owen's "Disabled," portray the alienation and rejection experienced by returning veterans who were wounded physically and psychologically in the trench warfare of World War I. Another series of texts here explores the arbitrariness of war by attacking the tradition of the blind hatred of the enemy. Although Thomas Hardy and Denise Levertov belong to different historical moments, each of these poets, in "The Man He Killed" and "What Were They Like?" evokes war's irrationality by attempting to portray the enemy as a human being with a personal and cultural identity. "The Sniper," a story that dramatizes the suspense of an urban guerrilla episode during civil war in Ireland, brings the concern of the "myth of the enemy" even closer to home.

One of the most devastating aspects of World War II was Hitler's attempt to exterminate the Jewish people in the death camps of the Third Reich. In "Silence," by Tadeusz Borowski, you will enter the bizarre world of the concentration camp, a terrifying reminder of human depravity. And in Yevtushenko's "Babiy Yar," written to commemorate the massacre of some thirty-four thousand Jews from Kiev, who were rounded up, stripped, shot one by one, and then tossed into a mass grave, you will share the courageous attempts of the poet to identify with the "enemy"—the Jewish victims of Hitler's massacre.

Other contemporary texts in Part Three focus on Latin America recreating conditions analogous to those of war: violence, torture, and dictatorship. During the 1980s alone, military right-wing forces took the lives of some eighty thousand people in El Salvador. Contemporary poet Carolyn Forché, writing about her experiences as an American human rights advocate in El Salvador, uses her poetry of witness to remind us that the human spirit can sometimes transcend the tortured body.

The Vietnam War and its aftermath is the subject of several texts by Vietnam veterans, including Tim O'Brien, who—in his short story "The Things They Carried"—communicates the soldiers' attitudes toward their war experiences by describing what they are carrying in their pockets, and on their shoulders, and in their hearts. Poets Jeffrey Harrison and Yusef Komunyakaa record their responses to the Vietnam War Memorial designed by Asian American Maya Lin; David W. Powell portrays the effects of posttraumatic stress disorder on Vietnam veterans. In "Warring Memories," American writer Kandi Tayebi shares her thoughts about her Iranian husband's recent war experiences in Iraq.

It is generally acknowledged that alienation, apathy, and boredom often lead to violence and that violent actions are frequently the result of feeling powerless or excluded. The often gratuitous acts of violence we read about daily are the subjects of "The Curse" and "Idle Hands," and in "The Destructors," British writer Graham Greene portrays the connection between the aftermath of World War II and the destructive acts of a gang of young boys. Racial violence, also a daily occurrence, is explored in "A Brother's Murder" and "Like a Winding Sheet."

As you ponder the complexities of war and violence in these and other texts, you may find yourself reexamining your presuppositions about them and considering other solutions to conflict. It is difficult to improve on the wisdom of Chris Hedges: "The covenant of love is such that it recognizes both the fragility and the sanctity of the individual. It recognizes itself in the other. It alone can save us."

FICTION

△△△△△△△△△△△△△△△△△△△△△△△△△△△△△△△△△△△△△△△

Graham Greene

The Destructors

1

It was on the eve of August Bank Holiday that the latest recruit became the leader of the Wormsley Common Gang. No one was surprised except Mike, but Mike at the age of nine was surprised by everything. "If you don't shut your mouth," somebody once said to him, "you'll get a frog down it." After that Mike kept his teeth tightly clamped except when the surprise was too great.

The new recruit had been with the gang since the beginning of the summer holidays, and there were possibilities about his brooding silence that all recognized. He never wasted a word even to tell his name until that was required of him by the rules. When he said "Trevor" it was a statement of fact, not as it would have been with the others a statement of shame or defiance. Nor did anyone laugh except Mike, who finding himself without support and meeting the dark gaze of the new-comer opened his mouth and was quiet again. There was every reason why T, as he was afterwards referred to, should have been an object of mockery—there was his name (and they substituted the initial because otherwise they had no excuse not to laugh at it), the fact that his father, a former architect and present clerk, had "come down in the world" and that his mother considered herself better than the neighbours. What but an odd quality of danger, of the unpredictable, established him in the gang without any ignoble ceremony of initiation?

The gang met every morning in an impromptu car-park, the site of the last bomb of the first blitz. The leader, who was known as Blackie, claimed to have heard it fall, and no one was precise enough in his dates to point out that he would have been one year old and fast asleep on the down platform of Wormsley Common Underground Station. On one side of the car-park leant the first occupied house, No. 3, of the shattered Northwood Terrace—literally leant, for it had suffered from the blast of the bomb and the side walls were supported on wooden struts. A smaller bomb and incendiaries had fallen beyond, so that the house stuck up like a jagged tooth and carried on the further wall relics of its neighbour, a dado, the remains of a fireplace. T, whose words were almost confined to voting "Yes" or "No" to the plan of operations proposed each day by Blackie, once startled the whole gang by saying broodingly, "Wren built that house, father says."

"Who's Wren?"

"The man who built St Paul's."

"Who cares?" Blackie said. "It's only Old Misery's."

Old Misery—whose real name was Thomas—had once been a builder and decorator. He lived alone in the crippled house, doing for himself: once a week you could see him coming back across the common with bread and vegetables, and once as the boys played in the car-park he put his head over the smashed wall of his garden and looked at them.

"Been to the lav," one of the boys said, for it was common knowledge that since the bombs fell something had gone wrong with the pipes of the house and Old Misery was too mean to spend money on the property. He could do the redecorating himself at cost price, but he had never learnt plumbing. The lav was a wooden shed at the bottom of the narrow garden with a star-shaped hole in the door: it had escaped the blast which had smashed the house next door and sucked out the window-frames of No. 3.

The next time the gang became aware of Mr Thomas was more surprising. Blackie, Mike and a thin yellow boy, who for some reason was called by his surname Summers, met him on the common coming back from the market. Mr Thomas stopped them. He said glumly, "You belong to the lot that play in the car-park?"

Mike was about to answer when Blackie stopped him. As the leader he had responsibilities. "Suppose we are?" he said ambiguously.

"I got some chocolates," Mr Thomas said. "Don't like 'em myself. Here you are. Not enough to go round, I don't suppose. There never is," he added with sombre conviction. He handed over three packets of Smarties.

The gang was puzzled and perturbed by this action and tried to explain it away. "Bet someone dropped them and he picked 'em up," somebody suggested.

"Pinched 'em and then got in a bleeding funk," another thought aloud.

"It's a bribe," Summers said. "He wants us to stop bouncing balls on his wall."

"We'll show him we don't take bribes," Blackie said, and they sacrificed the whole morning to the game of bouncing that only Mike was young enough to enjoy. There was no sign from Mr Thomas.

Next day T astonished them all. He was late at the rendezvous, and the voting for that day's exploit took place without him. At Blackie's suggestion the gang was to disperse in pairs, take buses at random and see how many free rides could be snatched from unwary conductors (the operation was to be carried out in pairs to avoid cheating). They were drawing lots for their companions when T arrived.

"Where you been, T?" Blackie asked. "You can't vote now. You know the rules."

"I've been *there*," T said. He looked at the ground, as though he had thoughts to hide.

"Where?"

"At Old Misery's." Mike's mouth opened and then hurriedly closed again with a click. He had remembered the frog.

"At Old Misery's?" Blackie said. There was nothing in the rules against it, but he had a sensation that T was treading on dangerous ground. He asked hopefully, "Did you break in?"

"No. I rang the bell."

"And what did you say?"

"I said I wanted to see his house."

"What did he do?"

"He showed it me."

"Pinch anything?"

"No."

"What did you do it for then?"

The gang had gathered round: it was as though an impromptu court were about to form and try some case of deviation. T said, "It's a beautiful house," and still watching the ground, meeting no one's eyes, he licked his lips first one way, then the other.

"What do you mean, a beautiful house?" Blackie asked with scorn.

"It's got a staircase two hundred years old like a corkscrew. Nothing holds it up."

"What do you mean, nothing holds it up. Does it float?"

"It's to do with opposite forces, Old Misery said."

"What else?"

"There's panelling."

"Like in the Blue Boar?"

"Two hundred years old."

"Is Old Misery two hundred years old?"

Mike laughed suddenly and then was quiet again. The meeting was in a serious mood. For the first time since T had strolled into the car-park on the first day of the holidays his position was in danger. It only needed a single use of his real name and the gang would be at his heels.

"What did you do it for?" Blackie asked. He was just, he had no jealousy, he was anxious to retain T in the gang if he could. It was the word "beautiful" that worried him—that belonged to a class world that you could still see parodied at the Wormsley Common Empire by a man wearing a top hat and a monocle, with a haw-haw accent. He was tempted to say, "My dear Trevor, old chap," and unleash his hell hounds. "If you'd broken in," he said sadly—that indeed would have been an exploit worthy of the gang.

"This was better," T said. "I found out things." He continued to stare at his feet, not meeting anybody's eye, as though he were absorbed in some dream he was unwilling—or ashamed—to share.

"What things?"

"Old Misery's going to be away all tomorrow and Bank Holiday."

Blackie said with relief, "You mean we could break in?"

"And pinch things?" somebody asked.

Blackie said, "Nobody's going to pinch things. Breaking in—that's good enough, isn't it? We don't want any court stuff."

"I don't want to pinch anything," T said. "I've got a better idea."

"What is it?"

T raised eyes, as grey and disturbed as the drab August day. "We'll pull it down," he said. "We'll destroy it."

Blackie gave a single hoot of laughter and then, like Mike, fell quiet, daunted by the serious implacable gaze. "What'd the police be doing all the time?" he said.

"They'd never know. We'd do it from inside. I've found a way in." He said with a sort of intensity, "We'd be like worms, don't you see, in an apple. When we came out again there'd be nothing there, no staircase, no panels, nothing but just walls, and then we'd make the walls fall down—somehow."

"We'd go to jug," Blackie said.

"Who's to prove? and anyway we wouldn't have pinched anything." He added without the smallest flicker of glee, "There wouldn't be anything to pinch after we'd finished."

"I've never heard of going to prison for breaking things," Summers said.

"There wouldn't be time," Blackie said. "I've seen house-breakers at work."

"There are twelve of us," T said. "We'd organize."

"None of us know how . . ."

"I know," T said. He looked across at Blackie. "Have you got a better plan?"

"Today," Mike said tactlessly, "we're pinching free rides . . ."

"Free rides," T said. "Kid stuff. You can stand down, Blackie, if you'd rather . . ."

"The gang's got to vote."

"Put it up then."

Blackie said uneasily, "It's proposed that tomorrow and Monday we destroy Old Misery's house."

"Here, here," said a fat boy called Joe.

"Who's in favour?"

T said, "It's carried."

"How do we start?" Summers asked.

"He'll tell you," Blackie said. It was the end of his leadership. He went away to the back of the car-park and began to kick a stone, dribbling it this way and that. There was only one old Morris in the park, for few cars were left there except lorries: without an attendant there was no safety. He took a flying kick at the car and scraped a little paint off the rear mudguard. Beyond, paying no more attention to him than to a stranger, the gang had gathered round T; Blackie was dimly aware of the fickleness of favour. He thought of going home, of never returning, of letting them all discover the hollowness of T's leadership, but suppose after all what T proposed was possible—nothing like it had ever been done before. The fame of the Wormsley Common car-park gang would surely reach around London. There would be headlines in the papers. Even the grown-up gangs who ran the betting at the all-in wrestling and the barrow-boys would hear with respect of how Old Misery's house had been destroyed. Driven by the pure, simple and altruistic ambition of fame for the gang, Blackie came back to where T stood in the shadow of Old Misery's wall.

T was giving his orders with decision: it was as though this plan had been with him all his life, pondered through the seasons, now in his fifteenth year crystallized with the pain of puberty. "You," he said to Mike, "bring some big nails, the biggest you can find, and a hammer. Anybody who can, better bring a hammer and a screwdriver. We'll need plenty of them. Chisels too. We can't have too many chisels. Can anybody bring a saw?"

"I can," Mike said.

"Not a child's saw," T said. "A real saw."

Blackie realized he had raised his hand like any ordinary member of the gang.

"Right, you bring one, Blackie. But now there's a difficulty. We want a hacksaw."

"What's a hacksaw?" someone asked.

"You can get 'em at Woolworth's," Summers said.

The fat boy called Joe said gloomily, "I knew it would end in a collection."

"I'll get one myself," T said. "I don't want your money. But I can't buy a sledge-hammer."

Blackie said, "They are working on No. 15. I know where they'll leave their stuff for Bank Holiday."

"Then that's all," T said. "We meet here at nine sharp."

"I've got to go to church," Mike said.

"Come over the wall and whistle. We'll let you in."

2

On Sunday morning all were punctual except Blackie, even Mike. Mike had a stroke of luck. His mother felt ill, his father was tired after Saturday night, and he was told to go to church alone with many warnings of what would happen if he strayed. Blackie had difficulty in smuggling out the saw, and then in finding the sledge-hammer at the back of No. 15. He approached the house from a lane at the rear of the garden, for fear of the policeman's beat along the main road. The tired ever-greens kept off a stormy sun: another wet Bank Holiday was being prepared over the Atlantic, beginning in swirls of dust under the trees. Blackie climbed the wall into Misery's garden.

There was no sign of anybody anywhere. The lav stood like a tomb in a neglected graveyard. The curtains were drawn. The house slept. Blackie lumbered nearer with the saw and the sledge-hammer. Perhaps after all nobody had turned up: the plan had been a wild invention: they had woken wiser. But when he came close to the back door he could hear a confusion of sound hardly louder than a hive in swarm: a clickety-clack, a bang bang, a scraping, a creaking, a sudden painful crack. He thought: it's true, and whistled.

They opened the back door to him and he came in. He had at once the impression of organization, very different from the old happy-go-lucky ways under his leadership. For a while he wandered up and down stairs looking for T. Nobody addressed him: he had a sense of great urgency, and already he could begin to see the plan. The interior of the house was being carefully demolished without touching the walls. Summers with hammer and chisel was ripping out the skirting-boards in the ground-floor dining-room: he had already smashed the panels of the door. In the same room Joe was heaving up the parquet blocks, exposing the soft wood floorboards over the cellar. Coils of wire came out of the damaged skirting and Mike sat happily on the floor clipping the wires.

On the curved stairs two of the gang were working hard with an inadequate child's saw on the banisters—when they saw Blackie's big saw they signalled for it wordlessly. When he next saw them a quarter of the banisters had been dropped into the hall. He found T at last in the bathroom—he sat moodily in the least cared-for room in the house, listening to the sounds coming up from below.

"You've really done it," Blackie said with awe. "What's going to happen?"

"We've only just begun," T said. He looked at the sledgehammer and gave his instructions. "You stay here and break the bath and the wash-basin. Don't bother about the pipes. They come later."

Mike appeared at the door. "I've finished the wires, T," he said.

"Good. You've just got to go wandering round now. The kitchen's in the basement. Smash all the china and glass and bottles you can lay hold of. Don't turn on the taps—we don't want a flood—yet. Then go into all the rooms and turn out the drawers. If they are locked get one of the others to break them open. Tear up any papers you find and smash all the ornaments. Better take a carving knife with you from the kitchen. The bedroom's opposite here. Open the pillows and tear up the sheets. That's enough for the moment. And you, Blackie, when you've finished in here crack the plaster in the passage up with your sledge-hammer."

"What are you going to do?" Blackie asked.

"I'm looking for something special," T said.

It was nearly lunch-time before Blackie had finished and went in search of T. Chaos had advanced. The kitchen was a shambles of broken glass and china. The dining-room was stripped of parquet, the skirting was up, the door had been taken off its hinges, and the destroyers had moved up a floor. Streaks of light came in through the closed shutters where they worked with the seriousness of creators—and destruction after all is a form of creation. A kind of imagination had seen this house as it had now become.

Mike said, "I've got to go home for dinner."

"Who else?" T asked, but all the others on one excuse or another had brought provisions with them.

They squatted in the ruins of the room and swapped unwanted sandwiches. Half an hour for lunch and they were at work again. By the time Mike returned they were on the top floor, and by six the superficial damage was completed. The doors were all off, all the skirtings raised, the furniture pillaged and ripped and smashed—no one could have slept in the house except on a bed of broken plaster. T gave his orders—eight o'clock next morning, and to escape notice they climbed singly over the garden wall, into the car-park. Only Blackie and T were left: the light had nearly gone, and when they touched a switch, nothing worked—Mike had done his job thoroughly.

"Did you find anything special?" Blackie asked.

T nodded. "Come over here," he said, "and look." Out of both pockets he drew bundles of pound notes. "Old Misery's savings," he said. "Mike ripped out the mattress, but he missed them."

"What are you going to do? Share them?"

"We aren't thieves," T said. "Nobody's going to steal anything from this house. I kept these for you and me—a celebration." He knelt down on the floor and counted them out—there were seventy in all. "We'll burn them," he said, "one by one," and taking it in turns they held a note upwards and lit the top corner, so that the flame burnt slowly towards their fingers. The grey ash floated above them and fell on their heads like age. "I'd like to see Old Misery's face when we are through," T said.

"You hate him a lot?" Blackie asked.

"Of course I don't hate him," T said. "There'd be no fun if I hated him." The last burning note illuminated his brooding face. "All this hate and love," he said, "it's soft, it's hooey. There's only things, Blackie," and he looked round the room crowded with the unfamiliar shadows of half things, broken things, former things. "I'll race you home, Blackie," he said.

3

Next morning the serious destruction started. Two were missing—Mike and another boy whose parents were off to Southend and Brighton in spite of the slow warm drops that had begun to fall and the rumble of thunder in the estuary like the first guns of the old blitz. "We've got to hurry," T said.

Summers was restive. "Haven't we done enough?" he asked. "I've been given a bob for slot machines. This is like work."

"We've hardly started," T said. "Why, there's all the floors left, and the stairs. We haven't taken out a single window. You voted like the others. We are going to *destroy* this house. There won't be anything left when we've finished."

They began again on the first floor picking up the top floorboards next the outer wall, leaving the joists exposed. Then they sawed through the joists and retreated into the hall, as what was left of the floor heeled and sank. They had learnt with practice, and the second floor collapsed more easily. By the evening an odd exhilaration seized them as they looked down the great hollow of the house. They ran risks and made mistakes: when they thought of the windows it was too late to reach them. "Cor," Joe said, and dropped a penny down into the dry rubble-filled well. It cracked and span amongst the broken glass.

"Why did we start this?" Summers asked with astonishment; T was already on the ground, digging at the rubble, clearing a space along the outer wall. "Turn on the taps," he said. "It's too dark for anyone to see now, and in the morning it won't matter." The water overtook them on the stairs and fell through the floorless rooms.

It was then they heard Mike's whistle at the back. "Something's wrong," Blackie said. They could hear his urgent breathing as they unlocked the door.

"The bogies?" Summers asked.

"Old Misery," Mike said. "He's on his way," he said with pride.

"But why?" T said. "He told me . . ." He protested with the fury of the child he had never been, "It isn't fair."

"He was down at Southend," Mike said, "and he was on the train coming back. Said it was too cold and wet." He paused and gazed at the water. "My, you've had a storm here. Is the roof leaking?"

"How long will he be?"

"Five minutes. I gave Ma the slip and ran."

"We better clear," Summers said. "We've done enough, anyway."

"Oh no, we haven't. Anybody could do this—" "this" was the shattered hollowed house with nothing left but the walls. Yet walls could be preserved. Façades were valuable. They could build inside again more beautifully than before. This could again be a home. He said angrily, "We've got to finish. Don't move. Let me think."

"There's no time," a boy said.

"There's got to be a way," T said. "We couldn't have got this far . . ."

"We've done a lot," Blackie said.

"No. No, we haven't. Somebody watch the front."

"We can't do any more."

"He may come in at the back."

"Watch the back too." T began to plead. "Just give me a minute and I'll fix it. I swear I'll fix it." But his authority had gone with his ambiguity. He was only one of the gang. "Please," he said.

"Please," Summers mimicked him, and then suddenly struck home with the fatal name. "Run along home, Trevor."

T stood with his back to the rubble like a boxer knocked groggy against the ropes. He had no words as his dreams shook and slid. Then Blackie acted before the gang had time to laugh, pushing Summers backward. "I'll watch the front, T," he said, and cautiously he opened the shutters of the hall. The grey wet common stretched ahead, and the lamps gleamed in the puddles. "Someone's coming, T. No, it's not him. What's your plan, T?"

"Tell Mike to go out to the lav and hide close beside it. When he hears me whistle he's got to count ten and start to shout."

"Shout what?"

"Oh, 'Help', anything."

"You hear, Mike," Blackie said. He was the leader again. He took a quick look between the shutters. "He's coming, T."

"Quick, Mike. The lav. Stay here, Blackie, all of you, till I yell."

"Where are you going, T?"

"Don't worry. I'll see to this. I said I would, didn't I?"

Old Misery came limping off the common. He had mud on his shoes and he stopped to scrape them on the pavement's edge. He didn't want to soil his house, which stood jagged and dark between the bomb-sites, saved so narrowly, as he believed, from destruction. Even the fan-light had been left unbroken by the bomb's blast. Somewhere somebody whistled. Old Misery looked sharply round. He didn't trust whistles. A child was shouting: it seemed to come from his own garden. Then a boy ran into the road from the car-park. "Mr Thomas," he called, "Mr Thomas."

"What is it?"

"I'm terribly sorry, Mr Thomas. One of us got taken short, and we thought you wouldn't mind, and now he can't get out."

"What do you mean, boy?"

"He's got stuck in your lav."

"He'd no business . . . Haven't I seen you before?"

"You showed me your house."

"So I did. So I did. That doesn't give you the right to . . ."

"Do hurry, Mr Thomas. He'll suffocate."

"Nonsense. He can't suffocate. Wait till I put my bag in."

"I'll carry your bag."

"Oh no, you don't. I carry my own."

"This way, Mr Thomas."

"I can't get in the garden that way. I've got to go through the house."

"But you *can* get in the garden this way, Mr Thomas. We often do."

"You often do?" He followed the boy with a scandalized fascination. "When? What right . . . ?"

"Do you see . . . ? the wall's low."

"I'm not going to climb walls into my own garden. It's absurd."

"This is how we do it. One foot here, one foot there, and over." The boy's face peered down, an arm shot out, and Mr Thomas found his bag taken and deposited on the other side of the wall.

"Give me back my bag," Mr Thomas said. From the loo a boy yelled and yelled. "I'll call the police."

"Your bag's all right, Mr Thomas. Look. One foot there. On your right. Now just above. To your left." Mr Thomas climbed over his own garden wall. "Here's your bag, Mr Thomas."

"I'll have the wall built up," Mr Thomas said, "I'll not have you boys coming over here, using my loo." He stumbled on the path, but the boy caught his elbow and supported him. "Thank you, thank you, my boy," he murmured automatically. Somebody shouted again through the dark. "I'm coming, I'm coming," Mr Thomas called. He said to the boy beside him, "I'm not unreasonable. Been a boy myself. As long as things are done regular. I don't mind you playing round the place Saturday mornings. Sometimes I like company. Only it's got to be regular. One of you asks leave and I say Yes. Sometimes I'll say No. Won't feel like it. And you come in at the front door and out at the back. No garden walls."

"Do get him out, Mr Thomas."

"He won't come to any harm in my loo," Mr Thomas said, stumbling slowly down the garden. "Oh, my rheumatics," he said. 'Always get 'em on Bank Holiday. I've got to be careful. There's loose stones here. Give me your hand. Do you know what my horoscope said yesterday? "Abstain from any dealings in first half of week. Danger of serious crash." That might be on this path,' Mr Thomas said. "They speak in parables and double meanings." He paused at the door of the loo. "What's the matter in there?" he called. There was no reply.

"Perhaps he's fainted," the boy said.

"Not in my loo. Here, you, come out," Mr Thomas said, and giving a great jerk at the door he nearly fell on his back when it swung easily open. A hand first supported him and then pushed him hard. His head hit the opposite wall and he sat heavily down. His bag hit his feet. A hand whipped the key out of the lock and the door slammed. "Let me out," he called, and heard the key turn in the lock. "A serious crash," he thought, and felt dithery and confused and old.

A voice spoke to him softly through the star-shaped hole in the door. "Don't worry, Mr Thomas," it said, "we won't hurt you, not if you stay quiet."

Mr Thomas put his head between his hands and pondered. He had noticed that there was only one lorry in the car-park, and he felt certain that the driver would not come for it before the morning. Nobody could hear him from the road in front, and the lane at the back was seldom used. Anyone who passed there would be hurrying home and would not pause for what they would certainly take to be drunken cries. And if he did call "Help," who, on a lonely Bank Holiday evening, would have the courage to investigate? Mr Thomas sat on the loo and pondered with the wisdom of age.

After a while it seemed to him that there were sounds in the silence—they were faint and came from the direction of his house. He stood up and peered through the ventilation-hole—between the cracks in one of the shutters he saw a light, not the light of a lamp, but the wavering light that a candle might give. Then he thought he heard the sound of hammering and scraping and chipping. He thought of burglars—perhaps they had employed the boy as a scout, but why should burglars engage in what sounded more and more like a stealthy form of carpentry? Mr Thomas let out an experimental yell, but nobody answered. The noise could not even have reached his enemies.

4

Mike had gone home to bed, but the rest stayed. The question of leadership no longer concerned the gang. With nails, chisels, screwdrivers, anything that was sharp and penetrating, they moved around the inner walls worrying at the mortar between the bricks. They started too high, and it was Blackie who hit on the damp course and realized the work could be halved if they weakened the joints immediately above. It was a long, tiring, unamusing job, but at last it was finished. The gutted house stood there balanced on a few inches of mortar between the damp course and the bricks.

There remained the most dangerous task of all, out in the open at the edge of the bomb-site. Summers was sent to watch the road for passers-by, and Mr Thomas, sitting on the loo, heard clearly now the sound of sawing. It no longer came from the house, and that a little reassured him. He felt less concerned. Perhaps the other noises too had no significance.

A voice spoke to him through the hole. "Mr Thomas."

"Let me out," Mr Thomas said sternly.

"Here's a blanket," the voice said, and a long grey sausage was worked through the hole and fell in swathes over Mr Thomas's head.

"There's nothing personal," the voice said. "We want you to be comfortable tonight."

"Tonight," Mr Thomas repeated incredulously.

"Catch," the voice said. "Penny buns—we've buttered them, and sausage-rolls. We don't want you to starve, Mr Thomas."

Mr Thomas pleaded desperately. "A joke's a joke, boy. Let me out and I won't say a thing. I've got rheumatics. I got to sleep comfortable."

"You wouldn't be comfortable, not in your house, you wouldn't. Not now."

"What do you mean, boy?" But the footsteps receded. There was only the silence of night: no sound of sawing. Mr Thomas tried one more yell, but he was daunted and rebuked by the silence—a long way off an owl hooted and made away again on its muffled flight through the soundless world.

At seven next morning the driver came to fetch his lorry. He climbed into the seat and tried to start the engine. He was vaguely aware of a voice shouting, but it didn't concern him. At last the engine responded and he backed the lorry until it touched the great wooden shore that supported Mr Thomas's house. That way he could drive right out and down the street without reversing. The lorry moved forward, was momentarily checked as though something were pulling it from behind, and then went on to the sound of a long rumbling crash. The driver was astonished to see bricks bouncing ahead of him, while stones hit the roof of his cab. He put on his brakes. When he climbed out the whole landscape had suddenly altered. There was no house beside the car-park, only a hill of rubble. He went round and examined the back of his lorry for damage, and found a rope tied there that was still twisted at the other end round part of a wooden strut.

The driver again became aware of somebody shouting. It came from the wooden erection which was the nearest thing to a house in that desolation of broken brick. The driver climbed the smashed wall and unlocked the door. Mr Thomas came out of the loo. He was wearing a grey blanket to which flakes of pastry adhered. He gave a sobbing cry. "My house," he said. "Where's my house?"

"Search me," the driver said. His eye lit on the remains of a bath and what had once been a dresser and he began to laugh. There wasn't anything left anywhere.

"How dare you laugh," Mr Thomas said. "It was my house. My house."

"I'm sorry," the driver said, making heroic efforts, but when he remembered the sudden check of his lorry, the crash of bricks falling, he became convulsed again. One moment the house had stood there with such dignity between the bomb-sites like a man in a top hat, and then, bang, crash, there wasn't anything left—not anything. He said, "I'm sorry. I can't help it, Mr Thomas. There's nothing personal, but you got to admit it's funny."

[1954]

Journal Entry

There is much evidence of gang violence throughout the United States. How would you contrast the gang violence of *The Destructors* with gang violence you are personally aware of or hear or read about in the media?

Textual Considerations

1. How does the author use paradox and metaphor in *The Destructors*? For example, the tools one normally thinks of being used to build a house, such as hammers, chisels and screwdrivers, are used to destroy a house (paradox of creation/destruction).
2. Blackie feels his role as leader of the gang is threatened by T's plan. Why does he feel this way? Why does he go along with the plan without a fight? When T heard Old Misery was on his way home early and the rest of the boys wanted to run off, leaving the destruction incomplete, why did Blackie stand by T's side?
3. Describe the scenario of the gang's hangout. What emotional responses does it create in the gang members? On you as a reader? Are they alienated from their surroundings? Cite evidence from the text to justify your point of view.
4. T's refusal to steal anything from the house may be understood because his plan was only to destroy the house, but why did he burn the money? What did T mean when he said, "All this hate and love [. . .] it's soft and hooey. There's only things, Blackie."
5. Graham Greene was quoted as saying, "There is always one moment in childhood when the door opens and lets the future in." How would you connect this to Blackie or Trevor?

Cultural Contexts

1. A gang can be viewed as a society within a society. Cite examples of how the Wormsley Common Gang behave like a society.
2. The story takes place in post–World War II England at a time of political and social transition. How does the author use *The Destructors* as a social commentary?

Liam O'Flaherty

The Sniper

The long June twilight faded into night. Dublin lay enveloped in darkness but for the dim light of the moon that shone through fleecy clouds, casting a pale light as of approaching dawn over the streets and the dark waters of the Liffey. Around the beleaguered Four Courts the heavy guns roared. Here and there through the city, machine-guns and rifles broke the silence of the night, spasmodically, like dogs barking on lone farms. Republicans and Free Staters were waging civil war.

On a roof-top near O'Connell Bridge, a Republican sniper lay watching. Beside him lay his rifle and over his shoulders were slung a pair of field glasses. His face was the face of a student, thin and ascetic, but his eyes had the cold gleam of the fanatic. They were deep and thoughtful, the eyes of a man who is used to looking at death.

He was eating a sandwich hungrily. He had eaten nothing since morning. He had been too excited to eat. He finished the sandwich, and, taking a flask of whiskey from his pocket, he took a short draught. Then he returned the flask to his pocket. He paused for a moment, considering whether he should risk a smoke. It was dangerous. The flash might be seen in the darkness and there were enemies watching. He decided to take the risk.

Placing a cigarette between his lips, he struck a match. There was a flash and a bullet whizzed over his head. He dropped immediately. He had seen the flash. It came from the opposite side of the street.

He rolled over the roof to a chimney stack in the rear, and slowly drew himself up behind it, until his eyes were level with the top of the parapet. There was nothing to be seen—just the dim outline of the opposite housetop against the blue sky. His enemy was under cover.

Just then an armored car came across the bridge and advanced slowly up the street. It stopped on the opposite of the street, fifty yards ahead. The sniper could hear the dull panting of the motor. His heart beat faster. It was an enemy car. He wanted to fire, but he knew it was useless. His bullets would never pierce the steel that covered the gray monster.

Then round the corner of a side street came an old woman, her head covered by a tattered shawl. She began to talk to the man in the turret of the car. She was pointing to the roof where the sniper lay. An informer.

The turret opened. A man's head and shoulders appeared, looking toward the sniper. The sniper raised his rifle and fired. The head fell heavily on the turret wall. The woman darted toward the side street. The sniper fired again. The woman whirled round and fell with a shriek into the gutter.

Suddenly from the opposite roof a shot rang out and the sniper dropped his rifle with a curse. The rifle clattered to the roof. The sniper thought the noise would wake the dead. He stopped to pick the rifle up. He couldn't lift it. His forearm was dead.

"Christ," he muttered, "I'm hit."

Dropping flat onto the roof, he crawled back to the parapet. With his left hand he felt the injured right forearm. There was no pain—just a deadened sensation, as if the arm had been cut off.

Quickly he drew his knife from his pocket, opened it on the breast-work of the parapet, and ripped open the sleeve. There was a small hole where the bullet had entered. On the other side there was no hole. The bullet had lodged in the bone. It must have fractured it. He bent the arm below the wound. The arm bent back easily. He ground his teeth to overcome the pain.

Then taking out the field dressing, he ripped open the packet with his knife. He broke the neck of the iodine bottle and let the bitter fluid drip into the wound. A paroxysm of pain swept through him. He placed the cotton wadding over the wound and wrapped the dressing over it. He tied the ends with his teeth.

Then he lay against the parapet, and, closing his eyes, he made an effort of will to overcome the pain.

In the street beneath all was still. The armored car had retired speedily over the bridge, with the machine-gunner's head hanging lifelessly over the turret. The woman's corpse lay still in the gutter.

The sniper lay still for a long time nursing his wounded arm and planning escape. Morning must not find him wounded on the roof. The enemy on the opposite roof covered his escape. He must kill that enemy and he could not use his rifle. He had only a revolver to do it. Then he thought of a plan.

Taking off his cap, he placed it over the muzzle of his rifle. Then he pushed the rifle slowly over the parapet, until the cap was visible from the opposite side of the street. Almost immediately there was a report, and a bullet pierced the center of the cap. The sniper slanted the rifle forward. The cap slipped down into the street. Then catching the rifle in the middle, the sniper dropped his left hand over the roof and let it hang, lifelessly. After a few moments he let the rifle drop to the street. Then he sank to the roof, dragging his hand with him.

Crawling quickly to the left, he peered up at the corner of the roof. His ruse had succeeded. The other sniper, seeing the cap and rifle fall, thought he had killed his man. He was now standing before a row of chimney pots, looking across, with his head clearly silhouetted against the western sky.

The Republican sniper smiled and lifted his revolver above the edge of the parapet. The distance was about fifty yards—a hard shot in the dim light, and his right arm was paining him like a thousand devils. He took a steady aim. His hand trembled with eagerness. Pressing his lips together, he took a deep breath through his nostrils and fired. He was almost deafened with the report and his arm shook with the recoil.

Then when the smoke cleared he peered across and uttered a cry of joy. His enemy had been hit. He was reeling over the parapet in his death agony. He struggled to keep his feet, but he was slowly falling forward, as if in a dream. The rifle fell from his grasp, hit the parapet, fell over, bounded off the pole of a barber's shop beneath and then clattered on the pavement.

Then the dying man on the roof crumpled up and fell forward. The body turned over and over in space and hit the ground with a dull thud. Then it lay still.

The sniper looked at his enemy falling and he shuddered. The lust of battle died in him. He became bitten by remorse. The sweat stood out in beads on his forehead. Weakened by his wound and the long summer day of fasting and watching on the roof, he revolted from the sight of the shattered mass of his dead enemy. His teeth chattered, he began to gibber to himself, cursing the war, cursing himself, cursing everybody.

He looked at the smoking revolver in his hand, and with an oath he hurled it to the roof at his feet. The revolver went off with the concussion and the bullet whizzed past the sniper's head. He was frightened back to his senses by the shock. His nerves steadied. The cloud of fear scattered from his mind and he laughed.

Taking the whiskey flask from his pocket, he emptied it at a draught. He felt reckless under the influence of the spirit. He decided to leave the roof now and look for his company commander, to report. Everywhere around was quiet. There was not much danger in going through the streets. He picked up his revolver and put it in his pocket. Then he crawled down through the sky-light to the house underneath.

When the sniper reached the laneway on the street level, he felt a sudden curiosity as to the identity of the enemy sniper whom he had killed. He decided that he was a good shot, whoever he was. He wondered did he know him. Perhaps he had been in his own company before the split in the army. He decided to risk going over to have a look at him. He peered round the corner into O'Connell Street. In the upper part of the street there was heavy firing, but around here all was quiet.

The sniper darted across the street. A machine-gun tore up the ground around him with a hail of bullets, but he escaped. He threw himself face downward beside the corpse. The machine-gun stopped.

Then the sniper turned over the dead body and looked into his brother's face.

[1923]

Journal Entry

Under what circumstances, if any, can you imagine killing your brother?

Textual Considerations

1. Analyze the opening paragraph of the story to discuss setting and atmosphere. How does O'Flaherty use setting in the opening paragraph and throughout the story?
2. Observe O'Flaherty's frequent use of irony in "The Sniper," and analyze its effects on the story's meaning, style, and tone. Cite examples from the text.

3. Investigate the effects of the narrative **point of view** on the development of the story. To what extent does the narrator's stance affect your evaluation of the sniper? Is the sniper given a voice of his own in the story? Explain.
4. Chart the stages in the sniper's responses to his situation, and evaluate their plausibility. Argue whether he is a political "fanatic," as the text suggests, or whether the reader can detect glimpses of his humanity behind his political commitment as a sniper.
5. Identify some of the internal and external actions in the plot development of the story. How does O'Flaherty combine both actions? What role does the "old woman" play in the story? Explain the meaning of the narrator's final words about the woman.

Cultural Contexts

1. To what extent do you share the sniper's fanatic commitment to a political cause? Argue in favor of or against the position he takes to become a sniper. You may engage in an imaginary dialogue with him about his commitment.
2. Working with your group, examine how the violence of civil wars, like that of the war between the Republicans and the Free Staters in Ireland (1921), compare to the violence that results from war among nations. Can your group reach a consensus about whether young people today are willing to die for their country or their religion?

Tadeusz Borowski

Silence

At last they seized him inside the German barracks, just as he was about to climb over the window ledge. In absolute silence they pulled him down to the floor and panting with hate dragged him into a dark alley. Here, closely surrounded by a silent mob, they began tearing at him with greedy hands.

Suddenly from the camp gate a whispered warning was passed from one mouth to another. A company of soldiers, their bodies leaning forward, their rifles on the ready, came running down the camp's main road, weaving between the clusters of men in stripes standing in the way. The crowd scattered and vanished inside the blocks. In the packed, noisy barracks the prisoners were cooking food pilfered during the night from neighbouring farmers. In the bunks and in the passageways between them, they were grinding grain in small flour-mills, slicing meat on heavy slabs of wood, peeling potatoes and throwing the peels on to the floor. They were playing cards for stolen cigars, stirring batter for pancakes, gulping down hot soup, and lazily killing fleas. A stifling odour of sweat hung in the air, mingled with the smell of food, with smoke and with steam that liquefied along the ceiling beams and fell on the men, the bunks and the food in large, heavy drops, like autumn rain.

There was a stir at the door. A young American officer with a tin helmet on his head entered the block and looked with curiosity at the bunks and the tables. He wore a freshly pressed uniform; his revolver was hanging down, strapped in an open holster that dangled against his thigh. He was assisted by the translator who wore a yellow band reading "interpreter" on the sleeve of his civilian coat, and by the chairman of the Prisoners' Committee, dressed in a white summer coat, a pair of tuxedo trousers and tennis shoes. The men in the barracks fell silent. Leaning out of their bunks and lifting their eyes from the kettles, bowls and cups, they gazed attentively into the officer's face.

"Gentlemen," said the officer with a friendly smile, taking off his helmet—and the interpreter proceeded at once to translate sentence after sentence—"I know, of course, that after what you have gone through and after what you have seen, you must feel a deep hate for your tormentors. But we, the soldiers of America, and you, the people of Europe, have fought so that law should prevail over lawlessness. We must show our respect for the law. I assure you that the guilty will be punished, in this camp as well as in all the others. You have already seen, for example, that the S.S. men were made to bury the dead."

". . . right, we could use the lot at the back of the hospital. A few of them are still around," whispered one of the men in a bottom bunk.

". . . or one of the pits," whispered another. He sat straddling the bunk, his fingers firmly clutching the blanket.

"Shut up! Can't you wait a little longer? Now listen to what the American has to say," a third man, stretched across the foot of the same bunk, spoke in an angry whisper. The American officer was now hidden from their view behind the thick crowd gathered at the other end of the block.

"Comrades, our new Kommandant gives you his word of honour that all the criminals of the S.S. as well as among the prisoners will be punished," said the translator. The men in the bunks broke into applause and shouts. In smiles and gestures they tried to convey their friendly approval of the young man from across the ocean.

"And so the Kommandant requests," went on the translator, his voice turning somewhat hoarse, "that you try to be patient and do not commit lawless deeds, which may only lead to trouble, and please pass the sons of bitches over to the camp guards. How about it, men?"

The block answered with a prolonged shout. The American thanked the translator and wished the prisoners a good rest and an early reunion with their dear ones. Accompanied by a friendly hum of voices, he left the block and proceeded to the next.

Not until after he had visited all the blocks and returned with the soldiers to his headquarters did we pull our man off the bunk—where covered with blankets and half-smothered with the weight of our bodies he lay gagged, his face buried in the straw mattress—and dragged him on to the cement floor under the stove, where the entire block, grunting and growling with hatred, trampled him to death.

[1967]

Journal Entry

Respond to the setting of the concentration camp in "Silence." Imagine yourself in the place of the survivors.

Textual Considerations

1. Explore the thematic nuances of the story's title. Consider, for example, the effects of juxtaposing the silence of the concentration camp survivors with the speech of the young American officer through his interpreter.
2. Review the story carefully, and discuss how Borowski uses the physical appearance and language of the survivors to reinforce their psychic distance from the outside world.
3. How successful is "Silence" in portraying not only the narrator's realistic recreation of a concentration camp but also his disillusionment and horror of war?
4. Analyze what "Silence" conveys about the survivors' need for revenge. Consider, too, what the text implies about the ability of the young American officer and other noninmates to judge the actions of the inmates.
5. Use arguments from the text to support or challenge the thesis that in killing one of their former oppressors, the inmates in "Silence" perpetuate the violence that victimized them.

Cultural Contexts

1. Review Borowski's brief biography on page 988 of this text. Then reread the story. What new insights did you discover? Can you imagine how you might behave in a place like Auschwitz? Use your journal entry to help you assess your viewpoint about this issue.
2. Working with your group, respond to this statement: "There is nothing one man will not do to another." Can you reach a consensus about this issue?

André Dubus

The Curse

Mitchell Hayes was forty-nine years old, but when the cops left him in the bar with Bob, the manager, he felt much older. He did not know what it was like to be very old, a shrunken and wrinkled man, but he assumed it was like this: fatigue beyond relieving by rest, by sleep. He also was not a small man. His weight moved up and down in the 170s, and he was five feet, ten inches tall. But now his body seemed short and thin. Bob stood at one end of the bar; he was a large, black-haired man, and there was nothing in front of him but an ashtray he was using. He looked at Mitchell at the cash register and said, "Forget it. You heard what Smitty said."

Mitchell looked away, at the front door. He had put the chairs upside down on the tables. He looked from the door past Bob to the empty space of floor at the rear; sometimes people danced there, to the jukebox. Opposite Bob, on the wall behind the bar, was a telephone; Mitchell looked at it. He had told Smitty there were five guys, and when he moved to the phone, one of them stepped around the corner of the bar and shoved him, one hand against Mitchell's chest, and it pushed him backward; he nearly fell. That was when they were getting rough with her at the bar. When they took her to the floor, Mitchell looked once toward her sounds, then looked down at the duckboard he stood on, or at the belly or chest of a young man in front of him.

He knew they were not drunk. They had been drinking before they came to his place, a loud popping of motorcycles outside, then walking into the empty bar, young and sunburned and carrying helmets and wearing thick leather jackets in August. They stood in front of Mitchell and drank drafts. When he took their first order, he thought they were on drugs, and later, watching them, he was certain. They were not relaxed in the way of most drinkers near closing time. Their eyes were quick, alert as wary animals, and they spoke loudly, with passion, but their passion was strange and disturbing, because they were only chatting, bantering. Mitchell knew nothing of the effects of drugs, so could not guess what was in their blood. He feared and hated drugs because of his work and because he was the stepfather of teenagers: a boy and a girl. He gave last call and served them and leaned against the counter behind him.

Then the door opened and the girl walked in from the night, a girl he had never seen, and she crossed the floor toward Mitchell. He stepped forward to tell her she had missed last call; but before he spoke, she asked for change for the cigarette machine. She was young—he guessed nineteen to twenty-one—and deeply tanned and had dark hair. She was sober and wore jeans and a dark-blue T-shirt. He gave her the quarters, but she was standing between two of the men and she did not get to the machine.

When it was over and she lay crying on the cleared circle of floor, he left the bar and picked up the jeans and T-shirt beside her and crouched and handed them to her. She did not look at him. She laid the clothes across her breasts and what Mitchell thought of now as her wound. He left her and dialed 911, then Bob's number. He woke up Bob. Then he picked up her sneakers from the floor and placed them beside her and squatted near her face, her crying. He wanted to speak to her and touch her, hold a hand or press her brow, but he could not.

The cruiser was there quickly, the siren coming east from town, then slowing and deepening as the car stopped outside. He was glad Smitty was one of them; he had gone to high school with Smitty. The other was Dave, and Mitchell knew him because it was a small town. When they saw the girl, Dave went out to the cruiser to call for an ambulance; and when he came back, he said two other cruisers had those scumbags and were taking them in. The girl was still crying and could not talk to Smitty and Dave. She was crying when a man and a woman lifted her onto a stretcher and rolled her out the door and she vanished forever in a siren.

Bob came in while Smitty and Dave were sitting at the bar drinking coffee and Smitty was writing his report; Mitchell stood behind the bar. Bob sat next to Dave as Mitchell said, "I could have stopped them, Smitty."

"That's our job," Smitty said. "You want to be in the hospital now?"

Mitchell did not answer. When Smitty and Dave left, he got a glass of Coke from the cobra and had a cigarette with Bob. They did not talk. Then Mitchell washed his glass and Bob's cup and they left, turning off the lights. Outside, Mitchell locked the front door, feeling the sudden night air after almost ten hours of air conditioning. When he had come to work, the day had been very hot, and now he thought it would not have happened in winter. They had stopped for a beer on their way somewhere from the beach; he had heard them say that. But the beach was not the reason. He did not know the reason, but he knew it would not have happened in winter. The night was cool, and now he could smell trees. He turned and looked at the road in front of the bar. Bob stood beside him on the small porch.

"If the regulars had been here . . ." Bob said.

He turned and with his hand resting on the wooden rail, he walked down the ramp to the ground. At his car, he stopped and looked over its roof at Mitchell.

"You take it easy," he said.

Mitchell nodded. When Bob got into his car and left, he went down the ramp and drove home to his house on a street that he thought was neither good nor bad. The houses were small, and there were old large houses used now as apartments for families. Most of the people had work, most of the mothers cared for their children and most of the children were clean and looked like they lived in homes, not caves like some he saw in town. He worried about the older kids, one group of them, anyway. They were idle. When he was a boy in a town farther up the Merrimack River, he and his friends committed every mischievous act he could recall on afternoons and nights when they were idle. His stepchildren were not part of that group. They had friends from the high school. The front-porch light was on for him and one in the kitchen at the rear of the house. He went in the front door and switched off the porch light and walked through the living and dining rooms to the kitchen. He got a can of beer from the refrigerator, turned out the light, and sat at the table. When he could see, he took a cigarette from Susan's pack in front of him.

Down the hall, he heard Susan move on the bed, then get up, and he hoped it wasn't for the bathroom but for him. He had met her eight years ago, when he had given up on ever marrying and having kids; then, one night, she came into the bar with two of her girlfriends from work. She made six dollars an hour going to homes of invalids, mostly what she called her little old ladies, and bathing them. She got the house from her marriage, and child support the guy paid for a few months till he left town and went south. She came barefoot down the hall and stood in the kitchen doorway and said, "Are you all right?"

"No."

She sat across from him, and he told her. Very soon, she held his hand. She was good. He knew if he had fought all five of them and was lying in pieces in the hospital bed, she would tell him he had done the right thing, as she was telling him now. He liked her strong hand on his. It was a professional hand, and he wanted from her something he had never wanted before: to lie in bed while she bathed him. When they went to bed, he did not think he would be able to sleep, but she knelt beside him and massaged his shoulders and rubbed his temples and pressed her hands on his forehead. He woke to the voices of Marty and Joyce in the kitchen. They had summer jobs, and always when they woke him, he went back to sleep till noon, but now he got up and dressed and went to the kitchen door. Susan was at the stove, her back to him, and Marty and Joyce were talking and smoking. He said, "Good morning," and stepped into the room.

"What are you doing up?" Joyce said.

She was a pretty girl with her mother's wide cheekbones, and Marty was a tall, good-looking boy, and Mitchell felt as old as he had before he slept. Susan was watching him. Then she poured him a cup of coffee and put it at his place and he sat. Marty said, "You getting up for the day?"

"Something happened last night. At the bar." They tried to conceal their excitement, but he saw it in their eyes. "I should have stopped it. I think I *could* have stopped it. That's the point. There were these five guys. They were on motorcycles, but they weren't bikers. Just punks. They came in late, when everybody else had gone home. It was a slow night, anyway. Everybody was at the beach."

"They rob you?" Marty asked.

"No. A girl came in. Young. Nice-looking. You know: just a girl, minding her business."

They nodded, and their eyes were apprehensive.

"She wanted cigarette change; that's all. Those guys were on dope. Coke or something. You know: They were flying in place."

"Did they rape her?" Joyce said.

"Yes, honey."

"The *fuckers*."

Susan opened her mouth, then closed it, and Joyce reached quickly for Susan's pack of cigarettes. Mitchell held his lighter for her and said, "When they started getting rough with her at the bar, I went for the phone. One of them stopped me. He shoved me; that's all. I should have hit him with a bottle."

Marty reached over the table with his big hand and held Mitchell's shoulder.

"No, Mitch. Five guys that mean. And coked up or whatever. No way. You wouldn't be here this morning."

"I don't know. There was always a guy with me. But just one guy, taking turns."

"Great," Joyce said. Marty's hand was on Mitchell's left shoulder; she put hers on his right hand.

"They took her to the hospital," he said. "The guys are in jail."

"They are?" Joyce said.

"I called the cops. When they left."

"You'll be a good witness," Joyce said.

He looked at her proud face.

"At the trial," she said.

The day was hot, but that night, most of the regulars came to the bar. Some of the younger ones came on motorcycles. They were a good crowd: They all worked, except the retired ones, and no one ever bothered the women, not even the young ones with their summer tans. Everyone talked about it: Some had read the news-paper story, some had heard the story in town, and they wanted to hear it from Mitchell. He told it as often as they asked, but he did not finish it, because he was working hard and could not stay with any group of customers long enough.

He watched their faces. Not one of them, even the women, looked at him as if he had not cared enough for the girl or was a coward. Many of them even appeared sympathetic, making him feel for moments that he was a survivor of something horrible; and when that feeling left him, he was ashamed. He felt tired and old, making drinks and change, talking and moving up and down the bar. At the stool at the far end, Bob drank coffee; and whenever Mitchell looked at him, he smiled or nodded and once raised his right fist, with the thumb up.

Reggie was drinking too much. He did that two or three times a month, and Mitchell had to shut him off, and Reggie always took it humbly. He was a big, gentle man with a long brown beard. But tonight, shutting off Reggie demanded from Mitchell an act of will, and when the eleven-o'clock news came on the television and Reggie ordered another shot and a draft, Mitchell pretended not to hear him. He served the customers at the other end of the bar, where Bob was. He could hear Reggie calling, "Hey, Mitch; shot and a draft, Mitch."

Mitchell was close to Bob now. Bob said softly, "He's had enough."

Mitchell nodded and went to Reggie, leaned closer to him, so he could speak quietly, and said, "Sorry, Reggie. Time for coffee. I don't want you dead out there."

Reggie blinked at him.

"OK, Mitch." He pulled some bills from his pocket and put them on the bar. Mitchell glanced at them and saw at least a ten-dollar tip. When he ran up Reggie's tab, the change was $16.50, and he dropped the coins and shoved the bills into the beer mug beside the cash register. The mug was full of bills, as it was on most nights, and he kept his hand in there, pressing Reggie's into the others, and saw the sunburned young men holding her down on the floor and one kneeling between her legs, spread and held, and he heard their cheering voices and her screaming and groaning and finally weeping and weeping and weeping, until she was the siren crying, then fading into the night. From the floor behind him, far across the room, he felt her pain and terror and grief, then her curse upon him. The curse moved into his back and spread down and up his spine, into his stomach and legs and arms and shoulders until he quivered with it. He wished he were alone so he could kneel to receive it.

[1988]

Journal Entry

How is it possible to be a rape victim without being raped?

Textual Considerations

1. Analyze Mitchell's character. Do you think he did the right thing? Explain.
2. Do you agree with his family and friends that his intervention would have accomplished nothing? Why or why not?
3. How does the author's choice of an omniscient narrator affect the meaning and tone of the story?
4. Why do we find out so little about the girl?
5. Review the last paragraph. What does it reveal about Mitchell's psychological state? How does it reinforce the implications of the story's title?

Cultural Contexts

1. Dubus wrote this story while recovering from an automobile accident that occurred when he stopped to help a woman with a flat tire. He was hit by a car and lost a leg. What new meanings does this biographical information add to your understanding of the text?
2. Discuss with your group the effects of being a witness to violence. To what extent should people get involved? Is action or inaction more likely to result in some psychological suffering for the witness? How might you have responded in Mitchell's situation?

Tim O'Brien

The Things They Carried

First Lieutenant Jimmy Cross carried letters from a girl named Martha, a junior at Mount Sebastian College in New Jersey. They were not love letters, but Lieutenant Cross was hoping, so he kept them folded in plastic at the bottom of his rucksack. In the late afternoon, after a day's march, he would dig his foxhole, wash his hands under a canteen, unwrap the letters, hold them with the tips of his fingers, and spend the last hour of light pretending. He would imagine romantic camping trips into the White Mountains in New Hampshire. He would sometimes taste the envelope flaps, knowing her tongue had been there. More than anything, he wanted Martha to love him as he loved her, but the letters were mostly chatty, elusive on the matter of love. She was a virgin, he was almost sure. She was an English major at Mount Sebastian, and she wrote beautifully about her professors and roommates and midterm exams, about her respect for Chaucer and her great affection for Virginia Woolf. She often quoted lines of poetry; she never mentioned the war, except to say, Jimmy, take care of yourself. The letters weighed ten ounces. They were signed "Love, Martha," but Lieutenant Cross understood that "Love" was only a way of signing and did not mean what he sometimes pretended it meant. At dusk, he would carefully return the letters to his rucksack. Slowly, a bit distracted, he would get up and move among his men, checking the perimeter, then at full dark he would return to his hole and watch the night and wonder if Martha was a virgin.

The things they carried were largely determined by necessity. Among the necessities or near necessities were P-38 can openers, pocket knives, heat tabs, wrist watches, dog tags, mosquito repellent, chewing gum, candy, cigarettes, salt tablets, packets of Kool-Aid, lighters, matches, sewing kits, Military Payment Certificates, C rations, and two or three canteens of water. Together, these items weighed between fifteen and twenty pounds, depending upon a man's habits or rate of metabolism. Henry Dobbins, who was a big man, carried extra rations; he was especially fond of canned peaches in heavy syrup over pound cake. Dave Jensen, who practiced field hygiene, carried a toothbrush, dental floss, and several hotel-size bars of soap he'd stolen on R&R in Sydney, Australia. Ted Lavender, who was scared, carried tranquilizers until he was shot in the head outside the village of

Than Khe in mid-April. By necessity, and because it was SOP,[1] they all carried steel helmets that weighed five pounds including the liner and camouflage cover. They carried the standard fatigue jackets and trousers. Very few carried underwear. On their feet they carried jungle boots—2.1 pounds—and Dave Jensen carried three pairs of socks and a can of Dr. Scholl's foot powder as a precaution against trench foot. Until he was shot, Ted Lavender carried six or seven ounces of premium dope, which for him was a necessity. Mitchell Sanders, the RTO,[2] carried condoms. Norman Bowker carried a diary. Rat Kiley carried comic books. Kiowa, a devout Baptist, carried an illustrated New Testament that had been presented to him by his father, who taught Sunday school in Oklahoma City, Oklahoma. As a hedge against bad times, however, Kiowa also carried his grandmother's distrust of the white man, his grandfather's old hunting hatchet. Necessity dictated. Because the land was mined and booby-trapped, it was SOP for each man to carry a steel-centered, nylon-covered flak jacket, which weighed 6.7 pounds, but which on hot days seemed much heavier. Because you could die so quickly, each man carried at least one large compress bandage, usually in the helmet band for easy access. Because the nights were cold, and because the monsoons were wet, each carried a green plastic poncho that could be used as a raincoat or ground sheet or makeshift tent. With its quilted liner, the poncho weighed almost two pounds, but it was worth every ounce. In April, for instance, when Ted Lavender was shot, they used his poncho to wrap him up, then to carry him across the paddy, then to lift him into the chopper that took him away.

They were called legs or grunts.

To carry something was to "hump" it, as when Lieutenant Jimmy Cross humped his love for Martha up the hills and through the swamps. In its intransitive form, "to hump" meant "to walk," or "to march," but it implied burdens far beyond the intransitive.

Almost everyone humped photographs. In his wallet, Lieutenant Cross carried two photographs of Martha. The first was a Kodachrome snapshot signed "Love," though he knew better. She stood against a brick wall. Her eyes were gray and neutral, her lips slightly open as she stared straight-on at the camera. At night, sometimes, Lieutenant Cross wondered who had taken the picture, because he knew she had boyfriends, because he loved her so much, and because he could see the shadow of the picture taker spreading out against the brick wall. The second photograph had been clipped from the 1968 Mount Sebastian yearbook. It was an action shot—women's volleyball—and Martha was bent horizontal to the floor, reaching, the palms of her hands in sharp focus, the tongue taut, the expression frank and competitive. There was no visible sweat. She wore white gym shorts. Her legs, he thought, were almost certainly the legs of a virgin, dry and without hair, the left knee cocked and carrying her entire weight, which was just over one hundred pounds. Lieutenant Cross remembered touching that left knee. A dark theater, he

---

[1] Standard operating procedure.
[2] Radiotelephone operator.

remembered, and the movie was *Bonnie and Clyde*, and Martha wore a tweed skirt, and during the final scene, when he touched her knee, she turned and looked at him in a sad, sober way that made him pull his hand back, but he would always remember the feel of the tweed skirt and the knee beneath it and the sound of the gunfire that killed Bonnie and Clyde, how embarrassing it was, how slow and oppressive. He remembered kissing her good night at the dorm door. Right then, he thought, he should've done something brave. He should've carried her up the stairs to her room and tied her to the bed and touched that left knee all night long. He should've risked it. Whenever he looked at the photographs, he thought of new things he should've done.

What they carried was partly a function of rank, partly of field specialty.

As a first lieutenant and platoon leader, Jimmy Cross carried a compass, maps, code books, binoculars, and a .45-caliber pistol that weighed 2.9 pounds fully loaded. He carried a strobe light and the responsibility for the lives of his men.

As an RTO, Mitchell Sanders carried the PRC-25 radio, a killer, twenty-six pounds with its battery.

As a medic, Rat Kiley carried a canvas satchel filled with morphine and plasma and malaria tablets and surgical tape and comic books and all the things a medic must carry, including M&M's for especially bad wounds, for a total weight of nearly twenty pounds.

As a big man, therefore a machine gunner, Henry Dobbins carried the M-60, which weighed twenty-three pounds unloaded, but which was almost always loaded. In addition, Dobbins carried between ten and fifteen pounds of ammunition draped in belts across his chest and shoulders.

As PFCs or Spec 4s, most of them were common grunts and carried the standard M-16 gas-operated assault rifle. The weapon weighed 7.5 pounds unloaded, 8.2 pounds with its full twenty-round magazine. Depending on numerous factors, such as topography and psychology, the riflemen carried anywhere from twelve to twenty magazines, usually in cloth bandoliers, adding on another 8.4 pounds at minimum, fourteen pounds at maximum. When it was available, they also carried M-16 maintenance gear—rods and steel brushes and swabs and tubes of LSA oil— all of which weighed about a pound. Among the grunts, some carried the M-79 grenade launcher, 5.9 pounds unloaded, a reasonably light weapon except for the ammunition, which was heavy. A single round weighed ten ounces. The typical load was twenty-five rounds. But Ted Lavender, who was scared, carried thirty-four rounds when he was shot and killed outside Than Khe, and he went down under an exceptional burden, more than twenty pounds of ammunition, plus the flak jacket and helmet and rations and water and toilet paper and tranquilizers and all the rest, plus the unweighed fear. He was dead weight. There was no twitching or flopping. Kiowa, who saw it happen, said it was like watching a rock fall, or a big sandbag or something—just boom, then down—not like the movies where the dead guy rolls around and does fancy spins and goes ass over teakettle—not like that, Kiowa said, the poor bastard just flat-fuck fell. Boom. Down. Nothing else. It was a bright morning in mid-April. Lieutenant Cross felt the pain. He blamed himself. They stripped off Lavender's canteens and ammo, all the heavy things, and Rat Kiley said the obvious, the guy's dead, and Mitchell Sanders used his radio to report one U.S. KIA[3] and to request a chopper. Then they wrapped Lavender in his poncho. They carried him out to a dry paddy, established security, and sat smoking the dead man's dope until the chopper came. Lieutenant Cross kept to himself. He pictured Martha's smooth young face, thinking he loved her more than anything, more than his men, and now Ted Lavender was dead because he loved her so much and could not stop thinking about her. When the dust-off arrived, they carried Lavender aboard. Afterward they burned Than Khe. They marched until dusk, then dug their holes, and that night Kiowa kept explaining how you had to be there, how fast it was, how the poor guy just dropped like so much concrete. Boom-down, he said. Like cement.

In addition to the three standard weapons—the M-60, M-16, and M-79—they carried whatever presented itself, or whatever seemed appropriate as a means of killing or staying alive. They carried catch-as-catch-can. At various times, in various situations, they carried M-14s and CAR-15s and Swedish Ks and grease guns and captured AK-47s and Chi-Coms and RPGs and Simonov carbines and black-market Uzis and .38-caliber Smith & Wesson handguns and 66 mm LAWs and shotguns and silencers and blackjacks and bayonets and C-4 plastic explosives. Lee Strunk carried a slingshot; a weapon of last resort, he called it. Mitchell Sanders carried brass knuckles. Kiowa carried his grandfather's feathered hatchet. Every third or fourth man carried a Claymore antipersonnel mine—3.5 pounds with its firing device. They all carried fragmentation grenades—fourteen ounces each. They all carried at least one M-18 colored smoke grenade—twenty-four ounces. Some carried CS or teargas grenades. Some carried white-phosphorus grenades. They carried all they could bear, and then some, including a silent awe for the terrible power of the things they carried.

In the first week of April, before Lavender died, Lieutenant Jimmy Cross received a good-luck charm from Martha. It was a simple pebble, an ounce at most. Smooth to the touch, it was a milky-white color with flecks of orange and violet, oval-shaped, like a miniature egg. In the accompanying letter, Martha wrote that she had found the pebble on the Jersey shoreline, precisely where the land touched water at high tide, where things came together but also separated. It was this separate-but-together quality, she wrote, that had inspired her to pick up the pebble and to carry it in her breast pocket for several days, where it seemed weightless, and then to send it through the mail, by air, as a token of her truest feelings for him. Lieutenant Cross found this romantic. But he wondered what her truest feelings were, exactly, and what she meant by separate-but-together. He wondered how the tides and waves had come into play on that afternoon along the Jersey shoreline when Martha saw the pebble and bent down to rescue it from geology. He imagined bare feet. Martha was a poet, with the poet's sensibilities, and her feet would be brown and bare, the toenails unpainted, the eyes chilly and somber like the ocean in March,

[3] Killed in action.

and though it was painful, he wondered who had been with her that afternoon. He imagined a pair of shadows moving along the strip of sand where things came together but also separated. It was phantom jealousy, he knew, but he couldn't help himself. He loved her so much. On the march, through the hot days of early April, he carried the pebble in his mouth, turning it with his tongue, tasting sea salts and moisture. His mind wandered. He had difficulty keeping his attention on the war. On occasion he would yell at his men to spread out the column, to keep their eyes open, but then he would slip away into daydreams, just pretending, walking barefoot along the Jersey shore, with Martha, carrying nothing. He would feel himself rising. Sun and waves and gentle winds, all love and lightness.

What they carried varied by mission.

When a mission took them to the mountains, they carried mosquito netting, machetes, canvas tarps, and extra bug juice.

If a mission seemed especially hazardous, or if it involved a place they knew to be bad, they carried everything they could. In certain heavily mined AOs,[4] where the land was dense with Toe Poppers and Bouncing Betties, they took turns humping a twenty-eight-pound mine detector. With its headphones and big sensing plate, the equipment was a stress on the lower back and shoulders, awkward to handle, often useless because of the shrapnel in the earth, but they carried it anyway, partly for safety, partly for the illusion of safety.

On ambush, or other night missions, they carried peculiar little odds and ends. Kiowa always took along his New Testament and a pair of moccasins for silence. Dave Jensen carried night-sight vitamins high in carotin. Lee Strunk carried his slingshot; ammo, he claimed, would never be a problem. Rat Kiley carried brandy and M&M's. Until he was shot, Ted Lavender carried the starlight scope, which weighed 6.3 pounds with its aluminum carrying case. Henry Dobbins carried his girlfriend's pantyhose wrapped around his neck as a comforter. They all carried ghosts. When dark came, they would move out single file across the meadows and paddies to their ambush coordinates, where they would quietly set up the Claymores and lie down and spend the night waiting.

Other missions were more complicated and required special equipment. In mid-April, it was their mission to search out and destroy the elaborate tunnel complexes in the Than Khe area south of Chu Lai. To blow the tunnels, they carried one-pound blocks of pentrite high explosives, four blocks to a man, sixty-eight pounds in all. They carried wiring, detonators, and battery-powered crackers. Dave Jensen carried earplugs. Most often, before blowing the tunnels, they were ordered by higher command to search them, which was considered bad news, but by and large they just shrugged and carried out orders. Because he was a big man, Henry Dobbins was excused from tunnel duty. The others would draw numbers. Before Lavender died there were seventeen men in the platoon, and whoever drew the number seventeen would strip off his gear and crawl in head first with a flashlight and Lieutenant Cross's .45-caliber pistol. The rest of them would fan out as security. They would sit

----

[4] Areas of operations.

down or kneel, not facing the hole, listening to the ground beneath them, imagining cobwebs and ghosts, whatever was down there—the tunnel walls squeezing in—how the flashlight seemed impossibly heavy in the hand and how it was tunnel vision in the very strictest sense, compression in all ways, even time, and how you had to wiggle in—ass and elbows—a swallowed-up feeling—and how you found yourself worrying about odd things—will your flashlight go dead? Do rats carry rabies? If you screamed, how far would the sound carry? Would your buddies hear it? Would they have the courage to drag you out? In some respects, though not many, the waiting was worse than the tunnel itself. Imagination was a killer.

On April 16, when Lee Strunk drew the number seventeen, he laughed and muttered something and went down quickly. The morning was hot and very still. Not good, Kiowa said. He looked at the tunnel opening, then out across a dry paddy toward the village of Than Khe. Nothing moved. No clouds or birds or people. As they waited, the men smoked and drank Kool-Aid, not talking much, feeling sympathy for Lee Strunk but also feeling the luck of the draw. You win some, you lose some, said Mitchell Sanders, and sometimes you settle for a rain check. It was a tired line and no one laughed.

Henry Dobbins ate a tropical chocolate bar. Ted Lavender popped a tranquilizer and went off to pee.

After five minutes, Lieutenant Jimmy Cross moved to the tunnel, leaned down, and examined the darkness. Trouble, he thought—a cave-in maybe. And then suddenly, without willing it, he was thinking about Martha. The stresses and fractures, the quick collapse, the two of them buried alive under all that weight. Dense, crushing love. Kneeling watching the hole, he tried to concentrate on Lee Strunk and the war, all the dangers, but his love was too much for him, he felt paralyzed, he wanted to sleep inside her lungs and breathe her blood and be smothered. He wanted her to be a virgin and not a virgin, all at once. He wanted to know her. Intimate secrets—why poetry? Why so sad? Why the grayness in her eyes? Why so alone? Not lonely, just alone—riding her bike across campus or sitting off by herself in the cafeteria. Even dancing, she danced alone—and it was the aloneness that filled him with love. He remembered telling her that one evening. How she nodded and looked away. And how, later, when he kissed her, she received the kiss without returning it, her eyes wide open, not afraid, not a virgin's eyes, just flat and uninvolved.

Lieutenant Cross gazed at the tunnel. But he was not there. He was buried with Martha under the white sand at the Jersey shore. They were pressed together, and the pebble in his mouth was her tongue. He was smiling. Vaguely, he was aware of how quiet the day was, the sullen paddies, yet he could not bring himself to worry about matters of security. He was beyond that. He was just a kid at war, in love. He was twenty-two years old. He couldn't help it. A few moments later Lee Strunk crawled out of the tunnel. He came up grinning, filthy but alive. Lieutenant Cross nodded and closed his eyes while the others clapped Strunk on the back and made jokes about rising from the dead.

Worms, Rat Kiley said. Right out of the grave. Fuckin' zombie.

The men laughed. They all felt great relief.

Spook City, said Mitchell Sanders.

Lee Strunk made a funny ghost sound, a kind of moaning, yet very happy, and right then, when Strunk made that high happy moaning sound, when he went *Ahhooooo*, right then Ted Lavender was shot in the head on his way back from peeing. He lay with his mouth open. The teeth were broken. There was a swollen black bruise under his left eye. The cheekbone was gone. Oh shit, Rat Kiley said, the guy's dead. The guy's dead, he kept saying which seemed profound—the guy's dead. I mean really.

The things they carried were determined to some extent by superstition. Lieutenant Cross carried his good-luck pebble. Dave Jensen carried a rabbit's foot. Norman Bowker, otherwise a very gentle person, carried a thumb that had been presented to him as a gift by Mitchell Sanders. The thumb was dark brown, rubbery to the touch, and weighed four ounces at most. It had been cut from a VC corpse, a boy of fifteen or sixteen. They'd found him at the bottom of an irrigation ditch, badly burned, flies in his mouth and eyes. The boy wore black shorts and sandals. At the time of his death he had been carrying a pouch of rice, a rifle, and three magazines of ammunition.

You want my opinion, Mitchell Sanders said, there's a definite moral here.

He put his hand on the dead boy's wrist. He was quiet for a time, as if counting a pulse, then he patted the stomach, almost affectionately, and used Kiowa's hunting hatchet to remove the thumb.

Henry Dobbins asked what the moral was.

Moral?

You know. *Moral*.

Sanders wrapped the thumb in toilet paper and handed it across to Norman Bowker. There was no blood. Smiling, he kicked the boy's head, watched the flies scatter, and said, It's like with that old TV show—Paladin. Have gun, will travel.

Henry Dobbins thought about it.

Yeah, well, he finally said. I don't see no moral.

There it *is*, man.

Fuck off.

They carried USO stationery and pencils and pens. They carried Sterno, safety pins, trip flares, signal flares, spools of wire, razor blades, chewing tobacco, liberated joss sticks and statuettes of the smiling Buddha, candies, grease pencils, *The Stars and Stripes*, fingernail clippers, Psy Ops[5] leaflets, bush hats, bolos, and much more. Twice a week, when the resupply choppers came in, they carried hot chow in green Mermite cans and large canvas bags filled with iced beer and soda pop. They carried plastic water containers, each with a two-gallon capacity. Mitchell Sanders carried a set of starched tiger fatigues for special occasions. Henry Dobbins carried Black Flag insecticide. Dave Jensen carried empty sandbags that could be filled at night for added protection. Lee Strunk carried tanning lotion. Some things they carried in common. Taking turns, they carried the big PRC-77 scrambler radio,

---

[5] Psychological operations.

which weighed thirty pounds with its battery. They shared the weight of memory. They took up what others could no longer bear. Often, they carried each other, the wounded or weak. They carried infections. They carried chess sets, basketballs, Vietnamese-English dictionaries, insignia of rank, Bronze Stars and Purple Hearts, plastic cards imprinted with the Code of Conduct. They carried diseases, among them malaria and dysentery. They carried lice and ringworm and leeches and paddy algae and various rots and molds. They carried the land itself—Vietnam, the place, the soil—a powdery orange-red dust that covered their boots and fatigues and faces. They carried the sky. The whole atmosphere, they carried it, the humidity, the monsoons, the stink of fungus and decay, all of it, they carried gravity. They moved like mules. By daylight they took sniper fire, at night they were mortared, but it was not battle, it was just the endless march, village to village, without purpose, nothing won or lost. They marched for the sake of the march. They plodded along slowly, dumbly, leaning forward against the heat, unthinking, all blood and bone, simple grunts, soldiering with their legs, toiling up the hills and down into the paddies and across the rivers and up again and down, just humping, one step and then the next and then another, but no volition, no will, because it was automatic, it was anatomy, and the war was entirely a matter of posture and carriage, the hump was everything, a kind of inertia, a kind of emptiness, a dullness of desire and intellect and con-science and hope and human sensibility. Their principles were in their feet. Their calculations were biological. They had no sense of strategy or mission. They searched the villages without knowing what to look for, not caring, kicking over jars of rice, frisking children and old men, blowing tunnels, sometimes setting fires and sometimes not, then forming up and moving on to the next village, then other vil-lages, where it would always be the same. They carried their own lives. The pres-sures were enormous. In the heat of early afternoon, they would remove their helmets and flak jackets, walking bare, which was dangerous but which helped ease the strain. They would often discard things along the route of march. Purely for comfort, they would throw away rations, blow their Claymores and grenades, no matter, because by nightfall the resupply choppers would arrive with more of the same, then a day or two later still more, fresh watermelons and crates of ammuni-tion and sunglasses and woolen sweaters— the resources were stunning—sparklers for the Fourth of July, colored eggs for Easter. It was the great American war chest—the fruits of science, the smokestacks, the canneries, the arsenals at Hart-ford, the Minnesota forests, the machine shops, the vast fields of corn and wheat— they carried like freight trains; they carried it on their backs and shoulders—and for all the ambiguities of Vietnam, all the mysteries and unknowns, there was at least the single abiding certainty that they would never be at a loss for things to carry.

After the chopper took Lavender away, Lieutenant Jimmy Cross led his men into the village of Than Khe. They burned everything. They shot chickens and dogs, they trashed the village well, they called in artillery and watched the wreck-age, then they marched for several hours through the hot afternoon, and then at dusk, while Kiowa explained how Lavender died, Lieutenant Cross found himself trembling.

He tried not to cry. With his entrenching tool, which weighed five pounds, he began digging a hole in the earth.

He felt shame. He hated himself. He had loved Martha more than his men, and as a consequence Lavender was now dead, and this was something he would have to carry like a stone in his stomach for the rest of the war.

All he could do was dig. He used his entrenching tool like an ax, slashing, feeling both love and hate, and then later, when it was full dark, he sat at the bottom of his foxhole and wept. It went on for a long while. In part, he was grieving for Ted Lavender, but mostly it was for Martha, and for himself, because she belonged to another world, which was not quite real, and because she was a junior at Mount Sebastian College in New Jersey, a poet and a virgin and uninvolved, and because he realized she did not love him and never would.

Like cement, Kiowa whispered in the dark. I swear to God—boom-down. Not a word.

I've heard this, said Norman Bowker.

A pisser, you know? Still zipping himself up. Zapped while zipping.

All right, fine. That's enough.

Yeah, but you had to see it, the guy just—

I *heard*, man. Cement. So why not shut the fuck *up*?

Kiowa shook his head sadly and glanced over at the hole where Lieutenant Jimmy Cross sat watching the night. The air was thick and wet. A warm, dense fog had settled over the paddies and there was the stillness that precedes rain.

After a time Kiowa sighed.

One thing for sure, he said. The Lieutenant's in some deep hurt. I mean that crying jag—the way he was carrying on—it wasn't fake or anything, it was real heavy-duty hurt. The man cares.

Sure, Norman Bowker said.

Say what you want, the man does care.

We all got problems.

Not Lavender.

No, I guess not, Bowker said. Do me a favor, though.

Shut up?

That's a smart Indian. Shut up.

Shrugging, Kiowa pulled off his boots. He wanted to say more, just to lighten up his sleep, but instead he opened his New Testament and arranged it beneath his head as a pillow. The fog made things seem hollow and unattached. He tried not to think about Ted Lavender, but then he was thinking how fast it was, no drama, down and dead, and how it was hard to feel anything except surprise. It seemed un-Christian. He wished he could find some great sadness, or even anger, but the emotion wasn't there and he couldn't make it happen. Mostly he felt pleased to be alive. He liked the smell of the New Testament under his cheek, the leather and ink and paper and glue, whatever the chemicals were. He liked hearing the sounds of night. Even his fatigue, it felt fine, the stiff muscles and the prickly awareness of his own body, a floating feeling. He enjoyed not being dead. Lying there, Kiowa admired

Lieutenant Jimmy Cross's capacity for grief. He wanted to share the man's pain, he wanted to care as Jimmy Cross cared. And yet when he closed his eyes, all he could think was Boom-down, and all he could feel was the pleasure of having his boots off and the fog curling in around him and the damp soil and the Bible smells and the plush comfort of night.

After a moment Norman Bowker sat up in the dark.

What the hell, he said. You want to talk, *talk*. Tell it to me.

Forget it.

No, man, go on. One thing I hate, it's a silent Indian.

For the most part they carried themselves with poise, a kind of dignity. Now and then, however, there were times of panic, when they squealed or wanted to squeal but couldn't, when they twitched and made moaning sounds and covered their heads and said Dear Jesus and flopped around on the earth and fired their weapons blindly and cringed and sobbed and begged for the noise to stop and went wild and made stupid promises to themselves and to God and to their mothers and fathers, hoping not to die. In different ways, it happened to all of them. Afterward, when the firing ended, they would blink and peek up. They would touch their bodies, feeling shame, then quickly hiding it. They would force themselves to stand. As if in slow motion, frame by frame, the world would take on the old logic—absolute silence, then the wind, then sunlight, then voices. It was the burden of being alive. Awkwardly, the men would reassemble themselves, first in private, then in groups, becoming soldiers again. They would repair the leaks in their eyes. They would check for casualties, call in dust-offs, light cigarettes, try to smile, clear their throats and spit and begin cleaning their weapons. After a time someone would shake his head and say, No lie, I almost shit my pants, and someone else would laugh, which meant it was bad, yes, but the guy had obviously not shit his pants, it wasn't that bad, and in any case nobody would ever do such a thing and then go ahead and talk about it. They would squint into the dense, oppressive sunlight. For a few moments, perhaps, they would fall silent, lighting a joint and tracking its passage from man to man, inhaling, holding in the humiliation. Scary stuff, one of them might say. But then someone else would grin or flick his eyebrows and say, Roger-dodger, almost cut me a new asshole, *almost*.

There were numerous such poses. Some carried themselves with a sort of wistful resignation, others with pride or stiff soldierly discipline or good humor or macho zeal. They were afraid of dying but they were even more afraid to show it.

They found jokes to tell.

They used a hard vocabulary to contain the terrible softness. *Greased*, they'd say. *Offed, lit up, zapped while zipping*. It wasn't cruelty, just stage presence. They were actors and the war came at them in 3-D. When someone died, it wasn't quite dying, because in a curious way it seemed scripted, and because they had their lines mostly memorized, irony mixed with tragedy, and because they called it by other names, as if to encyst and destroy the reality of death itself. They kicked corpses. They cut off thumbs. They talked grunt lingo. They told stories about Ted Lavender's supply of tranquilizers, how the poor guy didn't feel a thing, how incredibly tranquil he was.

There's a moral here, said Mitchell Sanders.

They were waiting for Lavender's chopper, smoking the dead man's dope.

The moral's pretty obvious, Sanders said, and winked. Stay away from drugs. No joke, they'll ruin your day every time.

Cute, said Henry Dobbins.

Mind-blower, get it? Talk about wiggy—nothing left, just blood and brains.

They made themselves laugh.

There it is, they'd say, over and over, as if the repetition itself were an act of poise, a balance between crazy and almost crazy, knowing without going. There it is, which meant be cool, let it ride, because oh yeah, man, you can't change what can't be changed, there it is, there it absolutely and positively and fucking well is.

They were tough.

They carried all the emotional baggage of men who might die. Grief, terror, love, longing—these were intangibles, but the intangibles had their own mass and specific gravity, they had tangible weight. They carried shameful memories. They carried the common secret of cowardice barely restrained, the instinct to run or freeze or hide, and in many respects this was the heaviest burden of all, for it could never be put down, it required perfect balance and perfect posture. They carried their reputations. They carried the soldier's greatest fear, which was the fear of blushing. Men killed, and died, because they were embarrassed not to. It was what had brought them to the war in the first place, nothing positive, no dreams of glory or honor, just to avoid the blush of dishonor. They died so as not to die of embarrassment. They crawled into tunnels and walked point and advanced under fire. Each morning, despite the unknowns, they made their legs move. They endured. They kept humping. They did not submit to the obvious alternative, which was simply to close the eyes and fail. So easy, really. Go limp and tumble to the ground and let the muscles unwind and not speak and not budge until your buddies picked you up and lifted you into the chopper that would roar and dip its nose and carry you off to the world. A mere matter of falling, yet no one ever fell. It was not courage, exactly; the object was not valor. Rather, they were too frightened to be cowards.

By and large they carried these things inside, maintaining the masks of composure. They sneered at sick call. They spoke bitterly about guys who had found release by shooting off their own toes or fingers. Pussies, they'd say. Candyasses. It was fierce, mocking talk, with only a trace of envy or awe, but even so, the image played itself out behind their eyes.

They imagined the muzzle against flesh. They imagined the quick, sweet pain, then the evacuation to Japan, then a hospital with warm beds and cute geisha nurses.

They dreamed of freedom birds.

At night, on guard, staring into the dark, they were carried away by jumbo jets. They felt the rush of takeoff. *Gone!* they yelled. And then velocity, wings and engines, a smiling stewardess—but it was more than a plane, it was a real bird, a big sleek silver bird with feathers and talons and high screeching. They were flying. The weights fell off, there was nothing to bear. They laughed and held on tight, feeling the cold slap of wind and altitude soaring, thinking *It's over, I'm gone!*—they were naked, they were light and free—it was all lightness, bright and fast and buoyant, light as light, a helium buzz in the brain, a giddy bubbling in the lungs as they were taken up over the clouds and the war, beyond duty, beyond gravity and mortification and global entanglements—*Sin loi!*[6] they yelled, *I'm sorry, motherfuckers, but I'm out of it, I'm goofed, I'm on a space cruise, I'm gone!*—and it was a restful, disencumbered sensation, just riding the light waves, sailing that big silver freedom bird over the mountains and oceans, over America, over the farms and great sleeping cities and cemeteries and highways and the golden arches of McDonald's. It was flight, a kind of fleeing, a kind of falling, falling higher and higher, spinning off the edge of the earth and beyond the sun and through the vast, silent vacuum where there were no burdens and where everything weighed exactly nothing. *Gone!* they screamed, *I'm sorry but I'm gone!* And so at night, not quite dreaming, they gave themselves over to lightness, they were carried, they were purely borne.

On the morning after Ted Lavender died, First Lieutenant Jimmy Cross crouched at the bottom of his foxhole and burned Martha's letters. Then he burned the two photographs. There was a steady rain falling, which made it difficult, but he used heat tabs and Sterno to build a small fire, screening it with his body, holding the photographs over the tight blue flame with the tips of his fingers.

He realized it was only a gesture. Stupid, he thought. Sentimental, too, but mostly just stupid.

Lavender was dead. You couldn't burn the blame.

Besides, the letters were in his head. And even now, without photographs, Lieutenant Cross could see Martha playing volleyball in her white gym shorts and yellow T-shirt. He could see her moving in the rain.

When the fire died out, Lieutenant Cross pulled his poncho over his shoulders and ate breakfast from a can.

There was no great mystery, he decided.

In those burned letters Martha had never mentioned the war, except to say, Jimmy, take care of yourself. She wasn't involved. She signed the letters "Love," but it wasn't love, and all the fine lines and technicalities did not matter.

The morning came up wet and blurry. Everything seemed part of everything else, the fog and Martha and the deepening rain.

It was a war, after all.

Half smiling, Lieutenant Jimmy Cross took out his maps. He shook his head hard, as if to clear it, then bent forward and began planning the day's march. In ten minutes, or maybe twenty, he would rouse the men and they would pack up and head west, where the maps showed the country to be green and inviting. They would do what they had always done. The rain might add some weight, but otherwise it would be one more day layered upon all the other days.

He was realistic about it. There was that new hardness in his stomach.

No more fantasies, he told himself.

Henceforth, when he thought about Martha, it would be only to think that she belonged elsewhere. He would shut down the daydreams. This was not Mount

---

[6] "Sorry about that!"

Sebastian, it was another world, where there were no pretty poems or midterm exams, a place where men died because of carelessness and gross stupidity. Kiowa was right. Boom-down, and you were dead, never partly dead.

Briefly, in the rain, Lieutenant Cross saw Martha's gray eyes gazing back at him. He understood.

It was very sad, he thought. The things men carried inside. The things men did or felt they had to do.

He almost nodded at her, but didn't.

Instead he went back to his maps. He was now determined to perform his duties firmly and without negligence. It wouldn't help Lavender, he knew that, but from this point on he would comport himself as a soldier. He would dispose of his good-luck pebble. Swallow it, maybe, or use Lee Strunk's slingshot, or just drop it along the trail. On the march he would impose strict field discipline. He would be careful to send out flank security, to prevent straggling or bunching up, to keep his troops moving at the proper pace and at the proper interval. He would insist on clean weapons. He would confiscate the remainder of Lavender's dope. Later in the day, perhaps, he would call the men together and speak to them plainly. He would accept the blame for what had happened to Ted Lavender. He would be a man about it. He would look them in the eyes, keeping his chin level, and he would issue the new SOPs in a calm, impersonal tone of voice, an officer's voice, leaving no room for argument or discussion. Commencing immediately, he'd tell them, they would no longer abandon equipment along the route of march. They would police up their acts. They would get their shit together, and keep it together, and maintain it neatly and in good working order.

He would not tolerate laxity. He would show strength, distancing himself.

Among the men there would be grumbling, of course, and maybe worse, because their days would seem longer and their loads heavier, but Lieutenant Cross reminded himself that his obligation was not to be loved but to lead. He would dispense with love; it was not now a factor. And if anyone quarreled or complained, he would simply tighten his lips and arrange his shoulders in the correct command posture. He might give a curt little nod. Or he might not. He might just shrug and say Carry on, then they would saddle up and form into a column and move out toward the villages of Than Khe.

                                                                              [1986]

Journal Entry

Empty the contents of your backpack and write a journal entry on what they reveal about your personality.

Textual Considerations

1. How does the author use repetition to enhance theme? Consider, for example, the effect of the many references to Lavender's death and to Martha's letters.

2. Each man carries other things in addition to "necessities." Review the second paragraph. Cite examples of what they carry, and discuss what these things reveal about them. The men also carry psychological "things." What is suggested in the following examples?

"They carried all they could bear, and then some, including a silent awe for the terrible power of the things they carried."
"They all carried ghosts."
"They carried all the emotional baggage of men who might die."

3. How does the author use variations in paragraph length to suggest the tedium of the soldiers' daily routines? Cite examples.
4. Why does Cross burn Martha's letter and photographs? What thematic roles does Martha play in the story?
5. What is the "moral" that Mitchell Sanders finds in the dead Vietcong boy in the irrigation ditch?

Cultural Contexts

1. Lieutenant Cross carried "the responsibility for the lives of his men." Did he feel responsible for Lavender's death? Do you think he was responsible for Lavender's death? How could Cross have prevented his death? How does Lavender's death affect the way Cross will command his troops in the future?
2. Using a dictionary and a thesaurus, list the various meanings and connotations of the word *carry*. Go through O'Brien's story with your group members, looking for examples that correspond to the meanings of *carry* on your lists. What multiple thematic roles does *carrying* play in the narrative?

Ann Petry

Like a Winding Sheet

He had planned to get up before Mae did and surprise her by fixing breakfast. Instead he went back to sleep and she got out of bed so quietly he didn't know she wasn't there beside him until he woke up and heard the queer soft gurgle of water running out of the sink in the bathroom.

He knew he ought to get up but instead he put his arms across his forehead to shut the afternoon sunlight out of his eyes, pulled his legs up close to his body, testing them to see if the ache was still in them.

Mae had finished in the bathroom. He could tell because she never closed the door when she was in there and now the sweet smell of talcum powder was drifting down the hall and into the bedroom. Then he heard her coming down the hall.

"Hi, babe," she said affectionately.

"Hum," he grunted, and moved his arms away from his head, opened one eye.

"It's a nice morning."

"Yeah," he rolled over and the sheet twisted around him, outlining his thighs, his chest. "You mean afternoon, don't ya?"

Mae looked at the twisted sheet and giggled. "Looks like a winding sheet," she said. "A shroud—." Laughter tangled with her words and she had to pause for a moment before she could continue. "You look like a huckleberry—in a winding sheet—"

"That's no way to talk. Early in the day like this," he protested.

He looked at his arms silhouetted against the white of the sheets. They were inky black by contrast and he had to smile in spite of himself and he lay there smiling and savouring the sweet sound of Mae's giggling.

"Early?" She pointed a finger at the alarm clock on the table near the bed, and giggled again. "It's almost four o'clock. And if you don't spring up out of there you're going to be late again."

"What do you mean 'again'?"

"Twice last week. Three times the week before. And once the week before and—"

"I can't get used to sleeping in the day time," he said fretfully. He pushed his legs out from under the covers experimentally. Some of the ache had gone out of them but they weren't really rested yet. "It's too light for good sleeping. And all that standing beats the hell out of my legs."

"After two years you oughtta be used to it," Mae said.

He watched her as she fixed her hair, powdered her face, slipping into a pair of blue denim overalls. She moved quickly and yet she didn't seem to hurry.

"You look like you'd had plenty of sleep," he said lazily. He had to get up but he kept putting the moment off, not wanting to move, yet he didn't dare let his legs go completely limp because if he did he'd go back to sleep. It was getting later and later but the thought of putting his weight on his legs kept him lying there.

When he finally got up he had to hurry and he gulped his breakfast so fast that he wondered if his stomach could possibly use food thrown at it at such a rate of speed. He was still wondering about it as he and Mae were putting their coats on in the hall.

Mae paused to look at the calendar. "It's the thirteenth," she said. Then a faint excitement in her voice. "Why it's Friday the thirteenth." She had one arm in her coat sleeve and she held it there while she stared at the calendar. "I oughtta stay home," she said. "I shouldn't go otta the house."

"Aw don't be a fool," he said. "To-day's payday. And payday is a good luck day everywhere, any way you look at it." And as she stood hesitating he said, "Aw, come on."

And he was late for work again because they spent fifteen minutes arguing before he could convince her she ought to go to work just the same. He had to talk persuasively, urging her gently and it took time. But he couldn't bring himself to talk to her roughly or threaten to strike her like a lot of men might have done. He wasn't made that way.

So when he reached the plant he was late and he had to wait to punch the time clock because the day shift workers were streaming out in long lines, in groups and bunches that impeded his progress.

Even now just starting his work-day his legs ached. He had to force himself to struggle past the out-going workers, punch the time clock, and get the little cart he pushed around all night because he kept toying with the idea of going home and getting back in bed.

He pushed the cart out on the concrete floor, thinking that if this was his plant he'd make a lot of changes in it. There were too many standing up jobs for one thing. He'd figure out some way most of 'em could be done sitting down and he'd put a lot more benches around. And this job he had—this job that forced him to walk ten hours a night, pushing this little cart, well, he'd turn it into a sittin'-down job. One of those little trucks they used around railroad stations would be good for a job like this. Guys sat on a seat and the thing moved easily, taking up little room and turning in hardly any space at all, like on a dime.

He pushed the cart near the foreman. He never could remember to refer to her as the forelady even in his mind. It was funny to have a woman for a boss in a plant like this one.

She was sore about something. He could tell by the way her face was red and her eyes were half shut until they were slits. Probably been out late and didn't get enough sleep. He avoided looking at her and hurried a little, head down, as he passed her though he couldn't resist stealing a glance at her out of the corner of his eyes. He saw the edge of the light colored slacks she wore and the tip end of a big tan shoe.

"Hey, Johnson!" the woman said.

The machines had started full blast. The whirr and the grinding made the building shake, made it impossible to hear conversations. The men and women at the machines talked to each other but looking at them from just a little distance away they appeared to be simply moving their lips because you couldn't hear what they were saying. Yet the woman's voice cut across the machine sounds—harsh, angry.

He turned his head slowly. "Good Evenin', Mrs. Scott," he said and waited.

"You're late again."

"That's right. My legs were bothering me."

The woman's face grew redder, angrier looking. "Half this shift comes in late," she said. "And you're the worst one of all. You're always late. Whatsa matter with ya?"

"It's my legs," he said. "Somehow they don't ever get rested. I don't seem to get used to sleeping days. And I just can't get started."

"Excuses. You guys always got excuses," her anger grew and spread. "Every guy comes in here late always has an excuse. His wife's sick or his grandmother died or somebody in the family had to go to the hospital," she paused, drew a deep breath. "And the niggers are the worse. I don't care what's wrong with your legs. You get in here on time. I'm sick of you niggers—"

"You got the right to get mad," he interrupted softly. "You got the right to cuss me four ways to Sunday but I ain't letting nobody call me a nigger."

He stepped closer to her. His fists were doubled. His lips were drawn back in a thin narrow line. A vein in his forehead stood out swollen, thick.

And the woman backed away from him, not hurriedly but slowly—two, three steps back.

"Aw, forget it," she said. "I didn't mean nothing by it. It slipped out. It was a accident." The red of her face deepened until the small blood vessels in her cheeks were purple. "Go on and get to work," she urged. And she took three more slow backward steps.

He stood motionless for a moment and then turned away from the red lipstick on her mouth that made him remember that the foreman was a woman. And he couldn't bring himself to hit a woman. He felt a curious tingling in his fingers and he looked down at his hands. They were clenched tight, hard, ready to smash some of those small purple veins in her face.

He pushed the cart ahead of him, walking slowly. When he turned his head, she was staring in his direction, mopping her forehead with a dark blue handkerchief. Their eyes met and then they both looked away.

He didn't glance in her direction again but moved past the long work benches, carefully collecting the finished parts, going slowly and steadily up and down, back and forth the length of the building and as he walked he forced himself to swallow his anger, get rid of it.

And he succeeded so that he was able to think about what had happened without getting upset about it. An hour went by but the tension stayed in his hands. They were clenched and knotted on the handles of the cart as though ready to aim a blow.

And he thought he should have hit her anyway, smacked her hard in the face, felt the soft flesh of her face give under the hardness of his hands. He tried to make his hands relax by offering them a description of what it would have been like to strike her because he had the queer feeling that his hands were not exactly a part of him any more—they had developed a separate life of their own over which he had no control. So he dwelt on the pleasure his hands would have felt—both of them cracking at her, first one and then the other. If he had done that his hands would have felt good now—relaxed, rested.

And he decided that even if he'd lost his job for it he should have let her have it and it would have been a long time, maybe the rest of her life before she called anybody else a nigger.

The only trouble was he couldn't hit a woman. A woman couldn't hit back the same way a man did. But it would have been a deeply satisfying thing to have cracked her narrow lips wide open with just one blow, beautifully timed and with all his weight in back of it. That way he would have gotten rid of all the energy and tension his anger had created in him. He kept remembering how his heart had started pumping blood so fast he had felt it tingle even in the tips of his fingers.

With the approach of night fatigue nibbled at him. The corners of his mouth dropped, the frown between his eyes deepened, his shoulders sagged; but his hands stayed tight and tense. As the hours dragged by he noticed that the women workers had started to snap and snarl at each other. He couldn't hear what they said because of the sound of machines but he could see the quick lip movements that sent words tumbling from the sides of their mouths. They gestured irritably with their hands and scowled as their mouths moved.

Their violent jerky motions told him that it was getting close on to quitting time but somehow he felt that the night still stretched ahead of him, composed of endless hours of steady walking on his aching legs. When the whistle finally blew he went on pushing the cart, unable to believe that it had sounded. The whirring of the machines died away to a murmur and he knew then that he'd really heard the whistle. He stood still for a moment filled with a relief that made him sigh.

Then he moved briskly, putting the cart in the store room, hurrying to take his place in the line forming before the paymaster. That was another thing he'd change, he thought. He'd have the pay envelopes handed to the people right at their benches so there wouldn't be ten or fifteen minutes lost waiting for the pay. He always got home about fifteen minutes late on payday. They did it better in the plant where Mae worked, brought the money right to them at their benches.

He stuck his pay envelope in his pants' pocket and followed the line of workers heading for the subway in a slow moving stream. He glanced up at the sky. It was a nice night, the sky looked packed full to running over with stars. And he thought if he and Mae would go right to bed when they got home from work they'd catch a few hours of darkness for sleeping. But they never did. They fooled around—cooking and eating and listening to the radio and he always stayed in a big chair in the living room and went almost but not quite to sleep and when they finally got to bed it was five or six in the morning and daylight was already seeping around the edges of the sky.

He walked slowly, putting off the movement when he would have to plunge into the crowd hurrying toward the subway. It was a long ride to Harlem and tonight the thought of it appalled him. He paused outside an all-night restaurant to kill time, so that some of the first rush of workers would be gone when he reached the subway.

The lights in the restaurant were brilliant, enticing. There was life and motion inside. And as he looked through the window he thought that everything within range of his eyes gleamed—the long imitation marble counter, the tall stools, the white porcelain topped tables and especially the big metal coffee urn right near the window. Steam issued from its top and a gas flame flickered under it—a lively, dancing, blue flame.

A lot of the workers from his shift—men and women—were lining up near the coffee urn. He watched them walk to the porcelain topped tables carrying steaming cups of coffee and he saw that just the smell of the coffee lessened the fatigue lines in their faces. After the first sip their faces softened, they smiled, they began to talk and laugh.

On a sudden impulse he shoved the door open and joined the line in front of the coffee urn. The line moved slowly. And as he stood there the smell of the coffee, the sound of the laughter and of the voices, helped dull the sharp ache in his legs.

He didn't pay any attention to the girl who was serving the coffee at the urn. He kept looking at the cups in the hands of the men who had been ahead of him. Each time a man stepped out of the line with one of the thick white cups the fragrant steam got in his nostrils. He saw that they walked carefully so as not to spill a single drop. There was a froth of bubbles at the top of each cup and he thought about how he would let the bubbles break against his lips before he actually took a big deep swallow.

Then it was his turn. "A cup of coffee," he said, just as he had heard the others say.

The girl looked past him, put her hands up to her head and gently lifted her hair away from the back of her neck, tossing her head back a little. "No more coffee for awhile," she said.

He wasn't certain he'd heard her correctly and he said, "What?" blankly.

"No more coffee for awhile," she repeated.

There was silence behind him and then uneasy movement. He thought some-one would say something, ask why or protest, but there was only silence and then a faint shuffling sound as though the men standing behind him had simultaneously shifted their weight from one foot to the other.

He looked at her without saying anything. He felt his hands begin to tingle and the tingling went all the way down to his finger tips so that he glanced down at them. They were clenched tight, hard, into fists. Then he looked at the girl again. What he wanted to do was hit her so hard that the scarlet lipstick on her mouth would smear and spread over her nose, her chin, out toward her cheeks; so hard that she would never toss her head again and refuse a man a cup of coffee because he was black.

He estimated the distance across the counter and reached forward, balancing his weight on the balls of his feet, ready to let the blow go. And then his hands fell back down to his sides because he forced himself to lower them, to unclench them and make them dangle loose. The effort took his breath away because his hands fought against him. But he couldn't hit her. He couldn't even now bring himself to hit a woman, not even this one, who had refused him a cup of coffee with a toss of her head. He kept seeing the gesture with which she had lifted the length of her blonde hair from the back of her neck as expressive of her contempt for him.

When he went out the door he didn't look back. If he had he would have seen the flickering blue flame under the shiny coffee urn being extinguished. The line of men who had stood behind him lingered a moment to watch the people drinking coffee at the tables and then they left just as he had without having had the coffee they wanted so badly. The girl behind the counter poured water in the urn and swabbed it out and as she waited for the water to run out she lifted her hair gently from the back of her neck and tossed her head before she began making a fresh lot of coffee.

But he walked away without a backward look, his head down, his hands in his pockets, raging at himself and whatever it was inside of him that had forced him to stand quiet and still when he wanted to strike out.

The subway was crowded and he had to stand. He tried grasping an overhead strap and his hands were too tense to grip it. So he moved near the train door and stood there swaying back and forth with the rocking of the train. The roar of the train beat inside his head, making it ache and throb, and the pain in his legs clawed up into his groin so that he seemed to be bursting with pain and he told himself that it was due to all that anger-born energy that had piled up in him and not been used and so it had spread through him like a poison—from his feet and legs all the way up to his head.

Mae was in the house before he was. He knew she was home before he put the key in the door of the apartment. The radio was going. She had it turned up loud and she was singing along with it.

"Hello, Babe," she called out as soon as he opened the door.

He tried to say "hello" and it came out half a grunt and half sigh.

"You sure sound cheerful," she said.

She was in the bedroom and he went and leaned against the door jamb. The denim overalls she wore to work were carefully draped over the back of a chair by the bed. She was standing in front of the dresser, tying the sash of a yellow house-coat around her waist and chewing gum vigorously as she admired her reflection in the mirror over the dresser.

"Whatsa matter?" she said. "You get bawled out by the boss or somep'n?"

"Just tired," he said slowly. "For God's sake do you have to crack that gum like that?"

"You don't have to lissen to me," she said complacently. She patted a curl in place near the side of her head and then lifted her hair away from the back of her neck, ducking her head forward and then back.

He winced away from the gesture. "What you got to be always fooling with your hair for?" he protested.

"Say, what's the matter with you, anyway?" she turned away from the mirror to face him, put her hands on her hips. "You ain't been in the house two minutes and you're picking on me."

He didn't answer her because her eyes were angry and he didn't want to quarrel with her. They'd been married too long and got along too well and so he walked all the way into the room and sat down in the chair by the bed and stretched his legs out in front of him, putting his weight on the heels of his shoes, leaning way back in the chair, not saying anything.

"Lissen," she said sharply. "I've got to wear those overalls again tomorrow. You're going to get them all wrinkled up leaning against them like that."

He didn't move. He was too tired and his legs were throbbing now that he had sat down. Besides the overalls were already wrinkled and dirty, he thought. They couldn't help but be for she'd worn them all week. He leaned further back in the chair.

"Come on, get up," she ordered.

"Oh, what the hell," he said wearily and got up from the chair. "I'd just as soon live in a subway. There'd be just as much place to sit down."

He saw that her sense of humor was struggling with her anger. But her sense of humor won because she giggled.

"Aw, come on and eat," she said. There was a coaxing note in her voice. "You're nothing but a old hungry nigger trying to act tough and—" she paused to giggle and then continued, "You—"

He had always found her giggling pleasant and deliberately said things that might amuse her and then waited, listening for the delicate sound to emerge from her throat. This time he didn't even hear the giggle. He didn't let her finish what she was saying. She was standing close to him and that funny tingling started in his finger tips, went fast up his arms and sent his fist shooting straight for her face.

There was the smacking sound of soft flesh being struck by a hard object and it wasn't until she screamed that he realized he had hit her in the mouth—so hard that the dark red lipstick had blurred and spread over her full lips, reaching up toward the tip of her nose, down toward her chin, out toward her cheeks.

The knowledge that he had struck her seeped through him slowly and he was appalled but he couldn't drag his hands away from her face. He kept striking her and he thought with horror that something inside him was holding him, binding him to this act, wrapping and twisting about him so that he had to continue it. He had lost all control over his hands. And he groped for a phrase, a word, something to describe what this thing was like that was happening to him and he thought it was like being enmeshed in a winding sheet—that was it—like a winding sheet. And even as the thought formed in his mind his hands reached for her face again and yet again.

[1971]

Journal Entry

Imagine yourself as a juror in Johnson's domestic violence trial. Would you vote to acquit or convict? On what evidence?

Textual Considerations

1. Explain the meaning of Mae's statement in the beginning of the story, "You look like a huckleberry—in a winding sheet."
2. What further significance does the phrase "like a winding sheet" acquire when Johnson uses it at the end?
3. What is the effect of beginning the story with a nebulous "he" when the reader doesn't really discover who the "he" is until much later? Is the same effect also achieved by using "he" instead of "Johnson" so often throughout the text?
4. What is the author's attitude toward Mae? Toward Johnson? How do the descriptive phrases and the thought patterns help you determine these differing attitudes?
5. The story is organized in a chronological sequence, but how does Petry keep it moving forward without making the time structure obtrusive?

Cultural Contexts

1. What role does color play in the relationships between the characters in the story: Johnson and Mrs. Scott; Johnson and the girl at the coffee shop; Johnson and Mae?
2. Which is the primary cause of Johnson's behavior—his race or his social class? Working with your group, indicate whether Johnson is justified in releasing his frustrations on his wife? Can your group reach a consensus about this issue?

ESSAYS

Brent Staples

A Brother's Murder

It has been more than two years since my telephone rang with the news that my younger brother Blake—just 22 years old—had been murdered. The young man who killed him was only 24. Wearing a ski mask, he emerged from a car, fired six times at close range with a massive .44 Magnum, then fled. The two had once been inseparable friends. A senseless rivalry—beginning, I think, with an argument over a girlfriend—escalated from posturing, to threats, to violence, to murder. The way the two were living, death could have come to either of them from anywhere. In fact, the assailant had already survived multiple gunshot wounds from an incident much like the one in which my brother lost his life.

As I wept for Blake I felt wrenched backward into events and circumstances that had seemed light-years gone. Though a decade apart, we both were raised in Chester, Pennsylvania, an angry, heavily black, heavily poor, industrial city southwest of Philadelphia. There, in the 1960's, I was introduced to mortality, not by the old and failing, but by beautiful young men who lay wrecked after sudden explosions of violence. The first, I remember from my 14th year—Johnny, brash lover of fast cars, stabbed to death two doors from my house in a fight over a pool game. The next year, my teenage cousin, Wesley, whom I loved very much, was shot dead. The summers blur. Milton, an angry young neighbor, shot a crosstown rival, wounding him badly. William, another teen-age neighbor, took a shotgun blast to the shoulder in some urban drama and displayed his bandages proudly. His brother, Leonard, severely beaten, lost an eye and donned a black patch. It went on.

I recall not long before I left for college, two local Vietnam veterans—one from the Marines, one from the Army—arguing fiercely, nearly at blows about which outfit had done the most in the war. The most killing, they meant. Not much later, I read a magazine article that set that dispute in a context. In the story, a noncommissioned officer—a sergeant, I believe—said he would pass up any number of affluent, suburban-born recruits to get hard-core soldiers from the inner city. They jumped into the rice paddies with "their manhood on their sleeves," I believe he said. These two items—the veterans arguing and the sergeant's words—still characterize for me the circumstances under which black men in their teens and twenties kill one another with such frequency. With a touchy paranoia born of living battered lives, they are desperate to be real men. Killing is only *machismo* taken to the extreme. Incursions to be punished by death were many and minor, and they remain so: they include stepping on the wrong toe, literally; cheating in a drug deal; simply saying "I dare you" to someone holding a gun; crossing territorial lines in a gang dispute. My brother grew up to wear his manhood on his sleeve. And when he died, he was in that group—black, male and in its teens and early twenties—that is far and away the most likely to murder or be murdered.

I left the East Coast after college, spent the mid- and late-1970s in Chicago as a graduate student, taught for a time, then became a journalist. Within ten years of leaving my hometown, I was overeducated and "upwardly mobile," ensconced on a quiet, tree-lined street where voices raised in anger were scarcely ever heard. The telephone, like some grim umbilical, kept me connected to the old world with news of deaths, imprisonings and misfortune. I felt emotionally beaten up. Perhaps to protect myself, I added a psychological dimension to the physical distance I had achieved. I rarely visited my hometown. I shut it out.

As I fled the past, so Blake embraced it. On Christmas of 1983, I traveled from Chicago to a black section of Roanoke, Virginia, where he then lived. The desolate public housing projects, the hopeless, idle young men crashing against one another—these reminded me of the embittered town we'd grown up in. It was a place where once I would have been comfortable, or at least sure of myself. Now, hearing of my brother's forays into crime, his scrapes with police and street thugs, I was scared, unsteady on foreign terrain.

I saw that Blake's romance with the street life and the hustler image had flowered dangerously. One evening that late December, standing in some Roanoke dive among drug dealers and grim, hair-trigger losers, I told him I feared for his life. He had affected the image of the tough he wanted to be. But behind the dark glasses and the swagger, I glimpsed the baby-faced toddler I'd once watched over. I nearly wept. I wanted desperately for him to live. The young think themselves immortal, and a dangerous light shone in his eyes as he spoke laughingly of making fools of the policemen who had raided his apartment looking for drugs. He cried out as I took his right hand. A line of stitches lay between the thumb and index finger. Kickback from a shotgun, he explained, nothing serious. Gunplay had become part of his life.

I lacked the language simply to say: Thousands have lived this for you and died. I fought the urge to lift him bodily and shake him. This place and the way you are living smells of death to me, I said. Take some time away, I said. Let's go downtown tomorrow and buy a plane ticket anywhere, take a bus trip, anything to get away and cool things off. He took my alarm casually. We arranged to meet the following night—an appointment he would not keep. We embraced as though through glass. I drove away.

As I stood in my apartment in Chicago holding the receiver that evening in February 1984, I felt as though part of my soul had been cut away. I questioned myself then, and I still do. Did I not reach back soon enough or earnestly enough for him? For weeks I awoke crying from a recurrent dream in which I chased him, urgently trying to get him to read a document I had, as though reading it would protect him from what had happened in waking life. His eyes shining like black diamonds, he smiled and danced just beyond my grasp. When I reached for him, I caught only the space where he had been.

[1986]

Journal Entry

What knowledge or experience of inner-city violence can you bring to your reading of Staples's text?

Textual Considerations

1. What do we learn about Blake's way of life from the essay's first paragraph?
2. How did the narrator escape the fate of the other young men in the ghetto? Does the fact that he did escape alter your opinion of those who didn't?
3. "As I fled the past, so Blake embraced it." How did this choice affect the brothers' relationship?
4. Staples uses several flashbacks in the essay. Identify examples, and discuss their impact on the essay's purpose.
5. Staples tries to maintain an objective tone. Are there points at which his tone becomes more personal? What examples can you cite? What is their effect?

Cultural Contexts

1. Respond to Staples's statement that he "was introduced to mortality, not by the old and failing, but by the beautiful young men who lay wrecked after sudden explosions of violence." Staples wrote this essay in 1986. Is his experience still relevant almost two decades later? Explain.
2. Discuss with your group Staples's reasons for including the argument between the Vietnam veterans. How does it add to your understanding of his thesis that "killing is only *machismo* taken to the extreme"? To what extent do you agree with this point of view?

David W. Powell

Vietnam: What I Remember[1]

The following events come to my conscious memory uninvited. I not only remember them vividly, I reexperience them with all my senses:

Froze with fright, standing up, the first time I was under fire

Watched two marines try to break open the skull of a dead Viet Cong with a large rock

Observed a marine intentionally shoot a girl four or six years of age

Watched the girl's grandfather carry her into our line of fire, sobbing

Had a lieutenant who delighted in sneaking up on me when I was on watch at night

Was offered a blood-soaked flak jacket and a helmet with a bullet hole through it as my first field equipment

---

[1] From "Patriotism Revisited," a memoir.

Had my boots rot off during an operation in the field
Observed two captured nurses being beaten and raped by marines
Rifle-butted a girl of twelve in the face when she would not move away
Strangled a captured Viet Cong for refusing to talk to an interpreter
Discovered brain matter on barbed wire I was stretching out
Observed a marine laugh as he stepped on the chest of a dead Viet Cong and
watched blood squirt out of the enemy's wounds
Awoke to find a buffalo leech on my leg
Was abandoned under fire when a rocket jammed in my launcher
Was abandoned under fire when I was shot
Hit head and fell in open field. Watched my fellow marines run by me to seek
cover for themselves
Received letter from wife telling me how much fun she and a girlfriend had on
Friday nights when they went out to bars to dance
Watched fellow marine shoot himself in the foot to get evacuated
Heard same man cry in his sleep when he was returned to the company
Found marine boot with foot in it in a hedgerow
Almost run over by retreating U.S. tank
Saw Lt. Spivey hit a head-high booby trap
Nearly murdered villager for stealing my laundry
Watched Prestridge test his new M-16 by shooting a woman getting water
from a nearby well
Identified Haas's remains
Exchanged letters with Haas's mother
Had an artillery canister fall six inches in front of my head
Was about to put on fresh boots when I discovered lice swimming in them
Saw seven-foot python climbing in ceiling just above my head
Bullets sounding like bees digging up ground all around me
Nearly trapped in Da Nang village my last night in Vietnam
Robbed by marines while I slept in Okinawa after tour was over
Circled over El Toro air base for two hours so that President Johnson could
land and be photographed greeting returning veterans

Since my return I have held eighteen different jobs and have been unemployed
for several six-month periods. This is a direct result of my Post Traumatic Stress
Disorder, specifically a disdain for being told to do tasks I do not want to do; an
exaggerated startle response, which is terribly embarrassing to me; and a lack of
control over emotional flooding.

I divorced my first wife two years after I got out of the service. I divorced my
second wife in 1982. I separated from a four year relationship in 1987. I have not
had a significant relationship with a woman since then. I have no significant male
or female friendships. I am aloof from my immediate family, who live in Tucson,
Arizona.

[1994]

Journal Entry

What knowledge, experience, associations, or images of the Vietnam War can you bring to your reading of this text?

Textual Considerations

1. How does Powell's cataloging the events that come to his "conscious memory uninvited" develop the memoir's meaning?
2. Powell uses the verbs *observed* and *watched* several times. In these instances, what do these memories have in common?
3. What is the tone of the last two paragraphs? Explain.
4. How do the last two paragraphs differ thematically and stylistically from the rest of the memoir?
5. Identify specific lines in which the speaker collapses war myths, such as the myth of war as a great romantic adventure with esprit de corps, or soldiers' solidarity.

Cultural Contexts

1. To what extent does Powell's memoir support or challenge the image of the Vietnam veteran as an **antihero**?
2. Brainstorm with your group on your associations with patriotism. Was Powell's choice of title appropriate? Why do you think he chose it for his memoir?

Kandi Tayebi

Warring Memories

"They should take off their rings," my husband stated matter-of-factly as we watched CNN broadcasting more trouble in the Middle East. For two years he had fought in the Iran-Iraq war, but he rarely shared his experiences with me, perhaps feeling that his American-born wife might have difficulty relating to the realities of warfare in one's homeland. On the television screen, eighteen-year-old soldiers displayed their bravery, shaking rifles and shooting into the air. Faces crushed too close to the camera triumphantly spoke of victory. Without the tanks lined behind the young men, or the rifles and camouflage, one could easily think the segment centered on a basketball tournament. One young man, sweat streaked across his T-shirt, held his rifle high in the air, tilted his head back, and whooped. His golden wedding ring covered skin not yet whitened by years of being hidden. I turned slowly to my husband after my eyes focused on the wedding ring encircling the finger of a dark, soft-eyed man, the gold scraping against the side of his MG3 and reflecting the sun into the camera lens.

My husband, mingling his words with those of the CNN announcer, said quietly, "When they die, their bodies will bloat in the heat. For gold, their fingers will be cut off." His words were almost drowned out by the victory calls of the young men on the screen.

For me, video-game graphics displaying a target and its destruction constitute war. Generals, in neatly pressed fatigues, stand in front of blackboards like coaches before the big game, explaining the strategic plans behind each assault against the enemy. Occasionally, a screaming mother, sister, or wife lies across someone's body, but the television screen separates her pain from my world, framing her in cinematic neutrality. I try to match my husband's stories with the only other version of war I know, those from the movie screen—*Saving Private Ryan, The Green Berets, Apocalypse Now.*

An olive-skinned boy with just the beginnings of a beard across his chin pushes his way to the front of the crowd and smiles. Two gold teeth define the border of his mouth, and I laugh cautiously, "Should he remove his teeth, too?" My husband tells about men shoving the butts of their rifles against a jaw, splintering bone across the sand, to remove gold teeth for souvenirs. The boy on the television looks fragile.

I want to nullify the horror of my husband's tales by believing these acts occur only in distant lands at the hands of people unlike me, but the boy's eyes look so much like my son's. The camera turns down to show his black and white Nikes. Suddenly, the lens pans through the crowd to a building in the back. Out of the window dangles what appears at first to be a bloody white cloth or, as the camera moves in, an effigy. Standing above the lifeless form, a boy not older than sixteen or seventeen waves his bloodied hands at the camera. Blood smears his white T-shirt, making abstract patterns over the face of an unidentifiable basketball player dunking a ball. The camera zooms in on the battered, pulpy mass of the dead man, now clearly distinguishable as he falls to the ground. The crowd grabs the body—kicking, pulling, tearing. My eyes remain focused on the screen; not even this violence makes me turn away.

I realize I see war as a snapshot—moments flashed across a screen or plastered on the page. Slowly over time, bits of the war have leaked out into the conversations between my husband and me. He informs me that the worst part of war is the waiting, something the snapshots don't show. During the moments when the fighting is most intense, one doesn't have time to think or to worry. Adrenaline pushes the body to action, and the surroundings seem surreal. Yet most of the day is spent listening and waiting. Stray shots go off in the distance, planes fly over, and soldiers practice by shooting rats. After awhile, the older soldiers learn to avoid thinking by filling the air with idle talk. It is the new men, the ones who haven't yet realized where they are, the ones who still dream about normal life, who begin the taboo discussions of home and family.

Almost a year after the CNN broadcast, my husband recounts one memory from the war as we sit watching our children play in the yard under the summer sun. One young soldier, away from home for the first time, sat on the hillside next to my husband during a late-night watch. As point men, they were to listen carefully for the enemy, then stand up and shoot when the enemy crested the hill. For hours they sat, telling stories of their families—an oldest sister's trip to college, a youngest brother's business, a mother's dream for her son to become a doctor. Silence stretched the night, forcing the two men into the thickness of loneliness. Just before dawn, a shot shattered the stillness, and my husband, the wizened experienced soldier at twenty-three, stood and began firing back.

"Stand up and shoot," he hollered at his partner, who shook with fear. Grabbing the boy by a shoulder soaked with sweat, my husband tried to force him onto his feet. Finally, in resignation, he dropped the boy back down onto the soft earth.

After the battle ended and the silence returned, my husband looked down at the boy lying across his boots. That first shot had drilled a hole through his forehead— his shaking was the last sign of life, the wetness on his shoulder the blood draining from his wound. Pushing the boy off his feet, my husband turned his eyes away.

A few weeks after my husband confides this war story to me, while I am cleaning out closets before the rush of the school year begins, I run across a box of old photos he brought with him from Iran. I thumb through pictures of my husband during the war, looking at all of the wan faces for signs of the man I've come to know. I've watched him walk for hours across our bedroom floor, our son cradled against his chest. As the fevered cries of our son filled the room, my husband would patiently sing Persian lullabies and stroke the baby's back. He has deftly bandaged skinned knees, extracted splinters, and chased away scary dreams. When we were refused housing after a woman saw my husband was from the Middle East, I angrily protested while he quietly walked away. When colleagues at work have called him "camel rider," asked him about all the abusive men in his country, and even discussed how they would bomb all those "Arabs," my husband has responded with humor and reminded me that people need time to change. In contrast, I have at times come close to hitting colleagues who have asked, "How could a bright woman like you marry a man from the Middle East?"

Yet in these war pictures, the muscular body and soft eyes of my husband are camouflaged by the gaunt, grizzled look of the young man staring out. His eyes sunk deep in his head glare back in desperation. One hand grips an MG 3; the other rests gently on the front of a tank. Men no more than twenty-five years old, aged by the sights of battle, surround him. In another more haunting photo, a soldier smiles childishly; an oddity among his serious compatriots. At his feet lies a body, the head bent awkwardly to the right as a boot steps down on the face. In the soldier's hand are the dog tags of the dead man. Another soldier distractedly tosses dirt clods onto the dead man's chest, already piled with rocks and trash thrown by others. In the background, my husband shares a sandwich with another young man.

This photo wakens my husband's sharpest memory from the war. Out of all the frightening scenes of the fighting, my husband's strongest recollection is of a tomato sandwich. As his unit entered a village devastated by recent bombings, they began to search for food and shelter. Entire walls and roofs were missing from most of the houses that remained. The streets were lined with rubble, stray chickens and goats, and body parts of women, men, and children. Chunks of blackened flesh checkered the cobblestones. Two fingers, still attached to the outside of an arm blown open and swollen by the sun, lay against one wall. Occasionally, around a corner or behind some bodies, a small piece of greenery pushed its way up through the broken stones and trash.

The soldiers were lucky enough to find a few tomatoes left behind by one house's occupants and somehow untouched by the blast that had leveled all of the walls and blown off the roof. In the kitchen, a loaf of freshbaked bread sat neatly on the counter above the body of an old woman still dressed in a white and red apron. Her arms were twisted awkwardly behind her back. The left side of her face smeared with ashes, her eyes staring at the cupboard, she seemed prepared to greet visitors—except for the large black hole ripped out of the right side of her head.

For weeks, the soldiers had had little but dried army rations to eat. Sitting on the rat-infested floor, the men devoured sandwiches, relishing the red juice streaking the white bread. The smell of yeast mixed with the stench of burnt flesh. The tomato sandwich amid the destruction was a delicacy.

Fall arrives again, bringing the frenzied activity of a new school year. I sip my last drop of tea, kiss my boys goodbye, and head off to teach at the university, where children the age of those in the photographs I looked at this past summer will struggle with their own sets of problems. One young man comes into my office to explain why he won't be able to complete my course. With vacant eyes, he explains that his two-year-old sister was killed in a drive-by shooting, and his mama needs him to help with his four- and five-year-old brothers. He apologizes for letting me down, shakes my hand, and walks out of the office wiping the nose of one of those brothers. I walk outside into the sunshine.

Fall in the South brings cool relief from the torching humidity of summer, and students sit beneath the old oak trees that line the paths winding throughout campus, taking advantage of the pleasant sun, breeze, and fragrant flowers. Walking across the landscaped lawns, I pause to enjoy the newly blossomed hibiscus, the squirrels chasing each other up one tree and around another, and the students clad in jeans and T-shirts sporting fashion designers' names. My mind drifts to scenes of my young son delighted by the pointy-nosed armadillos that dig up slugs in our yard. He and the neighborhood cats chase the armadillos, which dodge their advances while appearing nonchalantly to ignore their existence. Coming from Colorado, we marvel at these unusual spotted creatures, watching them for hours from our porch and finally resorting to the video camera to record their images for those left behind in the Rockies. Texas has exposed us to a whole new array of animals—slimy, slinking, furry, flying, wrinkled, skittering—that are unfamiliar and enticing.

Only the playful squirrels seem a familiar sight. Today, they race through the crabgrass and roll down the hills, enjoying the newly crisp air. Almost like a shooting star, seen briefly in one's peripheral vision and then gone, a squirrel falls from the tallest tree in the middle of the courtyard. Unsure what it really was, I join the increasing number of students gathered closely around the damaged body. The squirrel sits on his hind legs, at first appearing to be a movie on pause. Then, with great effort, it thrusts its front legs as if to scurry up the tree. The back legs drag for only an inch, the top half of its body collapses on the ground, and its breaths come in forced bursts. Back broken, the squirrel continues to struggle as I look away. Even after calling someone to come help the animal, I have flashbacks of the squirrel staring at me, reaching towards me with its front paws only to be pulled back against its useless rear legs.

When I return home from the university, I find my husband preparing sandwiches for a picnic in the park. Our two boys chase each other up and down the stairs, giggling and screaming. I tell my husband about the slow death of the squirrel, and after a moment of silence, he responds, "Imagine if that were a human being." For an instant I can vaguely comprehend the war he lived.

At the park, I find our neighborhood celebrating Safety Night, an event that helps citizens and local police officers come together to protect our children. While the kids play cowboys and Indians, climb on the monkey bars, and collect police officer trading cards, the adults eat and talk. At sundown the fireworks begin, filling the sky with color. My husband cringes at the first few flashes of light and the accompanying loud booms before he can settle in. My youngest son sits on his lap, leans against his chest, and sees only beauty in the explosions.

[2001]

Journal Entry

Review the first and last paragraphs of Tayebi's memoir. How do they complement each other structurally and thematically? Record your response to each.

Textual Considerations

1. Although "Warring Memories" is told from the author's point of view, she quotes her husband directly several times in the memoir. What do these passages reveal about him? His war experiences? His attitude toward war?
2. The author makes frequent references to various media, including CNN, video games, war movies, and to a box of old photographs. To what extent do these images reinforce and enhance the theme? Which did you find most effective?
3. The author makes the distinction several times between being a spectator in war as opposed to a participant. How does her encounter with the squirrel relate to this point?

Cultural Considerations

1. Settings change frequently in "Warring Memories," including the author's home, workplace, neighborhood, and various war zones. Discuss with your group the effects of juxtaposing these various sites.
2. The catalyst for "Warring Memories" was a July Fourth picnic as Tayebi watched her husband cradling their infant son while he himself cringed each time fireworks exploded. She wrote the piece in the hope it can "help the healing process for a world torn by violence and remind each of us of our humanity." To what extent does she succeed? Record your group's responses.

Seth Mydans

Not Just the Inner City: Well-to-Do Join Gangs

In suburban Hawthorne, social workers tell of the police officers who responded to a report of gang violence, only to let the instigators drive away in expensive cars, thinking they were a group of teenagers on their way to the beach.

In Tucson, Ariz., a white middle-class teenager wearing gang colors died, a victim of a drive-by shooting, as he stood with black and Hispanic members of the Bloods gang.

At Antelope Valley High School in Lancaster, Calif., about 50 miles north of Los Angeles, 200 students threw stones at a policeman who had been called to help enforce a ban on the gang outfits that have become a fad on some campuses.

Around the country, a growing number of well-to-do youths have begun flirting with gangs in a dalliance that can be as innocent as a fashion statement or as deadly as hard-core drug dealing and violence.

The phenomenon is emerging in a variety of forms. Some affluent white youths are joining established black or Hispanic gangs like the Crips and Bloods; others are forming what are sometimes called "copy-cat" or "mutant" or "yuppie" gangs.

The development seems to defy the usual socioeconomic explanations for the growth of gangs in inner cities, and it appears to have caught parents, teachers, and law-enforcement officers off guard.

Police experts and social workers offer an array of reasons: a misguided sense of the romance of gangs; pursuit of the easy money of drugs; self-defense against the spread of established hard-core gangs. And they note that well-to-do families in the suburbs can be as empty and loveless as poor families in the inner city, leaving young people searching for a sense of group identity.

Furthermore, "kids have always tried to shock their parents," said Marianne Diaz-Parton, a social worker who works with young gang members in the Los Angeles suburb of Lawndale, "and these days becoming a gang member is one way to do it."

A member of the South Bay Family gang in Hermosa Beach, a twenty-one-year-old surfer called Road Dog who said his family owned a chain of pharmacies, put it this way: "This is the nineties, man. We're the type of people who don't take no for an answer. If your mom says no to a kid in the nineties, the kid's just going to laugh." He and his friends shouted in appreciation as another gang member lifted his long hair to reveal a tattoo on a bare shoulder. "Mama tried."

Separating their gang identities from their home lives, the South Bay Family members give themselves nicknames that they carry in elaborate tattoos around the backs of their necks. They consented to interviews on the condition that only these gang names be used.

The gang's leader, who said he was the son of a bank vice president, flexed a bicep so the tattooed figure of a nearly naked woman moved suggestively. Voicing his own version of the basic street philosophy of gang solidarity, the leader, who is called Thumper, said, "If you want to be able to walk the mall, you have to know you've got your boys behind you."

From Cool to Dead

For young people who have not been hardened by the inner city, an attitude like this, if taken into the streets, can be dangerous, said Sgt. Wes McBride of the Los Angeles Sherriff's Department, who has gathered reports on the phenomenon from around the country.

"They start out thinking it's real cool to be a gang member," he said. "They are 'wannabes' with nothing happening around them to show them it's real dangerous, until they run afoul of real gang members, and then they end up dead."

In California's palm-fringed San Fernando Valley, said Manuel Velasquez, a social worker with Community Youth Gang Services, a private agency, "there are a lot of kids who have no business being in gangs who all of a sudden are going around acting like gang members."

"They play the part," he went on. "They vandalize. They do graffiti. They do all kinds of stuff. But when it comes down to the big stuff, it's: 'Wait a minute. That's enough for me. I want to change the rules.' And then they realize it's a little bit too late."

There are few statistics on middle-class involvement in gangs, and officials are reluctant to generalize about its extent or the form it is taking. But reports of middle-class gang activity come from places as disparate as Denver, Seattle, Tucson, Portland, Dallas, Phoenix, Chicago, Minneapolis, Omaha, and Honolulu.

Sgt. John Galea, until recently the head of the youth gang intelligence unit of the New York City Police Department, said that although there was no lack of youth violence in the city, organized street gangs as such were not a serious problem.

The South Bay Family, in Hermosa Beach, has evolved over the past five years from a group of bouncers for a rock band to a full-fledged street-wise, well-armed gang. But for the most part, white gangs, or white members of minority gangs, have just begun to be noticed in the past few months.

"Parents Are Totally Unaware"

"I think it's a new trend just since the latter part of 1989, and it's really interesting how it's getting out to suburban areas," said Dorothy Elmore, a gang intelligence officer for the Portland Police Bureau in Oregon. "We've got teachers calling up and saying: 'We've got some Bloods and Crips here. What's going on?'

"It's definitely coming from two-parent families, working class to middle class to upper middle class, predominantly white," she went on. "The parents are totally unaware of the kind of activity these kids are doing."

In Tucson, Sgt. Ron Zimmerling, who heads the Police Department's gang unit, said that "Kids from even our country-club areas were suddenly joining gangs."

After the drive-by shooting last summer in which a white teenager was killed, he said, he asked a black gang member about another white youth who had attached himself to the gang. "I don't know," the black member replied. "He just likes to hang out."

The phenomenon is better established but still relatively new in the Los Angeles area, the nation's gang capital.

"We have covered parties where I'm totally shocked at the mixture of people who are there," said Mrs. Diaz-Parton, of Community Youth Gang Services in Lawndale. "Your traditional Hispanic gang member is next to this disco-looking person who is next to a preppie guy who looks like he's getting straight A's on his way to college."

Bandannas and Baseball Caps

Irving G. Spergel, a sociology professor at the University of Chicago who studies gangs, emphasized that the phenomenon accounts for a very small part of the nation's gang problem, which is centered in inner cities. He said the four thousand to five thousand neo-Nazi skinhead groups around the country, which have their own style and ideology, were a separate and worrisome problem.

More trivial, but still troubling to school officials, is a trend toward gang fashions in some high schools and junior high schools. In Los Angeles, Phoenix, Tucson, and several California suburbs, students have staged demonstrations to protest bans on wearing certain colors, bandannas, jewelry, or baseball caps that can be a mark of gang membership.

Bare chests, tattoos, Budweiser beer, and a televised hockey game seemed to be the fashion one recent Saturday evening at an extremely noisy gathering of members of the South Bay Family in a small house in a middle-class neighborhood near the Pacific Coast Highway in Hermosa Beach. There were knives and a deer rifle in evidence, and some said they had pistols.

Asked about the gang's philosophy, Bam Bam, the son of a professor at the University of Southern California, shouted, "Right or wrong, your bros are your bros!"

"Another thing that goes good here is peace," said Road Dog loudly.

"Peace by force, man," shouted Porgy, who said his father was vice president of a plastics company.

"No drug dealing!" shouted Tomcat, the son of a stockbroker.

"Quit lying to him, man," said Little Smith. "There's drugs everywhere."

On a more reflective note, away from the crowd in a small back room, Porgy said: "There is no justification. We do what we do because we want to. I don't blame my mother. She did the best she could."

[1990]

Journal Entry

Brainstorm on your associations with gangs. What images, emotions, or ideas does the word *gang* evoke? Are gangs and violence synonymous in your experience?

Textual Considerations

1. Review the first section of Mydans's essay, and list the reasons cited for the growing popularity of gangs in suburbia.

2. Respond to Sgt. McBride's statement: "They are 'wannabes' with nothing happening around them to show them it's real dangerous, until they run afoul of real gang members, and then they end up dead."
3. Comment on the attitudes toward parents expressed by several gang members. Why are the parents "totally unaware of the kind of activity these kids are doing"?
4. Analyze Mydans's tone. Is it consistent with his purpose? Is he mainly trying to inform his audience? Explain.
5. To analyze the relation between fashion, identity, and politics, consider what Mydans's text reveals about gang centrality. Do you agree with students' protest demonstrations about the control of fashion? To what extent does fashion forge the gang's image and identity?

Cultural Contexts

1. Respond to Thumper's statement: "If you want to be able to walk the mall, you have to know you've got your boys behind you."
2. Are suburban gangs mainly making fashion statements, or are they potentially violent? What is your response to their bonding rituals? Write a summary of your group's responses to Mydans's essay.

POETRY

Jeffrey Harrison

Reflection on the Vietnam War Memorial

Here it is, the back porch of the dead.
You can see them milling around in there,
   screened in by their own names,
   looking at us in the same
vague and serious way we look at them.   5

An underground house, a roof of grass—
one version of the underworld. It's all
   we know of death, a world
   like our own (but darker, blurred)
inhabited by beings like ourselves.   10

The location of the name you're looking for
can be looked up in a book whose resemblance
   to a phone book seems to claim
   some contact can be made
through the simple act of finding a name.   15

As we touch the name the stone absorbs our grief.
It takes us in—we see ourselves inside it.
   And yet we feel it as a wall
   and realize the dead are all
just names now, the separation final.   20

[1987]

518

Yusef Komunyakaa

Facing It

My black face fades,
hiding inside the black granite.
I said I wouldn't,
dammit: No tears.
I'm stone. I'm flesh.   5
My clouded reflection eyes me
like a bird of prey, the profile of night
slanted against morning. I turn
this way—the stone lets me go.
I turn that way—I'm inside   10
the Vietnam Veterans Memorial
again, depending on the light
to make a difference.
I go down the 58,022 names,
half-expecting to find   15
my own in letters like smoke.
I touch the name Andrew Johnson;
I see the booby trap's white flash.
Names shimmer on a woman's blouse
but when she walks away   20
the names stay on the wall.
Brushstrokes flash, a red bird's
wings cutting across my stare.
The sky. A plane in the sky.
A white vet's image floats   25
closer to me, then his pale eyes
look through mine. I'm a window.
He's lost his right arm
inside the stone. In the black mirror
a woman's trying to erase names: 30
No, she's brushing a boy's hair.

[1988]

Journal Entry

You will need a picture of the Vietnam Memorial in Washington, D.C., to appreciate these
poems. What functions do war memorials serve? Record your responses to any war memorial
that you have visited in the United States or elsewhere.

Textual Considerations

1. In the first two stanzas of Harrison's text, the wall is portrayed as though it were transparent. What reactions to the wall does the speaker express in these lines? Compare his reactions to the reactions of the speaker in "Facing It."
2. What is the effect of comparing looking for the names on the memorial with looking up names in a phone book?
3. How is the wall portrayed in the last stanza of Harrison's poem? How does touching the names affect the speaker?
4. What lines in the beginning of "Facing It" best capture the speaker's emotional response to visiting the memorial?
5. Explain lines 15 and 16 of "Facing It." What happened to Andrew Johnson? How does the speaker know him?

Cultural Contexts

1. Discuss the thematic significance of the images in lines 19 through 30 of "Facing It." What might they be suggesting about the memorial and the dead veterans?
2. Why does the speaker in "Facing It" mention that 58,022 names appear on the memorial? To what extent did that affect your group's response to the text?

JARRELL AND HARDY

Randall Jarrell

The Death of the Ball Turret Gunner*

From my mother's sleep I fell into the State
And I hunched in its belly till my wet fur froze.°
Six miles from earth, loosed from its dream of life,
I woke to black flak° and the nightmare fighters.
When I died they washed me out of the turret with a hose.   5

[1945]

---

*Ball Turret Gunner: High-altitude bombers in World War II (1941–45) contained a revolvable gun turret both at the top and at the bottom, from which a machine-gunner could shoot at attacking fighter planes. Gunners in these turrets were sometimes mutilated by the gunfire of attacking planes. **2 Froze:** The stratospheric below-zero temperatures caused the moisture in the gunner's breath to freeze as it contacted the collar of his flight jacket.   **4 flak:** the round black explosions of antiaircraft shells fired at bombers from the ground, an acronym of the German word *Fliergerabwehrkanone.*

Thomas Hardy

The Man He Killed

"Had he and I but met
    By some old ancient inn,
We should have sat us down to wet
    Right many a nipperkin!

"But ranged as infantry,   5
    And staring face to face,
I shot at him as he at me,
    And killed him in his place.

"I shot him dead because—
    Because he was my foe,   10
Just so: my foe of course he was;
    That's clear enough; although

> "He thought he'd 'list, perhaps,
>   Off-hand like—just as I—
> Was out of work—had sold his traps—   15
>   No other reason why.
>
> "Yes; quaint and curious war is!
>   You shoot a fellow down
> You'd treat if met where any bar is,
>   Or help to half-a-crown."   20

[1902]

Journal Entry

Brainstorm on your associations with war. What images, ideas, or emotions does the word *war* evoke? What experiences, your own or others, can you draw on?

Textual Considerations

1. How does the speaker in Jarrell's text connect sleeping and waking, dreams and nightmares, and life and death?
2. Who is the speaker in Jarrell's poem? In what has he been involved? How do you respond to the last line of the poem?
3. Who is the speaker in Hardy's poem? What story is he recalling? How does the poet use setting to enhance theme?
4. How does the sentence structure of Hardy's text convey the attitude of the speaker to his so-called foe?
5. What indications are there that the speaker is trying to clarify for himself his reasons for killing in Hardy's poem? Consider the repetition of "because" in lines 9 and 10 as well as the significance of "although" in line 12.

Cultural Contexts

1. Jarrell's text portrays the carnage that resulted from aerial combat during World War II; Hardy's focus is on how war disrupts everyday human relationships. Discuss the effectiveness of these texts as antiwar poems.
2. Discuss with your group the effect of point of view on theme in both poems. Do you respond differently to Jarrell's text, lamenting the loss of a generation of young men, as opposed to the account of how the speaker killed his "enemy" in Hardy's text? Record your discussion.

LEVERTOV AND YEVTUSHENKO

Denise Levertov

What Were They Like?

1) Did the people of Vietnam
    use lanterns of stone?
2) Did they hold ceremonies
    to reverence the opening of buds?
3) Were they inclined to quiet laughter?   5
4) Did they use bone and ivory,
    jade and silver, for ornament?
5) Had they an epic poem?
6) Did they distinguish between speech and singing?

1) Sir, their light hearts turned to stone.   10
    It is not remembered whether in gardens
    stone lanterns illumined pleasant ways.
2) Perhaps they gathered once to delight in blossom,
    but after the children were killed
    there were no more buds.   15
3) Sir, laughter is bitter to the burned mouth.
4) A dream ago, perhaps. Ornament is for joy.
    All the bones were charred.
5) It is not remembered. Remember,
    most were peasants; their life   20
    was in rice and bamboo.
    When peaceful clouds were reflected in the paddies
    and the water buffalo stepped surely along terraces,
    maybe fathers told their sons old tales.
    When bombs smashed those mirrors   25
    there was time only to scream.
6) There is no echo yet
    of their speech which was like a song.
    It was reported their singing resembled
    the flight of moths in moonlight.   30
    Who can say? It is silent now.

                                                            [1966]

Yevgeny Yevtushenko

Babiy Yar

Over Babiy Yar
there are no memorials.
The steep hillside like a rough inscription.
I am frightened.
Today I am as old as the Jewish race. 5
I seem to myself a Jew at this moment.
I, wandering in Egypt.
I, crucified. I perishing.
Even today the mark of the nails.
I think also of Dreyfus. I am he. 10
The Philistine my judge and my accuser.
Cut off by bars and cornered,
ringed round, spat at, lied about;
the screaming ladies with the Brussels lace
poke me in the face with parasols. 15
I am also a boy in Belostok,
the dropping blood spreads across the floor,
the public-bar heroes are rioting
in an equal stench of garlic and of drink.
I have no strength, go spinning from a boot, 20
shriek useless prayers that they don't listen to;
with a cackle of "Thrash the kikes and save Russia!"
the corn-chandler is beating up my mother.
I seem to myself like Anna Frank
to be transparent as an April twig 25
and am in love, I have no need for words,
I need for us to look at one another.
How little we have to see or to smell
separated from foliage and the sky,
how much, how much in the dark room 30
gently embracing each other.
They're coming. Don't be afraid.
The booming and banging of the spring.
It's coming this way. Come to me.
Quickly, give me your lips. 35
They're battering in the door. Roar of the ice.

Over Babiy Yar
rustle of the wild grass.
The trees look threatening, look like judges.
And everything is one silent cry. 40

Taking my hat off
I feel myself slowly going grey.
And I am one silent cry
over the many thousands of the buried;
am every old man killed here,   45
every child killed here.
O my Russian people, I know you.
Your nature is international.
Foul hands rattle your clean name.
I know the goodness of my country.   50
How horrible it is that pompous title
the anti-semites calmly call themselves,
Society of the Russian People.
No part of me can ever forget it.
When the last anti-semite on the earth   55
is buried for ever
let the International ring out.
No Jewish blood runs among my blood,
but I am as bitterly and hardly hated
by every anti-semite   60
as if I were a Jew. By this
I am a Russian.

[1962]

Journal Entry

Levertov portrays the destruction of the Vietnamese people and their culture, whereas Yevtushenko is concerned with anti-Semitism and the genocide of Russian Jews. What contribution can you make to this conversation?

Textual Considerations

1. How does setting reinforce theme in Levertov's and Yevtushenko's texts?
2. What is the effect of Levertov's series of questions followed by a series of answers? Who might the questioner be? Is his or her occupation important?
3. In Levertov's poem, who is answering? Does his or her nationality matter? Characterize the attitude of the person answering the questions, the questions themselves, the people of Vietnam, and the war in this poem.
4. Yevtushenko uses literary techniques such as flashbacks, first-person narrator, and two relatively long stanzas to reinforce the meanings in "Babiy Yar." What aspects of this formal organization do you find most effective thematically? Explain.
5. In the latter part of "Babiy Yar," Yevtushenko addresses the Russian people. Characterize his attitude toward them. Does it surprise you that Yevtushenko's poem was originally banned in Russia because he was regarded as a traitor? Explain.

Cultural Contexts

1. In "Babiy Yar," Yevtushenko refers to historical places and people. Review the poem and research the significance of his allusions to Dreyfus, Brussels, Belostok, and so on. Discuss what these references have in common.

2. Discuss with your group your responses to these protest poems. Should poetry be concerned with issues of war and violence? Under what circumstances can you imagine being involved in social protest?

Janice Mirikitani

Prisons of Silence

1.
The strongest prisons are built
with walls of silence.

2.
Morning light falls between us
like a wall.
We have laid beside each other   5
as we have for years.
Before the war, when life
would clamor through our windows,
we woke joyfully to the work.

I keep those moments   10
like a living silent seed.

After day's work, I would
smell the damp soil in his hands,
his hands that felt the outlines
of my body in the velvet   15
night of summers.

I hold his warm hands to this
cold wall of flesh
as I have for years.

   3.
Jap!   20
Filthy Jap!

Who lives within me?

Abandoned homes, confiscated land,
loyalty oaths, barbed wire prisons
in a strange wasteland.   25

Go home, Jap!
Where is home?

A country of betrayal.
No one speaks to us.

We would not speak to each other.   30

We were accused.

Hands in our hair,
hands that spread our legs
and searched our thighs for secret weapons,
hands that knit barbed wire   35
to cripple our flight.

Giant hot hands flung me,
fluttering, speechless into
barbed wire, thorns in a broken wing.

The strongest prisons are built   40
with walls of silence.

4.
I watched him depart that day
from the tedious wall of wire,
the humps of barracks,
handsome in his uniform.   45

I would look each day for letters
from a wall of time,
waiting for approach of my deliverance
from a wall of dust.

I do not remember   50
reading about his death
only the wall of wind
that encased me, as I turned my head.

5.
U.S. Japs hailed as heroes!

I do not know the face of this country   55
it is inhabited by strangers
who call me obscene names.

Jap. Go home.
Where is home?

I am alone wandering   60
in this desert.
Where is home?
Who lives within me?

A stranger with a knife in her tongue
and broken wing,   65

mad from separations and losses cruel
as hunger.

Walls suffocate her as a tomb,
encasing history.

6.

I have kept myself contained   70
within these walls shaped to my body
and buried my rage.
I rebuilt my life
like a wall, unquestioning.
Obeyed their laws . . . their laws.   75

    7.

    All persons of Japanese ancestry
      filthy jap.
    Both alien and non-alien
      japs are enemy aliens.
    To be incarcerated   80
      for their own good
    A military necessity
      The army to handle only the japs
    Where is home?
    A country of betrayal.   85

8.

This wall of silence crumbles
from the bigness of their crimes.
This silent wall
crushed by living memory.

He awakens from the tomb   90
I have made for myself
and unearths my rage.

I must speak.

9.

He faces me in this small
room of myself.   95
I find the windows
where light escapes.
From this cell of history
this mute grave,
we birth our rage.   100

We heal our tongues.

We listen to ourselves

     Korematsu, Hirabayashi, Yasui.

We ignite the syllables of our names.

We give testimony.   105

We hear the bigness of our sounds freed
like many clapping hands,
thundering for reparations.

We give testimony.

Our noise is dangerous.   110

10.
We beat our hands
like wings healed.

We soar
from these walls of silence.

                                                    [1987]

Wilfred Owen

Disabled

He sat in a wheeled chair, waiting for dark,
And shivered in his ghastly suit of grey,
Legless, sewn short at elbow. Through the park
Voices of boys rang saddening like a hymn,
Voices of play and pleasure after day,   5
Till gathering sleep had mothered them from him.

            ...

About this time Town used to swing so gay
When glow-lamps budded in the light blue trees,
And girls glanced lovelier as the air grew dim,—
In the old times, before he threw away his knees.   10
Now he will never feel again how slim
Girls' waists are, or how warm their subtle hands.
All of them touch him like some queer disease.

            ...

There was an artist silly for his face,
For it was younger than his youth, last year.   15

Now, he is old; his back will never brace;
He's lost his colour very far from here,
Poured it down shell-holes till the veins ran dry,
And half his lifetime lapsed in the hot race
And leap of purple spurted from his thigh.   20

...

One time he liked a blood-smear down his leg,
After the matches, carried shoulder-high.
It was after football, when he'd drunk a peg,
He thought he'd better join.—He wonders why.
Someone had said he'd look a god in kilts,   25
That's why; and maybe, too, to please his Meg,
Aye, that was it, to please the giddy jilts
He asked to join. He didn't have to beg;
Smiling they wrote his lie: aged nineteen years.
Germans he scarcely thought of; all their guilt,   30
And Austria's, did not move him. And no fears
Of Fear came yet. He thought of jewelled hilts
For daggers in plaid socks; of smart salutes;
And care of arms; and leave; and pay arrears;
Esprit de corps; and hints for young recruits.   35
And soon, he was drafted out with drums and cheers.

...

Some cheered him home, but not as crowds cheer Goal.
Only a solemn man who brought him fruits
Thanked him; and then enquired about his soul.

...

Now, he will spend a few sick years in institutes,   40
And do what things the rules consider wise,
And take whatever pity they may dole.
Tonight he noticed how the women's eyes
Passed from him to the strong men that were whole.
How cold and late it is! Why don't they come   45
And put him into bed? Why don't they come?

[1920]

Journal Entry

What knowledge of the merciless trench warfare of World War I or of the decision of the
United States to relegate Americans of Japanese ancestry to prison camps after the Japanese
attack on Pearl Harbor can you bring to your reading of these texts?

Textual Considerations

1. Review sections 3, 8, and 9 of "Prisons of Silence," and find examples from the poem to answer the following questions: What enables the victims to break through their silence? To what extent does their testimony make possible their transformation from victims to victors?
2. The narrator of "Prisons of Silence" frequently juxtaposes the discourses of silence and speech. Investigate the various relationships between silence and powerlessness and between speech and power in the poem.
3. Analyze the effects of Owen's juxtaposing images from the soldier's past and present life.
4. Characterize the tone of "Disabled." Is the speaker angry, bitter, resigned? How does tone reinforce theme?
5. How does society's attitude toward the soldier change after his injury? On what aspects of war and people's attitude toward war does the speaker comment?

Cultural Contexts

1. "Prisons of Silence" dramatizes the decision of the United States to relegate Americans of Japanese ancestry to prison camps after the Japanese attack on Pearl Harbor during World War II. Identify the images that most effectively chart the progression of their physical displacement and psychological alienation.
2. Examine the relationship between war and sex by analyzing the gender-related issues explored in lines 9–13, 25–28, and 43–44 of "Disabled." Debate with your group the extent to which the military uniform is still considered a magnet of sexual attraction.

RUKEYSER AND WHITMAN

Muriel Rukeyser

Waking This Morning

Waking this morning,
a violent woman in the violent day
Laughing.

        Past the line of memory
along the long body of your life,   5
in which move childhood, youth, your lifetime of touch,
eyes, lips, chest, belly, sex, legs, to the waves of the sheet.
I look past the little plant
on the city windowsill
to the tall towers bookshaped, crushed together in greed,   10
the river flashing flowing corroded,
the intricate harbor and the sea, the wars, the moon, the planets, all
    who people space

in the sun visible invisible.
African violets in the light
breathing, in a breathing universe.   I want strong peace, and delight, 15
the wild good.
I want to make my touch poems:
to find my morning, to find you entire
alive moving among the anti-touch people.

        I say across the waves of the air to you: 20
today once more
I will try to be non-violent
one more day
this morning, waking the world away
in the violent day.   25

                          [1973]

Walt Whitman

The Dying Veteran

(A Long Island incident—early part of the nineteenth century)

Amid these days of order, ease, prosperity,
Amid the current songs of beauty, peace, decorum,
I cast a reminiscence—(likely 'twill offend you,
I heard it in my boyhood;)—More than a generation since,
A queer old savage man, a fighter under Washington himself,   5
(Large, brave, cleanly, hot-blooded, no talker, rather spiritualistic,
Had fought in the ranks—fought well—had been all through the
    Revolutionary war,)
Lay dying—sons, daughters, church-deacons, lovingly tending him,
Sharping their sense, their ears, towards his murmuring, half-caught
    words:
"Let me return again to my war-days,   10
To the sights and scenes—to forming the line of battle,
To the scouts ahead reconnoitering,
To the cannons, the grim artillery,
To the galloping aids, carrying orders,
To the wounded, the fallen, the heat, the suspense,   15
The perfume strong, the smoke, the deafening noise;
Away with your life of peace!—your joys of peace!
Give me my old wild battle-life again!"

                                                                        [1892]

Walt Whitman

The Artilleryman's Vision*

While my wife at my side lies slumbering, and the wars are over long,
And my head on the pillow rests at home, and the vacant midnight
    passes,
And through the stillness, through the dark, I hear, just hear, the breath
    of my infant,
There in the room as I wake from sleep this vision presses upon me;
The engagement opens there and then in fantasy unreal,   5
The skirmishers begin, they crawl cautiously ahead, I hear the irregular
    snap! snap!

I hear the sounds of the different missiles, the short *t-h-t! t-h-t!* of the
    rifle-balls,
I see the shells exploding leaving small white clouds, I hear the great
    shells shrieking as they pass,
The grape like the hum and whirr of wind through the trees,
    (tumultuous now the contest rages,)
All the scenes at the batteries rise in detail before me again,   10
The crashing and smoking, the pride of the men in their pieces,
The chief-gunner ranges and sights his piece and selects a fuse of the
    right time,
After firing I see him lean aside and look eagerly off to note the effect;
Elsewhere I hear the cry of a regiment charging, (the young colonel
    leads himself this time with brandish'd sword,)
I see the gaps cut by the enemy's volleys, (quickly fill'd up, no delay,)   15
I breathe the suffocating smoke, then the flat clouds hover low
    concealing all;
Now a strange lull for a few seconds, not a shot fired on either side,

Then resumed the chaos louder than ever, with eager calls and orders
of officers,
While from some distant part of the field the wind wafts to my ears a
    shout of applause, (some special success,)
And ever the sound of the cannon far or near, (rousing even in dreams a
    devilish exultation and all the old mad joy in the depths of my soul,)   20
And ever the hastening of infantry shifting positions, batteries, cavalry,
    moving hither and thither,
(The falling, dying, I heed not, the wounded dripping and red I heed
    not, some to the rear are hobbling,)
(Grime, heat, rush, aide-de-camps galloping by or on a full run,
With the patter of small arms, the warning *s-s-t* of the rifles, (these in
    my vision I hear or see,)
And bombs bursting in air, and at night the vari-color'd rockets.   25

                               [1886]

---

*The Artilleryman's Vision: First published as "The Veteran's Vision" in the 1865 edition of *Leaves of Grass* and with this title in the 1871 edition.

Journal Entry

Freewrite on your associations with the word *peace*. What visual images come to mind? Are there colors, situations, or experiences that you link to the word?

Textual Considerations

1. What is the effect of the speaker's juxtaposing images of past and present and touch and antitouch in a poem about peace? Identify those you consider most effective in "Waking This Morning."
2. What is the speaker's attitude toward violence in Rukeyser's poem? Explain. Analyze the speaker's tone in the last stanza. What does it reveal about the speaker?
3. Identify images of peace in Whitman's "The Dying Veteran." What do they imply about the speaker's perspectives on peace? To what extent are they similar to yours?
4. Most of Whitman's lines in "The Dying Veteran" focus on images of war. What do they reveal about the experiences the veteran values so much?
5. Analyze the effect of repetition in the speaker's lines 11–15 of "The Dying Veteran." What do they add to the overall theme of the poem? What kinds of images do they highlight? What is their impact on the reader?.
6. Evaluate Whitman's use of visual imagery in "The Artilleryman's Vision." To what other sense does the poem appeal?
7. Explain the effects of the contrasting images of war, peace, and violence in Rukeyser's and Whitman's poems.

Cultural Contexts

1. Rukeyser's speaker focuses on the joys of peace, whereas Whitman's dying veteran extols the thrills of war. With whose perspective do you agree? Why is it more difficult to write poems about peace?
2. Discuss with your group your responses to the veteran's postwar traumatic "vision" in "The Artilleryman's Vision." To what extent has he "survived" the war?

EMERSON AND TENNYSON

Ralph Waldo Emerson

Concord Hymn

Sung at the Completion of the Battle
Monument, July 4, 1837

By the rude bridge that arched the flood,
   Their flag to April's breeze unfurled,
Here once the embattled farmers stood
   And fired the shot heard round the world.

The foe long since in silence slept;   5
   Alike the conqueror silent sleeps;
And Time the ruined bridge has swept
Down the dark stream which seaward creeps.

On this green bank, by this soft stream,   10
   We set to-day a votive stone;
That memory may their deed redeem,
   When, like our sires, our sons are gone.

Spirit, that made those heroes dare   15
   To die, and leave their children free,
Bid Time and Nature gently spare
   The shaft we raise to them and thee.

                                                    [1836]

Alfred, Lord Tennyson

The Charge of the Light Brigade

I
Half a league, half a league,
Half a league onward,
All in the valley of Death,
   Rode the six hundred.   5

"Forward, the Light Brigade!
Charge for the guns!" he said.
Into the valley of Death
 Rode the six hundred.

II

"Forward, the Light Brigade!"
Was there a man dismay'd?   10
Not tho' the soldier knew
 Some one had blunder'd.
Theirs not to make reply,
Theirs not to reason why,
Theirs but to do and die.   15
Into the valley of Death
 Rode the six hundred.

III

Cannon to the right of them,
Cannon to the left of them,
Cannon in front of them   20
 Volley'd and thunder'd;
Storm'd at with shot and shell,
Boldly they rode and well,
Into the jaws of Death,
Into the mouth of hell   25
 Rode the six hundred.

IV

Flash'd all their sabres bare,
Flash'd as they turn'd in air
Sabring the gunners there,
Charging an army, while   30
 All the world wonder'd.
Plunged into the battery-smoke
Right thro' the line they broke;
Cossack and Russian
Reel'd from the sabre-stroke   35
 Shatter'd and sunder'd.
Then they rode back, but not,
 Not the six hundred.

V

Cannon to the right of them,
Cannon to the left of them,   40
Cannon behind them,
 Volley'd and thunder'd;

> Storm'd at with shot and shell,
> While horse and hero fell,
> They that had fought so well
> Came thro' the jaws of Death,
> Back from the mouth of hell,
> All that was left of them,
>   Left of six hundred.
>
> **VI**
>
> When can their glory fade?
> O the wild charge they made!
>   All the world wonder'd.
> Honour the charge they made!
> Honour the Light Brigade,
>   Noble six hundred!

45

50

55

[1854]

Journal Entry

What does patriotism, or love of country, mean to you? Compare and contrast your view of patriotism with the views of Emerson and Tennyson.

Textual Considerations

1. How does Emerson's use of alliteration contribute to the unity of the poem? What ideas does alliteration emphasize in lines 2, 5, 6, 8 and 11? Characterize the poem's tone.
2. Discuss the theme of Emerson's poem. What is the effect of waiting until the last stanza to introduce it? How does Emerson introduce it? Explain.
3. Consider how Tennyson explores the effects of sound and rhythm to convey the emotional intensity of the charge of the light brigade. Focus specifically on the patterns of rhythm and the phonic symbolism of the galloping of the horses in stanzas I and III.
4. How does the refrain of each stanza of "The Charge of the Light Brigade" contribute to the development of its dramatic action? What does it reveal about the light brigade's response to their commander's "blunder"?
5. Compare and contrast the last stanzas of the two poems. To whom are they addressed? How does Emerson's "those heroes dare / To die" compare with Tennyson's second-stanza "Theirs but to do and die"? Explain.

Cultural Contexts

1. To what extent is Tennyson's poem an expression of patriotism or a critique of Britain's attitude toward the Crimean War (1854–56)? In your opinion, does "The Charge of the Light Brigade" display a prowar or an antiwar sensibility? Explain.
2. What is the purpose of war memorials for Emerson? Does your group think that the building of war memorials helps restore the intellectual and moral stamina of younger generations? What is the purpose of war memorials for your group? Is there a war memorial that has inspired your group? Describe it.

Gabriel Spera

Idle Hands

We're shoveling the sheetrock, bricks, and planks
the builders couldn't use into a pocked
and rusted pickup, settling in the clay
outside the condos springing up around
what will be cul-de-sacs, when all at once   5
we see this snake come trickling through the gutter
licking slackly over tire treads sunk
from lumbering machines, and one of our
small crew, career odd-jobber, Keith, jumps up,
runs over, plants his steel-toed shoes, and hoists   10
his shovel, set to hack its head clean off—
but not yet, not before he watches it
recoil from where his shadow falls, almost
not smiling his first smile all day, and from
somebody else's mouth it seems I hear   15
my voice say, "Wait, it's just a garter snake,
it's harmless, just forget it, let it go."
And so he turns to me, his face the face
of someone stopped from beating something
he clearly feels he owns, he turns and says,   20
"S'that so? Well now, if you're so fucking sure
go pick it up. Go 'head, right now." I can't
begin to guess how many snakes I held
when I was younger, treadmilling my hands
beneath their waterfalling bodies, but   25
enough. Time was, I'd prowl through sagging barns
looking for them, and knew the bleached flat stones
where they'd be scrawled out, knew exactly where
to grab them to keep that trap of fishhook teeth
from clamping on my thumb, yet now I can't   30
be sure of anything, except how bad
Keith wants it dead, and not because he thinks
it's poisonous. Snakes I know, but hate
like Keith's is hard to figure. So I keep
my peace until he jabs, "Time's up," and watch   35

him work his shovel like a butter churn,
catching, scritching, shredding the luckless thing
in bows and ribbons into dirt.

[1992]

Gabriel Spera

Kindness

It's the small acts of kindness I take strength in, acts
of grace so beautiful and true, they make me weep
despite myself. Just take this story of the five
who went out cruising in the canyons after dark
and found a car parked on an empty stretch of road.   5
They smashed the windshield, slashed the tires, jammed the locks
and drove away—but then turned back to see if there
were anything inside the car worth taking. It's then
they find the owners, two young couples, early teens
who'd sneaked away from home to watch the stars come out   10
and kiss. They rush them, beat the boys, and drag the girls
into the brush. The one, her skirt half torn away,
pinned down, looks up and begs the stranger straddling her,
don't kill me, please, don't kill me. Shut your mouth, he says,
don't look me in the face, you'll be alright, and moves   15
a hand down to his belt. She turns her head, and says
as though to no one in the world, then kiss my cheek,
as a promise you won't kill me when it's done. And so
he pauses, perched above her, silent, though the dark
is queasy with the sound of muffled sobs, he stops   20
and kisses her wet cheek, and I, who've judged my kind
most harshly always, I with no good word for men,
can only hang my head to know the emptiness,
the pity, in this small and stunning act of grace.

[1992]

Journal Entry

What emotions, reactions, memories, or images of being in a situation in which you felt
powerless can you bring to your reading of these texts?

Textual Considerations

1. How does the speaker explore the dichotomy between town and nature in "Idle Hands"? Which images best evoke this contrast? What meaning would have been lost if the speaker had focused exclusively on one or the other?
2. Characterize Keith. How does his reaction to the snake mirror his attitude toward life in "Idle Hands"?
3. Explain the speaker's lines, "Snakes I know, but hate / like Keith's is hard to figure." Can you "figure" it? How do these lines reinforce the meaning of "Idle Hands"?
4. What is your response to the last five lines of "Kindness"? How is the poem's meaning enhanced by their phonic and rhythmic effects?
5. Analyze the speaker's roles in "Idle Hands" and "Kindness." When does their presence emerge most powerfully? What point of view do they express about the events in the poems?

Cultural Contexts

1. How does the snake function symbolically in "Idle Hands"? Is it important that the snake was harmless? Can you speculate on the origin of the title? Does the title help us better understand the poem? Explain.
2. Argue for or against the speaker's conclusion that the rapist's kiss on his victim's cheek becomes a "small and stunning act of grace." How does your group react to this provocative idea? Did you reach a consensus? Read the last two lines of the poem to fully understand the words that modify the poem's concluding statement.

FORCHÉ

Carolyn Forché

The Colonel

What you have heard is true. I was in his house. His wife carried a tray
of coffee and sugar. His daughter filed her nails, his son went out for the
night. There were daily papers, pet dogs, a pistol on the cushion beside him.
The moon swung bare on its black cord over the house. On the television
was a cop show. It was in English. Broken bottles were embedded in the 5
walls around the house to scoop the kneecaps from a man's legs or cut his
hands to lace. On the windows there were gratings like those in liquor
stores. We had dinner, rack of lamb, good wine, a gold bell was on the table
for calling the maid. The maid brought green mangoes, salt, a type of bread.
I was asked how I enjoyed the country. There was a brief commercial in 10
Spanish. His wife took everything away. There was some talk then of how
difficult it had become to govern. The parrot said hello on the terrace. The
colonel told it to shut up, and pushed himself from the table. My friend said
to me with his eyes: say nothing. The colonel returned with a sack used to
bring groceries home. He spilled many human ears on the table. They were 15
like dried peach halves. There is no other way to say this. He took one of
them in his hands, shook it in our faces, dropped it into a water glass. It came
alive there. I am tired of fooling around he said. As for the rights of anyone,
tell your people they can go fuck themselves. He swept the ears to the floor
with his arm and held the last of his wine in the air. Something for your 20
poetry, no? he said. Some of the ears on the floor caught this scrap of his
voice. Some of the ears on the floor were pressed to the ground.

[1978]

Carolyn Forché

The Visitor

In Spanish he whispers there is no time left.
It is the sound of scythes arcing in wheat,
the ache of some field song in Salvador.
The wind along the prison, cautious
as Francisco's hands on the inside, touching

the walls as he walks, it is his wife's breath
slipping into his cell each night while he
imagines his hand to be hers. It is a small country.

There is nothing one man will not do to another.

[1979]

Carolyn Forché

The Memory of Elena

We spend our morning
in the flower stalls counting
the dark tongues of bells
that hang from the ropes waiting
for the silence of an hour.   5
We find a table, ask for *paella*,
cold soup and wine, where a calm
light trembles years behind us.

In Buenos Aires only three
years ago, it was the last time his hand   10
slipped into her dress, with pearls
cooling her throat and bells like
these, chipping at the night—

As she talks, the hollow
clopping of a horse, the sound   15
of bones touches together.
The *paella* comes, a bed of rice
and *camarones*, fingers and shells,
the lips of those whose lips
have been removed, mussels   20
the soft blue of a leg socket.

This is not *paella*, this is what
has become of those who remained
in Buenos Aires. This is the ring
of a rifle report on the stones,   25
her hand over his mouth,
her husband falling against her.

These are the flowers we bought
this morning, the dahlias tossed

on his grave and bells
waiting with their tongues cut out
for this particular silence.   30

[1977]

Carolyn Forché

As Children Together

Under the sloped snow
pinned all winter with Christmas
lights, we waited for your father
to whittle his soap cakes
away, finish the whisky,   5
your mother to carry her coffee
from room to room closing lights
cubed in the snow at our feet.
Holding each other's
coat sleeves we slid down   10
the roads in our tight
black dresses, past
crystal swamps and the death
face of each dark house,
over the golden ice   15
of tobacco spit, the blue
quiet of ponds, with town
glowing behind the blind
white hills and a scant
snow ticking in the stars.   20
You hummed *blanche comme
la neige°* and spoke of Montreal
where a québecoise could sing,
take any man's face
to her unfastened blouse   25
and wake to wine
on the bedside table.
I always believed this,
Victoria, that there might
be a way to get out.   30

You were ashamed of that house,
its round tins of surplus flour,

22 **blanche comme la neige:** white as the snow.

chipped beef and white beans,
relief checks and winter trips
that always ended in deer   35
tied stiff to the car rack,
the accordion breath of your uncles
down from the north, and what
you called the stupidity
of the Michigan French.   40

Your mirror grew ringed
with photos of servicemen
who had taken your breasts
in their hands, the buttons
of your blouses in their teeth,   45
who had given you the silk
tassles of their graduation,
jackets embroidered with dragons
from the Far East. You kept
the corks that had fired   50
from the bottles over their beds,
their letters with each city
blackened, envelopes of hair
from their shaved heads.

I am going to have it, you said.   55
Flowers wrapped in paper from carts
in Montreal, a plane lifting out
of Detroit, a satin bed, a table
cluttered with bottles of scent.

So standing in a platter of ice   60
outside a Catholic dance hall
you took their collars
in your fine chilled hands
and lied your age to adulthood.

I did not then have breasts of my own,   65
nor any letters from bootcamp
and when one of the men who had
gathered around you took my mouth
to his own there was nothing
other than the dance hall music   70
rising to the arms of iced trees.

I don't know where you are now, Victoria.
They say you have children, a trailer
in the snow near our town,

and the husband you found as a girl   75
returned from the Far East broken
cursing holy blood at the table
where nightly a pile of white shavings
is paid from the edge of his knife.

If you read this poem, write to me.   80
I have been to Paris since we parted.

[1980]

Journal Entry

The catalyst for Forché's poems was the two years she spent in El Salvador in the late 1970s. What knowledge of the atrocities of this dictatorship can you bring to your reading of these texts?

Textual Considerations

1. Forché refers to "The Colonel" as a "documentary poem." What stylistic aspects of the text suggest journalistic prose?
2. What portrait of the colonel emerges in the poem? How does Forché's ironic juxtaposition of domestic and violent images affect that portrayal? Cite three examples you find most effective.
3. Explain the meaning of the last line in "The Colonel."
4. The setting for "The Visitor" is the dark recesses of a Salvadoran prison. Cite images that best evoke the sense of individual tragedy and impending violence in Forché's other poems.
5. The speaker in "The Memory of Elena" addresses an imaginary listener to whom she shows several significant objects. What story emerges from the descriptions of the flowers and *paella*?
6. How does the juxtaposition of past and present in Elena's memories reinforce the horror of personal destruction caused by political dictatorships?
7. Forché's autobiographical poem "As Children Together" focuses on her own childhood and her friendship with Victoria. What portrait of Victoria emerges in the text?
8. What economic realities contribute to Victoria's inability to fulfill her dream to go to Montreal in "As Children Together"?

Cultural Contexts

1. React to Forché's conviction that "the twentieth-century human condition demands a poetry of witness." To what events might she be referring besides the dictatorship of El Salvador? Do you think it is essential that poets bear witness to atrocities? Explain.
2. Forché went to El Salvador as a journalist, poet, and human rights observer (1979–80). She is committed to the concept that poetry should link the political and the personal, and that one function of the poet is to inform the audience of the horrors of the twentieth-century atrocities. With your group, share your journal entries on Forché's poems as well as your response to her concept of the poet's responsibility.

DRAMA

Fernando Arrabal

Picnic on the Battlefield

CHARACTERS

ZAPO, *a soldier*
MONSIEUR TÉPAN, *the soldier's father*
MADAME TÉPAN, *the soldier's mother*
ZÉPO, *an enemy soldier*
First Stretcher Bearer
Second Stretcher Bearer

A battlefield. The stage is covered with barbed wire and sandbags. The battle is at its height. Rifle shots, exploding bombs and machine guns can be heard.
 ZAPO *is alone on the stage; flat on his stomach, hidden among the sandbags. He is very frightened. The sound of the fighting stops. Silence.*
 ZAPO *takes a ball of wool and some needles out of a canvas workbag and starts knitting a pullover, which is already quite far advanced. The field telephone, which is by his side, suddenly starts ringing.*

ZAPO: Hallo, hallo . . . yes, Captain . . . yes, I'm the sentry of sector 47 . . . Nothing new, Captain . . . Excuse me, Captain, but when's the fighting going to start again? And what am I supposed to do with the hand-grenades? Do I chuck them in front of me or behind me? . . . Don't get me wrong. I didn't mean to annoy you . . . Captain, I really feel terribly lonely, couldn't you send me someone to keep me company? . . . even if it's only a nanny-goat? (*The* CAPTAIN *is obviously severely reprimanding him.*) Whatever you say, Captain, whatever you say. (ZAPO *hangs up. He mutters to himself. Silence. Enter* MONSIEUR *and* MADAME TÉPAN *carrying baskets as if they were going on a picnic. They address their son, who has his back turned and doesn't see them come in.*)

MONS. T (*ceremoniously*): Stand up, my son, and kiss your mother on the brow. (ZAPO, *surprised, gets up and kisses his mother very respectfully on the forehead. He is about to speak, but his father doesn't give him a chance.*) And now, kiss *me.*

ZAPO: But, dear Father and dear Mother, how did you dare to come all this way, to such a dangerous place? You must leave at once.

MONS. T: So you think you've got something to teach your father about war and danger, do you? All this is just a game to me. How many times—to take the

548

first example that comes to mind—have I got off an underground train while it
was still moving.

MME. T: We thought you must be bored, so we came to pay you a little visit. This
war must be a bit tedious, after all.

ZAPO: It all depends.

MONS. T: I know exactly what happens. To start with you're attracted by the nov-
elty of it all. It's fun to kill people, and throw hand-grenades about, and wear
uniforms—you feel smart, but in the end you get bored stiff. You'd have found
it much more interesting in my day. Wars were much more lively, much more
highly colored. And then, the best thing was that there were horses, plenty of
horses. It was a real pleasure; if the Captain ordered us to attack, there we all
were immediately, on horseback, in our red uniforms. It was a sight to be seen.
And then there were the charges at the gallop, sword in hand, and suddenly
you found yourself face to face with the enemy, and he was equal to the occasion too—with his horses—there were always horses, lots of horses, with their
well-rounded rumps—in his highly-polished boots, and his green uniform.

MME. T: No, no, the enemy uniform wasn't green. It was blue. I remember distinctly
that it was blue.

MONS. T: I tell you it was green.

MME. T: When I was little, how many times did I go out to the balcony to watch
the battle and say to the neighbour's little boy: "I bet you a gum-drop the blues
win." And the blues were our enemies.

MONS. T: Oh, well, you must be right, then.

MME. T: I've always liked battles. As a child I always said that when I grew up I
wanted to be a Colonel of dragoons. But my mother wouldn't hear of it, you
know how she will stick to her principles at all costs.

MONS. T: Your mother's just a half-wit.

ZAPO: I'm sorry, but you really must go. You can't come into a war unless you're a
soldier.

MONS. T: I don't give a damn, we came here to have a picnic with you in the country and to enjoy our Sunday.

MME. T: And I've prepared an excellent meal, too. Sausage, hard-boiled eggs—
you know how you like them!—ham sandwiches, red wine, salad, and cakes.

ZAPO: All right, let's have it your way. But if the Captain comes he'll be absolutely
furious. Because he isn't at all keen on us having visits when we're at the front.
He never stops telling us: "Discipline and hand-grenades are what's wanted in
war, not visits."

MONS. T: Don't worry, I'll have a few words to say to your Captain.

ZAPO: And what if we have to start fighting again?

MONS. T: You needn't think that'll frighten me, it won't be the first fighting I've
seen. Now if only it was battles on horseback! Times have changed, you can't
understand. (*Pause.*) We came by motor bike. No one said a word to us.

ZAPO: They must have thought you were the referees.

MONS. T: We had enough trouble getting through, though. What with all the
tanks and jeeps.

MME. T: And do you remember the bottle-neck that cannon caused, just when we got here?

MONS. T: You mustn't be surprised at anything in wartime, everyone knows that.

MME. T: Good, let's start our meal.

MONS. T: You're quite right, I feel as hungry as a hunter. It's the smell of gunpowder.

MME. T: We'll sit on the rug while we're eating.

ZAPO: Can I bring my rifle with me?

MME. T: You leave your rifle alone. It's not good manners to bring your rifle to table with you. (*Pause.*) But you're absolutely filthy, my boy. How on earth did you get into such a state? Let's have a look at your hands.

ZAPO (*ashamed, holding out his hands*):   I had to crawl about on the ground during the manoeuvres.

MME. T: And what about your ears?

ZAPO: I washed them this morning.

MME. T: Well that's all right, then. And your teeth? (*He shows them.*) Very good. Who's going to give her little boy a great big kiss for cleaning his teeth so nicely? (*To her husband.*) Well, go on, kiss your son for cleaning his teeth so nicely. (*M. TÉPAN kisses his son.*) Because, you know, there's one thing I *will* not have, and that's making fighting a war an excuse for not washing.

ZAPO: Yes, mother. (*They eat.*)

MONS. T: Well, my boy, did you make a good score?

ZAPO: When?

MONS. T: In the last few days, of course.

ZAPO: Where?

MONS. T: At the moment, since you're fighting a war.

ZAPO: No, nothing much. I didn't make a good score. Hardly ever scored a bull.

MONS. T: Which are you best at shooting, enemy horses or soldiers?

ZAPO: No, not horses, there aren't any horses any more.

MONS. T: Well, soldiers then?

ZAPO: Could be.

MONS. T: Could be? Aren't you sure?

ZAPO: Well you see . . . I shoot without taking aim, (*pause*) and at the same time I say a Pater Noster for the chap I've shot.

MONS. T: You must be braver than that. Like your father.

MME. T: I'm going to put a record on. (*She puts a record on the gramophone—a pasodoble. All three are sitting on the ground, listening.*)

MONS. T: That really is music. Yes indeed, ole! (*The music continues. Enter an enemy soldier: ZÉPO. He is dressed like ZAPO. The only difference is the colour of their uniforms. ZÉPO is in green and ZAPO is in grey. ZÉPO listens to the music open-mouthed. He is behind the family so they can't see him. The record ends. As he gets up ZAPO discovers ZÉPO. Both put their hands up. M. and MME. TÉPAN look at them in surprise.*) What's going on? (*ZAPO reacts—he hesitates. Finally, looking as if he's made up his mind, he points his rifle at ZÉPO.*)

ZAPO: Hands up! (*ZÉPO puts his hands up even higher, looking even more terrified. ZAPO doesn't know what to do. Suddenly he goes over quickly to ZÉPO and touches him gently on the shoulder, like a child playing a game of "tag".)* Got you! *(To his father, very pleased.)* There we are! A prisoner!

MONS. T: Fine. And now what're you going to do with him?

ZAPO: I don't know, but, well, could be—they might make me a corporal.

MONS. T: In the meantime, you'd better tie him up.

ZAPO: Tie him up? Why?

MONS. T: Prisoners always get tied up!

ZAPO: How?

MONS. T: Tie up his hands.

MME. T: Yes, there's no doubt about it, you must tie up his hands, I've always seen them do that.

ZAPO: Right. *(To his prisoner.)* Put your hands together, if you please.

ZÉPO: Don't hurt me too much.

ZAPO: I won't.

ZÉPO: Ow! You're hurting me.

MONS. T: Now, now, don't maltreat your prisoner.

MME. T: Is that the way I brought you up? How many times have I told you that we must be considerate of our fellow-men?

ZAPO: I didn't do it on purpose. *(To Zépo.)* And like that, does it hurt?

ZÉPO: No, it's all right like that.

MONS. T: Tell him straight out, say what you mean, don't mind us.

ZÉPO: It's all right like that.

MONS. T: Now his feet.

ZAPO: His feet as well, whatever next?

MONS. T: Didn't they teach you the rules?

ZAPO: Yes.

MONS. T: Well then!

ZAPO *(very politely, to* ZÉPO*)*: Would you be good enough to sit on the ground, please?

ZÉPO: Yes, but don't hurt me.

MME. T: You'll see, he'll take a dislike to you.

ZAPO: No he won't, no he won't. I'm not hurting you, am I?

ZÉPO: No, that's perfect.

ZAPO: Papa, why don't you take a photo of the prisoner on the ground and me with my foot on his stomach?

MONS. T: Oh, yes that'd look good.

ZÉPO: Oh no, not that!

MME. T: Say yes, don't be obstinate.

ZÉPO: No, I said no, and no it is.

MME. T: But just a little teeny weeny photo, what harm could that do you? And we could put it in the dining room, next to the life-saving certificate my husband won thirteen years ago.

ZÉPO: No—you won't shift me.

ZAPO: But why won't you let us?

ZÉPO: I'm engaged. And if she sees the photo one day, she'll say I don't know how to fight a war properly.

ZAPO: No she won't, all you'll need to say is that it isn't you, it's a panther.

MME. T: Come on, do say yes.

ZÉPO: All right then. But only to please you.

ZAPO: Lie down flat. (ZÉPO *lies down.* ZAPO *puts a foot on his stomach and grabs his rifle with a martial air.*)

MME. T: Stick your chest out a bit further.

ZAPO: Like this?

MME. T: Yes like that, and don't breathe.

MONS. T: Try to look like a hero.

ZAPO: What d'you mean, like a hero?

MONS. T: It's quite simple; try and look like the butcher does when he's boasting about his successes with the girls.

ZAPO: Like this?

MONS. T: Yes, like that.

MME. T: The most important thing is to puff your chest out and not breathe.

ZÉPO: Have you nearly finished?

MONS. T: Just be patient a moment. One . . . two . . . three.

ZAPO: I hope I'll come out well.

MME. T: Yes, you looked very martial.

MONS. T: You were fine.

MME. T: It makes me want to have my photo taken with you.

MONS. T: Now there's a good idea.

ZAPO: Right. I'll take it if you like.

MME. T: Give me your helmet to make me look like a soldier.

ZÉPO: I don't want any more photos. Even one's far too many.

ZAPO: Don't take it like that. After all, what harm can it do you?

ZÉPO: It's my last word.

MONS. T (*to his wife*):   Don't press the point, prisoners are always very sensitive. If we go on he'll get cross and spoil our fun.

ZAPO: Right, what're we going to do with him, then?

MME. T: We could invite him to lunch. What do you say?

MONS. T: I don't see why not.

ZAPO (*to* ZÉPO):   Well, will you have lunch with us, then?

ZÉPO: Er . . .

MONS. T: We brought a good bottle with us.

ZÉPO: Oh well, all right then.

MME. T: Make yourself at home, don't be afraid to ask for anything you want.

ZÉPO: All right.

MONS. T: And what about you, did you make a good score?

ZÉPO: When?

MONS. T: In the last few days, of course.

ZÉPO: Where?

Mons. T: At the moment, since you're fighting a war.

Zépo: No, nothing much. I didn't make a good score, hardly ever scored a bull.

Mons. T: Which are you best at shooting? Enemy horses or soldiers?

Zépo: No, not horses, they aren't any horses any more.

Mons. T: Well, soldiers, then?

Zépo: Could be.

Mons. T: Could be? Aren't you sure?

Zépo: Well you see . . . I shoot without taking aim, (*pause*) and at the same time I say an Ave Maria for the chap I've shot.

Zapo: An Ave Maria? I'd have thought you'd have said a Pater Noster.

Zépo: No, always an Ave Maria. (*Pause*) It's shorter.

Mons. T: Come come, my dear fellow, you must be brave.

Mme. T (*to* Zépo): We can untie you if you like.

Zépo: No, don't bother, it doesn't matter.

Mons. T: Don't start getting stand-offish with us now. If you'd like us to untie you, say so.

Mme. T: Make yourself comfortable.

Zépo: Well, if that's how you feel, you can untie my feet, but it's only to please you.

Mons. T: Zapo, untie him. (Zapo *unties him.*)

Mme. T: Well, do you feel better?

Zépo: Yes, of course. I really am putting you to a lot of inconvenience.

Mons. T: Not at all, just make yourself at home. And if you'd like us to untie your hands you only have to say so.

Zépo: No, not my hands, I don't want to impose upon you.

Mons. T: No no, my dear chap, no no. I tell you, it's no trouble at all.

Zépo: Right . . . Well then, untie my hands too. But only for lunch, eh? I don't want you to think that you give me an inch and I take an ell.[1]

Mons. T: Untie his hands, son.

Mme. T: Well, since our distinguished prisoner is so charming, we're going to have a marvelous day in the country.

Zépo: Don't call me your distinguished prisoner; just call me your prisoner.

Mme. T: Won't that embarrass you?

Zépo: No, no, not at all.

Mons. T: Well, I must say you're modest. (*Noise of aeroplanes.*)

Zapo: Aeroplanes. They're sure to be coming to bomb us. (Zapo *and* Zépo *throw themselves on the sandbags and hide.*) (*To his parents.*) Take cover. The bombs will fall on you. (*The noise of the aeroplanes overpowers all the other noises. Bombs immediately start to fall. Shells explode very near the stage but not on it. A deafening noise.* Zapo *and* Zépo *are cowering down between the sandbags. M.* Tépan *goes on talking calmly to his wife, and she answers in the same unruffled way. We can't hear what they are saying because of the bombing.* Mme. Tépan *goes over to one of the baskets and takes an umbrella out of it. She opens it.* M. *and* Mme. Tépan *shelter under it as if it*

---

[1] **ell:** a unit of measure equal to 45 inches.

were raining. They are standing up. They shift rhythmically from one foot to the other and talk about their personal affairs. The bombing continues. Finally the aeroplanes go away. Silence. M. TÉPAN *stretches an arm outside the umbrella to make sure that nothing more is falling from the heavens.*)

MONS. T (*to his wife*):   You can shut your umbrella. (MME. TÉPAN *does so. They both go over to their son and tap him lightly on the behind with the umbrella.*) Come on, out you come. The bombing's over. (ZAPO *and* ZÉPO *come out of their hiding place.*)

ZAPO: Didn't you get hit?

MONS. T: What d'you think could happen to your father? (*Proudly.*) Little bombs like that! Don't make me laugh! (*Enter, left, two Red Cross Soldiers. They are carrying a stretcher.*)

1ST STRETCHER BEARER: Any dead here?

ZAPO: No, no one around these parts.

1ST STRETCHER BEARER: Are you sure you've looked properly?

ZAPO: Sure.

1ST STRETCHER BEARER: And there isn't a single person dead?

ZAPO: I've already told you there isn't.

1ST STRETCHER BEARER: No one wounded, even?

ZAPO: Not even that.

2ND STRETCHER BEARER (*to the* 1ST S. B.):   Well, now we're in a mess! (*To* ZAPO *persuasively.*) Just look again, search everywhere, and see if you can't find us a stiff.

1ST STRETCHER BEARER: Don't keep on about it, they've told you quite clearly there aren't any.

2ND STRETCHER BEARER: What a lousy trick!

ZAPO: I'm terribly sorry. I promise you I didn't do it on purpose.

2ND STRETCHER BEARER: That's what they all say. That no one's dead and that they didn't do it on purpose.

1ST STRETCHER BEARER: Oh, let the chap alone!

MONS. T (*obligingly*):   We should be only too pleased to help you. At your service.

2ND STRETCHER BEARER: Well, really, if things go on like this I don't know what the Captain will say to us.

MONS. T: But what's it all about?

2ND STRETCHER BEARER: Quite simply that the others' wrists are aching with carting so many corpses and wounded men about, and that we haven't found any yet. And it's not because we haven't looked!

MONS. T: Well, yes, that really is annoying. (*To* ZAPO.) Are you quite sure no one's dead?

ZAPO: Obviously, Papa.

MONS. T: Have you looked under all the sandbags?

ZAPO: Yes, Papa.

MONS. T (*angrily*):   Well then, you might as well say straight out that you don't want to lift a finger to help these gentlemen, when they're so nice, too!

1ST STRETCHER BEARER: Don't be angry with him. Let him be. We must just hope we'll have more luck in another trench and that all the lot'll be dead.

MONS. T:　I should be delighted.

MME. T:　Me too. There's nothing I like more than people who put their hearts into their work.

MONS. T (*indignantly, addressing his remarks to the wings*):　Then is no one going to do anything for these gentlemen?

ZAPO:　If it only rested with me, it'd already be done.

ZÉPO:　I can say the same.

MONS. T:　But look here, is neither of you even wounded?

ZAPO (*ashamed*):　No, not me.

MONS. T (*to* ZÉPO):　What about you?

ZÉPO (*ashamed*):　Me neither. I never have any luck.

MME. T (*pleased*):　Now I remember! This morning, when I was peeling the onions, I cut my finger. Will that do you?

MONS. T:　Of course it will! (*Enthusiastically.*) They'll take you off at once!

1ST STRETCHER BEARER:　No, that won't work. With ladies it doesn't work.

MONS. T:　We're no further advanced, then.

1ST STRETCHER BEARER:　Never mind.

2ND STRETCHER BEARER:　We may be able to make up for it in the other trenches. (*They start to go off.*)

MONS. T:　Don't worry! If we find a dead man we'll keep him for you! No fear of us giving him to anyone else!

2ND STRETCHER BEARER:　Thank you very much, sir.

MONS. T:　Quite all right, old chap, think nothing of it. (*The two* STRETCHER BEARERS *say goodbye. All four answer them. The* STRETCHER BEARERS *go out.*)

MME. T:　That's what's so pleasant about spending a Sunday in the country. You always meet such nice people.

MONS. T (*pause*):　But why are you enemies?

MME. T:　Your father is the only one who's capable of thinking such ideas; don't forget he's a former student of the Ecole Normale, *and* a philatelist.[2]

ZÉPO:　I don't know, I'm not very well educated.

MME. T:　Was it by birth, or did you become enemies afterwards?

ZÉPO:　I don't know, I don't know anything about it.

MONS. T:　Well then, how did you come to be in the war?

ZÉPO:　One day, at home, I was just mending my mother's iron, a man came and asked me: "Are you Zépo?" "Yes." "Right, you must come to the war." And so I asked him: "But what war?" and he said: "Don't you read the papers then? You're just a peasant!" I told him I did read the papers but not the war bits. . . .

ZAPO:　Just how it was with me—exactly how it was with me.

MONS. T:　Yes, they came to fetch you too.

MME. T:　No, it wasn't quite the same; that day you weren't mending an iron, you were mending the car.

MONS. T:　I was talking about the rest of it. (*To* ZÉPO.) Go on, what happened then?

[2]**Ecole Normale . . . philatelist:** student of the Teacher's College and a stamp collector.

ZÉPO: Then I told him I had a fiancée and that if I didn't take her to the pictures on Sundays she wouldn't like it. He said that wasn't the least bit important.

ZAPO: Just how it was with me—exactly how it was with me.

ZÉPO: And then my father came down, and he said I couldn't go to the war because I didn't have a horse.

ZAPO: Just what my father said.

ZÉPO: The man said you didn't need a horse any more, and I asked him if I could take my fiancée with me. He said no. Then I asked whether I could take my aunt with me so that she could make me one of her custards on Thursdays; I'm very fond of them.

MME. T (*realizing that she'd forgotten it*):   Oh! The custard!

ZÉPO: He said no again.

ZAPO: Same as with me.

ZÉPO: And ever since then I've been alone in the trench nearly all the time.

MME. T: I think you and your distinguished prisoner might play together this afternoon, as you're so close to each other and so bored.

ZAPO: Oh no, Mother, I'm too afraid, he's an enemy.

MONS. T: Now now, you mustn't be afraid.

ZAPO: If you only knew what the General was saying about the enemy!

MME. T: What did he say?

ZAPO: He said the enemy are very nasty people. When they take prisoners they put little stones in their shoes so that it hurts them to walk.

MME. T: How awful! What barbarians!

MONS. T (*indignantly, to* ZÉPO):   And aren't you ashamed to belong to an army of criminals?

ZÉPO: I haven't done anything. I don't do anybody any harm.

MME. T: He was trying to take us in, pretending to be such a little saint!

MONS. T: We oughtn't to have untied him. You never know, we only need to turn our backs and he'll be putting a stone in our shoes.

ZÉPO: Don't be so nasty to me.

MONS. T: What'd you think we *should* be, then? I'm indignant. I know what I'll do. I'll go and find the Captain and ask him to let me fight in the war.

ZAPO: He won't let you, you're too old.

MONS. T: Then I'll buy myself a horse and a sword and come and fight on my own account.

MME. T: Bravo! If I were a man I'd do the same.

ZÉPO: Don't be like that with me, Madame. Anyway I'll tell you something—our General told us the same thing about you.

MME. T: How could he dare tell such a lie!

ZAPO: No—but the same thing really?

ZÉPO: Yes, the same thing.

MONS. T: Perhaps it was the same man who talked to you both?

MME. T: Well if it was the same man he might at least have said something different. That's a fine thing—saying the same thing to everyone!

MONS. T (*to* ZÉPO *in a different tone of voice*):   Another little drink?

MME. T: I hope you liked our lunch?

MONS. T: In any case, it was better than last Sunday.

ZÉPO: What happened?

MONS. T: Well, we went to the country and we put the food on the rug. While we'd got our backs turned a cow ate up all our lunch, and the napkins as well.

ZÉPO: What a greedy cow!

MONS. T: Yes, but afterwards, to get our own back, we ate the cow. (*They laugh.*)

ZAPO (*to* ZÉPO):   They couldn't have been very hungry after that!

MONS. T: Cheers! (*They all drink.*)

MME. T (*to* ZÉPO):   And what do you do to amuse yourself in the trench?

ZÉPO: I spend my time making flowers out of rags, to amuse myself. I get terribly bored.

MME. T: And what do you do with the flowers?

ZÉPO: At the beginning I used to send them to my fiancée, but one day she told me that the greenhouse and the cellar were already full of them and that she didn't know what to do with them any more, and she asked me, if I didn't mind, to send her something else.

MME. T: And what did you do?

ZÉPO: I go on making rag flowers to pass the time.

MME. T: Do you throw them away afterwards, then?

ZÉPO: No, I've found a way to use them now. I give one flower for each pal who dies. That way I know that even if I make an awful lot there'll never be enough.

MONS. T: That's a good solution you've hit on.

ZÉPO (*shyly*):   Yes.

ZAPO: Well, what I do is knit, so as not to get bored.

MME. T: But tell me, are all the soldiers as bored as you?

ZÉPO: It all depends on what they do to amuse themselves.

ZAPO: It's the same on our side.

MONS. T: Then let's stop the war.

ZÉPO: How?

MONS. T: It's very simple. (*To* ZAPO.) You just tell your pals that the enemy soldiers don't want to fight a war, and you (*to* ZÉPO) say the same to your comrades. And then everyone goes home.

ZAPO: Marvellous!

MME. T: And then you'll be able to finish mending the iron.

ZAPO: How is it that no one thought of such a good idea before?

MME. T: Your father is the only one who's capable of thinking such ideas; don't forget he's a former student of the Ecole Normale, *and* a philatelist.

ZÉPO: But what will the sergeant-majors and corporals do?

MONS. T: We'll give them some guitars and castanets to keep them quiet!

ZÉPO: Very good idea.

MONS. T: You see how easy it is. Everything's fixed.

ZÉPO: We shall have a tremendous success.

ZAPO: My pals will be terribly pleased.

MME. T: What d'you say to putting on the pasodoble we were playing just now, to celebrate?

ZÉPO: Perfect.

ZAPO: Yes, put the record on, Mother. (MME. TÉPAN *puts a record on. She turns the handle. She waits. Nothing can be heard.*)

MONS. T: I can't hear a thing.

MME. T: Oh, how silly of me! Instead of putting a record on I put on a beret. (*She puts the record on. A gay pasodoble is heard. ZAPO dances with ZÉPO and MME. TÉPAN with her husband. They are all very gay. The field telephone rings. None of the four hears it. They go on dancing busily. The telephone rings again. The dance continues.*

The battle starts up again with a terrific din of bombs, shots and bursts of machine-gun fire. None of the four has seen anything and they go on dancing merrily. A burst of machine-gun fire mows them all down. They fall to the ground, stone dead. A shot must have grazed the gramophone; the record keeps repeating the same thing, like a scratched record. The music of the scratched record can be heard till the end of the play. The two STRETCHER BEARERS *enter left. They are carrying the empty stretcher.*)

SUDDEN CURTAIN

[1967]

Journal Entry

What images, ideas, or associations does the word *absurd* evoke for you? What elements of Arrabal's drama fit your lists? How would you define "theater of the absurd"?

Textual Considerations

1. Describe the phonic and visual images of war in the play. How does Arrabal convey them? Cite the impact of these effects and explain how they contribute to meaning.
2. What attitudes about war does the playwright convey by having Zépo and Zapo double and mirror each other? What role do the parents play in the drama? Contrast their views of war with those of Zépo and Zapo.
3. The sense of the absurdity of life in *Picnic on the Battlefield* is usually ascribed to the characters' inability to control their own lives. To examine how Arrabal communicates his view of the absurd to the audience, make a list of the contradictions, paradoxes, and contrast devices that dominate his characters' use of language.
4. How do you respond to the play's title and its ending? Why does Arrabal juxtapose *picnic* and *battlefield* in the play's title? Does the author foreshadow the end at an earlier point in the play? Cite evidence for your answer.
5. What role do the stretcher bearers play in *Picnic in the Battlefield*? Analyze the degree to which their presence advances or increases the dramatic action. What does their presence add to the war theme?

Cultural Contexts

1. Arrabal, who wrote this play when he was only fourteen, describes it as "panic theater." What aspects of *Picnic on the Battlefield* best fit his description?

2. Select examples of prowar or antiwar attitude in *Picnic on the Battlefield* to analyze the cultural conventions, war myths, and sensibilities that Monsieur and Madame Tépan, Zépo, Zapo, and the government officials exhibit regarding war. Discuss whether you and your classmates support these conventions and sensibilities.

Performance Exercises

PERFORMANCE EXPRESS (45 MINUTES)

Select a comic dialogue from *Picnic on the Battlefield*—Zapo's imprisonment of Zépo and the dialogue that follows would be a good choice—and deliver it in a way that emphasizes the dehumanization of the characters. Invite the whole class to direct and advise the actors by suggesting facial movements, gestures, and voice qualities that highlight comic effects. Should the actors playing Zapo and Zépo be interchangeable in your staging of this scene? As costume designers, how would you dress them?

PERFORMANCE PROJECTS

1. Stage *Picnic on the Battlefield* in a way that would bring out the absurdity of its comic one-dimensional characters and the wordplay of their disjointed dialogues. Consider the settings, props, costumes, and the phonic effects you would use in the stage directions. What challenges do the roles of these "absurd" characters present to traditional staging conventions?
2. To help you focus on *Picnic on the Battlefield* as a "theater of the absurd" play, use the Internet to access an English-language production of this play. Read about it, and then stage Arrabal's play using sets, costumes, and music to evoke a twentieth-century war scenario. Discuss with your group which lines you would cut out to ensure the dramatic impact you want your postmodern production to have on the audience.

STUDENT RESEARCH PAPER

James Geasor
Professor Callender
EN102 D 15
November 2006

Silent Echoes of War

All wars throughout history have left in their
wake countless soldiers who had taken home with
them the effects of their experiences with death
and brutality. The Vietnam War was different. If
lucky enough to escape the war with his life, the
average American soldier would indeed find himself
back home, but instead of feeling pride for
serving his country, he would feel alienated from
the country he went risking his life to serve.
What would cause this isolation? By the second
half of the 1960s the Vietnam War was being fought
on two fronts: in Southeast Asia by the military,
and at home in the United States between the
government and an increasingly hostile American
public. And who would be the ones forced to live
with the scars of this two-front war? The American
soldier. The American soldier in the Vietnam War
faced the enemy on the battlefield and the enmity
of the American public at home. For the soldier
that survived this gruesome conflict, the
psychological scars of war made the transition
back to civilian life an unbearable burden.

America's involvement in the Vietnam
conflict began a few years after the failed

Geasor 2

attempt at reunification between North Vietnam
and South Vietnam. Albert Marrin's historical
overview reveals that in 1954 the country was
split along the 17th Parallel after a cease-fire
was arranged by the Geneva conference that set
apart Ho Chi Minh's communist north from emperor
Bao Dai's democratic south. Conflict ensued, and
by 1956 the United States began sending aid to
South Vietnam with the hope of building South
Vietnam into a strong enough nation to win its
fight against Ho Chi Minh's communist aggression.
Before long a largely disproportionate amount
of that aid was given militarily (Marrin 53-63).
By the time Lyndon B. Johnson's presidency was
nearing its end, the struggle had developed into
a full-fledged war. An undeclared war, but a war
nonetheless.

Up until this time the conflict was more a
series of small skirmishes and "firefights" than
any actual large-scale battles. These clashes
would normally have been small U.S. patrols going
against small pockets of Viet Cong or NVA (North
Vietnamese Army) resistance. When the NVA crossed
into South Vietnam in November 1965 with the
intent of splitting the country in half, the
first large-scale battle followed, which signaled
the coming escalation in fighting, and newfound
intensity, to which most ensuing battles would be
pitched. This became known as the Battle of Ia
Drang Valley. As recounted by Ron Steinman, a
rather large force of 430 American troops entered
the Ia Drang Valley via helicopter drop to cut
off the supply train of the NVA. They didn't

Geasor 3

realize until they hit the ground that they had
nearly landed on top of 2,000 battle-ready NVA
regulars (29). Fierce combat soon gave way to
hand to hand fighting, and once they realized
the gravity of their situation, the U.S. Army
captains on the ground called in for air support,
which meant napalm. By the next morning a
severely wounded Jack Smith of the 2nd Battalion,
7th Cavalry, would remember, "The grass and
ground were literally covered with blood.
Everywhere you put your hand was sticky with
blood and the place smelled of gunpowder, blood,
and urine. . . . There were body parts lying all
around me. The dead were stacked on top of each
other. . . . It looked like the devil's butcher
shop" (Steinman 41-42). Other accounts of this
battle have been documented and have become a
source for the understanding of the brutality and
excessive violence that was created by guerrilla
warfare, including the shooting to death of the
other sides wounded, which was done by both the
American and NVA troops. The fighting being waged
between the U.S. Army and the Viet Cong and NVA
would become increasingly bloody and would have
a profound psychological effect on the American
troops.

As the war progressed similar battles were
becoming more frequent, and some lacked proper
military coordination. Many of the battles were
fought in the jungles of Vietnam, which made
getting into the battles and effectively fighting
the battles difficult and deadly. At times there
was confusion to the point that many American

Geasor 4

troops were killed by "friendly fire," which is in essence being shot by your own side. One well-documented account of this happened to an army outfit called the Black Lions. Writer David Maraniss recalls in great detail how the unit walked into an ambush and after being pinned down were attacked by a second wave of Viet Cong. In the ensuing firefight they were disoriented as to where they were situated and to whom they were firing at (268-270). He noted, "A machine gun pounding at the [American] battalion command area from the east sounded like an American gun and further confused the situation. First Sergeant Barrow heard Terry Allen and other officers shout, 'Cease fire! Cease fire! You're shooting your own men'" (Maraniss 270). The devastating psychological effect of realizing you were shooting at or being shot by our own men was not too uncommon in the dense jungles of Vietnam. As the battles increased in frequency and the war intensified, the military was calling for additional troops from Washington to reinforce those already there fighting. The Johnson administration escalated the bombing but was hesitant to send more troops. By 1967, while the politicians in the United States were beginning to consider the wisdom of escalating the violence in Vietnam, a determined counterculture began to emerge that vehemently protested the war in Vietnam and America's involvement in it.

Sprouting up mostly on college campuses, which was once fertile ground for recruiting potential military officers, there began instead

Geasor 5

a breed of contempt not only for the military
itself, but the U.S. government and their
stubbornness to escalate the war. Writer David
Maraniss's book deftly juxtaposes the above
mentioned Black Lions' battle with the increasing
unrest on one particular Midwest campus, the
University of Wisconsin. The University of
Wisconsin would explode in protest and violence
to the growing war and the use of the campus to
recruit not only military volunteers but
recruiting students for jobs in companies that
manufactured weapons of war, and in particular
napalm (233-242). His book reveals in chilling
detail that as the war abroad was building in
intensity and violence, the burgeoning conflict
at home regarding the war was also building in
intensity and violence. The American soldier
began being emotionally ambushed at home as well
as physically ambushed in the field, and most
psychologically scarring of all, he was being
condemned for his hapless involvement in the
Vietnam War by his own generation. That
television, via live coverage of the situation in
Vietnam showing its protracted violence and its
effect on Vietnamese civilians, would bring
further angst to the Johnson administration by
the American public only exacerbated and made
more prominent the situation abroad for those
fighting the war. As the protests in America grew
in intensity there would begin a backlash against
the returning American troops to the point of
calling them murderers and baby killers. American
soldiers also began to feel betrayed by their own

Geasor 6

government for not adequately supporting them.
Veteran John Wilson noted, "The controversy over
the war as well as their experiences in it led
many veterans to feel stigmatized for their
actions in Vietnam and cynical about the honesty,
integrity, and trustworthiness of authority and
political leaders" (Mason 196).

For the returning American soldier there was
a deep resentment for his government and his
fellow citizens. The contempt for his fellow
citizens could be summed up as noted by A. D.
Horne: "A 1971 Harris survey found that most
Americans believed that those who went to Vietnam
were 'suckers, having to risk their lives in the
wrong war, in the wrong place, at the wrong
time'" (8). In a sad indictment of America for
its role in the Vietnam conflict we only need to
contemplate the words of writer Patience Mason,
"We the people sent eighteen-year-olds to die
in a foreign country we had no intention of
conquering, as cogs in a military machine run on
principles that guaranteed we couldn't win. And
when we couldn't win, we left" (8).

We are now thirty years removed from the
Vietnam War, and the scars still haven't
completely healed. The psychological damage done
to these brave fighting men and the difficulty of
their reintegration into an antagonistic society
is something no soldier who defends his country's
honor should ever have to go through. That these
scars are not only from a foreign battlefield but
from the home front as well should give us all
pause.

Geasor 7

Works Cited

Horne, A. D., ed. *The Wounded Generation: America After Vietnam.* Englewood Cliffs: Prentice Hall, 1981. Print.

Maraniss, David. *They Marched into Sunlight: War and Peace Vietnam and America October 1967.* New York: Simon & Schuster, 2003. Print.

Marrin, Albert. *America and Vietnam: The Elephant and the Tiger.* New York: Viking, 1992. Print.

Mason, Patience. *Recovering from the War: A Woman's Guide to Helping Your Vietnam Vet, Your Family, and Yourself.* New York: Penguin, 1990. Print.

Steinman, Ron. *The Soldier's Story: Vietnam in Their Own Words.* New York: TV Books, 1999. Print.

TOPICS FOR DISCUSSION AND WRITING

▽▽▽▽▽▽▽▽▽▽▽▽▽▽▽▽▽▽▽▽▽▽▽▽▽▽▽▽

Writing Topics

1. In "A Brother's Murder," Staples cites many examples of the violence and dangers inherent in ghetto life. Write an essay discussing the impressions that his brother's experiences made on you, including any stereotypes you had to modify as a result of reading about them. Clarify your purpose and meaning. Think of a provocative statement to begin your essay, and end with an effective conclusion.

2. Many sociologists have argued that the news media, particularly television, contribute to a romanticization of war, portraying it as high drama. How do the texts by Jarrell, Owen, Levertov, or Yevtushenko refute the media's point of view?

3. Plot and suspense are considered essential elements of a successful story, yet "The Things They Carried" is virtually plotless and offers little suspense. How does O'Brien compensate for the lack of a traditional plot? What elements does he use instead to capture the reader's interest? Why does he deemphasize plot in this story? To what effect?

4. Write an essay in which you analyze the causes and effects of the violent actions of the young boys in "The Destructors" that includes your attitudes toward their behavior.

5. The Vietnam War and its aftermath is the subject of several texts in this part. Compare and contrast the portrayals of this theme. With whose perspective were you most in tune? Explain.

6. "The Sniper," "Silence," and "The Curse" make use of the literary convention of the surprise ending. Review the last paragraphs of the three stories, and write an analysis of the meanings they introduce or the ironies they reinforce.

7. Several texts explore the relationship between the discourses of speech and silence. To what extent do Levertov, Yevtushenko, and Forché make it possible for you to listen to the "voice of silence"? Write a postscript expressing what you "heard."

8. Apply the notion of physical and psychological violence in the stories by Dubus and Petry.

9. Antiheroism is the focus of the texts by Powell and Arrabal. With whose point of view are you most in agreement? Cite evidence you found most convincing.

10. According to the Russian American pacifist Emma Goldman, "Organized violence at the top . . . creates individual violence at the bottom." Test the validity of her hypothesis by applying it to any three texts in Part Three.

11. Consider the relationship of gender and violence in "Kindness," "The Curse," and "Like a Winding Sheet." What do the texts also imply about the interplay of sexuality and violence?

12. Write an essay discussing the idea that *Picnic on the Battlefield* portrays war as a private, social, and political game devoid of moral purpose. Argue whether Arrabal's play also explores other issues besides the war topic. Does *Picnic on the Battlefield* make statements about human beings? What kinds of statements? Cite evidence from the play.

13. Compare and contrast war images you encounter in such texts as "The Dying Veteran," *Picnic on the Battlefield*, "Concord Hymn," "Charge of the Light Brigade," and "The Things They Carried." How do they compare with the war images provided by network television? Limit yourself to three texts.

14. Write an essay analyzing the images of violence in Spera's poems. Is he raising issues about the causes of violence? What do his portrayals of violence suggest about our post-modern culture?

15. In "The Destructors," Graham uses multiple points of view to enhance theme. Write an essay that analyzes what the house means to the following characters: Old Misery, T, the other gang members, and the lorry driver. What is he suggesting about the dichotomy between our capacity for creativity or destruction?

Research Topics

1. War songs such as "Lili Marlene," "For Johnny," "When This Bleeding War Is Over," and "Hymn of Hate"—and many others that emphasize either the patriotic view of war or various forms of war protest—became an important part of the tradition of the two world wars. Research some lyrics from World Wars I and II, the Vietnam War, the Persian Gulf War, or the current "war on terrorism" to write a documented paper analyzing their function as war poetry or war propaganda. Speculate on other functions they may have served.

2. Write a documented paper summarizing the history of women in World Wars I and II, the Vietnam War, the Persian Gulf War, or the current antiterrorist "war." Starting with the domestic view of women as lovers, mothers, and peacemakers, as well as the image of women as "stepdaughters" of war—nurses, doctors, ambulance drivers—move to the current view of women as actively engaged in war.

3. Recent research on the First World War focuses on the treatment of thousands of soldiers whose lives were devastated and sometimes destroyed by shell shock. Explore this topic using selected poems and correspondence of Wilfred Owen, and include a brief description of the revolutionary treatment developed by Arthur Hurst at Seale Hayne convalescent home in Devonshire, England. Use library and Internet sources for your research.

FILM ANGLES

ᗐᗐᗐᗐᗐᗐᗐ

INTRODUCTION

This unit, like Part Four, "Race and Culture," is divided into two sections because it deals with two subjects. That is, although all wars are violent, not all violence is linked to war. As a perusal of any newspaper or news program on television attests, violence occurs in every society every day in a variety of ways. A distinction between war and violence is evident in the literature selections of this unit as well. Many focus on war, whereas the short stories "The Curse" and "The Destructors" and several poems deal with domestic and social violence and its effects on the individual.

Do movies have anything new or significant to add to our knowledge and awareness of war and violence? Actually, more than any other thematic unit in this book, war and violence have a long and intimate connection to film history. The words themselves conjure up concrete mental images and allude to actions, the heart and soul of motion pictures. But although it may be easy to understand why movies have represented war and violence, it is also true that, along with television, they have perpetuated the fascination Americans seem to have with violent subjects. Novelist Scott Turow remarked, "[We] need only glance at a TV screen to realize that murder remains an American preoccupation." This affinity between film and television media and violent subject matter is itself an important subject in need of investigation.

The ease and directness with which movies deal with war and violence often make it difficult to grasp the moral perspective from which we judge the action in some films. Even if a filmmaker's point of view is highly critical of war or violence, that perspective is often overshadowed by the powerful impressions induced by graphic images. This problem has caused many critics and censoring groups to accuse filmmakers who graphically depict violent subject matter of exploiting or glorifying war and violence rather than denouncing them.

For example, the first thirty minutes of Steven Spielberg's *Saving Private Ryan* (1998), which recounts the Allied invasion of Europe in World War II, is filled with images of bloodied limbs, dismemberment, and heads being blown off in vivid color and close-ups. Yet neither Spielberg nor those who have written about the film would contend that the film glorifies war. Several key questions arise, then, concerning the moral perspective of films that deal with war or violence and how the viewer should incorporate brutal imagery in an overall understanding of a film's narrative and theme.

Questions to Consider

1. What purpose is served by graphic detail in a war film? Is it justified by an aim for "greater realism"? Are the images designed to repel us and show how horrific war is? If so, is this aim consistent with the rest of the movie, which, in the case of *Saving Private Ryan*, seems to celebrate the heroism of American soldiers?
2. Think of a movie that contains realistic depictions of violent actions. What was your reaction to the violence? Do you think the way it was presented helped or hindered your appreciation and understanding of the film's theme?

WAR

Film History

Genre

Many films include war as a backdrop to the characters' lives—including such classics as *Gone with the Wind* (1939) and *Casablanca* (1942). Others focus on individuals or societies that are the victims of war, such as the Italian film *Life Is Beautiful* (1997). None of these belongs to the **genre** of the war film, per se, which emerged in the silent period as a response to the First World War. As a genre, the war film often treats war as a phenomenon that societies are forced to engage in from time to time to defend freedom or suppress a hostile leader or regime. Most of the war films of the 1940s and 1950s depicting the fight against Hitler and Nazi Germany are examples of the genre.

Not every war film was or is antiwar, any more than every novel about war is inherently against it. Neither James Jones's *From Here to Eternity* (made into a film in 1953) nor Norman Mailer's *The Naked and the Dead* (made into a film in 1958) is primarily against war. No doubt this is because both were about World War II, generally considered a "just" war because it was fought against the spread of Nazism and fascism in Europe. The typical war film treats going to war as an unfortunate necessity, but it generally does not take a critical stance against war. This is because such films often have a direct correlation to the sentiments in society contemporaneous to the war in question.

In films about the Second World War, for example, American soldiers, it was assumed, fought with the confidence that the enemy was clear and their country was behind their efforts. The viewer was encouraged to identify with the soldier risking his life to rid the world of "evil" ideologies and the tyrants who enforce them. Identification is an important element in narrative filmmaking, encouraging the viewer to become emotionally and psychologically bound to the principal character or characters often to endorse values he or they represent. In this sense, a typical war film that follows the so-called "rules" of the genre is in accord with the audience's feelings and values.

In a classical example of the war film genre, therefore, the following features are usually found:

1. Soldiers in combat situations fight a clearly defined enemy.
2. The film usually has an unambiguous moral perspective.
3. The viewer easily identifies with the central protagonist(s).
4. There is a credible sense that the war is fought for a clear purpose, that the battles waged by fighting men serve this purpose, and that even the lives of soldiers are a justifiable sacrifice.
5. The film has narrative closure and a relatively cathartic effect based on imminent victory or the success of a particular mission.

Question to Consider

Think of any war film you have seen in terms of how many of these genre features it contains.

The Antiwar Film

How is the relative compatibility between the viewer and the model war film affected when a film takes a critical stance against war? This, too, has a long history, as far back as *All Quiet on the Western Front* (d. Lewis Milestone, 1930), based on a famous novel by Erich Maria

Remarque. And despite the general view that World War II was a just war, it has been less than gloriously presented in such films as *The Bridge on the River Kwai* (d. David Lean, Great Britain, 1957) and *The Thin Red Line* (d. Terrence Malick, 1998). More overtly antiwar films were made about the Vietnam War, consistent with the conflicted social attitudes about that war—*The Deer Hunter* (1978), *Platoon* (1986), and *Full Metal Jacket* (d. Stanley Kubrick, Great Britain, 1987), being among the most well known. An important indication that a film is taking a critical position toward war is that it problematizes or violates one or more of the standard rules or features of the genre just listed.

The question raised earlier—namely, how do we determine what perspective or point of view a film takes toward its subject—is relevant in this context. It is generally easier to resolve that question in a work of literature because it is the work of one author who shapes the plot, develops the theme, selects the language, and controls the tone and mood of the piece. Whether blatant or subtle, ironic or nonjudgmental, the moral perspective is established by the intention of the author, whether his or her view is in the third person or channeled through a first-person narrator. In Liam O'Flaherty's story "The Sniper," for example, the author adopts a deceptively simple and neutral tone, restricting our knowledge to the experience of the sniper, but it is exactly that control and tone that allows the surprise ending to resonate with such powerful effect.

Films present us with a complex variation of the ruling voice of a narrative—its **point of view**. Because the medium uses means other than language to communicate, the filmmaker's intentions are often misunderstood. We see and hear much more than any one "voice" can control, which means we must pay as much attention to a film's audio and visual "texts" as we do to its screenplay and dialogue. The student must look closely at the director's other instruments—the images on the screen and the way they are framed, composed, lit, and filmed by the camera, what is known as a film's **mise-en-scène**—as equally powerful expressive aspects, embodying ideas that may or may not be put into words. To determine whether a film is antiwar, then, we need to examine not only how it departs from the basic conventions and rules of the genre but how it employs cinematic elements.

Questions to Consider

1. What characteristics of the classic war film are missing from *All Quiet on the Western Front*, *The Bridge on the River Kwai*, *The Deer Hunter*, *Platoon*, or *The Thin Red Line*? Does the absence of these features make any of these films antiwar?
2. What aspects of the mise-en-scène in any of these films can be interpreted as establishing or reinforcing an antiwar message?

Case Studies

Paths of Glory and *Full Metal Jacket*

The director Stanley Kubrick made two extraordinary war films—*Paths of Glory* (1957), set during World War I, and *Full Metal Jacket*, set during the Vietnam War. A comparison of these two films and their protagonists is an enlightening lesson in understanding how the convention of providing a protagonist with whom the viewer can identify can make an important difference in how we understand the film and recognize its perspective.

Paths of Glory, based on a novel by Humphrey Cobb, focuses more on the corruption of the officers who run wars and the way the military system victimizes the soldiers in the trenches. The clear moral perspective that allows us to judge this situation is provided by the protagonist, Colonel Dax, whose courage, integrity, and loyalty to his men are never in question. *Full Metal Jacket*, based on the novel *The Short-Timers* by ex-marine Gustav Hasford, follows the training of a group of marines from boot camp to their assignment in Vietnam. Contrary to the situation as presented in the earlier film, however, Kubrick makes it difficult for the viewer to identify with the protagonist, Joker, whose behavior and thinking is ambivalent and morally questionable.

In addition to the problematizing of viewer identification, the film's mise-en-scène is an important key to Kubrick's intentions. Especially in the first half, many shots are composed and designed to underline the rigidity and uniformity of the basic training process. The recruits are often lined up symmetrically in a manner that stresses the need for group behavior and thinking at the expense of the individual.

Sound and music are additional important elements in a movie. Kubrick always used music that belonged to the period in which the film is set. In *Full Metal Jacket*, many popular songs from the 1960s, some linked directly to the war, contribute to the ironic tone of the film. For example, the film's abrupt transition from the bloody climax of Part One to the Vietnam section is bridged by the song, "These Boots Are Made for Walking," sung over a shot of a prostitute on the streets of Saigon. This use of **audio/visual montage** can be a rich source of probing a film's multilayered meanings.

Questions to Consider

1. List the character features of Colonel Dax, the protagonist of *Paths of Glory*. Which of these seem crucial to the viewer's ability to identify with the character? What are his views toward war?
2. What are the features of the main protagonist in *Full Metal Jacket*? What does his nickname "Joker" suggest about him? What other clues does Kubrick provide to show how Joker might reflect the moral, political, and social ambivalences that characterized the Vietnam War?
3. How do the visual compositions in *Full Metal Jacket* serve the director's overall point of view? What other cinematic features can you identify in the film that suggest how we can interpret character behavior or action?
4. Note the lyrics of "These Boots Are Made for Walking" and other songs, and discuss how they interact directly with the images and scenes depicted in each case. What do you make of this juxtaposition of music and image? What does it add to our understanding of the director's point of view?

Flags of Our Fathers and Letters from Iwo Jima

Two recent war films, *Flags of Our Fathers* and *Letters from Iwo Jima* (both 2006 and directed by Clint Eastwood), deserve serious attention in relation to the topics of this section because they constitute an unprecedented phenomenon in the history of the war film. Each film approaches the same historic World War II battle for the Pacific island of Iwo Jima, but from the perspective of each side of the conflict. *Flags of Our Fathers* depicts the seizure of the island by United States marines, alternating images of this event with the fortunes of three marines who are exploited by the media back home as the heroes who raised the flag on the island—an image that became one of the most famous photographs of all time. The film exposes the hypocrisy and lies of the media and the government that for many decades hid the fact that the real marines who raised the flag had died in combat and that the photograph was the result of a second raising, staged for the camera.

Letters from Iwo Jima follows the actions of the Japanese soldiers who knew they were outnumbered and doomed to die. In his concern for authenticity, the director used Japanese actors speaking Japanese so that the film required subtitles. He also photographed the battle scenes in both films in ashen-gray tones that stresses the rock and soil terrain of the island and gives these scenes a bitter, documentary look as opposed to the vivid colors of most war films. Examine these two groundbreaking films in terms of (a) the conventions of the war film as listed earlier, (b) the importance of the viewer's ability to identify with the protagonist(s), and (c) the attitude toward war that each film displays as detected in its representation of action, its dialogue, the photography, and the mise-en-scène. In the case of *Flags of Our Fathers*, there is an additional dimension to consider: the need for American society to glorify American victory in war time, even at the cost of the truth.

Questions to Consider

1. Who are the protagonists of *Flags of Our Fathers* and *Letters from Iwo Jima*? Is there one in each case or several? Does either film depend on our ability to identify with a protagonist? If not, how does this affect the way the viewer becomes involved in each narrative?
2. World War II has often been declared a just war. Does either *Flags of Our Fathers* or *Letters from Iwo Jima* challenge that viewpoint?

Research Topics

1. Compare *Saving Private Ryan* and *Full Metal Jacket* as war films. How does each film fit or not fit the mold of the genre? If an identification figure is an essential component of the genre, how does the protagonist in each of these films function in this capacity? Does the specific war in each case have any bearing on its relationship to the genre or to your reactions?
2. Compare *Full Metal Jacket* with other films about the Vietnam War (e.g., *The Deer Hunter* or *Platoon*). Do they present similar views of that war? If not, how are they different? How do the main characters in each work function as identification figures?
3. Both *Saving Private Ryan* and *The Thin Red Line* deal with World War II from a contemporary perspective. How does each film represent the war? What role does the **imagery** play in each film?
4. Both Tim O'Brien's short story "The Things They Carried" and Gustav Hasford's *The Short-Timers*, the novel on which *Full Metal Jacket* is based, are written by men who fought in Vietnam. The screenplay for the film was also co-written by Hasford and Michael Herr, another Vietnam War veteran. Compare the O'Brien story to the Vietnam section of either the Hasford novel or the film in terms of how each depicts the experience of the soldier in that war.
5. With the help of a VHS or DVD player, watch *Full Metal Jacket*, *The Thin Red Line*, or *Paths of Glory* several times and stop it at selected images to study the way the director has deliberately framed and composed images. See if you can detect *patterns of such imagery* and interpret what those patterns reveal about the director's intentions and the meaning of the film.
6. Compare the first-person point of view in *Full Metal Jacket* or *The Thin Red Line* with a war story or novel in the first person in terms of how each guides our perceptions and feelings.
7. Watch the DVD or video of one of the many documentaries on war (e.g., *War Photographer*, d. Christian Frei, 2002; *First Kill*, d. Coco Schrijber, Holland, 2002; *Gunner Palace*,

d. Michael Tucker and Petra Epperlein, 2005; *Why We Fight*?, d. Eugene Jarecki, 2006; or *The War Tapes*, d. Deborah Scranton, 2006), and compare the film's methods and techniques with those used in a fictionalized war film. What differences can you discern between narrative films and documentaries? Without such conventions as a dramatic story line and character involvement, how does a documentary engage the viewer? Do we learn more about the subject of war from a documentary? Is the representation of violence more or less justified in a documentary than it is in a narrative film?

8. Not many feature films have been made about the first Persian Gulf War or the more recent and controversial war in Iraq. Nor does it seem that such films would fit neatly into the category of either the classical war film or the antiwar film. For example, in *Jarhead* (d. Sam Mendes, 2005), based on a memoir of the first Gulf War, marines who have been trained to fight and kill are frustrated because they never get the opportunity to do either. The focus is on the gung-ho attitude of those trained for war rather than on the war itself. Consider the point of view of this film. What does it tell us about war mentality?

9. Often in war films the enemy is depicted in stereotypical terms that make it easier for the viewer to demonize him and identify with the "official" hero or heroes of the film. How does presenting the point of view of the Japanese enemy in *Letters from Iwo Jima* affect the viewer's feelings and perceptions? Does the director Eastwood succeed in humanizing the "enemy"? If so, how does this affect arguments for war and the traditional positions of war films? Would it be possible to make a film today that asks the viewer to identify with whatever persons or group current events have declared to be enemies?

VIOLENCE

Introduction

Unlike war, which is a specific event, violence is a behavioral phenomenon of many events—individual and group, private and social—and crosses all class, cultural, national, and racial lines. Many philosophers and psychologists—including Friedrich Nietzsche and Sigmund Freud—believe that violence is inherent in human nature and will always present a problem for the individual and society as a whole.

Stanley Kubrick's *A Clockwork Orange* (1971), based on the novel by Anthony Burgess, seems to endorse this view by implying that to deal with violence, societies often resort to other forms of it. David Fincher's *Fight Club* (1999), based on the novel by Chuck Palahniuk, associates violence with men and suggests that it is connected to the primal instincts of the race. Its protagonist, enraged and bored with the world and his own failures, begins a "fight club," in which similarly disillusioned single men meet late at night for boxing matches in which they pummel each other brutally. The twist in the story concerns the identity of the main character and suggests that every man has a "double" who carries his deeply repressed rage. Unlike the character in *A Clockwork Orange*, however, the protagonist in *Fight Club* turns his aggression inward.

Question to Consider

Think of some recent films containing violence. How is it presented in each case? Can you identify a viewpoint that represents what the director wants you to think about the violence in each case? Does it suggest that nothing can be done to eliminate violence and aggression? What does the film suggest about society's responsibility? Is society the cause of violence? If so, is it responsible for finding a cure?

History and Genre

Violence has a long history in the movies and can be found in many genres other than war, such as westerns, crime and detective films, horror and science fiction thrillers, and ordinary melodramas. Even Tom and Jerry cartoons have come under fire for treating violence as a subject for laughter, thus providing a dangerous model for children. To talk about violence in movies, we should distinguish between films that are about violent actions or situations— such as riots, serial killings, rape, or domestic violence—and films about any number of subjects that include violence and represent it in a disturbing manner.

Some filmmakers have made the question of violence the theme of their films. Arthur Penn's *Bonnie and Clyde* (1967), about bank robbers during the Depression, ends in a shocking bloodbath as the title characters are riddled with bullets in slow motion. Historians now read the film as a displaced expression of the underlying violence of American society. This theme continues to be explored by filmmakers, most recently in David Cronenberg's *A History of Violence* (2005), in which a character we assume is an ordinary family man, when forced to confront his past as a hired killer, resorts to the very violence he had allegedly renounced in order to return to the domestic life he has built.

In Sam Peckinpah's *Straw Dogs* (1971), the protagonist, a mild-mannered mathematician played by Dustin Hoffman, is forced to confront his avowed pacifism when he and his wife are assaulted by local thugs. Some critics interpreted this film, as well as Peckinpah's *The Wild Bunch* (1969) as **allegories** about the inherent violence of American society and the ongoing debate during the late 1960s and early 1970s between advocates of the Vietnam War, known as "hawks," and advocates of peace, known as "doves."

Whereas a war film's graphic violence may be justified by the message the film conveys, other films that indulge in excessive violence are sometimes said to appeal to bloodthirsty viewers who enjoy spectacles of carnage. Accusations along this line were made against the grisly Colosseum combats in *Gladiator* (d. Ridley Scott, 2000), in which men, enslaved by the Roman Empire, are sent into the arena with the barest minimum of weapons to defend themselves against impossible odds and an almost certain bloody death—all for the purpose of entertaining the emperor and Roman citizens. The line between artistic edification and exploitation is often a thin one, and films like *Gladiator* reopen that debate.

Some filmmakers, for various reasons; and according to the taste and permissiveness of the times, leave the violence off-screen entirely, somewhat in the tradition of Greek tragedy in which representations of violence on the stage were considered morally and aesthetically inappropriate. A subject like rape, for example, once considered too distressing to show on the screen, is only implied in *Johnny Belinda* (1948) but is depicted more graphically in *The Accused* (1988). Greater tolerance and changes in cultural and social attitudes over forty years no doubt affect what is shown on the screen, but this does not preclude there being other reasons for the differences in the treatment of such subjects.

The tragic events of 9/11 have brought the violence of terrorism closer to home for millions of people in America and elsewhere. The hijacking of airplanes that led to the destruction of lives on that day have so far been dramatized in two films released in 2006, each approaching the events from a distinct point of view. *United 93* (d. Paul Greengrass) uses telephone transcripts and other evidence to imagine how passengers aboard one of the planes acted under the circumstances and fought against the terrorists. *World Trade Center* (d. Oliver Stone) balances the scale of the event with an intimate focus on the individual lives of two firefighters trapped under tons of debris in one of the towers of the trade center and the attempts of rescuers and families to reach them.

Finally, the depiction of violence may not only be justified but may illuminate an important dimension of a character's personality or demonstrate the extremes to which both criminals and the police who pursue them resort to achieve their respective ends. An example of the former is Martin Scorsese's *Raging Bull* (1980), in which the protagonist, famous prize-fighter Jake La Motta, uses the boxing ring to act out his anger and rage against others as well as a form of punishing himself for doing so. The character is portrayed as so insecure and inarticulate that the bloody rituals of the boxing ring become his only form of expression. An example of the latter is the same director's *The Departed* (2006) in which excessive violence exists on both sides of the law. The film suggests that unchecked indulgence in such behavior often obliterates the line between law and order, on the one hand, and the criminal world, on the other, and corrodes the well-being and private lives of even the most dedicated champions of the law.

Questions to Consider

1. Consider the merits, if any, of these conflicting views of *Gladiator:* (1) That the film's unrestrained violence is justified because it shows that the Roman Empire, although allegedly civilized, indulged in blood sports and was indifferent to the value of human life. (2) That the excessive violence is just an excuse to show what special effects, digital filmmaking, and editing can achieve in the endless effort to gratify spectators who like bloody action.

2. Often genre films like *The Wild Bunch* (a western) and *Bonnie and Clyde* (a crime drama) are indirect reflections of social and political realities occurring at the time they were made. Can you think of any genre films that you have seen over the past few years—crime, science fiction, or horror films—that can be interpreted in a similar way?

3. Many social critics believe media violence has a direct relation to violence in society. Consider the series of teenage horror films and their sequels—sometimes referred to as "slasher" films: *Friday the 13th, Halloween, The Nightmare on Elm Street, Scream,* and *I Know What You Did Last Summer*—as examples of increasingly graphic violence on the screen. What does the popularity of such films, both in theaters and in video and DVD formats, say about American audiences and the filmmakers who continue to gratify the appetite for such films? Are they merely entertaining, or do they reflect an indifference to violence in society in general?

4. The rape scene is left out of Andre Dubus's story "The Curse" somewhat like actions that "occur" off-screen in a movie. Compare this to the treatment of the rape in *The Accused.* What are the artistic, narrative, psychological, and thematic reasons behind the treatment in each case? Do they seem justified to you?

Case Study

A Clockwork Orange

A Clockwork Orange created a scandal when it was released in 1971 and was the cause of such outcry in Great Britain, where it was blamed as the cause of copycat crimes, that its director, Stanley Kubrick, withdrew it from distribution for over twenty-five years. Its shock effect had to do, in part, with the fact that, as presented, the viewer can neither identify with nor approve of either the individual who commits violence nor the society that attempts to correct his behavior. Alex, the main character of a futuristic society, is a sociopath addicted to violence and criminal behavior. Upon his arrest and incarceration, he is subject to an experimental technique, called the Lodovico method. He is constrained like a mental patient, his eyes clipped open, and forced to watch acts of violence on a movie screen in the hope he will develop conditioned reflexes that will suppress his violent instincts.

The film raises disturbing ethical questions about the limits to which a society will go to protect itself. The viewer is presented with an impossible choice: Should the state be granted unlimited license to prevent crime by any means necessary, even at the expense of the individual? Or should we condemn such excessive measures in the name of libertarian values even though this leaves the perpetrators of violence license to trample on those very values?

No small part of the film's shock effect, still felt by audiences today, is the style with which everything is presented—a fusion of audio and visual excess that in itself does a kind of violence by assaulting the senses, rendering the action both hyperreal and surreal. The exuberance with which Alex and his "droogs" brutalize others disturbed many viewers, who concluded it meant the director endorsed such behavior. The same style, however, characterizes the Lodovico method, equating its sanitized form of brainwashing with a violence to the spirit every bit as brutal as the behavior it purports to correct. All in all, the film can be understood as a dark social satire, mocking the extremes of liberalism as well as the abuses and follies of the society that tries to control them. For some viewers, however, the film's assault on the mind and the senses made it difficult to be amused.

Questions to Consider

1. How would you characterize the violence in *A Clockwork Orange*? Is it an expression of youthful rebellion against a corrupt society, or is it mindless and random?
2. The end of the film implies that the Lodovico method ultimately fails. Does this suggest it was the wrong method or that society simply lacks the ability to deal with Alex's kind of violence?
3. Although originally *A Clockwork Orange* took place in the future, we have now arrived at that point. How does its vision of the "future" accord with the present state of society? How does it compare with other visions of the future in science fiction films?
4. The film, like the novel, is presented in the first person, from Alex's point of view. How does this affect the viewer's involvement and ability to identify? Are there aspects of Alex's personality that redeem him in ethical or human terms?
5. Analyze a sequence from the film that illustrates the director's visual style. How does the mise-en-scène contribute to this style and to the film's atmosphere?
6. The language in the film closely follows that in the Anthony Burgess novel, much of it made up of invented words and composites of familiar ones. What is the function and effect of this language? Can this language be seen as an expression or instrument of the individual's rebellious stance against society?

Research Topics

1. Consider one or more of the following films—*Unforgiven* (d. Clint Eastwood, 1992), *Gangs of New York* (d. Martin Scorsese, 2002), *Bloody Sunday* (d. Paul Greengrass United Kingdom/Ireland, 2002), *Mystic River* (d. Clint Eastwood, 2003), *A History of Violence* (d. David Cronenberg, 2005), and *The Departed* (d. Martin Scorsese, 2006)—in which the use of violence may be, as in the case of *Raging Bull*, both distressing and enlightening. Look at each film carefully and analyze specific examples that illustrate either (a) how the representation of violence is necessary to a full understanding of the film's subject and theme; or (b) that excessive violence tends to obstruct any positive aims the filmmaker might have.
2. Critics and censoring bodies argue that depictions of violence in movies and television help create a permissive atmosphere in society in which people accept it as a legitimate means of dealing with anger and frustration against individuals who have harmed them or

against perceived injustices of society itself. Do some library research on this topic and evaluate the merits or flaws of this viewpoint. Use references to specific movies or television programs to support your points.

3. Choose one of the films discussed in this section that is based on a novel—*A Clockwork Orange* or *Fight Club*—and compare the movie to the novel specifically in relation to the different ways that violence is represented. Does a literary description of violence evoke strong emotions comparable to those evoked by a film? If not, what does this say about the way each medium affects the impact of violence? Does the very nature of film imply it is more difficult to retain an objective viewpoint toward a depiction of graphic violence?

4. Compare the two films based on the events of 9/11 in terms of how each treats the subject. What is the nature of the violence, and how is it approached and understood in each film? Is one approach more effective than the other? Does either film suggest that terrorism and suicide bombings have introduced a new level of violence in the world that justifies retaliation? If so, what are the implications of such an idea?

PART FOUR

RACE AND CULTURE

Fiction

The Moment Before the Gun Went Off, Nadine Gordimer ◆ *Still*, John Talbird ◆ *And the Soul Shall Dance*, Wakako Yamauchi ◆ *Puertoricanness*, Aurora Levins Morales ◆ *The Lesson*, Toni Cade Bambara ◆ *I Stand Here Ironing*, Tillie Olsen ◆ *Désirée's Baby*, Kate Chopin

Essays

Silent Dancing, Judith Ortiz Cofer ◆ *How I Learned to Read and Write*, Frederick Douglass ◆ *Black Hair*, Gary Soto ◆ *A Chinaman's Chance: Reflections on the American Dream*, Eric Liu

Poetry

I Hear America Singing, Walt Whitman ◆ *Poet Power*, Denise Levertov ◆ *Indian Boarding School: The Runaways*, Louise Erdrich ◆ *Public School No. 18: Paterson, New Jersey*, Maria Mazziotti Gillan ◆ *The Weary Blues*, Langston Hughes ◆ *Dream Variations*, Langston Hughes ◆ *Harlem (A Dream Deferred)*, Langston Hughes ◆ *Telephone Conversation*, Wole Soyinka ◆ *On the Subway*, Sharon Olds ◆ *Chinese Fireworks Banned in Hawaii*, Eric Chock ◆ *Latero Story*, Tato Laviera ◆ *Child of the Americas*, Aurora Levin Morales ◆ *Legal Alien*, Pat Mora ◆ *Elena*, Pat Mora ◆ *Lost Sister*, Cathy Song ◆ *Cross Plains, Wisconsin*, Martín Espada ◆ *Federico's Ghost*, Martín Espada ◆ *Tony Went to the Bodega but He Didn't Buy Anything*, Martín Espada

Drama

Othello, The Moor of Venice, William Shakespeare

"Ours is the only nation to have a dream and give its name to one—
the American Dream," wrote the literary critic Lionel Trilling more
than fifty years ago. Although the United States continues to be a
nation of immigrants in search of that dream, many groups have felt
excluded from the right to equality promised in the Declaration of
Independence of 1776. These groups are challenging the ideal of
the "melting pot," which was first expressed in Hector St. Jean de
Crevecoeur's 1781 statement that "individuals of all nations are melted
down in a new race of men" and has shaped the collective consciousness
of North Americans for more than two centuries.

The metaphor of the melting pot, however, has been challenged
by many contemporary writers in the United States including Asian
American Bharati Mukherjee. She suggests that a "fusion chamber"
in which elements interact but do not melt is a more appropriate
metaphor to describe the new multiracial democracy of the twenty-first
century. African American novelist Toni Morrison concurs. "We have
to acknowledge that the thing we call 'literature' is pluralistic now just
as society ought to be. The melting pot never worked." Henry Louis
Gates Jr., professor and critic, extends the conversation: "Pluralism
isn't supposed to be about leaping the boundaries, it's supposed to be
about breaking those boundaries down, acknowledging the fluid and
interactive nature of all our identities."

Much of the literature in Part Four portrays the irrationality of
racism and the politics of exclusion and examines their effects on
the groups that continue to challenge the myths of assimilation and
justice for all. Walt Whitman's poem "I Hear America Singing"
(1867), for instance, celebrates the delight of diversity in what
Whitman envisions as a truly democratic America. In a strong epic
voice, Whitman communicates to all Americans, regardless of class
and race, the idealized vision of democracy engraved in the
Declaration of Independence (1776) and the Gettysburg Address
(1863). However, in the poems by Langston Hughes written over
two decades, we hear the voices of exclusion. In "The Weary
Blues," set in a bar in Harlem in the 1920s, the singer finds a
catharsis in the blues songs of his people, in spite of his poverty
and personal pain; and in "Dream Variations," the speaker sounds
an optimistic note as he imagines himself flinging his arms wide and
dancing in the sunlight. In "Harlem," however, written in the
1940s, the speaker sounds an ominous note as he explores the
consequences of deferring the dreams of African Americans. In
very few lines, Hughes presents possible responses to hope denied
and ends with the possibility of explosion, foreshadowing the race
riots of the 1960s.

Kate Chopin's "Désirée's Baby" brings us in touch with
characters whose marital relations across racial lines end in a crude

awareness of their ethnic heritage. On the wife's side, her oppressed female condition makes her the primary victim of a racist drama after the discovery of visible signs of color in her baby. On the husband's side, the reader can only speculate that his chance encounter with his own black identity will exacerbate the roots of his male-centered racism, leading to the only possible solution— ethnic self-hatred. Chopin's story articulates and historicizes issues related to ethnic origins, racial prejudice, and interracial marriage in the late nineteenth century that are still pertinent today.

The effects of economic inequities are poignantly recorded in Tillie Olsen's story, "I Stand Here Ironing," as the speaker reveals how a lifetime of poverty and drudgery limited her own choices as well as the decisions she made that adversely affected the life of her daughter. In "The Lesson," Toni Cade Bambara exposes the economic realities of ghetto life through a visit by a group of African American grade school children to an expensive toy store in Manhattan. One of them concluded, "This is not much of a democracy if you ask me. Equal chance to pursue happiness means an equal crack at the dough, don't it?"

Other writers, including Tato Laviera, Judith Ortiz Cofer, and Aurora Levins Morales, present the conflicts between ethnic identification and cultural assimilation as they question what it means to be bilingual and bicultural writers in the United States. They wrestle with such issues as the linguistic pain of transition from the public world to the private, whether their oral traditions will remain in the past, hidden in the memories of childhood, and if mastery of the dominant language will erase the stories of their multilingual indigenous cultures. Morales, for example, in "Child of the Americas" portrays the cross-fertilization of her Jewish/Puerto Rican ancestry and analyzes and critiques her two cultures.

In "Public School No. 18: Paterson, New Jersey," the Italian American speaker finally learns as an adult to find her own voice and an identity strong enough to confront and challenge the myth of Anglo-Saxon superiority reinforced by the educational institutions she attended.

Eric Liu, in contrast, offers a different perspective in his 1994 essay "A Chinaman's Chance: Reflections on the American Dream," in which he urges his peers to share his faith in the "unique destiny" of the United States to absorb "hyphenates" like himself who will contribute to "an ever more vibrant future for *all* Americans."

As you read these and other texts in "Race and Culture," consider how factors such as race and social class have contributed to or detracted from your own position in contemporary society. As you wrestle with your own issues with respect to individual, ethnic, economic, and culture identity in the highly complex world of the twenty-first century, you might consider formulating a new definition of the American Dream appropriate for our more diverse world.

FICTION

Nadine Gordimer

The Moment Before the Gun Went Off

Marais Van der Vyver shot one of his farm laborers, dead. An accident, there are accidents with guns every day of the week—children playing a fatal game with a father's revolver in the cities where guns are domestic objects, nowadays, hunting mishaps like this one, in the country—but these won't be reported all over the world. Van der Vyver knows his will be. He knows that the story of the Afrikaner farmer—regional leader of the National Party and commandant of the local security commando—shooting a black man who worked for him will fit exactly *their* version of South Africa, it's made for them. They'll be able to use it in their boycott and divestment campaigns, it'll be another piece of evidence in their truth about the country. The papers at home will quote the story as it has appeared in the overseas press, and in the back and forth he and the black man will become those crudely drawn figures on anti-apartheid banners, units in statistics of white brutality against blacks quoted at the United Nations—he, whom they will gleefully be able to call "a leading member" of the ruling Party.

People in the farming community understand how he must feel. Bad enough to have killed a man, without helping the Party's, the government's, the country's enemies as well. They see the truth of that. They know, reading the Sunday papers, that when Van der Vyver is quoted saying he is "terribly shocked," he will "look after the wife and children," none of those Americans and English, and none of those people at home who want to destroy the white man's power will believe him. And how they will sneer when he even says of the farm boy (according to one paper, if you can trust any of those reporters), "He was my friend, I always took him hunting with me." Those city and overseas people don't know it's true: farmers usually have one particular black boy they like to take along with them in the lands; you could call it a kind of friend, yes, friends are not only your own white people, like yourself, whom you take into your house, pray with in church, and work with on the Party committee. But how can those others know that? They don't want to know it. They think all blacks are like the bigmouth agitators in town. And Van der Vyver's face in the photographs, strangely opened by distress—everyone in the district remembers Marais Van der Vyver as a little boy who would go away and hide himself if he caught you smiling at him, and everyone knows him now as a man who hides any change of expression round his mouth behind a thick, soft mustache, and in his eyes by always looking at some object in hand, a leaf or a crop fingered, pen or stone picked up, while concentrating on what he is saying, or while listening to you.

It just goes to show what shock can do; when you look at the newspaper photographs you feel like apologizing, as if you had stared in on some room where you should not be.

There will be an inquiry; there had better be, to stop the assumption of yet another case of brutality against farm workers, although there's nothing in doubt—an accident, and all the facts fully admitted by Van der Vyver. He made a statement when he arrived at the police station with the dead man in his *bakkie*. Captain Beetge knows him well, of course; he gave him brandy. He was shaking, this big, calm, clever son of Willem Van der Vyver, who inherited the old man's best farm. The black was stone dead, nothing to be done for him. Beetge will not tell anyone that after the brandy Van der Vyver wept. He sobbed, snot running onto his hands, like a dirty kid. The captain was ashamed for him, and walked out to give him a chance to recover himself.

Marais Van der Vyver left his house at three in the afternoon to cull a buck from the family of kudu he protects in the bush areas of his farm. He is interested in wildlife and sees it as the farmers' sacred duty to raise game as well as cattle. As usual, he called at his shed to pick up Lucas, a twenty-year-old farmhand who had shown mechanical aptitude and whom Van der Vyver himself had taught to maintain tractors and other farm machinery. He hooted, and Lucas followed the familiar routine, jumping onto the back of the truck. He liked to travel standing up there, spotting game before his employer did. He would lean forward, bracing against the cab below him.

Van der Vyver had a rifle and .30 caliber ammunition beside him in the cab. The rifle was one of his father's, because his own was at the gunsmith's in town. Since his father died (Beetge's sergeant wrote "passed on") no one had used the rifle, and so when he took it from a cupboard he was sure it was not loaded. His father had never allowed a loaded gun in the house, he himself had been taught since childhood never to ride with a loaded weapon in a vehicle. But this gun was loaded. On a dirt track, Lucas thumped his fist on the cab roof three times to signal: look left. Having seen the white-ripple-marked flank of a kudu, and its fine horns raking through disguising bush, Van der Vyver drove rather fast over a pothole. The jolt fired the rifle. Upright, it was pointing straight through the cab roof at the head of Lucas. The bullet pierced the roof and entered Lucas's brain by way of his throat.

That is the statement of what happened. Although a man of such standing in the district, Van der Vyver had to go through the ritual of swearing that it was the truth. It has gone on record, and will be there in the archive of the local police station as long as Van der Vyver lives, and beyond that, through the lives of his children, Magnus, Helena, and Karel—unless things in the country get worse, the example of black mobs in the town spreads to the rural areas and the place is burned down as many urban police stations have been. Because nothing the government can do will appease the agitators and the whites who encourage them. Nothing satisfies them, in the cities: blacks can sit and drink in white hotels now, the Immorality Act has gone, blacks can sleep with whites . . . It's not even a crime anymore.

◆ ◆ ◆

Van der Vyver has a high, barbed security fence round his farmhouse and garden which his wife, Alida, thinks spoils completely the effect of her artificial stream with its tree ferns beneath the jacarandas. There is an aerial soaring like a flagpole in the backyard. All his vehicles, including the truck in which the black man died, have aerials that swing their whips when the driver hits a pothole: they are part of the security system the farmers in the district maintain, each farm in touch with every other by radio, twenty-four hours out of twenty-four. It has already happened that infiltrators from over the border have mined remote farm roads, killing white farmers and their families out on their own property for a Sunday picnic. The pothole could have set off a land mine, and Van der Vyver might have died with his farm boy. When neighbors use the communications system to call up and say they are sorry about "that business" with one of Van der Vyver's boys, there goes unsaid: it could have been worse.

It is obvious from the quality and fittings of the coffin that the farmer has provided money for the funeral. And an elaborate funeral means a great deal to blacks; look how they will deprive themselves of the little they have, in their lifetime, keeping up payments to a burial society so they won't go in boxwood to an unmarked grave. The young wife is pregnant (of course) and another little one, a boy wearing red shoes several sizes too large, leans under her jutting belly. He is too young to understand what has happened, what he is witnessing that day, but neither whines nor plays about; he is solemn without knowing why. Blacks expose small children to everything, they don't protect them from the sight of fear and pain the way whites do theirs. It is the young wife who rolls her head and cries like a child, sobbing on the breast of this relative and that. All present work for Van der Vyver or are the families of those who work; in the weeding and harvest seasons, the women and children work for him too, carried at sunrise to the fields, wrapped in their blankets, on a truck, singing. The dead man's mother is a woman who can't be more than in her late thirties (they start bearing children at puberty), but she is heavily mature in a black dress, standing between her own parents, who were already working for old Van der Vyver when Marais, like their daughter, was a child. The parents hold her as if she were a prisoner or a crazy woman to be restrained. But she says nothing, does nothing. She does not look up; she does not look at Van der Vyver, whose gun went off in the truck, she stares at the grave. Nothing will make her look up; there need be no fear that she will look up, at him. His wife, Alida, is beside him. To show the proper respect, as for any white funeral, she is wearing the navy blue and cream hat she wears to church this summer. She is always supportive, although he doesn't seem to notice it; this coldness and reserve—his mother says he didn't mix well as a child—she accepts for herself but regrets that it has prevented him from being nominated, as he should be, to stand as the Party's parliamentary candidate for the district. He does not let her clothing, or that of anyone else gathered closely, make contact with him. He, too, stares at the grave. The dead man's mother and he stare at the grave in communication like that between the black man outside and the white man inside the cab the moment before the gun went off.

The moment before the gun went off was a moment of high excitement shared through the roof of the cab, as the bullet was to pass, between the young black man outside and the white farmer inside the vehicle. There were such moments, without explanation, between them, although often around the farm the farmer would pass the young man without returning a greeting, as if he did not recognize him. When the bullet went off what Van der Vyver saw was the kudu stumble in fright at the report and gallop away. Then he heard the thud behind him, and past the window saw the young man fall out of the vehicle. He was sure he had leapt up and toppled—in fright, like the buck. The farmer was almost laughing with relief, ready to tease, as he opened his door, it did not seem possible that a bullet passing through the roof could have done harm.

The young man did not laugh with him at his own fright. The farmer carried him in his arms, to the truck. He was sure, sure he could not be dead. But the young black man's blood was all over the farmer's clothes, soaking against his flesh as he drove.

How will they ever know, when they file newspaper clippings, evidence, proof, when they look at the photographs and see his face—guilty! guilty! they are right!—how will they know, when the police stations burn with all the evidence of what has happened now, and what the law made a crime in the past? How could they know that *they do not know*. Anything. The young black callously shot through the negligence of the white man was not the farmer's boy; he was his son.

[1972]

Journal Entry

Choices can sometimes involve pain. Write a journal entry on a choice that you made involving pain—your own or others. What did you learn from the experience?

Textual Considerations

1. From whose point of view is the story told? How and why does the author put the reader in an awkward position?
2. How does Van der Vyver's wife view her husband's emotional state?
3. Why will the captain not tell anyone that Van der Vyver wept? How does Van der Vyver's weeping confirm or refute his wife's opinion of him?
4. What is ironic about the statement that "blacks can sleep with whites now"?
5. What important choices has Van der Vyver made in the past? What does he now face as a result?

Cultural Contexts

1. Gordimer's protagonist assumes financial responsibility for the family of the young man he shot accidentally. How does this affect your view of him? Would he have done this had the young man not also been his illegitimate son? Why or why not?
2. Analyze with your group the public and private lives of Van der Vyver. To what extent was his public life the result of a personal choice or a response to the political system of apartheid?

John Talbird

Still

Sidney Closkey is a bald man with a beard. He's short too, can't be five-five. It's hot as hell today, but he's buttoned up to the neck: coat, tie and vest. He's the kind that gestures when he talks, closes his eyes to concentrate. His hand is out, raised above his head like he's fixing to shake a giant's hand. The guy he's talking to—skinny fellow, leaning back against the cinder block wall, no-teeth mouth—is slouched so low he seems shorter than Closkey. He turns a Skoal tin in his dirty palm, sporting a nasty cracked thumbnail, head tilted sideways to hear. Apparently, this Sidney Closkey is stirring up the brick workers, trying to organize. Word is he's a communist.

"Mr. Closkey?"

"Yes?" Closkey says, turning to me, hand still raised, opening his eyes.

"Your son is dead. I'm sorry."

I'm almost off, so instead of going back to the station, I flirt with Angie down the hall at the hospital's water cooler.

"Why don't you come around no more?" she asks straightening her stockings.

"Guess I haven't had so many homicides." I nod toward Closkey who carefully puts his pointer into the round holes of the phone dial, traces the circle, watches it click back, does it again. He sits behind the receptionist's cluttered desk. The lamp glows on the top of his head and the way it shines he looks blessed. He's got an almost smile on his face and you might think he was asking his wife to come out to dinner.

"That's so sad," says Angie. "That boy didn't have a chance." She scratches my cheek softly. "You need a shave, honey."

Momma makes a big meal seven days a week. There's fried chicken tonight, mashed potatoes, creamed corn, rolls. She serves on her good china, and we drink sweet tea out of crystal. My full plate's surrounded by silverware: two forks, two knives, two spoons. There's also a plate of cold cuts with a prong thingy for picking them up, another fork to poke the chicken, a big old spoon for the bowl of corn, a different kind of spoon for the taters, another scoopy thing for the rolls, and a platter of pickles and olives and okra—what she calls "relishes"—with their own tiny fork. Everything shines under the chandelier except what's not supposed to. Momma's hair's done up and she wears a purple dress.

"Boy got killed today. Beat up by some other fellows after school. Kicked his head in."

"Oh, that's awful."

I pour gravy from its boat over a roll, dribble some over the taters. "Yep, well he probably asked for it."

"Now, Benjamin, no one asks to have . . . well, to be killed."

"No," I say, stifling a belch. "I imagine not. His daddy probably got him killed though—accidentally, of course. He's a communist. A Jew too, I think."

"Well, still, honey," she says and I nod, cause, *yeah, still.*

After dinner, I kiss my momma's cheek, and help her carry the dishes to the kitchen and make my usual move to clean up. But she steers me away, says, "Have yourself a piece of pie. I've got blueberry and cherry."

I slap my belly. "Sorry, honey. Too damn full."

"Now, Benjamin, don't talk that way."

"No, ma'am," I say, kissing her cheek before sitting on the trunk in the pantry to put on my rubbers. My belly hangs over my belt, and I'm full enough to throw up. I must've gained fifty pounds since Daddy died last spring. I stare at two stacks of gleaming pots setting on the floor, listening to it rain outside, water drumming on the storage shed's tin roof out back. Momma's clearing the table and humming, clinking all that flatware. Finally, I haul myself to my big feet, a groan coming from my chest and belly, and take my umbrella, tapping it on the kitchen floor.

"You drive careful, baby," she says when I kiss her again.

"I will, you precious old thing."

I go to the Stream Bed for a whiskey and beer since I can't ever sleep when Momma's fed me so full. The caramel-colored whiskey is smooth and makes me frown good. I can feel it working in my chest and I close my eyes for a second. On the jukebox, there's a country song I recognize and my friend Alex is telling me about the Dawgs' chances for beating the Gators next Saturday and I'm nodding and nursing my beer cause I'm too stuffed to drink fast. Sidney Closkey comes through the swinging doors and right up to me.

"You must arrest them."

"I did arrest them, Mr. Closkey." I consider introducing him to Alex, but decide not.

"No," he says, shaking his finger in my face. "You arrested three."

"Yes, I did. Please move your hand out of my face." He does, and I tick the names off on my fingers: "Art Bunco, John South, and Pete Skin. They're all in jail, except South who was the only one to make bail. Hell, I just made me a little rhyme," I say to Alex, and we tap glasses. I sip the beer, wipe my chin. "Manslaughter. I assume you agree: they were boys fighting, it was not no premeditated thing."

"No, *no*," he says, gripping my arm.

I pry his fingers loose and there's a grunt of pain coming from him when I bend back his pinky. "Now, Mr. Closkey, you should know better than to grab an officer of the law."

He takes a step back and his bottom lip is quivering, eyes wet like he might bawl. He's been shaken, definitely less put together than this afternoon. He's got the same suit on, but it looks like it's been through the rain with no umbrella. His tie is crooked and hanging over the pocket of his jacket is a wet newspaper full of gibberish. Or Russian. I guess they've got a different alphabet than's usual.

"Not three," he says, in his thick accent, "three *plus* seven." He raises both palms at me, like he wants to play paddy cake, "three plus seven! Sergei said it was three plus seven." I have no idea who Sergei is.

"Well, then, Mr. Closkey, ask Mr. Sergei to come down to the station tomorrow and make a statement. I'm drinking now. Would you care for a whiskey? Or vodka?" I can hear him muttering to himself as he heads to the door. His voice has a lilt like he might sing. But I'm thinking it's probably tears.

I stumble through the door and knock over the lamp turning it on. It throws a sick glow on the wall, and the shade is bent, maybe torn. The cat, shiny flat eyes, looks at me like she always does: I can almost see a thought bubble floating over her head, no words, just a question mark. Or maybe an exclamation point. The fish tank light glows blue through the water and the filter hums, blowing bubbles behind the two fish who swim and pucker and have no expressions, no thought bubbles. The bag of Krystals is kind of greasy in my hand and no longer warm. I burp an onion taste and sit at my Daddy's check-writing desk which he left for me, and I call my ex-wife. The big numbers take forever to get back to the starting place on the dial and I can hear my heart in my chest, and the drip of sweat and rain falling on the wood floor. The bag of burgers falls too with a loud plop as Sherrie answers.

"Hello?"

"Hello, honey, may I speak to our son, the fruit of our loins?"

There's a pause, just a little one, then, "Are you drinking again, Benjy?"

"Well, no. Not really. I mean, I have. Tonight. But to answer, 'Am I drinking again?' I would have to say, 'No, not really.'"

"I'm hanging up. You should know not to call when you're like this."

"I was hoping that I could see my son again, honey. You know, Max? I moved out of Momma's and I'm living in my own place now. I got a fish tank with two fish. Tropical."

"Uh-huh." She yawns.

"And a cat. Also a little plant in a pot. Jade. I got a leaf cutting from Patty. You remember Patty, our secretary down at the station? If I was an alcoholic, I don't think I could nurse a piece of leaf into . . ."

"He's allergic."

"What? Who is? To jade?"

She sighs, speaks slowly: "Max. He's allergic to cats, remember? We had one. When he was two. We had to take Max to the hospital cause of an asthma attack. He can *die* from being around a cat."

I listen to the phone hum. She's in Valdosta. Two-and-a-half hours down seventy-five. The fish tank gurgles. The jade plant holds perfectly still in its little clay pot on the sill. The cat licks a paw, runs it behind her head. I want to say, *She's got short black and white fur. She's very sweet. She'll sleep on your chest in the morning*.

"I've got to go, Benjy. Your son's asleep. Call back when it's not two in the morning. And when you're sober."

She hangs up and I listen to the dial tone for a while, but the operator comes on and says, "Did you want to make a call, hon?"

"No, I'm sorry. I forgot the number. Good night." I hang up and get slowly on my knees, put my arms around the waste basket as if it might hug back. I stare down its cool, black throat and wait, but the food I've eaten is like a cinder block in my stomach and it's not going nowhere. The cat licks my hand and there's a light sweat on my neck and it takes me forever to roll onto my back, but somehow I make it.

Outside, the first bird is singing. It's a lonely sound. I'm perfectly still, so the cat crawls up on my chest and its legs seem to disappear inside itself. It closes its eyes and purrs. "Sweet kitty," I say. "Sweet kitty."

[2006]

Journal Entry

Write a journal entry exploring sympathy in this story. Benjamin doesn't appear to sympathize with Sidney Closkey for the loss of his son. Why do you think this is? Who do *you* sympathize with and why?

Textual Considerations

1. Where is the setting of this story? When, historically, is the story set? How do we learn these details?
2. How would you describe Benjamin's relationship with women?
3. What role does food and drink play in the story? Krystal is a popular and inexpensive hamburger chain in the American South. Why does Benjamin arrive home with a bag of burgers at the end of the story? How would you contrast this scene with the feast he has earlier with his mother?
4. How are parent–child relationships depicted? Can you make connections between the different parents and their children?

Cultural Contests

1. What is the connection between the violence and Closkey's politics and religion? Why does Benjamin first refer to the Russian alphabet as "gibberish"?
2. We see both Benjamin's public life, as a police officer, and his private life (son, ex-husband, father, drinking buddy). Discuss with your group how one informs the other. Where are these two roles distinct? Where do they blur?

Wakako Yamauchi

And the Soul Shall Dance

It's all right to talk about it now. Most of the principals are dead, except of course, me and my younger brother, and possibly Kiyoko Oka, who might be near forty-five now, because, yes, I'm sure of it, she was fourteen then. I was nine, and my brother about four, so he hardly counts at all. Kiyoko's mother is dead, my father is dead, my mother is dead, and her father could not have lasted all these years with his tremendous appetite for alcohol and pickled chilies—those little yellow ones, so hot they could make your mouth hurt; he'd eat them like peanuts and tears would surge from his bulging thyroid eyes in great waves and stream down the dark coarse terrain of his face.

My father farmed then in the desert basin resolutely named Imperial Valley, in the township called Westmoreland; twenty acres of tomatoes, ten of summer squash, or vice versa, and the Okas lived maybe a mile, mile and a half, across an alkaline road, a stretch of greasewood, tumbleweed and white sand, to the south of us. We didn't hobnob much with them, because you see, they were a childless couple and we were a family: father, mother, daughter, and son, and we went to the Buddhist church on Sundays where my mother taught Japanese, and the Okas kept pretty much to themselves. I don't mean they were unfriendly; Mr. Oka would sometimes walk over (he rarely drove) on rainy days, all dripping wet, short and squat under a soggy news-paper, pretending to need a plow-blade or a file, and he would spend the afternoon in our kitchen drinking sake and eating chilies with my father. As he got progressively drunker, his large mouth would draw down and with the stream of tears, he looked like a kindly weeping bullfrog.

Not only were they childless, impractical in an area where large families were looked upon as labor potentials, but there was a certain strangeness about them. I became aware of it the summer our bathhouse burned down, and my father didn't get right down to building another, and a Japanese without a bathhouse . . . well, Mr. Oka offered us the use of his. So every night that summer we drove to the Okas for our bath, and we came in frequent contact with Mrs. Oka, and this is where I found the strangeness.

Mrs. Oka was small and spare. Her clothes hung on her like loose skin and when she walked, the skirt about her legs gave her a sort of webbed look. She was pretty in spite of the boniness and the dull calico and the barren look; I know now that she couldn't have been over thirty. Her eyes were large and a little vacant, although once I saw them fill with tears; the time I insisted we take the old Victrola over and we played our Japanese records for her. Some of the songs were sad, and I imagined the nostalgia she felt, but my mother said the tears were probably from yawning or from the smoke of her cigarettes. I thought my mother resented her for not being more hospitable; indeed, never a cup of tea appeared before us, and between them the conversation of women was totally absent: the rise and fall of gentle voices, the arched eyebrows, the croon of polite surprise. But more than this, Mrs. Oka was *different*.

Obviously she was shy, but some nights she disappeared altogether. She would see us drive into her yard and then lurch from sight. She was gone all evening. Where could she have hidden in that two-roomed house—where in that silent desert? Some nights she would wait out our visit with enormous forbearance, quietly pushing wisps of stray hair behind her ears and waving gnats away from her great moist eyes, and some nights she moved about with nervous agitation, her khaki canvas shoes slapping loudly as she walked. And sometimes there appeared to be welts and bruises on her usually smooth brown face, and she would sit solemnly, hands on lap, eyes large and intent on us. My mother hurried us home then: "Hurry, Masako, no need to wash well; hurry."

You see, being so poky, I was always last to bathe. I think the Okas bathed after we left because my mother often reminded me to keep the water clean. The routine was to lather outside the tub (there were buckets and pans and a small wooden stool), rinse off the soil and soap, and then soak in the tub of hot water and contemplate. Rivulets of perspiration would run down the scalp.

When my mother pushed me like this, I dispensed with ritual, rushed a bar of soap around me and splashed about a pan of water. So hastily toweled, my wet skin strapped the clothes to me, impeding my already clumsy progress. Outside, my mother would be murmuring her many apologies and my father, I knew, would be carrying my brother whose feet were already sandy. We would hurry home.

I thought Mrs. Oka might be insane and I asked my mother about it, but she shook her head and smiled with her mouth drawn down and said that Mrs. Oka loved her sake. This was unusual, yes, but there were other unusual women we knew. Mrs. Nagai was brought by her husband from a geisha house; Mrs. Tani was a militant Christian Scientist; Mrs. Abe, the midwife, was occult. My mother's statement explained much: sometimes Mrs. Oka was drunk and sometimes not. Her taste for liquor and cigarettes was a step in the realm of men; unusual for a Japanese wife, but at the time, in that place, and to me, Mrs. Oka loved her sake the way my father loved his, in the way of Mr. Oka, and the way I loved my candy. That her psychology may have demanded this anesthetic, that she lived with something unendurable, did not occur to me. Nor did I perceive the violence of emotions that the purple welts indicated—or the masochism that permitted her to display these wounds to us.

In spite of her masculine habits, Mrs. Oka was never less than a woman. She was no lady in the area of social amenities; but the feminine in her was innate and never left her. Even in her disgrace, she was a small broken sparrow, slightly floppy, too slowly enunciating her few words, too carefully rolling her Bull Durham, cocking her small head and moistening the ocher tissue. Her aberration was a protest of the life assigned her; it was obstinate, but unobserved, alas, unheeded. "Strange" was the only concession we granted her.

Toward the end of summer, my mother said we couldn't continue bathing at the Okas'; when winter set in we'd catch our death from the commuting and she'd always felt dreadful about our imposition on Mrs. Oka. So my father took the corrugated tin sheets he'd found on the highway and had been saving for some other use and built up our bathhouse again. Mr. Oka came to help.

While they raised the quivering tin walls, Mr. Oka began to talk. His voice was sharp and clear above the low thunder of the metal sheets.

He told my father he had been married in Japan previously to the present Mrs. Oka's older sister. He had a child by the marriage, Kiyoko, a girl. He had left the two to come to America intending to send for them soon, but shortly after his departure, his wife passed away from an obscure stomach ailment. At the time, the present Mrs. Oka was young and had foolishly become involved with a man of poor reputation. The family was anxious to part the lovers and conveniently arranged a marriage by proxy and sent him his dead wife's sister. Well that was all right, after all, they were kin, and it would be good for the child when she came to join them. But things didn't work out that way, year after year he postponed calling for his daughter, couldn't get the price of fare together, and the wife—ahhh, the wife, Mr. Oka's groan was lost in the rumble of his hammering.

He cleared his throat. The girl was now fourteen, he said, and begged to come to America to be with her own real family. Those relatives had forgotten the favor he'd done in accepting a slightly used bride, and now tormented his daughter for being forsaken. True, he'd not sent much money, but if they knew, if they only knew how it was here.

"Well," he sighed, "who could be blamed? It's only right she be with me anyway."

"That's right," my father said.

"Well, I sold the horse and some other things and managed to buy a third-class ticket on the Taiyo-Maru. Kiyoko will get here the first week of September." Mr. Oka glanced toward my father, but my father was peering into a bag of nails. "I'd be much obliged to you if your wife and little girl," he rolled his eyes toward me, "would take kindly to her. She'll be lonely."

Kiyoko-San came in September. I was surprised to see so very nearly a woman; short, robust, buxom: the female counterpart of her father; thyroid eyes and pro-truding teeth, straight black hair banded impudently into two bristly shucks, Cuban heels and white socks. Mr. Oka brought her proudly to us.

"Little Masako here," for the first time to my recollection, he touched me; he put his rough fat hand on the top of my head, "is very smart in school. She will help you with your school work, Kiyoko," he said.

I had so looked forward to Kiyoko-san's arrival. She would be my soul mate; in my mind I had conjured a girl of my own proportion: thin and tall, but with refine-ment and beauty I didn't yet possess that would surely someday come to the fore. My disappointment was keen and apparent. Kiyoko-san stepped forward shyly, then retreated with a short bow and small giggle, her fingers pressed to her mouth.

My mother took her away. They talked for a long time—about Japan, about enrollment in American school, the clothes Kiyoko-san would need, and where to look for the best values. As I watched them, it occurred to me that I had been deceived: this was not a child, this was a woman. The smile pressed behind her fin-gers, the way of her nod, so brief, like my mother when father scolded her: the face inscrutable, but something—maybe spirit—shrank visibly, like a piece of silk in water. I was disappointed; Kiyoko-san's soul was barricaded in her unenchanting appearance and the smile she fenced behind her fingers.

She started school from third grade, one below me, and as it turned out, she quickly passed me by. There wasn't much I could help her with except to drill her on pronunciation—the "L" and "R" sounds. Every morning walking to our rural school: land, leg, library, loan, lot; every afternoon returning home: ran, rabbit, rim, rinse, roll. That was the extent of our communication; friendly but uninteresting.

One particularly cold November night—the wind outside was icy; I was sitting on my bed, my brother's and mine, oiling the cracks in my chapped hands by lamplight—someone rapped urgently at our door. It was Kiyoko-san; she was hysterical, she wore no wrap, her teeth were chattering, and except for the thin straw zori, her feet were bare. My mother led her to the kitchen, started a pot of tea, and gestured to my brother and me to retire. I lay very still but because of my brother's restless tossing and my father's snoring, was unable to hear much. I was aware, though, that drunken and sav-age brawling had brought Kiyoko-san to us. Presently they came to the bedroom. I feigned sleep. My mother gave Kiyoko-san a gown and pushed me over to make room for her. My mother spoke firmly: "Tomorrow you will return to them; you must not leave them again. They are your people." I could almost feel Kiyoko-san's short nod.

All night long I lay cramped and still, afraid to intrude into her hulking back. Two or three times her icy feet jabbed into mine and quickly retreated. In the morning I found my mother's gown neatly folded on the spare pillow. Kiyoko-san's place in bed was cold.

She never came to weep at our house again but I know she cried: her eyes were often swollen and red. She stopped much of her giggling and routinely pressed her fingers to her mouth. Our daily pronunciation drill petered off from lack of interest. She walked silently with her shoulders hunched, grasping her books with both arms, and when I spoke to her in my halting Japanese, she absently corrected my prepositions.

Spring comes early in the Valley; in February the skies are clear though the air is still cold. By March, winds are vigorous and warm and wild flowers dot the desert floor, cockleburs are green and not yet tenacious, the sand is crusty underfoot, everywhere there is a smell of things growing and the first tomatoes are showing green and bald.

As the weather changed, Kiyoko-san became noticeably more cheerful, Mr. Oka, who hated so to drive, could often be seen steering his dusty old Ford over the road that passes our house, and Kiyoko-san sitting in front would sometimes wave gaily to us. Mrs. Oka was never with them. I thought of these trips as the westernizing of Kiyoko-san: with a permanent wave, her straight black hair became tangles of tiny frantic curls; between her textbooks she carried copies of *Modern Screen* and *Photoplay*, her clothes were gay with print and piping, and she bought a pair of brown suede shoes with alligator trim. I can see her now picking her way gingerly over the deceptive white peaks of alkaline crust.

At first my mother watched their coming and going with vicarious pleasure, "Probably off to a picture show; the stores are all closed at this hour," she might say. Later her eyes would get distant and she would muse, "They've left her home again; Mrs. Oka is alone again, the poor woman."

Now when Kiyoko-san passed by or came in with me on her way home, my mother would ask about Mrs. Oka—how is she, how does she occupy herself these rainy days, or these windy or warm or cool days. Often the answers were polite: "Thank you, we are fine," but sometimes Kiyoko-san's upper lip would pull over her teeth, and her voice would become very soft and she would say, "Drink, always drinking and fighting." And those times my mother would invariably say, "Endure, soon you will be marrying and going away."

Once a young truck driver delivered crates at the Oka farm and he dropped back to our place to tell my father that Mrs. Oka had lurched behind his truck while he was backing up, and very nearly let him kill her. Only the daughter pulling her away saved her, he said. Thoroughly unnerved, he stopped to rest himself and talk about it. Never, never, he said in wide-eyed wonder, had he seen a drunken Japanese woman. My father nodded gravely, "Yes, it's unusual," he said and drummed his knee with his fingers.

Evenings were longer now, and when my mother's migraines drove me from the house in unbearable self-pity, I would take walks in the desert. One night with the warm wind against me, the dune primrose and yellow poppies closed and fluttering, the greasewood swaying in languid orbit, I lay on the white sand beneath a shrub and tried to disappear.

A voice sweet and clear cut through the half-dark of the evening:

> Red lips press against a glass
> Drink the purple wine
> And the soul shall dance

Mrs. Oka appeared to be gathering flowers. Bending, plucking, standing, searching, she added to a small bouquet she clasped. She held them away; she looked at them slyly, lids lowered, demure, then in a sudden and sinuous movement, she broke into a stately dance. She stopped, gathered more flowers, and breathed deeply into them. Tossing her head, she laughed—softly, beautifully, from her dark throat. The picture of her imagined grandeur was lost to me, but the delusion that transformed the bouquet of tattered petals and sandy leaves, and the aloneness of a desert twilight into a fantasy that brought such joy and abandon made me stir with discomfort. The sound broke Mrs. Oka's dance. Her eyes grew large and her neck tense—like a cat on the prowl. She spied me in the bushes. A peculiar chill ran through me. Then abruptly and with child-like delight, she scattered the flowers around her and walked away singing:

> Falling, falling, petals on a wind . . .

That was the last time I saw Mrs. Oka. She died before the spring harvest. It was pneumonia. I didn't attend the funeral, but my mother said it was sad. Mrs. Oka looked peaceful, and the minister expressed the irony of the long separation of Mother and Child and the short-lived reunion; hardly a year together, she said. We went to help Kiyoko-san address and stamp those black-bordered acknowledgments.

When harvest was over, Mr. Oka and Kiyoko-san moved out of the Valley. We never heard from them or saw them again, and I suppose in a large city, Mr. Oka found some sort of work, perhaps a janitor or dishwasher and Kiyoko-san grew up and found someone to marry.

[1974]

Journal Entry

Respond to the portrayals of the Japanese American immigrant experience in the story.

Textual Considerations

1. Masako characterizes Mrs. Oka as "different." Do you agree? What makes her different? How do the narrator's impressions of her change as the story develops?
2. What new aspects of Mrs. Oka's personality are revealed as the narrator watches her dance and sing at the end of the story? How does this scene reinforce the multiple meanings of the story's title?
3. Characterize the narrator's mother. What is her attitude toward Mrs. Oka? Is there any evidence that she is oppressed by her environment? Explain.
4. What is Kiyoko-san's role in the story? How does the narrator's mother relate to her? What part does she play in the narrator's life? Is she in any sense a **foil** to Masako? Cite evidence.

5. Describe the setting of Yamauchi's story and its many references to time elements. To what extent does place and time relate to the characters' identity and expectations?

Cultural Contexts

1. Discuss with your group the nature of the conflicts that emerge in the story. To what extent would your group classify them as cultural, as Mrs. Oka's inability to fit in her Japanese community, or as generational—illustrated by Mrs. Oka's relationship with her husband's daughter? Can your group reach a consensus about the nature of the conflicts?
2. What significance is there in Masako's decision, as the only Nisei (children of immigrant Japanese parents, second generation) to break the silence and tell Mrs. Oka's story? What makes her story worth telling? How do you interpret the last paragraph of the narrative?

Aurora Levins Morales

Puertoricanness

It was Puerto Rico waking up inside her. Puerto Rico waking her up at 6:00 A.M., remembering the rooster that used to crow over on 59th Street and the neighbors all cursed "that damn rooster," but she loved him, waited to hear his harsh voice carving up the Oakland sky and eating it like chopped corn, so obliviously sure of himself, crowing all alone with miles of houses around him. She was like that rooster.

Often she could hear them in her dreams. Not the lone rooster of 59th Street (or some street nearby . . . she had never found the exact yard though she had tried), but the wild careening hysterical roosters of 3:00 A.M. in Bartolo, screaming at the night and screaming again at the day.

It was Puerto Rico waking up inside her, uncurling and shoving open the door she had kept neatly shut for years and years. Maybe since the first time she was an immigrant, when she refused to speak Spanish in nursery school. Certainly since the last time, when at thirteen she found herself between languages, between countries, with no land feeling at all solid under her feet. The mulberry trees of Chicago, that first summer, had looked so utterly pitiful beside her memory of flamboyan and banana and. . . . No, not even the individual trees and bushes but the mass of them, the overwhelming profusion of green life that was the home of her comfort and nest of her dreams.

The door was opening. She could no longer keep her accent under lock and key. It seeped out, masquerading as dyslexia, stuttering, halting, unable to speak the word which will surely come out in the wrong language, wearing the wrong clothes. Doesn't that girl know how to dress? Doesn't she know how to date, what to say to a professor, how to behave at a dinner table laid with silver and crystal and too many forks?

Yesterday she answered her husband's request that she listen to the whole of his thoughts before commenting by screaming. "This is how we talk. I will not wait sedately for you to finish. Interrupt me back!" She drank pineapple juice three or four times a day. Not Lotus, just Co-op brand, but it was *piña*,[1] and it was sweet and yellow. And she was letting the clock slip away from her into a world of morning and afternoon and night, instead of "five-forty-one-and-twenty seconds—beep."

There were things she noticed about herself, the Puertoricanness of which she had kept hidden all these years, but which had persisted as habits, as idiosyncrasies of her nature. The way she left a pot of food on the stove all day, eating out of it whenever hunger struck her, liking to have something ready. The way she had lacked food to offer Elena in the old days and had stamped on the desire to do so because it *was* Puerto Rican: Come, mija . . . ¿quieres café?[2] The way she was embarrassed and irritated by Ana's unannounced visits, just dropping by, keeping the country habits after a generation of city life. So unlike the cluttered datebooks of all her friends, making appointments to speak to each other on the phone days in advance. Now she yearned for that clocklessness, for the perpetual food pots of her childhood. Even in the poorest houses a plate of white rice and brown beans with calabaza[3] or green bananas and oil.

She had told Sally that Puerto Ricans lived as if they were all in a small town still, a small town of six million spread out over tens of thousands of square miles, and that the small town that was her country needed to include Manila Avenue in Oakland now, because she was moving back into it. She would not fight the waking early anymore, or the eating all day, or the desire to let time slip between her fingers and allow her work to shape it. Work, eating, sleep, lovemaking, play—to let them shape the day instead of letting the day shape them. Since she could not right now, in the endless bartering of a woman with two countries, bring herself to trade in one-half of her heart for the other, exchange this loneliness for another perhaps harsher one, she would live as a Puerto Rican lives en la isla,[4] right here in north Oakland, plant the bananales[5] and cafetales[6] of her heart around her bedroom door, sleep under the shadow of their bloom and the carving hoarseness of the roosters, wake to blue-rimmed white enamel cups of jugo de piña[7] and plates of guineo verde,[8] and heat pots of rice with bits of meat in them on the stove all day.

There was a woman in her who had never had the chance to move through this house the way she wanted to, a woman raised to be like those women of her childhood, hardworking and humorous and clear. That woman was yawning up out of sleep and into this cluttered daily routine of a Northern California writer living at the edges of Berkeley. She was taking over, putting doilies on the word processor,

[1] Pineapple.
[2] "Eat, darling, you want some coffee?"
[3] Pumpkin.
[4] On the island.
[5] Banana plants.
[6] Coffee trees.
[7] Pineapple juice.
[8] Green bananas, or plantains.

not bothering to make appointments, talking to the neighbors, riding miles on the bus to buy bacalao,[9] making her presence felt . . . and she was all Puerto Rican, every bit of her.

[1986]

Journal Entry

Respond to the juxtaposition of chronological and psychological time in "Puertoricanness." How are they similar? Different?

Textual Considerations

1. Evaluate the effectiveness of Morales's use of the metaphor of a house to suggest multiple identities. What prompts her to open the doors of her Puertorican self? To what extent does identity encompass multiple selves? Explain.
2. Morales uses repetition to enhance theme. Cite examples you found particularly effective.
3. Describe the new self that the speaker constructs. How is it different from her former selves? With which self do you most empathize? Explain.

Cultural Contexts

1. Discuss with your group the speaker's desire to live again in a "clockless world." How does it differ from your world? Is it possible or even desirable to live without an awareness of time? What might be gained? Lost?
2. Review the last paragraph of the story. What does it imply about the costs of cultural displacement? Are ethnic identification and cultural assimilation mutually exclusive? Record your group's responses.

[9] Codfish.

Toni Cade Bambara

The Lesson

Back in the days when everyone was old and stupid or young and foolish and me and Sugar were the only ones just right, this lady moved on our block with nappy hair and proper speech and no makeup. And quite naturally we laughed at her, laughed the way we did at the junk man who went about his business like he was some big-time president and his sorry-ass horse his secretary. And we kinda hated her too, hated the way we did the winos who cluttered up our parks and pissed on our handball walls and stank up our hallways and stairs so you couldn't halfway play hide-and-seek without a goddamn gas mask. Miss Moore was her name. The only woman on the block with no first name. And she was black as hell, cept for her feet, which were fish-white and spooky. And she was always planning these boring-ass things for us to do, us being my cousin, mostly, who lived on the block cause we all moved North the same time and to the same apartment then spread out gradual to breathe. And our parents would yank our heads into some kinda shape and crisp up our clothes so we'd be presentable for travel with Miss Moore, who always looked like she was going to church, though she never did. Which is just one of the things the grownups talked about when they talked behind her back like a dog. But when she came calling with some sachet she'd sewed up or some gingerbread she'd made or some book, why then they'd all be too embarrassed to turn her down and we'd get handed over all spruced up. She'd been to college and said it was only right that she should take responsibility for the young ones' education, and she not even related by marriage or blood. So they'd go for it. Specially Aunt Gretchen. She was the main gofer in the family. You got some ole dumb shit foolishness you want somebody to go for, you send for Aunt Gretchen. She been screwed into the go-along for so long, it's a blood-deep natural thing with her. Which is how she got saddled with me and Sugar and Junior in the first place while our mothers were in a la-de-da apartment up the block having a good ole time.

So this one day Miss Moore rounds us all up at the mailbox and it's puredee hot and she's knockin herself out about arithmetic. And school suppose to let up in summer I heard, but she don't never let up. And the starch in my pinafore scratching the shit outta me and I'm really hating this nappy-head bitch and her goddamn college degree. I'd much rather go to the pool or to the show where it's cool. So me and Sugar leaning on the mailbox being surly, which is a Miss Moore word. And Flyboy checking out what everybody brought for lunch. And Fat Butt already wasting his peanut-butter-and-jelly sandwich like the pig he is. And Junebug punchin on Q.T.'s arm for potato chips. And Rosie Giraffe shifting from one hip to the other waiting for somebody to step on her foot or ask her if she from Georgia so she can kick ass, preferably Mercedes'. And Miss Moore asking us do we know what money is, like we a bunch of retards. I mean real money, she say, like it's only poker chips or monopoly papers we lay on the grocer. So right away I'm tired of this and say so. And would much rather snatch Sugar and go to the Sunset and terrorize the West Indian kids and take their hair ribbons and their money too. And Miss Moore files that remark away for next week's lesson on brotherhood, I can tell. And finally I say we oughta get to the subway cause it's cooler and besides we might meet some cute boys. Sugar done swiped her mama's lipstick, so we ready.

So we heading down the street and she's boring us silly about what things cost and what our parents make and how much goes for rent and how money ain't divided up right in this country. And then she gets to the part about we all poor and live in the slums, which I don't feature. And I'm ready to speak on that, but she steps out in the street and hails two cabs just like that. Then she hustles half the crew in with her and hands me a five-dollar bill and tells me to calculate 10 percent tip for the driver. And we're off. Me and Sugar and Junebug and Flyboy hangin out the window and hollering to everybody, putting lipstick on each other cause Flyboy a faggot anyway, and making farts with our sweaty armpits. But I'm mostly trying to figure how to spend this money. But they all fascinated with the meter ticking and Junebug starts laying bets as to how much it'll read when Flyboy can't hold his breath no more. Then Sugar lays bets as to how much it'll be when we get there. So I'm stuck. Don't nobody want to go for my plan, which is to jump out at the next light and run off to the first bar-b-que we can find. Then the driver tells us to get the hell out cause we there already. And the meter reads eighty-five cents. And I'm stalling to figure out the tip and Sugar say give him a dime. And I decide he don't need it bad as I do, so later for him. But then he tries to take off with Junebug foot still in the door so we talk about his mama something ferocious. Then we check out that we on Fifth Avenue and everybody dressed up in stockings. One lady in a fur coat, hot as it is. White folks crazy.

"This is the place," Miss Moore say, presenting it to us in the voice she uses at the museum. "Let's look in the windows before we go in."

"Can we steal?" Sugar asks very serious like she's getting the ground rules squared away before she plays. "I beg your pardon," say Miss Moore, and we fall out. So she leads us around the windows of the toy store and me and Sugar screamin, "This is mine, that's mine, I gotta have that, that was made for me, I was born for that," till Big Butt drowns us out.

"Hey, I'm goin to buy that there."

"That there? You don't even know what it is, stupid."

"I do so," he say punchin on Rosie Giraffe. "It's a microscope."

"Whatcha gonna do with a microscope, fool?"

"Look at things."

"Like what, Ronald?" ask Miss Moore. And Big Butt ain't got the first notion. So here go Miss Moore gabbing about the thousands of bacteria in a drop of water and the somethinorother in a speck of blood and the million and one living things in the air around us is invisible to the naked eye. And what she say that for? Junebug go to town on that "naked" and we rolling. Then Miss Moore ask what it cost. So we all jam into the window smudgin it up and the price tag say $300. So then she ask how long'd take for Big Butt and Junebug to save up their allowances. "Too long," I say. "Yeh," adds Sugar, "outgrown it by that time." And Miss Moore say no, you never outgrow learning instruments. "Why, even medical students and interns and," blah, blah, blah. And we ready to choke Big Butt for bringing it up in the first damn place.

"This here costs four hundred eighty dollars," says Rosie Giraffe. So we pile up all over her to see what she pointin out. My eyes tell me it's a chunk of glass cracked with something heavy, and different-color inks dripped into the splits, then the whole thing put into a oven or something. But for $480 it don't make sense.

"That's a paperweight made of semi-precious stones fused together under tremendous pressure," she explains slowly, with her hands doing the mining and all the factory work.

"So what's a paperweight?" asks Rosie Giraffe.

"To weigh paper with, dumbbell," say Flyboy, the wise man from the East.

"Not exactly," say Miss Moore, which is what she say when you warm or way off too. "It's to weigh paper down so it won't scatter and make your desk untidy." So right away me and Sugar curtsy to each other and then to Mercedes who is more the tidy type.

"We don't keep paper on top of the desk in my class," say Junebug, figuring Miss Moore crazy or lyin one.

"At home, then," she say. "Don't you have a calendar and pencil case and a blotter and a letter-opener on your desk at home where you do your homework?" And she know damn well what our homes look like cause she nosys around in them every chance she gets.

"I don't even have a desk," say Junebug. "Do we?"

"No. And I don't get no homework neither," says Big Butt.

"And I don't even have a home," say Flyboy like he do at school to keep the white folks off his back and sorry for him. Send this poor kid to camp posters, is his specialty.

"I do," says Mercedes. "I have a box of stationery on my desk and a picture of my cat. My godmother bought the stationery and the desk. There's a big rose on each sheet and the envelopes smell like roses."

"Who wants to know about your smelly-ass stationery," say Rosie Giraffe fore I can get my two cents in.

"It's important to have a work area all your own so that . . ."

"Will you look at this sailboat, please," say Flyboy, cuttin her off and pointin to the thing like it was his. So once again we tumble all over each other to gaze at this magnificent thing in the toy store which is just big enough to maybe sail two kittens across the pond if you strap them to the posts tight. We all start reciting the price tag like we in assembly. "Handcrafted sailboat of fiberglass at one thousand one hundred ninety-five dollars."

"Unbelievable," I hear myself say and am really stunned. I read it again for myself just in case the group recitation put me in a trance. Same thing. For some reason this pisses me off. We look at Miss Moore and she lookin at us, waiting for I dunno what.

"Who'd pay all that when you can buy a sailboat set for a quarter at Pop's, a tube of glue for a dime, and a ball of string for eight cents? It must have a motor and a whole lot else besides," I say. "My sailboat cost me about fifty cents."

"But will it take water?" say Mercedes with her smart ass.

"Took mine to Alley Pond Park once," say Flyboy. "String broke. Lost it. Pity."

"Sailed mine in Central Park and it keeled over and sank. Had to ask my father for another dollar."

"And you got the strap," laugh Big Butt. "The jerk didn't even have a string on it. My old man wailed on his behind."

Little Q.T. was staring hard at the sailboat and you could see he wanted it bad. But he too little and somebody'd just take it from him. So what the hell. "This boat for kids, Miss Moore?"

"Parents silly to buy something like that just to get all broke up," say Rosie Giraffe.

"That much money it should last forever," I figure.

"My father'd buy it for me if I wanted it."

"Your father, my ass," say Rosie Giraffe getting a chance to finally push Mercedes.

"Must be rich people shop here," say Q.T.

"You are a very bright boy," say Flyboy. "What was your first clue?" And he rap him on the head with the back of his knuckles, since Q.T. the only one he could get away with. Though Q.T. liable to come up behind you years later and get his licks in when you half expect it.

"What I want to know is," I says to Miss Moore though I never talk to her, I wouldn't give the bitch that satisfaction, "is how much a real boat costs? I figure a thousand'd get you a yacht any day."

"Why don't you check that out," she says, "and report back to the group?" Which really pains my ass. If you gonna mess up a perfectly good swim day least you could do is have some answers. "Let's go in," she say like she got something up her sleeve. Only she don't lead the way. So me and Sugar turn the corner to where the entrance is, but when we get there I kinda hang back. Not that I'm scared, what's there to be afraid of, just a toy store. But I feel funny, shame. But what I got to be shamed about? Got as much right to go in as anybody. But somehow I can't seem to get hold of the door, so I step away for Sugar to lead. But she hangs back too. And I look at her and she looks at me and this is ridiculous. I mean, damn, I have never ever been shy about doing nothing or going nowhere. But then Mercedes steps up and then Rosie Giraffe and Big Butt crowd in behind and shove, and next thing we all stuffed into the doorway with only Mercedes squeezing past us, smoothing out her jumper and walking right down the aisle. Then the rest of us tumble in like a glued-together jigsaw done all wrong. And people lookin at us. And it's like the time me and Sugar crashed into the Catholic church on a dare. But once we got in there and everything so hushed and holy and the candles and the bowin and the handkerchiefs on all the drooping heads, I just couldn't go through with the plan. Which was for me to run up to the altar and do a tap dance while Sugar played the nose flute and messed around in the holy water. And Sugar kept givin me the elbow. Then later teased me so bad I tied her up in the shower and turned it on and locked her in. And she'd be there till this day if Aunt Gretchen hadn't finally figured I was lyin about the boarder takin a shower.

Same thing in the store. We all walkin on tiptoe and hardly touchin the games and puzzles and things. And I watched Miss Moore who is steady watchin us like she waitin for a sign. Like Mama Drewery watches the sky and sniffs the air and takes note of just how much slant is in the bird formation. Then me and Sugar bump smack into each other, so busy gazing at the toys, specially the sailboat. But we don't laugh and go into our fat-lady bump-stomach routine. We just stare at that price tag. Then Sugar run a finger over the whole boat. And I'm jealous and want to hit her. Maybe not her, but I sure want to punch somebody in the mouth.

"Watcha bring us here for, Miss Moore?"

"You sound angry, Sylvia. Are you mad about something?" Givin me one of them grins like she tellin a grown-up joke that never turns out to be funny. And she's lookin very closely at me like maybe she planning to do my portrait from memory. I'm mad, but I won't give her that satisfaction. So I slouch around the store bein very bored and say, "Let's go."

Me and Sugar at the back of the train watchin the tracks whizzin by large then small then getting gobbled up in the dark. I'm thinkin about this tricky toy I saw in the store. A clown that somersaults on a bar then does chin-ups just cause you yank lightly at his leg. Cost $35. I could see me askin my mother for a $35 birthday clown. "You wanna who that costs what?" she'd say, cocking her head to the side to get a better view of the hole in my head. Thirty-five dollars could buy new bunk beds for Junior and Gretchen's boy. Thirty-five dollars and the whole household could go visit Granddaddy Nelson in the country. Thirty-five dollars would pay for the rent and the piano bill too. Who are these people that spend that much for performing clowns and $1000 for toy sailboats? What kinda work they do and how they live and how come we ain't in on it? Where we are is who we are, Miss Moore always pointin out. But it don't necessarily have to be that way, she always adds then waits for somebody to say that poor people have to wake up and demand their share of the pie and don't none of us know what kind of pie she talking about in the first damn place. But she ain't so smart cause I still got her four dollars from the taxi and she sure ain't gettin it. Messin up my day with this shit. Sugar nudges me in my pocket and winks.

Miss Moore lines us up in front of the mailbox where we started from, seem like years ago, and I got a headache for thinkin so hard. And we lean all over each other so we can hold up under the draggy-ass lecture she always finishes us off with at the end before we thank her for borin us to tears. But she just looks at us like she readin tea leaves. Finally she say, "Well, what did you think of F. A. O. Schwarz?"

Rosie Giraffe mumbles, "White folks crazy."

"I'd like to go there again when I get my birthday money," says Mercedes, and we shove her out the pack so she has to lean on the mailbox by herself.

"I'd like a shower. Tiring day," say Flyboy.

Then Sugar surprises me by sayin, "You know, Miss Moore, I don't think all of us here put together eat in a year what that sailboat costs." And Miss Moore lights up like somebody goosed her. "And?" she say, urging Sugar on. Only I'm standin on her foot so she don't continue.

"Imagine for a minute what kind of society it is in which some people can spend on a toy what it would cost to feed a family of six or seven. What do you think?"

"I think," say Sugar pushing me off her feet like she never done before, cause I whip her ass in a minute, "that this is not much of a democracy if you ask me. Equal chance to pursue happiness means an equal crack at the dough, don't it?" Miss Moore is beside herself and I am disgusted with Sugar's treachery. So I stand on her foot one more time to see if she'll shove me. She shuts up, and Miss Moore looks at me, sorrowfully I'm thinkin. And somethin weird is goin on, I can feel it in my chest.

"Anybody else learn anything today?" lookin dead at me. I walk away and Sugar has to run to catch up and don't even seem to notice when I shrug her arm off my shoulder.

"Well, we got four dollars anyway," she says.

"Uh hunh."

"We could go to Hascombs and get half a chocolate layer and then go to the Sunset and still have plenty money for potato chips and ice cream sodas."

"Un hunh."

"Race you to Hascombs," she say.

We start down the block and she gets ahead which is O.K. by me cause I'm going to the West End and then over to the Drive to think this day through. She can run if she want to and even run faster. But ain't nobody gonna beat me at nuthin.

[1972]

Journal Entry

According to Miss Moore, "Where we are is who we are." To what extent do you agree? Do you consider yourself the product of your social class? What other factors have contributed to your identity?

Textual Considerations

1. What does Miss Moore hope to accomplish during the class outing? What lesson does she want to teach? Does it need teaching? Why? To what extent does Miss Moore's method of teaching succeed?
2. Although the reader knows that Sylvia is angry, she will not admit her feelings to Miss Moore. Why not? Does Sylvia know what has made her angry? Explain.
3. With which character in the story do you most empathize? Why?
4. How does your attitude toward the expensive toys compare to that of the children? How do you account for similarities and/or differences in your responses?
5. How does Bambara use humor to enhance meaning in "The Lesson"? Cite examples.

Cultural Contexts

1. "White folks crazy" appears twice in "The Lesson." What situations give rise to this conclusion? What emotions are the children expressing through these words? What is the significance of Sylvia's resolve: "ain't nobody gonna beat me at nuthin"?
2. Working with your group, react to Miss Moore's assessment: "Imagine for a minute what kind of society it is in which some people can spend on a toy what it would cost to feed a family of six or seven." What does your group think?

Tillie Olsen

I Stand Here Ironing

I stand here ironing, and what you asked me moves tormented back and forth with the iron.

"I wish you would manage the time to come in and talk with me about your daughter. I'm sure you can help me understand her. She's a youngster who needs help and whom I'm deeply interested in helping."

"Who needs help." Even if I came, what good would it do? You think because I am her mother I have a key, or that in some way you could use me as a key? She has lived for nineteen years. There is all that life that has happened outside of me, beyond me.

And when is there time to remember, to sift, to weigh, to estimate, to total? I will start and there will be an interruption and I will have to gather it all together again. Or I will become engulfed with all I did or did not do, with what should have been and what cannot be helped.

She was a beautiful baby. The first and only one of our five that was beautiful at birth. You do not guess how new and uneasy her tenancy in her now-loveliness. You did not know her all those years she was thought homely, or see her poring over her baby pictures, making me tell her over and over how beautiful she had been—and would be, I would tell her—and was now, to the seeing eye. But the seeing eyes were few or non-existent. Including mine.

I nursed her. They feel that's important nowadays. I nursed all the children, but with her, with all the fierce rigidity of first motherhood, I did like the books then said. Though her cries battered me to trembling and my breasts ached with swollenness, I waited till the clock decreed.

Why do I put that first? I do not even know if it matters, or if it explains anything.

She was a beautiful baby. She blew shining bubbles of sound. She loved motion, loved light, loved colour and music and textures. She would lie on the floor in her blue overalls patting the surface so hard in ecstasy her hands and feet would blur. She was a miracle to me, but when she was eight months old I had to leave her daytimes with the woman downstairs to whom she was no miracle at all, for I worked or looked for work and for Emily's father, who "could no longer endure" (he wrote in his good-bye note) "sharing want with us."

I was nineteen. It was the pre-relief, pre-WPA world of the depression. I would start running as soon as I got off the street-car, running up the stairs, the place smelling sour, and awake or asleep to startle awake, when she saw me she would break into a clogged weeping that could not be comforted, a weeping I can yet hear.

After a while I found a job hashing at night so I could be with her days, and it was better. But it came to where I had to bring her to his family and leave her.

It took a long time to raise the money for her fare back. Then she got chicken pox and I had to wait longer. When she finally came, I hardly knew her, walking quick and nervous like her father, looking like her father, thin, and dressed in a shoddy red that yellowed her skin and glared at the pock marks. All the baby loveliness gone.

She was two. Old enough for nursery school they said, and I did not know then what I know now—the fatigue of the long day, and the lacerations of group life in nurseries that are only parking places for children.

Except that it would have made no difference if I had known. It was the only place there was. It was the only way we could be together, the only way I could hold a job.

And even without knowing, I knew. I knew the teacher that was evil because all these years it has curdled into my memory, the little boy hunched in the corner, her rasp, "why aren't you outside, because Alvin hits you? that's no reason, go out, scaredy." I knew Emily hated it even if she did not clutch and implore "don't go Mommy" like the other children, mornings.

She always had a reason why we should stay home. Momma, you look sick, Momma. I feel sick. Momma, the teachers aren't there today, they're sick. Momma, we can't go, there was a fire there last night. Momma, it's a holiday today, no school, they told me.

But never a direct protest, never rebellion. I think of our others in their three-, four-year-oldness—the explosions, the tempers, the denunciations, the demands—and I feel suddenly ill. I put the iron down. What in me demanded that goodness in her? And what was the cost, the cost to her of such goodness?

The old man living in the back once said in his gentle way: "You should smile at Emily more when you look at her." What *was* in my face when I looked at her? I loved her. There were all the acts of love.

It was only with the others I remembered what he said, and it was the face of joy, and not of care or tightness or worry I turned to them—too late for Emily. She does not smile easily, let alone almost always as her brothers and sisters do. Her face is closed and sombre, but when she wants, how fluid. You must have seen it in her pantomimes, you spoke of her rare gift for comedy on the stage that rouses a laughter out of the audience so dear they applaud and applaud and do not want to let her go.

Where does it come from, that comedy? There was none of it in her when she came back to me that second time, after I had had to send her away again. She had a new daddy now to learn to love, and I think perhaps it was a better time. Except when we left her alone nights, telling ourselves she was old enough.

"Can't you go some other time, Mommy, like tomorrow?" she would ask. "Will it be just a little while you'll be gone? Do you promise?"

The time we came back, the front door open, the clock on the floor in the hall. She rigid awake. "It wasn't just a little while. I didn't cry. Three times I called you, just three times, and then I ran downstairs to open the door so you could come faster. The clock talked loud. I threw it away, it scared me what it talked."

She said the clock talked loud again that night I went to the hospital to have Susan. She was delirious with the fever that comes before red measles, but she was fully conscious all the week I was gone and the week after we were home when she could not come near the new baby or me.

She did not get well. She stayed skeleton thin, not wanting to eat, and night after night she had nightmares. She would call for me, and I would rouse from exhaustion to sleepily call back: "You're all right, darling, go to sleep, it's just a dream," and if she still called, in a sterner voice, "now go to sleep, Emily, there's nothing to hurt you." Twice, only twice, when I had to get up for Susan anyhow, I went in to sit with her.

Now when it is too late (as if she would let me hold and comfort her like I do the others) I get up and go to her at once at her moan or restless stirring. "Are you awake, Emily? Can I get you something, dear?" And the answer is always the same: "No, I'm all right, go back to sleep, Mother."

They persuaded me at the clinic to send her away to a convalescent home in the country where "she can have the kind of food and care you can't manage for her, and you'll be free to concentrate on the new baby." They still send children to that place. I see pictures on the society page of sleek young women planning affairs to raise money for it, or dancing at the affairs, or decorating Easter eggs or filling Christmas stockings for the children.

They never have a picture of the children so I do not know if the girls still wear those gigantic red bows and the ravaged looks on the every other Sunday when parents can come to visit "unless otherwise notified"—as we were notified the first six weeks.

Oh it is a handsome place, green lawns and tall trees and fluted flower beds. High up on the balconies of each cottage the children stand, the girls in their red bows and white dresses, the boys in white suits and giant red ties. The parents stand below shrieking up to be heard and the children shriek down to be heard, and between them the invisible wall "Not To Be Contaminated by Parental Germs or Physical Affection."

There was a tiny girl who always stood hand in hand with Emily. Her parents never came. One visit she was gone. "They moved her to Rose Cottage," Emily shouted in explanation. "They don't like you to love anybody here."

She wrote once a week, the laboured writing of a seven-year-old. "I am fine. How is the baby. If I write my letter nicely I will have a star. Love." There never was a star. We wrote every other day, letters she could never hold or keep but only hear read—once. "We simply do not have room for children to keep any personal possessions," they patiently explained when we pieced one Sunday's shrieking together to plead how much it would mean to Emily, who loved so to keep things, to be allowed to keep her letters and cards.

Each visit she looked frailer. "She isn't eating," they told us.

(They had runny eggs for breakfast or mush with lumps, Emily said later, I'd hold it in my mouth and not swallow. Nothing ever tasted good, just when they had chicken.)

It took us eight months to get her released home, and only the fact that she gained back so little of her seven lost pounds convinced the social worker.

I used to try to hold and love her after she came back, but her body would stay stiff, and after a while she'd push away. She ate little. Food sickened her, and I think much of life too. Oh she had physical lightness and brightness, twinkling by on skates, bouncing like a ball up and down up and down over the jump rope, skimming over the hill; but these were momentary.

She fretted about her appearance, thin and dark and foreign-looking at a time when every little girl was supposed to look or thought she should look like a chubby blonde replica of Shirley Temple. The door-bell sometimes rang for her, but no one seemed to come and play in the house or be a best friend. Maybe because we moved so much.

There was a boy she loved painfully through two school semesters. Months later she told me how she had taken pennies from my purse to buy him candy. "Liquorice was his favourite and I brought him some every day, but he still liked Jennifer better'n me. Why, Mommy?" The kind of question for which there is no answer.

School was a worry to her. She was not glib or quick in a world where glibness and quickness were easily confused with ability to learn. To her overworked and exasperated teachers she was an overconscientious "slow learner" who kept trying to catch up and was absent entirely too often.

I let her be absent, though sometimes the illness was imaginary. How different from my now-strictness about attendance with the others. I wasn't working. We had a new baby, I was home anyhow. Sometimes, after Susan grew old enough, I would keep her home from school, too, to have them all together.

Mostly Emily had asthma, and her breathing, harsh and laboured, would fill the house with a curiously tranquil sound. I would bring the two old dresser mirrors and her boxes of collections to her bed. She would select beads and single earrings, bottle tops and shells, dried flowers and pebbles, old postcards and scraps, all sorts of oddments; then she and Susan would play Kingdom, setting up landscapes and furniture, peopling them with action.

Those were the only times of peaceful companionship between her and Susan. I have edged away from it, that poisonous feeling between them, that terrible balancing of hurts and needs I had to do between the two, and did so badly, those earlier years.

Oh there are conflicts between the others too, each one human, needing, demanding, hurting, taking—but only between Emily and Susan, no, Emily toward Susan that corroding resentment. It seems so obvious on the surface, yet it is not obvious. Susan, the second child, Susan, golden- and curly-haired and chubby, quick and articulate and assured, everything in appearance and manner Emily was not; Susan, not able to resist Emily's precious things, losing or sometimes clumsily breaking them; Susan telling jokes and riddles to company for applause while Emily sat silent (to say to me later: that was *my* riddle, Mother, I told it to Susan); Susan, who for all the five years' difference in age was just a year behind Emily in developing physically.

I am glad for that slow physical development that widened the difference between her and her contemporaries, though she suffered over it. She was too vulnerable for that terrible world of youthful competition, of preening and parading, of constant measuring of yourself against every other, of envy, "If I had that copper hair," or "If I had that skin. . . ." She tormented herself enough about not looking like the others, there was enough of the unsureness, the having to be conscious of words before you speak, the constant caring—what are they thinking of me? What kind of an impression am I making?—there was enough without having it all magnified by the merciless physical drives.

Ronnie is calling. He is wet and I change him. It is rare there is such a cry now. That time of motherhood is almost behind me when the ear is not one's own but must always be racked and listening for the child cry, the child call. We sit for a while and I hold him, looking out over the city spread in charcoal with its soft aisles of light. "*Shoogily*," he breathes and curls closer. I carry him back to bed, asleep. *Shoogily*. A funny word, a family word, inherited from Emily, invented by her to say: *comfort*.

In this and other ways she leaves her seal, I say aloud. And startle at my saying it. What do I mean? What did I start to gather together, to try and make coherent? I was at the terrible, growing years. War years. I do not remember them well. I was working, there were four smaller ones now, there was not time for her. She had to help be a mother, and housekeeper, and shopper. She had to set her seal. Mornings of crisis and near hysteria trying to get lunches packed, hair combed, coats and shoes found, everyone to school or Child Care on time, the baby ready for transportation. And always the paper scribbled on by a smaller one, the book looked at by Susan then mislaid, the homework not done. Running out to that huge school where she was one, she was lost, she was a drop; suffering over the unpreparedness, stammering and unsure in her classes.

There was so little time left at night after the kids were bedded down. She would struggle over books, always eating (it was in those years she developed her enormous appetite that is legendary in our family) and I would be ironing, or preparing food for the next day, or writing V-mail to Bill, or tending the baby. Sometimes, to make me laugh, or out of her despair, she would imitate happenings or types at school.

I think I said once: "Why don't you do something like this in the school amateur show?" One morning she phoned me at work, hardly understandable through the weeping: "Mother, I did it. I won, I won; they gave me first prize; they clapped and clapped and wouldn't let me go."

Now suddenly she was Somebody, and as imprisoned in her difference as she had been in anonymity.

She began to be asked to perform at other high schools, even in colleges, then at city and state-wide affairs. The first one we went to, I only recognized her that first moment when thin, shy, she almost drowned herself into the curtains. Then: Was this Emily? The control, the command, the convulsing and deadly clowning, the spell, then the roaring, stamping audience, unwilling to let this rare and precious laughter out of their lives.

Afterwards: You ought to do something about her with a gift like that—but without money or knowing how, what does one do? We have left it all to her, and the gift has as often eddied inside, clogged and clotted, as been used and growing.

She is coming. She runs up the stairs two at a time with her light graceful step, and I know she is happy tonight. Whatever it was that occasioned your call did not happen today.

"Aren't you ever going to finish the ironing, Mother? Whistler painted his mother in a rocker. I'd have to paint mine standing over an ironing-board." This is one of her communicative nights and she tells me everything and nothing as she fixes herself a plate of food out of the icebox.

She is so lovely. Why did you want me to come in at all? Why were you concerned? She will find her way.

She starts up the stairs to bed. "Don't get me up with the rest in the morning." "But I thought you were having midterms." "Oh, those," she comes back in, kisses me, and says quite lightly, "in a couple of years when we'll all be atom-dead they won't matter a bit."

She has said it before. She *believes* it. But because I have been dredging the past, and all that compounds a human being is so heavy and meaningful in me, I cannot endure it tonight.

I will never total it all. I will never come in to say: She was a child seldom smiled at. Her father left me before she was a year old. I had to work her first six years when there was work, or I sent her home and to his relatives. There were years she had care she hated. She was dark and thin and foreign-looking in a world where the prestige went to blondness and curly hair and dimples, she was slow where glibness was prized. She was a child of anxious, not proud, love. We were poor and could not afford for her the soil of easy growth. I was a young mother, I was a distracted mother. There were the other children pushing up, demanding. Her younger sister seemed all that she was not. There were years she did not want me to touch her. She kept too much in herself, her life was such she had to keep too much in herself. My wisdom came too late. She has much to her and probably nothing will come of it. She is a child of her age, of depression, of war, of fear.

Let her be. So all that is in her will not bloom—but in how many does it? There is still enough left to live by. Only help her to know—help make it so there is cause for her to know that she is more than this dress on the ironing-board, helpless before the iron.

[1956]

Journal Entry

Write a journal entry describing how your relationship with your parents defined your process of coming of age. What feelings, emotions, and conflicts do you remember most?

Textual Considerations

1. Relate the title of the story to the events that occur. To what extent is the iron the dominant symbol of the story? What does it symbolize? What other symbols can you identify?
2. Examine the bonds that tie mother and daughter in Olsen's text. How well does the mother succeed in building a good relationship with her daughter? What kind of resentment might Emily feel toward her mother?
3. How does point of view function in the story? To what extent might the narrative be considered an interior monologue? What does the narrator reveal about herself? About her understanding of Emily?
4. What does the mother's statement "My wisdom came too late" mean? What kind of "wisdom" does she refer to? Explain.
5. What does the daughter's comment "Whistler painted his mother in a rocker. I'd have to paint mine standing over an ironing-board" reveal about the daughter's cultural background?

Cultural Contexts

1. Emily's mother represents the plight of single parents in the 1930s. What can be done to help young distracted mothers of the twenty-first century who are trying to raise children by themselves? Consider, also, what these mothers might do to help themselves.
2. Olsen's story is set partly during the Depression, when the child star Shirley Temple dominated American movies. Share with your group what you feel about the narrator's criticism of that time in expressions such as "She was dark and thin and foreign-looking in a world where the prestige went to blondness and curly hair and dimples" and "She is a child of her age, of depression, of war, of fear." To what extent do you consider Emily a victim of socioeconomic circumstances?

Kate Chopin

Désirée's Baby

As the day was pleasant, Madame Valmondé drove over to L'Abri to see Désirée and the baby.

It made her laugh to think of Désirée with a baby. Why, it seemed but yesterday that Désirée was little more than a baby herself; when Monsieur in riding through the gateway of Valmondé had found her lying asleep in the shadow of the big stone pillar.

The little one awoke in his arms and began to cry for "Dada." That was as much as she could do or say. Some people thought she might have strayed there of her own accord, for she was of the toddling age. The prevailing belief was that she had been purposely left by a party of Texans, whose canvas-covered wagon, late in the day, had crossed the ferry that Coton Maïs kept, just below the plantation. In time Madame Valmondé abandoned every speculation but the one that Désirée had been sent to her by a beneficent Providence to be the child of her affection, seeing that she was without child of the flesh. For the girl grew to be beautiful and gentle, affectionate and sincere—the idol of Valmondé.

It was no wonder, when she stood one day against the stone pillar in whose shadow she had lain asleep, eighteen years before, that Armand Aubigny riding by and seeing her there, had fallen in love with her. That was the way all the Aubignys fell in love, as if struck by a pistol shot. The wonder was that he had not loved her before; for he had known her since his father brought him home from Paris, a boy of eight, after his mother died there. The passion that awoke in him that day, when he saw her at the gate, swept along like an avalanche, or like a prairie fire, or like anything that drives headlong over all obstacles.

Monsieur Valmondé grew practical and wanted things well considered; that is, the girl's obscure origin. Armand looked into her eyes and did not care. He was reminded that she was nameless. What did it matter about a name when he could give her one of the oldest and proudest in Louisiana? He ordered the *corbeille*[1] from Paris, and contained himself with what patience he could until it arrived; then they were married.

Madame Valmondé had not seen Désirée and the baby for four weeks. When she reached L'Abri she shuddered at the first sight of it, as she always did. It was a sad looking place, which for many years had not known the gentle presence of a mistress, old Monsieur Aubigny having married and buried his wife in France, and she having loved her own land too well ever to leave it. The roof came down steep and black like a cowl, reaching out beyond the wide galleries that encircled the yellow stuccoed house. Big, solemn oaks grew close to it, and their thick-leaved, far-reaching branches shadowed it like a pall. Young Aubigny's rule was a strict one, too, and under it his

---

[1] Wedding presents given by the groom.

negroes had forgotten how to be gay, as they had been during the old master's easy-going and indulgent lifetime.

The young mother was recovering slowly, and lay full length, in her soft white muslins and laces, upon a couch. The baby was beside her, upon her arm, where he had fallen asleep, at her breast. The yellow nurse woman sat beside a window fanning herself.

Madame Valmondé bent her portly figure over Désirée and kissed her, holding her an instant tenderly in her arms. Then she turned to the child.

"This is not the baby!" she exclaimed, in startled tones. French was the language spoken at Valmondé in those days.

"I knew you would be astonished," laughed Désirée, "at the way he has grown. The little *cochon de lait!*[2] Look at his legs, mamma, and his hands and finger-nails,—real finger-nails. Zandrine had to cut them this morning. Isn't it true, Zandrine?"

The woman bowed her turbaned head majestically, "Mais si, Madame."

"And the way he cries," went on Désirée, "is deafening. Armand heard him the other day as far away as La Blanche's cabin."

Madame Valmondé had never removed her eyes from the child. She lifted it and walked with it over to the window that was lightest. She scanned the baby narrowly, then looked as searchingly at Zandrine, whose face was turned to gaze across the fields.

"Yes, the child has grown, has changed," said Madame Valmondé, slowly, as she replaced it beside its mother. "What does Armand say?"

Désirée's face became suffused with a glow that was happiness itself.

"Oh, Armand is the proudest father in the parish, I believe, chiefly because it is a boy, to bear his name; though he says not,—that he would have loved a girl as well. But I know it isn't true. I know he says that to please me. And mamma," she added, drawing Madame Valmondé's head down to her, and speaking in a whisper, "he hasn't punished one of them—not one of them—since baby is born. Even Négrillon, who pretended to have burnt his leg that he might rest from work—he only laughed, and said Négrillon was a great scamp. Oh, mamma, I'm so happy; it frightens me."

What Désirée said was true. Marriage, and later the birth of his son, had softened Armand Aubigny's imperious and exacting nature greatly. This was what made the gentle Désirée so happy, for she loved him desperately. When he frowned she trembled, but loved him. When he smiled, she asked no greater blessing of God. But Armand's dark, handsome face had not often been disfigured by frowns since the day he fell in love with her.

When the baby was about three months old, Désirée awoke one day to the conviction that there was something in the air menacing her peace. It was at first too subtle to grasp. It had only been a disquieting suggestion; an air of mystery among the blacks; unexpected visits from far-off neighbors who could hardly account for their coming. Then a strange, an awful change in her husband's manner, which she dared not ask him to explain. When he spoke to her, it was with averted eyes, from which the old love-light seemed to have gone out. He absented himself from home;

---

[2] Suckling pig.

and when there, avoided her presence and that of her child, without excuse. And the very spirit of Satan seemed suddenly to take hold of him in his dealings with the slaves. Désirée was miserable enough to die.

She sat in her room, one hot afternoon, in her *peignoir*,[3] listlessly drawing through her fingers the strands of her long, silky brown hair that hung about her shoulders. The baby, half naked, lay asleep upon her own great mahogany bed, that was like a sumptuous throne, with its satin-lined half-canopy. One of La Blanche's little quadroon boys—half naked too—stood fanning the child slowly with a fan of peacock feathers. Désirée's eyes had been fixed absently and sadly upon the baby, while she was striving to penetrate the threatening mist that she felt closing about her. She looked from her child to the boy who stood beside him, and back again; over and over. "Ah!" It was a cry that she could not help; which she was not conscious of having uttered. The blood turned like ice in her veins, and a clammy moisture gathered upon her face.

She tried to speak to the little quadroon boy; but no sound would come, at first. When he heard his name uttered, he looked up, and his mistress was pointing to the door. He laid aside the great, soft fan, and obediently stole away, over the polished floor, on his bare tiptoes.

She stayed motionless, with gaze riveted upon her child, and her face the picture of fright.

Presently her husband entered the room, and without noticing her, went to a table and began to search among some papers which covered it.

"Armand," she called to him, in a voice which must have stabbed him, if he was human. But he did not notice. "Armand," she said again. Then she rose and tottered towards him. "Armand," she panted once more, clutching his arm, "look at our child. What does it mean? Tell me."

He coldly but gently loosened her fingers from about his arm and thrust the hand away from him. "Tell me what it means!" she cried despairingly.

"It means," he answered lightly, "that the child is not white; it means that you are not white."

A quick conception of all that this accusation meant for her nerved her with unwonted courage to deny it, "It is a lie; it is not true, I am white! Look at my hair, it is brown; and my eyes are gray, Armand, you know they are gray. And my skin is fair," seizing his wrist. "Look at my hand; whiter than yours, Armand," she laughed hysterically.

"As white as La Blanche's," he returned cruelly; and went away leaving her alone with their child.

When she could hold a pen in her hand, she sent a despairing letter to Madame Valmondé.

"My mother, they tell me I am not white. Armand has told me I am not white. For God's sake tell them it is not true. You must know it is not true. I shall die. I must die. I cannot be so unhappy and live."

---

[3] Dressing gown.

The answer that came was as brief:

"My own Désirée: Come home to Valmondé; back to your mother who loves you. Come with your child."

When the letter reached Désirée she went with it to her husband's study, and laid it open upon the desk before which he sat. She was like a stone image: silent, white, motionless after she placed it there.

In silence he ran his cold eyes over the written words. He said nothing. "Shall I go, Armand?" she asked in tones sharp with agonized suspense.

"Yes, go."

"Do you want me to go?"

He thought Almighty God had dealt cruelly and unjustly with him; and felt, somehow, that he was paying Him back in kind when he stabbed thus into his wife's soul. Moreover, he no longer loved her, because of the unconscious injury she had brought upon his home and his name.

She turned away like one stunned by a blow, and walked slowly towards the door, hoping he could call her back.

"Good-by, Armand," she moaned.

He did not answer her. That was his last blow at fate.

Désirée went in search of her child. Zandrine was pacing the sombre gallery with it. She took the little one from the nurse's arms with no word of explanation, and descending the steps, walked away, under the live-oak branches.

It was an October afternoon; the sun was just sinking. Out in the still fields the negroes were picking cotton.

Désirée had not changed the thin white garment nor the slippers she wore. Her hair was uncovered and the sun's rays brought a golden gleam from its brown meshes. She did not take the broad, beaten road which led to the far-off plantation of Valmondé. She walked across a deserted field, where the stubble bruised her tender feet, so delicately shod, and tore her thin gown to shreds.

She disappeared among the reeds and willows that grew thick along the banks of the deep, sluggish bayou; and she did not come back again.

Some weeks later there was a curious scene at L'Abri. In the centre of the smoothly swept back yard was a great bonfire. Armand Aubigny sat in the wide hallway that commanded a view of the spectacle; and it was he who dealt out to a half dozen negroes the material which kept this fire ablaze.

A graceful cradle of willow, with all its dainty furbishings, was laid upon the pyre, which had already been fed with the richness of a priceless *layette*.[4] Then there were silk gowns, and velvet and satin ones added to these; laces, too, and embroideries; bonnets and gloves; for the *corbeille* had been of rare quality.

The last thing to go was a tiny bundle of letters; innocent little scribblings that Désirée had sent to him during the days of their espousal. There was the remnant of one back in the drawer from which he took them. But it was not Désirée's; it was

---

[4] A complete outfit of clothing and equipment for a newborn infant.

part of an old letter from his mother to his father. He read it. She was thanking God for the blessing of her husband's love:—

"But, above all," she wrote, "night and day, I thank God for having so arranged our lives that our dear Armand will never know that his mother, who adores him, belongs to the race that is cursed with the brand of slavery."

[1893]

Journal Entry

What knowledge and experience of interracial marriages do you bring to the reading of this text? Do you believe that interracial marriages have the same chance of succeeding as marriages of people with the same ethnic origins?

Textual Considerations

1. Characterize Désirée and Armand. What specific images and descriptions does Chopin use to portray them? How similar or different are they?
2. Ancestry and heritage play an important role in Chopin's story. How do these issues apply to Armand and Désirée? Is it important to the development of the story that Désirée was a foundling, adopted by the Valmondés? How does this issue connect with the theme of racism in the story?
3. Describe the setting of L'Abri. What does its dilapidated condition and "solemn oaks" indicate about the Aubigny property? What other symbols can you cite in the story? How do you interpret them?
4. What do the background characters, including Négrillon, and the quadroon's boys add to the reader's understanding of the story?
5. How do you view the "letter device" Chopin uses in "Désirée's Baby"? Do you consider it effective from the narrative point of view? Can you think of any other narrative tool Chopin could have used to reveal to Armand the truth about his own black ancestry?

Cultural Contexts

1. Examine the extent to which the presence of the French, American, and African elements in L'Abri contribute to its ethnic and cultural diversity. How integrated are they?
2. How does Chopin explore the issue of racial prejudice in her story? Discuss with your group whether Armand Aubigny's values—placing racial prejudices above marriage, love, and family ties—in the late nineteenth century still exist today. How does your group react toward interracial marriage?

ESSAYS

Judith Ortiz Cofer

Silent Dancing

We have a home movie of this party. Several times my mother and I have watched it together, and I have asked questions about the silent revelers coming in and out of focus. It is grainy and of short duration, but it's a great visual aid to my memory of life at that time. And it is in color—the only complete scene in color I can recall from those years.

We lived in Puerto Rico until my brother was born in 1954. Soon after, because of economic pressures on our growing family, my father joined the United States Navy. He was assigned to duty on a ship in Brooklyn Yard—a place of cement and steel that was to be his home base in the States until his retirement more than twenty years later. He left the Island first, alone, going to New York City and tracking down his uncle who lived with his family across the Hudson River in Paterson, New Jersey. There my father found a tiny apartment in a huge tenement that had once housed Jewish families but was just being taken over and transformed by Puerto Ricans, overflowing from New York City. In 1953 he sent for us. My mother was only twenty years old, I was not quite three, and my brother was a toddler when we arrived at El Building, as the place had been christened by its newest residents.

My memories of life in Paterson during those first few years are all in shades of gray. Maybe I was too young to absorb vivid colors and details, or to discriminate between the slate blue of the winter sky and the darker hues of the snow-bearing clouds, but that single color washes over the whole period. The building we lived in was gray, as were the streets, filled with slush the first few months of my life there. The coat my father had bought for me was similar in color and too big; it sat heavily on my thin frame.

I do remember the way the heater pipes banged and rattled, startling all of us out of sleep until we got so used to the sound that we automatically shut it out or raised our voices above the racket. The hiss from the valve punctuated my sleep (which has always been fitful) like a nonhuman presence in the room—a dragon sleeping at the entrance of my childhood. But the pipes were also a connection to all the other lives being lived around us. Having come from a house designed for a single family back in Puerto Rico—my mother's extended-family home—it was curious to know that strangers lived under our floor and above our heads, and that the heater pipe went through everyone's apartment. (My first spanking in Paterson came as a result of playing tunes on the pipes in my room to see if there would be an answer.) My mother was as new to this concept of beehive life as I was, but she had been given strict orders by my father to keep the doors locked, the noise down, ourselves to ourselves.

It seems that Father had learned some painful lessons about prejudice while searching for an apartment in Paterson. Not until years later did I hear how much resistance he had encountered with landlords who were panicking at the influx of Latinos into a neighborhood that had been Jewish for a couple of generations. It made no difference that it was the American phenomenon of ethnic turnover which was changing the urban core of Paterson, and that the human flood could not be held back with an accusing finger.

"You Cuban?" one man had asked my father, pointing at his name tag on the navy uniform—even though my father had the fair skin and light brown hair of his northern Spanish background, and the name Ortiz is as common in Puerto Rico as Johnson is in the United States.

"No," my father had answered, looking past the finger into his adversary's angry eyes. "I'm Puerto Rican."

"Same shit." And the door closed.

My father could have passed as European, but we couldn't. My brother and I both have our mother's black hair and olive skin, and so we lived in El Building and visited our great-uncle and his fair children on the next block. It was their private joke that they were the German branch of the family. Not many years later that area too would be mainly Puerto Rican. It was as if the heart of the city map were being gradually colored brown—*café con leche* brown. Our color.

The movie opens with a sweep of the living room. It is a "typical" immigrant Puerto Rican decor for the time: the sofa and chairs are square and hard-looking, upholstered in bright colors (blue and yellow in this instance) and covered with the transparent plastic that furniture salesmen then were so adept at convincing women to buy. The linoleum on the floor is light blue; where it had been subjected to spike heels, as it was in most places, there were dime-size indentations all over it that cannot be seen in this movie. The room is full of people dressed up: dark suits for the men, red dresses for the women. When I have asked my mother why most of the women are in red that night, she has shrugged and said, "I don't remember. Just a coincidence." She doesn't have my obsession for assigning symbolism to everything.

The three women in red sitting on the couch are my mother, my eighteen-year-old cousin, and her brother's girlfriend. The novia *is just up from the Island, which is apparent in her body language. She sits up formally, her dress pulled over her knees. She is a pretty girl, but her posture makes her look insecure, lost in her full-skirted dress, which she has carefully tucked around her to make room for my gorgeous cousin, her future sister-in-law. My cousin has grown up in Paterson and is in her last year of high school. She doesn't have a trace of what Puerto Ricans call* la mancha *(literally, the stain: the mark of the new immigrant— something about the posture, the voice, or the humble demeanor that makes it obvious to everyone the person has just arrived on the mainland). My cousin is wearing a tight, sequined, cocktail dress. Her brown hair has been lightened with peroxide around the bangs, and she is holding a cigarette expertly between her fingers, bringing it up to her mouth in a sensuous arc of her arm as she talks animatedly. My mother, who has come up to sit between the two women, both only a few years younger than herself, is somewhere between the poles they represent in our culture.*

• • •

It became my father's obsession to get out of the barrio, and thus we were never permitted to form bonds with the place or with the people who lived there. Yet El Building was a comfort to my mother, who never got over yearning for *la isla*. She felt surrounded by her language: the walls were thin, and voices speaking and arguing in Spanish could be heard all day. *Salsas* blasted out of radios, turned on early in the morning and left on for company. Women seemed to cook rice and beans perpetually—the strong aroma of boiling red kidney beans permeated the hallways.

Though Father preferred that we do our grocery shopping at the supermarket when he came home on weekend leaves, my mother insisted that she could cook only with products whose labels she could read. Consequently, during the week I accompanied her and my little brother to La Bodega—a hole-in-the-wall grocery store across the street from El Building. There we squeezed down three narrow aisles jammed with various products. Goya and Libby's—those were the trademarks that were trusted by her *mamá*, so my mother bought many cans of Goya beans, soups, and condiments, as well as little cans of Libby's fruit juices for us. And she also bought Colgate toothpaste and Palmolive soap. (The final *e* is pronounced in both these products in Spanish, so for many years I believed that they were manufactured on the Island. I remember my surprise at first hearing a commercial on television in which "Colgate" rhymed with "ate.") We always lingered at La Bodega, for it was there that Mother breathed best, taking in the familiar aromas of the foods she knew from Mamá's kitchen. It was also there that she got to speak to the other women of El Building without violating outright Father's dictates against fraternizing with our neighbors.

Yet Father did his best to make our "assimilation" painless. I can still see him carrying a real Christmas tree up several flights of stairs to our apartment, leaving a trail of aromatic pine. He carried it formally, as if it were a flag in a parade. We were the only ones in El Building that I knew of who got presents on both Christmas and *día de Reyes*, the day when the Three Kings brought gifts to Christ and Hispanic children.

Our supreme luxury in El Building was having our own television set. It must have been a result of Father's guilt feelings over the isolation he had imposed on us, but we were among the first in the barrio to have one. My brother quickly became an avid watcher of Captain Kangaroo and Jungle Jim, while I loved all the series showing families. By the time I started first grade, I could have drawn a map of Middle America as exemplified by the lives of characters in *Father Knows Best*, *The Donna Reed Show*, *Leave It to Beaver*, *My Three Sons*, and (my favorite) *Bachelor Father*, where John Forsythe treated his adopted teenage daughter like a princess because he was rich and had a Chinese houseboy to do everything for him. In truth, compared to our neighbors in El Building *we* were rich. My father's navy check provided us with financial security and a standard of living that the factory workers envied. The only thing his money could not buy us was a place to live away from the barrio—his greatest wish, Mother's greatest fear.

In the home movie the men are shown next, sitting around a card table set up in one corner of the living room, playing dominoes. The clack of the ivory pieces was a familiar sound. I heard it in many houses on the Island and in many apartments in Paterson. In

Leave It to Beaver, *the Cleavers played bridge in every other episode; in my childhood, the men started every social occasion with a hotly debated round of dominoes. The women would sit around and watch, but they never participated in the games.*

Here and there you can see a small child. Children were always brought to parties and, whenever they got sleepy, were put to bed in the host's bedroom. Babysitting was a concept unrecognized by the Puerto Rican women I knew: a responsible mother did not leave her children with any stranger. And in a culture where children are not considered intrusive, there was no need to leave the children at home. We went where our mother went.

Of my preschool years I have only impressions: the sharp bite of the wind in December as we walked with our parents toward the brightly lit stores downtown; how I felt like a stuffed doll in my heavy coat, boots, and mittens; how good it was to walk into the five-and-dime and to sit at the counter drinking hot chocolate. On Saturdays our whole family would walk downtown to shop at the big department stores on Broadway. Mother bought all our clothes at Penney's and Sears, and she liked to buy her dresses at the women's specialty shops like Lerner's and Diana's. At some point we'd go into Woolworth's and sit at the soda fountain to eat.

We never ran into other Latinos at these stores or when eating out, and it became clear to me only years later that the women from El Building shopped mainly in other places—stores owned by other Puerto Ricans or by Jewish merchants who had philosophically accepted our presence in the city and decided to make us their good customers, if not real neighbors and friends. These establishments were located not downtown but in the blocks around our street, and they were referred to generically as La Tienda, El Bazar, La Bodega, La Botánica. Everyone knew what was meant. These were the stores where your face did not turn a clerk to stone, where your money was as green as anyone else's.

One New Year's Eve we were dressed up like child models in the Sears catalogue: my brother in a miniature man's suit and bow tie, and I in black patent-leather shoes and a frilly dress with several layers of crinoline underneath. My mother wore a bright red dress that night, I remember, and spike heels; her long black hair hung to her waist. Father, who usually wore his navy uniform during his short visits home, had put on a dark civilian suit for the occasion: we had been invited to his uncle's house for a big celebration. Everyone was excited because my mother's brother Hernan—a bachelor who could indulge himself with luxuries—had bought a home movie camera, which he would be trying out that night.

Even the home movie cannot fill in the sensory details such a gathering left imprinted in a child's brain. The thick sweetness of women's perfumes mixing with the ever-present smells of food cooking in the kitchen: meat and plantain *pasteles*, as well as the ubiquitous rice dish made special with pigeon peas—*gandules*—and seasoned with precious *sofrito* sent up from the Island by somebody's mother or smuggled in by a recent traveler. *Sofrito* was one of the items that women hoarded, since it was hardly ever in stock at La Bodega. It was the flavor of Puerto Rico.

The men drank Palo Viejo rum, and some of the younger ones got weepy. The first time I saw a grown man cry was at a New Year's Eve party: he had been reminded of his mother by the smells in the kitchen. But what I remember most were the boiled *pasteles*, plantain or yucca rectangles stuffed with corned beef or other meats, olives, and many other savory ingredients, all wrapped in banana leaves. Everybody had to fish one out with a fork. There was always a "trick" *pastel*—one without stuffing—and whoever got that one was the "New Year's Fool."

There was also the music. Long-playing albums were treated like precious china in these homes. Mexican recordings were popular, but the songs that brought tears to my mother's eyes were sung by the melancholy Daniel Santos, whose life as a drug addict was the stuff of legend. Felipe Rodriguez was a particular favorite of couples, since he sang about faithless women and brokenhearted men. There is a snatch of one lyric that has stuck in my mind like a needle on a worn groove: *De piedra ha de ser mi cama, de piedra la cabezera . . . la mujer que a mi me quiera . . . ha de quererme de veras. Ay, Ay, Ay, corazón, porque no amas . . .* I must have heard it a thousand times since the idea of a bed made of stone, and its connection to love, first troubled me with its disturbing images.

The five-minute home movie ends with people dancing in a circle—the creative filmmaker must have set it up, so that all of them could file past him. It is both comical and sad to watch silent dancing. Since there is no justification for the absurd movements that music provides for some of us, people appear frantic, their faces embarrassingly intense. It's as if you were watching sex. Yet for years, I've had dreams in the form of this home movie. In a recurring scene, familiar faces push themselves forward into my mind's eye, plastering their features into distorted close-ups. And I'm asking them: "Who is *she*? Who is the old woman I don't recognize? Is she an aunt? Somebody's wife? Tell me who she is."

"See the beauty mark on her cheek as big as a hill on the lunar landscape of her face—well, that runs in the family. The women on your father's side of the family wrinkle early; it's the price they pay for that fair skin. The young girl with the green stain on her wedding dress is *la novia*—just up from the Island. See, she lowers her eyes when she approaches the camera, as she's supposed to. Decent girls never look at you directly in the face. *Humilde*, humble, a girl should express humility in all her actions. She will make a good wife for your cousin. He should consider himself lucky to have met her only weeks after she arrived here. If he marries her quickly, she will make him a good Puerto Rican–style wife; but if he waits too long, she will be corrupted by the city, just like your cousin there."

"She means me, I do what I want. This is not some primitive island I live on. Do they expect me to wear a black mantilla on my head and go to mass every day? Not me. I'm an American woman, and I will do as I please. I can type faster than anyone in my senior class at Central High, and I'm going to be a secretary to a lawyer when I graduate. I can pass for an American girl anywhere—I've tried it. At least for Italian, anyway—I never speak Spanish in public. I hate these parties, but I wanted the dress. I look better than any of these *humildes* here. *My* life is going to be different. I have an American boyfriend. He is older and has a car. My parents don't know it, but I sneak out of the house late at night sometimes to be with him. If I marry him, even my name will be American. I hate rice and beans—that's what makes these women fat."

"Your *prima* is pregnant by that man she's been sneaking around with. Would I lie to you? I'm your *tía política*, your great-uncle's common-law wife—the one he abandoned on the Island to go marry your cousin's mother. *I* was not invited to this party, of course, but I came anyway. I came to tell you that story about your cousin that you've always wanted to hear. Do you remember the comment your mother made to a neighbor that has always haunted you? The only thing you heard was your cousin's name, and then you saw your mother pick up your doll from the couch and say: 'It was as big as this doll when they flushed it down the toilet.' This image has bothered you for years, hasn't it? You had nightmares about babies being flushed down the toilet, and you wondered why anyone would do such a horrible thing. You didn't dare ask your mother about it. She would only tell you that you had not heard her right, and yell at you for listening to adult conversations. But later, when you were old enough to know about abortions, you suspected."

"I am here to tell you that you were right. Your cousin was growing an *americanito* in her belly when this movie was made. Soon after, she put something long and pointy into her pretty self, thinking maybe she could get rid of the problem before breakfast and still make it to her first class at the high school. Well, *niña*, her screams could be heard downtown. Your aunt, her *mamá*, who had been a midwife on the Island, managed to pull the little thing out. Yes, they probably flushed it down the toilet. What else could they do with it—give it a Christian burial in a little white casket with blue bows and ribbons? Nobody wanted that baby—least of all the father, a teacher at her school with a house in West Paterson that he was filling with real children, and a wife who was a natural blonde."

"Girl, the scandal sent your uncle back to the bottle. And guess where your cousin ended up? Irony of ironies. She was sent to a village in Puerto Rico to live with a relative on her mother's side: a place so far away from civilization that you have to ride a mule to reach it. A real change in scenery. She found a man there—women like that cannot live without male company—but believe me, the men in Puerto Rico know how to put a saddle on a woman like her. *La gringa*, they call her. Ha, ha, ha. *La gringa* is what she always wanted to be . . . "

The old woman's mouth becomes a cavernous black hole I fall into. And as I fall, I can feel the reverberations of her laughter. I hear the echoes of her last mocking words: *la gringa, la gringa!* And the conga line keeps moving silently past me. There is no music in my dream for the dancers.

When Odysseus visits Hades to see the spirit of his mother, he makes an offering of sacrificial blood, but since all the souls crave an audience with the living, he has to listen to many of them before he can ask questions. I, too, have to hear the dead and the forgotten speak in my dream. Those who are still part of my life remain silent, going around and around in their dance. The others keep pressing their faces forward to say things about the past.

My father's uncle is last in line. He is dying of alcoholism, shrunken and shriveled like a monkey, his face a mass of wrinkles and broken arteries. As he comes closer I realize that in his features I can see my whole family. If you were to stretch that rubbery flesh, you could find my father's face, and deep within *that* face—my own. I don't want to look into those eyes ringed in purple. In a few years he will retreat into silence, and take a long, long time to die. *Move back. Tio*, I tell him. *I don't want to hear what you have to say. Give the dancers room to move. Soon it will be midnight. Who is the New Year's Fool this time?*

[1990]

Journal Entry

Brainstorm on your associations with "whiteness." Are your responses in part attributable to your ethnicity? Explain.

Textual Considerations

1. How did Cofer's father's policy of isolating his family affect the family, and Cofer specifically? Was assimilation the goal of this policy of isolation? If so, how would you have expected Cofer's father to regard the cousin—as, for example, a model for his family?
2. Can you find evidence to show Cofer's own attitude toward this policy of isolation?
3. How do you interpret the statement "*La Gringa* is what she always wanted to be"? What point about assimilation does the cousin's life make?
4. Why do you think Cofer sees her whole family in her alcoholic uncle's face?
5. What would you say are Cofer's feelings about the dead and the forgotten relations that make her think of Odysseus in Hades? If she identifies or sympathizes with them, why does she say, "I don't want to hear what you have to say"?

Cultural Contexts

1. Cofer's father rejected his Puerto Rican culture, whereas her mother embraced it. How well does Cofer understand both parents? How have their attitudes toward assimilation affected hers? With whose view on assimilation do you agree? Why?
2. Cofer describes the family home movie as a powerful visual aid to her childhood memories. Working with your group, examine how her visual recollections affect the meaning of her essay. Where in her descriptions do you also find Cofer appealing to taste and smell? How do these relate to her cultural heritage?

Frederick Douglass

How I Learned to Read and Write

I lived in Master Hugh's family about seven years. During this time, I succeeded in learning to read and write. In accomplishing this, I was compelled to resort to various stratagems. I had no regular teacher. My mistress, who had kindly commenced to instruct me, had, in compliance with the advice and direction of her husband, not only ceased to instruct, but had set her face against my being instructed by any one else. It is due, however, to my mistress to say of her, that she did not adopt this course of treatment immediately. She at first lacked the depravity indispensable to shutting me up in mental darkness. It was at least necessary for her to have some training in the exercise of irresponsible power, to make her equal to the task of treating me as though I were a brute.

My mistress was, as I have said, a kind and tender-hearted woman; and in the simplicity of her soul she commenced, when I first went to live with her, to treat me as she supposed one human being ought to treat another. In entering upon the duties of a slaveholder, she did not seem to perceive that I sustained to her the relation of a mere chattel, and that for her to treat me as a human being was not only wrong, but dangerously so. Slavery proved as injurious to her as it did to me. When I went there, she was a pious, warm, and tenderhearted woman. There was no sorrow or suffering for which she had not a tear. She had bread for the hungry, clothes for the naked, and comfort for every mourner that came within her reach. Slavery soon proved its ability to divest her of these heavenly qualities. Under its influence, the tender heart became stone, and the lamblike disposition gave way to one of tiger-like fierceness. The first step in her downward course was in her ceasing to instruct me. She now commenced to practise her husband's precepts. She finally became even more violent in her opposition than her husband himself. She was not satisfied with simply doing as well as he had commanded; she seemed anxious to do better. Nothing seemed to make her more angry than to see me with a newspaper. She seemed to think that here lay the danger. I have had her rush at me with a face made all up of fury, and snatch from me a newspaper, in a manner that fully revealed her apprehension. She was an apt woman; and a little experience soon demonstrated, to her satisfaction, that education and slavery were incompatible with each other.

From this time I was most narrowly watched. If I was in a separate room any considerable length of time, I was sure to be suspected of having a book, and was at once called to give an account of myself. All this, however, was too late. The first step had been taken. Mistress, in teaching me the alphabet, had given me the *inch*, and no precaution could prevent me from taking the *ell*.

The plan which I adopted, and the one by which I was most successful, was that of making friends of all the little white boys whom I met in the street. As many of these as I could, I converted into teachers. With their kindly aid, obtained at different times and in different places, I finally succeeded in learning to read. When I was sent on errands, I always took my book with me, and by doing one part of my errand quickly, I found time to get a lesson before my return. I used also to carry bread with me, enough of which was always in the house, and to which I was always welcome; for I was much better off in this regard than many of the poor white children in our neighborhood. This bread I used to bestow upon the hungry little urchins, who, in return, would give me that more valuable bread of knowledge. I am strongly tempted to give the names of two or three of those little boys, as a testimonial of the gratitude and affection I bear them; but prudence forbids;—not that it would injure me, but it might embarrass them; for it is almost an unpardonable offence to teach slaves to read in this Christian country. It is enough to say of the dear little fellows, that they lived on Philpot Street, very near Durgin and Bailey's shipyard. I used to talk this matter of slavery over with them. I would sometimes say to them, I wished I could be as free as they would be when they got to be men. "You will be free as soon as you are twenty-one, *but I am a slave for life!* Have not I as good a right to be free as you have?" These words used to trouble them; they would express for me the liveliest sympathy, and console me with the hope that something would occur by which I might be free.

I was now about twelve years old, and the thought of being *a slave for life* began to bear heavily upon my heart. Just about this time, I got hold of a book entitled "The Columbian Orator." Every opportunity I got, I used to read this book. Among much of other interesting matter, I found in it a dialogue between a master and his slave. The slave was represented as having run away from his master three times. The dialogue represented the conversation which took place between them, when the slave was retaken the third time. In this dialogue, the whole argument in behalf of slavery was brought forward by the master, all of which was disposed of by the slave. The slave was made to say some very smart as well as impressive things in reply to his master—things which had the desired though unexpected effect; for the conversation resulted in the voluntary emancipation of the slave on the part of the master.

In the same book, I met with one of Sheridan's mighty speeches on and in behalf of Catholic emancipation. These were choice documents to me. I read them over and over again with unabated interest. They gave tongue to interesting thoughts of my own soul, which had frequently flashed through my mind, and died away for want of utterance. The moral which I gained from the dialogue was the power of truth over the conscience of even a slaveholder. What I got from Sheridan was a bold denunciation of slavery, and a powerful vindication of human rights. The reading of these documents enabled me to utter my thoughts, and to meet the arguments brought forward to sustain slavery; but while they relieved me of one difficulty, they brought on another even more painful than the one of which I was relieved. The more I read, the more I was led to abhor and detest my enslavers. I could regard them in no other light than a band of successful robbers, who had left their homes, and gone to Africa, and stolen us from our homes, and in a strange land reduced us to slavery. I loathed them as being the meanest as well as the most wicked of men. As I read and contemplated the subject, behold! that very discontentment which Master Hugh had predicted would follow my learning to read had already come, to torment and sting my soul to unutterable anguish. As I writhed under it, I would at times feel that learning to read had been a curse rather than a blessing. It had given me a view of my wretched condition, without the remedy. It opened my eyes to the horrible pit, but to no ladder upon which to get out. In moments of agony, I envied my fellow-slaves for their stupidity. I have often wished myself a beast. I preferred the condition of the meanest reptile to my own. Any thing, no matter what, to get rid of thinking! It was this ever-lasting thinking of my condition that tormented me. There was no getting rid of it. It was pressed upon me by every object within sight or hearing, animate or inanimate. The silver trump of freedom had roused my soul to eternal wakefulness. Freedom now appeared, to disappear no more forever. It was heard in every sound, and seen in every thing. It was ever present to torment me with a sense of my wretched condition. I saw nothing without seeing it, I heard nothing without hearing it, and felt nothing without feeling it. It looked from every star, it smiled in every calm, breathed in every wind, and moved in every storm.

I often found myself regretting my own existence, and wishing myself dead; and but for the hope of being free, I have no doubt but that I should have killed myself, or done something for which I should have been killed. While in this state of mind, I was eager to hear any one speak of slavery. I was a ready listener. Every little while, I could hear something about the abolitionists. It was some time before I found what the word meant. It was always used in such connections as to make it an interesting word to me. If a slave ran away and succeeded in getting clear, or if a slave killed his master, set fire to a barn, or did any thing very wrong in the mind of a slaveholder, it was spoken of as the fruit of *abolition*. Hearing the word in this connection very often, I set about learning what it meant. The dictionary afforded me little or no help. I found it was "the act of abolishing"; but then I did not know what was to be abolished. Here I was perplexed. I did not dare to ask any one about its meaning, for I was satisfied that it was something they wanted me to know very little about. After a patient waiting, I got one of our city papers, containing an account of the number of petitions from the north, praying for the abolition of slavery in the District of Columbia, and of the slave trade between the States. From this time I understood the words *abolition* and *abolitionist*, and always drew near when that word was spoken, expecting to hear something of importance to myself and fellow-slaves. The light broke in upon me by degrees. I went one day down to the wharf of Mr. Waters; and seeing two Irishmen unloading a scow of stone, I went, unasked, and helped them. When we had finished, one of them came to me and asked me if I were a slave. I told him I was. He asked, "Are ye a slave for life?" I told him that I was. The good Irishman seemed to be deeply affected by the statement. He said to the other that it was a pity so fine a little fellow as myself should be a slave for life. He said it was a shame to hold me. They both advised me to run away to the north; that I should find friends there, and that I should be free. I pretended not to be interested in what they said, and treated them as if I did not understand them; for I feared they might be treacherous. White men have been known to encourage slaves to escape, and then, to get the reward, catch them and return them to their masters. I was afraid that these seemingly good men might use me so; but I nevertheless remembered their advice, and from that time I resolved to run away. I looked forward to a time at which it would be safe for me to escape. I was too young to think of doing so immediately; besides, I wished to learn how to write, as I might have occasion to write my own pass. I consoled myself with the hope that I should one day find a good chance. Meanwhile, I would learn to write.

The idea as to how I might learn to write was suggested to me by being in Durgin and Bailey's ship-yard, and frequently seeing the ship carpenters, after hewing, and getting a piece of timber ready for use, write on the timber the name of that part of the ship for which it was intended. When a piece of timber was intended for the larboard side, it would be marked thus—"L." When a piece was for the starboard side, it would be marked thus—"S." A piece for the larboard side forward, would be marked thus—"L. F." When a piece was for starboard side forward, it would be marked thus—"S. F." For larboard aft, it would be marked thus—"L. A." For starboard aft, it would be marked thus—"S. A." I soon learned the names of these letters, and for what they were intended when placed upon a piece of timber in the ship-yard. I immediately commenced copying them, and in a short time was able to make the four letters named. After that, when I met with any boy who I knew could write, I would tell him I could write as well as he. The next word would be, "I don't believe you. Let me see you try it." I would then make the letters which I had been so fortunate as to learn, and ask him to beat that. In this way I got a good many lessons in writing, which it is quite possible I should never have gotten in any other way. During this time, my copy-book was the board fence, brick wall, and pavement; my pen and ink was a lump of chalk. With these, I learned mainly how to write. I then commenced and continued copying the Italics in Webster's Spelling Book, until I could make them all without looking on the book. By this time, my little Master Thomas had gone to school, and learned how to write, and had written over a number of copy-books. These had been brought home, and shown to some of our near neighbors, and then laid aside. My mistress used to go to class meeting at the Wilk Street meetinghouse every Monday afternoon, and leave me to take care of the house. When left thus, I used to spend the time in writing in the spaces left in Master Thomas's copy-book, copying what he had written. I continued to do this until I could write a hand very similar to that of Master Thomas. Thus, after a long, tedious effort for years, I finally succeeded in learning how to write.

[1845]

Journal Entry

What is your first reading or writing memory, either at home or at school? When was the first time you realized that something you wrote had an effect on someone?

Textual Considerations

1. What portrait of Douglass's mistress emerges from paragraphs 1 and 2?
2. Why would slaveholders wish slaves to remain illiterate?
3. What does Douglass learn from reading "The Columbian Orator"?
4. Select two or three paragraphs from Douglass's essay and show how his examples support his thesis in each case.
5. How does Douglass use the statement in paragraph 1, "I was compelled to resort to various stratagems," to organize his account of learning to read and write?

6. How many examples of such stratagems can you find? Why do you think Douglass chose this particular word?
7. Douglass uses irony and **figurative language** to enhance his narrative. Cite examples.

Cultural Contexts

1. Douglass's determination to educate himself involves acts of rebellion and self-reliance. To what extent does he succeed in challenging and refuting racial stereotypes about African American slaves? Can you imagine sacrificing as he does to acquire an education?
2. How did language acquisition change Douglass's concept of himself? Do you think of language as empowerment? Were there obstacles you had to overcome? Discuss these issues with your group and compare your responses.

Gary Soto

Black Hair

There are two kinds of work: One uses the mind and the other uses muscle. As a kid I found out about the latter. I'm thinking of the summer of 1969 when I was a seventeen-year-old runaway who ended up in Glendale, California, to work for Valley Tire Factory. To answer an ad in the newspaper I walked miles in the afternoon sun, my stomach slowly knotting on a doughnut that was breakfast, my teeth like bright candles gone yellow.

I walked in the door sweating and feeling ugly because my hair was still stiff from a swim at the Santa Monica beach the day before. Jules, the accountant and part owner, looked droopily through his bifocals at my application and then at me. He tipped his cigar in the ashtray, asked my age as if he didn't believe I was seventeen, but finally after a moment of silence, said, "Come back tomorrow. Eight-thirty."

I thanked him, left the office, and went around to the chain link fence to watch the workers heave tires into a bin; others carted uneven stacks of tires on hand trucks. Their faces were black from tire dust and when they talked—or cussed— their mouths showed a bright pink.

From there I walked up a commercial street, past a cleaners, a motorcycle shop, and a gas station where I washed my face and hands; before leaving I took a bottle that hung on the side of the Coke machine, filled it with water, and stopped it with a scrap of paper and a rubber band.

The next morning I arrived early at work. The assistant foreman, a potbellied Hungarian, showed me a timecard and how to punch in. He showed me the Coke machine, the locker room with its slimy shower, and also pointed out the places where I shouldn't go: The ovens where the tires were recapped and the customer service area which had a slashed couch, a coffee table with greasy magazines, and an ashtray. He introduced me to Tully, a fat man with one ear, who worked the buffers that resur- faced the white walls. I was handed an apron and a face mask and shown how to use the buffer: Lift the tire and center, inflate it with a footpedal, press the buffer against the white band until cleaned, and then deflate and blow off the tire with an air hose.

With a paint brush he stirred a can of industrial preserver. "Then slap this blue stuff on." While he was talking a co-worker came up quietly from behind him and goosed him with the air hose. Tully jumped as if he had been struck by a bullet and then turned around cussing and cupping his genitals in his hands as the other worker walked away calling out foul names. When Tully turned to me smiling his gray teeth, I lifted my mouth into a smile because I wanted to get along. He has to be on my side, I thought. He's the one who'll tell the foreman how I'm doing.

I worked carefully that day, setting the tires on the machine as if they were babies, since it was easy to catch a finger in the rim that expanded to inflate the tire. At the day's end we swept up the tire dust and emptied the trash into bins.

At five the workers scattered for their cars and motorcycles while I crossed the street to wash at a burger stand. My hair was stiff with dust and my mouth showed pink against the backdrop of my dirty face. I then ordered a hotdog and walked slowly in the direction of the abandoned house where I had stayed the night before. I lay under the trees and within minutes was asleep. When I woke my shoulders were sore and my eyes burned when I squeezed the lids together.

From the backyard I walked dully through a residential street, and as evening came on, the TV glare in the living rooms and the headlights of passing cars showed against the blue drift of dusk. I saw two children coming up the street with snow cones, their tongues darting at the packed ice. I saw a boy with a peach and wanted to stop him, but felt embarrassed by my hunger. I walked for an hour only to return and discover the house lit brightly. Behind the fence I heard voices and saw a flashlight poking at the garage door. A man on the back steps mumbled something about the refrigerator to the one with the flashlight.

I waited for them to leave, but had the feeling they wouldn't because there was the commotion of furniture being moved. Tired, even more desperate, I started walking again with a great urge to kick things and tear the day from my life. I felt weak and my mind kept drifting because of hunger. I crossed the street to a gas station where I sipped at the water fountain and searched the Coke machine for change. I started walking again, first up a commercial street, then into a residential area where I lay down on someone's lawn and replayed a scene at home—my Mother crying at the kitchen table, my stepfather yelling with food in his mouth. They're cruel, I thought, and warned myself that I should never forgive them. How could they do this to me.

When I got up from the lawn it was late. I searched out a place to sleep and found an unlocked car that seemed safe. In the back seat, with my shoes off, I fell asleep but woke up startled about four in the morning when the owner, a nurse on her way to work, opened the door. She got in and was about to start the engine when I raised my head up from the backseat to explain my presence. She screamed so loudly when I said "I'm sorry" that I sprinted from the car with my shoes in hand. Her screams faded, then stopped altogether, as I ran down the block where I hid behind a trash bin and waited for a police siren to sound. Nothing. I crossed the street to a church where I slept stiffly on cardboard in the balcony.

I woke up feeling tired and greasy. It was early and a few street lights were still lit, the east growing pink with dawn. I washed myself from a garden hose and returned to the church to break into what looked like a kitchen. Paper cups, plastic spoons, a coffee pot littered on a table. I found a box of Nabisco crackers which I ate until I was full.

At work I spent the morning at the buffer, but was then told to help Iggy, an old Mexican, who was responsible for choosing tires that could be recapped without the risk of exploding at high speeds. Every morning a truck would deliver used tires, and after I unloaded them Iggy would step among the tires to inspect them for punctures and rips on the side walls.

With a yellow chalk he marked circles and Xs to indicate damage and called out "junk." For those tires that could be recapped, he said "goody" and I placed them on my hand truck.

When I had a stack of eight I kicked the truck at an angle and balanced them to another work area where Iggy again inspected the tires, scratching Xs and calling out "junk."

Iggy worked only until three in the afternoon, at which time he went to the locker room to wash and shave and to dress in a two-piece suit. When he came out he glowed with a bracelet, watch, rings, and a shiny fountain pen in his breast pocket. His shoes sounded against the asphalt. He was the image of a banker stepping into sunlight with millions on his mind. He said a few low words to workers with whom he was friendly and none to people like me.

I was seventeen, stupid because I couldn't figure out the difference between an F 78 14 and 750 14 at sight. Iggy shook his head when I brought him the wrong tires, especially since I had expressed interest in being his understudy. "Mexican, how can you be so stupid?" he would yell at me, slapping a tire from my hands. But within weeks I learned a lot about tires, from sizes and makes to how they are molded in iron forms to how Valley stole from other companies. Now and then we received a truckload of tires, most of them new or nearly new, and they were taken to our warehouse in the back where the serial numbers were ground off with a sander. On those days the foreman handed out Cokes and joked with us as we worked to get the numbers off.

Most of the workers were Mexican or black, though a few redneck whites worked there. The base pay was a dollar sixty-five, but the average was three dollars. Of the black workers, I knew Sugar Daddy the best. His body carried two hundred and fifty pounds, armfuls of scars, and a long knife that made me jump when he brought it out from his boot without warning. At one time he had been a singer, and had cut a record in 1967 called *Love's Chance*, which broke into the R and B charts. But nothing came of it. No big contract, no club dates, no tours. He made very little from the sales, only enough for an operation to pull a steering wheel from his gut when, drunk and mad at a lady friend, he slammed his Mustang into a row of parked cars.

"Touch it," he smiled at me one afternoon as he raised his shirt, his black belly kinked with hair. Scared, I traced the scar that ran from his chest to the left of his belly button, and I was repelled but hid my disgust.

Among the Mexicans I had few friends because I was different, a *pocho*[1] who spoke bad Spanish. At lunch they sat in tires and laughed over burritos, looking up at me to laugh even harder. I also sat in tires while nursing a Coke and felt dirty and sticky because I was still living on the street and had not had a real bath in over a week. Nevertheless, when the border patrol came to round up the nationals, I ran with them as they scrambled for the fence or hid among the tires behind the warehouse. The foreman, who thought I was an undocumented worker, yelled at me to run, to get away. I did just that. At the time it seemed fun because there was no risk, only a goodhearted feeling of hide-and-seek, and besides it meant an hour away from work on company time. When the police left we came back and some of the nationals made up stories of how they were almost caught—how they out-raced the police. Some of the stories were so convoluted and unconvincing that everyone laughed *mentiras*[2], especially when one described how he overpowered a policeman, took his gun away, and sold the patrol car. We laughed and he laughed, happy to be there to make up a story.

If work was difficult, so were the nights. I still had not gathered enough money to rent a room, so I spent the nights sleeping in parked cars or in the balcony of a church. After a week I found a newspaper ad for room for rent, phoned, and was given directions. Finished with work, I walked the five miles down Mission Road looking back into the traffic with my thumb out. No rides. After eight hours of handling tires, I was frightening, I suppose, to drivers since they seldom looked at me; if they did, it was a quick glance. For the next six weeks I would try to hitchhike, but the only person to stop was a Mexican woman who gave me two dollars to take the bus. I told her it was too much and that no bus ran from Mission Road to where I lived, but she insisted that I keep the money and trotted back to her idling car. It must have hurt her to see me day after day walking in the heat and looking very much the dirty Mexican to the many minds that didn't know what it meant to work at hard labor. That woman knew. Her eyes met mine as she opened the car door, and there was a tenderness that was surprisingly true—one for which you wait for years but when it comes it doesn't help. Nothing changes. You continue on in rags, with the sun still above you.

I rented a room from a middle-aged couple whose lives were a mess. She was a school teacher and he was a fireman. A perfect set up, I thought. But during my stay there they would argue with one another for hours in their bedroom.

When I rang at the front door both Mr. and Mrs. Van Deusen answered and didn't bother to disguise their shock at how awful I looked. But they let me in all the same. Mrs. Van Deusen showed me around the house, from the kitchen and bathroom to the living room with its grand piano. On her fingers she counted out the house rules as she walked me to my room. It was a girl's room with lace curtains, scenic wallpaper of a Victorian couple enjoying a stroll, canopied bed, and stuffed animals in a corner. Leaving, she turned and asked if she could do laundry for me and, feeling shy and hurt, I told her no; perhaps the next day. She left and I undressed to take a bath, exhausted as I sat on the edge of the bed probing my aches and my

---

[1] a derogatory term for Mexicans living in the United States who have forgotten their cultural heritage.

bruised places. With a towel around my waist I hurried down the hallway to the bathroom where Mrs. Van Deusen had set out an additional towel with a tube of shampoo. I ran the water in the tub and sat on the toilet, lid down, watching the steam curl toward the ceiling. When I lowered myself into the tub I felt my body sting. I soaped a wash cloth and scrubbed my arms until they lightened, even glowed pink, but still I looked unwashed around my neck and face no matter how hard I rubbed. Back in the room I sat in bed reading a magazine, happy and thinking of no better luxury than a girl's sheets, especially after nearly two weeks of sleeping on cardboard at the church.

I was too tired to sleep, so I sat at the window watching the neighbors move about in pajamas, and, curious about the room, looked through the bureau drawers to search out personal things—snapshots, a messy diary, and a high school year-book. I looked up the Van Deusen's daughter, Barbara, and studied her face as if I recognized her from my own school—a face that said "promise," "college," "nice clothes in the closet." She was a skater and a member of the German Club; her greatest ambition was to sing at the Hollywood Bowl.

After awhile I got into bed and as I drifted toward sleep I thought about her. In my mind I played a love scene again and again and altered it slightly each time. She comes home from college and at first is indifferent to my presence in her home, but finally I overwhelm her with deep pity when I come home hurt from work, with blood on my shirt. Then there was another version: Home from college she is immediately taken with me, in spite of my work-darkened face, and invites me into the family car for a milkshake across town. Later, back at the house, we sit in the living room talking about school until we're so close I'm holding her hand. The truth of the matter was that Barbara did come home for a week, but was bitter toward her parents for taking in boarders (two others besides me). During that time she spoke to me only twice: Once, while searching the refrigerator, she asked if we had any mustard; the other time she asked if I had seen her car keys.

But it was a place to stay. Work had become more and more difficult. I not only worked with Iggy, but also with the assistant foreman who was in charge of unloading trucks. After they backed in I hopped on top to pass the tires down by bouncing them on the tailgate to give them an extra spring so they would be less difficult to handle on the other end. Each truck was weighed down with more than two hundred tires, each averaging twenty pounds, so that by the time the truck was emptied and swept clean I glistened with sweat and my T-shirt stuck to my body. I blew snot threaded with tire dust onto the asphalt, indifferent to the customers who watched from the waiting room.

The days were dull. I did what there was to do from morning until the bell sounded at five; I tugged, pulled, and cussed at tires until I was listless and my mind drifted and caught on small things, from cold sodas to shoes to stupid talk about what we would do with a million dollars. I remember unloading a truck with Hamp, a black man.

"What's better than a sharp lady?" he asked me as I stood sweaty on a pile of junked tires. "Water. With ice," I said.

He laughed with his mouth open wide. With his fingers he pinched the sweat from his chin and flicked at me. "You be too young, boy. A woman can make you a god."

As a kid I had chopped cotton and picked grapes, so I knew work. I knew the fatigue and the boredom and the feeling that there was a good possibility you might have to do such work for years, if not for a lifetime. In fact, as a kid I imagined a dark fate: To marry Mexican poor, work Mexican hours, and in the end die a Mexican death, broke and in despair.

But this job at Valley Tire Company confirmed that there was something worse than field work, and I was doing it. We were all doing it, from foreman to the newcomers like me, and what I felt heaving tires for eight hours a day was felt by everyone—black, Mexican, redneck. We all despised those hours but didn't know what else to do. The workers were unskilled, some undocumented and fearful of deportation, and all struck with an uncertainty at what to do with their lives. Although everyone bitched about work, no one left. Some had worked there for as long as twelve years; some had sons working there. Few quit; no one was ever fired. It amazed me that no one gave up when the border patrol jumped from their vans, baton in hand, because I couldn't imagine any work that could be worse—or any life. What was out there, in the world, that made men run for the fence in fear?

How we arrived at such a place is a mystery to me. Why anyone would stay for years is even a deeper concern. You showed up, but from where? What broken life? What ugly past? The foreman showed you the Coke machine, the washroom, and the yard where you'd work. When you picked up a tire, you were amazed at the black it could give off.

Journal Entry

What associations, emotions, or attitudes toward illegal immigrants do you bring to your reading of Soto's memoir?

Textual Considerations

1. "There are two kinds of work: One uses the mind and the other uses muscle." To what extent do you agree? What evidence does Soto offer to support his thesis?
2. Soto catalogs his first day of his summer job in great detail. How do his sensory and visual descriptions enhance his essay? Cite examples.
3. Review paragraph 13. What did the woman "know"? How does her knowing affect Soto?
4. Explain Iggy's role in Soto's summer work experience. How is Iggy different from his co-workers? Does Soto ever resolve his doubts about Iggy's "dignity"? Explain.
5. What does the inclusion of the van Deusens add to the issues of ethnicity and social class that they represent? To what extent do you agree that "their lives were a mess"?

Cultural Contexts

1. Discuss with your group the significance of Soto's contrasting experiences as a field worker and his summer job in the tire factory. Do you agree that although field work pays less, it is preferable to the tire factory? Why or why not?
2. Soto was seventeen the summer he worked at the tire factory. Review the questions he raises in his conclusion. What do they reveal about Soto's knowledge of life and people? Write a summary of your group's responses.

Eric Liu

A Chinaman's Chance: Reflections on the American Dream

A lot of people my age seem to think that the American Dream is dead. I think they're dead wrong.

Or at least only partly right. It is true that for those of us in our twenties and early thirties, job opportunities are scarce. There looms a real threat that we will be the first American generation to have a lower standard of living than our parents.

But what is it that we mean when we invoke the American Dream?

In the past, the American Dream was something that held people of all races, religions, and identities together. As James Comer has written, it represented a shared aspiration among all Americans—black, white, or any other color—"to provide well for themselves and their families as valued members of a democratic society." Now, all too often, it seems the American Dream means merely some guarantee of affluence, a birthright of wealth.

At a basic level, of course, the American Dream is about prosperity and the pursuit of material happiness. But to me, its meaning extends beyond such concerns. To me, the dream is not just about buying a bigger house than the one I grew up in or having shinier stuff now than I had as a kid. It also represents a sense of opportunity that binds generations together in commitment, so that the young inherit not only property but also perseverance, not only money but also a mission to make good on the strivings of their parents and grandparents.

The poet Robert Browning once wrote that "a man's reach must exceed his grasp—else what's a heaven for?" So it is in America. Every generation will strive, and often fail. Every generation will reach for success, and often miss the mark. But Americans rely as much on the next generation as on the next life to prove that such struggles and frustrations are not in vain. There may be temporary setbacks, cutbacks, recessions, depressions. But this is a nation of second chances. So long as there are young Americans who do not take what they have—or what they can do—for granted, progress is always possible.

My conception of the American Dream does not take progress for granted. But it does demand the *opportunity* to achieve progress—and values the opportunity as much as the achievement. I come at this question as the son of immigrants. I see just as clearly as anyone else the cracks in the idealist vision of fulfillment for all. But because my parents came here with virtually nothing, because they did build something, I see the enormous potential inherent in the ideal.

I happen still to believe in our national creed: freedom and opportunity, and our common responsibility to uphold them. This creed is what makes America unique. More than any demographic statistic or economic indicator, it animates the American Dream. It infuses our mundane struggles—to plan a career, do good work, get ahead—with purpose and possibility. It makes America the only country that could produce heroes like Colin Powell—heroes who rise from nothing, who overcome the odds.

I think of the sacrifices made by my own parents. I appreciate the hardship of the long road traveled by my father—one of whose first jobs in America was painting the yellow line down a South Dakota interstate—and by my mother—whose first job here was filing pay stubs for a New York restaurant. From such beginnings, they were able to build a comfortable life and provide me with a breadth of resources—through arts, travel, and an Ivy League education. It was an unspoken obligation for them to do so.

I think of my boss in my first job after college, on Capitol Hill. George is a smart, feisty, cigar-chomping, take-no-shit Greek-American. He is about fifteen years older than I, has different interests, a very different personality. But like me, he is the son of immigrants, and he would joke with me that the Greek-Chinese mafia was going to take over one day. He was only half joking. We'd worked harder, our parents doubly harder, than almost anyone else we knew. To people like George, talk of the withering of the American Dream seems foreign.

It's undeniable that principles like freedom and opportunity, no matter how dearly held, are not enough. They can inspire a multiracial March on Washington, but they can not bring black salaries in alignment with white salaries. They can draw wave after wave of immigrants here, but they can not provide them the means to get out of our ghettos and barrios and Chinatowns. They are not sufficient for fulfillment of the American Dream.

But they are necessary. They are vital. And not just to the children of immigrants. These ideals form the durable thread that weaves us all in union. Put another way, they are one of the few things that keep America from disintegrating into a loose confederation of zip codes and walled-in communities.

What alarms me is how many people my age look at our nation's ideals with a rising sense of irony. What good is such a creed if you are working for hourly wages in a deadend job? What value do such platitudes have if you live in an urban war zone? When the only apparent link between homeboys and housepainters and bike messengers and investment bankers is pop culture—MTV, the NBA, movies, dance music—then the social fabric is flimsy indeed.

My generation has come of age at a time when the country is fighting off bouts of defeatism and self-doubt, at a time when racism and social inequities seem not only persistent but intractable. At a time like this, the retreat to one's own kind is seen by more and more of my peers as an advance. And that retreat has given rise again to the notion that there are essential and irreconcilable differences among the races—a notion that was supposed to have disappeared from American discourse by the time my peers and I were born in the sixties.

Not long ago, for instance, my sister called me a "banana."

I was needling her about her passion for rap and hip-hop music. Every time I saw her, it seemed, she was jumping and twisting to Arrested Development or Chubb Rock or some other funky group. She joked that despite being the daughter of Chinese immigrants, she was indeed "black at heart." And then she added, lightheartedly,

"You, on the other hand—well, you're basically a banana." Yellow on the outside, but white inside.

I protested, denied her charge vehemently. But it was too late. She was back to dancing. And I stood accused.

Ever since then, I have wondered what it means to be black, or white, or Asian "at heart"—particularly for my generation. Growing up, when other kids would ask whether I was Chinese or Korean or Japanese, I would reply, a little petulantly, "American." Assimilation can still be a sensitive subject. I recall reading about a Korean-born Congressman who had gone out of his way to say that Asian-Americans should expect nothing special from him. He added that he was taking speech lessons "to get rid of this accent." I winced at his palpable self-hate. But then it hit me: Is this how my sister sees me?

There is no doubt that minorities like me can draw strength from our communities. But in today's environment, anything other than ostentatious tribal fealty is taken in some communities as a sign of moral weakness, a disappointing dilution of character. In times that demand ever-clearer thinking, it has become too easy for people to shut off their brains: "It's a black/Asian/Latino/white thing," says the variable T-shirt. "You wouldn't understand." Increasingly, we don't.

The civil-rights triumphs of the sixties and the cultural revolutions that followed made it possible for minorities to celebrate our diverse heritages. I can appreciate that. But I know, too, that the sixties—or at least, my generation's grainy, hazy vision of the decade—also bequeathed to young Americans a legacy of near-pathological race consciousness.

Today's culture of entitlement—and of race entitlement in particular—tells us plenty about what we get if we are black or white or female or male or old or young.

It is silent, though, on some other important issues. For instance: What do we "get" for being American? And just as importantly, What do we owe? These are questions around which young people like myself must tread carefully, since talk of common interests, civic culture, responsibility, and integration sounds a little too "white" for some people. To the new segregationists, the "American Dream" is like the old myth of the "Melting Pot": an oppressive fiction, an opiate for the unhappy colored masses.

How have we allowed our thinking about race to become so twisted? The formal obstacles and the hateful opposition to civil rights have long faded into memory. By most external measures, life for minorities is better than it was a quarter century ago. It would seem that the opportunities for tolerance and cooperation are commonplace. Why, then, are so many of my peers so cynical about our ability to get along with one another?

The reasons are frustratingly ambiguous. I got a glimpse of this when I was in college. It was late in my junior year, and as the editor of a campus magazine, I was sitting on a panel to discuss "The White Press at Yale: What Is to Be Done?" The assembly hall was packed, a diverse and noisy crowd. The air was heavy, nervously electric.

Why weren't there more stories about "minority issues" in the Yale *Daily News*? Why weren't there more stories on Africa in my magazine, the foreign affairs journal? How many "editors of color" served on the boards of each of the major publications? The questions were volleyed like artillery, one round after another, punctuated only by the applause of an audience spoiling for a fight. The questions were not at all unfair. But it seemed that no one—not even those of us on the panel who *were* people of color—could provide, in this context, satisfactory answers.

Toward the end of the discussion, I made a brief appeal for reason and moderation. And afterward, as students milled around restlessly, I was attacked: for my narrow-mindedness—How dare you suggest that Yale is not a fundamentally prejudiced place!—for my simplemindedness—Have you, too, been co-opted?

And for my betrayal—Are you just white inside?

My eyes were opened that uncomfortably warm early summer evening. Not only to the cynical posturing and the combustible opportunism of campus racial politics. But more importantly, to the larger question of identity—my identity—in America. Never mind that the aim of many of the loudest critics was to generate headlines in the very publications they denounced. In spite of themselves—against, it would seem, their true intentions—they got me to think about who I am.

In our society today, and especially among people of my generation, we are congealing into clots of narrow commonality. We stick with racial and religious comrades. This tribal consciousness-raising can be empowering for some. But while America was conceived in liberty—the liberty, for instance, to associate with whomever we like—it was never designed to be a mere collection of subcultures. We forget that there is in fact such a thing as a unique American identity that transcends our sundry tribes, sets, gangs, and cliques.

I have grappled, wittingly or not, with these questions of identity and allegiance all my life. When I was in my early teens, I would invite my buddies overnight to watch movies, play video games, and beat one another up. Before too long, my dad would come downstairs and start hamming it up—telling stories, asking gently nosy questions, making corny jokes, all with his distinct Chinese accent. I would stand back, quietly gauging everyone's reaction. Of course, the guys loved it. But I would feel uneasy.

What was then cause for discomfort is now a source of strength. Looking back on such episodes, I take pride in my father's accented English; I feel awe at his courage to laugh loudly in a language not really his own.

It was around the same time that I decided that continued attendance at the community Chinese school on Sundays was uncool. There was no fanfare; I simply stopped going. As a child, I'd been too blissfully unaware to think of Chinese school as anything more than a weekly chore, with an annual festival (dumplings and spring rolls, games and prizes). But by the time I was a peer-pressured adolescent, Chinese school seemed like a badge of the woefully unassimilated. I turned my back on it.

Even as I write these words now, it feels as though I am revealing a long-held secret. I am proud that my ancestors—scholars, soldiers, farmers—came from one of the world's great civilizations. I am proud that my grandfather served in the Chinese Air Force. I am proud to speak even my clumsy brand of Mandarin, and I feel blessed to be able to think idiomatically in Chinese, a language so much richer in nuance and subtle poetry than English.

Belatedly, I appreciate the good fortune I've had to be the son of immigrants. As a kid, I could play Thomas Jefferson in the bicentennial school play one week and the next week play the poet Li Bai at the Chinese school festival. I could come home from an afternoon of teen slang at the mall and sit down to dinner for a rollicking conversation in our family's hybrid of Chinese and English. I understood, when I went over to visit friends, that my life was different. At the time, I just never fully appreciated how rich it was.

Yet I know that this pride in my heritage does not cross into prejudice against others. What it reflects is pride in what my country represents. That became clear to me when I went through Marine Corps Officer Candidates' School. During the summers after my sophomore and junior years of college, I volunteered for OCS, a grueling boot camp for potential officers in the swamps and foothills of Quantico, Virginia.

And once I arrived—standing 5'4", 135 pounds, bespectacled, a Chinese Ivy League Democrat—I was a target straight out of central casting. The wiry, raspy-voiced drill sergeant, though he was perhaps only an inch or two taller than I, called me "Little One" with as much venom as can be squeezed into such a moniker. He heaped verbal abuse on me, he laughed when I stumbled, he screamed when I hesitated. But he also never failed to remind me that just because I was a little shit didn't mean I shouldn't run farther, climb higher, think faster, hit harder than anyone else.

That was the funny thing about the Marine Corps. It is, ostensibly, one of the most conservative institutions in the United States. And yet, for those twelve weeks, it represented the kind of color-blind equality of opportunity that the rest of society struggles to match. I did not feel uncomfortable at OCS to be of Chinese descent. Indeed, I drew strength from it. My platoon was a veritable cross section of America: forty young men of all backgrounds, all regions, all races, all levels of intelligence and ability, displaced from our lives (if only for a few weeks) with nowhere else to go.

Going down the list of names—Courtemanche, Dougherty, Grella, Hunt, Liu, Reeves, Schwarzman, and so on— brought to mind a line from a World War II documentary I once saw, which went something like this: The reason why it seemed during the war that America was as good as the rest of the world put together was that America *was* the rest of the world put together.

Ultimately, I decided that the Marines was not what I wanted to do for four years and I did not accept the second lieutenant's commission. But I will never forget the day of the graduation parade: bright sunshine, brisk winds, the band playing Sousa as my company passed in review. As my mom and dad watched and photographed the parade from the rafters, I thought to myself: this is the American Dream in all its cheesy earnestness. I felt the thrill of truly being part of something larger and greater than myself.

I do know that American life is not all Sousa marches and flag-waving. I know that those with reactionary agendas often find it convenient to cloak their motives in the language of Americanism. The "American Party" was the name of a major nativist organization in the nineteenth century. "America First" is the siren song of the isolationists who would withdraw this country from the world and expel the world from this country. I know that our national immigration laws were once designed explicitly to cut off the influx from Asia.

I also know that discrimination is real. I am reminded of a gentle old man who, after Pearl Harbor, was stripped of his possessions without warning, taken from his home, and thrown into a Japanese internment camp. He survived, and by many measures has thrived, serving as a community leader and political activist. But I am reluctant to share with him my wide-eyed patriotism.

I know the bittersweet irony that my own father—a strong and optimistic man—would sometimes feel when he was alive. When he came across a comically lost cause—if the Yankees were behind 14–0 in the ninth, or if Dukakis was down ten points in the polls with a week left—he would often joke that the doomed party had "a Chinaman's chance" of success. It was one of those insensitive idioms of a generation ago, and it must have lodged in his impressionable young mind when he first came to America. It spoke of a perceived stacked deck.

I know, too, that for many other immigrants, the dream simply does not work out. Fae Myenne Ng, the author of *Bone*, writes about how her father ventured here from China under a false identity and arrived at Angel Island, the detention center outside the "Gold Mountain" of San Francisco. He got out, he labored, he struggled, and he suffered "a bitter no-luck life" in America. There was no glory. For him, Ng suggests, the journey was not worth it.

But it is precisely because I know these things that I want to prove that in the long run, over generations and across ethnicities, it *is* worth it. For the second-generation American, opportunity is obligation. I have seen and faced racism. I understand the dull pain of dreams deferred or unmet. But I believe still that there is so little stopping me from building the life that I want. I was given, through my parents' labors, the chance to bridge that gap between ideals and reality. Who am I to throw away that chance?

Plainly, I am subject to the criticism that I speak too much from my own experience. Not everyone can relate to the second-generation American story. When I have spoken like this with some friends, the issue has been my perspective. *What you say is fine for you. But unless you grew up where I did, unless you've had people avoid you because of the color of your skin, don't talk to me about common dreams.*

But are we then to be paralyzed? Is respect for different experiences supposed to obviate the possibility of shared aspirations? Does the diversity of life in America doom us to a fractured understanding of one another? The question is basic: Should the failure of this nation thus far to fulfill its stated ideals incapacitate its young people, or motivate us?

Our country was built on, and remains glued by, the idea that everybody deserves a fair shot and that we must work together to guarantee that opportunity—the original American Dream. It was this idea, in some inchoate form, that drew every immigrant here. It was this idea, however sullied by slavery and racism, that motivated the civil-rights movement. To write this idea off—even when its execution is spotty— to let American life descend into squabbles among separatist tribes would not just be sad. It would be a total mishandling of a legacy, the squandering of a great historical inheritance.

Mine must not be the first generation of Americans to lose America. Just as so many of our parents journeyed here to find their version of the American Dream, so must young Americans today journey across boundaries of race and class to rediscover one another. We are the first American generation to be born into an integrated society, and we are accustomed to more race mixing than any generation before us. We started open-minded, and it's not too late for us to stay that way.

Time is of the essence. For in our national political culture today, the watchwords seem to be *decline* and *end*. Apocalyptic visions and dark millennial predictions abound. The end of history. The end of progress. The end of equality. Even something as ostensibly positive as the end of the Cold War has a bittersweet tinge, because for the life of us, no one in America can get a handle on the big question, "What Next?"

For my generation, this fixation on endings is particularly enervating. One's twenties are supposed to be a time of widening horizons, of bright possibilities. Instead, America seems to have entered an era of limits. Whether it is the difficulty of finding jobs from some place other than a temp agency, or the mountains of debt that darken our future, the message to my peers is often that this nation's time has come and gone; let's bow out with grace and dignity.

A friend once observed that while the Chinese seek to adapt to nature and yield to circumstance, Americans seek to conquer both. She meant that as a criticism of America. But I interpreted her remark differently. I *do* believe that America is exceptional. And I believe it is up to my generation to revive that spirit, that sense that we do in fact have control over our own destiny—as individuals and as a nation.

If we are to reclaim a common destiny, we must also reach out to other generations for help. It was Franklin Roosevelt who said that while America can't always build the future for its youth, it can—and must—build its youth for the future. That commitment across generations is as central to the American Dream as any I have enunciated. We are linked, black and white, old and young, one and inseparable.

I know how my words sound. I am old enough to perceive my own naïveté but young enough still to cherish it. I realize that I am coming of age just as the American Dream is showing its age. Yet I still have faith in this country's unique destiny—to create generation after generation of hyphenates like me, to channel this new blood, this resilience and energy into an ever more vibrant future for *all* Americans.

And I want to prove—for my sake, for my father's sake, and for my country's sake—that a Chinaman's chance is as good as anyone else's.

[1994]

Journal Entry

What concepts, experiences, associations, or images of the American Dream can you bring to your reading of Liu's text?

Textual Considerations

1. Why does Liu include so many details about his parents' experience? How does this affect his argument?

2. "What alarms me is how many people my age look at our nation's ideals with a rising sense of irony" (paragraph 13). What evidence does Liu offer to support his thesis? To what extent do you agree with him?

3. Liu is an assimilationist, yet he is proud of his Chinese American heritage. How does he reconcile these different aspects of his philosophy?

4. Liu's essay was originally published in 1994 in a collection of essays titled *Next: Young American Writers on the New Generation*, which he edited. Who was his intended audience?

5. Characterize your response to Liu's essay. Was his purpose in his essay to inform or persuade? Explain.

Cultural Contexts

1. Liu is disturbed by the fact that in recent times, "America seems to have entered an era of limits." What challenges does he issue to his own generation? How do you respond to his call to action? Does his summons transcend generational limitations? How?

2. If you were forced to emigrate from your country and found yourself raising a family in another culture, what aspects of your native culture would you attempt to preserve and share with your children? Discuss this issue with members of your group.

POETRY

Walt Whitman

I Hear America Singing

I hear America singing, the varied carols I hear,
Those of mechanics, each one singing his as it should be blithe and strong,
The carpenter singing his as he measures his plank or beam,
The mason singing his as he makes ready for work, or leaves off work,
The boatman singing what belongs to him on his boat, the deck-hand
    singing on the steamboat deck,   5
The shoemaker singing as he sits on his bench, the hatter singing as he
    stands,
The wood-cutter's song, the ploughboy's on his way in the morning, or
    at noon intermission or at sundown,
The delicious singing of the mother, or of the young wife at work, or of
    the girl sewing or washing,
Each singing what belongs to him or her and to none else,
The day what belongs to the day—at night the party of young fellows,
    robust, friendly,   10
Singing with open mouths their strong melodious songs.

[1865]

Denise Levertov

Poet Power

Riding by taxi, Brooklyn to Queens,
a grey spring day. The Hispanic driver,
when I ask, 'Es usted Mexicano?' tells me
No, he's an exile from Uruguay. And I say,
'The only other Uraguayan I've met   5

was a writer—maybe
you know his name?—
                         Mario Benedetti?
   And he takes both hands
off the wheel and swings round,   10
glittering with joy: '*Benedetti!*
Mario Benedetti!!'
                         There are
hallelujahs in his voice—
we execute a perfect   15
figure 8 on the shining highway,
and rise aloft, high above traffic, flying
all the rest of the way in the blue sky, azul, azul!

                                                    [1987]

Journal Entry

Whitman and Levertov celebrate the diversity of the United States. What experiences or knowledge of ethnic or cultural diversity can you bring to your reading of these texts?

Textual Considerations

1. What is the thematic significance of the titles of the two poems?
2. Discuss the effectiveness of the metaphor of song to reinforce meaning in Whitman's text. Which "songs" did you find most appealing?
3. What images in Levertov's text best express the joy of the taxi driver?
4. What emotions is Levertov trying to capture in this poem? Explain.
5. Discuss the parallel structure of Whitman's poem. How does it contribute to rhythm, imagery, and idea? How does it compare to the stanzaic structure of Levertov's poem?

Cultural Considerations

1. Whitman was the first American poet who tried to express and celebrate democracy and cultural diversity in the language of the people. Is his concept of social equality applicable to the twenty-first century? Explain.
2. According to fiction writer Grace Paley, "If you say what's on your mind in the language that comes to you from your parents and your street and your friends, you'll probably say something beautiful." Test Paley's thesis with your group members and write a short poem in your own language.

ERDRICH AND GILLAN

Louise Erdrich

Indian Boarding School: The Runaways

Home's the place we head for in our sleep.
Boxcars stumbling north in dreams
don't wait for us. We catch them on the run.
The rails, old lacerations that we love,
shoot parallel across the face and break   5
just under Turtle Mountains. Riding scars
you can't get lost. Home is the place they cross.

The lame guard strikes a match and makes the dark
less tolerant. We watch through cracks in boards
as the land starts rolling, rolling till it hurts   10
to be here, cold in regulation clothes.
We know the sheriff's waiting at midrun
to take us back. His car is dumb and warm.
The highway doesn't rock, it only hums
like a wing of long insults. The worn-down welts   15
of ancient punishments lead back and forth.

All runaways wear dresses, long green ones,
the color you would think shame was. We scrub
the sidewalks down because it's shameful work.
Our brushes cut the stone in watered arcs   20
and in the soak frail outlines shiver clear
a moment, things us kids pressed on the dark
face before it hardened, place, remembering
delicate old injuries, the spines of names and leaves.

[1984]

Maria Mazziotti Gillan

Public School No. 18:
Paterson, New Jersey

Miss Wilson's eyes, opaque
as blue glass, fix on me:
"We must speak English.
We're in America now."
I want to say, "I am American,"   5
but the evidence is stacked against me.

My mother scrubs my scalp raw, wraps
my shining hair in white rags
to make it curl; Miss Wilson
drags me to the window, checks my hair   10
for lice. My face wants to hide.

At home, my words smooth in my mouth,
I chatter and am proud. In school,
I am silent; I grope for the right English
words, fear the Italian word will sprout   15
from my mouth like a rose.

I fear the progression of teachers
in their sprigged dresses,
their Anglo-Saxon faces.

Without words, they tell me   20
to be ashamed.
I am.
I deny that booted country
even from myself,
want to be still   25
and untouchable
as these women
who teach me to hate myself.

Years later, in a white
Kansas City house,   30
the psychology professor tells me
I remind him of the Mafia leader
on the cover of *Time* magazine.
My anger spits
venomous from my mouth: 35

I am proud of my mother,
dressed all in black,
proud of my father
with his broken tongue,
proud of the laughter
and noise of our house.   40

Remember me, ladies,
the silent one?
I have found my voice
and my rage will blow   45
your house down.

[1984]

Journal Entry

What experiences, memories, or emotions of being an ethnic outsider in a classroom can you bring to your reading of these texts?

Textual Considerations

1. Describe the situation in Erdrich's text. Is it imagined or real? Explain.
2. What images of home in the first stanza of "Indian Boarding School: The Runaways" do you find most effective? Identify them and explain how they relate to the full meaning of the poem. What kinds of experiences do they evoke?
3. Why do the children in Erdrich's poem run away if they know they will be caught?
4. How do the railroad tracks, work uniform, and highways function literally and symbolically in "Indian Boarding School: The Runaways"?
5. Why does the speaker in Gillan's poem feel like an outsider?
6. How do the teachers in Gillan's poem contribute to her humiliation and exclusion?
7. Characterize the tone of Gillan's poem. Is it consistent throughout? How does it compare with the tone of Erdrich's poem?

Cultural Contexts

1. Erdrich is a Native American of German and Chippewa heritage. What preconceptions about Native Americans and reservations did you bring to this text? Did you modify them in any way after this experience? How?
2. Should a schoolteacher serve as a role model for students? How important is it that he or she be a member of the students' ethnic group? Do teachers have too much or too little influence on their students? Discuss these issues with your group and record your responses.

Langston Hughes

The Weary Blues

Droning a drowsy syncopated tune,
Rocking back and forth to a mellow croon,
    I heard a Negro play.
Down on Lenox Avenue° the other night
By the pale dull pallor of an old gas light   5
    He did a lazy sway . . .
    He did a lazy sway . . .
To the tune o' those Weary Blues.
With his ebony hands on each ivory key
He made that poor piano moan with melody.   10
    O Blues!
Swaying to and fro on his rickety stool
He played that sad raggy tune like a musical fool.
    Sweet Blues!
Coming from a black man's soul.   15
    O Blues!

    In a deep song voice with a melancholy tone
    I heard that Negro sing, that old piano moan—
        "Ain't got nobody in all this world,
        Ain't got nobody but ma self.   20
        I's gwine° to quit ma frownin'
        And put ma troubles on the shelf."
Thump, thump, thump, went his foot on the floor.
He played a few chords then he sang some more—
        "I got the Weary Blues   25
        And I can't be satisfied.
        Got the Weary Blues
        And can't be satisfied—
        I ain't happy no mo'
        And I wish that I had died."   30
And far into the night he crooned that tune.
The stars went out and so did the moon.
The singer stopped playing and went to bed
While the Weary Blues echoed through his head.
He slept like a rock or a man that's dead.   35

                                                                [1923]

---

4 Lenox Avenue: was a main street in Harlem.   **21 "gwine":** "going."

Langston Hughes

Dream Variations

To fling my arms wide
In some place of the sun,
To whirl and to dance
Till the white day is done.
Then rest at cool evening   5
Beneath a tall tree
While night comes on gently,
    Dark like me—
That is my dream!

To fling my arms wide   10
In the face of the sun,
Dance! Whirl! Whirl!
Till the quick day is done.
Rest at pale evening . . .

A tall, slim tree . . .   15
Night coming tenderly
    Black like me.

[1926]

Langston Hughes

Harlem (A Dream Deferred)

What happens to a dream deferred?

    Does it dry up
    like a raisin in the sun?
    Or fester like a sore—
    And then run?
    Does it stink like rotten meat?   5
    Or crust and sugar over—
    like a syrupy sweet?

    Maybe it just sags
    like a heavy load.   10

    Or does it explode?

[1951]

Journal Entry

What knowledge of jazz, blues, or Harlem can you bring to your reading of these poems?

Textual Considerations

1. How does the speaker use color imagery to enhance theme in "Dream Variations"?
2. What does the second stanza of "The Weary Blues" add to the first? To what extent does the poem's structure underline meaning?
3. What strategies does the speaker of "The Weary Blues" use to reinforce the influence of blues and jazz in his poetry?
4. To what extent does the speaker of "The Weary Blues" find refuge in the blues?
5. How does setting function in "Dream Variations"?
6. Evaluate the effectiveness of the speakers' voices in "The Weary Blues," "Dream Variations," and "Harlem." Consider tone, direct speech, punctuation, and the use of questions and answers.

Cultural Contexts

1. Hughes published "Harlem" in 1951 in response to his having witnessed the gradual erosion of the dreams of his people in the previous two decades. To what extent was his prophecy of violence fulfilled? Does the poem have any relevance to the dreams of your generation? Explain.
2. In the 1920s, during the Harlem Renaissance, many critics, both black and white, criticized Hughes's poetry because it reflected the seedy side of Harlem with its portrayals of musicians in bars and bordellos, suggestive of the lowdown aspects of the jazz life. How do your group members respond to that criticism? Are musicians particularly vulnerable to societal critiques? How did you respond to Hughes's poetry?

SOYINKA AND OLDS

Wole Soyinka

Telephone Conversation

The price seemed reasonable, location
Indifferent. The landlady swore she lived
Off premises. Nothing remained
But self-confession. "Madam," I warned,
"I hate a wasted journey—I am African."   5
Silence. Silenced transmission of
Pressurized good-breeding. Voice, when it came,
Lipstick coated, long gold-rolled
Cigarette-holder pipped. Caught I was, foully.
"HOW DARK?" . . . I had not misheard . . . "ARE YOU LIGHT   10
OR VERY DARK?" Button B. Button A. Stench
Of rancid breath of public hide-and-speak.
Red booth. Red pillar-box. Red double-tiered
Omnibus squelching tar. It *was* real! Shamed
By ill-mannered silence, surrender   15
Pushed dumbfoundment to beg simplification.
Considerate she was, varying the emphasis—
"ARE YOU DARK? OR VERY LIGHT?" Revelation came.
"You mean—like plain or milk chocolate?"
Her assent was clinical, crushing in its light   20
Impersonality. Rapidly, wave-length adjusted,
I chose. "West African sepia"—and as afterthought,
"Down in my passport." Silence for spectroscopic
Flight of fancy, till truthfulness clanged her accent
Hard on the mouthpiece. "WHAT'S THAT?" conceding   25
"DON'T KNOW WHAT THAT IS." "Like brunette."
"THAT'S DARK, ISN'T IT?" "Not altogether.
Facially, I am brunette, but madam, you should see
The rest of me. Palm of my hand, soles of my feet
Are a peroxide blonde. Friction, caused—   30
Foolishly madam—by sitting down, has turned
My bottom raven black—One moment madam!"—sensing
Her receiver rearing on the thunderclap
About my ears—"Madam," I pleaded, "wouldn't you rather
See for yourself?"   35

[1960]

Sharon Olds

On the Subway

The boy and I face each other.
His feet are huge, in black sneakers
laced with white in a complex pattern like a
set of intentional scars. We are stuck on
opposite sides of the car, a couple of   5
molecules stuck in a rod of light
rapidly moving through darkness. He has the
casual cold look of a mugger,
alert under hooded lids. He is wearing
red, like the inside of the body   10
exposed. I am wearing dark fur, the
whole skin of an animal taken and
used. I look at his raw face,
he looks at my fur coat, and I don't
know if I am in his power—   15
he could take my coat so easily, my
briefcase, my life—
or if he is in my power, the way I am
living off his life, eating the steak
he does not eat, as if I am taking   20
the food from his mouth. And he is black
and I am white, and without meaning or
trying to I must profit from his darkness,
the way he absorbs the murderous beams of the
nation's heart, as black cotton   25
absorbs the heat of the sun and holds it. There is
no way to know how easy this
white skin makes my life, this
life he could take so easily and
break across his knee like a stick the way his   30
own back is being broken, the
rod of his soul that at birth was dark and
fluid and rich as the heart of a seedling
ready to thrust up into any available light.

[1987]

Journal Entry

Define racism and stereotyping. How do they differ in meaning and connotation?

Textual Considerations

1. Create a profile of the landlady in "Telephone Conversation." How does the speaker use visual and sensory imagery to communicate her attitude toward skin color? Cite examples.
2. What profile of the speaker emerges in Soyinka's poem? How do the poet's stylistic techniques, such as short sentences and unusual syntax, enhance theme? How do you interpret the last four lines?
3. How does Olds use color to heighten differences in race and social class in "On the Subway"?
4. Explain lines 20–25 of "On the Subway." To what extent do you agree with the speaker that exploitation on the basis of race continues today as it did in the days of slavery?
5. Compare and contrast the conflict in each poem. Is it between the speaker and an antagonist? Or within the speaker himself/herself? Explain.

Cultural Contexts

1. In addition to race, both poems address class, social injustice, power, and powerlessness. Who wins or loses in each text?
2. Is the community in which you are currently living integrated, or are there ethnic groups that would make you feel unwelcome? If so, how would your group explain or change the situation?

CHOCK AND LAVIERA

Eric Chock

Chinese Fireworks Banned in Hawaii
for Uncle Wongie, 1987

Almost midnight, and the aunties
are wiping the dinner dishes
back to their shelves,
cousins eat jook° from the huge vat
in the kitchen, and small fingers   5
help to mix the clicking ocean
of mah jong tiles, so the uncles can play
through another round of seasons.
And you put down your whiskey
and go outside to find your long bamboo pole   10
so Uncle Al can help you tie on
a ten foot string of good luck,
red as the raw fish we want
on our plates every New Year's.
As you hang this fish over the railing   15
Uncle Al walks down the steps
and with his cigarette lighter
ignites it and jumps out of the way.
You lean back and jam the pole
into the bottom of your guts,   20
waving it across the sky,
whipping sparks of light from its tail,
your face in a laughing Buddha smile
as you trace your name in the stars
the way we teach our kids to do   25
with their sparklers.
This is the family picture
that never gets taken, everyone
drawn from dishes and food and games
and frozen at the sound   30
of 10,000 wishes filling our bodies
and sparkling our eyes.
You play the fish till its head explodes
into a silence that echoes,
scattering red scales to remind us of spirits   35

that live with us in Hawaii.
Then, as we clap and cheer,
the collected smoke of our consciousness
floats over Honolulu, as it has
each year for the last century.   40
But tonight, as we leave,
Ghislaine stuffs her styrofoam tea cup
full of red paper from the ground.
This is going to be history, she says.
Let's take some home.   45

[1989]

4 jook: Asian rice dish

Tato Laviera

Latero° Story

i am a twentieth-century welfare recipient
moonlighting in the sun as a latero
a job invented by national state laws
designed to re-cycle aluminum cans
returned to consumer's acid laden   5
gastric inflammation pituitary glands
coca diet rites low cal godsons
of artificially flavored malignant
indigestions somewhere down the line
of a cancerous cell   10

i collect garbage cans in outdoor facilities
congested with putrid residues
my hands shelving themselves
opening plastic bags never knowing
what they'll encounter   15

several times a day i touch evil rituals
cut throats of chickens
tongues of poisoned rats
salivating my index finger
smells of month old rotten foods   20

next to pamper's diarrhea
    dry blood infectious diseases
hypodermic needles tissued with
heroin water drops pilfered in
slimy greases hazardous waste materials   25
but i cannot use rubber gloves
they undermine my daily profits

i am a twentieth-century welfare recipient
moonlighting in the day as a latero
that is the only opportunity i have   30
to make it big in america
some day i might become experienced enough
to offer technical assistance
to other lateros
i am thinking of publishing   35
my own guide to latero's collection
and a latero's union offering
medical dental benefits

i am a twentieth-century welfare recipient
moonlighting in the night as a latero   40
i am considered some kind of expert
at collecting cans during fifth avenue parades
i can now hire workers at twenty
five cents an hour guaranteed salary
and fifty per cent two and one half cents   45
profit on each can collected

i am a twentieth-century welfare recipient
moonlighting in midnight as a latero
i am becoming an entrepreneur
an american success story   50
i have hired bag ladies to keep peddlers
from my territories
i have read in some guide to success
that in order to get rich
to make it big   55
i have to sacrifice myself
moonlighting until dawn by digging
deeper into the extra can
margin of profit
i am on my way up the opportunistic   60
ladder of success
in ten years i will quit welfare
to become a legitimate businessman

> i'll soon become a latero executive
> with corporate conglomerate intents
> god bless america

65

[1988]

Latero: From Spanish *lata*: can. A man who picks up cans from garbage containers and the streets.

Journal Entry

What associations, images, experiences, or memories of alienation or displacement can you bring to your reading of these texts?

Textual Considerations

1. Who is the speaker addressing in Chock's poem, and on what occasion?
2. Speculate on the significance and identity of the spirits in Chock's poem.
3. How do you interpret the next-to-last line of "Chinese Fireworks Banned in Hawaii"?
4. Laviera uses irony and repetition to satirize the values of corporate America in "Latero Story." Cite lines you find most effective. What is your response to his point of view?
5. Much of Laviera's poetry belongs to oral tradition. What does that suggest about his purpose and audience? How does it compare to the purpose and audience in Chock's poem?

Cultural Contexts

1. Chock and Laviera use poetry to transmit individual and cultural experiences. Experiment with writing a short poem about an experience, image, or emotion that has cultural implications for you.
2. Chock is an Asian of Hawaiian descent; Laviera is an immigrant from Puerto Rico. Why might the preservation of their ethnic and cultural heritage inform their poetry? What does it mean to break traditions? How important is it to transmit and preserve communal rituals? Did your group reach a consensus?

MORALES AND MORA

Aurora Levin Morales

Child of the Americas

I am a child of the Americas,
a light-skinned mestiza of the Caribbean,
a child of many diaspora.° born into this continent at a crossroads.

I am a U.S. Puerto Rican Jew.
a product of the ghettos of New York I have never known.   5
An immigrant and the daughter and granddaughter of immigrants.
I speak English with passion: it's the tongue of my consciousness,
a flashing knife blade of crystal, my tool my craft.

I am Caribeña,° island grown. Spanish is in my flesh.
ripples from my tongue lodges in my hips: 10

the language of garlic and mangoes,
the singing in my poetry, the flying gestures of my hands.

I am of Latinoamerica, rooted in the history of my continent:
I speak from that body.

I am not african. African is in me, but I cannot return.   15
I am not taína.° Taíno is in me, but there is no way back.
I am not european. Europe lives in me, but I have no home there.

I am new. History made me. My first language was spanglish.°
I was born at the crossroads
and I am whole.   20

[1986]

3 diaspora: literally, "scattering": the term is used especially to refer to the dispersion of the Jews outside of Israel from the sixth century, when they were exiled to Babylonia, to the present time.
9 Caribeña: Caribbean woman

Pat Mora

Legal Alien

Bi-lingual, Bi-cultural,
able to slip from "How's life?"
to "*Me'stan volviendo loca,*"°

able to sit in a paneled office
drafting memos in smooth English,   5
able to order in fluent Spanish
at a Mexican restaurant,
American but hyphenated,
viewed by Anglos as perhaps exotic,
perhaps inferior, definitely different,   10
viewed by Mexicans as alien,
(their eyes say, "You may speak
Spanish but you're not like me")
an American to Mexicans
a Mexican to Americans   15
a handy token
sliding back and forth
between the fringes of both worlds
by smiling
by masking the discomfort   20
of being pre-judged
Bi-laterally.

[1985]

3 Me'stan . . . loca: They are driving me crazy.

Journal Entry

Respond to the statement: "The past that constitutes our identity cannot be erased." How does it apply to the poems by Mora and Morales?

Textual Considerations

1. What aspects of Mora's being "American but hyphenated" most impressed or surprised you?
2. Explain the emotional, literal, and symbolic implications of the poem's title.
3. Select images/phrases that support Morales's claim that she "was born at the crossroads."
4. Morales uses repetition to enhance theme. Select examples you find most effective.
5. Compare and contrast the tone of each poem. How does tone enhance theme in both texts?

Cultural Contexts

1. Mora and Morales wrestle with the emotional and cultural complexities of their multicultural heritages. To what extent is it possible to resolve the tensions of assimilation into the larger culture while preserving the songs, stories, and language of their indigenous cultures?
2. Both poets are part of a large number of contemporary linguistically gifted artists who are seeking a space where cultural mixing and interaction occurs. To what extent is it desirable that a multi- ethnic concept of America replace the traditional metaphor of the melting pot? Record your group's responses.

Pat Mora

Elena

My Spanish isn't enough.
I remember how I'd smile
listening to my little ones,
understanding every word they'd say,
their jokes, their songs, their plots.   5
        Vamos a pedirle dulces a mamá. Vamos.°
But that was in Mexico.
Now my children go to American high schools.
They speak English. At night they sit around
the kitchen table, laugh with one another.   10
I stand by the stove and feel dumb, alone.
I bought a book to learn English.
My husband frowned, drank more beer.
My oldest said, "*Mamá*, he doesn't want you
to be smarter than he is." I'm forty,   15
embarrassed at mispronouncing words,
embarrassed at the laughter of my children,
the grocer, the mailman. Sometimes I take
my English book and lock myself in the bathroom,
say the thick words softly,   20
for if I stop trying, I will be deaf
when my children need my help.

[1986]

6 Vamos a pedirle. . . . Vamos: Let's ask *mamá* for candy. Come on.

Cathy Song

Lost Sister

1

In China,
even the peasants
named their first daughters
Jade—
the stone that in the far fields   5
could moisten the dry season,
could make men move mountains
for the healing green of the inner hills
glistening like slices of winter melon.

And the daughters were grateful: 10
they never left home.
To move freely was a luxury
stolen from them at birth.
Instead, they gathered patience,
learning to walk in shoes   15
the size of teacups,°
without breaking—
the arc of their movements
as dormant as the rooted willow,
as redundant as the farmyard hens.   20

But they traveled far
in surviving,
learning to stretch the family rice,
to quiet the demons,
the noisy stomachs.   25

2

There is a sister
across the ocean,
who relinquished her name,
diluting jade green
with the blue of the Pacific.   30
Rising with a tide of locusts,
she swarmed with others
to inundate another shore.
In America,

there are many roads   35
and women can stride along with men.

But in another wilderness,
the possibilities,
the loneliness,
can strangulate like jungle vines.   40
The meager provisions and sentiments
of once belonging—
fermented roots, Mah-Jongg° tiles and firecrackers—
set but a flimsy household
in a forest of nightless cities.   45
A giant snake rattles above,
spewing black clouds into your kitchen.
Dough-faced landlords
slip in and out of your keyholes,
making claims you don't understand,   50
tapping into your communication systems
of laundry lines and restaurant chains.
You find you need China:
your one fragile identification,
a jade link   55
handcuffed to your wrist.

You remember your mother
who walked for centuries,
footless—
and like her,   60

you have left no footprints,
but only because
there is an ocean in between,
the unremitting space of your rebellion.

[1987]

16 teacups: A reference to the practice of binding young girls' feet so that they remain small. This practice was common in China until the Communist revolution.   **43 Mah-Jongg:** Or mahjong, an ancient Chinese game played with dice and tiles.

Journal Entry

Respond to the causes of the emotional and cultural displacement of the speakers in both poems. To what extent can you identify with them? Explain.

Textual Considerations

1. How has Elena's inability to read English and therefore converse with her children contributed to her powerlessness as a mother, person, and member of her community?

2. Comment on the thematic significance of the speaker's use of "But" in line 7. What has replaced the "jokes," "smiles" and "understanding" in line 4? Consider Lines 11 and 21–22.
3. Do you agree with the comment of her oldest child? Why does the speaker mention her age? What is your response to that information?
4. State the conflict at the heart of Song's poem.
5. Why does the speaker include the reference to footbinding in the first stanza?
6. How do you respond to the description of where she lives in the United States?
7. Explain why the lost sister and her mother have left no footprints.

Cultural Contexts

1. Review Song's biographical endnote and discuss with your group the following statement made by another Asian immigrant: "Oh Asia, that nets its children in ties of blood so binding that they cut the spirit." To what extent does this apply to Song's poem? Explain.
2. Discuss with your group why both speakers are ambivalent about their choice to leave their countries of origin? Have their losses outweighed their gains? Summarize your group's responses.

Martín Espada

Cross Plains, Wisconsin

Blue bandanna
across the forehead,
beard bristling
like a straw broom,
sleeveless T-shirt   5
of the Puerto Rican flag
with Puerto Rico stamped
across the chest,
a foreign name on the license,
evidence enough   10
for the cop to announce
that the choice is cash or jail,
that today
the fine for speeding
is exactly   15
sixty-seven dollars,
and his car
will follow my car
out of town

[1990]

Martín Espada

Federico's Ghost

The story is
that whole families of fruitpickers
still crept between the furrows
of the field at dusk,
when for reasons of whiskey or whatever   5
the cropduster plane sprayed anyway,
floating a pesticide drizzle
over the pickers

who thrashed like dark birds
in a glistening white net,   10
except for Federico,
a skinny boy who stood apart
in his own green row,
and, knowing the pilot
would not understand in Spanish   15
that he was the son of a whore,
instead jerked his arm
and thrust an obscene finger.

The pilot understood.   20
He circled the plane and sprayed again,
watching a fine gauze of poison
drift over the brown bodies
that cowered and scurried on the ground,
and aiming for Federico,
leaving the skin beneath his shirt   25
wet and blistered,
but still pumping his finger at the sky.

After Federico died,
rumors at the labor camp
told of tomatoes picked and smashed at night,   30
growers muttering of vandal children
or communists in camp,
first threatening to call Immigration,
then promising every Sunday off
if only the smashing of tomatoes would stop.

Still tomatoes were picked and squashed   35
in the dark,
and the old women in camp
said it was Federico,
laboring after sundown
to cool the burns on his arms,   40
flinging tomatoes
at the cropduster
that hummed like a mosquito
lost in his ear,   45
and kept his soul awake.

                                                    [1990]

Martín Espada

Tony Went to the Bodega° but He Didn't Buy Anything
para° Angel Guadalupe

Tony's father left the family
and the Long Island city projects,
leaving a mongrel-skinny puertorriqueño boy
nine years old
who had to find work.   5

Makengo the Cuban
let him work at the bodega.
In grocery aisles
he learned the steps of the dry-mop mambo,
banging the cash register   10
like piano percussion
in the spotlight of Machito's orchestra,
polite with the abuelas° who bought on credit,
practicing the grin on customers
he'd seen Makengo grin   15
with his bad yellow teeth.

Tony left the projects too,
with a scholarship for law school.
But he cursed the cold primavera°
in Boston;   20
the cooking of his neighbors
left no smell in the hallway,
and no one spoke Spanish
(not even the radio).

So Tony walked without a map   25
through the city,
a landscape of hostile condominiums
and the darkness of white faces,
sidewalk-searcher lost
till he discovered the projects.   30

Tony went to the bodega
but he didn't buy anything:
he sat by the doorway satisfied
to watch la gente° (people
island-brown as him)   35

crowd in and out,
hablando español,°
thought: this is beautiful,
and grinned
his bodega grin.

40

This is a rice and beans
success story:
Today Tony lives on Tremont Street,
above the bodega.

[1987]

Bodega: Grocery and liquor store. **para:** in the dedication, after the title, means "for." **13 abuelas:** Grandmothers. **19 primavera:** Spring season. **34 la gente:** The people. **37 hablando español:** Speaking Spanish.

Journal Entry

How does Espada's philosophy that "any oppressive social condition, before it can be changed, must be named and condemned in words that pervade by stirring the emotions, awakening the senses" apply to his poetry?

Textual Considerations

1. Analyze the effects of withholding the use of the personal pronouns until the end of "Cross Plains, Wisconsin." Describe the meaning of the dramatic contrasts imposed by the use of the pronouns.
2. What factors contributed to the fine imposed by the police officer in "Cross Plains, Wisconsin"? Identify them and interpret the meaning they acquire in the context of the poem.
3. Characterize the speaker's tone in "Cross Plains, Wisconsin." How does the cop react to him and the collection of physical traits that identify his ethnic origin? Does the fact the incident takes place in Cross Plains, Wisconsin, affect the cop's decision? Why or why not?
4. Why does Federico act as he does in "Federico's Ghost"? What is your response to his actions? Explain.
5. How do the growers modify their first reactions to the migrant workers in "Federico's Ghost"? Why?
6. Explain the significance of the final simile in "Federico's Ghost."
7. Characterize Tony. Why does he return to his roots? How do you respond to that decision?
8. Why does Espada mention Tony's father in the first part of the poem?

Cultural Contexts

1. Espada's poems—poems of political imagination—document racism, dehumanizing labor, and personal and political resistance. To what extent do you agree or disagree that the poet should protest social injustices?
2. Debate with your group the idea that Espada's poems present life well by transforming everyday reality into art but that their lack of commitment to a clearly imposed poetic form make them inferior to poems that excel in both—a fusion of form, elegance, and artistic structure with the imaginative transformation of reality into art. Record your findings.

DRAMA

<figure>
Decorative border
</figure>

William Shakespeare

Othello, the Moor of Venice

CHARACTERS

OTHELLO, *the Moor*
BRABANTIO, *a senator, father to* DESDEMONA
CASSIO, *an honourable lieutenant to* OTHELLO
IAGO, OTHELLO's *ancient, a villain.*
RODERIGO, *a gulled gentleman.*
DUKE OF VENICE
SENATORS *of Venice.*
MONTANO, *governor of Cyprus.*
LODOVICO *and* GRATIANO, *kinsmen to* BRABANTIO, *two noble Venetians*
Sailors
Clown
DESDEMONA, *daughter to* BRABANTIO *and wife to* OTHELLO
EMILIA, *wife to* IAGO
BIANCA, *a courtesan and mistress to* CASSIO
Messenger, Herald, Officers, Gentlemen, Musicians, and Attendants

(SCENE: *Venice: a sea-port in Cyprus*)

ACT I

SCENE I

Venice. A Street.

(*Enter* RODERIGO *and* IAGO.)

ROD: Tush! never tell me; I take it much unkindly
That thou, Iago, who hast had my purse
As if the strings were thine, shouldst know of this.

IAGO: 'Sblood,° but you'll not hear me:
If ever I did dream of such a matter,
Abhor me.

ROD: Thou told'st me thou didst hold him in thy hate.

IAGO: Despise me, if I do not. Three great ones of the city,° 5

I.i. 4. 'Sblood: an oath, "by God's blood."   **8. great ones of the city:** Iago means to indicate his importance in the community; this is suggested also by his use of the word *worth* in line 11.

In personal suit to make me his lieutenant,
Off-capp'd to him°: and, by the faith of man,   10
I know my price, I am worth no worse a place:
But he, as loving his own pride and purposes,
Evades them, with a bombast circumstance
Horribly stuff'd with epithets of war;
And, in conclusion,   15
Nonsuits° my mediators; for, "Certes," says he,
"I have already chose my officer."
And what was he?
Forsooth, a great arithmetician,°
One Michael Cassio, a Florentine,   20
A fellow almost damn'd in a fair wife°;
That never set a squadron in the field,
Nor the division° of a battle knows
More than a spinster; unless the bookish theoric,°
Wherein the toged° consuls can propose°   25
As masterly as he: mere prattle, without practice,
Is all his soldiership. But he, sir, had th' election:
And I, of whom his eyes had seen the proof
At Rhodes, at Cyprus° and on other grounds
Christian and heathen, must be be-lee'd and calm'd   30
By debitor and creditor: this counter-caster,°
He, in good time,° must his lieutenant be,
And I—God bless the mark!°—his Moorship's ancient.°
ROD: By heaven, I rather would have been his hangman.
IAGO: Why, there's no remedy; 'tis the curse of service,   35
Preferment goes by letter and affection,
And not by old gradation,° where each second
Stood heir to th' first. Now, sir, be judge yourself,
Whether I in any just term am affin'd°
To love the Moor.
ROD: I would not follow then.   40
IAGO: O, sir, content you;
I follow him to serve my turn upon him:
We cannot all be masters, nor all masters

---

10. him: Othello.   **16. Nonsuits:** rejects.   **19. arithmetician:** a man whose military knowledge was merely theoretical, based on books of tactics.   **21. A . . . wife:** Cassio does not seem to be married, but his counterpart in Shakespeare's source did have a wife.   **23. division:** disposition of a battle line.   **24. theoric:** theory.   **25. toged:** wearing the toga.   **25. propose:** discuss.   **29. Rhodes, Cyprus:** islands in the Mediterranean south of Asia Minor, long subject to contention between the Venetians and the Turks.   **31. counter-caster:** a sort of bookkeeper; contemptuous term.   **32. in good time:** forsooth.   **33. God bless the mark:** anciently, a pious interjection to avert evil omens.   **33. ancient:** standard-bearer, ensign.   **37. old gradation:** seniority; Iago here expresses a characteristic prejudice of professional soldiers.   **39. affin'd:** bound.

Cannot be truly follow'd. You shall mark
Many a duteous and knee-crooking knave,   45
That, doting on his own obsequious bondage,
Wears out his time, much like his master's ass,
For nought but provender, and when he's old, cashier'd:
Whip me such honest knaves. Others there are
Who, trimm'd in forms and visages of duty,   50
Keep yet their hearts attending on themselves,
And, throwing but shows of service on their lords,
Do well thrive by them and when they have lin'd their coats
Do themselves homage: these fellows have some soul;
And such a one do I profess myself. For, sir,   55
It is as sure as you are Roderigo,
Were I the Moor, I would not be Iago°:
In following him, I follow but myself;
Heaven is my judge, nor I for love and duty,
But seeming so, for my peculiar end: 60
For when my outward action doth demonstrate
The native act and figure of my heart
In compliment extern,° 'tis not long after
But I will wear my heart upon my sleeve
For daws to peck at: I am not what I am.   65
Rod: What a full fortune does the thick-lips° owe,
          If he can carry 't thus!
Iago: Call up her father,
          Rouse him: make after him, poison his delight,
          Proclaim him in the streets; incense her kinsmen,
          And, though he in a fertile climate dwell,   70
          Plague him with flies: though that his joy be joy,
          Yet throw such changes of vexation on 't,
          As it may lose some colour.
Rod: Here is her father's house; I'll call aloud.
Iago: Do, with like timorous° accent and dire yell   75
          As when, by night and negligence, the fire
          Is spied in populous cities.
Rod: What, ho, Brabantio! Signior Brabantio, ho!
Iago: Awake! what, ho, Brabantio! thieves! thieves! thieves!
          Look to your house, your daughter and your bags!   80
          Thieves! thieves!

(Brabantio *appears above at a window*.)

---

57. Were . . . Iago: Were I in the position of the Moor, I should not feel as Iago feels.   **63. compliment extern:** outward civility.   **66. thick-lips:** Elizabethans often applied the term *Moor* to Africans.
75. timorous: frightening.

BRA: What is the reason of this terrible summons?
   What is the matter there?
ROD: Signior, is all your family within?
IAGO: Are your doors lock'd?
BRA: Why, wherefore ask you this?   85
IAGO: 'Zounds, sir, y' are robb'd; for shame, put on your gown;
   Your heart is burst, you have lost half your soul;
   Even now, now, very now, an old black ram
   Is tupping your white ewe. Arise, arise:
   Awake the snorting° citizens with the bell,   90
   Or else the devil will make a grandsire of you:
   Arise, I say.
BRA: What, have you lost your wits?
ROD: Most reverend signior, do you know my voice?
BRA: Not I: what are you?
ROD: My name is Roderigo.
BRA: The worser welcome: 95
   I have charg'd thee not to haunt about my doors:
   In honest plainness thou has heard me say
   My daughter is not for thee; and now, in madness,
   Being full of supper and distemp'ring draughts,
   Upon malicious bravery,° doest thou come   100
   To start° my quiet.
ROD: Sir, sir, sir,—
BRA: But thou must needs be sure
   My spirit and my place have in them power
   To make this bitter to thee.°
ROD: Patience, good sir.
BRA: What tell'st thou me of robbing? this is Venice;   105
   My house is not a grange.°
ROD: Most grave Brabantio,
   In simple and pure soul I come to you.
IAGO: 'Zounds, sir, you are one of those that will not serve God, if the devil bid
   you. Because we come to do you service and you think we are ruffians, you'll have
   your daughter covered with a Barbary horse, you'll have your nephews° neigh to   110
   you; you'll have coursers for cousins and gennets° for germans.°
BRA: What profane wretch art thou?
IAGO: I am one, sir, that comes to tell you your daughter and the Moor are now
   making the beast with two backs.
BRA: Thou art a villain.
IAGO: You are—a senator.   115

---

90. snorting: snoring.   **100. bravery:** defiance, bravado.   **101. start:** disrupt.   **106. grange:** isolated
farmhouse.   **110. nephews:** grandsons.   **111. gennets:** small Spanish horses.   **111. germans:** near
relatives.

BRA: This thou shalt answer; I know thee, Roderigo.
ROD: Sir, I will answer any thing. But, I beseech you,
    If 't be your pleasure and most wise consent,
    As partly I find it is, that your fair daughter,
    At this odd-even° and dull watch o' th' night,   120
    Transported, with no worse nor better guard
    But with a knave of common hire, a gondolier,
    To the gross clasps of a lascivious Moor,—
    If this be known to you and your allowance,°
    We then have done you bold and saucy wrongs;   125
    But if you know not this, my manners tell me
    We have your wrong rebuke. Do not believe
    That, from° the sense of all civility,
    I thus would play and trifle with your reverence:
    Your daughter, if you have not given her leave,   130
    I say again, hath made a gross revolt;
    Tying her duty, beauty, wit and fortunes
    In an extravagant° and wheeling° stranger
    Of here and every where. Straight satisfy yourself:
    If she be in her chamber or your house,   135
    Let loose on me the justice of the state
    For thus deluding you.
BRA: Strike on the tinder,° ho!
    Give me a taper! call up my people!
    This accident° is not unlike my dream:
    Belief of it oppresses me already.   140
    Light, I say! light?   *(Exit above.)*
IAGO: Farewell; for I must leave you:
    It seems not meet, nor wholesome to my place,
    To be produc'd—as, if I stay, I shall—
    Against the Moor: for I do know the state,
    However this may gall him with some check,°   145
    Cannot with safety cast° him, for he's embark'd
    With such loud reason to the Cyprus wars,
    Which even now stand in act,° that, for their souls,
    Another of his fathom° they have none,
    To lead their business: in which regard,   150
    Though I do hate him as I do hell-pains,
    Yet, for necessity of present life,
    I must show out a flag and sign of love,

---

120. odd-even: between night and morning.   **124. allowance:** permission.   **128. from:** contrary to.
133. extravagant: wandering.   **133. wheeling:** vagabond.   **137. tinder:** charred linen kept in a metal box, and ignited by a spark from flint and steel.   **139. accident:** occurrence, event.   **145. check:** rebuke.   **146. cast:** dismiss.   **148. stand in act:** are going on.   **149. fathom:** ability.

Which is indeed but sign. That you shall surely find him,
Lead to the Sagittary° the raised search:
And there will I be with him. So, farewell.   *(Exit.)*   155

    (Enter below BRABANTIO *with* SERVANTS *and torches.)*

BRA: It is too true an evil; gone she is;
And what's to come of my despised time
Is nought but bitterness. Now, Roderigo,
Where didst thou see her? O unhappy girl!
With the Moor, say'st thou? Who would be a father!   160
How didst thou know 'twas she? O, she deceives me
Past thought! What said she to you? Get moe° tapers:
Raise all my kindred. Are they married, think you?

ROD: Truly, I think they are.   165

BRA: O heaven! How got she out? O treason of the blood!
Fathers, from hence trust not your daughters' minds
By what you see them act. Is° there not charms
By which the property° of youth and maidhood
May be abus'd? Have you not read, Roderigo,   170
Of some such thing?

ROD: Yes, sir, I have indeed.

BRA: Call up my brother. O, would you° had had her!
Some one way, some another. Do you know
Where we may apprehend her and the Moor?

ROD: I think I can discover him, if you please   175
To get good guard and go along with me.

BRA: Pray you, lead on. At every house I'll call;
I may command at most. Get weapons, ho!
And raise some special officers of night.°   *(Exeunt.)*
On, good Roderigo: I will deserve your pains.   180

    SCENE II

    Another street.

    (Enter OTHELLO, IAGO, ATTENDANTS *with torches.)*

IAGO: Though in the trade of war I have slain men,
Yet do I hold it very stuff o' th' conscience
To do no contriv'd murder: I lack iniquity
Sometime to do me service: nine or ten times
I had thought t' have yerk'd° him here under the ribs.   5

OTH: 'Tis better as it is.

IAGO: Nay, but he prated,

---

155. Sagittary: probably an inn. **163. moe:** more. **168. Is:** are. **169. property:** special quality.
172. you: Roderigo. **179. officers of night:** police. **I.ii. 5. yerk'd:** stabbed.

And spoke such scurvy and provoking terms
Against your honour
That, with the little godliness I have,
I did full hard forbear him. But, I pray you, sir,   10
Are you fast married? Be assur'd of this,
That the magnifico° is much belov'd,
And hath in his effect° a voice potential°
As double° as the duke's: he will divorce you;
Or put upon you what restraint and grievance   15
The law, with all his might to enforce it on,
Will give him cable.

OTH: Let him do his spite;
My services, which I have done the signiory°
Shall out-tongue hhis complaints. 'Tis yet to know—   20
Which, when I know that boasting is an honour,
I shall promulgate—I fetch my life and being
From men of royal siege,° and my demerits°
May speak unbonneted° to as proud a fortune
As this that I have reach'd: for know, Iago,
But that I love the gentle Desdemona,   25
I would not my unhoused free condition
Put into circumscription and confine
For the sea's worth. But, look! what lights come yond?

IAGO: Those are the raised father and his friends:
You were best go in.

OTH: Not I; I must be found: 30
My parts, my title and my perfect soul°
Shall manifest me rightly. Is it they?

IAGO: By Janus, I think no.

(*Enter* CASSIO *and certain* OFFICERS *with torches.*)

OTH: The servants of the duke, and my lieutenant.
The goodness of the night upon you, friends!   35
What is the news?

CAS: The duke does greet you, general,
And he requires your haste-post-haste appearance,
Even on the instant.

OTH: What is the matter, think you?

CAS: Something from Cyprus, as I may divine:
It is a business of some heat: the galleys   40
Have sent a dozen sequent° messengers

---

12. **magnifico:** Venetian grandee (i.e., Brabantio).   13. **effect:** influence.   13. **potential:** powerful.
14. **double:** twice as influential as most men's.   18. **signiory:** Venetian government.   22. **siege:** rank.
22. **demerits:** deserts.   23. **unbonneted:** on equal terms.   31. **perfect soul:** unflawed conscience.
41. **sequent:** successive.

This very night at one another's heels,
And many of the consuls,° rais'd and met,
Are at the duke's already: you have been hotly call'd for;
When, being not at your lodging to be found,   45
The senate hath sent about three several° quests
To search you out.
OTH: 'Tis well I am found by you.
I will but spend a word here in the house.
And go with you.   (*Exit.*)
CAS: Ancient, what makes he here?
IAGO: 'Faith, he to-night hath boarded a land carack°:   50
If it prove lawful prize, he's made for ever.
CAS: I do not understand.
IAGO: He's married.
CAS: To who?

         (*Enter* OTHELLO.)

IAGO: Marry, to—Come, captain, will you go?
OTH: Have with you.
CAS: Here comes another troop to seek for you.

         (*Enter* BRABANTIO, RODERIGO, *with* OFFICERS *and torches.*)

IAGO: It is Brabantio. General, be advis'd;   55
He comes to bad intent.
OTH: Holla! stand there!
ROD: Signior, it is the Moor.
BRA: Down with him, thief!   (*They draw on both sides.*)
IAGO: You, Roderigo! come, sir, I am for you.
OTH: Keep up your bright swords, for the dew will rust them.
Good Signior, you shall more command with years   60
Than with your weapons.
BRA: O thou foul thief, where hast thou stow'd my daughter?
Damn'd as thou art, thou has enchanted her;
For I'll refer me to all things of sense,°
If she in chains of magic were not bound,   65
Whether a maid so tender, fair and happy,
So opposite to marriage that she shunn'd
The wealthy curled darlings of our nation,
Would ever have, t' incur a general mock
Run from her guardage° to the sooty bosom   70
Of such a thing as thou, to fear, not to delight
Judge me the world, if 'tis not gross in sense°

---

43. consuls: senators.   **46. several:** separate.   **50. carack:** large merchant ship.   **64. things of sense:** commonsense understandings of the natural order.   **70. guardage:** guardianship.   **72. gross in sense:** easily discernible in apprehension or perception.

That thou has practis'd on her with foul charms,
Abus'd her delicate youth with drugs or minerals°
That weaken motion°: I'll have't disputed on°;   75
'Tis probable and palpable to thinking.
I therefore apprehend and do attach thee
For an abuser of the world,° a practiser
Of arts inhibited° and out of warrant.
Lay hold upon him: if he do resist,   80
Subdue him at his peril.

OTH: Hold your hands,
Both you of my inclining,° and the rest:
Were it my cue to fight, I should have known it
Without a prompter. Whither will you that I go
To answer this charge?

BRA: To prison, till fit time   85
Of law and course of direct session°
Call thee to answer.

OTH: What if I do obey?
How may the duke be therewith satisfied,
Whose messengers are here about my side,
Upon some present business of the state   90
To bring me to him?

FIRST OFF: 'Tis true, most worthy signior;
The duke's in council, and your noble self,
I am sure, is sent for.

BRA: How! the duke in council!
In this time of night! Bring him away:
Mine's not an idle cause: the duke himself,   95
Or any of my brothers of the state
Cannot but feel this wrong as 'twere their own;
For if such actions may have passage free,
Bond-slaves and pagans° shall our statesmen be.   [*Exeunt.*]

SCENE III

A council-chamber.

(*Enter* DUKE, SENATORS *and* OFFICERS *set at a table, with lights and* ATTENDANTS.)

DUKE: There is no composition in these news
That gives them credit.

FIRST SEN: Indeed, they are disproportion'd°;

---

74. **minerals:** medicine, poison.   75. **motion:** thought, reason.   75. **disputed on:** argued in court by professional counsel.   78. **abuser of the world:** corrupter of society.   79. **inhibited:** prohibited. 82. **inclining:** following, party.   86. **course of direct session:** regular legal proceedings.   99. **Bond-slaves and pagans:** contemptuous reference to Othello's past history.   I. iii. 2. **disproportion'd:** inconsistent.

My letters say a hundred and seven galleys.
DUKE: And mine, a hundred forty.
SEC. SEN: And mine, two hundred:
  But though they jump° not on a just account,—   5
  As in these cases, where the aim° reports,
  'Tis oft with difference—yet do they all confirm
  A Turkish fleet, and bearing up to Cyprus.
DUKE: Nay, it is possible enough to judgment:
  I do not so secure me° in the error,   10
  But the main article° I do approve
  In fearful sense.
SAILOR (*Within*):   What, ho! what, ho! what, ho!
FIRST OFF: A messenger from the galleys.

          (*Enter* SAILOR.)

DUKE: Now, what's the business?
SAIL: The Turkish preparation makes for Rhodes;
  So was I bid report here to the state   15
  By Signior Angelo.
DUKE: How say you by this change?
FIRST SEN: This cannot be,
  By no assay° of reason: 'tis a pageant,
  To keep us in false gaze. When we consider
  Th' importancy of Cyprus to the Turk,   20
  And let ourselves again but understand,
  That as it more concerns the Turk than Rhodes,
  So may he with more facile question° bear it,
  For that it stands not in such warlike brace,°
  But altogether lacks th' abilities   25
  That Rhodes is dress'd in: if we make thought of this,
  We must not think the Turk is so unskilful
  To leave that latest which concerns him first,
  Neglecting an attempt of ease and gain,
  To wake and wage a danger profitless.   30
DUKE: Nay, in all confidence, he's not for Rhodes.
FIRST OFF: Here is more news.

          (*Enter a* MESSENGER.)

MESS: The Ottomites, reverend and gracious,
  Steering with due course toward the isle of Rhodes,
  Have there injointed them with an after fleet.   35

---

5. jump: agree.   **6. aim:** conjecture.   **10. secure me:** feel myself secure.   **11. main article:** i.e., that
the Turkish fleet is threatening.   **18. assay:** test.   **23. more facile question:** greater facility of effort.
24. brace: state of defense.

FIRST SEN: Ay, so I thought. How many, as you guess?

MESS: Of thirty sail: and now they do re-stem°

  Their backward course, bearing with frank appearance

  Their purposes toward Cyprus. Signior Montano,

  Your trusty and most valiant servitor,   40

  With his free duty recommends you thus,

  And prays you to believe him.

DUKE: 'Tis certain, then, for Cyprus.

  Marcus Luccicos, is not he in town?

FIRST SEN: He's now in Florence.   45

DUKE: Write from us to him; post-posthaste dispatch.

FIRST SEN: Here comes Brabantio and the valiant Moor.

(*Enter* BRABANTIO, OTHELLO, CASSIO, IAGO, RODERIGO, *and* OFFICERS.)

DUKE: Valiant Othello, we must straight employ you

  Against the general enemy Ottoman.

  (*To* BRABANTIO) I did not see you; welcome, gentle signior;   50

  We lack'd your counsel and your help to-night.

BRA: So did I yours. Good your grace, pardon me;

  Neither my place nor aught I heard of business

  Hath rais'd me from my bed, nor does the general care

  Take hold on me, for my particular grief   55

  Is of so flood-gate and o'erbearing nature

  That it engluts° and swallows other sorrows

  And it is still itself.

DUKE: Why, what's the matter?

BRA: My daughter! O, my daughter!

DUKE *and* SEN: Dead?

BRA: Ay, to me;

  She is abus'd, stol'n from me, and corrupted   60

  By spells and medicines bought of mountebanks;

  For nature so preposterously to err,

  Being not deficient, blind, or lame of sense,

  Sans witchcraft could not.

DUKE: Whoe'er he be that in this foul proceeding   65

  Hath thus beguil'd your daughter of herself

  And you of her, the bloody book of law

  You shall yourself read in the bitter letter

  After your own sense, yea, though our proper son

  Stood in your action.°   70

BRA: Humbly I thank your grace.

  Here is the man, this Moor, whom now, it seems,

---

37. re-stem: steer again.   **57. engluts:** engulfs.   **70. Stood . . . action:** was under your accusation.

Your special mandate for the state-affairs
Hath hither brought.

DUKE *and* SEN: We are very sorry for 't.

DUKE (*To* OTHELLO):   What, in your own part, can you say to this?

BRA: Nothing, but this is so.   75

OTH: Most potent, grave, and reverend signiors,
My very noble and approv'd good masters,
That I have ta'en away this old man's daughter,
It is most true; true, I have married her:
The very head and front of my offending   80
Hath this extent, no more. Rude am I in my speech,
And little bless'd with the soft phrase of peace;
For since these arms of mine had seven years' pith,°
Till now some nine moons wasted, they have us'd
Their dearest action in the tented field,   85
And little of this great world can I speak,
More than pertains to feats of broil and battle,
And therefore little shall I grace my cause
In speaking for myself. Yet, by your gracious patience,°
I will a round unvarnish'd tale deliver   90
Of my whole course of love; what drugs, what charms,
What conjuration and what mighty magic,
For such proceeding I am charg'd withal,
I won his daughter.

BRA: A maiden never bold;
Of spirit so still and quiet, that her motion   95
Blush'd at herself°; and she, in spite of nature,
Of years, of country, credit, every thing,
To fall in love with what she fear'd to look on!
It is a judgement maim'd and most imperfect
That will confess perfection so could err   100
Against all rules of nature, and must be driven
To find our practices of cunning hell,
Why this should be. I therefore vouch° again
That with some mixtures pow'rful o'er the blood,
Or with some dram conjur'd to this effect,   105
He wrought upon her.

DUKE: To vouch this, is no proof,
Without more wider and more overt test
Than these thin habits and poor likelihoods
Of modern seeming do prefer against him.

FIRST SEN: But, Othello, speak: 110

---

83. pith: strength, vigor. **89. patience:** suffering, permission. **96. motion . . . herself:** inward impulses blushed at themselves. **103. vouch:** assert.

Did you by indirect and forced courses
Subdue and poison this young maid's affections?
Or came it by request and such fair question
As soul to soul affordeth?

OTH: I do beseech you,
    Send for the lady to the Sagittary,   115
    And let her speak of me before her father:
    If you do find me foul in her report,
    The trust, the office I do hold of you,
    Not only take away, but let your sentence
    Even fall upon my life.

DUKE: Fetch Desdemona hither.   120

OTH: Ancient, conduct them; you best know the place.

                              (*Exeunt* IAGO *and* ATTENDANTS.)

    And, till she come, as truly as to heaven
    I do confess the vices of my blood,
    So justly to your grave ear I'll present
    How I did thrive in this fair lady's love,   125
    And she in mine.

DUKE: Say it, Othello.

OTH: Her father lov'd me; oft invited me;
    Still question'd me the story of my life,
    From year to year, the battles, sieges, fortunes,   130
    That I have pass'd.
    I ran it through, even from my boyish days,
    To th' very moment that he bade me tell it;
    Wherein I spake of most disastrous chances,
    Of moving accidents by flood and field,   135
    Of hair-breadth scapes i' th' imminent° deadly breach,
    Of being taken by the insolent foe
    And sold to slavery, of my redemption thence
    And portance° in my travels' history:
    Wherein of antres° vast and deserts idle,°   140
    Rough quarries, rocks and hills whose heads touch heaven,
    It was my hint° to speak,—such was the process;
    And of the Cannibals that each other eat,°
    The Anthropophagi° and men whose heads
    Do grow beneath their shoulders. This to hear   145
    Would Desdemona seriously incline:
    But still the house-affairs would draw her thence:
    Which ever as she could with haste dispatch,

---

136. imminent: i.e., impending parts when a gap has been made in a fortification.   **139. portance:**
conduct.   **140. antres:** caverns.   **140. idle:** barren, unprofitable.   **142. hint:** occasion.   **143. eat:**
ate.   **144. Anthropophagi:** man-eaters.

She 'ld come again, and with a greedy ear
Devour up my discourse: which I observing, 150
Took once a pliant hour, and found good means
To draw from her a prayer of earnest heart
That I would all my pilgrimage dilate,°
Whereof by parcels she had something heard,
But not intentively°; I did consent, 155
And often did beguile her of her tears,
When I did speak some distressful stroke
That my youth suffer'd. My story being done,
She gave me for my pains a world of sighs:
She swore, in faith, 'twas strange, 'twas passing strange, 160
'Twas pitiful, 'twas wondrous pitiful:
She wish'd she had not heard it, yet she wish'd
That heaven had made her such a man: she thank'd me,
And bade me, if I had a friend that lov'd her,
I should but teach him how to tell my story, 165
And that would woo her. Upon this hint I spake:
She lov'd me for the dangers I had pass'd,
And I lov'd her that she did pity them.
This only is the witchcraft I have us'd:
Here comes the lady; let her witness it. 170

(*Enter* DESDEMONA, IAGO *and* ATTENDANTS.)

DUKE: I think this tale would win my daughter too.
Good Brabantio,
Take up this mangled matter at the best:
Men do their broken weapons rather use
Than their bare hands.
BRA: I pray you, hear her speak: 175
If she confess that she was half the wooer,
Destruction on my head, if my bad blame
Light on the man! Come hither, gentle mistress:
Do you perceive in all this noble company
Where most you owe obedience?
DES: My noble father, 180
I do perceive here a divided duty°:
To you I am bound for life and education;
My life and education both do learn me
How to respect you; you are the lord of duty;
I am hitherto your daughter: but here's my husband, 185
And so much duty as my mother show'd

---

153. dilate: relate in detail.   **155. intentively:** with full attention.   **181. divided duty:** Desdemona recognizes that she still owes a duty to her father even after marriage.

To you, preferring you before her father,
So much I challenge that I may profess
Due to the Moor my lord.
BRA: God be with you! I have done.
Please it your grace, on to° the state-affairs: 190
I had rather to adopt a child than get° it.
Come hither, Moor:
I here do give thee that with all my heart
Which, but thou hast already, with all my heart
I would keep from thee. For your sake,° jewel,   195
I am glad at soul I have no other child;
For thy escape would teach me tyranny,
To hang clogs on them. I have done, my lord.
DUKE: Let me speak like yourself,° and lay a sentence,°
Which, as a grise° or step, may help these lovers   200
Into your favour.
When remedies are past, the griefs are ended
By seeing the worst, which late on hopes depended.
To mourn a mischief that is past and gone
Is the next° way to draw new mischief on.   205
Which cannot be preserv'd when fortune takes,
Patience her injury a mock'ry makes.
The robb'd that smiles steals something from the thief;
He robs himself that spends a bootless grief.
BRA: So let the Turk of Cyprus us beguile;   210
We lost it now, so long as we can smile.
He bears the sentence well that nothing bears
But the free comfort° which from thence he hears,
But he bears both the sentence and the sorrow
That, to pay grief, must of poor patience borrow.   215
These sentences, to sugar, or to gall,
Being strong on both sides, are equivocal:
But words are words; I never yet did hear
That the bruis'd heart was pierced through the ear.
I humbly beseech you, proceed to th' affairs of state.   220
DUKE: The Turk with a most mighty preparation makes for Cyprus. Othello, the
fortitude° of the place is best known to you; and though we have there a substi-
tute of most allowed° sufficiency, yet opinion, a sovereign mistress of effects,
throws a more safer voice on you°: you must therefore be content to slubber° the
gloss of your new fortunes with this more stubborn and boist'rous expedition.   225

190. on to: i.e., proceed with.   **191. get:** beget.   **195. For your sake:** on your account.   **199. like yourself:** i.e., as you would, in your proper temper.   **199. sentence:** maxim.   **200. grise:** step.   **205. next:** nearest.   **213. comfort:** i.e., the consolation that it may be borne with patience.   **222. fortitude:** strength.   **223. allowed:** acknowledged.   **223–224. opinion . . . on you:** public opinion, an important determiner of affairs, chooses you as the best man.   **224. slubber:** soil, sully.

OTH: The tyrant custom, most grave senators,
    Hath made the flinty and steel couch of war
    My thrice-driven° bed of down: I do agnize°
    A natural and prompt alacrity
    I find in hardness° and do undertake   230
    These present wars against the Ottomites.
    Most humbly therefore bending to your state,
    I crave fit disposition for my wife,
    Due reference of place and exhibition,°
    With such accommodation and besort°   235
    As levels with her breeding.

DUKE: If you please,
    Be 't at her father's.

BRA: I'll not have it so.

OTH: Nor I.

DES: Nor I; I would not there reside,
    To put my father in impatient thoughts
    By being in his eye. Most gracious duke,   240
    To my unfolding lend your prosperous° ear
    And let me find a charter° in your voice,
    T' assist my simpleness.°

DUKE: What would you, Desdemona?

DES: That I did love the Moor to live with him,   245
    My downright violence and storm of fortunes
    May trumpet to the world: my heart's subdu'd
    Even to the very quality of my lord:
    I saw Othello's visage in his mind,
    And to his honours and his valiant parts   250
    Did I my soul and fortunes consecrate.
    So that, dear lords, if I be left behind,
    A moth of peace, and he go to the war,
    The rites for why I love him are bereft me,
    And I a heavy interim shall support   255
    By his dear absence. Let me go with him.

OTH: Let her have your voices.
    Vouch with me, heaven, I therefore beg it not,
    To please the palate of my appetite,
    Nor to comply with heat—the young affects°   260
    In me defunct—and proper satisfaction,
    But to be free and bounteous to her mind:
    And heaven defend your good souls, that you think

---

228. thrice-driven: thrice sifted. **228. agnize:** know in myself. **230. hardness:** hardship.
234. exhibition: allowance. **235. besort:** suitable company. **241. prosperous:** propitious.
242. charter: privilege. **243. simpleness:** simplicity. **260. affects:** inclinations, desires.

I will your serious and great business scant
When she is with me: no, when light-wing'd toys   265
Of feather'd Cupid seel° with wanton dullness
My speculative and offic'd instruments,°
That° my disports° corrupt and taint° my business,
Let housewives make a skillet of my helm,
And all indign° and base adversities   270
Make head against my estimation!°

DUKE: Be it as you shall privately determine,
        Either for her stay or going: th' affair cries haste,
        And speed must answer for it.

FIRST SEN: You must away to-night.

OTH: With all my heart.   275

DUKE: At nine i' th' morning here we'll meet again.
        Othello, leave some officer behind,
        And he shall our commission bring to you;
        With such things else of quality and respect
        As doth import° you.

OTH: So please your grace, my ancient;   280
        A man he is of honesty and trust:
        To his conveyance I assign my wife,
        With what else needful your good grace shall think
        To be sent after me.

DUKE: Let it be so.
        Good night to every one. (*To* BRA.) And, noble signior,   285
        If virtue no delighted° beauty lack,
        Your son-in-law is far more fair than black.

FIRST SEN: Adieu, brave Moor; use Desdemona well.

BRA: Look to her, Moor, if thou hast eyes to see;
       She has deceiv'd her father, and may thee.   290

                    (*Exeunt* DUKE, SENATORS, OFFICERS, *&c.*)

OTH: My life upon her faith! Honest Iago,°
       My Desdemona must I leave to thee:
       I prithee, let thy wife attend on her;
       And bring them after in the best advantage.
       Come, Desdemona; I have but an hour   295
       Of love, of worldly matters and direction,
       To spend with thee: we must obey the time.   (*Exit with* DESDEMONA.)

ROD: Iago—

---

266. seel: in falconry, to make blind by sewing up the eyes of the hawk in training.   **267. speculative . . . instruments:** ability to see and reason clearly.   **268. That:** so that.   **268. disports:** pastimes.   **268. taint:** impair.   **270. indign:** unworthy, shameful.   **271. estimation:** reputation.   **280. import:** concern.   **286. delighted:** delightful.   **291. Honest Iago:** an evidence of Iago's carefully built reputation.

Iago: What say'st thou, noble heart?

Rod: What will I do, thinkest thou?

Iago: Why, go to bed, and sleep.

Rod: I will incontinently° drown myself.

Iago: If thou dost, I shall never love thee after. Why, thou silly gentleman!

Rod: It is silliness to live when to live is torment; and then have we a prescription to die when death is our physician.

Iago: O villainous! I have looked upon the world for four times seven years; and since I could distinguish betwixt a benefit and an injury, I never found man that knew how to love himself. Ere I would say, I would drown myself for the love of a guinea-hen, I would change my humanity with a baboon.

Rod: What should I do? I confess it is my shame to be so fond; but it is not in my virtue° to amend it.

Iago: Virtue! a fig! 'tis in ourselves that we are thus or thus. Our bodies are our gardens, to the which our wills are gardeners; so that if we will plant nettles, or sow lettuce, set hyssop° and weed up thyme, supply it with one gender° of herbs, or distract it with many, either to have it sterile with idleness,° or manured with industry, why, the power and corrigible authority° of this lies in our wills. If the balance of our lives had not one scale of reason to poise another of sensuality, the blood and baseness of our natures would conduct us to most preposterous conclusions°: but we have reason to cool our raging motions,° our carnal stings, our unbitted° lusts, whereof I take this that you call love to be a sect° or scion.

Rod: It cannot be.

Iago: It is merely a lust of the blood and a permission of the will. Come, be a man. Drown thyself! drown cats and blind puppies. I have professed me thy friend and I confess me knit to thy deserving with cables of perdurable° toughness; I could never better stead thee than now. Put money in thy purse; follow thou the wars; defeat thy favour° with an usurped beard; I say, put money in thy purse. It cannot be that Desdemona should long continue her love to the Moor,—put money in thy purse,—nor he his to her: it was a violent commencement in her, and thou shalt see an answerable sequestration°:—put but money in thy purse. These Moors are changeable in their wills:—fill thy purse with money:—the food that to him now is as luscious as locusts,° shall be to him shortly as bitter as coloquintida.° She must change for youth: when she is sated with his body, she will find the error of her choice: she must have change, she must: therefore put money in thy purse. If thou wilt needs damn

---

302. incontinently: immediately. **311. virtue:** strength. **314. hyssop:** an herb of the mint family. **314. gender:** kind. **315. idleness:** want of cultivation. **316. corrigible authority:** the power to correct. **317–319. reason . . . conclusions:** Iago understands the warfare between reason and sensuality, but his ethics are totally inverted; reason works in him not good, as it should according to natural law, but evil, which he has chosen for his good. **319. motions:** appetites. **320. unbitted:** uncontrolled. **321. sect:** cutting. **325. perdurable:** very durable. **327. defeat thy favour:** disguise and disfigure thy face. **330. answerable sequestration:** a separation corresponding. **332. locusts:** of doubtful meaning; defined as fruit of the carob tree, as honeysuckle, and as lollipops or sugar sticks. **333. coloquintida:** colocynth, or bitter apple, a purgative.

thyself, do it a more delicate way than drowning. Make all the money thou canst:
if sanctimony and a frail vow betwixt an erring° barbarian and a super-subtle
Venetian be not too hard for my wits and all the tribe of hell, thou shalt enjoy her;
therefore make money. A pox of drowning thyself! it is clean out of the way: seek
thou rather to be hanged in compassing thy joy than to be drowned and go with-   340
out her.

ROD: Wilt thou be fast to my hopes, if I depend on the issue?

IAGO: Thou art sure of me:—go, make money:—I have told thee often, and I retell thee again and again, I hate the Moor: my cause is hearted°; thine hath no less
reason. Let us be conjunctive° in our revenge against him; if thou canst cuckold   345
him, thou dost thyself a pleasure, me a sport. There are many events in the womb
of time which will be delivered. Traverse!° go, provide thy money. We shall have
more of this to-morrow. Adieu.

ROD: Where shall we meet i' the morning?

IAGO: At my lodging.   350

ROD: I'll be with thee betimes.

IAGO: Go to; farewell. Do you hear, Roderigo?

ROD: What say you?

IAGO: No more of drowning, do you hear?

ROD: I am changed: I'll go sell all my land.   *(Exit.)*   355

IAGO: Thus do I ever make my fool my purse;
For I mine own gain'd knowledge should profane,
If I would time expend with such a snipe,°
But for my sport and profit. I hate the Moor;
And it is thought abroad, that 'twixt my sheets   360
H' as done my office: I know not if 't be true;
But I, for mere suspicion in that kind,
Will do as if for surety. He holds me well;
The better shall my purpose work on him.
Cassio's a proper man: let me see now: 365
To get his place and to plume up° my will
In double knavery—How, how?—Let's see:—
After some time, to abuse Othello's ears
That he° is too familiar with his wife.
He hath a person and a smooth dispose°   370
To be suspected, fram'd to make women false.
The Moor is of a free° and open nature,
That thinks men honest that but seem to be so,
And will as tenderly be led by th' nose
As asses are.   375
I have 't. It is engend'red. Hell and night
Must bring this monstrous birth to the world's light.   *(Exit.)*

---

337. erring: wandering.   **344. hearted:** fixed in the heart.   **345. conjunctive:** united.   **347. Traverse:**
go (military term).   **358. snipe:** gull, fool.   **366. plume up:** glorify, gratify.   **369. he:** i.e., Cassio
370. dispose: external manner.   **372. free:** frank.

ACT II

SCENE I

A Sea-port in Cyprus. An open place near the quay.

(*Enter* MONTANO *and two* GENTLEMEN.)

MON: What from the cape can you discern at sea?

FIRST GENT: Nothing at all: it is a high-wrought flood;
  I cannot, 'twixt the heaven and the main,
  Descry a sail.

MON: Methinks the wind hath spoke aloud at land;   5
  A fuller blast ne'er shook our battlements:
  If it hath ruffian'd° so upon the sea,
  What ribs of oak, what mountains melt on them,
  Can hold the mortise?° What shall we hear of this?

SEC. GENT: A segregation° of the Turkish fleet: 10
  For do but stand upon the foaming shore,
  The chidden billow seems to pelt the clouds:
  The wind-shak'd surge, with high and monstrous mane,
  Seems to cast water on the burning bear,°
  And quench the guards° of th' ever-fixed pole: 15
  I never did like molestation view
  On the enchafed° flood.

MON: If that the Turkish fleet
  Be not enshelter'd and embay'd, they are drown'd;
  It is impossible they bear it out.

(*Enter a third* GENTLEMAN.)

THIRD GENT: News, lads! our wars are done   20
  The desperate tempest hath so bang'd the Turks,
  That their designment° halts: a noble ship of Venice
  Hath seen a grievous wrack and sufferance°
  On most part of their fleet.

MON: How! is this true?

THIRD GENT: The ship is here put in,   25
  A Veronesa; Michael Cassio,
  Lieutenant to the warlike Moor Othello,
  Is come on shore: the Moor himself at sea,
  And is in full commission here for Cyprus.

MON: I am glad on 't; 'tis a worthy governor.   30

II.i. **7. ruffian'd:** raged.   **9. mortise:** the socket hollowed out in fitting timbers.   **10. segregation:** dispersion.   **14. bear:** a constellation.   **15. quench the guards:** overwhelm the stars near the polestar.   **17. enchafed:** angry.   **22. designment:** enterprise.   **23. sufferance:** disaster.

THIRD GENT: But this same Cassio, though he speak of comfort
　　　Touching the Turkish loss, yet he looks sadly,
　　　And prays the Moor be safe; for they were parted
　　　With foul and violent tempest.
MON:　　　　　　　　　　Pray heavens he be;
　　　For I have serv'd him, and the man commands　　　　　　35
　　　Like a full° soldier. Let's to the seaside, ho!
　　　As well to see the vessel that's come in
　　　As to throw out our eyes for brave Othello,
　　　Even till we make the main and th' aerial blue
　　　And indistinct regard.°
THIRD GENT:　　　　　　Come, let's do so;　　　　　　　40
　　　For every minute is expectancy
　　　Of more arrivance.°

　　　　　　(*Enter* CASSIO.)

CAS: Thanks, you the valiant of this warlike isle,
　　　That so approve the Moor! O, let the heavens
　　　Give him defence against the elements,　　　　　　　　45
　　　For I have lost him on a dangerous sea.
MON: Is he well shipp'd?
CAS: His bark is stoutly timber'd, and his pilot
　　　Of very expert and approv'd allowance°;
　　　Therefore my hopes, not surfeited to death,　　　　　　50
　　　Stand in bold cure. (*A cry within.*) "A sail, a sail, a sail!"

　　　　　　(*Enter a fourth* GENTLEMAN.)

CAS: What noise?
FOURTH GENT: The town is empty; on the brow o' th' sea
　　　Stand ranks of people, and they cry "A sail!"
CAS: My hopes do shape him for the governor.　　(*Guns heard.*) 55
SEC. GENT: They do discharge their shot of courtesy:
　　　Our friends at least.
CAS:　　　　　　　　I pray you, sir, go forth,
　　　And give us truth who 'tis that is arriv'd.
SEC. GENT: I shall.　　　　　　　　　　　　　　　(*Exit.*)
MON: But, good lieutenant, is your general wiv'd?　　　　60
CAS: Most fortunately: he hath achiev'd a maid
　　　That paragons° description and wild fame;
　　　One that excels the quirks° of blazoning° pens,

---

36. **full**: perfect.　**39–40. make . . . regard**: cause the blue of the sea and the air to grow indistinguishable in our view.　**42. arrivance**: arrival.　**49. allowance**: reputation.　**62. paragons**: surpasses.
63. quirks: witty conceits.　**63. blazoning**: setting forth honorably in words.

And in th' essential vesture of creation°
Does tire the ingener.°

      (*Enter second* GENTLEMAN.)

            How now! who has put in?   65
SEC. GENT: 'Tis one Iago, ancient to the general.
CAS: Has had most favourable and happy speed:
  Tempests themselves, high seas and howling winds,
  The gutter'd° rocks and congregated sands,—
  Traitors ensteep'd° to clog the guiltless keel,—   70
  As having sense of beauty, do omit
  Their mortal° natures, letting go safely by
  The divine Desdemona.
MON: What is she?
CAS: She that I spake of, our great captain's captain,
  Left in the conduct of the bold Iago,   75
  Whose footing here anticipates our thoughts
  A se'nnight's° speed. Great Jove, Othello guard,
  And swell his sail with thine own powr'ful breath,
  That he may bless this bay with his tall ship,
  Make love's quick pants in Desdemona's arms,   80
  Give renew'd fire to our extincted spirits,
  And bring all Cyprus comfort!

      (*Enter* DESDEMONA, IAGO, RODERIGO, *and* EMILIA *with* ATTENDANTS.)

              O, behold!
  The riches of the ship is come on shore!
  You men of Cyprus, let her have your knees.
  Hail to thee, lady! and the grace of heaven,   85
  Before, behind thee and on every hand,
  Enwheel thou round!
DES: I thank you, valiant Cassio.
  What tidings can you tell me of my lord?
CAS: He is not yet arriv'd: nor know I aught
  But that he's well and will be shortly here.   90
DES: O, but I fear—How lost you company?
CAS: The great contention of the sea and skies
  Parted our fellowship—But, hark! a sail.
  (*Within*) "A sail, a sail!" (*Guns heard.*)
SEC. GENT: They give their greeting to the citadel: 95
  This likewise is a friend.

---

64. vesture of creation: the real qualities with which creation has invested her. **65. ingener:** inventor, praiser. **69. gutter'd:** jagged, trenched. **70. ensteep'd:** lying under water. **72. mortal:** deadly. **77. se'nnight's:** week's.

CAS: See for the news.   (*Exit* GENTLEMAN.)
  Good ancient, you are welcome. (*To* EMILIA) Welcome, mistress:
  Let it not gall your patience, good Iago,
  That I extend my manners; 'tis my breeding
  That gives me this bold show of courtesy. (*Kissing her.*)   100
IAGO: Sir, would she give you so much of her lips
  As of her tongue she oft bestows on me,
  You would have enough.
DES: Alas, she has no speech.
IAGO: In faith, too much;
  I find it still, when I have list to sleep: 105
  Marry, before your ladyship, I grant,
  She puts her tongue a little in her heart,
  And chides with thinking.
EMIL: You have little cause to say so.
IAGO: Come on, come on; you are pictures out of doors,   110
  Bells in your parlours, wild-cats in your kitchens,
  Saints in your injuries, devils being offended,
  Players in your housewifery, and housewives° in your beds.
DES: O, fie upon thee, slanderer!
IAGO: Nay, it is true, or else I am a Turk: 115
  You rise to play and go to bed to work.
EMIL: You shall not write my praise.
IAGO: No, let me not.
DES: What wouldst thou write of me, if thou shouldst praise me?
IAGO: O gentle lady, do not put me to 't;
  For I am nothing, if not critical.°   120
DES: Come on, assay. There's one gone to the harbour?
IAGO: Ay, madam.
DES: I am not merry; but I do beguile
  The thing I am, by seeming otherwise.
  Come, how wouldst thou praise me?   125
IAGO: I am about it; but indeed my invention
  Comes from my pate as birdlime° does from frieze°;
  It plucks out brains and all: but my Muse labours,
  And thus she is deliver'd.
  If she be fair and wise, fairness and wit,   130
  The one's for use, the other useth it.
DES: Well praised! How if she be black and witty?
IAGO: If she be black, and thereto have a wit,
  She'll find a white° that shall her blackness fit.

---

113. housewives: hussies. **120. critical:** censorious. **127. birdlime:** sticky substance smeared on twigs to catch small birds. **127. frieze:** coarse woolen cloth. **134. white:** a fair person, with a word-play on *wight*.

DES: Worse and worse. 135

EMIL: How if fair and foolish?

IAGO: She never yet was foolish that was fair;
For even her folly help'd her to an heir.

DES: These are old fond° paradoxes to make fools laugh i' the alehouse.
What miserable praise hast thou for her that's foul and foolish? 140

IAGO: There's none so foul and foolish thereunto,
But does foul pranks which fair and wise ones do.

DES: O heavy ignorance! thou praisest the worst best. But what praise couldst
thou bestow on a deserving woman indeed, one that, in the authority of her
merit, did justly put on the vouch° of her malice itself? 145

IAGO: She that was ever fair and never proud,
Had tongue at will and yet was never loud,
Never lack'd gold and yet went never gay,
Fled from her wish and yet said "Now I may,"
She that being ang'rd, her revenge being nigh, 150
Bade her wrong stay and her displeasure fly,
She that in wisdom never was so frail
To change the cod's head for the salmon's tail,°
She that could think and ne'er disclose her mind,
See suitors following and not look behind, 155
She was a wight, if ever such wight were,—

DES: To do what?

IAGO: To suckle fools and chronicle small beer.°

DES: O most lame and impotent conclusion! Do not learn of him, Emilia, though
he be thy husband. How say you, Cassio? is he not a most profane and liberal° 160
counsellor?

CAS: He speaks home,° madam: you may relish him more in the soldier than in the
scholar.

IAGO (*Aside*): He takes her by the palm: ay, well said, whisper: with as little a web as
this will I ensnare as great a fly as Cassio. Ay, smile upon her, do; I will gyve° thee 165
in thine own courtship.° You say true; 'tis so, indeed: if such tricks as these strip
you out of your lieutenantry, it had been better you had not kissed your three fin-
gers° so oft, which now again you are most apt to play the sir° in. Very good; well
kissed! an excellent courtesy! 'tis so, indeed. Yet again your fingers to your lips?
would they were clyster-pipes° for your sake. (*Trumpet within.*) The Moor! I 170
know his trumpet.

CAS: 'Tis truly so.

DES: Let's meet him and receive him.

CAS: Lo, where he comes!

---

139. fond: foolish.   **145. put on the vouch:** compel the approval.   **153. To change . . . tail:** to exchange
a delicacy for mere refuse.   **158. chronicle small beer:** keep petty household accounts.   **160. liberal:**
licentious.   **162. speaks home:** i.e., without reserve.   **165. gyve:** fetter, shackle.   **166. courtship:** courtesy.   **167–168. kissed your three fingers:** he kisses his own hand as a token of reverence.   **168. the sir:**
i.e., the fine gentleman.   **170. clyster-pipes:** tubes used for enemas.

(*Enter* OTHELLO *and* ATTENDANTS.)

OTH: O my fair warrior!
DES: My dear Othello!   175
OTH: It gives me wonder great as my content
     To see you here before me. O my soul's joy!
     If after every tempest come such calms,
     May the winds blow till they have waken'd death!
     And let the labouring bark climb hills of seas   180
     Olympus-high and duck again as low
     As hell 's from heaven! If it were now to die,
     'Twere now to be most happy; for, I fear,
     My soul hath her content so absolute
     That not another comfort like to this   185
     Succeeds in unknown fate.
DES: The heavens forbid
     But that our loves and comforts should increase,
     Even as our days grow!
OTH: Amen to that, sweet powers!
     I cannot speak enough of this content;
     It stops me here; it is too much of joy;   190
     And this, and this, the greatest discords be (*Kissing her*)
     That e'er our hearts shall make!
IAGO (*Aside*):   O, you are well tun'd now!
     But I'll set down the pegs° that make this music,
     As honest as I am.
OTH: Come, let us to the castle.
     News, friends, our wars are done, the Turks are drowned.   195
     How does my old acquaintance of this isle?
     Honey, you shall be well desir'd in Cyprus;
     I have found greatest love amongst them. O my sweet,
     I prattle out of fashion, and I dote
     In mine own comforts. I prithee, good Iago,   200
     Go to the bay and disembark my coffers:
     Bring thou the master to the citadel;
     He is a good one, and his worthiness
     Does challenge much respect. Come, Desdemona,
     Once more, well met at Cyprus.   205
          (*Exeunt* OTHELLO *and* DESDEMONA *and all but* IAGO *and* RODERIGO.)
IAGO (*to an* ATTENDANT):   Do thou meet me presently at the harbour. (*To* ROD.)
     Come hither. If thou be'st valiant,—as, they say, base men being in love have
     then a nobility in their natures more than is native to them,—list me. The lieu-
     tenant tonight watches on the court of guard.°—First, I must tell thee this—
     Desdemona is directly in love with him.   210

193. set down the pegs: lower the pitch of the strings, i.e., disturb the harmony.   **209. court of guard:**
guardhouse.

Rod: With him! why 'tis not possible.

Iago: Lay thy finger thus, and let thy soul be instructed. Mark me with what violence she first loved the Moor, but for bragging and telling her fantastical lies: and will she love him still for prating? let not thy discreet heart think it. Her eye must be fed; and what delight shall she have to look on the devil? When the blood   215
is made dull with the act of sport, there should be, again to inflame it and to give satiety a fresh appetite, loveliness in favour, sympathy in years, manners and beauties; all which the Moor is defective in: now, for want of these required conveniences, her delicate tenderness will find itself abused, begin to heave the gorge, disrelish and abhor the Moor; very nature will instruct her in it and compel   220
her to some second choice. Now, sir, this granted,—as it is a most pregnant and unforced position—who stands so eminent in the degree of this fortune as Cassio does? a knave very voluble; no further conscionable° than in putting on the mere form of civil and humane seeming, for the better compassing of his salt° and most hidden loose affection? why, none; why, none: a slipper° and subtle   225
knave, a finder of occasions, that has an eye can stamp and counterfeit advantages, though true advantage never present itself; a devilish knave. Besides, the knave is handsome, young, and hath all those requisites in him that folly and green minds look after: a pestilent complete knave; and the woman hath found him already.   230

Rod: I cannot believe that in her; she's full of most blessed condition.

Iago: Blessed fig's-end! the wine she drinks is made of grapes: if she had been blessed, she would never have loved the Moor. Blessed pudding! Didst thou not see her paddle with the palm of his hand? didst not mark that?

Rod: Yes, that I did; but that was but courtesy.   235

Iago: Lechery, by this hand; an index and obscure prologue to the history of lust and foul thoughts. They met so near with their lips that their breaths embraced together. Villainous thoughts, Roderigo! when these mutualities so marshall the way, hard at hand comes the master and main exercise, the incorporate conclusion. Pish! But, sir, be you ruled by me: I have brought you from Venice. Watch   240
you to-night; for the command, I'll lay't upon you. Cassio knows you not. I'll not be far from you: do you find some occasion to anger Cassio, either by speaking too loud, or tainting° his discipline; or from what other course you please, which the time shall more favourably minister.

Rod: Well.   245

Iago: Sir, he is rash and very sudden in choler, and haply may strike at you: provoke him, that he may; for even out of that will I cause these of Cyprus to mutiny; whose qualification° shall come into no true taste again but by the displanting of Cassio. So shall you have a shorter journey to your desires by the means I shall then have to prefer them; and the impediment most profitably removed, without   250
the which there were no expectation of our prosperity.

---

223. conscionable: conscientious.   **224. salt:** licentious.   **225. slipper:** slippery.   **243. tainting:** disparaging.   **248. qualification:** appeasement.

ROD: I will do this if I can bring it to any opportunity.

IAGO: I warrant thee. Meet me by and by° at the citadel: I must fetch his necessaries ashore. Farewell.

ROD: Adieu.   (*Exit.*) 255

IAGO: That Cassio loves her, I do well believe 't;
That she loves him, 'tis apt° and of great credit°:
The Moor, howbeit that I endure him not,
Is of a constant, loving, noble nature,
And I dare think he'll prove to Desdemona   260
A most dear husband. Now I do love her too;
Not out of absolute lust, though peradventure
I stand accountant for as great a sin,
But partly led to diet my revenge,
For that I do suspect the lusty Moor   265
Hath leap'd into my seat; the thought whereof
Doth, like a poisonous mineral, gnaw my inwards;
And nothing can or shall content my soul
Till I am even'd with him, wife for wife,
Or failing so, yet that I put the Moor   270
At least into a jealousy so strong
That judgement cannot cure. Which thing to do,
If this poor trash° of Venice, whom I trash°
For his quick hunting, stand the putting on,°
I'll have Michael Cassio on the hip,°   275
Abuse him to the Moor in the rank garb—
For I fear Cassio with my night-cap too—
Make the Moor thank me, love me and reward me,
For making him egregiously an ass
And practicing upon his peace and quiet   280
Even to madness. 'Tis here, but yet confus'd:
Knavery's plain face is never seen till us'd.   (*Exit.*)

SCENE II

A street.

(*Enter* OTHELLO'S HERALD *with a proclamation.*)

HER: It is Othello's pleasure, our noble and valiant general, that, upon certain tidings now arrived, importing the mere perdition° of the Turkish fleet, every man
put himself into triumph; some to dance, some to make bonfires, each man to
what sport and revels his addiction leads him: for, besides these beneficial news, it

---

253. **by and by:** immediately.   257. **apt:** probable.   257. **credit:** credibility.   273. **trash:** worthless
thing (Roderigo).   273. **trash:** hold in check.   274. **putting on:** incitement to quarrel.   275. **on the
hip:** at my mercy (wrestling term).   **II.ii. 2. mere perdition:** complete destruction.

is the celebration of his nuptial. So much was his pleasure should be proclaimed. 5
All offices° are open, and there is full liberty of feasting from this present hour of
five till the bell have told eleven. Heaven bless the isle of Cyprus and our general
Othello! (*Exit.*)

SCENE III

A hall in the castle.

(*Enter* OTHELLO, DESDEMONA, CASSIO, *and* ATTENDANTS.)

OTH: Good Michael, look you to the guard to-night:
Let's teach ourselves that honourable stop,°
Not to outsport discretion.
CAS: Iago hath direction what to do;
But, notwithstanding, with my personal eye 5
Will I look to 't.
OTH: Iago is most honest.
Michael, goodnight: to-morrow with your earliest
Let me have speech with you. (*To* DESDEMONA) Come, my dear love,
The purchase made, the fruits to ensue;
That profit's yet to come 'tween me and you. 10
Good night. (*Exit* OTHELLO, *with* DESDEMONA *and* ATTENDANTS.]

(*Enter* IAGO.)

CAS: Welcome, Iago; we must to the watch.
IAGO: Not this hour, lieutenant; 'tis not yet ten o' the clock. Our general cast° us
thus early for the love of his Desdemona; who let us not therefore blame: he hath
not yet made wanton the night with her; and she is sport for Jove. 15
CAS: She's a most exquisite lady.
IAGO: And, I'll warrant her, full of game.
CAS: Indeed, she's a most fresh and delicate creature.
IAGO: What an eye she has! methinks it sounds a parley of provocation.
CAS: An inviting eye; and yet methinks right modest. 20
IAGO: And when she speaks, is it not an alarum to love?
CAS: She is indeed perfection.
IAGO: Well, happiness to their sheets! Come, lieutenant, I have a stoup° of wine;
and here without are a brace of Cyprus gallants that would fain have a measure to
the health of black Othello. 25
CAS: Not to-night, good Iago: I have very poor and unhappy brains for drinking: I
could well wish courtesy would invent some other custom of entertainment.
IAGO: O, they are our friends; but one cup: I'll drink for you.

---

6. offices: rooms where food and drink were kept. **II.iii. 2. stop:** restraint. **13. cast:** dismissed.
23. stoup: measure of liquor, two quarts.

CAS: I have drunk but one cup to-night, and that was craftily qualified° too, and,
behold, what innovation° it makes here°: I am unfortunate in the infirmity, and   30
dare not task my weakness with any more.

IAGO: What, man! 'tis a night of revels: the gallants desire it.

CAS: Where are they?

IAGO: Here at the door; I pray you, call them in.

CAS: I'll do 't; but it dislikes me.   (*Exit.*)   35

IAGO: If I can fasten but one cup upon him,
With that which he hath drunk to-night already,
He'll be as full of quarrel and offence
As my young mistress' dog. Now, my sick fool Roderigo,
Whom love hath turn'd almost the wrong side out,   40
To Desdemona hath to-night carous'd
Potations pottle-deep°; and he's to watch:
Three lads of Cyprus, noble swelling spirits,
That hold their honours in a wary distance,°
The very elements° of this warlike isle,   45
Have I to-night fluster'd with flowing cups,
And they watch° too. Now, 'mongst this flock of drunkards,
Am I to put our Cassio in some action
That may offend the isle.—But here they come:

(*Enter* CASSIO, MONTANO, *and* GENTLEMEN; SERVANTS *following with wine.*)

If consequence do but approve° my dream,   50
My boat sails freely, both with wind and stream.

CAS: 'Fore God, they have given me a rouse° already.

MON: Good faith, a little one; not past a pint, as I am a soldier.

IAGO: Some wine, ho!
(*Sings*) And let me the canakin° clink, clink;   55
      And let me the canakin clink:
      A soldier's a man;
      A life's but a span;
      Why, then, let a soldier drink.

Some wine, boys!   60

CAS: 'Fore God, an excellent song.

IAGO: I learned it in England, where, indeed, they are most potent in potting: your
Dane, your German, and your swag-bellied Hollander—Drink, ho!—are nothing to your English.

CAS: Is your Englishman so expert in his drinking?   65

29. qualified: diluted.   **30. innovation:** disturbance.   **30. here:** i.e., in Cassio's head.   **42. pottle-
deep:** to the bottom of the tankard.   **44. hold . . . distance:** i.e., are extremely sensitive of their honor.
45. very elements: true representatives.   **47. watch:** are members of the guard.   **50. approve:** confirm.   **52. rouse:** full draft of liquor.   **55. canakin:** small drinking vessel.

IAGO: Why, he drinks you, with facility, your Dane dead drunk; he sweats not to overthrow your Almain°; he gives your Hollander a vomit, ere the next pottle can be filled.

CAS: To the health of our general!

MON: I am for it, lieutenant; and I'll do you justice.° 70

IAGO: O sweet England! (*Sings.*)
    King Stephen was a worthy peer,
        His breeches cost him but a crown;
    He held them sixpence all too dear,
        With that he call'd the tailor lown.° 75
    He was a wight of high renown,
        And thou art but of low degree:
    'Tis pride that pulls the country down;
        Then take thine auld cloak about thee.
    Some wine, ho! 80

CAS: Why, this is a more exquisite song than the other.

IAGO: Will you hear't again?

CAS: No; for I hold him to be unworthy of his place that does those things. Well, God's above all; and there be souls must be saved, and there be souls must not be saved. 85

IAGO: It's true, good lieutenant.

CAS: For mine own part,—no offence to the general, nor any man of quality,—I hope to be saved.

IAGO: And so do I too, lieutenant.

CAS: Ay, but, by your leave, not before me; the lieutenant is to be saved before the 90 ancient. Let's have no more of this; let 's to our affairs.—God forgive us our sins!—Gentlemen, let's look to our business. Do not think, gentlemen, I am drunk: this is my ancient; this is my right hand, and this is my left: I am not drunk now; I can stand well enough, and speak well enough.

ALL: Excellent well. 95

CAS: Why, very well then; you must not think then that I am drunk.   (*Exit.*)

MON: To th' platform, masters; come, let's set the watch.

IAGO: You see this fellow that is gone before;
    He's soldier fit to stand by Caesar
    And give direction: and do but see his vice; 100
    'Tis to his virtue a just equinox,°
    The one as long as th' other: 'tis pity of him.
    I fear the trust Othello puts him in,
    On some odd time of his infirmity,
    Will shake this island.

MON: But is he often thus? 105

IAGO: 'Tis evermore the prologue to his sleep:

---

67. Almain: German. **70. I'll . . . justice:** i.e., drink as much as you. **75. lown:** lout, loon.
101. equinox: equal length of days and nights; used figuratively to mean "counterpart."

He'll watch the horologe° a double set,°
If drink rock not his cradle.
MON: It were well
The general were put in mind of it.
Perhaps he sees it not; or his good nature   110
Prizes the virtue that appears in Cassio,
And looks not on his evils: is not this true?

   (*Enter* RODERIGO.)

IAGO (*Aside to him*):   How now, Roderigo!
I pray you, after the lieutenant; go.   (*Exit* RODERIGO.)
MON: And 'tis great pity that the noble Moor   115
Should hazard such a place as his own second
With one of an ingraft° infirmity:
It were an honest action to say
So to the Moor.
IAGO: Not I, for this fair island:
I do love Cassio well; and would do much   120
To cure him of this evil—But, hark! what noise? (*Cry within:* "Help! help!")

   (*Enter* CASSIO, *pursuing* RODERIGO.)

CAS: 'Zounds, you rogue! you rascal!
MON: What's the matter, lieutenant?
CAS: A knave teach me my duty!
I'll beat the knave into a twiggen° bottle.
ROD: Beat me!
CAS: Dost thou prate, rogue? (*Striking* RODERIGO.)
MON: Nay, good lieutenant; (*Staying him.*)   125
I pray you, sir, hold your hand.
CAS: Let me go, sir,
Or I'll knock you o'er the mazzard.°
MON: Come, come, you're drunk.
CAS: Drunk! (*They fight.*)
IAGO (*aside to* RODERIGO):   Away, I say; go out, and cry a mutiny.

   (*Exit* RODERIGO.)
                                        130
Nay, good lieutenant,—God's will, gentlemen;—
Help, ho!—Lieutenant,—sir,—Montano,—sir,—
Help, masters!—Here's a goodly watch indeed! (*Bell rings.*)
Who's that which rings the bell?—Diablo,° ho!
The town will rise°: God's will, lieutenant, hold!
You'll be asham'd for ever.

107. horologe: clock.   **107. double set:** twice around.   **117. ingraft:** ingrafted, inveterate.
124. twiggen: covered with woven twigs.   **127. mazzard:** head.   **133. Diablo:** the devil.   **134. rise:**
grow riotous.

(*Enter* OTHELLO *and* ATTENDANTS.)

OTH: What is the matter here?   135

MON: 'Zounds, I bleed still; I am hurt to th' death.
He dies! (*Thrusts at* CASSIO.)

OTH: Hold, for your lives!

IAGO: Hold, ho! Lieutenant,—sir,—Montano,—gentlemen,—
Have your forgot all sense of place and duty?   140
Hold! the general speaks to you; hold, for shame!

OTH: Why, how now, ho! from whence ariseth this?
Are we turn'd Turks° and to ourselves do that
Which heaven hath forbid the Ottomites?
For Christian shame, put by this barbarous brawl: 145
He that stirs next to carve for° his own rage
Holds his soul light; he dies upon his motion.
Silence that dreadful bell: it frights the isle
From her propriety.° What is the matter, masters?
Honest Iago, that looks dead with grieving,   150
Speak, who began this? on thy love, I charge thee.

IAGO: I do not know: friends all but now, even now,
In quarter,° and in terms like bride and groom
Devesting them for bed; and then, but now—
As if some planet had unwitted men—   155
Swords out, and tilting one at other's breast,
In opposition bloody. I cannot speak
Any beginning to this peevish odds°;
And would in action glorious I had lost
Those legs that brought me to a part of it!   160

OTH: How comes it, Michael, you are thus forgot?

CAS: I pray you, pardon me; I cannot speak.

OTH: Worthy Montano, you were wont to be civil;
The gravity and stillness of your youth
The world hath noted, and your name is great   165
In mouths of wisest censure°: what's the matter,
That you unlace° your reputation thus
And spend your rich opinion for the name
Of a night-brawler? give me answer to it.

MON: Worthy Othello, I am hurt to danger: 170
Your officer, Iago, can inform you,—
While I spare speech, which something now offends me,—
Of all that I do know: nor know I aught

---

143. turn'd Turks: changed completely for the worse; proverbial. **146. carve for:** indulge.
149. propriety: proper state or condition. **153. In quarter:** on terms. **158. peevish odds:** childish
quarrel. **166. censure:** judgment. **167. unlace:** degrade.

By me that's said or done amiss this night;
Unless self-charity be sometimes a vice, 175
And to defend ourselves it be a sin
When violence assails us.

OTH: Now, by heaven,
My blood begins my safer guides to rule;
And passion, having my best judgement collied,°
Assays to lead the way: if I once stir, 180
Or do but lift this arm, the best of you
Shall sink in my rebuke. Give me to know
How this foul rout began, who set it on;
And he that is approv'd in° this offence,
Though he had twinn'd with me, both at birth, 185
Shall lose me. What! in a town of war,
Yet wild, the people's hearts brimful of fear,
To manage private and domestic quarrel,
In night, and on the court and guard° of safety!
'Tis monstrous. Iago, who began 't? 190

MON: If partially affin'd,° or leagu'd in office,
Thou dost deliver more or less than truth,
Thou art no soldier.

IAGO: Touch me not so near:
I had rather have this tongue cut from my mouth
Than it should do offence to Michael Cassio; 195
Yet, I persuade myself, to speak the truth,
Shall nothing wrong him. Thus it is, general.
Montano and myself being in speech,
There comes a fellow crying out for help;
And Cassio following him with determin'd sword, 200
To execute° upon him. Sir, this gentleman
Steps in to Cassio, and entreats his pause;
Myself the crying fellow did pursue,
Lest by his clamour—as it so fell out—
The town might fall in fright: he, swift of foot, 205
Outran my purpose; and I return'd the rather
For that I heard the clink and fall of swords,
And Cassio high in oath; which till to-night
I ne'er might say before. When I came back—
For this was brief—I found them close together, 210
At blow and thrust; even as again they were
When you yourself did part them.
More of this matter cannot I report:

179. **collied:** darkened.   184. **approv'd in:** found guilty of.   189. **court and guard:** spot and guarding place, i.e., the main guardhouse.   191. **affin'd:** bound by a tie.   201. **execute:** give effect to (his anger).

But men are men; the best sometimes forget:
Though Cassio did some little wrong to him, 215
As men in rage strike those that wish them best,
Yet surely, Cassio, I believe, receive'd
From him that fled some strange indignity,
Which patience could not pass.

OTH: I know, Iago,
Thy honesty and love doth mince this matter, 220
Making it light to Cassio. Cassio, I love thee;
But never more be officer of mine.

          (*Enter* DESDEMONA, *attended.*)

Look, if my gentle love be not rais'd up!
I'll make thee an example.

DES: What's the matter?

OTH: All's well now, sweeting; come away to bed. 225
Sir, for your hurts, myself will be your surgeon:
Lead him off. (*To* MONTANO, *who is led off.*)
Iago, look with care about the town,
And silence those whom this vile brawl distracted.
Come, Desdemona: 'tis the soldier's life 230
To have their balmy slumbers wak'd with strife.

         (*Exit with all but* IAGO *and* CASSIO.)

IAGO: What, are you hurt, lieutenant?

CAS: Ay, past all surgery.

IAGO: Marry, God forbid!

CAS: Reputation, reputation, reputation! O, I have lost my reputation! I have lost 235
the immortal part of myself, and what remains is bestial. My reputation, Iago, my
reputation!

IAGO: As I am an honest man, I thought you had received some bodily wound;
there is more sense in that than in reputation. Reputation is an idle and most false
imposition; oft got without merit, and lost without deserving: you have lost no 240
reputation at all, unless you repute yourself such a loser. What, man! there are
ways to recover the general again: you are but now cast in his mood, a punishment more in policy than in malice; even so as one would beat his offenceless dog
to affright an imperious lion: sue to him again, and he 's yours.

CAS: I will rather sue to be despised than to deceive so good a commander with so 245
slight, so drunken, and so indiscreet an officer. Drunk? and speak parrot?° and
squabble? swagger? swear? and discourse fustian° with one's own shadow? O
thou invisible spirit of wine, if thou has no name to be known by, let us call thee
devil!

IAGO: What was he that you followed with your sword? What had he done to you? 250

CAS: I know not.

---

246. speak parrot: talk nonsense.   **247. discourse fustian:** talk nonsense.

IAGO: Is't possible?

CAS: I remember a mass of things, but nothing distinctly; a quarrel, but nothing wherefore. O God, that men should put an enemy in their mouths to steal away their brains! that we should, with joy, pleasance, revel and applause, transform ourselves into beasts! 255

IAGO: Why, but you are now well enough: how came you thus recovered?

CAS: It hath pleased the devil drunkenness to give place to the devil wrath: one unperfectness° shows me another, to make me frankly despise myself.

IAGO: Come, you are too severe a moraler: as the time, the place, and the condi- 260 tion of this country stands, I could heartily wish this had not befallen; but, since it is as it is, mend it for your own good.

CAS: I will ask him for my place again; he shall tell me I am a drunkard! Had I as many mouths as Hydra,° such an answer would stop them all. To be now a sen- sible man, by and by a fool, and presently a beast! O strange! Every inordinate 265 cup is unblessed and the ingredient is a devil.

IAGO: Come, come, good wine is a good familiar creature, if it be well used: exclaim no more against it. And, good lieutenant, I think you think I love you.

CAS: I have well approved° it, sir. I drunk!

IAGO: You or any man living may be a drunk at a time, man. I'll tell you what you 270 shall do. Our general's wife is now the general: I may say so in this respect, for that he hath devoted and given up himself to the contemplation, mark, and denotement° of her parts and graces: confess yourself freely to her; importune her help to put you in your place again: she is of so free, so kind, so apt, so blessed a dispositon, she holds it a vice in her goodness not to do more than she is 275 requested: this broken joint between you and her husband entreat her to splin- ter°; and, my fortunes against any lay° worth naming, this crack of your love shall grow stronger than it was before.

CAS: You advise me well.

IAGO: I protest, in the sincerity of love and honest kindness. 280

CAS: I think it freely; and betimes in the morning I will beseech the virtuous Des- demona to undertake for me: I am desperate of my fortunes if they check° me here.

IAGO: You are in the right. Good night, lieutenant; I must to the watch.

CAS: Good night, honest Iago.   (*Exit* CASSIO.) 285

IAGO: And what 's he then that says I play the villain?
    When this advice is free I give and honest,
    Probal° to thinking and indeed the course
    To win the Moor again? For 'tis most easy
    Th' inclining° Desdemona to subdue° 290
    In any honest suit: she 's fram'd as fruitful

---

259. unperfectness: imperfection.   **264. Hydra:** a monster with many heads, slain by Hercules as the second of his twelve labors.   **269. approved:** proved.   **273. denotement:** observation.   **277. splin- ter:** bind with splints.   **277. lay:** stake, wager.   **282. check:** repulse.   **288. Probal:** probable. **290. inclining:** favorably disposed.   **290. subdue:** persuade.

As the free elements. And then for her
To win the Moor—were 't to renounce his baptism,
All seals and symbols of redeemed sin,
His soul is so enfetter'd to her love,   295
That she may make, unmake, do what she list,
Even as her appetite shall play the god
With his weak function. How am I then a villain
To counsel Cassio to this parallel° course,
Directly to his good? Divinity of hell!   300
When devils will the blackest sins put on,°
They do suggest° at first with heavenly shows,
As I do now; for whiles this honest fool
Plies Desdemona to repair his fortunes
And she for him pleads strongly to the Moor,   305
I'll pour this pestilence into his ear,
That she repeals him° for her body's lust;
And by how much she strives to do him good,
She shall under her credit with the Moor,
So will I turn her virtue into pitch,   310
And out of her own goodness make the net
That shall enmesh them all.

               (*Enter* RODERIGO.)

               How now, Roderigo!

ROD: I do not follow here in the chase, not like a hound that hunts, but one that fills
up the cry.° My money is almost spent; I have been tonight exceedingly well
cudgelléd; and I think the issue will be, I shall have so much experience for my   315
pains, and so, with no money at all and a little more wit, return again to Venice.

IAGO: How poor are they that have not patience!
What wound did ever heal but by degrees?
Thou know'st we work by wit, and not by witchcraft;   320
And wit depends on dilatory time.
Does 't not go well? Cassio hath beaten thee,
And thou, by that small hurt, hast cashier'd° Cassio:
Though other things grow fair against the sun,
Yet fruits that blossom first will first be ripe: 325
Content thyself awhile. By th' mass, 'tis morning;
Pleasure and action make the hours seem short.
Retire thee; go where thou art billeted:
Away, I say; thou shalt know more hereafter:
Nay, get thee gone.   (*Exit* RODERIGO.)

---

299. parallel: probably, corresponding to his best interest.   **301. put on:** further.   **302. suggest:**
tempt.   **307. repeals him:** i.e., attempts to get him restored.   **314. cry:** pack.   **323. cashier'd:** dismissed from service.

Two things are to be done: 330
My wife must move for Cassio to her mistress;
I'll set her on;
Myself the while to draw the Moor apart,
And bring him jump° when he may Cassio find
Soliciting his wife: ay, that's the way: 335
Dull not device by coldness and delay.   (*Exit.*)

ACT III

Scene I

Before the castle.

(*Enter* Cassio *and* Musicians.)

Cas: Masters, play here; I will content° your pains;
        Something that's brief; and bid "Good morrow, general." (*They play.*)

(*Enter* Clown.)

Clo: Why, masters, have your instruments been in Naples, that they speak i' the
        nose° thus?

First Mus: How, sir, how!   5

Clo: Are these, I pray you, wind-instruments?

First Mus: Ay, marry, are they, sir.

Clo: O, thereby hangs a tail.

First Mus: Whereby hangs a tale,° sir?

Clo: Marry, sir, by many a wind-instrument that I know. But, masters, here's   10
        money for you: and the general so likes your music, that he desires you, for love's
        sake, to make no more noise with it.

First Mus: Well, sir, we will not.

Clo: If you have any music that may not be heard, to 't again: but, as they say, to
        hear music the general does not greatly care.   15

First Mus: We have none such, sir.

Clo: Then put up your pipes in your bag, for I'll away: go; vanish into air;
        away!   (*Exeunt* Musicians.)

Cas: Dost thou hear, my honest friend?

Clo: No, I hear not your honest friend; I hear you.   20

Cas: Prithee, keep up thy quillets. There's a poor piece of gold for thee: if the gen-
        tlewoman that attends the general's wife be stirring, tell her there's one Cassio
        entreats her a little favour of speech: wilt thou do this?

Clo: She is stirring, sir: if she will stir hither, I shall seem to notify unto her.

Cas: Do, good my friend.   (*Exit* Clown.)

---

334. jump: precisely.   **III.i. 1. content:** reward.   **3–4. speak i' the nose:** i.e., like Neapolitans, who
spoke a nasal dialect (with a joke on syphilis, which attacks the nose).   **9. tale:** pun on *tail*, a wind instrument of sorts.

(*Enter* IAGO.)

In happy time, Iago. 25

IAGO: You have not been a-bed, then?

CAS: Why, no; the day had broke
Before we parted. I have made bold, Iago,
To send in to your wife: my suit to her
Is, that she will to virtuous Desdemona 30
Procure me some access.

IAGO: I'll send her to you presently;
And I'll devise a means to draw the Moor
Out of the way, that your converse and business
May be more free.

CAS: I humbly thank you for 't. (*Exit* IAGO.)
I never knew 35
A Florentine more kind and honest.

(*Enter* EMILIA.)

EMIL: Good morrow, good lieutenant: I am sorry
For your displeasure; but all will sure be well.
The general and his wife are talking of it;
And she speaks for you stoutly: the Moor replies, 40
That he you hurt is of great fame in Cyprus
And great affinity° and that in wholesome wisdom
He might not but refuse you, but he protests he loves you
And needs no other suitor but his likings
To take the safest occasion by the front° 45
To bring you in again.

CAS: Yet, I beseech you,
If you think fit, or that it may be done,
Give me advantage of some brief discourse
With Desdemona alone.

EMIL: Pray you, come in:
I will bestow you where you shall have time 50
To speak your bosom freely.

CAS: I am much bound to you. (*Exeunt.*)

SCENE II

A room in the castle.

(*Enter* OTHELLO, IAGO, *and* GENTLEMEN.)

OTH: These letters give, Iago, to the pilot;
And by him do my duties to the senate:

---

42. affinity: kindred, family connection.   **45. by the front:** i.e., by the forelock.

That done, I will be walking on the works°:
Repair there to me.

IAGO: Well, my good lord, I'll do 't.

OTH: This fortification, gentlemen, shall we see't?   5

GENT: We'll wait upon your lordship.   (*Exeunt.*)

SCENE III

The garden of the castle.

(*Enter* DESDEMONA, CASSIO, *and* EMILIA.)

DES: Be thou assur'd, good Cassio, I will do
All my abilities in thy behalf.

EMIL: Good madam, do: I warrant it grieves my husband,
As if the case were his.

DES: O, that 's an honest fellow. Do not doubt, Cassio,   5
But I will have my lord and you again
As friendly as you were.

CAS: Bounteous madam,
Whatever shall become of Michael Cassio,
He's never any thing but your true servant.

DES: I know't; I thank you. You do love my lord: 10
You have known him long; and be you well assur'd
He shall in strangeness° stand no farther off
Than in a politic distance.

CAS: Ay, but lady,
That policy may either last so long
Or feed upon such nice and waterish diet,
Or breed itself so out of circumstance,°   15
That, I being absent and my place supplied,
My general will forget my love and service.

DES: Do not doubt° that; before Emilia here
I give thee warrant of thy place: assure thee,   20
If I do vow a friendship, I'll perform it
To the last article: my lord shall never rest;
I'll watch him tame° and talk him out of patience;
His bed shall seem a school, his board a shrift°;
I'll intermingle every thing he does   25
With Cassio's suit: therefore be merry, Cassio;
For thy solicitor shall rather die
Than give thy cause away.°

III.ii. 3. works: earthworks, fortifications.   **III.iii. 12. strangeness:** distant behavior.   **16. breed . . .
circumstance:** increase itself so on account of accidents.   **19. doubt:** fear.   **23. watch him tame:** tame
him by keeping him from sleeping (a term from falconry).   **24. shrift:** confessional.   **28. away:** up.

(*Enter* Othello *and* Iago *at a distance*.)

EMIL: Madam, here comes my lord.

CAS: Madam, I'll take my leave.

DES: Why, stay, and hear me speak. 30

CAS: Madam, not now: I am very ill at ease,
Unfit for mine own purposes.

DES: Well, do your discretion. (*Exit* Cassio.)

IAGO: Ha! I like not that.

OTH: What dost thou say? 35

IAGO: Nothing, my lord: or if—I know not what.

OTH: Was not that Cassio parted from my wife?

IAGO: Cassio, my lord! No, sure, I cannot think it,
That he would steal away so guilty-like,
Seeing you coming.

OTH: I do believe 'twas he. 40

DES: How now, my lord!
I have been talking with a suitor here,
A man that languishes in your displeasure.

OTH: Who is 't you mean?

DES: Why, your lieutenant, Cassio. Good my lord, 45
If I have any grace or power to move you,
His present reconciliation take;
For if he be not one that truly loves you,
That errs in ignorance and not in cunning,
I have no judgement in an honest face: 50
I prithee, call him back.

OTH: Went he hence now?

DES: Ay, sooth; so humbled
That he hath left part of his grief with me,
To suffer with him. Good love, call him back.

OTH: Not now, sweet Desdemona; some other time. 55

DES: But shall 't be shortly?

OTH: The sooner, sweet, for you.

DES: Shall 't be to-night at supper?

OTH: No, not to-night.

DES: To-morrow dinner, then?

OTH: I shall not dine at home;
I meet the captains at the citadel.

DES: Why, then, to-morrow night; or Tuesday morn; 60
On Tuesday noon, or night; on Wednesday morn:
I prithee, name the time, but let it not
Exceed three days: in faith, he's penitent;
And yet his trespass, in our common reason°—

---

64. common reason: everyday judgments.

Save that, they say, the wars must make examples   65
Out of their best—is not almost a fault
T' incur a private check. When shall he come?
Tell me, Othello: I wonder in my soul,
What you would ask me, that I should deny,
Or stand so mamm'ring on.° What! Michael Cassio,   70
That came a-wooing with you, and so many a time,
When I have spoke of you dispraisingly,
Hath ta'en your part; to have so much to do
To bring him in! Trust me, I could do much,—

OTH: Prithee, no more: let him come when he will;   75
I will deny thee nothing.

DES: Why, this is not a boon;
'Tis as I should entreat you wear your gloves,
Or feed on nourishing dishes, or keep you warm,
Or sue to you to do a peculiar profit
To your own person: nay, when I have a suit   80
Wherein I mean to touch your love indeed,
It shall be full of poise° and difficult weight
And fearful to be granted.

OTH: I will deny thee nothing:
Whereon, I do beseech thee, grant me this,
To leave me but a little to myself.   85

DES: Shall I deny you? no: farewell, my lord.

OTH: Farewell, my Desdemona: I'll come to thee straight.

DES: Emilia, come. Be as your fancies teach you;
Whate'er you be, I am obedient.

                                        (*Exit with* EMILIA.)

OTH: Excellent wretch!° Perdition catch my soul,   90
But I do love thee! and when I love thee not,
Chaos is come again.

IAGO: My noble lord,—

OTH: What dost thou say, Iago?

IAGO: Did Michael Cassio, when you woo'd my lady,
Know of your love?   95

OTH: He did, from first to last: why dost thou ask?

IAGO: But for a satisfaction of my thought;
No further harm.

OTH: Why of thy thought, Iago?

IAGO: I did not think he had been acquainted with her.

OTH: O, yes; and went between us very oft.   100

IAGO: Indeed!

OTH: Indeed! ay, indeed: discern'st thou aught in that?
Is he not honest?

---

70. mamm'ring on: wavering.   **82. poise:** weight, heaviness.   **90. wretch:** term of affectionate endearment with a connotation of pity.

IAGO: Honest, my lord!

OTH: Honest! ay, honest.

IAGO: My lord, for aught I know.

OTH: What dost thou think?

IAGO: Think, my lord!

OTH: Think, my lord!   105
By heaven, he echoes me,
As if there were some monster in his thought
Too hideous to be shown. Thou dost mean something:
I heard thee say even now, thou lik'st not that,
When Cassio left my wife: what didst not like?   110
And when I told thee he was of my counsel
In my whole course of wooing, thou criedst "Indeed!"
And didst contract and purse thy brow together,
As if thou then hadst shut up in thy brain
Some horrible conceit: if thou dost love me,   115
Show me thy thought.

IAGO: My lord, you know I love you.

OTH: I think thou dost;
And, for I know thou 'rt full of love and honesty,
And weigh'st thy words before thou giv'st them breath,
Therefore these stops of thine fright me more: 120
For such things in a false disloyal knave
Are tricks of custom, but in a man that's just
They 're close delations,° working from the heart
That passion cannot rule.

IAGO: For Michael Cassio,
I dare be sworn I think that he is honest.   125

OTH: I think so too.

IAGO: Men should be what they seem;
Or those that be not, would they might seem none!

OTH: Certain, men should be what they seem.

IAGO: Why, then, I think Cassio 's an honest man.

OTH: Nay, yet there 's more in this: 130
I prithee, speak to me as to thy thinkings,
As thou dost ruminate, and give thy worst of thoughts
The worst of words.

IAGO: Good my lord, pardon me:
Though I am bound to every act of duty,
I am not bound to that all slaves are free to.   135
Utter my thoughts? Why, say they are vile and false:
As where 's that palace whereinto foul things
Sometimes intrude not? who has a breast so pure,

---

123. close delations: secret or involuntary accusations.

But some uncleanly apprehensions
    Keep leets° and law-days° and in sessions sit   140
    With meditations lawful?

OTH: Thou dost conspire against thy friend, Iago,
    If thou but think'st him wrong'd and mak'st his ear
    A stranger to thy thoughts.

IAGO: I do beseech you—
    Though I perchance am vicious° in my guess,   145
    As, I confess, it is my nature's plague
    To spy into abuses, and oft my jealousy°
    Shapes faults that are not—that your wisdom yet,
    From one that so imperfectly conceits,°
    Would take no notice, nor build yourself a trouble   150
    Out of his scattering and unsure observance.
    It were not for your quiet nor your good,
    Nor for my manhood, honesty, or wisdom,
    To let you know my thoughts.

OTH: What dost thou mean?

IAGO: Good name in man and woman, dear my lord,   155
    Is the immediate jewel of their souls:
    Who steals my purse steals trash: 'tis something, nothing;
    'Twas mine, 'tis his, and has been slave to thousands;
    But he that filches from me my good name
    Robs me of that which not enriches him   160
    And makes me poor indeed.

OTH: By heaven, I'll know thy thoughts.

IAGO: You cannot, if my heart were in your hand;
    Nor shall not, whilst 'tis in my custody.

OTH: Ha!

IAGO: Oh, beware, my lord, of jealousy;   165
    It is the green-ey'd monster which doth mock
    The meat it feeds on: that cuckhold lives in bliss
    Who certain of his fate, loves not his wronger;
    But, O, what damned minutes tells her o'er
    Who dotes, yet doubts, suspects, yet strongly loves!   170

OTH: O misery!

IAGO: Poor and content is rich and rich enough,
    But riches fineless° is as poor as winter
    To him that ever fears he shall be poor.
    Good God, the souls of all my tribe defend   175
    From jealousy!

OTH: Why, why is this?

---

140. Keep leets: hold courts.   **140. law-days:** court days.   **145. vicious:** wrong.   **147. jealousy:** suspicion of evil.   **149. conceits:** judges.   **173. fineless:** boundless.

Think'st thou I'd make a life of jealousy,
To follow still the changes of the moon
With fresh suspicions? No; to be once in doubt
Is once to be resolv'd: exchange me for a goat, 180
When I shall turn the business of my soul
To such exsufflicate and blown° surmises,
Matching thy inference. 'Tis not to make me jealous
To say my wife is fair, feeds well, loves company,
Is free of speech, sings, plays and dances well; 185
Where virtue is, these are more virtuous;
Nor from mine own weak merits will I draw
The smallest fear or doubt of her revolt:
For she had eyes, and chose me. No, Iago;
I'll see before I doubt; when I doubt, prove; 190
And on the proof, there is no more but this,—
Away at once with love or jealousy!

IAGO: I am glad of this; for now I shall have reason
To show the love and duty that I bear you
With franker spirit: therefore, as I am bound, 195
Receive it from me. I speak not yet of proof.
Look to your wife; observe her well with Cassio;
Wear your eye thus, not jealous nor secure.°
I would not have your free and noble nature,
Out of self-bounty,° be abus'd; look to 't: 200
I know our country disposition well;
In Venice they do let heaven see the pranks
They dare not show their husbands; their best conscience
Is not to leave 't undone, but keep 't unknown.

OTH: Dost thou say so? 205

IAGO: She did deceive her father, marrying you;
And when she seem'd to shake and fear your looks,
She lov'd them most.

OTH: And so she did.

IAGO: Why, go to then;
She that, so young, could give out such a seeming,°
To seel° her father's eyes up close as oak— 210
He thought 'twas witchcraft—but I am much to blame;
I humbly do beseech you of your pardon
For too much loving you.

OTH: I am bound to thee for ever.

IAGO: I see this hath a little dash'd your spirits.

---

182. exsufflicate and blown: unsubstantial and inflated, flyblown. **198. secure:** free from uneasiness.
200. self-bounty: inherent or natural goodness. **209. seeming:** false appearance. **210. seel:** blind
(a term from falconry).

OTH: Not a jot, not a jot.

IAGO: I' faith, I fear it has.   215
> I hope you will consider what is spoke
> Comes from my love. But I do see y' are mov'd:
> I am to pray you not to strain my speech
> To grosser issues nor to larger reach°
> Than to suspicion.   220

OTH: I will not.

IAGO: Should you do so, my lord,
> My speech would fall into such vile success
> As my thoughts aim not at. Cassio 's my worthy friend—
> My lord, I see y' are mov'd.

OTH: No, not much mov'd:
> I do not think but Desdemona's honest.   225

IAGO: Long live she so! and long live you to think so!

OTH: And yet, how nature erring from itself,—

IAGO: Ay, there's the point: as—to be bold with you—
> Not to affect many proposed matches
> Of her own clime, complexion, and degree,   230
> Whereto we see in all things nature tends—
> Foh! one may smell in such a will° most rank,
> Foul disproportion,° thoughts unnatural.
> But pardon me; I do not in position°
> Distinctly speak of her; though I may fear   235
> Her will, recoiling to° her better judgment,
> May fall to match you with her country forms°
> And happily repent.°

OTH: Farewell, farewell:
> If more thou dost perceive, let me know more;
> Set on thy wife to observe: leave me, Iago.   240

IAGO (*going*):   My lord I take my leave.

OTH: Why did I marry? This honest creature doubtless
> Sees and knows more, much more, than he unfolds.

IAGO (*returning*):   My lord, I would I might entreat your honour
> To scan this thing no farther; leave it to time: 245
> Although 'tis fit that Cassio have his place,
> For, sure, he fills it up with great ability,
> Yet, if you please to hold him off awhile,
> You shall by that perceive him and his means:
> Note, if your lady strain his entertainment°   250

---

219. reach: meaning.   **232. will:** sensuality.   **233. disproportion:** abnormality.   **234. position:** general argument.   **236. recoiling to:** falling back upon, or recoiling against.   **237. fall . . . forms:** happen to compare you with Venetian norms of handsomeness.   **238. repent:** i.e., of her marriage. **250. strain his entertainment:** urge his reinstatement.

With any strong or vehement importunity;
Much will be seen in that. In the mean time,
Let me be thought too busy in my fears—
As worthy cause I have to fear I am—
And hold her free,° I do beseech your honour.   255

OTH: Fear not my government.°

IAGO: I once more take my leave.   *(Exit.)*

OTH: This fellow 's of exceeding honesty,
And knows all qualities, with a learned spirit,
Of human dealings. If I do prove her haggard,°   260
Though that her jesses° were my dear heartstrings,
I 'ld whistle her off and let her down the wind,
To prey at fortune.° Haply, for I am black
And have not those soft parts of conversation
That chamberers° have, or for I am declin'd   265
Into the vale of years,—yet that 's not much—
She 's gone. I am abus'd: and my relief
Must be to loathe her. O curse of marriage,
That we can call these delicate creatures ours,
And not their appetites! I had rather be a toad,   270
And live upon the vapour of a dungeon,
Than keep a corner in the thing I love
For others' uses. Yet, 'tis the plague of great ones;
Prerogativ'd° are they less than the base;
'Tis destiny unshunnable, like death: 275
Even then this forked° plague is fated to us
When we do quicken.° Look where she comes:

(*Enter* DESDEMONA *and* EMILIA.)

If she be false, O, then heaven mocks itself!
I'll not believe 't.

DES: How now, my dear Othello!
Your dinner, and the generous° islanders   280
By you invited, do attend your presence.

OTH: I am to blame.

DES: Why do you speak so faintly?
Are you not well?

OTH: I have a pain upon my forehead here.

DES: 'Faith, that 's with watching°; 'twill away again: 285

---

255. hold her free: regard her as innocent.   **256. government:** self-control.   **260. haggard:** a wild female duck.   **261. jesses:** straps fastened around the legs of a trained hawk.   **263. at fortune:** at random.   **265. chamberers:** gallants.   **274. Prerogativ'd:** privileged.   **276. forked:** an allusion to the horns of the cuckold.   **277. quicken:** receive life.   **280. generous:** noble.   **285. watching:** working late.

Let me but bind it hard, within this hour
It will be well.
OTH: Your napkin is too little: (*He puts the handkerchief from him; and it drops.*)
Let it alone. Come, I'll go in with you.
DES: I am very sorry that you are not well.   (*Exit with* OTHELLO.)
EMIL: I am glad I have found this napkin: 290
This was her first remembrance from the Moor:
My wayward husband hath a hundred times
Woo'd me to steal it; but she so loves the token,
For he conjur'd her she should ever keep it,
That she reserves it evermore about her   295
To kiss and talk to. I'll have the work ta'en out,°
And give 't Iago: what he will do with it
Heaven knows, not I;
I nothing but to please his fantasy.

            (*Enter* IAGO.)

IAGO: How now! what do you here alone?   300
EMIL: Do not you chide; I have a thing for you.
IAGO: A thing for me? it is a common thing°—
EMIL: Ha!
IAGO: To have a foolish wife.
EMIL: O, is that all? What will you give me now   305
For that same handkerchief?
IAGO: What handkerchief?
EMIL: What handkerchief!
Why, that the Moor first gave Desdemona;
That which so often you did bid me steal.
IAGO: Hast stol'n it from her?   310
EMIL: No, 'faith; she let it drop by negligence,
And, to th' advantage, I, being here, took 't up.
Look, here it is.
IAGO: A good wench; give it to me.
EMIL: What will you do with 't, that you have been so earnest
To have me filch it?
IAGO: (*Snatching it*) Why, what is that to you?   315
EMIL: If it be not for some purpose of import,
Give 't me again: poor lady, she'll run mad
When she shall lack it.
IAGO: Be not acknown on 't°; I have use for it.
Go, leave me.   (*Exit* EMILIA.) 320

---

296. work ta'en out: design copied.   **302. common thing:** *common* suggests coarseness and availability to all, and *thing* is slang for female sexual organs.   **319. Be . . . on 't:** do not confess knowledge of it.

I will in Cassio's lodging lose this napkin,
And let him find it. Trifles light as air
Are to the jealous confirmations strong
As proofs of holy writ: this may do something.
The Moor already changes with my poison:
Dangerous conceits are, in their natures, poisons,   325
Which at the first are scarce found to distaste,
But with a little act° upon the blood,
Burn like the mines of sulphur. I did say so:

       (*Enter* OTHELLO.)

Look, where he comes! Not poppy, nor mandragora,   330
Nor all the drowsy syrups of the world,
Shall ever medicine thee to that sweet sleep
Which thou owedst yesterday.

OTH: Ha! ha! false to me?
IAGO: Why, how now, general! no more of that.
OTH: Avaunt! be gone! thou has set me on the rack;   335
   I swear 'tis better to be much abus'd
   Than but to know 't a little.
IAGO: How now, my lord!
OTH: What sense had I of her stol'n hours of lust?
   I saw 't not, thought it not, it harm'd not me:
   I slept the next night well, fed well, was free and merry;   340
   I found not Cassio's kisses on her lips:
   He that is robb'd, not wanting what is stol'n,
   Let him not know 't, and he 's not robb'd at all.
IAGO: I am sorry to hear this.
OTH: I had been happy, if the general camp,   345
   Pioners° and all, had tasted her sweet body,
   So I had nothing known. O, now, for ever
   Farewell the tranquil mind! farewell content!
   Farewell the plumed troop, and the big wars,
   That make ambition virtue! O, farewell!   350
   Farewell the neighing steed, and the shrill trump,
   The spirit-stirring drum, th' ear-piercing fife,
   The royal banner, and all quality,
   Pride, pomp and circumstance° of glorious war!
   And, O you mortal engines,° whose rude throats   355
   Th' immortal Jove's dread clamours counterfeit,
   Farewell! Othello's occupation 's gone!
IAGO: Is 't possible, my lord?

---

328. act: action, working.   **346. Pioners:** sappers, a low grade of soldiers.   **354. circumstance:** attendant fact; here, formal display.   **355. mortal engines:** i.e., cannon.

OTH: Villain, be sure thou prove my love a whore,
   Be sure of it; give me the ocular proof;   360
   Or, by the worth of mine eternal soul,
   Thou hadst been better have been born a dog
   Than answer my wak'd wrath!
IAGO: Is 't come to this?
OTH: Make me to see 't; or, at the least, so prove it,
   That the probation bear no hinge nor loop   365
   To hang a doubt on; or woe upon thy life!
IAGO: My noble lord,—
OTH: If thou dost slander her and torture me,
   Never pray more; abandon all remorse;
   On horror's head horrors° accumulate;   370
   Do deeds to make heaven weep, all earth amaz'd;
   For nothing canst thou to damnation add
   Greater than that.
IAGO: O grace! O heaven forgive me!
   Are you a man? have you a soul or sense?
   God be wi' you; take mine office. O wretched fool,   375
   That liv'st to make thine honesty a vice!
   O monstrous world! Take note, take note, O world,
   To be direct and honest is not safe.
   I thank you for this profit; and from hence
   I'll love no friend, sith love breeds such offence.   380
OTH: Nay, stay: thou shouldst be honest.
IAGO: I should be wise, for honesty 's a fool
   and loses that it works for.
OTH: By the world,
   I think my wife be honest and think she is not;
   I think thou are just and think thou are not.   385
   I'll have some proof. Her name, that was as fresh
   As Dian's visage, is now begrim'd and black
   As mine own face. If there be cords, or knives,
   Poison, or fire, or suffocating streams,
   I'll not endure it. Would I were satisfied!   390
IAGO: I see, sir, you are eaten up with passion:
   I do repent me that I put it to you.
   You would be satisfied!
OTH: Would! nay, I will.
IAGO: And may: but, how? how satisfied, my lord?
   Would you, the supervisor, grossly gape on—   395
   Behold her topp'd?
OTH: Death and damnation! O!

370. horrors: object of *accumulate*.

IAGO: It were a tedious difficulty, I think,
  To bring them to that prospect: damn them then,
  If ever mortal eyes do see them bolster°
  More than their own! What then? how then?   400
  What shall I say? Where 's satisfaction?
  It is impossible you should see this,
  Were they as prime as goats, as hot as monkeys,
  As salt° as wolves in pride, and fools as gross
  As ignorance made drunk. But yet, I say,   405
  If imputation° and strong circumstances,
  Which lead directly to the door of truth,
  Will give you satisfaction, you may have 't.
OTH: Give me a living reason she 's disloyal.
IAGO: I do not like the office: 410
  But, sith I am ent'red in this cause so far,
  Prick'd to 't by foolish honesty and love,
  I will go on. I lay with Cassio lately;
  And, being troubled with a raging tooth,
  I could not sleep.   415
  There are a kind of men so loose of soul,
  That in their sleeps will mutter their affairs:
  One of this kind is Cassio:
  In sleep I heard him say "Sweet Desdemona,
  Let us be wary, let us hide our loves";   420
  And then, sir, would he grip and wring my hand,
  Cry, "O sweet creature!" and then kiss me hard,
  As if he pluck'd up kisses by the roots
  That grew upon my lips: then laid his leg
  Over my thigh, and sigh'd, and kiss'd; and then   425
  Cried "Cursed fate that gave thee to the Moor!"
OTH: O monstrous! monstrous!
IAGO: Nay, this was but his dream.
OTH: But this denoted a foregone conclusion°:
  'Tis a shrewd doubt, though it be but a dream.
IAGO: And this may help to thicken other proofs   430
  That do demonstrate thinly.
OTH: I'll tear her all to pieces.
IAGO: Nay, but be wise; yet we see nothing done;
  She may be honest yet. Tell me but this,
  Have you not sometimes seen a handkerchief
  Spotted with strawberries in your wife's hand?   435

---

399. bolster: lie together.   **404. salt:** wanton, sexual.   **406. imputation:** i.e., opinion founded on strong circumstantial evidence.   **428. foregone conclusion:** previous trial or experience (not used in our sense).

OTH: I gave her such a one; 'twas my first gift.

IAGO: I know not that: but such a handkerchief—
I am sure it was your wife's—did I to-day
See Cassio wipe his beard with.

OTH: If it be that,—

IAGO: If it be that, or any that was hers,   440
It speaks against her with the other proofs.

OTH: O, that the slave had forty thousand lives!
One is too poor, too weak for my revenge.
Now do I see 'tis true. Look here, Iago;
All my fond love thus do I blow to heaven.   445
'Tis gone.
Arise, black vengeance, from the hollow hell!
Yield up, O love, thy crown and hearted° throne
To tyrannous hate! Swell, bosom, with thy fraught,°
For 'tis of aspics'° tongues!

IAGO: Yet be content.   450

OTH: O, blood, blood, blood!

IAGO: Patience, I say; your mind perhaps may change.

OTH: Never, Iago. Like to the Pontic sea,
Whose icy current and compulsive course
Ne'er feels retiring ebb, but keeps due on   455
To the Propontic and the Hellespont,
Even so my bloody thoughts, with violent pace,
Shall ne'er look back, ne'er ebb to humble love,
Till that a capable and wide revenge
Swallow them up. Now, by yond marble° heaven,   460
(*Kneels*) In the due reverence of a sacred vow
I here engage my words.

IAGO: Do not rise yet.
(*Kneels*) Witness, you ever-burning lights above,
You elements that clip us round about,
Witness that here Iago doth give up   465
The execution° of his wit, hands, heart,
To wrong'd Othello's service! Let him command,
And to obey shall be in me remorse,°
What bloody business ever. (*They rise*.)

OTH: I greet thy love,
Not with vain thanks, but with acceptance bounteous,   470
And will upon the instant put thee to 't:
Within these three days let me hear thee say

---

448. hearted: fixed in the heart.   **449. fraught:** freight, burden.   **450. aspics':** venomous serpents'.   **460. marble:** i.e., gleaming like marble.   **466. execution:** exercise.   **468. remorse:** pity for Othello's wrongs.

That Cassio 's not alive.

IAGO: My friend is dead; 'tis done at your request:
But let her live.   475

OTH: Damn her, lewd minx! O, damn her! damn her!
Come, go with me apart; I will withdraw,
To furnish me with some swift means of death
For the fair devil. Now art thou my lieutenant.

IAGO: I am your own for ever.   *(Exeunt.)*   480

    SCENE IV

    Before the castle.

    (*Enter* DESDEMONA, EMILIA, *and* CLOWN.)

DES: Do you know, sirrah, where Lieutenant Cassio lies?

CLO: I dare not say he lies any where.

DES: Why, man?

CLO: He's a soldier, and for one to say a soldier lies, is stabbing.

DES: Go to; where lodges he?   5

CLO: To tell you where he lodges, is to tell you where I lie.

DES: Can any thing be made of this?

CLO: I know not where he lodges, and for me to devise a lodging and say he lies
here or he lies there, were to lie in mine own throat.

DES: Can you inquire him out, and be edified by report?   10

CLO: I will catechize the world for him, that is, make questions, and by them
answer.

DES: Seek him, bid him come hither: tell him I have moved my lord on his behalf,
and hope all will be well.

CLO: To do this is within the compass of man's wit; and therefore I will attempt   15
the doing it.   (*Exit* CLOWN.)

DES: Where should I lose that handkerchief, Emilia?

EMIL: I know not, madam.

DES: Believe me, I had rather lost my purse
Full of crusadoes°: and, but my noble Moor   20
Is true of mind and made of no such baseness
As jealous creatures are, it were enough
To put him to ill thinking.

EMIL: Is he not jealous?

DES: Who, he? I think the sun where he was born
Drew all such humours from him.

EMIL: Look, where he comes.   25

    (*Enter* OTHELLO.)

DES: I will not leave him now till Cassio
Be call'd to him.—How is 't with you, my lord?

II.iv. 20. crusadoes: Portuguese gold coins.

OTH: Well, my good lady. (*Aside*) O, hardness, to dissemble!—
        How do you do, Desdemona?
DES: Well, my good lord.
OTH: Give me your hand: this hand is moist, my lady.   30
DES: It yet hath felt no age nor known no sorrow.
OTH: This argues fruitfulness and liberal heart:
        Hot, hot, and moist: this hand of yours requires
        A sequester° from liberty, fasting and prayer,
        Much castigation, exercise devout;   35
        For here 's a young and sweating devil here,
        That commonly rebels. 'Tis a good hand,
        A frank one.
DES: You may, indeed, say so:
        For 'twas that hand that gave away my heart.
OTH: A liberal hand: the hearts of old gave hands;   40
        But our new heraldry is hands, not hearts.°
DES: I cannot speak of this. Come now, your promise.
OTH: What promise, chuck?
DES: I have sent to bid Cassio come speak with you.
OTH: I have a salt and sorry rheum° offends me;   45
        Lend me thy handkerchief.
DES: Here, my lord.
OTH: That which I gave you.
DES: I have it not about me.
OTH: Not?
DES: No, indeed, my lord.
OTH: That 's a fault.
        That handkerchief
        Did an Egyptian° to my mother give;
        She was a charmer, and could almost read   50
        The thoughts of people: she told her, while she kept it,
        'Twould make her amiable and subdue my father
        Entirely to her love, but if she lost it
        Or made a gift of it, my father's eye   55
        Should hold her loathed and his spirits should hunt
        After new fancies: she, dying, gave it me;
        And bid me, when my fate would have me wive,
        To give it her. I did so: and take heed on 't;
        Make it a darling like your precious eye;   60
        To lose 't or give 't away were such perdition
        As nothing else could match.
DES: Is 't possible?

34. **sequester:** separation, sequestration.   41. **new . . . hearts:** a current expression referring to marriages in which there is a joining of hands without the giving of hearts.   45. **sorry rheum:** distressful
head cold.   50. **Egyptian:** gypsy.

OTH: 'Tis true: there 's magic in the web of it:
 A sibyl, that had numb'red in the world
 The sun to course two hundred compasses,   65
 In her prophetic fury sew'd the work;
 The worms were hallow'd that did breed the silk;
 And it was dy'd in mummy° which the skilful
 Conserv'd of° maidens' hearts.

DES: Indeed! is 't true?

OTH: Most veritable; therefore look 't well.   70

DES: Then would to God that I had never seen 't!

OTH: Ha! wherefore?

DES: Why do you speak so startingly and rash?

OTH: Is 't lost? is 't gone? speak, is it out o' the way?

DES: Heaven bless us!   75

OTH: Say you?

DES: It is not lost; but what if it were?

OTH: How!

DES: I say, it is not lost.

OTH: Fetch 't, let me see 't.

DES: Why, so I can sir, but I will not now.   80
 This is a trick to put me from my suit:
 Pray you, let Cassio be receiv'd again.

OTH: Fetch me the handkerchief: my mind misgives.

DES: Come, come:
 You'll never meet a more sufficient man.   85

OTH: The handkerchief!

DES: I pray, talk me of Cassio.

OTH: The handkerchief!

DES: A man that all his time
 Hath founded his good fortunes on your love,
 Shar'd dangers with you,—

OTH: The handkerchief!   90

DES: In sooth, you are to blame.

OTH: Away!   (*Exit* OTHELLO.)

EMIL: Is not this man jealous?

DES: I ne'er saw this before.
 Sure, there 's some wonder in this handkerchief: 95
 I am most unhappy in the loss of it.

EMIL: 'Tis not a year or two shows us a man:
 They are all but stomachs, and we all but food;
 They eat us hungerly, and when they are full,
 They belch us.

---

68. mummy: medicinal or magical preparation drained from the flesh of mummified bodies.   **69. Conserv'd of:** preserved out of.

(*Enter* IAGO *and* CASSIO.)

Look you, Cassio and my husband!   100

IAGO: There is no other way; 'tis she must do 't:
And, lo, the happiness! go, and importune her.

DES: How now, good Cassio! what 's the news with you?

CAS: Madam, my former suit: I do beseech you
That by your virtuous means I may again   105
Exist, and be a member of his love
Whom I with all the office of my heart
Entirely honour: I would not be delay'd.
If my offence be of such mortal kind
That nor my service past, nor present sorrows,   110
Nor purpos'd merit in futurity,
Can ransom me into his love again,
But to know so much be my benefit°;
So shall I clothe me in a forc'd content,
And shut myself up in some other course,   115
To fortune's alms.

DES: Alas, thrice-gentle Cassio!
My advocation° is not now in tune;
My lord is not my lord; nor should I know him,
Were he in favour as in humour alter'd.
So help me every spirit sanctified   120
As I have spoken for you all my best
And stood within the blank° of his displeasure
For my free speech! You must awhile be patient:
What I can do I will; and more I will
Than for myself I dare: let that suffice you.   125

IAGO: Is my lord angry?

EMIL: He went hence but now,
And certainly in strange unquietness.

IAGO: Can he be angry? I have seen the cannon,
When it hath blown his ranks into the air,
And, like the devil, from his very arm   130
Puff'd his own brother:—and can he be angry?
Something of moment then: I will go meet him:
There 's matter in 't indeed, if he be angry.

DES: I prithee, do so.   (*Exit* IAGO.)
                     Something, sure, of state,
Either from Venice, or some unhatch'd practice   135
Made demonstrable here in Cyprus to him,

---

113. to know . . . benefit: to know that my case is hopeless will end my vain endeavor.   **117. advocation:** advocacy.   **122. blank:** white spot in the center of a target; here, range.

Hath puddled° his clear spirit; and in such cases
Men's natures wrangle with inferior things,
Though great ones are their object. 'Tis even so;
For let our finger ache, and it indues°   140
Our other healthful members even to a sense
Of pain: nay, we must think men are not gods,
Nor of them look for such observancy
As fits the bridal. Beshrew me much, Emilia,
I was, unhandsome° warrior as I am,   145
Arraigning his unkindness with my soul;
But now I find I had suborn'd the witness,
And he 's indicted falsely.

EMIL: Pray heaven it be state-matters, as you think,
And no conception° nor no jealous toy   150
Concerning you.

DES: Alas the day! I never gave him cause.

EMIL: But jealous souls will not be answer'd so;
They are not ever jealous for the cause,
But jealous for they are jealous: 'tis a monster   155
Begot upon itself, born on itself.

DES: Heaven keep that monster from Othello's mind!

EMIL: Lady, amen.

DES: I will go seek him. Cassio, walk here about:
If I do find him fit, I'll move your suit   160
And seek to effect it to my uttermost.

CAS: I humbly thank your ladyship.   (*Exit* DESDEMONA *with* EMILIA.)

      (*Enter* BIANCA.)

BIAN: Save you, friend Cassio!

CAS: What make you from home?
How is 't with you, my most fair Bianca?
I' faith, sweet love, I was coming to your house.   165

BIAN: And I was going to your lodging, Cassio.
What, keep a week away? seven days and nights?
Eight score eight hours? and lovers' absent hours,
More tedious than the dial eight score times?
O weary reck'ning!

CAS: Pardon me, Bianca.   170
I have this while with leaden thoughts been press'd;
But I shall, in a more continuate° time,
Strike off this score of absence. Sweet Bianca, (*Giving her* DESDEMONA's
handkerchief.)

---

137. puddled: sullied the purity of.   **140. indues:** brings to the same condition.   **145. unhandsome:** unfair.   **150. conception:** mere fancy.   **172. continuate:** uninterrupted.

Take me this work out.°

BIAN: O Cassio, whence came this?
 This is some token from a newer friend: 175
 To the felt absence now I feel a cause:
 Is 't come to this? Well, well.

CAS: Go to, woman!
 Throw your vile guesses in the devil's teeth,
 From whence you have them. You are jealous now
 That this is from some mistress, some remembrance: 180
 No, in good troth, Bianca.

BIAN: Why, whose is it?

CAS: I know not, sweet: I found it in my chamber.
 I like the work well: ere it be demanded—
 As like enough it will—I would have it copied:
 Take it, and do 't; and leave me for this time.   185

BIAN: Leave you! wherefore?

CAS: I do attend here on the general;
 And think it no addition, nor my wish,
 To have him see me woman'd.

BIAN: Why, I pray you?

CAS: Not that I love you not.

BIAN: But that you do not love me.   190
 I pray you, bring me on the way a little,
 And say if I shall see you soon at night.

CAS: 'Tis but a little way that I can bring you;
 For I attend here: but I'll see you soon.

BIAN: 'Tis very good; I must be circumstance'd.°   (*Exeunt omnes.*)   195

ACT IV

SCENE I

Cyprus. Before the castle.

(*Enter* OTHELLO *and* IAGO.)

IAGO: Will you think so?

OTH: Think so, Iago!

IAGO: What,
 To kiss in private?

OTH: An unauthoriz'd kiss.

IAGO: Or to be naked with her friend in bed
 An hour or more, not meaning any harm?

OTH: Naked in bed, Iago, and not mean harm!   5

---

174. Take . . . out: i.e., copy this embroidery for me.   **195. circumstance'd:** governed by circumstances.

It is hypocrisy against the devil:
They that mean virtuously, and yet do so,
The devil their virtue tempts, and they tempt heaven.

IAGO: So° they do nothing, 'tis a venial slip:
But if I give my wife a handkerchief,—   10

OTH: What then?

IAGO: Why, then, 'tis hers, my lord: and, being hers,
She may, I think, bestow 't on any man.

OTH: She is protectress of her honour too:
May she give that?   15

IAGO: Her honour is an essence that 's not seen;
They have it very oft that have it not:
But, for the handkerchief,—

OTH: By heaven, I would most gladly have forgot it.
Thou said'st—O, it comes o'er my memory,   20
As doth the raven o'er the infected house,°
Boding to all—he had my handkerchief.

IAGO: Ay, what of that?

OTH: That's not so good now.

IAGO: What,
If I had said I had seen him do you wrong?
Or hear him say,—as knaves be such abroad,   25
Who having, by their own importunate suit,
Or voluntary dotage of some mistress,
Convinced or supplied° them, cannot choose
But they must blab—

OTH: Hath he said anything?

IAGO: He hath, my lord; but be you well assur'd,   30
No more than he'll unswear.

OTH: What hath he said?

IAGO: 'Faith, that he did—I know not what he did.

OTH: What? What?

IAGO: Lie—

OTH: With her?

IAGO: With her, on her; what you will.

OTH: Lie with her! lie on her! We say lie on her, when they belie her. Lie with her!   35
that's fulsome.—Handkerchief—confessions—handkerchief!—To confess, and
be hanged for his labour;—first, to be hanged, and then to confess.— I tremble at
it. Nature would not invest herself in such shadowing passion without some
instruction.° It is not words that shake me thus. Pish! Noses, ears, and lips.—Is 't
possible?—Confess—handkerchief—O devil! (*Falls in a trance.*)   40

IV.i. **9. So:** as long as.   **21. raven . . . house:** allusion to the belief that the raven hovered over a house
of sickness or infection.   **28. Convinced or supplied:** i.e., mistresses gained by importunity and those
who doted voluntarily.   **38–39. Nature . . . instruction:** i.e., my jealousy cannot be merely the result of
natural imagination, but must have some foundation in fact.

IAGO: Work on,
My medicine, work! Thus credulous fools are caught;
And many worthy and chaste dames even thus,
All guiltless, meet reproach. What, ho! my lord!
My lord, I say! Othello!

(*Enter* CASSIO.)

                    How now, Cassio!   45
CAS: What's the matter?
IAGO: My lord is fall'n into an epilepsy:
This is his second fit; he had one yesterday.
CAS: Rub him about the temples.
IAGO: No, forbear;
The lethargy° must have his quiet course: 50
If not, he foams at mouth and by and by
Breaks out to savage madness. Look, he stirs:
Do you withdraw yourself a little while,
He will recover straight: when he is gone,
I would on great occasion speak with you.   (*Exit* CASSIO.) 55
How is it, general? have you not hurt your head?
OTH: Dost thou mock me?
IAGO: I mock you! no, by heaven.
Would you would bear your fortune like a man!
OTH: A horned man's a monster and a beast.
IAGO: There's many a beast then in a populous city,   60
And many a civil° monster.
OTH: Did he confess it?
IAGO: Good sir, be a man;
Think every bearded fellow that's but yok'd
May draw with you°: there's millions now alive
That nightly lie in those unproper° beds   65
Which they dare swear peculiar°: your case is better.
O, 'tis the spite of hell, the fiend's arch-mock,
To lip a wanton in a secure couch,
And to suppose her chaste! No, let me know;
And knowing what I am, I know what she shall be.   70
OTH: O, thou art wise; 'tis certain.
IAGO: Stand you awhile apart;
Confine yourself but in a patient list.°
Whilst you were here o'erwhelmed with your grief—
A passion most unsuiting such a man—
Cassio came hither: I shifted him away,   75

50. **lethargy:** unconscious condition.   61. **civil:** i.e., in civilized society.   64. **draw with you:** i.e., share
your fate as cuckold.   65. **unproper:** not belonging exclusively to an individual.   66. **peculiar:** private,
one's own.   72. **patient list:** within the bounds of patience.

And laid good 'scuse upon your ecstasy,
Bade him anon return and here speak with me;
The which he promis'd. Do but encave° yourself,
And mark the fleers,° the gibes, and notable scorns,
That dwell in every region of his face;   80
For I will make him tell the tale anew,
Where, how, how oft, how long ago, and when
He hath, and is again to cope your wife:
I say, but mark his gesture. Marry, patience;
Or I shall say y' are all in all in spleen,   85
And nothing of a man.
OTH: Dost thou hear, Iago?
I will be found most cunning in my patience;
But—dost thou hear?—most bloody.
IAGO: That 's not amiss;
But yet keep time° in all. Will you withdraw? (OTHELLO *retires*.)
Now will I question Cassio of Bianca,   90
A housewife that by selling her desires
Buys herself bread and clothes: it is a creature
That dotes on Cassio; as 'tis the strumpet's plague
To beguile many and be beguil'd by one:
He, when he hears of her, cannot refrain   95
From the excess of laughter. Here he comes:

            (*Enter* CASSIO.)

As he shall smile, Othello shall go mad;
And his unbookish° jealousy must conster°
Poor Cassio's smiles, gestures and light behaviour,
Quite in the wrong. How do you now, lieutenant?   100
CAS: The worser that you give me the addition°
Whose want even kills me.
IAGO: Ply Desdemona well, and you are sure on 't.
(*Speaking lower*) Now, if this suit lay in Bianca's power,
How quickly should you speed!
CAS: Alas, poor caitiff!   105
OTH: Look, how he laughs already!
IAGO: I never knew woman love man so.
CAS: Alas, poor rogue! I think, i' faith, she loves me.
OTH: Now he denies it faintly, and laughs it out.
IAGO: Do you hear, Cassio?
OTH: Now he importunes him   110
To tell o'er: go to; well said, well said.

---

78. encave: conceal.   **79. fleers:** sneers.   **89. keep time:** use judgment and order.   **98. unbookish:** uninstructed.   **98. conster:** construe.   **101. addition:** title.

IAGO: She gives it out that you shall marry her:
  Do you intend it?

CAS: Ha, ha, ha!

OTH: Do you triumph, Roman?° do you triumph?   115

CAS: I marry her! what? a customer!° Prithee, bear some charity to my wit; do not
  think it so unwholesome. Ha, ha, ha!

OTH: So, so, so, so: they laugh that win.

IAGO: 'Faith, the cry goes that you shall marry her.

CAS: Prithee, say true.   120

IAGO: I am a very villain else.

OTH: Have you scored me?° Well.

CAS: This is the monkey's own giving out: she is persuaded I will marry her, out of
  her own love and flattery, not out of my promise.

OTH: Iago beckons me; now he begins the story.   125

CAS: She was here even now; she haunts me in every place. I was the other day
  talking on the seabank with certain Venetians; and thither comes the bauble,°
  and, by this hand, she falls me thus about my neck—

OTH: Crying, 'O dear Cassio!' as it were: his gesture imports it.

CAS: So hangs, and lolls, and weeps upon me; so shakes, and pulls me: ha, ha, ha!   130

OTH: Now he tells how she plucked him to my chamber. O, I see that nose of
  yours, but not that dog I shall throw it to.

CAS: Well, I must leave her company.

IAGO: Before me!° look, where she comes.

           (*Enter* BIANCA.)

CAS: 'Tis such another fitchew!° marry, a perfumed one.—What do you mean by   135
  this haunting of me?

BIAN: Let the devil and his dam haunt you! What did you mean by that same
  handkerchief you gave me even now? I was a fine fool to take it. I must take out
  the work?—A likely piece of work, that you should find it in your chamber, and
  not know who left it there! This is some minx's token, and I must take out the   140
  work? There; give it your hobby-horse°: wheresoever you had it, I'll take out
  no work on 't.

CAS: How now, my sweet Bianca! how now! how now!

OTH: By heaven, that should be my handkerchief!

BIAN: An you'll come to supper to-night, you may; an' you will not, come when   145
  you are next prepared for.   (*Exit.*)

IAGO: After her, after her.

CAS: 'Faith, I must; she'll rail in the street else.

IAGO: Will you sup there?

---

115. Roman: epithet arising from the association of the Romans with the idea of triumph.   **116. customer:** prostitute.   **122. scored me:** made up my reckoning, or branded me.   **127. bauble:** plaything.
134. Before me!: On my soul!   **135. fitchew:** polecat (because of her strong perfume; also, slang word
for a prostitute).   **141. hobby-horse:** harlot.

CAS: Yes, I intend so.   150
IAGO: Well, I may chance to see you; for I would very fain speak with you.
CAS: Prithee, come; will you?
IAGO: Go to; say no more.   (*Exit* CASSIO.)
OTH (*advancing*):   How shall I murder him, Iago?
IAGO: Did you perceive how he laughed at his vice?   155
OTH: O Iago!
IAGO: And did you see the handkerchief?
OTH: Was that mine?
IAGO: Yours, by this hand: and to see how he prizes the foolish woman your wife!
   She gave it him, and he hath given it his whore.   160
OTH: I would have him nine years a-killing. A fine woman! a fair woman! a sweet
   woman!
IAGO: Nay, you must forget that.
OTH: Ay, let her rot, and perish, and be damned to-night; for she shall not live: no,
   my heart is turned to stone; I strike it, and it hurts my hand. O, the world hath   165
   not a sweeter creature: she might lie by an emperor's side and command him
   tasks.
IAGO: Nay, that 's not your way.°
OTH: Hang her! I do but say what she is: so delicate with her needle: an admirable
   musician: O! she will sing the savageness out of a bear: of so high and plenteous   170
   wit and invention:—
IAGO: She 's the worse for all this.
OTH: O, a thousand thousand times: and then, of so gentle a condition!
IAGO: Ay, too gentle.
OTH: Nay, that 's certain: but yet the pity of it, Iago! O Iago, the pity of it, Iago!   175
IAGO: If you are so fond over her iniquity, give her patent° to offend; for, if it touch
   not you, it comes near nobody.
OTH: I will chop her into messes°; cuckold me!
IAGO: O, 'tis foul in her.
OTH: With mine officer!   180
IAGO: That 's fouler.
OTH: Get me some poison, Iago; this night: I'll not expostulate with her, lest her
   body and beauty unprovide° my mind again: this night, Iago.
IAGO: Do it not with poison, strangle her in her bed, even the bed she hath
   contaminated.   185
OTH: Good, good: the justice of it pleases: very good.
IAGO: And for Cassio, let me be his undertaker°: you shall hear more by midnight.
OTH: Excellent good. (*A trumpet within.*) What trumpet is that same?
IAGO: I warrant something from Venice.

   (*Enter* LODOVICO, DESDEMONA, *and* ATTENDANTS.)

---

168. your way: i.e., the way you should think of her.   **176. patent:** license.   **178. messes:** dishes of
food.   **183. unprovide:** weaken, unfit.   **187. let . . . undertaker:** i.e., let me settle with him.

                           'Tis Lodovico.

This comes from the duke: and, see, your wife's with him.   190

LOD: God save you, worthy general!

OTH: With all my heart, sir.

LOD: The duke and the senators of Venice greet you. (*Gives him a letter.*)

OTH: I kiss the instrument of their pleasures. (*Opens the letter, and reads.*)

DES: And what 's the news, good cousin Lodovico?

IAGO: I am very glad to see you, signior;   195

    Welcome to Cyprus.

LOD: I thank you. How does Lieutenant Cassio?

IAGO: Lives, sir.

DES: Cousin, there 's fall'n between him and my lord

    An unkind breach: but you shall make all well.   200

OTH: Are you sure of that?

DES: My lord?

OTH (*reads*):   "This fail you not to do, as you will—"

LOD: He did not call; he 's busy in the paper.

    Is there division 'twixt my lord and Cassio?   205

DES: A most unhappy one: I would do much

    T' atone them, for the love I bear to Cassio.

OTH: Fire and brimstone!

DES: My lord?

OTH: Are you wise?

DES: What, is he angry?

LOD: May be the letter mov'd him:

    For, as I think, they do command him home,   210

    Deputing Cassio in his government.°

DES: Trust me, I am glad on 't.

OTH: Indeed!

DES: My lord?

OTH: I am glad to see you mad.

DES: Why, sweet Othello,—

OTH (*striking her*):   Devil!

DES: I have not deserv'd this.   215

LOD: My lord, this would not be believ'd in Venice,

    Though I should swear I saw 't; 'tis very much:

    Make her amends; she weeps.

OTH: O devil, devil!

    If that the earth could teem with woman's tears,

    Each drop she falls would prove a crocodile.°   220

    Out of my sight!

DES: I will not stay to offend you. (*Going.*)

---

211. government: office.   **220. prove a crocodile:** i.e., by weeping crocodile tears; it was believed the crocodile shed tears over the body of the person it was eating.

LOD: Truly, an obedient lady:
    I do beseech your lordship, call her back.
OTH: Mistress!
DES: My lord?
OTH: What would you with her, sir?
LOD: Who, I, my lord?   225
OTH: Ay; you did wish that I would make her turn:
    Sir, she can turn, and turn, and yet go on,
    And turn again; and she can weep, sir, weep;
    And she 's obedient, as you say, obedient,
    Very obedient. Proceed you in your tears.   230
    Concerning this, sir,—O well-painted passion,°—
    I am commanded home. Get you away;
    I'll send for you anon. Sir, I obey the mandate,
    And will return to Venice. Hence, avaunt!   (*Exit* DESDEMONA.)
    Cassio shall have my place. And, sir, to-night,   235
    I do entreat that we may sup together:
    You are welcome, sir, to Cyprus.—Goats and monkeys!   (*Exit.*)
LOD: Is this the noble Moor whom our full senate
    Call all in all sufficient? Is this the nature
    Whom passion could not shake? whose solid virtue   240
    The shot of accident, nor dart of chance,
    Could neither graze nor pierce?
IAGO: He is much chang'd.
LOD: Are his wits safe? is he not light of brain?
IAGO: He 's that he is: I may not breathe my censure
    What he might be: if what he might he is not,   245
    I would to heaven he were!
LOD: What, strike his wife!
IAGO: 'Faith, that was not so well; yet would I knew
    That stroke would prove the worst!
LOD: Is it his use?
    Or did the letters work upon his blood,
    And new-create this fault?   250
IAGO: Alas, alas!
    It is not honesty in me to speak
    What I have seen and known. You shall observe him,
    And his own courses will denote him so
    That I may save my speech: do but go after,
    And mark how he continues.   255
LOD: I am sorry that I am deceiv'd in him.   (*Exeunt.*)

---

231. well-painted passion: well-simulated emotion.

SCENE II

A room in the castle.

(*Enter* OTHELLO *and* EMILIA.)

OTH:	You have seen nothing then?
EMIL:	Nor ever heard, nor ever did suspect.
OTH:	Yes, you have seen Cassio and she together.
EMIL:	But then I saw no harm, and then I heard
	Each syllable that breath made up between them.

OTH: What, did they never whisper?
EMIL: Never, my lord.
OTH: Nor send you out 'o th' way?
EMIL: Never.
OTH: To fetch her fan, her gloves, her mask, nor nothing?
EMIL: Never, my lord.
OTH: That 's strange.
EMIL: I durst, my lord, to wager she is honest,
    Lay down my soul at stake: if you think other,
    Remove your thought: it doth abuse your bosom.
    If any wretch have put this in your head,
    Let heaven requite it with the serpent's curse!
    For, if she be not honest, chaste, and true,
    There 's no man happy; the purest of their wives
    Is foul as slander.
OTH: Bid her come hither: go.   (*Exit* EMILIA.)
    She says enough; yet she 's a simple bawd
    That cannot say as much. This is a subtle whore,
    A closet lock and key° of villainous secrets:
    And yet she'll kneel and pray; I have seen her do 't.

(*Enter* DESDEMONA *and* EMILIA.)

DES: My lord, what is your will?
OTH: Pray, chuck, come hither.
DES: What is your pleasure?
OTH: Let me see your eyes;
    Look in my face.
DES: What horrible fancy 's this?
OTH (*to* EMILIA):   Some of your function,° mistress;
    Leave procreants° alone and shut the door;
    Cough, or cry "hem," if any body come:
    Your mystery, your mystery°: nay, dispatch.   (*Exit* EMILIA.)   30

5

10

15

20

25

IV.ii. 22. closet lock and key: complete storeroom.   **27. Some . . . function:** i.e., set to work in your chosen profession, that of bawd.   **28. procreants:** mating couples.   **30. mystery:** trade, occupation.

DES: Upon my knees, what doth your speech import?
    I understand a fury in your words,
    But not the words.
OTH: Why, what art thou?
DES: Your wife, my lord; your true
    And loyal wife.
OTH: Come, swear it, damn thyself;   35
    Lest, being like one of heaven, the devils themselves
    Should fear to seize thee: therefore be double damn'd:
    Swear thou are honest.
DES: Heaven doth truly know it.
OTH: Heaven truly knows that thou art false as hell.
DES: To whom, my lord? with whom? how am I false?   40
OTH: O Desdemona! away! away! away!
DES: Alas the heavy day! Why do you weep?
    Am I the motive of these tears, my lord?
    If haply you my father do suspect
    An instrument of this your calling back,   45
    Lay not your blame on me: if you have lost him,
    Why, I have lost him too.
OTH: Had it pleas'd heaven
    To try me with affliction; had they° rain'd
    All kinds of sores and shames on my bare head,
    Steep'd me in poverty to the very lips,   50
    Given to captivity me and my utmost hopes,
    I should have found in some place of my soul
    A drop of patience: but, alas, to make me
    A fixed figure for the time of scorn
    To point his slow unmoving finger at!°   55
    Yet could I bear that too; well, very well:
    But there, where I have garner'd up my heart,
    Where either I must live, or bear no life;
    The fountain from the which my current runs,
    Or else dries up; to be discarded thence!   60
    Or keep it as a cistern for foul toads
    To knot and gender° in! Turn thy complexion° there,
    Patience, thou young and rose-lipp'd cherubin,—
    Ay, there, look grim as hell!
DES: I hope my noble lord esteems me honest.   65

---

48. they: heavenly powers.   **54–55. A . . . at:** Othello possibly thinks of himself as a man set in a pillory at whom the scornful world points in mockery. There seems to be a comparison with the sundial, whose gnomon, or indicator, becomes the finger of scornful time.   **62. gender:** engender.   **62. Turn thy complexion:** grow pale.

OTH: O, ay; as summer flies are in the shambles,°
    That quicken° even with blowing. O thou weed,
    Who are so lovely fair and smell'st so sweet
    That the sense aches at thee, would thou hads't ne'er been born!
DES: Alas, what ignorant sin have I committed?   70
OTH: Was this fair paper, this most goodly book,
    Made to write "whore" upon? What committed!
    Committed! O thou public commoner!°
    I should make very forges of my cheeks,
    That would to cinders burn up modesty,   75
    Did I but speak thy deeds. What committed!
    Heaven stops the nose at it and the moon winks,
    The bawdy wind that kisses all it meets
    Is hush'd within the hollow mine of earth,
    And will not hear it. What committed!   80
    Impudent strumpet!
DES: By heaven, you do me wrong.
OTH: Are not you a strumpet?
DES: No, as I am a Christian:
    If to preserve this vessel° for my lord
    From any other foul unlawful touch
    Be not to be a strumpet, I am none.   85
OTH: What, not a whore?
DES: No, as I shall be sav'd.
OTH: Is 't possible?
DES: O, heaven forgive us!
OTH: I cry you mercy, then:
    I took you for the cunning whore of Venice
    That married with Othello. (*Raising his voice.*) You, mistress,   90
    That have the office opposite to Saint Peter,
    And keep the gate of hell!

             (*Enter* EMILIA.)

                  You, you, ay, you!
    We have done our course; there's money for your pains:
    I pray you, turn the key and keep our counsel.   (*Exit.*)
EMIL: Alas, what does this gentleman conceive?   95
    How do you, madam? how do you, my good lady?
DES: 'Faith, half asleep.
EMIL: Good madam, what's the matter with my lord?
DES: With who?

---

66. shambles: slaughterhouse.   **67. quicken:** come to life.   **73. commoner:** prostitute.   **83. vessel:** body.

EMIL: Why, with my lord, madam. 100
DES: Who is thy lord?
EMIL: He that is yours, sweet lady.
DES: I have none: do not talk to me, Emilia;
    I cannot weep; nor answers have I none,
    But what should go by water.° Prithee, tonight
    Lay on my bed my wedding sheets: remember; 105
    And call thy husband hither.
EMIL: Here's a change indeed!   (*Exit.*)
DES: 'Tis meet I should be us'd so, very meet.
    How have I been behav'd, that he might stick
    The small'st opinion on my least misuse?°

        (*Enter* IAGO *and* EMILIA.)

IAGO: What is your pleasure, madam? How is 't with you? 110
DES: I cannot tell. Those that do teach young babes
    Do it with gentle means and easy tasks:
    He might have chid me so; for, in good faith,
    I am a child to chiding.
IAGO: What is the matter, lady?
EMIL: Alas, Iago, my lord hath so bewhor'd her, 115
    Thrown such despite° and heavy terms upon her,
    As true hearts cannot bear.
DES: Am I that name, Iago?
IAGO: What name, fair lady?
DES: Such as she said my lord did say I was.
EMIL: He call'd her whore: a beggar in his drink 120
    Could not have laid such terms upon his callet.°
IAGO: Why did he so?
DES: I do not know; I am sure I am none such.
IAGO: Do not weep, do not weep. Alas the day!
EMIL: Hath she forsook so many noble matches,
    Her father and her country and her friends, 125
    To be call'd whore? would it not make one weep?
DES: It is my wretched fortune.
IAGO: Beshrew him for 't!
    How comes this trick upon him?
DES: Nay, heaven doth know.
EMIL: I will be hang'd, if some eternal villain, 130
    Some busy and insinuating rogue,
    Some cogging,° cozening slave, to get some office,
    Have not devis'd this slander; I will be hang'd else.

---

104. go by water: be expressed by tears.   **109. misuse:** evil conduct.   **116. despite:** contempt, scorn.
121. callet: lewd woman.   **132. cogging:** cheating.

IAGO: Fie, there is no such man; it is impossible.

DES: If any such there be, heaven pardon him!   135

EMIL: A halter pardon him! and hell gnaw his bones!

Why should he call her whore? who keeps her company?

What place? what time? what form? what likelihood?

The Moor's abus'd by some most villainous knave,

Some base notorious knave, some scurvy fellow.   140

O heaven, that such companions thou 'ldst unfold,

And put in every honest hand a whip

To lash the rascals naked through the world

Even from the east to th' west!

IAGO: Speak within door.°

EMIL: O, fie upon them! Some such squire he was   145

That turn'd your wit the seamy side without,

And made you to suspect me with the Moor.

IAGO: You are a fool; go to.

DES: Alas, Iago.

What shall I do to win my lord again?

Good friend, go to him; for, by this light of heaven,   150

I know not how I lost him. Here I kneel:

If e'er by will did trespass 'gainst his love,

Either in discourse of thought or actual deed,

Or that mine eyes, mine ears, or any sense,

Delighted them in any other form;   155

Or that I do not yet, and ever did,

And ever will—though he do shake me off

To beggarly divorcement—love him dearly,

Comfort forswear me! Unkindness may do much;

And his unkindness may defeat my life,   160

But never taint my love. I cannot say "whore":

It doth abhor me now I speak the word;

To do the act that might the addition° earn

Not the world's mass of vanity could make me.

IAGO: I pray you, be content; 'tis but his humour: 165

The business of the state does him offence,

And he does chide with you.

DES: If 'twere no other,—

IAGO: 'Tis but so, I warrant. (*Trumpets within.*)

Hark, how these instruments summon to supper!

The messengers of Venice stay the meat°;   170

Go in, and weep not; all things shall be well.   (*Exeunt* DESDEMONA *and* EMILIA.)

---

144. Speak ... door: i.e., not so loud.   **163. addition:** title.   **170. stay the meat:** are waiting for supper.

(*Enter* RODERIGO.)

How now, Roderigo!

ROD: I do not find that thou dealest justly with me.

IAGO: What in the contrary?

ROD: Everyday thou daffest me° with some device, Iago; and rather, as it seems to   175
me now, keepest from me all conveniency° than suppliest me with the least
advantage of hope. I will indeed no longer endure it, nor am I yet persuaded to
put up° in peace what already I have foolishly suffered.

IAGO: Will you hear me, Roderigo?

ROD: 'Faith, I have heard too much, for your words and performances are no kin   180
together.

IAGO: You charge me most unjustly.

ROD: With nought but truth. I have wasted myself out of my means. The jewels you
have had from me to deliver to Desdemona would half have corrupted a votarist°:
you have told me she hath received them and returned me expectations and com-   185
forts of sudden respect and acquaintance, but I find none.

IAGO: Well; go to; very well.

ROD: Very well! go to! I cannot go to, man; nor 'tis not very well: nay, I think it is
scurvy, and begin to find myself fopped° in it.

IAGO: Very well.   190

ROD: I tell you 'tis not very well. I will make myself known to Desdemona: if she
will return me my jewels, I will give over my suit and repent my unlawful solicita-
tion; if not, assure yourself I will seek satisfaction of you.

IAGO: You have said now.°

ROD: Ay, and said nothing but what I protest intendment° of doing.   195

IAGO: Why, now I see there's mettle in thee, and even from this instant do build
on thee a better opinion than ever before. Give me thy hand, Roderigo: thou hast
taken against me a most just exception; but yet, I protest, I have dealt most
directly in thy affair.

ROD: It hath not appeared.   200

IAGO: I grant indeed it had not appeared, and your suspicion is not without wit and
judgement. But, Roderigo, if thou hast that in thee indeed, which I have greater
reason to believe now than ever, I mean purpose, courage and valour, this night
show it: if thou the next night following enjoy not Desdemona, take me from this
world with treachery and devise engines for° my life.   205

ROD: Well, what is it? is it within reason and compass?

IAGO: Sir, there is especial commission come from Venice to depute Cassio in
Othello's place.

ROD: Is that true? why, then Othello and Desdemona return again to Venice.

---

175. daffest me: puts me off with an excuse. **176. conveniency:** advantage, opportunity. **178. put
up:** submit to. **185. votarist:** nun. **189. fopped:** fooled. **194. You . . . now:** well said, quite right.
195. intendment: purpose, intention. **205. engines for:** plots against.

IAGO: O, no; he goes into Mauritania° and takes away with him the fair Desde-   210
mona, unless his abode be lingered here by some accident: wherein none can be
so determinate° as the removing of Cassio.

ROD: How do you mean, removing of him?

IAGO: Why, by making him uncapable of Othello's place; knocking out his brains.

ROD: And that you would have me to do?   215

IAGO: Ay, if you dare do yourself a profit and a right. He sups to-night with a harlotry,° and thither will I go to him: he knows not yet of his honourable fortune. If
you will watch his going thence, which I will fashion to fall out between twelve
and one, you may take him at your pleasure: I will be near to second your attempt,
and he shall fall between us. Come, stand not amazed at it, but go along with   220
me; I will show you such a necessity in his death that you shall think yourself
bound to put it to him. It is now high° supper-time, and the night grows to waste:
about it.

ROD: I will hear further reason for this.

IAGO: And you shall be satisfied.   (*Exeunt.*)   225

SCENE III

Another room in the castle.

(*Enter* OTHELLO, LODOVICO, DESDEMONA, EMILIA, *and* ATTENDANTS.)

LOD: I do beseech you, sir, trouble yourself no further.

OTH: O, pardon me; 'twill do me good to walk.

LOD: Madam, good night; I humbly thank your ladyship.

DES: Your honour is most welcome.

OTH: Will you walk, sir?
O,—Desdemona,—   5

DES: My lord?

OTH: Get you to bed on th' instant; I will be returned forthwith: dismiss your
attendant there: look 't be done.

DES: I will, my lord.   (*Exit* OTHELLLO, *with* LODOVICO *and* ATTENDANTS.)

EMIL: How goes it now? he looks gentler than he did.   10

DES: He says he will return incontinent°:
He hath commanded me to go to bed,
And bade me to dismiss you.

EMIL: Dismiss me!

DES: It was his bidding; therefore, good Emilia,
Give me my nightly wearing, and adieu: 15
We must not now displease him.

EMIL: I would you had never seen him!

DES: So would not I: my love doth so approve him,

---

210. Mauritania: Roman name of northwest Africa, supposed land of the Moors.   **212. determinate:**
decisive.   **216–217. harlotry:** courtesan.   **222. high:** quite.   **IV.iii. 11. incontinent:** immediately.

That even his stubbornness,° his checks,° his frowns,—
Prithee, unpin me,—have grace and favour in them.   20

EMIL: I have laid those sheets you bade me on the bed.

DES: All 's one. Good faith, how foolish are our minds!
If I do die before thee, prithee, shroud me
In one of those same sheets.

EMIL: Come, come, you talk.

DES: My mother had a maid call'd Barbary: 25
She was in love, and he she lov'd prov'd mad
And did forsake her: she had a song of 'willow';
An old thing 'twas, but it express'd her fortune,
And she died singing it: that song to-night
Will not go from my mind; I have much to do,   30
But to° go hang my head all at one side,
And sing it like poor Barbary. Prithee, dispatch.

EMIL: Shall I go fetch your night-gown?°

DES: No, unpin me here.
This Lodovico is a proper man.

EMIL: A very handsome man.   35

DES: He speaks well.

EMIL: I know a lady in Venice would have walked barefoot to Palestine for a touch
of his nether lip.

DES (*Singing*):   The poor soul sat sighing by a sycamore tree,
Sing all a green willow;   40
Her hand on her bosom, her head on her knee,
Sing willow, willow, willow:
The fresh streams ran by her, and murmur'd her moans;
Sing willow, willow, willow;
Her salt tears fell from her, and soft'ned the stones;—   45
Lay by these:—
(*Singing*) Sing willow, willow, willow;
Prithee, hie thee; he'll come anon:—
(*Singing*) Sing all a green willow must be my garland.
Let nobody blame him; his scorn I approve,—   50
Nay, that 's not next.—Hark! who is 't that knocks?

EMIL: It 's the wind.

DES (*Singing*):   I call'd my love false love; but what said he then?
Sing willow, willow, willow:
If I court moe women, you'll couch with moe men.—   55
So, get thee gone; good night. Mine eyes do itch;
Doth that bode weeping?

EMIL: 'Tis neither here nor there.

---

19. stubbornness: harshness.   **19. checks:** rebukes.   **31. But to:** not to.   **33. night-gown:** dressing gown.

DES: I have heard it said so. O, these men, these men!
    Dost thou in conscience think,—tell me, Emilia,—
    That there be women do abuse their husbands   60
    In such gross kind?

EMIL: There be some such, no question.

DES: Wouldst thou do such a deed for all the world?

EMIL: Why, would not you?

DES: No, by this heavenly light!

EMIL: Nor I neither by this heavenly light; I might do 't as well i' the dark.

DES: Wouldst thou do such a deed for all the world?   65

EMIL: The world 's a huge thing: it is a great price
    For a small vice.

DES: In troth, I think thou wouldst not.

EMIL: In troth, I think I should; and undo 't when I had done. Marry, I would not
    do such a thing for a joint-ring,° nor for measures of lawn, nor for gowns, petti-   70
    coats, nor caps, nor any petty exhibition°; but, for all the whole world,—why,
    who would not make her husband a cuckold to make him a monarch? I should
    venture purgatory for 't.

DES: Beshrew me, if I would do such a wrong
    For the whole world.   75

EMIL: Why, the wrong is but a wrong i' the world; and having the world for your
    labour, 'tis a wrong in your own world, and you might quickly make it right.

DES: I do not think there is any such woman.

EMIL: Yes, a dozen; and as many to the vantage° as would store the world they
      played for.   80
    But I do think it is their husband's faults
    If wives do fall: say that they slack their duties,
    And pour our treasures into foreign laps,°
    Or else break out in peevish jealousies,
    Throwing restraint upon us; or say they strike us,   85
    Or scant our former having in despite°;
    Why, we have galls,° and though we have some grace,
    Yet have we some revenge. Let husbands know
    Their wives have sense like them: they see and smell
    And have their palates both for sweet and sour,   90
    As husbands have. What is it that they do
    When they change us for others? Is it sport?
    I think it is: and doth affection breed it?
    I think it doth: is 't frailty that thus errs?
    It is so too: and have not we affections,   95
    Desires for sport, and frailty, as men have?

---

70. joint-ring: a ring made in separable halves as a lover's token.   **71. exhibition:** gift, present.   **79. to
the vantage:** in addition.   **83. pour . . . laps:** i.e., are unfaithful.   **86. scant . . . despite:** reduce our
allowance to spite us.   **87. have galls:** are capable of resenting injury and insult.

Then let them use us well: else let them know,
The ills we do, their ills instruct us so.

DES: Good night, good night: heaven me such uses send,
Not to pick bad from bad, but by bad mend!   *(Exeunt.)* 100

ACT V

SCENE I

Cyprus. A street.

(Enter IAGO *and* RODERIGO.*)*

IAGO: Here stand behind this bulk°; straight will he come:
Wear thy good rapier bare, and put it home:
Quick, quick; fear nothing; I'll be at they elbow:
It makes us, or it mars us; think on that,
And fix most firm thy resolution.   5

ROD: Be near at hand; I may miscarry in 't.

IAGO: Here, at thy hand: be bold, and take thy stand. *(Retires.)*

ROD: I have no great devotion to the deed;
And yet he hath given me satisfying reasons:
'Tis but a man gone. Forth, my sword: he dies.   10

IAGO: I have rubb'd this young quat° almost to the sense,°
And he grows angry. Now, whether he kill Cassio,
Or Cassio him, or each do kill the other,
Every way makes my gain: live Roderigo,
He calls me to a restitution large   15
Of gold and jewels that I bobb'd° from him,
As gifts to Desdemona;
It must not be: if Cassio do remain,
He hath a daily beauty in his life
That makes me ugly; and, besides, the Moor   20
May unfold me to him; there stand I in much peril:
No, he must die. But so: I hear him coming.

        (Enter CASSIO.*)*

ROD: I know his gait, 'tis he.—Villain, thou diest! *(Makes a pass at* CASSIO.*)*

CAS: That thrust had been mine enemy indeed,
But that my coat° is better than thou know'st: 25
I will make proof of thine. *(Draws, and wounds* RODERIGO.*)*

ROD: O, I am slain!

      *(*IAGO *from behind wounds* CASSIO *in the leg, and exits.)*

CAS: I am maim'd for ever. Help, ho! murder! murder! *(Falls.)*

V.i. 1. bulk: framework projecting from the front of a shop.   **11. quat:** pimple, pustule; used contemptuously.   **11. to the sense:** to the quick.   **16. bobb'd:** filched cunningly.   **25. coat:** coat of mail.

(*Enter* OTHELLO.)

OTH: The voice of Cassio: Iago keeps his word.
ROD: O, villain that I am!
OTH: It is even so.
CAS: O, help, ho! light! a surgeon!   30
OTH: 'Tis he:—O brave Iago, honest and just,
   That hast such noble sense of thy friend's wrong!
   Thou teachest me. Minion, your dear lies dead,
   And your unblest fate hies: strumpet, I come.
   Forth of my heart those charms, thine eyes, are blotted;   35
   Thy bed, lust-stain'd, shall with lust's blood be spotted.   (*Exit* OTHELLO.)

       (*Enter* LODOVICO *and* GRATIANO.)

CAS: What, ho! no watch? no passage?° murder! murder!
GRA: 'Tis some mischance; the cry is very direful.
CAS: O, help!
LOD: Hark!   40
ROD: O wretched villain!
LOD: Two or three groan: it is a heavy° night;
   These may be counterfeits: let's think 't unsafe
   To come in to the cry without more help.
ROD: Nobody come? then shall I bleed to death.   45
LOD: Hark!

       (*Enter* IAGO *with a light.*)

GRA: Here's one comes in his shirt, with light and weapons.
IAGO: Who's there? whose noise is this that cries on° murder?
LOD: We do not know.
IAGO: Did not you hear a cry?
CAS: Here, here! for heaven's sake, help me!
IAGO: What's the matter?   50
GRA: This is Othello's ancient, as I take it.
LOD: The same indeed; a very valiant fellow.
IAGO: What are you here that cry so grievously?
CAS: Iago? O, I am spoil'd, undone by villains!
   Give me some help.   55
IAGO: O me, lieutenant! what villains have done this?
CAS: I think that one of them is hereabout,
   And cannot make away.
IAGO: O treacherous villains!
   What are you there? come in, and give some help. (*To* LODOVICO *and* GRATIANO.)
ROD: O, help me here!   60
CAS: That 's one of them.

37. passage: people passing.   **42. heavy:** thick, cloudy.   **48. cries on:** cries out.

IAGO: O murd'rous slave! O villain! (*Stabs* RODERIGO.)

ROD: O damn'd Iago! O inhuman dog!

IAGO: Kill men i' th' dark!—Where be these bloody thieves?—
How silent is this town!—Ho! murder! murder!—
What° may you be? are you of good or evil?   65

LOD: As you shall prove us, praise us.

IAGO: Signior Lodovico?

LOD: He, sir.

IAGO: I cry you mercy. Here 's Cassio hurt by villains.

GRA: Cassio!   70

IAGO: How is 't, brother!

CAS: My leg is cut in two.

IAGO: Marry, heaven forbid!
Light, gentlemen: I'll bind it with my shirt.

        (*Enter* BIANCA.)

BIAN: What is the matter, ho? who is 't that cried?

IAGO: Who is 't that cried?   75

BIAN: O my dear Cassio! my sweet Cassio!
O Cassio, Cassio, Cassio!

IAGO: O notable strumpet! Cassio, may you suspect
Who they should be that have thus mangled you?

CAS: No.   80

GRA: I am sorry to find you thus: I have been to seek you.

IAGO: Lend me a garter. So. O, for a chair,°
To bear him easily hence!

BIAN: Alas, he faints! O Cassio, Cassio, Cassio!

IAGO: Gentlemen all, I do suspect this trash°   85
To be a party in this injury.
Patience awhile, good Cassio. Come, come;
Lend me a light. Know we this face or no?
Alas, my friend and my dear countryman
Roderigo! no:—yes, sure:—O heaven! Roderigo.   90

GRA: What, of Venice?

IAGO: Even he, sir: did you know him?

GRA: Know him! ay.

IAGO: Signior Gratiano? I cry your gentle pardon;
These bloody accidents must excuse my manners,
That so neglected you.

GRA: I am so glad to see you.   95

IAGO: How do you, Cassio? O, a chair, a chair!

GRA: Roderigo!

IAGO: He, he, 'tis he. (*A chair brought in.*) O, that's well said; the chair.
Some good man bear him carefully from hence;

---

65. What: who.   **82. chair:** sedan chair.   **85. trash:** worthless thing, i.e., Bianca.

I'll fetch the general's surgeon. (*To* BIANCA) For you, mistress,   100
Save you your labour. He that lies slain here, Cassio,
Was my dear friend: what malice was between you?
CAS: None in the world; nor do I know the man.
IAGO (*To* BIAN.):   What, look you pale? O, bear him out o' th' air.

(CASSIO *and* RODERIGO *are borne off.*)

Stay you, good gentlemen. Look you pale, mistress?   105
Do you perceive the gastness° of her eye?
Nay, if you stare, we shall hear more anon.
Behold her well; I pray you, look upon her:
Do you see, gentlemen? nay, guiltiness will speak,
Though tongues were out of use.   110

(*Enter* EMILIA.)

EMIL: 'Las, what's the matter? what's the matter, husband?
IAGO: Cassio hath here been set on in the dark
    By Roderigo and fellows that are scap'd:
    He's almost slain, and Roderigo dead.
EMIL: Alas, good gentlemen! alas, good Cassio!   115
IAGO: This is the fruit of whoring. Prithee, Emilia,
    Go know of Cassio where he supp'd to-night.
    (*To* BIANCA) What, do you shake at that?
BIAN: He supp'd at my house; but I therefore shake not.
IAGO: O, did he so? I charge you, go with me.   120
EMIL: Fie, fie upon thee, strumpet!
BIAN: I am no strumpet; but of life as honest
    As you that thus abuse me.
EMIL: As I! foh! fie upon thee!
IAGO: Kind gentlemen, let's go see poor Cassio dress'd.
    Come, mistress, you must tell 's another tale.   125
    Emilia, run you to the citadel,
    And tell my lord and lady what hath happ'd.
    Will you go on afore? (*Aside*) This is the night
    That either makes me or fordoes° me quite.

(*Exeunt.*)

SCENE II

A bedchamber in the castle.

(*Enter* OTHELLO *with a light;* DESDEMONA *in her bed.*)

OTH: It is the cause, it is the cause,° my soul,—
    Let me not name it to you, you chaste stars!—

---

106. gastness: terror, ghastliness.   **129. fordoes:** undoes, ruins.   **V.ii. 1. It is the cause:** i.e., the cause
of justice on which Othello must act, Desdemona's deed, which is too unmentionable to be named to the
chaste stars.

It is the cause. Yet I'll not shed her blood;
Nor scar that whiter skin of hers than snow,
And smooth as monumental alabaster.   5
Yet she must die, else she'll betray more men.
Put out the light, and then put out the light:
If I quench thee, thou flaming minister,
I can again thy former light restore,
Should I repent me: but once put out thy light,   10
Thou cunning'st pattern of excelling nature,
I know not where is that Promethean heat°
That can thy light relume.° When I have pluck'd the rose,
I cannot give it vital growth again,
It needs must wither: I'll smell thee on the tree. (*Kissing her.*)   15
O balmy breath, that dost almost persuade
Justice to break her sword! One more, one more.
Be thus when thou art dead, and I will kill thee,
And love thee after. One more, and that's the last:
So sweet was ne'er so fatal. I must weep,   20
But they are cruel tears: this sorrow's heavenly°;
It strikes where it doth love. She wakes.
DES: Who's there? Othello?
OTH: Ay, Desdemona.
DES: Will you come to bed, my lord?
OTH: Have you pray'd to-night, Desdemona?
DES: Ay, my lord.   25
OTH: If you bethink yourself of any crime
    Unreconcil'd as yet to heaven and grace,
    Solicit for it straight.
DES: Alack, my lord, what may you mean by that?
OTH: Well, do it, and be brief; I will walk by: 30
    I would not kill thy unprepared spirit;
    No; heaven forfend! I would not kill thy soul.
DES: Talk you of killing?
OTH: Ay, I do.
DES: Then heaven
    Have mercy on me!
OTH: Amen, with all my heart!
DES: If you say so, I hope you will not kill me.   35
OTH: Hum!
DES: And yet I fear you; for you're fatal then
    When your eyes roll so: why I should fear I know not,

---

12. Promethean heat: divine fire; allusion to the theft of fire from heaven by Prometheus.
13. relume: rekindle.   **21. this . . . heavenly:** this tenderness, with which I lament the punishment
which justice compels me to inflict, is a holy passion.

Since guiltiness I know not; but yet I feel I fear.

OTH: Think on thy sins.

DES: They are loves I bear to you.   40

OTH: Ay, and for that thou diest.

DES: That death 's unnatural that kills for loving.
    Alas, why gnaw you so your nether lip?
    Some bloody passion shakes your very frame:
    These are portents; but yet I hope, I hope,   45
    They do not point on me.

OTH: Peace, and be still!

DES: I will so. What 's the matter?

OTH: That handkerchief which I so lov'd and gave thee
    Thou gav'st to Cassio.

DES: No, by my life and soul!
    Send for the man, and ask him.

OTH: Sweet soul, take heed,   50
    Take heed of perjury; thou are on thy deathbed.

DES: Ay, but not yet to die.

OTH: Yes, presently:
    Therefore confess thee freely of thy sin;
    For to deny each article with oath
    Cannot remove nor choke the strong conception°   55
    That I do groan withal. Thou art to die.

DES: Then Lord have mercy on me!

OTH: I say, amen.

DES: And have you mercy too! I never did
    Offend you in my life; never lov'd Cassio
    But with such general warranty of heaven   60
    As I might love; I never gave him token.

OTH: By heaven, I saw my handkerchief in 's hand.
    O perjur'd woman! thou dost stone° my heart,
    And makest me call what I intend to do
    A murder, which I thought a sacrifice: 65
    I saw the handkerchief.

DES: He found it then;
    I never gave it him: send for him hither;
    Let him confess a truth.

OTH: He hath confess'd.

DES: What, my Lord?

OTH: That he hath us'd thee.

DES: How? unlawfully?

OTH: Ay.   70

---

55. conception: plan, intention.   **63. stone:** turn to stone, harden; Othello means that he will be tempted to kill her in sheer anger because of her perjury.

DES: He will not say so.

OTH: No, his mouth is stopp'd;
Honest Iago hath ta'en order° for 't.

DES: O! my fear interprets: what, is he dead?

OTH: Had all his hairs been lives, my great revenge
Had stomach for them all.   75

DES: Alas! he is betray'd and I undone.

OTH: Out, strumpet! weep'st thou for him to my face?

DES: O, banish me, my lord, but kill me not!

OTH: Down, strumpet!

DES: Kill me to-morrow: let me live to-night!   80

OTH: Nay, if you strive,—

DES: But half an hour!

OTH: Being done, there is no pause.°

DES: But while I say one prayer!

OTH: It is too late. (*Smothers her.*)

EMIL (*at the door*): My lord, my lord! what, ho! my lord, my lord!

OTH: What noise is this? Not dead? not yet quite dead?   85
I that am cruel am yet merciful;
I would not have thee linger in thy pain:
So, so.

EMIL (*within*): What, ho! my lord, my lord!

OTH: Who's there?

EMIL (*within*): O, good my lord, I would speak a word with you!   90

OTH: Yes: 'tis Emilia. By and by. She 's dead.
'Tis like she comes to speak of Cassio's death.—
The noise was here. Ha! no more moving?
Still as the grave. Shall she come in? were 't good?—
I think she stirs again:—no. What 's best to do?   95
If she come in, she'll sure speak to my wife:
My wife! my wife! what wife? I have no wife.
O, insupportable! O heavy hour!
Methinks it should be now a huge eclipse
Of sun and moon, and that th' affrighted globe
Should yawn° at alteration.°   100

EMIL: (*Within*) I do beseech you
That I may speak with you, O, good my lord!

OTH: I had forgot thee: O, come in, Emilia:
Soft; by and by. Let me the curtains draw.
Where art thou? (*Closes bed-curtains and opens door.*)

72. ta'en order: taken measures.   82. Being . . . pause: i.e., when the execution of the deed has once begun, there is no stopping.   101. yawn: gape in amazement.   101. at alteration: at the change.

(*Enter* EMILIA.)

| | What 's the matter with thee now? | 105 |

EMIL: O, my good lord, yonder's foul murders done!

OTH: What, now?

EMIL: But now, my lord.

OTH: It is the very error° of the moon;
She comes more nearer earth than she was wont, 110
And makes men mad.

EMIL: Cassio, my lord, hath kill'd a young Venetian
Call'd Roderigo.

OTH: Roderigo kill'd!
And Cassio kill'd!

EMIL: No, Cassio is not kill'd.

OTH: Not Cassio kill'd! then murder 's out of tune, 115
And sweet revenge grows harsh.

DES: O, falsely, falsely murder'd!

EMIL: Alas, what cry is that?

OTH: That! what!

EMIL: Out, and alas! that was my lady's voice.
Help, help, ho! help. O lady, speak again! 120
Sweet Desdemona! O sweet mistress, speak!

DES: A guiltless death I die.

EMIL: O, who hath done this deed?

DES: Nobody; I myself. Farewell:
Commend me to my kind lord: O, farewell! (*Dies.*) 125

OTH: Why, how should she be murd'red?

EMIL: Alas, who knows?

OTH: You heard her say herself, it was not I.

EMIL: She said so: I must needs report the truth.

OTH: She's, like a liar, gone to burning hell:
'Twas I that kill'd her.

EMIL: O, the more angel she, 130
And you the blacker devil!

OTH: She turn'd to folly,° and she was a whore.

EMIL: Thou dost belie her, and thou art a devil.

OTH: She was false as water.

EMIL: Thou art rash as fire, to say
That she was false: O, she was heavenly true! 135

OTH: Cassio did top her; ask thy husband else.
O, I were damned beneath all depth in hell,
But that I did proceed upon just grounds

---

109. error: irregularity.   **132. folly:** unchastity.

To this extremity. Thy husband knew it all.

EMIL: My husband!   140

OTH: Thy husband.

EMIL: That she was false to wedlock?

OTH: Ay, with Cassio. Nay, had she been true,
If heaven would make me such another world
Of one entire and perfect chrysolite,°   145
I'ld not have sold her for it.

EMIL: My husband!

OTH: Ay, 'twas he that told me first:
An honest man he is, and hates the slime
That sticks on filthy deeds.

EMIL: My husband!

OTH: What needs this iterance,° woman? I say thy husband.   150

EMIL: O mistress, villainy hath made mocks with° love!
My husband say that she was false!

OTH: He, woman;
I say thy husband: dost understand the word?
My friend, thy husband, honest, honest Iago.

EMIL: If he say so, may his pernicious soul   155
Rot half a grain a day! he lies to th' heart:
She was too fond of her most filthy bargain.

OTH: Ha!

EMIL: Do thy worst:
This deed of thine is no more worthy heaven   160
Than thou wast worthy her.

OTH: Peace, you were best.

EMIL: Thou hast not half that power to do me harm
As I have to be hurt.° O gull! O dolt!
As ignorant as dirt! thou hast done a deed—
I care not for thy sword; I'll make thee known,   165
Though I lost twenty lives.—Help! help, ho! help!
The Moor hath kill'd my mistress! Murder! murder!

(*Enter* MONTANO, GRATIANO, *and* IAGO *with others.*)

MON: What is the matter! How now, general!

EMIL: O, are you come, Iago? you have done well,
That men must lay their murders on your neck.   170

GRA: What is the matter?

EMIL: Disprove this villain, if thou be'st a man:
He says thou told'st him that his wife was false:

145. **chrysolite:** the golden stone; a name given to various precious stones of green color.   150. **iterance:** iteration, repetition.   151. **made mocks with:** derided, made sport of.   163. **to be hurt:** i.e., to endure hurting.

I know thou didst not, thou 'rt not such a villain:
Speak, for my heart is full.   175

IAGO: I told him what I thought, and told no more
Than what he found himself was apt° and true.

EMIL: But did you ever tell him she was false?

IAGO: I did.

EMIL: You told a lie; an odious, damned lie;   180
Upon my soul, a lie, a wicked lie.
She false with Cassio!—did you say with Cassio?

IAGO: With Cassio, mistress. Go to, charm° your tongue.

EMIL: I will not charm my tongue; I am bound to speak:
My mistress here lies murdered in her bed,—   185

ALL: O heavens forfend!

EMIL: And your reports have set the murder on.

OTH: Nay, stare not, masters: it is true, indeed.

GRA: 'Tis a strange truth.

MON: O monstrous act!

EMIL: Villainy, villainy, villainy!   190
I think upon 't, I think: I smell 't: O villainy—
I thought so then°: I'll kill myself for grief:—
O villainy, villainy!

IAGO: What, are you mad? I charge you, get you home.

EMIL: Good gentlemen, let me have leave to speak: 195
'Tis proper I obey him, but not now.
Perchance, Iago, I will ne'er go home.

OTH: O! O! O! (*He falls on the bed.*)

EMIL: Nay, lay thee down and roar;
For thou hast kill'd the sweetest innocent
That e'er did lift up eye.

OTH: (*Rising*) O, she was foul!   200
I scarce did know you, uncle: there lies your niece,
Whose breath, indeed, these hands have newly stopp'd:
I know this act shows horrible and grim.

GRA: Poor Desdemona! I am glad thy father's dead:
Thy match was mortal to him, and pure grief   205
Shore° his old thread in twain: did he live now,
This sight would make him do a desperate turn,
Yea, curse his better angel from his side,
And fall to reprobation.°

OTH: 'Tis pitiful; but yet Iago knows   210
That she with Cassio hath the act of shame

---

177. apt: natural, likely.   **183. charm:** keep silent.   **192. then:** i.e., at some earlier time, probably IV, ii, when she suspected the machinations of *some eternal villain*; she did not, however, know that villain to be Iago until this moment.   **206. Shore:** cut   **209. reprobation:** damnation, rejection by God.

A thousand times committed; Cassio confess'd it:
And she did gratify his amorous works
With that recognizance° and pledge of love
Which I first gave her; I saw it in his hand: 215
It was a handkerchief, an antique token
My father gave my mother.

EMIL: O heaven! O heavenly pow'rs!

IAGO: Come, hold your peace.

EMIL: 'Twill out, 'twill out: I peace!
No, I will speak as liberal as the north°:   220
Let heaven and men and devils, let them all,
All, all, cry shame against me, yet I'll speak.

IAGO: Be wise, and get you home.

EMIL: I will not! (IAGO *offers to stab* EMILIA.)

GRA: Fie!
Your sword upon a woman?

EMIL: O thou dull Moor! that handkerchief thou speak'st of   225
I found by fortune° and did give my husband;
For often, with solemn earnestness,
More than indeed belong'd to such a trifle,
He begg'd me to steal it.

IAGO: Villainous whore!

EMIL: She give it Cassio! no, alas! I found it,   230
And I did give 't my husband.

IAGO: Filth, thou liest!

EMIL: By heaven, I do not, I do not, gentlemen.
O murd'rous coxcomb!° what should such a fool
Do with so good a wife!

OTH: Are there no stones in heaven°
But what serves for the thunder?—Precious villain!   235
            (*He runs at* IAGO: IAGO, *from behind, stabs* EMILIA, *and exits.*)

GRA: The woman falls; sure, he hath kill'd his wife.

EMIL: Ay, ay: O, lay me by my mistress' side.

GRA: He 's gone, but his wife 's kill'd.

MON: 'Tis a notorious villain. Take you this weapon,
Which I have here recover'd from the Moor: 240
Come, guard the door without; let him not pass,
But kill him rather. I'll after that same villain,
For 'tis a damned slave.   (*Exit with all but* OTHELLO *and* EMILIA.)

OTH: I am not valiant neither,
But every puny whipster° gets my sword:

---

214. recognizance: token.   **220. liberal as the north:** freely as the north wind.   **226. fortune:** chance.
233. coxcomb: fool; addressed to Othello.   **234. stones in heaven:** thunderbolts. It was supposed that
real stones fell with the thunder and caused the damage.   **244. whipster:** contemptible fellow.

But why should honour outlive honesty?°   245
    Let it go all.
EMIL: What did thy song bode, lady?
    Hark, canst thou hear me? I will play the swan,
    And die in music. (*Singing*) Willow, willow, willow.—
    Moor, she was chaste; she lov'd thee, cruel Moor;
    So come my soul to bliss, as I speak true;   250
    So speaking as I think, I die, I die. (*Dies.*)
OTH: I have another weapon in this chamber;
    It is a sword of Spain, the ice-brook's temper°:—
    O, here it is. Uncle, I must come forth.
GRA (*within*):   If thou attempt it, it will cost thee dear: 255
    Thou hast no weapon, and perforce must suffer.
OTH: Look in upon me then and speak with me,
    Or, naked° as I am, I will assault thee.

              (*Enter* GRATIANO.)

GRA: What is the matter?
OTH: Behold, I have a weapon;
    A better never did itself sustain   260
    Upon a soldier's thigh: I have seen the day,
    That, with this little arm and this good sword,
    I have made my way through more impediments
    Than twenty times your stop°: but, O vain boast!
    Who can control his fate? 'tis not so now.   265
    Be not afraid, though you do see me weapon'd;
    Here is my journey's end, here is my butt,°
    And very sea-mark° of my utmost sail.
    Do you go back dismay'd? 'tis a lost fear;
    Man° but a rush° against Othello's breast,   270
    And he retires. Where should Othello go?
    Now, how dost thou look now? O ill-starr'd wench!
    Pale as thy smock! when we shall meet at compt,°
    This look of thine will hurl my soul from heaven,
    And fiends will snatch at it. Cold, cold, my girl!   275
    Even like thy chastity. O cursed, cursed slave!
    Whip me, ye devils,
    From the possession of this heavenly sight!
    Blow me about in winds! roast me in sulphur!
    Wash me in steep-down gulfs of liquid fire!   280

---

245. honour outlive honesty: Othello realizes that he has done a shameful deed; he asks why his reputation for valor should endure.   **253. ice-brook's temper:** usually defined as "tempered in ice-cold
water."   **258. naked:** unarmed.   **264. stop:** power.   **267. butt:** mark for archery, goal, limit.
268. sea-mark: beacon (marking his destination or limit).   **270. Man:** provide, as in manning a gun.
270. rush: reed.   **273. compt:** account, judgment day.

O Desdemona! Dead Desdemona! dead!
Oh! Oh!

    (*Enter* Lodovico, Cassio, *carried in a chair*, Montano, *and* Iago, *prisoner,*
    with Officers.)

Lod:	Where is this rash and most unfortunate man?
Oth:	That 's he that was Othello: here I am.
Lod:	Where is that viper? bring the villain forth.

Oth: I look down towards his feet°; but that 's a fable.
     If that thou be'st a devil, I cannot kill thee. (*Wounds* Iago.]
Lod: Wrench his sword from him.
Iago: I bleed sir; but not kill'd.
Oth: I am not sorry neither: I 'ld have thee live;
     For, in my sense, 'tis happiness to die.
Lod: O thou Othello, that wert once so good,
     Fall'n in the practice of a damned slave,
     What shall be said to thee?
Oth: Why, any thing:
     An honourable murder, if you will;
     For nought I did in hate, but all in honour.
Lod: This wretch hath part confess'd his villainy:
     Did you and he consent in Cassio's death?
Oth: Ay.
Cas: Dear general, I never gave you cause.
Oth: I do believe it, and I ask your pardon.
     Will you, I pray, demand that demi-devil
     Why he hath thus ensnar'd my soul and body?
Iago: Demand me nothing: what you know, you know:
     From this time forth I never will speak word.
Lod: What, not to pray?
Gra: Torments will ope your lips.
Oth: Well, thou dost best.
Lod: Sir, you shall understand what hath befall'n,
     Which, as I think, you know not. Here is a letter
     Found in the pocket of the slain Roderigo;
     And here another: the one of them imports
     The death of Cassio to be undertook
     By Roderigo.
Oth: O villain!
Cas: Most heathenish and most gross!
Lod: Now here 's another discontented° paper,
     Found in his pocket too; and this, it seems,
     Roderigo meant t' have sent this damned villain;

285

290

295

300

305

310

315

286. towards his feet: i.e., to see if they were cloven like a devil's.   **314. discontented:** expressing
dissatisfaction.

But that belike Iago in the interim
Came in and satisfied him.

OTH: O thou pernicious caitiff!°—
How came you, Cassio, by that handkerchief
That was my wife's?

CAS: I found it in my chamber: 320
And he himself confess'd but even now
That there he dropp'd it for a special purpose
Which wrought to his desire.

OTH: O fool! O fool! fool!

CAS: There is besides in Roderigo's letter,
How he upbraids Iago, that he made him   325
Brave° me upon the watch; whereon it came
That I was cast°: and even but now he spake,
After long seeming dead, Iago hurt him,
Iago set him on.

LOD: You must forsake this room, and go with us: 330
Your power and your command is taken off,°
And Cassio rules in Cyprus. For this slave,
If there be any cunning cruelty
That can torment him much and hold him long,
It shall be his. You shall close prisoner rest,   335
Till that the nature of your fault be known
To the Venetian state. Come, bring him away.

OTH: Soft you; a word or two before you go.
I have done the state some service, and they know 't.
No more of that. I pray you, in your letters,   340
When you shall these unlucky deeds relate,
Speak of me as I am; nothing extenuate,°
Nor set down aught in malice: then must you speak
Of one that lov'd not wisely but too well;
Of one not easily jealous, but being wrought,   345
Perplex'd° in the extreme; of one whose hand,
Like the base Judean,° threw a pearl away
Richer than all his tribe; of one whose subdu'd eyes,
Albeit unused to the melting mood,
Drop tears as fast as the Arabian trees   350
Their medicinal gum. Set you down this;
And say besides, that in Aleppo° once,

318. **caitiff:** wretch.   326. **Brave:** defy.   327. **cast:** dismissed.   331. **taken off:** taken away.
342. **extenuate:** diminish, depreciate; the idea is contrasted with the thought of *malice* in the following
line.   346. **Perplex'd:** confounded, distracted.   347. **Judean:** infidel or disbeliever.   352. **Aleppo:** a
Turkish city where the Venetians had special trading privileges. It is stated that it was immediate death
for a Christian to strike a Turk in Aleppo; Othello risked his life for the honor of Venice.

Where a malignant and a turban'd Turk
Beat a Venetian and traduc'd the state,
I took by th' throat the circumcised dog,   355
And smote him, thus. (*Stabs himself.*)
LOD: O bloody period!°
GRA: All that is spoke is marr'd.
OTH: I kiss'd thee ere I kill'd thee: no way but this;
Killing myself, to die upon a kiss.

     (*Falls on the bed, and dies.*)

CAS: This did I fear, but thought he had no weapon;   360
For he was great of heart.
LOD: (*To* IAGO) O Spartan dog,°
More fell than anguish, hunger, or the sea!
Look on the tragic loading of this bed;
This is thy work: the object poisons sight;
Let it be hid, Gratiano, keep the house,   365
And seize upon the fortunes of the Moor,
For they succeed on you. To you, lord governor,
Remains the censure of this hellish villain;
The time, the place, the torture: O, enforce it!
Myself will straight abroad; and to the state   370
This heavy act with heavy heart relate.   (*Exeunt.*)

                [1604]

357. period: termination, conclusion.   **361. Spartan dog:** Spartan dogs were noted for their savagery.

Journal Entry

How effective is Shakespeare's play in portraying the presence of a black moor in a white society? Consider Brabantio's, the Duke's, Iago's, and Othello's various attitudes toward the issue of race relations.

Textual Considerations

1. To analyze the structural development of *Othello*, consider Othello's autobiographical speeches in act 1, scene 3. Explain how Othello's portrait of himself and his cultural background might have contributed to his manipulation by Iago.
2. Analyze the images of women in *Othello* from the viewpoint of gender and class. What role do the women fulfill in the patriarchal system? What position do they occupy in Venetian society?. Don't overlook Cassio's treatment of Desdemona and Bianca as well as the various images of women with which Iago entertains his audience in act 2, scene 1.
3. Consider the extent to which the settings of the play suggest a symbolic contrast between the social and political orders of Venice and Cyprus. To what extent do these symbolic settings reflect psychological changes in Othello?

4. What kinds of responses do Iago's soliloquies and asides elicit from the audience? Consider the audience's feelings of comfort, discomfort, fear, sympathy, repulsion, expectation, and suspense.

5. Analyze the images of women that Desdemona uses in act 1, scene 3, lines 185–88, and in act 4, scene 3, lines 25–32. To what extent do these images help Desdemona justify her actions and communicate her feelings and emotions? How effective is Desdemona's use of language in both passages?

Cultural Contexts

1. The explanations behind Iago's motives for destroying Othello have ranged from Iago's dissatisfaction with Othello's poor distribution of power within the ranks of his army, to Iago's pleasure and excitement in manipulating people, to Iago's "motiveless malignity." What other motives can you and your classmates attribute to Iago? How effective are these motives in view of the closure Iago imposes on this issue at the end of the play: "what you know, you know: From this time forth I never will speak a word" (act 5, scene 2, lines 303–304)?

2. Some of the lines in *Othello*, such as "Were I the Moor, I would not be Iago" (act 1, scene 1, line 57), suggest Iago's dissatisfaction with his sense of self. Identify other lines and speeches that support the viewpoint that Iago is continuously fashioning a new identity for himself.

Performance Exercises

PERFORMANCE EXPRESS (45 MINUTES)

Propose a cast for all the roles in *Othello*, using your classmates as actors. To identify themselves to their audience, ask actors to stick paper tags with their names to their garments. After a brief (ten-minute) rehearsal, bring them in front of the classroom audience to talk about their characters and discuss their roles in the play. Encourage the actors to explore voice, physical action, and the emotional possibilities of their roles. To create a good dynamic *ensemble*, invite the class to interact with the actors.

PERFORMANCE PROJECTS

1. One of the most reputable Shakespearean critics, A.C. Bradley (1851–1935), defined Othello as "by far the most romantic figure among Shakespeare's heroes." Working with your group, search for character traits that emphasize Othello's romantic background in his famous speech, "Her father lov'd me" (1.3.128–70). Break the script into its smallest parts and devise the character's intention for each part or beat. Discuss and encourage the actors cast in the role of Othello to present a variety of vocal, physical, and emotion choices. The group should also decide on scenic design, music, and costume to support this romantic staging of Othello's speech.

2. Iago was cast as a gloomy malcontent and self-centered individualist in the film adaptations of *Othello* by Orson Welles (1952) and Oliver Parker (1995). Working with your group, stage a production of Iago's soliloquies to show your own dramatic interpretation of Iago. Consider the importance of voice, movement, constumes, and emotional focus, as well as the context or situation in which Iago finds himself for his solo performance of each soliloquy.

STUDENT JOURNAL ENTRY

on "Black Hair"

I enjoyed reading Gary Soto's essay "Black Hair" because I have also worked at summer jobs that I did not like, although none was as bad as working in that tire factory. The points that I intend to emphasize in my essay include the horrible working conditions, the monotony of their daily routine, and what I learned about being an undocumented worker. The fact that none of the men tried to escape made me rethink some of my ideas about how we treat illegal workers and how we need to modify our immigration policies. I was also amazed that some of my group members thought illegal immigrants were taking jobs away from American citizens. Who would want to work in a tire factory or pick produce?

TOPICS FOR DISCUSSION
AND WRITING

Writing Topics

1. Identify and analyze the sources of racial hostility in "Cross Plains, Wisconsin," "Telephone Conversation," and "On the Subway." To what extent do the poems reinforce or negate the concept that people can modify ingrained assumptions about race?

2. Poverty, economic inequity, immigration, exile, and displacement are subtexts in the poems by Espada and Laviera. Compare and contrast their speakers' responses to their situations. What knowledge do they bring to this topic?

3. Compare and contrast the portrayals of the American Dream in the texts by Hughes, Lui, Soto, and Yamauchi. What factors might account for differences in their points of view? Limit your discussion to three texts.

4. Compare and contrast the themes of ethnic identification and cultural assimilation in the texts by Lui, Douglass, Hughes, Morales, and Mora. What circumstances might account for differences in their points of view? Choose any three texts.

5. Compare and contrast images of whiteness in the poems by Soyinka, Olds, and Hughes and the short stories by Bambara, Chopin, and Gordimer. Limit yourself to three texts.

6. Several texts use stereotypes to show how one racial group envisions the other. Write an essay in which you test these stereotypes against reality by comparing them to facts or to your own observations about stereotypes.

7. Using texts by Soto, Mora, and/or Espada, write an analysis of the costs of being an undocumented worker in the United States. To what extent do these authors further the current debate on immigration? How do their ideas compare with yours?

8. Choose two or three texts that support or refute African American critic Shelby Steele's thesis that "black anger always in a way flatters white power."

9. Several texts focus on the relation between exclusion and social class. Discuss their portrayal in "I Stand Here Ironing," "Latero Story," and "On the Subway."

10. A lack of awareness of cultural differences or the assumption by one cultural group that another is inferior often results in painful personal and social encounters. Apply this thesis to any three texts.

11. Personal and cultural alienation is a motif in the poetry of Gillan, Erdrich, Espada, Mora, and Morales. Analyze the causes and effects of the various speakers' sense of exclusion. To what extent are anger and rebellion part of their responses? To what effect? Choose any two poets.

12. Because of their brevity, stories like "Still" have to suggest as much as they say. What happens "outside" the story here? What happens after the story ends? Write the next scene.

13. Write an essay on the issue of race in *Othello*. Identify the racists in the play, and discuss their effect on Othello. Pay particular attention to Iago's determination to undermine

Othello's self-confidence by focusing on his being not only black but also an outsider in Venetian society.

14. Discuss the issue of gender relations in *Othello*. Consider, for example, how social class and the patriarchal tradition have shaped the personal identities of Iago, Emilia, and Desdemona.

Research Topics

1. Research part of the history of an ethnic group (your own or another you wish to know more about). Possibilities include Japanese internment camps in which Japanese American citizens were placed during World War II, Cesar Chavez and the struggles of Mexican American farmworkers against economic exploitation, or Indian reservations in the 1930s notorious for their high mortality rate, alcohol abuse, and chronic unemployment and the disintegration of the fabric of Native American culture and traditions.

2. Do some research on the Internet on the history of labor activism in the American South after World War II. In which instances did activism lead to violence and why? Who were the adversaries? What did each side want? What were some of the outcomes?

3. Focus on the contributions African Americans have made to arts, movies, literature, television, business, sports, government, and the armed forces. Research biographical material on one prominent African American of your choice, and write a profile of that individual that highlights the nature of his or her contribution: Toni Morrison, Wynton Marsalis, Tiger Woods, Oprah Winfrey, the Williams sisters (Venus and Serena), Alice Walker, or Colin Powell are just some of the people you could consider.

FILM ANGLES

As the literary selections of this part affirm, both race and culture often concern the existence of the "other," an individual or group considered to be outside the so-called norm. Such people are either denied the rights of the majority or excluded from entrance to the ruling minority. In the former circumstance, the other is often perceived as a threat to the beliefs, values, and institutions that sustain society; in the latter, the other's exclusion reinforces the segregation of society into class groups, especially the elitist nature of the "upper" or moneyed class. As two classic novels—Theodore Dreiser's *An American Tragedy* and John Steinbeck's *The Grapes of Wrath*—powerfully demonstrate, this division is true even in America, which purports to be democratic and free of class distinctions. Both novels have been made into strong films worth studying in this context: *A Place in the Sun* (d. George Stevens, 1951) is a version of the former, and *The Grapes of Wrath* (d. John Ford, 1940) an adaptation of the latter.

History is strewn with ugly illustrations of how societies have dealt with such phenomena as racial and religious difference. Examples include the history of slavery and segregation in America, the Holocaust in Nazi Germany, and the colonial occupations of Africa, Asia, and South America by various European nations. Although mainstream filmmakers have addressed these subjects, they tend to sanitize or understate their more horrific aspects to appeal to a mass audience. For example, neither Steven Spielberg's *Amistad* (1997) nor his *The Color Purple* (1985), both dealing with slavery, avoids typical Hollywood production values and clichés. The black protagonist of the former, for example, is saved by a white Anglo-Saxon hero. The same is true of Spielberg's *Schindler's List* (1993), which is less about the fate of the millions of Jews who died in the Holocaust than it is about the rescue of the fortunate few by a "good" Nazi.

By avoiding the more troubling aspects of these subjects, popular movies have often perpetuated ignorance and prejudice. For the greater part of its history, Hollywood characterized black people, Jews, Italians, Hispanics, Arabs, and Asians as negative or comic stereotypes rather than full-bodied three-dimensional individuals. As social attitudes have replaced ignorance and prejudice with knowledge and tolerance, movies have projected more enlightened views.

A foreign film, *Nowhere in Africa* (d. Caroline Link, Germany, 2002), poses the question of the other in an intriguing cross-cultural context. Based on an autobiographical novel by Stefanie Zweig, the story concerns a German/Jewish couple who flee to Africa with their young daughter in 1938—just before Jews were sent to concentration camps. Although the couple's marriage and lifestyle suffer from the uprooting, the daughter learns various tribal languages in Kenya and assimilates cultural values completely foreign to her European/Judaic roots. Although her mother treats the Africans as outsiders, it is she and her family, as Europeans, who are the real "others."

Spike Lee's powerful documentary, *When the Levees Broke: A Requiem in Four Acts*, made for television in 2006, brings together both themes of this unit. The film persuasively demonstrates that the federal government's failure to act quickly and effectively to address the catastrophe wrought by Hurricane Katrina was precisely because of its indifference to the plight of those most affected: African and poor white Americans.

Questions to Consider

1. Spike Lee's epic film *When the Levees Broke* is composed of many small narratives of the lives and fortunes of those who survived Hurricane Katrina only to face continued economic and psychological devastation. Many of these people are as memorable as characters in works of fiction. Select one or two vignettes from this film that illustrate Lee's method, and discuss how those interviewed dealt with the disaster. What have their experiences taught them about the continued problems of race and culture in this country? What has studying the film taught you?

2. Examine several scenes in *Nowhere in Africa* that illustrate the different attitudes of members of the family. Do these attitudes change in the course of the film? What lessons do the daughter, her mother, and father learn about living with the "other"? What do they learn about themselves?

RACE AND ETHNIC DIFFERENCE: HISTORY AND GENRE

Representations of Blacks in Movies

No better film example of the racial conflict that has stained American history and continues to divide society can be found than D. W. Griffith's controversial Civil War epic *The Birth of a Nation* (1915). The film made instant cultural history: It advanced the art of narrative filmmaking exponentially with its complex interweaving of characters against an historical backdrop, yet it also espoused a racist ideology with its regressive depiction of blacks and heroic images of the Ku Klux Klan as preservers of racial purity. Upon its release, it aroused vociferous protests across America, signaling the astounding impact movies would have on society. Although film historians do not deny the film's artistic achievement, neither can they deny its undisguised racism. Many object to public screenings of the film; others argue that suppressing it is equivalent to denying the existence of the disturbing circumstances and sentiments it reflects. If we want to learn from the past, scholars and historians assert, we cannot ignore the records and artworks that document it—however unpleasant they may be.

For decades popular movies reflected an ingrained prejudice toward African Americans by perpetuating stereotypical images. Until the 1950s, it was the rare film that did not restrict them to menial character roles (e.g., maids, butlers, bellhops) or treat them as objects of humor. The only black actor to win an Academy Award between 1929 and 1963 was Hattie McDaniel as Scarlett O'Hara's Mammy in *Gone with the Wind* (d. Victor Fleming, 1939).

This tendency began to change after World War II, with films like *Pinky* (d. Elia Kazan), *Home of the Brave* (d. Mark Robson), *Intruder in the Dust* (d. Clarence Brown), and *Lost Boundaries* (d. Alfred L. Werker), all released in 1949—all with more fully developed black characters. Independent films in the 1960s, such as *Nothing But a Man* (d. Michael Roemer, 1964) and *One Potato, Two Potato* (d. Larry Peerce, 1964), dealt more openly with the effect of prejudice on the everyday worker and with interracial marriage, a theme tackled by Hollywood three years later in the popular *Guess Who's Coming to Dinner* (d. Stanley Kramer, 1967).

Today African Americans are actively engaged in filmmaking. Spike Lee's films range from depictions of racial conflict in New York neighborhoods (*Do the Right Thing*, 1989; *Clockers*, 1995), to biographical drama (*Malcolm X*, 1972), and satire (*Bamboozled*, 2002). Comedies and melodramas with all-black casts are commonplace; documentaries like Lee's *When the Levees Broke* and *Love and Diane* (d. Jennifer Dworkin, 2003) deal with ongoing social problems that beset the black community.

Questions to Consider

1. Compare any two films from different decades with black characters. Do you discern any changes in the way the characters are represented?
2. Compare the social situations depicted in *Clockers* and *Do the Right Thing*. Do the different settings and intercultural circumstances have any effect on character behavior and race relations in each case?

Representations of Other Ethnic Groups

From the treatment of the Native American in countless westerns to stereotypes of Jews, Italians, Asians, Irish, and others, Hollywood movies are rife with examples of how ethnicity is represented in films. Many groups protest what they believe are negative images. Some Italian Americans object to films like *The Godfather* (d. Francis Ford Coppola, 1972) and *Goodfellas* (d. Martin Scorsese, 1990), and the TV series *The Sopranos* because they allegedly reinforce the belief that all Italians are associated with crime and the Mafia.

Genres often perpetuate **character types** and formulaic images of ethnic groups (e.g., the Italian mobster, the Irish cop, the Jewish businessman). Perhaps the best illustration of how genre has shaped popular conceptions of an ethnic group is the western. Westerns proliferated from the 1910s through the 1950s, moved to television in the 1950s and 1960s, and made a sporadic return with *Dances with Wolves* (d. Kevin Costner, 1990), *Unforgiven* (d. Clint Eastwood, 1992), *The Missing* (d. Ron Howard, 2004), and, less typically, *The Three Burials of Mechilades Estrada* (d. Tommy Lee Jones, 2005) and *Brokeback Mountain* (d. Ang Lee, 2005). Many traditional westerns exploited the image of the Native American as a threat to civilized life who had to be eradicated to make way for progress. It was through the western that generations of children learned to play "cowboys and Indians," a game that not so innocently reenacted the history of territorial expansion and communal settlement across America— both at the expense of the cultures and peoples of Indian nations. As in the history and the films, so with the games: The Indians never won.

John Ford, the most revered director in Hollywood's history, did as much as anyone to propagate this myth, symbolized in his westerns as the clash between the "garden" (civilization) and the "wilderness" (untamed nature). Yet he also made *The Searchers* (1956)—judged by film scholars to be among the ten greatest movies ever made—whose hero's pathological hatred of the Indian is scrutinized in the film.

Pathological hatred also underlies anti-Semitic sentiments in America, Europe, and other parts of the world. The Holocaust has been the subject of documentaries (e.g., Claude Lanzmann's *Shoah*, 1985) and narrative films (e.g., Sidney Lumet's *The Pawnbroker*, 1965; *Schindler's List*; and Roman Polanski's *The Pianist*, 2002). Unfortunately, anti-Semitism did not end with the horrors of the Holocaust. It was treated in such Hollywood films as *Gentleman's Agreement* (d. Elia Kazan, 1947) and *Crossfire* (d. Edward Dmytryk, 1947) and continues to be an important subject.

Questions to Consider

1. Stereotypes use features familiar to viewers from various aspects of a culture. Can you think of a recent film that uses stereotypes in this way? What are the familiar features it relies on?
2. Think of a recent film in which an individual or a group is treated unjustly because of their racial or ethnic difference. How are these people characterized in the film? Does the film resort to stereotyping? Is the difference treated as a "problem" that the community must deal with?

3. Think of a recent film, TV movie, or series that might invite the kind of controversy that surrounded *The Birth of a Nation*. Should a film be denied public exhibition because it may offend certain members of the audience? Is this what is meant by "political correctness"? If so, how does that differ from censorship? Doesn't freedom of speech and of the press preclude censorship?

4. What is the difference between a character type and a three-dimensional character? Can you think of a recent movie that illustrates the difference? What is the effect of each of these on your impressions of a character of a particular race or ethnic group?

5. Although *The Godfather* films and *Goodfellas* are heirs to the crime drama and gangster genre movies of the 1930s, they aspire to be more complex works of film art. This means the characters are more complicated both morally and psychologically, which can make it harder to judge the rightness or wrongness of their actions. Do you find it difficult to identify with any of the characters in these films? If so, does that have anything to do with the conflict between your values and theirs?

CASE STUDIES

To Kill a Mockingbird and *The Searchers*

Films about outsiders raise questions about viewer **identification** discussed in earlier units. It is generally assumed that the viewer will identify with the most admirable character, either because we approve how that character acts in a given situation or because the character's principles and ideas provide the most lucid and morally acceptable guide through whatever controversies the film presents. In *To Kill a Mockingbird* (d. Robert Mulligan, 1962), the film version of Harper Lee's novel, this character is the courageous lawyer who defends a black man on trial for rape.

Imagine a black member of the audience in the South, however—someone who had been directly or indirectly affected by events like the one in the film. Would this person identify with the film's "hero"—the white lawyer—or the accused black man? Assuming the latter would be a form of stereotyping because it would presume that a black member of the audience would naturally identify with the underdog. Suppose, however, this same viewer had aspirations to improve society—perhaps to become a lawyer or to help his or her son or grandson to become a lawyer and fight the hatred, prejudice, and stereotyping that led to many such situations. Might not such a person also identify with the white lawyer?

Having to split one's identification is not an uncommon effect of movies. Ethan Edwards, the ostensible hero in *The Searchers*, is both the courageous, experienced, and knowledgeable character determined to track down the Indians who murdered his family and abducted his nieces *and* a person consumed by blinding hatred of Indians. Although we respect his positive features, we may be repelled by his irrational ones. The film provides us with a younger, less experienced character, no less determined and courageous, who accompanies Ethan on the search and, like the viewer, aligns himself with Ethan's good features while repudiating the bad.

Questions to Consider

1. Both *To Kill a Mockingbird* and *The Searchers* confirm that the more complex a character's makeup and situation, the more complex the viewer's reaction and ability to identify will be. Why might this be an appropriate position for the viewer of a film dealing with race and difference?

2. Consider the film *Training Day* (d. Antoine Farqua, 2001) from the perspective of viewer identification. How is the Denzel Washington character initially presented? Do your first

impressions change as the film progresses? Why? Does the Ethan Hawke character act as the surrogate for the viewer's ambivalence?

OTHELLO

As a play, *Othello* has a more direct, visceral appeal than *Hamlet*—its plot and passions less ambiguous. A study of the play demonstrates that its protagonist's life and downfall are affected by both aspects of the other, as stated at the beginning of this Film Angles section. That is, he is subject to the restrictions of both race and culture because his admission to high society depends, as the play makes clear, on his use value as a military defender of the Venetian state. Therefore, despite his preeminent position as commander of the Venetian fleet, he remains a stranger to that culture, racially and otherwise, which is why he is doubly vulnerable to Iago's attacks on his peace of mind. Othello is both a man of status and the ultimate outsider, so ignorant of the ways of the Venetian court that he cannot contradict Iago's shrewd, licentious characterizations of Venetian women, including his wife. Othello's innocence and naïveté about such things, coupled with his military reputation and presumed sexual prowess, no doubt feed Iago's jealousy and hatred, well beyond the motives Shakespeare provides for his evil machinations.

Yet Iago's plan of destruction extends to Desdemona and Cassio, and to his own wife Emilia as well. As his soliloquies reveal, his is a philosophically grounded hatred of virtue, the manifestation of which in other people makes his life and person meaner by contrast. In this sense, the play explores the psychological underpinnings of hatred of the other, whose difference acts as a foil, exposing the inadequacies and inferiority of the one who hates. To varying degrees, each film version of *Othello* explores these facets of the characters.

The Range of Film Treatments

Like *Hamlet*, *Othello* was filmed in abridged and wordless form in silent movies. Understandably, its most notable film treatments have been those of Shakespearean actor/directors Laurence Olivier and Orson Welles. Opera and film director Franco Zeffirelli also made a film in 1986 of Verdi's opera *Otello* with Placido Domingo as the Moor. The opera is a consummate fusion of music and drama, thanks to the play's tight construction and generous supply of dramatic high points. Zeffirelli's film, however, illustrates how filmmakers, to make a play more cinematic, often mislead the viewer. In the scene in which Iago is trying to convince Othello that Desdemona and Cassio are lovers, Zeffirelli shows us Iago sleeping next to Cassio as the latter tosses and turns, presumably "dreaming" of Desdemona. This is not only gratuitous, but it tends to validate as fact what the play presents as fabrication.

In Oliver Parker's film (1995), Laurence Fishburne is a physically imposing Othello, and Shakespearean actor Kenneth Branagh a convincingly menacing Iago, yet neither seems to have grasped the complexities of the characters. Fishburne's forcefulness, for example, is unrelenting even when he should convey Othello's susceptibility to Iago's schemes. Huge close-ups of Branagh in his soliloquies misfire, giving undue stress to Iago's motives, reducing this most ambiguous of Shakespeare's villains to simpler sentiments.

Othello has also been modernized in various ways. In a production made for British television in 2001, directed by Geoffrey Saxe, the protagonist is a police lieutenant elevated to captain because he has the clout, and is of the complexion, to calm protests in black communities. His nemesis is jealous that he has been overlooked, and, as in the play, believes the captain has seduced his wife. In *O* (d. Tim Blake Nelson, 2001), the protagonist is Odin, a star basketball player at a private school, loved by everyone, including his coach, whose son

Hugo (Iago) becomes jealous. Although it stretches credibility, the film, in making the villain the coach's son, infuses his motives with a convincing sense of fraternal rivalry.

Both Orson Welles and Laurence Olivier were experienced Shakespearean artists whose knowledge of film and theater made them especially suited to transpose Shakespeare to the screen. Welles directed the Negro Theater's production of *Macbeth* in Harlem in 1936, a landmark work in the history of the American theater. Like his other film treatments of Shakespeare (*Macbeth* in 1948, *Falstaff* [aka *Chimes at Midnight*] in 1966), his *Othello* is more than a simple rendering of the play. He explores the tensions between language (the strength of the theater) and the visual (the strength of the cinema). His *Othello*, therefore, is as much a rich cinematic experience as it is a powerful interpretation of the play. This is immediately evident in the brief, wordless prologue—a flash forward scene of Welles's invention—in which the bodies of Othello and Desdemona are carried aloft to their burial, the funeral procession etched in stark black-and-white images against the sky. He condenses the play—one of Shakespeare's most dramatically focused—to a fast-moving ninety-two minutes, eliminating many lines, including most of Iago's soliloquies, and transposing others to different scenes. Through ingenious editing and overlapping dialogue, much of the action is collapsed into brief passages. Although purists have objected to these changes, key speeches and dramatic exchanges retain their privileged places, and the performances are strong, especially those by Welles, a larger-than-life Othello with a grave, sonorous voice, and Michael MacLiammoir, who, although not quite a physically imposing Iago, is credibly malevolent.

Olivier's film, running close to three hours, follows the play's action more faithfully and offers the most controversial portrait of the Moor. Neither noble nor admirable, Olivier's Othello is a pompous, self-centered figure whose blackness is flamboyantly, even crudely emphasized. Although no doubt politically incorrect, this version stresses Othello's otherness more bluntly and disturbingly than any other. Indeed, in putting Othello's race front and center, Olivier seems to answer scholar E. A. J. Honigmann's remark, "Who would dare to say, in the more liberal 1990s, that we have changed so completely that Othello's 'otherness' no longer affects us in the theatre?" (Introduction to the Arden edition of the play, 1997). The boldness of Olivier's portrayal, raising issues of the visibility or invisibility of blackness, is reason enough for classroom viewing and discussion.

Comparing Interpretive and Cinematic Features

Like many filmed versions of plays, Olivier's *Othello* is more concerned with preserving on film the interpretation and performance of a famous actor. It is more an archival treasure than a work of cinematic imagination. Such records are important because the texts of Shakespeare's plays lack directions as to how lines should be delivered, or who might be listening to a verbal exchange, and concerning various aspects of stage design that affect the audience's understanding of the action.

For a more cinematically minded director, a convention such as the soliloquy poses a problem. Welles gets around it by virtually eliminating Iago's soliloquies—in which the character tells us his true intentions and lays out his evil plans—by incorporating sections of them into his interactions with Roderigo. Othello's first soliloquy, declaring that he could stand almost anything but Desdemona's betrayal, is spoken as part of a scene with Desdemona, and his final one is spoken as a voice-over/interior monologue because he is in shadows and we never see his mouth moving. Thus Welles converts the stage convention into the more realistic terms of film language.

Such cinematographic elements as camera angles, camera movements, and lighting enhance aspects of the text and create specific moods that either intensify or counteract what characters are doing and saying. Welles makes frequent use of these features to make the space in which the play occurs a dynamic character in itself, subject to the shifts and turns of the action. Examples of this are when the camera revolves from ground level and peruses the sky to express Othello's collapse into an epileptic fit, as if from his point of view, and the way it spins dizzily at the end to mimic Othello's reeling condition in his final moments.

Equally expressive is Welles's way of filming and lighting the architecture and set, making them eloquent participants in the action rather than static backdrops. At the height of his rage over the thought of his wife's infidelity, Othello moves quickly with Iago through the castle's spaces and outdoors, in each shot framed and caught in a web of crisscrossing beams and shadows that increasingly express not only the distortions of his mind but his inability to free himself from what Iago calls the "net that shall enmesh them all." In such ways, Welles, as great a filmmaker as he was a Shakespearean, creates cinematic imagery to match the play's verse. To fully appreciate what a filmmaker can add to a work of literature requires close scrutiny of the film's parallel visual text, rich in connotative meanings and metaphorical implications.

Questions to Consider

1. What problems are there in trying to adapt a Shakespearean play to a contemporary setting—as in *O* and the British television film *Othello*? Do you think these problems have been solved in either film? Are there advantages to being introduced to the play in such forms?

2. What effect do you think the emphasis on Othello's blackness—as in Olivier's film— would have on today's viewers? Would it distract from other aspects of the play? Would it distort the play's meaning in any way? Do you think black viewers and white viewers would form different impressions of the characters or the play?

3. In Welles's film, in the scene when Iago makes Othello doubt why Desdemona married him, Othello looks into a mirror in three different shots. What is the significance of this gesture in this context? What idea does the mirror visualize? Is it related to Othello's awareness of his blackness?

Research Topics

1. In his critical study *Shakespeare: The Invention of the Human*, Harold Bloom argues that a major reason for Othello's vulnerability to Iago's lies is that he has not consummated his marriage to Desdemona. If, Bloom suggests, in addition to Othello's lack of experience of Venetian women, he has no physical verification of his wife's virginity, then he cannot know for certain that she has been faithful. Because no scene in the play absolutely confirms the issue one way or the other, use Bloom's thesis as a guide and look for evidence in several of the films that would indicate where each filmmaker stands on the issue.

2. Compare any two performances of actors or actresses in film versions of *Othello*. What are the strong or weak points in each? Which seem to lend themselves better to the film medium as opposed to the stage?

3. Two interesting films use *Othello* as a sustained backdrop to the lives and careers of theater actors. In both, what is going on in their private lives is partially fused with and reflected in performances of the play. The first, *A Double Life* (d. George Cukor, 1947), is a powerful drama about an actor on the New York stage who constantly confuses his real life with his theatrical life and ultimately acts out his jealous rage in reality during a performance. The actor, Ronald Colman, won the Oscar as Best Actor of 1947. The second film, *Stage Beauty* (d. Richard Eyre, 2004), is a period drama set during Restoration England when the rule

against women acting on the stage was relaxed, permanently changing the dynamics of theatrical realism. Watch either or both of these films, and consider how Othello's murder of Desdemona functions in each one.

CULTURE

Many films have explored the ramifications of class and culture in different societies. General audiences seem to enjoy watching the behavior of members of a class with which they presumably would have no contact throughout their lives. Perhaps this is the appeal of such films, allowing us, on the one hand, to envy the privileges upper-class people enjoy while, on the other hand, observing that despite such status they experience the same errors, foibles, and tragedies that befall the rest of us. The popularity of film and television versions of Jane Austen's novels testifies to the appeal of seeing people struggling to improve their class through marriage. No fewer than five versions of *Pride and Prejudice*, for example, have appeared over the last twenty years.

The desire to peer into the private lives of royalty is another aspect of this interest. Stephen Frears's intelligently written and brilliantly acted film *The Queen* (2006) exemplifies the phenomenon by depicting the insular lives of the English royal family as it comes to grips with the tragic death of the former Princess Diana and its impact on the population. The essence of the public relations scandal that ensued became a contest between Queen Elizabeth's traditional reserve and the need of her "subjects" to see her mourn with them a figure who they believed had erased the cultural and economic distance between royalty and the general populace by becoming what prime minister Tony Blair called "the people's princess."

Some works parody the notion of class divisions by drawing attention to the superficiality of what determines who belongs to what class. A famous example is George Bernard Shaw's play *Pygmalion*, turned into the highly successful musical and film *My Fair Lady* (d. George Cukor, 1964). In this story, a language professor turns the guttersnipe Eliza Doolittle into a lady simply by teaching her how to speak and walk, and he manages to deceive the royal heads of Europe. The cultivation of language and manners is also the means by which a young servant girl is transformed into a sophisticated woman in *Sabrina* (d. Billy Wilder, 1954), thus exposing the thin line that separates class divisions in a society, like America, based on money.

Although Americans tend to think of official royalty and aristocracy as outworn residues of old European cultures, biographers, historians, and popular media have repeatedly characterized family dynasties in our own history in aristocratic terms. For example, hardly a year goes by without a new book or television series on the Kennedys or the Roosevelts. Although from its beginnings, America has prided itself as a country in which every citizen has equal opportunities to achieve the so-called "American Dream," our society has been torn—also from its beginnings—by racial strife and cultural divides that have placed this achievement out of reach for the majority of its population.

CASE STUDIES

A Place in the Sun

Some of America's foremost writers have been preoccupied with the subject of class and culture. In novels such as *Sister Carrie* and *An American Tragedy*, Theodore Dreiser analyzes the role played by social conditions and class divisions in the lives of his protagonists. *An American Tragedy* is perhaps the most prominent example of the American Dream turning into a nightmare as it tells the story of Clyde Griffiths, a young man who leaves his poverty-stricken family and Bible-obsessed mother of the Midwest to try his fortunes in the East. He secures a job in a rich uncle's factory and, against company policy, becomes involved with a female factory worker. Unexpectedly, he meets and falls in love with a wealthy young debutante, who symbolizes the life of money, glamour, and privilege that has always been beyond his reach. His pursuit of her and plans to marry are interrupted when the factory girl becomes pregnant and threatens to expose him. Confused and desperate, he first thinks of killing her during a boat ride in a secluded location. Although he changes his mind, she drowns accidentally, and he is tried for murder and eventually sentenced to death.

The novel was made into a film of the same title in 1931 and later as *A Place in the Sun* (d. George Stevens, 1951), a hugely successful film that garnished many awards. Although the film changes the title and the names of the characters, it is true to the thrust of the plot and to the tragic turn of events. From the first scene, it signals the central theme as the protagonist (now called George Eastman) hitchhikes his way to a new life against the backdrop of a huge billboard, which shows a beautiful girl in a bathing suit enjoying a life of leisure, over which the words "It's an Eastman" are sprawled. The phrase refers to the successful company owned by his uncle where he will be employed, as well as to the kind of life that briefly but teasingly seems within his grasp. In retrospect, the advertisement is an especially biting and ironic visual commentary on the aspirations of the protagonist whose pursuit of the American Dream ends not only in failure but in ignominious death.

The film makes use of such techniques as the fade and the dissolve to amplify other aspects of the story and theme through visual effects. For example, as the factory girl threatens George in a telephone conversation, the transition to the following scene is via a dissolve that shows her standing in the telephone booth as a shot of the lake where she will drown slowly comes into view. The momentary impression is that she is already immersed in the water. Such techniques raise a question about the perspective the film takes on human life and free will. To telegraph future events in this way might suggest that everything is predestined and George is doomed from the start. If so, this would provide a dark commentary on the entire notion of the American Dream.

Questions to Consider

1. How are the differences in class and culture implied in the film represented in characters and situations? Do the looks and behavior of each of the women in George's life define these differences? Do you think the film reduces such "class" distinctions to stereotypes of any kind?
2. Find other visual and optical effects that draw attention to aspects of the story or the theme. Are these always ironic? Do they clarify the film's ideas or overstate them? How do they affect our impressions of the characters' behavior and whether they act out of freedom of choice?

Far from Heaven

Todd Haynes's *Far from Heaven* (2002), a melodrama set in the 1950s, is, among other things, an homage to and partial remake of Douglas Sirk's *All That Heaven Allows*, a classic of the genre that dealt with class difference, gender expectations, and social alienation. Haynes's film deliberately imitates the look and style of Sirk's, and even much of its plot. Here, a young couple's picture-perfect, middle-class life in a New England (Connecticut) community is shattered when the wife discovers that her husband, a successful sales executive, is living a secret life as a homosexual. She finds solace temporarily with her black gardener, a relationship that deepens into a possible romance, only to realize in the end that a future together would be impossible. The film touches more explicitly on many aspects of difference—class, racial, and sexual—than was typical in a Hollywood film of the 1950s.

The film is a good example of how an important film genre adjusts to the changing views of a contemporary audience without violating genre "rules" or renouncing the style of the original. By evoking Sirk's film in its use of rich autumnal New England colors and interior shadows, Haynes's film provides a dialogue not only with that film but with the genre of the melodrama and film history. The added tension provided by the racial and sexual themes implies that middle-class life was—and perhaps is still—precariously sustained through the suppression of certain feelings and desires and illustrates how the surface gloss of melodramas of the 1950s reflected these realities.

Questions to Consider

1. How is the subject of race handled in *Far from Heaven*? Given their social roles, do you think the wife and the gardener behave in credible ways? If the film were set in present day, how different would their behavior be? What does the film imply prevents their having a future together? Is it race or class? Does the film imply that race and class were, or are, synonymous?
2. How is the homosexual issue treated in the film? Which elements in the film—acting, dialogue, mise-en-scène—seem most effective in presenting this theme? Do we sympathize with the husband's dilemma as much as the wife's? Why or why not? Does the film suggest that homosexuality is incompatible with middle-class life of the period? How and why?
3. On the surface the domestic situation presented in the film seems to perfectly embody the ideal American Dream—until race and forbidden sexuality enter the picture. What message does the film convey about such concepts as the American Dream? What point do you think the director wants to make about what lies under the surface of middle-class life?

Research Topics

1. Do a little library research on the concept of class and how it is applied to any understanding of American society. Then examine one or two contemporary films that illustrate your findings.
2. Find a good definition of the American Dream. Is this theme out of date? If not, has it been transformed or disguised in contemporary society? Can you find recent films or television programs that still reflect the idea of the American Dream?
3. The famous American film *The Grapes of Wrath* deals with the plight of poverty-stricken families during the Depression, for whom the very notion of the American Dream is foreign. Watch this film (and if possible read the Steinbeck novel on which it is based), and consider the vision it presents of the poor and disenfranchised of American society. Are the conditions depicted strictly tied to the Depression and have they now been eliminated from American society? If not, how can we reconcile the existence of so many poor and uneducated people in a country that claims there is equal opportunity for all?
4. Study Spike Lee's film *When the Levees Broke* in light of the questions raised about the American Dream. Examine the lives and fortunes of several of the people tracked in the film and compare their situations. Compare the way they handle the effects of Hurricane Katrina on their lives. What profile of the society they all share emerges?

PART FIVE

INDIVIDUALISM AND COMMUNITY

"Postmodern life will place a premium on relationships, not individualism," predicted a contemporary psychologist as he looked ahead to the new century. Yet at the beginning of the twenty-first century, many sociological studies show marked variations in Americans' attitudes toward their roles in traditional communities such as the family, neighborhood, workplace, and religious institution. According to Robert Bellah, a contemporary American sociologist, ours "is a society in which the individual can rarely and with difficulty understand himself and his activities as interrelated in morally meaningful ways with those of other, different Americans."

Novelist Toni Morrison views the issue of individualism from a different perspective in her speech to the 2001 graduates of Smith College in which she urges them to resist conformity and focus on their individuality:

> You need not settle for any defining category: taxpayers, consumers, minority, majority. Of course, you are general. But you're also specific. Of course, you're more citizen than consumer. But you are also a person like no other on the planet. Nobody has your exact memory but you. You are your own stories and therefore, free to imagine, to discover, and to implement what it is to be human without wealth. What it feels like to be human without dominion over others, without reckless arrogance, without fear and without plundering others unlike you. Without rotating, rehearsing, and reinventing the hatreds learned in the sandbox. And although you don't have complete control of the narrative—no author does—you can, nevertheless, create it.

How do we resolve the issues of individualism and community in the complex and diverse society of the twenty-first century? What questions about the relation between our private and communal selves do we need to answer? How can we reconcile our individual quests for identity with the sometimes conflicting demands of social responsibility? To what extent should we rebel against social conformity? What kinds of threats, if any, do individuals pose to the community? Are individual rights and social responsibility irreconcilable? What are the necessary preconditions for individual participation in any society? According to anthropologist Bronislaw Malinowski, culture is the "artificial, secondary environment" that human beings superimpose on nature. We human beings, then, are in both nature and culture, and both influence our choices. A diversity of cultures, which the following selections illustrate, creates many opportunities for choices and sometimes leads to great difficulty in actually choosing. While nature is passively selecting the fittest organisms for survival, we humans are actively, sometimes painfully, making a variety of choices—personal, ethical, political, economic—for a number of reasons, both rational and emotional. Many of these choices concern other people and our relations to them; others involve coming to terms with our cultural or institutional pasts. Are cultural and historical factors limitations on freedom of choice, or do they allow more opportunity for individual action and imagination? Do we increase our individual choices to the degree that we free ourselves from history and culture?

Several stories in Part Five will also engage you in various debates raised by the voices of the individual and the community in different historical and cross-cultural contexts. To what extent, for example, are the choices of the protagonist in "Eveline," set in Dublin at the turn of the last century, shaped by the religious, economic, familial, and communal forces? How have the lives and choices of two sisters in "A Red Sweater," a contemporary story about a Chinese American family living in California, been influenced by the immigrant experiences and marriage of their parents and the suicide of their middle sister?

The way in which communities deal with threats against their authority is the subject of "The Guest," which takes place in Algeria in the 1950s and explores the choice of the protagonist to treat a murderer as a guest and allow him to make his own decision about handing himself over to the authorities. And in "Dead Men's Path," set in Africa in the 1970s, you will witness the consequences of cultural clashes between the old and the new.

The poems by William Blake and William Wordsworth portray their concern with social problems in nineteenth-century London, including child labor, and the degree to which religious and political institutions failed to respond to these problems, whereas the texts by Dickinson, Stevens, and Cummings focus on the cost to individuals who conform to rigidly assigned societal roles. "People" and "Danse Russe" extend the discussion of individualism and community through their celebration of the uniqueness of human beings; other texts, such as "Constantly Risking Absurdity" and "The Writer," explore the dual paradoxical role of the artist who needs solitude to create and society to respond to his or her creations.

The dramas in Part Five explore issues related to civil disobedience and alienation. Although Sophocles' *Antigone* presents conflicts such as those between male and female, youth and age, and religious and secular beliefs, the main issue is the decision of Antigone to insist on obeying her conscience, even if it means violating the laws of the state. Edward Albee's *The Zoo Story*, set in New York's central park in the 1970s, belongs to the theater of the absurd, a movement developed in the second half of the twentieth century. Through strong and imaginative language, Albee highlights the poverty of interpersonal relationships and communication and the devastating results of extreme alienation.

As you read these and other texts in this part, you, too, will be asked to make judgments about issues such as personal freedom and social responsibility, rebellion and conformity, the right of an individual to participate in acts of civil disobedience, the conflicting demands of individual preference and familial obligation, and the extent to which personal identity is shaped by external social forces.

FICTION

Shirley Jackson

The Lottery

The morning of June 27th was clear and sunny, with the fresh warmth of a full-summer day; the flowers were blossoming profusely and the grass was richly green. The people of the village began to gather in the square, between the post office and the bank, around ten o'clock; in some towns there were so many people that the lottery took two days and had to be started on June 26th, but in this village, where there were only about three hundred people, the whole lottery took less than two hours, so it could begin at ten o'clock in the morning and still be through in time to allow the villagers to get home for noon dinner.

The children assembled first, of course. School was recently over for the summer, and the feeling of liberty sat uneasily on most of them; they tended to gather together quietly for a while before they broke into boisterous play, and their talk was still of the classroom and the teacher, of books and reprimands. Bobby Martin had already stuffed his pockets full of stones, and the other boys soon followed his example, selecting the smoothest and roundest stones; Bobby and Harry Jones and Dickie Delacroix—the villagers pronounced this name "Dellacroy"—eventually made a great pile of stones in one corner of the square and guarded it against the raids of the other boys. The girls stood aside, talking among themselves, looking over their shoulders at the boys, and the very small children rolled in the dust or clung to the hands of their older brothers or sisters.

Soon the men began to gather, surveying their own children, speaking of planting and rain, tractors and taxes. They stood together, away from the pile of stones in the corner, and their jokes were quiet and they smiled rather than laughed. The women, wearing faded house dresses and sweaters, came shortly after their menfolk. They greeted one another and exchanged bits of gossip as they went to join their husbands. Soon the women, standing by their husbands, began to call to their children, and the children came reluctantly, having to be called four or five times. Bobby Martin ducked under his mother's grasping hand and ran, laughing, back to the pile of stones. His father spoke up sharply, and Bobby came quickly and took his place between his father and his oldest brother.

The lottery was conducted—as were the square dances, the teenage club, the Halloween program—by Mr. Summers, who had time and energy to devote to civic activities. He was a round-faced, jovial man and he ran the coal business, and people were sorry for him, because he had no children and his wife was a scold. When he arrived in the square, carrying the black wooden box, there was a murmur of conversation among the villagers, and he waved and called, "Little late today, folks."

The postmaster, Mr. Graves, followed him, carrying a three-legged stool, and the stool was put in the center of the square and Mr. Summers set the black box down on it. The villagers kept their distance, leaving a space between themselves and the stool, and when Mr. Summers said, "Some of you fellows want to give me a hand?" there was a hesitation before two men, Mr. Martin and his oldest son, Baxter, came forward to hold the box steady on the stool while Mr. Summers stirred up the papers inside it.

The original paraphernalia for the lottery had been lost long ago, and the black box now resting on the stool had been put into use even before Old Man Warner, the oldest man in town, was born. Mr. Summers spoke frequently to the villagers about making a new box, but no one liked to upset even as much tradition as was represented by the black box. There was a story that the present box had been made with some pieces of the box that had preceded it, the one that had been constructed when the first people settled down to make a village here. Every year, after the lottery, Mr. Summers began talking again about a new box, but every year the subject was allowed to fade off without anything's being done. The black box grew shabbier each year; by now it was no longer completely black but splintered badly along one side to show the original wood color, and in some places faded or stained.

Mr. Martin and his oldest son, Baxter, held the black box securely on the stool until Mr. Summers had stirred the papers thoroughly with his hand. Because so much of the ritual had been forgotten or discarded, Mr. Summers had been successful in having slips of paper substituted for the chips of wood that had been used for generations. Chips of wood, Mr. Summers had argued, had been all very well when the village was tiny, but now that the population was more than three hundred and likely to keep on growing, it was necessary to use something that would fit more easily into the black box. The night before the lottery, Mr. Summers and Mr. Graves made up the slips of paper and put them in the box, and it was then taken to the safe of Mr. Summers's coal company and locked up until Mr. Summers was ready to take it to the square next morning. The rest of the year, the box was put away, sometimes one place, sometimes another; it had spent one year in Mr. Graves's barn and another year underfoot in the post office, and sometimes it was set on a shelf in the Martin grocery and left there.

There was a great deal of fussing to be done before Mr. Summers declared the lottery open. There were the lists to make up—of heads of families, heads of households in each family, members of each household in each family. There was the proper swearing-in of Mr. Summers by the postmaster, as the official of the lottery; at one time, some people remembered, there had been a recital of some sort, performed by the official of the lottery, a perfunctory, tuneless chant that had been rattled off duly each year; some people believed that the official of the lottery used to stand just so when he said or sang it, others believed that he was supposed to walk among the people, but years and years ago this part of the ritual had been allowed to lapse. There had been, also, a ritual salute, which the official of the lottery had had to use in addressing each person who came up to draw from the box, but this also had changed with time, until now it was felt necessary only for the official to speak to each person approaching. Mr. Summers was very good at all this; in his clean white shirt and blue jeans, with one hand resting carelessly on the black box, he seemed very proper and important as he talked interminably to Mr. Graves and the Martins.

Just as Mr. Summers finally left off talking and turned to the assembled villagers, Mrs. Hutchinson came hurriedly along the path to the square, her sweater thrown over her shoulders, and slid into place in the back of the crowd. "Clean forgot what day it was," she said to Mrs. Delacroix, who stood next to her, and they both laughed softly. "Thought my old man was out back stacking wood," Mrs. Hutchinson went on, "and then I looked out the window and the kids was gone, and then I remembered it was the twenty-seventh and came a-running." She dried her hands on her apron, and Mrs. Delacroix said, "You're in time, though. They're still talking away up there."

Mrs. Hutchinson craned her neck to see through the crowd and found her husband and children standing near the front. She tapped Mrs. Delacroix on the arm as a farewell and began to make her way through the crowd. The people separated good-humoredly to let her through; two or three people said, in voices just loud enough to be heard across the crowd, "Here comes your Missus, Hutchinson," and "Bill, she made it after all." Mrs. Hutchinson reached her husband, and Mr. Summers, who had been waiting, said cheerfully. "Thought we were going to have to get on without you, Tessie." Mrs. Hutchinson said, grinning, "Wouldn't have me leave m'dishes in the sink, now, would you, Joe?" and soft laughter ran through the crowd as the people stirred back into position after Mrs. Hutchinson's arrival.

"Well, now," Mr. Summers said soberly, "guess we better get started, get this over with, so's we can go back to work. Anybody ain't here?"

"Dunbar," several people said. "Dunbar, Dunbar."

Mr. Summers consulted his list. "Clyde Dunbar," he said. "That's right. He's broke his leg, hasn't he? Who's drawing for him?"

"Me, I guess," a woman said, and Mr. Summers turned to look at her. "Wife draws for her husband," Mr. Summers said. "Don't you have a grown boy to do it for you, Janey?" Although Mr. Summers and everyone else in the village knew the answer perfectly well, it was the business of the official of the lottery to ask such questions formally. Mr. Summers waited with an expression of polite interest while Mrs. Dunbar answered.

"Horace's not but sixteen yet," Mrs. Dunbar said regretfully. "Guess I gotta fill in for the old man this year."

"Right," Mr. Summers said. He made a note on the list he was holding. Then he asked, "Watson boy drawing this year?"

A tall boy in the crowd raised his hand. "Here," he said. "I'm drawing for m'mother and me." He blinked his eyes nervously and ducked his head as several voices in the crowd said things like "Good fellow, Jack," and "Glad to see your mother's got a man to do it."

"Well," Mr. Summers said, "guess that's everyone. Old Man Warner make it?"

"Here," a voice said, and Mr. Summers nodded.

A sudden hush fell on the crowd as Mr. Summers cleared his throat and looked at the list. "All ready?" he called. "Now, I'll read the names—heads of families first—and the men come up and take a paper out of the box. Keep the paper folded in your hand without looking at it until everyone has had a turn. Everything clear?"

The people had done it so many times that they only half listened to the directions; most of them were quiet, wetting their lips, not looking around. Then Mr. Summers raised one hand high and said, "Adams." A man disengaged himself from the crowd and came forward. "Hi, Steve," Mr. Summers said, and Mr. Adams said, "Hi, Joe." They grinned at one another humorlessly and nervously. Then Mr. Adams reached into the black box and took out a folded paper. He held it firmly by one corner as he turned and went hastily back to his place in the crowd, where he stood a little apart from his family, not looking down at his hand.

"Allen," Mr. Summers said, "Anderson . . . Bentham."

"Seems like there's no time at all between lotteries any more," Mrs. Delacroix said to Mrs. Graves in the back row. "Seems like we got through with the last one only last week."

"Time sure goes fast," Mrs. Graves said.

"Clark . . . Delacroix."

"There goes my old man," Mrs. Delacroix said. She held her breath while her husband went forward.

"Dunbar," Mr. Summers said, and Mrs. Dunbar went steadily to the box while one of the women said, "Go on, Janey," and another said, "There she goes."

"We're next," Mrs. Graves said. She watched while Mr. Graves came around from the side of the box, greeted Mr. Summers gravely, and selected a slip of paper from the box. By now, all through the crowd there were men holding the small folded papers in their large hands, turning them over and over nervously. Mrs. Dunbar and her two sons stood together, Mrs. Dunbar holding the slip of paper.

"Harburt . . . Hutchinson."

"Get up there, Bill," Mrs. Hutchinson said, and the people near her laughed.

"Jones."

"They do say," Mr. Adams said to Old Man Warner, who stood next to him, "that over in the north village they're talking of giving up the lottery."

Old Man Warner snorted. "Pack of crazy fools," he said. "Listening to the young folks, nothing's good enough for *them*. Next thing you know, they'll be wanting to go back to living in caves, nobody work any more, live *that* way for a while. Used to be a saying about 'Lottery in June, corn be heavy soon.' First thing you know, we'd all be eating stewed chickweed and acorns. There's *always* been a lottery," he added petulantly. "Bad enough to see young Joe Summers up there joking with everybody."

"Some places have already quit lotteries," Mrs. Adams said.

"Nothing but trouble in *that*," Old Man Warner said stoutly. "Pack of young fools."

"Martin." And Bobby Martin watched his father go forward. "Overdyke . . . Percy."

"I wish they'd hurry," Mrs. Dunbar said to her oldest son. "I wish they'd hurry."

"They're almost through," her son said.

"You get ready to run tell Dad," Mrs. Dunbar said.

Mr. Summers called his own name and then stepped forward precisely and selected a slip from the box. Then he called, "Warner."

"Seventy-seventh year I been in the lottery," Old Man Warner said as he went through the crowd. "Seventy-seventh time."

"Watson." The tall boy came awkwardly through the crowd. Someone said, "Don't be nervous, Jack," and Mr. Summers said, "Take your time, son."

"Zanini."

After that, there was a long pause, a breathless pause, until Mr. Summers, holding his slip of paper in the air, said, "All right, fellows." For a minute, no one moved, and then all the slips of paper were opened. Suddenly, all the women began to speak at once, saying, "Who is it?" "Who's got it?" "Is it the Dunbars?" "Is it the Watsons?" Then the voices began to say, "It's Hutchinson. It's Bill." "Bill Hutchinson's got it."

"Go tell your father," Mrs. Dunbar said to her older son.

People began to look around to see the Hutchinsons. Bill Hutchinson was standing quiet, staring down at the paper in his hand. Suddenly, Tessie Hutchinson shouted to Mr. Summers, "You didn't give him time enough to take any paper he wanted. I saw you. It wasn't fair!"

"Be a good sport, Tessie," Mrs. Delacroix called, and Mrs. Graves said, "All of us took the same chance."

"Shut up, Tessie," Bill Hutchinson said.

"Well, everyone," Mr. Summers said, "that was done pretty fast, and now we've got to be hurrying a little more to get done in time." He consulted his next list. "Bill," he said, "you draw for the Hutchinson family. You got any other households in the Hutchinsons?"

"There's Don and Eva," Mrs. Hutchinson yelled. "Make *them* take their chance!"

"Daughters drew with their husbands' families, Tessie," Mr. Summers said gently. "You know that as well as anyone else."

"It wasn't *fair*," Tessie said.

"I guess not, Joe," Bill Hutchinson said regretfully. "My daughter draws with her husband's family, that's only fair, And I've got no other family except the kids."

"Then, as far as drawing for families is concerned, it's you," Mr. Summers said in explanation, "and as far as drawing for households is concerned, that's you, too. Right?"

"Right," Bill Hutchinson said.

"How many kids, Bill?" Mr. Summers asked formally.

"Three," Bill Hutchinson said. "There's Bill, Jr., and Nancy, and little Dave. And Tessie and me."

"All right, then," Mr. Summers said. "Harry, you got their tickets back?"

Mr. Graves nodded and held up the slips of paper. "Put them in the box, then," Mr. Summers directed. "Take Bill's and put it in."

"I think we ought to start over," Mrs. Hutchinson said, as quietly as she could. "I tell you it wasn't *fair*. You didn't give him time enough to choose. *Every*body saw that."

Mr. Graves had selected the five slips and put them in the box, and he dropped all the papers but those onto the ground, where the breeze caught them and lifted them off.

"Listen, everybody," Mrs. Hutchinson was saying to the people around her.

"Ready, Bill?" Mr. Summers asked, and Bill Hutchinson, with one quick glance around at his wife and children, nodded.

"Remember," Mr. Summers said, "take the slips and keep them folded until each person has taken one. Harry, you help little Dave." Mr. Graves took the hand of the little boy, who came willingly with him up to the box. "Take a paper out of the box, Davy," Mr. Summers said. Davy put his hand into the box and laughed. "Take just *one* paper," Mr. Summers said. "Harry, you hold it for him." Mr. Graves took the child's hand and removed the folded paper from the tight fist and held it while little Dave stood next to him and looked up at him wonderingly.

"Nancy next," Mr. Summers said. Nancy was twelve, and her school friends breathed heavily as she went forward, switching her skirt, and took a slip daintily from the box. "Bill, Jr.," Mr. Summers said, and Billy, his face red and his feet over-large, nearly knocked the box over as he got a paper out. "Tessie," Mr. Summers said. She hesitated for a minute, looking around defiantly, and then set her lips and went up to the box. She snatched a paper out and held it behind her.

"Bill," Mr. Summers said, and Bill Hutchinson reached into the box and felt around, bringing his hand out at last with the slip of paper in it.

The crowd was quiet. A girl whispered, "I hope it's not Nancy," and the sound of the whisper reached the edges of the crowd.

"It's not the way it used to be," Old Man Warner said clearly. "People ain't the way they used to be."

"All right," Mr. Summers said. "Open the papers. Harry, you open little Dave's."

Mr. Graves opened the slip of paper and there was a general sigh through the crowd as he held it up and everyone could see that it was blank. Nancy and Bill, Jr., opened theirs at the same time, and both beamed and laughed, turning around to the crowd and holding their slips of paper above their heads.

"Tessie," Mr. Summers said. There was a pause, and then Mr. Summers looked at Bill Hutchinson, and Bill unfolded his paper and showed it. It was blank.

"It's Tessie," Mr. Summers said, and his voice was hushed. "Show us her paper, Bill."

Bill Hutchinson went over to his wife and forced the slip of paper out of her hand. It had a black spot on it, the black spot Mr. Summers had made the night before with the heavy pencil in the coal-company office. Bill Hutchinson held it up and there was a stir in the crowd.

"All right, folks," Mr. Summers said. "Let's finish quickly."

Although the villagers had forgotten the ritual and lost the original black box, they still remembered to use stones. The pile of stones the boys had made earlier was ready; there were stones on the ground with the blowing scraps of paper that had come out of the box. Mrs. Delacroix selected a stone so large she had to pick it up with both hands and turned to Mrs. Dunbar, "Come on," she said. "Hurry up."

Mrs. Dunbar had small stones in both hands, and she said, gasping for breath, "I can't run at all. You'll have to go ahead and I'll catch up with you."

The children had stones already, and someone gave little Davy Hutchinson a few pebbles.

Tessie Hutchinson was in the center of a cleared space by now, and she held her hands out desperately as the villagers moved in on her. "It isn't fair," she said. A stone hit her on the side of the head.

Old Man Warner was saying, "Come on, come on, everyone." Steve Adams was in the front of the crowd of villagers, with Mrs. Graves beside him.

"It isn't fair, it isn't right," Mrs. Hutchinson screamed and then they were upon her.

[1948]

Journal Entry

What are your associations with a lottery? What images and situations does the word evoke?

Textual Considerations

1. What do the villagers mean by "fairness"? What is implied by the fact that the only villager to complain about the lottery's consequences is Tessie Hutchinson?
2. Why does Jackson use a flat reportorial style to describe an event that would normally be headline news?
3. Consider the role of irony in the story.
4. How important is it that the story is set in New England in the mid-1950s? How, for example, would its influence differ if it were set in Aztec Mexico, a culture that routinely practiced human sacrifice?
5. What indications are there that the villagers have lost interest in the process that leads up to the choosing of the slip?

Cultural Contexts

1. When Jackson's story was first published in the *New Yorker* in 1948, she received hundreds of letters from people "who wanted to know where the lotteries were held, and whether they could go there and watch." Examine what these responses reveal about human nature. What is your own response to the story?
2. By showing the process involved in the lottery, what is Jackson implying about traditions, mass psychology, and social pressure? How did your group's response to this question compare with that of other groups in your class?

Franz Kafka

The Metamorphosis

Translated by Will and Edwin Muir

I

As Gregor Samsa awoke one morning from uneasy dreams he found himself transformed in his bed into a gigantic insect. He was lying on his hard, as it were armor-plated, back and when he lifted his head a little he could see his dome-like brown belly divided into stiff arched segments on top of which the bed quilt could hardly keep in position and was about to slide off completely. His numerous legs, which were pitifully thin compared to the rest of his bulk, waved helplessly before his eyes.

What has happened to me? he thought. It was no dream. His room, a regular human bedroom, only rather too small, lay quiet between the four familiar walls. Above the table on which a collection of cloth samples was unpacked and spread out—Samsa was a commercial traveler—hung the picture which he had recently cut out of an illustrated magazine and put into a pretty gilt frame. It showed a lady, with a fur cap on and a fur stole, sitting upright and holding out to the spectator a huge fur muff into which the whole of her forearm had vanished!

Gregor's eyes turned next to the window, and the overcast sky—one could hear rain drops beating on the window gutter—made him quite melancholy. What about sleeping a little longer and forgetting all this nonsense, he thought, but it could not be done, for he was accustomed to sleep on his right side and in his present condition he could not turn himself over. However violently he forced himself towards his right side he always rolled on to his back again. He tried it at least a hundred times, shutting his eyes to keep from seeing his struggling legs, and only desisted when he began to feel in his side a faint dull ache he had never experienced before.

Oh God, he thought, what an exhausting job I've picked on! Traveling about day in, day out. It's much more irritating work than doing the actual business in the office, and on top of that there's the trouble of constant traveling, of worrying about train connections, the bed and irregular meals, casual acquaintances that are always new and never become intimate friends. The devil take it all! He felt a slight itching up on his belly; slowly pushed himself on his back nearer to the top of the bed so that he could lift his head more easily; identified the itching place which was surrounded by many small white spots the nature of which he could not understand and made to touch it with a leg, but drew the leg back immediately, for the contact made a cold shiver run through him.

He slid down again into his former position. This getting up early, he thought, makes one quite stupid. A man needs his sleep. Other commercials live like harem women. For instance, when I come back to the hotel of a morning to write up the orders I've got, these others are only sitting down to breakfast. Let me just try that with my chief; I'd be sacked on the spot. Anyhow, that might be quite a good thing for me, who can tell? If I didn't have to hold my hand because of my parents I'd have given notice long ago. I'd have gone to the chief and told him exactly what I think of him. That would knock him endways from his desk! It's a queer way of doing, too, this sitting on high at a desk and talking down to employees, especially when they have to come quite near because the chief is hard of hearing. Well, there's still hope; once I've saved enough money to pay back my parents' debts to him—that should take another five or six years—I'll do it without fail. I'll cut myself completely loose then. For the moment, though, I'd better get up, since my train goes at five.

He looked at the alarm clock ticking on the chest. Heavenly Father! he thought. It was half-past six o'clock and the hands were quietly moving on, it was even past the half-hour, it was getting on toward a quarter to seven. Had the alarm clock not gone off? From the bed one could see that it had been properly set for four o'clock; of course it must have gone off. Yes, but was it possible to sleep quietly through that ear-splitting noise? Well, he had not slept quietly, yet apparently all the more soundly for that. But what was he to do now? The next train went at seven o'clock; to catch that he would need to hurry like mad and his samples weren't even packed up, and he himself wasn't feeling particularly fresh and active. And even if he did catch the train he wouldn't avoid a row with the chief, since the firm's porter would have been waiting for the five o'clock train and would long since have reported his failure to turn up. The porter was a creature of the chief's, spineless and stupid. Well, supposing he were to say he was sick? But that would be most unpleasant and would look suspicious, since during his five years' employment he had not been ill once. The chief himself would be sure to come with the sick-insurance doctor, would reproach his parents with their son's laziness and would cut all excuses short by referring to the insurance doctor, who of course regarded all mankind as perfectly healthy malingerers. And would he be so far wrong on this occasion? Gregor really felt quite well, apart from a drowsiness that was utterly superfluous after such a long sleep, and he was even unusually hungry.

As all this was running through his mind at top speed without his being able to decide to leave his bed—the alarm clock had just struck a quarter to seven—there came a cautious tap at the door behind the head of his bed. "Gregor," said a voice—it was his mother's—"it's a quarter to seven. Hadn't you a train to catch?" That gentle voice! Gregor had a shock as he heard his own voice answering hers, unmistakably his own voice, it was true, but with a persistent horrible twittering squeak behind it like an undertone, that left the words in their clear shape only for the first moment and then rose up reverberating round them to destroy their sense, so that one could not be sure one had heard them rightly. Gregor wanted to answer at length and explain everything, but in the circumstances he confined himself to saying: "Yes, yes, thank you, Mother, I'm getting up now." The wooden door between them must have kept the change in his voice from being noticeable outside, for his mother contented herself with this statement and shuffled away. Yet this brief exchange of words had made the other members of the family aware that Gregor was still in the house, as they had not expected, and at one of the side doors his father was already knocking, gently, yet with his fist. "Gregor, Gregor," he called, "what's the matter with you?" And after a little while he called again in a deeper voice: "Gregor! Gregor!" At the other side door his sister was saying in a low, plaintive tone: "Gregor? Aren't you well? Are you needing anything?" He answered them both at once: "I'm just ready," and did his best to make his voice sound as normal as possible by enunciating the words very clearly and leaving long pauses between them. So his father went back to his breakfast, but his sister whispered: "Gregor, open the door, do." However, he was not thinking of opening the door, and felt thankful for the prudent habit he had acquired in traveling of locking all doors during the night, even at home.

His immediate attention was to get up quietly without being disturbed, to put on his clothes and above all eat his breakfast, and only then to consider what else was to be done, since in bed, he was well aware, his meditations would come to no sensible conclusion. He remembered that often enough in bed he had felt small aches and pains, probably caused by awkward postures, which had proved purely imaginary once he got up, and he looked forward eagerly to seeing this morning's delusions gradually fall away. That the change in his voice was nothing but the precursor of a severe chill, a standing ailment of commercial travelers, he had not the least possible doubt.

To get rid of the quilt was quite easy; he had only to inflate himself a little and it fell off by itself. But the next move was difficult, especially because he was so uncommonly broad. He would have needed arms and hands to hoist himself up; instead he had only the numerous little legs which never stopped waving in all directions and which he could not control in the least. When he tried to bend one of them it was the first to stretch itself straight; and did he succeed at last in making it do what he wanted, all the other legs meanwhile waved the more wildly in a high degree of unpleasant agitation. "But what's the use of lying idle in bed," said Gregor to himself.

He thought that he might get out of bed with the lower part of his body first, but this lower part, which he had not yet seen and of which he could form no clear conception, proved too difficult to move; it shifted so slowly, and when finally, almost wild with annoyance, he gathered his forces together and thrust out recklessly, he had miscalculated the direction and bumped heavily against the lower end of the bed, and the stinging pain he felt informed him that precisely this lower part of his body was at the moment probably the most sensitive.

So he tried to get the top part of himself out first, and cautiously moved his head towards the edge of the bed. That proved easy enough, and despite its breadth and mass the bulk of his body at last slowly followed the movement of his head. Still, when he finally got his head free over the edge of the bed he felt too scared to go on advancing, for after all if he let himself fall in this way it would take a miracle to keep his head from being injured. And at all costs he must not lose consciousness now, precisely now; he would rather stay in bed.

But when after a repetition of the same efforts he lay in his former position again, sighing, and watched his little legs struggling against each other more wildly than ever, if that were possible, and saw no way of bringing any order into this arbitrary confusion, he told himself again that it was impossible to stay in bed and that the most sensible course was to risk everything for the smallest hope of getting away from it. At the same time he did not forget meanwhile to remind himself that cool reflection, the coolest possible, was much better than desperate resolves. In such moments he focused his eyes as sharply as possible on the window, but, unfortunately, the prospect of the morning fog, which muffled even the other side of the narrow street, brought him little encouragement and comfort. "Seven o'clock already," he said to himself when the alarm clock chimed again, "seven o'clock already and still such a thick fog." And for a little while he lay quiet, breathing lightly, as if perhaps expecting such complete repose to restore all things to their real and normal condition.

But then he said to himself: "Before it strikes a quarter past seven I must be quite out of this bed, without fail. Anyhow, by that time someone will have come from the office to ask for me, since it opens before seven." And he set himself to rocking his whole body at once in a regular rhythm, with the idea of swinging it out of the bed. If he tipped himself out in that way he could keep his head from injury by lifting it at an acute angle when he fell. His back seemed to be hard and was not likely to suffer from a fall on the carpet. His biggest worry was the loud crash he would not be able to help making, which would probably cause anxiety, if not terror, behind all the doors. Still, he must take the risk.

When he was already half out of the bed—the new method was more a game than an effort, for he needed only to hitch himself across by rocking to and fro—it struck him how simple it would be if he could get help. Two strong people—he thought of his father and the servant girl—would be amply sufficient; they would only have to thrust their arms under his convex back, lever him out of the bed, bend down with their burden and then be patient enough to let him turn himself right over on to the floor, where it was to be hoped his legs would then find their proper function. Well, ignoring the fact that the doors were all locked, ought he really to call for help? In spite of his misery he could not suppress a smile at the very idea of it.

He had got so far that he could barely keep his equilibrium when he rocked himself strongly, and he would have to nerve himself very soon for the final decision since in five minutes' time it would be a quarter past seven—when the front door bell rang. "That's someone from the office," he said to himself, and grew almost rigid, while his little legs jigged about all the faster. For a moment everything stayed quiet. "They're not going to open the door," said Gregor to himself, catching at some kind of irrational hope. But then of course the servant girl went as usual to the door with her heavy tread and opened it. Gregor needed only to hear the first good morning of the visitor to know immediately who it was—the chief clerk himself. What a fate, to be condemned to work for a firm where the smallest omission at once gave rise to the gravest suspicion! Were all employees in a body nothing but scoundrels, was there not among them one single loyal devoted man who, had he wasted only an hour or so of the firm's time in a morning, was so tormented by conscience as to be driven out of his mind and actually incapable of leaving his bed? Wouldn't it really have been sufficient to send an apprentice to inquire—if any inquiry were necessary at all—did the chief clerk himself have to come and thus indicate to the entire family, an innocent family, that this suspicious circumstance could be investigated by no one less versed in affairs than himself? And more through the agitation caused by these reflections than through any act of will Gregor swung himself out of bed with all his strength. There was a loud thump, but it was not really a crash. His fall was broken to some extent by the carpet, his back, too, was less stiff than he thought, and so there was merely a dull thud, not so very startling. Only he had not lifted his head carefully enough and had hit it; he turned it and rubbed it on the carpet in pain and irritation.

"That was something falling down in there," said the chief clerk in the next room to the left. Gregor tried to suppose to himself that something like what had happened to him today might some day happen to the chief clerk; one really could not deny that it was possible. But as if in brusque reply to this supposition the chief clerk took a couple of firm steps in the next-door room and his patent leather boots creaked. From the right-hand room his sister was whispering to inform him of the situation: "Gregor, the chief clerk's here." "I know," muttered Gregor to himself; but he didn't dare to make his voice loud enough for his sister to hear it.

"Gregor," said his father now from the left-hand room, "the chief clerk has come and wants to know why you didn't catch the early train. We don't know what to say to him. Besides, he wants to talk to you in person. So open the door, please. He will be good enough to excuse the untidiness of your room." "Good morning, Mr. Samsa," the chief clerk was calling amiably meanwhile. "He's not well," said his mother to the visitor, while his father was still speaking through the door, "he's not well, sir, believe me. What else would make him miss a train! The boy thinks about nothing but his work. It makes me almost cross the way he never goes out in the evenings; he's been here the last eight days and has stayed at home every single evening. He just sits there quietly at the table reading a newspaper or looking through railway timetables. The only amusement he gets is doing fretwork. For instance, he spent two or three evenings cutting out a little picture frame; you would be surprised to see how pretty it is; it's hanging in his room; you'll see it in a minute when Gregor opens the door. I must say I'm glad you've come, sir; we should never have got him to unlock the door by ourselves; he's so obstinate; and I'm sure he's unwell, though he wouldn't have it to be so this morning." "I'm just coming," said Gregor slowly and carefully, not moving an inch for fear of losing one word of the conversation. "I can't think of any other explanation, madam," said the chief clerk, "I hope it's nothing serious. Although on the other hand I must say that we men of business—fortunately or unfortunately—very often simply have to ignore any slight indisposition, since business must be attended to." "Well, can the chief clerk come in now?" asked Gregor's father impatiently, again knocking on the door. "No," said Gregor. In the left-hand room a painful silence followed this refusal, in the right-hand room his sister began to sob.

Why didn't his sister join the others? She was probably newly out of bed and hadn't even begun to put on her clothes yet. Well, why was she crying? Because he wouldn't get up and let the chief clerk come in, because he was in danger of losing his job, and because the chief would begin dunning his parents again for the old debts? Surely these were things one didn't need to worry about for the present. Gregor was still at home and not in the least thinking of deserting the family. At the moment, true, he was lying on the carpet and no one who knew the condition he was in could seriously expect him to admit the chief clerk. But for such a small discourtesy, which could plausibly be explained away somehow later on, Gregor could hardly be dismissed on the spot. And it seemed to Gregor that it would be much more sensible to leave him in peace for the present than to trouble him with tears and entreaties. Still, of course, their uncertainty bewildered them all and excused their behavior.

"Mr. Samsa," the chief clerk called now in a louder voice, "what's the matter with you? Here you are, barricading yourself in your room, giving only 'yes' and 'no' for answers, causing your parents a lot of unnecessary trouble and neglecting— I mention this only in passing—neglecting your business duties in an incredible fashion. I am speaking here in the name of your parents and of your chief, and I beg you quite seriously to give me an immediate and precise explanation. You amaze me, you amaze me. I thought you were a quiet, dependable person, and now all at once you seem bent on making a disgraceful exhibition of yourself. The chief did hint to me early this morning a possible explanation for your disappearance—with reference to the cash payments that were entrusted to you recently—but I almost pledged my solemn word of honor that this could not be so. But now that I see how incredibly obstinate you are, I no longer have the slightest desire to take your part at all. And your position in the firm is not so unassailable. I came with the intention of telling you all this in private, but since you are wasting my time so needlessly I don't see why your parents shouldn't hear it too. For some time past your work has been most unsatisfactory; this is not the season of the year for a business boom, of course, we admit that, but a season of the year for doing no business at all, that does not exist, Mr. Samsa, must not exist."

"But sir," cried Gregor, beside himself and in his agitation forgetting everything else, "I'm just going to open the door this very minute. A slight illness, an attack of giddiness, has kept me from getting up. I'm still lying in bed. But I feel all right again. I'm getting out of bed now. Just give me a moment or two longer! I'm not quite so well as I thought. But I'm all right, really. How a thing like that can suddenly strike one down! Only last night I was quite well, my parents can tell you, or rather I did have a slight presentiment. I must have showed some sign of it. Why didn't I report it at the office! But one always thinks that an indisposition can be got over without staying in the house. Oh sir, do spare my parents! All that you're reproaching me with now has no foundation; no one has ever said a word to me about it. Perhaps you haven't looked at the last orders I sent in. Anyhow, I can still catch the eight o'clock train, I'm much the better for my few hours' rest. Don't let me detain you here, sir; I'll be attending to business very soon, and do be good enough to tell the chief so and to make my excuses to him!"

And while all this was tumbling out pell-mell and Gregor hardly knew what he was saying, he had reached the chest quite easily, perhaps because of the practice he had had in bed, and was now trying to lever himself upright by means of it. He meant actually to open the door, actually to show himself and speak to the chief clerk; he was eager to find out what the others, after all their insistence, would say at the sight of him. If they were horrified then the responsibility was no longer his and he could stay quiet. But if they took it calmly, then he had no reason either to be upset, and could really get to the station for the eight o'clock train if he hurried. At first he slipped down a few times from the polished surface of the chest, but at length with a last heave he stood upright; he paid no more attention to the pains in the lower part of his body, however they smarted. Then he let himself fall against the back of a near-by chair, and clung with his little legs to the edges of it. That brought him into control of himself again and he stopped speaking, for now he could listen to what the chief clerk was saying.

"Did you understand a word of it?" the chief clerk was asking; "surely he can't be trying to make fools of us?" "Oh dear," cried his mother, in tears, "perhaps he's terribly ill and we're tormenting him. Grete! Grete!" she called out then. "Yes Mother?" called his sister from the other side. They were calling to each other across Gregor's room. "You must go this minute for the doctor. Gregor is ill. Go for the doctor, quick. Did you hear how he was speaking?" "That was no human voice," said the chief clerk in a voice noticeably low beside the shrillness of the mother's. "Anna! Anna!" his father was calling through the hall to the kitchen, clapping his hands, "get a locksmith at once!" And the two girls were already running through the hall with a swish of skirts—how could his sister have got dressed so quickly?—and were tearing the front door open. There was no sound of its closing again; they had evidently left it open, as one does in houses where some great misfortune has happened.

But Gregor was now much calmer. The words he uttered were no longer understandable, apparently, although they seemed clear enough to him, even clearer than before, perhaps because his ear had grown accustomed to the sound of them. Yet at any rate people now believed that something was wrong with him, and were ready to help him. The positive certainty with which these first measures had been taken comforted him. He felt himself drawn once more into the human circle and hoped for great and remarkable results from both the doctor and the locksmith, without really distinguishing precisely between them. To make his voice as clear as possible for the decisive conversation that was now imminent he coughed a little, as quietly as he could, of course, since this noise too might not sound like a human cough for all he was able to judge. In the next room meanwhile there was complete silence. Perhaps his parents were sitting at the table with the chief clerk, whispering, perhaps they were all leaning against the door and listening.

Slowly Gregor pushed the chair towards the door, then let go of it, caught hold of the door for support—the soles at the end of his little legs were somewhat sticky—and rested against it for a moment after his efforts. Then he set himself to turning the key in the lock with his mouth. It seemed, unhappily, that he hadn't really any teeth—what could he grip the key with?—but on the other hand his jaws were certainly very strong; with their help he did manage to set the key in motion, heedless of the fact that he was undoubtedly damaging them somewhere, since a brown fluid issued from his mouth, flowed over the key and dripped on the floor. "Just listen to that," said the chief clerk next door; "he's turning the key." That was a great encouragement to Gregor; but they should all have shouted encouragement to him, his father and mother too: "Go on, Gregor," they should have called out, "keep going, hold on to that key!" And in the belief that they were all following his efforts intensely, he clenched his jaws recklessly on the key with all the force at his command. As the turning of the key progressed he circled round the lock, holding on now only with his mouth, pushing on the key, as required, or pulling it down again with all the weight of his body. The louder click of the finally yielding lock literally quickened Gregor. With a deep breath of relief he said to himself: "So I didn't need the locksmith," and laid his head on the handle to open the door wide.

Since he had to pull the door towards him, he was still invisible when it was really wide open. He had to edge himself slowly round the near half of the double door, and to do it very carefully if he was not to fall plump upon his back just on the threshold. He was still carrying out this difficult manoeuvre, with no time to observe anything else, when he heard the chief clerk utter a loud "Oh!"—it sounded like a gust of wind—and now he could see the man, standing as he was nearest to the door, clapping one hand before his open mouth and slowly backing away as if driven by some invisible steady pressure. His mother—in spite of the chief clerk's being there her hair was still undone and sticking up in all directions—first clasped her hands and looked at his father, then took two steps towards Gregor and fell on the floor among her outspread skirts, her face quite hidden on her breast. His father knotted his fist with a fierce expression on his face as if he meant to knock Gregor back into his room, then looked uncertainly round the living room, covered his eyes with his hands and wept till his great chest heaved.

Gregor did not go now into the living room, but leaned against the inside of the firmly shut wing of the door, so that only half his body was visible and his head above it bending sideways to look at the others. The light had meanwhile strengthened; on the other side of the street one could see clearly a section of the endlessly long, dark gray building opposite—it was a hospital—abruptly punctuated by its row of regular windows; the rain was still falling, but only in large singly discernible and literally singly splashing drops. The breakfast dishes were set out on the table lavishly, for breakfast was the most important meal of the day to Gregor's father, who lingered it out for hours over various newspapers. Right opposite Gregor on the wall hung a photograph of himself on military service, as a lieutenant, hand on sword, a carefree smile on his face, inviting one to respect his uniform and military bearing. The door leading to the hall was open, and one could see that the front door stood open too, showing the landing beyond and the beginning of the stairs going down.

"Well," said Gregor, knowing perfectly that he was the only one who had retained any composure, "I'll put my clothes on at once, pack up my samples and start off. Will you only let me go? You see, sir, I'm not obstinate, and I'm willing to work; traveling is a hard life, but I couldn't live without it. Where are you going, sir? To the office? Yes? Will you give a true account of all this? One can be temporarily incapacitated, but that's just the moment for remembering former services and bearing in mind that later on, when the incapacity has been got over, one will certainly work with all the more industry and concentration. I'm loyally bound to serve the chief, you know that very well. Besides, I have to provide for my parents and my sister. I'm in great difficulties, but I'll get out of them again. Don't make things any worse for me than they are. Stand up for me in the firm. Travelers are not popular there, I know. People think they earn sacks of money and just have a good time. A prejudice there's no particular reason for revising. But you, sir, have a more comprehensive view of affairs than the rest of the staff, yes, let me tell you in confidence, a more comprehensive view than the chief himself, who, being the owner, lets his judgment easily be swayed against one of his employees. And you know very well that the traveler, who is never seen in the office almost the whole year round, can so easily fall a victim to gossip and ill luck and unfounded complaints, which he mostly knows nothing about, except when he comes back exhausted from his rounds, and only then suffers in person from their evil consequences, which he can no longer trace back to the original causes. Sir, sir, don't go away without a word to me to show that you think me in the right at least to some extent!"

But at Gregor's very first words the chief clerk had already backed away and only stared at him with parted lips over one twitching shoulder. And while Gregor was speaking he did not stand still one moment but stole away towards the door, without taking his eyes off Gregor, yet only an inch at a time, as if obeying some secret injunction to leave the room. He was already at the hall, and the suddenness with which he took his last step out of the living room would have made one believe he had burned the sole of his foot. Once in the hall he stretched his right arm before him towards the staircase, as if some supernatural power were waiting there to deliver him.

Gregor perceived that the chief clerk must on no account be allowed to go away in this frame of mind if his position in the firm were not to be endangered to the utmost. His parents did not understand this so well; they had convinced themselves in the course of years that Gregor was settled for life in this firm, and besides they were so occupied with their immediate troubles that all foresight had forsaken them. Yet Gregor had this foresight. The chief clerk must be detained, soothed, persuaded and finally won over; the whole future of Gregor and his family depended on it! If only his sister had been there! She was intelligent; she had begun to cry while Gregor was still lying on his back. And no doubt the chief clerk, so partial to ladies, would have been guided by her; she would have shut the door of the flat and in the hall talked him out of his horror. But she was not there, and Gregor would have to handle the situation himself. And without remembering that he was still unaware what powers of movement he possessed, without even remembering that his words in all possibility, indeed in all likelihood, would again be unintelligible, he let go of the wing of the door, pushed himself through the opening, started to walk towards the chief clerk, who was already ridiculously clinging with both hands to the railing on the landing; but immediately, as he was feeling for a support, he fell down with a little cry upon all his numerous legs. Hardly was he down when he experienced for the first time a sense of physical comfort; his legs had firm ground under them; they were completely obedient, as he noted with joy; they even strove to carry him forward in whatever direction he chose; and he was inclined to believe that a final relief from all his sufferings was at hand. But in the same moment as he found himself on the floor, rocking with suppressed eagerness to move, not far from his mother, indeed just in front of her, she, who had seemed so completely crushed, sprang all at once to her feet, her arms and fingers outspread, cried: "Help, for God's sake, help!" bent her head down as if to see Gregor better, yet on the contrary kept backing senselessly away; had quite forgotten that the laden table stood behind her; sat upon it hastily, as if in absence of mind, when she bumped into it; and seemed altogether unaware that the big coffee pot beside her was upset and pouring coffee in a flood over the carpet.

"Mother, Mother," said Gregor in a low voice, and looked up at her. The chief clerk, for the moment, had quite slipped from his mind; instead, he could not resist snapping his jaws together at the sight of the streaming coffee. That made his mother scream again, she fled from the table and fell into the arms of his father, who hastened to catch her. But Gregor had now no time to spare for his parents; the chief clerk was already on the stairs; with his chin on the banisters he was taking one last backward look. Gregor made a spring, to be as sure as possible of overtaking him; the chief clerk must have divined his intention, for he leaped down several steps and vanished; he was still yelling "Ugh!" and it echoed through the whole staircase.

Unfortunately, the flight of the chief clerk seemed completely to upset Gregor's father, who had remained relatively calm until now, for instead of running after the man himself, or at least not hindering Gregor in his pursuit, he seized in his right hand the walking stick which the chief clerk had left behind on a chair, together with a hat and greatcoat, snatched in his left hand a large newspaper from the table and began stamping his feet and flourishing the stick and the newspaper to drive Gregor back into his room. No entreaty of Gregor's availed, indeed no entreaty was even understood, however humbly he bent his head his father only stamped on the floor the more loudly. Behind his father his mother had torn open a window, despite the cold weather, and was leaning far out of it with her face in her hands. A strong draught set in from the street to the staircase, the window curtains blew in, the newspapers on the table fluttered, stray pages whisked over the floor. Pitilessly Gregor's father drove him back, hissing and crying "Shoo!" like a savage. But Gregor was quite unpracticed in walking backwards, it really was a slow business. If he only had a chance to turn round he could get back to his room at once, but he was afraid of exasperating his father by the slowness of such a rotation and at any moment the stick in his father's hand might hit him a fatal blow on the back or on the head. In the end, however, nothing else was left for him to do since to his horror he observed that in moving backwards he could not even control the direction he took; and so, keeping an anxious eye on his father all the time over his shoulder, he began to turn round as quickly as he could, which was in reality very slowly. Perhaps his father noted his good intentions, for he did not interfere except every now and then to help him in the manoeuvre from a distance with the point of the stick. If only he would have stopped making that unbearable hissing noise! It made Gregor quite lose his head. He had turned almost completely round when the hissing noise so distracted him that he even turned a little the wrong way again. But when at last his head was fortunately right in front of the doorway, it appeared that his body was too broad simply to get through the opening. His father, of course, in his present mood was far from thinking of such a thing as opening the other half of the door, to let Gregor have enough space. He had merely the fixed idea of driving Gregor back into his room as quickly as possible. He would never have suffered Gregor to make the circumstantial preparations for standing up on end and perhaps slipping his way through the door. Maybe he was now making more noise than ever to urge Gregor forward, as if no obstacle impeded him; to Gregor, anyhow, the noise in his rear sounded no longer like the voice of one single father; this was really no joke, and Gregor thrust himself—come what might—into the doorway. One side of his body rose up, he was tilted at an angle in the doorway, his flank was quite bruised, horrid blotches stained the white door, soon he was stuck fast and, left to himself, could not have moved at all, his legs on one side fluttered trembling in the air, those on the other were crushed painfully to the floor—when from behind his father gave him a strong push which was literally a deliverance and he flew far into the room, bleeding freely. The door was slammed behind him with the stick, and then at last there was silence.

II

Not until it was twilight did Gregor awake out of a deep sleep, more like a swoon than a sleep. He would certainly have waked up of his own accord not much later, for he felt himself sufficiently rested and well-slept, but it seemed to him as if a fleeting step and a cautious shutting of the door leading into the hall had aroused him. The electric lights in the street cast a pale sheen here and there on the ceiling and the upper surfaces of the furniture, but down below, where he lay, it was dark. Slowly, awkwardly trying out his feelers, which he now first learned to appreciate, he pushed his way to the door to see what had been happening there. His left side felt like one single long, unpleasantly tense scar, and he had actually to limp on his two rows of legs. One little leg, moreover, had been severely damaged in the course of that morning's events—it was almost a miracle that only one had been damaged— and trailed uselessly behind him.

He had reached the door before he discovered what had really drawn him to it: the smell of food. For there stood a basin filled with fresh milk in which floated little sops of white bread. He could almost have laughed with joy, since he was now still hungrier than in the morning, and he dipped his head almost over the eyes straight into the milk. But soon in disappointment he withdrew it again; not only did he find it difficult to feed because of his tender left side—and he could only feed with the palpitating collaboration of his whole body—he did not like the milk either, although milk had been his favorite drink and that was certainly why his sister had set it there for him, indeed it was almost with repulsion that he turned away from the basin and crawled back to the middle of the room.

He could see through the crack of the door that the gas was turned on in the living room, but while usually at this time his father made a habit of reading the afternoon newspaper in a loud voice to his mother and occasionally to his sister as well, not a sound was now to be heard. Well, perhaps his father had recently given up this habit of reading aloud, which his sister had mentioned so often in conversation and in her letters. But there was the same silence all around, although the flat was certainly not empty of occupants. "What a quiet life our family has been leading," said Gregor to himself, and as he sat there motionless staring into the darkness he felt great pride in the fact that he had been able to provide such a life for his parents and sister in such a fine flat. But what if all the quiet, the comfort, the content- ment were now to end in horror? To keep himself from being lost in such thoughts Gregor took refuge in movement and crawled up and down the room.

Once during the long evening one of the side doors was opened a little and quickly shut again, later the other side door too; someone had apparently wanted to come in and then thought better of it. Gregor now stationed himself immediately before the living room door, determined to persuade any hesitating visitor to come in or at least to discover who it might be; but the door was not opened again and he waited in vain. In the early morning, when the doors were locked, they had all wanted to come in, now that he had opened one door and the other had apparently been opened during the day, no one came in and even the keys were on the other side of the doors.

It was late at night before the gas went out in the living room, and Gregor could easily tell that his parents and his sister had all stayed awake until then, for he could clearly hear the three of them stealing away on tiptoe. No one was likely to visit him, not until the morning, that was certain; so he had plenty of time to meditate at his leisure on how he was to arrange his life afresh. But the lofty, empty room in which he had to lie flat on the floor filled him with an apprehension he could not account for, since it had been his very own room for the past five years—and with a half-unconscious action, not without a slight feeling of shame, he scuttled under the sofa, where he felt comfortable at once, although his back was a little cramped and he could not lift his head up, and his only regret was that his body was too broad to get the whole of it under the sofa.

He stayed there all night, spending his time partly in a light slumber, from which his hunger kept waking him up with a start, and partly in worrying and sketching vague hopes, which all led to the same conclusion, that he must lie low for the present and, by exercising patience and the utmost consideration, help the family to bear the inconvenience he was bound to cause them in his present condition.

Very early in the morning, it was still almost night, Gregor had the chance to test the strength of his new resolutions, for his sister, nearly fully dressed, opened the door from the hall and peered in. She did not see him at once, yet when she caught sight of him under the sofa—well, he had to be somewhere, he couldn't have flown away, could he?—she was so startled that without being able to help it she slammed the door shut again. But as if regretting her behavior she opened the door again immediately and came in on tiptoe, as if she were visiting an invalid or even a stranger. Gregor had pushed his head forward to the very edge of the sofa and watched her. Would she notice that he had left the milk standing, and not for lack of hunger, and would she bring in some other kind of food more to his taste? If she did not do it of her own accord, he would rather starve than draw her attention to the fact, although he felt a wild impulse to dart out from under the sofa, throw himself at her feet and beg her for something to eat. But his sister at once noticed, with surprise, that the basin was still full, except for a little milk that had been spilt all around it, she lifted it immediately, not with her bare hands, true, but with a cloth and carried it away. Gregor was wildly curious to know what she would bring instead, and made various speculations about it. Yet what she actually did next, in the goodness of her heart, he could never have guessed at. To find out what he liked she brought him a whole selection of food, all set out on an old newspaper. There were old, half-decayed vegetables, bones from last night's supper covered with a white sauce that had thickened; some raisins and almonds; a piece of cheese that Gregor would have called uneatable two days ago; a dry roll of bread, a buttered roll, and a roll both buttered and salted. Besides all that, she set down again the same basin, into which she had poured some water, and which was apparently to be reserved for his exclusive use. And with fine tact, knowing that Gregor would not eat in her presence, she withdrew quickly and even turned the key, to let him understand that he could take his ease as much as he liked. Gregor's legs all whizzed towards the food. His wounds must have healed completely, moreover, for he felt no disability, which amazed him and made him reflect how more than a month ago he had cut one finger a little with a knife and had still suffered pain from the wound only the day before yesterday. Am I less sensitive now? he thought, and sucked greedily at the cheese, which above all the other edibles attracted him at once and strongly. One after another and with tears of satisfaction in his eyes he quickly devoured the cheese, the vegetables and the sauce; the fresh food, on the other hand, had no charms for him, he could not even stand the smell of it and actually dragged away to some little distance the things he could eat. He had long finished his meal and was only lying lazily on the same spot when his sister turned the key slowly as a sign for him to retreat. That roused him at once, although he was nearly asleep, and he hurried under the sofa again. But it took considerable self-control for him to stay under the sofa, even for the short time his sister was in the room, since the large meal had swollen his body somewhat and he was so cramped he could hardly breathe. Slight attacks of breathlessness afflicted him and his eyes were starting a little out of his head as he watched his unsuspecting sister sweeping together with a broom not only the remains of what he had eaten but even the things he had not touched, as if these were now of no use to anyone, and hastily shoveling it all into a bucket, which she covered with a wooden lid and carried away. Hardly had she turned her back when Gregor came from under the sofa and stretched and puffed himself out.

In this manner Gregor was fed, once in the early morning while his parents and the servant girl were still asleep, and a second time after they had all had their mid-day dinner, for then his parents took a short nap and the servant girl could be sent out on some errand or other by his sister. Not that they would have wanted him to starve, of course, but perhaps they could not have borne to know more about his feeding than from hearsay, perhaps too his sister wanted to spare them such little anxieties wherever possible, since they had quite enough to bear as it was.

Under what pretext the doctor and the locksmith had been got rid of on that first morning Gregor could not discover, for since what he said was not understood by the others it never struck any of them, not even his sister, that he could understand what they said, and so whenever his sister came into his room he had to content himself with hearing her utter only a sigh now and then and an occasional appeal to the saints. Later on, when she had got a little used to the situation—of course she could never get completely used to it—she sometimes threw out a remark which was kindly meant or could be so interpreted. "Well, he liked his dinner today," she would say when Gregor had made a good clearance of his food; and when he had not eaten, which gradually happened more and more often, she would say almost sadly: "Everything's been left standing again."

But although Gregor could get no news directly, he overheard a lot from the neighboring rooms, and as soon as voices were audible, he would run to the door of the room concerned and press his whole body against it. In the first few days especially there was no conversation that did not refer to him somehow, even if only indirectly. For two whole days there were family consultations at every mealtime about what should be done; but also between meals the same subject was discussed, for there were always at least two members of the family at home, since no one wanted to be alone in the flat and to leave it quite empty was unthinkable. And on the very first of these days the household cook—it was not quite clear what and how much she knew of the situation—went down on her knees to his mother and begged leave to go, and when she departed, a quarter of an hour later, gave thanks for her dismissal with tears in her eyes as if for the greatest benefit that could have been conferred on her, and without any prompting swore a solemn oath that she would never say a single word to anyone about what had happened.

Now Gregor's sister had to cook too, helping her mother; true, the cooking did not amount to much, for they ate scarcely anything. Gregor was always hearing one of the family vainly urging another to eat and getting no answer but: "Thanks, I've had all I want," or something similar. Perhaps they drank nothing either. Time and again his sister kept asking his father if he wouldn't like some beer and offered kindly to go and fetch it herself, and when he made no answer suggested that she could ask the concierge to fetch it, so that he need feel no sense of obligation, but then a round "No" came from his father and no more was said about it.

In the course of that very first day Gregor's father explained the family's financial position and prospects to both his mother and his sister. Now and then he rose from the table to get some voucher or memorandum out of the small safe he had rescued from the collapse of his business five years earlier. One could hear him opening the complicated lock and rustling papers out and shutting it again. This statement made by his father was the first cheerful information Gregor had heard since his imprisonment. He had been of the opinion that nothing at all was left over from his father's business, at least his father had never said anything to the contrary, and of course he had not asked him directly. At that time Gregor's sole desire was to do his utmost to help the family to forget as soon as possible the catastrophe which had overwhelmed the business and thrown them all into a state of complete despair. And so he had set to work with unusual ardor and almost overnight had become a commercial traveler instead of a little clerk, with of course much greater chances of earning money, and his success was immediately translated into good round coin which he could lay on the table for his amazed and happy family. These had been fine times, and they had never recurred, at least not with the same sense of glory, although later on Gregor had earned so much money that he was able to meet the expenses of the whole household and did so. They had simply got used to it, both the family and Gregor; the money was gratefully accepted and gladly given, but there was no special uprush of warm feeling. With his sister alone had he remained intimate, and it was a secret plan of his that she, who loved music, unlike himself, and could play movingly on the violin, should be sent next year to study at the Conservatorium, despite the great expense that would entail, which must be made up in some other way. During his brief visits home the Conservatorium was often mentioned in the talks he had with his sister, but always merely as a beautiful dream which could never come true, and his parents discouraged even those innocent references to it; yet Gregor had made up his mind firmly about it and meant to announce the fact with due solemnity on Christmas Day.

Such were the thoughts, completely futile in his present condition, that went through his head as he stood clinging upright to the door and listening. Sometimes out of sheer weariness he had to give up listening and let his head fall negligently against the door, but he always had to pull himself together again at once, for even the slight sound his head made was audible next door and brought all conversation to a stop. "What can he be doing now?" his father would say after a while, obviously turning towards the door, and only then would the interrupted conversation gradually be set going again.

Gregor was now informed as amply as he could wish—for his father tended to repeat himself in his explanations, partly because it was a long time since he had handled such matters and partly because his mother could not always grasp things at once—that a certain amount of investments, a very small amount it was true, had survived the wreck of their fortunes and had even increased a little because the dividends had not been touched meanwhile. And besides that, the money Gregor brought home every month—he had kept only a few dollars for himself—had never been quite used up and now amounted to a small capital sum. Behind the door Gregor nodded his head eagerly, rejoiced at this evidence of unexpected thrift and foresight. True, he could really have paid off some more of his father's debts to the chief with his extra money, and so brought much nearer the day on which he could quit his job, but doubtless it was better the way his father had arranged it.

Yet this capital was by no means sufficient to let the family live on the interest of it; for one year, perhaps, or at the most two, they could live on the principal, that was all. It was simply a sum that ought not to be touched and should be kept for a rainy day; money for living expenses would have to be earned. Now his father was still hale enough but an old man, and he had done no work for the past five years and could not be expected to do much; during these five years, the first years of leisure in his laborious though unsuccessful life, he had grown rather fat and become sluggish. And Gregor's old mother, how was she to earn a living with her asthma, which troubled her even when she walked through the flat and kept her lying on a sofa every other day panting for breath beside an open window? And was his sister to earn her bread, she who was still a child of seventeen and whose life hitherto had been so pleasant, consisting as it did in dressing herself nicely, sleeping long, helping in the housekeeping, going out to a few modest entertainments and above all playing the violin? At first whenever the need for earning money was mentioned Gregor let go his hold on the door and threw himself down on the cool leather sofa beside it, he felt so hot with shame and grief.

Often he just lay there the long nights through without sleeping at all, scrabbling for long hours on the leather. Or he nerved himself to the great effort of pushing an armchair to the window, then crawled up over the window sill and, braced against the chair, leaned against the window panes, obviously in some recollection of the sense of freedom that looking out of a window always used to give him. For in reality day by day things that were even a little way off were growing dimmer to his sight; the hospital across the street, which he used to execrate for being all too often before his eyes, was now quite beyond his range of vision, and if he had not known that he lived in Charlotte Street, a quiet street but still a city street, he might have believed that his window gave on a desert waste where gray sky and gray land blended indistinguishably into each other. His quick-witted sister only needed to observe twice that the armchair stood by the window; after that whenever she had tidied the room she always pushed the chair back to the same place at the window and even left the inner casements open.

If he could have spoken to her and thanked her for all she had to do for him, he could have borne her ministrations better; as it was, they oppressed him. She certainly tried to make as light as possible of whatever was disagreeable in her task, and as time went on she succeeded, of course, more and more, but time brought more enlightenment to Gregor too. The very way she came in distressed him. Hardly was she in the room when she rushed to the window, without even taking time to shut the door, careful as she was usually to shield the sight of Gregor's room from the others, and as if she were almost suffocating tore the casements open with hasty fingers, standing then in the open draught for a while even in the bitterest cold and drawing deep breaths. This noisy scurry of hers upset Gregor twice a day; he would crouch trembling under the sofa all the time, knowing quite well that she would certainly have spared him such a disturbance had she found it at all possible to stay in his presence without opening the window.

On one occasion, about a month after Gregor's metamorphosis, when there was surely no reason for her to be still startled at his appearance, she came a little earlier than usual and found him gazing out the window, quite motionless, and thus well placed to look like a bogey. Gregor would not have been surprised had she not come in at all, for she could not immediately open the window while he was there, but not only did she retreat, she jumped back as if in alarm and banged the door shut; a stranger might well have thought that he had been lying in wait for her there meaning to bite her. Of course he hid himself under the sofa at once, but he had to wait until midday before she came again, and seemed more ill at ease than usual. This made him realize how repulsive the sight of him still was to her, and that it was bound to go on being repulsive, and what an effort it must cost her not to run away even from the sight of the small portion of his body that stuck out from under the sofa. In order to spare her that, therefore, one day he carried a sheet on his back to the sofa—it cost him four hours' labor—and arranged it there in such a way as to hide him completely, so that even if she were to bend down she could not see him. Had she considered the sheet unnecessary, she would certainly have stripped it off the sofa again, for it was clear enough that this curtaining and confining of himself was not likely to conduce Gregor's comfort, but she left it where it was, and Gregor even fancied that he caught a thankful glance from her eye when he lifted the sheet carefully a very little with his head to see how she was taking the new arrangement.

For the first fortnight his parents could not bring themselves to the point of entering his room, and he often heard them expressing their appreciation of his sister's activities, whereas formerly they had frequently scolded her for being as they thought a somewhat useless daughter. But now, both of them often waited outside the door, his father and his mother, while his sister tidied his room, and as soon as she came out she had to tell them exactly how things were in the room, what Gregor had eaten, how he had conducted himself this time and whether there was not perhaps some slight improvement in his condition. His mother, moreover, began relatively soon to want to visit him, but his father and sister dissuaded her at first with arguments which Gregor listened to very attentively and altogether approved. Later, however, she had to be held back by main force, and when she cried out: "Do let me in to Gregor, he is my unfortunate son! Can't you understand that I must go in to him?" Gregor thought that it might be well to have her come in, not every day, of course, but perhaps once a week; she understood things, after all, much better than his sister, who was only a child despite the efforts she was making and had perhaps taken on so difficult a task merely out of childish thoughtlessness.

Gregor's desire to see his mother was soon fulfilled. During the daytime he did not want to show himself at the window, out of consideration for his parents, but he could not crawl very far around the few square yards of floor space he had, nor could he bear lying quietly at rest all during the night, while he was fast losing any interest he had ever taken in food, so that for mere recreation he had formed the habit of crawling crisscross over the walls and ceiling. He especially enjoyed hanging suspended from the ceiling; it was much better than lying on the floor; one could breathe more freely; one's body swung and rocked lightly; and in the almost blissful absorption induced by this suspension it could happen to his own surprise that he let go and fell plump on the floor. Yet he now had his body much better under control than formerly, and even such a big fall did him no harm. His sister at once remarked the new distraction Gregor had found for himself—he left traces behind him of the sticky stuff on his soles wherever he crawled—and she got the idea in her head of giving him as wide a field as possible to crawl in and of removing the pieces of furniture that hindered him, above all the chest of drawers and the writing desk. But that was more than she could manage all by herself; she did not dare ask her father to help her; and as for the servant girl, a young creature of sixteen who had had the courage to stay on after the cook's departure, she could not be asked to help, for she had begged as an especial favor that she might keep the kitchen door locked and open it only on a definite summons; so there was nothing left but to apply to her mother at an hour when her father was out. And the old lady did come, with exclamations of joyful eagerness, which, however, died away at the door of Gregor's room. Gregor's sister, of course, went in first, to see that everything was in order before letting his mother enter. In great haste Gregor pulled the sheet lower and rucked it more in folds so that it really looked as if it had been thrown accidentally over the sofa. And this time he did not peer out from under it; he renounced the pleasure of seeing his mother on this occasion and was only glad that she had come at all. "Come in, he's out of sight," said his sister, obviously leading her mother in by the hand. Gregor could now hear the two women struggling to shift the heavy old chest from its place, and his sister claiming the greater part of the labor for herself, without listening to the admonitions of her mother who feared she might overstrain herself. It took a long time. After at least a quarter of an hour's tugging his mother objected that the chest had better be left where it was, for in the first place it was too heavy and could never be got out before his father came home, and standing in the middle of the room like that it would only hamper Gregor's movements, while in the second place it was not at all certain that removing the furniture would be doing a service to Gregor. She was inclined to think to the contrary; the sight of the naked walls made her own heart heavy, and why shouldn't Gregor have the same feeling, considering that he had been used to his furniture for so long and might feel forlorn without it. "And doesn't it look," she concluded in a low voice—in fact she had been almost whispering all the time as if to avoid letting Gregor, whose exact whereabouts she did not know, hear even the tones of her voice, for she was convinced that he could not understand her words—"doesn't it look as if we were showing him, by taking away his furniture, that we have given up hope of his ever getting better and are just leaving him coldly to himself? I think it would be best to keep his room exactly as it has always been, so that when he comes back to us he will find everything unchanged and be able all the more easily to forget what has happened in between."

On hearing these words from his mother Gregor realized that the lack of all direct human speech for the past two months together with the monotony of family life must have confused his mind, otherwise he could not account for the fact that he had quite earnestly looked forward to having his room emptied of furnishing. Did he really want his warm room, so comfortably fitted with old family furniture, to be turned into a naked den in which he would certainly be able to crawl unhampered in all directions but at the price of shedding simultaneously all recollection of his human background? He had indeed been so near the brink of forgetfulness that only the voice of his mother, which he had not heard for so long, had drawn him back from it. Nothing should be taken out of his room; everything must stay as it was; he could not dispense with the good influence of the furniture on his state of mind; and even if the furniture did hamper him in his senseless crawling round and round, that was no drawback but a great advantage.

Unfortunately his sister was of the contrary opinion; she had grown accustomed, and not without reason, to consider herself an expert in Gregor's affairs as against her parents, and so her mother's advice was now enough to make her determined on the removal not only of the chest and the writing desk, which had been her first intention, but of all the furniture except the indispensable sofa. This determination was not, of course, merely the outcome of childish recalcitrance and of the self-confidence she had recently developed so unexpectedly and at such cost; she had in fact perceived that Gregor needed a lot of space to crawl about in, while on the other hand he never used the furniture at all, so far as could be seen. Another factor might have been also the enthusiastic temperament of an adolescent girl, which seeks to indulge itself on every opportunity and which now tempted Grete to exaggerate the horror of her brother's circumstances in order that she might do all the more for him. In a room where Gregor lorded it all alone over empty walls no one save herself was likely ever to set foot.

And so she was not to be moved from her resolve by her mother who seemed moreover to be ill at ease in Gregor's room and therefore unsure of herself, was soon reduced to silence and helped her daughter as best she could to push the chest outside. Now, Gregor could do without the chest, if need be, but the writing desk he must retain. As soon as the two women had got the chest out of his room, groaning as they pushed it, Gregor stuck his head out from under the sofa to see how he might intervene as kindly and cautiously as possible. But as bad luck would have it, his mother was the first to return, leaving Grete clasping the chest in the room next door where she was trying to shift it all by herself, without of course moving it from the spot. His mother however was not accustomed to the sight of him, it might sicken her and so in alarm Gregor backed quickly to the other end of the sofa, yet could not prevent the sheet from swaying a little in front. That was enough to put her on the alert. She paused, stood still for a moment and then went back to Grete.

Although Gregor kept reassuring himself that nothing out of the way was happening, but only a few bits of furniture were being changed around, he soon had to admit that all this trotting to and fro of the two women, their little ejaculations and the scraping of furniture along the floor affected him like a vast disturbance coming from all sides at once, and however much he tucked in his head and legs and cowered to the very floor he was bound to confess that he would not be able to stand it for long. They were clearing his room out; taking away everything he loved; the chest in which he kept his fret saw and other tools was already dragged off; they were now loosening the writing desk which had almost sunk into the floor, the desk at which he had done all his homework when he was at the commercial academy, at the grammar school before that, and, yes, even at the primary school—he had no more time to waste in weighing the good intentions of the two women, whose existence he had by now forgotten, for they were so exhausted that they were laboring in silence and nothing could be heard but the heavy scuffling of their feet.

And so he rushed out—the women were just leaning against the writing desk in the next room to give themselves a breather—and four times changed his direction, since he really did not know what to rescue first, then on the wall opposite, which was already otherwise cleared, he was struck by the picture of the lady muffled in so much fur and quickly crawled up to it and pressed himself to the glass, which was a good surface to hold on to and comforted his hot belly. This picture at least, which was entirely hidden beneath him, was going to be removed by nobody. He turned his head towards the door of the living room so as to observe the women when they came back.

They had not allowed themselves much of a rest and were already coming; Grete had twined her arm round her mother and was almost supporting her. "Well, what shall we take now?" said Grete, looking round. Her eyes met Gregor's from the wall. She kept her composure, presumably because of her mother, bent her head down to her mother, to keep her from looking up, and said, although in a fluttering, unpremeditated voice: "Come, hadn't we better go back to the living room for a moment?" Her intentions were clear enough to Gregor, she wanted to bestow her mother in safety and then chase him down from the wall. Well, just let her try it! He clung to his picture and would not give it up. He would rather fly in Grete's face.

But Grete's words had succeeded in disquieting her mother, who took a step to one side, caught sight of the huge brown mass on the flowered wallpaper, and before she was really conscious that what she saw was Gregor screamed in a loud, hoarse voice: "Oh God, oh God!" fell with outspread arms over the sofa as if giving up and did not move. "Gregor!" cried his sister, shaking her fist and glaring at him. This was the first time she had directly addressed him since his metamorphosis. She ran into the next room for some aromatic essence with which to rouse her mother from her fainting fit. Gregor wanted to help too—there was still time to rescue the picture—but he was stuck fast to the glass and had to tear himself loose; he then ran after his sister into the next room as if he could advise her, as he used to do; but then had to stand helplessly behind her; she meanwhile searched among various small bottles and when she turned round started in alarm at the sight of him; one bottle fell on the floor and broke; a splinter of glass cut Gregor's face and some kind of corrosive medicine splashed him; without pausing a moment longer Grete gathered up all the bottles she could carry and ran to her mother with them; she banged the door shut with her foot. Gregor was now cut off from his mother, who was perhaps nearly dying because of him; he dared not open the door for fear of frightening away his sister, who had to stay with her mother; there was nothing he could do but wait; and harassed by self-reproach and worry he began now to crawl to and fro, over everything, walls, furniture, and ceiling, and finally in his despair, when the noble room seemed to be reeling round him, fell down on to the middle of the big table.

A little while elapsed. Gregor was still lying there feebly and all around was quiet, perhaps that was a good omen. Then the doorbell rang. The servant girl was of course locked in her kitchen, and Grete would have to open the door. It was his father. "What's been happening?" were his first words; Grete's face must have told him everything. Grete answered in a muffled voice, apparently hiding her head on his breast: "Mother has been fainting, but she's better now. Gregor's broken loose." "Just what I expected," said his father, "just what I've been telling you, but you women would never listen." It was clear to Gregor that his father had taken the worst interpretation of Grete's all too brief statement and was assuming that Gregor had been guilty of some violent act. Therefore Gregor must now try to propitiate his father, since he had neither time nor means for an explanation. And so he fled to the door of his own room and crouched against it, to let his father see as soon as he came in from the hall that his son had the good intention of getting back into his room immediately and that it was not necessary to drive him there, but that if only the door were opened he would disappear at once.

Yet his father was not in the mood to perceive such fine distinctions. "Ah!" he cried as soon as he appeared, in a tone which sounded at once angry and exultant. Gregor drew his head back from the door and lifted it to look at his father. Truly, this was not the father he had imagined to himself; admittedly he had been too absorbed of late in his new recreation of crawling over the ceiling to take the same interest as before in what was happening elsewhere in the flat, and he ought really to be prepared for some changes. And yet, and yet, could that be his father? The man who used to lie wearily sunk in bed whenever Gregor set out on a business journey; who welcomed him back of an evening lying in a long chair in a dressing gown; who could not really rise to his feet but only lifted his arms in greeting, and on the rare occasions when he did go out with his family, on one or two Sundays a year and on high holidays, walked between Gregor and his mother, who were slow walkers anyhow, even more slowly than they did, muffled in his old greatcoat, shuffling laboriously forward with the help of his crook-handled stick which he set down most cautiously at every step and, whenever he wanted to say anything, nearly always came to a full stop and gathered his escort around him? Now he was standing there in fine shape; dressed in a smart blue uniform with gold buttons, such as bank messengers wear; his strong double chin bulged over the stiff high collar of his jacket; from under his bushy eyebrows his black eyes darted fresh and penetrating glances; his onetime tangled white hair had been combed flat on either side of a shining and carefully exact parting. He pitched his cap, which bore a gold monogram, probably the badge of some bank, in a wide sweep across the whole room on to a sofa and with the tail-ends of his jacket thrown back, his hands in his trouser pockets, advanced with a grim visage towards Gregor. Likely enough he did not himself know what he meant to do; at any rate he lifted his feet uncommonly high, and Gregor was dumbfounded at the enormous size of his shoe soles. But Gregor could not risk standing up to him, aware as he had been from the very first day of his new life that his father believed only the severest measures suitable for dealing with him. And so he ran before his father, stopping when he stopped and scuttling forward again when his father made any kind of move. In this way they circled the room several times without anything decisive happening; indeed the whole operation did not even look like a pursuit because it was carried out so slowly. And so Gregor did not leave the floor, for he feared that his father might take as a piece of peculiar wickedness any excursion of his over the walls or the ceiling. All the same, he could not stay this course much longer, for while his father took one step he had to carry out a whole series of movements. He was already beginning to feel breathless, just as in his former life his lungs had not been very dependable. As he was staggering along, trying to concentrate his energy on running, hardly keeping his eyes open; in his dazed state never even thinking of any other escape than simply going forward; and having almost forgotten that the walls were free to him, which in this room were well provided with finely carved pieces of furniture full of knobs and crevices—suddenly something lightly flung landed close behind him and rolled before him. It was an apple; a second apple followed immediately; Gregor came to a stop in alarm; there was no point in running on, for his father was determined to bombard him. He had filled his pockets with fruit from the dish on the sideboard and was now shying apple after apple, without taking particularly good aim for the moment. The small red apples rolled about the floor as if magnetized and cannoned into each other. An apple thrown without much force grazed Gregor's back and glanced off harmlessly. But another following immediately landed right on his back and sank in; Gregor wanted to drag himself forward, as if this startling, incredible pain could be left behind him; but he felt as if nailed to the spot and flattened himself out in a complete derangement of all his senses. With his last conscious look he saw the door of his room being torn open and his mother rushing out ahead of his screaming sister, in her underbodice, for her daughter had loosened her clothing to let her breathe more freely and recover from her swoon, he saw his mother rushing toward his father, leaving one after another behind her on the floor her loosened petticoats, stumbling over her petticoats straight to his father and embracing him, in complete union with him—but here Gregor's sight began to fail—with her hands clasped round his father's neck as she begged for her son's life.

III

The serious injury done to Gregor, which disabled him for more than a month—the apple went on sticking in his body as a visible reminder, since no one bothered to remove it—seemed to have made even his father recollect that Gregor was a member of the family, despite his present unfortunate and repulsive shape, and ought not to be treated as an enemy, that, on the contrary, family duty required the suppression of disgust and the exercise of patience, nothing but patience.

And although his injury had impaired, probably for ever, his power of movement, and for the time being it took him long, long minutes to creep across his room like an old invalid—there was no question now of crawling up the wall—yet in his own opinion he was sufficiently compensated for this worsening of his condition by the fact that towards evening the living-room door, which he used to watch intently for an hour or two beforehand, was always thrown open, so that lying in the darkness of his room, invisible to the family, he could see them all at the lamp-lit table and listen to their talk, by general consent as it were, very different from his earlier eavesdropping.

True, their intercourse lacked the lively character of former times, which he had always called to mind with a certain wistfulness in the small hotel bedrooms where he had been wont to throw himself down, tired out, on damp bedding. They were now mostly very silent. Soon after supper his father would fall asleep in his armchair; his mother and sister would admonish each other to be silent; his mother, bending low over the lamp, stitched at fine sewing for an underwear firm; his sister, who had taken a job as a salesgirl, was learning shorthand and French in the evenings on the chance of bettering herself. Sometimes his father woke up, and as if quite unaware that he had been sleeping said to his mother: "What a lot of sewing you're doing today!" and at once fell asleep again, while the two women exchanged a tired smile.

With a kind of mulishness his father persisted in keeping his uniform on even in the house; his dressing gown hung uselessly on its peg and he slept fully dressed where he sat, as if he were ready for service at any moment and even here only at the beck and call of his superior. As a result, his uniform, which was not brand-new to start with, began to look dirty, despite all the loving care of the mother and sister to keep it clean, and Gregor often spent whole evenings gazing at the many greasy spots on the garment, gleaming with gold buttons always in a high state of polish, in which the old man sat sleeping in extreme discomfort and yet quite peacefully.

As soon as the clock struck ten his mother tried to rouse his father with gentle words and to persuade him after that to get into bed, for sitting there he could not have a proper sleep and that was what he needed most, since he had to go to duty at six. But with the mulishness that had obsessed him since he became a bank messenger he always insisted on staying longer at the table, although he regularly fell asleep again and in the end only with the greatest trouble could be got out of his armchair and into his bed. However insistently Gregor's mother and sister kept urging him with gentle reminders, he would go on slowly shaking his head for a quarter of an hour, keeping his eyes shut, and refuse to get to his feet. The mother plucked at his sleeve, whispering endearments in his ear, the sister left her lessons to come to her mother's help, but Gregor's father was not to be caught. He would only sink down deeper in his chair. Not until the two women hoisted him up by the armpits did he open his eyes and look at them both, one after the other, usually with the remark: "This is a life. This is the peace and quiet of my old age." And leaning on the two of them he would heave himself up, with difficulty, as if he were a great burden to himself, suffer them to lead him as far as the door and then wave them off and go on alone, while the mother abandoned her needlework and the sister her pen in order to run after him and help him farther.

Who could find time, in this overworked and tired-out family, to bother about Gregor more than was absolutely needful? The household was reduced more and more; the servant girl was turned off; a gigantic bony charwoman with white hair flying round her head came in morning and evening to do the rough work; everything else was done by Gregor's mother, as well as great piles of sewing. Even various family ornaments, which his mother and sister used to wear with pride at parties and celebrations, had to be sold, as Gregor discovered of an evening from hearing them all discuss the prices obtained. But what they lamented most was the fact that they could not leave the flat which was much too big for their present circumstances, because they could not think of any way to shift Gregor. Yet Gregor saw well enough that consideration for him was not the main difficulty preventing the removal, for they could have easily shifted him in some suitable box with a few air holes in it; what really kept them from moving into another flat was rather their own complete hopelessness and the belief that they had been singled out for a misfortune such as had never happened to any of their relations or acquaintances. They fulfilled to the uttermost all that the world demands of poor people, the father fetched breakfast for the small clerks in the bank, the mother devoted her energy to making underwear for strangers, the sister trotted to and fro behind the counter at the behest of customers, but more than this they had not the strength to do. And the wound in Gregor's back began to nag at him afresh when his mother and sister, after getting his father into bed, came back again, left their work lying, drew close to each other and sat cheek by cheek; when his mother, pointing towards his room, said: "Shut that door now, Grete," and he was left again in darkness, while next door the women mingled their tears or perhaps sat dry-eyed staring at the table.

Gregor hardly slept at all by night or by day. He was often haunted by the idea that next time the door opened he would take the family's affairs in hand again just as he used to do; once more, after this long interval, there appeared in his thoughts the figures of the chief and the chief clerk, the commercial travelers and the apprentices, the porter who was so dull-witted, two or three friends in other firms, a chambermaid in one of the rural hotels, a sweet and fleeting memory, a cashier in a milliner's shop, whom he had wooed earnestly but too slowly—they all appeared, together with strangers or people he had quite forgotten, but instead of helping him and his family they were one and all unapproachable and he was glad when they vanished. At other times he would not be in the mood to bother about his family, he was only filled with rage at the way they were neglecting him, and although he had no clear idea of what he might care to eat he would make plans for getting into the larder to take the food that was after all his due, even if he were not hungry. His sister no longer took thought to bring him what might especially please him, but in the morning and at noon before she went to business hurriedly pushed into his room with her foot any food that was available, and in the evening cleared it out again with one sweep of the broom, heedless of whether it had been merely tasted, or—as most frequently happened—left untouched. The cleaning of his room, which she now always did in the evenings, could not have been more hastily done. Streaks of dirt stretched along the walls, here and there lay balls of dust and filth. At first Gregor used to station himself in some particularly filthy corner when his sister arrived, in order to reproach her with it, so to speak. But he could have sat there for weeks without getting her to make any improvements; she could see the dirt as well as he did, but she had simply made up her mind to leave it alone. And yet, with a touchiness that was new to her, which seemed anyhow to have infected the whole family, she jealously guarded her claim to be the sole caretaker of Gregor's room. His mother once subjected his room to a thorough cleaning, which was achieved only by means of several buckets of water—all this dampness of course upset Gregor too and he lay widespread, sulky and motionless on the sofa—but she was well punished for it. Hardly had his sister noticed the changed aspect of his room that evening than she rushed in high dudgeon into the living room and, despite the imploringly raised hands of her mother, burst into a storm of weeping, while her parents—her father had of course been startled out of his chair—looked on at first in helpless amazement; then they too began to go into action; the father reproached the mother on his right for not having left the cleaning of Gregor's room to his sister; shrieked at the sister on his left that never again was she allowed to clean Gregor's room; while the mother tried to pull the father into his bedroom, since he was beyond himself with agitation; the sister, shaken with sobs, then beat upon the table with her small fists; and Gregor hissed loudly with rage because not one of them thought of shutting the door to spare him such a spectacle and so much noise.

Still, even if the sister, exhausted by her daily work, had grown tired of looking after Gregor as she did formerly, there was no need for his mother's intervention or for Gregor's being neglected at all. The charwoman was there. This old widow, whose strong bony frame had enabled her to survive the worst a long life could offer, by no means recoiled from Gregor. Without being in the least curious she had once by chance opened the door of his room and at the sight of Gregor, who, taken by surprise, began to rush to and fro although no one was chasing him, merely stood there with her arms folded. From that time she never failed to open his door a little for a moment, morning and evening, to have a look at him. At first she even used to call him to her, with words which apparently she took to be friendly, such as: "Come along, then, you old dung beetle!" or "Look at the old dung beetle, then!" To such allocutions Gregor made no answer, but stayed motionless where he was, as if the door had never been opened. Instead of being allowed to disturb him so senselessly whenever the whim took her, she should rather have been ordered to clean out his room daily, that charwoman! Once, early in the morning—heavy rain was lashing on the windowpanes, perhaps a sign that spring was on the way— Gregor was so exasperated when she began addressing him again that he ran at her, as if to attack her, although slowly and feebly enough. But the charwoman instead of showing fright merely lifted high a chair that happened to be beside the door, and as she stood there with her mouth wide open it was clear that she meant to shut it only when she brought the chair down on Gregor's back. "So you're not coming any nearer?" she asked, as Gregor turned away again, and quietly put the chair back into the corner.

Gregor was now eating hardly anything. Only when he happened to pass the food laid out for him did he take a bit of something in his mouth as a pastime, kept it there for an hour at a time and usually spat it out again. At first he thought it was chagrin over the state of his room that prevented him from eating, yet he soon got used to the various changes in his room. It had become a habit in the family to push into his room things there was no room for elsewhere, and there were plenty of these now, since one of the rooms had been let to three lodgers. Three serious gentlemen—all three of them with full beards, as Gregor once observed through a crack in the door—had a passion for order, not only in their own room but, since they were now members of the household, in all its arrangements, especially in the kitchen. Superfluous, not to say dirty, objects they could not bear. Besides, they had brought with them most of the furnishings they needed. For this reason many things could be dispensed with that it was no use trying to sell but that should not be thrown away either. All of them found their way into Gregor's room. The ash can likewise and the kitchen garbage can. Anything that was not needed for the moment was simply flung into Gregor's room by the charwoman, who did everything in a hurry; fortunately Gregor usually saw only the object, whatever it was, and the hand that held it. Perhaps she intended to take the things away again as time and opportunity offered, or to collect them until she could throw them all out in a heap, but in fact they just lay wherever she happened to throw them, except when Gregor pushed his way through the junk heap and shifted it somewhat, at first out of necessity, because he had not room enough to crawl, but later with increasing enjoyment, although after such excursions, being sad and weary to death, he would lie motionless for hours. And since the lodgers often ate their supper at home in the common living room, the living-room door stayed shut many an evening, yet Gregor reconciled himself quite easily to the shutting of the door, for often enough on evenings when it was opened he had disregarded it entirely and lain in the darkest corner of his room, quite unnoticed by the family. But on one occasion the charwoman left the door open a little and it stayed ajar even when the lodgers came in for supper and the lamp was lit. They set themselves at the top end of the table where formerly Gregor and his father and mother had eaten their meals, unfolded their napkins and took knife and fork in hand. At once his mother appeared in the other doorway with a dish of meat and close behind her his sister with a dish of potatoes piled high. The food steamed with a thick vapor. The lodgers bent over the food set before them as if to scrutinize it before eating, in fact the man in the middle, who seemed to pass for an authority with the other two, cut a piece of meat as it lay on the dish, obviously to discover if it were tender or should be sent back to the kitchen. He showed satisfaction, and Gregor's mother and sister, who had been watching anxiously, breathed freely and began to smile.

The family itself took its meals in the kitchen. None the less, Gregor's father came into the living room before going into the kitchen and with one prolonged bow, cap in hand, made a round of the table. The lodgers all stood up and murmured something in their beards. When they were alone again they ate their food in almost complete silence. It seemed remarkable to Gregor that among the various noises coming from the table he could always distinguish the sound of their masticating teeth, as if this were a sign to Gregor that one needed teeth in order to eat, and that with toothless jaws even of the finest make one could do nothing. "I'm hungry enough," said Gregor sadly to himself, "but not for that kind of food. How these lodgers are stuffing themselves, and here am I dying of starvation!"

On that very evening—during the whole of his time there Gregor could not remember ever having heard the violin—the sound of violin-playing came from the kitchen. The lodgers had already finished their supper, the one in the middle had brought out a newspaper and given the other two a page apiece, and now they were leaning back at ease reading and smoking. When the violin began to play they pricked up their ears, got to their feet, and went on tiptoe to the hall door where they stood huddled together. Their movements must have been heard in the kitchen, for Gregor's father called out: "Is the violin-playing disturbing you, gentlemen? It can be stopped at once." "On the contrary," said the middle lodger, "could not Fräulein Samsa come and play in this room, beside us, where it is much more convenient and comfortable?" "Oh certainly," cried Gregor's father, as if he were the violin-player. The lodgers came back into the living room and waited. Presently Gregor's father arrived with the music stand, his mother carrying the music and his sister with the violin. His sister quietly made everything ready to start playing; his parents, who had never let rooms before and so had an exaggerated idea of the courtesy due to lodgers, did not venture to sit down on their own chairs; his father leaned against the door, the right hand thrust between two buttons of his livery coat, which was formally buttoned up; but his mother was offered a chair by one of the lodgers and, since she left the chair just where he had happened to put it, sat down in a corner to one side.

Gregor's sister began to play; the father and mother, from either side, intently watched the movements of her hands. Gregor, attracted by the playing, ventured to move forward a little until his head was actually inside the living room. He felt hardly any surprise at his growing lack of consideration for the others; there had been a time when he prided himself on being considerate. And yet just on this occasion he had more reason than ever to hide himself, since owing to the amount of dust which lay thick in his room and rose into the air at the slightest movement, he too was covered with dust; fluff and hair and remnants of food trailed with him, caught on his back and along his sides; his indifference to everything was much too great for him to turn on his back and scrape himself clean on the carpet, as once he had several times a day. And in spite of his condition, no shame deterred him from advancing a little over the spotless floor of the living room.

To be sure, no one was aware of him. The family was entirely absorbed in the violin-playing; the lodgers, however, who first of all had stationed themselves, hands in pockets, much too close behind the music stand so that they could all have read the music, which must have bothered his sister, had soon retreated to the window, half-whispering with downbent heads, and stayed there while his father turned an anxious eye on them. Indeed, they were making it more than obvious that they had been disappointed in their expectation of hearing good or enjoyable violin-playing, that they had had more than enough of the performance and only out of courtesy suffered a continued disturbance of their peace. From the way they all kept blowing the smoke of their cigars high in the air through nose and mouth one could divine their irritation. And yet Gregor's sister was playing so beautifully. Her face leaned sideways, intently and sadly her eyes followed the notes of music. Gregor crawled a little farther forward and lowered his head to the ground so that it might be possible for his eyes to meet hers. Was he an animal, that music had such an effect upon him? He felt as if the way were opening before him to the unknown nourishment he craved. He was determined to push forward till he reached his sister, to pull at her skirt and so let her know that she was to come into his room with her violin, for no one here appreciated her playing as he would appreciate it. He would never let her out of his room, at least, not so long as he lived; his frightful appearance would become, for the first time, useful to him; he would watch all the doors of his room at night and spit at intruders; but his sister should need no constraint, she should stay with him of her own free will; she should sit beside him on the sofa, bend down her ear to him and hear him confide that he had had the firm intention of sending her to the Conservatorium, and that, but for his mishap, last Christmas—surely Christmas was long past?—he would have announced it to everybody without allowing a single objection. After this confession his sister would be so touched that she would burst into tears, and Gregor would then raise himself to her shoulder and kiss her on the neck, which, now that she went to business, she kept free of any ribbon or collar.

"Mr. Samsa!" cried the middle lodger, to Gregor's father, and pointed, without wasting any more words, at Gregor, now working himself slowly forwards. The violin fell silent, the middle lodger first smiled to his friends with a shake of the head and then looked at Gregor again. Instead of driving Gregor out, his father seemed to think it more needful to begin by soothing the lodgers, although they were not at all agitated and apparently found Gregor more entertaining than the violin-playing. He hurried towards them and, spreading out his arms, tried to urge them back into their own room and at the same time to block their view of Gregor. They now began to be really a little angry, one could not tell whether because of the old man's behavior or because it had just dawned on them that all unwittingly they had such a neighbor as Gregor next door. They demanded explanations of his father, they waved their arms like him, tugged uneasily at their beards, and only with reluctance backed towards their room. Meanwhile Gregor's sister, who stood there as if lost when her playing was so abruptly broken off, came to life again, pulled herself together all at once after standing for a while holding violin and bow in nervelessly hanging hands and staring at her music, pushed her violin into the lap of her mother, who was still sitting in her chair fighting asthmatically for breath, and ran into the lodgers' room to which they were now being shepherded by her father more quickly than before. One could see the pillows and blankets on the beds flying under her accustomed fingers and being laid in order. Before the lodgers had actually reached their room she had finished making the beds and slipped out.

The old man seemed once more to be so possessed by his mulish self-assertiveness that he was forgetting all the respect he should show to his lodgers. He kept driving them on and driving them on until in the very door of the bedroom the middle lodger stamped his foot loudly on the floor and so brought him to a halt. "I beg to announce," said the lodger, lifting one hand and looking also at Gregor's mother and sister, "that because of the disgusting conditions prevailing in this household and family"—here he spat on the floor with emphatic brevity—"I give you notice on the spot. Naturally I won't pay you a penny for the days I have lived here, on the contrary I shall consider bringing an action for damages against you, based on claims—believe me—that will be easily susceptible of proof." He ceased and stared straight in front of him, as if he expected something. In fact his two friends at once rushed into the breach with these words: "And we too give notice on the spot." On that he seized the door-handle and shut the door with a slam.

Gregor's father, groping with his hands, staggered forward and fell from his chair; it looked as if he were stretching himself there for his ordinary evening nap, but the marked jerkings of his head, which was as if uncontrollable, showed that he was far from asleep. Gregor had simply stayed quietly all the time on the spot where the lodgers had espied him. Disappointment at the failure of his plan, perhaps also the weakness arising from extreme hunger, made it impossible for him to move. He feared, with a fair degree of certainty, that at any moment the general tension would discharge itself in a combined attack upon him, and he lay waiting. He did not react even to the noise made by the violin as it fell off his mother's lap from under her trembling fingers and gave out a resonant note.

"My dear parents," said his sister, slapping her hand on the table by way of introduction, "things can't go on like this. Perhaps you don't realize that, but I do. I won't utter my brother's name in the presence of this creature, and so all I say is: we must try to get rid of it. We've tried to look after it and to put up with it as far as is humanly possible, and I don't think anyone could reproach us in the slightest."

"She is more than right," said Gregor's father to himself. His mother, who was still choking for lack of breath, began to cough hollowly into her hand with a wild look in her eyes.

His sister rushed over to her and held her forehead. His father's thoughts seemed to have lost their vagueness at Grete's words, he sat more upright, fingering his service cap that lay among the plates still lying on the table from the lodgers' supper, and from time to time looked at the still form of Gregor.

"We must try to get rid of it," his sister now said explicitly to her father, since her mother was coughing too much to hear a word, "it will be the death of both of you, I can see that coming. When one has to work as hard as we do, all of us, one can't stand this continual torment at home on top of it. At least I can't stand it any longer." And she burst into such a passion of sobbing that her tears dropped on her mother's face, where she wiped them off mechanically.

"My dear," said the old man sympathetically, and with evident understanding, "but what can we do?"

Gregor's sister merely shrugged her shoulders to indicate the feeling of help-lessness that had now overmastered her during her weeping fit, in contrast to her former confidence.

"If he could understand us," said her father, half questioningly; Grete, still sob-bing, vehemently waved a hand to show how unthinkable that was.

"If he could understand us," repeated the old man, shutting his eyes to consider his daughter's conviction that understanding was impossible, "then perhaps we might come to some agreement with him. But as it is—"

"He must go," cried Gregor's sister, "that's the only solution, Father. You must just try to get rid of the idea that this is Gregor. The fact that we've believed it for so long is the root of all our trouble. But how can it be Gregor? If this were Gregor, he would have realized long ago that human beings can't live with such a creature, and he'd have gone away on his own accord. Then we wouldn't have any brother, but we'd be able to go on living and keep his memory in honor. As it is, this creature persecutes us, drives away our lodgers, obviously wants the whole apartment to himself and would have us all sleep in the gutter. Just look, Father," she shrieked all at once, "he's at it again!" And in an access of panic that was quite incomprehensible to Gregor she even quitted her mother, literally thrusting the chair from her as if she would rather sacrifice her mother than stay so near to Gregor, and rushed behind her father, who also rose up, being simply upset by her agitation, and half-spread his arms out as if to protect her.

Yet Gregor had not the slightest intention of frightening anyone, far less his sister. He had only begun to turn round in order to crawl back to his room, but it was certainly a startling operation to watch, since because of his disabled condition he could not execute the difficult turning movements except by lifting his head and then bracing it against the floor over and over again. He paused and looked round. His good intentions seemed to have been recognized; the alarm had been only momentary. Now they were all watching him in melancholy silence. His mother lay in her chair, her legs stiffly outstretched and pressed together, her eyes almost clos-ing for sheer weariness; his father and his sister were sitting beside each other, his sister's arm around the old man's neck.

Perhaps I can go on turning round now, thought Gregor, and began his labors again. He could not stop himself from panting with the effort, and had to pause now and then to take breath. Nor did anyone harass him, he was left entirely to himself. When he had completed the turn-round he began at once to crawl straight back. He was amazed at the distance separating him from his room and could not under-stand how in his weak state he had managed to accomplish the same journey so recently, almost without remarking it. Intent on crawling as fast as possible, he barely noticed that not a single word, not an ejaculation from his family, interfered with his progress. Only when he was already in the doorway did he turn his head round, not completely, for his neck muscles were getting stiff, but enough to see that nothing had changed behind him except that his sister had risen to her feet. His last glance fell on his mother, who was now quite overcome by sleep.

Hardly was he well inside his room when the door was hastily pushed shut, bolted and locked. The sudden noise in his rear startled him so much that his little legs gave beneath him. It was his sister who had shown such haste. She had been standing ready waiting and had made a light spring forward, Gregor had not even heard her coming, and she cried "At last!" to her parents as she turned the key in the lock.

"And what now?" said Gregor to himself, looking round in the darkness. Soon he made the discovery that he was unable to stir a limb. This did not surprise him, rather it seemed unnatural that he should ever actually have been able to move on these feeble little legs. Otherwise he felt relatively comfortable. True, his whole body was aching, but it seemed that the pain was gradually growing less and would finally pass away. The rotting apple in his back and the inflamed area around it, all covered with soft dust, already hardly troubled him. He thought of his family with tenderness and love. The decision that he must disappear was one that he held to even more strongly than his sister, if that were possible. In this state of vacant and peaceful meditation he remained until the tower clock struck three in the morning. The first broadening of light in the world outside the window entered his consciousness once more. Then his head sank to the floor of its own accord and from his nostrils came the last faint flicker of his breath.

When the charwoman arrived early in the morning—what between her strength and her impatience she slammed all the doors so loudly, never mind how often she had been begged not to do so, that no one in the whole apartment could enjoy any quiet sleep after her arrival—she noticed nothing unusual as she took her customary peep into Gregor's room. She thought he was lying motionless on purpose, pretending to be in the sulks; she credited him with every kind of intelligence. Since she happened to have the long-handled broom in her hand she tried to tickle him up with it from the doorway. When that too produced no reaction she felt provoked and poked at him a little harder, and only when she had pushed him along the floor without meeting any resistance was her attention aroused. It did not take her long to establish the truth of the matter, and her eyes widened, she let out a whistle, yet did not waste much time over it but tore open the door of the Samsas' bedroom and yelled into the darkness at the top of her voice: "Just look at this, it's dead; it's lying here dead and done for!"

Mr. and Mrs. Samsa started up in their double bed and before they realized the nature of the charwoman's announcement had some difficulty in overcoming the shock of it. But then they got out of bed quickly, one on either side, Mr. Samsa throwing a blanket over his shoulders, Mrs. Samsa in nothing but her nightgown; in this array they entered Gregor's room. Meanwhile the door of the living room opened, too, where Grete had been sleeping since the advent of the lodgers; she was completely dressed as if she had not been to bed, which seemed to be confirmed also by the paleness of her face. "Dead?" said Mrs. Samsa, looking questioningly at the charwoman, although she could have investigated for herself, and the fact was obvious enough without investigation. "I should say so," said the charwoman, proving her words by pushing Gregor's corpse a long way to one side with her broomstick. Mrs. Samsa made a movement as if to stop her, but checked it. "Well," said Mr. Samsa, "now thanks be to God." He crossed himself, and the three women followed his example. Grete, whose eyes never left the corpse, said: "Just see how thin he was. It's such a long time since he's eaten anything. The food came out again just as it went in." Indeed, Gregor's body was completely flat and dry, as could only now be seen when it was no longer supported by the legs and nothing prevented one from looking closely at it.

"Come in beside us, Grete, for a little while," said Mrs. Samsa with a tremulous smile, and Grete, not without looking back at the corpse, followed her parents into their bedroom. The charwoman shut the door and opened the window wide. Although it was so early in the morning a certain softness was perceptible in the fresh air. After all, it was already the end of March.

The three lodgers emerged from their room and were surprised to see no breakfast; they had been forgotten. "Where's our breakfast?" said the middle lodger peevishly to the charwoman. But she put her finger to her lips and hastily, without a word, indicated by gestures that they should go into Gregor's room. They did so and stood, their hands in the pockets of their somewhat shabby coats, around Gregor's corpse in the room where it was now fully light.

At that the door of the Samsas' bedroom opened and Mr. Samsa appeared in his uniform, his wife on one arm, his daughter on the other. They all looked a little as if they had been crying; from time to time Grete hid her face on her father's arm.

"Leave my house at once!" said Mr. Samsa, and pointed to the door without disengaging himself from the women. "What do you mean by that?" said the middle lodger, taken somewhat aback, with a feeble smile. The two others put their hands behind them and kept rubbing them together, as if in gleeful expectation of a fine set-to in which they were bound to come off the winners. "I mean just what I say," answered Mr. Samsa, and advanced in a straight line with his two companions towards the lodger. He stood his ground at first quietly, looking at the floor as if his thoughts were taking a new pattern in his head. "Then let us go, by all means," he said, and looked up at Mr. Samsa as if in a sudden access of humility he were expecting some renewed sanction for this decision. Mr. Samsa merely nodded briefly once or twice with meaning eyes. Upon that the lodger really did go with long strides into the hall, his two friends had been listening and had quite stopped rubbing their hands for some moments and now went scuttling after him as if afraid that Mr. Samsa might get into the hall before them and cut them off from their leader. In the hall they all three took their hats from the rack, their sticks from the umbrella stand, bowed in silence and quitted the apartment. With a suspiciousness which proved quite unfounded Mr. Samsa and the two women followed them out to the landing; leaning over the banister they watched the three figures slowly but surely going down the long stairs, vanishing from sight at a certain turn of the staircase on every floor and coming into view again after a moment or so; the more they dwindled, the more the Samsa family's interest in them dwindled, and when a butcher's boy met them and passed them on the stairs coming up proudly with a tray on his head, Mr. Samsa and the two women soon left the landing and as if a burden had been lifted from them went back into their apartment.

They decided to spend this day in resting and going for a stroll; they had not only deserved such a respite from work, but absolutely needed it. And so they sat down at the table and wrote three notes of excuse, Mr. Samsa to his board of management, Mrs. Samsa to her employer and Grete to the head of her firm. While they were writing, the charwoman came in to say that she was going now, since her morning's work was finished. At first they only nodded without looking up, but as she kept hovering there they eyed her irritably. "Well?" said Mr. Samsa. The charwoman stood grinning in the doorway as if she had good news to impart to the family but meant not to say a word unless properly questioned. The small ostrich feather standing upright on her hat, which had annoyed Mr. Samsa ever since she was engaged, was waving gaily in all directions. "Well, what is it, then?" asked Mrs. Samsa, who obtained more respect from the charwoman than the others. "Oh," said the charwoman, giggling so amiably that she could not at once continue, "just this, you don't need to bother about how to get rid of the thing next door. It's been seen to already." Mrs. Samsa and Grete bent over their letters again, as if preoccupied; Mr. Samsa, who perceived that she was eager to begin describing it all in detail, stopped her with a decisive hand. But since she was not allowed to tell her story, she remembered the great hurry she was in, being obviously deeply huffed: "Bye, everybody," she said, whirling off violently, and departed with a frightful slamming of doors.

"She'll be given notice tonight," said Mr. Samsa, but neither from his wife nor his daughter did he get any answer, for the charwoman seemed to have shattered again the composure they had barely achieved. They rose, went to the window and stayed there, clasping each other tight. Mr. Samsa turned in his chair to look at them and quietly observed them for a little. Then he called out: "Come along, now, do. Let bygones be bygones. And you might have some consideration for me." The two of them complied at once, hastened to him, caressed him and quickly finished their letters.

Then they all three left the apartment together, which was more than they had done for months, and went by tram into the open country outside the town. The tram, in which they were the only passengers, was filled with warm sunshine. Leaning comfortably back in their seats they canvassed their prospects for the future, and it appeared on closer inspection that these were not at all bad, for the jobs they had got, which so far they had never really discussed with each other, were all three admirable and likely to lead to better things later on. The greatest immediate improvement in their condition would of course arise from moving to another house; they wanted to take a smaller and cheaper but also better situated and more easily run apartment than the one they had, which Gregor had selected. While they were thus conversing, it struck both Mr. and Mrs. Samsa, almost at the same moment, as they became aware of their daughter's increasing vivacity, that in spite of all the sorrow of recent times, which had made her cheeks pale, she had bloomed into a pretty girl with a good figure. They grew quieter and half unconsciously exchanged glances of complete agreement, having come to the conclusion that it would soon be time to find a good husband for her. And it was like a confirmation of their new dreams and excellent intentions that at the end of their journey their daughter sprang to her feet first and stretched her young body.

[1915]

Journal Entry

How do you respond to the first sentence of "The Metamorphosis"? Characterize the narrator's tone.

Textual Considerations

1. Characterize the narrator's attitude toward Gregor. What does he reveal about Gregor, his job, and his relationship with his boss?
2. Analyze Gregor's relationship with his sister. Explain how her treatment of Gregor changes as the story continues. To what extent is her final betrayal inevitable?
3. Food plays an important role in the story. How does it affect the main ideas Kafka explores in the story? Explain.
4. Characterize Gregor's father. To what extent has he exploited Gregor? Why is it ironic that as Gregor's situation deteriorates that of his family improves?
5. Consider the roles of the three lodgers and the charwoman. How are their attitudes toward Gregor similar to or different from those of his family?
6. Compare and contrast Kafka's treatment of time in parts I and II. How is it reflective of Gregor's psychological state?
7. How many "metamorphoses" occur in the story? Consider, for example, the final scene. How does it differ stylistically from the rest of the story?

Cultural Contexts

1. Analyze the extent to which Gregor is responsible for his sense of alienation. Does he deserve his fate? Of what is he guilty? Is he a victim of the selfishness or manipulation of others? What might Kafka be implying about one's relationship to oneself versus responsibility to family and community?
2. Many critics attribute Kafka's thematic preoccupation with exile and alienation to his biographical circumstances. Kafka was a Jew raised in a Gentile world, suffered from tuberculosis, was terrified of his domineering and judgmental father, and was a sensitive artist in a typical middle-class society. Debate with your group the degree to which Gregor's sense of isolation may be explained solely by these circumstances.

James Joyce

Eveline

She sat at the window watching the evening invade the avenue. Her head was leaned against the window curtains and in her nostrils was the odor of dusty cretonne. She was tired.

Few people passed. The man out of the last house passed on his way home; she heard his footsteps clicking along the concrete pavement and afterwards crunching on the cinder path before the new red houses. One time there used to be a field there in which they used to play every evening with other people's children. Then a man from Belfast bought the field and built houses in it—not like their little brown houses but bright brick houses with shining roofs. The children of the avenue used to play together in that field—the Devines, the Waters, the Dunns, little Keogh the cripple, she and her brothers and sisters. Ernest, however, never played: he was too grown up. Her father used often to hunt them in out of the field with his blackthorn stick; but usually little Keogh used to keep *nix* and call out when he saw her father coming. Still they seemed to have been rather happy then. Her father was not so bad then; and besides, her mother was alive. That was a long time ago; she and her brothers and sisters were all grown up; her mother was dead. Tizzie Dunn was dead, too, and the Waters had gone back to England. Everything changes. Now she was going to go away like the others, to leave her home.

Home! She looked round the room, reviewing all its familiar objects which she had dusted once a week for so many years, wondering where on earth all the dust came from. Perhaps she would never see again those familiar objects from which she had never dreamed of being divided. And yet during all those years she had never found out the name of the priest whose yellowing photograph hung on the wall above the broken harmonium beside the colored print of the promises made to Blessed Margaret Mary Alacoque. He had been a school friend of her father. Whenever he showed the photograph to a visitor her father used to pass it with a casual word:

—He is in Melbourne now.

She had consented to go away, to leave her home. Was that wise? She tried to weigh each side of the question. In her home anyway she had shelter and food; she had those whom she had known all her life about her. Of course she had to work hard both in the house and at business. What would they say of her in the Stores when they found out that she had run away with a fellow? Say she was a fool, perhaps; and her place would be filled up by advertisement. Miss Gavan would be glad. She had always had an edge on her, especially whenever there were people listening.

—Miss Hill, don't you see these ladies are waiting?

—Look lively, Miss Hill, please.

She would not cry many tears at leaving the Stores.

But in her new home, in a distant unknown country, it would not be like that. Then she would be married—she, Eveline. People would treat her with respect then. She would not be treated as her mother had been. Even now, though she was over nineteen, she sometimes felt herself in danger of her father's violence. She knew it was that that had given her the palpitations. When they were growing up he had never gone for her, like he used to go for Harry and Ernest, because she was a girl; but latterly he had begun to threaten her and say what he would do to her only for her dead mother's sake. And now she had nobody to protect her. Ernest was dead and Harry, who was in the church decorating business, was nearly always down somewhere in the country. Besides, the invariable squabble for money on Saturday nights had begun to weary her unspeakably. She always gave her entire wages—seven shillings—and Harry always sent up what he could but the trouble was to get any money from her father. He said she used to squander the money, that she had no head, that he wasn't going to give her his hard-earned money to throw about the streets, and much more, for he was usually fairly bad of a Saturday night.

In the end he would give her the money and ask her had she any intention of buying Sunday's dinner. Then she had to rush out as quickly as she could and do her marketing, holding her black leather purse tightly in her hand as she elbowed her way through the crowds and returning home late under her load of provisions. She had hard work to keep the house together and to see that the two young children who had been left to her charge went to school regularly and got their meals regularly. It was hard work—a hard life—but now that she was about to leave it she did not find it a wholly undesirable life.

She was about to explore another life with Frank. Frank was very kind, manly, open-hearted. She was to go away with him by the night-boat to be his wife and to live with him in Buenos Ayres where he had a home waiting for her. How well she remembered the first time she had seen him; he was lodging in a house on the main road where she used to visit. It seemed a few weeks ago. He was standing at the gate, his peaked cap pushed back on his head and his hair tumbled forward over a face of bronze. Then they had come to know each other. He used to meet her outside the Stores every evening and see her home. He took her to see *The Bohemian Girl* and she felt elated as she sat in an unaccustomed part of the theatre with him. He was awfully fond of music and sang a little. People knew that they were courting and, when he sang about the lass that loves a sailor, she always felt pleasantly confused. He used to call her Poppens out of fun. First of all it had been an excitement for her to have a fellow and then she had begun to like him. He had tales of distant countries. He had started as a deck boy at a pound a month on a ship of the Allan Line going out to Canada. He told her the names of the ships he had been on and the names of the different services. He had sailed through the Straits of Magellan and he told her stories of the terrible Patagonians. He had fallen on his feet in Buenos Ayres, he said, and had come over to the old country just for a holiday. Of course, her father had found out the affair and had forbidden her to have anything to say to him.

—I know these sailor chaps, he said.

One day he had quarrelled with Frank and after that she had to meet her lover secretly.

The evening deepened in the avenue. The white of two letters in her lap grew indistinct. One was to Harry; the other was to her father. Ernest had been her favorite but she liked Harry too. Her father was becoming old lately, she noticed; he would miss her. Sometimes he could be very nice. Not long before, when she had been laid up for a day, he had read her out a ghost story and made toast for her at the fire. Another day, when their mother was alive, they had all gone for a picnic to the Hill of Howth. She remembered her father putting on her mother's bonnet to make the children laugh.

Her time was running out but she continued to sit by the window, leaning her head against the window curtain, inhaling the odor of dusty cretonne. Down far in the avenue she could hear a street organ playing. She knew the air. Strange that it should come that very night to remind her of the promise to her mother, her promise to keep the home together as long as she could. She remembered the last night of her mother's illness; she was again in the close dark room at the other side of the hall and outside she heard a melancholy air of Italy. The organ-player had been ordered to go away and given sixpence. She remembered her father strutting back into the sickroom saying:

—Damned Italians! coming over here!

As she mused, the pitiful vision of her mother's life laid its spell on the very quick of her being—that life of commonplace sacrifices closing in final craziness. She trembled as she heard again her mother's voice saying constantly with foolish insistence:

—Derevaun Seraun! Derevaun Seraun!

She stood up in a sudden impulse of terror. Escape! She must escape! Frank would save her. He would give her life, perhaps love, too. But she wanted to live. Why should she be unhappy? She had a right to happiness. Frank would take her in his arms, fold her in his arms. He would save her.

She stood among the swaying crowd in the station at the North Wall. He held her hand and she knew that he was speaking to her, saying something about the passage over and over again. The station was full of soldiers with brown baggages. Through the wide doors of the sheds she caught a glimpse of the black mass of the boat, lying in beside the quay wall, with illumined portholes. She answered nothing. She felt her cheek pale and cold and, out of a maze of distress, she prayed to God to direct her, to show her what was her duty. The boat blew a long mournful whistle into the mist. If she went, tomorrow she would be on the sea with Frank, steaming towards Buenos Ayres. Their passage had been booked. Could she still draw back after all he had done for her? Her distress awoke a nausea in her body and she kept moving her lips in silent fervent prayer.

A bell clanged upon her heart. She felt him seize her hand:

—Come!

All the seas of the world tumbled about her heart. He was drawing her into them: he would drown her. She gripped with both hands at the iron railing.

—Come!

No! No! No! It was impossible. Her hands clutched the iron in frenzy. Amid the seas she sent a cry of anguish!

—Eveline! Evvy!

He rushed beyond the barrier and called to her to follow. He was shouted at to go on but he still called to her. She set her white face to him, passive, like a helpless animal. Her eyes gave him no sign of love or farewell or recognition.

[1916]

Journal Entry

Imagine yourself in Eveline's position and defend the choice you have made. How might your choice be similar or different from hers? Explain.

Textual Considerations

1. How does Eveline define "home" in paragraphs 3–5 of Joyce's story? To what extent does her definition of home differ from or contrast with her definition of "new home"?

2. What do the first paragraphs of the story reveal about Eveline? How emotionally connected is she to her physical surroundings?
3. Characterize Frank. To what extent is he a romantic figure? Identify the romantic elements he uses to court Eveline. How does Eveline's father react to Frank? Why is Frank unable to persuade Eveline to overcome her "fixed gender identity?"
4. Discuss the appropriateness of dust as the dominant symbol in "Eveline." Can you find other symbols in that story?
5. To what extent is Eveline's inability to choose her own happiness attributable to her role as daughter and as a single woman in an Irish Catholic environment at the turn of the century? What other factors might have contributed to her sense of paralysis?

Cultural Contexts

1. Compare and contrast Frank's philosophy of life with the view Eveline's mother expresses through her insistent statement that "the end of pleasure is pain" ("Deveraun Seraun").
2. Initiate a group discussion of "Eveline" by locating the conflict between the forces of tradition and change in Joyce's story.

Fae Myenne Ng

A Red Sweater

I chose red for my sister. Fierce, dark red. Made in Hong Kong. Hand Wash Only because it's got that skin of fuzz. She'll look happy. That's good. Everything's perfect, for a minute. That seems enough.

Red. For Good Luck. Of course. This fire-red sweater is swollen with good cheer. Wear it, I will tell her. You'll look lucky.

We're a family of three girls. By Chinese standards, that's not lucky. "Too bad," outsiders whisper, ". . . nothing but daughters. A failed family."

First, Middle, and End girl. Our order of birth marked us. That came to tell more than our given names.

My eldest sister, Lisa, lives at home. She quit San Francisco State, one semester short of a psychology degree. One day she said, "Forget about it, I'm tired." She's working full time at Pacific Bell now. Nine hundred a month with benefits. Mah and Deh think it's a great deal. They tell everybody, "Yes, our Number One makes good pay, but that's not even counting the discount. If we call Hong Kong, China even, there's forty percent off!" As if anyone in their part of China had a telephone.

Number Two, the in-between, jumped off the "M" floor three years ago. Not true! What happened? Why? Too sad! All we say about that is, "It was her choice."

We sent Mah to Hong Kong. When she left Hong Kong thirty years ago, she was the envy of all: "Lucky girl! You'll never have to work." To marry a sojourner was to have a future. Thirty years in the land of gold and good fortune, and then she returned to tell the story: three daughters, one dead, one unmarried, another who-cares-where, the thirty years in sweatshops, and the prince of the Golden Mountain turned into a toad. I'm glad I didn't have to go with her. I felt her shame and regret. To return, seeking solace and comfort, instead of offering banquets and stories of the good life.

I'm the youngest. I started flying with American the year Mah returned to Hong Kong, so I got her a good discount. She thought I was good for something then. But when she returned, I was pregnant.

"Get an abortion," she said. "Drop the baby," she screamed.

"No."

"Then get married."

"No. I don't want to."

I was going to get an abortion all along. I just didn't like the way they talked about the whole thing. They made me feel like dirt, that I was a disgrace. Now I can see how I used it as an opportunity. Sometimes I wonder if there wasn't another way. Everything about those years was so steamy and angry. There didn't seem to be any answers.

"I have no eyes for you," Mah said.

"Don't call us," Deh said.

They wouldn't talk to me. They ranted idioms to each other for days. The apartment was filled with images and curses I couldn't perceive. I got the general idea: I was a rotten, no-good, dead thing. I would die in a gutter without rice in my belly. My spirit—if I had one—wouldn't be fed. I wouldn't see good days in this life or the next.

My parents always had a special way of saying things.

Now I'm based in Honolulu. When our middle sister jumped, she kind of closed the world. The family just sort of fell apart. I left. Now, I try to make up for it; the folks still won't see me, but I try to keep in touch with them through Lisa. Flying cuts up your life, hits hardest during the holidays. I'm always sensitive then. I feel like I'm missing something, that people are doing something really important while I'm up in the sky, flying through time zones.

So I like to see Lisa around the beginning of the year. January, New Year's, and February, New Year's again, double luckiness with our birthdays in between. With so much going on, there's always something to talk about.

"You pick the place this year," I tell her.

"Around here?"

"No," I say. "Around here" means the food is good and the living hard. You eat a steaming rice plate, and then you feel like rushing home to sew garments or assemble radio parts or something. We eat together only once a year, so I feel we should splurge. Besides, at the Chinatown places, you have nothing to talk about except the bare issues. In American restaurants, the atmosphere helps you along. I want nice light and a view and handsome waiters.

"Let's go somewhere with a view," I say.

We decide to go to Following Sea, a new place on the Pier 39 track. We're early, the restaurant isn't crowded. It's been clear all day, so I think the sunset will be nice. I ask for a window table. I turn to talk to my sister, but she's already talking to a waiter. He's got that dark island tone that she likes. He's looking her up and down. My sister does not blink at it. She holds his look and orders two Johnny Walkers. I pick up a fork, turn it around in my hand. I seldom use chopsticks now. At home, I eat my rice in a plate, with a fork. The only chopsticks I own, I wear in my hair. For a moment, I feel strange sitting here at this unfamiliar table. I don't know this tablecloth, this linen, these candles. Everything seems foreign. It feels like we should be different people. But each time I look up, she's the same. I know this person. She's my sister. We sat together with chopsticks, mismatched bowls, braids, and braces, across the formica tabletop.

"I like three-pronged forks," I say, pressing my thumb against the sharp points.

My sister rolls her eyes. She lights a cigarette.

I ask for one.

I finally say, "So, what's new?"

"Not much." Her voice is sullen. She doesn't look at me. Once a year, I come in, asking questions. She's got the answers, but she hates them. For me, I think she's got the peace of heart, knowing that she's done her share for Mah and Deh. She thinks I have the peace, not caring. Her life is full of questions, too, but I have no answers.

I look around the restaurant. The sunset is not spectacular, and we don't comment on it. The waiters are lighting candles. Ours is bringing the drinks. He stops very close to my sister, seems to breathe her in. She raises her face toward him. "Ready?" he asks. My sister orders for us. The waiter struts off.

"Tight ass," I say.

"The best," she says.

My scotch tastes good. It reminds me of Deh. Johnny Walker or Seagrams 7, that's what they served at Chinese banquets. Nine courses and a bottle. No ice. We learned to drink it Chinese style, in teacups. Deh drank from his rice bowl, sipping it like hot soup. By the end of the meal, he took it like cool tea, in bold mouthfuls. We sat watching, our teacups in our laps, his three giggly girls.

Relaxed, I'm thinking there's a connection. Johnny Walker then and Johnny Walker now. I ask for another cigarette and this one I enjoy. Now my Johnny Walker pops with ice. I twirl the glass to make the ice tinkle.

We clink glasses. Three times for good luck. She giggles. I feel better.

"Nice sweater," I say.

"Michael Owyang," she says. She laughs. The light from the candle makes her eyes shimmer. She's got Mah's eyes. Eyes that make you want to talk. Lisa is reed thin and tall. She's got a body that clothes look good on. My sister slips something on, and it wraps her like skin. Fabric has pulse on her.

"Happy birthday, soon," I say.

"Thanks, and to yours too, just as soon."

"Here's to Johnny Walker in shark's fin soup," I say.

"And squab dinners."

"'I Love Lucy,'" I say.

We laugh. It makes us feel like children again. We remember how to be sisters.

I raise my glass, "To 'I Love Lucy,' squab dinners, and brown bags."

"To bones," she says.

"Bones," I repeat. This is a funny story that gets sad, and knowing it, I keep laughing. I am surprised how much memory there is in one word. Pigeons. Only recently did I learn they're called squab. Our word for them was pigeon—on a plate or flying over Portsmouth Square. A good meal at forty cents a bird. In line by dawn, we waited at the butcher's listening for the slow churning motor of the trucks. We watched the live fish flushing out of the tanks into the garbage pails. We smelled the honey-crushed cha sui bows baking. When the white laundry truck turned into Wentworth, there was a puffing trail of feathers following it. A stench filled the alley. The crowd squeezed in around the truck. Old ladies reached into the crates, squeezing and tugging for the plumpest pigeons.

My sister and I picked the white ones, those with the most expressive eyes. Dove birds, we called them. We fed them leftover rice in water, and as long as they stayed plump, they were our pets, our baby dove birds. And then one day we'd come home from school and find them cooked. They were a special, nutritious treat. Mah let us fill our bowls high with little pigeon parts: legs, breasts, and wings, and take them out to the front room to watch "I Love Lucy." We took brown bags for the bones. We balanced our bowls on our laps and laughed at Lucy. We leaned forward, our chopsticks crossed in mid-air, and called out, "Mah! Mah! Come watch! Watch Lucy cry!"

But she always sat alone in the kitchen sucking out the sweetness of the lesser parts: necks, backs, and the head. "Bones are sweeter than you know," she always said. She came out to check the bags. "Clean bones," she said, shaking the bags. "No waste," she said.

Our dinners come with a warning. "Plate's hot. Don't touch." My sister orders a carafe of house white. "Enjoy," he says, smiling at my sister. She doesn't look up.

I can't remember how to say scallops in Chinese. I ask my sister, she doesn't know either. The food isn't great. Or maybe we just don't have the taste buds in us to go crazy over it. Sometimes I get very hungry for Chinese flavors: black beans, garlic and ginger, shrimp paste and sesame oil. These are tastes we grew up with, still dream about. Crave. Run around town after. Duck liver sausage, bean curd, jook, salted fish, and fried dace with black beans. Western flavors don't stand out, the surroundings do. Three pronged forks. Pink tablecloths. Fresh flowers. Cute waiters. An odd difference.

"Maybe we should have gone to Sun Hung Heung. At least the vegetables are real," I say.

"Hung toh-yee-foo-won-tun!" she says.

"Yeah, yum!" I say.

I remember Deh teaching us how to pick bok choy, his favorite vegetable. "Stick your fingernail into the stem. Juicy and firm, good. Limp and tough, no good." The three of us followed Deh, punching our thumbnails into every stem of bok choy we saw.

"Deh still eating bok choy?"

"Breakfast, lunch and dinner." My sister throws her head back, and laughs. It is Deh's motion. She recites in a mimic tone. "Your Deh, all he needs is a good hot bowl of rice and a plate full of greens. A good monk."

There was always bok choy. Even though it was nonstop for Mah—rushing to the sweatshop in the morning, out to shop on break, and then home to cook by evening—she did this for him. A plate of bok choy, steaming with the taste of ginger and garlic. He said she made good rice. Timed full-fire until the first boil, medium until the grains formed a crust along the sides of the pot, and then low-flamed to let the rice steam. Firm, that's how Deh liked his rice.

The waiter brings the wine, asks if everything is all right.

"Everything," my sister says.

There's something else about this meeting. I can hear it in the edge of her voice. She doesn't say anything and I don't ask. Her lips make a contorting line; her face looks sour. She lets out a breath. It sounds like she's been holding it in too long.

"Another fight. The bank line," she says. "He waited four times in the bank line. Mah ran around outside shopping. He was doing her a favor. She was doing him a favor. Mah wouldn't stop yelling. 'Get out and go die! Useless Thing! Stinking Corpse!'"

I know he answered. His voice must have had that fortune teller's tone to it. You listened because you knew it was a warning.

He always threatened to disappear, jump off the Golden Gate. His thousand-year-old threat. I've heard it all before. "I will go. Even when dead, I won't be far enough away. Curse the good will that blinded me into taking you as wife!"

I give Lisa some of my scallops. "Eat," I tell her.

She keeps talking. "Of course, you know how Mah thinks, that nobody should complain because she's been the one working all these years."

I nod. I start eating, hoping she'll follow.

Don't start that again! Everything I make at that dead place I hand . . .

How come . . .
What about . . .
So . . .

It was obvious. The stories themselves mean little. It was how hot and furious they could become.

Is there no end to it? What makes their ugliness so alive, so thick and impossible to let go of?

"I don't want to think about it anymore." The way she says it surprises me. This time I listen. I imagine what it would be like to take her place. It will be my turn one day.

"Ron," she says, wiggling her fingers above the candle. "A fun thing."

The opal flickers above the flame. I tell her that I want to get her something special for her birthday, ". . . next trip I get abroad." She looks up at me, smiles.

For a minute, my sister seems happy. But she won't be able to hold onto it. She grabs at things out of despair, out of fear. Gifts grow old for her. Emotions never ripen, they sour. Everything slips away from her. Nothing sustains her. Her beauty has made her fragile.

We should have eaten in Chinatown. We could have gone for coffee in North Beach, then for jook at Sam Wo's.

"No work, it's been like that for months, just odd jobs," she says.

I'm thinking, it's not like I haven't done my share. I was a kid once, I did things because I felt I should. I helped fill out forms at the Chinatown employment agencies. I went with him to the Seaman's Union. I waited too, listening and hoping for those calls: "Busboy! Presser! Prep Man!" His bags were packed, he was always ready to go. "On standby," he said.

Every week. All the same. Quitting and looking to start all over again. In the end, it was like never having gone anywhere. It was like the bank line, waiting for nothing.

How many times did my sister and I have to hold them apart? The flat *ting!* sound as the blade slapped onto the linoleum floor, the wooden handle of the knife slamming into the corner. Was it she or I who screamed, repeating all of their ugliest words? Who shook them? Who made them stop?

The waiter comes to take the plates. He stands by my sister for a moment. I raise my glass to the waiter.

"You two Chinese?" he asks.

"No," I say, finishing off my wine. I roll my eyes. I wish I had another Johnny Walker. Suddenly I don't care.

"We're two sisters," I say. I laugh. I ask for the check, leave a good tip. I see him slip my sister a box of matches.

Outside, the air is cool and brisk. My sister links her arm into mine. We walk up Bay onto Chestnut. We pass Galileo High School and then turn down Van Ness to head toward the pier. The bay is black. The foghorns sound far away. We walk the whole length of the pier without talking.

The water is white where it slaps against the wooden stakes.

For a long time Lisa's wanted out. She can stay at that point of endurance forever. Desire that becomes old feels too good, it's seductive. I know how hard it is to go.

The heart never travels. You have to be heartless. My sister holds that heart, too close and for too long. This is her weakness, and I like to think, used to be mine. Lisa endures too much.

We're lucky, not like the bondmaids growing up in service, or the newborn daughters whose mouths were stuffed with ashes. Courtesans with the three-inch feet, beardless, soft-shouldered eunuchs, and the frightened child-brides, they're all stories to us. We're the lucky generation. Our parents forced themselves to live through the humiliation in this country so that we could have it better. We know so little of the old country. We repeat names of Grandfathers and Uncles, but they will always be strangers to us. Family exists only because somebody has a story, and knowing the story connects us to a history. To us, the deformed man is oddly compelling, the forgotten man is a good story. A beautiful woman suffers.

I want her beauty to buy her out.

◆   ◆   ◆

The sweater cost two weeks pay. Like the forty-cent birds that are now a delicacy, this is a special treat. The money doesn't mean anything. It is, if anything, time. Time is what I would like to give her.

A red sweater. One hundred percent angora. The skin of fuzz will be a fierce rouge on her naked breasts.

Red. Lucky. Wear it. Find that man. The new one. Wrap yourself around him. Feel the pulsing between you. Fuck him and think about it. One hundred percent. Hand Wash Only. Worn Once.

[1987]

Journal Entry

Respond to the following: "We're a family of three girls. By Chinese standards, that's not lucky. 'Too bad,' outsiders whisper, . . . nothing but daughters. A failed family.'"

Textual Considerations

1. The author uses irony to reinforce meaning in "A Red Sweater." One example is the discrepancy between Mah's and the community's experience when she left Hong Kong and the disappointing reality of her situation on her return thirty years later. Cite at least two other examples of irony and show how they enhance theme.
2. Analyze the role of the parents. How has their marital relationship affected each of them? How has it influenced the narrator and Lisa? How would you characterize their relationship? With whom do you empathize?
3. The red sweater is the dominant symbol in the story. List the several references to the title, paying particular attention to the last three paragraphs. How does its meaning change in the course of the narrative? What conscious and unconscious meanings does it acquire?

Cultural Contexts

1. React to the protagonist's statement that "I am surprised how much memory there is in one word." How do her memories contribute to her sense of self? How are they related to the advice she gives Lisa at the end of the story?
2. "We're the lucky generation. Our parents forced themselves to live through the humiliation in this country so we could have it better." Are they, in fact, the lucky ones? Explain. Consider, for example, if the narrator and her sister have a sense of their extended family and if they have experienced a feeling of community in the United States.

Albert Camus

The Guest

Translated by Justin O'Brien

The schoolmaster was watching the two men climb toward him. One was on horseback, the other on foot. They had not yet tackled the abrupt rise leading to the schoolhouse built on the hillside. They were toiling onward, making slow progress in the snow, among the stones, on the vast expanse of the high, deserted plateau. From time to time the horse stumbled. Without hearing anything yet, he could see the breath issuing from the horse's nostrils. One of the men, at least, knew the region. They were following the trail although it had disappeared days ago under a layer of dirty white snow. The schoolmaster calculated that it would take them half an hour to get onto the hill. It was cold; he went back into the school to get a sweater.

He crossed the empty, frigid classroom. On the blackboard the four rivers of France, drawn with four different colored chalks, had been flowing toward their estuaries for the past three days. Snow had suddenly fallen in mid-October after eight months of drought without the transition of rain, and the twenty pupils, more or less, who lived in the villages scattered over the plateau had stopped coming. With fair weather they would return. Daru now heated only the single room that was his lodging, adjoining the classroom and giving also onto the plateau to the east. Like the class windows, his window looked to the south too. On that side the school was a few kilometers from the point where the plateau began to slope toward the south. In clear weather could be seen the purple mass of the mountain range where the gap opened onto the desert.

Somewhat warmed, Daru returned to the window from which he had first seen the two men. They were no longer visible. Hence they must have tackled the rise. The sky was not so dark, for the snow had stopped falling during the night. The morning had opened with a dirty light which had scarcely become brighter as the ceiling of clouds lifted. At two in the afternoon it seemed as if the day were merely beginning. But still this was better than those three days when the thick snow was falling amidst unbroken darkness with little gusts of wind that rattled the double door of the classroom. Then Daru had spent long hours in his room, leaving it only to go to the shed and feed the chickens or get some coal. Fortunately the delivery truck from Tadjid, the nearest village to the north, had brought his supplies two days before the blizzard. It would return in forty-eight hours.

Besides, he had enough to resist a siege, for the little room was cluttered with bags of wheat that the administration left as a stock to distribute to those of his pupils whose families had suffered from the drought. Actually they had all been victims because they were all poor. Every day Daru would distribute a ration to the children. They had missed it, he knew, during these bad days. Possibly one of the fathers or big brothers would come this afternoon and he could supply them with grain. It was just a matter of carrying them over to the next harvest. Now shiploads of wheat were arriving from France and the worst was over. But it would be hard to forget that poverty, that army of ragged ghosts wandering in the sunlight, the plateaus burned to a cinder month after month, the earth shriveled up little by little, literally scorched, every stone bursting into dust under one's foot. The sheep had died then by thousands and even a few men, here and there, sometimes without anyone's knowing.

In contrast with such poverty, he who lived almost like a monk in his remote schoolhouse, nonetheless satisfied with the little he had and with the rough life, had felt like a lord with his white-washed walls, his narrow couch, his unpainted shelves, his well, and his provision of water and food. And suddenly this snow, without warning, without the foretaste of rain. This is the way the region was, cruel to live in, even without men—who didn't help matters either. But Daru had been born here. Everywhere else, he felt exiled.

He stepped out onto the terrace in front of the schoolhouse. The two men were now halfway up the slope. He recognized the horseman as Balducci, the old gendarme he had known for a long time. Balducci was holding on the end of a rope an Arab who was walking behind him with hands bound and head lowered. The gendarme waved a greeting to which Daru did not reply, lost as he was in contemplation of the Arab dressed in a faded blue jellaba, his feet in sandals but covered with socks of heavy raw wool, his head surmounted by a narrow, short *chèche*. They were approaching. Balducci was holding back his horse in order not to hurt the Arab and the group was advancing slowly.

Within earshot, Balducci shouted: "One hour to do the three kilometers from El Ameur!" Daru did not answer. Short and square in his thick sweater, he watched them climb. Not once had the Arab raised his head. "Hello," said Daru when they got up onto the terrace. "Come in and warm up." Balducci painfully got down from his horse without letting go the rope. From under his bristling mustache he smiled at the schoolmaster. His little dark eyes, deep-set under a tanned forehead, and his mouth surrounded with wrinkles made him look attentive and studious. Daru took the bridle, led the horse to the shed, and came back to the two men, who were now waiting for him in the school. He led them into his room. "I am going to heat up the classroom," he said. "We'll be more comfortable there." When he entered the room again, Balducci was on the couch. He had undone the rope tying him to the Arab, who had squatted near the stove. His hands still bound, the *chèche* pushed back on his head, he was looking toward the window. At first Daru noticed only his huge lips, fat, smooth, almost Negroid; yet his nose was straight, his eyes were dark and full of fever. The *chèche* revealed an obstinate forehead and, under the weathered skin now rather discolored by the cold, the whole face had a restless and rebellious look that struck Daru when the Arab, turning his face toward him, looked him straight in the eyes. "Go into the other room," said the schoolmaster, "and I'll make you some mint tea." "Thanks," Balducci said. "What a chore! How I long for retirement." And addressing his prisoner in Arabic: "Come on, you." The Arab got up and, slowly, holding his bound wrists in front of him, went into the classroom.

With the tea, Daru brought a chair. But Balducci was already enthroned on the nearest pupil's desk and the Arab had squatted against the teacher's platform facing the stove, which stood between the desk and the window. When he held out the glass of tea to the prisoner, Daru hesitated at the sight of his bound hands. "He might perhaps be untied." "Sure," said Balducci. "That was for the trip." He started to get to his feet. But Daru, setting the glass on the floor, had knelt beside the Arab. Without saying anything, the Arab watched him with his feverish eyes. Once his hands were free, he rubbed his swollen wrists against each other, took the glass of tea, and sucked up the burning liquid in swift little sips.

"Good," said Daru. "And where are you headed?"

Balducci withdrew his mustache from the tea. "Here, son."

"Odd pupils! And you're spending the night?"

"No. I'm going back to El Ameur. And you will deliver this fellow to Tinguit. He is expected at police headquarters."

Balducci was looking at Daru with a friendly little smile.

"What's this story?" asked the schoolmaster. "Are you pulling my leg?"

"No, son. Those are the orders."

"The orders? I'm not . . ." Daru hesitated, not wanting to hurt the old Corsican. "I mean, that's not my job."

"What! What's the meaning of that? In wartime people do all kinds of jobs."

"Then I'll wait for the declaration of war!"

Balducci nodded.

"O.K. But the orders exist and they concern you too. Things are brewing, it appears. There is talk of a forthcoming revolt. We are mobilized, in a way."

Daru still had his obstinate look.

"Listen, son," Balducci said. "I like you and you must understand. There's only a dozen of us at El Ameur to patrol throughout the whole territory of a small department and I must get back in a hurry. I was told to hand this guy over to you and return without delay. He couldn't be kept there. His village was beginning to stir; they wanted to take him back. You must take him to Tinguit tomorrow before the day is over. Twenty kilometers shouldn't faze a husky fellow like you. After that, all will be over. You'll come back to your pupils and your comfortable life."

Behind the wall the horse could be heard snorting and pawing the earth. Daru was looking out the window. Decidedly, the weather was clearing and the light was increasing over the snowy plateau. When all the snow was melted, the sun would take over again and once more would burn the fields of stone. For days, still, the unchanging sky would shed its dry light on the solitary expanse where nothing had any connection with man.

"After all," he said, turning around toward Balducci, "what did he do?" And, before the gendarme had opened his mouth, he asked: "Does he speak French?"

"No, not a word. We had been looking for him for a month, but they were hiding him. He killed his cousin."

"Is he against us?"

"I don't think so. But you can never be sure."

"Why did he kill?"

"A family squabble, I think. One owed the other grain, it seems. It's not at all clear. In short, he killed his cousin with a billhook. You know, like a sheep, *kreezk*!"

Balducci made the gesture of drawing a blade across his throat and the Arab, his attention attracted, watched him with a sort of anxiety. Daru felt a sudden wrath against the man, against all men with their rotten spite, their tireless hates, their blood lust.

But the kettle was singing on the stove. He served Balducci more tea, hesitated, then served the Arab again, who, a second time, drank avidly. His raised arms made the jellaba fall open and the schoolmaster saw his thin, muscular chest.

"Thanks, kid," Balducci said. "And now, I'm off."

He got up and went toward the Arab, taking a small rope from his pocket.

"What are you doing?" Daru asked dryly.

Balducci, disconcerted, showed him the rope.

"Don't bother."

The old gendarme hesitated. "It's up to you. Of course, you are armed?"

"I have my shotgun."

"Where?"

"In the trunk."

"You ought to have it near your bed."

"Why? I have nothing to fear."

"You're crazy, son. If there's an uprising, no one is safe, we're all in the same boat."

"I'll defend myself. I'll have time to see them coming."

Balducci began to laugh, then suddenly the mustache covered the white teeth.

"You'll have time? O.K. That's just what I was saying. You have always been a little cracked. That's why I like you, my son was like that."

At the same time he took out his revolver and put it on the desk.

"Keep it; I don't need two weapons from here to El Ameur."

The revolver shone against the black paint of the table. When the gendarme turned toward him, the schoolmaster caught the smell of leather and horseflesh.

"Listen, Balducci," Daru said suddenly, "every bit of this disgusts me, and first of all your fellow here. But I won't hand him over. Fight, yes, if I have to. But not that."

The old gendarme stood in front of him and looked at him severely.

"You're being a fool," he said slowly. "I don't like it either. You don't get used to putting a rope on a man even after years of it, and you're even ashamed—yes, ashamed. But you can't let them have their way."

"I won't hand him over," Daru said again.

"It's an order, son, and I repeat it."

"That's right. Repeat to them what I've said to you: I won't hand him over."

Balducci made a visible effort to reflect. He looked at the Arab and at Daru. At last he decided.

"No, I won't tell them anything. If you want to drop us, go ahead; I'll not denounce you. I have an order to deliver the prisoner and I'm doing so. And now you'll just sign this paper for me."

"There's no need. I'll not deny that you left him with me."

"Don't be mean with me. I know you'll tell the truth. You're from hereabouts and you are a man. But you must sign, that's the rule."

Daru opened his drawer, took out a little square bottle of purple ink, the red wooden penholder with the "sergeant-major" pen he used for making models of penmanship, and signed. The gendarme carefully folded the paper and put it into his wallet. Then he moved toward the door.

"I'll see you off," Daru said.

"No," said Balducci. "There's no use being polite. You insulted me."

He looked at the Arab, motionless in the same spot, sniffed peevishly, and turned away toward the door. "Good-by, son," he said. The door shut behind him. Balducci appeared suddenly outside the window and then disappeared. His footsteps were muffled by the snow. The house stirred on the other side of the wall and several chickens fluttered in fright. A moment later Balducci reappeared outside the window leading the horse by the bridle. He walked toward the little rise without turning around and disappeared from sight with the horse following him. A big stone could be heard bouncing down. Daru walked back toward the prisoner, who, without stirring, never took his eyes off him. "Wait," the schoolmaster said in Arabic and went toward the bedroom. As he was going through the door, he had a second thought, went to the desk, took the revolver, and stuck it in his pocket. Then, without looking back, he went into his room.

For some time he lay on his couch watching the sky gradually close over, listening to the silence. It was this silence that had seemed painful to him during the first days here, after the war. He had requested a post in the little town at the base of the foothills separating the upper plateaus from the desert. There, rocky walls, green and black to the north, pink and lavender to the south, marked the frontier of eternal summer. He had been named to a post farther north, on the plateau itself. In the beginning, the solitude and the silence had been hard for him on those wastelands peopled only by stones. Occasionally, furrows suggested cultivation, but they had been dug to uncover a certain kind of stone good for building. The only plowing here was to harvest rocks. Elsewhere a thin layer of soil accumulated in the hollows would be scraped out to enrich paltry village gardens. This is the way it was: bare rock covered three quarters of the region. Towns sprang up, flourished, then disappeared; men came by, loved one another or fought bitterly, then died. No one in this desert, neither he nor his guest, mattered. And yet, outside this desert neither of them, Daru knew, could have really lived.

When he got up, no noise came from the classroom. He was amazed at the unmixed joy he derived from the mere thought that the Arab might have fled and that he would be alone with no decision to make. But the prisoner was there. He had merely stretched out between the stove and the desk. With eyes open, he was staring at the ceiling. In that position, his thick lips were particularly noticeable, giving him a pouting look. "Come," said Daru. The Arab got up and followed him. In the bedroom, the schoolmaster pointed to a chair near the table under the window. The Arab sat down without taking his eyes off Daru.

"Are you hungry?"

"Yes," the prisoner said.

Daru set the table for two. He took flour and oil, shaped a cake in a frying-pan, and lighted the little stove that functioned on bottled gas. While the cake was cooking, he went out to the shed to get cheese, eggs, dates, and condensed milk. When the cake was done he set it on the window sill to cool, heated some condensed milk diluted with water, and beat up the eggs into an omelette. In one of his motions he knocked against the revolver stuck in his right pocket. He set the bowl down, went into the classroom, and put the revolver in his desk drawer. When he came back to the room, night was falling. He put on the light and served the Arab. "Eat," he said. The Arab took a piece of the cake, lifted it eagerly to his mouth, and stopped short.

"And you?" he asked.

"After you. I'll eat too."

The thick lips opened slightly. The Arab hesitated, then bit into the cake determinedly.

The meal over, the Arab looked at the schoolmaster. "Are you the judge?"

"No, I'm simply keeping you until tomorrow."

"Why do you eat with me?"

"I'm hungry."

The Arab fell silent. Daru got up and went out. He brought back a folding bed from the shed, set it up between the table and the stove, perpendicular to his own bed. From a large suitcase which, upright in a corner, served as a shelf for papers, he took two blankets and arranged them on the camp bed. Then he stopped, felt useless, and sat down on his bed. There was nothing more to do or to get ready. He had to look at this man. He looked at him, therefore, trying to imagine his face bursting with rage. He couldn't do so. He could see nothing but the dark yet shining eyes and the animal mouth.

"Why did you kill him?" he asked in a voice whose hostile tone surprised him.

The Arab looked away.

"He ran away. I ran after him."

He raised his eyes to Daru again and they were full of a sort of woeful interrogation. "Now what will they do to me?"

"Are you afraid?"

He stiffened, turning his eyes away.

"Are you sorry?"

The Arab stared at him openmouthed. Obviously he did not understand. Daru's annoyance was growing. At the same time he felt awkward and self-conscious with his big body wedged between the two beds.

"Lie down there," he said impatiently. "That's your bed."

The Arab didn't move. He called to Daru:

"Tell me!"

The schoolmaster looked at him.

"Is the gendarme coming back tomorrow?"

"I don't know."

"Are you coming with us?"

"I don't know. Why?"

The prisoner got up and stretched out on top of the blankets, his feet toward the window. The light from the electric bulb shone straight into his eyes and he closed them at once.

"Why?" Daru repeated, standing beside the bed.

The Arab opened his eyes under the blinding light and looked at him, trying not to blink.

"Come with us," he said.

In the middle of the night, Daru was still not asleep. He had gone to bed after undressing completely; he generally slept naked. But when he suddenly realized that he had nothing on, he hesitated. He felt vulnerable and the temptation came to him to put his clothes back on. Then he shrugged his shoulders; after all, he wasn't a child and, if need be, he could break his adversary in two. From his bed he could observe him, lying on his back, still motionless with his eyes closed under the harsh light. When Daru turned out the light, the darkness seemed to coagulate all of a sudden. Little by little, the night came back to life in the window where the starless sky was stirring gently. The schoolmaster soon made out the body lying at his feet. The Arab still did not move, but his eyes seemed open. A faint wind was prowling around the schoolhouse. Perhaps it would drive away the clouds and the sun would reappear.

During the night the wind increased. The hens fluttered a little and then were silent. The Arab turned over on his side with his back to Daru, who thought he heard him moan. Then he listened for his guest's breathing; it became heavier and more regular. He listened to that breath so close to him and mused without being able to go to sleep. In this room where he had been sleeping alone for a year, this presence bothered him. But it bothered him also by imposing on him a sort of brotherhood he knew well but refused to accept in the present circumstances. Men who share the same rooms, soldiers or prisoners, develop a strange alliance as if, having cast off their armor with their clothing, they fraternized every evening, over and above their differences, in the ancient community of dream and fatigue. But Daru shook himself; he didn't like such musings, and it was essential to sleep.

A little later, however, when the Arab stirred slightly, the schoolmaster was still not asleep. When the prisoner made a second move, he stiffened, on the alert. The Arab was lifting himself slowly on his arms with almost the motion of a sleepwalker. Seated upright in bed, he waited motionless without turning his head toward Daru, as if he were listening attentively. Daru did not stir; it had just occurred to him that the revolver was still in the drawer of his desk. It was better to act at once. Yet he continued to observe the prisoner, who, with the same slithery motion, put his feet on the ground, waited again, then began to stand up slowly. Daru was about to call out to him when the Arab began to walk, in a quite natural but extraordinarily silent way. He was heading toward the door at the end of the room that opened into the shed. He lifted the latch with precaution and went out, pushing the door behind him but without shutting it. Daru had not stirred. "He is running away," he merely thought. "Good riddance!" Yet he listened attentively. The hens were not fluttering; the guest must be on the plateau. A faint sound of water reached him, and he didn't know what it was until the Arab again stood framed in the doorway, closed the door carefully, and came back to bed without a sound. Then Daru turned his back on him and fell asleep. Still later he seemed, from the depths of his sleep, to hear furtive steps around the schoolhouse. "I'm dreaming! I'm dreaming!" he repeated to himself. And he went on sleeping. When he awoke, the sky was clear; the loose window let in a cold, pure air. The Arab was asleep, hunched up under the blankets now, his mouth open, utterly relaxed. But when Daru shook him, he started dreadfully, staring at Daru with wild eyes as if he had never seen him and such a frightened expression that the schoolmaster stepped back. "Don't be afraid. It's me. You must eat." The Arab nodded his head and said yes. Calm had returned to his face, but his expression was vacant and listless.

The coffee was ready. They drank it together on the folding bed as they munched their pieces of the cake. Then Daru led the Arab under the shed and showed him the faucet where he washed. He went back into the room, folded the blankets and the bed, made his own bed and put the room in order. Then he went through the classroom and out onto the terrace. The sun was already rising in the blue sky; a soft, bright light was bathing the deserted plateau. On the ridge the snow was melting in spots. The stones were about to reappear. Crouched on the edge of the plateau, the schoolmaster looked at the deserted expanse. He thought of Balducci. He had hurt him, for he had sent him off in a way as if he didn't want to be associated with him. He could still hear the gendarme's farewell and, without knowing why, he felt strangely empty and vulnerable. At that moment, from the other side of the schoolhouse, the prisoner coughed. Daru listened to him almost despite himself and then, furious, threw a pebble that whistled through the air before sinking in the snow. That man's stupid crime revolted him, but to hand him over was contrary to honor. Merely thinking of it made him smart with humiliation. And he cursed at one and the same time his own people who had sent him this Arab and the Arab too who had dared to kill and not managed to get away. Daru got up, walked in a circle on the terrace, waited motionless, and then went back into the schoolhouse.

The Arab, leaning over the cement floor of the shed, was washing his teeth with two fingers. Daru looked at him and said: "Come." He went back into the room ahead of the prisoner. He slipped a hunting-jacket on over his sweater and put on walking-shoes. Standing, he waited until the Arab had put on his *chèche* and sandals. They went into the classroom and the schoolmaster pointed to the exit, saying: "Go head." The fellow didn't budge. "I'm coming," said Daru. The Arab went out. Daru went back into the room and made a package of pieces of rusk, dates, and sugar. In the classroom, before going out, he hesitated a second in front of his desk, then crossed the threshold and locked the door. "That's the way," he said. He started toward the east, followed by the prisoner. But, a short distance from the schoolhouse, he thought he heard a slight sound behind them. He retraced his steps and examined the surroundings of the house; there was no one there. The Arab watched him without seeming to understand. "Come on," said Daru.

They walked for an hour and rested beside a sharp peak of limestone. The snow was melting faster and faster and the sun was drinking up the puddles at once, rapidly cleaning the plateau, which gradually dried and vibrated like the air itself. When they resumed walking, the ground rang under their feet. From time to time a bird rent the space in front of them with a joyful cry. Daru breathed in deeply the fresh morning light. He felt a sort of rapture before the vast familiar expanse, now almost entirely yellow under its dome of blue sky. They walked an hour more, descending toward the south. They reached a level height made up of crumbly rocks. From there on, the plateau sloped down, eastward, toward a low plain where there were a few spindly trees and, to the south, toward outcroppings of rock that gave the landscape a chaotic look.

Daru surveyed the two directions. There was nothing but the sky on the horizon. Not a man could be seen. He turned toward the Arab, who was looking at him blankly. Daru held out the package to him. "Take it," he said. "There are dates, bread, and sugar. You can hold out for two days. Here are a thousand francs too." The Arab took the package and the money but kept his full hands at chest level as if he didn't know what to do with what was being given him. "Now look," the schoolmaster said as he pointed in the direction of the east, "there's the way to Tinguit. You have a two-hour walk. At Tinguit you'll find the administration and the police. They are expecting you." The Arab looked toward the east, still holding the package and the money against his chest. Daru took his elbow and turned him rather roughly toward the south. At the foot of the height on which they stood could be seen a faint path. "That's the trail across the plateau. In a day's walk from here you'll find pasturelands and the first nomads. They'll take you in and shelter you according to their law." The Arab had now turned toward Daru and a sort of panic was visible in his expression. "Listen," he said. Daru shook his head: "No, be quiet. Now I'm leaving you." He turned his back on him, took two long steps in the direction of the school, looked hesitantly at the motionless Arab, and started off again. For a few minutes he heard nothing but his own step resounding on the cold ground and did not turn his head. A moment later, however, he turned around. The Arab was still there on the edge of the hill, his arms hanging now, and he was looking at the schoolmaster. Daru felt something rise in his throat. But he swore with impatience, waved vaguely, and started off again. He had already gone some distance when he again stopped and looked. There was no longer anyone on the hill.

Daru hesitated. The sun was now rather high in the sky and was beginning to beat down on his head. The schoolmaster retraced his steps, at first somewhat uncertainly, then with decision. When he reached the little hill, he was bathed in sweat. He climbed it as fast as he could and stopped, out of breath, at the top. The rock-fields to the south stood out sharply against the blue sky, but on the plain to the east a steamy heat was already rising. And in that slight haze, Daru, with heavy heart, made out the Arab walking slowly on the road to prison.

A little later, standing before the window of the classroom, the schoolmaster was watching the clear light bathing the whole surface of the plateau, but he hardly saw it. Behind him on the blackboard, among the winding French rivers, sprawled the clumsily chalked-up words he had just read: "You handed over our brother. You will pay for this." Daru looked at the sky, the plateau, and, beyond, the invisible lands stretching all the way to the sea. In this vast landscape he had loved so much, he was alone.

[1957]

Journal Entry

Assume the persona of the Arab and record your impressions of Daru.

Textual Considerations

1. The narrator describes this part of Algeria as "cruel to live in." What details reinforce this description? Why doesn't Daru leave? Where in the story does he indicate his attitude toward the land?
2. What does Daru think of humanity? What connection is there between his attitude toward people and his profession?
3. Describe the relationship between Balducci and Daru. To what extent are they foils for each other?
4. Daru, the French Algerian, must play host to an Arab. How does he behave toward his guest? How does the guest respond to his host?
5. To what extent do we see the action through Daru's eyes? Do we enter the mind of any character other than Daru? Could the story have been written in the first person? What different effects would a first-person narration create?

Cultural Contexts

1. "That stupid man's crime revolted him, but to hand him over was contrary to honor." Why does Daru's philosophy make it dishonorable to turn in a murderer? What is your response to such a philosophy?
2. Why does Daru give the Arab a choice, rather than setting him on the path to freedom? Why does Daru observe the Arab's choice with "heavy heart"? What is your group's response? What irony is implicit in the last paragraph?

Chinua Achebe

Dead Men's Path

Michael Obi's hopes were fulfilled much earlier than he had expected. He was appointed headmaster of Ndume Central School in January 1949. It had always been an unprogressive school, so the Mission authorities decided to send a young and energetic man to run it. Obi accepted this responsibility with enthusiasm. He had many wonderful ideas and this was an opportunity to put them into practice. He had had sound secondary school education which designated him a "pivotal teacher" in the official records and set him apart from the other headmasters in the mission field. He was outspoken in his condemnation of the narrow views of these older and often less-educated ones.

"We shall make a good job of it, shan't we?" he asked his young wife when they first heard the joyful news of his promotion.

"We shall do our best," she replied. "We shall have such beautiful gardens and everything will be just *modern* and delightful . . ." In their two years of married life she had become completely infected by his passion for "modern methods" and his denigration of "these old and superannuated people in the teaching field who would be better employed as traders in the Onitsha market." She began to see herself already as the admired wife of the young headmaster, the queen of the school.

The wives of the other teachers would envy her position. She would set the fashion in everything . . . Then, suddenly, it occurred to her that there might not be other wives. Wavering between hope and fear, she asked her husband, looking anxiously at him.

"All our colleagues are young and unmarried," he said with enthusiasm which for once she did not share. "Which is a good thing," he continued.

"Why?"

"Why? They will give all their time and energy to the school."

Nancy was downcast. For a few minutes she became skeptical about the new school; but it was only for a few minutes. Her little personal misfortune could not blind her to her husband's happy prospects. She looked at him as he sat folded up in a chair. He was stoop-shouldered and looked frail. But he sometimes surprised people with sudden bursts of physical energy. In his present posture, however, all his bodily strength seemed to have retired behind his deep-set eyes, giving them an extraordinary power of penetration. He was only twenty-six, but looked thirty or more. On the whole, he was not unhandsome.

"A penny for your thoughts, Mike," said Nancy after a while, imitating the woman's magazine she read.

"I was thinking what a grand opportunity we've got at last to show these people how a school should be run."

Ndume School was backward in every sense of the word. Mr. Obi put his whole life into the work, and his wife hers too. He had two aims. A high standard of teaching was insisted upon, and the school compound was to be turned into a place of beauty. Nancy's dream-gardens came to life with the coming of the rains, and blossomed. Beautiful hibiscus and allamanda hedges in brilliant red and yellow marked out the carefully tended school compound from the rank neighbourhood bushes.

One evening as Obi was admiring his work he was scandalized to see an old woman from the village hobble right across the compound, through a marigold flower-bed and the hedges. On going up there he found faint signs of an almost disused path from the village across the school compound to the bush on the other side.

"It amazes me," said Obi to one of his teachers who had been three years in the school, "that you people allowed the villagers to make use of this footpath. It is simply incredible." He shook his head.

"The path," said the teacher apologetically, "appears to be very important to them. Although it is hardly used, it connects the village shrine with their place of burial."

"And what has that got to do with the school?" asked the headmaster.

"Well, I don't know," replied the other with a shrug of the shoulders. "But I remember there was a big row some time ago when we attempted to close it."

"That was some time ago. But it will not be used now," said Obi as he walked away. "What will the Government Education Officer think of this when he comes to inspect the school next week? The villagers might, for all I know, decide to use the schoolroom for a pagan ritual during the inspection."

Heavy sticks were planted closely across the path at the two places where it entered and left the school premises. These were further strengthened with barbed wire.

Three days later the village priest of *Ani* called on the headmaster. He was an old man and walked with a slight stoop. He carried a stout walking-stick which he usually tapped on the floor, by way of emphasis, each time he made a new point in his argument.

"I have heard," he said after the usual exchange of cordialities, "that our ancestral footpath has recently been closed . . ."

"Yes," replied Mr. Obi. "We cannot allow people to make a highway of our school compound."

"Look here, my son," said the priest bringing down his walking-stick, "this path was here before you were born and before your father was born. The whole life of this village depends on it. Our dead relatives depart by it and our ancestors visit us by it. But most important, it is the path of children coming in to be born . . ."

Mr. Obi listened with a satisfied smile on his face.

"The whole purpose of our school," he said finally, "is to eradicate just such beliefs as that. Dead men do not require footpaths. The whole idea is just fantastic. Our duty is to teach your children to laugh at such ideas."

"What you say may be true," replied the priest, "but we follow the practices of our fathers. If you re-open the path we shall have nothing to quarrel about. What I always say is: let the hawk perch and let the eagle perch." He rose to go.

"I am sorry," said the young headmaster. "But the school compound cannot be a thoroughfare. It is against our regulations. I would suggest your constructing another path, skirting our premises. We can even get our boys to help in building it. I don't suppose the ancestors will find the little detour too burdensome."

"I have no more words to say," said the old priest, already outside.

Two days later a young woman in the village died in childbed. A diviner was immediately consulted and he prescribed heavy sacrifices to propitiate ancestors insulted by the fence.

Obi woke up next morning among the ruins of his work. The beautiful hedges were torn up not just near the path but right round the school, the flowers trampled to death and one of the school buildings pulled down . . . That day, the white Supervisor came to inspect the school and wrote a nasty report on the state of the premises but more seriously about the "tribal-war situation developing between the school and the village, arising in part from the misguided zeal of the new headmaster."

[1972]

Journal Entry

With which characters in Chinua Achebe's story do you identify most? Explain.

Textual Considerations

1. Characterize Obi's attitude toward the teachers and the people in the community.
2. Speculate on the implications of the story's title. To what extent do you agree with Obi's reasons for closing the path?
3. Explain what the supervisor means by "misguided zeal." What is ironic about this statement? Does Obi deserve his censure? Why or why not?
4. Draw a character sketch of Nancy, including an analysis of her personality traits and her attitude toward life.
5. How does the story explore the cultural clash between two different kinds of knowledge, experience, and attitudes toward life? Identify them and explain why they oppose each other.

Cultural Contexts

1. The conflict between individual aspirations and communal rites is central to this story. With whom do you empathize—Obi, who insisted on "civilizing the pagans," or the villagers, who used the path that "connects the village shrine with their place of burial"?
2. Consider with your group why Obi and the village priest are unable to negotiate a compromise. Explain the implications of the priest's plea to "let the hawk perch and let the eagle perch."

ESSAYS

May Sarton

The Rewards of Living a Solitary Life

The other day an acquaintance of mine, a gregarious and charming man, told me he had found himself unexpectedly alone in New York for an hour or two between appointments. He went to the Whitney and spent the "empty" time looking at things in solitary bliss. For him it proved to be a shock nearly as great as falling in love to discover that he could enjoy himself so much alone.

What had he been afraid of, I asked myself? That, suddenly alone, he would discover that he bored himself, or that there was, quite simply, no self there to meet? But having taken the plunge, he is now on the brink of adventure; he is about to be launched into his own inner space, space as immense, unexplored, and sometimes frightening as outer space to the astronaut. His every perception will come to him with a new freshness and, for a time, seem startlingly original. For anyone who can see things for himself with a naked eye becomes, for a moment or two, something of a genius. With another human being present vision becomes double vision, inevitably. We are busy wondering, what does my companion see or think of this, and what do I think of it? The original impact gets lost, or diffused.

"Music I heard with you was more than music."[1] Exactly. And therefore music *itself* can only be heard alone. Solitude is the salt of personhood. It brings out the authentic flavor of every experience.

"Alone one is never lonely: the spirit adventures, walking/In a quiet garden, in a cool house, abiding single there."

Loneliness is most acutely felt with other people, for with others, even with a lover sometimes, we suffer from our differences of taste, temperament, mood. Human intercourse often demands that we soften the edge of perception, or withdraw at the very instant of personal truth for fear of hurting, or of being inappropriately present, which is to say naked, in a social situation. Alone we can afford to be wholly whatever we are, and to feel whatever we feel absolutely. That is a great luxury!

For me the most interesting thing about a solitary life, and mine has been that for the last twenty years, is that it becomes increasingly rewarding. When I can wake up and watch the sun rise over the ocean, as I do most days, and know that I have an entire day ahead, uninterrupted, in which to write a few pages, take a walk with my dog, lie down in the afternoon for a long think (why does one think better in a horizontal position?), read and listen to music, I am flooded with happiness.

I am lonely only when I am overtired, when I have worked too long without a break, when for the time being I feel empty and need filling up. And I am lonely

---

[1] A line from Conrad Aiken's *Bread and Music* (1914).

836

sometimes when I come back home after a lecture trip, when I have seen a lot of people and talked a lot, and am full to the brim with experience that needs to be sorted out.

Then for a little while the house feels huge and empty, and I wonder where my self is hiding. It has to be recaptured slowly by watering the plants, perhaps, and looking again at each one as though it were a person, by feeding the two cats, by cooking a meal.

It takes a while, as I watch the surf blowing up in fountains at the end of the field, but the moment comes when the world falls away, and the self emerges again from the deep unconscious; bringing back all I have recently experienced to be explored and slowly understood, when I can converse again with my hidden powers, and so grow, and so be renewed, till death do us part.

[1990]

Journal Entry

To what extent do you agree with the author's statement: "Loneliness is most acutely felt with other people"?

Textual Considerations

1. Explain the statement that "anyone who can see things for himself with a naked eye becomes, for a moment or two, something of a genius."
2. What evidence is there to support Sarton's thesis that solitude is rewarding?
3. How does Sarton's conclusion connect with her introduction?
4. Is Sarton seeking to inform or persuade her audience? To what extent does she persuade you?
5. How does Sarton describe loneliness in paragraph 7?

Cultural Contexts

1. Explain the differences between being *alone* and being *lonely*. Is it possible to feel alone in a room full of people? Why or why not?
2. Can your group reach a consensus about what would happen to "relatedness" and community values if everybody established "loneliness" as an ideal?

Thomas Jefferson

The Declaration of Independence

When in the course of human events, it becomes necessary for one people to dissolve the political bands which have connected them with another, and to assume among the Powers of the earth, the separate and equal station to which the Laws of Nature and of Nature's God entitle them, a decent respect to the opinions of mankind requires that they should declare the causes which impel them to the separation.

We hold these truths to be self-evident, that all men are created equal, that they are endowed by their Creator with certain unalienable Rights, that among these are Life, Liberty and the pursuit of Happiness. That to secure these rights, Governments are instituted among Men deriving their just powers from the consent of the governed. That whenever any Form of Government becomes destructive of these ends, it is the Right of the People to alter or to abolish it, and to institute new Government, laying its foundation on such principles and organizing its powers in such form, as to them shall seem most likely to effect their Safety and Happiness. Prudence, indeed, will dictate that Governments long established should not be changed for light and transient causes; and accordingly all experience hath shown, that mankind are more disposed to suffer, while evils are sufferable, than to right themselves by abolishing the forms to which they are accustomed. But when a long train of abuses and usurpations pursuing invariably the same Object evinces a design to reduce them under absolute Despotism, it is their right, it is their duty, to throw off such government, and to provide new Guards for their future security. Such has been the patient sufferance of these Colonies; and such is now the necessity which constrains them to alter their former Systems of Government. The history of the present King of Great Britain is a history of repeated injuries and usurpations, all having in direct object the establishment of an absolute Tyranny over these States. To prove this, let Facts be submitted to a candid world.

He has refused his Assent to laws, the most wholesome and necessary for the public good.

He has forbidden his Governors to pass Laws of immediate and pressing importance, unless suspended in their operation till his Assent should be obtained; and when so suspended, he has utterly neglected to attend to them.

He has refused to pass other Laws for the accommodation of large districts of people, unless those people would relinquish the right of Representation in the Legislature, a right inestimable to them and formidable to tyrants only.

He has called together legislative bodies at places unusual, uncomfortable, and distant from the depository of their Public Records, for the sole purpose of fatiguing them into compliance with his measures.

He has dissolved Representative Houses repeatedly, for opposing with manly firmness his invasions on the rights of the people.

He has refused for a long time, after such dissolutions, to cause others to be elected; whereby the Legislative Powers, incapable of Annihilation, have returned to the People at large for their exercise; the State remaining in the mean time exposed to all the dangers of invasion from without, and convulsions within.

He has endeavoured to prevent the population of these States; for that purpose obstructing the Laws of Naturalization of Foreigners; refusing to pass others to encourage their migration hither, and raising the conditions of new Appropriations of Lands.

He has obstructed the Administration of Justice, by refusing his Assent to Laws for establishing Judiciary Powers.

He has made Judges dependent on his Will alone, for the tenure of their offices, and the amount and payment of their salaries.

He has erected a multitude of New Offices, and sent hither swarms of Officers to harass our People, and eat out their substance.

He has kept among us, in time of peace. Standing Armies without the Consent of our Legislature.

He has affected to render the Military independent of and superior to the Civil Power.

He has combined with others to subject us to jurisdictions foreign to our constitution, and unacknowledged by our laws: giving his Assent to their acts of pretended Legislation:

For quartering large bodies of armed troops among us:

For protecting them, by a mock Trial, from Punishment for any Murders which they should commit on the Inhabitants of these States:

For cutting off our Trade with all parts of the world:

For imposing Taxes on us without our Consent:

For depriving us in many cases, of the benefits of Trial by Jury:

For transporting us beyond Seas to be tried for pretended offenses:

For abolishing the free System of English Laws in a Neighbouring Province, establishing therein an Arbitrary government, and enlarging its boundaries so as to render it at once an example and fit instrument for introducing the same absolute rule into these Colonies:

For taking away our Charters, abolishing our most valuable Laws, and altering fundamentally the Forms of our Governments:

For suspending our own Legislatures, and declaring themselves invested with Power to legislate for us in all cases whatsoever.

He has abdicated Government here, by declaring us out of his Protection and waging War against us.

He has plundered our seas, ravaged our Coasts, burnt our towns and destroyed the Lives of our people.

He is at this time transporting large Armies of foreign Mercenaries to compleat works of death, desolation and tyranny, already begun with circumstances of Cruelty & perfidy scarcely paralleled in the most barbarous ages, and totally unworthy the Head of a civilized nation.

He has constrained our fellow Citizens taken Captive on the high Seas to bear Arms against their Country, to become the executioners of their friends and Brethren, or to fall themselves by their Hands.

He has excited domestic insurrections amongst us, and has endeavoured to bring on the inhabitants of our frontiers, the merciless Indian Savages, whose known rule of warfare, is an undistinguished destruction of all ages, sexes and conditions.

In every stage of these Oppressions We have Petitioned for Redress in the most humble terms: Our repeated Petitions have been answered only by repeated injury. A Prince, whose character is thus marked by every act which may define a Tyrant, is unfit to be the ruler of a free People.

Nor have We been wanting in attention to our British brethren. We have warned them from time to time of attempts by their legislature to extend an unwarrantable jurisdiction over us. We have reminded them of the circumstances of our emigration and settlement here. We have appealed to their native justice and magnanimity, and we have conjured them by the ties of our common kindred to disavow these usurpations, which would inevitably interrupt our connections and correspondence. They too have been deaf to the voice of justice and of consanguinity. We must, therefore, acquiesce in the necessity, which denounces our Separation, and hold them, as we hold the rest of mankind, Enemies in War, in Peace Friends.

We, therefore, the Representatives of the united States of America, in General Congress, Assembled, appealing to the Supreme Judge of the world for the rectitude of our intentions, do, in the Name, and by Authority of the good People of these Colonies, solemnly publish and declare, That these United Colonies are, and of Right ought to be Free and Independent States; that they are Absolved from all Allegiance to the British Crown, and that all political connection between them and the State of Great Britain, is and ought to be totally dissolved; and that as Free and Independent States, they have full Power to levy War, conclude Peace, contract Alliances, establish Commerce, and to do all other Acts and Things which Independent States may of right do. And for the support of this Declaration, with a firm reliance on the Protection of Divine Providence, we mutually pledge to each other our Lives, our Fortunes and our sacred Honor.

[1776]

Journal Entry

Freewrite on your associations with *democracy*. What images, emotions, and ideas does the word evoke?

Textual Considerations

1. According to the Declaration, what is the purpose of government? How is this point important in the Declaration?
2. What is Jefferson's purpose in drafting the Declaration of Independence?
3. Does the Declaration of Independence appeal primarily to the reader's intellect, emotions, or both? Explain.
4. According to the Declaration, what are people more likely to do—rebel or put up with injustice?
5. What does the last paragraph of the Declaration proclaim? How is it related to the rest of the document?

Cultural Contexts

1. We have all heard the phrase "all men are created equal" so often that we don't really hear it anymore. What does it mean in this context? Is it true outside this context? In what sense is it true or not true?
2. Collaborate with your group in writing your own Declaration of Independence for the twenty-first century. What focus would you include that is not present in the original document?

Martin Luther King Jr.

I Have a Dream

I am happy to join with you today in what will go down in history as the greatest demonstration for freedom in the history of our nation.

Five score years ago, a great American in whose symbolic shadow we stand today, signed the Emancipation Proclamation. This momentous decree came as a great beacon light of hope to millions of Negro slaves who had been seared in the flames of withering injustice. It came as a joyous daybreak to end the long night of their captivity. But one hundred years later, the Negro still is not free. One hundred years later, the life of the Negro is still sadly crippled by the manacles of segregation and the chains of discrimination. One hundred years later, the Negro lives on a lonely island of poverty in the midst of a vast ocean of material prosperity. One hundred years later, the Negro is still anguished in the corners of American society and finds himself in exile in his own land. And so we have come here today to dramatize a shameful condition.

In a sense we have come to our nation's capital to cash a check. When the architects of our republic wrote the magnificent words of the Constitution and the Declaration of Independence, they were signing a promissory note to which every American was to fall heir. This note was the promise that all men—yes, Black men as well as white men—would be guaranteed the inalienable rights of life, liberty, and the pursuit of happiness.

It is obvious today that America has defaulted on this promissory note insofar as her citizens of color are concerned. Instead of honoring this sacred obligation, America has given the Negro people a bad check, a check which has come back marked "insufficient funds." But we refuse to believe that the bank of justice is bankrupt. We refuse to believe that there are insufficient funds in the great vaults of opportunity of this nation; and so we have come to cash this check, a check that will give us upon demand the riches of freedom and the security of justice.

We have also come to this hallowed spot to remind America of the fierce urgency of *now*. This is no time to engage in the luxury of cooling off or to take the tranquilizing drug of gradualism. *Now* is the time to make real the promises of democracy. *Now* is the time to rise from the dark and desolate valley of segregation to the sunlit path of racial justice. *Now* is the time to lift our nation from the quicksands of racial injustice to the solid rock of brotherhood. Now is the time to make justice a reality for all of God's children.

It would be fatal for the nation to overlook the urgency of the moment. This sweltering summer of the Negro's legitimate discontent will not pass until there is an invigorating autumn of freedom and equality. Nineteen Sixty-three is not an end, but a beginning. And those who hope that the Negro needed to blow off steam and will now be content will have a rude awakening if the nation returns to business as usual. There will be neither rest nor tranquility in America until the Negro is granted his citizenship rights. The whirlwinds of revolt will continue to shake the foundations of our nation until the bright day of justice emerges.

But there is something that I must say to my people who stand on the warm threshold which leads into the palace of justice. In the process of gaining our rightful place, we must not be guilty of wrongful deeds. Let us not seek to satisfy our thirst for freedom by drinking from the cup of bitterness and hatred. We must forever conduct our struggle on the high plane of dignity and discipline. We must not allow our creative protest to degenerate into physical violence. Again and again we must rise to the majestic heights of meeting physical force with soul force. And the marvelous new militancy which has engulfed the Negro community must not lead us to a distrust of all white people; for many of our white brothers, as evidenced by their presence here today, have come to realize that their destiny is tied up with our destiny, and they have come to realize that their freedom is inextricably bound to our freedom.

We cannot walk alone. And as we walk we must make the pledge that we shall always march ahead. We cannot turn back. There are those who are asking the devotees of civil rights, "When will you be satisfied?" We can never be satisfied as long as the Negro is the victim of the unspeakable horrors of police brutality. We can never be satisfied as long as our bodies, heavy with the fatigue of travel, cannot gain lodging in the motels of the highways and the hotels of the cities. We cannot be satisfied as long as the Negro's basic mobility is from a smaller ghetto to a larger one. We can never be satisfied as long as our children are stripped of their selfhood and robbed of their dignity by signs stating "For Whites Only." We cannot be satisfied as long as the Negro in Mississippi cannot vote and a Negro in New York believes he has nothing for which to vote. No, no, we are not satisfied, and we will not be satisfied until justice rolls down like waters and righteousness like a mighty stream.

I am not unmindful that some of you have come here out of great trials and tribulations. Some of you have come fresh from narrow jail cells. Some of you have come from areas where your quest for freedom left you battered by the storms of persecution and staggered by the winds of police brutality. You have been the veterans of creative suffering. Continue to work with the faith that unearned suffering is redemptive.

Go back to Mississippi, and go back to Alabama. Go back to South Carolina. Go back to Georgia. Go back to Louisiana. Go back to the slums and ghettos of our Northern cities, knowing that somehow this situation can and will be changed. Let us not wallow in the valley of despair.

I say to you today, my friends, even though we face the difficulties of today and tomorrow, I still have a dream. It is a dream deeply rooted in the American dream. I have a dream that one day this nation will rise up and live out the true meaning of its creed: "We hold these truths to be self-evident, that all men are created equal." I have a dream that one day, on the red hills of Georgia, sons of former slaves and the sons of former slave owners will be able to sit down together at the table of brotherhood. I have a dream that one day even the state of Mississippi, a state sweltering with the heat of injustice, sweltering with the heat of oppression, will be transformed into an oasis of freedom and justice. I have a dream that my four children will one day live in a nation where they will not be judged by the color of their skin, but by the content of their character.

I have a dream today. I have a dream that one day down in Alabama—with its vicious racists, with its governor's lips dripping with the words of interposition and nullification—one day right there in Alabama, little Black boys and Black girls will be able to join hands with little white boys and white girls as sisters and brothers.

I have a dream today. I have a dream that one day every valley shall be exalted and every hill and mountain shall be made low, the rough places will be made plain and the crooked places will be made straight, and the glory of the Lord shall be revealed, and all flesh shall see it together.

This is our hope. This is the faith that I go back to the South with. And with this faith we will be able to hew out of the mountain of despair a stone of hope. With this faith we will be able to transform the jangling discords of our nation into a beautiful symphony of brotherhood. With this faith we will be able to work together, to play together, to struggle together, to go to jail together, to stand up for freedom together, knowing that we will be free one day.

And this will be the day—this will be the day when all God's children will be able to sing with new meaning:

> My country, 'tis of thee,
>   Sweet land of liberty;
>   Of thee I sing;
>   Land where my fathers died,
>   Land of the Pilgrims' pride,
>   From every Mountainside
>   Let freedom ring.

And if America is to be a great nation, this must become true.

And so let freedom ring from the prodigious hilltops of New Hampshire. Let freedom ring from the mighty mountains of New York. Let freedom ring from the heightening Alleghenies of Pennsylvania. Let freedom ring from the snowcapped Rockies of Colorado. Let freedom ring from the curvaceous slopes of California.

But not only that. Let freedom ring from Stone Mountain of Georgia. Let freedom ring from Lookout Mountain of Tennessee. Let freedom ring from every hill and molehill of Mississippi. "From every Mountainside let freedom ring."

And when this happens—when we allow freedom to ring, when we let it ring from every village and every hamlet, from every state and every city—we will be able to speed up that day when all of God's children, Black men and white men, Jews and Gentiles, Protestants and Catholics, will be able to join hands and sing in the words of the old Negro spiritual: "Free at last! Free at last! Thank God Almighty. We are free at last!"

[1963]

Journal Entry

King uses the word *freedom* several times in his speech. What do you think he means by it? Consider the different possible meanings of freedom to the various members of his audience. What does it mean to you?

Textual Considerations

1. Why is the phrase "Five score years ago" more appropriate than "a hundred years ago" or "in 1863"? Why does King later repeat the phrase "one hundred years later" so often?
2. When King speaks of "cash [ing] a check" or "insufficient funds," is he talking about money? Explain.
3. What evidence is there that King is writing for an audience that includes whites?
4. King states, "You have been the veterans of creative suffering." Can suffering be creative? How?
5. One characteristic of persuasion is that it uses connotative diction and figurative language to appeal to the reader's emotions. What words or expressions do you find in this speech that make you react emotionally?
6. Characterize the tone of the speech. Is it objective, angry, neutral? Explain your answer.

Cultural Contexts

1. King says his dream is "rooted in the American dream." What is that? Explain King's quotation, and connect it with the Declaration of Independence. Is the American Dream more than the hopes and rights expressed in that document? If so, in what way?
2. Working with your group, discuss what events in Mississippi in the early 1960s might have caused King to single out that state. Why would he specifically mention Georgia? Why Alabama?

POETRY

James Wright

A Blessing

Just off the highway to Rochester, Minnesota,
Twilight bounds softly forth on the grass.
And the eyes of those two Indian ponies
Darken with kindness.
They have come gladly out of the willows   5
To welcome my friend and me.
We step over the barbed wire into the pasture
Where they have been grazing all day, alone.
They ripple tensely, they can hardly contain their happiness
That we have come.   10
They bow shyly as wet swans. They love each other.
There is no loneliness like theirs.
At home once more,
They begin munching the young tufts of spring in the darkness.
I would like to hold the slenderer one in my arms,   15
For she has walked over to me
And nuzzled my left hand.
She is black and white,
Her mane falls wild on her forehead,
And the light breeze moves me to caress her long ear   20
That is delicate as the skin over a girl's wrist.
Suddenly I realize
That if I stepped out of my body I would break
Into blossom.

[1961]

845

William Carlos Williams

Danse Russe

If when my wife is sleeping
and the baby and Kathleen
are sleeping
and the sun is a flame-white disc
in silken mists   5
above shining trees,—
if I in my north room
dance naked, grotesquely
before my mirror
waving my shirt round my head   10
and singing softly to myself:

"I am lonely, lonely.
I was born to be lonely,
I am best so!"
If I admire my arms, my face,   15
my shoulders, flanks, buttocks
against the yellow drawn shades,—
Who shall say I am not
the happy genius of my household?

[1938]

Journal Entry

Freewrite on your associations, experiences, memories, or images of loneliness. Is it possible to be alone and not be lonely? Explain.

Textual Considerations

1. What figures of speech enhance the poet's descriptions of the ponies and the setting in Wright's text?
2. How do you interpret the juxtaposition of lines 11 and 12 in "A Blessing"?
3. What blessing is referred to in the title of Wright's poem?
4. What several connotations do the speakers in "A Blessing" and "Danse Russe" give to the words *blessing* and *lonely*, respectively?
5. What effect does the place of the sun as well as its description have on the speaker's Russian dance? What are his motivations for dancing?
6. Why does the speaker dance in front of the mirror? Is he narcissistic? Explain.

Cultural Contexts

1. Explain the connotations of the word *epiphany* in the contexts "A Blessing" and "Danse Russe." What kinds of experiences are both poets celebrating? How do you respond to the concluding lines of both texts?
2. Discuss with your group the metaphor "solitude is the salt of personhood." Did you reach a consensus?

CUMMINGS AND STEVENS

E. E. Cummings

the Cambridge ladies
who live in furnished souls

the Cambridge ladies who live in furnished souls
are unbeautiful and have comfortable minds
(also, with the church's protestant blessings
daughters, unscented shapeless spirited)
they believe in Christ and Longfellow, both dead,   5
are invariably interested in so many things—
at the present writing one still finds
delighted fingers knitting for the is it Poles?
perhaps. While permanent faces coyly bandy
scandal of Mrs. N. and Professor D   10
. . . . the Cambridge ladies do not care, above
Cambridge if sometimes in its box of
sky lavender and cornerless, the
moon rattles like a fragment of angry candy

[1923]

Wallace Stevens

Disillusionment of Ten O'Clock

The houses are haunted
By white night-gowns.
None are green,
Or purple with green rings,
Or green with yellow rings,   5
Or yellow with blue rings.
None of them are strange,
With socks of lace
And beaded ceintures.
People are not going   10
To dream of baboons and periwinkles.

Only, here and there, an old sailor,
Drunk and asleep in his boots,
Catches tigers
In red weather.

[1951]

Journal Entry

How would you define yourself? Are you a curious person? Can curiosity be dangerous? Explain.

Textual Considerations

1. What does the speaker in "the Cambridge ladies" mean by "live in furnished souls"?
2. What effect has the church had on these women in E. E. Cummings's poem?
3. Does the speaker in the Cummings poem reverse his attitude toward the women in the line "[they] are invariably interested in so many things"? Explain.
4. Explain lines 7–10 in the Cummings poem. What is their motivation for what they do and say?
5. Analyze the double meanings of the image in the first two lines of Stevens's text.
6. What attitude does the speaker convey toward dreaming of "baboons and periwinkles" in "Disillusionment of Ten O'Clock"?
7. Compare the functions that the Cambridge ladies and the old sailor have in the Cummings and Stevens poems.
8. What is the effect of listing the colored nightgowns in the Stevens poem?

Cultural Contexts

1. What kind of people wear white nightgowns and have "furnished souls"? Would you enjoy a conversation with them? Why or why not?
2. Do you consider yourself a dreamer? Do you have a "dream"? How do you and your group interpret the last four lines of the Cummings text? What connection do they have to dreaming?

Walt Whitman

What Is the Grass?

A child said *What is the grass?* fetching it to me with full hands,
How could I answer the child? I do not know what it is any more
    than he.

I guess it must be the flag of my disposition, out of hopeful green stuff
    woven.

Or I guess it is the handkerchief of the Lord,
A scented gift and remembrancer designedly dropt,   5

Bearing the owner's name someway in the corners, that we may see and
    remark, and say *Whose?*

Or I guess the grass is itself a child, the produced babe of the
    vegetation.

Or I guess it is a uniform hieroglyphic,
And it means, Sprouting alike in broad zones and narrow zones,
Growing among black folks as among white,   10
Kanuck, Tuckahoe, Congressman, Cuff, I give them the same, I receive
    them the same.

And now it seems to me the beautiful uncut hair of graves.

Tenderly will I use you curling grass,
It may be you transpire from the breasts of young men,
It may be if I had known them I would have loved them,   15
It may be you are from old people, or from offspring taken soon out of
    their mothers' laps,
And here you are the mothers' laps.
This grass is very dark to be from the white heads of old mothers,
Darker than the colorless beards of old men,
Dark to come from under the faint red roofs of mouths.   20
O I perceive after all so many uttering tongues,
And I perceive they do not come from the roofs of mouths for nothing.

I wish I could translate the hints about the dead young men and
    women,
And the hints about old men and mothers, and the offspring taken soon
    out of their laps.

What do you think has become of the young and old men?   25
And what do you think has become of the women and children?

They are alive and well somewhere,
The smallest sprout shows there is really no death,
And if ever there was it led forward life, and does not wait at the end to
     arrest it,
And ceas'd the moment life appear'd.   30
All goes onward and outward, nothing collapses,
And to die is different from what any one supposed, and luckier.

                                                                              [1886]

Percy Bysshe Shelley

Ozymandias°

I met a traveller from an antique land
Who said: Two vast and trunkless legs of stone
Stand in the desert . . . Near them, on the sand,
Half sunk, a shattered visage lies, whose frown,
And wrinkled lip, and sneer of cold command,   5
Tell that its sculptor well those passions read
Which yet survive, stamped on these lifeless things,
The hand that mocked them, and the heart that fed:
And on the pedestal these words appear:
"My name is Ozymandias, king of kings: 10
Look on my works, ye Mighty, and despair!"
Nothing beside remains. Round the decay
Of that colossal wreck, boundless and bare
The lone and level sands stretch far away.

                                                                              [1818]

Ozymandias: Egyptian monarch of the thirteenth century B.C., said to have erected a huge statue of himself.

Journal Entry

How would you answer the question in Whitman's title?

Textual Considerations

1. The speaker in "What Is the Grass?" strikes the pose of an old man pondering the questions of youth. What evidence in the poem indicates that he is probing for answers?

2. In responding to the child's question, the speaker in Whitman's poem postulates several answers. What are they?

3. One answer seems more satisfactory to the speaker in "What Is the Grass?" than the others because he emphasizes it in an obvious way. Which answer is it, and how does the speaker emphasize it?

4. How do the structures of "What Is the Grass?" and "Ozymandias" emphasize meaning? What is the significance of the lines printed completely separate from the others in "What Is the Grass?"? What is the significance of the compact stanza of Shelley's poem?

5. How is the sculptor depicted in "Ozymandias"?

6. In what condition is this ancient statue? Why is it located alone in an empty desert?

7. What irony is implied in the inscription on the pedestal of Ozymandias?

Cultural Contexts

1. Discuss with your group Whitman's philosophy of death as he presents it in the poem. How does his point of view compare to yours? Explain.

2. Shelley was an English Romantic poet who rebelled against authority. What evidence of this do you find in the poem? To what extent does your group agree or disagree with his point of view?

BLAKE AND WORDSWORTH

William Blake

London

I wander through each chartered° street,
Near where the chartered Thames does flow
And mark in every face I meet
Marks of weakness, marks of woe.

In every cry of every man, 5
In every infant's cry of fear,
In every voice; in every ban,
The mind-forged manacles I hear:

How the chimney-sweeper's cry
Every blackening church appalls, 10
And the hapless soldier's sigh
Runs in blood down palace-walls.

But most, through midnight streets I hear
How the youthful harlot's curse
Blasts the new-born infant's tear, 15
And blights with plagues the marriage-hearse.

[1794]

1 chartered: Preempted by the state and leased out under royal patent.

William Wordsworth

London, 1802

Milton! thou should'st be living at this hour:
England hath need of thee: she is a fen
Of stagnant waters: altar, sword, and pen,
Fireside, the heroic wealth of hall and bower,
Have forfeited their ancient English dower 5
Of inward happiness. We are selfish men;
Oh! raise us up, return to us again;
And give us manners, virtue, freedom, power.

Thy soul was like a Star, and dwelt apart:
Thou hadst a voice whose sound was like the sea: 10
Pure as the naked heavens, majestic, free,
So didst thou travel on life's common way,
In cheerful godliness; and yet thy heart
The lowliest duties on herself did lay.

[1802]

William Wordsworth

The World Is Too Much with Us

The world is too much with us; late and soon,
Getting and spending, we lay waste our powers:
Little we see in Nature that is ours;
We have given our hearts away, a sordid boon!
This Sea that bares her bosom to the moon;   5
The winds that will be howling at all hours,
And are up-gathered now like sleeping flowers;
For this, for every thing, we are out of tune;
It moves us not.—Great God! I'd rather be
A Pagan suckled in a creed outworn;   10
So might I, standing on this pleasant lea,
Have glimpses that would make me less forlorn;
Have sight of Proteus° rising from the sea;
Or hear old Triton blow his wreathéd horn.°

[1807]

13 Proteus: An old man of the sea who (in the *Odyssey*) could assume a variety of shapes.
14 Triton: A sea deity, usually represented as blowing on a conch shell.

Journal Entry

What associations, attitudes, or ideas about institutions do you bring to your reading of these poems?

Textual Considerations

1. What pictures of London do Blake and Wordsworth present? Which aspects of the speakers' descriptions are not meant literally? How do these pictures compare with Wordsworth's picture of the world in "The World Is Too Much with Us"?
2. Why does Blake use the word *chartered* twice? Explain the meaning in each case.

3. What effect does Blake achieve through repetition of words from line to line and sometimes within the same line? How does repetition affect the mood of the poem?
4. What aspects of English life and institutions does the speaker portray as stagnant in Wordsworth's "London, 1802"?
5. What evidence does he offer in the first six lines of "London, 1802" to support this charge? Summarize the theme of the last eight lines of Wordsworth's sonnet.
6. What contrasts between "The world" and "Nature" does the speaker make in "The World Is Too Much with Us"?

Cultural Contexts

1. In both poems about London, the speakers lament the demise of institutions and their suppression of the human spirit. To what extent do their critiques apply to life in urban centers today? Are these poems anti-city? Explain.
2. Why does Wordsworth invoke Milton in "London, 1802" and Proteus and Triton in "The World Is Too Much with Us," whereas Blake invokes the images of "the chimney-sweeper's cry," "the hapless soldier's sigh," and "the youthful harlot's curse"? Which belief do you tend to share—that human beings can rekindle humanity's sense of awe or that they themselves are responsible for the creation of evil?

YEVTUSHENKO AND REID

Yevgeny Yevtushenko

People

No people are uninteresting.
Their fate is like the chronicle of planets.

Nothing in them is not particular,
and planet is dissimilar from planet.

And if a man lived in obscurity   5
making his friends in that obscurity
obscurity is not uninteresting.

To each his world is private,
and in that world one excellent minute.

And in that world one tragic minute.   10
These are private.

In any man who dies there dies with him
his first snow and kiss and fight.
It goes with him.

They are left books and bridges   15
and painted canvas and machinery.

Whose fate is to survive.
But what has gone is also not nothing:

by the rule of the game something has gone.
Not people die but worlds die in them.   20

Whom we knew as faulty, the earth's creatures.
Of whom, essentially, what did we know?

Brother of a brother? Friend of friends?
Lover of lover?

We who knew our fathers   25
in everything, in nothing.

They perish. They cannot be brought back.
The secret worlds are not regenerated.

And every time again and again
I make my lament against destruction.   30

[1962]

Alastair Reid

Curiosity

may have killed the cat. More likely,
the cat was just unlucky, or else curious
to see what death was like, having no cause
to go on licking paws, or fathering
litter on litter of kittens, predictably.   5

Nevertheless, to be curious
is dangerous enough. To distrust
what is always said, what seems;
to ask odd questions, interfere in dreams,
smell rats, leave home, have hunches,   10
does not endear cats to those doggy circles
where well-smelt baskets, suitable wives, good lunches
are the order of things, and where prevails
much wagging of incurious heads and tails.

Face it. Curiosity   15
will not cause us to die—
only lack of it will.
Never to want to see
the other side of the hill
or that improbable country   20
where living is an idyll
(although a probable hell)
would kill us all.
Only the curious
have if they live a tale   25
worth telling at all.

Dogs say cats love too much, are irresponsible,
are dangerous, marry too many wives,
desert their children, chill all dinner tables
with tales of their nine lives.   30
Well, they are lucky. Let them be
nine-lived and contradictory,
curious enough to change, prepared to pay
the cat-price, which is to die
and die again and again,   35
each time with no less pain.
A cat-minority of one
is all that can be counted on

to tell the truth; and what cats have to tell
on each return from hell   40
is this: that dying is what the living do,
that dying is what the loving do,
and that dead dogs are those who never know
that dying is what, to live, each has to do.

[1959]

Journal Entry

Create a conversation between Yevtushenko and Reid on what makes a person interesting.

Textual Considerations

1. Analyze Yevtushenko's use of symbolism in "People." To what events might the "excellent minute" and the "tragic minute" refer? What other examples reinforce the poem's meanings about individual uniqueness, mortality, and our ability to know another person?
2. What is the significance of the contrast between "first snow and kiss and fight" and "books and bridges and painted canvas and machinery" in "People"?
3. Explain the line "Not people die but worlds die in them" in Yevtushenko's poem. Characterize your response to it.
4. Explain Reid's statement that "Only the curious/have, they live, a tale/worth telling at all."
5. What kind of people are dogs? What criticism do they have of cats? What does living entail, according to Reid?
6. The title of Reid's poem also serves as the first line. Why might he choose to structure the poem in this way?

Cultural Contexts

1. Discuss with your group Yevtushenko's idea that "obscurity is not uninteresting." What does he mean by obscurity? Is there an ordinary person that you consider interesting? What makes a person interesting? Did your group reach a consensus?
2. Often writers use paradoxes to generate multiple meanings. Explore with your group possible meanings for the paradox "dying is what the living do." Before beginning, review that section of Reid's poem.

Sharon Olds

Summer Solstice, New York City

By the end of the longest day of the year he could not stand it,
he went up the iron stairs through the roof of the building
and over the soft, tarry surface
to the edge, put one leg over the complex green tin cornice
and said if they came a step closer that was it.   5
Then the huge machinery of the earth began to work for his life,
the cops came in their suits blue-gray as the sky on a cloudy evening,
and one put on a bulletproof vest, a
black shell around his own life,
life of his children's father, in case   10
the man was armed, and one, slung with a
rope like the sign of his bounden duty,
came up out of a hole in the top of the neighboring building,
like the gold hole they say is in the top of the head,
and began to lurk toward the man who wanted to die.   15
The tallest cop approached him directly,
softly, slowly, talking to him, talking, talking,
while the man's leg hung over the lip of the next world,
and the crowd gathered in the street, silent, and the
dark hairy net with its implacable grid was   20
unfolded near the curb and spread out and
stretched as the sheet is prepared to receive at a birth.
Then they all came a little closer
where he squatted next to his death, his shirt
glowing its milky glow like something   25
growing in a dish at night in the dark in a lab, and then
everything stopped
as his body jerked and he
stepped down from the parapet and went toward them
and they closed on him, I thought they were going to   30
beat him up, as a mother whose child has been
lost will scream at the child when it's found, they
took him by the arms and held him up and
leaned him against the wall of the chimney and the
tall cop lit a cigarette   35
in his own mouth, and gave it to him, and

then they all lit cigarettes, and the
red glowing ends burned like the
tiny campfires we lit at night
back at the beginning of the world.

[1987]   40

Leo Romero

What the Gossips Saw

Everyone pitied Escolastica, her leg
had swollen like a watermelon in the summer
It had practically happened over night
She was seventeen, beautiful and soon
to be married to Guillermo who was working   5
in the mines at Terreros, eighty miles away
far up in the mountains, in the wilderness
Poor Escolastica, the old women would say
on seeing her hobble to the well with a bucket
carrying her leg as if it were the weight   10
of the devil, surely it was a curse from heaven
for some misdeed, the young women who were
jealous would murmur, yet they were grieved too
having heard that the doctor might cut
her leg, one of a pair of the most perfect legs   15
in the valley, and it was a topic of great
interest and conjecture among the villagers
whether Guillermo would still marry her
if she were crippled, a one-legged woman—
as if life weren't hard enough for a woman   20
with two legs—how could she manage

Guillermo returned and married Escolastica
even though she had but one leg, the sound
of her wooden leg pounding down the wooden aisle
stayed in everyone's memory for as long   25
as they lived, women cried at the sight
of her beauty, black hair so dark
that the night could get lost in it, a face
more alluring than a full moon

Escolastica went to the dances with her husband
and watched and laughed but never danced   30

though once she had been the best dancer
and could wear holes in a pair of shoes
in a matter of a night, and her waist had been
as light to the touch as a hummingbird's flight   35
And Escolastica bore five children, only half
what most women bore, yet they were healthy
In Escolastica's presence, no one would mention
the absence of her leg, though she walked heavily
And it was not long before the gossips   40
spread their poison, that she must be in cahoots
with the devil, had given him her leg
for the power to bewitch Guillermo's heart
and cloud his eyes so that he could not see
what was so clear to them all   45

[1981]

Journal Entry

What associations or attitudes toward suicide can you bring to your reading of Olds's text?

Textual Considerations

1. How does setting contribute to the theme of "Summer Solstice, New York City"?
2. How are the cops portrayed in Olds's poem? Cite specific lines.
3. Explain the last three lines of "Summer Solstice, New York City."
4. Consider the importance of the word *saw* in Romero's title. What other allusions to sight do you find in the poem?
5. What issue seems to be of greatest concern to the communities in Olds's and Romero's texts? Chart the course of the speakers' reactions to the suicidal man in Olds's poem and to Escolastica and Guillermo in Romero's poem.

Cultural Contexts

1. Olds and Romero address the issue of boundaries, or fences, in relationships—our often conflicting needs for solitude and solidarity, identity and community, and personal space and relatedness. What new meanings about relationships can you draw from these poems?
2. Working with your group, reconstruct the circumstances under which each of you would risk your life to save another's. Can you imagine yourself in the place of the cops in Olds's poem? How does the poem address the conflict between individual rights and the claims of communal obligation? Were the cops only doing their jobs? Explain.

FERLINGHETTI AND WILBUR

Lawrence Ferlinghetti

Constantly Risking Absurdity

Constantly risking absurdity
               and death
        whenever he performs
            above the heads
                  of his audience   5
     the poet like an acrobat
              climbs on rime
                    to a high wire of his own making
    and balancing on eyebeams
             above a sea of faces   10
       paces his way
            to the other side of day
     performing entrechats
          and sleight-of-foot tricks
   and other high theatrics   15
          and all without mistaking
     any thing
         for what it may not be
For he's the super realist
          who must perforce perceive   20
     taut truth
         before the taking of each stance or step
   in his supposed advance
         toward that still higher perch
where Beauty stands and waits   25
       with gravity
            to start her death-defying leap
And he
   a little charleychaplin man
        who may or may not catch   30
    her fair eternal form
       spreadeagled in the empty air
  of existence

[1958]

Richard Wilbur

The Writer

In her room at the prow of the house
Where light breaks, and the windows are tossed with linden,
My daughter is writing a story.

I pause in the stairwell, hearing
From her shut door a commotion of typewriter-keys   5
Like a chain hauled over a gunwale.

Young as she is, the stuff
Of her life is a great cargo, and some of it heavy:
I wish her a lucky passage.

But now it is she who pauses,   10
As if to reject my thought and its easy figure.
A stillness greatens, in which

The whole house seems to be thinking,
And then she is at it again with a bunched clamor
Of strokes, and again is silent.   15

I remember the dazed starling
Which was trapped in that very room, two years ago;
How we stole in, lifted a sash

And retreated, not to affright it;
And how for a helpless hour, through the crack of the door,   20
We watched the sleek, wild, dark

And iridescent creature
Batter against the brilliance, drop like a glove
To the hard floor, or the desk-top,

And wait then, humped and bloody,   25
For the wits to try it again; and how our spirits
Rose when, suddenly sure,

It lifted off from a chair-back,
Beating a smooth course for the right window
And clearing the sill of the world.   30

It is always a matter, my darling,
Of life or death, as I had forgotten. I wish
What I wished you before, but harder.

[1971]

Journal Entry

What is your concept of a poet or a writer? Do you think of yourself as a creative person? How do you define creativity?

Textual Considerations

1. Ferlinghetti's poem is based on the simile of the poet as acrobat. Why is it an appropriate comparison for the poem's subject?
2. How does the structure of Ferlinghetti's poem contribute to its meaning?
3. Respond to the concept of the poet as "the super realist" in "Constantly Risking Absurdity." Why does the poet sometimes "not catch" Beauty? Who is the writer in "The Writer"? How does he compare with the poet in "Constantly Risking Absurdity"?
4. The beginning of "The Writer" draws an elaborate comparison between the daughter's writing and a sea voyage. Review the poem and explain each of the sea images.
5. What is the similarity between the daughter's effort to write and the starling's effort to escape? What does the speaker learn from the example of the starling?

Cultural Contexts

1. Discuss the artist's relationship to audience in both poems. What attitude toward himself is the speaker expressing in calling himself "a little charleychaplin man"? Why is he constantly risking absurdity? What is "always a matter, . . . /Of life or death" in "The Writer"? What do both poems suggest about the creative process? Explain the role of community in both texts.
2. Discuss with your group the significance of the allusions to death in both poems. In what sense do artists, writers, and musicians defy death?

Emily Dickinson

Volcanoes be in Sicily

Volcanoes be in Sicily
And South America
I judge from my Geography—
Volcanos nearer here
A Lava step at any time   5
Am I inclined to climb—
A Crater I may contemplate
Vesuvius at Home.

[c. 1914]

Emily Dickinson

The Soul selects her own society–

The Soul selects her own Society—
Then—shuts the Door—
To her divine Majority—
Present no more—

Unmoved—she notes the Chariots—pausing—   5
At her low Gate—
Unmoved—an Emperor be kneeling
Upon her Mat—

I've known her—from an ample nation—
Choose One—   10
Then—close the Valves of her attention—
Like Stone—

[c. 1862]

Emily Dickinson

Much madness is divinest sense–

Much Madness is divinest Sense—
To a discerning Eye—
Much Sense—the starkest Madness—
'Tis the Majority
In this, as All, prevail—   5
Assent—and you are sane—
Demur—you're straightway dangerous—
And handled with a Chain—

[c. 1862]

Emily Dickinson

Tell all the Truth but tell it slant–

Tell all the Truth but tell it slant—
Success in Circuit lies
Too bright for our infirm Delight
To Truth's superb surprise
As Lightning to the Children eased   5
With explanation kind
The Truth must dazzle gradually
Or every man be blind—

[c. 1868]

Journal Entry

What associations with volcanoes or with madness can you bring to your reading of Dickinson's texts?

Textual Considerations

1. Explain the paradox in the first four lines of "Volcanoes be in Sicily."
2. Analyze the literal and symbolic significance of volcanoes in the poem.
3. Explain how Dickinson's use of door imagery contributes to the unity and meaning of "The Soul selects her own society—."
4. What does the poet's use of active verbs imply about the "soul's" anatomy?

5. Analyze Dickinson's use of paradox to enhance meaning in "Much madness is divinest sense—."
6. Do you agree that the majority decides what is sane or insane?
7. To what extent do you agree with the speaker in "Tell all the Truth but tell it slant—"?
8. How do you respond to the speaker's description of truth? Explain the last two lines of "Tell all the Truth but tell it slant—."
9. Select one image from each poem and explain how the images enhance meaning. Explain.

Cultural Contexts

1. In 1991, May Sarton, a twentieth-century American poet, described the function of poetry as follows:

> For poetry exists to break through
> to below the level of reason
> where the angels and monsters
> that the amenities keep in the cellar
> may come out to dance,
> to rove and roar,
> growling and singing,
> to bring life back to the enclosed rooms
> where too often we are only
> living and partly living.

What might Sarton mean by juxtaposing "angels" and "monsters"? What does her choice of verbs suggest about the function of poetry? Why are the rooms "enclosed?" Explain the last two lines. To what extent does Sarton's concept of poetry apply to Dickinson's texts? What is your response to Sarton's description of the role of poetry in people's lives?

2. To what extent do your group members agree with Dickinson that it is dangerous to be a nonconformist? What examples from history or from your own experience can you think of?

DRAMA

Sophocles

Antigone

English version by Dudley Fitts and Robert Fitzgerald

CHARACTERS

ANTIGONE
ISMENE
EURYDICE
CREON
HAIMON
TEIRESIAS
A Sentry
A Messenger
Chorus

SCENE: *Before the palace of* CREON, *King of Thebes. A central double door, and two lateral doors. A platform extends the length of the façade, and from this platform three steps lead down into the "orchestra," or chorus-ground.* TIME: *dawn of the day after the repulse of the Argive army from the assault on Thebes.*

PROLOGUE

(ANTIGONE *and* ISMENE° *enter from the central door of the Palace.*)

ANTIGONE: Ismenê, dear sister,
   You would think that we had already suffered enough
   For the curse on Oedipus:
   I cannot imagine any grief
   That you and I have not gone through. And now—
   Have they told you of the new decree of our King Creon?   5
ISMENE: I have heard nothing: I know
   That two sisters lost two brothers, a double death
   In a single hour; and I know that the Argive army
   Fled in the night; but beyond this, nothing.
ANTIGONE: I thought so. And that is why I wanted you   10

Prologue. S.d. Antigone and Ismene: daughters of Oedipus.

To come out here with me. There is something we must do.
ISMENE: Why do you speak so strangely?
ANTIGONE: Listen, Ismenê:
    Creon buried our brother Eteoclês   15
    With military honors, gave him a soldier's funeral,
    And it was right that he should; but Polyneicês,
    Who fought as bravely and died as miserably,—
    They say that Creon has sworn
    No one shall bury him, no one mourn for him,   20
    But his body must lie in the fields, a sweet treasure
    For carrion birds to find as they search for food.
    That is what they say, and our good Creon is coming here
    To announce it publicly; and the penalty—
    Stoning to death in the public square!
                                            There it is,   25
    And now you can prove what you are:
    A true sister, or a traitor to your family.
ISMENE: Antigonê, you are mad! What could I possibly do?
ANTIGONE: You must decide whether you will help me or not.
ISMENE: I do not understand you. Help you in what?   30
ANTIGONE: Ismenê, I am going to bury him. Will you come?
ISMENE: Bury him! You have just said the new law forbids it.
ANTIGONE: He is my brother. And he is your brother, too.
ISMENE: But think of the danger! Think what Creon will do!
ANTIGONE: Creon is not strong enough to stand in my way.   35
ISMENE: Ah sister!
    Oedipus died, everyone hating him
    For what his own search brought to light, his eyes
    Ripped out by his own hand; and Iocastê died,
    His mother and wife at once: she twisted the cords   40
    That strangled her life; and our two brothers died,
    Each killed by the other's sword. And we are left:
    But oh, Antigonê!
    Think how much more terrible than these
    Our own death would be if we should go against Creon   45
    And do what he has forbidden! We are only women,
    We cannot fight with men, Antigonê!
    The law is strong, we must give in to the law
    In this thing, and in worse. I beg the Dead
    To forgive me, but I am helpless: I must yield   50
    To those in authority. And I think it is dangerous business
    To be always meddling.
ANTIGONE: If that is what you think,
    I should not want you, even if you asked to come.
    You have made your choice, you can be what you want to be.

But I will bury him; and if I must die,   55
I say that this crime is holy: I shall lie down
With him in death, and I shall be as dear
To him as he to me.
                              It is the dead,
Not the living, who make the longest demands:
We die for ever . . .
                              You may do as you like,   60
Since apparently the laws of the gods mean nothing to you.

ISMENE: They mean a great deal to me; but I have no strength
To break laws that were made for the public good.

ANTIGONE: That must be your excuse, I suppose. But as for me,
I will bury the brother I love.

ISMENE: Antigonê,   65
I am so afraid for you!

ANTIGONE: You need not be:
You have yourself to consider, after all.

ISMENE: But no one must hear of this, you must tell no one!
I will keep it a secret, I promise!

ANTIGONE: Oh tell it! Tell everyone!
Think how they'll hate you when it all comes out   70
If they learn that you knew about it all the time!

ISMENE: So fiery! You should be cold with fear.

ANTIGONE: Perhaps. But I am only doing what I must.

ISMENE: But can you do it? I say that you cannot.

ANTIGONE: Very well: when my strength gives out, I shall do no more.   75

ISMENE: Impossible things should not be tried at all.

ANTIGONE: Go away, Ismenê:
I shall be hating you soon, and the dead will too,
For your words are hateful. Leave me my foolish plan:
I am not afraid of the danger; if it means death,   80
It will not be the worst of deaths—death without honor.

ISMENE: Go then, if you feel that you must.
You are unwise,
But a loyal friend indeed to those who love you.

                    (*Exit into the Palace.* ANTIGONE *goes off*, L. *Enter the* CHORUS.)

PÁRODOS

CHORUS: Now the long blade of the sun, lying   (STROPHE 1)
Level east to west, touches with glory
Thebes of the Seven Gates. Open, unlidded
Eye of golden day! O marching light
Across the eddy and rush of Dircê's stream,   5
Striking the white shields of the enemy

Thrown headlong backward from the blaze of morning!

CHORAGOS: Polyneicês their commander
   Roused them with windy phrases,
   He the wild eagle screaming   10
   Insults above our land,
   His wings their shields of snow,
   His crest their marshalled helms.

CHORUS: Against our seven gates in a yawning ring   (ANTISTROPHE 1)
   The famished spears came onward in the night;   15
   But before his jaws were sated with our blood,
   Or pinefire took the garland of our towers,
   He was thrown back; and as he turned, great Thebes—
   No tender victim for his noisy power—
   Rose like a dragon behind him, shouting war.   20

CHORAGOS: For God hates utterly
   The bray of bragging tongues;
   And when he beheld their smiling,
   Their swagger of golden helms,
   The frown of his thunder blasted   25
   Their first man from our walls.

CHORUS: We heard his shout of triumph high in the air   (STROPHE 2)
   Turn to a scream; far out in a flaming arc
   He fell with his windy torch, and the earth struck him.
   And others storming in fury no less than his   30
   Found shock of death in the dusty joy of battle.

CHORAGOS: Seven captains at seven gates
   Yielded their clanging arms to the god
   That bends the battle-line and breaks it.
   These two only, brothers in blood,   35
   Face to face in matchless rage,
   Mirroring each the other's death,
   Clashed in long combat.

CHORUS: But now in the beautiful morning of victory   (ANTISTROPHE 2)
   Let Thebes of the many chariots sing for joy!   40
   With hearts for dancing we'll take leave of war:
   Our temples shall be sweet with hymns of praise,
   And the long night shall echo with our chorus.

SCENE I

CHORAGOS: But now at last our new King is coming:
   Creon of Thebes, Menoikeus' son.
   In this auspicious dawn of his reign
   What are the new complexities
   That shifting Fate has woven for him?   5

What is his counsel? Why has he summoned
The old men to hear him?

(Enter CREON *from the Palace, C. He addresses the* CHORUS *from the top step.)*

CREON: Gentlemen: I have the honor to inform you that our Ship of State, which
recent storms have threatened to destroy, has come safely to harbor at last,
guided by the merciful wisdom of Heaven. I have summoned you here this   10
morning because I know that I can depend upon you: your devotion to King
Laïos was absolute; you never hesitated in your duty to our late ruler Oedipus;
and when Oedipus died, your loyalty was transferred to his children. Unfortunately, as you know, his two sons, the princes Eteoclês and Polyneicês, have
killed each other in battle; and I, as the next in blood, have succeeded to the full   15
power of the throne.

I am aware, of course, that no Ruler can expect complete loyalty from his
subjects until he has been tested in office. Nevertheless, I say to you at the very
outset that I have nothing but contempt for the kind of Governor who is afraid,
for whatever reason, to follow the course that he knows is best for the State;   20
and as for the man who sets private friendship above the public welfare,—I
have no use for him, either. I call God to witness that if I saw my country
headed for ruin, I should not be afraid to speak out plainly; and I need hardly
remind you that I would never have any dealings with an enemy of the people.
No one values friendship more highly than I; but we must remember that   25
friends made at the risk of wrecking our Ship are not real friends at all.

These are my principles, at any rate, and that is why I have made the following decision concerning the sons of Oedipus: Eteoclês, who died as a man
should die, fighting for his country, is to be buried with full military honors,
with all the ceremony that is usual when the greatest heroes die; but his   30
brother Polyneicês, who broke his exile to come back with fire and sword
against his native city and the shrines of his fathers' gods, whose one idea was
to spill the blood of his blood and sell his own people into slavery—Polyneicês,
I say, is to have no burial: no man is to touch him or say the least prayer for
him; he shall lie on the plain, unburied; and the birds and the scavenging dogs   35
can do with him whatever they like.

This is my command, and you can see the wisdom behind it. As long as I am
King, no traitor is going to be honored with the loyal man. But whoever shows
by word and deed that he is on the side of the State,—he shall have my respect
while he is living, and my reverence when he is dead.   40

CHORAGOS: If that is your will, Creon son of Menoikeus,
You have the right to enforce it: we are yours.

CREON: That is my will. Take care that you do your part.

CHORAGOS: We are old men: let the younger ones carry it out.

CREON: I do not mean that: the sentries have been appointed.   45

CHORAGOS: Then what is it that you would have us do?

CREON: You will give no support to whoever breaks this law.

CHORAGOS: Only a crazy man is in love with death!

CREON: And death it is; yet money talks, and the wisest
      Have sometimes been known to count a few coins too many.   50

            (*Enter* SENTRY *from L.*)

SENTRY: I'll not say that I'm out of breath from running, King, because every time
      I stopped to think about what I have to tell you, I felt like going back. And all
      the time a voice kept saying, "You fool, don't you know you're walking straight
      into trouble?"; and then another voice: "Yes, but if you let somebody else get
      the news to Creon first, it will be even worse than that for you!" But good sense   55
      won out, at least I hope it was good sense, and here I am with a story that
      makes no sense at all; but I'll tell it anyhow, because, as they say, what's going to
      happen's going to happen, and—
CREON: Come to the point. What have you to say?
SENTRY: I did not do it. I did not see who did it. You must not punish me for what   60
      someone else has done.
CREON: A comprehensive defense! More effective, perhaps,
      If I knew its purpose. Come: what is it?
SENTRY: A dreadful thing . . . I don't know how to put it—
CREON: Out with it!
SENTRY: Well, then;   65
      The dead man—
                Polyneicês—

            (*Pause. The* SENTRY *is overcome, fumbles for words.* CREON *waits impassively.*)

                          out there—
                                    someone,—
      New dust on the slimy flesh!

            (*Pause. No sign from* CREON.)

      Someone has given it burial that way, and
      Gone . . .

            (*Long pause. Creon finally speaks with deadly control:*)

CREON: And the man who dared do this?   70
SENTRY: I swear I
      Do not know! You must believe me!
                          Listen:
      The ground was dry, not a sign of digging, no,
      Not a wheeltrack in the dust, no trace of anyone.
      It was when they relieved us this morning: and one of them,   75
      The corporal, pointed to it.
                          There it was,
      The strangest—
                Look:
      The body, just mounded over with light dust: you see?
      Not buried really, but as if they'd covered it

Just enough for the ghost's peace. And no sign   80
Of dogs or any wild animal that had been there.

And then what a scene there was! Every man of us
Accusing the other: we all proved the other man did it,
We all had proof that we could not have done it.
We were ready to take hot iron in our hands,   85
Walk through fire, swear by all the gods,
It was not I!
I do not know who it was, but it was not I!

> (CREON'S *rage has been mounting steadily, but the* SENTRY *is too intent upon his story to notice it*)

And then, when this came to nothing, someone said
A thing that silenced us and made us stare   90
Down at the ground: you had to be told the news,
And one of us had to do it! We threw the dice,
And the bad luck fell to me. So here I am,
No happier to be here than you are to have me:
Nobody likes the man who brings bad news.   95

CHORAGOS: I have been wondering, King: can it be that the gods have done this?
CREON (*Furiously*):   Stop!
  Must you doddering wrecks
  Go out of your heads entirely? "The gods!"
  Intolerable!   100
  The gods favor this corpse? Why? How had he served them?
  Tried to loot their temples, burn their images,
  Yes, and the whole State, and its laws with it!
  Is it your senile opinion that the gods love to honor bad men?
  A pious thought!—
                        No, from the very beginning   105
  There have been those who have whispered together,
  Stiff-necked anarchists, putting their heads together,
  Scheming against me in alleys. These are the men,
  And they have bribed my own guard to do this thing.

  Money!   (*Sententiously*)   110
  There's nothing in the world so demoralizing as money.
  Down go your cities,
  Homes gone, men gone, honest hearts corrupted,
  Crookedness of all kinds, and all for money!   (*To* SENTRY)
                        But you—!   115
  I swear by God and by the throne of God,
  The man who has done this thing shall pay for it!
  Find that man, bring him here to me, or your death
  Will be the least of your problems: I'll string you up

Alive, and there will be certain ways to make you 120
Discover your employer before you die;
And the process may teach you a lesson you seem to have missed:
The dearest profit is sometimes all too dear:
That depends on the source. Do you understand me?
A fortune won is often misfortune. 125

SENTRY: King, may I speak?
CREON: Your very voice distresses me.
SENTRY: Are you sure that it is my voice, and not your conscience?
CREON: By God, he wants to analyze me now!
SENTRY: It is not what I say, but what has been done, that hurts you.
CREON: You talk too much.
SENTRY: Maybe; but I've done nothing. 130
CREON: Sold your soul for some silver: that's all you've done.
SENTRY: How dreadful it is when the right judge judges wrong!
CREON: Your figures of speech
May entertain you now; but unless you bring me the man,
You will get little profit from them in the end.   (*Exit* CREON *into the Palace.*) 135
SENTRY: "Bring me the man"—!
I'd like nothing better than bringing him the man!
But bring him or not, you have seen the last of me here.
At any rate, I am safe!   (*Exit* SENTRY)

ODE I

CHORUS: (STROPHE 1)
Numberless are the world's wonders, but none
More wonderful than man; the stormgray sea
Yields to his prows, the huge crests bear him high;
Earth, holy and inexhaustible, is graven
With shining furrows where his plows have gone 5
Year after year, the timeless labor of stallions.

The lightboned birds and beasts that cling to cover,   (ANTISTROPHE 1)
The lithe fish lighting their reaches of dim water,
All are taken, tamed in the net of his mind;
The lion on the hill, the wild horse windy-maned, 10
Resign to him; and his blunt yoke has broken
The sultry shoulders of the mountain bull.

Words also, and thought as rapid as air,   (STROPHE 2)
He fashions to his good use; statecraft is his,
And his the skill that deflects the arrows of snow, 15
The spears of winter rain: from every wind
He has made himself secure—from all but one:
In the late wind of death he cannot stand.

O clear intelligence, force beyond all measure!   (ANTISTROPHE 2)
O fate of man, working both good and evil!   20
When the laws are kept, how proudly his city stands!
When the laws are broken, what of his city then?
Never may the anárchic man find rest at my hearth,
Never be it said that my thoughts are his thoughts.

SCENE II

(*Re-enter* SENTRY *leading* ANTIGONE.)

CHORAGOS: What does this mean? Surely this captive woman
    Is the Princess, Antigonê. Why should she be taken?
SENTRY: Here is the one who did it! We caught her
    In the very act of burying him.—Where is Creon?
CHORAGOS: Just coming from the house.   5

(*Enter* CREON, *C.*)

CREON: What has happened?
    Why have you come back so soon?
SENTRY: (*Expansively*)   O King,
    A man should never be too sure of anything:
    I would have sworn
    That you'd not see me here again: your anger   10
    Frightened me so, and the things you threatened me with;
    But how could I tell then
    That I'd be able to solve the case so soon?

    No dice-throwing this time: I was only too glad to come!

    Here is this woman. She is the guilty one: 15
    We found her trying to bury him.
    Take her, then; question her; judge her as you will.
    I am through with the whole thing now, and glád óf it.
CREON: But this is Antigonê! Why have you brought her here?
SENTRY: She was burying him, I tell you!
CREON: (*Severely*)   Is this the truth?   20
SENTRY: I saw her with my own eyes. Can I say more?
CREON: The details: come, tell me quickly!
SENTRY: It was like this:
    After those terrible threats of yours, King,
    We went back and brushed the dust away from the body.
    The flesh was soft by now, and stinking,   25
    So we sat on a hill to windward and kept guard.
    No napping this time! We kept each other awake.
    But nothing happened until the white round sun
    Whirled in the center of the round sky over us:

Then, suddenly,
A storm of dust roared up from the earth, and the sky
Went out, the plain vanished with all its trees
In the stinging dark. We closed our eyes and endured it.
The whirlwind lasted a long time, but it passed;
And then we looked, and there was Antigonê!
I have seen
A mother bird come back to a stripped nest, heard
Her crying bitterly a broken note or two
For the young ones stolen. Just so, when this girl
Found the bare corpse, and all her love's work wasted,
She wept, and cried on heaven to damn the hands
That had done this thing.
                And then she brought more dust
And sprinkled wine three times for her brother's ghost.

We ran and took her at once. She was not afraid,
Not even when we charged her with what she had done.
She denied nothing.
           And this was a comfort to me,
And some uneasiness: for it is a good thing
To escape from death, but it is no great pleasure
To bring death to a friend.
              Yet I always say
There is nothing so comfortable as your own safe skin!
CREON: (*Slowly, dangerously*) And you, Antigonê,
You with your head hanging,—do you confess this thing?
ANTIGONE: I do. I deny nothing.
CREON (*To* SENTRY):   You may go.   (*Exit* SENTRY)

    (*To* ANTIGONE:)

Tell me, tell me briefly:
Had you heard my proclamation touching this matter?
ANTIGONE: It was public. Could I help hearing it?
CREON: And yet you dared defy the law.
ANTIGONE: I dared.
It was not God's proclamation. That final Justice
That rules the world below makes no such laws.
Your edict, King, was strong,
But all your strength is weakness itself against
The immortal unrecorded laws of God.
They are not merely now: they were, and shall be,
Operative for ever, beyond man utterly.

I knew I must die, even without your decree:
I am only mortal. And if I must die

30

35

40

45

50

55

60

65

Now, before it is my time to die,
Surely this is no hardship: can anyone
Living, as I live, with evil all about me,
Think Death less than a friend? This death of mine   70
Is of no importance; but if I had left my brother
Lying in death unburied, I should have suffered.
Now I do not.
                    You smile at me. Ah Creon,
Think me a fool, if you like; but it may well be
That a fool convicts me of folly.   75

CHORAGOS: Like father, like daughter: both headstrong, deaf to reason!
She has never learned to yield.

CREON: She has much to learn.
The inflexible heart breaks first, the toughest iron
Cracks first, and the wildest horses bend their necks
At the pull of the smallest curb.

                              Pride? In a slave?   80
This girl is guilty of double insolence,
Breaking the given laws and boasting of it.
Who is the man here,
She or I, if this crime goes unpunished?
Sister's child, or more than sister's child,   85
Or closer yet in blood—she and her sister
Win bitter death for this!

          (*To* SERVANTS:)

                    Go, some of you,
Arrest Ismenê. I accuse her equally.
Bring her: you will find her sniffling in the house there.

Her mind's a traitor: crimes kept in the dark   90
Cry for light, and the guardian brain shudders;
But how much worse than this
Is brazen boasting of barefaced anarchy!

ANTIGONE: Creon, what more do you want than my death?

CREON: Nothing.
That gives me everything.

ANTIGONE: Then I beg you: kill me.   95
This talking is a great weariness: your words
Are distasteful to me, and I am sure that mine
Seem so to you. And yet they should not seem so:
I should have praise and honor for what I have done.
All these men here would praise me   100
Were their lips not frozen shut with fear of you.   (*Bitterly*)
Ah the good fortune of kings,
Licensed to say and do whatever they please!

CREON: You are alone here in that opinion.

ANTIGONE: No, they are with me. But they keep their tongues in leash.   105

CREON: Maybe. But you are guilty, and they are not.

ANTIGONE: There is no guilt in reverence for the dead.

CREON: But Eteoclês—was he not your brother too?

ANTIGONE: My brother too.

CREON: And you insult his memory?

ANTIGONE (*Softly*):   The dead man would not say that I insult it.   110

CREON: He would: for you honor a traitor as much as him.

ANTIGONE: His own brother, traitor or not, and equal in blood.

CREON: He made war on his country. Eteoclês defended it.

ANTIGONE: Nevertheless, there are honors due all the dead.

CREON: But not the same for the wicked as for the just.   115

ANTIGONE: Ah Creon, Creon,
    Which of us can say what the gods hold wicked?

CREON: An enemy is an enemy, even dead.

ANTIGONE: It is my nature to join in love, not hate.

CREON (*Finally losing patience*):   Go join him, then; if you must have your love,   120
    Find it in hell!

CHORAGOS: But see, Ismenê comes:

          (*Enter* ISMENE, *guarded*)

    Those tears are sisterly, the cloud
    That shadows her eyes rains down gentle sorrow.

CREON: You, too, Ismenê,   125
    Snake in my ordered house, sucking my blood
    Stealthily—and all the time I never knew
    That these two sisters were aiming at my throne!
                                        Ismenê,
    Do you confess your share in this crime, or deny it?
    Answer me.   130

ISMENE: Yes, if she will let me say so. I am guilty.

ANTIGONE (*Coldly*):   No, Ismenê. You have no right to say so.
    You would not help me, and I will not have you help me.

ISMENE: But now I know what you meant; and I am here
    To join you, to take my share of punishment.   135

ANTIGONE: The dead man and the gods who rule the dead
    Know whose act this was. Words are not friends.

ISMENE: Do you refuse me, Antigonê? I want to die with you:
    I too have a duty that I must discharge to the dead.

ANTIGONE: You shall not lessen my death by sharing it.   140

ISMENE: What do I care for life when you are dead?

ANTIGONE: Ask Creon. You're always hanging on his opinions.

ISMENE: You are laughing at me. Why, Antigonê?

ANTIGONE: It's a joyless laughter, Ismenê.

ISMENE: But can I do nothing?

ANTIGONE: Yes. Save yourself. I shall not envy you.   145
    There are others who will praise you; I shall have honor, too.

ISMENE: But we are equally guilty!

ANTIGONE: No more, Ismenê.
    You are alive, but I belong to Death.

CREON (*To the* CHORUS):   Gentlemen, I beg you to observe these girls:
    One has just now lost her mind; the other,   150
    It seems, has never had a mind at all.

ISMENE: Grief teaches the steadiest minds to waver, King.

CREON: Yours certainly did, when you assumed guilt with the guilty!

ISMENE: But how could I go on living without her?

CREON: You are.
    She is already dead.

ISMENE: But your own son's bride!   155

CREON: There are places enough for him to push his plow.
    I want no wicked women for my sons!

ISMENE: O dearest Haimon, how your father wrongs you!

CREON: I've had enough of your childish talk of marriage!

CHORAGOS: Do you really intend to steal this girl from your son?   160

CREON: No; Death will do that for me.

CHORAGOS: Then she must die?

CREON (*Ironically*):   You dazzle me.
                         —But enough of this talk!

      (*To* GUARDS:)

You, there, take them away and guard them well:
For they are but women, and even brave men run
When they see Death coming.   (*Exeunt* ISMENE, ANTIGONE, *and* GUARDS)   165

ODE II

CHORUS: Fortunate is the man who has never tasted God's vengeance!   (STROPHE 1)
Where once the anger of heaven has struck, that house is shaken
For ever: damnation rises behind each child
Like a wave cresting out of the black northeast,
When the long darkness under sea roars up   5
And bursts drumming death upon the whirlwhipped sand.

I have seen this gathering sorrow from time long past   (ANTISTROPHE 1)
Loom upon Oedipus' children: generation from generation
Takes the compulsive rage of the enemy god.
So lately this last flower of Oedipus' line   10
Drank the sunlight! but now a passionate word
And a handful of dust have closed up all its beauty.

What mortal arrogance   (STROPHE 2)
  Transcends the wrath of Zeus?
Sleep cannot lull him, nor the effortless long months   15
Of the timeless gods: but he is young for ever,
And his house is the shining day of high Olympos.
  All that is and shall be,
  And all the past, is his.
No pride on earth is free of the curse of heaven.   20

  The straying dreams of men   (ANTISTROPHE 2)
  May bring them ghosts of joy:
But as they drowse, the waking embers burn them;
Or they walk with fixed éyes, as blind men walk.
But the ancient wisdom speaks for our own time: 25
  Fate works most for woe
  With Folly's fairest show.
Man's little pleasure is the spring of sorrow.

SCENE III

CHORAGOS: But here is Haimon, King, the last of all your sons.
  Is it grief for Antigonê that brings him here,
  And bitterness at being robbed of his bride?

  (*Enter* HAIMON)

CREON: We shall soon see, and no need of diviners.
                                              —Son,
  You have heard my final judgment on that girl: 5
  Have you come here hating me, or have you come
  With deference and with love, whatever I do?
HAIMON: I am your son, father. You are my guide.
  You make things clear for me, and I obey you.
  No marriage means more to me than your continuing wisdom. 10
CREON: Good. That is the way to behave: subordinate
  Everything else, my son, to your father's will.
  This is what a man prays for, that he may get
  Sons attentive and dutiful in his house,
  Each hating his father's enemies,   15
  Honoring his father's friends. But if his sons
  Fail him, if they turn out unprofitably,
  What has he fathered but trouble for himself
  And amusement for the malicious?
                            So you are right
  Not to lose your head over this woman.   20
  Your pleasure with her would soon grow cold, Haimon,
  And then you'd have a hellcat in bed and elsewhere.

Let her find her husband in Hell!
Of all the people in this city, only she
Has had contempt for my law and broken it.   25

Do you want me to show myself weak before the people?
Or to break my sworn word? No, and I will not.
The woman dies.
I suppose she'll plead "family ties." Well, let her.
If I permit my own family to rebel,   30
How shall I earn the world's obedience?
Show me the man who keeps his house in hand,
He's fit for public authority.
                         I'll have no dealings
With law-breakers, critics of the government:
Whoever is chosen to govern should be obeyed—   35
Must be obeyed, in all things, great and small,
Just and unjust! O Haimon,
The man who knows how to obey, and that man only,
Knows how to give commands when the time comes.
You can depend on him, no matter how fast   40
The spears come: he's a good soldier, he'll stick it out.

Anarchy, anarchy! Show me a greater evil!
This is why cities tumble and the great houses rain down,
This is what scatters armies!

No, no: good lives are made so by discipline.   45
We keep the laws then, and the lawmakers,
And no woman shall seduce us. If we must lose,
Let's lose to a man, at least! Is a woman stronger than we?
CHORAGOS: Unless time has rusted my wits,
What you say, King, is said with point and dignity.   50
HAIMON (*Boyishly earnest*):   Father:
Reason is God's crowning gift to man, and you are right
To warn me against losing mine. I cannot say—
I hope that I shall never want to say!—that you
Have reasoned badly. Yet there are other men   55
Who can reason too; and their opinions might be helpful.
You are not in a position to know everything
That people say or do, or what they feel:
Your temper terrifies them—everyone
Will tell you only what you like to hear.   60
But I, at any rate, can listen; and I have heard them
Muttering and whispering in the dark about this girl.
They say no woman has ever, so unreasonably,
Died so shameful a death for a generous act:

"She covered her brother's body. Is this indecent?   65
She kept him from dogs and vultures. Is this a crime?
Death?—She should have all the honor that we can give her!"

This is the way they talk out there in the city.

You must believe me:
Nothing is closer to me than your happiness.   70
What could be closer? Must not any son
Value his father's fortune as his father does his?
I beg you, do not be unchangeable:
Do not believe that you alone can be right.
The man who thinks that,   75
The man who maintains that only he has the power
To reason correctly, the gift to speak, the soul—
A man like that, when you know him, turns out empty.

It is not reason never to yield to reason!

In flood time you can see how some trees bend,   80
And because they bend, even their twigs are safe,
While stubborn trees are torn up, roots and all.
And the same thing happens in sailing:
Make your sheet fast, never slacken,—and over you go,
Head over heels and under: and there's your voyage.   85

Forget you are angry! Let yourself be moved!
I know I am young; but please let me say this:
The ideal condition
Would be, I admit, that men should be right by instinct;
But since we are all too likely to go astray,   90
The reasonable thing is to learn from those who can teach.

CHORAGOS: You will do well to listen to him, King,
If what he says is sensible. And you, Haimon,
Must listen to your father.—Both speak well.

CREON: You consider it right for a man of my years and experience 95
To go to school to a boy?

HAIMON: It is not right
If I am wrong. But if I am young, and right,
What does my age matter?

CREON: You think it right to stand up for an anarchist?

HAIMON: Not at all. I pay no respect to criminals.   100

CREON: Then she is not a criminal?

HAIMON: The City would deny it, to a man.

CREON: And the City proposes to teach me how to rule?

HAIMON: Ah. Who is it that's talking like a boy now?

CREON: My voice is the one voice giving orders in this City!   105
HAIMON: It is no City if it takes orders from one voice.
CREON: The State is the King!
HAIMON: Yes, if the State is a desert.   (*Pause*)
CREON: This boy, it seems, has sold out to a woman.
HAIMON: If you are a woman: my concern is only for you.
CREON: So? Your "concern"! In a public brawl with your father!   110
HAIMON: How about you, in a public brawl with justice?
CREON: With justice, when all that I do is within my rights?
HAIMON: You have no right to trample on God's right.
CREON (*Completely out of control*):   Fool, adolescent fool! Taken in by a woman!
HAIMON: You'll never see me taken in by anything vile.   115
CREON: Every word you say is for her!
HAIMON (*Quietly darkly*):   And for you.
    And for me. And for the gods under the earth.
CREON: You'll never marry her while she lives.
HAIMON: Then she must die.—But her death will cause another.
CREON: Another?   120
    Have you lost your senses? Is this an open threat?
HAIMON: There is no threat in speaking to emptiness.
CREON: I swear you'll regret this superior tone of yours!
    You are the empty one!
HAIMON: If you were not my father,
    I'd say you were perverse.   125
CREON: You girlstruck fool, don't play at words with me!
HAIMON: I am sorry. You prefer silence.
CREON: Now, by God—!
    I swear, by all the gods in heaven above us,
    You'll watch it, I swear you shall!

            (*To the* SERVANTS:)

                            Bring her out!
    Bring the woman out! Let her die before his eyes!   130
    Here, this instant, with her bridegroom beside her!
HAIMON: Not here, no; she will not die here, King.
    And you will never see my face again.
    Go on raving as long as you've a friend to endure you.   (*Exit* HAIMON)
CHORAGOS: Gone, gone.   135
    Creon, a young man in a rage is dangerous!
CREON: Let him do, or dream to do, more than a man can.
    He shall not save these girls from death.
CHORAGOS: These girls?
    You have sentenced them both?
CREON: No, you are right.
    I will not kill the one whose hands are clean.   140

CHORAGOS: But Antigonê?
CREON: (*Somberly*)   I will carry her far away
    Out there in the wilderness, and lock her
    Living in a vault of stone. She shall have food,
    As the custom is, to absolve the State of her death.
    And there let her pray to the gods of hell: 145
    They are her only gods:
    Perhaps they will show her an escape from death
    Or she may learn,
                        though late,
    That piety shown the dead is pity in vain.   (*Exit* CREON)

ODE III

CHORUS: Love, unconquerable   (STROPHE)
    Waster of rich men, keeper
    Of warm lights and all-night vigil
    In the soft face of a girl:
    Sea-wanderer, forest-visitor!   5
    Even the pure Immortals cannot escape you,
    And mortal man, in his one day's dusk,
    Trembles before your glory.

    Surely you swerve upon ruin   (ANTISTROPHE)
    The just man's consenting heart,   10
    As here you have made bright anger
    Strike between father and son—
    And none has conquered but Love!
    A girl's glánce wórking the will of heaven:
    Pleasure to her alone who mocks us,   15
    Merciless Aphroditê.

SCENE IV

CHORAGOS (*As* ANTIGONE *enters guarded*): But I can no longer stand in awe of this,
    Nor, seeing what I see, keep back my tears.
    Here is Antigonê, passing to that chamber
    Where we all find sleep at last.
ANTIGONE: Look upon me, friends, and pity me   (STROPHE 1) 5
    Turning back at the night's edge to say
    Good-by to the sun that shines for me no longer;
    Now sleepy Death
    Summons me down to Acheron,° that cold shore:
    There is no bridesong there, nor any music.   10

III.iv. 9. Acheron: river in Hades, the home of the dead.

CHORUS: Yet not unpraised, not without a kind of honor,
    You walk at last into the underworld;
    Untouched by sickness, broken by no sword.
    What woman has ever found your way to death?

ANTIGONE: How often I have heard the story of Niobê,°   (ANTISTROPHE 1)   15
    Tantalos' wretched daughter, how the stone
    Clung fast about her, ivy-close: and they say
    The rain falls endlessly
    And sifting soft snow; her tears are never done.
    I feel the loneliness of her death in mine.   20

CHORUS: But she was born of heaven, and you
    Are woman, woman-born. If her death is yours,
    A mortal woman's, is this not for you
    Glory in our world and in the world beyond?

ANTIGONE: You laugh at me. Ah, friends, friends,   (STROPHE 2)   25
    Can you not wait until I am dead? O Thebes,
    O men many-charioted, in love with Fortune,
    Dear springs of Dircê, sacred Theban grove,
    Be witnesses for me, denied all pity,
    Unjustly judged! and think a word of love   30
    For her whose path turns
    Under dark earth, where there are no more tears.

CHORUS: You have passed beyond human daring and come at last
    Into a place of stone where Justice sits.
    I cannot tell   35
    What shape of your father's guilt appears in this.

ANTIGONE: You have touched it at last: that bridal bed   (ANTISTROPHE 2)
    Unspeakable, horror of son and mother mingling:
    Their crime, infection of all our family!
    O Oedipus, father and brother!   40
    Your marriage strikes from the grave to murder mine.
    I have been a stranger here in my own land:
    All my life
    The blasphemy of my birth has followed me.

CHORUS: Reverence is a virtue, but strength   45
    Lives in established law: that must prevail.
    You have made your choice,
    Your death is the doing of your conscious hand.

ANTIGONE: Then let me go, since all your words are bitter,   (EPODE)
    And the very light of the sun is cold to me.   50
    Lead me to my vigil, where I must have
    Neither love nor lamentation; no song, but silence.

---

15. Niobe: her several children were slain in punishment for their mother's boastfulness. She was turned into stone on Mount Sipylus, and her tears became the stream of the mountain.

(CREON *interrupts impatiently*)

CREON: If dirges and planned lamentations could put off death,
   Men would be singing for ever.

(*To the* SERVANTS:)

                    Take her, go!
   You know your orders: take her to the vault   55
   And leave her alone there. And if she lives or dies,
   That's her affair, not ours: our hands are clean.
ANTIGONE: O tomb, vaulted bride-bed in eternal rock,
   Soon I shall be with my own again
   Where Persephonê welcomes the thin ghosts underground: 60
   And I shall see my father again, and you, mother,
   And dearest Polyneicês—
                    dearest indeed
   To me, since it was my hand
   That washed him clean and poured the ritual wine:
   And my reward is death before my time!   65

   And yet, as men's hearts know, I have done no wrong,
   I have not sinned before God. Or if I have,
   I shall know the truth in death. But if the guilt
   Lies upon Creon who judged me, then, I pray,
   May his punishment equal my own.
CHORAGOS: O passionate heart,   70
   Unyielding, tormented still by the same winds!
CREON: Her guards shall have good cause to regret their delaying.
ANTIGONE: Ah! That voice is like the voice of death!
CREON: I can give you no reason to think you are mistaken.
ANTIGONE: Thebes, and you my fathers' gods,   75
   And rulers of Thebes, you see me now, the last
   Unhappy daughter of a line of kings,
   Your kings, led away to death. You will remember
   What things I suffer, and at what men's hands,
   Because I would not transgress the laws of heaven.   80

(*To the* GUARDS, *simply:*)

Come: let us wait no longer.   (*Exit* ANTIGONE, *L.*, *guarded*)

ODE IV

CHORUS: All Danaê's° beauty was locked away   (STROPHE 1)
In a brazen cell where the sunlight could not come:
A small room, still as any grave, enclosed her.
Yet she was a princess too,
And Zeus in a rain of gold poured love upon her.   5
O child, child,
No power in wealth or war
Or tough sea-blackened ships
Can prevail against untiring Destiny!

And Dryas' son° also, that furious king,   (ANTISTROPHE 1)   10
Bore the god's prisoning anger for his pride:
Sealed up by Dionysos in deaf stone,
His madness died among echoes.
So at the last he learned what dreadful power
His tongue had mocked: 15
For he had profaned the revels,
And fired the wrath of the nine
Implacable Sisters° that love the sound of the flute.

And old men tell a half-remembered tale   (STROPHE 2)
Of horror done where a dark ledge splits the sea   20
And a double surf beats on the gráy shóres:
How a king's new woman, sick
With hatred for the queen he had imprisoned,
Ripped out his two sons' eyes with her bloody hands
While grinning Arês watched the shuttle plunge   25
Four times: four blind wounds crying for revenge,

Crying, tears and blood mingled.—Piteously born,   (ANTISTROPHE 2)
Those sons whose mother was of heavenly birth!
Her father was the god of the North Wind
And she was cradled by gales,   30
She raced with young colts on the glittering hills
And walked untrammeled in the open light:
But in her marriage deathless Fate found means
To build a tomb like yours for all her joy.

Ode IV. 1. Danae: she was locked away to prevent the fulfillment of a prophecy that she would bear a son who would kill her father. Despite this, she was impregnated by Zeus, who came to her in a shower of gold. **10. Dryas's son:** King Lycurgus, whom Dionysus, the god of wine, caused to be stricken with madness. **17–18. nine . . . Sisters:** the nine muses who presided over poetry, music, and the arts and sciences.

Scene V

(Enter blind Teiresias, *led by a boy. The opening speeches of* Teiresias *should be in singsong contrast to the realistic lines of* Creon.)

Teiresias: This is the way the blind man comes, Princes, Princes,
  Lock-step, two heads lit by the eyes of one.
Creon: What new thing have you to tell us, old Teiresias?
Teiresias: I have much to tell you: listen to the prophet, Creon.
Creon: I am not aware that I have ever failed to listen.   5
Teiresias: Then you have done wisely, King, and ruled well.
Creon: I admit my debt to you. But what have you to say?
Teiresias: This, Creon: you stand once more on the edge of fate.
Creon: What do you mean? Your words are a kind of dread.
Teiresias: Listen, Creon: 10
  I was sitting in my chair of augury, at the place
  Where the birds gather about me. They were all a-chatter,
  As is their habit, when suddenly I heard
  A strange note in their jangling, a scream, a
  Whirring fury; I knew that they were fighting,   15
  Tearing each other, dying
  In a whirlwind of wings clashing. And I was afraid.
  I began the rites of burnt-offering at the altar,
  But Hephaistos failed me: instead of bright flame,
  There was only the sputtering slime of the fat thigh-flesh   20
  Melting: the entrails dissolved in gray smoke,
  The bare bone burst from the welter. And no blaze!

  This was a sign from heaven. My boy described it,
  Seeing for me as I see for others.

  I tell you, Creon, you yourself have brought   25
  This new calamity upon us. Our hearths and altars
  Are stained with the corruption of dogs and carrion birds
  That glut themselves on the corpse of Oedipus' son.
  The gods are deaf when we pray to them, their fire
  Recoils from our offering, their birds of omen   30
  Have no cry of comfort, for they are gorged
  With the thick blood of the dead.
                                    O my son,
  These are no trifles! Think: all men make mistakes,
  But a good man yields when he knows his course is wrong,
  And repairs the evil. The only crime is pride.   35

  Give in to the dead man, then: do not fight with a corpse—
  What glory is it to kill a man who is dead?

Think, I beg you:
It is for your own good that I speak as I do.
You should be able to yield for your own good.   40
CREON: It seems that prophets have made me their especial province.
All my life long
I have been a kind of butt for the dull arrows
Of doddering fortune-tellers!
                              No, Teiresias:
If your birds—if the great eagles of God himself   45
Should carry him stinking bit by bit to heaven,
I would not yield. I am not afraid of pollution:
No man can defile the gods.
                              Do what you will,
Go into business, make money, speculate
In India gold or that synthetic gold from Sardis,   50
Get rich otherwise than by my consent to bury him.
Teiresias, it is a sorry thing when a wise man
Sells his wisdom, lets out his words for hire!
TEIRESIAS: Ah Creon! Is there no man left in the world—
CREON: To do what?—Come, let's have the aphorism!   55
TEIRESIAS: No man who knows that wisdom outweighs any wealth?
CREON: As surely as bribes are baser than any baseness.
TEIRESIAS: You are sick, Creon! You are deathly sick!
CREON: As you say: it is not my place to challenge a prophet.
TEIRESIAS: Yet you have said my prophecy is for sale.   60
CREON: The generation of prophets has always loved gold.
TEIRESIAS: The generation of kings has always loved brass.
CREON: You forget yourself! You are speaking to your King.
TEIRESIAS: I know it. You are a king because of me.
CREON: You have a certain skill; but you have sold out.   65
TEIRESIAS: King, you will drive me to words that—
CREON: Say them, say them!
Only remember: I will not pay you for them.
TEIRESIAS: No, you will find them too costly.
CREON: No doubt. Speak:
Whatever you say, you will not change my will.
TEIRESIAS: Then take this, and take it to heart!   70
The time is not far off when you shall pay back
Corpse for corpse, flesh of your own flesh.
You have thrust the child of this world into living night,
You have kept from the gods below the child that is theirs:
The one in a grave before her death, the other,   75
Dead, denied the grave. This is your crime:
And the Furies and the dark gods of Hell
Are swift with terrible punishment for you.

Do you want to buy me now, Creon?

                                  Not many days,
And your house will be full of men and women weeping,   80
And curses will be hurled at you from far
Cities grieving for sons unburied, left to rot
Before the walls of Thebes.

These are my arrows, Creon: they are all for you.
But come, child: lead me home.   (*To* BOY:)   85
Let him waste his fine anger upon younger men.
Maybe he will learn at last
To control a wiser tongue in a better head.   (*Exit* TEIRESIAS)

CHORAGOS: The old man has gone, King, but his words
    Remain to plague us. I am old, too,   90
    But I cannot remember that he was ever false.

CREON: That is true. . . . It troubles me.
    Oh it is hard to give in! but it is worse
    To risk everything for stubborn pride.

CHORAGOS: Creon: take my advice.

CREON: What shall I do?   95

CHORAGOS: Go quickly: free Antigonê from her vault
    And build a tomb for the body of Polyneicês.

CREON: You would have me do this?

CHORAGOS: Creon, yes!
    And it must be done at once: God moves
    Swiftly to cancel the folly of stubborn men.   100

CREON: It is hard to deny the heart! But I
    Will do it: I will not fight with destiny.

CHORAGOS: You must go yourself, you cannot leave it to others.

CREON: I will go.
              —Bring axes, servants:
Come with me to the tomb. I buried her, I   105
Will set her free.
            Oh quickly!
My mind misgives—
The laws of the gods are mighty, and a man must serve them
To the last day of his life!   (*Exit* CREON)

PÆAN

CHORAGOS: God of many names   (STROPHE 1)

CHORUS: O Iacchos
                     son
of Kadmeian Sémelê
          O born of the Thunder!

Guardian of the West
                    Regent
of Eleusis' plain
                    O Prince of maenad Thebes
and the Dragon Field by rippling Ismenos: 5
CHORAGOS: God of many names   (ANTISTROPHE 1)
CHORUS: the flame of torches
  flares on our hills
                    the nymphs of Iacchos
  dance at the spring of Castalia:

  from the vine-close mountain
                          come ah come in ivy:
  Evohé evohé! sings through the streets of Thebes   10
CHORAGOS: God of many names   (STROPHE 2)
CHORUS: Iacchos of Thebes
  heavenly Child
            of Sémelê bride of the Thunderer!
  The shadow of plague is upon us:
                          come
  with clement feet
                    oh come from Parnasos
  down the long slopes
                    across the lamenting water   15
CHORAGOS: Iô Fire! Chorister of the throbbing stars!   (ANTISTROPHE 2)
  O purest among the voices of the night!
  Thou son of God, blaze for us!
CHORUS: Come with choric rapture of circling Maenads
  Who cry *Iô Iacche!*

                    God of many names!   20

  ## ÉXODOS

  (*Enter* MESSENGER, *L.*)

MESSENGER: Men of the line of Kadmos, you who live
  Near Amphion's citadel:
                    I cannot say
  Of any condition of human life "This is fixed,
  This is clearly good, or bad." Fate raises up,
  And Fate casts down the happy and unhappy alike: 5
  No man can foretell his Fate.
                    Take the case of Creon:
  Creon was happy once, as I count happiness:
  Victorious in battle, sole governor of the land,
  Fortunate father of children nobly born.
  And now it has all gone from him! Who can say   10

That a man is still alive when his life's joy fails?
He is a walking dead man. Grant him rich,
Let him live like a king in his great house:
If his pleasure is gone, I would not give
So much as the shadow of smoke for all he owns.   15
CHORAGOS: Your words hint at sorrow: what is your news for us?
MESSENGER: They are dead. The living are guilty of their death.
CHORAGOS: Who is guilty? Who is dead? Speak!
MESSENGER: Haimon.
    Haimon is dead; and the hand that killed him
    Is his own hand.
CHORAGOS: His father's? or his own?   20
MESSENGER: His own, driven mad by the murder his father had done.
CHORAGOS: Teiresias, Teiresias, how clearly you saw it all!
MESSENGER: This is my news: you must draw what conclusions you can from it.
CHORAGOS: But look: Eurydicê, our Queen:
    Has she overheard us?   25

(*Enter* EURYDICE *from the Palace, C.*)

EURYDICE: I have heard something, friends:
    As I was unlocking the gate of Pallas' shrine,
    For I needed her help today, I heard a voice
    Telling of some new sorrow. And I fainted
    There at the temple with all my maidens about me.   30
    But speak again: whatever it is, I can bear it:
    Grief and I are no strangers.
MESSENGER: Dearest Lady,
    I will tell you plainly all that I have seen.
    I shall not try to comfort you: what is the use,
    Since comfort could lie only in what is not true?   35
    The truth is always best.
            I went with Creon
    To the outer plain where Polyneicês was lying,
    No friend to pity him, his body shredded by dogs.
    We made our prayers in that place to Hecatê
    And Pluto, that they would be merciful. And we bathed   40
    The corpse with holy water, and we brought
    Fresh-broken branches to burn what was left of it,
    And upon the urn we heaped up a towering barrow
    Of the earth of his own land.
          When we were done, we ran
    To the vault where Antigonê lay on her couch of stone.   45
    One of the servants had gone ahead,
    And while he was yet far off he heard a voice
    Grieving within the chamber, and he came back

And told Creon. And as the King went closer,
The air was full of wailing, the words lost,   50
And he begged us to make all haste. "Am I a prophet?"
He said, weeping, "And must I walk this road,
The saddest of all that I have gone before?
My son's voice calls me on. Oh quickly, quickly!
Look through the crevice there, and tell me   55
If it is Haimon, or some deception of the gods!"

We obeyed; and in the cavern's farthest corner
We saw her lying:
She had made a noose of her fine linen veil
And hanged herself. Haimon lay beside her,   60
His arms about her waist, lamenting her,
His love lost under ground, crying out
That his father had stolen her away from him.

When Creon saw him the tears rushed to his eyes
And he called to him: "What have you done, child? Speak to me.   65
What are you thinking that makes your eyes so strange?
O my son, my son, I come to you on my knees!"
But Haimon spat in his face. He said not a word,
Staring—
        And suddenly drew his sword
And lunged. Creon shrank back, the blade missed; and the boy,   70
Desperate against himself, drove it half its length
Into his own side, and fell. And as he died
He gathered Antigonê close in his arms again,
Choking, his blood bright red on her white cheek.
And now he lies dead with the dead, and she is his   75
At last, his bride in the houses of the dead.   (*Exit* EURYDICE *into the Palace*)

CHORAGOS: She has left us without a word. What can this mean?
MESSENGER: It troubles me, too; yet she knows what is best,
Her grief is too great for public lamentation,
And doubtless she has gone to her chamber to weep   80
For her dead son, leading her maidens in his dirge.

CHORAGOS: It may be so: but I fear this deep silence.   (*Pause*)
MESSENGER: I will see what she is doing. I will go in.

(*Exit* MESSENGER *into the Palace*)

(*Enter* CREON *with attendants, bearing* HAIMON's *body*)

CHORAGOS: But here is the King himself: oh look at him,
Bearing his own damnation in his arms.   85
CREON: Nothing you say can touch me any more.
My own blind heart has brought me

From darkness to final darkness. Here you see
The father murdering, the murdered son—
And all my civic wisdom!   90

Haimon my son, so young, so young to die,
I was the fool, not you; and you died for me.
CHORAGOS: That is the truth; but you were late in learning it.
CREON: This truth is hard to bear. Surely a god
Has crushed me beneath the hugest weight of heaven,
And driven me headlong a barbaric way   95
To trample out the thing I held most dear.

The pains that men will take to come to pain!

(*Enter* MESSENGER *from the Palace*)

MESSENGER: The burden you carry in your hands is heavy,
But it is not all: you will find more in your house.
CREON: What burden worse than this shall I find there?   100
MESSENGER: The Queen is dead.
CREON: O port of death, deaf world,
Is there no pity for me? And you, Angel of evil,
I was dead, and your words are death again.
Is it true, boy? Can it be true?   105
Is my wife dead? Has death bred death?
MESSENGER: You can see for yourself.

(*The doors are opened, and the body of* EURYDICE *is disclosed within.*)

CREON: Oh pity!
All true, all true, and more than I can bear!   110
O my wife, my son!
MESSENGER: She stood before the altar, and her heart
Welcomed the knife her own hand guided,
And a great cry burst from her lips for Megareus dead,
And for Haimon dead, her sons; and her last breath   115
Was a curse for their father, the murderer of her sons.
And she fell, and the dark flowed in through her closing eyes.
CREON: O god, I am sick with fear.
Are there no swords here? Has no one a blow for me?
MESSENGER: Her curse is upon you for the deaths of both.   120
CREON: It is right that it should be. I alone am guilty.
I know it, and I say it. Lead me in,
Quickly, friends.
I have neither life nor substance. Lead me in.
CHORAGOS: You are right, if there can be right in so much wrong.   125
The briefest way is best in a world of sorrow.

CREON: Let it come,
  Let death come quickly, and be kind to me.
  I would not ever see the sun again.
CHORAGOS: All that will come when it will; but we, meanwhile,   130
  Have much to do. Leave the future to itself.
CREON: All my heart was in that prayer!
CHORAGOS: Then do not pray any more: the sky is deaf.
CREON: Lead me away. I have been rash and foolish.
  I have killed my son and my wife.   135
  I look for comfort; my comfort lies here dead.
  Whatever my hands have touched has come to nothing.
  Fate has brought all my pride to a thought of dust.

  (*As* CREON *is being led into the house, the* CHORAGOS *advances and speaks
  directly to the audience*)

CHORAGOS: There is no happiness where there is no wisdom;
  No wisdom but in submission to the gods.   140
  Big words are always punished,
  And proud men in old age learn to be wise.

                                                    [441 B.C.]

Journal Entry

What knowledge of Greek history and culture do you bring to your reading of this play?
Should individuals obey the law under any circumstances, or in what cases can you justify
expressions of civil disobedience?

Textual Considerations

1. A "foil" is a contrasting character that helps to define another. To what extent is Ismene a
   foil to Antigone? What arguments do the sisters communicate in the opening debate of
   the play? Which side of the argument do you support?
2. What is the function of the Chorus? Summarize the argument of the *Párodos*, the entrance
   of the chanting Chorus. What does this poetic ode add to the play as a whole? Can you
   explain how a tragic event like the brothers' death in *Antigone* or the attacks of September 11, 2001, in the United States have been or eventually will be transmuted into poetry,
   legend, and myth?
3. Read Creon's speech to the Chorus in scene I and summarize the main principles of
   Creon's political philosophy. Compare Creon's political platform with that of your city's
   mayor, the governor of your state, the president of your country, or any other current
   ruler. Have Creon's principles changed much?
4. What arguments do Creon and Teiresias use against each other? What does their debate
   express about their physical characteristics, their personality traits, and the position they
   occupy as ruler and subject? After careful reading of this debate, do you understand the
   position prophets occupied in ancient Greece? What function did Teiresias fulfill in
   ancient Greek society?

5. What does the debate between Creon and Haimon reveal about their father–son relationship? About their political ideas? About their concern for Antigone? What does Haimon mean when he says that his concern is not only for Antigone but "for you (Creon), / And for me. And for the gods under the earth." Analyze this in view of the Greeks' ideal of individual and social harmony.

Cultural Contexts

1. Debate whether Creon's right to legislate and maintain order versus Antigone's right to bury her brother, follow her conscience, and defend the gods might represent equal dangers to the state. Can you think of two leaders, two nations, or two cultures or civilizations that demonstrate the same inability to negotiate, cooperate with each other, or use a political language? What is your assessment of people's inability to interact, engage in dialogue, or understand each other? Identify the voices of moderation in the play and in your society.

2. Discuss the interplay of gender and power with your group. How do gender relations between Creon and Antigone shape the outcome of Creon's decision about his enemy? Does the fact that Creon's enemy is a woman bother him? What does gender reveal about Creon's real power?

Performance Exercises

PERFORMANCE EXPRESS (45 MINUTES)

Prepare an improvisational and spontaneous dialogue from *Antigone*; Creon's and Haimon's debate would be a good choice. Use classroom props to simulate the set of the palace. Present the dialogue to the whole class.

PERFORMANCE PROJECTS

1. French playwright Jean Anouilh communicates in his reinterpretation of *Antigone*, written in occupied France in 1944, the major struggle of his generation: the war of the French resistance against the Nazi invaders. Discuss what Antigone means for your generation. Then stage a production of one scene, which your group has rewritten and adapted to highlight what you consider one of the major concerns of your generation. You may also think in terms of current conflicts between individual autonomy versus American identity or individual freedom versus public security. Decide on the casting of classmates for the main roles, the size of the chorus, and its choreography.

2. Stage an all-male performance of *Antigone* in which the brothers, Eteoclês and Polyneicês, are cast as the survivors of the House of Oedipus and the sisters, Antigone and Ismene, are referred to as the dead warriors. Rewrite one scene of the play; after staging it, discuss whether your gender-reversal production has changed your classmates' dramatic expectations about the play.

Edward Albee

The Zoo Story

THE PLAYERS

PETER: *A man in his early forties, neither fat nor gaunt, neither handsome nor homely. He wears tweeds, smokes a pipe, carries hornrimmed glasses. Although he is moving into middle age, his dress and his manner would suggest a man younger.*

JERRY: *A man in his late thirties, not poorly dressed, but carelessly. What was once a trim and lightly muscled body has begun to go to fat; and while he is no longer handsome, it is evident that he once was. His fall from physical grace should not suggest debauchery; he has, to come closest to it, a great weariness.*

THE SCENE:

It is Central Park; a Sunday afternoon in summer; the present. There are two park benches, one toward either side of the stage; they both face the audience. Behind them: foliage, trees, sky. At the beginning, Peter is sealed on one of the benches.

    Stage Directions: As the curtain rises, PETER *is seated on the bench stage-right. He is reading a book. He stops reading, cleans his glasses, goes back to reading.* JERRY *enters.*

JERRY: I've been to the zoo. (PETER *doesn't notice*) I said, I've been to the zoo. MISTER, I'VE BEEN TO THE ZOO!

PETER: Hm? . . .[1] What? . . . I'm sorry, were you talking to me?

JERRY: I went to the zoo, and then I walked until I came here. Have I been walking north?

PETER: (*Puzzled*) North? Why . . . I . . . I think so. Let me see.

JERRY: (*Pointing past the audience*) Is that Fifth Avenue?

PETER: Why yes; yes, it is.

JERRY: And what is that cross street there; that one, to the right?

PETER: That? Oh, that's Seventy-fourth Street.

JERRY: And the zoo is around Sixty-fifth Street; so, I've been walking north.

PETER: (*Anxious to get back to his reading*) Yes; it would seem so.

JERRY: Good old north.

PETER: (*Lightly, by reflex*) Ha, ha.

JERRY: (*After a slight pause*) But not due north.

PETER: I . . . well, no, not due north: but, we . . . call it north. It's northerly.

---

[1] Here, and throughout, the ellipsis points are Albee's.

JERRY: (*Watches as* PETER, *anxious to dismiss him, prepares his pipe*) Well, boy; you're not going to get lung cancer, are you?

PETER: (*Looks up, a little annoyed, then smiles*) No, sir. Not from this.

JERRY: No, sir. What you'll probably get is cancer of the mouth, and then you'll have to wear one of those things Freud wore after they took one whole side of his jaw away. What do they call those things?

PETER: (*Uncomfortable*) A prosthesis?

JERRY: The very thing! A prosthesis. You're an educated man, aren't you? Are you a doctor?

PETER: Oh, no; no. I read about it somewhere; *Time* magazine, I think. (*He turns to his book*)

JERRY: Well, *Time Magazine* isn't for blockheads.

PETER: No, I suppose not.

JERRY: (*After a pause*) Boy, I'm glad that's Fifth Avenue there.

PETER: (*Vagaely*) Yes.

JERRY: I don't like the west side of the park much.

PETER: Oh? (*Then, slightly wary, but interested*) Why?

JERRY: (*Offhand*) I don't know.

PETER: Oh. (*He returns to his book*)

JERRY: (*He stands for a few seconds, looking at* PETER, *who finally looks up again, puzzled*) Do you mind if we talk?

PETER: (*Obviously minding*) Why . . . no, no.

JERRY: Yes you do; you do.

PETER: (*Puts his book down, his pipe out and away, smiling*) No, really; I don't mind.

JERRY: Yes you do.

PETER: (*Finally decided*) No; I don't mind at all, really.

JERRY: It's . . . it's a nice day.

PETER: (*Stares unnecessarily at the sky*) Yes. Yes, it is; lovely.

JERRY: I've been to the zoo.

PETER: Yes, I think you said so . . . didn't you?

JERRY: You'll read about it in the papers tomorrow, if you don't see it on your TV tonight. You have TV, haven't you?

PETER: Why yes, we have two; one for the children.

JERRY: You're married!

PETER: (*With pleased emphasis*) Why, certainly.

JERRY: It isn't a law, for God's sake.

PETER: No . . . no, of course not.

JERRY: And you have a wife.

PETER: (*Bewildered by the seeming lack of communication*) Yes!

JERRY: And you have children.

PETER: Yes; two.

JERRY: Boys?

PETER: No, girls . . . both girls.

JERRY: But you wanted boys.

PETER: Well . . . naturally, every man wants a son, but . . .

JERRY: (*Lightly mocking*) But that's the way the cookie crumbles?

PETER: (*Annoyed*) I wasn't going to say that.

JERRY: And you're not going to have any more kids, are you?

PETER: (*A bit distantly*) No. No more. (*Then back, and irksome*) Why did you say that? How would you know about that?

JERRY: The way you cross your legs, perhaps; something in the voice. Or maybe I'm just guessing. Is it your wife?

PETER: (*Furious*) That's none of your business! (*A silence*) Do you understand? (JERRY *nods.* PETER *is quiet now*) Well, you're right. We'll have no more children.

JERRY: (*Softly*) That *is* the way the cookie crumbles.

PETER: (*Forgiving*) Yes . . . I guess so.

JERRY: Well, now; what else?

PETER: What were you saying about the zoo . . . that I'd read about it, or see . . . ?

JERRY: I'll tell you about it, soon. Do you mind if I ask you questions?

PETER: Oh, not really.

JERRY: I'll tell you why I do it; I don't talk to many people—except to say like: give me a beer, or where's the john, or what time does the feature go on, or keep your hands to yourself, buddy. You know—things like that.

PETER: I must say I don't . . .

JERRY: But every once in a while I like to talk to somebody, really *talk*; like to get to know somebody, know all about him.

PETER: (*Lightly laughing, still a little uncomfortable*) And am I the guinea pig for today?

JERRY: On a sun-drenched afternoon like this? Who better than a nice married man with two daughters and . . . uh . . . a dog? (PETER *shakes his head*) No? Two dogs. (PETER *shakes his head again*) Hm. No dogs? (PETER *shakes his head, sadly*) Oh, that's a shame. But you look like an animal man. CATS? (PETER *nods his head, ruefully*) Cats! But, that can't be your idea. No, sir. Your wife and daughters? (PETER *nods his head*) Is there anything else I should know?

PETER: (*He has to clear his throat*) There are . . . there are two parakeets. One . . . uh . . . one for each of my daughters.

JERRY: Birds.

PETER: My daughters keep them in a cage in their bedroom.

JERRY: Do they carry disease? The birds?

PETER: I don't believe so.

JERRY: That's too bad. If they did you could set them loose in the house and the cats could eat them and die, maybe. (PETER *looks blank for a moment, then laughs*) And what else? What do you do to support your enormous household?

PETER: I . . . uh . . . I have an executive position with a . . . a small publishing house. We . . . uh . . . we publish textbooks.

JERRY: That sounds nice; very nice. What do you make?

PETER: (*Still cheerful*) Now look here!

JERRY: Oh, come on.

PETER: Well, I make around eighteen thousand a year, but I don't carry more than forty dollars at any one time . . . in case you're a . . . a holdup man . . . ha, ha, ha.

JERRY: (*Ignoring the above*) Where do you live? (PETER *is reluctant*) Oh, look; I'm not going to rob you, and I'm not going to kidnap your parakeets, your cats, or your daughters.

PETER: (*Too loud*) I live between Lexington and Third Avenue, on Seventy-fourth Street.

JERRY: That wasn't so hard, was it?

PETER: I didn't mean to seem . . . ah . . . it's that you don't really carry on a conversation; you just ask questions. And I'm . . . I'm normally . . . uh . . . reticent. Why do you just stand there?

JERRY: I'll start walking around in a little while, and eventually I'll sit down. (*Recalling*) Wait until you see the expression on his face.

PETER: What? Whose face? Look here; is this something about the zoo?

JERRY: (*Distantly*) The what?

PETER: The zoo; the zoo. Something about the zoo.

JERRY: The zoo?

PETER: You mentioned it several times.

JERRY: (*Still distant, but returning abruptly*) The zoo? Oh, yes; the zoo. I was there before I came here. I told you that. Say, what's the dividing line between upper-middle-class and lower-upper-middle-class?

PETER: My dear fellow, I . . .

JERRY: Don't my dear fellow me.

PETER: (*Unhappily*) Was I patronizing? I believe I was; I'm sorry. But, you see, your question about the classes bewildered me.

JERRY: And when you're bewildered you become patronizing?

PETER: I . . . I don't express myself too well, sometimes. (*He attempts a joke on himself*) I'm in publishing, not writing.

JERRY: (*Amused, but not at the humor*) So be it. The truth *is: I* was being patronizing.

PETER: Oh, now; you needn't say that. (*It is at this point that* JERRY *may begin to move about the stage with slowly increasing determination and authority, but pacing himself, so that the long speech about the dog comes at the high point of the arc*).

JERRY: All right. Who are your favorite writers? Baudelaire and J. P. Marquand?[2]

PETER: (*Wary*) Well, I like a great many writers; I have a considerable . . . catholicity of taste, if I may say so. Those two men are fine, each in his way. (*Warming up*) Baudelaire, of course . . . uh . . . is by far the finer of the two, but Marquand has a place . . . in our . . . uh . . . national . . .

JERRY: Skip it.

PETER: I . . . sorry.

JERRY: Do you know what I did before I went to the zoo today? I walked all the way up Fifth Avenue from Washington Square; all the way.

PETER: Oh; you live in the Village! (*This seems to enlighten* PETER)

JERRY: No, I don't. I took the subway down to the Village so I could walk all the way up Fifth Avenue to the zoo. It's one of those things a person has to do;

---

[2] American popular novelist (1893–1960).

sometimes a person has to go a very long distance out of his way to come back a short distance correctly.

PETER: (*Almost pouting*) Oh, I thought you lived in the Village.

JERRY: What were you trying to do? Make sense out of things? Bring order? The old pigeonhole bit? Well, that's easy; I'll tell you. I live in a four-story brownstone rooming-house on the upper West Side between Columbus Avenue and Central Park West. I live on the top floor; rear; west. It's a laughably small room, and one of my walls is made of beaverboard; this beaverboard separates my room from another laughably small room, so I assume that the two rooms were once one room, a small room, but not necessarily laughable. The room beyond my beaverboard wall is occupied by a colored queen who always keeps his door open; well, not always but *always* when he's plucking his eyebrows, which he does with Buddhist concentration. This colored queen has rotten teeth, which is rare, and he has a Japanese kimono, which is also pretty rare; and he wears this kimono to and from the john in the hall, which is pretty frequent. I mean, he goes to the john a lot. He never bothers me, and he never brings anyone up to his room. All he does is pluck his eyebrows, wear his kimono and go to the john. Now, the two front rooms on my floor are a little larger, I guess; but they're pretty small, too. There's a Puerto Rican family in one of them, a husband, a wife, and some kids; I don't know how many. These people entertain a lot. And in the other front room, there's somebody living there, but I don't know who it is. I've never seen who it is. Never. Never ever.

PETER: (*Embarrassed*) Why . . . why do you live there?

JERRY: (*From a distance again*) I don't know.

PETER: It doesn't sound like a very nice place . . . where you live.

JERRY: Well, no; it isn't an apartment in the East Seventies. But, then again, I don't have one wife, two daughters, two cats and two parakeets. What I do have, I have toilet articles, a few clothes, a hot plate that I'm not supposed to have, a can opener, one that works with a key, you know; a knife, two forks, and two spoons, one small, one large; three plates, a cup, a saucer, a drinking glass, two picture frames, both empty, eight or nine books, a pack of pornographic playing cards, regular deck, an old Western Union typewriter that prints nothing but capital letters, and a small strongbox without a lock which has in it . . . what? Rocks! Some rocks . . . sea-rounded rocks I picked up on the beach when I was a kid. Under which . . . weighed down . . . are some letters . . . please letters . . . please why don't you do this, and please when will you do that letters. And when letters, too. When will you write? When will you come? When? These letters are from more recent years.

PETER: (*Stares glumly at his shoes, then*) About those two empty picture frames . . . ?

JERRY: I don't see why they need any explanation at all. Isn't it clear? I don't have pictures of anyone to put in them.

PETER: Your parents . . . perhaps . . . a girl friend . . .

JERRY: You're a very sweet man, and you're possessed of a truly enviable innocence. But good old Mom and good old Pop are dead . . . you know? . . . I'm broken up about it, too . . . I mean really, BUT. That particular vaudeville act is playing the cloud circuit now, so I don't see how I can look at them, all neat and framed. Besides, or, rather, to be pointed about it, good old Mom walked out on good old Pop when I was ten and a half years old; she embarked on an adulterous turn of our southern states . . . a journey of a year's duration . . . and her most constant companion . . . among others, among many others . . . was a Mr. Barleycorn. At least, that's what good old Pop told me after he went down . . . came back . . . brought her body north. We'd received the news between Christmas and New Year's, you see, that good old Mom had parted with the ghost in some dump in Alabama. And, without the ghost . . . she was less welcome. I mean, what was she? A stiff . . . a northern stiff. At any rate, good old Pop celebrated the New Year for an even two weeks and then slapped into the front of a somewhat moving city omnibus, which sort of cleaned things out family-wise. Well no; then there was Mom's sister, who was given neither to sin nor the consolations of the bottle. I moved in on her, and my memory of her is slight excepting I remember still that she did all things dourly: sleeping, eating, working, praying. She dropped dead on the stairs to her apartment, my apartment then, too, on the afternoon of my high school graduation. A terribly middle-European joke, if you ask me.

PETER: Oh, my; oh, my.

JERRY: Oh, your what? But that was a long time ago, and I have no feeling about any of it that I care to admit to myself. Perhaps you can see, though, why good old Mom and good old Pop are frameless. What's your name? Your first name?

PETER: I'm Peter.

JERRY: I'd forgotten to ask you. I'm Jerry.

PETER: (*With a slight, nervous laugh*) Hello, Jerry.

JERRY: (*Nods his hello*) And let's see now; what's the point of having a girl's picture, especially in two frames? I have two picture frames, you remember. I never see the pretty little ladies more than once, and most of them wouldn't be caught in the same room with a camera. It's odd, and I wonder if it's sad.

PETER: The girls?

JERRY: No. I wonder if it's sad that I never see the little ladies more than once. I've never been able to have sex with, or, how is it put? . . . make love to anybody more than once. Once; that's it. . . . Oh, wait; for a week and a half, when I was fifteen . . . and I hang my head in shame that puberty was late . . . I was a h-o-m-o-s-e-x-u-a-l. I mean, I was queer . . . (*Very fast*) . . . queer, queer, queer . . . with bells ringing, banners snapping in the wind. And for those eleven days, I met at least twice a day with the park superintendent's son . . . a Greek boy, whose birthday was the same as mine, except he was a year older. I think I was very much in love . . . maybe just with sex. But that was the jazz of a very special hotel, wasn't it? And now; oh, do I love the little ladies; really, I love them. For about an hour.

PETER: Well, it seems perfectly simple to me. . . .

JERRY: (*Angry*) Look! Are you going to tell me to get married and have parakeets?

PETER: (*Angry himself*) Forget the parakeets! And stay single if you want to. It's no business of mine. I didn't start this conversation in the . . .

JERRY: All right, all right. I'm sorry. All right? You're not angry?

PETER: (*Laughing*) No, I'm not angry.

JERRY: (*Relieved*) Good. (*Now back to his previous tone*) Interesting that you asked me about the picture frames. I would have thought that you would have asked me about the pornographic playing cards.

PETER: (*With a knowing smile*) Oh, I've seen those cards.

JERRY: That's not the point. (*Laughs*) I suppose when you were a kid you and your pals passed them around, or you had a pack of your own.

PETER: Well, I guess a lot of us did.

JERRY: And you threw them away just before you got married.

PETER: Oh, now; look here. I didn't *need* anything like that when I got older.

JERRY: No?

PETER: (*Embarrassed*) I'd rather not talk about these things.

JERRY: So? Don't. Besides, I wasn't trying to plumb your postadolescent sexual life and hard times; what I wanted to get at is the value difference between pornographic playing cards when you're a kid, and pornographic playing cards when you're older. It's that when you're a kid you use the cards as a substitute for a real experience, and when you're older you use real experience as a substitute for the fantasy. But I imagine you'd rather hear about what happened at the zoo.

PETER: (*Enthusiastic*) Oh, yes; the zoo.(*Then, awkward*) That is . . . if you. . . .

JERRY: Let me tell you about why I went . . . well, let me tell you some things. I've told you about the fourth floor of the roominghouse where I live. I think the rooms are better as you go down, floor by floor. I guess they are; I don't know. I don't know any of the people on the third and second floors. Oh, wait! I do know that there's a lady living on the third floor, in the front. I know because she cries all the time. Whenever I go out or come back in, whenever I pass her door, I always hear her crying, muffled, but . . . very determined. Very determined indeed. But the one I'm getting to, and all about the dog, is the landlady. I don't like to use words that are too harsh in describing people. I don't like to. But the landlady is a fat, ugly, mean, stupid, unwashed, misanthropic, cheap, drunken bag of garbage. And you may have noticed that I very seldom use profanity, so I can't describe her as well as I might.

PETER: You describe her . . . vividly.

JERRY: Well, thanks. Anyway, she has a dog, and I will tell you about the dog, and she and her dog are the gatekeepers of my dwelling. The woman is bad enough; she leans around in the entrance hall, spying to see that I don't bring in things or people, and when she's had her midafternoon pint of lemon-flavored gin she always stops me in the hall, and grabs ahold of my coat or my arm, and she presses her disgusting body up against me to keep me in a corner so she can talk to me. The smell of her body and her breath . . . you can't imagine it . . . and somewhere, somewhere in the back of that pea-sized brain of hers, an organ developed just enough to let her eat, drink, and emit, she has some foul parody of sexual desire. And I, Peter, I am the object of her sweaty lust.

PETER: That's disgusting. That's . . . horrible.

JERRY: But I have found a way to keep her off. When she talks to me, when she presses herself to my body and mumbles about her room and how I should come there, I merely say: but, Love; wasn't yesterday enough for you, and the day before? Then she puzzles, she makes slits of her tiny eyes, she sways a little, and then, Peter . . . and it is at this moment that I think I might be doing some good in that tormented house . . . a simple-minded smile begins to form on her unthinkable face, and she giggles and groans as she thinks about yesterday and the day before; as she believes and relives what never happened. Then, she motions to that black monster of a dog she has, and she goes back to her room. And I am safe until our next meeting.

PETER: It's so . . . unthinkable. I find it hard to believe that people such as that really *are*.

JERRY: (*Lightly mocking*) It's for reading about, isn't it?

PETER: (*Seriously*) Yes.

JERRY: And fact is better left to fiction. You're right, Peter. Well, what I have been meaning to tell you about is the dog; I shall, now.

PETER: (*Nervously*) Oh, yes; the dog.

JERRY: Don't go. You're not thinking of going, are you?

PETER: Well . . . no, I don't think so.

JERRY: (*As if to a child*) Because after I tell you about the dog, do you know what then? Then . . . then I'll tell you about what happened at the zoo.

PETER: (*Laughing faintly*) You're . . . you're full of stories, aren't you?

JERRY: You don't *have* to listen. Nobody is holding you here; remember that. Keep that in your mind.

PETER: (*Irritably*) I know that.

JERRY: You do? Good. (*The following long speech, it seems to me, should be done with a great deal of action, to achieve a hypnotic effect on* PETER, *and on the audience, too. Some specific actions have been suggested, but the director and the actor playing* JERRY *might best work it out for themselves*) ALL RIGHT. (*As if reading from a huge billboard*) THE STORY OF JERRY AND THE DOG! (*Natural again*) What I am going to tell you has something to do with how sometimes it's necessary to go a long distance out of the way in order to come back a short distance correctly; or, maybe I only think that it has something to do with that. But, it's why I went to the zoo today, and why I walked north . . . northerly, rather . . . until I came here. All right. The dog, I think I told you, is a black monster of a beast: an oversized head, tiny, tiny ears, and eyes . . . bloodshot, infected, maybe; and a body you can see the ribs through the skin. The dog is black, all black; all black except for the bloodshot eyes, and . . . yes . . . and open sore on its . . . *right* forepaw; that is red, too. And, oh yes; the poor monster, and I do believe it's an old dog . . . it's certainly a misused one . . . almost always has an erection . . . of sorts. That's red, too. And . . . what else? . . . oh, yes; there's a gray-yellow-white color, too, when he bares his fangs. Like this: Grrrrrr! Which is what he did when he saw me for the first time . . . the day I moved in. I worried about that animal the very first minute I met him. Now, animals don't take to me like Saint Francis had birds hanging off him all the time. What I mean is: animals are indifferent to me . . . like people (*He smiles slightly*) . . . most of the time. But this dog wasn't indifferent. From the very beginning he'd snarl and then go for me, to get one of my legs. Not like he was rabid, you know; he was sort of a stumbly dog, but he wasn't half-assed, either. It was a good, stumbly run; but I always got away. He got a piece of my trouser leg, look, you can see right here, where it's mended; he got that the second day I lived there; but, I kicked free and got upstairs fast, so that was that. (*Puzzles*) I still don't know to this day how the other roomers manage it, but you know what I *think:* I think it had to do only with me. Cozy. So. Anyway, this went on for over a week, whenever I came in; but never when I went out. That's funny. Or, it *was* funny. I could pack up and live in the street for all the dog cared. Well, I thought about it up in my room one day, one of the times after I'd bolted upstairs, and I made up my mind. I decided: First, I'll kill the dog with kindness, and if that doesn't work . . . I'll just kill him. (PETER *winces*) Don't react, Peter; just listen. So, the next day I went out and bought a bag of hamburgers, medium rare, no catsup, no onion; and on the way home I threw away the rolls and kept just the meat. (*Action for the following, perhaps*) When I got back to the roominghouse the dog was waiting for me. I half-opened the door that led into the entrance hall, and there he was; waiting for me. It figured. I went in, very cautiously, and I had the hamburgers, you remember; I opened the bag, and I set the meat down about twelve feet from where the dog was snarling at me. Like so! He snarled; stopped snarling; sniffed; moved slowly; then faster; then faster toward the meat. Well, when he got to it he stopped, and he looked at me. I smiled; but tentatively, you understand. He turned his face back to the hamburgers, smelled, sniffed some more, and then . . . RRRAAAAGGGGGHHHH, like that . . . he tore into them. It was as if he had never eaten anything in his life before, except like garbage. Which might very well have been the truth. I don't think the landlady ever eats anything but garbage. But. He ate all the hamburgers, almost all at once, making sounds in his throat like a woman. *Then*, when he'd finished the meat, the hamburger, and tried to eat the paper, too, he sat down and smiled. I think he smiled; I know cats do. It was a very gratifying few moments. Then, BAM, he snarled and made for me again. He didn't get me this time, either. So, I got upstairs, and I lay down on my bed and started to think about the dog again. To be truthful, I was offended, and I was damn mad, too. It was six perfectly good hamburgers with not enough pork in them to make it disgusting. I was offended. But, after a while, I decided to try it for a few more days. If you think about it, this dog had what amounted to an antipathy toward me; really. And, I wondered if I mightn't overcome this antipathy. So, I tried it for five more days, but it was always the same: snarl; sniff: move; faster; stare; gobble; RAAGGGHHH; smile; snarl; BAM. Well, now; by this time Columbus Avenue was strewn with hamburger rolls and I was less offended than disgusted. So, I decided to kill the dog. (PETER *raises a hand in protest*) Oh, don't be so alarmed, Peter; I didn't succeed. The day I tried to kill the dog I bought only one hamburger and what I thought was a murderous portion of rat poison. When I bought the hamburger I asked the man not to bother with the roll, all I wanted was the meat. I expected some reaction from him, like: we don't sell no hamburgers without rolls; or, wha' d'ya wanna do, eat it out'a ya han's? But no; he smiled benignly, wrapped up the hamburger in waxed paper, and said: A bite for ya pussy-cat? I wanted to say: No, not really; it's part of a plan to poison a dog I know. But, you can't say "a dog I know" without sounding funny; so I said, a little too loud, I'm afraid, and too formally: YES, A BITE FOR MY PUSSY-CAT. People looked up. It always happens when I try to simplify things: people look up. But that's neither hither nor thither. So. On my way back to the roominghouse, I kneaded the hamburger and the rat poison together between my hands, at that point feeling as much sadness as disgust. I opened the door to the entrance hall, and there the monster was, waiting to take the offering and then jump me. Poor bastard; he never learned that the moment he took to smile before he went for me gave me time enough to get out of range. BUT, there he was; malevolence with an erection, waiting. I put the poison patty down, moved toward the stairs and watched. The poor animal gobbled the food down as usual, smiled, which made me almost sick, and then, BAM. But, I sprinted up the stairs, as usual, and the dog didn't get me, as usual. AND IT CAME TO PASS THAT THE BEAST WAS DEATHLY ILL. I knew this because he no longer attended me, and because the landlady sobered up. She stopped me in the hall the same evening of the attempted murder and confided the information that God had struck her puppy-dog a surely fatal blow. She had forgotten her bewildered lust, and her eyes were wide open for the first time. They looked like the dog's eyes. She sniveled and implored me to pray for the animal. I wanted to say to her: Madam, I have myself to pray for, the colored queen, the Puerto Rican family, the person in the front room whom I've never seen, the woman who cries deliberately behind her closed door, and the rest of the people in all rooming-houses, everywhere; besides, Madam, I don't understand how to pray. But . . . to simplify things . . . I told her I would pray. She looked up. She said that I was a liar, and that I probably wanted the dog to die. I told her, and there was so much truth here, that I didn't want the dog to die. I didn't, and not just because I'd poisoned him. I'm afraid that I must tell you I wanted the dog to live so that I could see what our new relationship might come to. (PETER *indicates his increasing displeasure and slowly growing antagonism*) Please understand, Peter; that sort of thing is important. You must believe me; it *is* important. We have to know the effect of our actions. (*Another deep sigh*) Well, anyway; the dog recovered. I have no idea why, unless he was a descendant of the puppy that guarded the gates of hell or some such resort. I'm not up on my mythology. (*He pronounces the word myth-o-*logy) Are you? (PETER *sets to thinking, but* JERRY *goes on*) At any rate, and you've missed the eight-thousand-dollar question, Peter; at any rate, the dog recovered his health and the landlady recovered her thirst, in no way altered by the bow-wow's deliverance. When I came home from a movie that was playing on Forty-second Street, a movie I'd seen, or one that was very much like one or several I'd seen, after the landlady told me puppykins was better, I was so hoping for the dog to be waiting for me.

I was . . . well, how would you put it . . . enticed? . . . fascinated? . . . no, I don't think so . . . heart-shatteringly anxious, that's it; I was heart-shatteringly anxious to confront my friend again. (PETER *reacts scoffingly*) Yes, Peter; friend. That's the only word for it. I was heart-shatteringly et cetera to confront my doggy friend again. I came in the door and advanced, unafraid, to the center of the entrance hall. The beast was there . . . looking at me. And, you know, he looked better for his scrape with the nevermind. I stopped; I looked at him; he looked at me. I think . . . I think we stayed a long time that way . . . still, stone-statue . . . just looking at one another. I looked more into his face than he looked into mine. I mean, I can concentrate longer at looking into a dog's face than a dog can concentrate at looking into mine, or into anybody else's face, for that matter. But during that twenty seconds or two hours that we looked into each other's face, we made contact. Now, here is what I had wanted to happen: I loved the dog now, and I wanted him to love me. I had tried to love, and I had tried to kill, and both had been unsuccessful by themselves. I hoped . . . and I don't really know why I expected the dog to understand anything, much less my motiva-tions . . . I hoped that the dog would understand. (PETER *seems to be hypnotized*) It's just . . . it's just that . . . (JERRY *is abnormally tense, now*) . . . it's just that if you can't deal with people, you have to make a start somewhere. WITH ANIMALS! (*Much faster now, and like a conspirator*) Don't you see? A person has to have some way of dealing with SOMETHING. If not with people . . . if not with people . . . SOMETHING. With a bed, with a cockroach, with a mirror . . . no, that's too hard, that's one of the last steps. With a cockroach, with a . . . with a . . . with a carpet, a roll of toilet paper . . . no, not that, either . . . that's a mirror, too; always check bleeding. You see how hard it is to find things? With a street corner, and too many lights, all colors reflecting on the oily-wet streets . . . with a wisp of smoke, a wisp . . . of smoke . . . with . . . with pornographic playing cards, with a strongbox . . . WITHOUT A LOCK . . . with love, with vomiting, with crying, with fury because the pretty little ladies aren't pretty little ladies, with making money with your body which is an act of love and I could prove it, with howling because you're alive; with God. How about that? WITH GOD WHO IS A COLORED QUEEN WHO WEARS A KIMONO AND PLUCKS HIS EYEBROWS, WHO IS A WOMAN WHO CRIES WITH DETERMINATION BEHIND HER CLOSED DOOR . . . with God who, I'm told, turned his back on the whole thing some time ago . . . with . . . some day, with people. (JERRY *sighs the next word heavily*) People. With an idea; a concept. And where better, where ever better in this humiliating excuse for a jail, where better to communicate one single, simple-minded idea than in an entrance hall? Where? It would be A START! Where better to make a begin-ning . . . to understand and just possibly be understood . . . a beginning of an understanding, that with . . . (Here JERRY *seems to fall into almost grotesque fatigue*) . . . than with A DOG. Just that; a dog. (Here *there is a silence that might be prolonged for a moment or so; then* JERRY *wearily finishes his story*) A dog. It seemed like a perfectly sensible idea. Man is a dog's best friend, remember. So: the dog and I looked at each other. I longer than the dog. And what I saw then has been the same ever since. Whenever the dog and I see each other we both stop where we are. We regard each other with a mixture of sadness and suspicion, and then we feign indifference. We walk past each other safely; we have an understanding. It's very sad, but you'll have to admit that it is an understanding. We had made many attempts at contact, and we had failed. The dog has returned to garbage, and I to solitary but free passage. I have not returned. I mean to say, I have *gained* solitary free passage, if that much further loss can be said to be gain. I have learned that neither kindness nor cruelty by themselves, independent of each other, creates any effect beyond themselves; and I have learned that the two combined, together, at the same time, are the teaching emotion. And what is gained is loss. And what has been the result: the dog and I have attained a compromise; more of a bargain, really. We neither love nor hurt because we do not try to reach each other. And, *was* trying to feed the dog an act of love? And, perhaps, was the dog's attempt to bite me *not* an act of love? If we can so misunderstand, well then, why have we invented the word love in the first place? (*There is silence.* JERRY *moves to* PETER'*s bench and sits down beside him. This is the first time* JERRY *has sat down during the play*) The Story of Jerry and the Dog; the end. (PETER *is silent*) Well, Peter? (JERRY *is suddenly cheerful*) Well, Peter? Do you think I could sell that story to the *Reader's Digest* and make a couple of hundred bucks for *The Most Unforgettable Character I've Ever Met?* Huh? (JERRY *is animated, but* PETER *is disturbed*) Oh, come on now, Peter; tell me what you think.

PETER: (*Numb*) I . . . I don't understand what . . . I don't think I . . . (*Now, almost tearfully*) Why did you tell me all of this?

JERRY: Why not?

PETER: I DON'T UNDERSTAND!

JERRY: (*Furious, but whispering*) That's a lie.

PETER: No. No, it's not.

JERRY: (*Quietly*) I tried to explain it to you as I went along. I went slowly; it all has to do with . . .

PETER: I DON'T WANT TO HEAR ANY MORE. I don't understand you, or your landlady, or her dog. . . .

JERRY: *Her* dog! I thought it was my . . . No. No, you're right. It *is* her dog. (*Looks at* PETER *intently, shaking his head*) I don't know what I was thinking about; of course you don't understand. (*In a monotone, wearily*) I don't live in your block; I'm not married to two parakeets, or whatever your setup is. I am a *permanent transient*, and my home is the sickening roominghouses on the West Side of New York City, which is the greatest city in the world. Amen.

PETER: I'm . . . I'm sorry; I didn't mean to . . .

JERRY: Forget it. I suppose you don't quite know what to make of me, eh?

PETER: (*A joke*) We get all kinds in publishing. (*Chuckles*)

JERRY: You're a funny man. (*He forces a laugh*) You know that? You're a very . . . a richly comic person.

PETER: (*Modestly, but amused*) Oh, now, not really. (*Still chuckling*)

JERRY: Peter, do I annoy you, or confuse you?

PETER: (*Lightly*) Well, I must confess that this wasn't the kind of afternoon I'd anticipated.

JERRY: You mean, I'm not the gentleman you were expecting.

PETER: I wasn't expecting anybody.

JERRY: No, I don't imagine you were. But I'm here, and I'm not leaving.

PETER: (*Consulting his watch*) Well, you may not be, but I must be getting home soon.

JERRY: Oh, come on; stay a while longer.

PETER: I really should get home; you see . . .

JERRY: (*Tickles* PETER'S *ribs with his fingers*) Oh, come on.

PETER: (*He is very ticklish; as* JERRY *continues to tickle him his voice becomes falsetto*) No, I . . . OHHHHH! Don't do that. Stop, Stop. Ohhh, no, no.

JERRY: Oh, come on.

PETER: (*As* JERRY *tickles*) Oh, hee, hee, hee. I must go. I . . . hee, hee, hee. After all, stop, stop, hee, hee, hee, after all, the parakeets will be getting dinner ready soon. Hee, hee. And the cats are setting the table. Stop, stop, and, and . . . (PETER *is beside himself now*) . . . and we're having . . . hee, hee . . . uh . . . ho, ho, ho. (JERRY *stops tickling* PETER, *but the combination of the tickling and his own mad whimsy has* PETER *laughing almost hysterically. As his laughter continues, then subsides,* JERRY *watches him, with a curious fixed smile*)

JERRY: Peter?

PETER: Oh, ha, ha, ha, ha, ha. What? What?

JERRY: Listen, now.

PETER: Oh, ho, ho. What . . . what is it, Jerry? Oh, my.

JERRY: (*Mysteriously*) Peter, do you want to know what happened at the zoo?

PETER: Ah, ha, ha. The what? Oh, yes; the zoo. Oh, ho, ho. Well, I had my own zoo there for a moment with . . . hee, hee, the parakeets getting dinner ready, and the . . . ha, ha, whatever it was, the . . .

JERRY: (*Calmly*) Yes, that was very funny, Peter. I wouldn't have expected it. But do you want to hear about what happened at the zoo, or not?

PETER: Yes. Yes, by all means; tell me what happened at the zoo. Oh, my. I don't know what happened to me.

JERRY: Now I'll let you in on what happened at the zoo; but first, I should tell you why I went to the zoo. I went to the zoo to find out more about the way people exist with animals, and the way animals exist with each other, and with people too. It probably wasn't a fair test, what with everyone separated by bars from everyone else, the animals for the most part from each other, and always the people from the animals. But, if it's a zoo, that's the way it is. (*He pokes* PETER *on the arm*) Move over.

PETER: (*Friendly*) I'm sorry, haven't you enough room? (*He shifts a little*)

JERRY: (*Smiling slightly*) Well, all the animals are there, and all the people are there, and it's Sunday and all the children are there. (*He pokes* PETER *again*) Move over.

PETER: (*Patiently, still friendly*) All right. (*He moves some more, and* JERRY *has all the room he might need*)

JERRY.   And it's a hot day, so all the stench is there, too, and all the balloon sellers, and all the ice cream sellers, and all the seals are barking; and all the birds are screaming. (*Pokes* PETER *harder*) Move over!

PETER: (*Beginning to be annoyed*) Look here, you have more than enough room! (*But he moves more, and is now fairly cramped at one end of the bench*)

JERRY: And I am there, and it's feeding time at the lions' house, and the lion keeper comes into the lion cage, one of the lion cages, to feed one of the lions. (*Punches* PETER *on the arm, hard*) MOVE OVER!

PETER: (*Very annoyed*) I can't move over any more, and stop hitting me. What's the matter with you?

JERRY: Do you want to hear the story? (*Punches* PETER'S *arm again*)

PETER: (*Flabbergasted*) I'm not so sure! I certainly don't want to be punched in the arm.

JERRY: (*Punches* PETER'S *arm again*) Like that?

PETER: Stop it! What's the matter with you?

JERRY: I'm crazy, you bastard.

PETER: That isn't funny.

JERRY: Listen to me, Peter. I want this bench. You go sit on the bench over there, and if you're good I'll tell you the rest of the story.

PETER: (*Flustered*) But . . . whatever for? What *is* the matter with you? Besides, I see no reason why I should give up this bench. I sit on this bench almost every Sunday afternoon, in good weather. It's secluded here; there's never anyone sitting here, so I have it all to myself.

JERRY: (*Softly*) Get off this bench, Peter; I want it.

PETER: (*Almost whining*) No.

JERRY: I said I want this bench, and I'm going to have it. Now get over there.

PETER: People can't have everything they want. You should know that; it's a rule; people can have some of the things they want, but they can't have everything.

JERRY: (*Laughs*) Imbecile! You're slow-witted!

PETER: Stop that!

JERRY: You're a vegetable! Go lie down on the ground.

PETER: (*Intense*) Now *you* listen to me. I've put up with you all afternoon.

JERRY: Not really.

PETER: LONG ENOUGH. I've put up with you long enough. I've listened to you because you seemed . . . well, because I thought you wanted to talk to somebody.

JERRY: You put things well; economically, and, yet . . . oh, what is the word I want to put justice to your . . . JESUS, you make me sick . . . get off here and give me my bench.

PETER: MY BENCH!

JERRY: (*Pushes* PETER *almost, but not quite, off the bench*) Get out of my sight.

PETER: (*Regarding his position*) God da . . . mn you. That's enough! I've had enough of you. I will not give up this bench; you can't have it, and that's that. Now, go away (JERRY *snorts but does not move*) Go away, I said. (JERRY *does not move*) Get away from here. If you don't move on . . . you're a bum . . . that's what you are. . . . If you don't move on, I'll get a policeman here and make you go. (JERRY *laughs, stays*) I warn you. I'll call a policeman.

JERRY: (*Softly*) You won't find a policeman around here; they're all over the west side of the park chasing fairies down from trees or out of the bushes. That's all they do. That's their function. So scream your head off; it won't do you any good.

PETER: POLICE! I warn you, I'll have you arrested. POLICE! (*Pause*) I said POLICE! (*Pause*) I feel ridiculous.

JERRY: You look ridiculous: a grown man screaming for the police on a bright Sunday afternoon in the park with nobody harming you. If a policeman *did* fill his quota and come sludging over this way he'd probably take you in as a nut.

PETER: (*With disgust and impotence*) Great God, I just came here to read, and now you want me to give up the bench. You're mad.

JERRY: Hey, I got news for you, as they say. I'm on your precious bench, and you're never going to have it for yourself again.

PETER: (*Furious*) Look, you; get off my bench. I don't care if it makes any sense or not. I want this bench to myself; I want you OFF IT!

JERRY: (*Mocking*) Aw . . . look who's mad.

PETER: GET OUT!

JERRY: No.

PETER: I WARN YOU!

JERRY: Do you know how ridiculous you look *now*?

PETER: (*His fury and self-consciousness have possessed him*) It doesn't matter. (*He is almost crying*) GET AWAY FROM MY BENCH!

JERRY: Why? You have everthing in the world you want; you've told me about your home, and your family, and *your own* little zoo. You have everything, and now you want this bench. Are these the things men fight for? Tell me, Peter, is this bench, this iron and this wood, is this your honor? Is this the thing in the world you'd fight for? Can you think of anything more absurd?

PETER: Absurd? Look, I'm not going to talk to you about honor, or even try to explain it to you. Besides, it isn't a question of honor; but even if it were, you wouldn't understand.

JERRY: (*Contemptuously*) You don't even know what you're saying, do you? This is probably the first time in your life you've had anything more trying to face than changing your cat's toilet box. Stupid! Don't you have any idea, not even the slightest, what other people *need*?

PETER: Oh, boy, listen to you; well, you don't need this bench. That's for sure.

JERRY: Yes; yes, I do.

PETER: (*Quivering*) I've come here for years; I have hours of great pleasure, great satisfaction, right here. And that's important to a man. I'm a responsible person, and I'm a GROWNUP. This is my bench, and you have no right to take it away from me.

JERRY: Fight for it, then. Defend yourself; defend your bench.

PETER: You've *pushed* me to it. Get up and fight.

JERRY: Like a man?

PETER: (*Still angry*) Yes, like a man, if you insist on mocking me even further.

JERRY: I'll have to give you credit for one thing; you *are* a vegetable, and a slightly nearsighted one, I think . . .

PETER: THAT'S ENOUGH.

JERRY: . . . but, you know, as they say on TV all the time—you know—and I mean this, Peter, you have a certain dignity; it surprises me. . . .

PETER: STOP!

JERRY: (*Rises lazily*) Very well, Peter, we'll battle for the bench, but we're not evenly matched. (*He takes out and clicks open an ugly-looking knife*)

PETER: (*Suddenly awakening to the reality of the situation*) You *are* mad! You're stark raving mad! YOU'RE GOING TO KILL ME! (*But before* PETER *has time to think what to do,* JERRY *tosses the knife at* PETER'S *feet*)

JERRY: There you go. Pick it up. You have the knife and we'll be more evenly matched.

PETER: (*Horrified*) No!

JERRY: (*Rushes over to* PETER, *grabs him by the collar*; PETER *rises; their faces almost touch*) Now you pick up that knife and you fight with me. You fight for your self-respect; you fight for that goddamned bench.

PETER: (*Struggling*) No! Let . . . let go of me! He . . . Help!

JERRY: (*Slaps* PETER *on each "fight"*) You fight, you miserable bastard; fight for that bench; fight for your parakeets; fight for your cats; fight for your two daughters; fight for your wife; fight for your manhood, you pathetic little vegetable. (*Spits in* PETER'S *face*) You couldn't even get your wife with a male child.

PETER: (*Breaks away, enraged*) It's a matter of genetics, not manhood, you . . . you monster. (*He darts down, picks up the knife and backs off a little; he is breathing heavily*) I'll give you one last chance; get out of here and leave me alone! (*He holds the knife with a firm arm, but far in front of him, not to attack, but to defend*)

JERRY: (*Sighs heavily*) So be it! (*With a rush he charges* PETER *and impales himself on the knife. Tableau: For just a moment, complete silence,* JERRY *impaled on the knife at the end of* PETER'S *still firm arm. Then* PETER *screams, pulls away, leaving the knife in* JERRY. JERRY *is motionless, on point. Then he, too, screams, and it must be the sound of an infuriated and fatally wounded animal. With the knife in him, he stumbles back to the bench that* PETER *had vacated. He crumbles there, sitting facing* PETER, *his eyes wide in agony, his mouth open*)

PETER: (*Whispering*) Oh my God, oh my God, oh my God. . . . (*He repeats these words many times, very rapidly*)

JERRY: (JERRY *is dying; but now his expression seems to change. His features relax, and while his voice varies, sometimes wrenched with pain, for the most part he seems removed from his dying. He smiles*) Thank you, Peter. I mean that, now; thank you very much. (PETER'S *mouth drops open. He cannot move; he is transfixed*) Oh, Peter, I was so afraid I'd drive you away. (*He laughs as best he can*) You don't know how afraid I was you'd go away and leave me. And now I'll tell you what happened at the zoo. I think . . . I think this is what happened at the zoo . . . I think. I think that while I was at the zoo I decided that I would walk north . . . northerly, rather . . . until I found you . . . or somebody . . . and I decided that I would talk to you . . . I would tell you things . . . and things that I would tell you would . . . Well, here we are. You see? Here we *are*. But . . . I don't know . . . could I have planned all this? No . . . no, I couldn't have. But I think I did. And now I've told you what you wanted to know, haven't I? And now you know all about what happened at the zoo. And now you know what you'll see in your TV, and the face I told you about . . . you remember . . . the face I told you about . . . my face, the face you see right now. Peter . . . Peter? . . . Peter . . . thank you. I came unto you (*He laughs, so faintly*) and you have comforted me. Dear Peter.

PETER: (*Almost fainting*) Oh my God!

JERRY: You'd better go now. Somebody might come by, and you don't want to be here when anyone comes.

PETER: (*Does not move, but begins to weep*) Oh my God, oh my God.

JERRY: (*Most faintly, now; he is very near death*) You won't be coming back here any more, Peter; you've been dispossessed. You've lost your bench, but you've defended your honor. And Peter, I'll tell you something now; you're not really a vegetable; it's all right, you're an animal. You're an animal, too. But you'd better hurry now, Peter. Hurry, you'd better go . . . see? (JERRY *takes a handkerchief and with great effort and pain wipes the knife handle clean of finger prints*) Hurry away, Peter. (PETER *begins to stagger away*) Wait . . . wait, Peter. Take your book . . . book. Right here . . . beside me . . . on your bench . . . my bench, rather. Come . . . take your book. (PETER *starts for the book, but retreats*) Hurry . . . Peter. (PETER *rushes to the bench, grabs the book, retreats*) Very good, Peter . . . very good. Now . . . hurry away. (PETER *hesitates for a moment, then flees, stage-left*) Hurry away . . . (*His eyes are closed now*) Hurry away, your parakeets are making the dinner . . . the cats . . . are setting the table . . .

PETER: (*Off stage*) (*A pitiful howl*) OH MY GOD!

JERRY: (*His eyes still closed, he shakes his head and speaks; a combination of scornful mimicry and supplication*) Oh . . . my . . . God. (*He is dead*)

CURTAIN

1958

Journal Entry

Brainstorm on the implications of the title of the play. How many possibilities of multiple meanings did you generate?

Textual Considerations

1. As you read *The Zoo Story*, list examples of humor and comical inadequacies to illustrate how Albee uses playful elements to juxtapose a truthful and painful view of life. Explain how humor and laughter characterize Jerry's and Peter's experience as trapped and caged human beings.

2. Why does Jerry insist on telling his "story" at the beginning of the play? To what extent does his role as a storyteller contrast with Peter's? What storytelling technique does he use to accomplish his goal?

3. To what extent are Jerry and Peter foils to each other? List the several contrasts between them, including their physical appearances, their psychological and social traits, and their philosophies of life. How successful is Albee in portraying these characters? With whom do you identify and why?

4. Besides the dog, Jerry's story also refers to people like the "colored queen," the landlady, and the lady who lives on the third floor. What do Jerry's comments about these people reveal about his own character? How relevant are they to your understanding of Jerry?

Cultural Contexts

1. Discuss with your group your responses to the ending of the play. How do you evaluate Peter's action? Does he release Jerry from his suffering? Is Albee suggesting that we are all capable of Peter's act? What consensus, if any, did your group reach?

2. Several critics have suggested that Albee uses religious and mythological parallels in the play. What examples can you cite? How does the play fit into the theme of Part Five, the individual and the community? At the outset of the play, for example, did you think of Peter as a "community" person? Explain.

Performance Exercises

PERFORMANCE EXPRESS (45 MINUTES)

To experience the power of Albee's language, your group may divide *The Zoo Story* into short scenes and cast two of your classmates in the roles of Peter and Jerry. Then deliver a spontaneous performance of the play for your whole class. Does the play require the verbal energy of Albee's language to sustain its dramatic impact? How much of its dramatic intensity was lost or gained in your improvised performance?

PERFORMANCE PROJECT

1. For your semester performance project of *The Zoo Story*, consider transferring the set of the play to your twenty-first-century college environment. What scenes, speeches, and monologues would you cut out to fit postmodern expectations of your college audience? Besides the use of Peter's book and Jerry's knife, what other props would you use?

2. To stage a gendered version of *The Zoo Story*, select two women to perform the roles of Peter and Jerry. Think about costumes and scenic designs. What aspects of the play have been lost or highlighted in this gender-related setting? Think about the dramatic purpose of the play and how you can best portray male defense of territorial rights by casting women in the male roles.

STUDENT JOURNAL ENTRY

BRAINSTORMING EXERCISE ON TOPIC 10:
ROMERO AND STEVENS

Significance of both titles
Romero's poem based on ironic use of sight
Gossips value Escolastica's beauty only
Sure Guillermo will not marry her after the amputation
Jealous of her happiness and birth of five children
Convinced her pact with the devil had "clouded" G's eyesight
Stevens use color symbolism throughout contrasting green, purple, yellow
with blandness of white
Also with the drunken sailor who has exotic dreams

My paper will explore the juxtaposition of what was "seen" and not "seen"
in Romero to expose the evil of the gossips and Stevens's use of contrasting colors to disclose the conformity of the unimaginative.

TOPICS FOR DISCUSSION AND WRITING

Writing Topics

1. Examine the images or metaphors of fences, boundaries, or walls in any three texts in Part Five. Consider, for example, walls within families as well as those between or within groups.

2. The limitations of conformity are explored in the poems by Dickinson, Stevens, Williams, and Cummings. Choose images from any three texts that express the speakers' attitudes toward the constraints of predictability and respectability. To what extent do you agree or disagree with their points of view?

3. Compared and contrast the role of the family in "The Metamorphosis," "Eveline," or "A Red Sweater." To what extent do members of the family contribute to or limit the autonomy of the protagonists in any two stories?

4. Analyze the functions of setting in "Eveline," "The Guest," and "Dead Men's Path." What role does setting play in shaping the protagonist's choices in any two stories?

5. Compare and contrast the portrayals of the community in "The Lottery," "The Guest," and "Dead Men's Path." What causes the members of both communities to behave as they do? Are they seeking to decrease or even to destroy the rights of the individual protagonists? Explain.

6. Would it be fair to describe Daru in "The Guest" or Antigone as rebels? Write an analysis of the causes and effects of their rebellion, including your attitude toward it.

7. Analyze the role of the forces of authority in the selections by Olds, Camus, or Sophocles. What positions do they take? How do they enhance or impede the dialogue between the individual and the law?

8. Discuss the role of tradition, mass psychology, and social pressure in "The Lottery" and "Dead Men's Path." Consider how human beings respond to stereotypes, tradition, and outside pressures and how they balance the clash of the old versus the new and of the autonomous versus the communal self.

9. Discuss images of life and death in the poems by Olds, Wilbur, Yevtushenko, and Ferlinghetti. Consider how form—defined by the diversity of stanzaic patterns, rhythm, tone, and rhymes—affects meanings and defines the speakers' philosophies of life.

10. Several texts in Part Five include people who are particularly unimaginative. What indications of lack of imagination do you find in the texts by Romero, Stevens, Cummings, or Achebe? Limit yourself to two texts.

11. The issue of alienation of the individual from society emerges in texts by Kafka, Camus, Dickinson, Stevens, and many others. Select three of these texts and write an essay in which you characterize the kind of alienation—physical, psychological, intellectual, social, political, religious, or artistic—that these texts explore.

12. Kafka described "The Metamorphosis" as a story in which "the dream reveals the reality." What does this comment suggest about the underlying psychological significance of Gregor's physical transformation?

13. Playwrights like Albee, writing in the tradition of the theater of the absurd, portray the human condition as illogical, irrational, and meaningless. Write an essay citing effective examples of these elements in *The Zoo Story*.

14. Blake and Wordsworth focus on social problems in nineteenth-century London as well as on the failure of church and state to respond to them. Write an essay focusing on what you consider to be important urban problems in the present. How responsive have contemporary political and religious leaders been in addressing these issues? Limit yourself to two or three issues.

Research Topics

1. Several texts, including *Antigone* and "The Guest," address civil disobedience and the historical right of the individual to engage in social protester. Working with your group, write a documented essay on this issue, consulting at least two of the following sources: Plato's *Crito*, Henry David Thoreau's *On Civil Disobedience*, Martin Luther King Jr.'s "Letter from a Birmingham Jail," Thomas Jefferson's Declaration of Independence, and/or Elizabeth Cady Stanton's "Declaration of Sentiments and Resolutions." Given a choice between a society in which individual rights come first and one in which community needs have priority, which would you choose?

2. From 1959 to 1962, Edward Albee wrote three one-act plays: *The Death of Bessie Smith*, *The Sand Box*, and *The American Dream*. Write a documented paper evaluating the effectiveness of these dramas in reexamining important social issues including individual rights and communal responsibilities.

3. Access the Nobel Prize speeches by Camus, Gordimer, and Morrison on the Internet, and analyze them. What do they reveal about the speakers' humanitarian, political, and social viewpoints? What do they portray about the speakers themselves and their view of art, literature, and history? How do you respond to these speeches? How do they challenge you as a reader?

FILM ANGLES

The relationship between the individual and the community is the basis of every society—the heart and pulse of what sustains it. If the relationship is a healthy one, both the individual and the community thrive. If the relationship is inhospitable, both suffer. Literature and art offer countless illustrations of the struggle between the two, sometimes igniting the hope that humanity might learn from its mistakes. Some authors imagine a utopia, in which all of society's abuses and errors are corrected and individuals live in harmony.

The range of literary works that express this theme is wide—from Sophocles' tragedy *Antigone*, in which the individual challenges the authority of the state, to Kafka's "The Metamorphosis," Joyce's "Eveline," and Albee's *The Zoo Story*, all of which concern characters doomed to lead eccentric insular lives by the cultural, familial, and social forces that have shaped them. So, too, the range of movies that can be discussed in the context of Part Five is broad and varied.

FILM HISTORY AND GENRES

The extraordinary excitement that motion pictures elicited in the early years of the twentieth century was because, like most new technologies, film generated a utopian spirit. Filmmakers and critics believed that because film was a more "democratic" art form, as opposed to elitist, it would fulfill the dream of uniting humanity: As a visual language transcending linguistic barriers and national cultures, film could reach the common ground that all beings share. Film, it was thought, would create a true communal theater of a scope undreamed of by the Greeks or the Elizabethans. Early pioneer filmmakers, such as D. W. Griffith and Cecil B. De Mille, approached the medium with a messianic spirit, making movies with an aim toward correcting social injustices and transforming the world.

Like all technologies, however, motion pictures also provided opportunities for disseminating propaganda on an unprecedented scale and were used to promote the policies and values of such twentieth-century political tyrants as Lenin, Stalin, and Hitler. For every movie that has advanced the cause of social justice and educated millions on subjects like the Holocaust and civil rights, there are dozens devoted to mindless entertainment and questionable values.

Perhaps no theme is more compelling than that of the heroic individual who struggles valiantly against a formidable opponent. Clearly, the theme is universal, appealing to the rebel in all of us, and can be discerned in many **genres**. In the costume epic *Gladiator* (d. Ridley Scott, 2000), the protagonist fights the corruption of the Roman Empire at the expense of his own life. In the biographical/historical drama *Gandhi* (d. Richard Attenborough, Great Britain, 1982), a public figure rouses millions to fight a colonialist empire. Yet another biographical drama, *The Trial of Joan of Arc* (d. Robert Bresson, France, 1962) explores how a young woman's refusal to yield her inner spiritual convictions to the forces of the medieval Catholic Church condemns her to death. In all cases, the protagonist refuses to compromise personal values or bow to authority, legitimate or not.

Often the heroic figure is larger than life, suggesting that only such individuals have the charisma and power to make a difference. In John Ford's *Young Mr. Lincoln* (1939), many visual and cinematic motifs in the film emphasize that even Lincoln's idiosyncrasies predestined him for greatness. In the film versions of Jean Anouilh's *Becket* (d. Peter Glenville, Great Britain, 1964) and Robert Bolt's *A Man for All Seasons* (d. Fred Zinneman, 1966), the protagonists—Archbishop Thomas Becket and Chancellor Thomas More, respectively—resist the manipulative autocratic powers of English kings, preferring to die rather than compromise their consciences. In Spike Lee's *Malcolm X* (1992), the protagonist's personal life is sacrificed to his determination to give voice to the needs of an unempowered community. *Good Night and Good Luck* (d. George Clooney, 2005) dramatizes the circumstances in which Edward R. Murrow, a renowned newsman and television personality of the 1950s, risked his career and reputation by attacking the methods used by Senator Joseph McCarthy to oust alleged communists from government.

Movies have also shown ordinary people acting on personal convictions in everyday situations and affecting the course of events. A fledgling U.S. senator stands up against political corruption in *Mr. Smith Goes to Washington* (d. Frank Capra, 1939); a housewife and factory worker fights unfair labor practices in *Norma Rae* (d. Martin Ritt, 1979); an office worker pursues the cover-up of environmental pollutions in *Erin Brockovich* (d. Steven Soderbergh, 2000); a writer risks alienating her family in her fight against apartheid in *A World Apart* (d. Chris Menges, 1988); an employee puts his life and family in jeopardy when he gives incriminating evidence against the tobacco industry in *The Insider* (d. Michael Mann, 1999).

Several films over the last few years are especially tuned to the theme of individualism and community. Perhaps the most familiar is *Crash* (d. Paul Haggis), which won the Academy Award for Best Picture of 2005. Set in Los Angeles, the film tracks a number of characters from different classes and ethnic backgrounds whose lives ironically but inevitably intersect. In the course of the narrative, both racism and sexism come into play, exploited by those on both sides of the law. The film illustrates the idea that "no man is an island unto himself," a phrase from one of John Donne's most famous poems. This theme and structure also characterize *Amores Perros* (2000), *21 Grams* (2003), and *Babel* (2006), three critically acclaimed works by Mexican director Alejandro González-Iñárritu. Collectively, these films are impelled by the notion that the actions of any individual, however small, can have unexpected, sometimes tragic, consequences for many others. The most recent example, *Babel*, carries these effects across international borders, setting its separate stories in Morocco, Mexico, and Tokyo and accentuating how language and cultural barriers both underline and complicate universal communal bonds.

Questions to Consider

1. Discuss any film in terms of how it dramatizes the relationship between the individual and the community. Is the individual portrayed as ordinary or extraordinary? If both, how does the film balance the character's human limitations with his or her heroic features? Is the character too good to be true? If so, how does this affect your ability to relate to the character or appreciate the film?

2. In Sophocles' *Antigone*, the heroine defies authority by burying her brother—against King Creon's ruling. Because her action springs from such a strong personal impulse, can it also be seen as an example of civil disobedience? Can you think of a character in a film whose actions are both very personal and of public consequence?

3. Some critics have interpreted the film *Good Night and Good Luck*, which deals with an outspoken critic of the witch hunt for communists in the 1950s, as a warning against contemporary violations of civil rights and attempts to intimidate and blackmail news reporters critical of government policy. Discuss this film in the context of its relevance to recent political and social events—for example, concerning the criticism of the Iraq war.

CASE STUDIES

12 Angry Men

The film *12 Angry Men* (d. Sidney Lumet, 1957) is one of the strongest movies ever made about the jury system. A tour de force with an all-star cast headed by Henry Fonda, the film is frequently shown on television and remains more popular than its remake, which was made for television in 1997. When the film opens, twelve members of a jury are directed by the judge to arrive at a unanimous verdict and decide the fate of a young Hispanic accused of killing his father; they are told that a guilty verdict automatically means the death penalty. At the initial vote, eleven jurors, convinced it is an open-and-shut case, find the defendant guilty and consider the holdout member a nuisance whose opposition will only prolong the inevitable verdict. Because the circumstances of the crime point convincingly to the defendant's guilt, it is no easy task to convince anyone that the case is worth discussing, much less that they should change their minds. Nevertheless, as the drama unfolds and the details of the evidence are scrutinized, each juror exposes the weaker features of his character, revealing personal motives and deep-seated prejudices that strongly determine his judgment.

The individual—whose name, Davis, we only learn at the very end—who acts as the catalyst for the reversal of judgment is neither a recalcitrant rebel nor a radical with his own agenda. He is an ordinary man in doubt, an independent thinker who refuses simply to go along with the majority unless he can live with his conscience. He claims to have neither greater insight nor higher moral standards, but it is his insistence that the evidence may be flawed that plants doubt in the others' minds and triggers a more rigorous analysis of the case. In this way, Davis is neither a hero nor a martyr to a cause, but a citizen who reminds others how democracy and the court system is supposed to work.

Except for brief scenes in the beginning and end, the entire film is set in a drab and impersonal room in lower Manhattan where the jury must sit until they reach a decision. This lends an air of authenticity and claustrophobia to the drama, which is appropriate to the experience the men must endure as strangers forced together in an insulated environment. The uncomfortable physical conditions—it is the "hottest day of the year" and the room has a malfunctioning fan—add to the growing tension and confrontational nature of the characters' interactions.

Questions to Consider

1. Why do you think we never learn the names or ethnic identities of the men? Why are they referred to only by their juror numbers?
2. Examine the interaction among the men. Do your first impressions of any of the characters change in the course of the film? How and why?
3. Describe Davis's personality. What features stand out? Why does he feel the way he does? Does he seem morally superior to the others? Does the actor convince you that Davis is an average man? If not, does this affect the impact of the drama?
4. Because the jury ultimately shifts its initial view, its status as a "community" also changes. What is this change? Does the film encourage you to examine further the role of the individual in relation to his or her community?
5. How does the restricted setting affect the overall atmosphere of the film?

The Crucible

Arthur Miller's play *The Crucible*, set in Salem, Massachusetts, in 1692 during the witch trials, was first produced on the stage in 1953. At the time, certain forces of the U.S. government were bent on rooting out communists who allegedly had infiltrated the U.S. Army and various departments of government. Although the hearings in Washington, under the leadership of Senator Joseph McCarthy, were criticized and lamented by many, even at the time, they created a national hysteria—a paranoid fear of communism—and destroyed many careers and lives in the process. For this reason, they were, then and now, referred to as a "witch hunt," a clear reference to witchcraft trials throughout history, including those at Salem. Not coincidentally, therefore, Miller's play was interpreted not just as a dramatization of the historical events of the seventeenth century but as an allegory about contemporary American life.

The 1996 film version of the play, directed by Nicholas Hytner and with a screenplay by Miller, is an intelligent, well-acted adaptation—compelling evidence that the story has not lost its relevance. It makes it clear that however much we like to imagine our own times as more enlightened than the past, the compulsion to look for scapegoats to conceal our own flaws and hunt down and destroy the "other" in the name of the welfare of the community or the safety of the state is always subject to resurgence.

The drama concerns the havoc wreaked on the town of Salem by a group of young sexually precocious women, led by Abigail Williams, who claim to be victims of the devil, and certain "witches" among various members of the community. Among those accused are Elizabeth, wife of John Proctor, with whom Abigail has had an affair. The drama demonstrates how hysteria rules over reason and how the combination of human corruption and superstition, when backed by authority, leads to tyranny.

Because witchcraft is an "invisible crime"—as Judge Danforth, the Massachusetts authority who must decide the case says—about which only the witch and her victim can testify, there is little that a lawyer can do. Therein lies another resemblance between the play's theme and the McCarthy hearings of the 1950s. The very *accusation* of witchcraft, like that of being a communist, virtually equaled guilt. There was no recourse but submission. In both cases, the only way to exonerate oneself was to "name" others. Under the absurdity of the circumstances, the challenge to the individual was either to confess to a crime of which he or she was innocent or deny it and be executed. John Proctor, the primary character faced with this dilemma in the film, has every reason to want to live, yet he finally refuses to lie and destroy his good name.

Questions to Consider

1. The film, unlike the play, begins with a scene in the forest. What is the significance of this scene? Is it simply one of the more realistic touches that films can provide over stage presentations of plays, or does it add something important to what we learn later through the dialogue in the play? What is the view of the forest as it is discussed by Miller in one of the commentaries in the play? What did it represent to the Christian community of Salem?

2. Describe John Proctor and Elizabeth Proctor as characters and as individuals who become the primary focus of the drama. What are their strengths and weaknesses? How do these contribute to our impressions of them? Are they average people or larger-than-life heroes?

3. Many minor characters in *The Crucible* help form the Salem community. Which of these characters reinforce the repressive atmosphere of the community and which of them resist it?

4. Much of the play and film's impact depends on the credibility of the Abigail Williams character. Do you think she is a convincing figure? Even if several members of the community "believe" her for their own personal reasons, how can we explain the effect she has on Judge Danforth, an outsider who seems intelligent, wise, and not easily manipulated?

5. Although the "community" seems to be a unified force with similar views of witchcraft's threat to security, there is disagreement even among the outside specialists and lawmakers

regarding how to arrive at the truth. Who are the contesting figures, and how can we incorporate their views in our general impression of the Salem community?

Research Topics

1. The protagonists of *Gandhi*, *Malcolm X*, *Gladiator*, *Lawrence of Arabia* (d. David Lean, Great Britain, 1962), and *Spartacus* (d. Stanley Kubrick, 1960) are involved on a grand scale with momentous historical events. Compare two or three of these films in terms of how the character balances his personal ambitions or desires with his role as a leader.

2. Violence can be a means of oppression as well as liberation. Both *Spartacus* and *Gladiator*, for example, depict violence as a means of entertainment mandated by the governing authority (ancient Rome in both cases) for the pleasure of its citizens. Bloodshed, dismemberment, and the deaths of the gladiators were essential to the experience. In both films, individual gladiators—Spartacus in the first case, Maximus in the latter—survive only by conforming to the game and biding their time, eventually turning the violence against their oppressors and freeing the enslaved portion of the community. (At one critical moment in the arena, Maximus tells his fellow gladiators that the way to survive is to stay together.) Do the themes of these films indicate that authoritarian states can never be overcome through peaceful means? Do they suggest that violence in itself is a neutral phenomenon, its ethical dimension determined by the purpose it serves? Is the individual ever permitted to use violence against a repressive community? If so, what is the moral basis of this "permission"?

3. Compare the visions of the future in *Bladerunner* (d. Ridley Scott, 1982), *Gattica* (d. Andrew Nicoll, 1997), and *1984* (d. Michael Radford, Great Britain, 1984). Are the societies fantasized in these films an improvement over the ones in existence today? Is the relationship of the individual and the community more or less as it is today? Discuss specific images and scenes in each film to illustrate your answers.

4. In some ways *American Beauty* (d. Sam Mendes, 1999), *Being There* (d. Hal Ashby, 1979), *Ordinary People* (d. Robert Redford, 1980), and *Pleasantville* (d. Gary Ross, 1998) represent the extremes of a less confrontational relationship between the individual and the community. Each poses questions about the nature of dependency in that relationship and the community's effects on the individual. What are these "extreme" positions, and how does each film treat the question of the individual's role within the community?

6. In some ways *12 Angry Men* presents a relatively optimistic viewpoint in dramatizing a situation in which individuals are forced to confront their prejudices and, by rising above them, make some difference in the way justice is meted out in society. Clearly, this can only occur in a democratic society. Discuss the role of the individual in how the law functions in the societies represented in such films as *City of God* (d. Fernando Meirelles, Brazil/Portugal, 2003), *The Magdalene Sisters* (d. Peter Mullan, Ireland, 2003), *Lagaan: Once Upon a Time in India* (d. Ashutush Gowariker, India, 2002), and *Lumumba* (d. Raoul Peck, France/Belgium/Haiti, 2001).

7. Arthur Miller's play *The Crucible* was first filmed in 1956 in a French/East German co-production directed by Raymond Rouleau with a screenplay by noted existentialist writer Jean-Paul Sartre. Just as Miller wrote the play as an allegory of contemporary America, Sartre adopted it to express sentiments in France following World War II. As a result, there are many differences between this version and the 1996 film, especially the ending. Watch the video of both versions and consider these differences with special attention to (a) which characters are most affected by the changes, (b) whether the changes affect the meaning of the story, and (c) whether the French version violates the spirit of Miller's play.

An Introduction to the Elements of Fiction, Nonfiction, Poetry, and Drama

FICTION

What do we mean by *fiction*? For the novelist Toni Morrison, "fiction, by definition, is distinct from fact. Presumably it's the product of imagination—invention—and it claims the freedom to dispense with 'what really happened' or where it really happened, or when it really happened, and nothing in it needs to be publicly verifiable, although much of it can be verified." Morrison goes on to say, however, that as a storyteller she is less interested in the distinction between fiction and fact than in that between fact and truth, "because facts can exist without human intelligence, but truth cannot." Fiction, then, is concerned with what the novelist William Faulkner calls "the verities and truths of the heart."

Tales, fables, parables, epic poems, and romances, and even the fairy tales you heard as a child, rank among the most ancient modes of fiction, kept alive by the power of the human voice to narrate and transmit the excitement and authenticity of imaginary actions and events. Short stories, however, belong to a more contemporary mode of narrative fiction and gained in recognition through the works of nineteenth-century American and European writers, including Edgar Allan Poe, Mary E. Wilkins Freeman, Anton Chekhov, and Guy de Maupassant.

This appendix introduces several technical terms, such as *character*, *plot*, *setting*, *theme*, *narrator*, *style*, and *tone*, that are used to describe the formal elements of a short story. Getting acquainted with these terms will help you to understand how short stories are put together and make it easier for you both to read them and to write about them.

Character

A *character* is a fictional person in a story, and readers' first reactions to him or her are usually based on their subjective capacity to empathize with the character's experiences. A character is often revealed through his or her actions, which provide readers with clues about the character's personality, motives, and expectations. Many stories present a conflict between the protagonist (the story's central character) and the antagonist (the opposing character or force); the conflict is revealed through the author's use of dialogue and narrative. In Alifa Rifaat's story "Another Evening at the Club" (p. 309), for instance, the main character or protagonist, Samia, is in conflict with her husband, the antagonist, because of her inability to liberate herself from his dominating behavior.

Fictional characters are sometimes referred to as round, flat, static, or dynamic. Round characters change, grow, and possess a credible personality, like the protagonist in Alice Walker's short story "Roselily" (p. 293). Flat characters, in contrast, are usually one dimensional, act predictably, and are often presented as stereotypes. The bridegroom in Walker's story, for example, is an unimaginative and inflexible individual portrayed through images of entrapment Roselily associates with him, including "ropes, chains, handcuffs, his religion." In fact, he is in many ways a foil to her because his values are antithetical to hers.

Plot

Plot is the arrangement of the events in a story according to a pattern devised by the writer and inferred by the reader. Often the plot develops when characters and situations oppose each other, creating conflicts that grow and eventually reach a climax, the point of highest intensity of the story. After this climactic turning point, the action of the story finally declines, moving toward a resolution of the conflict.

Although the time frame in a story may vary from recapturing an intense, momentary experience to narrating an event that covers a much longer period, the storyteller must focus on what Poe terms the "single effect" as the action of the story moves toward a resolution of the conflict.

"Another Evening at the Club" provides an example of a plot centered on a conflict between Samia and her husband. The action starts to rise in dramatic intensity (*the rising action*) when Samia's loss of her emerald ring destabilizes her relationship with her husband. After this initial exposition, or narrative introduction of characters and situation, the action reaches its crisis (the *climax* of the action) when Samia's husband refuses to exonerate the maid, even though he knows she is innocent. Notice that this external conflict also parallels the internal conflict of the protagonist when she recognizes the degree of the husband's control over her and her inability to oppose him. The action of the story moves toward the resolution of its conflict (*the falling action*) when Samia yields to her husband's authority.

Although many writers continue to follow this traditional model of plot development, some authors deviate from it. Liam O'Flaherty, in "The Sniper," for example, and Sandip Roy, in "The Smells of Home," prefer the surprise ending, whereas André Dubus in "The Curse" ends his story without a resolution of the protagonist's inner conflict.

Although the typical fictional plot has a beginning, a middle, and an end, authors may also vary their patterns of narration. In "The Sniper," the story's events unfold in the order in which they took place, following a *chronological* development. In "Another Evening at the Club," Rifaat uses *flashbacks*, selecting a few episodes to build a plot that moves backward and forward in time: the action begins in the present with Samia's anguish at her husband's decision to blame the maid for the theft of the ring; then, through the use of flashbacks, the author reports past events that illustrate the position that women like Samia occupy in a patriarchal culture. Rifaat also uses *suspense* or uncertainty, creating a sense of anticipation and curiosity about what the protagonist will do next. Will she defend the servant accused of stealing the ring? How will her husband react when he finds out that the ring was not stolen?

Many stories also use foreshadowing, providing details and hints about what will happen next. In Edith Wharton's "Roman Fever," the title functions as a foreshadowing anticipating the outcome of the story. Fictional devices such as flashback and foreshadowing do not operate in isolation but rather work together with characterization, setting, point of view, style, and tone to create a unified effect.

Setting

The time, place, and social context of a story constitute its setting. Nadine Gordimer's "The Moment Before the Gun Went Off," for example, takes place in South Africa during Apartheid and narrates the accidental shooting of a farm laborer by an Afrikaner farmer who is also the regional leader of the National Party. Although distraught by the shooting, he is initially more concerned about the news coverage that will describe him as "a leading member" of the Ruling Party, a response that changes radically in the last sentence of the story.

The setting of Lan Samantha Chang's "The Unforgetting," transports readers to the American Midwest in the 1950s where Chinese immigrant parents fleeing from the communist regime decide to raise their son by blocking out all memories of their traumatic past. As you read a short story, watch for details related to time, place, and social context that reveal the motivation of the protagonist and establish the story's credibility. Pay particular attention to the writer's use of visual imagery aimed at helping you create mental pictures of the setting and assessing its effects on the characters' actions.

Theme

Theme may be defined as the central or dominant idea of the story reinforced by the interaction of fictional devices such as character, plot, setting, and point of view. The theme is the overall generalization we can make about the story's meaning and significance. Sometimes the theme can be stated in a short phrase. For instance, "the rights of the community versus those of an individual" is one theme that emerges in Achebe's short story "Dead Men's Path." The theme of Graham Greene's "The Destructors" is more complex: the story takes place in England after World War II and links the effects of that devastating event to the destructive actions of the young members of the Wormsley Common Gang.

To define the theme of a story, look for clues provided by the author such as the title, imagery, symbolism, and dialogue between the characters. A story may evoke a range of meanings. And readers—because of their diverse interests, cultural backgrounds, and expectations—will react individually and produce varied meanings. Meanings should be supported by evidence from the story, however.

Narrator

The voice that narrates a story is not necessarily the writer's; whereas the author writes the story, the narrator tells it. The *narrator* is a technique that writers use to create a particular point of view from which they will tell the story, present the actions, and shape the readers' responses. Narrators can report external and internal events, but most important, they express the narrative angle that writers use to tell the story.

Narrators that are *omniscient* know everything or almost everything that happens in the story, including what goes on inside the minds of the characters. They are presumed to be *reliable*. In "The Storm" by Kate Chopin, the narrator penetrates the minds of several people: Calixta, the wife who faces the storm at home; Bobinôt, the absent husband, who is especially concerned about his wife's safety; Alcée, Calixta's seducer; and Clarisse, Alcée's wife. By exposing the effect of the storm on these characters, the omniscient narrator provides glimpses of their different views of life and marriage. By exposing their interior thoughts, the omniscient narrator provides glimpses of a dramatic dialogue between two opposing points of view. Omniscient narrators tend to be objective—emotionally removed from the action—and to use the third-person *he, she, it,* and *they* to create a *third-person* point of view.

First-person narrators report the events from the point of view of the I, or first person. A first-person narrator differs from an omniscient narrator because the I both participates in the action and communicates a single point of view. This type of narrator usually creates a greater degree of intimacy with the reader as in "On Seeing the 100% Perfect Girl One Beautiful April Morning." The writer's choice of a narrator is important because it determines the point of view (or the voice and angle from which the narrator tells the story) and thereby affects the story's tone and meaning.

Style and Tone

Style refers to the way writers express themselves. Style depends on *diction* (the writer's choice of vocabulary), *syntax* (grammar and sentence structure), as well as *voice* and *rhythm*. Style reveals the writer's linguistic choices or preferences and therefore is as private and unique as their personalities and identities. Notice the sharp contrast, for example between Kate's Chopin's dramatic use of words and images to infuse them with symbolic significance in "The Storm" and Edith Wharton's straightforward, concise style, created to evoke the rhythm of a colloquial conversation in "Roman Fever." To make their language unique and particular, writers also use other devices, such as the following:

- *Irony* is the discrepancy between what is expected and what actually happens. The title of Franz Kafka's story "The Metamorphosis" is ironic because it reverses the reader's expectations of a positive change from an inferior to a superior state. Verbal irony is the discrepancy between what words convey and what they actually mean, as in the title of Albert Camus's "The Guest."
- A *symbol* is something—a word or an object—that stands for an idea beyond a literal meaning. In Elie Wiesel's "The Watch," the watch may function as a symbol of "the soul and memory" of the past.
- A *metaphor* is a figure of speech that compares two dissimilar elements without using *like* or *as:* "The rain was coming down in sheets" ("The Storm"). A *simile* is a comparison using *like* or *as:* "Her lips were as red and moist as pomegranate seed" ("The Storm").
- *Tone* is the manner, mood, or pervading attitude that writers establish for characters, situations, and readers. Authors use a variety of different tones such as intimate or distant, ironic or direct, hostile or sympathetic, formal or casual, humorous or serious, and emotional or objective.

In "A Red Sweater," for example, Fae Myenne Ng uses a straight, concise style to evoke the rhythm of a colloquial conversation and create a degree of intimacy with the reader. Haruki Murakami uses humor in his short story "On Seeing the 100% Perfect Girl One Beautiful April Morning" to communicate his protagonist's indecision and resulting regrets, whereas in "The Unforgetting," Lan Samantha Chang uses irony to portray the devastating results of the decision of her protagonists to erase their memories of their native China, thereby depriving their only son with any knowledge of his ethnic history.

That successful creators of short fiction must be involved with the intricacies of their craft is clear, but remember also that their primary purpose is to use language to communicate to you. As the novelist William Faulkner reminded us, in his 1950 Nobel Prize acceptance speech, writers like to tell and retell stories about "love and honor and pity and pride and compassion and sacrifice"—in other words, stories about the lives and experiences of all human beings.

CREATIVE OR LITERARY NONFICTION: THE ESSAY

Creative or literary nonfiction—such as memoirs, personal writing, journalism, and cultural and academic criticism—is often defined as writing that is neither imaginary nor inhabited by fictional characters like the literary offspring of fiction, poetry, and drama. The essay, a creative or literary nonfiction prose, emphasizes writers' tendency toward self-analysis, their casual free flow of thoughts, the range of their personal experiences, and the reliability of their voices.

The history of the essay takes us back to French writer Michel de Montaigne, a retired French magistrate, who in 1570 wrote in a flexible prose discourse a series of personal meditations on subjects like cannibalism, friendship, repentance, physiognomy, and experience. He referred to this informal, casual kind of writing as "*essai*," from the French word meaning "experiment," "trial," or "attempt." Montaigne's essays first reached England through John Florio's translation in 1580, and since then this creative nonfiction form has been widely used. Joseph Addison (1672–1719) and Sir Richard Steele (1672–1729) excelled in the creation of the "magazine" essay in England, showing how the essay could serve cultural needs and fulfill the moral, social, and political expectations of the average reader. In the twentieth century, the essay form proliferated in the hands of such outstanding essayists as Virginia Woolf and George Orwell. Following Montaigne's personal, digressive writing style, Woolf explored a wide range of subjects related to the position of women, and Orwell exposed in his essays the challenge of political, ideological, and social flaws. Woolf wrote more than five hundred literary reviews and essays, creating what rhetorician Thomas J. Farrell has called a "female mode of rhetoric"—a style of writing highlighted by association of ideas, a light tone, and personal experience. Its purpose is to oppose what Woolf viewed as the hierarchical, logical discourse of male literary tradition.

In the United States, the essay reached its great heights in the hands of Ralph Waldo Emerson and Henry David Thoreau, who explored issues related to self-reliance, transcendentalism, and civil disobedience in nineteenth-century New England. The essay then suffered a steady decline when readers in the twentieth century tended to favor creative fiction. In the late 1970s, American essayist E. B. White called attention to the role the essay played as a "second-class citizen" in relation to poetry, fiction, and drama. However, in the 1980s and 1990s, the contemporary American essay—whether formal, informal, or in the guise of personal memoir or criticism—gained momentum and new literary energy in journals, reviews, and book collections. As Joseph Epstein, noted Chicago essayist says, "Don't spread it around but it's a sweet time to be an essayist." Several features may account for the "rebirth" of the American essay:

1. Essayists use creative literary tools such as symbols, metaphors, and images; they also feel free to use the essay form to express their emotions. Thus, by collapsing the boundaries between fiction and nonfiction, essayists are being accorded the same recognition as writers of fiction.
2. Philosophers, mathematicians, and other professionals have been adopting the personal essay form to combine intimate recollections with factual evidence of scientific discourse.
3. Essayists also use the essay to combine their private and public voices to create texts that possess a sense of journalistic immediacy.

Audiences are especially receptive to the essay form as a personal, informal way of absorbing genuine intimate experience.

Form

In view of the diverse literary possibilities open to the contemporary essay, it is impossible to come up with a precise definition of its form. However, essayists' tentative exploration of a topic, their personal engagement in the process of self-analysis, their use of a nonauthoritative tone and such fictional devices as symbols and metaphors, as well as their intimate address to an audience, have emerged as some of the most notable features of essays.

The following classification is based on four fundamental modes of argumentation, which will help you analyze some of the most prominent features of the essays in this book. Notice, however, that any rigid classification of essay type tends to blur because of writers' lively, dynamic use of this creative nonfiction. As Susan Sontag, a prominent essayist on modern culture, has said, "In contrast to poetry and fiction, the nature of the essay is diversity—diversity of level, subject, tone, diction."

Narrative

Narratives essays tend to make a point by creating a sense of personal immediacy in an autobiographical narrative, in which writers disclose their own experiences and their self-discoveries about the way they relate to a specific topic. Narrative essays usually follow a chronological pattern.

Example: Brent Staples's "A Brother's Murder" and May Sarton's "The Rewards of Living a Solitary Life"

Staples's personal incursion into the past narrates the obstacles he encountered to save his brother from the terrifying threats of street life in the inner city. The essay's thesis, "I wanted desperately for him to live," also underscores the tone of urgency with which Staples fashions his biography to persuade the reader of his role as a devoted brother and a remorseful survivor of the dangers of urban street life. By concluding the essay with his own reaction to Blake's death, Staples places his experience into a larger social context: Should society feel guilty about the Blakes of the ghetto?

In contrast, Sarton's biographical narrative about the joys of a solitary life doesn't aim to persuade the reader; rather it reaffirms her enjoyment of the solitary life by committing it to writing. Frederick Douglass's "How I Learned to Read and Write" and Salman Rushdie's "From *Imaginary Homelands*" are also examples of memoirs and prose naratives.

Descriptive

Writers use descriptive essays to appeal primarily to the readers' sensory perception of sight, sound, touch, taste, and smell in order to transport them to a visual setting or to create a mental picture.

Example: Plato's "The Allegory of the Cave"

In "The Allegory of the Cave," Plato uses visual images to challenge his listener's imaginary eyes to "see," to "behold" the prisoner in the cave with the same sensory acuteness of his own eyes. Responding to the power of the speaker's description, Glaucon, student listener, also begins to look with the prisoner's eyes as he ascends into sunlight and descends back into the cave. Eventually, Glaucon finally "sees" the allegorical meaning of Plato's argument about the human capacity to understand reality. In "The Allegory of the Cave," descriptions function on the physical level of visual sight, the imaginative level of the mind's eye, and the allegorical level of abstraction.

Expository

Writers use expository essays to analyze, inform, argue, explain and clarify ideas, expose arguments, and propose solutions.

Example: Eric Liu's "A Chinaman's Chance: Reflections on the American Dream"

In this essay, Liu adopts a polemic initial tone to refute the idea that "the American Dream is dead." Throughout the essay, he analyzes and exposes his viewpoint by adding more arguments about immigrant expectations of America. Like a classical rhetorician who relies on the presentation of proofs, Liu wants to "prove" in his expository essay that the immigrants' journey to America is worth it. Liu's proofs increase his support of his topic, in such references as "my sister called me a 'banana,'" and he combines exposition with personal experience. Much of the energy of Liu's essay derives from his effective fusion of analysis and personal viewpoint.

Argumentative

Writers craft persuasive arguments to expose a problem, present evidence, reinforce or refute solutions, and convince the reader about a controversial issue. When writing persuasive essays, they also consider the audience's attitude toward a problem and their possible interpretation of the evidence presented.

Example: Deborah Tannen's "Sex, Lies and Conversation: Why Is It So Hard for Men and Women to Talk to Each Other?" and Virginia Woolf's "Professions for Women."

In these essays, Tannen and Woolf attempt to persuade readers about their theses. Tannen's scientific method reveals the imbalance in gender communication as a sociocultural phenomenon. Her conclusion—"Like charity, successful cross-cultural communication should begin at home"—fully reveals, however, that she uses a rigorous inductive method to reach and persuade her audience.

Woolf, in contrast, organizes her expository essay around two specific points: her conscious murder of the "angel of the house" and her inability to tell "the truth about my own experiences as a body." In the course of her analysis she uses other rhetorical devices, such as comparison and contrast (herself versus the "angel," man versus woman) and cause and effect (the consequences of the angel's death). Like Tannen, however, she also ends with a personal challenge to the audience, whom she dares to answer the questions she has posed to them. Notice that such a challenge also betrays to a great extent the degree of emotional commitment that sustains the rigorous clarity of Woolf's argumentative method.

Rhetorical Strategies

Writers use a host of rhetorical strategies to narrate, to analyze, to argue, and to persuade. If you become familiar with them, they will help you examine and analyze the argumentative possibilities of the essay form. The following texts illustrate some of these rhetorical devices, such as comparison and contrast, cause and effect, and process analysis.

Through comparison and contrast, Gary Soto in his essay "Black Hair" supports his thesis statement: "There are two kinds of work: One uses the mind and the other uses muscle" by citing examples throughout his memoir. Soto also moves from the concrete to the abstract, summing up the discrepancies between the ideals of the traditional American Dream with the realities of being Mexican American in dead-end jobs that "few quit; no one was ever fired." The young Soto "couldn't imagine any work that could be worse—or any life."

Seth Mydans and Martin Luther King Jr. use cause and effect. In "Not Just the Inner City: Well-to-Do Join Gangs," Mydans explains the reason for the growing popularity of gangs in U.S. suburbia; in "I Have a Dream," King delivers his emotional plea for a shared view of the promises of the American Dream through an analysis of the causes and consequences of its failure.

POETRY

What is poetry? The nineteenth-century poet William Wordsworth defines it as "an overflow of powerful feelings." For the contemporary poet Jeffrey Harrison, "Poetry is the lens through which the soul looks at the world, thereby keeping the soul alive." For E. E. Cummings, "Poetry is being, not doing."

Poets, like other artists, regardless of their historical moment, write for a variety of different reasons, but they share an imaginative view of language and a belief in the power of words. Compare, for example, Emily Dickinson's thoughts on words expressed in her poem number 1212:

> A word is dead
> When it is said,
> Some say.
> I say it just
> Begins to live
> That day.

with those of Lawrence Ferlinghetti in his poem "Constantly Risking Absurdity," written a century later:

> the poet like an acrobat
> climbs on rime
> to a high wire of his own making.

Both poets focus on the possibilities and power of words, emphasizing the ability of language to shape and express human experiences. Despite the contradictory claims and concerns with which different generations define poetry, there is some consensus that poetry combines emotional expression, meanings, and experiences through rhythm, images, structural form, and, above all, words.

Voice and Tone

The voice that communicates the feelings, emotions, and meanings of the poem is called the speaker. The speaker's voice is not the voice of the poet but a created voice, or *persona*. Robert Browning, in "My Last Duchess," creates the persona of a Renaissance duke to draw a portrait of his former wife. The speaker's voice, like that of a real person, may change and may express different tones throughout the poem as his or her attitudes vary toward the subject, toward himself or herself, and toward the reader. In "Idle Hands" by Gabriel Spera, the speaker's tone is at first meditative, but in the last lines it becomes angry and polemic.

The Poetic Elements: Images, Simile, Metaphor, Symbol, Personification, Paradox

Notice that the language of poetry is especially rich in creating images that evoke the senses of sight, smell, hearing, taste, and touch. To achieve their purposes, writers use not only language that communicates images literally but also figurative language that compares objects, describes emotions, and appeals to the reader's imagination through figures of speech such as simile, metaphor, symbol, personification, and paradox. To become an effective reader of poetry, learn to recognize how these elements reinforce poetic meaning.

Images are words and phrases that communicate sensory experiences and convey moods and emotions. Notice in "To His Coy Mistress," for example, how Andrew Marvell uses visual images such as "The Indian Ganges" and "Deserts of vast eternity" as well as auditory images, like "Time's winged chariot hurrying near," to evoke an exotic view of the romantic urgency of passion and desire.

A *simile* is a direct comparison between two explicit terms, usually introduced by *like* or *as*. In "London, 1802," the patriotic speaker of William Wordsworth's poem compares Milton's soul to a "star" and the "sound" of his voice to the sea: "Thy soul was like a Star . . . Thou hadst a voice whose sound was like the sea." Through these similes, the speaker endows Milton's soul and voice with emblematic naturelike qualities that place him above the "selfish men."

A *metaphor* is an implicit comparison that omits *like* or *as*. Wordsworth ends "London, 1802" with the metaphor of England as "a fen / Of stagnant waters" to criticize the inertia and stagnation in which the country had fallen in the beginning of the nineteenth century. Much of the meaning of this poem depends on the contrast that the speaker, who includes himself among the "selfish men," established between himself and Milton.

A *symbol* is a sign that points to meanings beyond its literal significance. The cross, for instance, is an archetype universally accepted as a symbol of Christianity. In John Keats's "Bright Star," the "bright star" points beyond the literal meaning the word suggests to function as a symbol that affirms and negates the idealized view of love.

Personification is the attribution of human qualities to animals, ideas, or inanimate things. It is used in these lines from Ralph Waldo Emerson's "Concord Hymn":

> Spirit that made those heroes dare
> To die and leave their children free

A *paradox* is a statement that appears to be contradictory and absurd but displays an element of truth. In Yevgeny Yevtushenko's poem "People," the paradox "We who knew our fathers / in everything, in nothing" suggests our inability to know or understand fully another human being, even a parent.

Types of Poetry: Lyric, Dramatic, and Narrative

A *lyric poem* is usually a short composition depicting the speaker's deepest emotions and feelings. Lyric poems are especially effective in arousing personal participation of readers and in stirring their sensations, feelings, and emotions. Songs, elegies, odes, and sonnets fall into this category.

A *dramatic poem* uses dramatic monologue or dialogue and assumes the presence of another character besides the speaker of the poem. In Robert Browning's "My Last Duchess" and also in Spera's poems "Idle Hands" and "Kindness," the speakers assume the presence of an audience.

A *narrative poem* usually emphasizes action or plot. "Home Burial" by Robert Frost qualifies as a narrative poem in which the action of the story—the loss of a child—creates the obstacle that impairs communication between husband and wife. The narrative is also dramatic because the action emerges though dialogue, not indirectly by description.

The Forms of Poetry

Some poems in this anthology use structural forms long established by literary history and tradition. In fact, for many poets a vision of poetic completion revolves around an idea of poetic structure or the formal beauty of a poetic pattern. Thus, to read a poem effectively and establish a dialogue with its poetic voice, you should be able to recognize some of the elements of poetic form.

Meter is the recurrent pattern of stressed and unstressed syllables in a poetic line. Together with elements such as rhyme and pause, meter determines the rhythm of the poem. One way to identify the metrical pattern of a poem is to mark the accented and unaccented syllables of the poetic line, as in the following example from a sonnet by Shakespeare:

My mistress' eyes are nothing like the sun

Next, divide the line into feet, the basic unit of measurement, according to patterns of accented and unaccented syllables. These are the five most common types of poetic feet:

iamb	(˘ ´)	forget
trochee	(´ ˘)	morning
anapest	(˘ ˘ ´)	at a house
dactyl	(´ ˘ ˘)	separate
spondee	(´ ´)	come, now

Shakespeare's line thus marked becomes five feet of iambs:

My mis/ tress' eyes/ are no/ thing like/ the sun/
    1   2   3   4   5

Notice that the length of the poetic lines depends on the number of poetic feet they possess, and they are defined by the following terms:

one foot   = monometer
two feet   = dimeter
three feet = trimeter
four feet = tetrameter
five feet = pentameter
six feet   = hexameter

Shakespeare's line "My mistress' eyes are nothing like the sun" is a good example of iambic pentameter, one of the most common patterns in English poetry.

Two other terms to recognize in relation to meter are *caesura*, a pause or pauses within the poetic line, and *enjambment*, a poetic line that carries its meaning and sound to the next line. The following lines, from the poem "Concord Hymn" by Ralph Waldo Emerson, provide us with a good example of an enjambment followed by a caesura:

> Bid Time and Nature gently spare
> The shaft we raise to them and thee.

A *stanza* is a group of two or more poetic lines forming the same metrical pattern or a closely similar pattern that is repeated throughout the poem. Most stanzas combine a fixed pattern of poetic lines with a fixed *rhyme scheme*. Thomas Hardy's poem "The Man He Killed" follows the traditional pattern of the *ballad stanza:* a quatrain (four-line stanza).

> Had he and I but met
> By some old ancient inn,
> We should have sat us down to wet
> Right many a nipperkin!

Notice that Hardy varies the typical rhyme scheme of the ballad stanza, in which only the second and fourth lines rhyme (which is called an *abcb* scheme), by also rhyming his first and third lines, to create an *abab* scheme.

Conventionally, the English *sonnet* is a poem of fourteen iambic pentameter lines. Immortalized by the fourteenth-century Italian poet Petrarch, the sonnet spread throughout Europe, becoming a major form across many cultures. Through it, sonneteers represented and explored the inward self and public life. Shakespeare and many other English poets used the *abab cdcd efef gg* rhyme scheme, which marks the division of a sonnet into three quatrains (four-line groupings) and a couplet (two rhyming lines). John Keats also uses this Shakespearean sonnet pattern in "Bright Star."

Blank verse is unrhymed iambic pentameter. Because it closely approximates the rhythm of human speech, blank verse was long considered an ideal dramatic medium, Shakespeare used it in many of his plays.

Free verse is poetry that does not follow a fixed pattern of rhythm, rhyme, and stanzaic arrangements. Like Walt Whitman, many poets have abandoned any kind of poetic structure for free verse, relying instead on a pattern based largely on repetition and parallel grammatical structure. The primary focus of free verse is not the external poetic form but the presence of an internal voice of address. One example is Whitman's "What Is the Grass?":

> What do you think has become of the young and old men?
> And what do you think has become of the women and children?

Most contemporary poets either use free verse or combine traditional and new patterns.

Poetry as Performance: The Sounds of Poetry

Reading a poem aloud is more than encountering actions and situations that the poet's creative imagination reshaped as meanings, rhythms, and emotions; it is an act of oral delivery conveying to the poetic discourse a special kind of situation and point of view comparable to the performance of a play. In fact, in most ancient cultures, and in some contemporary ones, poetry had strong ties to the oral tradition, and it was often meant to be sung and accompanied by musical instruments like the lyre. Although the oral delivery of poetry has been widely replaced by silent reading, reading a poem aloud will allow you to recover the emotional and phonic potential through which poetry expresses its relation to music and to life's dramatic possibilities. You will encounter the poetic voice—the voice that speaks the poem—in the act of expressing the poem's full potentiality.

To form layers of poetic meaning, poets throughout the centuries have explored several phonic devices, such as alliteration, repetition, onomatopoeia, assonance, as well as effects of orchestration, the clash of consonants. Here are some of the most common poetic devices.

Alliteration is the repetition of the initial sounds of the words in a poetic line. In "Federico's Ghost," Martín Espada uses alliteration (repetition of the plosive sound {p}) along three poetic lines:

> The pilot understood.
> He circled the plane and sprayed again,
> watching a fine gauze of poison . . .

Repetition refers to the repetition of a single word or phrase, the repetition of a refrain or a specific line or lines in a poem, or the repetition of a slightly changed version of a poetic line.

Onomatopoeia is the use of words that evoke or imitate the sounds they describe, such as *slam*, *murmur*, and *splash*.

DRAMA

Unlike fiction and most poetry, plays are intended to be performed before an audience, making drama primarily a communal art form in which the playwright collaborates with actors, director, and designers of set, lighting, and costume to produce an aural, visual, and social experience. If you are unable to see a performance of the plays included in this book, try to view a video production of *Antigone, Medea, Hamlet,* or *Tartuffe.*

What is the function of drama? Although its purpose and functions have evolved from ancient Greece to the present, according to contemporary playwright Arthur Miller, "all plays we call great, let alone those we call serious, are ultimately involved with some aspects of a single problem. It is this. How may man make of the outside world a home?" Unlike Greek playwrights or Shakespeare, many modern dramatists, like Miller, are most concerned with presenting social issues on stage. In the last decade, for example, several dramas have focused on the suffering and death caused by two contemporary forms of plague, cancer and AIDS, demonstrating the playwright's commitment to exploring the relation between the individual and society and to urging the audience to consider its personal and social commitment.

The Basic Elements of Drama

Characterization

Dramatis personae are the characters in a play. Usually the names of the persons who appear in a play, the dramatic characters, are listed at the beginning, often with a brief description. Read this list carefully to understand who the characters are.

As you read the play, pay attention not only to the dialogue of the characters but also to what the *stage directions* say about their entrances and exits, clothing, tone of voice, facial expressions, gestures, and movements.

As in fiction, the *protagonist*, or main character, of a play opposes the *antagonist*, or the character or other elements that defy his or her stability. In some plays there is a fairly simple contrast, as between Medea and Jason and between Medea and Athenian law; in others, as in *Antigone*, there is a more complex or involved contrast—not just between Antigone and Creon but also between Antigone and Ismene, Creon and Haimon, and religious and civil law. Often, if you recognize different sides of the conflict between a protagonist and an antagonist, you will be able to identify the core of the dramatic action of the play.

It is also important to notice that characters and dramatic action are intrinsically connected. In *Othello*, for instance, dramatic action emerges from Iago's inner motivation and goals to bring about Othello's downfall.

Plot

Plot may be defined as the arrangement of the dramatic action of a play. A typical plot structure follows a pattern of rising and falling action along five major steps: the exposition (or presentation of the dramatic situation), the rising action, the climax, the falling action, and the conclusion. The arrangement of the dramatic action in *Hamlet* may be illustrated by the so-called pyramid pattern, which is not always as symmetrical as the following diagram suggests.

Plot Structure of *Hamlet*				
Exposition	Rising action	Climax	Falling action	Conclusion
Death of old Hamlet	Appearance of ghost	From the play within the play to the killing of Polonius	Ophelia's death	Hamlet's death
Accession of Claudius	Hamlet's promise of revenge		Hamlet's return	
Gertrude's marriage				

To understand how the plot develops, consider the dramatic crisis that follows the major conflict, as well as subplots, or secondary lines of action connected with the main plot. In Hamlet, for example, the relationship between Hamlet and Ophelia, reflects and comments on the major conflicts between Hamlet and Claudius and Hamlet and Gertrude.

One can look at the plot arrangement of Greek plays such as *Antigone* and *Medea* from the point of view of the conventions of *time*, *place*, and *action* (the three unities). According to these conventions, traditionally attributed to Aristotle and the later dramatic theorists of the Renaissance (although Shakespeare did not observe them), the action of a play should not exceed a period of twenty-four hours (unity of time). Its locale should always remain the same (unity of place), and its actions and incidents should all contribute to the resolution of the plot (unity of action). An analysis of *Antigone* and *Medea* from the viewpoint of these conventions will reveal the dramatic freedom taken in the film versions of these classical plays.

Theme

Theme is the central idea or ideas dramatized in a play. Although you can look for a play's theme in the title, conflict, characters, or scenery, the ideas and the meanings you identify with will depend on your own set of beliefs, assumptions, and experiences. The play *Kiss of the Spider Woman*, for instance, explores what happens when two male characters, a revolutionary and a homosexual, liberate themselves from the oppressive constrictions of their own psyches.

Types of Plays: Tragedy, Comedy, and Tragicomedy

According to Aristotle, whose *Poetics* provides an analysis of the nature of classical drama, *tragedy* is the highest form of literary art. It deals with protagonists who are better than we are because of their engagement in honorable or dignified actions and their capacity to maintain their human dignity when withstanding adversity and suffering. Tragic protagonists are often also somehow connected with the religious and political destiny of their country. *Antigone*, for example, asks deeply religious questions about an individual's responsibility to the laws of God and the laws of the state. Greek and Shakespearean tragedies such as *Antigone*, *Medea*, and *Hamlet* are centered on the struggle that the protagonists, the *tragic heroes* and *heroines*, conduct against antagonistic forces.

The major event in a tragedy is the downfall that the protagonist suffers as a result of external causes (fate, coincidence), internal causes (ambition, excessive pride or hubris), or some error or frailty for which he or she is at least partially responsible. According to Aristotle, the spectators are purged of the emotions of "pity and fear" as they watch the hero or the heroine fall from greatness and as they witness the self-knowledge that the tragic protagonist gains in the process. The term *catharsis* refers to the emotional process that spectators undergo when they view a tragedy.

For modern playwrights, the protagonists of tragedies are no longer extraordinary beings but ordinary human beings caught in the struggle to shape their identities amid the crude realities of external and internal circumstances. In *Kiss of the Spider Woman*, for instance, Manuel Puig explores the causes and effects of political and sexual violence on Valentin and Molina. In the modern tragedy, the audience is urged to confront the corresponding social issues. Sometimes, in contemporary plays, the audience is also asked to participate in the actual performance of the play, or to construct meanings that determine the conclusion of the play.

In its ancient origins, *comedy* was a type of drama, designed to celebrate the renewal of life. Classical comedies usually dealt with the lives of ordinary people caught in personal and social conflicts, which they attempted to overcome through wit and humor. Unlike classical tragedies, which focus on heroes and heroines who are greater than ordinary human beings, classical comedies such as *Tartuffe* explore the lives of ordinary people facing the realities of love, sex, and class. Tragedies usually lead to a sense of wasted human potential in the death of the protagonist, whereas comedies tend to promote a happy ending through the reestablishment of social norms. Most contemporary plays, however, are tragicomedies combining the hilarious ingredients of comedy with the dramatic overtones of tragedy, as seen in *Picnic on the Battlefield*, Fernando Arrabal's humorous portrayal of the irrationality of war.

Kinds of Theater

Greek theater developed in Athens in connection with religious celebrations in honor of Dionysus, the god of wine and revelry. Athenian drama festivals also gained social and political meaning, becoming an intrinsic part of Athenian cultural life.

Plays such as *Medea* and *Antigone* were performed in large semicircular amphitheaters like the Theater of Dionysus at Athens, which could hold about seventeen thousand spectators. To cope with the physical conditions of such huge amphitheaters, actors had to look larger than life by wearing masks, padded costumes, elevated shoes, and mouthpieces that amplified their voices. Women's roles were performed by male actors because in Greek culture, as in many other early cultures, performances by women were taboo.

Greek plays such as *Antigone* usually alternate dramatic episodes with choral odes, following a five-part dramatic structure:

Prologue	Parados	Episodia/Stasimon	Exodos
Background information	Chorus; evaluation of situation	Debates followed by choral odes	Last scene

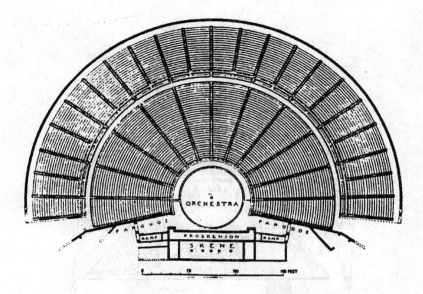

Illustration of the Greek Amphitheater at Epidaurus

The *chorus* consisted of a group of about twelve actors (often led by a leader, or *choragos*) who sang and danced in the *orchestra*, an area at the foot of the amphitheater. The chorus served several other functions as well: it represented the voice of the community, commented on the events of the play, provided background information about the story, and sometimes participated in the dramatic action. As part of its choreography, the chorus moved from right to left across the orchestra, the "dancing place" of the stage, as they sang the *strophe*, or the choral lyric, of the ode, and from left to right as they sang the *antistrophe*.

When reading a Greek play, keep in mind the following theatrical conventions:

Comic relief is provided by comic speeches or scenes that occur in a serious play. Consider, for example, the relief from dramatic action that the character of the sentry provides in *Antigone*.

Dramatic irony is a double meaning that occurs when the audience possesses foreknowledge of the situation and is therefore better informed than the characters. An effective example of dramatic irony occurs when Creon says after Haimon's death that nothing else could hurt him. However, he speaks this moments before he finds out about his wife's death, of which the audience is already aware.

Elizabethan theater, including Shakespearean theater, refers to plays written during the reign of Queen Elizabeth I of England (1558–1603). Compared to the huge Greek amphitheaters, the Elizabethan playhouse was small, seating a maximum of three thousand spectators. Its stage, as the nearby illustration shows, protruded into the orchestra so that the audience and actors could enjoy a more intimate theatrical atmosphere. Because Elizabethan theater used little setting, it was the power of Shakespeare's poetic language that stimulated the spectators to exercise their imagination and visualize places like the platform of the watch at the royal castle at Elsinore in *Hamlet*.

Although the text of *Hamlet* shows a series of structural divisions into acts and scenes, in Shakespeare's day *Hamlet* and the other Shakespearean plays were performed without any intermission. In Elizabethan theater, as in Greek theater, male actors performed female roles. The first actresses appeared on the English stage only after the Restoration of Charles II in 1660.

Illustration of a Shakespearean Playhouse

Shakespearean plays employ the theatrical conventions of soliloquy and aside:

A *soliloquy* is a speech delivered by a character who is alone on the stage. Through these speeches, such as Hamlet's famous soliloquy "O, what a rogue and peasant slave am I!" (act 2, scene 2, line 475), actors reveal their thoughts, feelings, inner struggles, and psychological complexity, securing their ties with the audience. The critic Ralph Berry believes that soliloquies permit the actors to establish a special kind of relationship with the audience. It is in his sequence of soliloquies, Berry argues, that Hamlet manages to seduce the audience.

An *aside* is a short speech that a character delivers in an undertone directly to the audience and that is not heard by the other actors on stage. For instance, Hamlet's aside "A little more than kin, and less than kind!" (act 1, scene 2, line 65) invites the audience to share the state of mind he has adopted toward Claudius.

In *neoclassical theater* the elegant and sophisticated dramas of Pierre Corneille (1606–84), Jean-Baptiste Poquelin Molière (1622–73), and Jean Racine (1639–99) established the principles of a new theatrical style. Dating from seventeenth-century France, neoclassical plays of the Golden Age of French drama were performed indoors in a proscenium theater (area located between the curtain and the orchestra) equipped with a raised stage and painted Italianate scenery. Mythological heroic figures and biblical sources became the subject matter of neoclassic tragedies, while the manners, values, and sexual intrigues of the upper and middle classes supplied the subject matter for comedies like Molière's *Tartuffe*.

Neoclassical theater employed several theatrical conventions, most of which were established as rules or formulas by which the Académie française, founded by Cardinal Richelieu in 1637, evaluated the artistic merits of a play. Molière uses many of the fundamental neoclassical conventions, such as the five-act structure, the principles of decorum (conformity to social conventions) and verisimilitude (the appearance of being true or near), and the unities of time, place, and action.

Realistic theater dates from nineteenth-century Europe. One of its purposes was to set the daily reality of middle-class life against antagonistic social conventions. The physical conditions of the picture-frame stage, with its proscenium arch, favored the exhibiting of realistic, lifelike pictures of everyday life. *Kiss of the Spider Woman*, by Manuel Puig, is a good example of a play that relies on the specific conditions of a realistic setting. The prison cell where the protagonists are confined conveys to the audience the degree to which its oppressive, degrading surroundings can influence and dominate human actions.

Theater of the absurd, which has developed in the second half of the twentieth century, portrays human beings as antiheroes caught in a world that is basically irrational, unpredictable, and illogical. Playwright Eugene Ionesco (1912–94) defined theater of the absurd as "that which has no purpose or goal or objective." Two major techniques of absurdist drama include the lack of logically connected events and the presence of characters whose fragmented language, personalities, and nihilistic attitudes undermine their ability to control their own destiny. *Picnic on the Battlefield*, Fernando Arrabal's absurdist play, provides a good example of a drama whose challenges to a rational view of life verge on the absurd. Instead of constructing a classical plot or creating characters with developed personalities, Arrabal presents one dramatic episode in which the characters Zapo and Zépo are so similar that they are practically interchangeable. Although absurdist theater can be performed on any kind of stage, contemporary dramatists prefer a stage with only a few props that are suggestive of a realistic setting or symbolic of the play's meaning.

FICTION, POETRY, AND DRAMA AS CULTURAL PRODUCTIONS

As part of your reading experience, *Literature Across Cultures* asks you not only to analyze the formal aspects of literature but also to integrate your study of the literary genres with a cultural focus that attempts to discover connections among literature, film, culture, and society. Such interactions will enable you not only to consider the interpretation of the literary text but to understand also its historical and cultural significance.

In addition to the Cultural Contexts questions after each reading selection in this anthology, the following topics will help you initiate a culturally oriented discussion of literature and film:

1. To examine the relation between the text and its social reality, consider the relation between writers and the cultural and historical issues of their times. Your focus here should be the literary text and its cultural (philosophical, religious, sociohistorical, and political) perspectives.
2. Focus on the physical and social aspects of the setting, attempting to define the tensions and relations between the setting and the speaker.
3. Notice how many plots, especially in fiction, tend to challenge or reinforce the conventional focus concerning the quest for individual identity and the sometimes competing values of the community.

4. When you study characterization, explore private and public attitudes toward race, class, gender, law, economics, and justice.

5. Think about the extent to which social and psychological forces such as heredity, environment, or fate control the action of individuals. Are individuals presented as victims of society? What kinds of responses do they develop to counteract the influence of society?

You may also consider the following topics:

6. The interplay of gender and power.
7. Gender differences.
8. Male gender construction.
9. The male patriarchal psyche and its definition of masculinity.
10. Sex role stereotypes supporting traditional notions of masculine aggression and feminine passivity.
11. The conflict between the individual and the social self.
12. Individuality and community as the core of American character.
13. Individual aspirations and community responsibility.
14. The psychological drama of the individual self.
15. The presence of the self in social, sexual, and cultural contexts.
16. The relation between war and violence.
17. Issues of cultural identity, gender, politics, and class. Their effects on individual and social identity.
18. Individuality and identity as products of a fixed historical era.
19. The forces of tradition and change and their effects on individual and communal lives.
20. The politics of domestic life; the organization of the family; the separation of private and public responsibility.
21. Changing concepts of the role of the family.
22. The politics of domestic life as affected by gender and class.
23. The significance of single-parent households.
24. The nature of mother–daughter, father–daughter, father–son, mother–son relations.
25. The role of the family in validating or manipulating one's sense of self.
26. The ethnic structure of the family and its effects on gender identity and communal relationships.
27. The literary text as a protest against racism or sexism.
28. The relation between war and sexual violence.
29. Immigration and its influence on contemporary culture.
30. The dominant ideology of the text: who has power, who benefits from portrayal of power.
31. The dynamics of male–female relations both within and outside of conventional social roles.
32. Women as creators and shapers of culture and history.
33. Evolving images and representations of women and men.
34. The causes and effects of sexism and domestic violence.
35. The sexual division of labor and its effects on gender relations.
36. Class distinction and class mobility within society; the causes of exclusion from the mainstream.

37. The interplay of class, race, and economics.
38. The causes and effects of segregation and integration.
39. Racial stereotypes, racial differences, and racial dominance; their effects on individuals and group identity.
40. Causes and effects of racial, sexual, and economic oppression.
41. Stereotypes of sexuality and race; the function of color in literary and social contexts.
42. The relation among racism, sexism, and violence; attitudes toward sexual preferences and sexual differences.
43. Concepts of the melting pot versus ethnic identity.
44. The notion of tragedy, moving away from Aristotelian stress on character and tragic flaw toward a concern for the sociopolitical roles of men and women.
45. Causes and effects of sociopolitical order and disorder.
46. AIDS; the discrimination imposed on AIDS victims; the effects of AIDS on the family and on gender relationships.
47. The attempt to understand our individualism and participate in it.
48. How writers situate their work in relation to the collective past.
49. The role that movies have assumed as powerful cultural agents in rewriting the past.
50. Films as articulators of gender roles; films, in which male–female relationships are central to the story, as a reflection of traditional and/or social perspectives on gender roles.
51. Gender, race, sex, violence, and identity as prominent cultural issues in films.
52. How a film that you believe addresses an important issue in contemporary society either endorses the standard criteria of values or questions how standards of behavior are created and applied.
53. Portrayals of World War II and the Vietnam War in film.
54. Literature and film as articulators of male and female experiences of war.
55. The interplay of war and terrorism.
56. Individual freedom and terrorism.
57. Wars of choice and wars of necessity.
58. Patriotism and terrorism.
59. Peacemaking and wars of necessity.
60. It takes two to make peace.
61. Pop culture icons of music, beauty, and filmmaking.
62. The biological foundations of gender differences.
63. The myths and realities of sensuality and sexuality in American, Arab, and Hispanic societies.
64. Memories, recollections, or being witness to the Holocaust.
65. The battle between human conscience and the law of dictatorship.
66. Biracial buddy films.

APPENDIX B

Writing a Research Paper

WHAT IS A LITERARY RESEARCH PAPER?

Writing a literary research paper involves gathering and examining evidence in relation to a text, a related group of texts, or an author's body of work. Literary research means not only analyzing a particular work, but also consulting literary criticism that enhances your understanding of the text within cultural and historical contexts.

Although the heart of a literary research paper is your in-depth examination of the primary source (the text or texts in question), the ideas resulting from this examination must also be supported by your analysis of researched secondary sources, including literary criticism. Your conclusions, based on your research and your own opinions, are then presented in a well-developed paper, supported by valid, fully documented evidence assembled from your research.

What Are Primary and Secondary Sources?

In doing research, you will typically analyze a primary source or sources, and you will utilize secondary sources that put your primary sources in context.

1. *Primary Sources:* The focuses of your research—the poems, plays, short stories, or novels you are investigating—are considered *primary* sources. If you were doing research on Walt Whitman, his writings (such as the poem "What Is the Grass?") would be your primary sources.
2. *Secondary Sources:* Analytical materials that comment on and interpret primary sources are *secondary* sources. Critical responses to Whitman's "What Is the Grass?," academic analyses of "What Is the Grass?," and any other writings that shed light on "What is the Grass?" are considered secondary sources for the poem.

Locating Materials

Knowing what to look for is the key to successfully locating pertinent materials for your literary research paper. Although it can seem daunting at first, two main tools are available to you, the library and the Internet. When starting to research a topic, you should consult the largest, most contemporary resource, the Internet. Although resources on the Internet vary widely in credibility, the act of searching for materials itself can be helpful. The results of your web searchers will give you a better idea as to the scope of your research and will better prepare you for research at the library. Details on researching materials using the library and the Internet can be found in Appendix C.

How to Choose a Topic

Most likely, your instructor will have specific instructions regarding the assignment. If not, do not be afraid to seek more specific guidance.

In an introductory literature course, you will focus on text(s) by an assigned author that can be covered in detail in the paper's length (a short story, a related group of poems). However, you often analyze long texts (such as *Hamlet*) and in cases like that you likely will explore a specific aspect or issue in the work you find interesting. You would not be able to write an in-depth analysis of the entire play in ten pages or less.

1. Generate a list of observations and questions raised while reading a text. An aspect of a work that interests you might be worth investigating further (a theme, a use of symbolism, an enigmatic character). Even a problem that arose during the reading of a text might make a good topic; investigating secondary sources that explore the same problem and comparing the author's viewpoints to your own can make for a compelling research paper.
2. Discuss with your instructor aspects of a potential text you find interesting. See if she or he has any advice regarding potential research avenues.
3. Pick a topic that you yourself find interesting. Why do you feel this issue deserves exploration? Why might analysis of this topic be enlightening to your readers?
4. Do some preliminary reading of secondary sources to gain a general idea of the aspects of the text that seem to be receiving the greatest response from accredited experts.
5. Formulate a thesis that you can deal with, given the limited amount of space and time; your paper must present an argument regarding an aspect of a text that is narrow enough to be covered in detail in the space allotted but not so narrow or lacking in interest that you will have nothing to say.

A thesis for a literary research paper is a sentence that makes an argument about a text or group of texts. It has to fit the pattern of something that needs to be proven and with which others may disagree.

```
Hamlet is not, despite his words to the contrary, feigning
his insanity throughout the play; he is, in fact, quite
insane from the moment he sees the ghost of his murdered
father.
```

The foregoing is an example of an adequate thesis for a literary paper. You would have to support this thesis by focusing on moments throughout the play in which Hamlet "appears" mad and analyze them. In a literary *research* paper, you would also have to scrutinize secondary sources that also investigate Hamlet's madness and either "argue" with them or use them in support of your argument.

ENGAGING IN DIALOGUE USING LITERARY CRITICISM

Writing is no less a form of communication than speech; throughout history, arguments have raged on the printed page. In this kind of assignment, you will generally enter into an academic "dialogue" with the authors of the researched texts. Your responsibility is not only to present their assertions to your readers, but to respond to them as well.

To support your thesis, you will be using secondary sources. However, not all secondary sources gathered during your research will agree with your interpretation. Do not ignore differing opinions. If you can make a solid case to disagree with a published opinion, using textual evidence from both your primary and secondary sources, it can be very effective and thought provoking.

Most secondary sources you will find fall under the heading of literary criticism. Literary criticism is the evaluation, analysis and interpretation of a specific literary work, a group of works, or an author's writings as a whole. By addressing the arguments put forth by these critics you will give your readers a more comprehensive understanding of your thesis and compel their respectful attention. Even if they ultimately disagree with your conclusions, you want them to find your presentation informed, thoughtful, and valid. That is to say, your paper must demonstrate your mastery of all relevant data, that you examine your sources critically, and that your conclusions follow sensibly from your presented evidence and arguments.

FOCUS: THE RESEARCH PROCESS

Critical to a successful literary research paper is the proper analysis of all your sources. Part of this process includes carefully organizing the information you gather and laying this information out to support your thesis coherently.

Taking Notes during the Research Process

Keep a running list in your word processor of all your sources, including the following details:

1. Name of the author, editor, and/or translator (if any)
2. Title of work (including book title as well as article or chapter title, if applicable)
3. Edition or volume of work
4. Place of publication
5. Publishing company
6. Date
7. Website URL (if applicable)

It is ideal to photocopy the original sources, so that you can highlight, underline, and comment on the text directly. Once you have read all the materials, go back through the text, typing all the relevant points in your word processor and taking note of the pages the points are taken from, making it easy to refer back to the original text.

Organizing Your Information

Once you have all your various ideas typed out, go through your notes and rearrange them, categorizing by major topic. This will make it easy for you to organize your research paper logically and coherently. While writing your paper, it is imperative to avoid listing one source's arguments on one page and another source's arguments on the next. Rather, mix and match information related to your thesis, and utilize your sources in a more dynamic and appealing manner. Your job is to shape the discussion so the reader is aware that this manuscript is solely your creation.

DRAFTING THE PAPER

Write an introduction that compels your reader to continue. The introduction, with few exceptions, should also provide the name and author of the primary work(s) and present your thesis statement.

The body of your paper should develop your thesis, supporting your assertions with evidence compiled from your primary source(s) and from your researched secondary sources. Use limited plot summary, only when necessary to clarify a point being made. A critical aspect of drafting a research paper is the flow of ideas. Be sure to spend time organizing your thoughts, arguments, and relevant sources. Your ideas should be grouped and follow logically and clearly. Do not jump around from idea to idea, which will only confuse your reader.

Incorporate all sources smoothly, using clear, precise transitions between your work and theirs, and cite them correctly.

Your conclusion should sum up your ideas and arguments and usually restate your thesis. Use your conclusion to give the reader a strong and satisfying last impression.

HOW TO DOCUMENT USING THE MLA FORMAT

A formal literary research paper involves citing, or documenting, the texts (both primary and secondary) you have employed. Presenting research means incorporating conclusions and ideas not originated by you. You must document all sources of information used, whether you quote the source directly using the exact words of the original author, or indirectly, rewriting the information in your own words. For general knowledge, such as the fact that Nathaniel Hawthorne wrote "Young Goodman Brown" or that Salem is in Massachusetts, you need not attribute such facts to a source. However, when you include information that you would not have known without referring to a particular source, such as the fact that Nathaniel Hawthorne's ancestors were involved in the Salem witch trials, you must credit the source. Therefore it is essential to take notes on all information you gather from your sources.

Once you've researched your sources, chosen the best ones, and organized your materials, there is still the matter of how to present the information properly within the text. The format for parenthetical citation used in this book follows the guidelines that the Modern Language Association of America (MLA) has established for research papers on literary subjects. See the *MLA Handbook for Writers of Research Papers* (seventh edition) for further information.

Both direct quotations and paraphrased information from sources should be cited throughout your manuscript. MLA style dictates that the last name of the author and the page number of the source are given in parentheses at the end of employment of the source. Such citations inform the reader which source is currently being quoted or paraphrased and guide the reader to the Works Cited page at the end of your manuscript, which provides further details regarding the source.

The following citation appearing at the end of a direct quote or paraphrase would alert the reader to the source being used:

`(Christian 72)`

Because this presents only the last name of the author and the page number of the source, the reader learns the full detail of the source utilized upon referencing the Works Cited page:

```
Christian, Barbara. Black Women Novelists: The Development
     of a Tradition, 1892-1976. Westport: Greenwood, 1980.
     Print.
```

Direct Quotation

Use an introductory phrase (or "signal phrase") before quoting a source in the body of your essay. If you mention the author's name in your signal phrase, then only the page number is required in the parenthetical citation at the end of the sentence. For example, if you mentioned Barbara Christian's name in your sentence before quoting her, you would have to put only the page number (72) in the parenthetical citation. If the quotation is taken from another author's work, you must make note in the parenthetical citation. For example, if you quote Toni Morrison in an interview she gave to Barbara Christian, you would alert the reader that you are quoting Morrison in your signal phrase, then note Christian in the citation:

```
As Toni Morrison feels, ". . . " (qtd. in Christian, 125).
```

If you have read your sources in depth, have organized a basic structure to your paper (following the guidelines for writing a literary essay in the introduction—it is the same basic pattern, only now you are offering opinions beyond your own), and are ready to write a draft that synthesizes your ideas with those of the experts you read, you still have to present the research smoothly.

Choose an organizing principle to your paper that makes the readers feel you are gracefully leading them on an "intellectual journey" to a logical conclusion. You can't just drop research onto a page in a disorganized manner, jerkily leading your reader through detours, down one-way and dead-end streets and to a sudden halt, also known as "The End."

Although you should have a basic idea of essay construction from previous composition classes (and from the discussion of literary essay writing in the introduction to this book), you still might be hesitant about how to present research within the body of your essay.

Signal Phrases

Be sure when you quote to use "signal phrases" that alert the reader the quote is coming and put the quotation in context with what preceded it. Just as you need strong transitions between paragraphs in any essay, you need strong transitions when shifting from your thoughts to another writer's. In the following examples of signal phrases, take note of the placement of your punctuation, especially quotation marks and end punctuation.

```
As Sigmund Freud has noted, ". . ." (134).
In the words of Tim O'Brien, ". . ." (qtd. in Lowell, 33).
In the late 1940s, Simone de Beauvoir encouraged her
readers to ". . ." (106).
". . .," suggests Diane Elizabeth Dreher (55).
```

Note that periods go after the citations.

To keep your research paper from sounding repetitive, vary the ways in which you present quotations. The following are further examples of signal phrases:

```
X confidently argues
According to X,
In the words of X
X agrees with Y by stating
Another point X makes is that
. . . suggests X.
X writes
X disagrees, stating
```

Although *says* and *writes* are perfectly acceptable, other verbs provide degrees of meaning that can be used in signal phrases: *acknowledge, agree, argue, ask, assert, believe, claim, comment, communicate, confirm, contend, declare, deny, emphasize, endorse, insist, note, observe, point out, propose, refute, reject, report, speculate, suggest, think,* and many others. Spend time finding that *perfect* way to translate your researched author's thoughts.

Short Quotations

A quotation need not always be a complete sentence. Your voice, guiding us to an author's opinion, can be quite effective, as long as you don't mislead the reader into a distortion of the original thought:

```
Among many other things, Barbara Christian suggests the
importance of "practical slave culture without which black
people as an abused race would not have been able to
survive" (72).
```

You can omit words within a quotation if they are not essential to your point and if they slow down the rhythm of your paper. Use an ellipsis (three spaced periods) with brackets around it (to differentiate from an ellipsis in the original source) as identification that something has been deleted:

```
Among many other things, Barbara Christian suggests the
importance of "practical slave culture without which black
people [. . . ] would not have been able to survive" (72).
```

Long Quotations

Your paper should not be overburdened with long quotations; with too many long quotations, the paper ceases to be yours—it's as if you are renting space to the authors of the original texts. On occasion, however, long quotations are necessary to present an author's complex theory or to set up a long analysis of the quoted material.

Any quotation of more than three lines should start on a new line and should be indented ten spaces. Because the indented format indicates that the words are taken from a secondary source, quotation marks are not necessary. The parenthetical citation should come two spaces after the period that ends the long quotation.

Note the difference in punctuation from short quotations that appear within the body of your paragraphs, where the parenthetical citation comes before the period ending the sentence.

> Randall Jarrell demonstrates his enthusiasm for Robert
> Frost's poetry when he asserts in *Poetry and the Age:*
>> Frost's virtues are extraordinary. No other living
>> poet has written so well about the actions of
>> ordinary men; his wonderful dramatic monologues or
>> dramatic scenes come out of a knowledge of people
>> that few poets have had, and they are written in a
>> verse that uses, sometimes with absolute mastery,
>> the rhythms of actual speech. (28)

Quoting from a Poem

When quoting from poetry, use slash marks to designate the end of a line, and duplicate the exact capitalization and punctuation of the poem. Give the line numbers in parentheses.

> In "Babiy Yar," Yevgeny Yevtushenko creates images that
> stimulate the imagination when he writes, "I, wandering in
> Egypt. / I crucified, I, perishing." (7-8).

If you are quoting more than a few lines of poetry, begin on a new line and indent ten spaces. Copy the quoted lines exactly. Do not follow the citation of line numbers with a period.

> In the following example, Martín Espada uses alliteration to
> paint a vivid picture of his protagonist in "Cross Plains,
> Wisconsin":
>> Blue bandana
>> across the forehead,
>> beard bristling
>> like a straw broom
>> sleeveless T-shirt
>> of the Puerto Rican flag (1-6)

Quoting from a Play

When quoting from a play, always give act, scene, and line numbers in Arabic (not Roman) numerals. Brief quotations may be placed within your main text. Start long quotations on a new line, and indent the quotation ten spaces.

> Hamlet observes Claudius and says, "Now might I do it pat,
> now he is praying, / And now I'll do it" (3.3.73-74).

Hamlet initially appears to feel confident that killing
Claudius as the King prays would fulfill his mandate for
revenge:

> Now might I do it pat, now he is praying,
> And now I'll do it. And so he goes to Heaven,
> And so I am revenged. That would be scanned:
> A villain kill my father, and for that
> I, his sole son, do this same villain send
> To Heaven. (3.3.73-78)

He sounds as if he is ready to act, but by repeating
himself in lines 73 and 74 ("I do it" and "I'll do it") it
appears he is not ready, but instead is trying to convince
himself to act. Twice repeating in lines 74 and 78 that
Claudius will be sent "to Heaven" is another indication
that this plan, despite being seemingly "scanned," is not
all that it initially appears: he has a creeping awareness
that Claudius going to heaven would hardly be a befitting
comeuppance.

Note that you return to the left margin to continue the paragraph in which you are utilizing the long quotation. Also note that if you do use a long quotation, you need to comment on it fully; here, the writer covers several lines from the passage quoted to justify the use of the long quote. If the writer were to analyze only lines 73 and 74, she or he would be justified in quoting only those two lines.

When quoting from plays that are not divided into acts, such as *Antigone*, give the scene and line numbers:

Creon asks his son Haimon a key question in relation to
his decision regarding Antigone: "You have heard my final
judgement on that girl: Have you come here hating me, or
have you come With difference and with love, whatever I
do?" (3.5-8)

Also indicate who is speaking if you are quoting dialogue or a passage in which more than two characters speak:

Hamlet, feeling betrayed, is suddenly aggressive toward
his love:

> HAMLET. Ha, ha! Are you honest?
> OPHELIA. My lord?
> HAMLET. Are you fair?

```
OPHELIA.  What means your lordship?
HAMLET.  That if you be honest and fair, your honesty
    should admit not discourse to your beauty?
    (3.1.103-107)
```

One sees that Ophelia, despite her betrayal of Hamlet, has no taste for it. When he begins questioning her honesty and fairness, she appears unsure of how to respond, as if in fact she has forgotten that she is currently deceiving him.

Again, note that when you quote, it is your responsibility to comment on the passage. Explain how it relates to the overall point you are trying to make in the paragraph. Don't expect a quotation to explain itself—it is your duty to assume that the reader needs assistance in assimilating the information.

Indirect Quotation: Paraphrasing

Instead of quoting a source directly, you can paraphrase, or give the information in your own words, using roughly the same number of words you found in the source. The key to paraphrasing is to relay the source's information without directly copying the original phrasing.

The following quotation by R.W.B. Lewis, regarding influences on Edith Wharton's *Ethan Frome*, is followed by a paraphrased version.

A certain Melvillian grandeur went into the configuration of her tragically conceived hero. Despite her early disclaimers, the spirit of Nathaniel Hawthorne pervades the New England landscape of the novella. . . . The role of the inquisitive city-born narrator is deployed with a good deal of the cunning and artistry of Henry James.

R.W.B. Lewis notes the influence of Herman Melville, Nathaniel Hawthorne, and Henry James on Edith Wharton's novel *Ethan Frome*. The nobility of the hero derives from the epic characters of Melville's style with the added urban outlook of the Jamesian protagonist. The atmosphere is similar to that found in Hawthorne's depiction of New England. (309)

The source would be listed in the Works Cited just like a directly quoted source:

Lewis, R.W.B. *Edith Wharton: A Biography*. New York: Harper, 1975. Print.

List of Works Cited

The Works Cited list contains information about all the works you referred to or cited in your paper. If you obtained information from a source but ultimately did not use it in the paper, do not list it in the Works Cited list. List only sources cited in the paper.

- The list should appear on a separate page at the end of your paper.
- The heading (Works Cited) should be centered.
- Citations should be listed alphabetically by author, last name first.
- Double-space entries.
- To help readers locate the citations more easily, indent all lines of an entry except the first by a half inch (or five spaces).

Print and Nonprint Sources

BOOK BY ONE AUTHOR

Allen, Jeffrey Renard. *Rails Under My Back*. New York:
    Farrar, 2000. Print.

BOOK BY TWO OR THREE AUTHORS

Gilbert, Sandra M., and Susan Gubar. *The Madwoman in the
    Attic: The Woman Writer and the Nineteenth-Century
    Literary Imagination*. New Haven: Yale UP, 1979. Print.

BOOK BY FOUR OR MORE AUTHORS

Gatto, Joseph, et al. *Exploring Visual Design*. 2nd ed.
    Worcester: Davis, 1987. Print.

BOOK WITH AN EDITOR

Gates, Henry Louis Jr., ed. *Classic Slave Narratives*.
    New York: NAL, 1987. Print.

TWO OR MORE BOOKS BY THE SAME AUTHOR

Frye, Northrup. *Anatomy of Criticism: Four Essays*.
    Princeton: Princeton UP, 1957. Print.

——.*The Myth of Deliverance: Reflections on Shakespeare's
    Problem Comedies*. Toronto: U of Toronto P, 1983. Print.

WORK IN AN ANTHOLOGY OR COLLECTION

Berghahn, Marion. "Images of Africa in the Writings of
    James Baldwin." *James Baldwin*. Ed. Harold Bloom. New
    York: Chelsea, 1986. Print.

MULTIVOLUME WORK

> Wimsatt, William K., and Cleanth Brooks. *Literary*
>   *Criticism: A Short History*. 2 vols. Chicago: U of
>   Chicago P, 1979. Print.

ARTICLE IN A JOURNAL

> Giles, Ronald K. "Archetype and Irony in *The Natural*."
>   *English Journal* 75.4 (1986): 49-54. Print.

ARTICLE IN A NEWSPAPER

> Mcdowell, Edwin. "Black Writers Gain Audience and
>   Visibility in Publishing." *New York Times* 12 Feb.
>   1991: C11. Print.

BOOK REVIEW

> Gonzales, Ray. Rev. of *City of Coughing and Dead Radiators*,
>   by Martín Espada. *The Nation* 30 Jan. 1994: 131-33.
>   Print.

FILM

> *Hamlet*. Dir. Campbell Scott. Perf. Campbell Scott and
>   Blair Brown. Artisan Entertainment, 2000. Film.

AUDIOTAPE

> *The Metamorphosis*. Read by James Mason. Caedmon/Harper,
>   1962. Audiocassette.

Electronic Sources

Citing electronic sources is an even more involved and complicated process than citing traditional print sources. Many online sources, particularly those of good repute, follow the practices of traditional publishing to some extent. The Works Cited page should list as much of the following information as possible regarding Internet sources:

- Author or editor name
- Title of article or document
- Print publication information, if any
- Name of online site, journal, or database
- Length in pages or paragraphs or section numbers, if applicable
- Date of online publication and volume or issue number, if applicable
- Medium, usually *Web*.
- Date you acquired the information
- URL (Uniform Resource Locater)—only included when necessary for locating the document.

The following examples will help you in documenting Internet sources:

ONLINE JOURNAL

> Loranger, Carol. "'This Book Spills Off the Page in All
>   Directions': What Is the Text of Naked Lunch?"
>   *Postmodern Culture* 10.1 (1999): n.p. Web. 10 Oct.
>   1998.

ABSTRACT OF A JOURNAL ARTICLE

> Poovey, M. "Beyond the Current Impasse in Literary
>   Studies." Abstract. *American Literary History* 11.2
>   (1999): 354–377. Web. 22 Dec. 2001.

ONLINE MAGAZINE

> Offman, Craig. "Book Publishers Don't Check Their Authors'
>   Facts." *Salon*. Salon, 25 Oct. 1999. Web. 25 Oct.
>   2002.

ONLINE MAGAZINE, NO AUTHOR LISTED

> "Complete Journals of Sylvia Plath Will Be Published."
>   *CNN*. Cable News Network, 14 Oct. 1999. Web. 21 Oct.
>   2002.

ONLINE GOVERNMENT DOCUMENT

> United States. National Endowment for the Arts. *NEA*
>   *Strategic Plan: 2006–2011*. NEA.gov, Nov. 2006. Web.
>   20 Dec. 2010.

ARTICLE IN A REFERENCE DATABASE

> "Alice Walker." *Encyclopaedia Britannica Online*.
>   Encyclopaedia Britannica, 1999. Web. 21 Sept. 1999.

Refer to the *MLA Handbook* or your college handbook for a more detailed listing of formats for the Works Cited list. These formats are also available at www.mla.org.

REVISING AND REWRITING

Writing is about rewriting. Especially in something as detailed as an analytical literary research paper, you cannot hope to put together something coherent the evening before the paper is due. Give yourself time to read and reread your primary source, building the case for your thesis. It will take effort to merge your ideas with those of the experts whose opinions you have researched, and again, your final draft should be an informed, valid, and thoughtful defense of your thesis.

Presenting Your Research Paper

A quality presentation is key to a successful research paper. A sloppily presented paper will make the reader suspicious of the diligence of your overall research. The following are some guidelines for the proper presentation of your research paper:

- Use standard 8½″ × 11″ paper and a 12-point font unless otherwise instructed.
- Make multiple print copies of your paper, in case one is misplaced.
- Double-space your document.
- Center the title of your essay. The title should be relevant to your paper's thesis; a "hook" to get a reader's attention, followed by a colon and a more in-depth announcement of your paper's intentions is often an effective choice, though not the only one:

```
"What Dreams May Come": The Afterlife as Explored in
Hamlet
```

or

```
How to Drive a Woman Insane Without Even Trying:
Wallpaper as a Prison in "The Yellow Wallpaper"
```

Both of these titles intrigue the reader while announcing the overall topic of the paper.

- Number every page, except the title page, in the upper right-hand corner.

After finishing your final draft, ask yourself the following questions:

1. Have I proofread for clarity of presentation?
2. Have I proofread for spelling and punctuation?
3. Are all sources credited?
4. Have I made clear which opinions are mine and which belong to other authors?
5. Does the information I have included relate directly to a clear thesis?
6. Have I cited my sources correctly?
7. Do I have a Works Cited page? Is it correctly formatted?

Isabel Pipolo
Professor Robson
Introduction to Literature
2 December 2005

Antigone: The Woman, the Heroine,
the Role Model

The character of Antigone in Sophocles' play
has many different facets to her. She can be
analyzed either as a woman, as a heroine, or as a
role model. However, upon closer examination, is it
necessary to unite all these facets to create a
unique character and personality? Or can we say
that if taken separately, any one of these
individual personal traits would be enough to
describe her?

Antigone is not only different from women in
today's society, she's unique among the Greek
society presented in Sophocles' play. She
especially contrasts with the law-abiding Ismene.
As Ismene is overwhelmed by Creon's power, she
expects Antigone to behave as a typical woman and
submit to men: "we must be sensible. Remember we
are women, / we're not born to contend with men.
Then too, / we're underlings, ruled by much
stronger hands, / so we must submit in this, and
things still worse" (2.74-77). Antigone, however,
is independent and believes that she has a right to
her own opinion. Moreover, she is willing to defend
them at all costs even if it means forsaking the
roles--traditionally assigned to women--of marriage
and children.

Thus, while Ismene views her womanhood in
traditional ways, Antigone discovers strength in
her female nature and uses it to her own advantage.

Unlike Ismene, Antigone is not afraid to defy her
king. As the passage below shows, she values
marriage and children, but she is willing to give
them up for the honor of burying her brother:

> And now he leads me off, a captive in his
> hands, with no part in the bridal-song,
> the bridal-bed, denied all joy of
> marriage, raising children--deserted so
> by loved ones, struck by fate, I descend
> alive to the caverns of the dead.
> (2.1008-12).

Unlike Creon's, Antigone's values seem to be deeply
rooted in her duties to the dead members of her
family. She values her emotional ties to brother
Polyneices over her ties to country and king.

As a woman, too, Antigone resents the way Creon
sexualizes the power hierarchy in Thebes. As Charles
Paul Segal writes in his essay "Sophocles' Praise of
Man and the Conflicts of the *Antigone*," "Antigone's
struggle is the woman's emotional resistance to the
ordered male reason of the state" (66). However,
the conflict between Antigone and Creon can go
beyond the debate between a woman and a man. It can
be further defined, as Segal mentions, as Creon's
inability to grasp the reasons, the motives, and
the nature of the "woman's resistance." In such
a debate, Antigone comes out as more "typically
female" or at least as representing the emotional
side of human nature.

Antigone's display of her female nature in
such a rash and unrelenting way can be better
understood when we realize that Antigone is still
a very young, impetuous woman. Bowra remarks in his
book *Sophoclean Tragedy* that Antigone "is young,
a girl on the verge of womanhood, not yet married,

with a girl's directness and refusal to compromise" (90). Because of her age, Antigone expresses her love for her brother in a less "rational" way than we might expect.

Antigone can also be considered a heroine, not only in the context of the play but also in a more universal sense. Even though she is oppressed and stifled by Creon and his laws, which she considers unjust, she shows a heroic kind of resilience, courage, and determination to fight him to the death to defend her own principles. If we see Creon representing the "state" in a more general sense, then Antigone symbolizes the heroic moral claims of individual conscience.

In the play, Creon is often portrayed as a blind, stubborn leader who is drunk on his own power: "The city is the king's--that's the law!" (1.825). As Rebecca Bushnell notes in her book *Prophesying Tragedy*, "Creon is tyrannical in his belief in the power of his own voice and his separation of himself from the claims of humanity" (54). He also raises the power of the city and his rule above the religious traditions of the people. According to the critic Gerald Else, this empowerment of the state defied what the Greeks considered the natural order: "Creon [exalts] the city above the gods and their laws, thus subverting the hierarchical order" (12).

Antigone is also portrayed in the play as an oppressed member of society who envisions power and glory as the outcome of her heroic struggle against impossible odds:

> Give me glory! What greater glory could
> I win than to give my own brother decent
> burial? These citizens here would all

Pipolo 4

agree, they would praise me too if their
lips weren't locked in fear. (2.562-65)
Antigone is a representative of the common people
who are unable to voice their opinions because of
the threat of political dictatorship. As she rises
as a heroic figure, she becomes an ideal for those
who are not strong enough to stand up on their own
and fight. Because of her strength, obstinate
personality, and moral convictions, she also becomes
a role model for her sister Ismene and for those who
believe she is right.

Even though Antigone has some influence over
Ismene, this is not enough to convince her sister to
defy Creon, his patriarchal system, and his public
policy. By the end of the play, however, after
Ismene has been convinced of the heroic purpose of
Antigone's madness and is willing to die with her,
Antigone will not let her. She feels that Ismene
would be sharing the glory for a courageous act in
which she had no part: "Never share my dying, /
don't lay claim to what you never touched. / My
death will be enough" (2.615-17)

Antigone also becomes a role model for Haimon,
her cousin and husband-to-be. In spite of his
initial assurance of his loyalty to his father,
Haimon proves that he and the people of Thebes
support Antigone. He tries to lend his support to
her by discussing the situation with his father,
but he fails to convince Creon of his error. His
support for Antigone unfailing, he ultimately has
no choice: "Haemon can join [Antigone] only by
joining in her death" (Scodel 50). Haimon's
suicide, in fact, may be seen as his final act in
support of Antigone.

Pipolo 5

What is most remarkable about Antigone's influence over Haimon is that her actions motivate him to challenge his father's private and public authority. It is to Antigone that Haimon owes his loyalty. Not only does Haimon betray his father to someone else, but he also betrays him for a woman, which is exactly what Creon seems to fear throughout. As Segal remarks in his essay,

> [Creon] sees in Antigone a challenge to his whole way of living and his basic attitudes toward the world. And of course he is right, for Antigone's full acceptance of her womanly nature, her absolute valuation of the bonds of blood and affection, is a total denial of Creon's obsessively masculine rationality. (70)

In betraying his father, therefore, and siding with Antigone, Haimon not only breaks his bonds of loyalty to father and family, but breaks them in conjunction with his affirmation of female power. His attitude especially antagonizes his father. The fact that Haimon takes such action against Creon's powerful voice may be considered a sign that Antigone functioned as a role model to him.

The individual traits that make up Antigone's character, portraying her as a woman, a heroine, and a role model, are all important factors in understanding her motivations and what she symbolizes as a whole. None of these categorizations on their own, however, is enough to completely explain her, since she has so many different sides. Bowra describes her character

as a complex one that can be seen from different
perspectives at different times:

> She is a human being, moved by deep
> affection and capable of true
> love. . . . . She is no embodiment of
> abstract devotion to duty, no martyr for
> martyrdom's sake, but a girl of strong
> character and strong feelings. Her
> motives are fundamentally simple, but are
> displayed now in one light, now in
> another, as her circumstances or her
> needs vary. (90)

However, together with each one of her individual
facets, Antigone also shows a dark and complex side
to her personality. It is this darkness and
complexity, in fact, that makes her so interesting.
She is also guided by what we might consider some
self-centered, negative drives.

She is inspired by her loyalty to her family
and to the gods, but what really drives her and what
enables her to stand resolute against Creon's decree
is her tragic inability to negotiate, compromise, or
see any kind of virtue in somebody else's argument.
Such personality traits make Antigone inflexible
and unable to relate well to others. Eventually
they lead to her death. However, they also are what
really makes Antigone different and noticeable in
this play. She is fighting for what she believes
in, and even though she is far from perfect, she is
carrying out her fight her own way.

Therefore, as a whole, we could say that what
Antigone really represents is a complete human
being. She means well when she defends her
individual conscience against Creon's public

policy. However, she is undone by her own frailties
and cannot overcome them. She becomes a heroine
because she is able to fight for what she believes
in, and in this process, she shows much strength as
a woman. She also becomes a role model for several
of the characters in the play. However, as she
cannot and does not try to meet anyone's
expectations of her, eventually her inability to
compromise causes her undoing.

Pipolo 8

Works Cited

Bowra, C. M. *Sophoclean Tragedy*. Oxford: Oxford
UP, 1944. Print.

Bushnell, Rebecca W. *Prophesying Tragedy*. Ithaca:
Cornell UP, 1988. Print.

Else, Gerald. *The Madness of Antigone*.
Heidelberg: Carl Winter, 1976. Print.

Scodel, Ruth. *Sophocles*. Boston: Twayne, 1984.
Print.

Segal, Charles Paul. "Sophocles' Praise of Man and
the Conflicts of the *Antigone*." *Sophocles*.
Ed. Thomas Woodard. Englewood Cliffs:
Prentice Hall, 1966. 62–85. Print.

Sophocles. *Antigone: The Three Theban Plays*.
Trans. Robert Fagles. Middlesex, Eng.:
Penguin, 1984. Print.

Researching Literary Sources

Organizing an informative and insightful research paper will say a lot about you as both a writer and researcher. To the reader, and especially your professor, how you present your paper and the content of the paper itself will determine not only your ability as a writer, it will be an indication of the amount of time you spent thinking about and exploring your topic. A finished research paper is something you should be proud of. Having pride in your work will go a long way toward not only your immediate grades, but your future as a college student and professional as well, regardless of what profession you choose.

Many reliable resources can be found in the library and online that will help you research your paper. Good writers use research tools to study their topic thoroughly.

- *The Library:* Not only are libraries the primary source of printed texts, they also provide computer terminals for online access, digital reference materials, and databases such as the *MLA International Bibliography*, which index texts that may relate to your topic.
- *The Internet:* There is still some debate among educators as to how far a student should go utilizing the Internet to prepare a research paper. It is undoubtedly an important resource tool, but the danger of the Internet lies in information overload (thus straying from your topic) and the false sense it may give you of knowing enough about your topic to present an informed paper. Never rely on the Internet exclusively. You may think of the Internet as a cyber-librarian, but the fact remains that the Internet can only provide information based on your input. A professional librarian (such as the one in your school) will be able to steer you more clearly to articles, essays and scholarly criticism that directly relate to your topic.

RESEARCH RESOURCES

By the time you are ready to do your research, you should have already established your topic and ideally your thesis too. A topic is broader than a thesis and may help when trying to do your research in that it will steer you toward various angles you can use to approach your thesis. Research occasionally may feel like searching for a needle in a haystack, but the process need not be so arbitrary. To find articles relating to your topic, first check a few Internet search engines as well as scholarly databases available at your school's library. Here are a few examples of reliable search engines:

- http://www.scholar.google.com
- http://www.ask.com

These are discussed in detail in the section on searching online sources. It is important when using the Internet that you don't just hit a few sites and try to squeeze the limited information you gather from a few Internet hits into your thesis. The point of doing research is to enrich your paper's content and enlighten your reader's perspective regarding your thesis. Never distort your research to fit your thesis. Research is not just a matter of gathering information; it includes evaluating your sources and analyzing their usefulness.

To help with your research, approach your topic by breaking it down into categories. Some examples of categories within literature are as follows:

- Genre (poetry, drama, short fiction, essays, etc.)
- Nationality (American, British, French, etc.)
- Period (the historical time in which the work was written—nineteenth century, medieval, etc.)
- Literary movement (realism, naturalism, etc.)

Try to think of your topic in categories. For example, Kate Chopin was a late nineteenth-century American novelist. A study of Kate Chopin would require using searches using her name, but you might also find useful information in studies of the novel in general, women in literature, southern literature, and realism. In print sources, you will often find bibliographies that lead you to further sources; on the Internet, you will often find links between various types of information.

It is not enough for a text to be tangentially related to your topic. It must relate specifically to your thesis and to other researched documents you are utilizing. The point of starting the search on the Internet is to gather a list of sources that you may bring to the library. It cannot be stressed enough that your number-one tool in pursuing research is the aid of the research librarians at your campus library. They are most aware of what the library holds, what the library does not hold but can access, and major changes to the library's holdings and databases in the recent past.

Reference Works

Once you have established a clear topic and gathered a few sources to bring to the library, start your research by exploring reference works. As noted in the excellent online resource Wikipedia, a reference work is a compendium of information giving brief yet comprehensive overviews of each individual topic. All of the articles you find in a reference work are authored by scholars in the given subject. These articles are listed in indexes, and the information presented is informative and based on facts. Your librarian will be able to help you search through the indexes of various reference works to better guide you in your search. Some indexes and bibliographies are all encompassing, and others specialize in subjects such as African American literature of the twentieth century or medieval English literature. Remember that if you are researching, for example, Kate Chopin, do not search only using her name as a subject. Use it as a key word as well, and with each source that comes up, see what subject headings it is listed under for hints about subject headings that could prove useful. Here are some basic titles and indexes to be aware of in a literature survey course:

- *MLA International Bibliography of Books and Articles in the Modern Languages and Literatures (1922–);* also available online and as a CD-ROM, which are more up to date.
- *Reader's Guide to Periodical Literature (1900–);* although this has been superseded by online databases such as *InfoTrac* for modern periodical (magazine, newspaper) articles, it is still a necessary tool for research of older periodical texts.
- *American Literary Scholarship (1965–)*
- *Oxford Companion to Contemporary Authors;* Oxford University Press has published many useful books in this reference series that could be helpful in literary research.
- *Dictionary of Literary Biography*
- *Masterplots* (print and CD-ROM)
- *Magill's Survey of Literature*
- *New Cambridge Bibliography of English Literature*
- *Reader's Guide to Literature in English*
- *Encyclopedia of American Literature*

Online Sources

The Reliability of Web-Based Information

Examine all your research sources carefully, and examine online sources with extra care. Remember that the point of quality literary research is to research the arguments of experts in the subject you are exploring. The primary goal of your online research is to look for Websites that provide both facts and scholarly opinions that will either support or challenge your thesis. With this in mind, you should be able to distinguish sites that provide the authoritative information you need from those that offer unsupported claims.

The lines are blurring regarding web addresses and what they signify, but it still holds true that a site ending in .edu is an educational domain. This does not guarantee a web page's quality, yet the majority of serious literary criticism available on the Internet will be found on .edu sites. Use common sense and good judgment in determining an online source's quality. If you are still unsure after a thorough investigation of the site, speak to your professor or a librarian about the potential source's suitability.

Searching Online Sources

It is impossible to deny that literary research has benefitted enormously from the Internet. A great deal of quality information and research on authors and texts can be found with a few keystrokes. The sites listed in the following sections are all serious attempts to gather useful information regarding all aspects of literature. Many provide links to other valuable sites. An incredible number of sites and indexes are available via the web although some sites may disappear or move to unannounced addresses without notice. The search engines just mentioned are a great place to start, but do not limit yourself to just one or two. It is also advisable to ask your professor, librarians and colleagues in class what tools they use to enhance their web searches. Everyone has their own methods of web research, and there is a good chance you may receive valuable input from the person sitting right next to you in class.

Some points to remember when searching online:

- If you are searching for a proper name, put it in quotation marks. Searching for "*Kate Chopin*" will give you sites that reference only the author; if you type *Kate* and *Chopin* you will still get sites related to the author, but you will also get sites that have the (common) names Kate and Chopin located anywhere on the search engine.
- Once you type in your keywords and hit enter, the initial page that comes up will have, on its right side, links to your subject (called *topic clusters*) that are related to your keywords. You may also want to type in whatever additional information is pertinent to your search. For example, if you are writing a paper on Kate Chopin's "The Story of an Hour," you can type in the search box "Kate Chopin and The Story of an Hour." This will immediately narrow your search to more relevant sites regarding your topic, but it adversely may limit the topic clusters about your subject.
- Remember to "bookmark" (save the location to your web browser) every page that seems useful, so you can find it again later.

Online Encyclopedias

Most search engines will steer you to an online encyclopedia, such as Wikipedia or the Encyclopedia Britannica, as your initial resource. This is done because of the value of an encyclopedia as a research tool. The encyclopedia is valuable for gaining information on authors and their works, and it is a great place to start. Note that in addition to online encyclopedias, there are many quality sites related to authors, some hosted by academic institutions and many by fans. They are often excellent as an overview of an author's life and work, and usually contain links to other sites of interest.

Online Literary Texts

- *The Bartleby Project*
  http://www.bartleby.com/index.html
- *Project Gutenberg*
  http://www.gutenberg.org
- *American Poetry*
  http://etext.lib.virginia.edu/ampo.html
- *The Internet Poetry Archives* (focusing on modern poets)
  http://www.ibiblio.org/ipa
- A library center and poetry archive
  http://www.poetshouse.org/

Literary Criticism Research Sites

- *The Voice of the Shuttle* is an outstanding place to start all research in the humanities.
  http://vos.ucsb.edu/
- Jack Lynch's *American Literature* page at Rutgers University is one of the best Web resources for literary studies.
  http://andromeda.rutgers.edu/~jlynch/Lit/american.html
- The *Internet Public Library* has a section devoted to literary criticism.
  http://www.ipl.org/div/litcrit/

- American literature—general resources:
  `http://bubl.ac.uk/link/a/americanliterature-general.htm`
- *Luminarium* is a resource for Middle English literature, Renaissance literature, and seventeenth-century literature.
  `http://www.luminarium.org/`
- The American Academy of Poets has an outstanding site dedicated to poets.
  `http://www.poets.org/`
- English poetry from the Anglo-Saxon times until the end of the nineteenth century:
  `http://etext.virginia.edu/epd.html`

Resource Guidelines

The sites just listed are just a few of the valuable resources available online, through subscription services, and in your library's holdings. Remember that locating and evaluating sources can be quite time consuming. Be aware, however, that the time you put into properly researching your topic will save you time later in the process of constructing your paper. Establishing excellent sources early on will make the actual writing of your paper much more engaging and satisfying for both you and your readers.

Final Thoughts

The proper usage of all available resources will lead to a successful paper. There is no lack of information available on any author you might research during your higher education career. The research process is time intensive, but as you begin to see your paper develop, a sense of satisfaction growing within you should help you maintain your focus and ultimately present a finished paper that will be rewarding to both you and your readers. Don't be afraid to ask for help from your librarian, your professor, other classmates, or anyone you think may help you prepare the materials you need to create a better and more informed final paper.

Critical Approaches: A Case Study of Hamlet

You probably have noticed that at times your response to a literary text may differ greatly from that of your classmates. Sometimes as you listen to these various voices in your literature class, you may even wonder whether you have all read the same text. Diverse factors such as your personalities, lifestyles, social environments, and experiences may lead you to adopt various kinds of value judgments, and to react differently to the stories, poems, and plays that you read. Like you, literary critics also come up with different responses to and diverse interpretations of the same literary work. Often they also adopt reading strategies that reflect a personal affiliation to various critical theories, such as formalism, psychoanalytic criticism, reader-response criticism, feminist criticism, and the new historicism.

The following selections highlight five different ways that literary critics have chosen to interpret Shakespeare's *Hamlet*. As you read them, you will discover how each can illuminate your reading of *Hamlet*, making you aware of new ways to delve into its literary complexity. Sigmund Freud once said that the poets and artists of the past had anticipated most of his findings about the unconscious. Freud's thesis may also be applied to *Hamlet*, whose the literary complexity seems to have anticipated the possibilities of various critical interpretations.

Notice that although none of the interpretations in this appendix claims to express an ideal evaluation of *Hamlet*, each will help you to uncover the rich complexity, ambiguity, and suggestiveness of Shakespeare's play.

PSYCHOANALYTIC CRITICISM

What Is the Focus of Psychoanalytic Criticism?

Psychoanalytic criticism takes the methods used to analyze the behavior of people in real-life situations and applies them to the dramatized patterns of human behavior in literature. Overall, it explores some basic assumptions devised by the pioneer of psychoanalysis, Sigmund Freud (1856–1939). Most important among these are Freud's fundamental ideas about the structure of the human psyche, his theory of repression, and the Oedipus complex model that Freud applied to his reading of *Hamlet*.

Freud's Theory of Repression

Freud viewed one part of the human psyche, the *id* or unconscious, as the site of our instincts, or the unconscious part of ourselves that is biologically rooted and is always pressing for some kind of satisfaction. For Freud, the id basically fulfilled the principle of life he called the "pleasure principle." The *ego* or the "*I*," in contrast, forms the rational part of the psyche. The ego opposes the id, as well as the *superego* or conscience. In a simplified view, the super-ego is that part of ourselves that regulates our moral judgment, telling us what is right or wrong. Based on this structural model, Freud developed his theory of *repression*. In his theory, the id becomes the repository of repressed material such as pain, sexual desires, wishes, and fears that the ego and superego tend to censor because of social mores, taboos, and other factors. As Freud viewed it, such repressed forces might eventually be reactivated to emerge either through our creative activities or through our fantasies, dreams, language, slips of the tongue, neuroses, repressed fears, and other sorts of mental conflicts.

The Oedipus Complex

The name Oedipus takes us back to the Greek hero Oedipus who unwittingly kills his father and marries his mother. By *Oedipus complex* Freud meant to define one of the major repressed wishes of a boy's childhood: his desire to identify with the father and replace him in the affection of the mother. Psychoanalysts who came after Freud constructed a feminine version of the Oedipus complex, called the *Electra complex*. Named after a Greek legend in which the heroine Electra kills her mother to avenge the death of her father, the Electra complex describes a girl's unconscious wish to take the mother's place in the affection of the father.

A Psychoanalytic Reading of *Hamlet*

In his analysis of *Hamlet*, which was later amplified by his disciple and biographer Ernest Jones, Freud used his theory of repression and his overall assessment of the Oedipus complex to raise the issue of how Hamlet's strong repressed desire for his mother prevents him from fulfilling the task assigned to him by his father's ghost.

Sigmund Freud

The Interpretation of Dreams

Another of the great creations of tragic poetry, Shakespeare's Hamlet, has its roots in the same soil as Oedipus Rex. But the changed treatment of the same material reveals the whole difference in the mental life of these two widely separated epochs of civilization: the secular advance of repression in the emotional life of mankind. In the Oedipus the child's wishful phantasy that underlies it is brought into the open and realized as it would be in a dream. In Hamlet it remains repressed; and—just as in the case of a neurosis—we only learn of its existence from its inhibiting consequences. Strangely enough, the overwhelming effect produced by the more modern tragedy has turned out to be compatible with the fact that people have remained completely in the dark as to the hero's character. The play is built up on

Hamlet's hesitations over fulfilling the task of revenge that is assigned to him; but its text offers no reasons or motives for these hesitations and an immense variety of attempts at interpreting them have failed to produce a result. According to the view which was originated by Goethe and is still the prevailing one to-day, Hamlet represents the type of man whose power of direct action is paralysed by an excessive development of his intellect. (He is "sicklied o'er with the pale cast of thought.") According to another view, the dramatist has tried to portray a pathologically irresolute character which might be classed as neurasthenic. The plot of the drama shows us, however, that Hamlet is far from being represented as a person incapable of taking any action. We see him doing so on two occasions: first in a sudden outburst of temper, when he runs his sword through the eavesdropper behind the arras, and secondly in a premeditated and even crafty fashion, when, with all the callousness of a Renaissance prince, he sends the two courtiers to the death that had been planned for himself. What is it, then, that inhibits him in fulfilling the task set him by his father's ghost? The answer, once again, is that it is the peculiar nature of the task. Hamlet is able to do anything—except take vengeance on the man who did away with his father and took that father's place with his mother, the man who shows him the repressed wishes of his own childhood realized. Thus the loathing which should drive him on to revenge is replaced in him by self-reproaches, by scruples of conscience, which remind him that he himself is literally no better than the sinner whom he is to punish.

Freud's psychoanalytic theories have been complemented, disputed, and revised by many of his followers. For instance, Carl Gustav Jung (1875–1961), Freud's student and later opponent, replaced Freud's main focus on sex with a theory of the *collective unconscious*. Unlike Freud, who highlights the individual history of repressed wishes, Jung emphasizes the importance of the collective unconscious, also known as racial memory, or the collective desires of the human race. The French psychoanalyst Jacques Lacan (1901–81) shifted Freud's view from mental processes to argue that the unconscious is structured like a language.

A Psychosocial Reading of *Hamlet*

Recent psychoanalytic thought, as well as some post-Freudian development in psychoanalysis, has opened up the criticism of *Hamlet* to different approaches. One such approach is known as the psychosocial. Without ignoring the psychosexual implications of the play, a *psychosocial approach* to *Hamlet*, such as the one David Leverenz adopts in his article "The Women in *Hamlet*: An Interpersonal View," emphasizes the role that culture plays in shaping Hamlet's identity. On the basis of such a rationale, Leverenz argues that the real tragedy of *Hamlet* is that Hamlet finally does act. He assumes the aggressive masculine role that the patriarchal structure of power imposes on him, even though he views it as quite meaningless.

David Leverenz

The Women in Hamlet: An Interpersonal View

Hamlet's tragedy is the forced triumph of filial duty over sensitivity to his own heart. To fulfil various fathers' commands, he has to deny his self-awareness, just as Gertrude and Ophelia have done. That denial is equivalent to suicide, as the language of the last act shows. His puritanical cries about whoredom in himself and others, his hysterical outbursts to Ophelia about nunneries and painted women, are the outer shell of a horror at what the nurtured, loving, and well-loved soul has been corrupted to. From a more modern perspective than the play allows, we can sense that the destruction of good mothering is the real issue, at least from Hamlet's point of view.

Freudians, too many of whom have their own paternal answers to "Who's there," see Hamlet as an unconscious Claudius-Oedipus, or as a man baffled by pre-Oedipal ambivalences about his weak-willed, passionate, fickle mother. While acknowledging Hamlet's parricidal and matricidal impulses, we should see these inchoate feelings as responses, not innate drives. Interpersonal expectations, more than self-contained desires, are what divide Hamlet from himself and conscript him to false social purposes. In this perspective, taken from Harry Stack Sullivan, R. D. Laing, and D. W. Winnicott, Hamlet's supposed delay is a natural reaction to overwhelming interpersonal confusion. His self-preoccupation is paradoxically grounded not so much in himself as in the extraordinary and unremitting array of "mixed signals" that separate role from self, reason from feeling, duty from love.

Hamlet has no way of unambiguously understanding what anyone says to him. The girl who supposedly loves him inexplicably refuses his attentions. His grieving mother suddenly marries. His dead father, suddenly alive, twice tells him to deny his anger at his mother's shocking change of heart. Two of his best friends "make love to this employment" of snooping against him (V.ii.57). Polonius, Claudius, and the Ghost all manifest themselves as loving fathers, yet expect the worst from their sons and spy on their children, either directly or through messengers. Who is this "uncle-father" and "aunt-mother" (II.ii.366), or this courtier-father, who preach the unity of being true to oneself and others yet are false to everyone, who can "smile, smile, and be a villain" (I.v.108)? Gertrude's inconstancy not only brings on disgust and incestuous feelings, it is also the sign of diseased doubleness in everyone who has accommodated to his or her social role. Usurping Claudius is the symbol of all those "pretenders," who are now trying to bring Hamlet into line. No wonder Hamlet weeps at the sight of a genuine actor—the irony reveals the problem—playing Hecuba's grief. The male expressing a woman's constancy once again mirrors Hamlet's need. And the role, though feigned, at least is openly played. The actor's tears are the play's one unambiguous reflection of the grief Hamlet thought his mother shared with him before the onset of so many multitudinous double-dealings.

To kill or not to kill cannot be entertained when one is not even sure of existing with any integrity. Being, not desiring or revenging, is the question. Freudians assume that everyone has strong desires blocked by stronger repressions, but contemporary work with schizophrenics reveals the tragic variety of people whose voices are only amalgams of other people's voices, with caustic self-observation or a still more terrifying vacuum as their incessant inward reality. This is Hamlet to a degree, as it is Ophelia completely. As Laing says of her in *The Divided Self*, "in her madness, there is no one there. She is not a person. There is no integral selfhood expressed through her actions or utterances. Incomprehensible statements are said by nothing. She has already died. There is now only a vacuum where there was once a person." Laing misrepresents her state only because there are many voices in Ophelia's madness speaking through her, all making sense, and none of them her own. She becomes the mirror for a madness-inducing world. Hamlet resists these pressures at the cost of a terrifying isolation. Once he thinks his mother has abandoned him, there is nothing and no one to "mirror" his feelings, as Winnicott puts it. Hamlet is utterly alone, beyond the loving semi- understanding of reasonable Horatio or obedient Ophelia.

A world of fathers and sons, ambition and lust, considers grief "unmanly," as Claudius preaches (I.ii.94). Hamlet seems to agree, at least to himself, citing his "whorish" doubts as the cause of his inability to take manly filial action. This female imagery, which reflects the play's male-centered world view, represents a covert homosexual fantasy, according to Freudian interpretation. Certainly Hamlet's idealisations of his father and of Horatio's friendship show a hunger for male closeness. Poisoning in the ear may unconsciously evoke anal intercourse. And the climactic swordplay with Laertes does lead to a brotherly understanding. But these instances of covert homosexual desire are responses to a lack. Poisoning in the ear evokes conscious and unconscious perversity to intimate the perversion of communication, especially between men. The woman in Hamlet is the source of his most acute perceptions about the diseased, disordered patriarchal society that tries to "play upon this pipe" of Hamlet's soul (III.ii.336), even as a ghost returning from the dead.

Reading Contexts

Freud's Text

1. Why, according to Freud, have Shakespeare's readers and critics remained completely in the dark in their attempts to interpret Hamlet's character?
2. Freud mentions that the Hamlet theory developed by the German poet Goethe (1749–1832) still prevailed in his time. Describe Goethe's theory, and summarize the arguments that Freud developed to refute Goethe's romantic interpretation of Hamlet's character. How does Freud's psychoanalytic interpretation differ from Goethe's romantic one?

Leverenz's Text

1. Explain the distinction between Freud's psychosexual interpretation and Leverenz's psychosocial interpretation of *Hamlet*, which highlights the idea that we are creatures of culture.
2. Leverenz argues that "interpersonal expectations, more than self-contained desires, are what divide Hamlet from himself and conscript him to false social purposes." In your opinion, is Leverenz's argument complex enough to explain the Hamlet problem?
3. One of the major arguments running through Leverenz's article supports the idea that Hamlet is manipulated and ultimately controlled by the male roles that patriarchal society imposes on him. Do you agree or disagree with Leverenz?

Psychoanalytic Criticism: Reading References

The reading references in this section include a series of works that, although not directly connected with *Hamlet*, highlight some of the critical ideas that inform the modern reading of *Hamlet*.

Erlich, Avi. *Hamlet's Absent Father*. Princeton: Princeton UP, 1977. Print.

Freud, Sigmund. "The Interpretation of Dreams." *The Standard Edition of the Complete Psychological Works*. Ed. James Strachey. London: Hogarth, 1953–74. Print.

Kurtzweil, Edith, and William Philips, eds. *Literature and Psychoanalysis*. New York: Columbia UP, 1983. Print.

Lacan, Jacques. "Desire and the Interpretation of Desire in *Hamlet*." *Literature and Psychoanalysis: The Question of Reading: Otherwise*. Ed. Shoshana Felman. Baltimore: Johns Hopkins UP, 1982. Print.

Leverenz, David. "The Women in *Hamlet:* An Interpersonal View." *Hamlet: Contemporary Critical Essays*. Ed. Martin Coyle. New York: St. Martin's, 1992. Print.

Sprengnether, Madelon. *The Spectral Mother: Freud, Feminism and Psychoanalysis*. Ithaca: Cornell UP, 1990. Print.

FORMALISM/NEW CRITICISM

What Is the Focus of Formalism?

Formalism seeks to emphasize the importance of the formal elements of literature or the formal qualities related to the language, form, and content of a literary text. It directly opposes any extrinsic kind of criticism that views the literary text as a product of the author's intentions or as a reflection of ethical and sociocultural forces. In modern formalist criticism, especially in the works of formalist critics known as *new critics*, literature is alienated and isolated from the actual world, seeking to fulfill the purposes of revealing deeper truths and embodying a unified vision of life in the shaped structure of a work of art.

Formalism flourished from the 1940s to the 1960s. To some extent, the close reading it advocates has remained a major goal not only for formalists but for all readers who rely on formal devices, such as imagery, irony, paradox, symbols, diction, plot, characterization, and narrative techniques, to understand the meanings of a literary text. A formalist reading of poetry can show, for instance, how a poem can integrate an ideal order of form and content by relating its phonic devices (aspects related to sounds, rhythm, and meter) to its images, symbols, and overall mode of poetic construction.

A New Critical Reading of *Hamlet*

Because a major focus of the New Critical method or formalism is the construction of literary craft, formalist critics have explored Shakespeare's use of character, language, and staging to validate the dramatic world of *Hamlet*. In "Hamlet and His Problems," T. S. Eliot applies formalist strategies to argue that feelings and emotions can be viewed as an objective mode of construction and be formally channeled in art. Shakespeare fails in *Hamlet*, Eliot argues, because he is unable to find "an objective correlative" or "a set of objects, a situation, a chain of events which shall be the formula of that *particular* emotion." Thus, as Eliot sees it, emotions and feelings in *Hamlet* exceed the literary form of Shakespeare's tragedy and cannot be expressed in art—they are "in excess of the facts." As to Gertrude, Eliot remarks that she "arouses in Hamlet the feeling which she is incapable of representing."

T. S. Eliot

Hamlet and His Problems

The only way of expressing emotion in the form of art is by finding an "objective correlative": in other words, a set of objects, a situation, a chain of events which shall be the formula of that *particular* emotion; such that when the external facts, which must terminate in sensory experience, are given, the emotion is immediately evoked. If you examine any of Shakespeare's more successful tragedies, you will find this exact equivalence; you will find that the state of mind of Lady Macbeth walking in her sleep has been communicated to you by a skilful accumulation of imagined sensory impressions; the words of Macbeth on hearing of his wife's death strike us as if, given the sequence of events, these words were automatically released by the last event in the series. The artistic "inevitability" lies in this complete adequacy of the external to the emotion; and this is precisely what is deficient in *Hamlet*. Hamlet (the man) is dominated by an emotion which is inexpressible, because it is in excess of the facts as they appear. And the supposed identity of Hamlet with his author is genuine to this point: that Hamlet's bafflement at the absence of objective equivalent to his feelings is a prolongation of the bafflement of his creator in the face of his artistic problem. Hamlet is up against the difficulty that his disgust is occasioned by his mother, but that his mother is not an adequate equivalent for it; his disgust envelops and exceeds her. It is thus a feeling which he cannot understand; he cannot objectify it, and it therefore remains to poison life and obstruct action. None of the possible actions can satisfy it; and nothing that Shakespeare can do with the plot can express Hamlet for him. And it must be noticed that the very nature of the *données* of the problem precludes objective equivalence. To have heightened the criminality of Gertrude would have been to provide the formula for a totally different emotion in Hamlet; it is just *because* her character is so negative and insignificant that she arouses in Hamlet the feeling which she is incapable of representing.

Reading Contexts

1. New criticism or formalism attempts to present a unified vision of a work of art in which every element, such as a word, an image, or a situation, contributes to a formal view of unity. With this in mind, analyze the use that Eliot makes of words such as *deficient, excess, not adequate,* and *negative* to support his reading of *Hamlet*.
2. According to Hazard Adams, what Eliot really meant by the "objective correlative" is not very clear. Examine Eliot's definition of this concept in the beginning of the first paragraph of his essay, and then decide whether you agree or disagree with Adams.

Formalism / New Criticism: Reading References

Brooks, Cleanth, and Robert Penn Warren. *Understanding Poetry*. New York: Henry Holt, 1938. Print.

Crane, Ronald Salmon. *The Languages of Criticism and the Structure of Poetry*. Toronto: U of Toronto P, 1953. Print.

Eliot, T. S. "Hamlet and His Problems." *Selected Essays*. New York: Harcourt, 1960. Print.

Warren, Austin. *Rage for Order: Essays in Criticism*. Ann Arbor: U of Michigan P, 1948. Print.

READER-RESPONSE CRITICISM
What is the Focus of Reader-Response Criticism?

Reader-response criticism places much emphasis on the literary experience of individual readers not only as interpreters of texts but as producers of meanings. One of its basic assumptions is that each reading of a text by a single reader will be different because the dynamic and subjective scope of the reader's responses makes each reader react in different ways. Thus the major focus of reader-response criticism is the diversity and plurality of the reader's interpretive experiences. Because individual readers are apt to be influenced by social, communal, cultural, and political values, reader-response criticism also focuses on how women, individuals, and groups, in different social settings and in different time periods, read texts. Some studies show, for instance, how readers can interact with the texts' gaps, ambiguities, and pluralities or use the reading process itself to revise and build up their own expectations as readers.

A Reader-Response Analysis of *Hamlet*

Reader-response criticism can make us understand why we encounter such diverse interpretive responses to our study of *Hamlet*. The critic Norman N. Holland, for instance, explains how three different readers can respond to *Hamlet* and construct the meaning of this play according to their emotional and psychological reactions to the concept of authority. For Holland, as for most reader-response critics, whenever a text threatens the identity of its readers, the readers question, rewrite, and project their feelings on it.

In the following passage, another reader-response critic, Stephen Booth, analyzes *Hamlet* in terms of the audience's response to the play. For Booth, the audience not only is involved in constructing the meaning of *Hamlet* but is also affected when its character and experience are altered and revised by the reading process itself. Thus at times *Hamlet*'s audience is invited to settle its mind, to get information, to develop double and contrary responses to Claudius, whereas at other times it gets frustrated, finding its focus shifted and its understanding threatened. At least once the audience is taken to the brink of intellectual terror. Most important, according to Booth, the audience never knows what it would have done in Hamlet's situation. Notice how Booth focuses on the position that the audience occupies in shaping the literary experience of act 2 of *Hamlet*.

Stephen Booth

On the Value of Hamlet

The audience sets out into Act II knowing what Hamlet knows, knowing Hamlet's plans, and secure in its superiority to the characters who do not. (Usually an audience is superior to the central characters: it knows that Desdemona is innocent, Othello does not; it knows what it would do when Lear foolishly divides his kingdom; it knows how Birnam Wood came to come to Dunsinane. In *Hamlet*, however, the audience never knows what it would have done in Hamlet's situation; in fact, since the King's successful plot in the duel with Laertes changes Hamlet's situation so that he becomes as much the avenger of his own death as of his father's, the audience never knows what Hamlet would have done. Except for brief periods near the end of the play, the audience never has insight or knowledge superior to Hamlet's or, indeed, different from Hamlet's. Instead of having superiority *to* Hamlet, the audience goes into the second act to share the superiority *of* Hamlet.) The audience knows that Hamlet will play mad, and its expectations are quickly confirmed. Just seventy-five lines into Act II, Ophelia comes in and describes a kind of behavior in Hamlet that sounds like the behavior of a young man of limited theatrical ability who is pretending to be mad (II.i.77–84). Our confidence that this behavior so puzzling to others is well within our grasp is strengthened by the reminder of the ghost, the immediate cause of the promised pretense, in Ophelia's comparison of Hamlet to a creature "loosed out of hell / To speak of horrors."

Before Ophelia's entrance, II.ii has presented an example of the baseness and foolishness of Polonius, the character upon whom both the audience and Hamlet exercise their superiority throughout Act II. Polonius seems base because he is arranging to spy on Laertes. He instructs his spy in ways to use the "bait of falsehood"—to find out directions by indirections (II.i.74). He is so sure that he knows everything, and so sure that his petty scheme is not only foolproof but brilliant, that he is as contemptible mentally as he is morally. The audience laughs at him because he loses his train of thought in pompous byways, so that, eventually, he forgets what he set out to say: "What was I about to say? . . . I was about to say something! Where did I leave?" (II.i.50–51). When Ophelia reports Hamlet's behavior, Polonius takes what is apparently Hamlet's bait: "Mad for thy love?" (II.i.85). He also thinks of (and then spends the rest of the act finding evidence for) a specific cause for Hamlet's madness: he is mad for love of Ophelia. The audience knows (1) Hamlet will pretend madness, (2) Polonius is a fool, and (3) what is actually bothering Hamlet. Through the rest of the act, the audience laughs at Polonius for being fooled by Hamlet. It continues to laugh at Polonius' inability to keep his mind on a track (II.ii.85–130); it also laughs at him for the opposite fault—he has a one-track mind and sees anything and everything as evidence that Hamlet is mad for love (II.ii.173–212; 394–402). Hamlet, whom the audience knows and understands, spends a good part of the rest of the scene making Polonius demonstrate his foolishness.

Reading Contexts

1. What kind of argument is Booth trying to make when he mentions that the audience in *Hamlet* "never knows what it would have done in Hamlet's situation"? Notice that whereas the formalist or new critical approach to *Hamlet* privileges character analysis, Booth's overall assumptions privilege the position of the audience.

2. How would you characterize Booth's portrayal of the audience in *Hamlet*? To what extent does the audience in *Hamlet* function as a reflection and a mirror of Hamlet's own frustrations and contradictions? Where do you stand in relation to this reader-response reading of *Hamlet*?

Reader-Response Criticism: Reference Readings

Booth, Stephen. "On the Value of *Hamlet*." *Reinterpretations of Elizabethan Drama*. Ed. Norman Rabkin. New York: Columbia UP, 1969. Print.

Eco, Umberto. *The Role of the Reader*. Bloomington: Indiana UP, 1979. Print.

Iser, Wolfgang. *Prospecting: From Reader Response to Literary Anthropology*. Baltimore: Johns Hopkins UP, 1989. Print.

Suleiman, Susan R., and Inge Crossman, eds. *The Reader in the Text: Essays on Audience and Interpretation*. Princeton: Princeton UP, 1980. Print.

Tompkins, Jane P. "An Introduction to Reader-Response Criticism." *Reader-Response Criticism: From Formalism to Post-Structuralism*. Ed. Jane P. Tompkins. Baltimore: Johns Hopkins UP, 1980. Print.

FEMINIST CRITICISM
What is the Focus of Feminist Criticism?

Modern *feminist criticism* emerged in the late 1960s and early 1970s out of a sociopolitical movement aimed at the defense of women's rights. It addressed the need women felt to reinterpret literature, to rewrite history, and to change the power structure that has traditionally defined male and female relationships in patriarchal societies. Like Marxist, African American, and the new historical criticism, the socially oriented perspective of feminist criticism has spread its voice in many directions. Among other things, it has promoted a reevaluation of the Freudian theory of sexual differences, a reassessment of female and male writing, a revision of the role of gender in literature, and a critique of the oppressive rationale of patriarchal ideology.

In her essay "This Sex Which Is Not One," the feminist critic Luce Irigaray revised Freud's theory of sex difference, protesting against the view of woman as a biological version of the male model. In following the assumptions of Jacques Lacan, French feminists have also criticized, among other things, the logic of language that associates positive qualities such as those related to creativity, light, logic, and power with masculinity. Many feminists like Hélène Cixous, who tend to draw a relationship between women's writing and women's bodies, have also attempted to create a language or a specific kind of women's writing (*écriture féminine*) that refuses participation in masculine discourse.

Other feminists have promoted a feminist critique of masculine ideology, protesting against the political marginalization women have suffered as blacks, chicanos, Asian Americans, and lesbians. For the feminist critic Catharine R. Stimpson, the defiance of sexual difference, the celebration of sexual difference, and the recognition of differences constitute the three major principles of feminist criticism. Many of the critical efforts of feminists have also been aimed at the study of women's history and the role of women in literary tradition.

Complementing feminism, lesbian and gay criticism, another by-product of a gender-centered approach, has sparked much recent debate in critical circles. One of its main premises, shaped by a feminist viewpoint, ponders whether lesbians and gays read and write the same way or differently from heterosexuals.

A Feminist Reading of *Hamlet*

One of the major contributions that feminist literary criticism has made to our reading of *Hamlet* has been its revisionist affirmation that female characters such as Gertrude and Ophelia possess a narrative of their own or a form of feminine discourse.

Notice in the following passage that Diane Elizabeth Dreher's feminist analysis of *Hamlet* opens new possibilities for an evaluation of Ophelia. By analyzing the forces that shaped Ophelia's identity as a "dominated daughter," Dreher liberates Ophelia from the rigid stereotypes that traditional criticism has ascribed to her. According to Dreher, because of the "fearful domination" that Polonius, Laertes, and Hamlet exercised on Ophelia, which cast her in the role of the "other," Ophelia is unable to grasp the full complexity of her self and resolve the crisis of her identity. As Dreher sees it, Ophelia is defined as a "simpleminded creature" only when evaluated from a male-oriented viewpoint.

Diane Elizabeth Dreher

Dominated Daughters

A feminist analysis of Ophelia's behavior demonstrates that she is not the simpleminded creature she seems. Traditional readings of her character have been as superficial as nineteenth-century productions, which portrayed her as a simple, pretty girl of flowers whose mad scenes were artfully sung and danced. As Helena Faucit realized and dared to play her to a stunned audience in 1844–45, Ophelia actually does go mad. There is pain and struggle beneath that sweet surface. Her misfortune merits not only our pity but our censure of traditional mores that make women repress themselves and behave like automatons.

Contrary to prevailing opinion, Ophelia is more than a simple girl, living in "a world of dumb ideas and feelings." The pity of it is that Ophelia *does* think and feel. A careful examination of the text in I.iii reveals that she loves Hamlet and thinks for herself, but is forced to repress all this at her father's command, conforming to the stifling patriarchal concept of female behavior that subordinates women to their "honor," their procreative function in male society.

Torn between what she feels and what she is told to be, Ophelia is tormented by the crisis of identity. As one critic pointed out long ago, "she is not aware of the nature of her own feelings; they are prematurely developed in their full force before she has strength to bear them." Caught in adolescent uncertainty between childhood and adulthood, she cannot enter the stage of intimacy and adult commitment because she does not yet know who she is. Carol Gilligan has pointed to the difficulties young women have in individuation. Raised with an emphasis on empathy rather than autonomy, girls tend to subordinate their own needs to those of others. Ophelia experiences severe role confusion in which her personal feelings are suppressed in favor of external expectations. . . .

Ophelia has been condemned for letting her father dominate her, for failing to "observe the fundamental responsibilities that hold together an existence." But let us consider the situation from her point of view. As a young woman, she is, first of all, more inclined to defer to the wishes of others than follow her own feelings. Ophelia errs in trusting her father, but she is not the only person in the play who has taken a parent at face value. Hamlet failed to recognize his mother's moral weakness until her marriage to Claudius. Furthermore, reverence for one's parents was expected of Renaissance youth. As Harley Granville-Barker emphasized, "we may call her docility a fault, when, as she is bid, she shuts herself away from Hamlet; but how not to trust to her brother's care for her and her father's wisdom?" Like Othello, Ophelia errs in trusting the wrong moral guide: in his case a friend who had shared dangers on the battlefield, in hers a father to whom convention bound her duty and obedience. Polonius' warning, seconded by her brother's, gains greater credibility. But most significant, her moral guides have not only told her how to behave; they have redefined her entire universe, inculcating in Ophelia a view of human sexuality as nasty and brutish as that which infects Othello. Ophelia sees herself in a world in which sexuality transforms human beings into beasts, with men the predators and women their prey.

Reading Contexts

1. Describe the traditional critical assumptions about Ophelia, and then contrast them with Dreher's. Explain how Dreher collapses the traditional view of Ophelia, offering insights into a new representation of this character.

2. To what extent does Dreher's argument about the rival claims of individuation and external expectations help to explain Ophelia's identity crisis? Where do you stand in relation to this argument?

Feminist Literary Criticism: Reading References

Abel, Elizabeth, ed. *Writing and Sexual Difference*. Chicago: UP, 1982. Print.

Abelove, Henry, et al., eds. *The Lesbian and Gay Studies Reader*. New York: Routledge, 1993. Print.

Carby, Hazel V. *Reconstructing Womanhood: The Emergence of the Afro-American Woman Novelist*. New York: Oxford UP, 1987. Print.

de Beauvoir, Simone. *The Second Sex*. Trans. and ed. H. M. Parshley. New York: Knopf, 1953. Print.

Dreher, Diane Elizabeth. *Dominance and Defiance: Fathers and Daughters in Shakespeare*. Kentucky: U of Kentucky P, 1986. Print.

Showalter, Elaine. "Representing Ophelia: Women, Madness, and the Responsibilities of Feminist Criticism." *Shakespeare and the Question of Theory*. Ed. Patricia Parker and Geoffrey Hartman. London: Methuen, 1985. Print.

THE NEW HISTORICISM
What is the Focus of the New Historicism?

The *new historicism*, or cultural poetics, may be defined as a form of political criticism closely related to Marxist criticism. One of its main goals is to focus on the critical study of power relations, politics, and ideology. For the new historicist critics, such as Stephen Greenblatt, who coined the term *new historical* in the early 1980s, this criticism displaces the traditional view of history as a discipline committed to an altruistic search for truth and to a faithful reconstruction of the dates and events of the past. Instead, the new historicist perspective advocates a focus on a historical dynamic or a view of history in action. Its aim is to erase the boundaries among disciplines such as literature, history, and the social sciences. The ideas of the French philosopher and historian Michel Foucault (1926–84) seem to inform much of the rationale that new historicism established for the complex relation among language, power, and knowledge.

New historical critics tend to view Shakespeare's plays as political acts reflecting and shaping the collective codes and beliefs of Shakespeare's times. New historicists also affirm the reciprocity between the text and the world, which they attempt to rewrite by showing how sociopolitical practices and institutions such as the theater can shape and transform cultural meanings. When considering the relation between text and reader, the new historicists advocate the reciprocity between these two elements, viewing them as dynamic forces interacting with and responding to each other.

A New Historical Reading of *Hamlet*

Leonard Tennenhouse's reading of *Hamlet* shows Shakespeare's play as a critique of power relations centered on a struggle for power between Hamlet and Claudius. According to Tennenhouse, the political struggle in *Hamlet* emerges from the clash between two different claims to the throne of Denmark: Hamlet's, which is based on blood and popular support, and Claudius's, which is based on his marriage to Gertrude and his use of force.

By approaching Shakespeare's tragedy through the critical lens traditionally applied in the criticism of history plays such as *Richard III*, *Richard II*, and *Henry IV*, Tennenhouse has erased the boundaries that traditional and formalist criticism insisted on establishing between Shakespeare's tragedies and his history plays. In his critique of the play-within-the-play in *Hamlet*, Tennenhouse also shifts the focus from Hamlet's goal of "catch[ing] the conscience of the King" to Hamlet's crime against the state. Tennenhouse also argues that in the play-within-the-play Hamlet fails because the political force he generates amounts to a mere symbolic gesture.

Leonard Tennenhouse

Power in Hamlet

Hamlet rehearses [the] dilemma of a state torn between two competitors, neither of whom can embody the mystical power of blood and land associated with the natural body. Hamlet's claim to power derives from his position as son in a patrilinear system as well as from "popular support." It is this support which Claudius consistently lacks and which, at the same time, prevents him from moving openly against Hamlet. Following the murder of Polonius, for example, Claudius says of Hamlet, "Yet must not we put the strong law on him. / He's lov'd of the distracted multitude . . ." (IV.iii.3–4). But this alone does not guarantee authority. Hamlet is not by nature capable of exercising force. To signal this lack, Shakespeare has given him the speech of Stoical writing, which shifts all action onto a mental plane where any show of force becomes self-inflicted aggression. We find this identification of force with self-assault made explicit in Hamlet's speeches on suicide as well as those in which he berates himself for his inability to act.

In contrast with Hamlet, Claudius's authority comes by way of his marriage to Gertrude. Where he would be second to Hamlet and Hamlet's line in a patrilineal system, the queen's husband and uncle of the king's son occupies the privileged male position in a matrilineal system. Like one of the successful figures from a history play, Claudius overthrew the reigning patriarch. Like one of the successful courtiers in a romantic comedy, he married into the aristocratic community. What is perhaps more important, he has taken the position through the effective use of force. Thus Shakespeare sets in opposition the two claims to authority—the exercise of force and the magic of blood—by means of these two members of the royal family. Because each has a claim, neither Hamlet nor Claudius achieves legitimate control over Denmark. Each one consequently assaults the aristocratic body in attempting to acquire the crown. It is to be expected that Claudius could not legally possess the crown, the matrilinear succession having the weaker claim on British political thinking. Thus the tragedy resides not in his failure but in the impossibility of Hamlet's rising according to Elizabethan strategies of state. This calls the relationship between the metaphysics of patriarchy and the force of law into question.

Reading Contexts

1. Find the sentences that best describe the two rival claims to power that Tennenhouse discusses in his text. Analyze the way these images of power reflect Tennenhouse's political views of *Hamlet*.

2. What conclusions can you draw from Tennenhouse's reading of this scene? Decide whether or not you agree or disagree with Tennenhouse's interpretation of *Hamlet*.

The New Historicism: Reading References

Brook, Thomas. *The New Historicism and Other Old-Fashioned Topics*. Princeton: Princeton UP, 1991. Print.

Greenblatt, Stephen J. *Renaissance Self-Fashioning: From More to Shakespeare*. Chicago: U of Chicago P, 1980. Print.

——, ed. *Representing the English Renaissance*. Berkeley: U of California P, 1988. Print.

Hunt, Lynn, ed. *The New Cultural History*. Berkeley: U of California P, 1989. Print.

Lindenberger, Herbert. "Toward a New History in Literature Studies." *Profession: Selected Articles from the Bulletin of the Association of Departments of English and the Association of Departments of Foreign Languages*. New York: MLA, 1984. Print.

Tennenhouse, Leonard. "Power in *Hamlet*." *Hamlet*. Ed. Martin Coyle. New York: St. Martin's, 1992. Print.

DECONSTRUCTIVE READING OF *HAMLET*

What Is the Focus of Deconstructive Criticism?

Deconstructive criticism seeks to disclose the binary opposition that exists in writing or in any system of literary, textual, cultural, and philosophical meanings. As the critic Terry Eagleton says, "Woman is the opposite, the 'other' of man: she is non-man, defective man, . . . Woman is not just an other in the sense of something beyond his ken, but an other intimately related to him as the image of what he is not, and therefore as an essential reminder of what he is (*Literary Theory: An Introduction* 132). By means of formal and structural analysis or strategies of the reading process, deconstructive critics explore the dichotomies, the mutually exclusive pairs of opposition in a text, revealing how each pair like "black/white," "male/female," "truth/error" undermines and destabilizes itself by inverting its corresponding binary opposite. Each term relates to the other as its essential part and is defined in relation to its opposite.

Deconstruction has been connected with the name of the French philosopher Jacques Derrida. Following Derrida's idea, these oppositions like the ones just cited or the binary pairs "speech/writing," "presence/absence" that also form hierarchies in which one term, favored by our culture as superior, contains the other, the inferior, with which it establishes a social relationship of power. There is also general consensus that deconstructive critics read "against the grain" or read against the text itself, demonstrating how it can support seemingly contradictory discourses, conflicting interpretations, and paradoxical meanings that destabilize themselves.

From this viewpoint, in deconstructive criticism meanings are unsettled, diffused, and subjected to change and instability. Thus the diverse and consequential antidualist deconstruction focuses on the "undoing" of the text, its subversion and unreliability, and its logical hegemony, as it bends toward a liberating critique of traditional textual practices.

Deconstruction has also caused a great impact on current theater practices of Shakespearean performances. Some contemporary directors have been casting Shakespeare's stage productions and film versions of his plays against their historical meanings, defining them in terms of the opposition that they establish with the Elizabethan cultural contexts. In the 2006

South Africa production of *Hamlet* at Stratford-Upon-Avon directed by Janet Suzman, the actors dressed in twentieth-century attire make use of a set in which the upper and lower levels suggest South Africa racial diversity. Film directors like Michael Almereyda in his film adaptation of *Hamlet* (2000) also attest to the way in which this contemporary staging conflicts with the so-called home-team view of Shakespeare's plays. Among other issues, Almereyda's film initiates a cultural/historical debate between his film's postmodern contemporary culture, immersed in a high-tech world, and the solid, political structures of Elizabethan culture that foreground Shakespeare's text. By the same token, Campbell Scott's film version of *Hamlet* (2000), set in America's Deep South, casts the Polonius family as African Americans, suggesting an approach where local, racial, and sexual sensibilities resist the solid traditional approach of the culturally centered Elizabethan *Hamlets*.

A Deconstructive Reading of *Hamlet*

James L. Calderwood applies deconstructive as well as metadramatic focus to argue that a negative quality or a negative mode shapes the development of Hamlet's delay. For critics like Calderwood, the digressions, imperfections, and inconsistencies are part of the play's artistic workmanship. As principle, such ambiguities emerge in line with Claudius's breakdown of the system of order and hierarchy that existed before the murder of King Hamlet. Calderwood's critical interest in metadrama (see his *Shakespearean Metadrama*, 1971) also appears in his criticism of *Hamlet* as he emphasizes that deconstruction surfaces in the play as part as part of its metadramatic condition. On the metadramatic level, Calderwood proposes that *Hamlet*'s audiences also respond to the play's internal system of negation, paradoxes, ironies, ambiguities, and contradictions.

James L. Calderwood

To Be or Not to Be: Negation and Metadrama in Hamlet

I offered in Part I a fairly positive, determinate, "centered" interpretation of the play. In Part II I want to suggest some of the ways in which the play resists positive interpretation, especially by its employment of the negative mode. Perhaps the most enticing entrance to this winding matter appears near the end of the Closet Scene when Gertrude, having been fairly thrust through by the verbal daggers of her son, asks Hamlet "What shall I do?" and is told:

> Not this, by no means, that I bid you do:
> Let the bloat king tempt you again to bed,
> Pinch wanton on your cheek, call you his mouse,
> And let him, for a pair of reechy kisses
> Or paddling in your neck with his damned fingers,
> Make you to travel all this matter out,
> That I essentially am not in madness
> But mad in craft.   (3.4.188–95)

To return to our textual crux: what, then, is Hamlet doing in his speech of advice to Gertrude? Many things, no doubt—some of them contradictory, some of them hard to distinguish from what Shakespeare is doing by means of Hamlet's speech. After all, the negative principle of "Not This," which in poetic employ becomes "Not This But Nevertheless This," would appear to license contradictions, ambiguities, multiplications of meaning. One could argue that Hamlet is indulging a voyeuristic Oedipal imagination within the self-exonerating safety zone of the double negative. Or that he is sublimating in repugnant but at least non-murderous language the matricidal impulses that were frustrated earlier in the scene by the arrival of the Ghost. Or that he is trying through magical force of speech to control the future. Or, to the contrary, that he is negating his own negations. His repellent images, that is, may be intended, not only to make Gertrude recoil into goodness, but also to express his own futility in a world so replete with evil that goodness itself withdraws into the unexpressive vacancy of "Not this, by no means."

Perhaps at some level of awareness Hamlet realizes that he is himself part of that corruption, even as in the speech itself he, the naysayer, is damned by what he denies. That is, if the poetic negative endows absence with presence, bringing "Not This" before us in the act of expressing it, then the naysayer must accept the guilt of his bringings-hither no less than the virtue of his forbiddings. "Nay, I had not known sin," Saint Paul said, "but by the law: for I had not known lust, except the law had said, 'Thou shalt not covet.'" If the fate of the naysaying lawgiver is to forbid crimes into existence, that of the moralist executioner is to become guilty not merely of saying evil to deny it but of doing evil to destroy it. Hamlet is well aware that this paradox has spun a web for his own revengeful actions. Pointing to the dead Polonius, he acknowledges that—

> heaven hath pleased it so,
> To punish me with this, and this with me,
> That I must be their scourge and minister.   (3.4.180–82)

Reading Contexts

1. Deconstructive criticism attempts to present a view of the literary text in which the open play of language, including words (or arbitrary "signifiers"), intended meanings, notions of representation, and authorial intentions, undermine and reverse a central, unified interpretation of the text. Analyze how Calderwood uses deconstructive strategies to reverse, dismantle, and unsettle the traditional criticism of *Hamlet* as a unified pattern of interpretation.

2. Examine how Calderwood explores contradictions and ambiguities in Hamlet's speech to Gertrude (3.4.188–95), to explain her inability to see the ghost; to portray the inversion of moral hierarchy in Denmark; and to support the argument of how "poetic negative" endows absence with presence.

Deconstructive Criticism: Reading References

Berrie, Robert. "Telmahs: Carnival Laughter in *Hamlet*." *New Essays on Hamlet*. Ed. Mark Thornton Burnet and John Manning. New York: AMS, 1994. 83–100. Print.

Calderwood, James L. *To Be and Not to Be: Negation and Metadrama in Hamlet*. New York: Columbia UP, 1983. Print.

Habib, Imtiaz. "'Never doubt I love': Misreading *Hamlet*." *College Literature* 21.2 (1994): 19–32. Print.

Hawkes, Terrence. *That Shakespearean Rag*. London: Methuen, 1986. Print.

Kerrigan, William. *Hamlet's Perfection*. Baltimore: Johns Hopkins UP, 1994. Print.

Biographical Endnotes

Achebe, Chinua (b. 1930)

Born in Nigeria, Achebe is considered one of Africa's most accomplished writers. He was educated at the University College of Ibadan and London University, and then took up a career in radio broadcasting. Dismayed with European writers' depiction of African life, he decided that Africans should tell their own stores and proceeded to write his first novel, *Things Fall Apart* (1958). The award-winning book, translated into forty-five languages, has been adapted for stage, television, and radio and is considered a classic in English. The novel's theme reflects Achebe's belief that outside influences eradicate traditional culture and values. When military forces took over Nigeria's government, Achebe left for the United States, taught at the University of Massachusetts, and lectured around the country. "Dead Men's Path" takes up his themes of loss of respect for tradition, and the past versus the present. He is currently a professor of languages and literature at Bard College, and his latest work includes *The Troubles with Nigeria* (1984), *Anthills of the Savannah* (1988), *Arrow of God* (1989), *A Man of the People* (1989), *Hopes and Impediments: Selected Essays* (1990), *Girls at War: And Other Stories* (1991), *Another Africa* (1998), *Home and Exile* (2000), and *Collected Poems* (2004).

Albee, Edward (b. 1928)

Following after the steps of American playwrights like Arthur Miller, Tennessee Williams, and Eugene O'Neill, Edward Albee took the American drama by surprise with a series of twenty-five plays that have placed him in a unique position as a playwright.

Born in Washington, D.C., Edward was adopted as an infant by Reid Albee, from a very wealthy family. However, despite having attended elite schools, the young Albee preferred to associate with artists and intellectuals in Greenwich Village in New York City, where he moved when he was twenty years old. His first success as a playwright came in 1959 when *The Zoo Story* was produced first in Europe and then in the United States. From 1959 to 1962 he wrote *The Death of Bessie Smith*, *The Sand Box*, and *The American Dream*, one-act plays that also received public acclaim. *Who's Afraid of Virginia Woolf?* (1962), a full-length play, captured the New York Drama Critics and Tony Awards for best play of the season, and it became a major box-office film starring Elizabeth Taylor and Richard Burton.

A Delicate Balance in 1967 received the Pulitzer Prize and *Three Tall Women* (1994) won him his third Pulitzer Prize besides receiving the Best Play award from the New York Drama Critics Circle and Outer Critics Circle.

Albee's rise to critical renown has to do with the seriousness with which his plays examine the existential questions of his time, through a dramatic medium he invigorated by his use of parody, humor, wit, and literary allusions. His language is strong and imaginative, and his social criticism of the American way of life a vehicle through which he probes into human suffering and alienation. On his connection with the theater of the absurd, Albee has remarked, "The Theatre of the Absurd is nothing more than the truly contemporary theatre, and it belongs to the playwright. . . . Most people unfortunately prefer theatre which uses basically the nineteenth century concept of the theater. They go to the theatre to have values, not examined, but reaffirmed" (Kolin, *Conversations with Edward Albee* 95).

Arrabal, Fernando (b. 1932)

Arrabal, born in Spanish Morocco, lived his early years in Madrid. At the age of twenty-three, finding life in Spain intolerable because of parental problems and the atmosphere of political oppression, he moved to Paris, where he still resides. Tuberculosis sapped his strength, and his early works mirror the despair he experienced because of his illness. He regained his health after an operation in 1957, and his plays were soon produced in Paris theaters. He refers to his work as "panic theater" in the tradition of the theater of the absurd. *Panic on the Battlefield* was written when he was fourteen and is the most frequently performed of his plays. Arrabal's concerns are the horrors of the civil war, betrayal, torture, tyranny, and human helplessness in an alien universe. Recent works includes *The Body-Builders Book of Love: Brevano de Amor de un Halterofilo* (translation by Lorenzo Mans) (1999), *Disparu* (2000), and *Champagne pour Tous* (2002).

Bambara, Toni Cade (1939–95)

Bambara grew up in New York City, deeply conscious of the inequities of race and class. A graduate of Queens College and City College of New York, she became a social worker, educator, and filmmaker. Her short story collections, such as *Gorilla, My Love* (1972), *The Sea Birds Are Still Alive* (1977), and *The Salt Eaters* (1980), deal particularly with the problems of women in urban environments. With humor and candor, she skillfully portrays the politics and culture of community life.

Behn, Aphra (1640?–89)

The early details of Behn's life have not been established conclusively, but most historians agree that she and her family probably sailed from England to Surinam in South America in 1663. Her father was to become lieutenant governor but died during the trip. Although she lived in Surinam less than a year, Behn had such a vivid impression of the country that she later incorporated them in a novel, *Oroonoko: or, The Royal Slave* (1688). On her return to England in 1664, she married a wealthy London merchant and became popular at the court of Charles II. Unfortunately, her husband died in 1666, and for reasons unknown she was left an impoverished widow. For a short time she became a spy for Charles II but was not remunerated for her work. In desperation, she turned to writing, an unheard-of female occupation. Her first play, *The Forced Marriage; or The Jealous Bridegroom*, proved successful, and she continued writing plays featuring sexual promiscuity and amorous intrigues in the mode of the day. Her poems are less coarse than many of those of her contemporaries, but she freely discusses female sexual desires and issues concerning gender roles. Critics charged her with indecency, but she fought back, claiming she was singled out because of her gender. Never possessing much wealth, she lived in less than healthy conditions, which led to an early death. Behn was honored by burial in Westminster Abbey and has won the admiration of many feminists, including Virginia Woolf.

Blake, William (1757–1827)

Born in Soho, London, Blake was apprenticed to James Basire, engraver to the Society of Antiquaries. His first poems appeared in *Poetical Sketches* in 1783, followed by *Songs of Innocence* (1789), a work in which he seeks to recapture the innocence and joy of childhood by manifesting his faith in human sympathy, integrity, and divine love. However, in his *Book of Thel* and his prose work entitled *The Marriage of Hell* (1790), Blake endorses a fiercely satiric outlook and a revolutionary position against issues such as the disintegration of personality, the abuse of authority, and the religious dogma of eternal punishment. His *Songs of Experience* (1794), centered on his deeper awareness of the state of experience and the mysterious power of evil, also contrasts with the joyful spontaneous assessment of the power of divine love in *Songs of Innocence*.

Today Blake is widely recognized as a great Christian, visionary, and mystical poet. In his own lifetime, however, he had to make a living by giving drawing lessons, working as an engraver, and illustrating books such as *The Divine Comedy*. He also illustrated his own books, some of which he colored by hand after applying a special color-printed process of his own invention.

In most of his works, Blake communicated his disgust for eighteenth-century scientific rationalism: "I will not reason and compare: my business is to create." In works such as *The Book of Los* (1795) and *The Four Zoas* (1797), he created his own mythological figures such as Los (imagination), Urizen (reason), Luvah (passions), and Tharmas (instincts). Blake became a spokesperson for a group of intellectual radicals and a great supporter of the French and American revolutions.

Borowski, Tadeusz (1922–51)

Born of Polish parents in the Soviet Ukraine, Borowski lived a life of poverty and oppression. When he was four, his father was sent to an Arctic labor camp. Four years later, his mother was sent to Siberia. The family was reunited in Warsaw before World War II. He was eventually arrested by the Gestapo for his political activities and sent to the concentration camp at Auschwitz. There he observed the horror and brutality perpetrated on the victims. He also witnessed prisoners betraying each other in order to survive. Borowski became a hospital orderly to escape extermination. The American forces freed him and his fellow prisoners in 1945. Borowski returned to Warsaw where he wrote short stories based on his experiences. His work has been criticized because he portrays some of the victims who resorted to betrayal and other criminal acts. Ironically, Borowski committed suicide using gas when he was twenty-nine.

Brooks, David (b. 1961)

Born in Toronto, Canada, Brooks grew up in New York City. He graduated from the University of Chicago in 1983 with a degree in history, served as a reporter for the *Wall Street Journal*, and has since been a senior editor at *The Weekly Standard*, a contributing editor at *Newsweek* and the *Atlantic Monthly*, and a commentator on NPR and *The NewsHour with*

Jim Lehrer. He is currently a columnist for the *New York Times* and considered one of the prominent voices of conservative politics in the United States. His publications include *Bobos in Paradise: The New Upper Class and How They Got There* (2000) and *On Paradise Drive: How We Live Now (and Always Have) in the Future Tense* (2004). He is also editor of the anthology *Backward and Upward: The New Conservative Writing* (1996). Originally a self-proclaimed liberal, Brooks surprised many when he wrote a column for the *New York Times* in 2003 in favor of gay marriage, featured here. Brooks will be teaching a course at Duke University's Terry Sanford Institute of Public Policy in the fall of 2006.

Browning, Robert (1812–89)

Born in England, Browning was a relatively unrecognized poet until his middle age. In fact, for a time he was better known for his dramatic rescue of Elizabeth Barrett from her tyrannical father. The couple had carried on a love affair through poetry and letters until they eloped and escaped to Italy where they lived until her death in 1861. During his life in Italy, Browning developed his dramatic monologues, in which a person reveals his or her motives and thoughts through speech. Browning researched many subjects of the Italian Renaissance. His most famous work is *The Ring and the Book* (1868–69), one of the longest poems in English literature.

Camus, Albert (1913–60)

An Algerian-born French writer of novels, essays, and plays, Camus is identified with the concept of absurdity, the problem of humans' desire for a rational universe as compared with the reality of its incoherence. Camus was only ten months old when his father was killed in World War I. Brought up in poverty by his illiterate mother, he fortunately encountered a teacher who encouraged his studies. Subsequently, he earned a scholarship to a *lycée* (secondary school) where he studied philosophy and read widely. In 1930, he had the first of many attacks of tuberculosis, and in the late 1930s he commenced his lifelong journals and completed his first novel, *A Happy Death*. During World War II, he lived in Paris and was editor of the French Resistance newspaper *Combat*. Throughout his life, he struggled to find a positive solution to the dilemma of the absurd. At age forty-four, he was awarded the Nobel Prize for Literature in recognition of his profound humanism.

Some of his most famous works include *The Stranger* (1942, tr. 1946), *The Myth of Sisyphus* (1942, tr. 1955), *The Plague* (1947, tr. 1948), *The Outsider* (1942, tr. 1946), *The Rebel* (1951, tr. 1953), and *The Fall* (1956, tr. 1957). His final novel, *The First Man*, was published posthumously in 1995. Camus died in an automobile crash in 1960.

Chang, Lan Samantha (b. 1965)

Born and raised in Appleton, Wisconsin, Chang received her B.A. at Yale University, her M.P.A. at Harvard University, and her M.F.A. at the University of Iowa. She held Wallace Stegner and Truman Capote fellowships at Stanford University and fellowships at Princeton University, the Radcliffe Institute for Advanced Study, and the National Endowment for the Arts. Her first novel, *Hunger: A Novella and Stories* (1998), was the winner of the California Book Award and the Southern Review Prize. Her most recent publication is *Inheritance* (2005). In her fiction, she focuses on the fragility of family relationships and the Chinese

American immigrant experience. Chang is currently director of the University of Iowa Writers' Workshop in the University of Iowa College of Liberal Arts and Sciences as well as fiction editor for the *Harvard Review*.

Chock, Eric (b. 1950)

Chock currently teaches in the Poets in the Schools program in Honolulu, Hawaii. His first book of poems, *Ten Thousand Wishes*, is now out of print. His second book of poems, *Last Days Here*, appeared in 1989. Chock is the editor or co-editor of several anthologies, including *The Best of Bamboo Ridge* (1986), *Small Kid Time Hawaii* (1981), and *Talk Story: An Anthology of Hawaii's Local Writers* (1978). An active member of the literary community, Chock has served on the board of directors of the Hawaii Literary Arts Council and the Honolulu Commission on Culture and the Arts. His most recent collections include *Growing Up Local* (1988) and *The Best of Honolulu Fiction* (1999).

Cofer, Judith Ortiz (b. 1952)

Cofer was born in Puerto Rico but moved with her family to New Jersey when she was a small child. Her work explores common challenges of the immigrant experience and the difficulties inherent in navigating between the values of her parents and those of the world in which she moves. As a graduate student at Florida Atlantic University she first began writing poetry and subsequently prose forms as well. Her 1989 novel, *The Line of the Sun*, received a Pulitzer Prize nomination. She has published many essays as well as a book of stories for young adults, and she has won a number of awards and prizes, including the 1990 Pushcart Prize for nonfiction and the 1994 O. Henry Prize for short stories. Her short story collection, *An Island Like You: Stories of the Barrio* (1995), was named Best Book of the Year by the American Library Association. Now Franklin Professor of English and Creative Writing at the University of Georgia, her recent publications are *The Meaning of Consuelo* (2003), *Call Me Maria* (2004), and *A Love Story Beginning in Spanish: Poems* (2005).

Cruz, Sor (Sister) Juana Inés de la (1651?–95)

Born in Nepantla, Mexico, to a Spanish father and a Creole mother, Cruz was one of the earliest authors in the Americas. At the age of three, she followed her sister to school and learned to read and write. With the guidance of her learned grandfather, she became educated far beyond many of her contemporaries. Cruz attracted the attention of the royal court in Mexico City, where she became a lady-in-waiting to the viceroy's wife. During those two years, she started writing poetry. Abruptly, at nineteen, she entered a convent. She continued to study and write, but her superiors demanded that she devote herself to church duties. When she refused to comply and argued that women should not have to submit to men's orders, she was accused of heresy. Sor Juana yielded and gave up her intellectual pursuits. While nursing her sister nuns during the plague in 1695, she contracted the disease and died.

Cummings, E. E. (Edward Estlin) (1894–1962)

A native of Cambridge, Massachusetts, Cummings received both a B.A. and M.A. from Harvard University and then volunteered as an ambulance driver in France during World War I.

There he was imprisoned on a treason charge for three months, which he described in *The Enormous Room* (1922), a prose narrative that won wide acclaim. Beginning with his first volume of poetry, *Tulips and Chimneys* (1923), his work has received both positive and negative attention for its unconventional language and punctuation, most famously his insistence on lowercase letters, even in his name. Cummings's influence on contemporary poetry is not limited to the widespread mimicry of his experiments with line breaks, punctuation, and capitalization. He published many volumes of poetry during his lifetime, including *No Thanks* (1935), *50 Poems* (1940), *1 × 1* (1944), *Xiape: Seventy-One Poems* (1950), *95 Poems* (1958), and *Selected Poems, 1923–1958* (1960). One of the many posthumous collections of his poetry, *Complete Poems: 1904–1962* (1994), contains more than a thousand poems.

Dickey, James (1923–97)

A World War II veteran born in Atlanta, Dickey's life was in some ways that of a typical mid-twentieth-century American man. He played football in college and upon returning from the war spent several years as an advertising copywriter before becoming a teacher, writer, and eventually poet in residence at the University of South Carolina. His work, fiction as well as poetry, is often brutal—like his famous novel *Deliverance* (1970)—and tends toward narrative. His books include the poetry volumes *Buckdancer's Choice* (1965) and *James Dickey: The Selected Poems* (1998), the novel *To the White Sea* (1993), and *Crux: The Letters of James Dickey*, published in 1998 after his death. Another posthumous collection is *The James Dickey Reader* (1999).

Dickinson, Emily (1830–86)

Born in Amherst, Massachusetts, Dickinson was educated at schools for females and then retired to her home. She rarely left it, and saw only family and a few friends during her lifetime. Although she wrote almost two thousand poems, only two were published while she lived. Many of her poems reflect her interest in the dialectic of private and public selves.

Donne, John (1572–1631)

Donne was born Catholic in England during a period of anti-Catholicism so severe that he was prevented from finishing his degree at Oxford. He eventually converted to Anglicanism but only after spending time as an adventurer, first on the high seas with Sir Walter Raleigh, among others, and then later in London. He studied law, became secretary to a powerful noble, served as a member of Parliament, and even went to jail briefly for a secret marriage, which ruined his chances for a civil career. Donne and his wife had twelve children; she died at thirty-three after the birth of their youngest. After his conversion to Anglicanism and subsequent ordination at age forty-two, Donne quickly became an extremely influential preacher and the dean of St. Paul's Cathedral in London. He was known as a wit and a man of letters, and although his poems were not published until after he died, more than 130 of his sermons appeared in print during his lifetime. In addition to the sermons and essays he produced in later life, he probably began writing poetry in his twenties, and his manuscripts were widely circulated among his friends. His work—dense and complicated sonnets, elegies, epigrams, and verse letters loaded with paradox, irony, and incongruity—was mostly ignored until the twentieth century. Beginning with his "rediscovery" by T. S. Eliot, Donne had an immense influence on the poetry of the twentieth century.

Douglass, Frederick (1817?–95)

Douglass was the illegitimate child of a white man and a black slave in Tuckahoe, Maryland. Upon his escape from slavery in 1838, he adopted the last name of Douglass and settled in New Bedford, Massachusetts. He so impressed the Massachusetts Anti-Slavery Society when he spoke before them in 1841 that they hired him. During the next four years, he toured the country, speaking out against slavery. Mobbed and beaten because of his views, he described his experiences in *Narrative of the Life of Frederick Douglass: An American Slave*. After a two-year visit to England, where he earned enough money to buy his freedom, he founded a newspaper, *The North Star*. For seventeen years he edited and wrote eloquent articles advocating the use of black troops during the Civil War and on civil rights for freedmen. Other autobiographical works included *My Bondage and My Freedom* (1855) and *Life and Times of Frederick Douglass* (1881). Abraham Lincoln consulted with him on matters pertaining to slavery. He held various public offices after the war, such as U.S. Marshal for the District of Columbia (1877–81), recorder of deeds for D.C., and U.S. Minister to Haiti (1889–91). Many of Douglass's writings, not available previously, have been collected in *Frederick Douglass: Selected Speeches and Writings* (1999).

Dubus, André (1936–99)

Born in Lake Charles, Louisiana, and educated in his home state, Dubus became an officer in the U.S. Marine Corps at age twenty-two. After five years, he resigned, resumed his education, and became a teacher of fiction and creative writing at Bradford College in Massachusetts. In 1970, one of his stories was chosen for the annual volume of *Best American Short Stories*. Dubus has written eight short story collections, including *The Times Are Never So Bad* (1983), *The Last Worthless Evening* (1986), *Collected Stories* (1988), *Dancing After Hours* (1996), and *Meditations from a Movable Chair* (1998). "The Curse" was written while he was convalescing from the loss of his leg in a highway accident. The themes of frailty and fallibility can be noted in Dubus's works. He died of a heart attack in 1999.

Eberhart, Richard (Ghormley) (1904–2005)

Born in Minnesota, Eberhart studied at Dartmouth College as well as Cambridge University. Over the course of a long life, in addition to teaching, he worked as a businessman, a naval officer, a cultural adviser, and a tutor to the son of the king of Siam. He won the Pulitzer Prize for Poetry in 1965 for his *Selected Poems, 1930–1965*. His many books include *Gifts of Being* (1968), *Collected Poems* (1930, 1976, 1988), *Uncollected Poems 1948–1983* (1984), *Maine Poems* (1988), and *New and Selected Poems: 1930–1990* (1990). Eberhart lived for many years in New Hampshire where he was poet laureate from 1979 to 1984 and was honored by the governor of that state, who proclaimed a Richard Eberhart Day in 1982.

Emanuel, James A. (b. 1921)

Born in Alliance, Nebraska, Emanuel was educated at Howard, Northwestern, and Columbia universities, and is professor emeritus at City College of the City University of New York. Poet, biographer, and critic, he has published several volumes of poetry, including *The Treehouse and Other Poems* (1961), *Panther Man* (1970), and *The Broken Bowl: New and Uncollected Poems* (1983). In the last decade he has written most of his poetry and prose in Europe. Some of his more recent publications include *Blues in Black and White*, with Godelieve

Simons (1992), *Reaching for Mumia: 16 Haiku* (1995), *JAZZ from the Haiku King* with artwork by Godelieve Simons (1999), and *The Force and the Reckoning* (2001).

Emerson, Ralph Waldo (1803–82)

Emerson was born in Boston and graduated from Harvard. He became a minister but resigned because he could not accept certain doctrines of the church. After traveling in Europe, where he met English philosophers and poets, he formulated the theory of transcendentalism, which stressed the divinity of humankind and relied on intuition to reveal life's truths. Although his prose writings were revolutionary, his poetry followed traditional form and content.

Erdrich, Louise (b. 1954)

A member of the Turtle Mountain Band of Chippewa, Erdrich was born in Minnesota and grew up in North Dakota. After getting her degree in anthropology from Dartmouth College, she taught in North Dakota for a while and then went to Johns Hopkins to study writing. Her work reflects her deep concern with Native American issues, both cultural and political, often depicting reservation life. She has won awards and prizes for both fiction and poetry, including the American Academy of Poets Prize when she was at Dartmouth. Her 1984 novel *Love Medicine* won the National Book Critics Circle Award. Her other novels have won both critical and popular success, establishing her as one of the country's major contemporary writers. They include *The Beet Queen* (1986), *Tracks* (1988), *The Bingo Palace* (1994), and *Tales of Burning Love* (1996), which continue various narrative threads she initiated with *Love Medicine*. The *Master Butchers Singing Club* (2003), *Four Souls* (2004), and *The Painted Drum* (2005) are her most recent publications. She has also published three volumes of poetry, *Jacklight* (1984), *Baptism of Desire* (1989), and *Original Fire: Selected and New Poems* (2003), and has collaborated with her husband, Michael Dorris, on two books: the nonfiction work *Broken Cord* (1989) and the novel *The Crown of Columbus* (1991). Erdrich lives in Minnesota with her daughters and is the owner of Birchbark Books, a small independent bookstore.

Espada, Martín (b. 1957)

Born in Brooklyn, New York, Espada is considered one of the leading poets of Puerto Rican heritage. Educated at the University of Wisconsin and Northeastern University, his work experience encompasses a variety of jobs from bouncer to radio journalist in Nicaragua to a tenant lawyer. At present he is professor at the University of Massachusetts—Amherst, where he teaches creative writing and Latino poetry. The themes of his poetry include immigrants, hard work, and poverty. His published works include *The Immigrant Iceboy's Bolero* (1982), *Trumpets from the Islands of Their Eviction* (1987), *Rebellion Is the Circle of a Lover's Hands* (1990), *City of Coughing and Dead Radiators* (1993), *Imagine the Angels of Bread* (1996), *Zapata's Disciple* (1998), and *A Mayan Astronomer in Hell's Kitchen: Poems* (2000). His more recent publications include *Alabanza: New and Selected Poems (1982–2002)* (2003) and a CD of poetry called *Now the Dead Will Dance the Mambo* (2004).

Euripides (480–406 B.C.)

Born on the Greek island of Salamis, Euripides was a writer of tragedies. Today he is considered as great a dramatist as Sophocles and Aeschylus, although during his lifetime he was not popular. His themes reflected a pessimistic view of life, and his criticism of social matters was not viewed approvingly. He attacked the inequalities of women's status in *Medea*, the emphasis on the glories of war in *The Trojan Women*, and the unjust treatment of illegitimate children in *Hippolytus*. Only nineteen of his eighty or ninety plays exist today, among them *Alcestis*, *Electra*, and *Ion*.

Ferlinghetti, Lawrence (b. 1919)

Poet, playwright, and editor, Ferlinghetti is co-owner of City Lights Books in San Francisco and founder and editor of City Lights Publishing House. He was an important figure in the beat movement of the 1950s whose adherents were primarily concerned with rebelling against society and taking strong stands on political issues. In 1994, the city of San Francisco celebrated Ferlinghetti's contributions by naming a street in his honor and followed up that tribute in 1998, crowning him the city's first poet laureate. Ferlinghetti writes in the language and speech rhythms of ordinary people, rather than in formal poetic language and structures. In his poem "Constantly Risking Absurdity" (1958), he speculates on the poet's responsibility to society. He is perhaps best known for *A Coney Island of the Mind: Poems* (1958). His recent works include *A Far Rockaway of the Heart* (1998), *How to Paint Sunlight* (2001), and *Americus: Part I* (2004).

Forché, Carolyn (b. 1950)

Born in Detroit, Michigan, and educated at Michigan State University, Forché is a poet, journalist, and educator. While a journalist in El Salvador from 1978 to 1980, she reported on human rights conditions for Amnesty International. This experience greatly affected her poetry, and she also lectured extensively on the subject when she returned to the United States. Her poetry collections include *Gathering the Tribes* (1976), *The Country Between Us* (1981), *The Angel of History* (1994), and *Star Quilt* (1998). Her fourth book of poems, *Blue Hour*, was published in 2003. Forché is currently a professor and director of creative writing at Skidmore College in Saratoga, New York.

Frost, Robert (1874–1963)

Born in San Francisco, Frost moved east with this family when he was a child, and his poems reflect New England life and people. He attended Dartmouth and Harvard for short periods, held a variety of jobs, and tried farming in New Hampshire. During these years, he wrote poetry but was rejected by publishers. Finally, he went to England where his poems were published. On his return to the United States, he met with more success. During his long life, he received four Pulitzer Prizes and many other awards. At President John F. Kennedy's inauguration in 1961, he read his poem "The Gift Outright." In many of his poems, Frost uses nature as the backdrop for his reflections on human behavior. In 1994, the Library of America published the most comprehensive collection of his works in a single volume— *Collected Poems, Prose & Plays*, which contains 1,036 pages.

Gillan, Maria Mazziotti

Born in New Jersey, Gillan has taught in a number of colleges. She is the founder and executive director of the Poetry Center at Passaic Country Community College in Paterson,

New Jersey, and editor of *The Paterson Literary Review*. In addition to the many anthologies in which her work appears, she has written eight books of poetry, including *Flowers from the Tree of Night* (1981) and *Where I Come From* (1995). With her daughter Jennifer, she has edited three anthologies, including *Unsettling America: An Anthology of Contemporary Multicultural Poetry* (1994). *Growing up Ethnic in America* was published in 1999. Her most recent work includes *Things My Mother Told Me* (1999), and *Italian Women in Black Dresses* (2002). Gillan is currently a professor and director of the creative writing program at Binghamton University, State University of New York.

Gilman, Charlotte Perkins (1860–1935)

Born in Hartford, Connecticut, and educated at the Rhode Island School of Design, Gilman was a social critic and feminist who wrote prolifically about the necessity of social and sexual equality, particularly about women's need for economic independence. Following a nervous breakdown after the birth of her daughter, Gilman divorced her husband and devoted her time to lecturing and writing about feminist issues. Her nonfiction includes *Women and Economics* (1898) and *The Man-Made World* (1911). Her novels include *Herland* (1915) and *With Her in Ourland* (1916). "The Yellow Wallpaper" (1899) is a fictionalized account of Gilman's own postpartum depression.

Gordimer, Nadine (b. 1923)

Born in Johannesburg, South Africa, and educated at the University of Witwatersrand, Gordimer was one of the few outspoken whites living in South Africa who protested the policy of apartheid (the restrictive laws that governed blacks and those of mixed race). Since her country's dismantling of apartheid in the 1990s, her work—both fiction and nonfiction—has continued to address with depth and nuance the personal and political complications of life in that racially and politically fraught society. She has written many novels and short stories and is the recipient of international awards, including the Nobel Prize for literature in 1991 and 1974 Booker Prize. Some of her recent works include *Writing and Being* (1995), *House Gun* (1998), *Living in Hope and History* (1999), *The Pickup* (2001), *Loot: And Other Stories* (2003), and *Get a Life* (2005).

Greene, Graham (1904–91)

British-born writer, novelist, playwright, and journalist, Greene is still one of the most widely read authors of the twentieth century. His first published work, *The Man Within* (1929), was received warmly by both critics and the public. In the 1930s, he began a career as film critic for London's *The Spectator* and was considered one of the finest reviewers of his time. Greene's interest in film led to his writing successful screenplays and adaptations for cinema, the most celebrated being *The Third Man*. During World War II, he worked for the British Secret Intelligence Service, and at this point his writings began leaning toward political concerns. After the war Greene traveled to political hot spots such as Stalinist Poland, Vietnam during the Indochina War, and Fidel Castro's Cuba. Although he claimed to be apolitical as a writer, most of his later novels were written expressly to support those he believed to be politically oppressed. Graham Greene was an interesting and enigmatic figure. He died in Vevey, Switzerland, in 1991. His novels include *The Ministry of Fear* (1943), *The End of the Affair* (1951), *The Quiet American* (1955), and *Collected Short Stories* (1973).

Hardy, Thomas (1860–1928)

Born in Dorset, England, Hardy became an architect but started writing in 1867. The success of one of his novels, *Far from the Madding Crowd* (1874), enabled him to give up architecture for a literary career. After two more successful novels, *Tess of the D'Urbervilles* (1891) and *Jude the Obscure* (1896), he gave up fiction for poetry. The bulk of his work is set in the semi-imaginary county of Wessex, named after the Anglo-Saxon kingdom that existed in the area. Hardy's first published volume of poetry is *Wessex Poems* (1898). Both Hardy's novels and poems are marked by poetic descriptions and fatalism.

Harrison, Jeffrey (b. 1957)

A native of Cincinnati, Ohio, Harrison once told an interviewer that, for him, poetry is "an effort to make sense of the world." He is a contributor to a wide variety of journals, both literary and general. He is the recipient of several fellowships including the John Simon Guggenheim Memorial Foundation and the National Endowment for the Arts. He is the author of *The Singing Underneath* (1988), *Signs of Arrival* (1996), and *Feeding the Fire* (2001). In 2005, *An Undertaking*, Harrison's sequence of poems about his brother's suicide, was published.

Hayden, Robert (1913–80)

Born and reared in a Detroit ghetto, Hayden not only suffered from the indignities of poverty but was ridiculed because of his poor eyesight. He immersed himself in books and attended Detroit City College and the University of Michigan, where he studied with poet W. H. Auden. His poetry was not widely appreciated until the 1960s. He was the first African American writer to serve as poetry consultant to the Library of Congress, and was a member of the American Academy and Institute of Arts and Letters. Among his important works are *Heart-Shape in the Dust* (1940), *Angle of Ascent* (1975), and *American Journal* (1979), in which he celebrates the triumphs of his people despite their years of slavery in the American South.

Heaney, Seamus (b. 1939)

Heaney was the first of nine children born on a farm near Belfast in County Derry, Northern Ireland. After local schooling he went to Queen's University in Belfast, where he earned first-class honors with his English degree. His work was first published as he worked toward his teacher's certificate in English at St. Joseph's College, also in Belfast. As a Catholic native of that strife-torn city, Heaney has been called the "laureate of violence." Heaney's poetry demonstrates the national preoccupation with the carnage in Northern Ireland; his work is consistently concerned with memorialization, and he has said that there is no other Heaney besides "the elegiac." He is considered the most important Irish poet since Yeats and, indeed, one of the greatest living poets, a distinction reflected in his many prizes and awards over the years, beginning with an early book of poems, *Death of a Naturalist* (1966), and culminating in the 1995 Nobel Prize for Literature. Not just an enormously popular poet, Heaney is an internationally sought-after teacher, having served at Oxford University, the University of California at Berkeley, and Harvard University. His 1999 verse translation of the Old English epic *Beowulf* was a commercial and critical success, and his many volumes of poetry include *Door into the Dark* (1969), *Wintering Out* (1973), *North* (1975), *Field Work* (1976), *Poems 1965–1975* (1980), *Station Island* (1985), *Poems 1966–1987* (1990), *Seeing Things* (1991), *The Spirit Level: Poems* (1996), and *Opened Ground: Selected Poems 1966–1996* (1999). His recent work includes *Electric Light* (2001) and *District and Circle* (2006). His prose work is collected in *Preoccupations: Selected Prose 1968–1978* (1980) and *The Government of the Tongue: Selected Prose 1978–1987.*

Hogan, Linda (b. 1947)

Hogan was born in Denver of Chickasaw heritage and earned a bachelor's degree from the University of Colorado. Her honors include the Five Civilized Tribes Playwriting Award in 1980 for *A Piece of Moon* and the 1986 Before Columbus Foundation's American Book Award for *Seeing through the Sun.* Presently, Hogan is an associate professor of American Indian studies at the University of Minnesota. Her poems reflect her interest in preserving the Chickasaw culture. She works as a volunteer with environmental and wildlife groups. Although Hogan published her first novel in 1990, she has been writing poetry since the 1970s. She was a finalist for the Pulitzer Prize for *Mean Spirit* (1994) as well as for a National Book Critics Circle Award for *The Book of Medicines* (1993). *Dwellings: A Spiritual History of the Living World* (1995) is a book of essays looking at the interconnectedness of nature, religion, and myth. Hogan's work is often concerned with the variety of complicated relationships between humans and the animal kingdom. She was co-editor of both *Between Species: Women and Animals* (1997) and *Intimate Nature: The Bond between Women and Animals* (1998). She received the Lifetime Achievement Award, Native Writers' Circle of the Americas in 1998. She published a novel, *Power*, in 1998, and *The Woman Who Watches over the World: A Native Memoir* in 2001. In 2004, she edited a collection on feminine spirituality, with Brenda Peterson, *Face to Face: Women Writers on Faith, Mysticism, and Awakening.*

Hughes, Langston (1902–67)

One of the most important African American literary figures of the twentieth century, Hughes was born in Missouri and grew up in Lawrence, Kansas, and Cleveland, Ohio, where he graduated from high school, having already begun to write. Enrolled at New York's Columbia University in 1921, he was not permitted to live in the racially restricted dormitories and so took up residence at the nearby Harlem YMCA, where he came across the budding Harlem Renaissance, of which he was to become a major figure. After a few years of international travel and work as a sailor, he graduated from Lincoln University in Pennsylvania and returned to New York City. His first book of poems, *The Weary Blues*, appeared in 1926. Besides poetry, Hughes wrote short stores, novels, plays, scripts for both radio and film, children's books, and works of humor and nonfiction. He also lectured frequently at black universities across the South. Hughes's poetry incorporated the conventions of black spirituals and the blues into more traditional verse forms, and his writing in general was celebratory of black life, artistic expression, and spirituality, in both structure and content. At the same time he addressed the pain, frustration, and loss inherent in the second-class citizenship to which African Americans were relegated. An exceedingly prolific writer, his many books include *Not without Laughter* (1930), *Dear Lovely Death* (1931), *The Negro Mother* (1931), *The Dream Keeper* (1932), *The Ways of White Folks* (1933), *A New Song* (1938), *One-Way Ticket* (1949), *The Sweet Flypaper of Life* (1955), *Ask Your Mama* (1961), *Simple's Uncle Sam* (1965), and many others.

Hurston, Zora Neale (1891–1960)

Born in 1891 in Eastonville, Florida, although she never finished grade school, Hurston was able to enter and complete her undergraduate studies at Howard University but left after a few years, unable to support herself. After a short story, "Drenched in Light," appeared in the New York African American magazine *Opportunity*, she decided to move to Harlem and pursue a literary career there. She was later offered a scholarship to Barnard College where she received her B.A. in anthropology in 1927 and received a fellowship to return to Florida and study the oral traditions of Eatonville. Thinking like a folklorist, Hurston strove to represent speech patterns of the period, which she documented through ethnographic research, but many readers objected to the representation of African American dialect in Hurston's novels, causing her work to slide into obscurity for decades. Her published works include *Jonah's Gourd Vine* (1934), *Mules and Men* (1935), *Their Eyes Were Watching God* (1937), and an autobiography entitled *Dust Tracks on a Road* (1942). Works published posthumously include *Mule Bone* (a play written with Langston Hughes) (1996) and *Spunk* (1985). The last decade of her life she lived in Florida, working from time to time as a maid. Hurston died penniless and was buried in an unmarked grave in Fort Pierce, Florida, until African American novelist Alice Walker and literary scholar Charlotte Hunt found and marked the grave in 1973, sparking a Hurston renaissance.

Jackson, Shirley (1916–65)

Best known for her macabre gothic fiction, of which "The Lottery" (1949) is the most famous example, Jackson's work often portrays the more sinister tendencies of people and communities. Her novels are psychological thrillers, often with a bizarre ironic twist. These novels include *The Haunting of Hill House* (1959) and *We Have Always Lived in the Castle* (1962), for which she received the National Book Award nomination. She is less widely known for her juvenile fiction and humorous books on family life—collections of short sketches usually first published in women's magazines and widely praised by contemporary critics.

Jarrell, Randall (1914–65)

A Tennessee native, Jarrell studied at Vanderbilt University, where he received both a B.A. and an M.A. His experience in the United States Air Corps in World War II formed his early collections of poetry. *Little Friend, Little Friend* (1945) and *Losses* (1948), which deal with the fears and moral struggles of soldiers, are considered to be among the most powerful American war commentaries. After the war he went back to work as a professor, poet, and critic, publishing several collections of verse, including *Selected Poems* (1955) and *The Woman at the Washington Zoo* (1960). He went on to write children's books, including *The Bat Poet* (1964). He was hit and killed by a car in 1965.

Jefferson, Thomas (1743–1826)

A governor, secretary of state, and president, he is best known for his draft of the Declaration of Independence. Although Benjamin Franklin and John Adams made some small revisions, the document is essentially Jefferson's. As you read it, speculate as to how the author's understanding of his audience contributed to his effective communication of his message.

Joyce, James (1882–1941)

Born in Dublin, Ireland, the eldest in a family of ten children, Joyce knew a life of poverty and efforts to maintain respectability. He was educated in Jesuit schools, where he was trained in Catholicism and the classics. However, he rebelled against his religion, his country, and his family, and at twenty he left Dublin for a life in Europe as an exile. By teaching languages and doing clerical work, he eked out a living for his common-law wife and their two children. In 1916, James published a semi-autobiographical work titled *A Portrait of the Artist as a Young Man*, which is ranked as the third greatest English-language novel of the twentieth century by the Modern Library, a division of Random House publishers. His novel *Ulysses* (1922), written in an innovative style, took seven years to complete. *Finnegan's Wake* (1939), his most experimental work, is written in a language he created. He also wrote poems, short stories, and one play. Despite his years of exile, all of his fiction is set in his native Dublin and portrays his attempt to free himself of religious and geographic restrictions.

Kafka, Franz (1883–1924)

Born in Prague, Czechoslovakia, Kafka spent an unhappy life as a victim of anti-Semitism and in a job he detested in an insurance company. His stories, such as "The Metamorphosis" (1915), and his three novels, *The Trial* (1925), *The Castle* (1926), and *Amerika* (1927), reflect his feelings of alienation from the community. When he died of tuberculosis at the age of forty-one, he left his unpublished manuscripts to a friend with instructions that they be destroyed. Instead, the friend edited and published them, thereby establishing the obscure clerk as a world-renowned author.

Keats, John (1795–1821)

Born in London, Keats studied to be a doctor but he never practiced medicine. His early interest in literature, and his friendship with poetry, inspired him to write poetry. Along with Lord Byron and Percy Bysshe Shelley, he established romantic poetry, with its emphasis on emotion and the imagination over reason and intelligence. Idealized love was the subject of many of his poems. In the spring and summer of 1819 he produced a series of odes, including "Ode on a Grecian Urn" and "Ode to a Nightingale," which are considered among the most important poetry ever written in English. At twenty-six, he died of tuberculosis.

Kenny, Maurice (b. 1929)

Born near the St. Lawrence River, the ancestral home of the Mohawk Indians, Kenny lived in New Jersey and in Watertown, New York, as a child. After high school he worked at a variety of jobs and lived in Mexico, Puerto Rico, and Chicago. Finally, he settled in Brooklyn and continued writing poetry until he experienced a near-fatal heart attack in 1974. Thereafter, he focused on his Native American roots as subjects for his poetry, and is now considered one of the leading Native American poets. As editor of a magazine and a publishing company, Kenny encourages other Native American writers. In 1984, he received the Before Columbus Foundation's American Book Award for *The Mama Poems*. He has taught writing in Oklahoma and is now a professor at North Country Community College in Saranac Lake, New York. Some of his two dozen books include *Between Two Rivers: Selected Poems* (1987), *Greyhounding This America* (1987), *Rain and Other Fictions* (1990), and *On Second Thought: A Compilation* (1995). He is the editor of *Stories for a Winter's Night* (2000).

King, Martin Luther Jr. (1929–68)

Born in Georgia, King was the son and grandson of Baptist ministers. He was educated at Morehouse College, Crozier Theologial Seminary, and Boston University. He was pastor of a Baptist church in Montgomery, Alabama, when Rosa Parks refused to relinquish her seat on a bus to a white person. King, influenced by the teachings of Mahatma Gandhi, led a nonviolent bus boycott in 1955 that attracted national attention. This boycott lasted for over a year and eventually led to the intervention of the U.S. Supreme Court, which ruled that Alabama's bus segregation was unconstitutional. King wrote of the experience in *Stride toward Freedom* (1958).

The message of passive resistance spread, and King and his followers organized many protests against segregation and injustice in the South. Although he was arrested, jailed, and stabbed, and his home was bombed, King continued to preach his philosophy and gained respect and admiration all over the world. In 1963, his *Letter from the Birmingham Jail* replied to those who criticized his methods and beliefs. King organized the March on Washington in 1963 and delivered his memorable "I Have a Dream" speech. He was awarded the Noble Peace Prize in 1964—at thirty-five, he was the youngest recipient. King continued to lead protests and coupled his message about segregation with opposition to the Vietnam War. While preparing to march with striking workers in Memphis, Tennessee, in 1968, he was assassinated.

Komunyakaa, Yusef (b. 1947)

Born in Bogalusa, Louisiana, Komunyakaa received the Bronze Star while serving with the U.S. Army in Vietnam from 1965 to 1967, as an information specialist and as editor of a military newspaper. On his return stateside, he went to college and graduate school in the West but went back to Louisiana to teach in the New Orleans schools at both the elementary and postsecondary levels. The winner of a number of awards, in 1994 he claimed the Pulitzer Prize and the $50,000 Kingsley Tufts Poetry Award for his *Neon Vernacular: New and Selected Poems*. His work weaves together the strands of his life experiences, from Louisiana to Vietnam, dealing variously with war, jazz, culture shock, and the power of American racism in history and the present. Some of his other books include *Copacetic* (1984), *Toys in a Field* (1986), *Dien Cai Dau* (1988), *Thieves of Paradise* (1998), *Talking Dirty to the Gods* (2000), *Pleasure Dome: New and Collected Poems* (2001), and *Taboo: The Wishbone Trilogy, Part 1* (2004). New York University has appointed Komunyakaa its Distinguished Senior Poet. He is currently part of NYU's faculty, teaching in their Graduate Creative Writing Program.

Lagerkvist, Pär (Fabian) (1891–1974)

This Swedish writer left his homeland as a young man for Paris, where he was intensely affected by the modern art movements of the time—fauvism, cubism, and naivism. *Anguish* (1916), his early book of poetry, is seen by some as the first expressionistic work in Swedish literature, and its publication established his reputation. Like many of his generation, he was deeply disturbed by World War I, and much of his work is concerned with the meaning of life and the conflict between good and evil. As he got older, his work became less pessimistic and more realistic, although in many ways his thematic concerns were the same. He was basically unknown in the United States until 1951, when he won the Nobel Prize for Literature and the English translation of his novel *Barabbas* (1950) appeared. Eleven years later, the movie adaptation of the book appreared, to wide acclaim. In the meantime he had written *The Eternal Smile and Other Stories* (1954) and *The Marriage Feast and Other Stories* (1955).

Lassell, Michael (b. 1947)

Born in New York City, Lassell has earned degrees from Colgate University, California Institute of the Arts, and the Yale School of Drama. Now living in Los Angeles, he is managing editor of *LA Style* magazine and has worked as a critic, photographer, teacher, and writer. His book *Poems for Lost and Un-Lost Boys* won the Amelia Chapbook Award in 1986. His latest published works are *Hard Way* (1995), *Flame for the Touch That Matters* (1998), *Certain Ecstasies* (1999), and *Celebration* (2004).

Laviera, Tato (b. 1951)

Laviera, born in Puerto Rico, has lived in New York City since 1960. He has taught creative writing at several northeastern universities, including Rutgers. His poetry and drama celebrate the ethnic diversity of New York City, and he often writes in English and Spanish as well as in "Spanglish," a mixture of the two languages used by several bilingual poets. He is deeply committed to preserving the oral traditions of Puerto Rico and the Caribbean, and, although his poetry is published in the written form, it is meant to be sung and celebrated by the community. He has written *AmeRican* (1985), *Enclave* (1986), *Mainstream Ethics=Etica Corriente* (1988), and *La Carreta Made a U-Turn* (1992).

Lee, Li-Young (b. 1957)

The Lee family's journey began in the early 1950s when they fled China's political turmoil for Indonesia. When anti-Chinese sentiment commenced in their new home, Lee's father was sent to prison. The family escaped to Hong Kong, and Mr. Lee rose to prominence as an evangelical preacher. The author, born in Jakarta, emigrated to America when he was six years old. Mr. Lee became the minister of an all-white Presbyterian church in a small town in western Pennsyslvania. The imposing, elusive, God-like figure of his father haunts Lee's work. He is the author of two award-winning volumes of poetry: *Rose* (1986) and *The City in Which I Love You* (1990). *The Winged Seed: A Remembrance* (1995) is an autobiographical work. Lee has taught in several universities including Northwestern and the University of Iowa. His most recent book is *Book of My Nights: Poems* (2001).

Levertov, Denise (1923–97)

Born in England of Welsh and Jewish parents, Levertov was a nurse in World War II. She married an American writer and moved to the United States in 1948. Her poetic style was influenced by her affiliation with the Black Mountain poets of North Carolina, who advocated a verse form that duplicates everyday speech patterns. Some of her poems focus on human relationships; many others express her commitment to social and environmental issues. Among her numerous collections of poetry are *Light up the Cave* (1981), *A Door in the Hive* (1989), *Evening Train* (1992), a memoir, *Tesserae: Memories and Suppositions* (1995), *The Life around Us: Selected Poems on Nature* (1997), and *The Stream & the Sapphire: Selected Poems on Religious Themes* (1997). The poet Kenneth Rexroth once wrote that she was "the most subtly skillful poet of her generation, the most profound, the most moving."

Liu, Eric (b. 1968)

The son of Taiwanese immigrants, Liu was born in Poughkeepsie, New York. A summa cum laude graduate of Yale University, he founded and edits *The Next Progressive*, a journal of opinion. He was a speechwriter for President Bill Clinton and has been a commentator on MSNBC. Liu edited the anthology *Next Young American Writers on the New Generation.*

His memoir, *The Accidental Asian: Notes of a Native Speaker* (1998), articulates the Asian American experience in defining one's identity. He also speaks eloquently of his father's struggles both in Taiwan and in America. His most recent book is *Guiding Lights: The People Who Lead Us toward Our Purpose in Life* (2004).

Lyman, Peter (b. 1940)

Lyman is a professor at the School of Information Management and Systems at the University of California at Berkeley. His research interests include the sociology of information, computer literacy, and electronic libraries. His most recent project is a study of how much new information was produced in 2002, titled *How Much Information 2003?* This study attempts to measure how much information is produced in the world each year.

Marvell, Andrew (1621–78)

Son of an Anglican clergyman, Marvell entered Cambridge and received his bachelor's degree in 1638. When his father died in 1640, he spent his inheritance on a four-year tour of the Continent. On his return, he tutored the daughter of a lord general and wrote poems on gardens and country life. For most of his life, Marvell took an active interst in politics and wrote many satirical pamphlets about the controversies of the times. A friend of John Milton, Marvell was influential in saving the poet from prison after the Restoration. During the last twenty years of his life, he was a representative in Parliament. His poetical works were virtually ignored until 1921. T. S. Eliot wrote an essay commemorating Marvell's birth, and interest in his lyric poetry flourished. Other poems include "To His Coy Mistress," "The Garden," "The Definition of Love," "An Horation Ode," "Upon Appleton House," and "A Dialogue between Body and Soul."

McKay, Claude (1890–1948)

Born on the island of Jamaica to peasant farmers, McKay heard African folk tales when he was a child and came to appreciate his racial heritage. He was encouraged in his literary ambitions by an Englishman through whose efforts two of his poetry collections were published in English. In 1912, he came to the United States to study agriculture. After a few years of school, he left for New York City to become a writer. Although he had experienced discrimination in Jamaica, he was unprepared for the extreme racism he encountered in the United States. McKay channeled his anger into a collection of poetry, *Harlem Shadows* (1922), which heralded the Harlem Renaissance (a period of unprecedented creativity by black writers centered in Harlem). His poetry reflects his concern over the treatment of African Americans in U.S. society. His other works include *Home to Harlem* (1928), *Banjo* (1929), *Songs of Jamaica* (1911), *Constab Ballads* (1912), and *Spring in New Hampshire and Other Poems* (1920). His book of collected poems, *Selected Poems* (1953), was published posthumously.

Millay, Edna St. Vincent (1892–1950)

Born in Rockland, Maine, her middle name is derived from St. Vincent's Hospital in New York, where her uncle's life had been saved just prior to her birth. Millay began to write poetry at an early age. Her first poem, "Renascence," was published during her senior year in college. During the 1920s, she lived a bohemian life in Greenwich Village, where she acted in plays and continued to write poetry. Her love sonnets, which advocated sexual and emotional freedom for women, were particularly popular. In 1923, she won the Pulitzer Prize in Poetry for *The Harp-Weaver and Other Poems*. She wrote infrequently during the last years of her life, and she died in relative obscurity.

Mirikitani, Janice (b. 1942)

A third-generation Japanese American, Mirikitani is currently the executive director of programs at the Glide and Urban Center, a community organization in California, and the president of the Glide Foundation, providing extensive outreach services to the lower income and homeless people of San Francisco. Her poetry illuminates contemporary urban life and also focuses on the injustices experienced by Japanese Americans who were interned in U.S. camps during World War II. Her published books include *Awake in the River* (1978), *Shedding Silence: Poetry and Prose* (1987), and *We, the Dangerous: New and Selected Poems* (1995). Her most recent works include *Love Works* (2001), and *What Matters: Young Writers and Artists Speak Out* (2004).

Mishima, Yukio (pseudonym of Kimitake Hiraoka) (1925–70)

Mishima was born in Tokyo, Japan. Twenty-nine days after he was born, he was taken from his mother by his grandmother who was related to the samurai of the Tokugawa era, and raised by her until he was twelve years old when he was returned to his parents. He attended the elite Peers school where his first short story *Hanazakari no Mori* (*The Forest in Full Bloom*) was published in 1944. Forbidden by his father to pursue a writing career, he was forced to study German law, graduating from the elite Tokyo University in 1947. He published his first novel, *Tōzoku* (*Thieves*) (1948), followed that same year by *Kamen no Kokuhaku* (*Confessions of a Mask*), an autobiographical work about a young homosexual who hides behind a mask in order to fit into society. The success of this novel made him a celebrity at the age of twenty-four with a following in Europe and America. He was nominated three times for the Nobel Prize for Literature.

True to the spirit of the samurai in which he was raised, Mishima was deeply troubled by the way in which Western modernization was changing Japan. Determined to restore the emperor to his rightful place, Mishima and four others entered the offices of the commandant of the eastern command in Tokyo with a list of demands. When his words fell on deaf years, he committed seppuku, a Japanese ritual suicide. The last pages of his final work, *The Sea of Fertility Tetralogy*, were delivered to his publisher on the day he committed suicide.

Momaday, N. Scott (b. 1934)

Born in Lawton, Oklahoma, and graduated from the University of New Mexico, Momaday spent a year teaching on an Apache reservation. He won a poetry fellowship to the creative writing program at Stanford University and earned a doctorate in 1963. After Momaday's first novel *House Made of Dawn* (1969), he was awarded the Pulitzer Prize for Fiction and began teaching at the University of California at Berkeley. His additional books include *Angle of Geese and Other Poems* (1974), *The Names* (1976), *The Ancient Child* (1989), *In the Presence of the Sun* (1991), *Circle of Wonder: A Native American Christmas Story* (1993), *The Native Americans: Indian Country* (1993), *The Man Made of Words: Essays, Stories, Passages* (1997), and

In the Bear's House (1999). Momaday recently retired from the University of Arizona where he had been a professor of English since 1982.

Mora, Pat (b. 1942)

Mora is a native of El Paso, Texas, the border city to which her grandparents migrated during the Mexican revolution. She received a bachelor's degree from Texas Western College and a master's degree from the University of Texas at El Paso. Her poetry reflects her Hispanic perspective, and she writes frequently on gender and political issues. Mora is now retired and lives in Santa Fe, New Mexico, and Cincinnati, Ohio. Her work has been collected in *Chants* (1984), *Borders* (1986), *Communion* (1991), *Aqua Santa—Holy Water* (1995), and *House of Houses* (1997). Among the most distinguished contemporary Hispanic writers, Mora receives praise for her cultural activism as well as her writing. She has also written many children's books, a book of autobiographical essays, *Nepantla: Essays from the Land in the Middle* (1993), and a memoir in essay form, *House of Houses* (1997). Her most recent volume of poetry for adults is *Aunt Carmen's Book of Practical Saints* (1997). In spring 1997, Mora's memoirs about her family, *Voices from the Garden: Voces del Jardin*, was published. Her upcoming books include *Adobe Odes* and *¡Marimba! Animales A–Z* (illustrated by Doug Cushman).

Morales, Aurora Levin (b. 1954)

Born in Castañer, Puerto Rico, to a Puerto Rican mother and a Jewish father, Morales came to the United States with her family in 1967 and lived in Chicago and New Hampshire. She attended Franconia College in New Hampshire in 1972, and then transferred to Oakland, California, where she earned an undergraduate degree in creative writing and ethnic studies. Morales also holds an M.A. and Ph.D. from The Union Institute in Cincinnati, Ohio. In 1981, she was published in *This Bridge Called My Back: Writings by Radical Women of Color*, the first anthology of Hispanic American women writers published in the United States, followed by a collection of short stories, essays, prose poems, and poetry (co-authored with her mother, Rosario Morales) entitled *Getting Home Alive* (1986). Her recent work includes *Remedios: Stories of Earth and Iron from the History of Puertorriquenas* (1998) and *Telling to Live: Latina Feminist Testimonios* (2001). In her writing Morales hopes to bring a voice to Latinas who are struggling to be heard. She presently lives and writes in the San Francisco Bay Area.

Morrison, Toni (pseudonym of Chloe Anthony Wofford) (b. 1931)

Born in an African community in Lorain, Ohio, Morrison earned her B.A. in English from the historically black Howard University in Washington, D.C., and an M.A. at Cornell University. Her continuing success as a novelist began in 1970 with the publication of *The Bluest Eye* and proceeded with *Sula* (1973), *Song of Solomon* (1977), and *Tar Baby* (1981). Recognition of her importance broadened when she won the 1987 Pulitzer Prize for Literature with the publication of *Beloved* and continued to grow with *Jazz* (1992), *Paradise* (1998), and *Love* (2003). Morrison's fiction is brilliantly written, sometimes fantastical, and preoccupied with the quest for self and with the personal and communal repercussions of African American history, which she paints as both seemingly painful and profoundly beautiful. Her work has universal artistic and social significance. That importance was acknowledged internationally in 1993 when she was awarded the Nobel Prize for Literature. Her book of essays, *Playing in the Dark; Whiteness and the Literary Imagination* (1992), addresses issues of importance across academic disciplines with a clarity and intellectual certainty rarely to be found in scholarly discussions of race. In 1989, Morrison became a professor of humanities at Princeton, a post she held until her retirement in May 2006. In 2002, Morrison began to write children's literature with her son Slade Morrison. Their collaborated works include *The Big Box* (2002), *The Book of Mean People* (2002), *Who's Got Game?: The Lion or the Mouse?* (2003), *Who's Got Game?: The Ant or the Grasshopper?* (2003), *Who's Got Game?: Poppy or the Snake?* (2004), and *Who's Got Game?: The Mirror or the Glass*, to be released in 2007.

Murakami, Haruki (b. 1949)

Murakami was born in Kyoto and raised in Kobe, Japan, by his parents, who were both teachers of Japanese literature. Since his early years as a child Murakami has been heavily influenced by Western culture, particularly in terms of Western music and literature. After finishing his studies at Waseda University in Tokyo, Murakami opened a jazz bar. Many of his novels have musical themes and titles referring to a particular song, including *Norwegian Wood* (1987) (after the Beatles song), *Dance, Dance, Dance* (1988) (from The Dells), and *South of the Border, West of the Sun* (1992) (the first part is the title of a song by Nat King Cole). Murakami's fiction is often criticized by Japan's literary establishment for being pop literature, criticizing the gap between Japan's capitalistic society and the Japanese people. Recent publications include *Sputnik Sweetheart* (1999), *Kafka on the Shore* (2002), and a collection of the English verions of twenty-five short stories titled *Blind Willow, Sleeping Woman* was published in 2006. The English version of his latest novel, *After Dark*, is scheduled to be released in 2007. Murakami taught at Princeton University in Princeton, New Jersey, and at Tufts University in Medford, Massachusetts. He presently lives in Kyoto, Japan.

Mydans, Seth (b. 1946)

Mydans is a veteran foreign correspondent who has served in England, the Philippines, Thailand, and the former Soviet Union. In 1983, he joined the *New York Times* as a reporter, after holding overseas posts for the Associated Press and *Newsweek*. He held the position of Southeast Asia bureau chief from 1996 through 2003. He presently works for the *International Herald Tribune* in Asia covering Southeast Asia from Bangkok.

Ng, Fae Myenne (b. 1957)

Born in San Francisco's Chinatown, Ng received her B.A. from the University of California at Berkeley and her M.F.A. from Columbia University School of Arts. She has lived in Brooklyn, New York, since 1989, where she worked as a waitress and teacher to support herself while she wrote the many drafts of her first novel *Bone* (1993), which took ten years to write. Ng received many awards and writing grants for *Bone*, including the Lila Wallace-Reader's Digest Literary Fellowship, the Pushcart Prize, a National Endowment for the Arts Award, a McDowell Fellowship, and a Fellowship in Literature from the American Academy of Arts and Letters. Her most recent publication is *Bound and Determined* (1994). Ng's primary goal as an author is to "write about true life" so that readers can see the kind of hard work immigrants have put into this country, to respect their choices, their desires, their courage.

Niatum, Duane (b. 1946)

Born in Seattle, this Native American poet was educated at the University of Washington and Johns Hopkins University. Niatum has worked as an editor, librarian, and teacher. The Pacific Northwest Writers Conference has awarded him first prize in poetry twice. His books include *Ascending Red Cedar Moon* (1969), *Songs for the Harvester of Dreams* (1982), and *Pieces* (1981). His poems express the disappointments and dreams of his people as they attempt to reconcile their private and communal selves. His most recent collection is *Drawings of the Song Animals: New and Selected Poems* (1991). His recent works are *The Crooked Beak of Love* (2000) and *Nesting Out for Stars: And other Stories* (2002). Recently Niatum returned to graduate school and received his Ph.D. from the University of Michigan in the Program in American Culture.

O'Brien, Tim (b. 1946)

Born in Austin, Minnesota, and educated at Macalester College, O'Brien graduated college in 1968 and received a draft notice. After serving in the Vietnam War, where he received the Purple Heart, he became a graduate student at Harvard University. He left Harvard to be an intern with the *Washington Post*. His war experiences have inspired both fiction and autobiography. *If I Die in a Combat Zone, Box Me Up and Ship Me Home* (1973) and *Northern Lights* (1974) preceded *Going after Cacciato* (1978), which won him the National Book Award. Many critics proclaim *Cacciato* to be the finest work written about the Vietnam War. The short story *The Things They Carried* deals with survival, lost innocence, and the war's lasting legacy for good and evil. It was excerpted from a collection of his works, *The Things They Carried* (1990) and was included in *The Best American Short Stories of 1987*. His recent publications include *In the Lake of the Woods* and *Twinkle, Twinkle* (both 1994), *Tomcat in Love* (1998), and *July, July* (2002). O'Brien is currently writer in residence at Southwest Texas State University in the Creative Writing Program.

O'Flaherty, Liam (1896–1984)

Born in the Aran Islands off the west coast of Ireland, O'Flaherty was educated for the priesthood but abandoned it and joined the Irish Guard before World War I. He was wounded and discharged in 1918. After completing his education, he traveled for several years, returning to Ireland in 1921 to fight with the Republicans against the Free Staters in the Irish civil war. He was exiled soon after, and while living in England he published his first short story, "The Sniper." His best known novel, *The Informer* (1925), became an Academy Award–winning film. However, *Famine* (1937), a novel based on the potato famine that claimed more than a million lives in Ireland during the 1840s, is considered his greatest work. Ireland's poor people were often the main characters in his stories.

Olds, Sharon (b. 1942)

Born in San Francisco, Olds graduated from Stanford University and received a doctorate from Columbia University. She has authored *Satan Says* (1980); *The Dead and the Living* (1984), for which she was awarded a National Book Critics Circle Award in poetry; and *The Gold Cell* (1987). Much of her work expresses her involvement with contemporary social issues and their effects on private and public selves. Her latest works include *The Father* (1992), *The Wellspring* (1996), *Blood, Tin, Straw* (1999), *The Unswept Room* (2002), and *Strike*

Sparks: Selected Poems (2004). Olds presently lives in New York where she is a professor of English at New York University.

Olsen, Tillie (b. 1913)

Olsen, born in Omaha, Nebraska, was determined to be a writer, although she worked at many jobs and raised four children. She began working on her novel *Yonnondio* in the 1920s and finished it in the 1970s. The subjects of her short stories and novels are people who have been denied their chance at creativity because of their sex, race, or class. Olsen's work is often anthologized. *Tell Me a Riddle* (1961), *Silences* (1978), and *Mothers & Daughters: That Special Quality: An Exploration in Photographs* (with Estelle Jussim) (1995) are among her published works. Olsen currently lives in Berkeley, California, where she continues to be an active lecturer, writer, and activist.

Owen, Wilfred (1893–1918)

Born in Shropshire, England, Owen is considered the most famous of the English poets of World War I. He expressed his hatred of war in descriptions of brutality and horror that he experienced on the battlefield. Owen died in action a week before the Armistice. "Above all this book is not concerned with Poetry, the subject of it is War, and the pity of War. The Poetry is in the pity. All a poet can do is warn," he wrote. Only five of Owen's poems had been published before his death, one of which was in fragmentary form. His best known poems include "Anthem for Doomed Youth," "Dulce Et Decorum Est," "The Parable of the Old Man and the Young," and "Strange Meeting."

Petry, Ann (1908–97)

Petry's was one of the few African American families in Old Saybrook, Connecticut, where she was born. She earned a pharmacy degree at the University of Connecticut and then went on to Columbia University, where she graduated in 1946. Her first novel, *The Street*, depicting the struggles of a young woman in Harlem, came out in 1946 to great success. She worked in New York as a reporter and editor for various newspapers while producing novels such as *The Country Place* (1947), and *The Narrows* (1953). A book of short stories, *Miss Muriel and Other Stories*, came out in 1971, just before she left New York to teach English for a few years at the University of Hawaii. Returning to New York, she worked as a teacher and an actress at the American Negro Theatre.

Plato (427–348 B.C.)

A Greek philosopher, teacher, and writer who became actively involved in the politics of the Athenian city-state, Plato vehemently protested the corruption that had permeated Athenian democracy, and the death of his teacher and friend Socrates impelled him to search for an alternative lifestyle. In "The Allegory of the Cave," one of his most famous philosophical dialogues, he talks about the human desire for illusion rather than truth.

Powell, David W. (b. 19-)

Powell served as a marine in Vietnam from 1965 to 1967. "Vietnam: What I Remember" is excerpted from Powell's memoir, "Patriotism Revisited," which he submitted to a creative writing class at the University of Arizona in Tucson. Powell recently published *My Tour in Hell: A Marine's Battle with Combat Trauma* (2006), which tells about his horrific experiences while serving in Vietnam and how posttraumatic stress disorder (PTSD) has drastically changed his life since his return.

Puig, Manuel (1932–90)

As a young boy in Argentina, Puig constantly watched North American and European films. He was so obsessed with movies that he wanted to become either a director or a screenwriter. Neither career suited him, and he turned to fiction. His work, however, is saturated with references to films and popular culture. Puig's autobiographical novel, *Betrayed by Rita Hayworth*, was completed in 1965 but wasn't published until three years later. It was translated into English in 1971 and found an appreciative audience in the United States. Life in Argentina became increasingly uncomfortable for Puig when Juan Peron returned to power in 1971. The writer left the country and lived in Mexico, Brazil, and New York.

His subsequent novels, *Heartbreak Tango* (1973) and *The Buenos Aires Affair: A Detective Novel* (1976), were not as popular, but his next novel, *Kiss of the Spider Woman* (1979), gained instant success and was subsequently made into a movie and a Broadway musical. It was recognized as an attack on the political and cultural corruption of Argentina. He also wrote *Blood of Unrequited Love* (1982) and *Tropical Night Falling* (1988). His novels and plays continue to attract attention from readers and critics alike. He died of a heart attack in 1990.

Reid, Alastair (b. 1926)

Born in Scotland, the son of a minister, Reid was an honors graduate of St. Andrews University. He taught at Sarah Lawrence College (1951–55) and was appointed as a staff writer at the *New Yorker* in 1959. He spent several years as a visiting professor at colleges in the United States, Latin American, and England teaching literature and Latin American studies. Reid is a published poet, translator, essayist, and author of children's books. He has lived in several countries, including Spain, Greece, Morocco, and Latin America.

Rifaat, Alifa (Fatma Abdalla) (1930–96)

Born in Cairo, Egypt, Rifaat wrote a short story when she was nine but was punished for doing so. She hoped to attend college, but her parents opposed this and arranged a marriage for her instead. Although opposition to her writing continued in her Muslim family, her first short stories were published in 1955. Obstacles prevented her from writing for fifteen years during her marriage, but she resumed work in 1975, and hundreds of her stories and a few novels have been published since. Themes related to the sexual and emotional problems encountered by married women in the Middle East dominate her fiction. Her collection *Distant View of a Minaret and Other Stories* was published in 1985. Her last novel was published a year before her death titled *Girls of Baurdin* (1995).

Roethke, Theodore (1908–63)

Roethke was born and raised in Saginaw, Michigan, where his father was the owner of a greenhouse. He studied at both the University of Michigan and Harvard University and went on to teach, settling finally at the University of Washington, where he was known as a great teacher. He was said never to have truly recovered from the death of his father when he was only fourteen, and indeed his work often has a mournful tone. His father's influence is also apparent in his frequent use of greenhouse imagery, as well as metaphors of nature. Roethke's work gained important recognition: *The Waking: Poems 1933–1953* won the 1954 Pulitzer Prize. Other honors included Guggenheim Fellowships in 1945 and 1950 as well as both a National Book Award and the Bollingen Prize in 1959 for *Words for the Wind* (1958). Other collections are *The Lost Son and Other Poems* (1948), *Praise to the End* (1951), *The Lost Field* (1964), and *Collected Poems* (1966). *The Far Field* (1964), *On Poetry & Craft* (1965), and *The Collected Poems of Theodore Roethke* (1966) were published poshumously.

Romero, Leo (b. 1950)

Born in New Mexico, Romero uses his home state as the setting for many of his poems. Educated at the University of New Mexico and New Mexico State University, he is a leading writer of Chicano poetry. His works include *During the Growing Season* (1978), *Celso* (1985), *Desert Nights* (1989), *Going Home Away Indian* (1990), and *Rita & Los Angeles* (1995) and its sequel, *Michael & Los Angeles* (1998). He has also produced a novel, *Crazy for Fabiola*, and more recent poetry collections, *San Fernandez Beat*, *Ravens Are Real*, *The God of Oranges*, and *At Dusk through the Canyon*. Romero and his partner, Elizabeth Cook Romero, presently own and operate a bookstore specializing in used books. The store, Books and More Books, is in Santa Fe, New Mexico, as is their home.

Roy, Sandip

Born in Calcutta, India, Roy's work has appeared in *India Currents Magazine* and *Christopher Street*, *A Magazine*, as well as in anthologies such as *Queer View Mirror* and *Men on Man 6*. He is currently an editor of Pacific News Service and host of "UpFront," the Pacific News Service weekly radio program in San Francisco about California's ethnic communities.

Rukeyser, Muriel (1913–80)

Born in New York City, Rukeyser was educated at Vassar College and Columbia University. A journalist as well as a poet, she reported from Spain on the Spanish civil war and was one of the journalists arrested at the Scottsboro trial in 1931, an important moment in the history of civil rights in the United States. Her poems, published over a period of forty years, reflect her commitment to her Jewish heritage, civil rights, and the antiwar movement. Since her death, two works have been published: *Out of Silence: Selected Poems* (1992) and *A Muriel Rukeyser Reader* (1996).

Rushdie, Salman (Ahmed) (b. 1947)

Rushdie was born in Bombay, India, and educated in his homeland and in England. He was an actor and an advertising copywriter before he began his writing career in the 1970s. His first novels received many prestigious awards. Among his works are *Grimus* (1975), *Midnight's Children* (1981), *Shame* (1983), and *The Satanic Verses* (1988). The latter work outraged Muslims around the world and was immediately banned in a dozen countries for his alleged blasphemy against Islam. Demonstrations and riots in India, Pakistan, and South Africa showed the depth of feeling against the book. Supporters of Rushdie have pointed out that all the objectionable sections take place in the dreams of a character who harbors insane delusions and are not necessarily the beliefs of the author. In 1989, Iran's religious leader, Ayatollah Khomeini, issued a death warrant and a $1 million reward to any Muslim who would assassinate the writer. Rushdie lived in hiding for several years but continued to write. Although the bounty on his life has been lifted, he still lives in semi-seclusion. Rushdie has also long mentored, although quietly, younger Indian (and ethnic Indian) writers, and he can be said to have influenced an entire generation of Indo-Anglican writers. His recent books include *Imaginary Homelands* (1991), *East, West* (1994), *The Moor's Last Sigh* (1996), *The Ground beneath her Feet* (1999), *Fury* (2001), *Conversations with Salman Rushdie* (edited by Michael Reder, 2000), *Step across This Line: Collected Nonfiction 1992–2002* (2002), and *The East Is Blue* (2004). His latest book, *Shalimar the Clown* (2005), was a finalist for the Whitbread Book Awards.

Sarton, May (1912–95)

Born in Belgium, Sarton was brought to the United States at the outbreak of World War I. Her early enthusiasms were poetry and acting. She joined Eva Le Gallienne's repertory theater in New York and later directed her own company. In the 1930s, she began to write poetry while supporting herself with teaching jobs, lecturing, and book reviewing. Sarton's main theme is the effect that love, in all its forms, has on personal relationships. Some of her works are *Encounter in April* (1937), *A Grain of Mustard Seed* (1971), *Collected Poems 1930–1973* (1974), *Halfway to Silence* (1980), and *The Silence Now: New and Uncollected Earlier Poems* (1988). Throughout her life she kept journals in which she recorded the events of everyday life. They have been published in *Journals of Solitude* (1973), *At Seventy* (1984), and *Encore: A Journal of the Eightieth Year* (1993).

Sexton, Anne (1928–74)

Born and raised in Newton, Massachusetts, Sexton studied with Robert Lowell at Boston College, going on to work for a year as a fashion model in Boston and then marrying and becoming a suburban housewife. At twenty-eight, she had a nervous breakdown and, having been encouraged by a therapist to write, saw wide success in 1960 with her first book of confessional poetry, *To Bedlam and Part Way Back*. Her second collection, *Live or Die*, won the Pulitzer Prize for 1967. Although she saw poetry as a form of therapy, saying "suicide is the opposite of the poem," she was not able to overcome her troubles, finally succeeding in 1974 after various attempts at taking her own life. A posthumous collection, *The Awful Rowing Toward God* (1975), describes in part the feelings that brought her to that point. Other collections include *All My Pretty Ones* (1962), *Love Poems* (1969), *Transformations* (1971), and *The Death Notebooks* (1974). Other posthumous works include *45 Mercy Street* (1976), and *Words for Dr. Y.* (1978). By no means limited to the contemplation of mental instability and death, her work also examines themes of love, motherhood, and daughterhood. She wrote about menstruation, abortion, masturbation, and adultery before such issues were openly discussed. Her work broke through many of the constraints on female poets with wit and style, opening doors for others to follow.

Shakespeare, William (1564–1616)

Born in Stratford-on-Avon, England, Shakespeare was a poet and dramatist of the Elizabethan Age. Relatively little is known about his personal life. He received a grammar school education and in 1594 was a member of the Lord Chamberlain's company of actors. By 1597, Shakespeare had written at least a dozen plays, including comedies, histories, and one tragedy. His greatest plays include the tragedies *Julius Caesar* (1600), *Hamlet* (1601), *Othello* (1604), *King Lear* (1605), and *Macbeth* (1606). He also composed a series of 154 sonnets between 1593 and 1601.

Shelley, Percy Bysshe (1792–1822)

One of the most important of the English Romantic poets, Shelley was a true revolutionary in life as well as work. He was expelled from Oxford in 1811 for a pamphlet he wrote, *The Necessity of Atheism*. In the same year he married sixteen-year-old Harriet Westbrook, leaving her just a few years later for Mary Wollstonecraft Godwin, who would later write *Franken-stein* (1818). The pair settled in Italy and were married after Harriet committed suicide in 1816. In company with other romantics, such as Keats, Byron, and Coleridge, Shelley broke down powerful conventions of social as well as literary behavior in his short life. His short lyric poems, such as "Ode to the West Wind," "To a Skylark," and "Ozymandias," and his elegy to Keats, "Adonais," stand high in the romantic pantheon. He also wrote plays and essays and was working on a long philosophical poem, "The Triumph of Life," when he was drowned in a boating accident at the age of thirty.

Song, Cathy (b. 1955)

Song was born in Honolulu. She attended the University of Hawaii, received a bachelor's degree from Wellesley College, and earned a master's degree at Boston University. Her first book, *Picture Bride* (1983), won the Yale Series of Younger Poets Award and was nominated for a National Book Critics Circle Award. Her poems reflect a deep awareness of her Asian heritage and the struggles of her people to find their own voices in contemporary culture. She has also written *Frameless Windows, Squares of Light* (1988), *School Figures* (1994), and *The Land of Bliss* (2001). She currently lives in Honolulu with her husband and three children and teaches at the University of Hawaii at Manoa.

Sophocles (496–406 B.C.)

Born near Athens, Greece, Sophocles was the most popular playwright of his day. He also held posts in the military and political life of Athens. Of the more than a hundred plays he wrote, only seven survive, among them three about Oedipus and his children, *Oedipus the King*, *Oedipus at Colonus*, and *Antigone*. Using mythology as the backdrop for his complex exploration of our private and public selves, Sophocles expressed the continuity of human experience.

Soto, Gary (b. 1952)

Born in Fresno, California, to working-class Mexican American parents, Soto grew up in the San Joaquin Valley where he worked as a migrant laborer. He attended Fresno City College, California State University, Fresno, and the University of California at Irvine, where he earned a masters in fine arts degree. Soto is the author of ten poetry collections. *New and Selected Poems* (1995) was a finalist for the Los Angeles Book Award and the National Book Award. *Living Up the Street*, Soto's memoir, received a Before Columbus Foundation American

Book Award in 1985. Recent publications include *Nerlandia: A Play* (1999), *A Fire in My Hands* (1999), *Nickel and Dimes* (2000), and *Poetry Lover* (2001). In addition to writing, Soto has produced a film and wrote a libretto for the Los Angeles Opera. Soto also serves as Young People's Ambassador for the California Rural Legal Assistance and the United Farm Workers of America. He presently lives in Berkeley, California.

Soyinka, Wole (b. 1934)

Born in Nigeria, Soyinka, a poet, playwright, novelist and essayist, was educated in his homeland and in England. Through his efforts, the theater in Nigeria has flourished. For his role in the political life of his country, he was imprisoned. Although denied the chance to write while in jail, he used scraps of cigarette and toilet papers to compose a collection of poems, which was smuggled out and published as *Poems from Prison* (1969). In 1986, he was awarded the Nobel Prize in Literature, the first person of African descent to be so honored. His themes, social injustice and the preservation of individual freedom, are developed with humor and satire. His works include *The Open Sore of a Continent: A Personal Narrative of the Nigerian Crisis* (1996), *The Burden of Memory, the Music of Forgiveness* (1998), *Arms and the Arts—a Continent's Unequal Dialogue* (1999), and *Conversations with Wole Soyinka* (edited by Biodun Jeyifo), which appeared in 2001. Recent publications include *Climate of Fear: The Quest for Dignity in a Dehumanized World* (2005), *African Theatre: Soyinka Blackout, Blowout & Beyond* (2005), and *You Must Set Forth at Dawn: A Memoir* is scheduled for publication in 2007.

Spera, Gabriel (b. 1966)

Spera received his B.A. from Cornell University and an M.F.A. from the University of North Carolina at Greensboro. He works as a technical editor in Los Angeles. His work has appeared in a number of journals, and his first collection of poems, *The Standing Wave*, was published in 2003. Selected for the 2002 National Poetry Series, the book also received the 2004 Literary Book Award for Poetry from PEN USA-West. Since 2001, Spera has been senior technical writer at the Aerospace Corporation in El Segundo, California.

Staples, Brent (b. 1951)

Staples is from Chester, Pennsylvania, and has a Ph.D. in psychology from the University of Chicago. He has been a reporter for the *Chicago Sun-Times* and the *New York Times* where he is currently on the editorial board and writes on culture and politics. His essay *Just Walk on By: A Black Man Ponders His Power to Alter Public Space* gained popularity when it was first published as "Black Men and Public Space" in *Ms. Magazine* in 1986. This essay deals with the issue of racism, stereotypes, and prejudice. His autobiography, *Parallel Time: Growing Up in Black and White* (1994), was the winner of the Anisfield-Wolff Book Award in 1995.

Stevens, Wallace (1879–1955)

Stevens was born in Reading, Pennsylvania, educated at Harvard University and New York University Law School, and an insurance executive for most of his life. He published his first book of poems, *Harmonium* in 1923, at the age of forty-four. Going on to become a vice president in his company in 1934, he continued to write poetry and became a central figure in twentieth-century American literature. His verse is musical, descriptive, and elegant, often giving weight and shape to abstract concepts. Among his collections of poetry are *Ideas of Order* (1935), *The Man with the Blue Guitar* (1937), *Parts of a World* (1942), *Transport to Summer* (1947), *Auroras of Autumn* (1950), and *Collected Poems* (1954), for which he won both the Pulitzer Prize and the National Book Award. His prose publications include *Notes toward a Supreme Fiction* (1942), and *The Necessary Angel* (1951). Publications printed posthumously include *Opus Posthumous* (1957), *The Palm at the End of the Mind* (1972), and *Collected Poetry and Prose* (Frank Kermode & Joan Richardson, editors) (1997).

Talbird, John (b. 1966)

Born in Atlanta, Georgia, Talbird lived his entire life in the American Southeast until 1999 when he moved to Lincoln, Nebraska, to earn his Ph.D. in English. Currently, he lives in Brooklyn, New York, and is assistant professor and assistant director of the writing program in the English Department at Queensborough Community College-CUNY where he teaches fiction writing, film studies, and composition. His stories have appeared in *Laurel Review*, *Berkeley Fiction Review*, *Coe Review*, and elsewhere. Talbird is also on the editorial board of *Green Hills Literary Lantern* and is a frequent contributor to *Quarterly Review of Film and Video*.

Tannen, Deborah (b. 1945)

Tannen attended Binghamton University as an undergraduate, then continued to earn her Ph.D. in Linguistics from the University of California at Berkeley. As a professor of sociolinguistics at Georgetown University, she has written scholarly works such as *Linguistics in Context* (1988), and *Framing in Discourse* (1993). She has also written many articles and books on linguistics that are easily accessible to the general public. *That's Not What I Meant: How Conversational Style Makes or Breaks Your Relations with Others* (1986), *You Just Don't Understand: Women and Men in Conversation* (1990), *Gender and Discourse* (1994), and *The Argument Culture* (1999) are her most well-known works. Her most recent books include *I Only Say This Because I Love You: How the Way We Talk Can Make or Break Family Relationships throughout Our Lives* (2001), and *You're Wearing That?: Understanding Mothers and Daughters in Conversation* (2006). She has also published a collection of short stories, *Greek Icons*.

Tayebi, Kandi (b. 19-)

Kandi Tayebi was born in San Francisco, California, to a career military man. Her family moved all over the United States and Germany before settling in Strasburg, Colorado, a small town of about 1,500 people on the eastern plains. She received her bachelor's and master's degrees from the University of North Colorado in Greeley, and her Ph.D. in English literature from the University of Denver. She is currently associate dean of humanities and social services at Sam Houston State University. In 1988, she married her husband, Javad, a native of Iran who was also a military man. He had served for two years on the frontline during his country's devastating war with Iraq. She and her husband have two sons, Bezhan and Shayon. Her research focuses on romantic women writers, feminist theory, technology, and Persian women's roles. She has published articles on romanticism, Persian folklore, and pedagogy, as well as creative writings. She is currently working on a book-length study about Charlotte Smith's poetics.

Tennyson, Alfred (1st Baron Tennyson, commonly called Alfred, Lord Tennyson) (1809–92)

Born in Somersby, Lincolnshire, England, Tennyson is considered representative of the Victorian era in his native country. His work encompasses the gamut of lyric, elegiac, dramatic, and epic poetry. His subject matter includes Arthurian legends, classical mythology, and the moral values of the upper classes. Among his best known poems are "The Lady of Shalot," "In Memoriam," and "Crossing the Bar."

Tesich, Steve (1943–66)

Born in Yugoslavia, Steve Tesich emigrated to the United States when he was fourteen. He frequently contributed articles to the now discontinued *About Men* column in the *New York Times Magazine* and often contributed to periodicals. He is best known for the original screenplay *Breaking Away* (1979), for which he won an Academy Award. He also wrote the screenplays *Eyewitness* (1981) and *Four Friends* (1981); many plays for the theater, including *Passing Game* (1977), *The Road* (1978), and *Division Street* (1980); and a novel, *Summer Crossing* (1982). A recurrent theme in Tesich's work is the plight of the outsider.

Thomas, Dylan (1914–53)

Thomas, born in Swansea, Wales, avoided formal education but began to write poems at an early age. By the age of twenty, he was a published poet. His voice impressed audiences who heard him read his works in lecture halls, on radio, and through recordings. His pastoral poems frequently reflect his joy in the frightening but beautiful processes of nature. "Do Not Go Gentle into That Good Night," "And Death Shall Have No Dominion," "A Refusal to Mourn Death, by Fire of a Child in London," and "Fern Hill" are among his best known poems. *Portrait of the Artist as a Young Dog* (1940) recalls his childhood and youth in Wales. *Under Milk Wood* (1954) is an inventive radio play for voices. In 2004, a new literary prize, the Dylan Thomas Prize, was created in honor of the poet. It will be awarded to the best published writer in English under the age of thirty.

Vigil-Piñón, Evangelina (b. 1952)

Vigil-Piñón, a Latina, produced a volume of poetry, *Thirty an' Seen a Lot* (1982), that reflects her explanations of the relation between past and present as it pertains to the preservation of family, myth, culture, and history. The role of the woman as lifegiver, literally as well as metaphorically, is central to her poetic vision. In addition to *The Computer Is Down* (1987), she has contributed to and edited two anthologies: *Woman of Her Word: Hispanic Women Writers* (1983) and *Decade II: An Anniversary Anthology* (1993). She has also written a children's book, *Nalina's Muumuu* (2001), and is a contributor to numerous literary periodicals.

Walker, Alice (b. 1944)

Born in Georgia to a family of sharecroppers, Walker was encouraged to excel in school and attended college in Atlanta and New York. Her first volume of poetry was published in 1968. In addition, she has written novels, short stories, and a book of essays. *The Color Purple* (1982) won a Pulitzer Prize and became a successful film (1985) as well as a 2005 Broadway musical play. Her fiction examines the role of black women in a world dominated by sexism and racial oppression. Walker was active in the civil rights movement in Mississippi. In addition to *The Color Purple*, her novels include *The Third Life of Grance Copeland* (1973), *Meridian* (1976), and *The Temple of My Familiar* (1989). Her short story collection includes *In Love and Trouble: Stories of Black Women* (1973) and *You Can't Keep a Good Woman Down* (1981). Her collected poetry appears in *Good Night, Willie Lee, I'll See You in the Morning* (1979), *Horses Make a Landscape More Beautiful* (1984), *Possessing the Secret of Joy* (1992), *Absolute Trust in the Goodness of the Earth* (2003), *A Poem Traveled Down My Arm: Poems and Drawings* (2003), and *Collected Poems* (2005). An autobiography, *The Same River Twice: Honoring the Difficult: A Meditation of Life, Spirit, and the Making of the Film, The Color Purple, Ten Years Later* was published in 1996. In 1994, the California State Board of Education removed two of Walker's short stories from one of its programs. "Roselily" was one of those banned because it concerned a teenage unwed mother. *Alice Walker Banned* (1996) relates the controversy and includes newspaper articles, letters, and assessment by Patricia Holt. Walker's recent nonfiction includes *Anything We Love Can Be Saved: A Writer's Activism* (1997) and *Dreads: Sacred Rites of the Natural Hair Revolution* (with Francesco Mastalia and Alfonse Pagano, 1999). Her latest works of fiction are *By the Light of My Father's Smile* (1998) and *The Way Forward Is with a Broken Heart* (2000). Publications in 2006 include *There Is a Flower at the Tip of My Nose Smelling Me* (Stefano Vitale illustrator) and *We Are the Ones We Have Been Waiting for: Light in a Time of Darkness*.

Wharton, Edith (1862–1937)

Wharton, born in New York City to wealthy and socially prominent parents, married a Boston banker in 1885. However, resenting the restrictions of a society matron, she pursued her own intellectual interests. She wrote novels such as *The House of Mirth* (1902) and *The Custom of the Country* (1913), which probed the emptiness of life in aristocratic New York society. A favorite theme was the rigid code of manners and conventions that denied personal happiness to both men and women. In 1907, she moved permanently to Europe but continued to write books with American settings and themes of the ironies and tragedies of life. *The Age of Innocence* (1920) won a Pulitzer Prize. The Cross of the Legion of Honor was awarded to her for relief work in World War I.

Whitman, Walt (1819–92)

Born near Huntington, Long Island, New York, Whitman held a variety of jobs, including office boy, carpenter, printer, schoolteacher, journalist, and editor. In 1855, he published a volume of poems entitled *Leaves of Grass*, but it was unfavorably reviewed because of its radical form and content. During the next thirty-five years, he revised and added to it in nine editions. When his brother was wounded in the Civil War, Whitman went to Virginia to nurse him. He stayed on in Washington, D.C., as a nurse in army hospitals. After the war, he was a clerk in a government office but was fired because *Leaves of Grass* was considered an immoral book. His verse was appreciated in Europe, however, and eventually he received recognition in his own country. "When Lilacs Last in the Dooryard Bloom'd" and "O Captain! My Captain!" commemorated the death of Abraham Lincoln. His war impressions appear in *Drum Taps and Specimen Days*. Some of his war poems reflect a nostalgic or romantic vision of war.

Wiesel, Elie (b. 1928)

Born Eliezer Wiesel in Rumania, he is a survivor of the Nazi concentration camps at Auschwitz and Buchenwald, where his parents and sister were killed. François Mauriac, the

French novelist and essayist, urged Wiesel to write of the horrors of the war, and Wiesel produced *Night* in 1956. This memoir-novel recounts his family's death-camp sufferings and his own guilt at surviving. Since then, he has completed over forty books. Many of his books are on Holocaust themes. Man's inhumanity to man, survival, and injustice are his subjects. In 1986, he was awarded the Nobel Peace Prize. *All Rivers Run to the Sea* (1995) contain his latest reflections on the Holocaust. *Untitled Memoirs* (1988), *And the Sea Is Never Full* (1999), *The Testament* (1999), *The Judges: A Novel* (2002), and *Night: With Related Readings* (2003), *Wise Men and Their Tales* (2003), and *The Time of the Uprooted* (2005) are his latest works. Wiesel lives in the United States where he holds the position of Andrew Mellon Professor of the Humanities at Boston University and professor of philosophy and religion, College of Arts and Sciences.

Wilbur, Richard (Purdy) (b. 1921)

A native of New York City, Wilbur earned his B.A. from Amherst College and an M.A. from Harvard, and he served in the U.S. Army in World War II. He has taught English at many Ivy League colleges. His poetry collections include *The Beautiful Changes* (1947), *Ceremony* (1950), *Things of This World* (Pulitzer Prize and National Book Award, 1956), *The Beastiary* (1955), *Advice to a Prophet* (1961), *The Poems of Richard Wilbur* (1963), *Walking to Sleep* (1960), and *The Mind Reader* (1971). He won his second Pulitzer Prize for *New and Collected Poems* in 1989. He has also translated many of Molière's plays into English, including *Tartuffe*. His work is collected in *The Poems of Richard Wilbur* (1988), *The Catbird's Songs: Prose Pieces, 1963–1995* (1997), and his most recent work includes *The Disappearing Alphabet* (illustrated by David Diaz, 1998), *Opposites, More Opposites, and a Few Differences* (2000), *Mayflies: New Poems and Translations* (2000), and *Collected Poems, 1943–2004* (2004).

Williams, William Carlos (1883–1963)

For most of his life, Williams lived and practiced medicine in his hometown of Rutherford, New Jersey. His patients' language often inspired his poems, which frequently focused on everyday objects and experiences. Although he lived and worked away from the literary world, he was friends with important writers of his time like Wallace Stevens, Ezra Pound and H. D. (Hilda Aldington), and he traced his roots to Whitman. His first book, *Poems*, appeared in 1909, followed by *The Tempers* (1913), *Kora in Hell* (1920), *Spring and All* (1923), and several volumes of *Collected Poems* (1963), which won a Pulitzer Prize. In addition to the five-volume epic *Paterson* (1946–58), Williams wrote *Autobiography* in 1951, several volumes of criticism, and a book of stories, *The Farmer's Daughter* (1961). Books published posthumously include *Imaginations* (1970), *Collected Poems: Volume I, 1909–1939* (1988), *Collected Poems: Volume II, 1939–1962* (1989) and *Early Poems* (1997).

Wolff, Tobias (b. 1945)

Tobias Wolff was born in Alabama and spent the larger part of his childhood moving about with his mother. After expulsion from high school he joined the army and did one tour of duty in Vietnam. After the military he enrolled in Oxford University in England and graduated with an honors degree in English. He came back to the United States and began a teaching career, which culminated with his appointment as Ward W. and Priscilla B. Woods Professor at Stanford in California, where he lives with his wife and three children. He has published numerous collections of short stories, including *In the Garden of North American Martyrs* (1981), *The Night in Question* (1997), and a recent novel, *Old School* (2004).

Woolf, Virginia (1882–1941)

Born in London, Woolf was reared in an upper-middle-class family dominated by her father, Sir Leslie Stephen, a noted scholar. Because of her delicate health and her father's views on the proper place of women, she was tutored at home and had free access to his extensive library. After her father's death, she and her sister Vanessa hosted gatherings at their home in the Bloomsbury section of London, attracting literary and intellectual figures of the day. Woolf kept diaries from an early age and soon began writing novels and short stories. At first conventional in form, she later wrote in an innovative and distinguished manner in such novels as *Jacob's Room* (1922), *To the Lighthouse* (1927), and *Orlando* (1928). She used stream of consciousness, a form of interior dialogue similar to the technique of her contemporary James Joyce. An absence of conventional plot and action characterized her distinctive style. She and her husband Leonard Woolf, a writer on politics and economics, started the Hogarth Press, and the success of their first ventures in publishing led to a series of works by the best and most original young authors such as T. S. Eliot and E. M. Forster. The first English edition of the works of Sigmund Freud, the originator of psychoanalysis, highlighted their endeavors. A strong advocate of women's rights, Woolf's views are expressed in a group of essays in *A Room of One's Own* (1929) and *Three Guineas* (1938). The essay "Professions for Women" was originally a talk delivered in 1931 to the Women's Service League. During her life, she suffered numerous nervous breakdowns and in 1941, the same year her last book *Between the Acts* was published, fearing the onset of another attack and the subsequent treatments, she committed suicide.

Wordsworth, William (1770–1850)

Wordsworth is considered the poet who introduced romanticism to England. Nurtured in the beautiful Lake District of England, Wordsworth experienced a life that led him to revere nature. He was educated at Cambridge University and lived for a short time in France where he became an advocate of the French Revolution. He believed the revolutionaries were interested in improving the life of the common people. On his return to England, he made the acquaintance of Samuel Taylor Coleridge and thus began a close friendship that lead to their collaboration on the *Lyrical Ballads* (1798). This volume included one of Wordsworth's most famous poems, "Tintern Abbey." In his celebrated preface to the second edition of this work, he declared himself a nature poet and one who was committed to democratic equality and the language of the common people. *The Prelude* was completed in 1805 but was not published until his death. His other works include *Poem in Two Volumes* (1807) and *The Excursion* (1814). In his later years, Wordsworth became more conservative in his beliefs and, although he continued to write, little of it is considered equal to his earlier works. In 1843, he was appointed poet laureate. When his daughter, Dora, died in 1847, his production of poetry came to a standstill.

Wright, James (1927–80)

Wright was born in Martins Ferry, Ohio, and studied with Theodore Roethke at the University of Washington, where he received his Ph.D. He taught at a number of colleges, finally settling at Hunter College in New York City, where he taught from 1966 until his death from cancer in 1980. A midwesterner who reviled his native soil, his work still relied for much of its inspiration on that region. His central image was that of a nomadic figure, alone in an overwhelming universe. *The Green Wall*, his first collection, appeared in 1957, followed by *Saint Judas* (1959), *The Lion's Tail and Eyes* (1962), *The Branch Will Not Break* (1963), *Shall We Gather at the River* (1968), the Pulitzer Prize–winning *Collected Poems* (1971), *Moments of the Italian Summer* (1976), and *To a Blossoming Pear Tree* (1977). Works published posthumously include *This Journey* (1982), *The Temple at Nimes* (1982), *Above the River—the Complete Poems* (1992), *Selected Poems* (2005), and *A Wild Perfection: The Selected Letters of James Wright* (2005).

Yamauchi, Wakako (b. 1924)

Yamauchi's parents left Japan and became farmers in Westmoreland, California, where Wakako was born in 1924. The family lived in a community of Japanese immigrants but she went to American public schools. At home the household looked back to Japan for its traditions, values, and rewards while the children were struggling to become Americans. In 1942, during World War II, she and her family were interned in a so-called relocation camp in Arizona. There Yamauchi worked on the camp newspaper and met the writer Hisaye Yamamoto. It was the first time she had "read a writer who spoke about things I knew about . . . the kinds of lives we led before the war. She taught me not to be ashamed or afraid of being Japanese in my writing, in my heart." Several years after her release from camp, Yamauchi started writing stories and plays, many of which deal with tensions between Japanese immigrant parents and their American-born children. They also address the universal elments of human endurance, survival, and strength. Her first play, *And the Soul Shall Dance*, was originally published as a short story in 1966, and has been republished eleven times since then. Her works have been collected in *Songs My Mother Taught Me: Stories, Plays, and Memoir* (1994).

Yevtushenko, Yevgeny (b. 1933)

Yevtushenko was born in Zima, Siberia, and had his first volume of poetry published when he was nineteen. He became prominent as the leader of the Soviet younger generation in its criticism of his country's policies. "Babiy Yar," his poem condemning the Nazis' murder of 96,000 Jews in Ukraine, caused consternation because it implied complicity on the part of the Soviet leadership. During the cold war thaw in the late 1950s, he was allowed to travel to the United States to give poetry readings, which attracted large audiences. In recent years, he again gained prominence for his support of Soviet president Mikhail Gorbachev's policy of *glasnost*. Some of his poems celebrate the everyday life of ordinary people. His works include *The Poetry of Yevgeny Yevtushenko* (1981), *Wild Berries* (1989), *Fatal Half Measures: The Cultures of Democracy in the Soviet Union* (1991), and *Don't Die before You're Dead* (1995). Most recently, he has published *Pre-Morning: A New Book of Poetry in English and Russian* (1995) and *The Best of the Best: A New Book of Poetry in English and Russian* (1999). Yevtushenko currently holds a position as distinguished professor in the Department of English at the University of Tulsa in Oklahoma and teaches European languages and literature at Queens College of the City University of New York.

Glossary

Abstract   Without physical, tangible existence in itself; a concept as opposed to an object. A "child" is a concrete object that our senses can perceive, but "childishness" is an abstract quality.

Act   A major division of the action of a play, usually subdivided into scenes—smaller units of action with no breaks in place or time.

Alienation   Emotional or intellectual separation from peer groups and/or society.

Allegory   A narrative that has a second meaning in addition to the obvious one. The meaning may be religious, moral, or political. Settings, objects, and events are only representational. Characters are incarnations of abstract ideas, for example, faith, hope, or desire.

Alliteration   Repetition of the same consonant sounds at the beginning of words on the same line or in close proximity—"Stole with soft step its shining archway through," for example.

Allusion   A reference to a familiar mythical, historical, or literary person, place, or thing.

Ambiguity   Intentional uncertainty or lack of clarity about meaning, where more than one meaning is possible.

Ambivalence   The existence of mutually conflicting attitudes or feelings.

Anachronism   Wrongful assignment of an event, person, or scene to a time when it did not exist.

Anecdote   Brief, unadorned narrative of an event or happening. It differs from a short story in that it is shorter, consists of a single episode, and has a simple plot.

Antagonist   The character in a drama, poem, or other fiction who opposes or rivals the protagonist.

Anticlimax   A trivial event immediately following significant events. The reader expects something greater or more serious to occur but finds a less striking event.

Antihero   A protagonist who is deficient in attributes usually attributed to a hero.

Anti-Semitism   Hostility toward Jews as a religious or racial minority group, often accompanied by social, economic, and/or political discrimination.

Apostrophe   A poetic figure of speech in which some abstract quality or personification is addressed, for example, "O ye Fountains, Meadows, Hills and Groves . . . "

Archetype   Primordial images from Jung's "collective unconscious" of the human race, often expressed in myths, religion, dreams, and literature. Can provoke a profound, resonating reader response.

Argumentation   In persuasive essays, a unit of discourse meant to prove a point or to convince; the process of proving or persuading.

Aside   Speech directed to the audience and, by convention, presumed inaudible to other characters on stage.

Assonance   In a line, sentence, or stanza, the repetition of similar vowel sounds, for example, *penitent* and *reticence*.

Atmosphere   The overall mood of a literary work, often created by the setting or landscape.

Audience   A work's intended readership, the author's perception of which directly affects style and tone. As a rule, the more limited or detailed the subject matter, the more specific the audience. An author may write more technically if the intended audience is composed of specialists in the field and may write less technically if the writing is for the general public.

Audio/Visual Montage   The relationship between visual material on the screen and a sound that does not belong to that material, for example, a shot of a woman about to scream accompanied by the loud sound of a train whistle instead of the scream.

Author (film)   The "author" of a film, as opposed to that of a novel or play, is considered to be the director, not the screenwriter, because the director must bring together and integrate all elements of a film, of which the screenplay is only one.

Ballad   A form that originated in the oral folk tradition as an anonymous shared song, usually terse, dramatic, and impersonal. Also, a literary poem deliberately written in the spirit and form of the folk ballad, for example, Keats's "La Belle Dame sans Merci."

Biographical Criticism   Based on the premise that knowledge of an author's life can enhance interpretation of his or her work.

Blank Verse   Unrhymed iambic pentameter. A fluid and common verse form close to the natural rhythms of English speech.

Burlesque   A form of comedy characterized by ridiculous and exaggerated actions.

Caesura   A pause in the meter and rhythm of a line of poetry, indicated in scansion by double straight slashes (//). See also *scansion*.

Camera movement   Can be anything from a brief *pan* or *tilt* of the camera to widen our view of a particular scene, to elaborate *tracking shots* in which the camera moves over a large expanse of space in any direction, for example, to follow the action in a continuous take rather than breaking it down through editing, to enhance the sense of the reality of a setting, or as directorial commentary on the action.

Canon   A criterion or standard of measurement; the generally accepted list of great works of literature or accepted list of an author's works.

Canto   A division or section of a long poem.

Carpe Diem   Latin for "seize the day," a popular literary theme stressing that life is all too brief and should be enjoyed as it unfolds.

Catharsis   The effect of tragedy in relieving or purging the emotions of an audience. Aristotle explains the theory in his *Poetics*.

Cause and Effect   A type of exposition used primarily to answer the questions "Why did this occur?" and "What will happen next?" The structure of a cause-and-effect essay is a series of events or conditions, the last of which (the effect) cannot occur without the preceding ones (causes). When you write a cause-and-effect essay, keep chronology clearly in mind. Remember, causes always create effects and effects are derived from causes.

Character Type   A standard, recognizable kind of secondary character, often stereotypical and found in many genre films, such as the country bumpkin or the good-hearted prostitute.

Chorus   In Greek drama, a group of performers who comment on the actions or characters in the play.

Classical Hollywood Filmmaking   This term refers to the collection of codes and stylistic conventions (such as *continuity editing* that preserves a logical sense of time and space from shot to shot) used in narrative filmmaking as established by Hollywood during the dominance of the studio system from the 1930s through the 1960s. It is not an evaluative term implying that every movie made in Hollywood during this time is a "classic" in the conventional sense of that word.

Classical Tragedy   Refers to the tragedy of the ancient Greeks and Romans. The rules of tragic composition are derived from Aristotle and Horace.

Climax   The point at which dramatic or narrative action builds to its highest point and the reader experiences the greatest emotional response.

Collective Unconscious   A foundational Jungian concept stemming from Jung's belief that racially inherited images and ideas persist in individual consciousness, and unconscious motivations are therefore collectively shared as well as personal.

Comedy   A dramatic work intended to engage and amuse the audience with the embarrassments and discomfitures endured by its main characters until a favorable ending is arrived at. High comedy, a comedy of manners and verbal wit, evokes intellectual laughter, and low comedy depends on physical antics, slapstick, or burlesque for humor.

Comedy of Manners   Realistic comedy concerned with the manners, fashion, and conventions of seventeenth-century high society. Usually characterized by witty dialogue, or repartee, and sexual innuendo.

Commedia dell'Arte   Italian low comedy from the mid-sixteenth century in which professional actors playing stock characters, performing in masks, improvised dialogue to fit a given scenario.

Comparison and Contrast   A type of exposition that states or suggests similarities and differences between two or more things. Two types of organization for comparison and contrast essays are point by point and subject by subject.

Complication   The part of the plot in which the conflict between opposing forces is developed.

Composition   The way visual material is organized in a film shot, such as foreground and background, and the arrangement of people and objects within the frame. Composition also includes the way the camera photographs the material—for example, from a high or low angle.

Conceit   A comparison between two very different objects.

Conflict   The struggle between opposing characters that causes tension or suspense.

Connotation   The implication(s) and overtones, qualities, feelings, and ideas that a word suggests. Connotation goes beyond literal meaning or dictionary definition.

Consensus   General agreement and/or collective opinion of a group.

Controlling Image   An image or metaphor that recurs in a literary work and symbolizes the theme, such as the wallpaper in Charlotte Perkins Gilman's "The Yellow Wallpaper."

Convention   Any device, style, or subject matter that has become, through its recurring use, an accepted element of technique.

Couplet   Two successive lines of verse that rhyme.

Cross-cutting   A form of film editing that repeatedly alternates between two or more different actions, often to imply simultaneity. It is commonly used in chase sequences, where the film cuts from shots of the pursuer to shots of the pursued throughout the progress of the chase.

Culture   The total pattern of human (learned) behavior embodied in thought, speech, action, and artifacts. It depends on the human capacity for learning and transmitting knowledge to succeeding generations through the use of tools, language, and systems of abstract thought.

Deconstructionism   A critical method of close textual analysis that explores the ambiguities of language and the many possible readings they suggest.

Definition   A type of exposition that explains the meaning of a word or concept by bringing its characteristics into sharp focus. An extended definition explores the feelings and ideas you attach to a word. Extended definitions are suited to words with complex meanings, words that are subject to interpretation, or words that evoke strong reactions. Such definitions are an appropriate basis for organizing exposition. A dictionary definition places a word in a class with similar items but also differentiates it from members of the same class.

Denotation   The literal meaning of a word as defined in a dictionary. It is distinct from connotation.

Denouement   A French word for the "unknotting" or falling action that follows the climax and leads to the resolution of the plot.

Description   A method of paragraph development that conveys sensory experience through one or more of the five senses: sight, hearing, touch, taste, and smell. Description is generally either objective or subjective and can be organized in three broad categories: spatial, chronological, or dramatic.

Diction   The writer's choice of words. In proper diction, word choice enhances the expression of the author's ideas; in poor diction, words get in the way of the author's intended meaning.

Discourse   Sets of statements that hold together around languages; any statements across culture that organize a mechanism, discipline, or sexuality; the social use of language.

Downstage   The area of the stage behind the proscenium, nearest the audience.

Drama   The literary form designed for the theater in which actors impersonate the characters and perform the dialogue and action.

Dramatic Irony   See *irony*.

Dramatic Monologue   A poetic form that presents one character speaking to a silent audience and revealing in the discourse personal temperament and a dramatic situation.

Dramatic Unities   See *three unities*.

Editing (film)   The process by which individual shots are joined to create meaning and develop the narrative. Editing can be of the "classical" type, following strict rules to sustain continuity and logic, or it can be experimental, creating ambiguous or provocative relationships between shots.

Ego   According to Freud, the rational and conscious part of the psyche that opposes the id as well as the superego.

Electra Complex   Female counterpart of the Oedipus complex. A daughter's unconscious competition with her mother for her father's affection. Based on the Greek myth of Electra and Agamemnon. See also *Oedipus complex*.

Elegy   A formal sustained expression of grief about the death of a particular person or the passing of a particular way of life.

Elizabethan Age   The English literary period named after Queen Elizabeth, lasting from 1558 until 1642, the year of the closing of the theaters. Notable names of the period include Shakespeare, Sidney, Spencer, and Marlowe.

Epic   A long narrative poem, dignified in theme and style with a hero who, through experiences of great adventure, accomplishes important deeds.

Epigram   A witty or clever saying, concisely expressed.

Epigraph   A quotation at the beginning of a work that is related to the theme.

Epilogue   A concluding statement, sometimes in verse, summarizing the themes of the work.

Epiphany   A moment of insight for a character, often the catalyst for a turning point in a narrative or drama.

Episode   An incident in the course of a series of events.

Erotic   Tending to excite sexual pleasure or desire.

Ethnicity   Ethnic quality or affiliation, physical or cultural characteristics that identify an individual with a particular race, religion, or cultural group.

Ethnocentrism   The tendency to judge other cultures by the standards of one's own.

Exclusion   The act of deliberately not including someone or something, or preventing entry into a place or activity.

Existentialism   A twentieth-century philosophy that denies the existence of a transcendent meaning to life and places the burden of justifying existence on individuals.

Exposition   A mode or form of discourse that conveys information, gives directions, or explains an idea that is difficult to understand.

Fable   A simple tale, either in prose or verse, told to illustrate a moral. The subject matter may be drawn from folklore.

Fantasy   An imaginative or fanciful work concerning supernatural or unnatural events or characters.

Farce   A dramatic piece intended to generate laughter through exaggerated or improbable situations.

Feminist Criticism   A mode of analysis, a method of approaching life and politics, rather than a set of political conclusions about the oppression of women; examines representations of the feminine in all literature and often focuses on works written by women.

Figurative Language   Words used to express meaning beyond the literal denotative level.

Figures of Speech   Language that departs from the standard denotation of words to achieve special meaning and effects. See also *metaphor, personification, simile*.

Film Genre   A kind of film, made in Hollywood and elsewhere, that follows established narrative, characterization, and thematic conventions and formulas—such as the melodrama, the western, the horror film, the war film, the musical, the crime or detective film, and science fiction.

Filmic Metaphor   The juxtaposition of two or more shots that establishes a likeness, similarity, or analogy among different elements, for example, a shot of people crowded in a subway during rush hour followed by a shot of sheep being herded into a pen.

Film Noir   A term introduced in the early 1940s to identify a style of Hollywood filmmaking, usually found in crime stories and melodramas, that relies on heavy use of shadows and dark, atmospheric cinematography.

Flashback   A device by which the chronology of events is interrupted by relating events from the past.

Flat Character or Stock Character   A person in a fictional or dramatic work who does not undergo individual development and who often embodies a stereotype.

Flash fiction   (also classified as "sudden fiction," "micro fiction," or "short-short," among other terms) A subgenre of the short story. Length is what distinguishes it from "traditional" stories. Flash fiction is customarily under two thousand words.

Foil   A term for any character who, through extreme contrast, intensifies the character of another.

Foot   A unit of stressed and unstressed syllables used in the scansion of poetry. The most common are the iamb, trochee, anapest, and dactyl. The predominant foot in a given line, together with the number of feet in the line, defines that line's meter. See also *iambic foot, meter, scansion*.

Foreshadowing   Subtle clues early in the narrative indicating what will happen later in the plot.

Formalist Criticism   A method of criticism in which the formal aspects of literature (such as figurative language and narrative techniques) and literary craft are the touchstones in studying a text.

Framing   The way a film shot is positioned in relation to the four borders of the screen; often used in conjunction with *composition*.

Free Verse   Verse that does not rhyme and uses open speech patterns and forms to create poetry.

Gay and Lesbian Criticism   A critical method that examines the representation of homosexuality in literature.

Gender   Characteristics and roles assigned by family and/or culture to establish preferred patterns of behavior based on sex; sets of social attributions, characteristics, behavior, appearance, dress, expectations, roles, and so on, expected of individuals based on gender assignment at birth.

Genre   Distinct categories of literature, such as the play, the short story, the poem, and the novel.

Hero/Heroine   See *tragic hero/heroine*.

Heterocentrism   The tendency to judge or treat as invisible any sexual or affectional relationship that does not conform to the dominant heterosexual or marriage standard.

High Comedy   See *comedy*.

Hubris   Excessive arrogance or pride that results in the downfall of the protagonist.

Hyperbole   Obvious exaggeration or an extravagant statement intended to create a memorable image. A fisherman who brags the one that got away was "as big as a whale" almost certainly is speaking hyperbolically.

Iambic Foot   A metrical foot in which an unstressed syllable is followed by a stressed syllable, for example, *away*.

Id   According to Freud, the driving force of the unconscious mind that is endowed with energy and is capable of motivating our actions.

Identity   The set of behavioral or personal characteristics by which an individual is recognizable as a member of a group.

Ideology   A system of belief used overtly or covertly to justify or legitimize preferred patterns of behavior.

Imagery   Used in descriptive passages in poetry to convey thematic mood and emotion. In film, a repeated use of related visual material, which accumulates important associations and illuminates some aspect of the story or theme (e.g., many shots of doors or rain or light).

Imperialism   The imposition of the power of one state over the territories of another, normally by military means, to exploit subjugated populations to extract economic and political advantages.

Institution   That which is established or accepted in society; an established way of behaving; established procedures and organizations—schools, for example.

Internal Rhyme   Rhyming words that appear within a line of poetry.

Irony   The undermining or contradicting of someone's expectations. Irony may be either verbal or dramatic. Verbal irony arises from a discrepancy, sometimes intentional and sometimes not, between what is said and what is meant, as when a dog jumps forward to bite you, and you say, "What a friendly dog!" Dramatic irony arises from a discrepancy between what someone expects to happen and what does happen, for example, if the dog that seemed so unfriendly to you saved your life.

Jargon   The vocabulary or phrases peculiar to a particular profession or group. It may also mean a language or word incomprehensible to others or garbled.

Journal   A daily written record of ideas, memories, experiences, or dreams. A journal can be used for prewriting and as a source for formal writing.

Literal   The ordinary or primary meaning of a word or expression. Strictly denotative language without imagination or embellishment.

Low Comedy   See *comedy*.

Lyric   A poem, usually brief, that expresses states of mind and emotion. See also *elegy, ode, sonnet*.

Marginalized   Not fully explored or realized.

Melodrama   A play written in a sensational manner, pitting a stereotypical hero and villain against one another in violent, suspenseful, and emotional scenes.

Metaphor   A comparison between unlike things that does not use *as* or *like*, such as "The road is a ribbon of moonlight."

Meter   The measurement establishing the rhythm of a line of poetry. The unit within the line is a foot, each being a set of accented and unaccented syllables. The number of feet in a line is also enumerated in the meter. For example, a line of five iambs is called iambic pentameter. See a specialized dictionary for a detailed explanation of meter. See also *foot*.

Metonymy   A figure of speech in which the name of one object or concept is substituted for that of a related one, for example, using "the bottle" to mean "strong drink" or "The White House" to refer to "the president."

Mise-en-Scène   A French term referring to the way a stage designer organizes the setting, lighting, and character movement in a play. In film, it refers to all visual components of the image: props, set design, color, lighting, organization of space, and character movement in relation to all of the above.

Misogyny   Women-hating; the belief that women are inferior to men mentally, emotionally, and physically.

Mixed Metaphor   An inconsistent and incongruous comparison between two things.

Modernism   A movement of the early twentieth century against the conventions of romantic literary representation. The modernists rejected what they viewed as the flowery and artificial language of Victorian literature and originated new techniques such as stream of consciousness in fiction and free verse in poetry.

Monoculturalism   Pertaining to one culture to the exclusion of all other cultures.

Montage   A form of editing developed by Russian filmmakers of the silent era, determined not by story logic and continuity, but by an idea the filmmaker wishes to suggest through a challenging and provocative juxtaposition of individual shots. In Sergei Eisenstein's *Battleship Potemkin*, the montage of a sword, a cross, and the czar's insignia suggests the collaboration of military, church, and state authorities.

Motif   A recurring character, theme, or situation that appears in many types of literature.

Motive   Whatever prompts a person to act in a particular way.

Multiculturalism   Assimilation of several cultures while allowing each culture to retain its separate identity.

Myth   A traditional or legendary story with roots in folk beliefs.

Narration   A narrative essay is a story with a point; narration is the technique used to tell the story. When writing a narrative essay, pay close attention to point of view, pacing, chronology, and transitions.

Narrative   The art, technique, or process of telling a story.

Narrator   The point of view from which the story is told. A first-person narrator is a character, not the author. A third-person narrator refers to an omniscient point of view. See also *omniscient narrator*.

Naturalism   A school of writing that tries to show human fate is controlled by environment and heredity, both of which humans do not understand.

Neoclassicism   Eighteenth-century literary theory and practice in theater and poetry with emphasis on tradition, form, and the social position and limitations of humanity. For example, the view that "the proper study of mankind is man."

Neurosis Emotional disturbance related to unresolved unconscious conflicts, typically involving anxiety and depression.

New Criticism An approach to criticism of literature that concentrates on textual criticism without referring to biographical or historical study.

New Historicism A politically oriented school of criticism, focusing on the power relations, ideologies, and political currents implicit in a text. It shares many of the tenets of Marxist criticism.

Ode A lyric poem that expresses exalted or enthusiastic emotion and often commemorates a person or event.

Oedipus Complex A male adult's repressed childhood wishes to identify with his father and to take his father's place in the affections of his mother. See also *Electra complex*.

Off-Screen Anything not seen on screen but whose existence is implied beyond the edges of the film's frame. It can be suggested by a sound, by the glance of a character in an off-screen direction, or by the viewer's preestablished knowledge of what lies in the off-screen space. Off-screen space is effectively used in horror and mystery films to create anxiety or suspense.

Omniscient Narrator A narrator who may reveal the consciousness of varying numbers of the story's characters. Three types of third-person narrators are frequently used by writers: *third-person omniscient*: thoughts and feelings of any number of characters are revealed; *third-person limited omniscient*: only one character's thoughts and feelings are revealed; and *third-person objective*: no character's thoughts and feelings are revealed.

Onomatopoeia A word whose pronunciation suggests its meaning, such as *hiss*, *buzz*, or *bang*.

Oppression The conditions and experience of subordination and injustice. Oppression is the condition of being overwhelmed or heavily burdened by another's exercise of wrongful authority or power, for example, the unjust or cruel treatment of subjects or inferiors; the imposition of unreasonable or unjust burdens.

Oxymoron A figure of speech that produces an effect of seeming contradiction, for example, "Make haste slowly."

Parable A short allegorical story designed to convey a truth or a moral lesson.

Paradox A seemingly contradictory statement that, upon examination, contains a truth, for example, "damn with faint praise."

Paraphrase The restatement of a passage using the reader's own words.

Pastoral Any literary work that celebrates the simple rural life or those who live close to nature.

Pathos The power of literature to evoke feelings of pity or compassion in the reader.

Patriarchy A system in which men have all or most of the power and importance in a society or group. The patriarchal system is preserved through marriage and the family; those who promote the system believe it is rooted in biology rather than in economics or history.

Pentameter A line of poetry that contains five metrical feet.

Persona The mask or voice that the author creates to tell a story.

Personification An abstract concept or inanimate object that is represented as having human qualities or characteristics. To write that "death rides a pale horse," for example, is to personify death.

Persuasion The art of moving someone else to act in a desired way or to believe in a chosen idea. Logic and reason are important tools of persuasion. Equally effective may be an appeal either to the emotions or to the ethical sensibilities.

Plagiarism Using the words or ideas of another writer and representing them as one's original work.

Poetic Justice   The ideal judgment that rewards virtue and punishes evil.

Point of View   The vantage point from which an author writes. For example, in expository writing, an author may adopt a first-person point of view. See also *narrator*.

Point of View Shot   A film shot that is seen from the perspective of a particular character. An entire narrative film may be from the viewpoint of one character, often reinforced by a narrative voice-over.

Postcolonial Criticism   See *new historicism*.

Postmodernism   Literary and artistic philosophy that rejects all formal constraints. The postmodern artist tends to accept the world as fragmented and incoherent and to represent those characteristics in art, typically in a comic and self-reflexive style.

Projection   The unconscious process of attributing one's own feelings and/or attitudes to others, especially as defense against guilt or feelings of inferiority.

Proscenium Arch   A picture-frame stage.

Protagonist   The main character in a play or story, also called the hero or heroine.

Psyche   The aggregate of the mental components of an individual, including both conscious and unconscious states and often regarded as an entity functioning apart from or independently of the body.

Psychoanalytic Criticism   Criticism using the theories of Freud and other psychologists to analyze human behavior in literature much as it is analyzed in real-life situations.

Pun   A play on words based on the similarity of sound between two words differing in meaning. For example, "Ask for me tomorrow and you will find me a grave man."

Purpose   A writer's reason for writing. A writer's purpose is clarified by his or her answer to the question, "*Why* am I writing?"

Quatrain   A four-line stanza employing various meters and rhyme patterns. The most common stanza in English poetry.

Reader-Response Criticism   Criticism that focuses on the reader's construction of meaning while experiencing a text, taking into account the wide range of responses a given text may produce.

Realism   A literary movement that lasted from approximately the mid-nineteenth century to the early twentieth century in America, England, and France. Realism is characterized by the attempt to depict the lives of ordinary people truthfully through accurate description and psychologically realistic characters.

Real Time   The actual concurrence of an action or event with the time it takes to unfold on film. For example, a performance of a dance photographed in a single uninterrupted, unedited shot preserves the actual time of the dance itself, thus adding to the viewer's appreciation of the performance skill of the dancers.

Refrain   A phrase or verse consisting of one or more lines repeated at intervals in a poem, usually at the end of each stanza.

Repression   The exclusion from consciousness of painful, unpleasant, or unacceptable memories, desires, and impulses.

Resolution   The conclusion to the major and minor subplots of a drama. The ending.

Rhetorical Question   A question not requiring a response. The answer is obvious and intended to produce an effect.

Rhyme   The repetition of similar or duplicate sounds at regular intervals—often the terminal sounds of the last words of lines of verse. For example, *girl, whirl*.

Rhythm   The pattern of recurrent strong and weak accents and long and short syllables in speech, music, and poetry. Rhythm creates sound patterns and accentuates meaning.

Romanticism   An artistic revolt of the late eighteenth and early nineteenth centuries against the traditional, formal, and orderly ideals of neoclassicism. The writers of this time dropped conventional poetic diction and forms in favor of freer forms and bolder language, and they explored the grotesque, nature, mysticism, and emotional psychology in their art.

Satire   A literary work in poetry or prose in which a subject or person is held up to scorn, derision, or ridicule with the intent of improving a situation.

Scansion   Counting the stresses in a line of poetry to establish its metrical pattern.

Scene   An episode that relates one part of a play's story. Acts are usually composed of more than one scene. The term may also refer to the setting of a work.

Script   A written text of a play used in preparation for performance. Includes dialogue, stage directions, and sometimes set, props, music, and lighting instructions.

Setting   The physical environment that is an element of a literary work, which can create atmosphere and mood and is closely related to the action and theme of the work. For example, psychological studies can gain in intensity if set in confined areas.

Sex   The anatomical and physiological characteristics that distinguish males from females. See also *gender*.

Simile   A comparison using *like* or *as*, such as *he ate like a pig; her heart felt as light as a feather*. A simile's effectiveness is determined by the contrast in the objects compared.

Social Class   Those having similar shares of power or wealth, thus forming a stratum in the hierarchy of possessions.

Social Structure   The organized patterns of human behavior in a society.

Soliloquy   A speech by one character in a play or other composition to disclose the speaker's innermost thoughts.

Sonnet   A fourteen-line poem with a set rhyme scheme. There are two main forms: the Italian (Petrarchan) and the English (Shakespearean). The Italian is divided into an eight-line stanza (octave) and a six-line stanza (sestet). The rhyme scheme in the octave is *abba, abba* and in the sestet is either *cde, cde* or *cdc, dcd*. The English form has four divisions: three quatrains and a rhymed couplet, *abab, cdcd, efef*, and *gg*.

Stage Directions   Written instructions to the actors and director regarding actions, body movements, and facial expressions during a play.

Stanza   A division in the formal pattern of a poem. Usually indicated by indentations or spaces.

Stream of Consciousness   A technique of writing in which a character's thoughts are presented as they occur in random sequence.

Subjective camera   In general, the sense that what we see is from the vantage point of a particular character. A sustained movement of the subjective camera through several spaces can convey the awkward or erratic moves of a character walking behind it. Used to stress the physical presence of a character or, as in a horror film, the unseen monster.

Subjectivity   The personal element in writing. The more subjective a piece of writing the more likely it is to be focused on the writer's opinions and feelings.

Subplot   A secondary line of action in a play or fiction often parallel with or in opposition to the main plot.

Superego   According to Freud, the part of the unconscious that regulates our moral judgment.

Surrealism   Influential movement in twentieth-century art and literature; it evolved in the mid-1920s from Dadaism. Taking inspiration from Freudian theories of the subconscious, the surrealists use bizarre imagery and strange juxtapositions to surprise and shock viewers.

Suspense   Uncertainty or excitement resulting from the reader's anxiety in awaiting a decision or outcome.

Symbol   Any word, image, description, name, character, or action that has a range of meanings and associations beyond its literal meaning. An eagle is a conventional symbol of the United States. It may also suggest freedom, power, or solitude.

Textual Criticism   A form of scholarship that attempts to establish an authentic text in the exact form the author wrote it.

Theatre of the Absurd   A type of twentieth-century avant-garde drama that presents the human condition as illogical, irrational, and meaningless. *Picnic on the Battlefield* is a good example of the genre.

Theme   The abstract concept embodied in the structure and imagery of a nondidactic or purely imaginative work.

Theory   A way of making sense of or explaining some social phenomenon.

Thesis   The main idea of an essay or other nonfiction work.

Thesis Statement   The part of an essay that clearly and directly states a writer's meaning— it tells what the essay will be about. A thesis statement should be one sentence long and is usually placed in the introduction.

Three Unities   Based on Aristotle's *Poetics*, the specification that a play's action should occur within one day (unity of time) and in a single locale (unity of place) and should reveal clearly ordered actions and plot incidents moving toward the plot's resolution (unity of action). Later scholars and critics, especially those in the neoclassical tradition, interpreted Aristotle's ideas as rules and established them as standards for drama.

Thrust stage   A stage extending beyond the *proscenium arch*, out to the audience so that patrons can be seated around three sides; similar to the Elizabethan stage.

Tone   An author's attitude toward his or her subject. It may be angry, resigned, humorous, serious, sentimental, mocking, ironic, sarcastic, satrical, reasoning, emotional, or philosophical. One tone may predominate, or many tones may be heard in a work.

Tragedy   Literary and particularly dramatic representations of serious actions that turn out disastrously for the chief character.

Tragic Hero/Heroine   In classical Greek drama, a noble character who possesses a tragic flaw that leads to his or her destruction.

Understatement   An obvious downplaying or underrating. It is the opposite of hyperbole, although either may create a memorable image or an ironic effect. To say that "after they ate the apple, Adam and Eve found life a bit tougher" is to understate their condition.

Unities   Aristotle's rules about action (a play should tell a single story); time (it should happen in a single day); and place (it should occupy a single setting).

Upstage   The area of the performance space farthest away from the audience.

Verse   A general term for a poem, often one with a metrical pattern and rhyme.

Verisimilitude   The appearance or semblance of truth.

Visual motif   Similar to the term *imagery*, but more inclusive in that it can refer not only to things contained within a shot but to camera angles, framings, and compositions of shots, which, when repeated in another context, take on additional meaning. For example, an expressive camera angle and composition in *Letter from an Unknown Woman* evokes the feelings of the female protagonist whose point of view was the initial motive for the shot.

Voice-Over   The technique by which a character's or a narrator's voice is heard over the images as a film progresses. If a film is a first-person narrative, it is used to establish and reinforce the first-person point of view.

Credits

Index of Authors
and Titles